EARLY
CHRISTIAN
READER

EARLY
CHRISTIAN
READER

Christian texts from the first and second centuries in
contemporary English translations, including the
NEW REVISED STANDARD VERSION OF THE NEW TESTAMENT

WITH INTRODUCTIONS AND ANNOTATIONS BY
STEVE MASON AND TOM ROBINSON

Society of Biblical Literature
Atlanta

Contents

CONTENTS

Preface to the Society of Biblical Literature Edition

As the church's foundational text, the New Testament will always have its largest reach in church circles. We have no desire to challenge that situation. But the earliest Christian texts, which are found within the New Testament, are also indispensable for anyone who wants to study the beginnings of Christianity historically, with or without any particular faith, as a crucial moment in the Western past. Many public universities and colleges offer courses from such a perspective. For them, the New Testament is not an ideal sourcebook.

After first working together as graduate teaching assistants (McMaster University) and then teaching Christian origins in different universities for some years, we decided to prepare a combined sourcebook and textbook that would be better suited to the questions and methods of our own courses and others like them. It would arrange the texts in a roughly historical order, include valuable early writings not found in the NT, and supply all the texts with historically oriented introductions and notes. Bearing in mind the many ways in which such courses could be structured, we also wanted to keep the format flexible.

The book before you is the result. Hendrickson Publishers brought it out in 2004, and we are grateful to the Society of Biblical Literature for taking it over. We also thank Bob Kraft, Jay Treat, and Stephen Patterson for allowing us to carry over their special contributions to this new edition.

The first *Reader* included reading lists after each introduction. We have left those intact because they are mentioned in the introductions. Much scholarship has been published since then, however, and we happily direct the reader to the regularly updated bibliographies on Mark Goodacre's gateway site: http://www.ntgateway.com/tools-and-resources/bibliography.

The first edition credited the authors of the special contributions but did not identify which of us wrote the other parts. We thought it might be a useful exercise in literary criticism for students to figure out which sections belonged together. That probably did not happen, so now we come clean. Tom Robinson prepared the sections connected with Peter and John, the Pastoral Letters, and most of Other Early Writings. Steve Mason prepared the general introduction, Paul and Paul-ish texts except the Pastorals, the Synoptic Gospels and Acts, and Hebrews.

We dedicate this book to students in their exciting first encounters with the early Christian texts from a historical point of view. The experience can be life-changing and relevant to the way we think about everything else. In our unbiased view, these are the most important courses on campus. If this edition helps more students open the doors to new ways of seeing, we will be pleased.

Steve Mason, University of Aberdeen, United Kingdom
Tom Robinson, University of Lethbridge, Canada

EARLY

CHRISTIAN

READER

Introduction

EARLIEST CHRISTIANITY IN HISTORICAL CONTEXT

INTRODUCTION

CONTEXT IS CRITICAL to interpretation. This may seem an obvious truth. After all, even visual perception is affected by context. Two lines of equal length will appear to be of different lengths if one has an arrow head at each end and the other has reversed arrow heads (the Müller-Lyer illusion). Such optical illusions demonstrate an important principle: even when we *know* that the reality is different from what we perceive, our perception is still skewed.

The same principle holds when we read the earliest Christian writings. Most of us have at least a vague notion that these are *ancient* texts, that they were not written in English, and that they come from a world very different from our own. Most of us would agree *in principle,* then, with the need to read these texts in their historical context—to try to put ourselves in the shoes of the first readers and hear the documents as they heard them. But instead we read them in an ahistorical context that has come to seem so natural and intuitive that it does not occur to us to question it.

What do we mean by an ahistorical context? We mean the context that is provided by the New Testament—the decisive part of the Christian Bible and the primary statement to faith and practice in the church. For nearly two thousand years, the NT context has predisposed readers to examine the earliest Christian writings for consistent ideas about Christian life in this world and the next. Rather than trying to understand the distinctive situation and context of each real-life author, Christians have usually devoted their energies to uncovering the timeless divine revelation in the NT. Their task was, in large measure, to arrange by subject what the NT had somewhat inconveniently filed under author. So they culled passages from *Matthew, John, Romans, Hebrews,* and *Revelation* as if from a single work. What the NT taught about such topics as anthropology (the human plight), soteriology (salvation), ecclesiology (the church), and eschatology (final things) became the stuff of systematic theology.

Perhaps many readers of this present book who know the early Christian texts mainly from their experience in church and devotional reading recognize this context well. But another kind of reading has developed over the last two centuries. This other approach recognizes that, in addition to the obvious value that the NT has for the church, it also contains within it the most important evidence about the origins of Christianity, the new faith that would decisively alter the direction of Western civilization after its adoption by the Emperor Constantine and his successors in the fourth century. In the public arena, therefore, the earliest Christian writings are understood as the property not only of the church but also of the culture as a whole. And they are considered susceptible of *historical* investigation.

Historical investigation differs in essential ways from religious or devotional (ahistorical) reading. Whereas the latter springs from an attitude of trust or faith, historians (no matter what the time and place of their interest) must assume a posture of suspicion, relentlessly asking questions and cross-examining their witnesses. They want to know the limitations, perspectives, and possible agendas of their sources. For example, it is not only Paul's thought that interests them, but also the views of Paul's opponents in various locales. So they must read between the lines as well as reading what is on the lines. Historians try to be alive to the differences, even small nuances, as well as the agreements in their material. They look for "unintentional evidence" that appears to run counter to an author's presentation of things. From this kind of material they hope to reconstruct plausible slices of real human life in early Christianity and to understand the aims of some key players.

Historical and faith-based approaches to the early Christian writings need not be mutually exclusive. Since the historical mode of reading was initiated in the eighteenth-century Enlightenment, aspects of it have been adopted by all serious scholars, whether they work in universities, seminaries, or Bible colleges. Each one will differ in his or her precise account of the ways in which faith and history interact, but every academic in the field must deal with their encounter. As we have said, almost every reader recognizes *at some level* that the early Christian writings are ancient texts and so require historical interpretation. But this historical interpretation is enormously difficult to carry through with the English Bible or NT, because the tool itself constantly reinforces the ahistorical context that we are trying to get around. That shortfall between message and medium is, in a nutshell, the reason for this *Reader*.

Let us try to clarify this point by discussing six issues, and these are only examples, that need to be unraveled for historical reading but that are rendered obscure by the context of the Christian Bible or NT.

Ancient Mediterranean Social Conditions

The eastern Mediterranean world of Jesus' and Paul's time had seen a succession of empires, from the neo-Babylonians and Persians (sixth to fourth centuries B.C.E.) to the Hellenistic kingdoms (fourth to first centuries B.C.E.) and now the Romans. Greek, however, had endured as the common language of communication and business. Judea was no longer governed by Jewish kings, but had recently fallen under the direct rule of a Roman prefect (from 6 C.E.). At the same time, until 39 C.E. Galilee remained under a prince of the old (quasi-) Jewish family of the Herods.

Although we rightly recognize the people of NT times as humans like us, facing many of the same fundamental issues of human existence, including the problem of finding happiness, we ought not to minimize the differences. They lived in a world that is difficult for us to imagine. To begin with, try to forget everything you know about such matters as health and wellness—for example, bacteria and personal hygiene; plumbing and sanitation; housing; basic principles of biology, chemistry, physics, and astronomy; the solar system and the universe; upward social mobility; equality of women and men; women's presence in public; justice for all; privacy and personal space; democratic representation in government; inalienable human rights; respect for individuals; intellectual growth; emotional well-being; diet, ways of eating, and exercise; mass production of goods; personal choice; financial credit and banks; the postal service; care of children; reading, writing, and public speaking; logic; public and private education; responsive police, ambulance, and fire services; free markets; weekends; easy travel and communication. If you can! (Of course, we cannot.)

Now try to imagine a world that you and most of your contemporaries understand as more or less flat: heaven above is the home of the gods; the underworld beneath is the home of departed spirits and destructive forces; the earth in the middle is the battleground between these arbitrary forces. Life is nasty and short: fifty is fairly old; health at forty is enviable. Infant mortality is extremely high: as many as one in three dies in birth or infancy. Sickness and suffering abound. In every small town or city you visit, you see the sick, the maimed, and the demon-possessed loitering in public places, often begging for food. You hope that this never happens to you. If you get sick, perhaps a magician, prophet, or exorcist will pass through your village, or you might visit a temple of the god Asclepius. But life seems cheap, as the judicial crucifixions by the dirt roads outside of town constantly remind you. Corpses covered in sheets, being carried to burial, are a common sight.

The bulk of the population have few civil rights because they are not Roman citizens, and slaves have none whatsoever. You can be arbitrarily arrested and executed by the governor on the mere suspicion of causing trouble. If you happen to live near a base of Roman or auxiliary soldiers, you are subject to the whims and outrages of the occupying armies. So, although you are still in your twenties, you have joined a club whose main purpose is to provide for the burial of its members.

The vast majority of the world's population are peasants working land that does not belong to them. Some are small landholders: whatever they produce beyond their family's immediate needs for survival goes to someone else. Sometimes you dream of living in a city, but you know that they have big problems too: poor sanitation, shoddily constructed buildings always susceptible to fire or collapse, crime-filled streets, ruthless and seemingly all-powerful bosses and landlords. In the city and in the countryside, slavery abounds: in Italy, the center of the world, one person in every four, in the eastern provinces perhaps one in every ten persons you encounter, belongs (literally and completely) to another human being.

You cannot read or write very well, though you can communicate adequately when you need to, and you can write a few numbers or words on a piece of broken pottery as a bill or receipt. Even those who can read and write well hardly ever do so; communication is mainly by speech. So what you say is extremely important and may commit you to an obligation every bit as binding as a written contract today.

A few powerful people control each city and region of the empire. They have all the land, all the money, and all the power. You never see these families, but only their agents, who come to collect rent or other dues from you. All you can do is attach yourself to someone on the next rung of the ladder, your "patron," and hope that your loyalty will pay off with some measure of security from life's worst outrages. Who knows, if you have a skill of some kind, perhaps you will be able to climb a bit yourself, maybe even buy Roman citizenship before you die. And at least you have your good name, your most treasured possession among your small circle of friends. Public shame, for any reason, would be infinitely worse than your unavoidable economic and social plight.

This was, in very broad strokes, the kind of world in which Christianity was born. It is fairly easy for modern Western readers to *say* that we acknowledge the strangeness of it, but quite another thing for us actually to admit that strangeness in our reading. Inevitably, we still want to pull the texts out of their world and into ours. In our sanitized churches, universities, seminaries, and Bible colleges, we tend to make the NT transparent for us today. So completely have we domesticated these texts, we seldom notice that they everywhere presuppose the "three-storey universe" described above (*1 Thess.* 4:17; *Phil.* 2:10; *Acts* 1:9–11), a cosmology that none of us would embrace in our ordinary lives. We hardly ever ponder who those "demon-possessed" people were, who seem to fill the hamlets of Galilee and the pages of the gospels. We do not care to understand what it meant to be "poor" or "mourning" or "sick" in this world. We gloss over the "Zealot" tag on one of Jesus' disciples' names as if it were merely a nickname like any other. Even such sharp and bloody images as crosses and sacrifices are somehow blended into happy Sunday school songs and university lectures. We dismiss references to the Pharisees or Herod Antipas or Pontius Pilate as mere set furniture behind the story.

Above all, we modern readers tend to privilege everything that Jesus or Paul said as if it were unique, simply because we have no easy way of knowing what else was being said and done in their world. Because Paul said that he had learned to be content with his lot in life (*Phil.* 4:12) and Jesus advised people not to be anxious (*Matt.* 6:25–34), many Christians remember these principles as "scriptural teaching." But Jesus and Paul probably did not mean to be particularly original here, since these were old principles of the Stoics, whose ideas had been popular for centuries. In these cases Jesus and Paul probably intended, rather, to say things that would resonate as obviously true with their audiences—much as if someone today should write another book advocating self-realization, exercise, and mental relaxation. It is successful not because the idea is original but, on the contrary, because it taps a vein (albeit in a new and interesting way) that already runs deep in our collective mind.

The earliest Christians wrote many different kinds or genres of writing: letters, life-stories or biographies, histories, argumentative essays, manuals of instruction, and apocalypses. Each of these writings has parallels of some kind in the Jewish, Greek, and Roman literature of the period. Paul's letters, for example, can be compared to other letters of the time, so we need to try to understand how letters were typically mailed, received, and read. The gospels and *Acts,* for their part, have affinities to ancient biographies, novels, and other kinds of historical writing. It is most useful to examine these parallel texts for their typical rhetorical features and for the light they shed on the early Christians' outlooks.

Ancient Mediterranean Languages and Modern Translations

A second kind of historical unraveling has to do with the language of our texts. The early Christians wrote in Greek.[1] Their Greek was the common language of the eastern Mediterranean at the time, with some special Christian vocabulary thrown in. This Greek was also influenced by Semitic (Hebrew and Aramaic) ways of speaking, such as the tendency to join clauses with "and," to use only simple verb tenses, and to speak in short (often parallel) sentences. The traditional Hebrew language of Judea was still known there, but after the Judean leadership was released from captivity in Babylon (beginning in the 530s B.C.E.), they naturally began to adopt the common Near Eastern language, Aramaic. Aramaic was a relative of Hebrew, in roughly the same way as English is a cousin to French. With the arrival of the Hellenistic kingdoms after Alexander the Great (late fourth century B.C.E.), Greek also began to play an important role in the area, and Greek cities were established both along the Palestinian coast and in the interior. So by the first century, even people living in rural Galilee spoke Aramaic, some elementary Greek, and possibly some Hebrew.

But the early Christians wrote in Greek. This presents a problem because, as anyone who has ever translated anything knows, every translation is an interpretation. The Greek word *logos,* for example, can mean everything from "single word" or "thing" to "message," "discourse," "teaching," "doctrine," and even "generative principle of the cosmos"! When a Greek author makes a deliberate play on words, the translator's task becomes impossible. The Greek word *genesis* in *Matt.* 1:1 can mean "origin," "beginning," "genealogy" (the NRSV choice there), "pedigree," or "birth" (the NRSV choice for the same word at *Matt.* 1:18). What is the "right" English translation? There is none. It is a matter of choice for the translator, which is why translations of ancient texts can read quite differently.

---

[1]Even though the full *Gospel of Thomas* exists only in fourth-century Coptic, enough of it is paralleled in second-century Gk fragments that we can establish an earlier Gk version.

Translators of the NT tend not to be as individualistic as they might be with other texts, however, for a reason peculiar to the context in which the NT is used. Because translators of the NT normally do their work with one eye on the church's use of these texts, they tend to preserve traditional translations where purely historical considerations might suggest something else. Let us mention a few. The word *euangelion,* signifying a "special announcement," was not common in first-century literature, but it did turn up in inscriptions praising the reforms brought by the Emperor Augustus (27 B.C.E.–14 C.E.). As far as we know, Paul was the first Christian to adopt this term as the watchword of his mission. He had a special announcement about Jesus' death, resurrection, and imminent return. It was an odd-sounding word, made into a kind of technical term by Paul. When we translate it as "gospel," a word that is safe and familiar to us from church preaching and even music, we rob it of the impact that it had on Paul's hearers. We intensify this problem when we apply the word to the first four documents of the NT, which do not claim to be "gospels." Similarly, when Paul took over the old Greek word for a political *assembly (ekklēsia)* for the little house groups of his followers, he had no idea that it would become ossified in English as "church," with all the connotations of organizations and stone buildings that word has for us. Why not recover the authors' original sense with a word such as "assembly"?

Other obvious cases of traditional language being preserved by translators are "baptism," "Lord," "disciple," "faith," and "Jew." Although the first rule of translation is to avoid simple transliteration (representing the letters of the foreign word in English) where possible, baptism is merely a transliteration of the Greek *baptismos.* But *baptismos* had a long history in Greek before Christianity was born, so when the first Christians used this word for their practice of "dipping" or "immersing" converts, it did not have the holy aura that "baptism" has for us. John was simply "the Dipper"—a bit of an odd-sounding expression then, as it would be now if we translated it this way.

The Greek *kyrios* had many applications in everyday life, but always for someone above oneself in the social pyramid: a husband, master, respected man, or patron. When we translate it as "Lord," once again we create a particularly religious aura that it did not have in antiquity.

Another English word with a big aura is "disciple," though it translates a Greek word *(mathētēs)* that simply meant "learner" or "student." That the early Christian writers would call Jesus' followers "students" is possibly significant for understanding how Jesus' group appeared to others, but we obscure all of this by using an unfamiliar or archaic word like *disciple.*

Likewise, the simple Greek words *pistis* and *pisteuō* ("trust" as noun and verb, respectively) have been permanently reconfigured in church English as "faith" and "believe," which again might evoke all sorts of images from our experience that were foreign to the first Christians.

And the Greek term *Ioudaios* was an ethnogeographical label, meaning "someone from *Ioudaia* (Judea)," a form precisely matching "Babylonian," "Egyptian," or

"Syrian." When we render it as "Jew" we obscure the ancient connotations of recent immigrant from the extreme East of the empire, member of a small subject nation made famous by the great King Herod, follower of the lawgiver Moses.

The NRSV translation, which we have chosen to use for the *Reader,* though it is excellent in many respects, and the product of international experts, preserves all these traditional but misleading translations. We nevertheless chose the NRSV for two main reasons. First, we did not want to make a new translation, both because of the excessive time required and because we did not want discussion of the translation to detract from the main idea of the book. Better to use a standard version, and the NRSV is as close as one comes to a new standard. Second, since this is a book principally designed to introduce the writings of early Christianity, we wanted it to be usable alongside the other main tools, such as gospel synopses and concordances, that exist for the NRSV but not for the more adventurous (though perhaps more literal) translations.

Even while the NRSV preserves customary translations of some key terms, it also makes a few innovations—also motivated by contemporary church use—that are equally problematic from a historical perspective. The world of the first Christians was pervasively patriarchal: adult males controlled almost everything. Ancient texts reflect this patriarchy, with their tendency to default to masculine words such as "man/men" and "brothers," masculine word endings (in languages in which all words are gendered), and masculine pronouns. This is the case even in the earliest Christian writings, though Paul (at least) gives some indications that women were welcomed on a more equal footing in his assemblies than in the world at large (see *1 Cor.* 1:11; 7:10–16; 11:12; *Gal.* 3:28; *Rom.* 16:1).

What to do, then, when early Christian authors address their hearers as "brothers"? The NRSV translators have responded by removing most of the NT's traditional masculine language. The argument for doing this is that, since Paul (for example) clearly included women in his assemblies with full status, he cannot have intended to address men only. So the NRSV usually renders the Greek *adelphoi* ("brothers") as "brothers and sisters," sometimes as "believers" (*1 Cor.* 6:5–8). Where Paul speaks of Christians as "sons" (Gk *huioi*) of God, the NRSV gives "children" (*Rom.* 8:14). As laudable as this translation practice may be in a church context, it creates problems when we set the texts in historical context. The Greek language was entirely capable of saying "sister" or "daughter" when that was intended, and therefore it is important that Paul still reflects his patriarchal environment in his language. When he speaks of "sons" of God in *Romans* 8, it is with intent, since (rightly or wrongly) the son was the heir in antiquity. An interesting case is *1 Cor.* 7:15, where Paul actually uses both "brother" and "sister," but since the NRSV has been routinely translating "brother" alone as "brother and sister," it cannot signal Paul's change of language.

Any translation is open to criticism because it is inevitably one *interpretation.* The comments above are not meant to heap blame on the NRSV translation that we have chosen to use: it is as good as any and better than most. Our purpose is merely to remind the reader that he or she is never seeing simply what the first Christians wrote but an interpretation of it, one that is necessarily conditioned by the translators' purposes.

What the First Christians Wrote and What We Read

An even more basic reason why what we read is not what the first Christians wrote is simply that what they wrote *no longer exists.* They wrote on papyrus rolls wrapped around sticks ("scrolls"). Papyrus was fairly durable, better than many kinds of paper today, but still it succumbed to humidity and eventually deteriorated. All the rolls on which the first Christians wrote their letters, essays, histories, and biographies have disappeared. Fortunately, some Christians took it upon themselves to copy those texts, and then at least from the time that Christianity became a state-sponsored religion in the fourth century it had large copy houses, known as *scriptoria,* at its disposal. In these rooms, one could achieve a kind of mass production by having someone read from a master copy while scribes seated in the room copied down what they heard. Predictably, this copying led to numerous errors, whether from the reader's oversight (missing or duplicating lines, or misreading an abbreviation) or from the copyists' misunderstanding (through lost concentration or in cases of sound-alikes). Also, some scribes took it upon themselves to "correct" what they took to be errors in the copies they saw.

The result of this long process is that, although we no longer possess the original texts of what the early Christians wrote, we have some 5,400 manuscripts (i.e., "handmade writings") that represent copies, dating from the second to the fifteenth centuries of this era. The very earliest known manuscript is a fragment of a few lines of *John* 18 ($\mathfrak{P}^{52}$), dating 125–150 C.E., and a few larger fragments exist from the late second and third centuries. But our earliest complete copies of the NT writings are on parchment (animal skin) and in book form, from the time at which Christianity began to enjoy governmental support (ca. 350 C.E.).[2]

From the middle of the fifteenth century, when Johannes Gutenberg invented the printing press, it was possible to make exact copies. But our 5,400 manuscripts from before that time are by no means identical; they include about 300,000 variations or "variant readings." The vast majority of these are of little significance, but some raise extremely significant questions. For example, the famous story of the woman caught in adultery (*John* 7:53–8:11) probably does not belong in *John* at all, since the best manuscripts either omit it or place it in *Luke.*

One might hope that the earliest manuscripts have the best chance of representing the originals, and that principle has some merit. The problem is that because our earliest complete manuscripts come only from the middle of the fourth century, we must still reckon with 250–300 years between the time of writing and our earliest copies. This is more than enough time for small changes to have crept in to

---

[2]Codex Sinaiticus (ℵ), dating from about 350, has the entire NT. Codex Vaticanus (B), dating from the same time, has all the main texts but is missing *1 Timothy, 2 Timothy, Titus, Philemon, Revelation,* and part of *Hebrews.*

even our "best" manuscripts. Sometimes a chronologically later manuscript might contain a less corrupted reading. Sometimes the original reading may be beyond our grasp altogether.

Therefore, although one often hears appeals to "the original Greek," this is quite a misleading expression. The Greek text used by all modern translations (NRSV, JB, NIV) is the creation of literary detectives who sift through the various manuscript readings and decide what was most likely in the original. Often they are unsure. But almost every reader of the NT, whether in church or elsewhere and whether reading in English, another modern language, or ancient Greek, is inescapably dependent upon the judgments of these historians. The "Greek NT" does not exist apart from their efforts.

So, what we read in English is but one interpretation of a Greek text that has itself been hypothetically reconstructed from thousands of manuscript variants. This observation should be a constant reminder as to just how far removed we are from the world of the first Christians. It should also prevent us from putting too much interpretative weight upon a single word or phrase until we verify the Greek text.

Scripture in Earliest Christianity

A fourth way in which use of the Christian Bible or NT dulls historical sensitivity is that it invites us to treat the writings of Paul or biographers of Jesus as scripture. Here are Paul's letters placed between the same covers as *Genesis, Exodus,* and *Isaiah!* Of course, these early Christian writings *are* now scripture for the church, and they have been for many centuries. But they were not scripture when they were written, not for their first readers. If our goal is to think historically about these texts, to put ourselves in the sandals of the first readers, then we too should abandon the designation "scripture" when reading them. But the use of the NT tends to entrench that hallowed designation.

Let us elaborate. When Paul and his contemporary Christians cited "scripture" or "what stands written," they invariably referred to the old and sacred writings of the Judeans. Their Bible was roughly equivalent to what Christians now call the Old Testament (OT). But it was not widely titled the Old Testament, of course, until there was a body of writing called the New Testament (NT), and that did not happen until Tertullian's time (ca. 200 C.E.). We say "roughly equivalent" because the early Christian authors show a marked preference for Greek translations of the Bible, though the Bible was originally written in Hebrew (with brief Aramaic sections). Moreover, it is not clear that the arrangement of the Greek Bibles known to the Christians were the same as the arrangement of the Hebrew Bible, if there was a single standard at all in the first century. And specialists are not yet in complete agreement as to whether all the books now in the Christian OT were recognized as scripture, or indeed whether more books might have been accepted as scripture by some significant Jewish groups. These are all thorny issues.

Nevertheless, it is clear that Jewish scripture served as scripture also for the first Christians. This does not mean that they all wished to observe the Torah brought down by Moses from Mount Sinai (see *Exodus* 20–40). Some did; some did not. But most Christians saw in Jesus, and so in their faith, the "fulfillment" of some age-old biblical hopes for restoration or the "reign of God." So they read this Bible through the lens, as it were, of Jesus—always looking for passages in it that might be applied to Jesus' birth, life, death, resurrection, or exaltation to heaven. Since the number of such passages cited by the first Christian authors is relatively small, and a few tend to be repeated often, it may be that most Christians did not consult the scriptures firsthand—physically difficult in any case, since they would have to manage numerous scrolls with no chapter, verse, or word divisions!—but rather cited from lists of favorite "proof texts." (See APPENDIX D.)

Whereas Jewish scripture was clearly authoritative for the first Christians, Paul's letters reveal that his letters did not hold the status of scripture when they were first read. Paul often struggles to convince his readers of a point, even to remain committed to his "announcement," and he expresses real fear that they will not do so (*Gal.* 1:6; 4:11). Sometimes Paul's readers have forthrightly challenged or even ridiculed him (*1 Cor.* 4:3–5, 18; *2 Cor.* 2:5; 7:12; 10:10). Not infrequently he expresses sharp anger, denouncing other Christian leaders (*2 Cor.* 11:4–5, 13; *Gal.* 1:8; 2:11). Although he perhaps tries his best to interpret God's will, he plainly admits that he is sometimes giving his opinion (*1 Cor.* 7:12, 25). Some other Christians even dismissed his right to call himself an apostle (*1 Cor.* 9:2). All this means that neither Paul nor his first readers understood his letters as immediate divine revelation.[3]

As we shall see in the introduction to BIOGRAPHY, ANECDOTE, AND HISTORY, none of those texts enjoyed any special recognition at their time of writing either. The author of *Luke* (1:1–4) explicitly sets out to improve on the other accounts in circulation, which he knows and uses. Even though he does not say it, the author of *Matthew* plainly does the same thing. How, then, did the earliest Christian texts achieve the status of sacred scripture for the church? That question brings us to our fifth major issue for historically minded readers.

---

[3]Thus, when the author of *2 Timothy* talks about the sacred writings that Timothy has known from childhood, which are valuable for instruction (3:1–16), he too means the Jewish scripture, as the context makes clear ("from childhood you have known" and the example in 3:8). *Second Peter* 3:16 presents a different case, for it includes Paul's writings among the "scriptures." Note first that the word rendered "scriptures" in English is an ordinary Gk word for "writings"; there is nothing explicit here about sacred or holy writings. The point may simply be that written statements by noted authorities are capable of being twisted, which is why many Christians did not like appeals to writings but preferred "living" oral traditions. (See Ignatius, *Philadelphians* 8; Papias in Eusebius, *Eccl. hist.* 3.39; Clement of Alexandria, *Miscellanies* 1, in Eusebius, *Eccl. hist.* 5.11.1.) Second, most scholars consider *2 Peter* a late document, not written by Peter. It assumes that Paul's letters already exist in a well-known collection and are used by various groups for their own purposes. This presumably dates the work well after Paul's death in the 60s. The discussion of the long delay of Jesus' return in 3:1–10, which assumes that the apostles belong to a bygone age, also points to a rather late, perhaps second-century, date.

The Scope of Early Christian Literature and Formation of the Canon

The writings of the NT collection do not reflect the complete range of early Christian viewpoints. Remember that documents from antiquity have survived only if someone had the interest and resources to copy them at appropriate junctures in history (i.e., before existing copies deteriorated too badly) or if they were hidden away in a very dry place (such as the Dead Sea coast or in parts of Egypt), where they might be discovered in our time. This means that the vast majority of ancient texts in general, and of Christian writings as a subset of those, have disappeared. If even some of Paul's own correspondence has been lost (see *1 Cor.* 5:9; *2 Cor.* 2:3; 7:8), we can understand how the writings of his opponents and of those who lost important debates in the following generations would have been neglected.

We know that there were such debates because, as we shall see in the introduction to THE LETTERS OF PAUL, his letters represent only one side of a conversation. And what he says makes it clear that he sharply disagreed with some other Christian leaders, perhaps on several fronts, about the significance of Jesus and what it meant to follow him properly. Since historians must attempt to create a picture of the way it was, not simply of the viewpoint that they might prefer, they must follow up on these differences of perspective. The clues within Paul's letters, from the first Christian generation, make it easier for us to discern differences of perspective in the second and later generations, even in the major gospels.

It is a fascinating historical exercise to try to reconstruct a full-bodied three-dimensional picture of Jesus' followers in the first three or four generations—a kind of virtual reality. Fortunately, in addition to the NT there happen to be a few early texts that survived intact because they were widely read in at least some Christian circles, but did not make it into the NT. Of these, *1 Clement* is the most obvious, since it is almost universally dated to the same period as some NT writings (the 90s); the letters of Ignatius of Antioch, written fifteen to twenty years later, are probably also contemporary with the latest NT writings. More controversial are the *Didache, Gospel of Thomas,* and *Epistle of Barnabas,* which come from later periods in their current forms but may well preserve Christian perspectives from the earliest period. Whether a secure case for early dating can be made or not, the historian is obligated to consider these and perhaps other texts in the effort to develop a responsible, complete picture of earliest Christian life and thought. And finally, we have numerous comments in the "church fathers," Christian leaders of the second to fifth centuries C.E., which allude to varieties of early Christianity that did not survive.

If the writings now found in the NT were not considered scripture from the first moment, and were only a few of the many Christian documents in circulation, why did they survive while most of the others perished? And how did they come to be considered scripture? To make a long story short, three things happened.

First, it was natural that over time some writings would receive more recognition, more citation, more use than others. These more widely used writings, especially those that were thought to originate in the first generation or two (from an apostle's authority), were gradually acquiring special status by about the middle of the second century.

Second, as some texts were naturally gaining relative prominence in this way, the churches were forced to begin to agree upon the precise nature of Christian teaching. Given the diversity of belief and practice among those who expressed allegiance to Jesus, what was essential, real "Christianity"? Christians faced bad press through much of the second and third centuries, especially with governments who considered their nighttime meetings of men and women a threat to social stability and perhaps morals. Wild stories about their behavior circulated, including claims that they practiced cannibalism and adultery—the same charges that had been made against the notorious secret cults of Dionysus long before. It did not help matters, perhaps, that some Christian groups appeared to take radical positions on the roles of women in church and relations between men and women. Questions of leadership, order, and belief were all wrapped up together: If Christians could agree in submitting to a kind of ordained leadership (in the bishops), then Christianity could hope to present a unified and respectable face to the world, some argued. The same tendencies that produced a hierarchical church leadership worked to identify some writings and not others as acceptable guides.

Third, while all of this was going on, a Christian leader named Marcion, from Pontus (northern Turkey), forced the issue whether the Christians should, after all, continue to use Jewish scripture. For Marcion this was a particular problem because he understood the religion of Jesus in a wholly non-Jewish way—as entirely spiritual, loving, and universal in contrast to what he perceived (lacking close knowledge) as an ethnic, vindictive, and material biblical religion. He went so far as to imagine that the creator God of the Jewish Bible was not the true God and father of Jesus, as Christianity elsewhere claimed. His passionate rejection of Jewish scripture as unsuited to Christianity provided the motive for him to assemble a purely Christian scripture. This consisted of Paul's letters and *Luke,* because he thought that these authors alone understood the non-Jewish character of Christianity, though he edited even these texts to remove what he saw as judaizing corruptions.

Marcion's writings have not survived except in snippets, sections quoted by his opponents for the purposes of rebuttal. That is because his radical disjunction between the God of the Bible and the father of Jesus was not widely shared. Most Christians considered the Jewish scripture indispensable, not because Gentile Christians actually observed its requirements (so far Marcion was right) but because it was thought to provide the ancient grounding for the appearance of Jesus; Christians understood it to point toward Jesus everywhere. This link with an ancient tradition was important in deflecting the criticism that Christianity was a "new superstition," as outsiders often remarked. Nevertheless, Marcion's challenge was an important catalyst in the definition of a new and Christian scripture. Although other Christians would add more to Marcion's meager list of authoritative texts in controversy with him, he was the one who forced the issue.

From the late second to the late fourth centuries, then, these three motives (and, no doubt, others) coalesced to produce a body of recognized "New Testament" writings. As some Christian texts were proving popular in many locations, and Christians were needing to decide which documents best reflected what they believed, they responded to Marcion's proposals by suggesting their own lists of authoritative books. It required two hundred years or more, however, for most Christians to agree on which texts were authoritative. We have a number of lists from the intervening period, but the first one that matches our NT comes in the Thirty-ninth Easter letter of Bishop Athanasius in 367 C.E.

To return to our original question: Much literature from the period of Christian origins has not survived to the present because it did not find a place in the "canon" (Gk *kanōn:* "rule" or "guide"). Here as elsewhere, the winners wrote history. This may be fine and understandable for the purposes of Christian tradition, but historians must try to reconstruct the full diversity of Christian perspectives as well as possible. They do this mainly by looking for small clues about other Christian groups and viewpoints. In addition, they turn to the small number of early texts that have survived from sheer popularity or chance discovery, even though they did not make it into the canon. All of this material together becomes evidence for a more realistic, three-dimensional historical picture.

The Historical Sequence of the Early Christian Texts

The final example of a historical issue that faces all NT readers is simply this: the NT's arrangement of books is not based on historical criteria. When we read the NT, it seems to present a logical order, for the biographies of Jesus (the gospels) come before the story of the first-generation church *(Acts)* and the major writings of the first Christian generation (Paul's and other apostolic letters). Every scholar in the field understands, however, that whereas Paul's letters come from the generation immediately following Jesus' life, the gospels and *Acts* were written in the second and possibly third generations. The evidence for this is in the documents themselves: Paul seems to have died during Nero's reign (54–68 C.E.), and the time periods he specifies in his letters make him active as a Christian missionary from the 30s. The gospels, by contrast, are anonymous texts that show many signs of later composition. (See the introductions to THE LETTERS OF PAUL and BIOGRAPHY, ANECDOTE, AND HISTORY, for details.)

Even within these major blocks of material, the historical sequence is different from that of the NT. The NT arranges Paul's letters from the longest to the shortest of those written to groups *(Romans to 2 Thessalonians)* and then from the longest to shortest of those written to individuals *(1 Timothy to Philemon)*. As we might expect, this scheme does not correspond to the events. Internal evidence shows that *1 Thessalonians* was (one of) the earliest and *Romans* (one of) the latest of his compositions. Although it might seem unimportant where one places the letters, as long as they are all included, the sequence *has* mattered a great deal in the past. The elaborate and sophisticated *Romans,* partly because it stands at the head of Paul's letter collection, has typically served as the gateway to understanding Paul; his other letters have been fit in around this "mature" statement. But *Romans* gives an unusual impression of the apostle, one that would not be obvious at all if one started with any other letter. Why not start with the earliest glimpse of Paul, *1 Thessalonians,* and build a historical picture from there?

With respect to the gospels and *Acts,* the NT also presents an ahistorical picture. Today the vast majority of scholars, whether conservative or liberal, agree that *Mark* was probably the first gospel written, though the NT puts *Matthew* first, and that *Luke* and *Acts* were composed by a single second-generation author. The NT's separation of *Luke* from *Acts* has its own logic (stories about Jesus come before stories about the church, and *Luke* belongs with *Matthew* and *Mark,* whereas *John* is different) but for historical purposes it is preferable by far to group texts by the same author and place them in proper sequence.

Making What Is Old and Familiar New Again

Here, then, is the problem in a nutshell. Everyone in the field of NT studies knows that treating these texts as scripture tends to obscure their historical significance. The NT is the church's sacred book, originally formulated and still used for guidance within specific Christian religious contexts. This was not a collection made for historical study of Christian origins. From that historical point of view, the NT collection is somewhat arbitrary and anachronistic. Its very *familiarity* to students, from the church context, actually makes historical study of Christian origins more difficult. Strangely—since everyone knows this, and instructors must spend several weeks of a course explaining the principles described above in order to help students reimagine the NT world—strangely, we still ask students to bring a Christian Bible or a NT to classes on Christian origins. Here is an example of the medium's contradicting the message.

To be sure, many such courses use one of the fine study Bibles available today. These study Bibles contain contributions from outstanding scholars, and they incorporate some historical information in their introductions and annotations. They also mention the most important textual variations—a function of the translations themselves. To the extent that they deal with the first three issues mentioned above, study Bibles go some distance toward helping students encounter these texts from a historical mindset. The problem is that, with respect to the latter three issues, the study Bibles actually undercut that significant accomplishment. They reinforce the anachronistic treatment of early Christian texts as scripture; they also anachronistically limit their scope to the canon; and they preserve the arbitrary canonical sequence of the included texts. It is difficult to see why these limitations need to be observed in textbooks designed for historical study in the public arena, at universities and colleges.

We prepared the *Early Christian Reader* because we found these restrictions unnecessary. Why not try to recover the range of early Christian viewpoints available by the early second century (the third Christian generation)? Why not include all the known texts from the period, ignoring the walls around the later canon, and put them in a plausible historical order? In making this innovation, we hope that we have taken over the best traditions of the study Bibles: adopting the translators' notes on manuscript variants; discussing translation issues from time to time; and providing some significant links to the cultural context of early Christianity. But if there is truth in the cliché that "a picture is worth a thousand words," then it simply makes good sense for those who study early Christian texts historically to use a sourcebook that is adequate to the task. Our primary aim has been to help such students read these documents in a new, historical light—to "taste them again for the first time."

In addition to this theoretical aim, we admit to a practical one. We have tried to include enough of an orientation to the texts that the *Reader* might serve as an introductory textbook as well as a sourcebook. It is a perennial difficulty for those who teach Christian origins to find the right textbook—not because we lack such books, but rather because each instructor's approach is so distinctive that existing books rarely seem to offer a close fit. Textbook authors must choose their own method around which to arrange their material, and this "angle" seldom matches the instructor's precisely.

Of course, we have our angles too, not to mention those of our special contributors Michael Holmes, Robert Kraft, Stephen Patterson, and Jay Treat. Because our main purpose in the *Reader* is to provide the texts themselves, however, we do not need to present a strong overall interpretation of early Christianity. Our format might conceivably fit any number of course designs. To make the book potentially useful as a course text, we have included extensive introductions not only to the individual documents but also to the major sections (e.g., Paul's letters, the gospels and *Acts,* Pauline tradition), so that students might gain a sense of the major scholarly developments in these areas.

Although the aims of the introductory essays should be self-evident, it might help if we clarify some issues pertaining to our notes. First, our goal has been minimalist: to facilitate historical reading of the texts. This has meant, first, explaining unfamiliar terms where we were able to do that. Second, we wanted to flag passages that have given rise to significant problems for interpreters. Third, even though we have made an effort to integrate the earliest Christian texts into their social environment, we obviously could not go far in this direction. Many excellent books introducing life in the Roman empire, the position of Jews and Christians within that world, and specific aspects of the environment (e.g., religious, philosophical, literary) already exist. We mention a few in the suggested reading below. Far from being comprehensive or even perfectly balanced, our notes are meant only to suggest a few important links. We hope that, in tracing them, curious readers will begin to discover the riches of the ancient world's legacy, which is not limited to the Christian texts.

A special problem was created by the early Christians' frequent citation of scripture. As all specialists know, these citations do not often match the Hebrew text that serves as the main basis for the Christian Old Testament. Although the texts in that collection were composed long before the birth of Christianity, and we now have extensive fragments of them among the Dead Sea Scrolls of Qumran (second century B.C.E. to first century C.E.), the text of the Hebrew Bible was formalized only in the ninth century C.E., in what is known as the Masoretic Text (MT). Since the early Christians lived in a Greek-speaking world, they preferred Greek translations of the Bible, which regularly differ from the Hebrew tradition that ended up in the MT. But their citations also disagree often with the "Septuagint" (abbreviated LXX), which is the classic form of the Greek Bible known to us from fourth-century C.E. manuscripts. Indeed, sometimes we cannot find a good parallel to the Christian citation in *any* known version of the Jewish Bible, whether the MT, the LXX, or other biblical traditions. Did the Christians deliberately change texts to make a point, or did they use texts (or oral traditions) that we do not know?

To complicate matters further, the Greek Bible (LXX) frequently uses a citation system (chapter and verse) that differs from the Hebrew Bible's (MT), and sometimes also from the Christian OT's, which is a hybrid.

Rather than comment on all these complexities in each case—an area of study all by itself—we have taken the following route. Where the Christian citation closely matches both MT and LXX, we simply give a reference to the passage in question. Where only the numbering system differs, we give both MT and LXX references. Where the Christian quotation matches the LXX, but not the MT, we give the reference(s) and also quote the pertinent section of the divergent MT. To help convey some sense of the original Hebrew idiom to the English-speaking student, we have used, with permission, the excellent translations of the Jewish Publication Society's *Tanakh: The Holy Scriptures.* Where the Christian citation differs from both MT and LXX, we quote the MT according to the JPS translation and also quote the LXX. In quoting the LXX, it made sense to follow the translation we used for the Christian author (usually NRSV) as long as the Greek matched; we used different English words only to highlight differences in Greek between the Christian citation and the LXX.

Our hope is that the *Early Christian Reader* will provide substantial help to all readers of early Christian literature who wish to think themselves back into the real circumstances of the authors and first readers.

For Further Reading

Ackroyd, P. R., and C. F. Evans. *From the Beginnings to Jerome.* Vol. 1 of *The Cambridge History of the Bible.* Cambridge: Cambridge University Press, 1970.
Boring, M. Eugene, Klaus Berger, and Carsten Colpe. *Hellenistic Commentary to the New Testament.* Nashville: Abingdon, 1995.

Crossan, John Dominic, and Jonathan L. Reed. *Excavating Jesus: Beneath the Stones, Behind the Texts.* London: SPCK, 2001.

Freedman, D. N., ed. *Anchor Bible Dictionary.* 6 vols. New York: Doubleday, 1992.

Freyne, Sean. *Galilee, from Alexander the Great to Hadrian, 323 B.C.E. to 135 C.E.: A Study of Second Temple Judaism.* Edinburgh: T&T Clark, 1998.

Garnsey, Peter, and Richard Saller. *The Roman Empire: Economy, Society and Culture.* Berkeley and Los Angeles: University of California Press, 1987.

Grabbe, Lester L. *Judaism from Cyrus to Hadrian.* 2 vols. Minneapolis: Fortress, 1992.

Grant, Robert M. *From Augustus to Constantine: The Rise and Triumph of Christianity in the Roman World.* San Francisco: Harper & Row, 1970.

Hanson, K. C., and Douglas E. Oakman. *Palestine in the Time of Jesus: Social Structures and Social Conflicts.* Minneapolis: Fortress Press, 1998.

Lewis, Naphtali, and Meyer Reinhold. *Roman Civilization.* 2 vols. 3d ed. New York: Columbia University Press, 1990.

McDonald, Lee Martin. *The Formation of the Christian Biblical Canon.* Rev. and enl. ed. Peabody, Mass.: Hendrickson 1995.

Meeks, Wayne, ed. The Library of Early Christianity. Philadelphia: Westminster Press, 1986–1987. This is an eight-volume set by various experts on aspects of the environment in which Christianity was born.

Meyers, Eric M., ed. *Galilee through the Centuries: Confluence of Cultures.* Winona Lake: Eisenbrauns, 1999.

Potter, D. S., and D. J. Mattingly, eds. *Life, Death, and Entertainment in the Roman Empire.* Ann Arbor: University of Michigan Press, 1998.

Shanks, Hershel, ed. *Christianity and Rabbinic Judaism: A Parallel History of Their Origins and Early Development.* Washington: Biblical Archaeology Society, 1992.

Shelton, Jo-Ann. *As the Romans Did: A Sourcebook on Roman Social History.* Oxford: Oxford University Press, 1988.

Theissen, Gerd. *The Shadow of the Galilean.* Philadelphia: Fortress, 1987.

Whittaker, Molly. *Jews and Christians: Graeco-Roman Views.* Cambridge: Cambridge University Press, 1984.

Wilken, Robert M. *The Christians As the Romans Saw Them.* New Haven: Yale University Press, 1984.

EARLY

CHRISTIAN

READER

THE LETTERS OF PAUL

PAUL'S LETTERS ARE THE EARLIEST known Christian writings. He was a leading missionary for the fledgling church from about 35 to 60 C.E. His letters are mainly addressed to the new Christian groups he established in the major cities of the eastern Mediterranean. Because they are the only documents that certainly come from the first Christian generation, his letters are of paramount importance for the study of Christian beginnings. It is especially fortunate for historians that he wrote letters and not essays, for their conversational nature illuminates not only Paul's thinking but also the viewpoints of the *other* first-generation Christians with whom Paul was in dialogue. Only in the last two centuries, however, have scholars really begun to read the letters in this way.

For most of their two-thousand-year history, Paul's writings were interpreted by virtue of their honored place in the Christian canon. Like other biblical documents, they were read as data for systematic theology, so that every statement became a timeless truth. Augustine, for example, took *Rom.* 5:12–21 as a basis for his doctrine of "original sin" without noticing that Paul never invokes such a doctrine elsewhere in his letters; this idea was arguably not even part of Paul's characteristic preaching. Or again, Augustine and Calvin drew an elaborate doctrine of "predestination" from *Romans* 9–11 without worrying much about the situation in which Paul wrote these paragraphs, how they functioned in the overall argument of *Romans,* or whether *Romans* itself was typical of Paul's preaching. That Paul's writings were real letters, written for particular situations in the first-generation church, was largely forgotten. Scholars entered the nineteenth century absorbed primarily with the content (or "what?") of Paul's letters as theological statements. It took the nineteenth and twentieth centuries to raise the equally important questions: Who really wrote the letters? When? Why? How? Five modern developments since that time are especially noteworthy.

The Unity of First-Generation Christianity

First came the work of Ferdinand Christian Baur, who began to teach at Tübingen, Germany, in the 1830s. Because he accepted the view of history formulated by G. W. F. Hegel, Baur was extremely sensitive to apparent conflicts among the NT writings; these antitheses, he thought, were the means by which history progressed. For Baur's interpretation of Paul, two conflicts were crucial. First, he found evidence that the traditional view of a harmonious early church, in which the leaders essentially agreed on the significance of Christ, was mistaken. He argued that Paul's letters revealed serious disagreements with those apostles (especially Peter and James) who wanted Christianity to remain Jewish. This contentious issue of the church's relationship to Judaism, Baur contended, preoccupied earliest Christianity. Another sort of conflict that he noticed was within the group of thirteen letters traditionally ascribed to Paul. The German critic's keen (perhaps overly intuitive) eye found irreconcilable differences of outlook among these letters. Accordingly, he declared only *Romans, 1* and *2 Corinthians,* and *Galatians* to be genuinely Pauline. The others, he claimed, were written in Paul's name by his admirers.

It is a tribute to Baur's insight that, although his Hegelian view of history has few supporters today, and most scholars now accept at least seven of the thirteen letters as authentic, the issues he raised have remained alive. Specialists are still disputing the degree and the possible causes of tension between Peter, Paul, and James. They generally consider *1 Timothy, 2 Timothy,* and *Titus* as non-Pauline, and they continue to debate the authenticity of *Colossians, 2 Thessalonians,* and *Ephesians* (see the introduction to LETTERS ATTRIBUTED TO PAUL).

What's in a Letter?

Still another of Baur's contributions was to focus attention on the occasion and purpose of each letter. Adolf Deissmann pursued this problem more thoroughly toward the end of the nineteenth century. One of the great discoveries of Deissmann's day was a cache of thousands of Greek letters, dating from 300 B.C.E. to 300 C.E., which had been preserved in the dry air of Oxyrhynchus in Egypt. These letters were generally brief, some written on broken pieces of pottery or wood, and they concerned everyday affairs—bills, receipts, friendly notes, and business arrangements. Deissmann's great contribution was to compare Paul's letters with this everyday correspondence. He reached three important conclusions.

He noted, first, that Paul used much the same style of Greek (*koinē* or "common" Greek) that was current among ordinary people in his day. Paul wrote the Greek of the street, used by merchants and businessmen throughout the Roman empire. Before Deissmann's time, Paul's letters could be compared only to the writings of upper-class composers who tended to use an old-fashioned "high" style. Scholars had concluded that NT Greek was unique; some even suggested that this was because of its inspired character. But the discovery of the "nonliterary papyri," as the ancient letters became known, enabled Deissmann to show that Paul wrote the language of the ordinary person.

Deissmann further observed that even the briefest letters discovered in Egypt followed a regular pattern, with a stylized opening, body, and closing. But the same pattern, he showed, was evident in Paul's letters. This meant that Paul's letters were genuine pieces of correspondence, not carefully planned literary productions. Although some famous writers of the ancient world, such as Cicero, did write literary epistles, designed for recital and publication as *belles lettres,* Paul's letters were not of this sort. They were conversational exchanges focused on the particular situation at hand.

Deissmann drew from this observation the consequence that readers should not expect the kind of consistency from Paul's letters that they find in theological essays. Though he had often been treated as the church's first theologian, Paul was in fact responding quickly and spontaneously to crises among his followers. The interpreter must, therefore, give full weight to the situation in which each letter was written and look for the distinctive features of each; one cannot simply lump them all together as if they were a single text.

Although scholars have since found that Deissmann overstated certain points— for example, we have not yet discovered *exact* parallels of Paul's letters in length— his legacy is a foundation of current Pauline studies. Treating Paul's writings as real letters opens our imagination to consider what was going on the other side of the letter: Who were Paul's conversation partners (friends or foes?) and what were they saying? Often, Paul leaves enough clues, sometimes even quoting his addressees (*1 Cor.* 8:1, 4), that we can reconstruct the others' positions with some confidence. And this exercise allows us to discover the views of Christians whose writings were not preserved.

Did Paul's Thinking Change?

Deissmann's insistence on reading each letter as a response to a unique situation led to a third major development: the recognition that Paul might have changed his views over time as a result of various crises in his life. The traditional view, in treating Paul's writings as a body of revealed truth, excluded the possibility of real shifts in his thinking. Truth, after all, does not change. But is it merely coincidence that Paul's earliest letters (*1 Thessalonians* and *1 Corinthians*) seem to stress the imminence of Jesus' return, during Paul's lifetime, while his later letters (*Philippians; 2 Corinthians*) raise the possibility of his own death? Many interpreters, from A. Sabatier in the nineteenth century to C. H. Dodd, C. H. Buck, G. Taylor, J. C. Hurd, and G. Lüdemann in recent years, have found significant lines of development in Paul's thinking. These include Paul's views on the time of Jesus' return relative to his own life, the nature of salvation in Christ, and the relationship between his gospel and Judaism. Those who find such developments insist that proper interpretation of Paul requires careful attention to the chronology of his life and letters.

PAUL'S CAREER IN *ACTS* AND IN HIS LETTERS

<table>
<tr><td align="center">ACTS</td><td align="center">THE LETTERS</td></tr>
</table>

Preaching

In normal fashion for Hellenistic history-writing, all the speeches reflect the author's perspective. E.g., in *Acts* 13:17–41, the first section (13:17–25) is like Stephen's earlier speech (7:1–43, a survey of Israel's history). The second part (13:26–41) is like Peter's sermons at 2:14–36 and 3:12–26. They all use the same themes and vocabulary: ignorance of the Jewish leaders in killing Jesus; Christ predestined to suffer; Christ as the "holy one"; Christ as David's descendant; citation of *Pss.* 2:7; 16:9; "forgiveness of sins" offered through Christ (see *Luke* 1:77; 3:3; 24:47; *Acts* 2:38; 5:31; 10:43; 13:38; 26:18); opening with Greek vocative "Men . . ." (1:11, 16; 2:14, 22; 3:12; 5:35; 7:2; 13:26; 15:7; 21:28; 22:1; 23:1).

Key terms include: in Christ; flesh/spirit; this present age/world; righteousness through faith; works of the law; sin (singular, as a power).

Paul connects faith in Christ with Abraham. He usually bypasses Moses and subsequent Jewish history as an aberration from the "promise."

Paul does not use the term "forgiveness of sins" in his (undisputed) letters, though it is characteristic of *Luke-Acts'* vocabulary.

Missionary Goals, Relation to Judaism

Paul always begins his preaching in the Jewish synagogue (13:14; 14:1; 17:1–4, 10; 19:8). He goes to the Gentiles only by default, when rejected by Jews (18:6). He is a Pharisee and strictly obeys the law, even as a Christian (16:1–4; 21:22–26; 24:14). He wants to demonstrate to Jews that Jesus is the Messiah (13:13ff.; 17:2; 18:5; 19:8). Many Gentiles are converted through Paul's preaching, but this happens in spite of his intention, which is to preach to Jews.

Paul declares that the law of Moses had a strictly limited purpose, and was nullified with the coming of Christ (*Gal.* 3:10–21). He places his life "in Judaism" and "under the law" in the past (*Gal.* 1:13). From the beginning, Paul was chosen to be apostle to the Gentiles (*Gal.* 1:15–16). A clear division of labor was understood, in which Paul preached to Gentiles and Peter to Jews (*Gal.* 2:7–10).

Apostleship

"Apostle" is an extremely important office. There are only twelve apostles in the proper sense. Qualifications are spelled out in 1:15–26, where a replacement is sought for Judas Iscariot. They must have been with Christ from his immersion by John until his ascension into heaven. The Twelve are the central authority of the young church, and all major decisions are made by them. Paul and Barnabas are not apostles with the Twelve, but only missionaries sent out under their authority (through the elders of Antioch).

Paul's self-understanding as an apostle is central to his preaching (see his letter openings). He claims full rights as an apostle, on the same level as the Twelve (*1 Corinthians* 9, 15; *2 Corinthians* 10–13) because he was granted a special resurrection appearance of the risen Jesus (*1 Cor.* 9:1; 15:8–11). His apostleship is not derivative, but was granted directly by divine revelation (*Gal.* 1:1, 12, 17). He knows, however, that many do not recognize his apostleship (*1 Cor.* 9:2; *2 Cor.* 12:12).

Conversion and First Jerusalem Visit

Paul is converted in Damascus (9:10–18). He begins preaching within days (9:20) but quickly runs into trouble with the Jews there, so he must escape to Jerusalem (9:23–26). In Jerusalem, he is introduced to "the apostles." He begins to travel with them, "preaching boldly" (9:29), until this public activity lands him in further trouble and he flees to Tarsus (9:30).

Paul is converted in Damascus, then immediately goes off to Arabia (*Gal.* 1:16), then back to Damascus. Only after three years does he first visit Jerusalem (*Gal.* 1:18). Even then, it is a short (two-week), private visit with Peter. He saw none of the other apostles, but did meet James (*Gal.* 1:18–19). Then he went off to Syria and Cilicia.

Later Visits to Jerusalem

Acts has Paul in Jerusalem five times: (1) soon after conversion, public visit (9:20); (2) famine visit soon thereafter (11:29; 12:25); (3) apostolic council, on Gentiles, resulting in several conditions for Gentile converts (ch. 15); (4) greeting the church (18:22); (5) final visit, with collection, leading to arrest and transfer to Rome (21; 24:17).

In *Galatians* 1–2, Paul insists that he has so far made only these visits to Jerusalem: (1) three years after conversion, private visit; (2) eleven or fourteen years after that, to settle the question of the Gentile Christians, resulting in a decision to take up an offering for Jerusalem (2:10; *1 Cor.* 16:4; *2 Corinthians* 8–9; *Rom.* 15:25–29), but no other conditions; so he expects: (3) a visit to convey the offering, which may bring trouble (*Rom.* 15:30–32).

Acts as a Source for the Chronology of Paul's Career

The effort to reconstruct Paul's chronology has led, further, to scholarly caution in using the book known as *Acts*. Since more than half of *Acts* is devoted to telling the story of Paul's career, from his conversion (ch. 9) through his missionary preaching to his final arrest (chs. 21–28), this book was traditionally welcomed as the key to charting the apostle's career. But when commentators began to scrutinize the details that Paul himself gives about his life, it soon became clear that his account could not easily be aligned with the picture offered in *Acts*.

John Knox, in particular, has pointed out that Paul's relationship to Jerusalem, his missionary goals, and the content of his preaching appear quite differently in the two sources. Consider the chart on the facing page.

In the face of such discrepancies, Knox argued that the interpreter must concede absolute priority to Paul's letters, since they are a primary source for Paul; *Acts* is, historiographically speaking, a secondary source, written by someone else a generation after Paul's time. Although some scholars have defended the trustworthiness of *Acts,* few today would *begin* a study of Paul with that book. Everyone realizes that Paul's own letters are the key to understanding him, even if *Acts* may be cautiously used in a supplementary way.

The Social Context of Paul's Preaching

Arguably the most important shift in interpreting Paul has come in the last two or three decades, with the growth of social-historical interest in Paul's world. "Social history" is an umbrella term that covers a wide range of problems related to the nitty-gritty details of human life. What did people eat? How did they study and speak and write? What were their assumptions about social roles (of males, females, children)? What sorts of groups existed among which social classes, and how were they organized? Until this time, even the most historically astute Pauline scholars had focused on the apostle's *ideas:* unwittingly assuming that his abstracted theology was the most important thing about him. In keeping with shifts in other academic disciplines, however, NT scholars have now begun to ask more about Paul's real social environment. Because words have meaning only in real-life contexts, those contexts must be recovered if we are to understand Paul.

The value of social-historical questions will be obvious. Given the standard types of social groups in antiquity—religious, professional, and burial societies, philosophical schools, ethnic-religious groups—how would outsiders view Pauline (Gentile) Christianity? Why does Paul defend himself against charges that were otherwise leveled at crooked philosophers (*1 Thess.* 2:3–12)? Was he seen, or did he present himself, as a philosopher? What were philosophers and philosophical schools like in the first century? How were Paul's followers organized socially? Who made decisions and how were policies carried out? If Paul's groups included those wealthy enough to own slaves, and to host large groups in their homes, how can we explain Paul's emphasis on their low status? If women had significant leadership functions, how can we explain a directive that women keep silent? If Paul writes for Gentiles, why does he bother to speak disparagingly of "the Jews" (*1 Thess.* 2:14)? In general, what were the conventions of writing in Paul's day, and what would the rhetorical effect of his letters, read aloud, have been? Recovering these real events in our imagination is a different kind of analysis from studying Paul's ideas with concordances and encyclopedias. How were Jewish communities constituted in the cities of the eastern Mediterranean, and what would it mean practically for Gentile Christians to "judaize" (*Gal.* 2:14)? What were Paul's conditions when he was "in chains"? What sort of prison should we envision him in (certainly not a modern penitentiary), and how might his conditions explain the language of *Philippians* or *Philemon*? Within the pervasive ancient networks of "patrons" and "clients," how should we understand Paul's social obligations, his self-understanding as a leader, his opponents' actions within his groups, and perhaps even the language (such as "Lord") that he uses of Christ? This sort of question effectively prevents us from abstracting every statement of Paul's as a theological position, and requires us instead to understand him within the real world of antiquity.

Recognition of rhetorically and socially conditioned features in Paul's letters has both negative and positive results. Negatively, it discourages us from treating some of his statements as purely theological propositions. For example, Paul's language about "edification" of the church may be not so much ponderously considered doctrine as a passing allusion to the major construction efforts ongoing in Corinth at the time. His dismissal of rhetoric (*1 Corinthians* 1–4), rather than being taken at face value, should perhaps be seen as itself a devastating rhetorical weapon, such as other masters of the art also used. And Paul may have intended it not as a universally true position but as a particular challenge to one competing teacher—a gifted orator. A barrage of scripture citations for Paul's Gentile hearers (*Galatians* 3–4) might have been intended to create a certain *aural effect* more than to reveal Paul's *theory* of scriptural interpretation. Positively, social history requires that we understand "saint" Paul's ideas such that they have legs and feet, in a way that would have made them intelligible to real people of the first century.

The Search for the "Center" of Paul's Thinking

What, then, was Paul all about? What was the message that he carried to the cities of the eastern Mediterranean? Answers to these questions have varied with the methods used to study Paul. For example, the canonical arrangement of Paul's letters, with *Romans* at its head, implies that this long letter is the gateway to the others, the fullest expression of Paul's thought. Consequently, many scholars take the apparently central themes of *Romans*, such as justification by faith in Christ and not by law, or union with Christ in death and resurrection, as the core of Paul's theology. The great Protestant thinkers have all had a particular fascination with the language of "righteousness (or justification) by faith" in *Romans,* and the influence of this tradition remains strong today.

Once interpreters began to take seriously the individual situation of each letter, however, they realized that "righteousness by faith" was not a prominent concern in most of Paul's letters: *1 Thessalonians, 1 Corinthians,* and *Philemon* do not discuss it at all (nor do *Colossians* and *Ephesians*); in *Philippians* and *2 Corinthians* the language of righteousness is incidental. It is particularly telling, scholars noted, that righteousness language is prominent only where Paul is in dialogue with Jewish perspectives. Against a claim that righteousness involves obedience to divine law, Paul argues for a new kind of righteousness, in Christ, apart from the law (*Rom.* 3:21). So the theme of righteousness by faith was perhaps not part of his essential message to Gentiles (who were not predisposed to observe Jewish law in the first place, and so might not have understood it), but was rather a later defensive statement against the claims of some who insisted on Torah observance.

If we concede that Paul's letters were written in different social situations, how are we to discover the center of Paul's thought, or indeed whether it has a center? A strictly logical approach is to look for the one fundamental position on which others are based. What is the most basic premise on which Paul depends for his claims? When we adopt this logical criterion, interestingly enough, righteousness by faith appears to be a *consequence* of Paul's thinking rather than a basis for it. Several scholars have observed that Paul grounds key arguments, rather, in the believer's union with Christ in death and resurrection. It is this union with Christ that explains Christian baptism (*Rom.* 6:4–6), constitutes his followers as a single "body" (*1 Cor.* 12:12–13), makes one dead to the world and to the law (*2 Cor.* 5:14–15; *Gal.* 2:19–20; *Rom.* 7:1–6), assures participation in his resurrection (*1 Thess.* 4:15–16; *1 Cor.* 15:20), and prevents other unions—with prostitutes (*1 Cor.* 6:15–17) or with demons (*1 Cor.* 10:20–21). Since Paul invokes the idea of union with Christ in all his letters, to explain quite different aspects of his teaching, many experts would consider this theme the heart of his theology. Jesus' death and resurrection mysteriously provide an opportunity for others to die to the world and rise to new life as a new creation.

Some commentators object that this account underestimates the roles of conceptual development and the particular situations in Paul's life. If it is true that some lines of his thought evolved over time, then it becomes essential to read his letters in their proper order. On this view, the most basic features of Paul's thinking would be those that he articulated at the beginning of his mission, before he became embroiled in intramural controversies—which might have colored the language of his later correspondence. Thus *1 Thessalonians* takes on special importance: most count it as the first of Paul's letters, and it is the only one that does not confront serious in-house differences. Paul's opposition is mainly external (2:1–16). In this correspondence, Paul and his followers seem preoccupied with the imminence of Jesus' return. He has convinced them that the risen Christ is about to descend from heaven, to rescue the faithful before divine wrath explodes (1:9–10).

This short letter affords many clues that the Thessalonians were already impatient about the delay of Christ's return, so that even the death of some believers before the end is cause for alarm (4:13).

With the "apocalyptic" theology of *1 Thessalonians* as a base, one might then understand Paul's development along the following lines. First, in *1 Corinthians* he confronts an alternative understanding of Christianity that sees Jesus as bringer of spiritual wisdom and knowledge. Perhaps influenced by stories of Jesus' proclamation of the present reality of the reign of God, these Christians were not attracted by a hope for the future alone. For them, the decisive moment in Christian experience was past: thanks to the work of Christ, one was *already* filled, happy, and free (*1 Cor.* 4:8–13). Against such a position, Paul relentlessly insists that full salvation was still in the future and dependent on Jesus' return; the present is a time of restraint, suffering, and personal sacrifice. This early conflict in Corinth then yielded ground to an even greater challenge. Paul's groups were increasingly attracted by those who saw commitment to Jesus as inextricably tied to Jewish life. Whether those teachers were themselves Jews by birth or Gentile converts to Judaism, they apparently contended that following Jesus authentically required one to become Jewish: to conform one's life to the covenant observed by Jews. If this problem was still peripheral when Paul wrote *Philippians* 3, it had become quite serious by the time that he composed *2 Corinthians* 3, 10–13. When he wrote to the *Galatians* he had to pull out all the stops to try to prevent them from adopting "Judean" ways. In the course of his career, however, Paul came to accept that Jesus' return might be indefinitely delayed well beyond his own death and so, paradoxically, began to move toward his former opponents' stress on the present benefits of salvation.

A perennial issue in the effort to find Paul's central views is his relationship to Judaism. Traditional Judaism and Christianity both saw him as someone who had thoroughly repudiated his native tradition for Christianity. But the question has become enormously complicated by recent study. First, most historians of the period would say that "Judaism" was not the homogeneous entity that earlier scholars assumed. We are discovering evidence for an array of Jewish groups, some of which may have reinterpreted circumcision and other aspects of the law much as Paul did. Second, if some of Paul's statements indicate his forthright repudiation of the Mosaic Torah, others (especially in *Romans*) show him eager to be thought of as faithful to his Jewish heritage. He also quotes Jewish scripture as an authority throughout his letters, and he continues to celebrate major Jewish festivals in some way. Third, it is not clear what it would mean in social terms for Paul to abandon "Judeanism" (Gk *Ioudaismos*), since that was not merely a religion but an ethnic-social category. Would he visit the synagogue or stay in the Jewish quarter when he visited a city? In asking whether Paul remained a Jew, one must deal with the thorny issues: (a) Could he have ceased to be a Jew (= "Judean") even if he had wanted to? (b) What would he have had to do to place himself beyond the pale of a diverse Judaism? (c) Are we asking about his personal views or his appearance to outsiders and status under law? (d) Where among the many statements in his letters do we find his *real* views about Judaism?

Debate on the center of Paul's thought continues. Interpreters must decide which letters are genuinely Pauline and, within each letter, which statements are central and which ones peripheral. Acceptance of *2 Thessalonians* as Paul's, for instance, might give more weight to an apocalyptic interpretation; acceptance of *Colossians* or *Ephesians* might support the union-with-Christ position. Or, developmentalists might place *2 Thessalonians* at the very beginning and argue that Paul's outlook moved one hundred eighty degrees from there to the irenic mysticism of *Ephesians.*

The net effect of these modern developments has been to render Paul an authentic human being. He wrote his letters in response to pressing needs in his newly founded churches. He often became angry with other Christians, sometimes denounced them with curses, even used four-letter words and crude imagery. But in the process, out of the urgency and conflict of his own life situations he managed to say some things that have resonated powerfully with many generations of Christians since his time.

For Further Reading

Baur, Ferdinand Christian. *Paul, the Apostle of Jesus Christ.* Translated by A. Menzies. 2 vols. London: Williams & Norgate, 1873–1875. Repr., 2 vols. in 1, Peabody, Mass.: Hendrickson, 2003.

Beker, J. Christiaan. *The Triumph of God: The Essence of Paul's Thought.* Translated by Loren T. Stuckenbruck. Minneapolis: Fortress, 1990.

Buck, Charles H., and Greer Taylor. *Saint Paul: A Study of the Development of His Thought.* New York: Scribners, 1969.

Dunn, J. D. G. *The Theology of Paul the Apostle.* Grand Rapids: Eerdmans, 1998.

Gager, John G. *Kingdom and Community: The Social World of Early Christianity.* Englewood Cliffs, N.J.: Prentice-Hall, 1975.

Hurd, John Coolidge Jr. *The Origin of I Corinthians.* Macon, Ga.: Mercer University Press, 1983.

Knox, John. *Chapters in a Life of Paul.* Nashville: Abingdon, 1950.

Lüdemann, Gerd. *Opposition to Paul in Jewish Christianity.* Translated by M. Eugene Boring. Minneapolis: Fortress, 1989.

Malherbe, Abraham. *Paul and the Popular Philosophers.* Minneapolis: Fortress, 1989.

Meeks, Wayne. *The First Urban Christians: The Social World of the Apostle Paul.* New Haven: Yale University Press, 1983.

Räisänen, Heikki. *Paul and the Law.* Philadelphia: Fortress, 1983.

Roetzel, Calvin. *The Letters of Paul: Conversations in Context.* 4th ed. Louisville: Westminster John Knox, 1998.

Sanders, E. P. *Paul.* Oxford: Oxford University Press, 1991.

———. *Paul and Palestinian Judaism: A Comparison of Patterns of Religion.* Philadelphia: Fortress, 1977.

Schweitzer, Albert. *The Mysticism of Paul the Apostle.* Translated by W. Montgomery. London: Adam and Charles Black, 1931.

Segal, Alan F. *Paul the Convert: The Apostolate and Apostasy of Saul the Pharisee.* New Haven: Yale University Press, 1990.

Stowers, Stanley K. *Letter-Writing in Greco-Roman Antiquity.* Philadelphia: Westminster, 1986.

Westerholm, Stephen. *Israel's Law and the Church's Faith: Paul and His Recent Interpreters.* Grand Rapids: Eerdmans, 1988.

To the Assembly of the Thessalonians

1 THESSALONIANS

Setting and Purpose

From 148 B.C.E., Thessalonica served as the capital city of Macedonia, the Roman province covering the northern part of Greece. It was an old and famous city by Paul's time, having come to prominence long before the Romans came on the scene. In about 315 B.C.E. one of Alexander the Great's successors, Cassander, took over the favorably situated village of Therma and renamed it after his wife and Alexander's sister *(Thessalonikē)*. Much later this increasingly prosperous city had served as a "second Rome" and home-in-exile of part of the Roman senate, in the civil war between Pompey and Julius Caesar (49 B.C.E.).

Although Macedonia was mainly a rural province with small towns scattered over a large area, the city of Thessalonica had become a busy center of trade in Paul's day. Situated at the juncture of the major east-west highway (*Via Egnatia* or Egnatian Road) with two north-south highways, it also enjoyed one of the best harbors in the Aegean Sea. So it was a bustling city, full of merchants and immigrants who brought their native cultures with them. Alongside the Roman imperial cult and worship of the traditional Greek gods Zeus, Apollo, Aphrodite, Castor and Pollux, and Dionysus, Egyptian religion also flourished (honoring Isis, Osiris, and Serapis) and there was a significant Jewish presence.

Thessalonica was not the first city Paul visited on his Christian mission. Since he would have needed to cross Asia Minor (modern Turkey) to reach Greece by land from Syria, where he had become a follower of Jesus, it is likely that he stopped in such cities as Ephesus before reaching Greece. Indeed the much later book of *Acts* (chs. 13–20) offers a fairly detailed itinerary within Asia Minor, but because it is difficult to square with Paul's letters it should not be relied upon too heavily.

In any case, the letter itself provides our best clues about Paul's situation at the time of writing. Before reaching Thessalonica he, Silvanus, and Timothy brought their special "announcement" *(euangelion)* about Jesus to the previous major stop on the highway, the Roman colony of Philippi. Although they established some believers there (see *Phil.* 4:15–16), they also faced considerable opposition from the townspeople, to the point of outright humiliation (*1 Thess.* 2:1–2); that abuse may have been the reason they left town. Nevertheless, the trio persevered and brought their announcement also to the people of Thessalonica (1:9), where too they established a group of "trusters" in the face of massive antagonism from others (1:6; 2:2). Once again they left town, perhaps under compulsion, and headed south toward Athens (3:1). After some time, however, fearing that the ongoing antagonism of the Thessalonians' compatriots (2:14) would sway these new converts to abandon their commitment, Paul asked Timothy to go back to them, both to ascertain their state and to strengthen their trust (3:2, 5).

The occasion of the letter, then, is essentially this: Timothy has now returned to Paul and Silvanus, and has brought them the good "announcement" that the Thessalonians have remained faithful to his announcement (3:6–10). So this brief letter contains a great deal of thanksgiving material. Paul writes to express his joy at their perseverance (1:2–10; 3:6–13).

But there is more to it than that. Timothy returns not only with good news, but also with a letter (or perhaps an oral report) from the Thessalonians containing certain questions for Paul. Among their concerns were, at a minimum, the perceived delay of Jesus' return from heaven and Paul's own failure to visit them again. While expressing his thanksgiving for their perseverance, therefore, Paul must deal with these issues. If we can understand better their questions and the reasons for the opposition to Paul in Thessalonica, we might hope for a clearer perception of what Paul had taught in this major city.

Overview and Major Themes

The letter offers us two ways of recovering what Paul taught in Thessalonica, his special "announcement." First, he makes several direct references to it. Second, from his responses to the Thessalonians' questions, we can work backward to the questions themselves and from there to Paul's original teaching.

His most telling direct statements are in 1:6–10; 2:19; 3:13; 4:1–8; and the concluding note in 5:23. In the first of these, Paul says that he made the radical demand that the Thessalonians abandon their native traditions—"turn from idols"—to serve the one true God, and to wait for God's son from heaven. This son of God is one Jesus, whom God raised from the dead and who will soon return to rescue or evacuate those who trust this announcement from the anger of God. They should wait for this event in expectant trust. The second, third, and fifth notices reiterate the imminence of Jesus' return, along with the hope that those who have believed at Thessalonica will be found "blameless" when the event occurs. The fourth passage clarifies further what is meant by blamelessness: Paul evidently emphasized sexual purity, controlling one's "vessel" and avoiding lust (4:3–5), for such activity is especially subject to punishment when Jesus returns (4:6).

In 4:9 to 5:11, Paul responds to three questions. We know this because he introduces each one with the Greek phrase *peri . . . de*, or "now concerning/about" (4:9, 13; 5:1). That phrase is a formula for responding to questions, as *1 Cor.* 7:1, 25; 8:1;

12:1 and other ancient Greek letters make clear. That is why in two of the three cases here, Paul dismisses the issue as soon as he raises it with the remark that he does not need to say anything more about it. These are responses to queries, not his own new proposals. What, then, were the issues on the minds of the Thessalonians?

The only question to which Paul responds with substantially new information is the second one, which concerns those who die before Jesus returns. Paul's answer of assurance (4:13–18), that the dead "in Christ" will not suffer disadvantage, confirms our understanding from his direct statements: he had left the impression that Jesus' return was extremely near. When someone in the group dies or perhaps becomes sick, the group becomes concerned at the delay of Jesus' return. Even now Paul speaks optimistically: "*we* who are alive, who are left until the coming of the Lord" (4:15, 17). That the Thessalonians were a bit troubled by the delay is also suggested by their third question (5:1), which seems merely to have been: *When* will it happen? Their first question, about the degree to which they needed to practice a heroic degree of brotherly love (4:9), perhaps also stemmed from their impatience with the wait for salvation.

So the combined evidence of *1 Thessalonians* indicates that Paul had left the new Christians in Thessalonica and elsewhere with the fervent hope that the risen Jesus would come back very soon to rescue them. This was his "announcement" (NRSV "gospel," 1:6; 2:2; 3:2), to which they responded with trust (NRSV "faith"). Except for his focus on Jesus as savior, much of his language is typical of the apocalyptic worldview that flourished in some Jewish circles of the time: a special truth revealed to a few faithful people about the imminent end of the age; a sharp distinction between the children of light, who will be saved, and the children of darkness, who will perish (5:4–7); and the activities of archdemons and archangels, who do constant battle for human souls (2:18; 3:5; 4:16).

With this understanding of Paul's announcement, we can better appreciate the nature of the opposition, which Paul recalls in 2:3–20. There he defends his entourage against very specific charges: falsehood (NRSV "deceit"), sexual immorality ("impure motives"), and deceit ("trickery"—2:3); trying to please people rather than speaking the truth (2:4); flattery and greed (2:5). He is also sensitive to the charge that he has left these believers in the lurch by not returning (2:17–18). It is unlikely that Paul's converts were making these accusations, or they would not have remained within him. The context (note the "for" following mention of the opposition in 2:2–3) suggests that these charges were the basis of the outsiders' antagonism. But the fact that Paul mounts such a sustained response invites the suspicion that his followers were not entirely immune to the outsiders' claims. In particular, his prolonged absence appears to have affected the believers. He must defend his reputation against both outsiders' charges and insiders' fears.

In other literature of the period, interestingly enough, we see similar accusations routinely made of wandering philosophers: they come into town, teach whatever nonsense will earn them some money—usually it requires flattery of their gullible hearers—and then leave town never to be seen again (Dio of Prusa,

Discourses 32.9). They might also use their influence for sexual advantage. Such impressions of wandering philosophers had been traditional for a long time in Paul's world, beginning with Plato's attack on the "sophists" of fifth-century B.C.E. Athens, who made their living teaching philosophical and moral relativism.

Paul responds to these stock charges by presenting himself in terms reminiscent of the ideal philosopher (Dio of Prusa, *Discourses* 32.11–12). Like Socrates of old, he protests that he cannot be sophistlike because he has taken no money for his teaching (2:9). We may note, however, that his opponents might be forgiven for supposing that Paul had taken money, since he had in fact accepted funds, even while in Thessalonica, from Philippi—as he later reveals (*Phil.* 4:15). In his defense, Paul also stresses his caring, gentle, and genuine concern for these followers. He insists that he has repeatedly tried to visit them personally, but has been prevented by Satan from doing so (2:17–19); he will nonetheless keep trying (3:10).

What was there in Paul's announcement that might have sounded like flattery and falsehood? Part of our problem as modern readers is that Christian teaching is so established in Western culture—indeed, it has for a long time been part of the Western establishment—that we have a hard time imagining how it sounded to the first people who heard about it. Imagine how might you feel, though, if a visitor to your town began to insist that someone who had recently been executed by the authorities in (say) Libya, was really God's son; he had risen from the dead and gone to heaven, from where he would soon return to rescue his followers from impending divine wrath. You must therefore give up your current lifestyle, including your Western family and religious traditions, trust this new teaching, and await his return. If you do this, you and a small group of believers will be saved, though everyone else will perish. Would you not think that this was nonsensical teaching, surely created for the profit of some cult leaders?

The second-century neo-Platonist philosopher Celsus ridiculed Christian teaching, which by his time was gaining some ground, in just these terms: "It is also foolish of them to think that when God, like a cook, applies fire, all the rest of mankind will be baked through and through, but they alone will survive."[1] He almost seems to be giving a caricature of Paul's teaching about Jesus when he writes:

> There are many nameless men who . . . become excited forsooth as if uttering an oracle. The formula that usually springs to their lips is: "I am God or Son of God or Holy Spirit. I have come, for the world is perishing and you, O men, are destroyed because of your sins. But I wish to save you and you shall see me again returning with heavenly power. Happy is he who has embraced my cult now, but on all other men and cities and countries I will hurl eternal fire."[2]

It was an easy assumption that preachers of such "flattering" messages were motivated by personal gain. So these charges may well have been the basis of the "great opposition" that Paul and his companions faced.

---

[1] Quoted by Origen in his *Against Celsus* 5.14; trans. Whittaker, 182–83.
[2] From Origen, *Against Celsus* 7.9; trans. Whittaker, 184.

Date

Evidence that *1 Thessalonians* is Paul's earliest letter is as follows. We have seen that, according to 2:1–2, Paul was beginning his missionary efforts in Greece. He and Silvanus have recently arrived in Achaia, the southern province that was home to Athens and Corinth. He enthusiastically reports that some people in Achaia have already heard of the Thessalonians' conversion (1:6–8).

Paul's other genuine letters seem to have been written after *1 Thessalonians.* The extensive Corinthian correspondence *(1* and *2 Corinthians),* for example, presupposes the settled existence of a Christian group in Corinth. But since Paul has only recently arrived in that southern region when he writes *1 Thessalonians,* the Corinthian letters must come later. *Philippians,* even if it is a composite letter (see the introduction to that letter), shows a mature Paul far removed from his founding visit (*Phil.* 4:15). *Galatians* has him reflecting on at least fifteen years of preaching to the Gentiles (*Gal.* 2:1–2). And *Romans* comes near the end of Paul's mission in the eastern Mediterranean (*Rom.* 15:19, 23). Only *Philemon* is difficult to place, but since Paul was in prison when he wrote it, most scholars would put it later than *1 Thessalonians.* Some who consider *2 Thessalonians* an authentic Pauline letter date it earlier than *1 Thessalonians* (see the introduction to *2 Thessalonians*), but that is a minority position.

We cannot yet determine the actual year in which Paul wrote *1 Thessalonians.* If he became a follower of Jesus in the mid-30s and was arrested in Jerusalem in the mid- to late 50s, when Antonius Felix was procurator (52–59 C.E.? see *Acts* 23:24), then we have a span of little more than twenty years for Paul's entire missionary career. Now *Acts* 18:12 seems to assert that Paul first visited Corinth when Junius Gallio was proconsul of Achaia. And a fragmentary inscription discovered in Corinth puts Gallio's proconsulship in 51/52. Since Paul wrote *1 Thessalonians* from the vicinity of Corinth, many scholars have accepted a date between 50 and 52 for this letter. But such a date would squeeze together all of Paul's writings, and the experiences that lie behind them, into a short period of perhaps five to seven years. The difficulties of deriving Paul's biography from *Acts* have already been discussed (see the introduction to THE LETTERS OF PAUL). In this case, the noticeable transition from *Acts* 18:1–11 (Paul's first visit to Corinth) to 18:12 (the reference to Gallio) invites speculation that the author has combined two distinct traditions about Paul's work in Corinth. In that case, Gallio need not have been governor at Paul's *first* visit.

If we were not constrained by the Gallio inscription and *Acts* 18, and we should not be, we might prefer to date *1 Thessalonians* closer to 40 C.E., to allow more time for the many imprisonments, conflicts, illnesses, and other challenges that would shape Paul's later letters. Some have even suggested that his reference in this letter to a decisive punishment of the Jews as a nation (*1 Thess.* 2:16) was occasioned by the Emperor Gaius Caligula's attempt to install his statue in the Jerusalem temple in 38 C.E. All things considered, a date in the 40s, perhaps even early 40s, seems plausible, though many would put it later.

Value and Relation to Other Early Christian Texts

This first glimpse of Paul establishes a framework for interpreting his career and a reference point for subsequent study of early Christianity. He tells Gentiles about Jesus' resurrection and imminent return from heaven. His virtual omission of biblical and Jewish themes (note the absence in this letter of the law and the prophets, Abraham, and Moses), and references to "the Jews" as if they were outsiders (2:13–16), may help to explain some of his later difficulties with Jewish Christianity (*2 Cor.* 10–13, *Philippians* 3, *Galatians*). His apocalyptic urgency may explain, on the other side, his later difficulties with Christians who stressed the present benefits of salvation (*1 Corinthians* 1–4). In subsequent writings, whether consciously or not, Paul will seem to relax his end-time urgency (*Phil.* 1:19–26; *2 Corinthians* 4–5) and he will discuss the biblical, Jewish content of Christian faith (*Galatians, Romans*) in contrast to *1 Thessalonians.* It is an ongoing debate among scholars whether Paul's thinking really changed much over time or whether the apparent changes result from new social and rhetorical situations. Opposition from nonbelievers, such as we see in *1 Thessalonians,* would hound him throughout his career, though internal Christian opposition would become more visible in his letters.

First Thessalonians shows us that Paul's allegiance to Jesus was marked from the beginning by an urgent hope for the new age to be inaugurated by Jesus' return. But already at this early stage, he must confront the challenge posed by the delay of Jesus' return. This tension between hope and delay would continue to shape many strains of Christianity in the second and third generations (see, notably, *2 Pet.* 3:3–7).

For Further Reading

Collins, R. F. *The Birth of the New Testament: The Origin and Development of the First Christian Generation.* New York: Crossroad, 1993.

Jewett, Robert K. *The Thessalonian Correspondence: Pauline Rhetoric and Millenarian Piety.* Philadelphia: Fortress, 1986.

Kloppenborg, John S. "*Philadelphia, Theodidaktos* and the Diosuri: The Rhetorical Situation of 1 Thess. 4:9–12." *New Testament Studies* 39, no. 2 (1993): 265–89.

Malherbe, Abraham J. *The Letters to the Thessalonians: A New Translation with Introduction and Commentary.* Anchor Bible 32B. New York: Doubleday, 2000.

———. *Paul and the Thessalonians: The Philosophic Tradition of Pastoral Care.* Philadelphia: Fortress, 1987.

———. *Paul and the Popular Philosophers.* Minneapolis: Fortress, 1989.

THE FIRST LETTER OF PAUL
TO THE THESSALONIANS

Salutation

1 Paul, Silvanus, and Timothy,
To the church of the Thessalonians in God the
Father and the Lord Jesus Christ:
Grace to you and peace.

The Thessalonians' Faith and Example

2We always give thanks to God for all of you and
mention you in our prayers, constantly 3remem-
bering before our God and Father your work of faith
and labor of love and steadfastness of hope in our
Lord Jesus Christ. 4For we know, brothers and sisters*a* beloved by God, that he has chosen you, 5be-
cause our message of the gospel came to you not in
word only, but also in power and in the Holy Spirit
and with full conviction; just as you know what kind
of persons we proved to be among you for your sake.
6And you became imitators of us and of the Lord, for
in spite of persecution you received the word with
joy inspired by the Holy Spirit, 7so that you became
an example to all the believers in Macedonia and in
Achaia. 8For the word of the Lord has sounded forth
from you not only in Macedonia and Achaia, but in
every place your faith in God has become known, so
that we have no need to speak about it. 9For the
people of those regions*b* report about us what kind
of welcome we had among you, and how you turned
to God from idols, to serve a living and true God,
10and to wait for his Son from heaven, whom he
raised from the dead—Jesus, who rescues us from
the wrath that is coming.

Paul's Ministry in Thessalonica

2 You yourselves know, brothers and sisters,*a* that
our coming to you was not in vain, 2but though
we had already suffered and been shamefully mistreated at Philippi, as you know, we had courage in
our God to declare to you the gospel of God in spite

---

a Gk *brothers*   *b* Gk *For they*

1:1 *Silvanus, and Timothy* Close associates of Paul. On Timothy, see, for example, 3:2, 6; *1 Cor.* 4:17; 16:10; on Silvanus,
also generally thought to be Silas, see, for example, *Acts* 15:22–40; 16:19–29; 17:1–15. *church* The Gk *ekklēsia* was
commonly used of political assemblies, originally the democratic assembly of male citizens in 5th-century B.C.E. Athens.
Paul adapts it to speak of his groups of converts. These assemblies, however, were small enough to meet in private homes.
The modern conception of *ekklēsia* as a large building did not arise for centuries. *Lord Jesus Christ* Paul usually distinguishes between God the Father and the "Lord"—Jesus. See *1 Cor.* 15:20–28. *peace* The common greeting in a Gk letter was a form of the word "grace." Paul typically combines this with the standard Jewish "peace" greeting. **1:2–10** The
first of Paul's letter-thanksgivings, which may extend all the way to 3:13, depending on how one reads it. Most forms of
Greek writing called for a prologue, in which the author would announce the themes of the work following. Although letters
were normally too brief and informal for prologues, Paul deftly uses an opening thanksgiving in most of his letters (*1 Cor.*
1:4–9; *Phil.* 1:3–11; *Phlm.* 4–7; *Rom.* 1:8–15; see *2 Cor.* 1:3–11) to announce his themes. In this case (*1 Thess.* 1:3), Paul mentions faith, love, and hope. As it happens, these words are featured in succession in *1 Thess.* 1:7–8; 2:4, 10, 14; 3:2, 5, 6, 7, 10
(faith); 4:9–12 (love); 4:13–5:11 (hope). All three are reprised in 5:8. **1:3** *faith . . . love . . . hope* These three terms seem
to represent Paul's early preaching about Jesus—his "three-point sermon." See also 5:8; *1 Cor.* 13:13. **1:5** *the gospel* This
is the first appearance in Paul's letters of a term that will be highly significant in his vocabulary. The Gk word *euangelion*
(see English, "evangelist"), "special announcement" or "good news," does not seem to have been widely used in other literature of Paul's day. It appears conspicuously, however, in inscriptions celebrating the achievements of Caesar Augustus, the
"savior" who rid the seas of piracy and brought stability and prosperity to the world. Paul takes over this term as the watchword of his mission. It does not seem to have been used by Jesus. *Luke*, the most historically sensitive gospel, omits the word.
Mark (1:1, 14) uses the term most often, and it is the most Pauline gospel. **1:7** *Macedonia and . . . Achaia* The northern
and southern Roman provinces that covered the bulk of Greece. **1:9** *turned to God from idols* This phrase suggests that
Paul's converts were Gentiles, in keeping with his self-understanding as apostle to Gentiles (*Gal.* 1:16; 2:7–9). But contrast
Acts 17:1–9. **1:10** *rescues* The Gk verb is commonly used for dragging off, carrying away, or evacuating an injured person
from the battlefield. **2:1** *You yourselves know* This phrase appears often in Paul's correspondence when he wishes to refer
back to his founding visit or to an earlier letter. **2:2** *Philippi* A colony established largely for Roman army veterans,
Paul's previous stop on the Egnatian Way. In a culture sensitive to honor and shame, Paul's "shameful mistreatment" could
have included a wide range of behavior—mild social disdain or ostracism, verbal ridicule, physical assault, imprisonment,
and corporal punishment. *the gospel* See note to 1:5.

of great opposition. 3For our appeal does not spring from deceit or impure motives or trickery, 4but just as we have been approved by God to be entrusted with the message of the gospel, even so we speak, not to please mortals, but to please God who tests our hearts. 5As you know and as God is our witness, we never came with words of flattery or with a pretext for greed; 6nor did we seek praise from mortals, whether from you or from others, 7though we might have made demands as apostles of Christ. But we were gentle*c* among you, like a nurse tenderly caring for her own children. 8So deeply do we care for you that we are determined to share with you not only the gospel of God but also our own selves, because you have become very dear to us.

9You remember our labor and toil, brothers and sisters;*d* we worked night and day, so that we might not burden any of you while we proclaimed to you the gospel of God. 10You are witnesses, and God also, how pure, upright, and blameless our conduct was toward you believers. 11As you know, we dealt with each one of you like a father with his children, 12urging and encouraging you and pleading that you lead a life worthy of God, who calls you into his own kingdom and glory.

13We also constantly give thanks to God for this, that when you received the word of God that you heard from us, you accepted it not as a human word but as what it really is, God's word, which is also at work in you believers. 14For you, brothers and sisters,*d* became imitators of the churches of God in Christ Jesus that are in Judea, for you suffered the same things from your own compatriots as they did from the Jews, 15who killed both the Lord Jesus and the prophets,*e* and drove us out; they displease God and oppose everyone 16by hindering us from speak-

---

c Other ancient authorities read *infants*
d Gk *brothers*

e Other ancient authorities read *their own prophets*

2:3–5 Evidently, the townspeople of Philippi and Thessalonica have accused Paul of being a kind of Sophist—an itinerant philosopher who took money for his teaching while propounding baseless and socially harmful ideas. See the criticisms of bad Cynics in Aelius Aristides, *Discourses* 4, and Dio Chrysostom, *Discourses* 32.9. **2:5–12** Paul's defense is along the lines of the ideal philosopher presented by Dio Chrysostom, *Disc.* 32.11–12. **2:7** Remarkably, at such an early stage, Paul has already accepted the notion that *apostles* are entitled to certain privileges, even though his claim to apostleship will come under attack (*1 Cor.* 9:2). Elsewhere he insists both that he is a genuine apostle (*1 Cor.* 9:1–2; 15:9–10; *2 Cor.* 12:12) and that nevertheless he has not made use of apostles' rights (*1 Cor.* 9:3–18; *2 Cor.* 2:17; 11:7–11). In the two generations following Paul, the rights of Christian teachers will become a standard topic of exhortation (*1 Tim.* 5:17–18; *Didache* 11–15). **2:9** See 2:5. Much as Socrates in Plato, *Apology* 19–21, Paul argues that he cannot be sophistlike because he did not ask for money but worked to support himself. When he goes to Corinth, in southern Greece, he will also make it a policy not to request payment for his teaching (see *1 Cor.* 9:3–18). Elsewhere, however, Paul allows that he did accept support from the Philippian community—his first preaching stop in Greece—and that the Philippians even subsidized the rest of his Greek mission, including his visit to Thessalonica (*Phil.* 4:15–16; *2 Cor.* 11:9). **2:14** *your own compatriots* The Christians' opponents in Thessalonica seem, then, to have been Greeks as well. The Christians themselves are Greek Gentiles, former worshipers of local gods (1:9), and the Gk phrase here implies an ethnic link between them and their opponents. Paul locates the Jewish persecution of Christians elsewhere, in Judea itself. *Acts* 17:1–9 implies, however, that Paul's Thessalonian opposition was primarily Jewish. This disparity may stem from the tendency of *Acts* to make Jewish intransigence a literary theme (see *Acts* 28:23–28). **2:15** *who killed both the Lord Jesus and the prophets* Although it will become a standard Christian claim that the Jews as a nation killed Jesus, thus continuing a long tradition (allegedly) of prophet killing (see *Matt.* 21:33–46; 23:29–36; *Acts* 3:14; 4:10; 5:3), both parts of this assertion are difficult to credit. The Jerusalem temple authorities may well have joined with the Roman authorities in seeking Jesus' removal for creating disturbances in the temple at a most sensitive feast time (*Mark* 11:15–19), but it was not "the Jews" as a nation who did this, any more than it was the Romans as a nation. The Roman governor Pilate had the final say. As for the prophets, it is entirely unclear, in spite of repeated Christian claims, which of the prophets were killed by any Jews or, if some Jews had killed a prophet in the 6th century B.C.E., what moral principle would connect those people with Jews of Paul's day. *displease God and oppose everyone* This broad accusation closely parallels common ancient charges against the Jews, namely: "atheism" and "misanthropy" (hatred of humanity). That is, they were perceived to reject the bedrock values of Greco-Roman civilization, which were piety toward the gods and generosity toward one's fellow human beings. The charge of atheism stemmed from the Jews' refusal to participate in the worship of gods (a refusal required by God). Their consequent withdrawal from many festivities of ancient life, which virtually all had religious associations, led to the charge of being antisocial. See, for example, Apollonius Molon in Josephus, *Ag. Ap.* 2.148, 258; Diodorus Siculus, *Historical Library* 34.1.1–5; 40.3.4; Cicero, *For Flaccus* 28.69; Tacitus, *Histories* 5.1–13. Although Paul was born a Jew, he here places himself over against the Jews, joining in these typical Gentile accusations. This trend continues in his later letters, where we see that, for him, trust in Christ means overthrowing both Judaism and observance of Torah (e.g., *Phil.* 3:4–11; *Gal.* 2:11–21; 3:23–29; 4:21–31). **2:16** *at last* Or "completely" or "forever." The word *God's* is supplied by the translators. Another translation could be, "But the end-time wrath overtook them!" The idea of impending wrath, from which Jesus will rescue those who believe in him, is part of Paul's basic preaching (see 1:10). He might be saying here that this end-time wrath has already overtaken the Jews in advance, because of their opposition to Christianity. Some scholars contend that since the largest national catastrophe for first-century Jews was the destruction of the

ing to the Gentiles so that they may be saved. Thus they have constantly been filling up the measure of their sins; but God's wrath has overtaken them at last.*f*

Paul's Desire to Visit the Thessalonians Again

17As for us, brothers and sisters,*g* when, for a short time, we were made orphans by being separated from you—in person, not in heart—we longed with great eagerness to see you face to face. 18For we wanted to come to you—certainly I, Paul, wanted to again and again—but Satan blocked our way. 19For what is our hope or joy or crown of boasting before our Lord Jesus at his coming? Is it not you? 20Yes, you are our glory and joy!

3 Therefore when we could bear it no longer, we decided to be left alone in Athens; 2and we sent Timothy, our brother and co-worker for God in proclaiming*h* the gospel of Christ, to strengthen and encourage you for the sake of your faith, 3so that no one would be shaken by these persecutions. Indeed, you yourselves know that this is what we are destined for. 4In fact, when we were with you, we told you beforehand that we were to suffer persecution; so it turned out, as you know. 5For this reason, when I could bear it no longer, I sent to find out about your faith; I was afraid that somehow the tempter had tempted you and that our labor had been in vain.

---

f Or *completely* or *forever*
g Gk *brothers*
h Gk lacks *proclaiming*

Timothy's Encouraging Report

6But Timothy has just now come to us from you, and has brought us the good news of your faith and love. He has told us also that you always remember us kindly and long to see us—just as we long to see you. 7For this reason, brothers and sisters,*g* during all our distress and persecution we have been encouraged about you through your faith. 8For we now live, if you continue to stand firm in the Lord. 9How can we thank God enough for you in return for all the joy that we feel before our God because of you? 10Night and day we pray most earnestly that we may see you face to face and restore whatever is lacking in your faith.

11Now may our God and Father himself and our Lord Jesus direct our way to you. 12And may the Lord make you increase and abound in love for one another and for all, just as we abound in love for you. 13And may he so strengthen your hearts in holiness that you may be blameless before our God and Father at the coming of our Lord Jesus with all his saints.

A Life Pleasing to God

4 Finally, brothers and sisters,*g* we ask and urge you in the Lord Jesus that, as you learned from us how you ought to live and to please God (as, in fact, you are doing), you should do so more and more. 2For you know what instructions we gave you through the Lord Jesus. 3For this is the will of God, your sanctification: that you abstain from fornication; 4that each

---

temple in 70 C.E., these lines (2:14–16 or at least 2:16c) must have been inserted into Paul's letter by a later hand, after 70. Were this true, it would absolve Paul of some rather disturbing remarks: the adoption of common anti-Jewish slander and the teaching that Jews were collectively responsible for the actions of a few. But manuscript evidence for such an omission is entirely lacking, and Paul's lifetime saw numerous catastrophes in Judea that he might have interpreted as the advance arrival of God's wrath—such as the great drought of the mid-40s. The dominant scholarly view is that Paul wrote these verses. **2:18 *again and again*** Paul's sudden departure from Thessalonica and his failure to return perhaps contributed to the opponents' case against him: "He flattered you with nonsensical stories and took your money [as they assumed], and now you'll never see him again!" This type of charge would explain Paul's emphatic response. ***Satan blocked our way*** In much Jewish and Christian literature of the period, evil and misfortune of all sorts were routinely blamed on diabolical powers that God had permitted to run amok for a short period before the end. As the *Rule of the Community* from Qumran says, "The Angel of Darkness leads all the children of righteousness astray, and, until his end, all their sin, iniquities, wickedness, and all their unlawful deeds are caused by his dominion . . . for all his allotted spirits seek the overthrow of the sons of light" (1QS 3.22–24; see *2 Cor.* 12:7–9). **3:2 *the gospel*** See note to 1:5. **3:3–4** On persecution and opposition, see 2:3–5. **3:5** Paul feared that his converts had abandoned their new faith in the face of disillusionment and opposition. Many other documents confirm that apostasy—defection from Christian circles—was an ongoing problem. See *Mark* 4:15–19; *Heb.* 6:1–12; 10:19–12:2. **3:6** For some reason, Paul omits here the third term of the triad (1:3; 5:8)—hope. **3:13** See 5:23. Here ends the thanksgiving, which seems to have been Paul's major purpose for writing. After consolidating his relationship with his faithful converts, he exhorts them to continue steadfast in the teachings that he originally gave them, then briefly takes up their questions. **4:1 *as you learned from us*** This direct reference to Paul's founding visit indicates that what follows on sexual purity (4:1–8) was a major part of Paul's original teaching in Thessalonica; here he defines what it means to be blameless at Jesus' coming (see 5:23). **4:2** Again Paul refers directly to his initial teaching. The Thessalonian Christians have already heard what he is about to say. **4:4 *body*** Lit. *vessel*. Older translations, including the RSV, take "vessel" to mean "wife" and so have Paul advocating that one "take a wife for himself." The resulting image is rather crude, however, even for a patriarchal society, and does not match Paul's advice in *1 Cor.* 7:25–31, which favors celibacy. Elsewhere Paul uses "vessel" as an image for one's body (*2 Cor.* 4:7), and in Greek literature of the period, "vessel" is sometimes a

one of you know how to control your own body*i* in holiness and honor, ⁵not with lustful passion, like the Gentiles who do not know God; ⁶that no one wrong or exploit a brother or sister*j* in this matter, because the Lord is an avenger in all these things, just as we have already told you beforehand and solemnly warned you. ⁷For God did not call us to impurity but in holiness. ⁸Therefore whoever rejects this rejects not human authority but God, who also gives his Holy Spirit to you.

⁹Now concerning love of the brothers and sisters,*k* you do not need to have anyone write to you, for you yourselves have been taught by God to love one another; ¹⁰and indeed you do love all the brothers and sisters*k* throughout Macedonia. But we urge you, beloved,*k* to do so more and more, ¹¹to aspire to live quietly, to mind your own affairs, and to work with your hands, as we directed you, ¹²so that you may behave properly toward outsiders and be dependent on no one.

The Coming of the Lord

¹³But we do not want you to be uninformed, brothers and sisters,*k* about those who have died,*l* so that you may not grieve as others do who have no hope. ¹⁴For since we believe that Jesus died and rose again, even so, through Jesus, God will bring with him those who have died.*l* ¹⁵For this we declare to you by the word of the Lord, that we who are alive, who are left until the coming of the Lord, will by no means precede those who have died.*l* ¹⁶For the Lord himself, with a cry of command, with the archangel's call and with the sound of God's trumpet, will descend from heaven, and the dead in Christ will rise first. ¹⁷Then we who are alive, who are left, will be caught up in the clouds together with them to meet the Lord in the air; and so we will be with the Lord forever. ¹⁸Therefore encourage one another with these words.

5 Now concerning the times and the seasons, brothers and sisters,*k* you do not need to have anything written to you. ²For you yourselves know very well that the day of the Lord will come like a thief in the night. ³When they say, "There is peace and security," then sudden destruction will come upon them, as labor pains come upon a pregnant woman, and there will be no escape! ⁴But you, beloved,*k* are not in darkness, for that day to surprise you like a thief; ⁵for you are all children of light and children of the day; we are not of the night or of darkness. ⁶So then let us not fall asleep as others do, but let us keep awake and be sober; ⁷for those who sleep sleep at night, and those

---

i Or *how to take a wife for himself*
j Gk *brother*
k Gk *brothers*
l Gk *fallen asleep*

---

euphemism for the male genital organ (Aelian, *Nat. an.* 17.11). The NRSV translation could be understood in either of these latter senses. **4:9 Now concerning** Paul turns here to the first of three questions raised by the Thessalonians, which they presumably sent through Timothy on his return trip. They are standing firm, but they still have some questions. The Gk phrase for *now concerning (peri de)* is identical to that in 5:1, where their third question is taken up. In 4:13, the two Gk words are separated (there translated "But . . . about"), but the sense is the same (see *1 Cor.* 7:1, 25 and introduction to *1 Thessalonians*). **taught by God** Lit. "god-taught." It is unclear whether Paul refers here to his own earlier teaching or perhaps to local tradition in Thessalonica, where the loving brother gods Castor and Pollux (Polydeuces), the so-called Dioscuri ("sons of Zeus"), were prominent. **4:13 But . . . about** Though broken up by several words, this is essentially the same Gk phrase as the one rendered "Now concerning" in 4:9 and 5:1. See note to 4:9. Thus Paul begins his response to the second of the three questions raised by the Thessalonians and conveyed by Timothy. **4:14** The distinction here between God and Jesus (the Lord) is characteristic of Paul; see 1:1, 3. **4:15** When did Jesus utter this *word*? The following description of the fate of believers who have died has no clear parallel in the gospels. Most scholars doubt that the apocalyptic scenario attending Jesus' return, the Parousia, was described in advance by Jesus of Nazareth. It is also unlikely that the fate of "those who have fallen asleep" was part of Paul's original preaching in Thessalonica; this is new information, as requested by the Thessalonians ("we do not want you to be ignorant" [4:13] means "we want you to know"—something new). Apparently, Paul is citing something that he has heard through his communication with the risen Jesus in prayer or through prophecy in the Christian community; elsewhere also he quotes sayings of the risen Lord (*2 Cor.* 12:9). Paul's lack of interest in distinguishing between sayings of Jesus of Nazareth (see *1 Cor.* 7:10, 25a) and those of the heavenly Lord (see *1 Cor.* 7:25b) raises significant questions about the general level of historical concern in early Christianity. See introduction to BIOGRAPHY, ANECDOTE, AND HISTORY. **4:16** Thus far Paul takes over the stock language of Jewish apocalyptic literature; see *Pss. Sol.* 11.1; *2 Bar.* 30; *4 Ezra* 6.23. **4:17 caught up in the clouds** For clouds as a means of heavenly transportation, see also *Dan.* 7:13; *Acts* 1:9. **5:1 Now concerning** The Gk connective phrase here *(peri de)* is identical to that in 4:9 and 4:13. See notes there. Paul begins his response to their third question. **5:2 you yourselves know** That is, this was part of Paul's original teaching. See 2:1. **thief in the night** See *Matt.* 24:42–44. **5:3 "There is peace and security."** This phrase is in quotation marks because Paul is apparently citing a slogan of the Roman world probably originating during the reign of the emperor Augustus, who was said to have brought "peace and security" *(pax et securitas)* by securing the empire's boundaries and eradicating piracy on land and sea. **5:5** These contrasting images—of light and darkness, wakefulness and sleep—were common in Paul's apocalyptic environment. See the Dead Sea Scrolls, especially the *War Scroll*, sometimes called *The War of the Sons of Light against the Sons of Darkness* (1QM), and also *John* 1:1–18.

who are drunk get drunk at night. [8]But since we belong to the day, let us be sober, and put on the breastplate of faith and love, and for a helmet the hope of salvation. [9]For God has destined us not for wrath but for obtaining salvation through our Lord Jesus Christ, [10]who died for us, so that whether we are awake or asleep we may live with him. [11]Therefore encourage one another and build up each other, as indeed you are doing.

Final Exhortations, Greetings, and Benediction

[12]But we appeal to you, brothers and sisters,[m] to respect those who labor among you, and have charge of you in the Lord and admonish you; [13]esteem them very highly in love because of their work. Be at peace among yourselves. [14]And we urge you, beloved,[m] to admonish the idlers, encourage the faint hearted, help the weak, be patient with all of them. [15]See that none of you repays evil for evil, but always seek to do good to one another and to all. [16]Rejoice always, [17]pray without ceasing, [18]give thanks in all circumstances; for this is the will of God in Christ Jesus for you. [19]Do not quench the Spirit. [20]Do not despise the words of prophets,[n] [21]but test everything; hold fast to what is good; [22]abstain from every form of evil.

[23]May the God of peace himself sanctify you entirely; and may your spirit and soul and body be kept sound[o] and blameless at the coming of our Lord Jesus Christ. [24]The one who calls you is faithful, and he will do this.

[25]Beloved,[p] pray for us.

[26]Greet all the brothers and sisters[m] with a holy kiss. [27]I solemnly command you by the Lord that this letter be read to all of them.[q]

[28]The grace of our Lord Jesus Christ be with you.[r]

---

m Gk *brothers*

n Gk *despise prophecies*
o Or *complete*
p Gk *Brothers*
q Gk *to all the brothers*
r Other ancient authorities add *Amen*

5:8 Paul here recapitulates the major themes of the letter: faith, love, and hope. See 1:3 and *1 Cor.* 13:13. **5:12** *appeal to you* Having finished responding to the Thessalonians' questions, Paul begins a series of final admonitions to faithfulness. Direct appeal to the reader by presenting the practical consequences of the preceding discussion was a standard rhetorical feature of ancient writing. *have charge of you* What kind of leadership did Paul leave in place in Thessalonica at this early stage? From the example of Corinth, where the leaders were the more prominent members, those who owned the houses that hosted the group, and those who could afford to travel (e.g., Chloe, Stephanas, Crispus, Gaius), we might suppose that leadership was still rather informal at this point, following obvious social categories. **5:20** Not the bygone prophets of the Bible. Among Paul's groups at least, divinely inspired (prophetic) speech by certain members of the group was common. See *1 Cor.* 12:28; 14:1–33; *Luke* 11:49; *Didache* 11–13. **5:23** This closing benediction brings together Paul's preaching and the thrust of the letter: persevere in blameless living as you await Jesus' imminent return. Paul implies that Jesus' coming is imminent and that his converts will witness that day. See 3:13. **5:24** Paul reassures them, in light of their questions, that Jesus is indeed coming soon. **5:26** *a holy kiss* See also *1 Pet.* 5:14. The Christian kiss, thus exchanged among men and women who met in private houses, often while it was dark, became an issue of scandal to some Roman observers of the 2d and 3d centuries. See Clement of Alexandria, *Christ the Educator* 3.11. **5:27** We do not know how many house groups composed the Christian assembly ("church") at Thessalonica, but this sentence implies that there were several.

To the Assembly in Corinth

1 CORINTHIANS

Setting

Although it was built over a famous old city, the Corinth of Paul's day was new and vibrant. The Romans had virtually destroyed the old Greek city in 146 B.C.E. because it took part in a regional rebellion against their rule. A century later (44 B.C.E.), Julius Caesar established the Roman colony of Corinth, and in 44 C.E. it was firmly designated the capital of the province of Achaia, after other political arrangements had been tried. So the city that Paul visited in the 40s and 50s was a boom-town, and one that offered rare economic opportunities for aggressive freedmen (former slaves). Building and urban expansion continued at a rapid pace through the mid-first century, which may help to explain Paul's fondness for building meta-phors when he writes to or from Corinth.[1]

Because of its location on the narrow isthmus connecting west-east and north-south trade routes, Corinth was quickly regaining its prominence as a center of international business. It was also becoming host to the many gods revered by its immigrants: archaeologists have found remains of several temples and a (later?) Jewish synagogue. Soon after leaving Thessalonica, Paul came to this bustling, cos-mopolitan city and gathered a group of converts to his announcement ("gospel").

Date

In spite of its traditional name, *1 Corinthians* was not the first letter that Paul wrote to his converts at Corinth. We know this because in *1 Cor.* 5:9–11 he refers to a previous letter that admonished the Corinthians to avoid immoral believers. That earlier letter is entirely lost to us unless, as some scholars have suggested, a fragment of it survives in *2 Cor.* 6:14–7:1. Whether the previous letter can be partially recov-ered or not, it is important for the reader to remember that *1 Corinthians* is at least Paul's second letter to this community. The correspondence presupposes a rela-tionship of some standing.

---

[1] *1 Cor.* 3:10; 8:1, 10; 10:23; 14:4, 17, 26; *2 Cor.* 5:1; 13:10; *Rom.* 14:19; 15:20.

First Corinthians must come before *2 Corinthians* and *Romans* because in it Paul has just begun his major collection for Jerusalem (16:12), whereas in the others that project is well under way. It is debated whether *1 Corinthians* should be placed before or after *Galatians*. But everyone agrees that *1 Corinthians* shows us a relatively early Paul, still actively engaged in establishing his churches.

Scholars have sometimes thought it possible to date *1 Corinthians* with even greater precision, for the following reason. According to *Acts* 18:12, when Paul was in Corinth he was brought before the proconsul Gallio. An inscription found in Delphi happens to mention Gallio's tenure as governor, and allows us to date his term to 51–52 C.E. Perhaps because this kind of external evidence is so rare, scholars have been eager to conclude that Paul's founding visit was during Gallio's term, and therefore to date *1 Corinthians* confidently between about 53 and 55 C.E.

But there are two problems with this conclusion. First, the chronological connections in *Luke-Acts* itself are problematic, from the census under Quirinius (*Luke* 3) to the Judas/Theudas episode (*Acts* 5) to the description of Paul's early years as a Christian (*Acts* 9). The fact that one of the characters mentioned in this story happens to turn up in an inscription, as some others turn up in Josephus's pages, does nothing to lessen the general problem of *Luke*'s chronology. The inscription confirms that the Gallio of *Acts* was a real proconsul of Achaia in 51–52; it would only help us to date Paul's founding visit, however, if we had good reason to believe that *Luke* was correct in placing that visit during Gallio's proconsulship. Second, *Acts* 18 shows some signs of having cobbled together two or three different traditions about Paul in Corinth. If 18:12 marks a seam joining two such traditions, then the Gallio episode may have occurred during a second or third visit. In that case, even if the tradition that Paul appeared before Gallio were reliable, Paul's founding visit to Corinth may have occurred somewhat earlier than Gallio's tenure as governor.

Apart from the Gallio inscription, there would be no reason to date *1 Corinthians* later than the 40s, which would allow more time for the many subsequent developments before Paul's arrest in the mid-50s, some time before the end of Felix's term as governor of Judea.[2]

Overview and Literary Features

The arrangement of *1 Corinthians* resembles that of *1 Thessalonians*. Paul's own issues, arising from an oral report, occupy the first part (chs. 1–6) and his responses to the Corinthians' written questions occupy the second (chs. 7–16). In this case,

---

[2]Of course, the link between Paul's arrest and Felix's term is also made only in *Acts* (24:27), and it might seem inconsistent to use that link as a datum. Our guess, however, is that the author has better information about the latter part of Paul's career—closer to his time and more widely known—than about earlier details, much as the events surrounding Jesus' death were preserved in much more coherent blocks than the order of events during his life. If the connection with Felix were given up, then we would have more time to work with in reconstructing Paul's career.

however, Paul's concerns arise from an unfavorable report on the Corinthian community that he has received from "Chloe's people" (1:11)—apparently the slaves of a wealthy woman in the Christian assembly. They have visited Paul in Ephesus (16:8) and reported to him: (a) that there is serious dissension in the church (chs. 1–4); (b) that a case of extreme sexual immorality has gone unchecked (ch. 5); and (c) that some believers are prosecuting others in secular courts (6:1–11). In the first part of the letter, therefore, Paul expresses his dismay over the unseemly conduct that has been reported.

One of the major interpretive problems arising from chapters 1 to 4 is to determine whether the factions at Corinth reflect only the inevitable tensions that arise within groups or whether they represent a principled opposition to Paul—a non-Pauline view of Christian faith. The way in which Paul moves easily back and forth from the dissension issue to a sustained attack on worldly wisdom and rhetoric suggests that the major faction in question had a stake in the themes of knowledge (gnōsis), wisdom (sophia), and power (dynamis). Moreover, although Paul begins the letter by denouncing all allegiance to human leaders, including himself (1:12–14; 3:4–9), he ends up insisting that his converts remain loyal to him, their master builder and father (3:10–15; 4:14–21). Evidently, Paul was not as much concerned with factionalism per se as with a particularly threatening alternative vision of Christianity, taught by other leaders, that emphasized the present benefits of the faith (see 4:8–13) and so undercut his apocalyptic urgency (see 3:13; 7:26, 29–31). Apparently, a significant faction within the community was openly critical of him and his teaching (4:3–5, 15–21).

In addition to the delegation from Chloe, a group consisting of Stephanas, Fortunatus, and Achaicus (16:17)—perhaps the leading members of the "household of Stephanas" (1:16)—has visited Paul in Ephesus. They were likely the bearers of the Corinthians' letter, to which Paul responds from 7:1 onward: "Now concerning (peri de) the matters about which you wrote." One can infer from Paul's responses that the main issues of concern to the Corinthians were: (a) marriage and sex (ch. 7); (b) the status of meat that had been used in pagan sacrifice (chs. 8–10); (c) spiritual gifts (chs. 12–14); (d) the future resurrection of Christian believers (ch. 15); (e) the collection for Jerusalem (16:1–4); and (f) the return of Apollos, a preacher who had spent some time in the church after Paul's departure (16:12). Since he does not introduce them with the usual formula "now concerning," it is uncertain whether Paul's discussions of women's decorum (11:2–16) and the Lord's Supper (11:17–34) were also prompted by the Corinthians' letter or whether he simply decided to interject at that point further responses to Chloe's information (or some other conduit of news about the community).

Themes and Issues

It is a matter of scholarly debate to what extent the issues raised by the Corinthians have a unifying theme. In several places, it appears that Paul quotes phrases from their letter in his response to them (see 6:12; 8:1, 4; 15:12). Study of these quoted phrases reveals that the Corinthians did not merely ask questions out of curiosity. With respect to "idol meat," resurrection, and probably also spiritual gifts, they seem to have known Paul's views and yet disagreed with him. For example, some of them denied future resurrection (15:12), though they must have known that this was essential to Paul's announcement (gospel), and others asserted that their knowledge permitted them to eat idol meat (8:1–13). In these cases, their questions were not so much inquisitive as provocative; they had already adopted counterpositions.

If there is a common thread in the Corinthians' counterpositions, it is that the believer has complete knowledge, freedom, and power at the present time (see 4:8–13). This view unavoidably influences their attitudes toward sexuality, idol meat, spiritual gifts, and resurrection, which occupy the bulk of the letter. Since Paul has dealt with the general problem of wisdom and knowledge in chapters 1 to 4, before proceeding to specific applications of it, it appears that he wrote much of this letter to combat one serious threat: a Christianity that had rejected his fervent eschatological hope in favor of what scholars call a "realized eschatology." Some Corinthians now preferred to see Jesus as one who had *already* ushered in an age of new possibilities: of freedom, knowledge, and a kind of "rule" or participation in God's reign. They wanted to revel in the present benefits of salvation.

If some Christians at Corinth valued Jesus especially as bringer of wisdom, what did they do with Jesus' saving death and resurrection, which were so pivotal to Paul's teaching? In Paul's view, at least, they did not place sufficient value on Jesus' death. He stresses that he proclaims not only Christ, but "him *crucified*" (1:23; 2:2). His language confirms that already within two decades of Jesus' death, different kinds of allegiance to Jesus had emerged. For Paul, Jesus' significance lay not in insightful teaching but in the *cross* (1:17–18), a disturbing image in Roman times, when people were accustomed to seeing convicts hanging in agony as they waited for death along the streets outside cities.

The Corinthians accepted, it seems, that Jesus had died and risen (in some way), but they do not appear to have attached the same value to those events as Paul did. They must have accepted Jesus' resurrection because Paul uses it as the basis for his argument about Jesus' return and Christian resurrection in the future: you cannot say "there is no resurrection" if Jesus was raised (15:12–18), and he is the first fruits; those who die trusting him will also be raised at his return (15:20–24). It was not so much Jesus' resurrection that troubled the Corinthians as the future bodily resurrection of Christians: they were inclined to live for the present rather than for some promise of future bliss (15:32–34), and they were put off by the notion that a physical body should be raised (15:35). Paul has to insist that the resurrection body is not physical but spiritual (15:32–50—something he had not apparently clarified before), and that is why even those who remain when Jesus returns will need to be transformed (15:51–57).

If these Corinthians dismissed the hope for their own future resurrection, how did they integrate Jesus' resurrection into their view of things? Although *1 Corinthians* does not spell this out, we have some ground for speculating that they understood their own resurrection to have taken place already, when they trusted Christ and joined him in mystical union; at that time they became beneficiaries of his new life. Such a hypothesis would explain how they could have moved, within a short space of time, from Paul's gospel to this new view: they saw it as an improvement of Paul's view to consider resurrection already accomplished. This approach would explain their apparent celebration of present life over against Paul's insistence on an orientation to the next world. Further, some other Christian texts that value present wisdom and knowledge also claim that the believer has already been raised (*Col.* 2:10–15; *Eph.* 2:6). And *2 Tim.* 2:18 will mention two Christian leaders "who have swerved from the truth by holding that the resurrection is past already." It is entirely plausible, though not provable, that Paul's Corinthian opponents first established the position, which would have considerable effect among later Christians, that believers' resurrection was past and spiritual.

Ideas never exist in a vacuum, and Paul's letter gives plenty of evidence that the theoretical issue of how one ought to follow Jesus was all tied up with the question: who is the rightful leader of the Christian community at Corinth? Paul knows that many are critical of him, but he boldly warns "someone else" who is building on his foundation (3:10).

Since the community is eager for the return of Apollos (16:12), but not of Paul (4:17–18), and since Apollos seems to be the prime target in chapters 1–4 (see 3:4–17; 4:1–6, 15; Cephas appears only in 1:12 and 3:22), some scholars have suggested that he was the one who taught the Corinthians this "de-eschatologized" Christianity that Paul so abhors. Notice that, in the biblical passage that Paul chooses for his attack on wisdom and cleverness (*1 Cor.* 1:19), the word for "I will destroy [the wisdom of the wise]" is *apolō*, which would sound very much like a form of Apollos's name *(Apollōs)*. It is hard to imagine that the pun was not intended by a writer with Paul's talents.

Apollos was remembered in Acts as a Jew from Alexandria, Egypt, who had embraced Christian teaching; *Acts* also knows a tradition that Apollos's views were challenged by others (*Acts* 18:24–27). The writings of Apollos's older contemporary Philo allow us to see some highly philosophical strains in Alexandrian Judaism, which in turn make it plausible that Apollos taught some of the positions held by the Corinthians—for example, concerning spiritual resurrection and idol meat. Self-knowledge as the way to interior freedom was a keynote of contemporary philosophical teaching, and it also permeated Philo's writing. Apollos might well have viewed Jesus as a teacher of such principles. Although some scholars object that Paul could not have been seriously at odds with Apollos if the two were still on speaking terms in Ephesus (*1 Cor.* 16:12), others find the evidence of the first four chapters more compelling. Let the reader decide.

Relation to Other Early Christian Texts

Whatever philosophical and personal bases the Corinthians' views may have had, they are most valuable to us because they reflect—albeit "in a mirror, dimly" (*1 Cor.* 13:12)—a way of following Jesus that is attested in several later Christian texts, though it was ultimately excluded by "orthodox" Christianity. *First Clement* indicates that the denial of future resurrection remained a major issue in Corinth long after Paul's death (*1 Clement* 23–27). Numerous traditions in the Synoptic Gospels present Jesus as one who taught moral wisdom through parable and proverb, and there he sometimes insists on present rather than future salvation (e.g., *Luke* 17:20–21), though this material has been incorporated in the service of a generally forward-looking narrative. Some specialists now think that the earliest layers of the lost sayings source that served as a basis for *Matthew* and *Luke* ("Q"; see the introduction to BIOGRAPHY, ANECDOTE, AND HISTORY) presented Jesus primarily as a wisdom teacher. Jesus also appears primarily as a teacher of proverbial wisdom in the letter of *James* and the first half (chs. 1–6) of the *Didache*.

The *Gospel of John* goes further in reorienting Jesus' mission to the past and present, and in making him a conduit of truth and knowledge, but the wisdom in question there is mainly cosmic rather than self-knowledge. In a similar vein, *Colossians* and *Ephesians* celebrate the "assured understanding and the knowledge of God's mystery" (*Col.* 2:2; see 1:26–28; *Eph.* 1:17–18) and a spiritual resurrection, already completed in the past, to fulness of life (*Col.* 2:10–15; *Eph.* 2:6).

By far the most thoroughgoing portrayal of Jesus as advocate of self-knowledge is the *Gospel of Thomas,* the earliest layers of which are now often dated to the first century. The *Gospel of Thomas* combines the mysterious qualities of *John's* Jesus with the pithy sayings of the synoptic tradition. Interestingly, in *1 Cor.* 2:9 Paul quotes as authoritative a saying that does not appear in either Jewish scripture or the canonical gospels, but does turn up in *Gospel of Thomas.* 17. This may indicate that the approach to Christianity recently adopted by some of his readers was in the tradition that would lead ultimately to the production of *Thomas*.

Perhaps because his opponents looked to Jesus' own teachings for their inspiration, Paul cites more sayings of Jesus in *1 Corinthians* than in any other letter. Therefore this letter also provides unique and concrete evidence of how Jesus' sayings were transmitted and used before they were grouped together in the gospel narratives. The most obvious examples come at *1 Cor.* 7:10, where Paul cites a word of the Lord forbidding divorce (see *Mark* 10:11 and par.); at 9:14, where Jesus is said to have mandated payment for those who live by preaching (see *Luke* 10:7); and at 11:23–25, where Paul cites the words of Jesus at the last supper (see *Mark* 14:22–25 and par.). It may be that Paul has Jesus traditions in mind in several other places as well—for example, in his description of the end of the age (*1 Cor.* 15:51; see *Mark* 13). In each case, he adapts a particular saying of Jesus to his point at the moment, much as he uses isolated passages of scripture, without awareness of the contexts that the synoptic writers will later introduce.

Like *1 Thessalonians, 1 Corinthians* shows us Paul declaring an announcement that is oriented almost entirely toward Jesus' imminent return and the passing away of the present age. His consistent retort to the Corinthians' realized eschatology, with all its implications, is that the end has *not yet* come: one cannot yet begin to rule, or enjoy complete knowledge or freedom now; resurrection too is still future. This age is a brief interval of intense suffering and self-denial, requiring absolute commitment, before Jesus returns to usher in the new age and judge the world; only then will knowledge, freedom, and Christian rule become a reality.

A significant difference from *1 Thessalonians* is Paul's new emphasis on Jewish scripture, especially the law, and Jewish customs. These features of the letter help to prepare us for reading *2 Corinthians, Philippians, Galatians,* and *Romans,* in which the question of Paul's relationship to Judaism becomes acute. The peculiar thing in *1 Corinthians,* however, is that this relationship does not yet seem to be a live issue: we see no evidence that anyone has been advocating circumcision or Torah observance to Paul's converts. Paul's followers seem to be mainly Gentiles (12:2), as they had been in Thessalonica.

It is interesting, then, that Paul adopts the language of Judaism in speaking of his converts: they are no longer "Gentiles" (12:2) and should consider it undesirable to be like a Gentile (5:1). These Christians also know about some major Jewish holidays and celebrate at least Passover and Pentecost—the former, apparently, according to the Jewish custom of removing leaven from the house (5:6–8). At least some of them appear to have been circumcised (7:18, though this might represent a merely rhetorical possibility). Most striking, Paul frequently cites Jewish scripture (with an amazing recall of even the most obscure passages), calls the Israelites "our ancestors" (10:1), and cites "the [Jewish] law" as if it were self-evidently authoritative for his readers (9:8–9). All of this stands in some tension with his later distancing of himself from Judaism (*Phil.* 3:3–11) and his relegation of the law to a bygone age (*Gal.* 3:1–26).

Value for the Study of Early Christianity

In *1 Corinthians,* Paul gives his views on a wide range of issues. Because of the range of problems that it covers, this letter is arguably the single best window we have into the real life of a first-generation Christian community.

For Further Reading

Barrett, C. K. *The First Epistle to the Corinthians.* Black's New Testament Commentary. London: A & C Black, 1968. Repr., Peabody, Mass.: Hendrickson, 1993.

Betz, Hans Dieter, and Margaret M. Mitchell. "Corinthians, First Epistle to the." Pages 1139–48 in vol. 1 of *Anchor Bible Dictionary.* Edited by D. N. Freedman. 6 vols. New York: Doubleday, 1992.

Conzelmann, Hans. *1 Corinthians: A Commentary on the First Epistle to the Corinthians.* Translated by James W. Leitch. Hermeneia. Philadelphia: Fortress, 1975.

Fee, Gordon D. *The First Epistle to the Corinthians.* New International Commentary on the New Testament. Grand Rapids: Eerdmans, 1987.

Gooch, Peter D. *Dangerous Food: 1 Corinthians 8–10 in its Context.* Waterloo: Wilfrid Laurier University Press, 1993.

Hurd, John Coolidge, Jr. *The Origin of I Corinthians.* Macon, Ga.: Mercer University Press, 1983 [London: SPCK, 1965].

Murphy-O'Connor, J. "Corinth." Pages 1134–39 in vol. 1 of *Anchor Bible Dictionary.* Edited by D. N. Freedman. 6 vols. New York: Doubleday, 1992.

Orr, William F., and James Arthur Walther. *I Corinthians: A New Translation.* Anchor Bible 32. Garden City, N.Y.: Doubleday, 1976.

Schmithals, Walter. *Gnosticism in Corinth.* Translated by John E. Steely. Nashville: Abingdon, 1971.

Thiselton, Anthony C. *The First Epistle to the Corinthians.* New International Greek Testament Commentary. Grand Rapids: Eerdmans, 2000.

Wills, W. L. *Idol Meat in Corinth.* Society of Biblical Literature Dissertation Series 68. Chico, Calif.: Scholars Press, 1985.

THE FIRST LETTER OF PAUL
TO THE CORINTHIANS

Salutation

1 Paul, called to be an apostle of Christ Jesus by the will of God, and our brother Sosthenes,

²To the church of God that is in Corinth, to those who are sanctified in Christ Jesus, called to be saints, together with all those who in every place call on the name of our Lord Jesus Christ, both their Lord*a* and ours:

³Grace to you and peace from God our Father and the Lord Jesus Christ.

⁴I give thanks to my*b* God always for you because of the grace of God that has been given you in Christ Jesus, ⁵for in every way you have been enriched in him, in speech and knowledge of every kind— ⁶just as the testimony of*c* Christ has been strengthened among you— ⁷so that you are not lacking in any spiritual gift as you wait for the revealing of our Lord Jesus Christ. ⁸He will also strengthen you to the end, so that you may be blameless on the day of our Lord Jesus Christ. ⁹God is faithful; by him you were called into the fellowship of his Son, Jesus Christ our Lord.

Divisions in the Church

¹⁰Now I appeal to you, brothers and sisters,*d* by the name of our Lord Jesus Christ, that all of you be in agreement and that there be no divisions among you, but that you be united in the same mind and the same purpose. ¹¹For it has been reported to me by Chloe's people that there are quarrels among you, my brothers and sisters.*e* ¹²What I mean is that each of you says, "I belong to Paul," or "I belong to Apollos," or "I belong to Cephas," or "I belong to Christ." ¹³Has Christ been divided? Was Paul crucified for you? Or were you baptized in the name of Paul? ¹⁴I thank God*f* that I baptized none of you except Crispus and Gaius, ¹⁵so that no one can say that you were baptized in my name. ¹⁶(I did baptize also the household of Stephanas; beyond that, I do not know whether I baptized anyone else.) ¹⁷For Christ did not send me to baptize but to proclaim the gospel, and not with eloquent wisdom, so that the cross of Christ might not be emptied of its power.

---

a Gk *theirs*
b Other ancient authorities lack *my*
c Or *to*

d Gk *brothers*
e Gk *my brothers*
f Other ancient authorities read *I am thankful*

1:1 *Sosthenes* A fairly common Gk name. *Acts* 18:17 mentions a Sosthenes, a synagogue president in Corinth who converted to Christianity. The Sosthenes mentioned here, who is with Paul in Ephesus, may be the same person. If some of Paul's converts in Corinth came from the synagogue, this would explain many of the letter's unusual emphases on scripture and Jewish custom. See note to 5:1. **1:4–9** In this diplomatic opening, Paul thanks God for the Corinthians' many abilities and their speech, knowledge, and spiritual gifts, even though in the body of the letter he will challenge all of their claims to these (see 1:17–20; 2:1; 3:18; 4:8–13; 8:1–2; 13:8–12). At the same time, he manages to establish his apocalyptic premise (1:7–8), which some of his readers have repudiated (4:8–11). And he introduces the theme of fellowship, sharing, or partnership, which will play a large role in several of his arguments (6:15; 10:16–21; 11:27–34; 12:12–26). **1:4** On the value of the thanksgiving for reading Paul's letters, see note to *1 Thess.* 1:2–10. **1:11** It is strange that Paul does not name these individuals; contrast his enumeration of the Corinthians' delegates (16:17) and his many personal greetings in other letters. Perhaps the best explanation is that the messengers were quite literally Chloe's people—slaves of a wealthy Corinthian woman. *Cephas* Probably Peter. Cephas is a Gk transliteration of the Aramaic *kefa*, meaning "rock." The equivalent Gk name is *Petros*, Peter (see *Matt.* 16:17). According to early Christian tradition, Peter founded the church at Rome and also died in the world capital. *1 Cor.* 9:5 implies that he had a mission outside Palestine (to Jews? *Gal.* 2:7–9) parallel to Paul's. Exactly how Peter's influence extended to Corinth is not clear. In the coming paragraphs, however, the confrontation between Paul and Apollos is central; Cephas is mentioned again only in 3:22. **1:12** *belong to Christ* Some see this as referring to a "Christ" group in Corinth. The problems with this reading are that (a) such a group will not be mentioned again and (b) Paul wants everyone to express allegiance only to Christ, in whose name they were all baptized (1:13), and so it would be *good* to say, "I belong to Christ." The Gk could also be understood as Paul's personal declaration, after listing the Corinthians' various allegiances: "But *I* belong to Christ. Has Christ been divided?" **1:14** *Crispus* and *Gaius* are Roman names, perhaps belonging to members of the upper social stratum in Corinth—freedmen or children of freedmen who colonized the city after its reestablishment in 44 B.C.E. Gaius had a house big enough to host the entire Christian community of the city (*Rom.* 16:23). Crispus is said (*Acts* 18:8) to have been the president of the Jewish synagogue. **1:16** This concession is humorous in view of Paul's emphatic denial in the preceding verse that he baptized anyone but Crispus and Gaius. Stephanas is apparently with him as he dictates the letter (16:17). Once Stephanas has corrected Paul, by reminding him of his own baptism, Paul can no longer recall the situation accurately and so forfeits his original point. The parentheses are supplied by the translators.

Christ the Power and Wisdom of God

[18]For the message about the cross is foolishness to those who are perishing, but to us who are being saved it is the power of God. [19]For it is written,

"I will destroy the wisdom of the wise,
    and the discernment of the discerning I will thwart."

[20]Where is the one who is wise? Where is the scribe? Where is the debater of this age? Has not God made foolish the wisdom of the world? [21]For since, in the wisdom of God, the world did not know God through wisdom, God decided, through the foolishness of our proclamation, to save those who believe. [22]For Jews demand signs and Greeks desire wisdom, [23]but we proclaim Christ crucified, a stumbling block to Jews and foolishness to Gentiles, [24]but to those who are the called, both Jews and Greeks, Christ the power of God and the wisdom of God. [25]For God's foolishness is wiser than human wisdom, and God's weakness is stronger than human strength.

[26]Consider your own call, brothers and sisters:[g] not many of you were wise by human standards,[h] not many were powerful, not many were of noble birth. [27]But God chose what is foolish in the world to shame the wise; God chose what is weak in the world to shame the strong; [28]God chose what is low and despised in the world, things that are not, to reduce to nothing things that are, [29]so that no one[i] might boast in the presence of God. [30]He is the source of your life in Christ Jesus, who became for us wisdom from God, and righteousness and sanctification and redemption, [31]in order that, as it is written, "Let the one who boasts, boast in[j] the Lord."

Proclaiming Christ Crucified

2 When I came to you, brothers and sisters,[g] I did not come proclaiming the mystery[k] of God to you in lofty words or wisdom. [2]For I decided to know nothing among you except Jesus Christ, and him crucified. [3]And I came to you in weakness and in fear and in much trembling. [4]My speech and my proclamation were not with plausible words of wisdom,[l] but with a demonstration of the Spirit and of power, [5]so that your faith might rest not on human wisdom but on the power of God.

The True Wisdom of God

[6]Yet among the mature we do speak wisdom, though it is not a wisdom of this age or of the rulers of this age, who are doomed to perish. [7]But we speak God's wisdom, secret and hidden, which God decreed before the ages for our glory. [8]None of the rulers of this age understood this; for if they had, they

---

g Gk brothers
h Gk according to the flesh

i Gk no flesh
j Or of
k Other ancient authorities read testimony
l Other ancient authorities read the persuasiveness of wisdom

---

1:19 *I will destroy* The Gk verb form *apolō* sounds exactly like Apollos's name in certain Gk constructions. Given Paul's fondness for wordplays, this is hardly a coincidence. He is taking a subtle jab at Apollos, whom he associates with wisdom and eloquence. Compare the description of Apollos in *Acts* 18:24–28. A further twist is that Apollo, the Gk god associated with reason, poetry, prophecy, and cures, among other things, was especially popular in Corinth and its surrounding region. *Isa.* 29:14. MT: "And the wisdom of its [that people's] wise shall fail, and the prudence of its prudent shall vanish." LXX: "I will destroy the wisdom of the wise, and the discernment of the discerning I will hide." **1:23** Some early Christian groups valued Jesus more as a teacher of wisdom than as a dying Savior. Paul's converts in Corinth have become attracted to such a view, represented elsewhere in the *Gospel of Thomas,* perhaps *James,* and Q. Paul here stresses the point of difference: he preaches Christ crucified and attacks all claims to wisdom. **1:26** *by human standards* Lit. "according to the flesh." *noble birth* This would serve as a general description of any ancient population, for wealth and privilege were concentrated in the hands of a minority. Still, Paul's followers in Corinth seem to have had their share of wealthier members, such as Chloe, Gaius and Crispus (see 1:16), Erastus, who held an important civic office (*Rom.* 16:23), and perhaps Stephanas with his companions (*1 Cor.* 16:15). **1:31** An adaptation of LXX *Jer.* 9:24. MT (9:23): "But only in this should one glory: in his earnest devotion to Me. For I the Lord act with kindness, justice, and equity in the world." LXX (9:24): "Let the one who boasts boast in this: understanding and knowing that I am the Lord who exercises mercy and judgment and righteousness upon the earth." Paul's adaptation omits the passage's support for "understanding and knowing" (also present in the literal Hebrew), which might play into his opponents' hands, and it assumes that the "Lord" in question is Jesus, the center of Paul's preaching. **2:4** In *Gal.* 3:1–5 Paul likewise appeals to the effective spiritual power of his gospel as proof of its legitimacy, in contrast to the claims of another gospel. **2:5** This contrast between human wisdom/eloquence and divine power is the dominant theme of *1 Cor.* 1–4 (see 1:20–21; 4:20). It was a very familiar contrast in Paul's day; see Socrates in Plato, *Apology* 1.17: "I shall prove that I am not a clever speaker in any way at all—unless, indeed, by a clever speaker they mean someone who speaks the truth." So, repeatedly, *Apology* 1.18; 6.21–22; 9.23: "Human wisdom is worth nothing." The two roles of eloquent speaker and truthteller seem here to be associated with Apollos and Paul, respectively (4:6). **2:6** *age* The Gk word *aiōn* for Paul means both a period of time and an evil regime; in the latter sense it is sometimes rendered as "world" (*2 Cor.* 4:4). Paul expects that this age, or aeon, will soon pass away (7:26–31; 10:11).

would not have crucified the Lord of glory. [9]But, as it is written,

> "What no eye has seen, nor ear heard,
>   nor the human heart conceived,
> what God has prepared for those who love
>   him"—

[10]these things God has revealed to us through the Spirit; for the Spirit searches everything, even the depths of God. [11]For what human being knows what is truly human except the human spirit that is within? So also no one comprehends what is truly God's except the Spirit of God. [12]Now we have received not the spirit of the world, but the Spirit that is from God, so that we may understand the gifts bestowed on us by God. [13]And we speak of these things in words not taught by human wisdom but taught by the Spirit, interpreting spiritual things to those who are spiritual.[m]

[14]Those who are unspiritual[n] do not receive the gifts of God's Spirit, for they are foolishness to them, and they are unable to understand them because they are spiritually discerned. [15]Those who are spiritual discern all things, and they are themselves subject to no one else's scrutiny.

[16]   "For who has known the mind of the Lord
            so as to instruct him?"
But we have the mind of Christ.

On Divisions in the Corinthian Church

3 And so, brothers and sisters,[o] I could not speak to you as spiritual people, but rather as people of the flesh, as infants in Christ. [2]I fed you with milk, not solid food, for you were not ready for solid food. Even now you are still not ready, [3]for you are still of the flesh. For as long as there is jealousy and quarreling among you, are you not of the flesh, and behaving according to human inclinations? [4]For when one says, "I belong to Paul," and another, "I belong to Apollos," are you not merely human?

[5]What then is Apollos? What is Paul? Servants through whom you came to believe, as the Lord assigned to each. [6]I planted, Apollos watered, but God gave the growth. [7]So neither the one who plants nor the one who waters is anything, but only God who gives the growth. [8]The one who plants and the one who waters have a common purpose, and each will receive wages according to the labor of each. [9]For we are God's servants, working together; you are God's field, God's building.

[10]According to the grace of God given to me, like a skilled master builder I laid a foundation, and someone else is building on it. Each builder must choose with care how to build on it. [11]For no one can lay any foundation other than the one that has been laid; that foundation is Jesus Christ. [12]Now if anyone

---

m Or *interpreting spiritual things in spiritual language,* or *comparing spiritual things with spiritual*

n Or *natural*

o Gk *brothers*

2:8 *rulers of this age* Compare "the god of this world" (see previous note) who has blinded unbelievers, in *2 Cor.* 4:4; also the "elemental spirits" of *Gal.* 4:8–9. In these passages Paul suggests a cosmic dualism, according to which humanity is enslaved by malevolent spiritual powers. He seems to differ with the Corinthians on the question of exactly what trust in Christ does (or will do, or has done) to remedy this situation.   Contrast this cosmic interpretation of Jesus' death, at the hands of spiritual powers, with Paul's earlier statement that the Judeans (or Jews) killed Jesus (*1 Thess.* 2:15).   **2:9** Although the first two phrases are vaguely reminiscent of LXX *Isa.* 64:4 (MT 64:3), this passage does not appear in the present texts of either the Hebrew or the Greek scriptures. It does, however, match a saying of Jesus in *Gospel of Thomas* 17: "Jesus said, 'I shall give you what no eye has seen, what no ear has heard, what no hand has touched, what has not arisen in the human heart.'" The community behind *Thomas,* like the Corinthians, understood these unspeakable benefits to be conferred to Jesus' followers in the present (see *1 Cor.* 4:8–13). Paul, who may be taking over one of the Corinthians' favorite lines, insisted that they would come only with Jesus' return.   **2:14** *unspiritual* Lit. "pertaining to the mind or soul *(psychē)."* In the context 1:19–27; 2:5–13, which attack human wisdom, Paul seems to be distinguishing intellectual from spiritual people. He thus evokes the two kinds of knowledge that are often discussed in both Western and Eastern philosophy.   **2:16** *Isa.* 40:13. MT: "Who has plumbed the mind of the Lord, What man could tell Him His plan?" LXX: "Who has known the mind of the Lord, and who has been his counselor, who has advised him?" Also cited by Paul in *Rom.* 11:34.   **3:1** Paul has now introduced three categories of person: spiritual, unspiritual, and *of the flesh.* Although the English translations must sometimes use several words, each adjective in Gk is a single word with the same *(-ikos)* construction. It may well be that these "fleshly" people are to be identified with the "mind-oriented" ones in 2:14, rather than forming a new group. In that case, Paul is adjusting his language as he goes along to make a new point: moving from a contrast between flesh and spirit to one between flesh and spirit.   **3:3** *inclinations* Supplied by the translators to complete the thought.   **3:4** Thus, Paul is still dealing with the set of issues introduced in 1:11. But he has gradually narrowed the discussion to the relation between himself and Apollos; Cephas has dropped out of the picture and will stay out except for 3:22. It may be, then, that Paul is not as much concerned with party strife in general as with the conflict that has developed between himself and Apollos.   **3:9** The switch of metaphor, from agriculture to construction, makes a new point: Paul has priority, as master builder, over Apollos, who is "building on top" (see next note).   **3:10** In these sentences Paul pointedly warns the *someone else* who is building over his foundation. That person, Paul's readers would readily understand, is Apollos (see 3:6).

builds on the foundation with gold, silver, precious stones, wood, hay, straw— 13the work of each builder will become visible, for the Day will disclose it, because it will be revealed with fire, and the fire will test what sort of work each has done. 14If what has been built on the foundation survives, the builder will receive a reward. 15If the work is burned up, the builder will suffer loss; the builder will be saved, but only as through fire.

16Do you not know that you are God's temple and that God's Spirit dwells in you?*p* 17If anyone destroys God's temple, God will destroy that person. For God's temple is holy, and you are that temple.

18Do not deceive yourselves. If you think that you are wise in this age, you should become fools so that you may become wise. 19For the wisdom of this world is foolishness with God. For it is written,

"He catches the wise in their craftiness,"

20and again,

"The Lord knows the thoughts of the wise,
    that they are futile."

21So let no one boast about human leaders. For all things are yours, 22whether Paul or Apollos or Cephas or the world or life or death or the present or the future—all belong to you, 23and you belong to Christ, and Christ belongs to God.

The Ministry of the Apostles

4 Think of us in this way, as servants of Christ and stewards of God's mysteries. 2Moreover, it is required of stewards that they be found trustworthy.

3But with me it is a very small thing that I should be judged by you or by any human court. I do not even judge myself. 4I am not aware of anything against myself, but I am not thereby acquitted. It is the Lord who judges me. 5Therefore do not pronounce judgment before the time, before the Lord comes, who will bring to light the things now hidden in darkness and will disclose the purposes of the heart. Then each one will receive commendation from God.

6I have applied all this to Apollos and myself for your benefit, brothers and sisters,*q* so that you may learn through us the meaning of the saying, "Nothing beyond what is written," so that none of you will be puffed up in favor of one against another. 7For who sees anything different in you?*r* What do you have that you did not receive? And if you received it, why do you boast as if it were not a gift?

8Already you have all you want! Already you have become rich! Quite apart from us you have become kings! Indeed, I wish that you had become kings, so that we might be kings with you! 9For I think that God has exhibited us apostles as last of all, as though sentenced to death, because we have become a spectacle to the world, to angels and to mortals. 10We are fools for the sake of Christ, but you are wise in Christ. We are weak, but you are strong. You are held in honor, but we in disrepute. 11To the present hour we are hungry and thirsty, we are poorly clothed and beaten and homeless, 12and we grow weary from the work of our own hands. When reviled, we bless; when persecuted, we endure; 13when slandered, we

---

p In verses 16 and 17 the Greek word for *you* is plural

q Gk *brothers*
r Or *Who makes you different from another?*

3:15 All of this is further warning to the one who is building over Paul's foundation.   **3:18** This is not a new topic, but it illustrates again the close connection between the leadership issue and the wisdom issue at Corinth: Paul's continual movement from one to the other in *1 Cor.* 1–4 suggests that his readers understood the connection. The Corinthians' claim to wisdom is linked to their teacher, whom Paul now warns not to destroy God's temple.   **3:19** *Job* 5:13. The MT and the LXX agree with Paul's wording.   **3:20** *Ps.* 94:11. MT: "The Lord knows the designs of men to be futile." LXX (93:11): "The Lord knows the thoughts of men, that they are futile." Observe Paul's ease in moving from book to book of the Jewish scriptures and pulling out passages concerning "wisdom" or "knowledge." He also adjusts the wording (e.g., by inserting *the wise* here) to stress his point.   **4:6** *Apollos* Paul confirms that the preceding discussion has been largely about himself and Apollos. Perhaps, then, it is those who prefer Apollos who have been "judging" or denigrating Paul in his absence (4:3).   *so that . . . what is written* Lit. "so that you may learn through us the 'not beyond what is written.'" The sentence structure, referent *(what is written)*, and meaning are unclear. "What is written" usually refers to scripture, but scholars have sought in vain for a biblical, philosophical, or rabbinic passage that Paul might have expected to use as an authority in this context. That he is giving a general admonition not to go beyond "scripture" seems unlikely both because of its vagueness and in view of Paul's own practice (i.e., he does not observe scriptural mandates). One scholar argues ingeniously that a Christian copyist made a small correction to the text by adding *not* before *puffed up* in the next line of the manuscript. The scribe then dutifully noted in the margin that "the not [goes] beyond what is written" (i.e., in the manuscript that he received), but his marginal note was later incorporated into the text itself. In any case, the following clause makes Paul's main point.   **4:8** *rich* This ongoing contrast between Paul and his readers fits with everything we have seen so far in the letter: he associates them with comfort, riches, power, wisdom, strength, and honor, while associating himself with humiliation, want, disrepute, ignorance, and suffering. The contrast seems to hinge on the word *Already* repeated at the outset. Paul does not believe that the full benefits of Christian life can be realized in this age.   *kings with you* Paul believes that Christians will reign and judge the world after Jesus returns (*1 Cor.* 6:2). He sees the Corinthians behaving as if they had already begun to rule.

speak kindly. We have become like the rubbish of the world, the dregs of all things, to this very day.

Fatherly Admonition

[14]I am not writing this to make you ashamed, but to admonish you as my beloved children. [15]For though you might have ten thousand guardians in Christ, you do not have many fathers. Indeed, in Christ Jesus I became your father through the gospel. [16]I appeal to you, then, be imitators of me. [17]For this reason I sent[s] you Timothy, who is my beloved and faithful child in the Lord, to remind you of my ways in Christ Jesus, as I teach them everywhere in every church. [18]But some of you, thinking that I am not coming to you, have become arrogant. [19]But I will come to you soon, if the Lord wills, and I will find out not the talk of these arrogant people but their power. [20]For the kingdom of God depends not on talk but on power. [21]What would you prefer? Am I to come to you with a stick, or with love in a spirit of gentleness?

Sexual Immorality Defiles the Church

5 It is actually reported that there is sexual immorality among you, and of a kind that is not found even among pagans; for a man is living with his father's wife. [2]And you are arrogant! Should you not rather have mourned, so that he who has done this would have been removed from among you?

[3]For though absent in body, I am present in spirit; and as if present I have already pronounced judgment [4]in the name of the Lord Jesus on the man who has done such a thing.[t] When you are assembled, and my spirit is present with the power of our Lord Jesus, [5]you are to hand this man over to Satan for the destruction of the flesh, so that his spirit may be saved in the day of the Lord.[u]

[6]Your boasting is not a good thing. Do you not know that a little yeast leavens the whole batch of dough? [7]Clean out the old yeast so that you may be a

---

s Or *am sending*

t Or *on the man who has done such a thing in the name of the Lord Jesus*

u Other ancient authorities add *Jesus*

4:15 Still another metaphor comparing Paul and Apollos: Paul is their only *father;* anyone who comes later, such as Apollos, is but one of the *ten thousand guardians* of the children. The guardian, of course, cannot compete with the father's authority. **4:17** See 16:10 and the note there. Either Timothy has already been dispatched or he will carry the letter from Paul (so that the past tense would anticipate his arrival with the letter). **everywhere in every church** Hyperbole. Although in *Phil.* 3:6 and *Gal.* 1:13 he implies that a church existed before his conversion, in *1 Cor.* 7:17; 11:16 and *Rom.* 16:16 he speaks, as here, on behalf of *all* the churches, almost as if "church" (Gk *ekklēsia*) was a unique term associated with his mission, not with other Christians. These lines confirm that Paul does want the Corinthians to follow him after all (contrast 1:11–13). Was the problem in Corinth, then, party strife per se, or was it defection from *Paul's* sphere of leadership? **4:20** A one-sentence summary of the entire argument in *1 Cor.* 1–4, which contrasts eloquent rhetoric, represented by Apollos, with the effective power claimed by Paul. In attacking empty speech and pretended wisdom, Paul agrees (albeit from his own perspective) with contemporary moral philosophers; see Plato, *Gorgias;* Epictetus, *Discourses* 2.19; 3.33. **kingdom of God** One of the few passages in Paul's letters that mention the kingdom (or "reign") of God, although this was apparently the dominant theme of Jesus' teaching (Mark 1:15). The other Pauline passages are *1 Thess.* 2:12; *1 Cor.* 6:9–10; 15:50; *Gal.* 5:21; *Rom.* 14:17. In every case Paul is speaking of general ethical concerns; the term does not appear central to his thought. **5:1 reported** Since this information comes from an observer of the Christian group at Corinth who is loyal to Paul and critical of problems in the church, it seems to have originated in the oral report from Chloe's people (1:11). **pagans** Lit. "nations," "Gentiles." This is the standard Jewish term for non-Jews. Although it might seem to confirm that a high proportion of the Corinthian Christians were native Jews—see also 5:8; 7:18; 10:1 and this letter's many citations of scripture as authoritative (e.g., 9:8)—Paul can also say that the Corinthian believers *were Gentiles* but are no longer (12:2). In other letters, he speaks of his Gentile followers as remaining "Gentiles": *Gal.* 2:12, 14; *Rom.* 15:9, 16; 16:4. **living with** Lit. "having," in the sexual sense. **father's wife** Such a liaison would violate Jewish law (*Lev.* 18:8), which expressly forbids union with one's "father's wife"—mentioned as someone distinct from the "mother" (18:7). The biblical law assumes the practice of polygamy, and so a "father's wife" could be any one of several wives who were not one's mother. In Greco-Roman society, which practiced monogamy, a woman described in this way would more naturally be understood as a stepmother. **5:5** Exactly what this involved is unclear. The anticipated outcome seems to be the man's death *(destruction of the flesh)* at the hands of Satan. Consider (a) Paul's view that misuse of the Eucharist also hastens sickness and death (11:30), so that perhaps depriving the man of the Eucharist would bring death; (b) the rabbinic view that death atones for one's sins during life (note Paul's *so that his spirit might be saved*); and (c) Josephus's claim that Essenes who were expelled from their group often died from starvation, being unable to eat ordinary food (*J.W.* 2.143). The passage could also be understood *(hand this man over to Satan)* to involve a curse; see *Gal.* 1:8–9. **5:7 paschal lamb** This is the earliest Christian statement linking Jesus' death with the Passover. The four canonical gospels will all develop this association in their narratives of Jesus' death, though in different ways. Note that Paul continues to celebrate Jewish festivals even though he has renounced many aspects of common Jewish identity (9:20b; *Gal.* 3:24–25). See 16:8, which confirms that Passover is approaching as Paul writes this letter. But contrast *Gal.* 4:9–11, where he seems to be upset with his Gentile converts for having

new batch, as you really are unleavened. For our paschal lamb, Christ, has been sacrificed. 8Therefore, let us celebrate the festival, not with the old yeast, the yeast of malice and evil, but with the unleavened bread of sincerity and truth.

Sexual Immorality Must Be Judged

9I wrote to you in my letter not to associate with sexually immoral persons— 10not at all meaning the immoral of this world, or the greedy and robbers, or idolaters, since you would then need to go out of the world. 11But now I am writing to you not to associate with anyone who bears the name of brother or sister*v* who is sexually immoral or greedy, or is an idolater, reviler, drunkard, or robber. Do not even eat with such a one. 12For what have I to do with judging those outside? Is it not those who are inside that you are to judge? 13God will judge those outside. "Drive out the wicked person from among you."

Lawsuits among Believers

6When any of you has a grievance against another, do you dare to take it to court before the unrigh-

teous, instead of taking it before the saints? 2Do you not know that the saints will judge the world? And if the world is to be judged by you, are you incompetent to try trivial cases? 3Do you not know that we are to judge angels—to say nothing of ordinary matters? 4If you have ordinary cases, then, do you appoint as judges those who have no standing in the church? 5I say this to your shame. Can it be that there is no one among you wise enough to decide between one believer*v* and another, 6but a believer*v* goes to court against a believer*v*—and before unbelievers at that?

7In fact, to have lawsuits at all with one another is already a defeat for you. Why not rather be wronged? Why not rather be defrauded? 8But you yourselves wrong and defraud—and believers*w* at that.

9Do you not know that wrongdoers will not inherit the kingdom of God? Do not be deceived! Fornicators, idolaters, adulterers, male prostitutes, sodomites, 10thieves, the greedy, drunkards, revilers, robbers—none of these will inherit the kingdom of God. 11And this is what some of you used to be. But you were washed, you were sanctified, you were

---

v Gk brother   *w* Gk brothers

---

begun to observe the Jewish calendar. It is unclear what it would mean in practical terms for Gentile Christians to celebrate the Passover. **5:8 old yeast** During the week following Passover, which commemorated Israel's deliverance from Egypt, all yeast had to be removed from the household in commemoration of the Israelites' hasty departure. This period was known in the 1st century as the Feast of Unleavened Bread. Later Judaism (and this may have been common earlier in some circles) has tended to call the entire eight-day celebration Passover. See *Exod.* 13:3–10; Philo, *On the Special Laws* 2.145–161; Josephus, *Ant.* 3.248–251. It is unclear whether Paul's Gentile converts in Corinth would have been expected to discard yeast from their homes. **5:9** Since Paul has not made a general statement about sexually immoral persons in this letter, it seems that he is referring to a previous letter to Corinth, which has been lost. A fragment of it may be preserved in *2 Cor.* 6:14–7:1, which deals with avoidance of unclean persons in the context of marriage. See the introduction to *2 Corinthians* and note to *2 Cor.* 6:14–7:1. **5:13** *Deut.* 17:7. MT: "Let the hands of the witnesses be the first against him [a convicted worshiper of other gods] to put him to death, and the hands of the rest of the people thereafter. Thus you will sweep out evil from your midst." LXX: "And the hand of the witnesses shall be [laid] on him, among the first to kill him, and finally the hand of the people. So drive out the wicked person from among you." To suit his purpose, Paul has changed the verb "drive out" from a singular (referring to Moses) to a plural and changed the issue to sexual immorality. **6:2** Although not developed elsewhere in Paul's writings, the idea that God's elect would rule and judge the world was common in Jewish literature of the period: *Dan.* 7:13–14; 12:3; *Wis.* 3:7–8; 4:16; and the *War Scroll* from Qumran (1QM). **6:3** Perhaps a reference to the "sons of God" in *Genesis* 6, who were a topic of some speculation in Paul's day. See *1 Enoch* 6–16, 64–71; *Jude* 6. **6:5 believer** The Gk word here *adelphos*, "brother." In most places the NRSV translates it as "brother and sister"; see the main introduction to the *Reader*. The root is not the same as that of the word translated "unbelievers" in the next verse. Paul apparently means to stress the familial relationship among his readers. **6:8 believers** Lit. "brothers." See previous note. **6:9 male prostitutes** Lit. "soft" or "dainty" (persons). The word can refer equally to physical or moral softness (including self-indulgence and cowardice), both of which were despicable by the standards of contemporary moral philosophy. Since only women were supposed to be soft, the word sometimes had the sense, perhaps indicated by the context here, of effeminacy or even homosexual activity. **sodomites** The Gk word *arsenokoitēs* is a compound from *arsēn* ("male") and *koitē* ("bed"): thus "one (a male) who beds a male." **6:10 robbers** For other lists of sundry moral evils in Paul, see *Gal.* 5:19–21; *Rom.* 1:29–31. Such lists were very common among the moral philosophers of the Greco-Roman world and in Greco-Jewish literature (see *Wis.* 14:24–26). As in *Galatians* 5, the vice lists were often set against lists of virtues. **kingdom of God** See the note to 4:20. It is striking that when Paul uses the phrase "kingdom of God" (rarely), he tends to use the verb "inherit" with it (*1 Cor.* 15:50; *Gal.* 5:21). In the synoptic tradition, Jesus more often speaks of inheriting eternal life; only *Matt.* 25:34 speaks of inheriting the "kingdom prepared for you." Hereditary rule was standard throughout the Greco-Roman world, so the image of inheriting a "reign" made sense. Paul may be preserving the language of Jesus and his earlier followers. **6:11 justified** In Gk, the verbal form of "righteous" or "just." To keep the same English word group, one might translate this verb "made righteous." **God** Here Paul finishes responding to the oral report from Chloe's people

justified in the name of the Lord Jesus Christ and in the Spirit of our God.

Glorify God in Body and Spirit

12"All things are lawful for me," but not all things are beneficial. "All things are lawful for me," but I will not be dominated by anything. 13"Food is meant for the stomach and the stomach for food,"x and God will destroy both one and the other. The body is meant not for fornication but for the Lord, and the Lord for the body. 14And God raised the Lord and will also raise us by his power. 15Do you not know that your bodies are members of Christ? Should I therefore take the members of Christ and make them members of a prostitute? Never! 16Do you not know that whoever is united to a prostitute becomes one body with her? For it is said, "The two shall be one flesh." 17But anyone united to the Lord becomes one spirit with him. 18Shun fornication! Every sin that a person commits is outside the body; but the fornicator sins against the body itself. 19Or do you not know that your body is a templey of the Holy Spirit within you, which you have from God, and that you are not your own? 20For you were bought with a price; therefore glorify God in your body.

---

x The quotation may extend to the word *other*
y Or *sanctuary*

Directions concerning Marriage

7Now concerning the matters about which you wrote: "It is well for a man not to touch a woman." 2But because of cases of sexual immorality, each man should have his own wife and each woman her own husband. 3The husband should give to his wife her conjugal rights, and likewise the wife to her husband. 4For the wife does not have authority over her own body, but the husband does; likewise the husband does not have authority over his own body, but the wife does. 5Do not deprive one another except perhaps by agreement for a set time, to devote yourselves to prayer, and then come together again, so that Satan may not tempt you because of your lack of self-control. 6This I say by way of concession, not of command. 7I wish that all were as I myself am. But each has a particular gift from God, one having one kind and another a different kind.

8To the unmarried and the widows I say that it is well for them to remain unmarried as I am. 9But if they are not practicing self-control, they should marry. For it is better to marry than to be aflame with passion.

10To the married I give this command—not I but the Lord—that the wife should not separate from

---

(1:11), which concerned the strong support for Apollos's wisdom-oriented Christianity (*Romans* 1–4), sexual immorality (*Romans* 5), and civil lawsuits (6:1–11). Paul will now turn to the Corinthians' own letter to him (7:1ff.). Before doing so, he includes the following paragraph, which is a sort of bridge to the next section: Paul criticizes the use of prostitutes (6:15–20), which may be another item from Chloe's negative report, but also raises the issues of appropriate diet (see *Romans* 8–10) and resurrection (see *Romans* 15). **6:12** The Gk text has no quotation marks. They are supplied by the translators, here and elsewhere, on the hypothesis that Paul sometimes quotes the Corinthians' slogans in order to qualify them. This conclusion arises in part because Paul frequently contradicts the words in quotation marks. But it is not always clear when Paul is quoting others (e.g., throughout *Romans* 8–10), and so we have a variety of interpretive possibilities, depending on where we insert the quotation marks. Here, the Corinthian position seems to be that, having entered a new age of wisdom, they are no longer bound by dietary and other laws. **6:13** *food* Anticipating the discussion of food in *1 Corinthians* 8–10. *fornication* The same Gk word is rendered "sexual immorality" elsewhere (5:1), and a cognate is rendered "sexually immoral persons" (5:9). This section seems to indicate that sexual activity and particularly the hire of prostitutes was a special problem among Paul's followers in Corinth. The city was notorious for its trade in prostitution. Words commonly used in antiquity for "to hire a prostitute" and "pimp" were built on the root word "Corinth." **6:14** Anticipating *1 Corinthians* 15. **6:15** *members of Christ* Anticipating *1 Corinthians* 12–14. **6:16** *Gen.* 2:24. MT: "and they will become one flesh." LXX: "and the two shall be one flesh." Also cited by Jesus; *Mark* 10:8; *Matt.* 19:5. **6:17** Paul uses the passage not to promote monogamy, as Jesus had, but to contrast fleshly and spiritual unions. For him, adultery is wrong not so much because it violates a man's prior union with his wife as because it violates the spiritual union with Christ. **6:19** Once again, Paul argues from a prior commitment not to one's wife but to the Holy Spirit. **7:1** *you wrote* Paul will now deal in order with the six issues (at least) that the Corinthians raised in their letter. Each response begins with the same Gk phrase *peri de*, translated here "now concerning." *not to touch a woman* Because this statement follows Paul's introduction of the Corinthians' concerns and because he immediately qualifies it, the translators have suggested that he is quoting the Corinthians' slogan rather than stating his own view. Nonetheless, 7:6–9 and 7:26–35 show that Paul's own preference is celibacy. The phrase *It is well* matches Paul's language in 7:8. Following the NRSV punctuation, many have supposed that the Corinthians favored "spiritual marriage," devoid of sex. This is hard to reconcile, however, with the dire warnings against adultery in *1 Corinthians* 6. Alternatively, the Corinthians' view of Christianity inclined them to unrestricted indulgence now (see 4:8–11), and Paul was the one who favored asceticism in view of the imminent end. **7:9** *to be aflame with passion* Lit. "to be burning [or 'aflame' or 'inflamed']." *With passion* is the translators' interpretation. Paul might be referring to the fire of future judgment (3:13–15). **7:10** Paul knows of Jesus' prohibition of divorce, or divorce and remarriage, which will be reported later in the Synoptic Gospels (*Mark* 10:11; *Matt.* 5:32; 19:9).

her husband 11(but if she does separate, let her remain unmarried or else be reconciled to her husband), and that the husband should not divorce his wife.

12To the rest I say—I and not the Lord—that if any believer*z* has a wife who is an unbeliever, and she consents to live with him, he should not divorce her. 13And if any woman has a husband who is an unbeliever, and he consents to live with her, she should not divorce him. 14For the unbelieving husband is made holy through his wife, and the unbelieving wife is made holy through her husband. Otherwise, your children would be unclean, but as it is, they are holy. 15But if the unbelieving partner separates, let it be so; in such a case the brother or sister is not bound. It is to peace that God has called you.*a* 16Wife, for all you know, you might save your husband. Husband, for all you know, you might save your wife.

The Life That the Lord Has Assigned

17However that may be, let each of you lead the life that the Lord has assigned, to which God called you. This is my rule in all the churches. 18Was anyone at the time of his call already circumcised? Let him not seek to remove the marks of circumcision. Was anyone at the time of his call uncircumcised? Let him not seek circumcision. 19Circumcision is nothing, and uncircumcision is nothing; but obeying the commandments of God is everything. 20Let each of you remain in the condition in which you were called.

21Were you a slave when called? Do not be concerned about it. Even if you can gain your freedom, make use of your present condition now more than ever.*b* 22For whoever was called in the Lord as a slave is a freed person belonging to the Lord, just as whoever was free when called is a slave of Christ. 23You were bought with a price; do not become slaves of human masters. 24In whatever condition you were called, brothers and sisters,*c* there remain with God.

The Unmarried and the Widows

25Now concerning virgins, I have no command of the Lord, but I give my opinion as one who by the Lord's mercy is trustworthy. 26I think that, in view of the impending*d* crisis, it is well for you to remain as you are. 27Are you bound to a wife? Do not seek to be free. Are you free from a wife? Do not seek a wife. 28But if you marry, you do not sin, and if a virgin marries, she does not sin. Yet those who marry will experience distress in this life,*e* and I would spare you that. 29I mean, brothers and sisters,*c* the appointed time has grown short; from now on, let even those who have wives be as though they had none, 30and those who mourn as though they were not mourning, and those who rejoice as though they were not rejoicing, and those who buy as though they had no possessions, 31and those who deal with the world as though they had no dealings with it. For the present form of this world is passing away.

32I want you to be free from anxieties. The unmarried man is anxious about the affairs of the Lord,

---

z Gk *brother*
a Other ancient authorities read *us*

b Or *avail yourself of the opportunity*
c Gk *brothers*
d Or *present*
e Gk *in the flesh*

7:11 Paul understands Jesus to have prohibited remarriage. Divorce is undesirable but remarriage is excluded. **7:14 *her husband*** Some manuscripts read "through the brother." ***holy*** If Paul is hinting at salvation by association here, his remark about proxy baptism (15:29) may be a significant parallel. **7:15 *brother or sister*** Although the translators regularly add "sisters" where Paul has only "brothers," in this case it is Paul who makes both cases explicit. **7:17 *all the churches*** See note to 4:17. **7:18 *circumcised*** Another indication that although Paul considered himself an apostle to Gentiles, at least some Jews were among his Corinthian converts. See 5:1, 7. ***marks of circumcision*** In the Greco-Roman world, various techniques, including surgical, were available for epispasm, the lengthening of the foreskin. Such procedures were used both by those born with short foreskins and by some Jews who wished to disguise their circumcision for one reason or another. **7:19** What exactly are *the commandments of God* here? The language *(obeying, commandments of God)* is biblical and is used by Jewish authors to speak of the Torah. Paul himself refers to the law of Moses as "the commandment" (*Rom.* 7:8–13). Here, however, he does not seem to be calling for Torah observance because (a) circumcision, which he dismisses as nothing, is one of the Torah's most fundamental requirements (*Genesis* 17) and (b) he elsewhere speaks as though the law were no longer in force (*Gal.* 3:24–25). Perhaps he means here the "law of Christ" (see *Gal.* 6:2), using "commandments" in a non-Jewish, Christian sense, but the meaning of the phrase remains unclear. **7:25** This is perhaps the second issue that Paul selects from the Corinthians' letter. Or they may have raised a series of related cases concerning sex and marriage (7:1, 8, 12) and Paul simply chooses to reinvoke the response formula "Now concerning" here. **7:29–35** A remarkably similar line of reasoning—that the devoted service of God suggests avoidance of marriage and family, especially under the present circumstances—is found in the Cynic-Stoic philosopher Epictetus at the end of the century (*Discourses* 3.65–82). The need for concentration was also a reason given for the requirement that Roman legionary soldiers remain celibate (Herodian, *Hist. Rom.* 3.8.5). **7:31** See *1 Thess.* 1:9–10; 4:13–18; *1 Cor.* 10:11; 15:12–58; 16:22. Paul, apparently in contrast to many of his readers (*1 Cor.* 4:8–13), eagerly awaits the end of this age.

how to please the Lord; 33but the married man is anxious about the affairs of the world, how to please his wife, 34and his interests are divided. And the unmarried woman and the virgin are anxious about the affairs of the Lord, so that they may be holy in body and spirit; but the married woman is anxious about the affairs of the world, how to please her husband. 35I say this for your own benefit, not to put any restraint upon you, but to promote good order and unhindered devotion to the Lord.

36If anyone thinks that he is not behaving properly toward his fiancée,*f* if his passions are strong, and so it has to be, let him marry as he wishes; it is no sin. Let them marry. 37But if someone stands firm in his resolve, being under no necessity but having his own desire under control, and has determined in his own mind to keep her as his fiancée,*f* he will do well. 38So then, he who marries his fiancée*f* does well; and he who refrains from marriage will do better.

39A wife is bound as long as her husband lives. But if the husband dies,*g* she is free to marry anyone she wishes, only in the Lord. 40But in my judgment she is more blessed if she remains as she is. And I think that I too have the Spirit of God.

Food Offered to Idols

8 Now concerning food sacrificed to idols: we know that "all of us possess knowledge." Knowledge puffs up, but love builds up. 2Anyone who claims to know something does not yet have the necessary knowledge; 3but anyone who loves God is known by him.

4Hence, as to the eating of food offered to idols, we know that "no idol in the world really exists," and that "there is no God but one." 5Indeed, even though there may be so-called gods in heaven or on earth— as in fact there are many gods and many lords— 6yet for us there is one God, the Father, from whom are all things and for whom we exist, and one Lord, Jesus Christ, through whom are all things and through whom we exist.

7It is not everyone, however, who has this knowledge. Since some have become so accustomed to idols until now, they still think of the food they eat as food offered to an idol; and their conscience, being weak, is defiled. 8"Food will not bring us close to God."*h* We are no worse off if we do not eat, and no better off if we do. 9But take care that this liberty of yours does not somehow become a stumbling block to the weak. 10For if others see you, who possess knowledge, eating in the temple of an idol, might they not, since their conscience is weak, be encouraged to the point of eating food sacrificed to idols? 11So by your knowledge those weak believers for whom Christ died are destroyed.*i* 12But when you thus sin against members of your family,*j* and wound their conscience when it is weak, you sin against

---

f Gk *virgin*
g Gk *falls asleep*

h The quotation may extend to the end of the verse
i Gk *the weak brother . . . is destroyed*
j Gk *against the brothers*

7:36 *let him marry as he wishes* Lit. "let him do what he wishes." In keeping with ancient social structures, Paul assumes that the man has the initiative in marriage. **7:39** Compare 7:15, where an unbelieving spouse departs and the believing spouse is "not bound." **8:1** *food sacrificed to idols* A new issue from the Corinthians' letter. In the ancient world, meat was relatively scarce and was eaten mainly on festive occasions. The usual place for such festivity was the local temple. No matter what the purpose of the celebration, it routinely included a sacrifice to the local god. In the sacrifice, some of the meat would be consumed in the flames, some would be set apart for the priests on the "table of the god," and some would be eaten by the celebrants. The priests could not eat all of the meat assigned to them, and the surplus was often sold in the marketplace—as choice meat, since it had been fit for sacrifice. Observant Jews would not eat this food because it had not been prepared according to biblical law (see, e.g., *Leviticus* 17; m. Avodah Zarah 2). It quickly became a problem for the Gentile church what position to take on sacrificial meat; see *Did.* 6.3. *all . . . knowledge* Apparently the Corinthians' slogan, given Paul's immediate rejection of claims to knowledge. **8:4** The translators take these to be further Corinthian slogans. Presumably, those who claimed that "all of us possess knowledge" would feel free to eat the meat, and this seems to be the Corinthian stance (see 8:9). **8:5–6** The emphatic tone seems to indicate that Paul is speaking here. He says that although *for us* there is only one (true) God, the other gods are real spiritual powers. See 10:20–22. See also the view in 8:4. **8:7** *Since some . . . to an idol* Or "But some people by custom until now eat sacrificial meat as if it were offered to an idol." *is defiled* It is usually supposed that these people of weak conscience are Gentiles who used to eat sacrificial meat readily. Now, having trusted Christ and abandoned their former lives, they face problems with such food because of its associations from their past. It may be, however, that the "custom" in question (in the alternative translation above) is Jewish tradition, which takes a pronounced stand against any association with *idols*. **8:8** *close to God* The NRSV's insertion of quotation marks departs from the earlier RSV translation. Perhaps in this translation the Corinthians are thought to be saying, "Observance of food laws will not bring us closer to God, so let us eat!" But the statement can also be read as Paul's own, since it seems coherent with what immediately follows. *We are . . . if we do* Paul does not say here that food is immaterial. Rather, both halves of the sentence challenge the claim that eating (sacrificial meat) is beneficial. Paul claims that abstinence will not hurt and indulgence will not help. He seems, therefore, to oppose eating this meat.

Christ. [13]Therefore, if food is a cause of their falling,[k] I will never eat meat, so that I may not cause one of them[l] to fall.

The Rights of an Apostle

9Am I not free? Am I not an apostle? Have I not seen Jesus our Lord? Are you not my work in the Lord? [2]If I am not an apostle to others, at least I am to you; for you are the seal of my apostleship in the Lord.

[3]This is my defense to those who would examine me. [4]Do we not have the right to our food and drink? [5]Do we not have the right to be accompanied by a believing wife,[m] as do the other apostles and the brothers of the Lord and Cephas? [6]Or is it only Barnabas and I who have no right to refrain from working for a living? [7]Who at any time pays the expenses for doing military service? Who plants a vineyard and does not eat any of its fruit? Or who tends a flock and does not get any of its milk?

[8]Do I say this on human authority? Does not the law also say the same? [9]For it is written in the law of Moses, "You shall not muzzle an ox while it is treading out the grain." Is it for oxen that God is concerned? [10]Or does he not speak entirely for our sake? It was indeed written for our sake, for whoever plows should plow in hope and whoever threshes should thresh in hope of a share in the crop. [11]If we have sown spiritual good among you, is it too much if we reap your material benefits? [12]If others share this rightful claim on you, do not we still more?

Nevertheless, we have not made use of this right, but we endure anything rather than put an obstacle in the way of the gospel of Christ. [13]Do you not know that those who are employed in the temple service get their food from the temple, and those who serve at the altar share in what is sacrificed on the altar? [14]In the same way, the Lord commanded that those who proclaim the gospel should get their living by the gospel.

[15]But I have made no use of any of these rights, nor am I writing this so that they may be applied in my case. Indeed, I would rather die than that—no one will deprive me of my ground for boasting! [16]If I proclaim the gospel, this gives me no ground for boasting, for an obligation is laid on me, and woe to me if I do not proclaim the gospel! [17]For if I do this of my own will, I have a reward; but if not of my own

---

k Gk *my brother's falling*
l Gk *cause my brother*
m Gk *a sister as wife*

8:13 I will never The Gk has an emphatic double negative—"I will never ever, for eternity"—stressing Paul's absolute commitment to the "weak" side (see 4:8–13). As with questions of sexuality, he is decidedly on the side of abstinence in view of the imminent end of the age. **9:1 free** First Corinthians 9 brings an abrupt shift of topic, although Paul will return to the idol meat issue in *1 Corinthians* 10. Because of the rupture, some scholars have suggested that *1 Corinthians* 9 is a fragment from another letter. But a careful reading shows a close connection between *1 Corinthians* 8 and 9; the issue in both is the contrast between rights and what is helpful. Just as Paul asks the Corinthians to forego their freedom to eat sacrificial idol meat, he now shows how he himself has forfeited his right to financial remuneration for his missionary work. He thus presents himself as an object lesson concerning rights not claimed. **seen Jesus** See 15:3–11. Paul insists that he has the full right to be called an apostle because he has encountered the risen Jesus in the same manner as the other apostles; he is the last one, he says, in this group (15:8). The author of *Acts,* on the other hand, makes Paul's experience of the risen Christ quite different from that of the apostles, who were with Jesus from his baptism by John through the forty-day period after his resurrection (*Acts* 1:2–3, 21–22). **9:2** Paul's apostleship was under frequent attack from other Christian leaders. See *2 Cor.* 10:7–12; 11:5; 12:11–12; *Gal.* 1:1. On the one hand, Paul did not limit the number of apostles to twelve as *Luke-Acts* did later (*Luke* 6:13; *Acts* 1:15–26), since he also includes himself and Barnabas at least (*1 Cor.* 9:5–6). On the other hand, he still sees the group as small: he is the *last* to be included (*1 Cor.* 15:10). Paul recognizes, as does the author of *Acts,* that any messenger may be called an apostle in a secondary sense (*2 Cor.* 8:23; *Phil.* 2:25). For *Acts,* however, Paul and Barnabas could be called apostles only in the secondary sense (*Acts* 14:4, 14), whereas Paul plainly considers himself one of the apostles in the primary sense. **9:5 brothers of the Lord** Other texts confirm that Jesus' brother James was a significant figure in the first-generation church (*Gal.* 1:19; 2:12; *Acts* 12:17; 15:13; 21:18); here is a rare indication that Jesus' other brothers (named at *Mark* 6:3) were also known outside Palestine for missionary work. **9:6** A valuable reference, along with *Gal.* 2:1–13, to Paul's companion Barnabas. See the traditions in *Acts* about Barnabas (*Acts* 4:36; 9:27; 11:22, 30; 12:25; 13:1–7, 43–50). **9:8** This appeal to Mosaic law as a direct, non-allegorical basis for behavior is unusual in Paul (contrast *Gal.* 3:23–25) and may be another indication that at least some of his readers had some Jewish background. See note to 5:1. **9:9** *Deut.* 25:4. The MT and the LXX agree, except that Paul's word for "muzzle" is different from that in the received LXX. **9:10** *Deut.* 25:4 appears amid a series of humane laws that protect the powerless, including orphans, widows, and foreigners (23:19–20); it seems that the concern there really *is* for the welfare of the animal. Paul's conviction that all scripture was in fact a coded book that spoke of his own climactic era (see 10:11; *Rom.* 4:23–24) was widely shared among early Christian writers. The closest parallel in Jewish circles is offered by the biblical commentaries among the Dead Sea Scrolls, whose authors saw in scripture references to their own era. **9:13** Further examples to supplement those in 9:4–11: Paul has a right to financial support. **9:14** Perhaps Paul has in mind the saying of Jesus, later preserved in *Luke* 10:7, "the laborer deserves to be paid."

will, I am entrusted with a commission. [18]What then is my reward? Just this: that in my proclamation I may make the gospel free of charge, so as not to make full use of my rights in the gospel.

[19]For though I am free with respect to all, I have made myself a slave to all, so that I might win more of them. [20]To the Jews I became as a Jew, in order to win Jews. To those under the law I became as one under the law (though I myself am not under the law) so that I might win those under the law. [21]To those outside the law I became as one outside the law (though I am not free from God's law but am under Christ's law) so that I might win those outside the law. [22]To the weak I became weak, so that I might win the weak. I have become all things to all people, that I might by all means save some. [23]I do it all for the sake of the gospel, so that I may share in its blessings.

[24]Do you not know that in a race the runners all compete, but only one receives the prize? Run in such a way that you may win it. [25]Athletes exercise self-control in all things; they do it to receive a perishable wreath, but we an imperishable one. [26]So I do not run aimlessly, nor do I box as though beating the air; [27]but I punish my body and enslave it, so that after proclaiming to others I myself should not be disqualified.

Warnings from Israel's History

10 I do not want you to be unaware, brothers and sisters,[n] that our ancestors were all under the cloud, and all passed through the sea, [2]and all were baptized into Moses in the cloud and in the sea, [3]and all ate the same spiritual food, [4]and all drank the same spiritual drink. For they drank from the spiritual rock that followed them, and the rock was Christ. [5]Nevertheless, God was not pleased with most of them, and they were struck down in the wilderness.

[6]Now these things occurred as examples for us, so that we might not desire evil as they did. [7]Do not become idolaters as some of them did; as it is written, "The people sat down to eat and drink, and they rose up to play." [8]We must not indulge in sexual immorality as some of them did, and twenty-three thousand fell in a single day. [9]We must not put Christ[o] to the

---

n Gk *brothers*

o Other ancient authorities read *the Lord*

9:18 But see *Phil.* 4:14–17, where Paul acknowledges the steady financial support of the Philippian church throughout the early phases of his Greek mission, both in Macedonia and in Achaia, where Corinth is located. Likewise, in *2 Cor.* 11:8 he will claim that he "robbed" other churches to support his mission in Corinth. **9:20** *Jew* and *one under the law* These two phrases appear synonymous. In spite of widespread diversity among 1st-century Jews, it was widely understood by outsiders that Jews ("Judeans") conducted their lives according to the law of Moses. *not under the law* On Paul's break with his Jewish past, see *Phil.* 3:4–9. **9:21** Paul does not deny being outside the law of Moses; rather, he has just affirmed his independence from it. But to keep the symmetry of his statement, he denies that he is without law altogether and invokes *Christ' law* (see *Gal.* 6:2; *Rom.* 8:2). **9:22** See Paul's championing of the "weak" in *1 Corinthians* 1–4 and 8. **9:24** Athletic imagery was commonly employed by moral philosophers of Paul's day; they generally held out virtue as a prize more worthy than the athlete's crown. See *Phil.* 3:14; Isocrates, *To Demonicus* 9–15; Plutarch, *On Listening to Lectures* 37F–38; Epictetus, *Discourses* 3.22.50–61; Dio Chrysostom, *Discourses* 8.9–16. **9:27** Just as he has given up all of his rights and just as an athlete gives up life's pleasures to win the prize, Paul wants his readers to give up even what they might think that they are entitled to, including sacrificial meat. **10:1** *I do not want you to be unaware* A formulaic phrase meaning "I want you to know" and used by Paul to indicate that new information follows. See *1 Thess.* 4:13; *1 Cor.* 12:1; *2 Cor.* 1:8; *Rom.* 1:13; 11:25. Contrast the phrase "you (yourselves) know," which assumes knowledge already shared (*1 Thess.* 2:1; 3:3; 4:2; 5:2; *1 Cor.* 12:2; *Phil.* 4:15; *Gal.* 4:13). Paul's interpretation of the wilderness wanderings will be new to his audience. **10:2** Paul takes over the story of Israel's deliverance from Egypt and subsequent rebellion in the desert under Moses as a negative example for his converts. To make the analogy secure, he suggests that the Israelites were *baptized into Moses,* evidently a reference to the crossing of the Sea of Reeds (*Exod.* 14:21–25), although the point of that story was that the Israelites did *not* get wet. The peculiar phrase *into Moses* seems to be chosen to parallel Christian baptism "into Christ" (*Gal.* 3:27; *Rom.* 6:3). **10:4** The Israelites' spiritual food was apparently the manna and quail of *Exod.* 16:4, 35. Their spiritual drink would, then, have been the water that miraculously issued from the rock: *Exod.* 17:6. Paul wants to link these phenomena to the bread and wine of the Christian Eucharist. Because *Exod.* 17:6 and *Num.* 20:1, 11 put the rock in different places, some Jewish interpreters reasoned that the rock must have followed the Israelites, although nothing in the text itself suggests this (*t. Sukkah* 3:11). Paul takes over this common legend and apparently expects his readers to make sense of it. **10:6** *examples for us* See note to 9:10. *desire evil as they did* Paul apparently intends to compare the Israelites to Christians, who participate in the sacraments of baptism and Eucharist and consider themselves safe as a result. He argues that, in spite of their "sacramental" legitimacy, so to speak, the Israelites were punished by God in the desert. His Christian converts, therefore, should expect the same fate if they displease God. A similar example is used by the author of Hebrews (*Heb.* 3:7–19). **10:7** *idolaters* See 10:14. **10:7** *Exod.* 32:6. This quotation matches our LXX exactly and is also a natural translation of the MT. But it is clear from the next verse that Paul takes the word *play* (or "make sport," "have fun") in a sexual sense. Characteristically, he appropriates biblical passages for the situation at hand. **10:8** See *Num.* 25:1–18, which describes the punishment of Israelites who sinned sexually with Moabite women; LXX and MT 25:9, however, put the number at twenty-four thousand. **10:9** See *Num.* 21:5–6.

test, as some of them did, and were destroyed by serpents. [10]And do not complain as some of them did,
and were destroyed by the destroyer. [11]These things
happened to them to serve as an example, and they
were written down to instruct us, on whom the ends
of the ages have come. [12]So if you think you are
standing, watch out that you do not fall. [13]No testing
has overtaken you that is not common to everyone.
God is faithful, and he will not let you be tested
beyond your strength, but with the testing he will
also provide the way out so that you may be able to
endure it.

[14]Therefore, my dear friends,[p] flee from the worship of idols. [15]I speak as to sensible people; judge for
yourselves what I say. [16]The cup of blessing that we
bless, is it not a sharing in the blood of Christ? The
bread that we break, is it not a sharing in the body of
Christ? [17]Because there is one bread, we who are
many are one body, for we all partake of the one
bread. [18]Consider the people of Israel;[q] are not those
who eat the sacrifices partners in the altar? [19]What do
I imply then? That food sacrificed to idols is anything,
or that an idol is anything? [20]No, I imply that what
pagans sacrifice, they sacrifice to demons and not to
God. I do not want you to be partners with demons.
[21]You cannot drink the cup of the Lord and the cup
of demons. You cannot partake of the table of the
Lord and the table of demons. [22]Or are we provoking
the Lord to jealousy? Are we stronger than he?

Do All to the Glory of God

[23]"All things are lawful," but not all things are beneficial. "All things are lawful," but not all things build
up. [24]Do not seek your own advantage, but that
of the other. [25]Eat whatever is sold in the meat market without raising any question on the ground of
conscience, [26]for "the earth and its fullness are the
Lord's." [27]If an unbeliever invites you to a meal and
you are disposed to go, eat whatever is set before you
without raising any question on the ground of conscience. [28]But if someone says to you, "This has been
offered in sacrifice," then do not eat it, out of consideration for the one who informed you, and for
the sake of conscience— [29]I mean the other's conscience, not your own. For why should my liberty
be subject to the judgment of someone else's conscience? [30]If I partake with thankfulness, why should
I be denounced because of that for which I give
thanks?

[31]So, whether you eat or drink, or whatever you
do, do everything for the glory of God. [32]Give no offense to Jews or to Greeks or to the church of God,
[33]just as I try to please everyone in everything I do,
not seeking my own advantage, but that of many, so
11 that they may be saved. [1]Be imitators of me, as I
am of Christ.

Head Coverings

[2]I commend you because you remember me in
everything and maintain the traditions just as I

p Gk *my beloved*
q Gk *Israel according to the flesh*

10:10 ***complain*** Or "do not continue to grumble." ***destroyed by the destroyer*** The verb *(apollymi)* and noun *(olothreutos)* have different Gk roots. The word for "destroyer" appears only here in Paul, but the cognate noun for "destruction" occurred in 5:5, where the destruction was to be accomplished by Satan. The biblical story of Israel lacks any reference to satanic power. Paul may have found Satan behind *Num.* 16:41–49 (MT: 17:6–15), which describes a plague that befell the Israelites as a result of their complaints. **10:11** See 9:10 and note. **10:14** Paul seems, after all, to equate the eating of meat offered to idols with idol worship, and so prohibits it. **10:17** Paul will further develop this *body* image in 11:29 and especially 12:14–26. **10:20** ***what pagans sacrifice*** Lit. "what they sacrifice"; *pagans* is supplied by the translators. **10:21** The Corinthians deny the reality of any other gods, so they feel free to eat idol meat. Paul does not argue that the other gods are real gods, but he does believe that they are demonic powers. Union with Christ through the Lord's Supper precludes spiritual union with these demons, just as it precludes union with a prostitute (6:12–20). Therefore, one must not participate in the Gentile feasts. **10:24** With these phrases Paul recapitulates the entire thrust of his argument on sacrificial meat, anticipated in 6:12–20 and developed in *1 Corinthians* 8–10. **10:25** Having thoroughly established his basic position, that one must not partake of sacrificial meat, Paul proceeds to discuss two specific cases: the innocent purchase of meat in the marketplace (should one refuse all meat on suspicion of its past?) and an invitation to dinner at someone else's house. **10:26** *Ps.* 23:1 (LXX: 24:1). Paul agrees exactly with the LXX, which parallels the MT. **10:29–30** These two questions seem to be in tension with the foregoing discussion, in which Paul has insisted that (a) his behavior is constrained by others' consciences, and (b) the demonic powers who receive the Gentile offerings are real. Perhaps he reverts without warning to the cases mentioned earlier, in which one does not know whether meat (purchased in the market or offered at another's home) has been offered to idols. **10:30** ***If I partake with thankfulness*** Or "If I participate in the blessing." **10:33** These lines, recalling 9:20–22, confirm that Paul meant for his own life to serve as an example on the issue of sacrificial meat. **11:2–16** The placement of this passage is problematic because, in view of 11:1 and especially 11:17, we would expect Paul to be discussing some point on which he agreed with the Corinthians' practices; instead 11:2–16 seems confrontational. Because of the passage's clear subordination of women to their husbands, some scholars have wondered hopefully whether it was added by a later church editor. But all of our manuscripts contain the passage, and in view of 14:33–36, we should hesitate to draw such a conclusion unless that, too, is an interpolation as some contend. Precise details of the situation behind

handed them on to you. [3]But I want you to understand that Christ is the head of every man, and the husband[r] is the head of his wife,[s] and God is the head of Christ. [4]Any man who prays or prophesies with something on his head disgraces his head, [5]but any woman who prays or prophesies with her head unveiled disgraces her head—it is one and the same thing as having her head shaved. [6]For if a woman will not veil herself, then she should cut off her hair; but if it is disgraceful for a woman to have her hair cut off or to be shaved, she should wear a veil. [7]For a man ought not to have his head veiled, since he is the image and reflection[t] of God; but woman is the reflection[t] of man. [8]Indeed, man was not made from woman, but woman from man. [9]Neither was man created for the sake of woman, but woman for the sake of man. [10]For this reason a woman ought to have a symbol of[u] authority on her head,[v] because

of the angels. [11]Nevertheless, in the Lord woman is not independent of man or man independent of woman. [12]For just as woman came from man, so man comes through woman; but all things come from God. [13]Judge for yourselves: is it proper for a woman to pray to God with her head unveiled? [14]Does not nature itself teach you that if a man wears long hair, it is degrading to him, [15]but if a woman has long hair, it is her glory? For her hair is given to her for a covering. [16]But if anyone is disposed to be contentious—we have no such custom, nor do the churches of God.

Abuses at the Lord's Supper

[17]Now in the following instructions I do not commend you, because when you come together it is not for the better but for the worse. [18]For, to begin with, when you come together as a church, I hear that there are divisions among you; and to some extent I believe it. [19]Indeed, there have to be factions among you, for only so will it become clear who among you

---

r The same Greek word means *man* or *husband*
s Or *head of the woman*
t Or *glory*
u Gk lacks *a symbol of*
v Or *have freedom of choice regarding her head*

---

this paragraph are lacking. It seems that whereas Corinthian and other Greek women wore veils in public, some Corinthian Christians thought that women should be able to remove their veils while worshiping. This position would fit with the Corinthians' general emphasis on freedom. Although the structure of Paul's argument is debated, his main point is clear: women must cover their hair even while praying or prophesying.   It is uncertain whether Paul is continuing his responses to the Corinthians' letter (see 12:1) or responding to an oral report.   **11:2** But see 4:3–21; 5:1–6; 6:1–8.   **11:4** Here and in the next verse, Paul uses "head" in at least two senses: physical head and superior authority. Some scholars have argued that he also means "source."   **11:5 disgraces her head** Paul seems to use "head" in different senses at the same time (see 11:3–4).   A difficult sentence, in view of the following claim (11:6) that an unveiled woman ought to shave her head— which would make no sense if indeed an uncovered head and a shaved head were the same thing. Paul seems to mean that an uncovered head is tantamount to a shaved head because the hair must be shaved if it is to be left uncovered.   **11:7** On man as the image of God, see *Gen.* 1:26–27, which, however, expressly includes both male and female. Paul shows no awareness of the later Jewish custom that requires men to wear a head covering at prayer. The historical origins of this custom are obscure, and it should probably be dated to a period later than Paul's.   **11:9** See the creation story of *Gen.* 2:18–23.   **11:10** A puzzling reference because it is not further explained. In the context, given Paul's concern that hair is a woman's distinctive sexual feature (11:15) and that failure to cover it up dishonors her husband (head) by attracting unwanted attention, it seems plausible that Paul has in mind the heavenly beings who were attracted to mortal women in *Gen.* 6:2; their sexual relations produced giants in the land, and all of this was part of the sinfulness that brought about the flood. These angels were the object of considerable speculation in some Jewish circles of Paul's day (see *Jude* 6 and *1 Enoch* 6–16, 64–71) and Paul may intend to prevent such angelic lust. Perhaps the angels are simply those who preside over Christian worship, whom one should not offend by impropriety. The reference is too allusive to permit solid conclusions.   **11:12** A rare statement of mutuality that seems to undercut what Paul has just said in 11:8–9. It is not uncommon for Paul to begin a thought that is counterproductive to his current argument and then drop it as he does here (see *1 Cor.* 1:14–16; *Rom.* 5:12).   **11:15 glory** Or "radiance," "splendor."   **covering** The Gk word here is different from that for "veiled" in the preceding verses.   **11:16 custom** If *custom* refers to women's covering their heads, then Paul is declaring his and the churches' willingness to abandon the position he has just supported if anyone makes an issue of it. But such a willingness would be uncharacteristic of Paul (see *1 Cor.* 4:17; *Gal.* 1:6) and difficult to square with either the force of his arguments in favor of women's head covering or the pejorative sense of *contentious*. More likely, *such [a] custom* refers back to the nearest antecedent, "being contentious." In this case, in keeping with the rest of the letter, Paul is dismissing those who would encourage dissension by challenging him: it is not our custom to be contentious.   **11:18 I hear that** This phrase indicates that Paul has interrupted his series of responses to the Corinthians' letter, which he will resume in 12:1. Now he is responding to a report about their bad behavior.   **to some extent I believe it** A rather tame statement in view of Paul's extended criticisms in 1:11–4:21. It seems, therefore, that the divisions in question here are not the same as those discussed earlier. These have to do only with wealthier cliques who celebrate the Lord's Supper in a way that humiliates the poor; the factionalism dealt with in *1 Corinthians* 1–4, however, revolved around fundamental issues of leadership and loyalty.

are genuine. 20When you come together, it is not really to eat the Lord's supper. 21For when the time comes to eat, each of you goes ahead with your own supper, and one goes hungry and another becomes drunk. 22What! Do you not have homes to eat and drink in? Or do you show contempt for the church of God and humiliate those who have nothing? What should I say to you? Should I commend you? In this matter I do not commend you!

The Institution of the Lord's Supper

23For I received from the Lord what I also handed on to you, that the Lord Jesus on the night when he was betrayed took a loaf of bread, 24and when he had given thanks, he broke it and said, "This is my body that is for*w* you. Do this in remembrance of me." 25In the same way he took the cup also, after supper, saying, "This cup is the new covenant in my blood. Do this, as often as you drink it, in remembrance of me." 26For as often as you eat this bread and drink the cup, you proclaim the Lord's death until he comes.

Partaking of the Supper Unworthily

27Whoever, therefore, eats the bread or drinks the cup of the Lord in an unworthy manner will be answerable for the body and blood of the Lord. 28Examine yourselves, and only then eat of the bread and drink of the cup. 29For all who eat and drink*x* without discerning the body,*y* eat and drink judgment against themselves. 30For this reason many of you are weak and ill, and some have died.*z* 31But if we judged ourselves, we would not be judged. 32But when we are judged by the Lord, we are disciplined*a* so that we may not be condemned along with the world.

33So then, my brothers and sisters,*b* when you come together to eat, wait for one another. 34If you are hungry, eat at home, so that when you come together, it will not be for your condemnation. About the other things I will give instructions when I come.

Spiritual Gifts

12 Now concerning spiritual gifts,*c* brothers and sisters,*b* I do not want you to be uninformed. 2You know that when you were pagans, you were

---

w Other ancient authorities read *is broken for*

---

x Other ancient authorities add *in an unworthy manner,*
y Other ancient authorities read *the Lord's body*
z Gk *fallen asleep*
a Or *When we are judged, we are being disciplined by the Lord*
b Gk *brothers*
c Or *spiritual persons*

11:20 The following passage is the earliest known reference to the most basic and enduring Christian celebration—the Lord's Supper, or Eucharist. Later the Synoptic Gospels will elaborate on the story of Jesus' final meal, which served as the basis for the Christian rite (*Mark* 14:12–26; *Matt.* 26:17–30; *Luke* 22:7–23). By the early 2d century, the Roman governor Pliny had ascertained that this common meal was at the heart of Christian identity (*Letters* 10.96). **11:22 *drink in*** These comments support Pliny's impression (see previous note) that the Lord's Supper did not include merely token amounts of bread and wine but was a full communal meal. In Corinth it seems that the membership brought the food, which gave rise to the problems discussed here. By the time of the *Didache* (9–10, 14) and Justin Martyr (*Apology* 1.65–66), the Eucharist had become a more formal and restricted ritual. **11:23 *Received . . . handed on*** Technical terms in contemporary Jewish literature for the transmission of tradition. This is one of the few places in Paul's letters in which he portrays himself as a bearer of tradition concerning Jesus of Nazareth (see also 15:3–7); more typically, he claims to have direct revelations from the risen Christ (see *Gal.* 1:11–17; *2 Cor.* 12:7–9). *betrayed* The earliest reference to Jesus' betrayal, and one of the very few details of Jesus' life mentioned by Paul. The gospels will later fill out this story in various ways. See *Mark* 14:43–50; *Matt.* 26:47–58; *Luke* 22:47–53; *John* 18:2–11. **11:24** The Gk word for "give thanks" is *eucharistō*, from which "Eucharist" derives. **11:25** See the later synoptic accounts: *Mark* 14:22–25; *Matt.* 26:26–29; *Luke* 22:17–20. **11:27 *body and blood*** Perhaps Paul is playing on different senses of the words at the same time (see 11:24; 12:13, 27; *John* 6:35–59). See note to 11:4. **11:29** See previous note. **11:30** For sleep as an image of death, see 15:6, 20. Paul's view that sickness and death are punishments is well established in both Jewish tradition (*Deut.* 28:15–46) and Greek tragedy. But his particular Christian interpretation may well be linked to his view that he and many others will still be alive when Jesus returns (*1 Thess.* 4:15, 17; *1 Cor.* 15:51). **12:1 *Now concerning spiritual gifts*** Paul now resumes his responses to the issues raised in the Corinthians' letter. *Gifts* has been added by the translators, probably correctly, in consideration of 12:4–11. The Gk word here translated *spiritual gifts* could by itself also mean "spiritual people" or "spiritual things." Details are debated, but Paul's emphasis indicates that some Corinthians considered certain people to have a spiritual advantage over others on the basis of the gifts that they exercised. ***I do not want you to be uninformed*** A formula in Paul's letters, introducing new material. See note to 10:1. **12:2 *pagans*** Lit. "nations," "peoples"; in Jewish usage, "Gentiles." See note to 5:1. Paul sometimes calls his followers Gentiles and sometimes distinguishes them from Gentiles. This is the only passage in which he speaks of their moving from Gentile to non-Gentile status. At least here, therefore, he has taken over Jewish vocabulary in the service of his Christian faith. *could not speak* A standard Jewish reproach against the gods of the Greco-Roman world. See *Wis.* 13–15; Philo, *On the Embassy to Gaius* 139, 163; Josephus, *Ag. Ap.* 2.239–256; *1 Thess.* 1:9; *Rom.* 1:20–23.

enticed and led astray to idols that could not speak. ³Therefore I want you to understand that no one speaking by the Spirit of God ever says "Let Jesus be cursed!" and no one can say "Jesus is Lord" except by the Holy Spirit.

⁴Now there are varieties of gifts, but the same Spirit; ⁵and there are varieties of services, but the same Lord; ⁶and there are varieties of activities, but it is the same God who activates all of them in everyone. ⁷To each is given the manifestation of the Spirit for the common good. ⁸To one is given through the Spirit the utterance of wisdom, and to another the utterance of knowledge according to the same Spirit, ⁹to another faith by the same Spirit, to another gifts of healing by the one Spirit, ¹⁰to another the working of miracles, to another prophecy, to another the discernment of spirits, to another various kinds of tongues, to another the interpretation of tongues. ¹¹All these are activated by one and the same Spirit, who allots to each one individually just as the Spirit chooses.

One Body with Many Members

¹²For just as the body is one and has many members, and all the members of the body, though many, are one body, so it is with Christ. ¹³For in the one Spirit we were all baptized into one body—Jews or Greeks, slaves or free—and we were all made to drink of one Spirit.

¹⁴Indeed, the body does not consist of one member but of many. ¹⁵If the foot would say, "Because I am not a hand, I do not belong to the body," that would not make it any less a part of the body. ¹⁶And if the ear would say, "Because I am not an eye, I do not belong to the body," that would not make it any less a part of the body. ¹⁷If the whole body were an eye, where would the hearing be? If the whole body were hearing, where would the sense of smell be? ¹⁸But as it is, God arranged the members in the body,

each one of them, as he chose. ¹⁹If all were a single member, where would the body be? ²⁰As it is, there are many members, yet one body. ²¹The eye cannot say to the hand, "I have no need of you," nor again the head to the feet, "I have no need of you." ²²On the contrary, the members of the body that seem to be weaker are indispensable, ²³and those members of the body that we think less honorable we clothe with greater honor, and our less respectable members are treated with greater respect; ²⁴whereas our more respectable members do not need this. But God has so arranged the body, giving the greater honor to the inferior member, ²⁵that there may be no dissension within the body, but the members may have the same care for one another. ²⁶If one member suffers, all suffer together with it; if one member is honored, all rejoice together with it.

²⁷Now you are the body of Christ and individually members of it. ²⁸And God has appointed in the church first apostles, second prophets, third teachers; then deeds of power, then gifts of healing, forms of assistance, forms of leadership, various kinds of tongues. ²⁹Are all apostles? Are all prophets? Are all teachers? Do all work miracles? ³⁰Do all possess gifts of healing? Do all speak in tongues? Do all interpret? ³¹But strive for the greater gifts. And I will show you a still more excellent way.

The Gift of Love

13 If I speak in the tongues of mortals and of angels, but do not have love, I am a noisy gong or a clanging cymbal. ²And if I have prophetic powers, and understand all mysteries and all knowledge, and if I have all faith, so as to remove mountains, but do not have love, I am nothing. ³If I give away all my possessions, and if I hand over my body so that I may boast,ᵈ but do not have love, I gain nothing.

---

d Other ancient authorities read *body to be burned*

12:3 Whether some Corinthian Christians really cursed Jesus is uncertain. Commentators have come up with ingenious explanations how this might have happened: for example, these might be gnostic Christians who rejected the man Jesus of Nazareth (see *1 John* 4:1–3), or the reference might be to trials before pagan authorities, where Christians might renounce Jesus under duress (Pliny, *Letters* 10.96). Paul's main point, however, seems to be in the following verses: all Christians have the Spirit; otherwise they could not declare Jesus Lord. It may be, then, that the *unreal* prospect of someone's cursing Jesus is introduced only to sharpen this point: Just as no one could curse Jesus by the Spirit (all agree), so none can praise him apart from the Spirit (Paul's point). Consequently, no one can claim superior status by virtue of having the Spirit, since all believers must have it. **12:10** *the working of miracles* Or "powerful activities." *tongues* From 13:1 and 14:2, 9, 14–16, 23, it seems that Paul refers here to a kind of prayer (addressed to God; 14:2) "in the Spirit" that is ordinarily unintelligible to others without the gift of interpretation. See *Rom.* 8:26. **12:12** Paul uses the analogy to much the same effect in *Rom.* 12:4–8. The comparison of a community with a human body, in which all of the parts must work together, was common in his world. In a famous passage the Roman historian Livy (*History* 2.32) had attributed the analogy to a 5th-century B.C.E. senator; philosophers such as Seneca (*Epistles* 92.30; 95.52), Epictetus (*Discourses* 2.10.3–6), and Marcus Aurelius (*Meditations* 2.1) compared the entire universe to a body. Note *Col.* 1:17–18. **12:13** See *Gal.* 3:28. As did some other clubs or voluntary associations in the Roman world, Paul's Christians rejected the most fundamental social distinction—between slaves and free persons. **12:28** See 12:4–10. **12:29** *miracles* The Gk word here is the same as that in the previous verse, translated correctly there as "deeds of power."

4Love is patient; love is kind; love is not envious or boastful or arrogant 5or rude. It does not insist on its own way; it is not irritable or resentful; 6it does not rejoice in wrongdoing, but rejoices in the truth. 7It bears all things, believes all things, hopes all things, endures all things.

8Love never ends. But as for prophecies, they will come to an end; as for tongues, they will cease; as for knowledge, it will come to an end. 9For we know only in part, and we prophesy only in part; 10but when the complete comes, the partial will come to an end. 11When I was a child, I spoke like a child, I thought like a child, I reasoned like a child; when I became an adult, I put an end to childish ways. 12For now we see in a mirror, dimly,*e* but then we will see face to face. Now I know only in part; then I will know fully, even as I have been fully known. 13And now faith, hope, and love abide, these three; and the greatest of these is love.

Gifts of Prophecy and Tongues

14 Pursue love and strive for the spiritual gifts, and especially that you may prophesy. 2For those who speak in a tongue do not speak to other people but to God; for nobody understands them, since they are speaking mysteries in the Spirit. 3On the other hand, those who prophesy speak to other people for their upbuilding and encouragement and consolation. 4Those who speak in a tongue build up themselves, but those who prophesy build up the church. 5Now I would like all of you to speak in tongues, but even more to prophesy. One who prophesies is greater than one who speaks in tongues, unless someone interprets, so that the church may be built up.

6Now, brothers and sisters,*f* if I come to you speaking in tongues, how will I benefit you unless I speak to you in some revelation or knowledge or prophecy or teaching? 7It is the same way with lifeless instruments that produce sound, such as the flute or the harp. If they do not give distinct notes, how will anyone know what is being played? 8And if the bugle gives an indistinct sound, who will get ready for battle? 9So with yourselves; if in a tongue you utter speech that is not intelligible, how will anyone know what is being said? For you will be speaking into the air. 10There are doubtless many different kinds of sounds in the world, and nothing is without sound. 11If then I do not know the meaning of a sound, I will be a foreigner to the speaker and the speaker a foreigner to me. 12So with yourselves; since you are eager for spiritual gifts, strive to excel in them for building up the church.

13Therefore, one who speaks in a tongue should pray for the power to interpret. 14For if I pray in a tongue, my spirit prays but my mind is unproductive. 15What should I do then? I will pray with the spirit, but I will pray with the mind also; I will sing praise with the spirit, but I will sing praise with the mind also. 16Otherwise, if you say a blessing with the spirit, how can anyone in the position of an outsider say the "Amen" to your thanksgiving, since the outsider does not know what you are saying? 17For you may give thanks well enough, but the other person is not built up. 18I thank God that I speak in tongues more than all of you; 19nevertheless, in church I would rather speak five words with my mind, in order to instruct others also, than ten thousand words in a tongue.

---

e Gk *in a riddle*   *f* Gk *brothers*

13:10 Against the Corinthians' view that they are already living with perfect knowledge and freedom (see 4:8–13; 6:12), Paul reasserts his apocalyptic principles: this age is about to pass away; only in the coming age will perfection come. **13:12** *dimly* Lit. "in a riddle" (thus, obscurely). 1st-century mirrors were usually made of highly polished metal, such as bronze. Glass with a lead backing (not mercury) was occasionally used. "Mirror images" were therefore indistinct in comparison with today's. **13:13** As we have seen, this triad forms the heart of Paul's basic preaching: put faith in Christ, wait for his imminent return, and in the meantime live in love (see *1 Thess.* 1:3, 9–10; 5:8). **14:2** *speaking mysteries* Ecstatic speech was familiar to the Corinthians from non-Christian sources: the nearby and world-famous oracle at Delphi, the followers of Dionysus, and the legendary Sibyl. **14:11** *a foreigner* Lit. "a barbarian." Writing to Greeks, Paul evokes the common Greek distinction between themselves and non–Gk speakers. **14:14** This is not a uniquely Christian observation. The 1st-century Jewish author Philo describes the prophet: "He is an interpreter prompted by Another in all his utterances, when knowing not what he does he is filled with inspiration, as the reason withdraws and surrenders the citadel of the soul to a new visitor and tenant, the Divine Spirit which plays upon the vocal organism and dictates words which clearly express the prophet's message" (*On the Special Laws* 4.49). **14:15** See note to 12:10. **14:16** *Amen* An old Hebrew and Aramaic word of affirmation (from a root meaning "trust" or "believe") that was characteristic of Jesus' speech, according to the gospel tradition. He used it to affirm his own sayings, not only in the liturgical setting of the synagogue. Paul uses it more conventionally, to close a doxology, or word of praise (*1 Thess.* 3:13; *1 Cor.* 16:24; *Phil.* 4:20; *Gal.* 1:5; 6:18; *Rom.* 1:25; 9:5; 16:24, etc.). He confirms here that the phrase has become a standard feature of Christian worship, even among Gk-speaking Gentiles (see also *1 Clem.* 20.12; 32.4; 38.4; etc.). By contrast, the LXX usually translates the phrase into a Gk equivalent; Philo and Josephus never use the word at all in their extensive writings for Gk-speaking audiences.

²⁰Brothers and sisters,^g do not be children in your thinking; rather, be infants in evil, but in thinking be adults. ²¹In the law it is written,

"By people of strange tongues
and by the lips of foreigners
I will speak to this people;
    yet even then they will not listen to me,"

says the Lord. ²²Tongues, then, are a sign not for believers but for unbelievers, while prophecy is not for unbelievers but for believers. ²³If, therefore, the whole church comes together and all speak in tongues, and outsiders or unbelievers enter, will they not say that you are out of your mind? ²⁴But if all prophesy, an unbeliever or outsider who enters is reproved by all and called to account by all. ²⁵After the secrets of the unbeliever's heart are disclosed, that person will bow down before God and worship him, declaring, "God is really among you."

Orderly Worship

²⁶What should be done then, my friends?^g When you come together, each one has a hymn, a lesson, a revelation, a tongue, or an interpretation. Let all things be done for building up. ²⁷If anyone speaks in a tongue, let there be only two or at most three, and each in turn; and let one interpret. ²⁸But if there is no one to interpret, let them be silent in church and speak to themselves and to God. ²⁹Let two or three prophets speak, and let the others weigh what is said. ³⁰If a revelation is made to someone else sitting nearby, let the first person be silent. ³¹For you can all prophesy one by one, so that all may learn and all be encouraged. ³²And the spirits of prophets are subject to the prophets, ³³for God is a God not of disorder but of peace.

(As in all the churches of the saints, ³⁴women should be silent in the churches. For they are not permitted to speak, but should be subordinate, as the law also says. ³⁵If there is anything they desire to know, let them ask their husbands at home. For it is shameful for a woman to speak in church.^h ³⁶Or did the word of God originate with you? Or are you the only ones it has reached?)

³⁷Anyone who claims to be a prophet, or to have spiritual powers, must acknowledge that what I am writing to you is a command of the Lord. ³⁸Anyone who does not recognize this is not to be recognized. ³⁹So, my friends,ⁱ be eager to prophesy, and do not forbid speaking in tongues; ⁴⁰but all things should be done decently and in order.

The Resurrection of Christ

15 Now I would remind you, brothers and sisters,^g of the good news^j that I proclaimed to you, which you in turn received, in which also you stand, ²through which also you are being saved, if you hold firmly to the message that I proclaimed to you—unless you have come to believe in vain.

³For I handed on to you as of first importance what I in turn had received: that Christ died for our

---

g Gk brothers

h Other ancient authorities put verses 34-35 after verse 40
i Gk my brothers
j Or gospel

14:21 *the law* Actually, the prophets. *listen to me* Isa. 28:11–12. MT: "Truly, as one who speaks to that people in a stammering jargon and an alien tongue is he who declares to them, 'This is the resting place, let the weary rest; this is the place of repose.' They refuse to listen." LXX (starting with v. 10): "Expect trouble upon trouble . . . on account of wickedness of the lips, by means of a different tongue; for they shall speak to this people, saying to them, 'This is rest for the one who is hungry, and this is the calamity'; but they did not want to hear." Paul's version is different in sense from both the Hebrew and the Greek texts. **14:34** *women* Or "wives." Possibly a reference to *Gen.* 3:16, where God says to the woman, "your urge shall be for your husband, and he shall rule over you." This is another appeal to the authority of the law, characteristic of this letter; see note to 5:1; 9:9. **14:35** The general point here—that a married woman's public presence must be mediated by her husband—supports the conservative tradition of Greek and Roman society (see Plutarch, *Advice to Brides and Grooms* 19, 31–32), although this had begun to be challenged in various quarters by the 1st century; it also matches Paul's concern that women keep themselves veiled in deference to their husbands (11:2–16). Still, the earlier passage plainly permitted women to pray or prophesy (11:4), and Paul's other letters show considerable evidence of women's activity in his churches (e.g., *1 Cor.* 1:11; *Phil.* 4:2; *Rom.* 16:1–6, 13, 15), whereas this sentence appears to be a blanket prohibition of women's speaking in church. The main options are that (a) this passage was added by a later hand, in keeping with the "Pauline" sentiments of *1 Tim.* 2:1–2; (b) the kind of speaking forbidden here is limited in some way (e.g., to public confrontation of one's husband); or (c) Paul simply allows the rhetorical need of the moment (a general statement on roles being taken by Corinthian Christian women) to exaggerate his true position. **14:36** As always, the parentheses have been supplied by the translators. · **14:38** Once again, Paul is aware of opposition to his views in Corinth; he deals with his opponents in his usual way (see 3:10–15; 4:17–21; 11:16). **15:1** Although he omits the characteristic phrase "Now concerning," it seems that Paul is now turning to another issue raised by the Corinthians' letter, for he will respond directly to some of their concerns (15:12, perhaps 15:35). The issue is resurrection, both that of Jesus in the past and that of Jesus' followers in the future. **15:3** As in 11:2, 23, Paul uses here the technical language of tradition—receiving and handing on. This language, along with the style of the following paragraph (consecutive *thats*, meter, and unusual vocabulary), suggests that he is quoting an earlier confession

sins in accordance with the scriptures, [4]and that he was buried, and that he was raised on the third day in accordance with the scriptures, [5]and that he appeared to Cephas, then to the twelve. [6]Then he appeared to more than five hundred brothers and sisters[k] at one time, most of whom are still alive, though some have died.[l] [7]Then he appeared to James, then to all the apostles. [8]Last of all, as to one untimely born, he appeared also to me. [9]For I am the least of the apostles, unfit to be called an apostle, because I persecuted the church of God. [10]But by the grace of God I am what I am, and his grace toward me has not been in vain. On the contrary, I worked harder than any of them—though it was not I, but the grace of God that is with me. [11]Whether then it was I or they, so we proclaim and so you have come to believe.

The Resurrection of the Dead

[12]Now if Christ is proclaimed as raised from the dead, how can some of you say there is no resurrection of the dead? [13]If there is no resurrection of the dead, then Christ has not been raised; [14]and if Christ has not been raised, then our proclamation has been in vain and your faith has been in vain. [15]We are even found to be misrepresenting God, because we testified of God that he raised Christ—whom he did not raise if it is true that the dead are not raised. [16]For if the dead are not raised, then Christ has not been raised. [17]If Christ has not been raised, your faith is futile and you are still in your sins. [18]Then those also who have died[l] in Christ have perished. [19]If for this life only we have hoped in Christ, we are of all people most to be pitied.

[20]But in fact Christ has been raised from the dead, the first fruits of those who have died.[l] [21]For since death came through a human being, the resurrection of the dead has also come through a human being; [22]for as all die in Adam, so all will be made alive in Christ. [23]But each in his own order: Christ the first fruits, then at his coming those who belong to Christ. [24]Then comes the end,[m] when he hands over the kingdom to God the Father, after he has destroyed every ruler and every authority and power. [25]For he must reign until he has put all his enemies under his feet. [26]The last enemy to be destroyed is death. [27]For "God[n] has put all things in subjection under his feet." But when it says, "All things are put in

---

k Gk *brothers*
l Gk *fallen asleep*

m Or *Then come the rest*
n Gk *he*

---

about Jesus' resurrection. Whether he is or not, this is the earliest extant statement of Jesus' postresurrection appearances; it is a generation earlier than the gospel accounts. **15:4** No scripture speaks plainly of either the death or the resurrection (especially after three days) of a messiah. Some Christians used the story of Jonah's three-day "burial" in the great fish and subsequent return to the land as a parable of Jesus' death and resurrection (see *Matt.* 12:40, although according to the gospels Jesus was buried only for two nights). Paul may have had this story in mind, or any of the general statements of God's vindication of the righteous that the church took over and applied to Jesus' resurrection (e.g., *Ps.* 118:22). As for resurrection *on the third day,* the closest verbal parallel in scripture is doubtless *Hos.* 6:2; remarkably, this passage is not cited in any Christian texts of the first two generations. **15:7** It is puzzling that Paul lists one appearance to the Twelve and then another to the *apostles;* although he uses the latter term loosely (see note to 9:1), he still considers it a small group, one that apparently includes the Twelve. Some scholars have suggested that Paul combines here two different lists of appearances: one from Peter (Cephas, the Twelve, and the five hundred) and one from Jesus' brother James (James and the apostles). See the accounts of Jesus' appearances in *Mark* 16 (no appearances listed); *Matthew* 28 (to the two Marys near the tomb, then the eleven in Galilee); *Luke* 24 (three appearances—to Cleopas and friend, to Peter, then to the eleven—within the vicinity of Jerusalem); and *John* 20–21 (to the eleven—without and with Thomas—in Jerusalem; to the eleven by the Sea of Galilee). None of these lists resembles Paul's. **15:8** *he appeared to me* Paul does not give the details of this event, but most scholars see here a reference to Paul's experience on the road to Damascus, related in *Acts* 9:3–9 (see *1 Cor.* 9:1; *Gal.* 1:12–16). The language here, however, may suggest a visionary experience. Of course, Paul wrote long before *Acts* was written. **15:9** See *Phil.* 3:6; *Gal.* 1:13. **15:10** Paul's feeling that he has worked harder and suffered more than the other apostles is reflected in *1 Cor.* 9:5–6 and perhaps *2 Cor.* 11:5–12:11—depending on the identity of those "super-apostles." **15:12** Some Corinthian Christians have begun to deny resurrection, even perhaps Jesus' resurrection. But Paul's appeal to Jesus' resurrection as the basis for his argument (15:12–20) would be puzzling if the latter were the case. His summary of evidence for Jesus' resurrection (note "remind" in 15:1) may serve to reestablish common ground for discussing Christian resurrection. Note 15:11: "you have come to believe." It seems, then, that Paul and the Corinthians both accept Jesus' resurrection in some form; the Corinthians have a problem with the future physical resurrection of Christians. Within a hundred years Justin Martyr (*Dialogue* 80) would likewise denounce those called Christians who did not believe in future resurrection but held that only the soul went to be with God at death. **15:16** A near repetition of 15:13. **15:19** Paul characteristically stresses the future benefits of faith in Christ. With the phrase *for this life only,* he may be hinting that the Corinthians' emphasis on the present benefits of salvation (see 4:8–13) is a factor in their repudiation of future resurrection. **15:22** See the expansion of a similar theme in *Rom.* 5:12–21. **15:27** *under his feet Ps.* 8:5–7. MT: "what is man that You have been mindful of him, mortal man that You have taken note of him, that You have made him little less than divine [or 'than the angels'], and adorned him with subjection," it is plain that this does not include the one who put all things in subjection under him. 28When all things are subjected to him, then the Son himself will also be subjected to the one who put all things in subjection under him, so that God may be all in all.

29Otherwise, what will those people do who receive baptism on behalf of the dead? If the dead are not raised at all, why are people baptized on their behalf?

30And why are we putting ourselves in danger every hour? 31I die every day! That is as certain, brothers and sisters,o as my boasting of you—a boast that I make in Christ Jesus our Lord. 32If with merely human hopes I fought with wild animals at Ephesus, what would I have gained by it? If the dead are not raised,

"Let us eat and drink,
    for tomorrow we die."

33Do not be deceived:

"Bad company ruins good morals."

34Come to a sober and right mind, and sin no more; for some people have no knowledge of God. I say this to your shame.

---

o Gk brothers

The Resurrection Body

35But someone will ask, "How are the dead raised? With what kind of body do they come?" 36Fool! What you sow does not come to life unless it dies. 37And as for what you sow, you do not sow the body that is to be, but a bare seed, perhaps of wheat or of some other grain. 38But God gives it a body as he has chosen, and to each kind of seed its own body. 39Not all flesh is alike, but there is one flesh for human beings, another for animals, another for birds, and another for fish. 40There are both heavenly bodies and earthly bodies, but the glory of the heavenly is one thing, and that of the earthly is another. 41There is one glory of the sun, and another glory of the moon, and another glory of the stars; indeed, star differs from star in glory.

42So it is with the resurrection of the dead. What is sown is perishable, what is raised is imperishable. 43It is sown in dishonor, it is raised in glory. It is sown in weakness, it is raised in power. 44It is sown a physical body, it is raised a spiritual body. If there is a

---

glory and majesty; You have made him master over Your handiwork, laying the world at his feet." The LXX (8:4–6) is very similar. Both the MT and the LXX end with the second person ("You have made him"). Paul's use of this psalm illustrates well his principle that all scripture really refers to Jesus and Jesus' end-time followers (1 Cor. 9:9; 10:11). Whereas the psalm plainly talks about the privileges given to human beings in creation, Paul takes this line as a theological statement about Jesus. This interpretation was doubtless facilitated by the Hebrew idiom "son of man," which is translated "mortal man" above, but which Paul takes as a reference to Jesus. *who put all things . . . under him* That is, God himself is not to be subject to Jesus. **15:28** *who put all things . . . under him* That is, Jesus will be subject to God. *all in all* Paul's terminology evokes the common Stoic position that God is the soul of the universe—in all and through all. See *Acts* 17:24–28 (a speech set before Stoic and Epicurean philosophers). **15:29** The only reference among 1st-century Christian writings to proxy baptism on behalf of those who have died without having been baptized. Myriad alternative explanations that have been proposed reflect more the interpreters' discomfort with the plain meaning of the words than any linguistic ambiguity. Paul simply uses this example without explanation and quickly discards it (see the angels of 11:10). We have no opportunity to determine what he thinks of the custom. **15:32** *Ephesus* Paul seems to have run into frequent trouble in Ephesus, the capital of Asia and his base of operations (see 2 Cor. 1:8–9; 11:23–27); he writes this letter from Ephesus (1 Cor. 16:8). Fighting with beasts is probably a metaphor, however, since Paul does not mention such encounters in his later detailed list of trials (2 Cor. 11:23ff.). Accused criminals who were consigned to wild animals in the amphitheater were not expected to survive, and even if Paul had somehow escaped, such an encounter should have made his list of major trials. Armed combatants would sometimes fight with animals for the entertainment of the audience, but Paul was hardly such a person. *we die* A proverb of the wicked, cited in *Isa.* 22:13 (MT and LXX). The force of the quotation comes from Paul's view that the Corinthians are behaving in the manner scorned by *Isaiah,* as if there were no future judgment to anticipate (see 4:8; 6:13). Paul may well not have expected his readers to understand the original context of the saying and may have used it only as a proverb. He displays again his astonishing ability to pull out obscure biblical passages that serve his immediate needs. **15:33** A popular Greek proverb, attributed to the poet Menander's (ca. 300 B.C.E.) lost comedy *Thais.* **15:35** Apparently, Paul now turns to one of the Corinthians' main reasons for denying resurrection—that they cannot conceive of a physical *body* being restored to life. Later Greek philosophers ridiculed the Jewish and Christian teaching on resurrection for precisely these reasons. See Celsus in Origen, *Against Celsus* 5.14 (cited in the introduction to *1 Thessalonians*); Augustine, *City of God* 22.4–5. Paul's following argument, in which he nuances the word "body," may be read as an attempt to remove the force of such objections. **15:36** Paul's misunderstanding of botany—common in the 1st century—nevertheless helps the analogy that he wants to establish for death and resurrection. Later Christian authors would use it to similar effect (1 Clement 24; John 12:24). **15:41** Paul tries to defuse Greek objections to the raising of decayed bodies (see note to 15:35) by arguing that "body" can mean many things and need not imply flesh and blood. **15:44** *physical* The same Gk word as in 2:14 and 15:46. Paul probably uses this word in anticipation of the scripture passage quoted in the next verse, where its noun form, *psychē,* often rendered "life" or "soul," is translated "living being." From what follows (15:50), it is clear that Paul wants to contrast a physical body with a spiritual one (hence the NRSV translation), although the language of the LXX does not help him much. He must force a word meaning "pertaining to the soul or mind" into the meaning "physical," in order to use *Gen.* 2:7 for support.

physical body, there is also a spiritual body. 45Thus it
is written, "The first man, Adam, became a living
being"; the last Adam became a life-giving spirit.
46But it is not the spiritual that is first, but the physical, and then the spiritual. 47The first man was from
the earth, a man of dust; the second man is[p] from
heaven. 48As was the man of dust, so are those who
are of the dust; and as is the man of heaven, so are
those who are of heaven. 49Just as we have borne the
image of the man of dust, we will[q] also bear the
image of the man of heaven.

50What I am saying, brothers and sisters,[r] is this:
flesh and blood cannot inherit the kingdom of God,
nor does the perishable inherit the imperishable.
51Listen, I will tell you a mystery! We will not all die,[s]
but we will all be changed, 52in a moment, in the
twinkling of an eye, at the last trumpet. For the
trumpet will sound, and the dead will be raised
imperishable, and we will be changed. 53For this perishable body must put on imperishability, and this
mortal body must put on immortality. 54When this
perishable body puts on imperishability, and this mortal body puts on immortality, then the saying that is
written will be fulfilled:

"Death has been swallowed up in victory."
55 "Where, O death, is your victory?
Where, O death, is your sting?"

56The sting of death is sin, and the power of sin is the
law. 57But thanks be to God, who gives us the victory
through our Lord Jesus Christ.

58Therefore, my beloved,[t] be steadfast, immovable, always excelling in the work of the Lord, because you know that in the Lord your labor is not
in vain.

The Collection for the Saints

16 Now concerning the collection for the saints:
you should follow the directions I gave to the
churches of Galatia. 2On the first day of every week,
each of you is to put aside and save whatever extra
you earn, so that collections need not be taken when I
come. 3And when I arrive, I will send any whom you
approve with letters to take your gift to Jerusalem. 4If
it seems advisable that I should go also, they will accompany me.

Plans for Travel

5I will visit you after passing through Macedonia—for I intend to pass through Macedonia— 6and
perhaps I will stay with you or even spend the winter,
so that you may send me on my way, wherever I go. 7I
do not want to see you now just in passing, for I hope
to spend some time with you, if the Lord permits.

p Other ancient authorities add *the Lord*
q Other ancient authorities read *let us*
r Gk *brothers*
s Gk *fall asleep*

t Gk *beloved brothers*

15:45 *Gen.* 2:7. MT: "The Lord God formed man [or 'Adam'] from the dust of the earth. He blew into his nostrils the breath of life, and man became a living being." LXX: "And God formed the man, dust of the earth. And he breathed into his face [the] breath of life, and the man became a living being." Paul has inserted *first* into the quotation to anticipate the "second" Adam, not mentioned in scripture. **15:46** ***physical*** Paul is still using the language of the scripture quotation, which does not really mean "physical," although that is the sense he needs to contrast Adam's entry into the flesh (*Gen.* 2:7) with Christ's departure from it, through resurrection. See note to 15:44. **15:50** Plainly, then, the resurrection for Paul is not to be understood as a physical, flesh-and-blood matter: Jesus became a "life-giving spirit" (15:45). Note also Paul's use of the word "appeared" (15:5) to describe postresurrection encounters with Jesus. Contrast Paul's view with that of the author of *Luke* (*Luke* 24:39). **15:51** Having established that the present physical body is not the one that will be raised, Paul must then explain what will happen to those who are still alive when Jesus returns, since their bodies will not have had the opportunity to be transformed through death. His answer is that they will be instantly transformed to become like resurrected bodies. **15:54** Loosely adapted from *Isa.* 25:8. MT: "He will destroy death forever. My Lord God will wipe the tears away from all faces and will put an end to the reproach of his people." LXX: "Death has prevailed and swallowed up [men] but again the Lord God has taken away every tear from every face. He has taken away the shame of the people from all the earth." **15:55** Loosely adapted from *Hos.* 13:14. MT: "From Sheol itself I shall save them, redeem them from very Death. Where, O Death, are your plagues? Your pestilence where, O Sheol?" LXX: "I shall rescue them from the hand of Hades, and shall redeem them from death. Where is your judgment, O Death? Where is your sting, O Hades? Consolation is hidden from my eyes." **15:56** See *Rom.* 7:11. The remark comes as a surprise here, since Paul has not been discussing the law except to quote it approvingly. **16:1** ***collection for the saints*** Another issue raised by the Corinthians' letter to Paul. Presumably, they have asked him how he would like the collection to be handled. This is the earliest reference to Paul's major collection from the Gentile churches for the church of Jerusalem. See also *2 Corinthians* 8–9; *Rom.* 15:25–32; and note to *Gal.* 2:10. ***churches of Galatia*** Paul probably began his mission in Asia Minor, including Galatia, before he proceeded to Greece. According to *Rom.* 15:25–32, however, the completed collection included gifts from Macedonia and Achaia. Perhaps the Galatians' ultimate defection from Paul's circle took them out of the collection project. **16:7** Compare these travel plans with the canceled trip discussed by Paul in *2 Cor.* 1:15–2:1.

8But I will stay in Ephesus until Pentecost, 9for a wide door for effective work has opened to me, and there are many adversaries.

10If Timothy comes, see that he has nothing to fear among you, for he is doing the work of the Lord just as I am; 11therefore let no one despise him. Send him on his way in peace, so that he may come to me; for I am expecting him with the brothers.

12Now concerning our brother Apollos, I strongly urged him to visit you with the other brothers, but he was not at all willing[u] to come now. He will come when he has the opportunity.

Final Messages and Greetings

13Keep alert, stand firm in your faith, be courageous, be strong. 14Let all that you do be done in love.

15Now, brothers and sisters,[v] you know that members of the household of Stephanas were the first converts in Achaia, and they have devoted themselves to the service of the saints; 16I urge you to put yourselves at the service of such people, and of everyone who works and toils with them. 17I rejoice at the coming of Stephanas and Fortunatus and Achaicus, because they have made up for your absence; 18for they refreshed my spirit as well as yours. So give recognition to such persons.

19The churches of Asia send greetings. Aquila and Prisca, together with the church in their house, greet you warmly in the Lord. 20All the brothers and sisters[v] send greetings. Greet one another with a holy kiss.

21I, Paul, write this greeting with my own hand. 22Let anyone be accursed who has no love for the Lord. Our Lord, come![w] 23The grace of the Lord Jesus be with you. 24My love be with all of you in Christ Jesus.[x]

---

u Or it was not at all God's will for him
v Gk brothers

w Gk Marana tha. These Aramaic words can also be read Maran atha, meaning Our Lord has come
x Other ancient authorities add Amen

16:8 Again, Paul's readers seem to know the significance of this Jewish feast (also called the Feast of Weeks, *Shabuoth*), seven weeks after Passover. See note to 5:1. **16:10** Although Timothy has already been dispatched (4:17), Paul *seems* to expect that the letter will arrive before him. Perhaps this means that the messengers from Corinth (16:17) will take Paul's letter back with them through the sea route, whereas Timothy has taken the circuitous land route. It is also possible, however, to interpret 4:17 in the sense that Timothy is now being dispatched with the letter. **16:12** *Apollos* The final issue that Paul addresses from the Corinthians' letter. Some have asked about Apollos, who is also now in Ephesus: they want him (but apparently not Paul; 4:18, 21) to return. It is not necessary to assume that Apollos was working in close cooperation with Paul. In the absence of a postal service, a letter hand-delivered to Paul in the large city of Ephesus might have included a personal request that he pass on the Corinthians' invitation to Apollos. We may speculate from *1 Corinthians* 1–4 that Paul felt some relief at Apollos's inability to return right away. **16:17** See 1:16, where Stephanas is mentioned alongside Crispus and Gaius as one of the few baptized by Paul in Corinth. Crispus and Gaius are Roman names and for other reasons (see note to 1:14) seem to belong to the higher social stratum. Stephanas's Gk name sets him apart as likely not one of the Roman colonists of Corinth. Still, he has a "household," and his freedom to travel may indicate some means. Achaicus must have received that name while living outside Achaia: perhaps he went to Rome as a slave from Achaia and has since returned as a freedman. **16:19** *Asia* Ephesus, from which Paul writes, was the capital of the Roman province of Asia. ***Aquila and Prisca*** Jewish Christian associates of Paul, remembered in traditions in *Acts* 18:1–4, 18–20, 26. They are now established in Ephesus, in some kind of house (perhaps a small flat joined to their place of business). By the time Paul writes *Romans,* however, they will be settled in Rome (*Rom.* 16:3). **16:20** See note to *1 Thess.* 5:26. **16:21** Paul often employed a stenographer, or amanuensis, to write his letters as he dictated (see *Rom.* 16:22). Here it seems to be only the greeting that Paul writes himself. The oral character of the letters helps to explain Paul's frequent qualifications of points just made (e.g., 1:14–16). **16:22** ***Our Lord, come!*** Although Paul writes in Gk, he includes this Aramaic phrase in transliteration: *Marana tha.* This is the only place in which Paul uses the phrase, which may further indicate a Jewish Christian influence on the Corinthian community. See note to 5:1.

To the Holy Ones in Philippi

PHILIPPIANS

Setting and Date

The city of Krenides was only about four years old when in 356 B.C.E. King Philip II of Macedon, father of Alexander the Great, took it over and renamed it after himself: Philippi. In the mid-second century B.C.E. the Romans conquered Philippi and, after the civil wars of the late first century B.C.E., made it the center of a large colony settled with army veterans. Archaeology has turned up inscriptions indicating that the city was run by Roman-style magistracies, that Latin was the dominant language (though Greek was also used), that Egyptian and Greco-Roman cults (Dionysus/Bacchus and Hercules) were popular, and that women worshipers were prominent in the latter.

We learned from *1 Thessalonians* that Philippi was the first city visited by Paul on his mission through Macedonia (*1 Thess.* 2:2); it lay on the main highway through the region (*Via Egnatia*). The Macedonian mission itself must have occurred early in Paul's career because he refers to that time as "the beginning of the gospel [announcement]" (*Phil.* 4:15). Nevertheless, his surviving letter to Philippi presupposes a later situation, for he is now in prison and facing the possibility of a death sentence (1:20; 2:17). At the end of this letter he fondly remembers his founding visits to Philippi and Thessalonica long before.

Scholars used to suppose that, since Paul wrote *Philippians* from prison, he must have done so from either Caesarea or Rome. This conclusion was drawn from *Acts*, which records only these two imprisonments outside Philippi itself (*Acts* 24:22–27; 28:16ff.). Further, Paul's references in the letter to the *praitōrion*, perhaps meaning the "imperial guard [at Rome]" (1:13),[1] and to "the emperor's household" (4:22) were taken to favor a Roman imprisonment. Finally, some scholars inferred from the evident threat of capital punishment in *Philippians* (1:20–26; 2:17; 3:10–11) that Paul must have been in Rome; were he anywhere else, he could have asked to be tried in Rome on account of his Roman citizenship.[2]

---

[1] An elite military unit in Rome, assigned to the protection of the emperor.

[2] Since *Acts* portrays Paul as a Roman citizen (22:25–28) who exploits his citizenship to request a trial in Rome (25:10–12), this view assumes that the prospect of capital punishment of which *Philippians* speaks is suited only to a Roman imprisonment.

But the traditional view faces numerous obstacles. First, Paul's technical language should not be pressed too far: the word *praitōrion* can mean not only "imperial guard" but also a "governor's residence" anywhere in the empire (as in *Matt.* 27:27). And "the emperor's household" signifies all those employed in the imperial civil service throughout the empire. Second, it is a false assumption that Paul faced serious imprisonments only at Caesarea and Rome. He himself declares that he has "fought with beasts" at Ephesus (*1 Cor.* 15:32),[3] that he is in peril "every hour" (*1 Cor.* 15:30), and that he thought he was facing a death sentence in Asia (*2 Cor.* 1:9). In *2 Cor.* 11:23–27, moreover, he claims to have been in prison numerous times, and "often near death," well before the Caesarean and Roman imprisonments. So there is no reason to assume that Paul wrote *Philippians* from either Caesarea or Rome, at the end of his career.

Indeed, the case against a Roman or Caesarean imprisonment as the setting of *Philippians* is strong. In *Phil.* 2:25–30, Paul discusses the welfare of Epaphroditus, who was sent from Philippi to deliver a substantial gift. After his arrival at Paul's place of imprisonment, Epaphroditus fell seriously ill (2:26). The Philippians have heard about his illness, and now Paul and Epaphroditus have heard about their concern (2:26); Paul writes in part to assure them of their messenger's regained health. But these frequent transfers of information require that Philippi and Paul's place of imprisonment were reasonably close. That Paul anticipates sending Timothy to Philippi and expects to hear back from him soon (2:19) confirms that he is not too far from the Macedonian city. Yet Rome and Caesarea were both at least five weeks' travel from Philippi under the most favorable conditions.

In view of these considerations, many recent scholars have posited Ephesus as the place from which Paul wrote *Philippians*. An Ephesian imprisonment would allow for rapid transfer of information. Since Ephesus was a base for Paul's activity (*1 Cor.* 16:8; *2 Cor.* 1:16) and since we know that he faced serious problems there (*1 Cor.* 15:32; *2 Cor.* 1:8), the Asian capital seems a plausible venue for the writing of *Philippians*.

This means that the letter need not be assigned to the end of Paul's career, when he was a prisoner in Caesarea or Rome. Although it cannot come from the earliest phase,[4] it may fall in the middle group of his letters. Some scholars have suggested that the Ephesian imprisonment reflected in *Philippians* was the great "affliction" in Asia that Paul had just survived when he wrote *2 Corinthians* (see *2 Cor.* 1:8–11). This would explain the many similarities between *Philippians* and *2 Corinthians* (see below).

Overview and Literary Features

So far we have spoken of *Philippians* as a single unit, but its structural peculiarities may indicate that it is really a composite of several letters. It begins normally

---

[3]On the meaning of this phrase, see notes to *1 Cor.* 15:32.
[4]He looks back on the "beginning of the gospel" as somewhat removed from his time of writing and recalls the numerous gifts sent to him by the Philippians during his mission (4:15).

enough, with a greeting, thanksgiving, letter body (1:12–30), ethical exhortations (2:1–18), and travel plans (2:30), and Paul seems to offer a closing farewell in 3:1. But then 3:2–4:7 brings an abrupt shift in topic, with its own argument (3:2–4:1) and final greetings (4:2–7). Most peculiar is the final section (4:10–20), because there Paul forthrightly and profusely thanks the Philippians for a gift that he has already mentioned twice in passing (1:5; 2:25) without any elaboration.

But if Paul wrote *Philippians* to thank the church for its gift, why did he hold his thanks until the end, when he had already seemed to close the letter body twice? This disjointed structure has led some to suppose that *Phil.* 4:10–20 is a fragment from an earlier letter of thanksgiving and that 3:2–4:7(9) comes from yet another letter to the Philippians. One's decision on the matter will depend largely on one's assessment of the analogies for both disjointed letter-writing and composite letters in Paul's repertoire.

Themes and Issues

However one solves the problem of letter structure, it does seem that all of *Philippians* pertains to a single situation in the lives of Paul and the Philippian community, namely: he is in prison and has recently received a gift from them. They are facing opposition. It is not clear, however, whether the opposition consists of one major group or several, and whether it is exclusively within the Christian community or also from outside.

Paul refers to an internal opposition when he mentions those who "preach Christ" from improper motives—envy, rivalry, and selfishness (1:15–18). These rhetorical descriptions tell us little about the real motives of his adversaries, but it does seem that they are adamantly, perhaps violently, opposed to his mission (see 1:17).

In 3:2–21, Paul castigates some Jewish teachers in Philippi. These people have evidently called for Paul's converts to identify fully with the Jewish community (*politeuma;* see 3:20) and to take on Jewish covenant responsibilities, especially circumcision and observance of the Torah. They have rebuked Paul for not raising these basic issues with his converts. Paul's response is that he has not neglected to teach Torah observance; rather, he has decisively repudiated his Jewish past, which he now labels "garbage" (3:8), in order to follow Christ. Because he believes only in a spiritual circumcision (3:3), spiritual righteousness (3:9), and a heavenly community (3:20), he scorns those who focus on the present world and Torah observance (3:2, 18–19). They will share in the coming destruction of the present world (3:19; see *1 Thess.* 1:10; *1 Cor.* 7:31).

Since many Jews in the first century welcomed and *perhaps* even solicited converts (Tacitus, *Hist.* 5.5; Josephus, *Ant.* 20.17–96), one might suppose that Paul's Jewish opponents, who invited his followers to be circumcised and join the Jewish community, were not Christian. But in *2 Corinthians* and *Galatians,* Paul will confront a strong judaizing movement that is clearly within the Christian sphere

(*2 Cor.* 11:22–23); it will even claim support from the Jerusalem apostles (*Gal.* 2:14). Moreover, the language used by Paul to describe the Philippian Jewish movement is closely paralleled by his attacks on the Christian Jews in *2 Corinthians* and *Galatians.*[5] It seems easiest to suppose, therefore, that the Jewish opposition at Philippi was also Christian, and part of the widespread movement that challenged Paul's repudiation of Judaism throughout his career. An in-house Christian-Jewish threat also best explains the vigor and sustained argument that Paul devotes to this issue.

An external conflict may be suggested by Paul's remarks in 1:27–30: The Philippians share in the same struggle faced by Paul himself. Since he is in prison, one thinks immediately of the earlier pagan opposition at Philippi and Thessalonica as a persistent source of aggravation for the Philippian Christians (see *1 Thess.* 1:10–2:14). But Paul's Christian opponents are (he thinks) taking advantage of his absence, and the "affliction" that they are causing him may have included a hand in having him arrested (see *Phil.* 1:17b). If so, the link between his situation and the Philippians' current straits could be explained on the basis of internal opposition alone: a single group of Jewish Christians was active in Philippi against Paul's mission. In any case, Paul consigns all of these opponents to destruction (1:28; 3:19).

A final observation concerns Paul's view of the future in *Philippians.* If this letter is properly positioned before *2 Corinthians* 1–9, then it is the first one in which Paul considers the prospect of his own death. Recall that in *1 Thess.* 4:13–18 he spoke as if Jesus would return during his lifetime and that in *1 Corinthians* he still believed that "we shall not all sleep [i.e., die]" (15:51). But at the writing of *Philippians* he has squarely faced the possibility of execution (1:20–26; 2:17). He is fully aware that he might die in prison.

Does this possibility affect his view of the future? On the one hand, *Philippians* abounds with Paul's typically eager expectation of the imminent "day of Christ" (1:6, 10; 2:16; 3:14, 20–21; 4:5). On the other hand, he also introduces some new features into his eschatology. First, Paul expresses the hope that he will participate in the resurrection of the dead (3:10–11), rather than being transformed alive at the moment of Jesus' return (see *1 Cor.* 15:51; *Phil.* 3:20–21). Second, he implies that death will bring him immediately into the presence of Christ (1:23) without, apparently, the necessity of his waiting for a resurrection. But resurrection was the whole basis of the Thessalonians' and Corinthians' hope (*1 Thess.* 4:16–17; see *1 Cor.* 15:18). Although it is possible that Paul had had always held to a belief in the "intermediate state" of the dead between death and resurrection, it is curious that he does not mention this to console the Thessalonians but seems to present resurrection as the only hope (*1 Thess.* 4:13–14). Scholars have wondered, therefore, whether Paul's thinking on this matter did not develop over time, stimulated by crises in his own life. According to such a developmental scheme, *2 Corinthians*

---

[5]Compare: "workers of evil" in *Phil.* 3:2 and *2 Cor.* 11:13; circumcision as "mutilation" in *Phil.* 3:2 and *Gal.* 5:12; and the general argument of *Phil.* 3:2–11 with *Gal.* 1:13–15.

would go even further in holding out the immortality of the soul with Christ, much more than resurrection, as the fundamental Christian hope (*2 Cor.* 4:7–5:8).

Relation to Other Early Christian Texts

In spite of its brevity, *Philippians* is a pivotal text among Paul's letters. Years have passed since the initial success of his Greek mission. The prospect of death here will continue to affect his outlook in *2 Corinthians, Galatians,* and *Romans.*

For Further Reading

Bockmuehl, Markus N. A. *The Epistle to the Philippians.* Peabody, Mass.: Hendrickson, 1998.

Fitzgerald, John T. "Philippians, Epistle to the." Pages 318–26 in vol. 5 of *Anchor Bible Dictionary.* Edited by D. N. Freedman. 6 vols. New York: Doubleday, 1992.

Hendrix, Holland L. "Philippi." Pages 313–17 in vol. 5 of *Anchor Bible Dictionary.* Edited by D. N. Freedman. 6 vols. New York: Doubleday, 1992.

Martin, Ralph P. *Carmen Christi: Philippians 2:5–11 in Recent Interpretation and in the Setting of Early Christian Worship.* Cambridge: Cambridge University Press, 1967.

Rapske, Brian. *Paul in Roman Custody.* Vol. 3 of *The Book of Acts in Its First-Century Setting.* Edited by Bruce W. Winter. Grand Rapids: Eerdmans, 1994.

THE LETTER OF PAUL
TO THE PHILIPPIANS

Salutation

1 Paul and Timothy, servants[a] of Christ Jesus,
To all the saints in Christ Jesus who are in Philippi, with the bishops[b] and deacons:[c]

[2]Grace to you and peace from God our Father and the Lord Jesus Christ.

Paul's Prayer for the Philippians

[3]I thank my God every time I remember you, [4]constantly praying with joy in every one of my prayers for all of you, [5]because of your sharing in the gospel from the first day until now. [6]I am confident of this, that the one who began a good work among you will bring it to completion by the day of Jesus Christ. [7]It is right for me to think this way about all of you, because you hold me in your heart,[d] for all of you share in God's grace[e] with me, both in my imprisonment and in the defense and confirmation of the gospel. [8]For God is my witness, how I long for all of you with the compassion of Christ Jesus. [9]And this is my prayer, that your love may overflow more and more with knowledge and full insight [10]to help you to determine what is best, so that in the day of Christ you may be pure and blameless, [11]having produced the harvest of righteousness that comes through Jesus Christ for the glory and praise of God.

Paul's Present Circumstances

[12]I want you to know, beloved,[f] that what has happened to me has actually helped to spread the gospel, [13]so that it has become known throughout the whole imperial guard[g] and to everyone else that my imprisonment is for Christ; [14]and most of the brothers and sisters,[f] having been made confident in the Lord by my imprisonment, dare to speak the word[h] with greater boldness and without fear.

[15]Some proclaim Christ from envy and rivalry, but others from goodwill. [16]These proclaim Christ out of love, knowing that I have been put here for the defense of the gospel; [17]the others proclaim Christ out of selfish ambition, not sincerely but intending to increase my suffering in my imprisonment. [18]What does it matter? Just this, that Christ is proclaimed in every way, whether out of false motives or true; and in that I rejoice.

Yes, and I will continue to rejoice, [19]for I know that through your prayers and the help of the Spirit of Jesus Christ this will turn out for my deliverance. [20]It is my eager expectation and hope that I will not be put to shame in any way, but that by my speaking with all boldness, Christ will be exalted now as always in my body, whether by life or by death. [21]For to

---

a Gk *slaves*
b Or *overseers*
c Or *overseers and helpers*
d Or *because I hold you in my heart*
e Gk *in grace*

f Gk *brothers*
g Gk *whole praetorium*
h Other ancient authorities read *word of God*

1:5 See 4:15, where Paul recalls the "early days of the gospel." This letter seems to belong to an advanced stage of his career. **1:6** Paul's concern to preserve his converts without blame until Jesus' imminent return is characteristic. See *1 Thess.* 1:10; 3:13; 4:6; 5:23; *1 Cor.* 1:8; 3:13; *Phil.* 1:10, 2:16. **1:7** *share in God's grace with me* See 2:25; 4:14–18: the Philippians have actively supported Paul's mission. *imprisonment* Paul's Gk here, "in my bonds," could cover a variety of situations, from chains in a state-run dungeon to less severe conditions, such as unchained confinement in a state prison; military custody, whether in a camp or in a provincial capital; temporary custody in a local jail; or various kinds of house arrest. In Paul's world, incarceration served mainly to hold the accused for trial or for execution of sentence but sometimes to enforce obedience. Although many governors appear to have used prison as a form of punishment in itself, formal prison sentences in the modern sense were unknown. Paul was apparently remanded to custody in a provincial capital or in Rome while awaiting trial (1:19, 25; 2:23). It is unclear on what charge he was imprisoned or who accused him. **1:10** See note to 1:6. **1:13** *the whole imperial guard* Either the praetorian guard—an elite military unit in Rome assigned to protect the emperor, which would mean that Paul is writing from Rome—or the personnel in the *praetorium,* the Roman governor's residence in a major city of a Roman province (*Mark* 15:16; *Matt.* 27:27; *Acts* 23:35). **1:17** See 3:18–19. **1:19** See 1:7. **1:20** *boldness* Although Paul does not call himself a philosopher, it was also the goal of philosophers in his day to attain such self-mastery that they could speak the truth with complete freedom, even in the face of death. **1:20** *by life or by death* Paul is evidently waiting to hear whether he will be executed or released. **1:21** Paul's statement is logically awkward. Although it could be understood in light of his Christ mysticism, some scholars have suggested that Paul's original Gk word might have been *chrēstos* ("beneficial") rather than *Christos (Christ)* and that the change to *Christ* crept into the manuscripts accidentally because the two words sounded similar to copyists. Thus, Paul would have been expressing a

me, living is Christ and dying is gain. ²²If I am to live in the flesh, that means fruitful labor for me; and I do not know which I prefer. ²³I am hard pressed between the two: my desire is to depart and be with Christ, for that is far better; ²⁴but to remain in the flesh is more necessary for you. ²⁵Since I am convinced of this, I know that I will remain and continue with all of you for your progress and joy in faith, ²⁶so that I may share abundantly in your boasting in Christ Jesus when I come to you again.

²⁷Only, live your life in a manner worthy of the gospel of Christ, so that, whether I come and see you or am absent and hear about you, I will know that you are standing firm in one spirit, striving side by side with one mind for the faith of the gospel, ²⁸and are in no way intimidated by your opponents. For them this is evidence of their destruction, but of your salvation. And this is God's doing. ²⁹For he has graciously granted you the privilege not only of believing in Christ, but of suffering for him as well—³⁰since you are having the same struggle that you saw I had and now hear that I still have.

Imitating Christ's Humility

2 If then there is any encouragement in Christ, any consolation from love, any sharing in the Spirit, any compassion and sympathy, ²make my joy complete: be of the same mind, having the same love, being in full accord and of one mind. ³Do nothing from selfish ambition or conceit, but in humility re-

gard others as better than yourselves. ⁴Let each of you look not to your own interests, but to the interests of others. ⁵Let the same mind be in you that wasⁱ in Christ Jesus,

6   who, though he was in the form of God,
      did not regard equality with God
      as something to be exploited,
7   but emptied himself,
      taking the form of a slave,
      being born in human likeness.
   And being found in human form,
8   he humbled himself
      and became obedient to the point of death—
      even death on a cross.
9   Therefore God also highly exalted him
      and gave him the name
      that is above every name,
10   so that at the name of Jesus
      every knee should bend,
      in heaven and on earth and under the earth,
11   and every tongue should confess
      that Jesus Christ is Lord,
      to the glory of God the Father.

Shining as Lights in the World

¹²Therefore, my beloved, just as you have always obeyed me, not only in my presence, but much more now in my absence, work out your own salvation

---

i Or *that you have*

---

genuine dilemma, as the context (1:22–24) suggests: living is useful but dying is gain. No manuscripts, however, support such a change in wording. **1:23** This is Paul's first reference (if the order of Paul's letters proposed in the *Reader* is correct) to a belief that the soul meets Christ immediately at death. In later letters he will elaborate this view (see *2 Cor.* 5:8). Earlier Paul insisted that if it were not for the hope in future resurrection, at Jesus' return, believers would have no hope (*1 Thess.* 4:13–14; *1 Cor.* 15:29–34). **1:27** *striving side by side . . . for the faith of the gospel* One of Paul's many athletic metaphors, to be repeated in 4:3. Perhaps Paul's appeal to unity in "the announcement" (or *the gospel*) indicates that he sees the term "announcement" *(euangelion)* as peculiar to his mission. See notes to *Rom.* 6:17; 16:17. **1:28** *opponents* So far Paul has mentioned only Christian opponents (1:15–17). *destruction . . . salvation* See 3:18–19. **1:30** See 1:15–17. **2:5** The following verses, known as the Philippian hymn or *carmen Christi,* have traditionally been interpreted, in keeping with the much later Christian creeds, as a statement of Christ's "self-emptying" (Gk *kenōsis*): although Christ was God, he emptied himself of divine attributes and became a man in order to save humanity. But if this is the point of the passage, then (a) Paul's use of Christ's action as a model to be followed (2:5) is puzzling (for how could any human emulate this kind of self-emptying?), and (b) the emphasis on Christ's exaltation as a *reward* for his humiliation (2:9–11) is difficult to understand, since his exaltation should have been simply a recovery of his original glory after the completion of his mission. Other scholars have argued that the hymn does not concern a preexistent Christ but Christ as the second Adam, a prominent theme in Paul's letters (*1 Cor.* 15:22, 45, 49; *Rom.* 5:12–21). Like Adam, Christ was made in the image of God (2:6). But unlike Adam, he did not grasp at equality with God (2:6); he accepted his human condition and served God's purpose faithfully (2:7–8). Therefore, God has exalted him. Thus Paul's point would apply to his readers: God rewards those who humbly serve others. This would mean, however, that Paul understood Jesus' status after his resurrection as new (see *Rom.* 1:3–4; *Acts* 2:36). Some interpreters claim that the rhythm of the passage marks it as a hymn that Paul borrowed or slightly edited; others think it just as plausible that Paul wrote the piece himself with a poetic cadence. **2:7** The Gk does not imply that the emptying consisted in taking the form of a servant. More literally it reads "he emptied himself, having taken the form of a servant." **2:11** A characteristic Pauline distinction between Jesus and God. **2:12** *work out* Perhaps the meaning is, "Work through to completion what you began with me"; see "holding fast to the word of life," 2:16. *fear and trembling* Although Paul may well be referring only to the fear of God, his other letters suggest that believers unfaithful to his original preaching also have something to fear from him as God's agent. See *1 Cor.* 4:17–21; *2 Cor.* 10:10:9–11; 13:2–10.

with fear and trembling; [13]for it is God who is at work in you, enabling you both to will and to work for his good pleasure.

[14]Do all things without murmuring and arguing, [15]so that you may be blameless and innocent, children of God without blemish in the midst of a crooked and perverse generation, in which you shine like stars in the world. [16]It is by your holding fast to the word of life that I can boast on the day of Christ that I did not run in vain or labor in vain. [17]But even if I am being poured out as a libation over the sacrifice and the offering of your faith, I am glad and rejoice with all of you— [18]and in the same way you also must be glad and rejoice with me.

Timothy and Epaphroditus

[19]I hope in the Lord Jesus to send Timothy to you soon, so that I may be cheered by news of you. [20]I have no one like him who will be genuinely concerned for your welfare. [21]All of them are seeking their own interests, not those of Jesus Christ. [22]But Timothy's[j] worth you know, how like a son with a father he has served with me in the work of the gospel. [23]I hope therefore to send him as soon as I see how things go with me; [24]and I trust in the Lord that I will also come soon.

[25]Still, I think it necessary to send to you Epaphroditus—my brother and co-worker and fellow soldier, your messenger[k] and minister to my need; [26]for he has been longing for[l] all of you, and has been distressed because you heard that he was ill. [27]He was indeed so ill that he nearly died. But God had mercy on him, and not only on him but on me also, so that I would not have one sorrow after another. [28]I am the more eager to send him, therefore, in order that you may rejoice at seeing him again, and that I may be less anxious. [29]Welcome him then in the Lord with all joy, and honor such people, [30]because he came close to death for the work of Christ,[m] risking his life to make up for those services that you could not give me.

3 Finally, my brothers and sisters,[n] rejoice[o] in the Lord.

Breaking with the Past

To write the same things to you is not troublesome to me, and for you it is a safeguard.

[2]Beware of the dogs, beware of the evil workers, beware of those who mutilate the flesh![p] [3]For it is we who are the circumcision, who worship in the Spirit of God[q] and boast in Christ Jesus and have no confidence in the flesh— [4]even though I, too, have reason for confidence in the flesh.

If anyone else has reason to be confident in the flesh, I have more: [5]circumcised on the eighth day, a member of the people of Israel, of the tribe of Benjamin, a Hebrew born of Hebrews; as to the law, a Pharisee; [6]as to zeal, a persecutor of the church; as to righteousness under the law, blameless.

---

j Gk *his*
k Gk *apostle*
l Other ancient authorities read *longing to see*

m Other ancient authorities read *of the Lord*
n Gk *my brothers*
o Or *farewell*
p Gk *the mutilation*
q Other ancient authorities read *worship God in spirit*

2:16 See note to 1:6. **2:17** A drink offering accompanied animal sacrifices in the ancient world. Here the image is of Paul's possible execution; perhaps he alludes also to corporal punishment that he is already enduring. **2:19–20** Timothy has the same trusted role in *1 Thess.* 1:3–10; *1 Cor.* 4:17; 16:10–11; *2 Cor.* 1:1. **2:22** See preceding note. **2:23** That is, once Paul hears the verdict in his case. **2:25** Epaphroditus brought the gift from the Philippian believers that occasioned this letter of gratitude from Paul; see 4:14–19. Many kinds of imprisonment in the Roman world allowed such gift visits; indeed, without such care from outside, the prisoner's life quickly became intolerable. Paul discusses Epaphroditus's well-being here long before he thanks the Philippians for the gift; this peculiarity supports theories that *Philippians* combines parts of two or more letters (see introduction). **2:30** *risking his life* Possibly a reference to Epaphroditus's illness. But since caregiving visitors were often harassed by guards and they sometimes risked imprisonment themselves if they could be associated with the same charges as the prisoner faced, Paul may be referring to more obvious risks. **3:1** *Finally* In view of the important material that is still to come, the term seems out of place. This apparent closure, along with the abrupt shifts in 3:2 and 4:10, supports theories that *Philippians* comprises fragments of several letters. See introduction. **3:2** *beware of those who mutilate the flesh* Lit. "look out for the flesh mutilation [group]." The Gk word for "mutilation," *katatomē*, is a deliberate play on the word for "circumcision," *peritomē*; changing the preposition from *peri* to *kata* alters the sense from "cutting around" to "cutting up," or "mutilating." Paul is here exploiting the common Greco-Roman revulsion at circumcision, which would be shared by his Gentile readers. Many Gentiles viewed it as a barbaric practice akin to castration. See 1:15–17, 27–28; 2:21. **3:3** *worship in the Spirit of God* Having ridiculed physical circumcision, Paul now claims that his converts need not worry about his opponents' demand—grounded in *Gen.* 17:9–14—for circumcision, because they are the spiritual circumcision. Throughout this section, Paul uses the common Greek contrast between transitory, unreliable flesh and eternal, truthful spirit to contrast Judaism and trust in Christ. **3:4–6** Paul reminds his readers that he knows all about the Torah and has fully accounted for it. His preaching is not defective (as his opponents have apparently charged).

⁷Yet whatever gains I had, these I have come to regard as loss because of Christ. ⁸More than that, I regard everything as loss because of the surpassing value of knowing Christ Jesus my Lord. For his sake I have suffered the loss of all things, and I regard them as rubbish, in order that I may gain Christ ⁹and be found in him, not having a righteousness of my own that comes from the law, but one that comes through faith in Christ,*ʳ* the righteousness from God based on faith. ¹⁰I want to know Christ*ˢ* and the power of his resurrection and the sharing of his sufferings by becoming like him in his death, ¹¹if somehow I may attain the resurrection from the dead.

Pressing toward the Goal

¹²Not that I have already obtained this or have already reached the goal;*ᵗ* but I press on to make it my own, because Christ Jesus has made me his own. ¹³Beloved,*ᵘ* I do not consider that I have made it my own;*ᵛ* but this one thing I do: forgetting what lies behind and straining forward to what lies ahead, ¹⁴I press on toward the goal for the prize of the heavenly*ʷ*

call of God in Christ Jesus. ¹⁵Let those of us then who are mature be of the same mind; and if you think differently about anything, this too God will reveal to you. ¹⁶Only let us hold fast to what we have attained.

¹⁷Brothers and sisters,*ᵘ* join in imitating me, and observe those who live according to the example you have in us. ¹⁸For many live as enemies of the cross of Christ; I have often told you of them, and now I tell you even with tears. ¹⁹Their end is destruction; their god is the belly; and their glory is in their shame; their minds are set on earthly things. ²⁰But our citizenship*ˣ* is in heaven, and it is from there that we are expecting a Savior, the Lord Jesus Christ. ²¹He will transform the body of our humiliation*ʸ* that it may be conformed to the body of his glory,*ᶻ* by the power that also enables him to make all things subject to himself. ¹Therefore, my brothers and sisters,*ᵃ* whom I love and long for, my joy and crown, stand firm in the Lord in this way, my beloved.

Exhortations

²I urge Euodia and I urge Syntyche to be of the same mind in the Lord. ³Yes, and I ask you also, my

---

r Or *through the faith of Christ*
s Gk *him*
t Or *have already been made perfect*
u Gk *Brothers*
v Other ancient authorities read *my own yet*
w Gk *upward*

x Or *commonwealth*
y Or *our humble bodies*
z Or *his glorious body*
a Gk *my brothers*

3:8 *surpassing value* Paul did not find Judaism inherently deficient; on the contrary, he prospered well in it. But his encounter with Christ brought him to repudiate his Torah observance and count it as *rubbish.* *rubbish* Paul uses a graphic word meaning "dung" or "manure." A contemporary English equivalent might be "crap." **3:9** In Jewish scripture and in Judaism the common meaning of "righteousness" is obedience to the commandments of God in the Torah. Paul takes the language of his Jewish-Christian opponents ("Why do you not begin to practice this righteousness?") and interprets it in terms of his gospel. **3:10** Participation in Jesus' death and resurrection seems to become an increasingly prominent theme in Paul's letters; see *1 Cor.* 6:14–17; *2 Cor.* 4:10–11; 5:14, 17; *Gal.* 2:19–20; 6:17; *Rom.* 6:4–6; 7:1–7. **3:11** Paul evidently considers resurrection to be only for believers; see *1 Thess.* 4:16. Others have no hope (*1 Thess.* 4:13; *1 Cor.* 15:18). Whereas Paul previously expected to be among those who survived until Jesus' return (*1 Thess.* 4:15, 17; *1 Cor.* 15:51), now that he encounters the prospect of his own death for the first time, he hopes for ultimate resurrection from the dead. See *Phil.* 1:23; *2 Cor.* 5:8. **3:14** *heavenly call of God* resurrection and glorification. Paul expects to be caught up in the air, in the clouds, when Jesus returns (*1 Thess.* 4:16–17; *1 Cor.* 15:51–54). **3:17** See note to 2:12. Paul often calls for imitation of his own behavior (2:12; 3:17). In antiquity, a teacher's manner of life was usually considered the acid test of his philosophy. In Paul's case, this appeal is also connected to his proprietary claim as founder of the community; it means, "Do not follow other teachers" (see *1 Cor.* 4:17). **3:18** Paul seems to be speaking of other Christians, as it is difficult to conceive of outsiders who *live as enemies of the cross of Christ.* Note the similarity in language in 1:28. **3:19** Paul continues the flesh-spirit contrast between Judaism and his gospel. Since *belly* could be a euphemism for genitalia, he may be continuing to make a point about the demand for circumcision of the genitals. In any case, it is unlikely that his opponents actually worship the "belly" as god. **3:20** *citizenship* Paul uses a Gk word often used for Jewish and other communities of the empire—*politeuma.* He may be responding to his opponents' charge that he has not brought his Gentile converts into the Jewish community by insisting that their community is spiritual. Paul continues to develop the scenario that lies at the base of his preaching: Jesus will return imminently. See *1 Thess.* 1:9–10. Paul describes this transformation more fully in *1 Cor.* 15:51–54. If one has not died before Jesus' return, then one's body must be transformed. **4:2** These two women are not mentioned elsewhere in Paul's letters. Both names, which are Gk, suggest that they came from slave (or freed) families in the Roman colony of Philippi. They seem now to be prominent figures in Paul's community; this accords with the portrayal in *Acts* 16:13, where women are featured in Philippian Christianity. Perhaps their disagreement, about which we know nothing, is related to the strife and partisanship that Paul has mentioned earlier (1:17; 2:1–4, 14). *To be of the same mind* recalls 2:2. **4:3** *companion* The person's identity is unknown. It is odd that Paul addresses him or her directly as if this were a personal letter. Perhaps the person was host, president, or overseer of the house church at which this letter was to be read aloud.

loyal companion,[b] help these women, for they have struggled beside me in the work of the gospel, together with Clement and the rest of my co-workers, whose names are in the book of life.

[4]Rejoice[c] in the Lord always; again I will say, Rejoice.[c] [5]Let your gentleness be known to everyone. The Lord is near. [6]Do not worry about anything, but in everything by prayer and supplication with thanksgiving let your requests be made known to God. [7]And the peace of God, which surpasses all understanding, will guard your hearts and your minds in Christ Jesus.

[8]Finally, beloved,[d] whatever is true, whatever is honorable, whatever is just, whatever is pure, whatever is pleasing, whatever is commendable, if there is any excellence and if there is anything worthy of praise, think about[e] these things. [9]Keep on doing the things that you have learned and received and heard and seen in me, and the God of peace will be with you.

Acknowledgment of the Philippians' Gift

[10]I rejoice[f] in the Lord greatly that now at last you have revived your concern for me; indeed, you were concerned for me, but had no opportunity to show it.[g] [11]Not that I am referring to being in need; for I have learned to be content with whatever I have. [12]I know what it is to have little, and I know what it is to have plenty. In any and all circumstances I have learned the secret of being well-fed and of going hungry, of having plenty and of being in need. [13]I can do all things through him who strengthens me. [14]In any case, it was kind of you to share my distress.

[15]You Philippians indeed know that in the early days of the gospel, when I left Macedonia, no church shared with me in the matter of giving and receiving, except you alone. [16]For even when I was in Thessalonica, you sent me help for my needs more than once. [17]Not that I seek the gift, but I seek the profit that accumulates to your account. [18]I have been paid in full and have more than enough; I am fully satisfied, now that I have received from Epaphroditus the gifts you sent, a fragrant offering, a sacrifice acceptable and pleasing to God. [19]And my God will fully satisfy every need of yours according to his riches in glory in Christ Jesus. [20]To our God and Father be glory forever and ever. Amen.

Final Greetings and Benediction

[21]Greet every saint in Christ Jesus. The friends[d] who are with me greet you. [22]All the saints greet you, especially those of the emperor's household.

[23]The grace of the Lord Jesus Christ be with your spirit.[h]

---

b Or *loyal Syzygus*
c Or *Farewell*
d Gk *brothers*
e Gk *take account of*
f Gk *I rejoiced*
g Gk lacks *to show it*

h Other ancient authorities add *Amen*

---

struggled beside me in the work of the gospel See note to 1:27. **Clement** A Roman Latin name *(Clemens),* suggesting a person of some social standing whose family was among the Roman colonists in Philippi. This person was identified from the 3d century onward with the Christian leader at Rome who wrote what we know as *1 Clement.* But the name was quite common. **book of life** It was a common belief in apocalyptic literature *(Dan.* 12:1; 1QM 12.2; *Rev.* 13:8; 21:27), no doubt grounded in biblical passages such as *Exod.* 32:32, that a heavenly book recorded the names of the saved or elect. Paul reflects many such features of apocalyptic thinking. **4:5** Jesus is about to return—a characteristic element of Paul's preaching (see *1 Thess.* 1:9–10; 4:13–18; *1 Cor.* 16:22; *Phil.* 3:20). **4:9 *seen in me*** See note to 3:17. **4:10 *concern for me*** The Philippians have sent a gift to Paul in prison through Epaphroditus (2:25–30; 4:18). On the abrupt shift to a new topic, after "final" greetings, see note to 3:1 and introduction. **4:12** Paul's words intersect with mainstream Greco-Roman philosophical, especially Stoic, thinking: the outward circumstances of one's life are irrelevant to inner peace. Paul grounds this outlook, however, in his Christian faith. **4:16** An important piece of information. Taken with *2 Cor.* 11:8–9, it shows that Paul's mission in both Thessalonica and southern Greece (Achaia) was subsidized by the Philippian church. Paul failed, however, to mention this support to his converts in Thessalonica and at first Corinth. In *1 Thess.* 2:9, he claims that he labored "night and day," with his own hands, so as not to burden the Thessalonians financially. In *1 Cor.* 9:15–18, he claims that he would rather die than relinquish his principle of not accepting payment for preaching. **4:21** A reference to some Christian members of the imperial civil service. Either they are prisoners with Paul or they have been in recent contact with him.

To Philemon, Apphia, Archippus, and Their Assembly

PHILEMON

Literary Features

Philemon offers the closest parallel among Paul's letters to the ordinary, everyday letter of the first century. It is short and personal, and it deals with a single issue—the slave Onesimus. It also exhibits a clear letter structure: sender (1a), recipient (1b-2), greeting (3); thanksgiving (4–7); body (8–20); closing commands (21–22); final greetings (23–24); and benediction (25). Although the purpose of the letter has not been fiercely debated because one interpretation has held the field, some recent challenges to the conventional view deserve attention.

Occasion and Purpose

The *Letter to Philemon* has usually been seen as Paul's admonition to a wealthy Christian named Philemon to take back his runaway slave (Onesimus) without any hard feelings. It is clear from the letter that Paul is in some sort of custody and that Philemon's slave Onesimus is with him (9–14). Against this background, the customary view takes verses 15–18 to mean: (a) that Onesimus is about to return to Philemon permanently (15—"Perhaps this is the reason he was separated from you for a while, so that you might have him back forever"); (b) that the runaway has become a Christian under Paul's supervision (16—"no longer as a slave but . . . a beloved brother"; see 11—"Formerly he was useless to you, but now he is indeed useful"); and (c) that Philemon should relinquish any claim to damages caused by Onesimus before he ran away (17–18—"If he has wronged you at all, or owes you anything, charge that to my account"). On the common view, then, Paul serves here as a counselor, intervening to restore a broken household relationship.

Commentators have noted several difficulties with this conventional hypothesis about the occasion for *Philemon*. First, although the thanksgiving section of a letter usually anticipates Paul's major arguments, here the thanksgiving is all about Philemon's giving or "sharing" to promote the Christian cause (vv. 6–7); it lacks any hint that he will *receive* Onesimus back. Second, Paul's appeal to Philemon in verses 8–14, which seems to be the heart of the letter, does not match the alleged purpose. Paul begins by asserting that, although he could require Philemon to do "your duty," he prefers to appeal to him "for (or concerning) my child Onesimus" (8–10). But what exactly is required? Although Paul is sending Onesimus back (12), he allows that he had wanted to keep him in the service of the gospel (13): "but I preferred to do nothing without your consent, in order that your good deed might be voluntary and not something forced" (14). If we take verses 8–14 as a distinct paragraph, therefore, the point seems to be that Philemon should allow Onesimus to join the apostle's entourage. Paul will send Onesimus back, so as not to presume upon Philemon (although he could do so), but he thinks that Philemon ought to donate Onesimus, as it were, to Paul's mission. This reading best explains Paul's command: "Yes, brother, let me have this benefit from you in the Lord!" (20). Notice that the Greek for "wanting some benefit" *(onaimēn)* is a pun on the name "Onesimus," which means "beneficial one." Paul evidently wants Onesimus to remain with him.

A recent examination of *Philemon* has shown, further, that the apparent allusions to Onesimus's running away and to his conversion under Paul may mean something else entirely (see Winter, below). First, Paul's statement, "If he has wronged you at all, or owes you anything, charge that to my account" (18), does not require that Paul knows of a specific wrong or debt incurred by Onesimus, such as theft, before escaping. It rather suggests Paul's attempt to secure a blanket release of the slave. Onesimus may not have been a runaway at all, then, but merely a messenger who had been sent by Philemon to assist Paul in prison. Although Paul generously offers to absorb the costs of Onesimus' release, he cannot resist noting that Philemon owes him his "very self" (19). Does he really expect Philemon to charge him?

Second, Paul's statements about the changed relationship between himself and Onesimus—"whose father I have become during my imprisonment" (10); formerly useless to you, now useful to me and you (11); no longer as a slave, but as a beloved brother (16)—may indicate simply the high esteem in which Paul has come to hold him. In that case, Paul would be implying a contrast to Philemon's view of Onesimus as merely one slave among many.

We note, finally, that there is something odd in the suggestion that a non-Christian runaway slave would first think of fleeing to visit the imprisoned Christian teacher, Paul. If he was already so minded before he was a believer, then his subsequent conversion under Paul could not have come as much of a surprise.

On this view of the letter's occasion, then, the well-to-do Philemon (or possibly Archippus) and the believers who meet in his house (1:2) send the slave Onesimus to assist Paul while he is in custody. This kind of private "Red Cross" service was often required to maintain imprisoned friends in the Roman world. But Paul has found Onesimus to be so helpful that he now sends him back to Philemon with a not-so-subtle appeal for the latter to release him into Paul's service. A remaining problem for this view is verse 15, in which Paul raises the prospect that Philemon will have Onesimus back "forever," but this may be only rhetorical on Paul's part.

Still another possibility is that Onesimus sought out Paul because he was having some difficulties with his master, and he knew that Philemon respected Paul. In this reconstruction, Onesimus would be following the common Roman practice of using a mutually acceptable arbiter to resolve a master-slave dispute (see Bartchy, below). This theory makes good sense in terms of the social background of Paul's day and it explains well much of Paul's language in verses 15–18. It does not explain as well Paul's remarks about wanting to keep Onesimus or about Philemon's obligation to obey and to do more than is required.

Remember, in any case, that we cannot simply read the situation out of Paul's own words, for his intended readers had much background that we lack; we must in every case reconstruct the backgrounds of Paul's letters according to the most likely hypothesis.

Themes

Perhaps the most obvious theme in *Philemon* is that of compassion, signified by the Greek plural *ta splanchna*—literally, "bowels" but figuratively the "seat of compassion." In English, we should perhaps translate, as the NRSV does, "heart." Paul uses this word only seven times in all of his undisputed correspondence, so it is remarkable that three of those occurrences fall within the scope of this short letter. Paul's opening gratitude for Philemon's work in "refreshing the hearts of the holy ones [= believers]" (7) is matched by his closing appeal that Philemon will "refresh my heart in Christ" (20). Between these two notices lies Paul's admission that the slave Onesimus *is* his own heart (12).

Paul's use of the "bowels [of compassion]" theme thus leaves open the question whether Paul is asking Philemon simply to take Onesimus back or to return him to Paul.

Date and Setting

The letter is difficult to date either absolutely or relative to Paul's other letters. Paul's imprisonment seems to be lengthy but perhaps not too severe, for he expresses confidence that he will soon be released (19, 22). This hope seems to favor Ephesus more than Caesarea or Rome as the place of imprisonment, since the last two (in succession) apparently led to his death. Strikingly, the list of Paul's companions in verse 23 closely matches that of *Col.* 4:10–14, where one of them (Epaphras) is identified as from Colossae, in the province of Asia (*Col.* 4:12). Even if Paul did not write *Colossians* (see the introductions to that letter and to LETTERS ATTRIBUTED TO PAUL), this additional connection with Asia (of which Ephesus was the capital) adds a bit of weight to the hypothesis of an Ephesian imprisonment. And the name of one of the letter's recipients, Apphia, seems to originate in Phrygia, the region of Asia where Colossae was located. Perhaps, then, Paul wrote this personal letter to Philemon during the same period in which he wrote the letter or letters we know as *Philippians*. But other dates are entirely possible, and one's interpretation of this little letter cannot depend on its exact date.

Value for the Study of Early Christianity

Though *Philemon* is all but ignored in discussions of Paul's life and thought, we should be grateful that it was preserved among his surviving letters. First, it shows us plainly that he did set out to write real letters according to the conventions of his time. This would not be so apparent if we had only the much longer and more involved letters, which now appear as extreme elaborations of the simple letter form. Second, this is the only letter that allows us to see Paul dealing with an almost completely nontheological issue: a straightforward matter of obligations, debts, and desires to be sorted out among the players concerned. The traditional interpretation of *Philemon* may have held sway for so long in part because it seemed to salvage a theological and ethical point from the letter concerning forgiveness and restoration. The background suggested above, however, would show Paul simply asking for a favor. Finally, if that proposed setting is the right one, then *Philemon* displays another aspect of Paul's rhetorical abilities: he couches his request in a variety of forms, alternating between reminders of debts owed, bold commands on the basis of authority, an offer to cover costs, and emotional appeals.

For Further Reading

Bartchy, S. Scott. Mallon Chrēsai: *First-Century Slavery and the Interpretation of 1 Corinthians 7:21*. Atlanta: Scholars Press, 1985.

Winter, Sara C. "Paul's Letter to Philemon." *New Testament Studies* 33 (1987): 1–15.

THE LETTER OF PAUL
TO PHILEMON

Salutation

[1]Paul, a prisoner of Christ Jesus, and Timothy our brother,[a]

To Philemon our dear friend and co-worker, [2]to Apphia our sister,[b] to Archippus our fellow soldier, and to the church in your house:

[3]Grace to you and peace from God our Father and the Lord Jesus Christ.

Philemon's Love and Faith

[4]When I remember you[c] in my prayers, I always thank my God [5]because I hear of your love for all the saints and your faith toward the Lord Jesus. [6]I pray that the sharing of your faith may become effective when you perceive all the good that we[d] may do for Christ. [7]I have indeed received much joy and encouragement from your love, because the hearts of the saints have been refreshed through you, my brother.

Paul's Plea for Onesimus

[8]For this reason, though I am bold enough in Christ to command you to do your duty, [9]yet I would rather appeal to you on the basis of love—and I, Paul, do this as an old man, and now also as a prisoner of Christ Jesus.[e] [10]I am appealing to you for my child, Onesimus, whose father I have become during my imprisonment. [11]Formerly he was useless to you, but now he is indeed useful[f] both to you and to me. [12]I am sending him, that is, my own heart, back to you. [13]I wanted to keep him with me, so that he might be of service to me in your place during my imprisonment for the gospel; [14]but I preferred to do nothing without your consent, in order that your good deed might be voluntary and not something forced. [15]Perhaps this is the reason he was separated from you for a while, so that you might have him back forever, [16]no longer as a slave but more than a slave, a beloved brother—especially to me but how much more to you, both in the flesh and in the Lord.

[17]So if you consider me your partner, welcome him as you would welcome me. [18]If he has wronged

---

a Gk *the brother*
b Gk *the sister*
c From verse 4 through verse 21, *you* is singular
d ancient authorities read *you* (plural)

e Or *as an ambassador of Christ Jesus, and now also his prisoner*
f The name Onesimus means *useful* or (compare verse 20) *beneficial*

---

1 *a prisoner of Christ Jesus* Paul often speaks of himself as a slave of Christ; now he is both a prisoner of the authorities (because of Christ) and *a prisoner of Christ*. Slavery and prison were two dreaded fates, and real possibilities for most people, in the ancient world. *Timothy our brother* Paul's closest associate, especially prominent in his early dealings with Thessalonica (*1 Thess.* 2:3, 6) and Corinth (*1 Cor.* 4:17) and later in Philippi (*Phil.* 2:19). *Philemon* Unknown outside this letter. **2** *Apphia* A name unknown outside this letter. The spelling of her name suggests that she is from Phrygia, where ancient Colossae was located. This strengthens the suggestion that Philemon's group lived in Colossae. That Paul singles her out for mention suggests that she plays a leading role in this local group of believers. The title he gives her, lit. "the sister," is entirely parallel to Timothy's "the brother." *Archippus* Appears elsewhere only at *Col.* 4:17. He, rather than Philemon, could be the one to whom the subsequent phrase *the church in your [singular] house* applies; if so, we should perhaps rename this letter Archippus. *the church* See *1 Cor.* 16:19; *Rom.* 15:23. At least through the first Christian century, "churches" (better: "assemblies") were small groups of Christians who met in the homes of their wealthier members. *in your house.* The possessive *your* is singular, usually taken to refer back to Philemon as the first mentioned, but quite possibly meant to connect with Archippus, the last mentioned. **3** Paul's standard greeting; see *1 Thess.* 1:1 and parallels. **7** *the hearts of the saints have been refreshed* First occurrence of a key phrase in this letter (*hearts*, lit. "bowels"); see verses 12 and 20, and also introduction to *Philemon*. **8** *do your duty* This may refer to Philemon's either receiving back his runaway slave or releasing him to Paul's service. **10** *for my child* Paul's Gk is conveniently vague: "concerning my child, Onesimus." The language suggests more "in the matter of Onesimus" than "for Onesimus's benefit." *whose father I have become* This figurative language might mean that Onesimus was converted under Paul's supervision or simply that he and Paul have become very close, as father and son. **11** An elaborate play on the name Onesimus, which means "useful" or "beneficial": when he was with you, he did not really live up to his name (as one of your numerous slaves), but he has indeed become "beneficial" to me. *my own heart* See note to verse 7. **13–14** This sentence supports the view that Paul really wants Onesimus back in his service. **15–18** These two sentences ground the view that Paul wants Philemon to accept his runaway slave, Onesimus, without exacting retribution. **18** *If he has wronged you...* The standard interpretation is that Paul offers compensation for the slave's damages. The phrasing may mean that Paul does not know of any specific damages caused by Onesimus; Paul might simply be offering to pay any such debts as a condition of having Onesimus delivered in his service.

you in any way, or owes you anything, charge that to my account. [19]I, Paul, am writing this with my own hand: I will repay it. I say nothing about your owing me even your own self. [20]Yes, brother, let me have this benefit from you in the Lord! Refresh my heart in Christ. [21]Confident of your obedience, I am writing to you, knowing that you will do even more than I say.

[22]One thing more—prepare a guest room for me, for I am hoping through your prayers to be restored to you.

Final Greetings and Benediction

[23]Epaphras, my fellow prisoner in Christ Jesus, sends greetings to you,[g] [24]and so do Mark, Aristarchus, Demas, and Luke, my fellow workers.

[25]The grace of the Lord Jesus Christ be with your spirit.[h]

---

g Here *you* is singular
h Other ancient authorities add *Amen*

---

20 ***this benefit*** The Gk lacks *this*: "I want a (some) benefit." ***Refresh my heart*** See note to verse 7. **23** ***Epaphras*** Mentioned elsewhere only in *Col.* 1:7; 4:12, where he appears as the founder of the Christian group at Colossae. Now he is with Paul at the time of writing. The name could be an abbreviation of Epaphroditus, but this person seems to be different from the Epaphroditus mentioned in *Phil.* 2, who was an emissary of the Philippian believers. **24** ***Mark, Aristarchus, Demas, and Luke*** All four are named among Paul's companions also in *Col.* 4:10, 14; all but Aristarchus appear in *2 Tim.* 4:9–12. Their appearance here strengthens the suggestion that Philemon's group was in Colossae. ***Mark*** A Jewish Christian and cousin of Barnabas according to *Col.* 4:10–11; son of one Mary according to *Acts* 12:12; sometime companion of Paul who deserted Paul en route (*Acts* 13:13) and so alienated him (15:36–41); close friend ("son") of Peter according to *1 Pet.* 5:13; identified by 2d-century Christians as the author of the anonymous gospel we now know as *Mark* (Eusebius, *Eccl. hist.* 2.15).

Aristarchus He appears in *Acts* (19:29; 20:4; 27:2) as a Macedonian from Thessalonica and Paul's travel companion from Ephesus to Judea to Rome. A Jewish Christian according to *Col.* 4:10–11. ***Demas*** A tradition in *2 Tim.* 4:10 claims that he abandoned Paul, having fallen "in love with this present world." The third chapter of the 2d-century *Acts of Paul,* perhaps roughly contemporary with *2 Timothy,* claims that Demas saw the resurrection as already past (3:14; see *1 Cor.* 15:12; *2 Tim.* 2:17–18). ***Luke*** According to *Col.* 4:14, a physician; mentioned as Paul's sole companion in *2 Tim.* 4:11; held by 2d-century and later tradition (Eusebius, *Eccl. hist.* 3.4) to have written the anonymous volumes we know as *Luke* and *Acts.*

Further to the Assembly in Corinth

2 CORINTHIANS

Setting

When he wrote his second letter to Corinth (i.e., *1 Corinthians*), Paul was already opposed by some within the church, and so he threatened to visit them with a "stick" (*1 Cor.* 4:18–21). The next letter to Corinth that we possess, traditionally known as *2 Corinthians,* is marked by a peculiar combination of Paul's strenuous efforts at reconciliation with the Corinthians (in chs. 1–7) on the one hand, and still further anguish and threats on the other (chs. 10–13). This odd combination has caused readers to wonder: (a) what has transpired between *1 Corinthians* and *2 Corinthians;* (b) whether our *2 Corinthians* was originally written as a single letter; and (c) whether the opposition that Paul confronts in *2 Corinthians* is the same that he faced in the earlier letter.

In the opening paragraphs of *2 Corinthians* Paul gives several clues about what has been happening in his life. First, although he had planned a double visit to Corinth—namely, on the way to *and* from Macedonia (*2 Cor.* 1:15–16)—he has canceled it in order to spare the church "another painful visit" (2:1). We recall, however, that he finished *1 Corinthians* by promising to visit Corinth only after passing through Macedonia (*1 Cor.* 16:5–6). So, either he has changed his travel plans in the interim or he has already made the trip anticipated in *1 Corinthians* and is now discussing additional planned visits that were canceled. Support for the second option comes from the phrase "another painful visit" in 2:1. It is unlikely that this phrase refers to Paul's founding visit to Corinth, since that visit produced the Christian community; they must have been on his side. It appears, then, that Paul has recently made a visit that turned out to be unpleasant (presumably, the one anticipated in *1 Corinthians* 16) and therefore has chosen to cancel further planned visits. What exactly made the visit painful is not clear. It seems, however, that one individual, in particular, deeply offended Paul while he was in Corinth (2:5–10; 7:12). So between *1 Corinthians* and *2 Corinthians* 1–7, Paul has paid an unpleasant visit to Corinth.

Second, in *2 Corinthians* 1–7 Paul repeatedly mentions his "harsh letter" to the Corinthians in order to bring them back to his side. Included there was a prescription for the punishment of the one who had offended Paul (2:5–9; 7:12). Evidently, Paul sent the letter with his companion Titus, whose job was both to present it to the church—perhaps read it aloud, elaborate on some points, and answer questions—and then to report back to Paul on its effectiveness (2:12–13; 7:6–9, 13–14). Paul would meet up with Titus in Troas to hear his report (2:12–13). All of these clues about the harsh letter indicate that it should not be identified with *1 Corinthians*. We must reckon, therefore, with the prospect that another important piece of the Corinthian correspondence has been lost, in addition to the "previous letter" that came before *1 Corinthians*.

Third, although Titus did not make it to Troas on schedule, which caused Paul some anxiety (2:12–13), the two eventually did meet (in Macedonia), and Titus had good news: Paul's harsh letter did serve its purpose and the Corinthian believers have shown some remorse for their actions. They have disciplined the offender (2:5–9; 7:5–12) and are now "longing" to see Paul again (7:7). All of this is gratifying for Paul. So the first seven chapters of *2 Corinthians* are dominated by the themes of "comfort" (or "consolation") and "reconciliation." He wants to consolidate his new relationship with the church. That this relationship is not yet entirely free of misgivings, however, is suggested at several points (5:20; 6:12).

The fourth significant event that has occurred in Paul's life is what he describes as a deadly peril in Asia (1:8–10). We do not know whether this was a serious illness, an imprisonment, or some other threat to his life. He has, however, recently faced the possibility of death. In this respect, *2 Corinthians* is similar to *Philippians*, where we found Paul in Asia (Ephesus appeared likely) and contemplating the possibility of a death sentence. And in both letters, interestingly enough, Paul seems to speak about the afterlife in terms that differ noticeably from those of his earlier letters, in which he thought that he would live to see Jesus' return. Thus in *2 Cor.* 5:1–5 he describes the body as a tent or "clay jar" (4:7) that is shed at death. Although he refers briefly to the idea of resurrection (4:14), he seems to view the afterlife, increasingly, according to the Greek understanding of the immortality of the soul (5:6–8). One is tempted by the thought that Paul's own struggles led him to reconsider his more optimistic views of both the timing and the nature of Jesus' return.

After chapter 7, *2 Corinthians* develops in ways that cast doubt on the literary integrity of the letter. First, chapters 8 and 9 are devoted to coaxing the Corinthians to contribute to Paul's collection for Jerusalem. In view of the deep wounds that Paul has so far been desperately trying to heal, this forthright and sustained appeal for money comes as a shock to the reader. The alternative is to infer that one of Paul's major motives in winning the Corinthians back was his fear of losing their contributions to the collection for Jerusalem. *First Corinthians* 16:2–4 indicates that Paul had planned to pick up the Corinthians' share of the collection when he visited; the rupture during that visit would likely have prevented him from doing so. This is supported by *2 Cor.* 8:10–11, where Paul admonishes the newly restored

Corinthians to finish what they had begun a year earlier, before the rift. The collection for Jerusalem must have been extremely important for Paul.

Even more perplexing is the function of chapters 10–13 in *2 Corinthians*. Whereas the first part of the letter reflects Paul's efforts at repairing the damage done by the painful visit, these last chapters show him once again in angry conflict with the church. He explosively chastises the Corinthians for belittling him (10:8–11; 11:5–6, 16; 12:11, 16) and for readily following other Christian leaders (11:1–4, 19), whom he now describes as fools (11:19), servants of Satan (11:15), and false apostles (11:13). In response to the perceived slanders of these teachers, Paul boasts at length of his own accomplishments (11:5–12:13). And he closes by declaring his intention to make a third visit to Corinth to set things straight (12:14; 13:1). He claims that he confronted some sinners already, on his second visit (13:2), and warns that he will do so again on his third. So the purpose of chapters 10–13 is to prepare for this planned third visit, so that he will not need to be "severe" when he comes (13:10).

Most expert readers agree that chapters 10–13 do not make much sense as a conclusion to the letter(s) represented by chapters 1–9. They seem to undo everything that has already been accomplished: Paul once again assumes the posture of the seriously aggrieved party, and he again plans an unpleasant visit. The two more likely possibilities are (a) that the relationship between Paul and the Corinthians deteriorated after *2 Corinthians* 1–9 was written, so that chapters 10–13 represent a much later and separate letter, or (b) that chapters 10–13 come earlier than chapters 1–9, from the period of conflict described there. In the latter case, they would be a fragment of the (otherwise lost) "severe letter" sent with Titus. This view has much in its favor,[1] although many scholars doubt that chapters 10–13 match what Paul reveals about his severe letter.[2]

One might summarize Paul's relationship with Corinth in the following stages:

1. Paul visits Corinth.

2. Paul writes Letter A to Corinth (lost; referred to in *1 Cor.* 5:9).

3. Chloe's slaves make an unfavorable report to Paul in Ephesus.

4. A letter from the Corinthians is conveyed to Paul in Ephesus by Stephanas, Fortunatus, and Achaicus.

5. Paul sends Letter B to Corinth, responding to their issues (= *1 Corinthians*).

---

[1]In other words: (a) *2 Corinthians* 10–13 is by any account a harsh letter. (b) It threatens, in effect, a second painful visit (third visit in total), which the letter is intended to prevent. (c) In *2 Corinthians* 1–7, the letter of reconciliation, Paul self-consciously asserts that he is not commending himself again (3:1; 5:12) and excuses his being "beside himself" (5:13). All of this works well if chapters 10–13 represent part of the missing harsh letter.

[2]On the one hand, chapters 1–7 make no mention of the "super-apostles," who are central to chapters 10–13, as an issue in the painful visit. On the other hand, chapters 10–13 do not mention the individual who has offended Paul and needs punishment. One could explain these divergences, of course, by the fragmentary nature of *2 Corinthians* 10–13.

6. Paul anticipates a painful visit to Corinth in *1 Cor.* 16:5–8. Paul confronts at least one offensive person (*2 Cor.* 2:5–11).

7. Paul returns to Ephesus in anger and writes a harsh letter to the Corinthians (*2 Cor.* 2:3–4, 9; Letter C = *2 Corinthians* 10–13?). He sends the letter with Titus, who will read it aloud and report back to Paul (in Troas) on the response of the Corinthians.

8. After a suspenseful delay, Titus meets Paul in Macedonia and gives him a favorable report about the Corinthians' response: the letter moved them to repentance and renewed allegiance to Paul (*2 Cor.* 7:5–13).

9. Letter D from Paul to Corinth (*2 Corinthians* 1–7 or 1–9) tries to consolidate this restored connection and possibly (if chs. 8–9 were part of it) to reinstate the Corinthians' participation in Paul's collection for Jerusalem.

10. Possibly additional letters are written from Paul to Corinth (on the collection and against the super-apostles, *2 Corinthians* 8, 9, 10–13).

If, as we have argued, there was a principled opposition to Paul in *1 Corinthians,* a group that tended toward "realized eschatology," such a group is scarcely visible in any part of *2 Corinthians.* To be sure, Paul mentions the themes of knowledge, wisdom, rhetoric, and power in chapters 10–13 (10:5, 10; 13:9), but these no longer appear to be central issues.

His current opponents are characterized chiefly by their apostolic accreditation (11:5, 13, 23; 12:11; see 3:1) and their Jewish background (11:22; see 3:4–18). Paul claims that they seek to enslave the Corinthians (11:20) and that they accuse him of worldliness (10:2). Taken together with his repudiation of Moses in 3:4–16, these data seem to indicate that his opponents were Jews (though also Christians) who sought to bring his followers within the orbit of observant Judaism. These opponents, then, would be somewhat similar to those who challenged Paul's teachings in Galatia (see next chapter).

One solution to the problem of Paul's Corinthian opponents is the hypothesis that the "Cephas" party, which was active but not yet significant when Paul wrote *1 Corinthians* (1:12; 3:22), came subsequently to displace Apollos's realized-eschatology group as Paul's most vigorous opponents. On the basis of *Gal.* 2:14, it would seem that any party devoted to Peter (Cephas) would have insisted on the Jewish character of Christianity. So, whereas *1 Corinthians* had been devoted to the repudiation of realized eschatology, *2 Corinthians* mainly confronts Christian Judaism (*2 Corinthians* 3, 10–13). This hypothesis would also explain Paul's greater concern in *2 Corinthians* with the apostolic credentials of his opponents (*2 Cor.* 3:1–2, 6; 10:12, 18; 11:5, 21–22; 12:11–12).

Some scholars, however, think that Paul's few allusions to the themes of rhetoric and wisdom in *2 Corinthians* require that his opponents in that letter be substantially the same group as his earlier adversaries in *1 Corinthians.* The result is that Paul's Corinthian opponents appear as a rather nebulous party of Hellenistic-Jewish gnostics who asserted strong ties to the Jerusalem church.

For Further Reading

In addition to the works cited for *1 Corinthians:*

Betz, Hans Dieter. "Corinthians, Second Epistle to the." Pages 1148–54 in vol. 1 of Anchor Bible Dictionary. Edited by D. N. Freedman. 6 vols. New York: Doubleday, 1992.

Garland, David E. *2 Corinthians.* New American Commentary. Nashville: Broadman and Holman, 1999.

Georgi, Dieter. *The Opponents of Paul in Second Corinthians.* Philadelphia: Fortress, 1986.

Welborn, L. L. *Politics and Rhetoric in the Corinthian Epistles.* Macon, Ga.: Mercer University Press, 1997.

THE SECOND LETTER OF PAUL
TO THE CORINTHIANS

Salutation

1 Paul, an apostle of Christ Jesus by the will of God, and Timothy our brother,

To the church of God that is in Corinth, including all the saints throughout Achaia:

²Grace to you and peace from God our Father and the Lord Jesus Christ.

Paul's Thanksgiving after Affliction

³Blessed be the God and Father of our Lord Jesus Christ, the Father of mercies and the God of all consolation, ⁴who consoles us in all our affliction, so that we may be able to console those who are in any affliction with the consolation with which we ourselves are consoled by God. ⁵For just as the sufferings of Christ are abundant for us, so also our consolation is abundant through Christ. ⁶If we are being afflicted, it is for your consolation and salvation; if we are being consoled, it is for your consolation, which you experience when you patiently endure the same sufferings that we are also suffering. ⁷Our hope for you is unshaken; for we know that as you share in our sufferings, so also you share in our consolation.

⁸We do not want you to be unaware, brothers and sisters,ᵃ of the affliction we experienced in Asia; for we were so utterly, unbearably crushed that we despaired of life itself. ⁹Indeed, we felt that we had received the sentence of death so that we would rely not on ourselves but on God who raises the dead. ¹⁰He who rescued us from so deadly a peril will continue to rescue us; on him we have set our hope that he will rescue us again, ¹¹as you also join in helping us by your prayers, so that many will give thanks on ourᵇ behalf for the blessing granted us through the prayers of many.

The Postponement of Paul's Visit

¹²Indeed, this is our boast, the testimony of our conscience: we have behaved in the world with franknessᶜ and godly sincerity, not by earthly wisdom but by the grace of God—and all the more toward you. ¹³For we write you nothing other than what you can read and also understand; I hope you will understand until the end— ¹⁴as you have already understood us in part—that on the day of the Lord Jesus we are your boast even as you are our boast.

¹⁵Since I was sure of this, I wanted to come to you first, so that you might have a double favor;ᵈ ¹⁶I

---

a Gk brothers

b Other ancient authorities read your
c Other ancient authorities read holiness
d Other ancient authorities read pleasure

1:1–2 grace . . . and peace This greeting is fairly standard in Paul's letters. On Timothy, see note to *1 Thess.* 1:1. Corinth was the capital of the Roman senatorial province of Achaia. Paul's greeting indicates that the large cities on which he focused his mission served as centers for the regions around them, where there were believers also. **1:3–11** This blessing substitutes for Paul's typical thanksgiving (see *1 Thess.* 1:2–10 and note; *1 Cor.* 1:4; *Phil.* 1:3; *Phlm.* 4; *Rom.* 1:8). Like the thanksgiving, it introduces the major themes of the letter (in this case, *2 Corinthians* 1–7 or 1–9; see introduction to *2 Corinthians*). The "consolation" word group appears ten times in these nine verses. The bulk of the letter (*2 Corinthians* 1–9) attempts to strengthen the new bond that has developed as a result of the letter that Paul sent with Titus (2:3–11). Having come through another kind of crisis at the same time, Paul appears full of *consolation.* This blessing contains no hint, however, of the antagonism that will be raised in *2 Corinthians* 10–13. **1:8 the affliction we experienced in Asia** Ephesus was the capital of this Roman senatorial province on the western side of Asia Minor (modern Turkey). See also *1 Cor.* 15:32, where Paul claims metaphorically to have fought wild beasts at Ephesus. **1:9 we felt that we had received the sentence of death** Since Paul was so often in danger of life and limb (11:23–27), we cannot be sure what kind of crisis occurred in Ephesus. The word *sentence* and the 1st-person plural suggest a serious legal problem; it is unlikely that Paul and his entourage all fell mortally ill at the same moment. He may be referring to the Ephesian imprisonment mentioned in *Phil.* 1:19–26; 2:17. *Acts* 19:23–41 tells of a riot in Ephesus, but it claims that Paul was able to leave without a trial. **rely on God who raises the dead** This line recalls *1 Corinthians* 15, where Paul responded at great length to Corinthians who claimed that there was no future resurrection (see *1 Cor.* 15:12). **1:12–14** These lines recall Paul's lengthy discussion, in *1 Corinthians* 1–4, of human wisdom and its opposition to God's spirit. Evidently, this battle is largely over in Paul's mind. Perhaps it was forced mainly by the one offensive person (an ardent partisan of Apollos?) whose views have now been disavowed by the group (2:5–11). Paul's protestations of frankness, simplicity, and honesty were typical of popular philosophers in his day; see also *1 Thess.* 2:3–12. **1:14 the day of the Lord Jesus** Paul still looks forward eagerly to Jesus' return from heaven in glory. See *1 Thess.* 1:9–10; 5:2, 23; *1 Cor.* 1:8; 5:5; *Phil.* 1:6, 10; 2:16. Paul also speaks of boasting (in his converts) on the day of Christ in *Phil.* 2:16. **1:15–2:2** Paul apparently has to explain why he has canceled announced plans to visit Corinth. He is not vacillating, he says; rather, he canceled the trip in order to avoid

wanted to visit you on my way to Macedonia, and to come back to you from Macedonia and have you send me on to Judea. [17]Was I vacillating when I wanted to do this? Do I make my plans according to ordinary human standards,[e] ready to say "Yes, yes" and "No, no" at the same time? [18]As surely as God is faithful, our word to you has not been "Yes and No." [19]For the Son of God, Jesus Christ, whom we proclaimed among you, Silvanus and Timothy and I, was not "Yes and No"; but in him it is always "Yes." [20]For in him every one of God's promises is a "Yes." For this reason it is through him that we say the "Amen," to the glory of God. [21]But it is God who establishes us with you in Christ and has anointed us, [22]by putting his seal on us and giving us his Spirit in our hearts as a first installment.

[23]But I call on God as witness against me: it was to spare you that I did not come again to Corinth. [24]I do not mean to imply that we lord it over your faith; rather, we are workers with you for your joy, because you stand firm in the faith. 2 [1]So I made up my mind not to make you another painful visit. [2]For if I cause you pain, who is there to make me glad but the one whom I have pained? [3]And I wrote as I did, so that when I came, I might not suffer pain from those

who should have made me rejoice; for I am confident about all of you, that my joy would be the joy of all of you. [4]For I wrote you out of much distress and anguish of heart and with many tears, not to cause you pain, but to let you know the abundant love that I have for you.

Forgiveness for the Offender

[5]But if anyone has caused pain, he has caused it not to me, but to some extent—not to exaggerate it—to all of you. [6]This punishment by the majority is enough for such a person; [7]so now instead you should forgive and console him, so that he may not be overwhelmed by excessive sorrow. [8]So I urge you to reaffirm your love for him. [9]I wrote for this reason: to test you and to know whether you are obedient in everything. [10]Anyone whom you forgive, I also forgive. What I have forgiven, if I have forgiven anything, has been for your sake in the presence of Christ. [11]And we do this so that we may not be outwitted by Satan; for we are not ignorant of his designs.

Paul's Anxiety in Troas

[12]When I came to Troas to proclaim the good news of Christ, a door was opened for me in the Lord; [13]but my mind could not rest because I did not find

---

e Gk *according to the flesh*

another unpleasant confrontation (2:1). It appears that he made the trip planned in *1 Cor.* 16:3–6 because he was expecting some trouble then (4:18–21). As it turned out, Paul was unable to collect the money for Jerusalem because of the unpleasantness he experienced during that visit, and so he planned a subsequent double visit, on the way to and from Macedonia. No doubt he had hoped to sort things out in Corinth on the way to Macedonia so that the collection would finally be ready on his way back. In the meantime, he also decided to send with Titus a letter that confronted the Corinthians over his last visit and perhaps included his plans for a third visit (2:3). But while he awaited Titus's report, he opted to postpone that next visit. **1:19 *Silvanus and Timothy and I*** See 1:1 and note to *1 Thess.* 1:1. *1 Thessalonians* confirms that these three men were together in Corinth, establishing the Christian community there, when Paul wrote to Thessalonica. But the last we heard of Timothy, Paul had sent him to "remind" the Corinthians of Paul's version of Christianity (*1 Cor.* 4:17) and had advised them to receive him warmly and not to despise him (16:10–11). Since Timothy will no longer figure in Paul's dealings with the Corinthians, having been replaced by Titus (2:14–17; 7:5–7; 8:6, 16), we may conjecture that he has lost the confidence of some Corinthians. **1:20 *we say the "Amen."*** One of several Aramaic words preserved in Paul's Gk-speaking Gentile communities in imitation of Jewish worship; see also notes to *1 Cor.* 16:22 and *Gal.* 4:6. "Amen" comes from the verb "to trust [or 'believe' or 'credit']," and it was used in later Jewish liturgy as a term of strong agreement. **1:22** See also 5:5. **2:3–11** Paul now describes for the first time the letter that he sent by the hand of Titus after his painful visit to Corinth. Evidently, he wrote in preparation for his next visit (2:3), which suggests that the cancellation of the visit (1:15–2:2) came afterward. *2 Corinthians* 10–13 also prepares for a painful visit to Corinth (12:20–21; 13:2–3, 10), which would have been Paul's third visit in total (13:2). **2:3** See 13:10. **2:4** See 12:14–16, 19. **2:5–8** In light of 7:12, it seems that Paul was confronted during his painful visit by some individual (perhaps one of the "arrogant people" mentioned in *1 Cor.* 4:19), who offended him deeply. But since the subsequent harsh letter was designed to bring the whole community to repentance (7:8–12), the offending man must have been speaking for a significant group in the church, as we might also have expected from *1 Corinthians*. At least the whole group was insufficiently supportive of Paul and disdainful of the offender. Paul's references to this man have no parallel in *2 Corinthians* 10–13. This could mean either that those chapters do not represent the harsh letter, after all, or that they are only a fragment of it (see introduction to *2 Corinthians*). **2:11** Like many people of his day, Paul sees the activity of Satan and his demons everywhere; see also 4:4; 11:14; 12:7; *1 Thess.* 2:18; *1 Cor.* 5:5; 7:5; *Rom.* 16:20; 1QS 3.22–23. **2:12–13** Paul had expected to meet Titus in Troas on the latter's return from delivering the harsh letter to Corinth. They would catch up with each other in Macedonia—presumably either Philippi or Thessalonica (7:5–6). Troas was a large city and a transportation hub on the western coast of Asia Minor, in the region known as Mysia. It lay about ten miles south of Troy, the city made famous by Homer and Virgil and whose name it preserved. See *Acts* 16:8. Since the itineraries of Paul and Titus follow coastal cities, it appears that they traveled by ship.

my brother Titus there. So I said farewell to them and went on to Macedonia.

¹⁴But thanks be to God, who in Christ always leads us in triumphal procession, and through us spreads in every place the fragrance that comes from knowing him. ¹⁵For we are the aroma of Christ to God among those who are being saved and among those who are perishing; ¹⁶to the one a fragrance from death to death, to the other a fragrance from life to life. Who is sufficient for these things? ¹⁷For we are not peddlers of God's word like so many;*f* but in Christ we speak as persons of sincerity, as persons sent from God and standing in his presence.

Ministers of the New Covenant

3 Are we beginning to commend ourselves again? Surely we do not need, as some do, letters of recommendation to you or from you, do we? ²You your-

selves are our letter, written on our*g* hearts, to be known and read by all; ³and you show that you are a letter of Christ, prepared by us, written not with ink but with the Spirit of the living God, not on tablets of stone but on tablets of human hearts.

⁴Such is the confidence that we have through Christ toward God. ⁵Not that we are competent of ourselves to claim anything as coming from us; our competence is from God, ⁶who has made us competent to be ministers of a new covenant, not of letter but of spirit; for the letter kills, but the Spirit gives life.

⁷Now if the ministry of death, chiseled in letters on stone tablets,*h* came in glory so that the people of Israel could not gaze at Moses' face because of the glory of his face, a glory now set aside, ⁸how much more will the ministry of the Spirit come in glory? ⁹For if there was glory in the ministry of condemnation, much more does the ministry of justification

---

f Other ancient authorities read *like the others*

g Other ancient authorities read *your*
h Gk *on stones*

2:14–17 This brief thanksgiving marks a transition from Paul's concrete discussion of his relationship with the Corinthian church to theological reflections occasioned by his criticism of his Christian opponents (2:17). He will return to the concrete issues, and the conclusion of his remarks about Titus and the harsh letter, in 7:5. **2:14–15** *always leads us in triumphal procession . . . aroma of Christ* The English sense is apt to mislead because it sounds rather happy. Paul, however, chooses shocking language: Leading in triumph was something done to slaves captured during war, who became a humiliated spectacle to the world (see *1 Cor.* 4:9), and the fragrance in question was the "sweet smell of sacrifice" enjoyed by both Israel's God (*Gen.* 8:21; *Lev.* 1:9, 13, 17) and the gods of the Gentiles. Paul characteristically inverts normal social virtues, celebrating his chosen slavery or captivity to Christ (*Phil.* 1:1). **2:17** In Paul's world there was a long-standing and widespread suspicion of Sophists, those who taught philosophy for profit (Plato, *Gorgias*). Paul repeatedly insists that he does not "peddle God's word" by asking for money as do other teachers (*1 Thess.* 2:3–12; *1 Cor.* 9:1–23; but see also *Phil.* 4:15 and *2 Cor.* 11:8–9). Those others apparently included Peter and Jesus' brothers James and Jude (*1 Cor.* 9:5–6). If *2 Corinthians* 10–13 has already been sent to the Corinthians as part of the harsh letter, then Paul is here recalling his strong words about his Corinthian opponents in 11:7–14. **3:1** *commend ourselves again* When has Paul commended himself earlier? He does so in 11:5–12:7. There, having ridiculed in 10:12–18 those who "commend themselves," he himself goes on to "boast," claiming a kind of temporary madness (11:16, 18, 21, 23, 30; 12:1). Then he expresses deep hurt that the community has not taken the initiative in commending him (12:11). This reference provides further evidence that *2 Corinthians* 10–13 came before *2 Corinthians* 1–9. See also 6:4–7. *letters of recommendation* See 10:12. Paul's opponents in *2 Corinthians* 10–13 come with impressive credentials, such that he must dismiss them as "false apostles" and "super-apostles" disguised as "angels of light" (11:5, 14). Also in Galatia, Paul's Jewish Christian opponents came with impressive support (1:8; 5:10). Because the ancient world functioned much more than ours does on the basis of social networks—there were few avenues for promoting an individual's ideas outside a particular group—these letters must have come from persons whom the Corinthians respected highly. Given that they knew Peter and Jesus' brothers (*1 Cor.* 9:5) and that these Jerusalem leaders appear to have expected Gentile Christians to convert to Judaism (*Gal.* 2:12, 14), it is entirely likely that Paul's judaizing opponents in Corinth had produced letters from the Jerusalem leaders. See note to 4:3–4. **3:3** *not on tablets of stone but on tablets of human hearts* Paul alludes to the new-covenant language of *Jer.* 31:31–34 (see *Ezek.* 11:17–20), a favorite passage of early Christians (see also *Heb.* 8:6–12; 9:15; 10:16–17). The original passage expressed hope for the time after Judah's return from exile in Babylon in the 6th century B.C.E.: the Torah would be written on people's hearts, so they would never violate God's will and face such punishment again. "New covenant" language was still in the air in Paul's day as various groups established communities more rigorous than the mainstream in hopes of fulfilling the passage's promise (e.g., CD 6.19). But Paul is unique in understanding the new covenant as one that *abandons* Torah observance altogether. **3:6** *a new covenant* See previous note. **3:7–9** God's giving the Torah to Moses on tablets of stone (*Exod.* 24:12) in itself implied nothing about death. On the contrary, God promises life to the righteous person who observes Torah (*Lev.* 18:5). Paul, however, identifies the entire culture of Torah observance with the image of cold stone used by Jeremiah (see note to 3:3). His argument here is that if even that covenant came with a certain *glory* (or "radiance"; Gk *doxa*), the new covenant will bring even more glory. In the first case, he is referring to the glowing of Moses' face after he received the Torah, which required him to veil himself (*Exod.* 34:29–35).

abound in glory! [10]Indeed, what once had glory has lost its glory because of the greater glory; [11]for if what was set aside came through glory, much more has the permanent come in glory!

[12]Since, then, we have such a hope, we act with great boldness, [13]not like Moses, who put a veil over his face to keep the people of Israel from gazing at the end of the glory that[i] was being set aside. [14]But their minds were hardened. Indeed, to this very day, when they hear the reading of the old covenant, that same veil is still there, since only in Christ is it set aside. [15]Indeed, to this very day whenever Moses is read, a veil lies over their minds; [16]but when one turns to the Lord, the veil is removed. [17]Now the Lord is the Spirit, and where the Spirit of the Lord is, there is freedom. [18]And all of us, with unveiled faces, seeing the glory of the Lord as though reflected in a mirror, are being transformed into the same image from one degree of glory to another; for this comes from the Lord, the Spirit.

Treasure in Clay Jars

4 Therefore, since it is by God's mercy that we are engaged in this ministry, we do not lose heart. [2]We have renounced the shameful things that one hides; we refuse to practice cunning or to falsify God's word; but by the open statement of the truth we commend ourselves to the conscience of everyone in the sight of God. [3]And even if our gospel is veiled, it is veiled to those who are perishing. [4]In their case the god of this world has blinded the minds of the unbelievers, to keep them from seeing the light of the gospel of the glory of Christ, who is the image of God. [5]For we do not proclaim ourselves; we proclaim Jesus Christ as Lord and ourselves as your slaves for Jesus' sake. [6]For it is the God who said, "Let light shine out of darkness," who has shone in our hearts to give the light of the knowledge of the glory of God in the face of Jesus Christ.

[7]But we have this treasure in clay jars, so that it may be made clear that this extraordinary power belongs to God and does not come from us. [8]We are afflicted in every way, but not crushed; perplexed, but not driven to despair; [9]persecuted, but not forsaken; struck down, but not destroyed; [10]always carrying in the body the death of Jesus, so that the life of Jesus may also be made visible in our bodies. [11]For while we live, we are always being given up to death for Jesus' sake, so that the life of Jesus may be made visible in our mortal flesh. [12]So death is at work in us, but life in you.

[13]But just as we have the same spirit of faith that is in accordance with scripture—"I believed, and so I

---

i Gk *of what*

3:10–11 Paul believes that the covenant of Torah has lost its validity because something better has replaced it (see also *Phil.* 3:7–8; *Gal.* 2:11–21; 3:19–29). He is perhaps here playing on the Gk word *doxa*, which means both "splendor" ("radiance," "glory") and "opinion" ("view," "judgment," as in "orthodoxy," lit. "correct view"). **3:12–13** According to *Exod.* 34:29–35, when Moses came down from Sinai after receiving the Torah, "the skin of his face shone because he had been talking with God." After allowing the people to see this radiance, he covered his face with a veil until his next encounter with God on the mountain. Whereas Jewish commentators took the veil as a safeguard for the people who could not tolerate his brilliance, Paul interprets the story to mean that Moses' radiance was *fading* in the interim and that Moses covered his face to prevent the people from seeing this fading. He then interprets the alleged fading of the glory on Moses' face as a symbol of the obsolescence of the Torah (see 3:7). **3:14–16** Paul is using word association: Moses' veil, which was required to protect the people from the divine glory (see previous note), is now construed as a negative thing—a cover over the eyes of the Jewish people, which needs to be removed. Those who maintain the veil, in Paul's view, are perishing (see 4:3–4). Thus, Paul sees the Torah not as a code that requires observance but only as a code that, properly understood (in the Spirit), speaks of Christ. **3:14** *reading of the old covenant* As far as we know, Paul was the first to describe the books of the Jewish Bible as the "old covenant" ("Old Testament"). This title would stick in Christian circles, but it was not until Tertullian, at the close of the 2d century C.E., that Christians began to call some of their own writings a "new covenant" ("New Testament"). **3:17–18** Paul characteristically returns to his rhetorical contrast, begun in 3:6–7, between words connected with spirit (life, freedom, superior glory) and those connected with flesh or matter (death, veil, darkness, blindness). See also *1 Cor.* 15:42–57; *Phil.* 3:3, 18–21; *Gal.* 3:1–5. **4:2** See note to 2:17. **4:3–4** Paul evidently continues his criticisms of Jews who have failed to accept Jesus (3:14–16) and even of his Jewish Christian opponents (4:2; see 3:1–3). He may well have thought that they, like non-Christian Jews, failed to appreciate the significance of Jesus' death and resurrection. This seems to be Paul's view in *Gal.* 2:15–21. **4:4** *the god of this world* See note to 2:11. *Christ, who is the image of God* This language recalls the description of the first humans in *Gen.* 1:27. Elsewhere Paul presents Jesus as a second Adam, who undoes the evil that Adam introduced (*1 Cor.* 15:44–49; *Phil.* 2:6–11; *Rom.* 5:12–21). **4:6** *Let light shine out of darkness* Recalling *Gen.* 1:3. Paul continues to appropriate language from the creation story for Christian believers; see also 5:17. **4:7** *we have this treasure in clay jars* Paul is no doubt continuing to refer to the creation story, in which God fashioned a man from the ground and then breathed into him (*Gen.* 2:7). But whereas the Bible tends to present the resulting human being as a single whole, Paul reads this story in typically Gk terms, such that the *clay* body houses the real *treasure,* which is the spirit. See especially 5:1–2. **4:10–11** See also *Gal.* 2:19–20; 6:17. **4:13** *I believed, and so I spoke. Ps.* 116:10. MT: "I trust [in the LORD]; / out of great suffering I spoke." LXX (115:10): "I believed, and so I spoke, but I was greatly humiliated." Presumably, Paul chose this obscure verse because it has the verb for "faith" (or "belief") linked with speaking.

spoke"—we also believe, and so we speak, [14]because we know that the one who raised the Lord Jesus will raise us also with Jesus, and will bring us with you into his presence. [15]Yes, everything is for your sake, so that grace, as it extends to more and more people, may increase thanksgiving, to the glory of God.

Living by Faith

[16]So we do not lose heart. Even though our outer nature is wasting away, our inner nature is being renewed day by day. [17]For this slight momentary affliction is preparing us for an eternal weight of glory beyond all measure, [18]because we look not at what can be seen but at what cannot be seen; for what can be seen is temporary, but what cannot be seen is eternal.

5 For we know that if the earthly tent we live in is destroyed, we have a building from God, a house not made with hands, eternal in the heavens. [2]For in this tent we groan, longing to be clothed with our heavenly dwelling— [3]if indeed, when we have taken it off[j] we will not be found naked. [4]For while we are still in this tent, we groan under our burden, because we wish not to be unclothed but to be further clothed, so that what is mortal may be swallowed up by life. [5]He who has prepared us for this very thing is God, who has given us the Spirit as a guarantee.

[6]So we are always confident; even though we know that while we are at home in the body we are away from the Lord— [7]for we walk by faith, not by sight. [8]Yes, we do have confidence, and we would rather be away from the body and at home with the Lord. [9]So whether we are at home or away, we make it our aim to please him. [10]For all of us must appear before the judgment seat of Christ, so that each may receive recompense for what has been done in the body, whether good or evil.

The Ministry of Reconciliation

[11]Therefore, knowing the fear of the Lord, we try to persuade others; but we ourselves are well known to God, and I hope that we are also well known to your consciences. [12]We are not commending ourselves to you again, but giving you an opportunity to boast about us, so that you may be able to answer those who boast in outward appearance and not in the heart. [13]For if we are beside ourselves, it is for God; if we are in our right mind, it is for you. [14]For the love of Christ urges us on, because we are convinced that one has died for all; therefore all have died. [15]And he died for all, so that those who live might live no longer for themselves, but for him who died and was raised for them.

[16]From now on, therefore, we regard no one from a human point of view;[k] even though we once knew Christ from a human point of view,[k] we know him no longer in that way. [17]So if anyone is in Christ,

---

j Other ancient authorities read *put it on*

k Gk *according to the flesh*

4:14 Paul characteristically considers resurrection with Jesus an exclusively future hope (*1 Thess.* 4:15–18; *1 Cor.* 15:35–51; *Rom.* 6:4–6). Contrast *Eph.* 2:6. **4:16–5:1** Paul begins to develop for the first time a classically Greek notion of immortality, namely, that the material body decays but the eternal spirit within remains intact. This view stands in some logical tension with his own notion of bodily resurrection, which depends on the idea that the dead sleep in the earth until the resurrection, such that if there were no resurrection, there would be no hope for them (*1 Thess.* 4:13, 18; *1 Cor.* 15:30–34). But the idea of the soul's immortality allows the one who dies to be in heaven immediately, present with Christ, at the moment of death (5:6–9; see *Phil.* 1:23–24). **5:2–4** Paul's talk of a new dwelling for the spirit, so that it will not remain naked after release from the body at death, seems to move toward the notion of an intermediate state: the spirit is immediately transported to its heavenly reward at death, where it awaits the resurrection of the body. Only the new, spiritual body will provide a suitable home for it. This scenario, which combines the Jewish idea of bodily resurrection with the Greek notion of the immortality of the spirit, became part of the mainstream Christian heritage. **5:5** *the Spirit as a guarantee* See also 1:22. Paul considers the Holy Spirit's presence obvious because it is manifested through various clear activities (*1 Cor.* 12:4–11). Thus, he can say that the Spirit's presence is a guarantee of things to come. **5:6–9** See note to 4:16–5:1. **5:10–11** Paul also mentions Christ's tribunal, the *bēma* that provincial governors sat upon when they judged cases, in *1 Cor.* 3:13 and *Rom.* 14:10. **5:12–13** These sentences, which close the discussion of commendation begun in 3:1, appear to presuppose the readers' knowledge of *2 Corinthians* 10–13. See 11:23, where Paul admits to speaking like a madman (5:13: *beside ourselves*), and note to 3:1 on self-commendation. **5:14–17** Paul here reinforces his view of the radically new character of Christian faith. In context, this is aimed particularly at his Jewish Christian opponents who seek some kind of continuity with Judaism. **5:14–15** Throughout his letters Paul conceives of Jesus' death not so much as a substitute for the death of others but as a means of enabling all to die (to the law and to the old world) in mystical union with Christ (see *Gal.* 2:20; 6:14; *Rom.* 6:3–6; 7:4). **5:16** Paul's exact meaning when he speaks of formerly knowing Christ *from a human point of view* (lit. "according to the flesh") is much debated. If he is referring to his preconversion days, then this human-style knowledge of Christ is what led him to act against the church (*Gal.* 1:13). Perhaps Paul is obliquely accusing his Jewish Christian opponents of remaining too much in Judaism in their approach to Christ; see note to 4:3–4. **5:17** One of Paul's clearest statements about the absolute change that Christ's death and resurrection effect in believers, whether Jewish or Gentile. He uses the same language in debate with Jewish Christian teachers in *Gal.* 6:15.

there is a new creation: everything old has passed away; see, everything has become new! 18All this is from God, who reconciled us to himself through Christ, and has given us the ministry of reconciliation; 19that is, in Christ God was reconciling the world to himself,*l* not counting their trespasses against them, and entrusting the message of reconciliation to us. 20So we are ambassadors for Christ, since God is making his appeal through us; we entreat you on behalf of Christ, be reconciled to God. 21For our sake he made him to be sin who knew no sin, so that in him we might become the righteousness of God.

6As we work together with him,*m* we urge you also not to accept the grace of God in vain. 2For he says,

"At an acceptable time I have listened to you,
and on a day of salvation I have helped you."

See, now is the acceptable time; see, now is the day of salvation! 3We are putting no obstacle in anyone's way, so that no fault may be found with our ministry, 4but as servants of God we have commended ourselves in every way: through great endurance, in afflictions, hardships, calamities, 5beatings, imprisonments, riots, labors, sleepless nights, hunger; 6by purity, knowledge, patience, kindness, holiness of spirit, genuine love, 7truthful speech, and the power of God; with the weapons of righteousness for the right hand and for the left; 8in honor and dishonor, in ill repute and good repute. We are treated as impostors, and yet are true; 9as unknown, and yet are well known; as dying, and see—we are alive; as punished, and yet not killed; 10as sorrowful, yet always rejoicing; as poor, yet making many rich; as having nothing, and yet possessing everything.

11We have spoken frankly to you Corinthians; our heart is wide open to you. 12There is no restriction in our affections, but only in yours. 13In return—I speak as to children—open wide your hearts also.

The Temple of the Living God

14Do not be mismatched with unbelievers. For what partnership is there between righteousness and lawlessness? Or what fellowship is there between light and darkness? 15What agreement does Christ have with Beliar? Or what does a believer share with an unbeliever? 16What agreement has the temple of God with idols? For we*n* are the temple of the living God; as God said,
"I will live in them and walk among them,
and I will be their God,
and they shall be my people.
17   Therefore come out from them,
and be separate from them, says the Lord,
and touch nothing unclean;
then I will welcome you,
18   and I will be your father,
and you shall be my sons and daughters,
says the Lord Almighty."

7Since we have these promises, beloved, let us cleanse ourselves from every defilement of body and of spirit, making holiness perfect in the fear of God.

Paul's Joy at the Church's Repentance

2Make room in your hearts*o* for us; we have wronged no one, we have corrupted no one, we have taken advantage of no one. 3I do not say this to

---

l Or *God was in Christ reconciling the world to himself*
m Gk *As we work together*

n Other ancient authorities read *you*
o Gk lacks *in your hearts*

5:18–6:2 Paul returns to his original theme (1:3–11) but now with the word *reconciliation* instead of "consolation." The new word is a bit more ambiguous about his relationship with the Corinthians. In spite of his earlier optimistic appraisal of their renewed friendship, much healing apparently remains (see also 6:12). **5:21** *sin* Possibly a "sin offering"—a biblical category (*Lev.* 5:14–6:7) in spite of what Paul has just said about the novelty of everything in Christ. **6:2** *Isa.* 49:8. **6:4–7** This repeated self-commendation (see 3:1) recalls Paul's list of hardships in 11:23–27, affording further evidence that *2 Corinthians* 10–13 belonged to an earlier letter. **6:8–10** See 4:8–10. **6:8** *we are treated as impostors* Paul's apostleship was rejected by his opponents (see *1 Cor.* 9:2–3; *2 Cor.* 11:5–12:11; *Gal.* 1:1). **6:12–13** Although Paul speaks optimistically of his healed relationship with the Corinthians (7:6, 11, 13–16), things remain less than perfectly settled. **6:14–7:1** Because *2 Corinthians* appears to be composed of at least two fragments from different letters (*2 Corinthians* 10–13 and 1–9) and since this passage interrupts Paul's appeal for acceptance (see 7:2: "Make room in your hearts for us"), many scholars suppose that 6:14–7:1 represents a fragment of a lost letter. Perhaps it comes from Paul's first letter to Corinth, recalled in *1 Cor.* 5:9, since that letter had to do with separation from sexual immorality. Here Paul could be speaking against remaining in marriages where one partner has converted and the other has not (but see *1 Cor.* 7:12–16), entering into marriage with an unbeliever, or engaging in illicit sexual unions with non-Christians. **6:15** *Beliar* One of the many names current in first-century Judaism for the devil or Satan. **6:16** *we are the temple of the living God* See *1 Cor.* 3:16; 6:19. **6:16–18** Paul does not quote the scripture here but roughly paraphrases several passages and cobbles them together as if they were one: *Lev.* 26:12, under the influence of *Jer.* 32:38 and/or *Ezek.* 37:37; *Isa.* 52:11, perhaps under the influence of *Ezek.* 20:41; *2 Sam.* 7:8, 14. **7:2** Paul resumes the theme of 6:13—his appeal for acceptance. His claim not to have wronged or corrupted anyone fits with his protest about rival Christian teachers in 11:20, which may have been written earlier.

condemn you, for I said before that you are in our hearts, to die together and to live together. 4I often boast about you; I have great pride in you; I am filled with consolation; I am overjoyed in all our affliction.

5For even when we came into Macedonia, our bodies had no rest, but we were afflicted in every way—disputes without and fears within. 6But God, who consoles the downcast, consoled us by the arrival of Titus, 7and not only by his coming, but also by the consolation with which he was consoled about you, as he told us of your longing, your mourning, your zeal for me, so that I rejoiced still more. 8For even if I made you sorry with my letter, I do not regret it (though I did regret it, for I see that I grieved you with that letter, though only briefly). 9Now I rejoice, not because you were grieved, but because your grief led to repentance; for you felt a godly grief, so that you were not harmed in any way by us. 10For godly grief produces a repentance that leads to salvation and brings no regret, but worldly grief produces death. 11For see what earnestness this godly grief has produced in you, what eagerness to clear yourselves, what indignation, what alarm, what longing, what zeal, what punishment! At every point you have proved yourselves guiltless in the matter. 12So although I wrote to you, it was not on account of the one who did the wrong, nor on account of the one who was wronged, but in order that your zeal for us might be made known to you before God. 13In this we find comfort.

In addition to our own consolation, we rejoiced still more at the joy of Titus, because his mind has been set at rest by all of you. 14For if I have been somewhat boastful about you to him, I was not disgraced; but just as everything we said to you was true, so our boasting to Titus has proved true as well. 15And his heart goes out all the more to you, as he remembers the obedience of all of you, and how you welcomed him with fear and trembling. 16I rejoice, because I have complete confidence in you.

Encouragement to Be Generous

8 We want you to know, brothers and sisters,[p] about the grace of God that has been granted to the churches of Macedonia; 2for during a severe ordeal of affliction, their abundant joy and their extreme poverty have overflowed in a wealth of generosity on their part. 3For, as I can testify, they voluntarily gave according to their means, and even beyond their means, 4begging us earnestly for the privilege[q] of sharing in this ministry to the saints— 5and this, not merely as we expected; they gave themselves first to the Lord and, by the will of God, to us, 6so that we might urge Titus that, as he had already made a beginning, so he should also complete this generous undertaking[r] among you. 7Now as you excel in everything—in faith, in speech, in knowledge, in utmost eagerness, and in our love for you[s]—so we want you to excel also in this generous undertaking.[r]

8I do not say this as a command, but I am testing the genuineness of your love against the earnestness of others. 9For you know the generous act[t] of our

p Gk *brothers*
q Gk *grace*
r Gk *this grace*
s Other ancient authorities read *your love for us*
t Gk *the grace*

7:4 Paul returns to the theme of 1:3–7—consolation in the midst of affliction. **7:5–7** Paul resumes the story that he suspended in 2:13: Paul could not rest his mind in Troas because he was waiting for word from Titus, who had taken his letter to Corinth; failing to meet him in Troas, Paul proceeded to Macedonia. There, at last, Titus returned from Corinth with a favorable report. These sentences show that Paul's consolation, emphasized in 1:3–7, resulted from Titus's positive report. **7:7** ***your longing, your mourning, your zeal for me*** In light of 5:20; 6:12, this appears to be an exaggeration. **7:12** ***the one who did the wrong*** See 2:5–11. Evidently, some individual confronted Paul on his second visit to Corinth. ***the one who was wronged*** That is, Paul (2:5). **7:16** Since Paul is able to express such confidence even in the most desperate circumstances (see *Gal.* 5:10) and since he expresses considerable reserve in 5:20; 6:12, it appears that his confidence is somewhat overstated here for rhetorical effect. **8:1–9:15** If *2 Corinthians* 8 and 9 are of one piece with *2 Corinthians* 1–7, they represent the main appeal of the letter (*2 Corinthians* 1–9). Therefore, one of Paul's major concerns in temporarily losing the Corinthians' allegiance was the resulting deficiency of his collection for Jerusalem (see *1 Cor.* 16:3; *2 Cor.* 1:16). The collection of this offering seems to have been laid upon him as a condition of the apostles' recognition of his mission; see *1 Cor.* 16:1–4; *Rom.* 15:25–32; and note to *Gal.* 2:10. As soon as he is sufficiently persuaded of the Corinthians' support, he once again presses the issue of the collection and offers seven reasons why they should give generously. In view of Paul's obviously strenuous efforts here to raise money, it is striking that in *Rom.* 15:27 he tells the Roman Christians how pleased the Achaians were to participate in the collection. **8:1–8** Paul's first argument is based on the example of the believers in the province of Macedonia (including Thessalonica and Philippi), to the north. Although hard pressed, they have given generously. The Corinthians seem to Paul relatively well off. **8:6** ***Titus*** Paul's trusted associate in current dealings with the Corinthians; he has delivered Paul's harsh letter and reported back (see 2:14–17; 7:5–7). See note to 1:19. ***already made a beginning*** That is, before the rift between Paul and the Corinthians one year earlier (8:10), during which the offering was put on hold. **8:7** ***in faith, in speech, in knowledge*** Curiously, the qualities that Paul seems to admire here (and in *1 Cor.* 1:5) are precisely what he criticizes in the Corinthians elsewhere (*1 Cor.* 1:17–20, 26–31; 2:1–4; *2 Cor.* 10:10). **8:9** Paul's second argument for giving is that they should imitate the example of Christ, who gave everything. See also *Phil.* 2:5–11. This could mean (a) that

Lord Jesus Christ, that though he was rich, yet for your sakes he became poor, so that by his poverty you might become rich. [10]And in this matter I am giving my advice: it is appropriate for you who began last year not only to do something but even to desire to do something— [11]now finish doing it, so that your eagerness may be matched by completing it according to your means. [12]For if the eagerness is there, the gift is acceptable according to what one has—not according to what one does not have. [13]I do not mean that there should be relief for others and pressure on you, but it is a question of a fair balance between [14]your present abundance and their need, so that their abundance may be for your need, in order that there may be a fair balance. [15]As it is written,

"The one who had much did not have too much, and the one who had little did not have too little."

Commendation of Titus

[16]But thanks be to God who put in the heart of Titus the same eagerness for you that I myself have. [17]For he not only accepted our appeal, but since he is more eager than ever, he is going to you of his own accord. [18]With him we are sending the brother who is famous among all the churches for his proclaiming the good news;[u] [19]and not only that, but he has also been appointed by the churches to travel with us while we are administering this generous undertaking[v] for the glory of the Lord himself[w] and to show our goodwill. [20]We intend that no one should blame us about this generous gift that we are administering, [21]for we intend to do what is right not only in the Lord's sight but also in the sight of others. [22]And with them we are sending our brother whom

we have often tested and found eager in many matters, but who is now more eager than ever because of his great confidence in you. [23]As for Titus, he is my partner and co-worker in your service; as for our brothers, they are messengers[x] of the churches, the glory of Christ. [24]Therefore openly before the churches, show them the proof of your love and of our reason for boasting about you.

The Collection for Christians at Jerusalem

9 Now it is not necessary for me to write you about the ministry to the saints, [2]for I know your eagerness, which is the subject of my boasting about you to the people of Macedonia, saying that Achaia has been ready since last year; and your zeal has stirred up most of them. [3]But I am sending the brothers in order that our boasting about you may not prove to have been empty in this case, so that you may be ready, as I said you would be; [4]otherwise, if some Macedonians come with me and find that you are not ready, we would be humiliated—to say nothing of you—in this undertaking.[y] [5]So I thought it necessary to urge the brothers to go on ahead to you, and arrange in advance for this bountiful gift that you have promised, so that it may be ready as a voluntary gift and not as an extortion.

[6]The point is this: the one who sows sparingly will also reap sparingly, and the one who sows bountifully will also reap bountifully. [7]Each of you must give as you have made up your mind, not reluctantly or under compulsion, for God loves a cheerful giver. [8]And God is able to provide you with every blessing in abundance, so that by always having enough of everything, you may share abundantly in every good work. [9]As it is written,

---

u Or *the gospel*
v Gk *this grace*
w Other ancient authorities lack *himself*

x Gk *apostles*
y Other ancient authorities add *of boasting*

Christ was a preexistent heavenly being who came to earth, or (b) that Paul knows Jesus to have been a man of some means who abandoned it all for his teaching ministry (*Luke*, which describes Jesus' poor family, was not yet written), or (c) simply that Jesus voluntarily gave up his life. **8:10–11** Paul's third argument is that they should finish what they started before they and Paul had the disagreement. **8:12–15** Paul's fourth argument is that he is not requesting an unreasonably large gift but simply a balancing out of resources among the Christians of the eastern Mediterranean. Evidently, the Christians of Jerusalem, for whom the gift is intended, are much poorer than the Corinthians; see also 9:12. He implies something similar in *Rom.* 15:26–27. It does not seem that the offering is intended to meet a specific crisis in Judea, since in that case the lengthy delay would make it pointless. **8:15** *Exod.* 16:18, which describes the abundance of food provided to the Israelites in the desert by the manna and the quail. **8:16–24** Paul's fifth argument, to which he devotes the greatest space, is that the money *will* reach its intended destination. It will be taken by Titus, Paul's associate, and two unnamed representatives of the other participating churches (in Macedonia? See 8:1; 9:2; *Rom.* 15:26). *2 Cor.* 12:16–18 confirms that the Corinthians did not trust Paul with their money. **9:1–5** Paul's sixth argument is that he has already boasted about the Corinthians' willingness to give and has even used this to spur the Macedonians to give (but see 8:1–7, where he does the reverse!). So the Corinthians must now give, if he and they are not to be embarrassed when the Macedonian representatives arrive with him to pick up their contribution. He is willing to send the couriers in advance so that when he arrives with the Macedonians it will all seem spontaneous. **9:6–15** Paul's final argument is that God rewards generous giving. This is the same point he made in response to the Philippians' gift to support him while he was in chains (*Phil.* 4:18–19). **9:9** *Ps.* 112:9 (LXX 111:9).

"He scatters abroad, he gives to the poor;
　　his righteousness[z] endures forever."
[10]He who supplies seed to the sower and bread for food will supply and multiply your seed for sowing and increase the harvest of your righteousness.[z] [11]You will be enriched in every way for your great generosity, which will produce thanksgiving to God through us; [12]for the rendering of this ministry not only supplies the needs of the saints but also overflows with many thanksgivings to God. [13]Through the testing of this ministry you glorify God by your obedience to the confession of the gospel of Christ and by the generosity of your sharing with them and with all others, [14]while they long for you and pray for you because of the surpassing grace of God that he has given you. [15]Thanks be to God for his indescribable gift!

Paul Defends His Ministry

10 I myself, Paul, appeal to you by the meekness and gentleness of Christ—I who am humble when face to face with you, but bold toward you when I am away!— [2]I ask that when I am present I need not show boldness by daring to oppose those who think we are acting according to human standards.[a] [3]Indeed, we live as human beings,[b] but we do not wage war according to human standards;[a] [4]for the weapons of our warfare are not merely human,[c] but they have divine power to destroy strongholds. We destroy arguments [5]and every proud obstacle raised up against the knowledge of God, and we take every thought captive to obey Christ. [6]We are ready to punish every disobedience when your obedience is complete.

[7]Look at what is before your eyes. If you are confident that you belong to Christ, remind yourself of this, that just as you belong to Christ, so also do we. [8]Now, even if I boast a little too much of our authority, which the Lord gave for building you up and not for tearing you down, I will not be ashamed of it. [9]I do not want to seem as though I am trying to frighten you with my letters. [10]For they say, "His letters are weighty and strong, but his bodily presence is weak, and his speech contemptible." [11]Let such people understand that what we say by letter when absent, we will also do when present.

[12]We do not dare to classify or compare ourselves with some of those who commend themselves. But when they measure themselves by one another, and compare themselves with one another, they do not show good sense. [13]We, however, will not boast beyond limits, but will keep within the field that God has assigned to us, to reach out even as far as you. [14]For we were not overstepping our limits when we reached you; we were the first to come all the way to you with the good news[d] of Christ. [15]We do not boast beyond limits, that is, in the labors of others; but our hope is that, as your faith increases, our sphere of action among you may be greatly enlarged, [16]so that we may proclaim the good news[d] in lands beyond you, without boasting of work already done in someone else's sphere of action. [17]"Let the one who boasts, boast in the Lord." [18]For it is not those who commend themselves that are approved, but those whom the Lord commends.

---

z Or *benevolence*
a Gk *according to the flesh*
b Gk *in the flesh*
c Gk *fleshly*

d Or *the gospel*

10:1–13:14 The final four chapters of *2 Corinthians* almost certainly represent a different letter from *2 Corinthians* 1–9; see introduction to *2 Corinthians*. **10:1** Paul refers to the Corinthians' view of him—a powerful letter writer but somewhat unimposing in person (see 10:10). **10:2** *when I am present* Paul contemplates another visit, his third (12:14; 13:1). This is the planned "painful visit" that was abandoned, according to 2:1, because Paul wished to spare the Corinthians. Since he has tried hard to mend his relationship with them in *2 Corinthians* 1–9, it is peculiar that he should now be planning another painful visit, unless this part of *2 Corinthians* either represents part of the harsh letter or was written somewhat later than *2 Corinthians* 1–9. *according to human standards* Lit. "according to the flesh." Perhaps Paul's opponents charge that his abandonment of circumcision and other biblical requirements merely capitulates to human weakness (see *Gal.* 1:10). **10:4** *We destroy arguments* Thus far, Paul's opponents sound rather like those denounced in *1 Corinthians* 1–4, who seem to have valued wisdom, knowledge, and rhetoric (*1 Cor.* 1:18–20). **10:7** The Gk puts all of this in the third person: "If anyone is confident . . ." Thus, Paul's opponents also express allegiance to Christ. **10:8** *building you up* Nouns and verbs of "building up" are particularly prominent in *1* and *2 Corinthians* (*1 Cor.* 3:9; 8:1, 10; 10:23; 14:3–5, 12, 17, 26; *2 Cor.* 5:1; 10:8; 12:9; 13:10)—letters written to a city that was still in the midst of massive rebuilding after its new foundation in 44 B.C.E. **10:9–10** These words presuppose that Paul has written often, even though we have only two authentic Pauline letters addressed to this community; see note to *1 Cor.* 5:9; see also the apocryphal *Epistles of Paul and Seneca* (5th century C.E.) and the *Epistle to the Laodiceans* (2d to 4th centuries C.E.). **10:10** See 10:1. **10:13–18** Paul is sensitive to the issue of territory, as *1 Cor.* 3:5–4:21 has made clear. In a society defined by networks of patron-client relationships, he believes that he has a special authority over his own churches and rejects the claims of all interlopers, no matter what their teachings, because they are building on his foundation (see *Gal.* 1:6–9; *Rom.* 15:20). **10:16** Perhaps an abbreviation of *Jer.* 9:24 (LXX; MT 9:22–23).

Paul and the False Apostles

11 I wish you would bear with me in a little foolishness. Do bear with me! ²I feel a divine jealousy for you, for I promised you in marriage to one husband, to present you as a chaste virgin to Christ. ³But I am afraid that as the serpent deceived Eve by its cunning, your thoughts will be led astray from a sincere and pure*e* devotion to Christ. ⁴For if someone comes and proclaims another Jesus than the one we proclaimed, or if you receive a different spirit from the one you received, or a different gospel from the one you accepted, you submit to it readily enough. ⁵I think that I am not in the least inferior to these super-apostles. ⁶I may be untrained in speech, but not in knowledge; certainly in every way and in all things we have made this evident to you.

⁷Did I commit a sin by humbling myself so that you might be exalted, because I proclaimed God's good news*f* to you free of charge? ⁸I robbed other churches by accepting support from them in order to serve you. ⁹And when I was with you and was in need, I did not burden anyone, for my needs were supplied by the friends*g* who came from Macedonia. So I refrained and will continue to refrain from burdening you in any way. ¹⁰As the truth of Christ is in me, this boast of mine will not be silenced in the regions of Achaia. ¹¹And why? Because I do not love you? God knows I do!

¹²And what I do I will also continue to do, in order to deny an opportunity to those who want an opportunity to be recognized as our equals in what they boast about. ¹³For such boasters are false apostles, deceitful workers, disguising themselves as apostles of Christ. ¹⁴And no wonder! Even Satan disguises himself as an angel of light. ¹⁵So it is not strange if his ministers also disguise themselves as ministers of righteousness. Their end will match their deeds.

Paul's Sufferings as an Apostle

¹⁶I repeat, let no one think that I am a fool; but if you do, then accept me as a fool, so that I too may boast a little. ¹⁷What I am saying in regard to this boastful confidence, I am saying not with the Lord's authority, but as a fool; ¹⁸since many boast according to human standards,*h* I will also boast. ¹⁹For you gladly put up with fools, being wise yourselves! ²⁰For you put up with it when someone makes slaves of you, or preys upon you, or takes advantage of you, or puts on airs, or gives you a slap in the face. ²¹To my shame, I must say, we were too weak for that!

But whatever anyone dares to boast of—I am speaking as a fool—I also dare to boast of that. ²²Are

---

e Other ancient authorities lack *and pure*
f Gk *the gospel of God*
g Gk *brothers*

h Gk *according to the flesh*

11:3 See *Gen.* 3:1–7. **11:4** *another Jesus . . . a different spirit . . . a different gospel* This language resembles that used by Paul of his Jewish Christian opponents in *Gal.* 1:6–9. **11:5–12:13** Paul carefully compares himself and the Christian teachers who have attracted the Corinthians. **11:5** *these super-apostles* The Gk uses two distinct words: "superlative apostles." It is curious that Paul describes them as apostles at all, for although he uses this word more freely than does the author of *Acts*—to include himself and Barnabas (*1 Cor.* 9:1–6)—he still regards himself as the last to join the group (*1 Cor.* 15:8–9). The group is still small, comprising the Jerusalem authorities (*Gal.* 1:17) and himself "as one untimely born" (*1 Cor.* 15:8). The title "false apostles" (11:13) is indeed puzzling. (He can use "apostle" in the banal sense of "messenger," as in 8:23, but he does not claim this sense of the word for himself nor would it explain his critique of his opponents.) Perhaps they included some of the Jerusalem apostles, or perhaps Paul is making fun of their letters of recommendation from Jerusalem (10:12; 3:1–2). **11:7–12** The first of Paul's three main arguments for his integrity is that he has taken no money from the Corinthians. See also *1 Cor.* 9:1–18, where he defends his apostleship in the same way (also *1 Thess.* 2:3–12). But in *1 Cor.* 9:5, 12 Paul names the other Christian teachers who do take money and are accompanied by wives: "the other apostles" and Jesus' brothers and Cephas (apparently Peter). Note the appearance of Cephas in *1 Cor.* 1:12; 3:22. The claim that accepting money created questions about the validity of one's teaching and that refusing money proved authenticity was an old saw by Paul's time. See Socrates in Plato, *Apology* 4.20, 18.31: "My accusers . . . have not had the shamelessness to say that I have either exacted or demanded payment." **11:8–9** Revealingly, Paul acknowledges that he did not request money from the Corinthians because he was being supported from Macedonia; see also *Phil.* 4:15, and contrast *1 Thess.* 2:9. **11:10** *in the regions of Achaia* In *1 Cor.* 9:15–18, however, Paul implied that his principle of not accepting funds was absolute. **11:11** *Because I do not love you?* It is not clear why the Corinthians should have criticized Paul for not accepting their money. Perhaps they did not, and he puts the matter like this in order to expose the injustice of their accusations. It may also be, however, that the Corinthians were suspicious of someone who came with independent financing. **11:13–15** Paul characteristically pronounces doom on even his Christian opponents; see also *Phil.* 1:28; 3:19; *Gal.* 1:8–9. **11:22–33** Paul now moves to his second appeal for acceptance: a point-for-point comparison with the "superlative apostles," the upshot of which is that he has worked harder and suffered more than any of them. This recalls his claim in *1 Cor.* 15:10 that he worked harder than the other apostles—though in that case he names them. **11:22** That Paul's opponents here make an issue of their Judaism suggests that they might have the same kind of outlook as his opponents in Galatia. This characteristic also fits with their connections to the Jerusalem apostles.

they Hebrews? So am I. Are they Israelites? So am I. Are they descendants of Abraham? So am I. 23Are they ministers of Christ? I am talking like a madman—I am a better one: with far greater labors, far more imprisonments, with countless floggings, and often near death. 24Five times I have received from the Jews the forty lashes minus one. 25Three times I was beaten with rods. Once I received a stoning. Three times I was shipwrecked; for a night and a day I was adrift at sea; 26on frequent journeys, in danger from rivers, danger from bandits, danger from my own people, danger from Gentiles, danger in the city, danger in the wilderness, danger at sea, danger from false brothers and sisters;i 27in toil and hardship, through many a sleepless night, hungry and thirsty, often without food, cold and naked. 28And, besides other things, I am under daily pressure because of my anxiety for all the churches. 29Who is weak, and I am not weak? Who is made to stumble, and I am not indignant?

30If I must boast, I will boast of the things that show my weakness. 31The God and Father of the Lord Jesus (blessed be he forever!) knows that I do not lie. 32In Damascus, the governorj under King Aretas guarded the city of Damascus in order tok seize me, 33but I was let down in a basket through a window in the wall,l and escaped from his hands.

Paul's Visions and Revelations

12It is necessary to boast; nothing is to be gained by it, but I will go on to visions and revelations of the Lord. 2I know a person in Christ who fourteen years ago was caught up to the third heaven—whether in the body or out of the body I do not know; God knows. 3And I know that such a person—whether in the body or out of the body I do not know; God knows— 4was caught up into Paradise and heard things that are not to be told, that no mortal is permitted to repeat. 5On behalf of such a one I will boast, but on my own behalf I will not boast, except of my weaknesses. 6But if I wish to boast, I will not be a fool, for I will be speaking the truth. But I refrain from it, so that no one may think better of me than what is seen in me or heard from me, 7even considering the exceptional character of the revelations. Therefore, to keepm me from being too elated, a thorn was given me in the flesh, a messenger of Satan to torment me, to keep me from being too elated.n 8Three times I appealed to the Lord about this, that it would leave me, 9but he said to me, "My grace is sufficient for you, for powero is made perfect in weakness." So, I will boast all the more gladly of my weaknesses, so that the power of Christ may dwell in me. 10Therefore I am content with weaknesses, insults, hardships, persecutions, and calamities for the sake of Christ; for whenever I am weak, then I am strong.

Paul's Concern for the Corinthian Church

11I have been a fool! You forced me to it. Indeed you should have been the ones commending me, for I am not at all inferior to these super-apostles, even though I am nothing. 12The signs of a true apostle

---

i Gk brothers
j Gk ethnarch
k Other ancient authorities read and wanted to
l Gk through the wall

m Other ancient authorities read To keep
n Other ancient authorities lack to keep me from being too elated
o Other ancient authorities read my power

11:24 *the forty lashes minus one* Deut. 25:2–3 prescribes *up to* forty lashes, not more, as the standard flogging. In its characteristic determination to err on the side of mercy and to avoid violating the commandment, later Jewish tradition specified thirty-nine lashes (*m. Makk.* 3:10). The Mishnah provides long lists of offenses meriting the thirty-nine lashes (*m. Makk.* 3:1–9). Perhaps Paul received them before he was driven out from Judea (see *1 Thess.* 2:14–15), perhaps during his journeys throughout the eastern Mediterranean. Perhaps the punishment stemmed from charges that he had misrepresented the Jewish people before the world or even advised Jews not to continue circumcision (*Acts* 21:21, 28; *1 Cor.* 7:18–19). **11:26** *false brothers and sisters* Paul reveals again how marginalized he was; even within the Christian world he had many enemies (see *Phil.* 1:15–17). **11:27** See also *1 Cor.* 4:10–13. **11:28** *my anxiety for all the churches* Paul typically speaks of *all* the churches as within his purview (*1 Cor.* 4:17; 11:16; 16:19; *2 Cor.* 8:18–19, 23; *Rom.* 16:1, 4, 16). But since many other Christian leaders and groups were not part of Paul's mission, it could be that the term "church" (Gk *ekklēsia*) was peculiar to him. **11:32–33** In Paul's time the Nabatean King Aretas IV controlled Damascus. *Acts* 9:23–25 also records the story of Paul's escape, but *Acts* typically asserts that it was the Jews of Damascus, not the governor, who sought to seize Paul. **12:1–10** Paul's final appeal for acceptance rests on mysterious revelations. The problem for interpreters is that although he wishes to use these encounters with Christ as grounds for boasting (12:1) and although he has had to suffer to keep from being too elated by these experiences (12:7), he describes the events in the third person, as if they occurred to someone else (see esp. 12:5). It is difficult to avoid the conclusion that he is speaking of himself. **12:2** *the third heaven* In ancient cosmologies the earth was seen as more or less flat, with ascending levels of heaven above. Paul apparently shares this view; see *1 Thess.* 4:13–18. **12:7** *a messenger of Satan to torment me* Early Judaism and Christianity commonly held that most evil and suffering in the world were caused by the devil and his minions; see 1QS 3.22; *1 Thess.* 2:18. The nature of Paul's affliction(s) has been much debated; *Gal.* 4:13–15 might suggest that he had serious eye problems. **12:11–15** Paul summarizes his case for acceptance, focusing on the claim that he has taken no money from the Corinthians.

were performed among you with utmost patience, signs and wonders and mighty works. 13How have you been worse off than the other churches, except that I myself did not burden you? Forgive me this wrong!

14Here I am, ready to come to you this third time. And I will not be a burden, because I do not want what is yours but you; for children ought not to lay up for their parents, but parents for their children. 15I will most gladly spend and be spent for you. If I love you more, am I to be loved less? 16Let it be assumed that I did not burden you. Nevertheless (you say) since I was crafty, I took you in by deceit. 17Did I take advantage of you through any of those whom I sent to you? 18I urged Titus to go, and sent the brother with him. Titus did not take advantage of you, did he? Did we not conduct ourselves with the same spirit? Did we not take the same steps?

19Have you been thinking all along that we have been defending ourselves before you? We are speaking in Christ before God. Everything we do, beloved, is for the sake of building you up. 20For I fear that when I come, I may find you not as I wish, and that you may find me not as you wish; I fear that there may perhaps be quarreling, jealousy, anger, selfishness, slander, gossip, conceit, and disorder. 21I fear that when I come again, my God may humble me before you, and that I may have to mourn over many who previously sinned and have not repented of the impurity, sexual immorality, and licentiousness that they have practiced.

Further Warning

13 This is the third time I am coming to you. "Any charge must be sustained by the evidence of two or three witnesses." 2I warned those who sinned previously and all the others, and I warn them now while absent, as I did when present on my second

visit, that if I come again, I will not be lenient— 3since you desire proof that Christ is speaking in me. He is not weak in dealing with you, but is powerful in you. 4For he was crucified in weakness, but lives by the power of God. For we are weak in him,p but in dealing with you we will live with him by the power of God.

5Examine yourselves to see whether you are living in the faith. Test yourselves. Do you not realize that Jesus Christ is in you?—unless, indeed, you fail to meet the test! 6I hope you will find out that we have not failed. 7But we pray to God that you may not do anything wrong—not that we may appear to have met the test, but that you may do what is right, though we may seem to have failed. 8For we cannot do anything against the truth, but only for the truth. 9For we rejoice when we are weak and you are strong. This is what we pray for, that you may become perfect. 10So I write these things while I am away from you, so that when I come, I may not have to be severe in using the authority that the Lord has given me for building up and not for tearing down.

Final Greetings and Benediction

11Finally, brothers and sisters,q farewell.r Put things in order, listen to my appeal,s agree with one another, live in peace; and the God of love and peace will be with you. 12Greet one another with a holy kiss. All the saints greet you.

13The grace of the Lord Jesus Christ, the love of God, and the communion oft the Holy Spirit be with all of you.

---

p Other ancient authorities read *with him*
q Gk *brothers*
r Or *rejoice*
s Or *encourage one another*
t Or *and the sharing in*

12:14 the third time See note to 10:2. **12:16–18** These sentences appear to refer to the collection that Paul was arranging in 8:16–23; the Corinthians perhaps feel that Paul deceived them in this enterprise. As in 8:20, he responds that his couriers were guarantors of decency. If this reading is correct, then this portion of the letter comes from a time somewhat later than *2 Corinthians* 1–9, when relations between Paul and the Corinthian Christians have again deteriorated. But since Titus also delivered the harsh letter (7:13–14), Paul may be referring here to other events. **12:19 building you up** See note to 10:8. **13:1 the third time** See note to 10:2. ***Any charge . . . witnesses*** *Deut.* 19:15. **13:2 my second visit** Evidently the painful visit anticipated in *1 Cor.* 4:21 and recalled in *2 Cor.* 2:1. **13:10 for building up** See note to 10:8. **13:12 a holy kiss** See *1 Cor.* 16:20. **13:13** Although this seems to modern ears a reference to the Trinity, it is most doubtful that Paul had a developed idea of the three divine persons in one essence—an idea that would be worked only much later and with great difficulty in the church councils of the third and fourth centuries.

To the Assemblies of Galatia

GALATIANS

Value for the Study of Early Christianity

Paul's letter to the Christian groups of Galatia is fascinating for many reasons. First, it is his most passionate writing. He was on the brink of losing many of his converts to other Christian leaders. More than in any other letter except perhaps *2 Corinthians* 10–13, therefore, we see him pleading, angry, and sarcastic—as a believable human being. Second, the issue at stake was the relationship between Christ and Judaism, for other Christian teachers were insisting that his Gentile converts be circumcised and embrace the Torah. In his response to their claims, Paul lays out fundamental arguments for the radical separation of Christianity from Judaism. The question of Jewish-Christian relations would come to dominate the entire period of Christian origins, and *Galatians* became central to that debate. Third, Paul's arguments include several appeals to scripture, which provide us with excellent examples of his interpretative and rhetorical art. Fourth, because *Galatians* offers a sustained argument on a single issue, it provides the material for a uniquely comprehensive picture of one group of Paul's opponents. On the basis of *Galatians* we can speak with some confidence about judaizing Christians in the first generation. Finally, it is in the course of his argument with judaizing Christians that Paul incidentally lays out a valuable (though still partial) chronological framework for his own career.

Date

Where to place *Galatians* among Paul's letters may seem like a trivial issue, but it is all tied up with larger questions: about the possibility of harmonizing Paul's letters with *Acts,* and about possible developments in Paul's thinking. Based on indicators within *Galatians* itself, many scholars prefer to place it fairly late in his career. For example, in his earliest letters *(1 Thessalonians* and *1 Corinthians)* Christian Judaism is not yet an evident concern, and in *Philippians* and *2 Corinthians* it appears as more of a potential threat than a consuming interest. But in *Galatians* we suddenly discover a whole region of Paul's churches turning to Judaism (1:6; 3:1; 4:10–11, 16, 21; 5:2–3, 7). So this letter seems to reflect the climax of a problem that has been developing for some time.

Paul's autobiographical statement in *Gal.* 1:15–2:10 appears to confirm the letter's relatively late date. He states there that he visited Jerusalem three years after his conversion and then again fourteen years "after that."[1] That would put his second visit seventeen years after his conversion. Since his second visit to Jerusalem was also somewhat in the past when he wrote *Galatians,* we need to allow for a minimum of at least eighteen years between Paul's conversion and his writing of *Galatians.* But Paul's active career probably came to a close between 56 and 58 C.E.[2] and his conversion could not have occurred much before 35 C.E.—since Jesus seems to have died only in 30 C.E., and we must allow some time for the early church to have begun and to have attracted Paul's attention as persecutor. This leaves little more than twenty years for Paul's entire Christian career. If he wrote *Galatians* at least eighteen years into that career, then this letter is among the latest of his writings.

The relative date of the letter is also connected with the identity of the Galatians in question. Galatia means "region of the Gauls." In 279 B.C.E. the Gauls (from what is now France) invaded and settled what is now north-central Turkey. When the Romans extended their influence eastward in 64 B.C.E., this kingdom of Galatia became one of their clients, what we might call a puppet regime. In 24 B.C.E., the Romans formally annexed Galatia to their empire as a province, but when they did so they included in the new province several southern, non-Galatian towns, including Iconium, Lystra, and Derbe. So by Paul's time, "Galatia" could signify either the traditional north-central region of the ethnic Gauls or the Roman province of Galatia with its added southern cities.

Why is this geographical information important for dating *Galatians?* Some scholars reconcile Paul's letters with the portrayal of his career in *Acts* (see the introduction to THE LETTERS OF PAUL) by proposing that the Galatia of *Galatians* was actually the southern region of the Roman province—including Iconium, Lystra, and Derbe. *Acts* places these cities on the itinerary of Paul's first "missionary journey" (*Acts* 13–14). Locating the readers of *Galatians* in these cities, then, puts the founding of the Galatian churches relatively early in Paul's career (in the scheme of *Acts*), well before his mission to Thessalonica and Corinth. An early founding visit allows more time for the judaizing problem to emerge, which means that Paul could write *Galatians* even before he wrote *1 Corinthians.* Many scholars who take this view also identify the second Jerusalem visit that Paul mentions in *Gal.* 2:1–10 with the "apostolic council" of *Acts* 15, and this permits them to date *Galatians* within a year, say, of that council. Since *Acts* has Paul beginning his Greek mission only after

---

[1]The phrase "after fourteen years" (2:1) could conceivably still be counting from Paul's conversion, but that is usually argued only to make an early date for *Galatians* more plausible. It is more natural to take it with "then," as indicating fourteen years from the first Jerusalem visit.

[2]That is, if *Acts* remembers correctly that Paul was imprisoned two years before the end of Felix's tenure in Palestine (*Acts* 23:33; 24:27), which is dated to 59 C.E. Not only is it antecedently probable that *Acts* has better information about the final phases of Paul's life than it does about his early preaching, but Paul's own letters tend to confirm the *Acts* account of the trouble and imprisonment in Judea (see *Rom.* 15:25, 30–33).

the council (*Acts* 16–17), the effect of this South Galatian hypothesis is to place *Galatians* before his letters to Corinth and Philippi. Not only does this scheme hope to create harmony between *Acts* and Paul's letters; it also precludes the notion of significant development in Paul's thinking, because the allegedly early *Galatians* has close parallels to *Romans,* which is plainly among Paul's latest letters.

The chief difficulties with the South Galatian hypothesis and the correspondingly early date for *Galatians* are as follows: (a) Identifying the second Jerusalem visit of *Galatians* 2 with the council of *Acts* 15 squeezes an improbable amount of Paul's missionary and literary activity (represented by *Acts* 16–21) into the last three years or so of his career.[3] (b) These two events, an emphatically private visit according to Paul and a public council according to *Acts* 15, should not be identified in any case. (c) Paul implies that his first visit to Galatia was *not* part of a scheduled missionary tour but was necessitated only by a "physical infirmity" (*Gal.* 4:13–15). (d) *Acts* itself reserves the term "Galatia" for the older north-central region of Turkey, excluding the southern part of the province (*Acts* 16:1–6; 18:23). (e) Paul's mocking address to his readers—"You foolish Galatians!" (3:1)—is best explained as a reference to ethnic Gauls rather than merely technical residents of the province Galatia. In the light of these objections and the internal evidence discussed above, we have followed those scholars who place *Galatians* late in Paul's career.

Setting

Whatever success commentators have had in reconstructing the setting of *Galatians* comes from the extensive material for "mirror reading" that the letter seems to provide. "Mirror reading" is the technique of using Paul's words to re-create the otherwise lost positions of the other participants. For example, when Paul abruptly asks, "Am I now seeking the favor of men, or of God? Or am I trying to please men?" (1:10), we might suppose that someone has accused him of pleasing men. Using this technique, we can establish the following points with some confidence: (a) Paul's opponents were Christians (see 1:6–7) who may have had an impressive status in Christian circles themselves (1:8; 5:10). They claimed the support of, or a connection with, the Jerusalem apostles (1:18; 2:6–10). (b) They called for the Galatian Christians, who were Gentiles (4:8–10), to become Jews by being circumcised and accepting the covenant of Moses (6:12–13; see 3:1–5, 10, 28; 4:21; 5:2–6). (c) They challenged the legitimacy of Paul's apostleship (1:1) and accused him of pleasing men rather than God (1:10).

One should use the technique of mirror reading with discrimination, however, and avoid the assumption that every statement of Paul's directly counters some alternate position. Although he asks, for example, "But if I, brethren, still preach circumcision, why am I still persecuted?" (5:11), it is hard to see how anyone could have accused him of still advocating circumcision! And when he denies that his

---

[3] See the autobiographical statement discussed above.

apostleship comes from men (1:2, 11–12), especially from the Jerusalem apostles (1:15–2:2), he cannot be saying this because his opponents have accused him of depending too heavily on the apostles; on the contrary, they have claimed that he is *out of step* with the Jerusalem authorities. Their accusation, apparently, is that he has taken the apostles' gospel and perverted it, in order to make it more palatable to Gentiles (= "please men") by removing its Jewish content. Paul's response, then, is that he could not have perverted the apostolic teaching because he did not get his gospel from the apostles. He received it directly from Christ, who called him to preach to the Gentiles (1:15–17). So Paul is not responding, as a mechanical mirror reading might suggest, to the charge that his gospel is human rather than divine in origin. He is defending his obvious divergence from the gospel of Jerusalem.

Themes and Overview

In short, then, we discover in *Galatians* a group of people claiming allegiance to Jesus who understand this trust in a rather different way from Paul. They see Paul telling Gentiles about Jesus as the dying, rising, and soon-returning savior who needs to be trusted for salvation, but they find this "announcement" (*euangelion*, "gospel") inadequate. From Jesus' original students ("disciples"), evidently, they have believed that one can live as Jesus' authentic student only if one is a Jew as he was, observing the divine commandments in the Bible. It is a matter of scholarly debate today whether or to what degree Jews in antiquity encouraged conversion to Judaism. If there were significant Jewish movements encouraging such conversion, that would help to explain the ease with which Paul's opponents seem to have expected it, and the apparently enthusiastic response of many Gentiles in Galatia.

Those Jewish or judaizing Christians apparently understood Jesus to be in direct continuity with Abraham, Moses, and the prophets. Perhaps they thought that, just as God often clarified his will in the past, from creation to his choosing of Abraham to the law of Moses to the prophetic interpretation of the law, so now he has sent Jesus as the final interpreter of the law. Paul takes a different view. He holds that Jesus' death and resurrection constituted a decisive moment in history. These events force one to reflect: if Jesus needed to die and rise to save the world, then the entire world needed saving; this means that everything that came before Jesus was insufficient and, in the light of Jesus' coming, is now irrelevant. This includes observance of the Torah (*Gal.* 2:21; 3:21). The only thing that matters now is trust in Jesus, which effects an entirely "new creation" (*Gal.* 6:15).

It is perhaps an index of Paul's opponents' arguments that he responds on two major issues: his own authority, in chapters 1 and 2, and the claims of scripture, in chapters 3 and 4. Chapters 5 and 6 comprise mainly ethical exhortations following from the other arguments, such as the appeal to freedom in 5:2–26: be free from slavery to the law, while at the same time exhibiting the "fruit of the Spirit," which far surpass the requirements of the law. Paul's biographical argument (chs. 1–2) is essentially that he could not have corrupted the apostles' teaching because he did not get his gospel from them, but directly from Christ. He is independent of the

Jerusalem church and, in any case, they acknowledged his gospel when he finally did have time to visit them (1:11–2:10). The chief characteristic of Paul's argument from scripture is rhetorical wordplay. Against the charges that he has neglected to tell his converts about the promises to Abraham, the circumcision requirement, the law of Moses, and the claims of scripture in general, Paul first adduces a set of passages (from all over the Bible) that superficially link "righteousness" with "trust" rather than "works of the law." In this way Paul tries to argue from the Bible itself that one need not observe the Bible's commands, and that those who trust in Jesus are righteous according to the Bible. He then drives a wedge between Abraham, whom he links directly with Christ, and Moses, whose law was a late and temporary departure from the main drift of the divine plan.

Relation to Other Early Christian Literature

Whether Paul was ultimately successful in preventing his Galatian churches from defecting to Christian Judaism may never be known. When he writes *Galatians,* the situation is already desperate and he is anxious that his work there might have been in vain (4:11–20). His lone statement of confidence that the Galatians will see things his way (5:10) seems to be rhetorical. It is noteworthy that, although the Galatian churches were among the first to participate in Paul's major collection for Jerusalem (see *1 Cor.* 16:1), Paul will not mention them when he describes, for outside observers, the final contributors to the collection (*Rom.* 15:26). Since only his churches participated in the collection—and even they withdrew their support when they were at odds with Paul (see *2 Cor.* 8:10–11)—the absence of the Galatians from the final list of contributors may well mean that they, or a significant group of them, found Paul's opponents more persuasive and, as a result, converted to (Christian) Judaism.

For Further Reading

Barclay, John M. G., "Mirror-Reading a Polemical Letter: Galatians as a Test Case." *Journal for the Study of the New Testament* 31 (1987): 73–93.

Betz, Hans Dieter. "Galatians, Epistle to the." Pages 872–75 in vol. 2 of *Anchor Bible Dictionary.* Edited by D. N. Freedman. 6 vols. New York: Doubleday, 1992.

Jervis, L. Ann. *Galatians.* New International Biblical Commentary. Peabody, Mass.: Hendrickson, 1999.

Longenecker, Richard N. *Galatians.* Word Biblical Commentary. Dallas: Word, 1990.

Lüdemann, Gerd. *Opposition to Paul in Jewish Christianity.* Translated by M. Eugene Boring. Minneapolis: Fortress, 1989.

Martyn, J. Louis. *Galatians: A New Translation with Introduction and Commentary.* Anchor Bible 33A. New York: Doubleday, 1997.

Matera, Frank J. *Galatians.* Collegeville, Minn.: Liturgical Press, 1992.

Mitchell, Stephen. "Galatia." Pages 870–72 in vol. 2 of *Anchor Bible Dictionary.* Edited by D. N. Freedman. 6 vols. New York: Doubleday, 1992.

Osiek, Carolyn. *Galatians.* Wilmington, Del.: Michael Glazier, 1980.

THE LETTER OF PAUL
TO THE GALATIANS

Salutation

1 Paul an apostle—sent neither by human commission nor from human authorities, but through Jesus Christ and God the Father, who raised him from the dead— 2and all the members of God's family*a* who are with me,

To the churches of Galatia:

3Grace to you and peace from God our Father and the Lord Jesus Christ, 4who gave himself for our sins to set us free from the present evil age, according to the will of our God and Father, 5to whom be the glory forever and ever. Amen.

There Is No Other Gospel

6I am astonished that you are so quickly deserting the one who called you in the grace of Christ and are turning to a different gospel— 7not that there is another gospel, but there are some who are confusing you and want to pervert the gospel of Christ. 8But even if we or an angel*b* from heaven should proclaim to you a gospel contrary to what we proclaimed to you, let that one be accursed! 9As we have said before, so now I repeat, if anyone proclaims to you a gospel contrary to what you received, let that one be accursed!

10Am I now seeking human approval, or God's approval? Or am I trying to please people? If I were still pleasing people, I would not be a servant*c* of Christ.

Paul's Vindication of His Apostleship

11For I want you to know, brothers and sisters,*d* that the gospel that was proclaimed by me is not of human origin; 12for I did not receive it from a human source, nor was I taught it, but I received it through a revelation of Jesus Christ.

13You have heard, no doubt, of my earlier life in Judaism. I was violently persecuting the church of

---

a Gk all the brothers

b Or a messenger
c Gk slave
d Gk brothers

1:1 an apostle—sent neither by human commission This unusual interruption of his opening identification indicates Paul's urgency to defend his apostleship. **1:2 churches of Galatia** This is the only one of Paul's letters addressed to a whole region, including perhaps several distinct groups. For the location of Galatia, see introduction to *Galatians*. **1:3** Paul's typical greeting. **1:4** A concise summary of Paul's gospel; see *1 Thess.* 1:9–10. **1:6 I am astonished . . .** This paragraph takes the place of Paul's usual opening thanksgiving (for the virtues of the church in question), which he includes even when he plans to raise contentious issues. See *1 Thess.* 1:2–3:13; *1 Cor.* 1:4–9; *Phil.* 1:3–11; *2 Cor.* 1:3–7. His abrupt confrontation of his readers here, without the diplomatic formality of a thanksgiving, reflects the seriousness of the situation in Galatia. **1:6 a different gospel** Paul's opponents are therefore rival Christian teachers. **1:7 not that there is another gospel** Paul uses different Gk words for the English *different* and *another*. We might expand: "You are turning to an altogether different announcement, which is not merely another variation of the announcement you received." **1:8** Paul seems to refer to the impressive credentials of the other teachers: even if they were angels, they should not be trusted. See also 5:10; 6:3. This indicates that they had a significant status for Paul's audience. **1:9** Since Paul knows full well that someone is preaching an alternative gospel, the force of the statement, taken with the preceding, seems to be, "If *anyone*, no matter what his status, is preaching another gospel" (see 5:10; 6:3). The curse is repeated to stress that he means it, no matter what rank these other teachers may have. **1:10** Evidently Paul has been accused before his own converts of having perverted the original teaching of Jesus' students out of a desire to please people. His omission of biblical/Jewish covenant obligations from his gospel, especially circumcision, would naturally lead to such a charge. **1:11–12** Thus Paul cannot have corrupted the apostles' teaching, for he did not receive his announcement from them. **1:13–2:10** This entire autobiographical section, mainly meant to support Paul's claim that he did not receive his announcement from any other person, points out his independence from Jerusalem: he was only there twice, briefly, and long after he had begun preaching. In any case, when they finally heard his announcement (2:2), they accepted it as valid for Gentiles (2:7, 9). **1:13** The grounds for this persecution are not obvious, since, prior to Paul's mission and especially in Judea, where he conducted the persecutions, most of Jesus' followers seem to have continued observing Jewish law and tradition. Of the numerous reasons for a Jewish persecution of Christianity suggested by *Acts*—among them Jewish jealousy (*Acts* 13:45; 17:5) and a Christian threat to destroy the temple and to change the customs delivered by Moses (*Acts* 6:13–14)—the most historically plausible may simply be the Christians' aggressive devotion to someone who was recently executed for political disturbance (see *Acts* 4:17; 5:28). The Judean authorities would doubtless have been irritated by a movement that continued to jeopardize their already difficult relations with the local Romans by revering a convicted and executed criminal.

God and was trying to destroy it. [14]I advanced in Judaism beyond many among my people of the same age, for I was far more zealous for the traditions of my ancestors. [15]But when God, who had set me apart before I was born and called me through his grace, was pleased [16]to reveal his Son to me,[e] so that I might proclaim him among the Gentiles, I did not confer with any human being, [17]nor did I go up to Jerusalem to those who were already apostles before me, but I went away at once into Arabia, and afterwards I returned to Damascus.

[18]Then after three years I did go up to Jerusalem to visit Cephas and stayed with him fifteen days; [19]but I did not see any other apostle except James the Lord's brother. [20]In what I am writing to you, before God, I do not lie! [21]Then I went into the regions of Syria and Cilicia, [22]and I was still unknown by sight to the churches of Judea that are in Christ; [23]they only heard it said, "The one who formerly was persecuting us is now proclaiming the faith he once tried to destroy." [24]And they glorified God because of me.

Paul and the Other Apostles

2 Then after fourteen years I went up again to Jerusalem with Barnabas, taking Titus along with me. [2]I went up in response to a revelation. Then I laid before them (though only in a private meeting with the acknowledged leaders) the gospel that I proclaim among the Gentiles, in order to make sure that I was not running, or had not run, in vain. [3]But even Titus, who was with me, was not compelled to be circumcised, though he was a Greek. [4]But because of false believers[f] secretly brought in, who slipped in to spy on the freedom we have in Christ Jesus, so that they might enslave us— [5]we did not submit to them even for a moment, so that the truth of the gospel might always remain with you. [6]And from those who were supposed to be acknowledged leaders (what they actually were makes no difference to me; God shows no partiality)—those leaders contributed nothing to me. [7]On the contrary, when they saw that I had been entrusted with the gospel for the uncircumcised, just as Peter had been entrusted with the gospel for the circumcised [8](for he who worked through Peter making him an apostle to the circumcised also

---

e Gk *in me*

f Gk *false brothers*

1:14 *the traditions of my ancestors* Although possibly a reference to Jewish tradition in general, this phrase more probably indicates the "tradition of the fathers" that was recognized by the Pharisees as a source of authority in addition to the Bible. See note to *Mark* 7:3; Josephus, *Ant.* 13.297–298. **1:17** *Arabia* The region dominated by the Nabateans, which in Paul's day virtually surrounded Palestine, to the south, east, and northeast, from Gaza around to Damascus. But since he distinguishes Damascus from Arabia, he probably means the more restricted region south and east of Palestine, with Petra as its capital. **1:18** *after three years* Contrast *Acts* 9:19–23, according to which Paul stayed only "some days" in Damascus (with no mention of a trip to Arabia) before his first trip to Jerusalem. *Cephas* That is, most scholars think, Peter. *Cephas* is a Gk transliteration of the Aramaic name *kefa* ("rock"), which was the nickname given to Simon by Jesus (see *Matt.* 16:17–18). The Gk translation of the same word (in masculine form) is *Petros*, or Peter. *James the Lord's brother* Although not himself an apostle in any early account that has survived, this brother of Jesus quickly assumed a dominant position in the early church; see *Acts* 12:17; 15:13; 21:18. The circumstances under which he did so are a matter of speculation. **1:22** Contrast *Acts* 9:26–30, according to which Paul's first visit to Jerusalem included both his introduction to the apostles as a group (not Cephas and James alone) and his *public* preaching. **2:1** *after fourteen years* Probably, fourteen years after Paul's first Jerusalem visit, therefore seventeen years after his conversion, although some have argued that the fourteen years is still counting from his conversion. *Barnabas* Aramaic name, meaning perhaps "son of [the god] Nebo" or "son of consolation." *Acts* describes him as Jewish, a leading figure in early Christian circles, and Paul's senior during Paul's early career (*Acts* 4:36; 9:27; 11:22, 30). *Titus* A close associate of Paul's, particularly prominent in one of Paul's later letters, *2 Corinthians*. Strangely, he does not appear in *Acts*. **2:2** *in response to a revelation* Contrast *Acts* 11:27–30, which claims that Paul's second trip to Jerusalem occurred early in his career, when he was delegated by the church of Antioch, along with Barnabas, to convey famine relief to Jerusalem. Curiously, *Acts* 15 connects Paul's *third* visit to Jerusalem with an apostolic council on the question of the Gentile mission. Even there, however, the details are different. **2:4** *false believers* Paul's sentence is ruptured here. He does not tell us what happened *because of false believers*. Perhaps he started to say that Titus was circumcised only because of the false brothers, but then decided, rather, to insist that if Titus was circumcised, it was not because of such pressure. Most scholars think, however, that Titus was not circumcised. **2:6** *those who were supposed to be acknowledged leaders* Paul develops here the contrast, famous in Greek thinking since Plato at least, between appearance and reality, between seeming and really being. See Plato, *Apology* 22 (33), 32 (41). Perhaps Paul is linking the Jerusalem leaders to the teachers in Galatia with whom he disagrees. **2:7** *uncircumcised . . . circumcised* Paul's Gk uses the jarring terms "the foreskin" (for the Gentiles, uncircumcised) and "the circumcision" (for the Jews, circumcised). Since circumcision was a common object of ridicule in Paul's world, his use of this term for Jews seems calculated to invite derision. His use of "the foreskin" for Gentiles seems intended to evoke a similar response. Because the categories Jew and Gentile no longer mean anything to Paul (see 3:28; 5:6), he can make fun of both genital conditions as inconsequential manifestations of the merely material world.

worked through me in sending me to the Gentiles), [9]and when James and Cephas and John, who were acknowledged pillars, recognized the grace that had been given to me, they gave to Barnabas and me the right hand of fellowship, agreeing that we should go to the Gentiles and they to the circumcised. [10]They asked only one thing, that we remember the poor, which was actually what I was[g] eager to do.

Paul Rebukes Peter at Antioch

[11]But when Cephas came to Antioch, I opposed him to his face, because he stood self-condemned; [12]for until certain people came from James, he used to eat with the Gentiles. But after they came, he drew back and kept himself separate for fear of the circumcision faction. [13]And the other Jews joined him in this hypocrisy, so that even Barnabas was led astray by their hypocrisy. [14]But when I saw that they were not acting consistently with the truth of the gospel, I said to Cephas before them all, "If you, though a Jew, live like a Gentile and not like a Jew, how can you compel the Gentiles to live like Jews?"[h]

Jews and Gentiles Are Saved by Faith

[15]We ourselves are Jews by birth and not Gentile sinners; [16]yet we know that a person is justified[i] not by the works of the law but through faith in Jesus Christ.[j] And we have come to believe in Christ Jesus,

---

g Or *had been*

h Some interpreters hold that the quotation extends into the following paragraph

i Or *reckoned as righteous;* and so elsewhere

j Or *the faith of Jesus Christ*

2:9 *James* Not the apostle, son of Zebedee, but Jesus' brother (see 1:19). *John* Presumably the student ("disciple") of Jesus and apostle of that name, son of Zebedee (*Mark* 1:19). Paul refutes the charge that he has corrupted the apostolic announcement. He argues (a) that he did not get his gospel from the Jerusalem apostles (1:17, 19) and (b) that when he finally met them, they consented to his non-Jewish, Gentile mission. **2:10** Probably not a general request to remember the plight of the poor, since the Gk tense suggests a particular activity of some kind that Paul was "eager to begin doing." Elsewhere in Paul's letters we see him deeply involved in gathering a collection for the Jerusalem church (*1 Cor.* 16:1–4; *2 Corinthians* 8–9; *Rom.* 15:25–32), which he once describes as for "the poor among the saints at Jerusalem" (*Rom.* 15:26); these may be the poor in question. It is not clear whether this offering for Jerusalem was a condition of the apostles' recognition of Paul's mission or merely a request. *Gal.* 2:10 could be interpreted either way, but the energy that Paul devotes to the offering and his fears that it might not be acceptable (*Rom.* 15:31) may suggest that the collection was a condition. It is also worth noting that although Paul seems to have in mind the real poor of Jerusalem, the term "poor" became a title for some groups within Jewish Christianity, such as the Ebionites (see *Matt.* 5:3; Eusebius, *Eccl. hist.* 3.27). **2:11** *when Cephas came to Antioch* Nothing is known of this incident beyond what Paul relates here. **2:12** *people came from James* Evidently, these people are *the circumcision faction*—those who advocate that Gentiles become Jews in order to follow Jesus. Here and elsewhere (*Acts* 21:18–26) Jesus' brother appears as one committed to Torah observance. James carries remarkable weight in Judean Christianity although he was not one of the original students of Jesus; both Peter and Barnabas are strongly influenced by him. One wonders whether and how these people from James are related to the false believers of 2:4 or even Paul's rival teachers in Galatia. *to eat with Gentiles* Although eating with Gentiles was not per se forbidden to Jews, they were only permitted to eat certain foods (see *Deut.* 14:3– 21), and even these had to be prepared in a certain way. Perhaps the assumption here is that eating with Gentiles entailed eating nonkosher food. *the circumcision faction* That is, the Torah-observant group from Jesus' brother. Given the standard Greco-Roman ridicule of circumcision, Paul's description of this group as "the circumcision" (as the Gk says) seems calculated to invite the derision of his Gentile readers. **2:13** *the other Jews* Paul does not include himself among "the Jews." **2:14** *you compel the Gentiles* The *you* is singular, indicating that, in Paul's view at least, Peter also supports the effort to have Gentile Christians convert to Judaism or *live like Jews.* Some scholars have suggested that Paul's confrontation of Peter must have occurred before the agreement described above (2:7–10), for surely after the agreement Peter would acknowledge Paul's mission and cease to require Gentile circumcision. But the agreement did not set a new course; it recognized what was already in place. Perhaps, then, Peter's recognition of Paul's law-free Gentile mission was not as forthright as Paul remembers it, and Peter really continued to view it as an aberration. It is common that when two opposing parties negotiate an agreement, they subsequently differ about what they agreed upon. We have only Paul's account. *to live like Jews* Since circumcision and Torah observance are involved, we should perhaps allow the Gk verb a stronger sense: "to become Jews." If Peter and Jesus' brother James required Gentiles to become Jewish proselytes when they became Christians, we have here clear evidence that Paul's opponents were not mistaken in thinking that they had formidable support for their Torah-observant Christianity. **2:15** *We ourselves are Jews* The Gk manuscripts have no quotation marks. Although the NRSV ends Paul's discussion with Peter at the preceding verse with closing quotation marks, supposing that 2:15–21 is addressed to the Galatian readers, it is equally plausible that these sentences continue the discussion with Peter, especially since Paul begins by identifying with someone else as a Jew by birth. In either case, 2:15–21 elaborates upon Paul's confrontation of Peter. **2:15–16** The opening premise is that both Peter and Paul are Jews by birth and yet both have become convinced of the need to follow Christ for salvation. This is what they have in common. Paul incorporates three words in Gk from *Ps.* 143:2 (LXX 142:2), "no one will be justified," and develops for law observance a negative implication with which Peter might not have agreed.

so that we might be justified by faith in Christ,^{k} and not by doing the works of the law, because no one will be justified by the works of the law. ^{17}But if, in our effort to be justified in Christ, we ourselves have been found to be sinners, is Christ then a servant of sin? Certainly not! ^{18}But if I build up again the very things that I once tore down, then I demonstrate that I am a transgressor. ^{19}For through the law I died to the law, so that I might live to God. I have been crucified with Christ; ^{20}and it is no longer I who live, but it is Christ who lives in me. And the life I now live in the flesh I live by faith in the Son of God,^{l} who loved me and gave himself for me. ^{21}I do not nullify the grace of God; for if justification^m comes through the law, then Christ died for nothing.

Law or Faith

3 You foolish Galatians! Who has bewitched you? It was before your eyes that Jesus Christ was publicly exhibited as crucified! ^{2}The only thing I want to learn from you is this: Did you receive the Spirit by doing the works of the law or by believing what you heard? ^{3}Are you so foolish? Having started with the Spirit, are you now ending with the flesh? ^{4}Did you experience so much for nothing?—if it really was for nothing. ^{5}Well then, does God^n supply you with the Spirit and work miracles among you by your doing the works of the law, or by your believing what you heard?

^{6}Just as Abraham "believed God, and it was reckoned to him as righteousness," ^{7}so, you see, those who believe are the descendants of Abraham. ^{8}And

---

k Or *the faith of Christ*
l Or *by the faith of the Son of God*
m Or *righteousness*

n Gk *he*

2:17 If Paul is addressing Peter's situation here, then his argument runs thus: In Peter's effort to live as a Christian, he felt inclined to eat with Gentile Christians in Antioch. But now he claims that this was sin, that he became a sinner, a transgressor of the Torah. Paul responds with a reduction-to-absurdity argument, that it was Christ, then, who led Peter into sin. This would be an untenable position for Peter. **2:18** The real *transgressor,* Paul says, is someone who rebuilds what he has already demolished. Such a transgressor Paul would be if he tried to re-create a life of Jewish observance after having "smashed it to pieces," as the Gk *(katalyō)* says. Paul's point is that Peter also, by seeking salvation in Christ and by consequently eating with Gentile Christians, has destroyed his Jewish past. Trying to rebuild it now would be a transgression of God's grace in sending Christ; see 2:21. Paul's exclusionary (either Christ or Torah) argument might not have conformed with other positions among early Christians. **2:19** Paul restates his own position regarding the law: he has died to it. A better punctuation would be the following: "For through the law, I died to the law so that I might live to God." That is, it was the demand of, in a sense, "life toward God" that brought Paul to abandon the Torah (see 3:21). It was not that the law itself had proven unsatisfactory (see 3:21; *Phil.* 3:5–10). **2:20** *no longer I who live* Such mystical statements—envisioning absorption of the self into a larger spiritual entity—are typical of Paul's later letters (e.g., *2 Cor.* 4:10–5:17; *Gal.* 6:14–17; *Rom.* 6:4–6). **2:21** Paul reasons from Christ's death, which he views as necessary for salvation, to the inadequacy of the Torah: if Christ had to die in order save humanity, then nothing before Christ (including the law) is critical any longer. Paul did not always feel some weakness in the law, but now that Christ has come, it has lost its significance (see *Phil.* 3:5–10). **3:1–5** Paul switches from an autobiographical argument for the legitimacy of his gospel to an argument from the Galatians' own experience: what they had was already complete and fulfilling before the rival teachers introduced their claims. **3:1** *foolish Galatians* This phrase suggests ethnic Gauls from the northern part of the province rather than "technical" Galatians, from the south. *bewitched you* The rival Christian teaching has proven extraordinarily attractive. **3:3** Paul sets up a contrast, between Christ, faith/trust, and Spirit, on the one hand, and law, works, and flesh, on the other. This is typical of his response to Christian Jews (see *Phil.* 3:2–21), and it connects with the Greek distinction, common since Plato, between the transient, material world and the real, spiritual world. For Paul, trust in Christ removes all concern about the physical, material world and therefore about physical acts such as Torah observance and circumcision. Many Jews, however, would not accept the faith-law dichotomy, since a person expresses trust in God through obedience to God's teaching. Among the Christian writings, see *Jas.* 2:18–20. **3:6** *Abraham* Paul turns now to his rivals' territory—argument from scripture. Whereas his opponents pointed out the demands of scripture, he must try to argue from scripture that salvation through Christ is the only thing that matters. Thus, whereas his opponents might well have noted that Abraham left his native traditions to become God's servant, obeying God's commands and accepting the requirement of circumcision (*Genesis* 17), Paul must show that Abraham serves mainly as a model of Christ. *believed God* Gen. 15:6. MT: "And because he put his trust in the LORD, He reckoned it to his merit." That is, Abraham accepted God's promise of numerous descendants when he and Sarah were beyond reproductive age, and he was accordingly reckoned "righteous" (where "righteousness" means obedience to God's commands). The LXX agrees, and Paul follows the wording of the LXX. *those who believe* In Gk, "believe" and "faith" are the verb and noun of the same word root (*pist-*); we might say "put [or 'have'] faith" instead of "believe." *descendants of Abraham* Paul's interpretation is that since Abraham is said to have been counted righteous because of his faithfulness/trust even without observing the Torah of Moses (for it had not yet been given), so also Christians are counted righteous and are his true descendants because of their faith/trust (in Christ). **3:8** A hodgepodge of *Gen.* 12:3; 18:18; 22:18. The idea in these passages of *Genesis* is that all nations (the Gentiles) will ultimately be blessed through Abraham's descendants (Israel), who will serve as a priestly people (*Exod.* 19:4–6) and therefore as a light to the other na-the scripture, foreseeing that God would justify the Gentiles by faith, declared the gospel beforehand to Abraham, saying, "All the Gentiles shall be blessed in you." [9]For this reason, those who believe are blessed with Abraham who believed.

[10]For all who rely on the works of the law are under a curse; for it is written, "Cursed is everyone who does not observe and obey all the things written in the book of the law." [11]Now it is evident that no one is justified before God by the law; for "The one who is righteous will live by faith."*o* [12]But the law does not rest on faith; on the contrary, "Whoever does the works of the law*p* will live by them." [13]Christ redeemed us from the curse of the law by becoming a curse for us—for it is written, "Cursed is everyone who hangs on a tree"— [14]in order that in Christ Jesus the blessing of Abraham might come to the Gentiles, so that we might receive the promise of the Spirit through faith.

The Promise to Abraham

[15]Brothers and sisters,*q* I give an example from daily life: once a person's will*r* has been ratified, no one adds to it or annuls it. [16]Now the promises were made to Abraham and to his offspring;*s* it does not say, "And to offsprings,"*t* as of many; but it says, "And to your offspring,"*s* that is, to one person, who is

---

o Or *The one who is righteous through faith will live*
p Gk *does them*

q Gk *Brothers*
r Or *covenant* (as in verse 17)
s Gk *seed*
t Gk *seeds*

---

tions. Paul's interpretation is that the Gentiles can achieve salvation by putting faith in Christ, following Abraham's example of faith (in God) without Torah observance, which came many centuries after Abraham. **3:10** *Deut.* 27:26. MT: "Cursed be he who will not uphold the terms of this Teaching and observe them." LXX: "Cursed is every human being who does not observe and obey all the words of this law." Whereas this sentence curses anyone who does not obey the law in question, Paul draws the lesson that anyone who *observes* the law is cursed. He stresses the phrase "all the words" and adapts the sentence to speak of the book of the law in general: since everyone will violate some provision of the Torah, anyone who tries to follow it is cursed. The Torah itself, however, envisions the prospect of failure, and so has a mechanism for repentance; the law claims that it is not too difficult to be observed (*Deut.* 30:11–20). Further, in the original context, the words "this law" refer to the preceding twelve curses on people who perform malicious acts such as leading the blind astray or taking bribes in order to condemn the innocent. It is those who commit such despicable crimes who are particularly cursed, not those who err or sin with respect to the law in general. **3:11** *Hab.* 2:4. MT: "But the righteous man is rewarded with life for his fidelity." More literally: "The righteous one through faith[fulness] will live." The original sense of the MT was that although wickedness (failure to observe Torah) prevails (1:4), the Lord promises that judgment will soon fall on the unrighteous, but "he who is righteous [i.e., obedient to God's Torah] will live [or 'survive']" on account of his faithfulness to God's laws. LXX: "The one who is righteous by my faith[fulness] will live." The LXX agrees with the MT but has the righteous person finding life through *God's* faithfulness. Paul, however, removes the verse entirely from the context of Torah observance and reads "He who is righteous through faith [in Christ, and therefore not through the law] will live [i.e., find spiritual life]." **3:12** *Lev.* 18:5. MT: "You shall keep My laws and My rules, by pursuit of which man shall live." LXX: "So you shall keep all my prescriptions and all my rules, and you shall do them; a person who does these things will live by them." Thus the Bible declares that faithfulness to the Torah is the way to life. Paul quotes only the last part—"does these things will live by them." Paul seems to be making a verbal play on the word "live": this statement about living by the commandments does not mention faith, so (assuming his earlier dichotomy between faith and works) according to the Bible itself Torah observance contradicts the principle just adduced from *Hab.* 2:4 (*Gal.* 3:11), that a person will find life only by faith/trust (in Christ). **3:13** *Deut.* 21:23. MT: "For an impaled [or 'hanged'] body is an affront to [or 'cursed by'] God." LXX: "For cursed by God is everyone who hangs on a tree." This sentence concludes a discussion of Israelite civil and criminal law. In Israelite law, hanging or impaling is not a technique of capital punishment, which is usually by stoning; it is, rather, intended for the exposure of a particularly heinous criminal's body (see *Josh.* 10:26). Because such a body is an affront to God, it must be buried by sundown to ensure that the land remains unpolluted. In Paul's hands, this verse serves to complete the chiastic pattern (A, B, B, A) begun in the three preceding quotations: cursed, live, live, cursed. To emphasize this chiasm, Paul changes the original participle, "cursed," to an adjective meaning the same, to match the adjective in 3:10 (this is not apparent in English translation). Having argued already that those who observe the Torah are cursed, Paul now asserts that Christ's death (hanging on a tree, so to speak) made him "cursed" and thereby removed the "curse of the law"—perhaps the curse that allegedly follows those who fail to live up to every detail (3:10). Paul omits the biblical phrase "by God" after "cursed." To understand Paul's argument here, it may be helpful to read it first without the scripture citations, as a series of assertions. The scriptural proofs are brought in because they contain the appropriate words ("righteous," "faith," "cursed," "live"), not because of their original sense in context. **3:15** *will* Paul uses a Gk word *(diathēkē)* that means both "a will" and "a covenant" or "a pact." He wants to distinguish between a variety of covenants in salvation history, especially between Abraham's and Moses', and so, employing the same word, uses the example of a human will. **3:16** *offspring* Paul refers to God's promise to Abraham in *Gen.* 22:18, which has perhaps been cited by his opponents. MT: "all the nations of the earth shall bless themselves by your descendants, because you have obeyed my command." LXX: "and in your offspring [lit. 'seed'] all the nations of the earth will be blessed." Although the word "seed" is singular, it is collective in sense, for God has

Christ. 17My point is this: the law, which came four hundred thirty years later, does not annul a covenant previously ratified by God, so as to nullify the promise. 18For if the inheritance comes from the law, it no longer comes from the promise; but God granted it to Abraham through the promise.

The Purpose of the Law

19Why then the law? It was added because of transgressions, until the offspring*u* would come to whom the promise had been made; and it was ordained through angels by a mediator. 20Now a mediator involves more than one party; but God is one.

21Is the law then opposed to the promises of God? Certainly not! For if a law had been given that could make alive, then righteousness would indeed come through the law. 22But the scripture has imprisoned all things under the power of sin, so that what was promised through faith in Jesus Christ*v* might be given to those who believe.

23Now before faith came, we were imprisoned and guarded under the law until faith would be revealed. 24Therefore the law was our disciplinarian until Christ came, so that we might be justified by faith. 25But now that faith has come, we are no longer subject to a disciplinarian, 26for in Christ Jesus you are all children of God through faith. 27As many of you as were baptized into Christ have clothed yourselves with Christ. 28There is no longer Jew or Greek, there is no longer slave or free, there is no longer male and female; for all of you are one in Christ Jesus. 29And if you belong to Christ, then you are Abraham's offspring,*u* heirs according to the promise.

4 My point is this: heirs, as long as they are minors, are no better than slaves, though they are the owners of all the property; 2but they remain under guardians and trustees until the date set by the father. 3So with us; while we were minors, we were enslaved to the elemental spirits*w* of the world. 4But when the fullness of time had come, God sent his Son, born of a woman, born under the law, 5in order to redeem

---

u Gk seed
v Or *through the faith of Jesus Christ*

w Or *the rudiments*

---

just promised Abraham that his offspring will be "as the stars of heaven and as the sand which is on the seashore" (*Gen.* 22:17). The word refers to Abraham's descendants, the nation of Israel. In 3:29 and *Rom.* 4:16–18, Paul will concede this point. But here he continues his wordplay with the claim that because the word "seed" is singular, it refers to a single person, Christ. Therefore, God's promises are to Abraham and Christ, bypassing Moses. **3:17 *covenant*** See note to 3:15. ***nullify the promise*** This verse refers back to the point begun in 3:15. Just as in a human will, Paul claims, subsequent additions do not cancel out the original terms, so in salvation history the later covenant brought by Moses (Torah) does not displace the original covenant (through faith alone, he alleges) made with Abraham. In Jewish writings of the period, by contrast, Moses' Torah appears as only the definitive statement of the covenant process begun with Noah (*Genesis* 9) and Abraham (*Genesis* 15–21). **3:18** Referring back to 3:16 and *Gen.* 22:18. **3:19** In Paul's day there was much speculation about angels, and many Jews had come to believe that angels were in attendance at the giving of the Torah on Sinai (see *Jub.* 1.29–2.1; *Acts* 7:53; *Heb.* 2:2). **3:20** Paul seems to be continuing his wordplay: The law came through a mediator. But the word *mediator* is associated with *more than one.* Yet *God is one.* Therefore, God should not be associated with the law! **3:21** Along with 2:21, a key to Paul's real criticism of the Torah: Christ provides the solution to a problem that the law did not address (death); in the light of his coming, the law is ineffectual. **3:24 *disciplinarian*** The Gk *paidagōgos* was much more than a disciplinarian; he was also the child's tutor, play supervisor (baby-sitter), and protector (from sexual abuse and vice in general). Paul seems more concerned here with the finite duration of this person's role than with the character of his duties. He claims that the Torah was such a temporary custodian, to keep things in check until Abraham's "seed" (Christ) should arrive, just as the *paidagōgos* should take care of the child only until the latter's maturity. Occasionally, custodians tried to continue their role past the appropriate time and drew the anger of their former charges; see Martial, *Epigrams* 11.39. **3:29** Paul's argument from 3:6 to this point suggests that his opponents had called for his converts to become children of Abraham by conversion to Judaism. **4:2** Rhetorical exaggeration, as far as we can tell from surviving texts. Heirs were usually much more highly valued than slaves; some were spoiled. Paul's main point, however, is that both slaves and child heirs live under careful supervision, without personal freedom. **4:3 *we were enslaved*** Paul switches metaphors here: not only are children like slaves; he and his readers really were slaves. This model prepares for the dominant images of adoption and freedom, rather than that of a child reaching maturity, that follow. ***elemental spirits*** Paul evidently includes his own Jewish upbringing, when he observed the law, under "slavery to elemental spirits." As in 3:19–20, therefore, he dissociates the law from God and attributes it, rather, to underlings, heavenly beings who kept things in order until God was ready to fulfill the promise to Abraham. See 4:9; *Col.* 2:8. Paul shared the view of many of his contemporaries, Jewish and Gentile, that the world was run by spiritual powers. **4:4** Paul concedes Jesus' Jewish environment but sees it as strictly preliminary to Jesus' real work, which entirely breaks out of its original Jewish context. **4:5 *those who were under the law*** Presumably, Paul and all other Jews. Since the regime of the law (Torah) has ended even for them, it makes no sense for his readers now to convert to Christian Judaism. ***adoption as children*** Paul has abandoned the original metaphor of the child heir and opted for that of adoption. It was common in his world for childless couples, especially if the husband was a

those who were under the law, so that we might receive adoption as children. 6And because you are children, God has sent the Spirit of his Son into our[x] hearts, crying, "Abba![y] Father!" 7So you are no longer a slave but a child, and if a child then also an heir, through God.[z]

Paul Reproves the Galatians

8Formerly, when you did not know God, you were enslaved to beings that by nature are not gods. 9Now, however, that you have come to know God, or rather to be known by God, how can you turn back again to the weak and beggarly elemental spirits?[a] How can you want to be enslaved to them again? 10You are observing special days, and months, and seasons, and years. 11I am afraid that my work for you may have been wasted.

12Friends,[b] I beg you, become as I am, for I also have become as you are. You have done me no wrong. 13You know that it was because of a physical infirmity that I first announced the gospel to you; 14though my condition put you to the test, you did not scorn or despise me, but welcomed me as an angel of God, as Christ Jesus. 15What has become of the goodwill you felt? For I testify that, had it been possible, you would have torn out your eyes and given them to me. 16Have I now become your enemy by telling you the truth? 17They make much of you, but for no good purpose; they want to exclude you, so that you may make much of them. 18It is good to be made much of for a good purpose at all times, and not only when I am present with you. 19My little children, for whom I am again in the pain of childbirth until Christ is formed in you, 20I wish I were present with you now and could change my tone, for I am perplexed about you.

The Allegory of Hagar and Sarah

21Tell me, you who desire to be subject to the law, will you not listen to the law? 22For it is written that Abraham had two sons, one by a slave woman and the other by a free woman. 23One, the child of the slave, was born according to the flesh; the other, the child of the free woman, was born through the promise. 24Now this is an allegory: these women are two covenants. One woman, in fact, is Hagar, from Mount Sinai, bearing children for slavery. 25Now Hagar is Mount Sinai in Arabia[c] and corresponds to the present Jerusalem, for she is in slavery with her children. 26But the other woman corresponds to the Jerusalem above; she is free, and she is our mother. 27For it is written,

> "Rejoice, you childless one, you who bear no children,
> burst into song and shout, you who endure no birth pangs;
> for the children of the desolate woman are more numerous
> than the children of the one who is married."

28Now you,[d] my friends,[e] are children of the promise, like Isaac. 29But just as at that time the child who was born according to the flesh persecuted the child who

---

x Other ancient authorities read *your*
y Aramaic for *Father*
z Other ancient authorities read *an heir of God through Christ*
a Or *beggarly rudiments*
b Gk *Brothers*

c Other ancient authorities read *For Sinai is a mountain in Arabia*
d Other ancient authorities read *we*
e Gk *brothers*

---

prominent figure, to adopt even young adults as heirs. Paul seems to be envisioning God's adoption of adult slaves, who immediately become heirs to his covenant; see 15–17. **4:6** *children* The Gk word in 4:5–7 means "sons," not children with respect to age. **4:7** *child* See previous note. **4:8** The Galatians, then, are Gentiles; they worshiped their traditional local gods before their conversion to Pauline Christianity. But Paul has already placed Jews in much the same category (4:3). **4:9** Paul equates his readers' acceptance of Judaism now with their former past as Gentiles, such that embarking upon a Jewish life now would be tantamount to a return to their past under the elemental spirits. See 4:3, 8. **4:10** That is, the Jewish calendar, the cornerstone of Jewish life. **4:13** In view of 4:15, it has often been suggested that Paul suffered from an eye disease (see *2 Cor.* 12:7–9). **4:15** See note to 4:13. **4:17** *exclude you* Or "hinder [or 'prevent'] you. **4:19** *little children* Here, in contrast to 4:4–7, Paul uses the Gk word for "children." *pain of childbirth* Paul uses a variety of such metaphors to describe his unique relationship to his own churches, against the claims of all interlopers; see *1 Cor.* 3:5–15; 4:14–17; *2 Cor.* 11:2; *Phlm.* 10. **4:22** See *Gen.* 16:15; 21:2, 9. The story of Abraham's relationship to Sarah (his wife) and Hagar (Sarah's slave) is fundamental to the biblical story of how God chose Israel. In all likelihood, Paul's opponents raised it in their appeal to the Galatians, since Paul has already taken up the Abraham question in some detail. Although Abraham produced a son (Ishmael) with Hagar in an attempt to fulfill God's promise of descendants, God intervened so that the elderly Sarah would produce the child of promise (Isaac). Israel is descended from Isaac and his son Jacob. **4:23** *allegory* A story in which each of the elements stands for something else, beyond its obvious sense. **4:27** *Isa.* 54:1. The MT and the LXX agree; Paul agrees with the LXX exactly. **4:29** *persecuted* The Bible does not suggest that Ishmael persecuted Isaac. *Gen.* 21:9, the only verse that brings them into contact, says that they played together. Perhaps Paul has some legend in mind.

was born according to the Spirit, so it is now also. [30]But what does the scripture say? "Drive out the slave and her child; for the child of the slave will not share the inheritance with the child of the free woman." [31]So then, friends,[f] we are children, not of the slave but of the free woman. 5 [1]For freedom Christ has set us free. Stand firm, therefore, and do not submit again to a yoke of slavery.

The Nature of Christian Freedom

[2]Listen! I, Paul, am telling you that if you let yourselves be circumcised, Christ will be of no benefit to you. [3]Once again I testify to every man who lets himself be circumcised that he is obliged to obey the entire law. [4]You who want to be justified by the law have cut yourselves off from Christ; you have fallen away from grace. [5]For through the Spirit, by faith, we eagerly wait for the hope of righteousness. [6]For in Christ Jesus neither circumcision nor uncircumcision counts for anything; the only thing that counts is faith working[g] through love.

[7]You were running well; who prevented you from obeying the truth? [8]Such persuasion does not come from the one who calls you. [9]A little yeast leavens the whole batch of dough. [10]I am confident about you in the Lord that you will not think otherwise. But whoever it is that is confusing you will pay the penalty. [11]But my friends,[f] why am I still being persecuted if I am still preaching circumcision? In that case the offense of the cross has been removed. [12]I wish those who unsettle you would castrate themselves!

[13]For you were called to freedom, brothers and sisters;[f] only do not use your freedom as an opportunity for self-indulgence,[h] but through love become slaves to one another. [14]For the whole law is summed up in a single commandment, "You shall love your neighbor as yourself." [15]If, however, you bite and devour one another, take care that you are not consumed by one another.

The Works of the Flesh

[16]Live by the Spirit, I say, and do not gratify the desires of the flesh. [17]For what the flesh desires is opposed to the Spirit, and what the Spirit desires is opposed to the flesh; for these are opposed to each other, to prevent you from doing what you want. [18]But if you are led by the Spirit, you are not subject to the law. [19]Now the works of the flesh are obvious: fornication, impurity, licentiousness, [20]idolatry, sorcery, enmities, strife, jealousy, anger, quarrels, dissensions, factions, [21]envy,[i] drunkenness, carousing, and things like these. I am warning you, as I warned you before: those who do such things will not inherit the kingdom of God.

The Fruit of the Spirit

[22]By contrast, the fruit of the Spirit is love, joy, peace, patience, kindness, generosity, faithfulness, [23]gentleness, and self-control. There is no law against such things. [24]And those who belong to Christ Jesus have crucified the flesh with its passions and desires. [25]If we live by the Spirit, let us also be guided by the Spirit. [26]Let us not become conceited, competing against one another, envying one another.

---

f Gk brothers
g Or made effective
h Gk the flesh

i Other ancient authorities add murder

4:30 *Gen.* 21:10. The MT and the LXX agree: "Drive out this slave and her child; for the child of this slave will not share the inheritance with my son Isaac." This is Sarah's command to her husband Abraham after she has seen Isaac and Ishmael playing together. Paul omits all references to this situation and replaces "my son Isaac" with *child of the free* in order to make Sarah's remark into a general principle. He also neglects the following verses in *Genesis*, in which, when Abraham is reluctant to agree to Sarah's harsh demands, God assures him that Hagar's child will also father a great nation. **5:1** *slavery* That is, to the Torah. **5:2** Contrast *Gen.* 17:14: "Any uncircumcised male who is not circumcised in the flesh of his foreskin shall be cut off from his people." See 2:21. **5:6** See 3:28; 6:15. For Paul, Christ's coming renders all previous ways of life irrelevant; all that matters now is the "new creation." **5:10** Either Paul does not know who the disturber is or the disturber has some impressive credentials and needs no introduction. In view of 1:6–9 and 2:14, the latter seems more probable. **5:11** Since it is unlikely that Paul has been accused of preaching circumcision, the precise meaning of this question is unclear. Its general point seems to be that if Paul did preach circumcision, this would make his opponents happy (see 6:12–13). **5:12** In the Greco-Roman world, circumcision was much ridiculed as a barbaric practice akin to castration, and it was especially associated with the Jews. Paul tries to rekindle what should have been his Gentile readers' aversion to circumcision. He does the same in *Phil.* 3:2. **5:14** *Lev.* 19:18. See the similar saying of Jesus in *Mark* 12:31 and parallels. **5:17–19** Paul evokes a common Greek distinction between transient, decaying matter, in this case flesh, and eternal, incorruptible spirit. As in *Phil.* 3:2–20, Judaism falls decidedly on the material and transient side, whereas trust in Christ is spiritual. **5:19–23** These lists are widely paralleled in ancient philosophers' lists of virtues and vices. **5:24** See 2:20.

Bear One Another's Burdens

6 My friends,[j] if anyone is detected in a transgression, you who have received the Spirit should restore such a one in a spirit of gentleness. Take care that you yourselves are not tempted. [2]Bear one another's burdens, and in this way you will fulfill[k] the law of Christ. [3]For if those who are nothing think they are something, they deceive themselves. [4]All must test their own work; then that work, rather than their neighbor's work, will become a cause for pride. [5]For all must carry their own loads.

[6]Those who are taught the word must share in all good things with their teacher.

[7]Do not be deceived; God is not mocked, for you reap whatever you sow. [8]If you sow to your own flesh, you will reap corruption from the flesh; but if you sow to the Spirit, you will reap eternal life from the Spirit. [9]So let us not grow weary in doing what is right, for we will reap at harvest time, if we do not give up. [10]So then, whenever we have an opportunity, let us work for the good of all, and especially for those of the family of faith.

Final Admonitions and Benediction

[11]See what large letters I make when I am writing in my own hand! [12]It is those who want to make a good showing in the flesh that try to compel you to be circumcised—only that they may not be persecuted for the cross of Christ. [13]Even the circumcised do not themselves obey the law, but they want you to be circumcised so that they may boast about your flesh. [14]May I never boast of anything except the cross of our Lord Jesus Christ, by which[l] the world has been crucified to me, and I to the world. [15]For[m] neither circumcision nor uncircumcision is anything; but a new creation is everything! [16]As for those who will follow this rule—peace be upon them, and mercy, and upon the Israel of God.

[17]From now on, let no one make trouble for me; for I carry the marks of Jesus branded on my body.

[18]May the grace of our Lord Jesus Christ be with your spirit, brothers and sisters.[n] Amen.

---

j Gk *Brothers*
k Other ancient authorities read *in this way fulfill*

l Or *through whom*
m Other ancient authorities add *in Christ Jesus*
n Gk *brothers*

6:2 *law of Christ* Paul may be using the phrase *law of Christ* sarcastically, in view of the issues raised in this letter. See 5:17–19 and note. That is, follow Paul's message and abandon inclinations toward Judaism. **6:11** Perhaps a further allusion to eye disease; see 4:13, 15. But this could simply be the point at which Paul took over the letter from the secretary, or amanuensis, to whom he dictated. See *1 Cor.* 16:21; *Rom.* 16:22. **6:12** See note to 5:11. Paul's opponents could no doubt have given a more principled rationale for their actions than the one Paul attributes to them. He claims that his opponents advocate Torah-observance in order to avoid persecution. But note that the young church was persecuted (by Paul the Pharisee, *Gal.* 1:13) before his Torah-free mission began. Complete observance of the Torah might have diminished Jewish hostility (see *Acts* 21:20–26), but there were also other reasons for this hostility (see note to 1:13). **6:14** See 2:20. **6:16** Although some scholars see this as a blessing on historic Israel, in context it seems to refer to the church as the true and spiritual Israel, the true children of Abraham (3:7, 9, 14, 29; 4:28, 31). **6:17** Although these stigmata were interpreted in the Middle Ages as Christ's wounds—Christians were said to have received nail wounds in their hands and feet—Paul may be referring to the many scars that he bears as a result of his frequent imprisonments and punishments (see *2 Cor.* 11:23–29).

To the Beloved of God in Rome

ROMANS

Setting and Purpose

Although everyone now accepts the principle that Paul's writings should be read as real letters and not timeless essays, that principle has proven hardest to apply in the case of *Romans*. Unlike his other missives, this one says little if anything about specific problems among the Roman Christians, such as leadership disputes, persecution from outside, judaizing, money, or sex. In spite of our hard-won principle that we should not read the letters as essays, therefore, this letter does appear at first to be a sort of essay in theology. It develops what might at first glance seem to be a highly abstract argument that seems to lack "the other side of the conversation" that is so interesting in Paul's other letters.

As soon as we begin to examine this "essay" closely, however, that first impression dissolves. For Paul provides just enough clues to indicate that he has a specific, perhaps urgent, reason for writing. Now in Corinth (16:1, 23), having essentially completed his work in the eastern Mediterranean (15:18–19), he is about to leave for Jerusalem with the offering that he has been collecting from his Gentile converts over some years (15:23–27). Pending the success of that trip, he hopes to proceed to the western Mediterranean, and will stop briefly in Rome en route (15:28–32). Why, then, does he write to Rome, which is west of Corinth, when he is about to head east?

If we turn to the main content of the letter for hints, we may be surprised to find that, although it looks superficially like a summary essay, it does not contain a comprehensive statement of Paul's theology from first principles. As far as we can tell from his other letters, Paul's theology begins with the death and resurrection of Jesus and places great stress on Jesus' imminent return. For him, discussion of Judaism or anything else belonging to the old world is secondary (*Gal.* 3:28); he engages those issues only when other teachers have raised them with his Gentile converts. *Romans,* however, says very little about Jesus' imminent return. It is rather focused on the defense of Paul's "gospel" or "announcement" in relation to Jewish questions. This defensiveness comes through already in the opening lines, where he suspends his usual greeting with a long sentence that grounds his special an-

nouncement and apostleship in the promises to Israel (1:1–6), and then resoundingly declares that he is not ashamed of this "gospel" (1:16). The remainder of the
letter is largely a development of the question: How does Israel figure in Paul's gospel? He insists upon his respect for Jewish law and culture (2:29; 3:1–2, 8, 31; 7:12),
circumcision (2:25; 3:1–2), and the historic role of Israel (9:3–5; 11:1). But he re-
acts, albeit diplomatically, against the assumption that Jews have any advantage in
Christian faith (2:17–29; 3:27–31; 4:11; 5:18; 8:1–8; 9:8, 23–24; 10:12; 15:8–12).

These common observations on the Jewish orientation of *Romans* might
seem to suggest, as F. C. Baur and many of his contemporaries thought, that Paul's
audience in Rome was Jewish-Christian. That conclusion would fit with a variety
of other evidence that Roman Christianity began in Jewish circles, for example:
Paul's notice that he did not establish the group (15:20–22), though non-Pauline
Christianity of the first generation was mainly Jewish (see *Gal.* 2:6–9); later Christian traditions that Peter preached in Rome in the 40s (Irenaeus, *Haer.* 3.1.1), and
that Christianity began there "according to a Jewish rite" (prologue of the fourth-
century "Ambrosiaster" to *Romans*); the continuing Jewish ambience of Roman
Christianity reflected in such texts as *Hebrews* (to Rome?) and *1 Clement* (from
Rome); and a notice in Suetonius that Claudius expelled from Rome "the Jews
who persisted in rioting at the instigation of Chrestus" (*Claudius* 25.4), where
"Chrestus" is often seen as an allusion to the introduction of Christian teaching in
the synagogues.

Most scholars, though they concede that Roman Christianity began in Jewish
circles, do not think that it was still Jewish when Paul wrote this letter. They observe
that in the letter opening (1:1–16) and closing (15:15–29; also 11:13), Paul refers to
his work among the Gentiles in such a way that implies that the readers are Gentiles
too. This reading of the passages is considered so obvious that the NRSV committee,
which is generally careful to avoid strong interpretations, has taken it for granted.
For example, we read in 1:5–6 (NRSV) that Paul works "among all the Gentiles . . . ,
including yourselves who are called to belong to Jesus Christ." What the Greek actually says, however, is that the Romans are "also among" the Gentiles, with the same
preposition *(en)* that Paul has just used of himself (v. 5)—though he is not, of
course, a Gentile. Space does not permit a thorough discussion of the relevant passages here (see the notes to the text). Suffice it to say that, although the Greek text
may be otherwise read, Paul's references to his Gentile mission are most commonly
taken to indicate that his readers at Rome, or at least a majority of them, were
Gentiles.

The supposition of a Gentile audience raises numerous problems. Why would
Paul send a letter dealing with Jewish concerns to a mainly Gentile community?
How could it be meaningful to them? And why would he do so when he is about to
depart for Jerusalem? Answering these related questions has become a large part of
the "*Romans* debate" of the past quarter century.

Scholarly opinion is divided into two main camps. Some argue that Paul addresses a problem within the Christian community of Rome. Such problems might

include: conflicts between Jewish and Gentile Christians; potential (not yet begun) judaizing activities; his tarnished reputation among Gentiles who have somehow been heavily influenced by Judaism; anti-Jewish feeling among Roman Gentiles; or the lack of an apostolic foundation for this group. Others think that Paul is not worried about the internal situation in Rome, of which he would not likely have intimate knowledge (since he has not been there yet). Perhaps, they argue, he writes only to present a mature summary of his theology, even a "circular" letter that could be sent to various churches, or to rehearse the conciliatory statement about Judaism that he will soon give in Jerusalem, or merely to introduce himself in Rome before he heads for Spain. None of these suggestions has gained widespread acceptance, however, in part because none of them explains why, if *Romans* is addressed to a Gentile community, it is so different from Paul's other letters to Gentiles. Why do these particular Gentiles get the most detailed and careful justification of his gospel in relation to Judaism?

Perhaps, then, we should reconsider the possibility of a Jewish-Christian audience. If Paul is writing to Jewish Christians, many peculiarities of the letter make better sense: his generally defensive posture over against Judaism; the urgency with which he identifies himself and his gospel with the Jewish heritage (1:2–6); his repeated address of a Jewish reader and response to Jewish questions; his emphatic assurances of commitment to Israel, its culture, laws, and history; his withholding of two bywords of his Gentile mission—"church" and "gospel"—from the community at Rome; his unique assumption that his readers know and are very concerned about the Bible; his almost consistent description of the Gentiles, even "all the churches of the Gentiles" (16:4), as a third party (see note to 11:13); his failure to invite the Romans to contribute to the collection from the Gentile churches; and the unusually long list of greetings in chapter 16, in which the most prominent figures (Prisca and Aquila, Andronicus and Junia, probably Mary and Herodion, possibly others) are Jewish Christians.

Indeed, the long list of greetings itself, which stresses Paul's familial relations and past friendship with some readers, coming at the end of such a careful defense of what he preaches, suggests his purpose. About to leave for Jerusalem, where he expects— and will indeed encounter—hostility from Jews and Jewish Christians (15:31–32; see *Acts* 21:21, 28), he wishes to enlist the support of an influential Jewish-Christian group outside Judea that might vouch for him in any future difficulties. He comes close to saying this in 15:30–33, when he asks for their prayers in view of his upcoming trip. Secondarily, should the Jerusalem trip go well, he would like to rely on the cooperation of these Roman Christians in his further ventures westward (15:24).

Overview and Themes

In defense of his announcement or gospel to the Gentiles, Paul wants to establish the universality of salvation in Christ: The coming of Christ shows that all human beings have the same basic problem, and this problem has the same solution. But his argument, as we have seen, is directed specifically against the assumption that Jews have some special status in Christian faith. In dealing with this issue he is diplomatically cautious, sliding back and forth between consolidation of his positive relationship with the readers (chs. 1, 5–6, 8, 12–13, 16) and intensive argumentation over against them (chs. 2–4, 7, 9–11, 14–15). This pattern of "attack and retreat," in which Paul deals with an issue from one angle, then seems to leave it for a moment, then returns to it from a different angle, is quite typical of his approach to other issues (see *1 Thessalonians* 1–3; *1 Corinthians* 1–4, 8–10, 12–14; *2 Corinthians* 1–7). What distinguishes *Romans* is that a single issue—how Paul's "announcement" relates to Judaism—dominates the entire long letter.

Paul's diplomacy is evident from the beginning, where he acknowledges his willingness to learn from his readers (1:12). After his greeting and thanksgiving, which anticipate his main points (1:1–16, 17), he begins by trying to win over his audience. Both he and they, who live in cosmopolitan Rome, can appreciate the unspeakable wickedness and perversity of the Gentile world, which he recalls with standard images from Alexandrian synagogue preaching (1:18–32; see *Wisdom of Solomon* 12–14). But then he subtly shifts the focus. Such sin is not a Gentile problem alone, he asserts, but a human problem (2:1–11), for God shows no partiality. Having reached this point, Paul makes his claim as clear as possible: the physical and cultural distinctions between Jews and Gentiles mean nothing in the context of Christian salvation, and Jews have no advantage. The righteousness of God through trust in Christ is not dependent upon Jewish culture, though Jewish scripture attests to it (3:21–22).

Once he has made his essential point, Paul moves around the issue of Israel's status from various perspectives. First, he deals with an obvious problem: what about the promises to Abraham, on which Israel's identity is based, and which involve the requirement of circumcision (*Gen.* 17:9–14)? In a subtle reinterpretation of scripture, Paul portrays Abraham as the father of both circumcised and uncircumcised—of all those who live by trust in Christ, whether Jews or not (4:11–12)—thus reinforcing his argument for a universal human condition. He then retreats to a positive, therapeutic statement of what Christ has accomplished for all humanity (ch. 5), which Christians appropriate through baptism into new life (6:1–14).

This upbeat pause prepares for another assault: what about the "law" or *Torah* that was given to Israel, which provides the basis for Jewish life. Does his gospel say that this God-given law was inadequate or even destructive? Paul is careful to disavow such positions (7:7, 13). His diplomacy sometimes makes his precise meaning difficult to recover. Clearly, however, he holds that all Christians, even Jewish Christians, have "died" to the regime of law (7:4). He plays with the word "law" a bit, to highlight once again the universality of the human plight (7:15–25).

This word association allows him to slide back into a positive statement of Christ's significance for all, in having delivered humanity from the realm of flesh (which includes the law, 8:1–8) into the realm of spirit (8:1–39). This resoundingly confident statement, for which he expects his readers' "Amen," prepares for his final engagement of the problem: what about God's choice of Israel as his light among the nations, his special people (*Exod.* 19:4–6)? Once again, Paul's exact meaning is not always clear. But he insists that he is personally committed to Israel; God is free to make decisions that may seem arbitrary; God has now made the inscrutable decision to welcome Gentiles through the gospel of Christ; Gentile salvation is in part a stimulus to make Israel jealous and finally accept the gospel; and, mysteriously, all Israel will ultimately be saved (chs. 9–11). Paul fills this section of the letter with citations from Jewish scripture about Israel's stubbornness and God's freedom in acting. Evidently he realizes that the continuing status of Israel, in a Christianity independent of Jewish culture, is the nub of the issue for his readers.

After this sustained appeal, Paul abruptly turns to general ethical exhortations of the sort that might apply to any of his churches (chs. 12–13). Perhaps his intent here is to provide some further breathing space, as in chapters 1, 5, and 8, by punctuating his serious discussion of Israel's place in salvation with nonthreatening statements aimed at consolidating the bond with his readers. Some of these exhortations seem particularly appropriate to the readers' situation: his unparalleled emphasis on respect for government (13:1–7) might have special significance for those living in the world capital, especially if they were influenced by rebel movements stirring in Judea at the time; and his insistence that Christian "love" fulfills the commandments of the law (13:8–10) seems directed toward those who are concerned about obeying the law of Moses.

With his theoretical arguments and exhortations in hand, Paul turns to his main practical goal, which is to win support for his message and his Gentile mission (chs. 14–16). Even here, he begins slowly (again), with a general point about how those who have trusted Christ, no matter how different they may be in diet, customs, and calendar, ought to get along (14:1–15:14). This all prepares for his direct plea: if all Christians should welcome one another in principle (15:15), then it is urgent now that the Gentiles of Paul's mission be welcomed into salvation (15:17–29). If the Romans can accept this, their support will be most valuable as Paul heads for Jerusalem (15:30–33). Paul concludes with a long list of greetings, in which he appeals to a close relationship with the Christians of Rome, some of whom he has met in his travels. Clearly, he needs their help.

Literary Features

Because *Romans* has seemed so different from Paul's typical letters, some scholars have wondered whether he has adopted a different genre here, such as the "letter essay." M. Luther Stirewalt, in particular, has tried to find parallels in ancient literature of something between a letter and an essay: a virtual essay cast in letter form. Such a shift in genre would fit well with proposals that Paul is writing a generic summary of his gospel in *Romans*.

But if he is writing to a Jewish-Christian community that he has never visited, that was founded by someone else, and that knows him only by his (oft-maligned) reputation, then we can understand *Romans* as a normal letter adapted to the situation. Because Paul and his readers do not have an established relationship in terms of a shared past, previous correspondence, or visits from Timothy and Titus, he must formulate issues more explicitly, giving the appearance of an essay. Yet on this reading, *Romans* would still be an urgent and serious letter, not an abstract treatise.

Two of this letter's other distinctive traits may likewise derive from its unique situation, namely, its unusual appeal to scriptural proof texts and its use of the "diatribe" form. Though marginally longer than *1 Corinthians, Romans* has some sixty quotations of scripture (not counting the many more allusions), whereas *1 Corinthians* has only seventeen. *Galatians* and *2 Corinthians,* which both deal extensively with Jewish issues, have only ten each. The number in *Romans* is strikingly disproportionate. Notice that fifty-four of the sixty quotations are concentrated in what we have called the argumentative sections of the letter (chs. 2–4, 7, 9–11, 15), whereas hardly any (six) appear in the "consolidation" sections (chs. 1, 5–6, 8, 12–13, 16). Evidently, Paul expects his Roman readers to have an especially high regard for the authority of scripture. Compare Ignatius's later complaint about Jewish Christians who refuse to believe what cannot be demonstrated from scripture (Ignatius, *Philadelphians* 8).

"Diatribe" is common shorthand among NT scholars for a style of discourse used by first-century philosophers in their lecture halls. It involved the use of rhetorical questions and other devices to raise a position that the speaker would debate, as if in dialogue with someone. It is striking that *Romans* uses this technique so frequently in comparison with Paul's other letters (e.g., 3:1, 3, 5, 8, 9, 27, 31; 4:1). But again, in the other letters Paul has little need of it, since he can assume the readers' knowledge of issues raised by their own letters to him *(1 Thessalonians, 1 Corinthians)* or by an oral report or visit *(1 Thessalonians, Philippians, Philemon, 2 Corinthians, Galatians).* The imaginary dialogue in *Romans* provides an economical way for Paul to raise an issue sharply: "What then shall we say? That the law is sin? By no means!" (7:7).

Date

Several factors converge to give a date of between 51 and 58 C.E., with highest probability favoring 54–57. Easiest is the question of where *Romans* fits in relation to the other letters. Paul has now completed his work in the eastern Mediterranean, during which period the letters to churches in Thessalonica, Corinth, Philippi, Galatia, and to the man Philemon were written, and he is about to go to Jerusalem (15:19–29); so *Romans* appears to be the last of his undisputed letters. If he became a follower of Christ in the early to mid-30s—allowing two or three years after Jesus' death for his persecution of the first Christians (*Gal.* 1:13) and the development of a few "pre-Pauline" Christian structures—then his own account places *Romans* some time after 50. In *Gal.* 2:1 he dates his second visit to Jerusalem either fourteen or (more naturally) seventeen years after his conversion, which would place that visit between 47 and 52. Then one must allow for the subsequent Galatian controversy itself and further activity leading up to the composition of *Romans*.

Paul's anticipation of trouble in Jerusalem (*Rom.* 15:30–32) fits well with the story in *Acts* that has him accused by Jewish leaders immediately upon his arrival (*Acts* 21:21, 28), and subsequently arrested. According to *Acts,* he was imprisoned under the governor Felix and ultimately sent off to Rome by Felix's successor Porcius Festus. It seems that Felix took office in 52, and that Festus died in office in 62, but we do not know when the change of governor took place. Most commonly scholars defend the year 59, though a date before 55 also has its supporters. Further questions concern: whether the phrase "two years" in *Acts* 24:27 refers to the duration of Felix's tenure or the length of Paul's imprisonment; whether the author known as Luke has accurate knowledge of either period; and the exact bearing of the "Gallio inscription" on Paul's career. An inscription found in Corinth places the tenure of Gallio in Achaia in 51–52, and *Acts* 18:12 claims that Paul appeared before Gallio. But the author of *Acts* may have telescoped different traditions about several Corinthian visits here, and it is not certain that *Romans* was written during the same visit as the Gallio hearing.

In view of the combined evidence, a date between 54 and 57 seems the safest bet.

Relation to Other Texts and Significance

The question of *Romans'* significance for understanding Paul depends upon its relation to Paul's other writings. If *Romans* is, as some think, a mature and general statement of Paul's theology for Gentiles, then it automatically takes on special importance. For example, his harsher statements about Judaism and the law in *Philippians, Galatians,* and *2 Corinthians* might be understood as momentary flashes of anger driven by particular situations, and not the "real Paul" such as we find in *Romans.* Or, if *Romans* is a careful essay in theology, then one might incline to bend every effort to plumb the depths of its paradoxes: faith upholds the law (3:31; 7:12) but at the same time frees one from the law (7:4; 8:1–8); Jews have a great advantage (3:1) but are no better off (3:9). On the basis that truth often seems paradoxical, many scholars have written large books attempting to fathom the senses in which Paul could make both kinds of assertions.

If, however, *Romans* is the only letter that Paul writes to an established Jewish-Christian community, whose help he urgently needs, then one might interpret his statements quite differently. His emphatic assertions of commitment to Israel and its culture might appear, for example, as rhetorical devices required by the situation. They would be intended to soften the blow of a viewpoint that sees the advent of Christ as so decisive that Judaism per se has become part of the old, pre-

Christian world associated with the flesh—the world that is passing away. On this reading, *Romans* would be extremely significant, but not in the way that is usually thought. It would not be a compendium of Paul's theology, but rather a vivid record of his predicament in relation to Judaism and an example of the strategy that he mentions to his Corinthian converts (*1 Cor.* 10:32–33; see 9:20): "Give no offense to Jews or to Greeks or to the church of God, just as I try to please everyone in everything I do, not seeking my own advantage, but that of many, so that they may be saved."

For Further Reading

Donfried, Karl P., ed. *The Romans Debate.* Rev. and enl. ed. Peabody, Mass.: Hendrickson, 1991.

Dunn, James D. G. *Romans.* 2 vols. Word Biblical Commentary. Dallas: Word, 1988.

Elliott, Neil. *The Rhetoric of Romans: Argumentative Constraint and Strategy in Paul's Dialogue with Judaism.* Sheffield: JSOT, 1990.

Fitzmyer, Joseph A. *Romans: A New Translation with Introduction and Commentary.* Anchor Bible 33. New York: Doubleday, 1993.

Mason, Steve. "'For I Am Not Ashamed of the Gospel' (Rom. 1.16): The Gospel and the First Readers of Romans." Pages 254–87 in L. Ann Jervis and Peter Richardson, *Gospel in Paul: Studies on Corinthians, Galatians, and Romans for Richard N. Longenecker.* Sheffield: Sheffield Academic Press, 1994.

Stowers, Stanley K. *The Diatribe and Paul's Letter to the Romans.* Chico, Calif.: Scholars Press, 1981.

THE LETTER OF PAUL
TO THE ROMANS

Salutation

1 Paul, a servant*a* of Jesus Christ, called to be an apostle, set apart for the gospel of God, ²which he promised beforehand through his prophets in the holy scriptures, ³the gospel concerning his Son, who was descended from David according to the flesh ⁴and was declared to be Son of God with power according to the spirit*b* of holiness by resurrection from the dead, Jesus Christ our Lord, ⁵through whom we have received grace and apostleship to bring about the obedience of faith among all the Gentiles for the sake of his name, ⁶including yourselves who are called to belong to Jesus Christ,

⁷To all God's beloved in Rome, who are called to be saints:

Grace to you and peace from God our Father and the Lord Jesus Christ.

Prayer of Thanksgiving

⁸First, I thank my God through Jesus Christ for all of you, because your faith is proclaimed throughout the world. ⁹For God, whom I serve with my spirit by announcing the gospel*c* of his Son, is my witness that without ceasing I remember you always in my prayers, ¹⁰asking that by God's will I may somehow at last succeed in coming to you. ¹¹For I am longing to see you so that I may share with you some spiritual gift to strengthen you— ¹²or rather so that we may be mutually encouraged by each other's faith, both yours and mine. ¹³I want you to know, brothers and sisters,*d* that I have often intended to come to you (but thus far have been prevented), in order that I may reap some harvest among you as I have among the rest of the Gentiles. ¹⁴I am a debtor both to Greeks and to barbarians, both to the wise and to the

---

a Gk *slave*
b Or *Spirit*

c Gk *my spirit in the gospel*
d Gk *brothers*

1:1 called ... Or "called to be an apostle set apart [or 'designated,' 'reserved'] for the gospel of God," without the comma after *apostle*. Such a reading would emphasize the distinctive character of Paul's apostleship—in connection with this "gospel" or "special announcement" that defined his teaching. **gospel of God** The *euangelion* or "special announcement"—of God (*1 Thess.* 2:2, 4, 8, 9) or of Christ (*1 Thess.* 3:2; *1 Cor.* 9:12)—appears to be a term that Paul considers distinctive of his presentation. Note his defensive statements about *his* gospel in this letter (1:16; 2:16; 16:25). Of the narrative gospels, significantly, only *Mark* (1:1, 14–15, etc.), the most Pauline (see the introduction to *Mark*), emphasizes the "gospel" theme. *Luke,* the most historically aware, never uses the term in connection with Jesus. **1:3 son** Because of the symmetrical form and meter of these verses, many scholars think that in 1:3–4 Paul quotes a faith statement familiar to his readers. **descended from David according to the flesh** Since, according to *Matt.* 1:20 and *Luke* 2:4, Joseph was the physical descendant of David but Jesus was *not* physically the son of Joseph (*Matt.* 1:16, 18, 20; *Luke* 3:23), it is difficult to reconcile this statement with the later virgin birth traditions. **1:4 by** The Gk preposition *(ek)* can also mean "out of" or "as a result of." **resurrection from the dead** Is Paul suggesting that Jesus' resurrection brought a change in Jesus' status? Some other early Christian texts seem to suggest that God raised and exalted Jesus in recognition of his unique righteousness, so that he became highly exalted (see *Phil.* 2:8–10; *Acts* 2:36; 10:38–42; 13:33; 17:31). Some later Christians would argue from such passages that divinity was accorded to Jesus only at the point of his resurrection, that he was a righteous man who was "adopted" by God. **1:6** The NRSV translation supposes that Paul's readers were Gentiles. But the Gk says literally "among whom you also are called of Jesus Christ." Paul has used the same language—"called" and "among the Gentiles"—of himself (1:1, 5), although he is not a Gentile. Both he and the Roman Christians, he says, are *called* by Jesus Christ to live *among* the Gentiles. **1:7 beloved in Rome** Notice the absence of the word "church" from this greeting and from the rest of this letter except *Romans* 16 in contrast to Paul's other letter openings (*1 Thess.* 1:1; *1 Cor.* 1:2; *Phil.* 4:15; *2 Cor.* 1:1; *Gal.* 1:2). Does Paul consciously refrain from calling these Christians a church, and if so, why? Scholars have offered an array of sociological (there was no coherent center to the group) and theological (there was some deficiency, according to Paul, in their faith) reasons. **Grace ... and peace** Only in *Romans* does Paul take so long to come to his greeting. **1:13 as I have among the rest of the Gentiles** By placing Paul's work *among the rest of the Gentiles* in the past ("as I have"), the NRSV interprets this clause as referring to his converts in the eastern Mediterranean (see 15:19). Thus, the Roman Christians are to be incorporated in some way within Paul's previous Gentile mission. But the Gk says literally "even as also among the remainder of the Gentiles." The "remainder of the Gentiles" are presumably those Paul has not yet met. In view of his travel plans, these Gentiles might well be those of the western Mediterranean (15:24). On this reading, Paul would have in view a stop in Rome *en route* to the West and "the remainder of the Gentiles"—in contrast to those of the eastern Mediterranean. **1:14** The terms "barbarian" and "foolish" are highly pejorative, so it is unlikely that Paul means to include his current readers in these categories. The terms make better sense as further references to his planned mission in the barbarian (i.e., non-Gk-speaking) West. He is explaining why he needs to go to the West, not why he needs to come to Rome.

foolish [15]—hence my eagerness to proclaim the gospel to you also who are in Rome.

The Power of the Gospel

[16]For I am not ashamed of the gospel; it is the power of God for salvation to everyone who has faith, to the Jew first and also to the Greek. [17]For in it the righteousness of God is revealed through faith for faith; as it is written, "The one who is righteous will live by faith."*e*

The Guilt of Humankind

[18]For the wrath of God is revealed from heaven against all ungodliness and wickedness of those who by their wickedness suppress the truth. [19]For what can be known about God is plain to them, because God has shown it to them. [20]Ever since the creation of the world his eternal power and divine nature, invisible though they are, have been understood and seen through the things he has made. So they are without excuse; [21]for though they knew God, they did not honor him as God or give thanks to him, but they became futile in their thinking, and their senseless minds were darkened. [22]Claiming to be wise, they became fools; [23]and they exchanged the glory of the immortal God for images resembling a mortal human being or birds or four-footed animals or reptiles.

[24]Therefore God gave them up in the lusts of their hearts to impurity, to the degrading of their bodies among themselves, [25]because they exchanged the truth about God for a lie and worshiped and served the creature rather than the Creator, who is blessed forever! Amen.

[26]For this reason God gave them up to degrading passions. Their women exchanged natural intercourse for unnatural, [27]and in the same way also the men, giving up natural intercourse with women, were consumed with passion for one another. Men committed shameless acts with men and received in their own persons the due penalty for their error.

[28]And since they did not see fit to acknowledge God, God gave them up to a debased mind and to things that should not be done. [29]They were filled with every kind of wickedness, evil, covetousness, malice. Full of envy, murder, strife, deceit, craftiness, they are gossips, [30]slanderers, God-haters,*f* insolent, haughty, boastful, inventors of evil, rebellious toward parents, [31]foolish, faithless, heartless, ruthless. [32]They know God's decree, that those who practice such things deserve to die—yet they not only do them but even applaud others who practice them.

The Righteous Judgment of God

2Therefore you have no excuse, whoever you are, when you judge others; for in passing judgment on another you condemn yourself, because you, the judge, are doing the very same things. [2]You say,*g* "We know that God's judgment on those who do such things is in accordance with truth." [3]Do you imagine,

---

e Or *The one who is righteous through faith will live*

f Or *God-hated*
g Gk lacks *You say*

1:15 my eagerness Lit. "the eagerness on my part." Paul's language may suggest that he is unsure about the Romans' eagerness to host him. This uncertainty is supported by his defensive tone ("I am not ashamed") from 1:16 following. **gospel** See 10:15, where Paul cites scripture (*Isa.* 52:7) about the beautiful feet of those who proclaim the gospel, and 15:20. **Rome** Having preached to the "Greeks" of the eastern Mediterranean, Paul now wishes to move to the "barbarian" West, and this move will finally afford him the opportunity to visit Rome. Hence *also*. **1:16 not ashamed** Paul perhaps has in mind *Isa.* 28:16, which he will quote twice in this letter (9:33; 10:11). That text promises that those who trust will not be ashamed. **gospel** See note to this word at 1:1. **Jew first** Paul's defensive tone in describing his gospel or "announcement" for the Gentiles will pervade the letter. Note other places in this letter where Paul insists that Jews have some kind of priority in salvation (2:9–10; 3:9; 10:12). Contrast *Gal.* 3:28; 4:24–25, 30. **1:17** *Hab.* 2:4. MT: "Lo, his [the unrighteous person's] spirit within him is puffed up, not upright, / But the righteous man is rewarded with life for his fidelity." LXX: "If he should draw back [from righteousness], my soul has no pleasure in him: but the righteous [i.e., law-observant] will live by my faithfulness." Paul reinterprets: "He who is righteous by faith [and not through faithfulness to the law!] will live [i.e., find spiritual life]." **1:20** See *Wis.* 13:1. **1:23** See *Wis.* 13:8–9. **1:27** Homosexual relations were common among the elite classes of Greek, and then Roman, society—typically involving a mature man and a teenage boy or young adult. Homosexual acts did not find the same toleration in the Jewish circles from which Paul came. See *Lev.* 18:22; Josephus, *Ag. Ap.* 2.199. **1:31** It appears that this long list of vices would not describe very many individuals, or Gentiles as a whole. Paul is using the rhetorical commonplaces of Jewish communities describing the world outside. *Wis.* 14:2–27 likewise makes idolatry the source of all wickedness. **1:32** This entire discourse on the perversion of Gentiles recalls standard themes of Alexandrian Jewish polemic; see *Wisdom of Solomon* 12–15; Philo, *Embassy to Gaius* 139, 163, 166. **2:1 whoever you are** Lit. "O human being." Paul now begins to address his readers as human beings, thus gradually removing the ground from the Jew-Gentile distinction that he has already acknowledged: all humans face the same problem. **very same things** How can Paul derive this conclusion from what precedes, since he has been joining his readers in judging sinners? Apparently, he has laid a trap: "The wicked deserve punishment, do they not?" "Yes indeed." "But who are *you* to judge?"

whoever you are, that when you judge those who do such things and yet do them yourself, you will escape the judgment of God? ⁴Or do you despise the riches of his kindness and forbearance and patience? Do you not realize that God's kindness is meant to lead you to repentance? ⁵But by your hard and impenitent heart you are storing up wrath for yourself on the day of wrath, when God's righteous judgment will be revealed. ⁶For he will repay according to each one's deeds: ⁷to those who by patiently doing good seek for glory and honor and immortality, he will give eternal life; ⁸while for those who are self-seeking and who obey not the truth but wickedness, there will be wrath and fury. ⁹There will be anguish and distress for everyone who does evil, the Jew first and also the Greek, ¹⁰but glory and honor and peace for everyone who does good, the Jew first and also the Greek. ¹¹For God shows no partiality.

¹²All who have sinned apart from the law will also perish apart from the law, and all who have sinned under the law will be judged by the law. ¹³For it is not the hearers of the law who are righteous in God's sight, but the doers of the law who will be justified. ¹⁴When Gentiles, who do not possess the law, do instinctively what the law requires, these, though not having the law, are a law to themselves. ¹⁵They show that what the law requires is written on their hearts, to which their own conscience also bears witness; and their conflicting thoughts will accuse or perhaps excuse them ¹⁶on the day when, according to my gospel, God, through Jesus Christ, will judge the secret thoughts of all.

The Jews and the Law

¹⁷But if you call yourself a Jew and rely on the law and boast of your relation to God ¹⁸and know his will and determine what is best because you are instructed in the law, ¹⁹and if you are sure that you

are a guide to the blind, a light to those who are in darkness, ²⁰a corrector of the foolish, a teacher of children, having in the law the embodiment of knowledge and truth, ²¹you, then, that teach others, will you not teach yourself? While you preach against stealing, do you steal? ²²You that forbid adultery, do you commit adultery? You that abhor idols, do you rob temples? ²³You that boast in the law, do you dishonor God by breaking the law? ²⁴For, as it is written, "The name of God is blasphemed among the Gentiles because of you."

²⁵Circumcision indeed is of value if you obey the law; but if you break the law, your circumcision has become uncircumcision. ²⁶So, if those who are uncircumcised keep the requirements of the law, will not their uncircumcision be regarded as circumcision? ²⁷Then those who are physically uncircumcised but keep the law will condemn you that have the written code and circumcision but break the law. ²⁸For a person is not a Jew who is one outwardly, nor is true circumcision something external and physical. ²⁹Rather, a person is a Jew who is one inwardly, and real circumcision is a matter of the heart—it is spiritual and not literal. Such a person receives praise not from others but from God.

3 Then what advantage has the Jew? Or what is the value of circumcision? ²Much, in every way. For in the first place the Jews^h were entrusted with the oracles of God. ³What if some were unfaithful? Will their faithlessness nullify the faithfulness of God? ⁴By no means! Although everyone is a liar, let God be proved true, as it is written,

"So that you may be justified in your words,
	and prevail in your judging."^i

⁵But if our injustice serves to confirm the justice of God, what should we say? That God is unjust to

---

h Gk *they*
i Gk *when you are being judged*

2:9 for everyone The Gk is emphatic: "for every human soul." **2:12** Having criticized his readers for taking a superior and judgmental posture in general, Paul now applies his general point to specific claims of Jewish advantage on the basis of the treasured law (2:12–16), the Jewish mission to the world (2:17–24), and the covenant sign of circumcision (2:25–26). Apparently addressing Jews, he tries to undermine any sense of security before God. **2:13 righteous . . . justified** The different English words "righteous(ness)" and "justice" translate forms of the same Gk root (*dik-*). **2:16 my gospel** Only in *Romans* (see also 16:25) does Paul use the phrase "my gospel." This may suggest that the "special announcement" *(euangelion)* is something distinctive to Paul's mission. See note at 1:1. **2:24** Isa. 52:5. MT: "For My people has been carried off for nothing, / Their mockers howl / —declares the Lord— / And constantly, unceasingly, My name is reviled." LXX: "Because my people was taken for nothing, wonder and howl! Declares the Lord: Because of you my name is continually blasphemed among the Gentiles." In its own context, the biblical passage does not support Paul's reading, for it stresses God's concern for his people, not their guilt. But few ancient readers worried about original context. **2:28 outwardly** Or "in appearance." It is unclear whether Jews looked or dressed much differently from others and whether they were more conspicuous in Rome than elsewhere in the eastern Mediterranean. **external and physical** Other Jews could easily agree with what Paul says about the importance of sincerity. But his claim that circumcision is spiritual and *not physical* was a problem, since the Torah makes it clear that circumcision is "in the flesh of the foreskin" (see *Gen.* 17:11, 14). See Philo, *On the Migration of Abraham* 89–93. **3:4** *Ps.* 51:4. MT (51:6): "so You are just in your sentence [or 'word'], / and right in Your judgment." The LXX (50:4) agrees verbally with Paul, except in the form of the verb "prevail." See note to 2:13. **3:5** See note to 2:13.

inflict wrath on us? (I speak in a human way.) ⁶By no means! For then how could God judge the world? ⁷But if through my falsehood God's truthfulness abounds to his glory, why am I still being condemned as a sinner? ⁸And why not say (as some people slander us by saying that we say), "Let us do evil so that good may come"? Their condemnation is deserved!

None Is Righteous

⁹What then? Are we any better off?*ʲ* No, not at all; for we have already charged that all, both Jews and Greeks, are under the power of sin, ¹⁰as it is written:

"There is no one who is righteous, not even one;
¹¹   there is no one who has understanding,
      there is no one who seeks God.
¹² All have turned aside, together they have become worthless;
      there is no one who shows kindness,
      there is not even one."
¹³ "Their throats are opened graves;
      they use their tongues to deceive."
   "The venom of vipers is under their lips."
¹⁴   "Their mouths are full of cursing and bitterness."
¹⁵ "Their feet are swift to shed blood;
¹⁶   ruin and misery are in their paths,

¹⁷   and the way of peace they have not known."
¹⁸   "There is no fear of God before their eyes."

¹⁹Now we know that whatever the law says, it speaks to those who are under the law, so that every mouth may be silenced, and the whole world may be held accountable to God. ²⁰For "no human being will be justified in his sight" by deeds prescribed by the law, for through the law comes the knowledge of sin.

Righteousness through Faith

²¹But now, apart from law, the righteousness of God has been disclosed, and is attested by the law and the prophets, ²²the righteousness of God through faith in Jesus Christ*ᵏ* for all who believe. For there is no distinction, ²³since all have sinned and fall short of the glory of God; ²⁴they are now justified by his grace as a gift, through the redemption that is in Christ Jesus, ²⁵whom God put forward as a sacrifice of atonement*ˡ* by his blood, effective through faith. He did this to show his righteousness, because in his divine forbearance he had passed over the sins previously committed; ²⁶it was to prove at the present time that he himself is righteous and that he justifies the one who has faith in Jesus.*ᵐ*

---

j Or *at any disadvantage?*

k Or *through the faith of Jesus Christ*
l Or *a place of atonement*
m Or *who has the faith of Jesus*

3:10 The following string of quotations from the psalms and the prophets is intended to show that all humanity, Israel included, inclines toward sin. The rabbis and presumably most Jews of Paul's day who thought about the issue would not have disagreed. But Judaism invited repentance and atonement for sin. The LXX includes all of what follows as part of *Ps.* 13:3, but since our LXX manuscripts come only from the 4th century C.E. and the MT does not include this material, most scholars think that the expanded LXX verse comes either from Paul's influence or from a pre-Pauline collection of such verses. **3:10–12** A conflation of ideas and statements from *Pss.* 14:1–3 and 53:1–3 (LXX 13:1–3 and 52:1–3), which are nearly identical with each other, and perhaps *Eccl.* 7:20 (LXX 7:21). Paul makes this statement of general human sinfulness a framework for the other quotations, which he also applies to all humanity. In their original contexts, however, most of these passages apply to sinners, or "the wicked," only. **3:13** *tongues to deceive Ps.* 5:10 (LXX 5:9). *under their lips Ps.* 140:4 (LXX 139:3). **3:14** *Ps.* 10:7. MT: "whose mouth is full of deceit and fraud." LXX (9:27): "whose mouth is full of cursing, bitterness, and fraud." **3:15–17** *Isa.* 59:7–8a. LXX (which is very close to the MT): "Their feet run after evil, swift to shed blood; their plans are plans driven by murder. Ruin and misery are in their paths, and the way of peace they do not know." Paul's language thus agrees closely with the LXX, but he omits some phrases. **3:18** *Ps.* 36:1 (MT 36:2; LXX 35:1). **3:19** *the law says* Although none of these passages is from the law in the strict sense (the Torah, the five books of Moses), Paul's use of this term to cover all scripture is paralleled among his Jewish contemporaries. See *1 Cor.* 14:21. *accountable to God* Paul insists, then, that the biblical texts themselves charge Israel with sin. **3:20** An allusion to *Ps.* 143:2 (LXX 142:2), although the psalmist is not dismissing *deeds prescribed by the law.* **3:21** *righteousness of God* Does Paul mean God's own uprightness or an uprightness that God bestows on others? Both are possible in Gk, and the debate continues. *the law and the prophets* Paul believes that Jewish scripture, although it does not mention Jesus explicitly, anticipates Christian faith and indeed relates ultimately to the cataclysmic events of Paul's own lifetime (see *1 Cor.* 9:9–10; 10:6, 11; 15:3–4; *2 Cor.* 3:14–16; *Gal.* 3:8, 16; 4:21–31). **3:24** Paul now moves to his positive point—the common solution to the common human problem. **3:25** *sacrifice of atonement* Or "mercy seat," the upper surface of the ark of the covenant in the tabernacle/temple, where the presence of God dwelt (*Exod.* 25:17). It seems that this allusion, unique in Paul's letters, would only be meaningful to Jewish readers or Gentiles who were thoroughly familiar with scripture. *sins previously committed* In Jewish scripture (esp. the Deuteronomistic History) it was asserted that God regularly punished sin with catastrophe and rewarded Israel when the nation repented (see *Deuteronomy* 28; *Judg.* 2:10–23, etc.; *Daniel* 9). **3:26** *justifies* In the Gk, the word for "justify" is the verb form of the adjective "righteous."

27Then what becomes of boasting? It is excluded. By what law? By that of works? No, but by the law of faith. 28For we hold that a person is justified by faith apart from works prescribed by the law. 29Or is God the God of Jews only? Is he not the God of Gentiles also? Yes, of Gentiles also, 30since God is one; and he will justify the circumcised on the ground of faith and the uncircumcised through that same faith. 31Do we then overthrow the law by this faith? By no means! On the contrary, we uphold the law.

The Example of Abraham

4 What then are we to say was gained by*n* Abraham, our ancestor according to the flesh? 2For if Abraham was justified by works, he has something to boast about, but not before God. 3For what does the scripture say? "Abraham believed God, and it was reckoned to him as righteousness." 4Now to one who works, wages are not reckoned as a gift but as something due. 5But to one who without works trusts him who justifies the ungodly, such faith is reckoned as righteousness. 6So also David speaks of the blessedness of those to whom God reckons righteousness apart from works:

7 "Blessed are those whose iniquities are forgiven,
   and whose sins are covered;
8 blessed is the one against whom the Lord will
   not reckon sin."

---

n Other ancient authorities read *say about*

9Is this blessedness, then, pronounced only on the circumcised, or also on the uncircumcised? We say, "Faith was reckoned to Abraham as righteousness." 10How then was it reckoned to him? Was it before or after he had been circumcised? It was not after, but before he was circumcised. 11He received the sign of circumcision as a seal of the righteousness that he had by faith while he was still uncircumcised. The purpose was to make him the ancestor of all who believe without being circumcised and who thus have righteousness reckoned to them, 12and likewise the ancestor of the circumcised who are not only circumcised but who also follow the example of the faith that our ancestor Abraham had before he was circumcised.

God's Promise Realized through Faith

13For the promise that he would inherit the world did not come to Abraham or to his descendants through the law but through the righteousness of faith. 14If it is the adherents of the law who are to be the heirs, faith is null and the promise is void. 15For the law brings wrath; but where there is no law, neither is there violation.

16For this reason it depends on faith, in order that the promise may rest on grace and be guaranteed to all his descendants, not only to the adherents of the law but also to those who share the faith of Abraham (for he is the father of all of us, 17as it is written, "I have made you the father of many nations")—in the

---

3:27 Here, as in *Romand* 7, Paul plays with various senses of *law:* law in general (or principle), law of works (commandments of Torah), and law of faith (not really a law but a principle). **3:30** A fitting conclusion to the entire argument from 1:18. Paul has asserted that if Gentiles are obviously sinful, so are Jews. The problem of sin is the same, and the solution—trust in Christ—is the same. **3:31** A natural question: If Jews and Gentiles are the same before God, what has become of the divine law that grounds Jewish culture and distinguishes it from the other nations? For the moment, Paul simply insists that he is not overthrowing the law, but he will not take up the issue until *Romans* 7. **4:1 *our ancestor according to the flesh*** Having completed his general argument that Jews and Gentiles stand in the same position, and having dismissed for now the question of Jewish law, Paul moves to the basic issue of descent from Abraham, with whom Israel's identity began. God made irrevocable promises of blessing to Abraham and his descendants (*Gen.* 12:2–3; 15:18–21; 17:6–8). Paul continues to assume a Jewish-Christian audience. Elsewhere he calls Abraham the ancestor of Gentiles also (*Gal.* 3:9, 29), but not *according to the flesh* as here. **4:3** *Gen.* 15:6. MT: "And because he put his trust in the Lord, He reckoned it to his merit." The LXX reads exactly as Paul. "Believe" is the verb corresponding to the noun "faith." In *Genesis,* the point seems to be that Abraham trusts God's promise of descendants although he is old and childless, and so God considers him righteous. Paul, however, wants to make Abraham's "faith" something absolute, in contrast to "works." **4:4** The contrast with a worker's wages seems suggested by the word "reckon," which was a common bookkeeping term, in *Gen.* 15:6. Paul plays with it a bit. **4:7** *Ps.* 32:1–2 (LXX 31:1–2). If, as seems likely, this passage suggested itself to Paul because it contained the word "reckon," then he must have had a concordancelike knowledge of the Bible, which allowed him to pull out such verses at will from even obscure places. **4:11** Paul has considerably revamped the argument of *Gal.* 3:15–18, which drove a sharp wedge between the Abrahamic covenant (of faith alone) and the Mosaic covenant (of commandments/works). That argument overlooked the fact that circumcision (which Paul associates with law and works) was already commanded to Abraham (*Gen.* 17:9–14); it did not originate with Moses. By contrast, Paul now distinguishes between Abraham's situation before and after the circumcision command: he is reckoned righteous in *Genesis* 15, but the circumcision command comes only in *Genesis* 17. **4:13** Thus the promises of special blessing made to Abraham do not challenge Paul's claim that Jews and Gentiles stand on an equal footing before God, for both Jews and Gentiles depend on a righteousness that comes through faith (in Christ). **4:14** See *Gal.* 2:21. **4:17 *many nations*** *Gen.* 17:5. ***who gives life to the dead*** Perhaps Paul is referring to the resurrection of Jesus and the wholly "new creation" (*2 Cor.* 5:17; *Gal.* 6:15) that has resulted.

presence of the God in whom he believed, who gives life to the dead and calls into existence the things that do not exist. [18]Hoping against hope, he believed that he would become "the father of many nations," according to what was said, "So numerous shall your descendants be." [19]He did not weaken in faith when he considered his own body, which was already[o] as good as dead (for he was about a hundred years old), or when he considered the barrenness of Sarah's womb. [20]No distrust made him waver concerning the promise of God, but he grew strong in his faith as he gave glory to God, [21]being fully convinced that God was able to do what he had promised. [22]Therefore his faith[p] "was reckoned to him as righteousness." [23]Now the words, "it was reckoned to him," were written not for his sake alone, [24]but for ours also. It will be reckoned to us who believe in him who raised Jesus our Lord from the dead, [25]who was handed over to death for our trespasses and was raised for our justification.

Results of Justification

5 Therefore, since we are justified by faith, we[q] have peace with God through our Lord Jesus Christ, [2]through whom we have obtained access[r] to this grace in which we stand; and we[s] boast in our hope of sharing the glory of God. [3]And not only that, but we[s] also boast in our sufferings, knowing that suffering produces endurance, [4]and endurance produces character, and character produces hope, [5]and hope does not disappoint us, because God's love has been poured

into our hearts through the Holy Spirit that has been given to us. [6]For while we were still weak, at the right time Christ died for the ungodly. [7]Indeed, rarely will anyone die for a righteous person—though perhaps for a good person someone might actually dare to die. [8]But God proves his love for us in that while we still were sinners Christ died for us. [9]Much more surely then, now that we have been justified by his blood, will we be saved through him from the wrath of God.[t] [10]For if while we were enemies, we were reconciled to God through the death of his Son, much more surely, having been reconciled, will we be saved by his life. [11]But more than that, we even boast in God through our Lord Jesus Christ, through whom we have now received reconciliation.

Adam and Christ

[12]Therefore, just as sin came into the world through one man, and death came through sin, and so death spread to all because all have sinned— [13]sin was indeed in the world before the law, but sin is not reckoned when there is no law. [14]Yet death exercised dominion from Adam to Moses, even over those whose sins were not like the transgression of Adam, who is a type of the one who was to come.

[15]But the free gift is not like the trespass. For if the many died through the one man's trespass, much more surely have the grace of God and the free gift in the grace of the one man, Jesus Christ, abounded for the many. [16]And the free gift is not like the effect of the one man's sin. For the judgment following one

---

o Other ancient authorities lack *already*
p Gk *Therefore it*
q Other ancient authorities read *let us*
r Other ancient authorities add *by faith*
s Or *let us*

t Gk *the wrath*

4:18 *Gen.* 15:5. Paul now rightly interprets the "seed" of *Gen.* 22:18 as a collective singular *(descendants)* rather than as a singular reference to Christ as he did in *Gal.* 3:16; see note to 4:11. **4:24** Having established at length the importance of faith for Abraham, Paul now fills the term with Christian content. Note his distinction between the ancient sense of the passage ("not for his sake alone"), which Paul concedes, and its application to Paul's day. Paul generally considers scripture to relate ultimately to his own time—the end of the age (see *1 Cor.* 9:9–10; 10:6). **5:2** Paul now seems to step back from subtle argumentation concerning Jewish culture to consolidate his bond with the reader in celebrating the benefits of Christian faith. **5:9** Except for references to the Eucharist in *1 Corinthians* (10:16; 11:25–27), *Romans* is the only letter in which Paul develops the idea of Jesus' death as a blood sacrifice; see 3:25. Perhaps this reflects Paul's Jewish audience. **5:12** A ruptured sentence that has caused endless discussion among commentators. Paul's view so far has been the typically Jewish one that all are sinners because all sin (3:9–19). He says this here also *(because all have sinned)*, but the point does not fit perfectly with the argument that he now wishes to make, concerning the legacy of *Adam's sin* for all humanity. This tension may be the cause of the ruptured sentence. **5:14** That is, if people died from Adam to Moses, as they did, even though their own sins were not counted (in the absence of any law), they must have died because of Adam's sin. This passage would be used by the 5th-century teacher Augustine as the basis for his doctrine of original sin, which subsequently assumed an important place in Christian theology. The problem is that (a) Paul does not elsewhere develop such an idea, (b) his main view is that people are sinners because they themselves sin (see 3:9–19; 5:12), and (c) he is not out to prove anything *new* about Adam here. Rather, Paul assumes his readers' knowledge of speculations about Adam (see *4 Ezra* 1.21–27), which he uses as a basis for his claim about the universality of Christ's benefits (5:15–21), his main point.

trespass brought condemnation, but the free gift following many trespasses brings justification. [17]If, because of the one man's trespass, death exercised dominion through that one, much more surely will those who receive the abundance of grace and the free gift of righteousness exercise dominion in life through the one man, Jesus Christ.

[18]Therefore just as one man's trespass led to condemnation for all, so one man's act of righteousness leads to justification and life for all. [19]For just as by the one man's disobedience the many were made sinners, so by the one man's obedience the many will be made righteous. [20]But law came in, with the result that the trespass multiplied; but where sin increased, grace abounded all the more, [21]so that, just as sin exercised dominion in death, so grace might also exercise dominion through justification[u] leading to eternal life through Jesus Christ our Lord.

Dying and Rising with Christ

6What then are we to say? Should we continue in sin in order that grace may abound? [2]By no means! How can we who died to sin go on living in it? [3]Do you not know that all of us who have been baptized into Christ Jesus were baptized into his death? [4]Therefore we have been buried with him by baptism into death, so that, just as Christ was raised from the dead by the glory of the Father, so we too might walk in newness of life.

[5]For if we have been united with him in a death like his, we will certainly be united with him in a resurrection like his. [6]We know that our old self was crucified with him so that the body of sin might be destroyed, and we might no longer be enslaved to sin. [7]For whoever has died is freed from sin. [8]But if we have died with Christ, we believe that we will also live with him. [9]We know that Christ, being raised from the dead, will never die again; death no longer has dominion over him. [10]The death he died, he died

to sin, once for all; but the life he lives, he lives to God. [11]So you also must consider yourselves dead to sin and alive to God in Christ Jesus.

[12]Therefore, do not let sin exercise dominion in your mortal bodies, to make you obey their passions. [13]No longer present your members to sin as instruments[v] of wickedness, but present yourselves to God as those who have been brought from death to life, and present your members to God as instruments[v] of righteousness. [14]For sin will have no dominion over you, since you are not under law but under grace.

Slaves of Righteousness

[15]What then? Should we sin because we are not under law but under grace? By no means! [16]Do you not know that if you present yourselves to anyone as obedient slaves, you are slaves of the one whom you obey, either of sin, which leads to death, or of obedience, which leads to righteousness? [17]But thanks be to God that you, having once been slaves of sin, have become obedient from the heart to the form of teaching to which you were entrusted, [18]and that you, having been set free from sin, have become slaves of righteousness. [19]I am speaking in human terms because of your natural limitations.[w] For just as you once presented your members as slaves to impurity and to greater and greater iniquity, so now present your members as slaves to righteousness for sanctification.

[20]When you were slaves of sin, you were free in regard to righteousness. [21]So what advantage did you then get from the things of which you now are ashamed? The end of those things is death. [22]But now that you have been freed from sin and enslaved to God, the advantage you get is sanctification. The end is eternal life. [23]For the wages of sin is death, but the free gift of God is eternal life in Christ Jesus our Lord.

---

u Or righteousness

v Or weapons
w Gk the weakness of your flesh

5:19 One finds a similar a fortiori argument in a rabbinic discussion of how good deeds outweigh bad—on the principle that God is more inclined to mercy than to punishment; see *Sifra Ḥovah* 12.10, which uses the same example of Adam. **6:2** Paul continues to fend off potential criticism (see 3:8; 13:8–10) that because he does not advocate Jewish law, he has no moral guidelines. **6:4** See *Gal.* 2:19–20. The absolute novelty of life in Christ, over against all other ways of life, is a basic theme of Paul's gospel, sometimes captured in the phrase "new creation" (*2 Cor.* 5:17; *Gal.* 6:15). **6:11** Paul's stress on dying to the old and rising to new life serves a critical function in the letter: it begins as a noncontroversial discussion of the meaning of baptism—a rite shared by all Christians, including Paul and his Roman readers. Paul elaborates first on the importance of death toward sin, which any Christian might also be expected to accept. But Paul will now gradually turn to the controversial climax of the argument: death toward *law*. **6:14** The first hint that Paul will turn the death/life theme against the regime of the Mosaic law. **6:17** An awkward and peculiar way to describe what the Romans believe, which he will not call "gospel"; see also 16:17. Apparently, Paul wants to preserve "gospel" (*euangelion*) as a special term for his Gentile mission. See 15:16, 19; 16:25. **6:23** The language of *wages* and *gift* recalls Paul's discussion of Abraham in 4:4. This passage brings to a head the entire theme of new life in Christ and its benefits, just before Paul applies it to the question of the Jewish law.

An Analogy from Marriage

7 Do you not know, brothers and sisters[x]—for I am speaking to those who know the law—that the law is binding on a person only during that person's lifetime? [2]Thus a married woman is bound by the law to her husband as long as he lives; but if her husband dies, she is discharged from the law concerning the husband. [3]Accordingly, she will be called an adulteress if she lives with another man while her husband is alive. But if her husband dies, she is free from that law, and if she marries another man, she is not an adulteress.

[4]In the same way, my friends,[x] you have died to the law through the body of Christ, so that you may belong to another, to him who has been raised from the dead in order that we may bear fruit for God. [5]While we were living in the flesh, our sinful passions, aroused by the law, were at work in our members to bear fruit for death. [6]But now we are discharged from the law, dead to that which held us captive, so that we are slaves not under the old written code but in the new life of the Spirit.

The Law and Sin

[7]What then should we say? That the law is sin? By no means! Yet, if it had not been for the law, I would not have known sin. I would not have known what it is to covet if the law had not said, "You shall not covet." [8]But sin, seizing an opportunity in the commandment, produced in me all kinds of covetousness. Apart from the law sin lies dead. [9]I was once alive apart from the law, but when the command-

ment came, sin revived [10]and I died, and the very commandment that promised life proved to be death to me. [11]For sin, seizing an opportunity in the commandment, deceived me and through it killed me. [12]So the law is holy, and the commandment is holy and just and good.

[13]Did what is good, then, bring death to me? By no means! It was sin, working death in me through what is good, in order that sin might be shown to be sin, and through the commandment might become sinful beyond measure.

The Inner Conflict

[14]For we know that the law is spiritual; but I am of the flesh, sold into slavery under sin.[y] [15]I do not understand my own actions. For I do not do what I want, but I do the very thing I hate. [16]Now if I do what I do not want, I agree that the law is good. [17]But in fact it is no longer I that do it, but sin that dwells within me. [18]For I know that nothing good dwells within me, that is, in my flesh. I can will what is right, but I cannot do it. [19]For I do not do the good I want, but the evil I do not want is what I do. [20]Now if I do what I do not want, it is no longer I that do it, but sin that dwells within me.

[21]So I find it to be a law that when I want to do what is good, evil lies close at hand. [22]For I delight in the law of God in my inmost self, [23]but I see in my members another law at war with the law of my mind, making me captive to the law of sin that dwells in my members. [24]Wretched man that I am! Who will rescue me from this body of death? [25]Thanks be to God through Jesus Christ our Lord!

---

x Gk *brothers*

y Gk *sold under sin*

7:1 *know the law* Another indicator of the audience's Jewish background: they know Torah. *lifetime* Paul now applies the death/life scheme to the fundamental question of the Jewish law: all believers have died to the law (see *Gal.* 2:19–20). **7:2** This analogy presents a logical problem: If the woman represents the believer, why does the *husband* (= the law?) die? **7:7** Is the equation of law with sin a natural consequence of Paul's argument? A more natural question might be whether the law is obsolete, to which Paul would presumably answer yes. Why does Paul, then, raise the extreme prospect that the law might be sin—a view that neither he nor his readers (as far as we know) has suggested? Perhaps so that he can dismiss it for its obvious absurdity, in a *reductio ad absurdium*. *You shall not covet.* Exod. 20:17. **7:9** A puzzling order, since Paul was born a Jew (*Phil.* 3:5). When was he alive before *the commandment came?* The order does fit, however, with his scheme of salvation history: Adam, Abraham (promise), Moses (law), Christ (faith). See *Gal.* 3:15–29; *Rom.* 5:13–14, 20. This correspondence suggests that Paul is talking about the history of salvation, using *I* as a symbol of humanity, not about his own life. **7:12** As in 3:31, Paul insists that he has nothing negative to say about the law per se. **7:13** Again, the negative consequences of the law were not the law's fault; sin used the law. **7:14** Paul assumes his readers' agreement: *We [Jews?] know that the law is spiritual.* But compare his statements elsewhere, which seem indeed to connect the law with flesh and sin (*Phil.* 3:2–20; *2 Cor.* 3:7–18; *Gal.* 3:1–5; *Rom.* 6:1–7:4; 8:1–8). It seems likely that the Roman Christians had heard of his remarks about Judaism and its code, which places him on the defensive. **7:18** Paul regularly appeals, as here, to a dichotomy, common in Greco-Roman antiquity, between the world of constantly decaying matter (including "flesh") and the world of unchanging truth ("spirit"). This distinction was fundamental to Plato's thought. **7:21** *I find it to be a law* It is typical of Paul, as we have already seen, to pick up a key word and give it a different sense as he shifts the focus of discussion. **7:24** If Paul were speaking of his pre-Christian past in Judaism, longing to be freed from slavery to the law, we would have to explain (a) the present tense here and (b) his other references to his former life (*Phil.* 3:5–6; *Gal.* 1:13–14), which indicate that he was prospering in Judaism before the decisive encounter with the risen Christ. Perhaps, then, he is still using *I* of humanity in general (see note to 7:9).

So then, with my mind I am a slave to the law of God, but with my flesh I am a slave to the law of sin.

Life in the Spirit

8 There is therefore now no condemnation for those who are in Christ Jesus. [2]For the law of the Spirit[z] of life in Christ Jesus has set you[a] free from the law of sin and of death. [3]For God has done what the law, weakened by the flesh, could not do: by sending his own Son in the likeness of sinful flesh, and to deal with sin,[b] he condemned sin in the flesh, [4]so that the just requirement of the law might be fulfilled in us, who walk not according to the flesh but according to the Spirit.[z] [5]For those who live according to the flesh set their minds on the things of the flesh, but those who live according to the Spirit[z] set their minds on the things of the Spirit.[z] [6]To set the mind on the flesh is death, but to set the mind on the Spirit[z] is life and peace. [7]For this reason the mind that is set on the flesh is hostile to God; it does not submit to God's law—indeed it cannot, [8]and those who are in the flesh cannot please God.

[9]But you are not in the flesh; you are in the Spirit,[z] since the Spirit of God dwells in you. Anyone who does not have the Spirit of Christ does not belong to him. [10]But if Christ is in you, though the body is dead because of sin, the Spirit[z] is life because of righteousness. [11]If the Spirit of him who raised Jesus from the dead dwells in you, he who raised Christ[c] from the dead will give life to your mortal bodies also through[d] his Spirit that dwells in you.

[12]So then, brothers and sisters,[e] we are debtors, not to the flesh, to live according to the flesh— [13]for if you live according to the flesh, you will die; but if by the Spirit you put to death the deeds of the body, you will live. [14]For all who are led by the Spirit of God are children of God. [15]For you did not receive a spirit of slavery to fall back into fear, but you have received a spirit of adoption. When we cry, "Abba![f] Father!" [16]it is that very Spirit bearing witness[g] with our spirit that we are children of God, [17]and if children, then heirs, heirs of God and joint heirs with Christ—if, in fact, we suffer with him so that we may also be glorified with him.

Future Glory

[18]I consider that the sufferings of this present time are not worth comparing with the glory about to be revealed to us. [19]For the creation waits with eager longing for the revealing of the children of God; [20]for the creation was subjected to futility, not of its own will but by the will of the one who subjected it, in hope [21]that the creation itself will be set free from its bondage to decay and will obtain the freedom of the glory of the children of God. [22]We know that the whole creation has been groaning in labor pains until now; [23]and not only the creation, but we ourselves, who have the first fruits of the Spirit, groan inwardly while we wait for adoption, the redemption of our bodies. [24]For in[h] hope we were saved. Now hope that is seen is not hope. For who hopes[i] for what is seen? [25]But if we hope for what we do not see, we wait for it with patience.

[26]Likewise the Spirit helps us in our weakness; for we do not know how to pray as we ought, but that very Spirit intercedes[j] with sighs too deep for words. [27]And God,[k] who searches the heart, knows what is the mind of the Spirit, because the Spirit[l] intercedes for the saints according to the will of God.[m]

---

z Or *spirit*

a Here the Greek word *you* is singular number; other ancient authorities read *me* or *us*

b Or *and as a sin offering*

c Other ancient authorities read *the Christ* or *Christ Jesus* or *Jesus Christ*

d Other ancient authorities read *on account of*

e Gk *brothers*

f Aramaic for *Father*

g Or [15]*a spirit of adoption, by which we cry, "Abba! Father!"*[16]*The Spirit itself bears witness*

h Or *by*

i Other ancient authorities read *awaits*

j Other ancient authorities add *for us*

k Gk *the one*

l Gk *he* or *it*

m Gk *according to God*

8:2 *Spirit* Capitalization is not used in the Gk manuscripts, so the translators must decide when it is appropriate in the English. Notice the further shift in the sense of "law." **8:3** *could not do* See *Gal.* 3:21. Paul effectively links the law with the flesh and sin, even though he is careful not to blame the law itself. The law has now been supplanted by the coming of Christ. *to deal with sin* If we translated this "and as a sin offering," which is plausible (note *b* above), the reference would be to *Lev.* 4:27–35. Such an allusion would be intelligible only to a Jewish audience or one familiar with Jewish scripture. **8:4** See 13:8–10; *Gal.* 5:15–6:2. **8:6** See notes to 7:14, 18. **8:8** Paul consistently associates observance of the law with the inferior, transient world of the flesh, as opposed to the enduring world of the Spirit; see *Phil.* 3:2–6, 19–20; *Gal.* 3:3. **8:9** Once again Paul stresses that all Christians share an entirely new life in the spirit (see 6:1–6). **8:12** Evidently, then, in spite of Paul's careful attempt to avoid criticizing the law, for him the law is finished. This is the view he expressed more directly in *Gal.* 3:23–25; 4:4–7, 21. **8:14–17** See *Gal.* 4:1–7, which uses similar language. **8:18** The following reflections recall *2 Cor.* 4:16–5:10, which also follows a discussion of the law. Paul begins to build here to a poetic crescendo, celebrating the benefits of trust in Christ (8:31–39), in an effort to cement the bond with his readers before he makes his final argument on the issue of Israel's election (chs. 9–11).

[28]We know that all things work together for good[n] for those who love God, who are called according to his purpose. [29]For those whom he foreknew he also predestined to be conformed to the image of his Son, in order that he might be the firstborn within a large family.[o] [30]And those whom he predestined he also called; and those whom he called he also justified; and those whom he justified he also glorified.

God's Love in Christ Jesus

[31]What then are we to say about these things? If God is for us, who is against us? [32]He who did not withhold his own Son, but gave him up for all of us, will he not with him also give us everything else? [33]Who will bring any charge against God's elect? It is God who justifies. [34]Who is to condemn? It is Christ Jesus, who died, yes, who was raised, who is at the right hand of God, who indeed intercedes for us.[p] [35]Who will separate us from the love of Christ? Will hardship, or distress, or persecution, or famine, or nakedness, or peril, or sword? [36]As it is written,

"For your sake we are being killed all day long;

    we are accounted as sheep to be slaughtered."

[37]No, in all these things we are more than conquerors through him who loved us. [38]For I am convinced that neither death, nor life, nor angels, nor rulers, nor things present, nor things to come, nor powers, [39]nor height, nor depth, nor anything else in all creation, will be able to separate us from the love of God in Christ Jesus our Lord.

God's Election of Israel

[9:1]I am speaking the truth in Christ—I am not lying; my conscience confirms it by the Holy Spirit— [2]I have great sorrow and unceasing anguish in my heart. [3]For I could wish that I myself were accursed and cut off from Christ for the sake of my own people,[q] my kindred according to the flesh. [4]They are Israelites, and to them belong the adoption, the glory, the covenants, the giving of the law, the worship, and the promises; [5]to them belong the patriarchs, and from them, according to the flesh, comes the Messiah,[r] who is over all, God blessed forever.[s] Amen.

[6]It is not as though the word of God had failed. For not all Israelites truly belong to Israel, [7]and not all of Abraham's children are his true descendants; but "It is through Isaac that descendants shall be named for you." [8]This means that it is not the children of the flesh who are the children of God, but the children of the promise are counted as descendants. [9]For this is what the promise said, "About this time I will return and Sarah shall have a son." [10]Nor is that all; something similar happened to Rebecca when she had conceived children by one husband, our ancestor Isaac. [11]Even before they had been born or had done anything good or bad (so that God's purpose of election might continue, [12]not by works but by his call) she was told, "The elder shall serve the younger." [13]As it is written,

"I have loved Jacob,

    but I have hated Esau."

---

n Other ancient authorities read *God makes all things work together for good*, or *in all things God works for good*

o Gk *among many brothers*

p Or *Is it Christ Jesus . . . for us?*

q Gk *my brothers*

r Or *the Christ*

s Or *Messiah, who is God over all, blessed forever*, or *Messiah. May he who is God over all be blessed forever*

8:36 Ps. 44:22 (LXX 43:22). Paul's Gk agrees with the LXX. **9:3** Paul here begins his most intensive appeal concerning the status of Israel's "election" (choice) by God, in the light of Jesus' coming. He has already argued that Jews and Gentiles share the same basis of salvation in Christ (*Romans* 1–4). He must now delicately explain what, then, has happened to God's choice of Israel in light of Christ's coming. This difficult argument (*Romans* 9–11) constitutes more than 20 percent of the letter by word count. **9:4** Israel's "advantages" were anticipated in 3:2. **9:5** *according to the flesh* See 1:3. *Messiah* The Gk word *Christos* is elsewhere rendered "Christ," which Paul normally uses as if it were one of Jesus' personal names (e.g., *Rom.* 1:1, 4; *1 Cor.* 1:1–3; *Gal.* 1:6–12). The translators properly treat it in context here as the title "Messiah," or "anointed one." Paul's unique usage here again suggests that his readers are Jews. *God* If Paul intends to call Jesus God, as one possible translation would read, it is the only place where he does so, and it would sound quite jarring immediately after *according to the flesh*. Even if he did mean to call Jesus God in this case, we should beware of reading later Christian content (concerning the divine nature of Christ) into such language. Other Jewish writers of the time, such as Philo, could describe various intermediaries as "God" without meaning that they were "coequal" and "coeternal" with the Creator. See Philo, *Somn.* 2.189. The Chalcedonian Definition of Christ's two natures required another 400 years to take shape (451 C.E.). **9:6** *the word of God* God's promises to Abraham, as the following makes clear; see *Romans* 4. **9:7** Gen. 21:12. **9:9** Gen. 18:10, 14. MT: "I will return to you next year, and your wife Sarah shall have a son [v. 10]. . . . I will return to you at the same season next year, and Sarah shall have a son [v. 14]." LXX: "About this time seasonally I will return and come to you [not Paul's words for 'return' and 'come'], and Sarah your wife will have a son [a different Gk construction from Paul's] [v. 10]. . . . About this time [a different Gk preposition from Paul's] seasonally I will return to you and Sarah shall have a son [the same construction as Paul's] [v. 14]." Thus, the chosen line was through Sarah (and her son Isaac) alone, not through Hagar's son Ishmael, who was already born. Paul's point is that, therefore, not all of Abraham's physical descendants are part of the line of promise. Many Jews would presumably have agreed with this point, but how does it help Paul's effort to transfer the promise to *spiritual* descendants of Abraham? See note to 9:29. **9:12** Gen. 25:23.

[14]What then are we to say? Is there injustice on God's part? By no means! [15]For he says to Moses,

"I will have mercy on whom I have mercy,
and I will have compassion on whom I have compassion."

[16]So it depends not on human will or exertion, but on God who shows mercy. [17]For the scripture says to Pharaoh, "I have raised you up for the very purpose of showing my power in you, so that my name may be proclaimed in all the earth." [18]So then he has mercy on whomever he chooses, and he hardens the heart of whomever he chooses.

God's Wrath and Mercy

[19]You will say to me then, "Why then does he still find fault? For who can resist his will?" [20]But who indeed are you, a human being, to argue with God? Will what is molded say to the one who molds it, "Why have you made me like this?" [21]Has the potter no right over the clay, to make out of the same lump one object for special use and another for ordinary use? [22]What if God, desiring to show his wrath and to make known his power, has endured with much patience the objects of wrath that are made for destruction; [23]and what if he has done so in order to make known the riches of his glory for the objects of mercy, which he has prepared beforehand for glory— [24]including us whom he has called, not from the Jews only but also from the Gentiles? [25]As indeed he says in Hosea,

"Those who were not my people I will call 'my people,'

and her who was not beloved I will call 'beloved.'"

[26] "And in the very place where it was said to them, 'You are not my people,'
there they shall be called children of the living God."

[27]And Isaiah cries out concerning Israel, "Though the number of the children of Israel were like the sand of the sea, only a remnant of them will be saved; [28]for the Lord will execute his sentence on the earth quickly and decisively."[t] [29]And as Isaiah predicted,

"If the Lord of hosts had not left survivors[u] to us,
we would have fared like Sodom
and been made like Gomorrah."

Israel's Unbelief

[30]What then are we to say? Gentiles, who did not strive for righteousness, have attained it, that is, righteousness through faith; [31]but Israel, who did strive for the righteousness that is based on the law, did not succeed in fulfilling that law. [32]Why not? Because they did not strive for it on the basis of faith, but as if it were based on works. They have stumbled over the stumbling stone, [33]as it is written,

"See, I am laying in Zion a stone that will make people stumble, a rock that will make them fall,

---

t Other ancient authorities read *for he will finish his work and cut it short in righteousness, because the Lord will make the sentence shortened on the earth*

u Or *descendants*; Gk *seed*

9:13 *Mal.* 1:2–3. These quotations demonstrate a further narrowing of the line of promise: God has made inscrutable choices among Abraham's descendants. Note again Paul's ability to find in obscure places verses with the language he needs. **9:15** *Exod.* 33:19. MT: "And I will grant the grace that I will grant and show the compassion that I will show." The LXX is exactly as Paul. **9:17** *Exod.* 9:16. **9:18** Thus, Paul has cited the narrowing of the physical line of Abraham's descendants mainly in order to support his point that God's free choice is not accountable to human judgment. Thus far, we should not expect disagreement from Jewish readers. **9:24** Paul now makes the decisive move, applying the general principle of God's free choice to his argument that God has freely chosen to include the Gentiles in salvation through Christ. **9:25** *Hos.* 2:23. MT (2:25): "And I will say to Lo-Ammi ['Not my people,' personified; see 1:9], 'You are My people,' / And he will respond, '[You are] my God.'" LXX (2:23): "To those who are not my people, I will say 'you are my people,' and they [lit. 'he'] will say, 'You are the Lord my God.'" **9:26** *Hos.* 1:10. MT (2:1), speaking of Israel: "instead of being told, 'You are Not-My-People,' they shall be called Children-of-the-Living-God." LXX (1:10) reads as Paul, except that the LXX adds an emphatic "even you." Paul applies to the Gentiles the metaphorical names given to Hosea's children because of God's temporary wrath toward Israel. **9:28** *Isa.* 10:22–23. MT: "Even if your people, O Israel, / Should be as the sands of the sea, / only a remnant of it shall return./ [two lines omitted] For my Lord God of Hosts is carrying out / A decree of destruction upon all the land." LXX: "Though the people of Israel should become as the sand of the sea, only the remnant of them will be saved; passing sentence quickly and decisively in righteousness, for the Lord will execute sentence decisively in the whole inhabited world." **9:29** *Isa.* 1:9. Paul's Gk agrees exactly with the LXX. To shore up his argument for the inclusion of Gentiles, Paul features passages that speak of the exclusion of part of Israel for unfaithfulness. **9:32** *faith* For a contrast to Paul's sharp distinction between faith and works, see *Jas.* 2:14–26. **9:33** *Isa.* 28:16. MT: "Behold, I will found in Zion, / Stone by stone, / A tower of precious cornerstones, / Exceedingly firm; / He who trusts [i.e., 'has faith'] need not fear." LXX: "See, I am establishing for the foundations of Zion a costly stone, a choice stone, a cornerstone, a precious stone for her foundations, and the one who trusts will in no way be ashamed." Paul now clarifies what faith means for him: trust in Christ. He adapts this text to his purpose by making the precious stone offensive (to match Jewish resistance to Christ) and by calling for belief (or faith, trust) *in him.*

and whoever believes in him[v] will not be put to shame."

10 Brothers and sisters,[w] my heart's desire and prayer to God for them is that they may be saved. [2]I can testify that they have a zeal for God, but it is not enlightened. [3]For, being ignorant of the righteousness that comes from God, and seeking to establish their own, they have not submitted to God's righteousness. [4]For Christ is the end of the law so that there may be righteousness for everyone who believes.

Salvation Is for All

[5]Moses writes concerning the righteousness that comes from the law, that "the person who does these things will live by them." [6]But the righteousness that comes from faith says, "Do not say in your heart, 'Who will ascend into heaven?'" (that is, to bring Christ down) [7]"or 'Who will descend into the abyss?'" (that is, to bring Christ up from the dead). [8]But what does it say?

"The word is near you,
     on your lips and in your heart"

(that is, the word of faith that we proclaim); [9]because[x] if you confess with your lips that Jesus is Lord and believe in your heart that God raised him from the dead, you will be saved. [10]For one believes with the heart and so is justified, and one confesses with the mouth and so is saved. [11]The scripture says, "No one who believes in him will be put to shame." [12]For there is no distinction between Jew and Greek; the same Lord is Lord of all and is generous to all who call on him. [13]For, "Everyone who calls on the name of the Lord shall be saved."

[14]But how are they to call on one in whom they have not believed? And how are they to believe in one of whom they have never heard? And how are they to hear without someone to proclaim him? [15]And how are they to proclaim him unless they are sent? As it is written, "How beautiful are the feet of those who bring good news!" [16]But not all have obeyed the good news;[y] for Isaiah says, "Lord, who has believed our message?" [17]So faith comes from what is heard, and what is heard comes through the word of Christ.[z]

[18]But I ask, have they not heard? Indeed they have; for

"Their voice has gone out to all the earth,
     and their words to the ends of the world."

[19]Again I ask, did Israel not understand? First Moses says,

"I will make you jealous of those who are not a
          nation;
     with a foolish nation I will make you angry."

---

v Or *trusts in it*
w Gk *Brothers*
x Or *namely, that*

y Or *gospel*
z Or *about Christ*; other ancient authorities read *of God*

10:1 *them* Evidently, non-Christian Jews. **10:3** *God's righteousness* That is, righteousness apart from the law, which has now been revealed in Christ. See 3:21–22. **10:4** *end of the law* Or "goal of the law." Paul here touches a main theme of the letter, reiterated in 10:12: Jews and Gentiles stand before God on the same basis of trust in Christ. **10:5** An inexact reference to *Lev.* 18:5. Whereas Moses presents the divine laws as the way to life, Paul cites Moses to make the opposite claim: the law involves *doing*, in contrast to trust (10:6). See Paul's use of the same verse in *Gal.* 3:10–12. **10:6** Paul here undertakes a bold reinterpretation of *Deut.* 30:12–14. There Moses insists that the divine law (Torah) is *within* Israel's reach and is *not* too difficult to observe (see *Deut.* 30:11). Paul, while claiming that the Torah is impossible to fulfill because of the weakness of the flesh (*Rom.* 7:13–25), refers this very passage to faith in Christ. His phrase-by-phrase reinterpretation reflects his view that the meaning of scripture becomes full only in light of Jesus' death and resurrection (see *1 Cor.* 9:9–10; 10:11; *Rom.* 4:23–24). The biblical commentaries of the Dead Sea Scrolls (e.g., *Pesher Habakkuk* [1QpHab]; 4Q169, 171, 173) show another community's efforts in the same period to interpret scripture in the light of its own situation. **10:7** *heaven Deut.* 30:12. LXX, which follows the MT: "it [the law just delivered by Moses] is not in heaven above, [as if one should] say, 'Who will go up into heaven for us, to get it for us, so that we might hear it and do it?'" *abyss Deut.* 30:13. LXX, which follows the MT: "Nor is it across the sea, [as if one should] say, 'Who will cross over to the other side of the sea for us, and get it for us, and make it audible to us so that we might do it?'" **10:8** Paul omits from the end of *Deut.* 30:14 "and in your hands, to do it [the law]." **10:11** Repeating the finale of his adaptation of *Isa.* 28:16 (see *Rom.* 9:33). Recall *Rom.* 1:16, where Paul insists that he is not "ashamed of the gospel" to the Gentiles. Perhaps he already had this verse in mind. **10:13** *Joel* 2:32 (MT 3:5). **10:14** Paul thus appeals for acceptance of his mission to the Gentiles. **10:15** *Isa.* 52:7. MT: "How welcome [or 'beautiful,' 'pleasant'] on the mountain / Are the footsteps [or 'feet'] of the herald / Announcing happiness, / Heralding good fortune, / Announcing victory, / Telling Zion, 'Your God is King!'" LXX: "I [the Lord] am present as a season of beauty upon the mountains, as the feet of one bringing good news of peace, as one proclaiming good news. For I will make known your [Israel's] salvation, saying, 'O Zion, your God shall reign!'" In the Gk, the verb "bring good news" is related to the noun "gospel." **10:16** *Isa.* 53:1. *our message* Lit. "our hearing" or "what we have heard"—the same Gk word as Paul takes up in 10:17: "what is heard." **10:18** *Ps.* 19:4 (MT 19:5; LXX 18:4), which describes heaven and earth's declaring God's glory. Paul's Gk matches the LXX exactly. **10:19** *Deut.* 32:21: Moses' prediction of Israel's temporary punishment by its enemies for having forsaken the law, before God finally vindicates Israel and punishes its enemies (32:26–43). Paul changes the third person of scripture ("them") to direct address.

20Then Isaiah is so bold as to say,

> "I have been found by those who did not seek
>   me;
> I have shown myself to those who did not ask
>   for me."

21But of Israel he says, "All day long I have held out my hands to a disobedient and contrary people."

Israel's Rejection Is Not Final

11 I ask, then, has God rejected his people? By no means! I myself am an Israelite, a descendant of Abraham, a member of the tribe of Benjamin. 2God has not rejected his people whom he foreknew. Do you not know what the scripture says of Elijah, how he pleads with God against Israel? 3"Lord, they have killed your prophets, they have demolished your altars; I alone am left, and they are seeking my life." 4But what is the divine reply to him? "I have kept for myself seven thousand who have not bowed the knee to Baal." 5So too at the present time there is a remnant, chosen by grace. 6But if it is by grace, it is no longer on the basis of works, otherwise grace would no longer be grace.a

7What then? Israel failed to obtain what it was seeking. The elect obtained it, but the rest were hardened, 8as it is written,

> "God gave them a sluggish spirit,
>   eyes that would not see
>   and ears that would not hear,
> down to this very day."

9And David says,

> "Let their table become a snare and a trap,
>   a stumbling block and a retribution for them;
> 10 let their eyes be darkened so that they cannot
>   see,
> and keep their backs forever bent."

The Salvation of the Gentiles

11So I ask, have they stumbled so as to fall? By no means! But through their stumblingb salvation has come to the Gentiles, so as to make Israelc jealous. 12Now if their stumblingb means riches for the world, and if their defeat means riches for Gentiles, how much more will their full inclusion mean!

13Now I am speaking to you Gentiles. Inasmuch then as I am an apostle to the Gentiles, I glorify my ministry 14in order to make my own peopled jealous, and thus save some of them. 15For if their rejection is the reconciliation of the world, what will their acceptance be but life from the dead! 16If the part of the dough offered as first fruits is holy, then the whole batch is holy; and if the root is holy, then the branches also are holy.

17But if some of the branches were broken off, and you, a wild olive shoot, were grafted in their place to share the rich roote of the olive tree, 18do not boast over the branches. If you do boast, remember that it is not you that support the root, but the root that supports you. 19You will say, "Branches were broken off so that I might be grafted in." 20That is true. They

---

a Other ancient authorities add *But if it is by works, it is no longer on the basis of grace, otherwise work would no longer be work*

b Gk *transgression*

c Gk *them*

d Gk *my flesh*

e Other ancient authorities read *the richness*

10:20 *Isa.* 65:1. Paul reverses the order of the two clauses but otherwise agrees with the LXX. In *Isaiah*, both this and the next verse (*Isa.* 65:2; see next note) relate to Israel's disobedience. **10:21** *Isa.* 65:2. MT: "I constantly [or 'all day long'] spread out My hands / To a disloyal people." The LXX reads exactly like Paul, except for word order. See previous note. **11:3** Elijah's complaint about Israel's worship of Baal; *1 Kgs.* (LXX *3 Kgdms*) 19:10. Paul reverses the "prophets" and "altars" clauses and omits "by the sword." In the Bible Elijah says this to illustrate his claim that Israel has forsaken God's covenant. **11:4** *seven thousand* The Gk has also "males" here. *Baal 1 Kgs.* 19:18. MT: "I [the Lord] will leave in Israel [i.e., spare from the sword] only seven thousand—every knee that has not knelt to Baal and every mouth that has not kissed him." LXX (*3 Kgdms* 19:18): "And you shall leave [i.e., and shall not have killed] seven thousand males, all the knees that have not bowed the knee to Baal, and every mouth that has not kissed him." The Bible identifies a remnant of Israelites who have not worshipped idols. Paul applies this "remnant" theme to the few Jews who have believed in Christ. **11:5** Paul here returns to the remnant theme anticipated in 9:27–29. **11:8** Closest to *Deut.* 29:4. LXX, which follows MT 29:3: "The Lord God has not given you a heart to know, or eyes to see, or ears to hear, to this day." But Paul's *sluggish spirit* and positive formulation (*God gave*) seem to be imported from *Isa.* 29:10, which is otherwise quite different. **11:10** *Ps.* 69:22–23, speaking of the king's enemies, in retaliation for their crimes against him. MT (69:23–24): "May their table be a trap for them, / a snare for their allies. / May their eyes grow dim so that they cannot see; / may their loins collapse continually." LXX (68:22–23): "Let their table before them become a snare, and a retribution, and a stumbling block [the remainder is exactly as in Paul]." **11:12** This is a common form of rabbinic and other argument, from the weaker or inferior case to the stronger, employed also in 11:15. Paul now begins to hint at the dramatic conclusion coming in 11:26. **11:13** *you Gentiles* These Gentiles are evidently not a local group in Rome (in view of what he will say about them) but the Gentiles of Paul's mission in the eastern Mediterranean, the ones he has been speaking about thus far, who have been "grafted" into salvation and for whom he considers himself the apostle. For rhetorical effect, he addresses his Gentile converts as if they were gathered together in one place. **11:15** See 11:12 and note. **11:16** For the benefit of Paul's Roman readers, the Gentile converts of his mission are cautioned that they have no special or permanent claim on faith in Christ.

were broken off because of their unbelief, but you stand only through faith. So do not become proud, but stand in awe. [21]For if God did not spare the natural branches, perhaps he will not spare you.*f* [22]Note then the kindness and the severity of God: severity toward those who have fallen, but God's kindness toward you, provided you continue in his kindness; otherwise you also will be cut off. [23]And even those of Israel,*g* if they do not persist in unbelief, will be grafted in, for God has the power to graft them in again. [24]For if you have been cut from what is by nature a wild olive tree and grafted, contrary to nature, into a cultivated olive tree, how much more will these natural branches be grafted back into their own olive tree.

All Israel Will Be Saved

[25]So that you may not claim to be wiser than you are, brothers and sisters,*h* I want you to understand this mystery: a hardening has come upon part of Israel, until the full number of the Gentiles has come in. [26]And so all Israel will be saved; as it is written,

"Out of Zion will come the Deliverer;
    he will banish ungodliness from Jacob."
[27] "And this is my covenant with them,
    when I take away their sins."

[28]As regards the gospel they are enemies of God*i* for your sake; but as regards election they are beloved, for the sake of their ancestors; [29]for the gifts and the calling of God are irrevocable. [30]Just as you were once disobedient to God but have now received mercy because of their disobedience, [31]so they have now been disobedient in order that, by the mercy shown to you,

they too may now*j* receive mercy. [32]For God has imprisoned all in disobedience so that he may be merciful to all.

[33]O the depth of the riches and wisdom and knowledge of God! How unsearchable are his judgments and how inscrutable his ways!

[34] "For who has known the mind of the Lord?
     Or who has been his counselor?"
[35] "Or who has given a gift to him,
     to receive a gift in return?"

[36]For from him and through him and to him are all things. To him be the glory forever. Amen.

The New Life in Christ

12 I appeal to you therefore, brothers and sisters,*h* by the mercies of God, to present your bodies as a living sacrifice, holy and acceptable to God, which is your spiritual*k* worship. [2]Do not be conformed to this world,*l* but be transformed by the renewing of your minds, so that you may discern what is the will of God—what is good and acceptable and perfect.*m*

[3]For by the grace given to me I say to everyone among you not to think of yourself more highly than you ought to think, but to think with sober judgment, each according to the measure of faith that God has assigned. [4]For as in one body we have many members, and not all the members have the same function, [5]so we, who are many, are one body in Christ, and individually we are members one of another. [6]We have gifts that differ according to the grace given to us: prophecy, in proportion to faith; [7]ministry, in ministering; the teacher, in teaching;

---

f Other ancient authorities read *neither will he spare you*
g Gk lacks *of Israel*
h Gk *brothers*
i Gk lacks *of God*

j Other ancient authorities lack *now*
k Or *reasonable*
l Gk *age*
m Or *what is the good and acceptable and perfect will of God*

11:24 See 11:12, 15 and note to 11:12. **11:25** *mystery* The closest parallel in the undisputed letters to this use of the word is perhaps *1 Cor.* 15:51, where it refers to something known by special revelation from God; see *1 Cor.* 4:1; *Rom.* 16:25. **11:26–27** *Isa.* 59:20–21. MT: "He shall come as redeemer to Zion, / To those in Jacob who turn back from sin / —declares the Lord. / And this shall be my covenant with them, said the Lord: My spirit which is upon you, and the words which I have placed in your mouth, shall not be absent from your mouth." LXX: "For the sake of Zion will come the Deliverer, and he will turn away ungodliness from Jacob. And this is my covenant with them, said the Lord: [the remainder is as in the MT]." The final clause *(when . . .)* recalls part of *Isa.* 27:9 and *Jer.* 31:33 (MT), which are otherwise different. **11:26** *Israel will be saved* Paul's strongest statement anywhere about the future of Israel. Although some scholars have proposed that Paul suddenly concedes Israel's salvation, as Israel, in much the same terms as rabbinic literature (*m. Sanh.* 10:1—"All Israel has a share in the world to come"), that position would not fit easily with Paul's entire case thus far. More likely, he expresses either a prediction or a hope that all Israel will come to trust Christ and *so* be saved. **11:29** These statements might suggest that Israel will be saved strictly on account of the ancient promises and covenants; but see 11:31. **11:31** This sentence seems to tie Israel's future to its repentance and faith in Christ as a result of the jealousy-producing salvation of the Gentiles. **11:34** *Isa.* 40:13. Paul's Gk agrees almost exactly with the LXX. **11:35** Perhaps loosely based on *Job* 35:7. **12:1** *therefore* Perhaps this section is less a continuation of the argument than it is a rest to consolidate his relationship with the reader by citing common ethical principles. **12:3** *grace given to me* Paul is self-conscious in using his authority in this community, which he did not establish; see 1:12; 15:15. *more highly than you ought* See *Phil.* 2:3. **12:5** See the similar analogy in *1 Cor.* 12:12–31 and the notes there.

8the exhorter, in exhortation; the giver, in generosity; the leader, in diligence; the compassionate, in cheerfulness.

Marks of the True Christian

9Let love be genuine; hate what is evil, hold fast to what is good; 10love one another with mutual affection; outdo one another in showing honor. 11Do not lag in zeal, be ardent in spirit, serve the Lord.*n* 12Rejoice in hope, be patient in suffering, persevere in prayer. 13Contribute to the needs of the saints; extend hospitality to strangers.

14Bless those who persecute you; bless and do not curse them. 15Rejoice with those who rejoice, weep with those who weep. 16Live in harmony with one another; do not be haughty, but associate with the lowly;*o* do not claim to be wiser than you are. 17Do not repay anyone evil for evil, but take thought for what is noble in the sight of all. 18If it is possible, so far as it depends on you, live peaceably with all. 19Beloved, never avenge yourselves, but leave room for the wrath of God;*p* for it is written, "Vengeance is mine, I will repay, says the Lord." 20No, "if your enemies are hungry, feed them; if they are thirsty, give them something to drink; for by doing this you will heap burning coals on their heads." 21Do not be overcome by evil, but overcome evil with good.

Being Subject to Authorities

13 Let every person be subject to the governing authorities; for there is no authority except from God, and those authorities that exist have been instituted by God. 2Therefore whoever resists authority resists what God has appointed, and those who resist will incur judgment. 3For rulers are not a terror to good conduct, but to bad. Do you wish to have no fear of the authority? Then do what is good, and you will receive its approval; 4for it is God's servant for your good. But if you do what is wrong, you should be afraid, for the authority*q* does not bear the sword in vain! It is the servant of God to execute wrath on the wrongdoer. 5Therefore one must be subject, not only because of wrath but also because of conscience. 6For the same reason you also pay taxes, for the authorities are God's servants, busy with this very thing. 7Pay to all what is due them—taxes to whom taxes are due, revenue to whom revenue is due, respect to whom respect is due, honor to whom honor is due.

Love for One Another

8Owe no one anything, except to love one another; for the one who loves another has fulfilled the law. 9The commandments, "You shall not commit adultery; You shall not murder; You shall not steal; You shall not covet"; and any other commandment, are summed up in this word, "Love your neighbor as yourself." 10Love does no wrong to a neighbor; therefore, love is the fulfilling of the law.

An Urgent Appeal

11Besides this, you know what time it is, how it is now the moment for you to wake from sleep. For salvation is nearer to us now than when we became believers; 12the night is far gone, the day is near. Let us then lay aside the works of darkness and put on the armor of light; 13let us live honorably as in the day, not in reveling and drunkenness, not in debauchery and licentiousness, not in quarreling and jealousy. 14Instead, put on the Lord Jesus Christ, and make no provision for the flesh, to gratify its desires.

Do Not Judge Another

14 Welcome those who are weak in faith,*r* but not for the purpose of quarreling over opinions. 2Some believe in eating anything, while the weak eat

---

n Other ancient authorities read *serve the opportune time*
o Or *give yourselves to humble tasks*
p Gk *the wrath*

q Gk it
r Or *conviction*

12:12 See *Phil.* 4:4–7; *1 Thess.* 5:12–22. **12:14** See Jesus' words according to *Matt.* 5:10–12, 44 and parallels. **12:19** Loosely based on *Lev.* 19:18; *Deut.* 32:35. **12:20** *Prov.* 25:21–22. Paul's Gk agrees exactly with the LXX. **13:9** *steal Exod.* 20:13–14; *Deut.* 5:17–18. The MT prohibits murder before adultery in both passages; the LXX has the prohibition of adultery and stealing before that of murder in *Exodus* 20. **yourself** *Lev.* 19:18. **13:12** See *1 Thess.* 5:4–11. See *1 Thess.* 1:9–10; 4:13–5:11; *1 Cor.* 7:25–31; 15:51. This is the only eschatological note, except for 16:20, in this long letter to Rome. **14:1** Paul begins now gradually to build toward his final appeal for the acceptance of his Gentile mission. He opens with general remarks about tolerance. Attempts to identify the *weak in faith* with some subgroup of the Roman Christians have not proved compelling (but see note to 14:14). **14:2** A vegetarian diet was admired by many, both Gentiles and Jews, in the 1st century as the most "philosophical" way to eat (Plutarch, *Advice about Keeping Well* 131e–132a). Further, many Jews opted for vegetarian diets when properly prepared (kosher) meat was unavailable (Josephus, *Ant.* 10.194; *Life* 14). And some Gentile Christians, out of concern for the origins of meat in local sacrifices, also abstained (*1 Corinthians* 8–10). Some commentators have attempted to identify these vegetarians as a Jewish subgroup among the Roman Christians (over against a Gentile majority), but the size of the Roman Jewish community—in the tens of thousands—would have ensured the availability of kosher food in several quarters of the city. Paul seems, rather, to be speaking of lifestyle conflicts that could arise within any Christian group, Jew or Gentile.

only vegetables. ³Those who eat must not despise those who abstain, and those who abstain must not pass judgment on those who eat; for God has welcomed them. ⁴Who are you to pass judgment on servants of another? It is before their own lord that they stand or fall. And they will be upheld, for the Lord*s* is able to make them stand.

⁵Some judge one day to be better than another, while others judge all days to be alike. Let all be fully convinced in their own minds. ⁶Those who observe the day, observe it in honor of the Lord. Also those who eat, eat in honor of the Lord, since they give thanks to God; while those who abstain, abstain in honor of the Lord and give thanks to God.

⁷We do not live to ourselves, and we do not die to ourselves. ⁸If we live, we live to the Lord, and if we die, we die to the Lord; so then, whether we live or whether we die, we are the Lord's. ⁹For to this end Christ died and lived again, so that he might be Lord of both the dead and the living.

¹⁰Why do you pass judgment on your brother or sister?*t* Or you, why do you despise your brother or sister?*t* For we will all stand before the judgment seat of God.*u* ¹¹For it is written,

"As I live, says the Lord, every knee shall bow to me,

and every tongue shall give praise to*v* God."
¹²So then, each of us will be accountable to God.*w*

Do Not Make Another Stumble

¹³Let us therefore no longer pass judgment on one another, but resolve instead never to put a stumbling block or hindrance in the way of another.*x* ¹⁴I know and am persuaded in the Lord Jesus that nothing is unclean in itself; but it is unclean for anyone who thinks it unclean. ¹⁵If your brother or sister*t* is being injured by what you eat, you are no longer walking in love. Do not let what you eat cause the ruin of one for whom Christ died. ¹⁶So do not let your good be spoken of as evil. ¹⁷For the kingdom of God is not food and drink but righteousness and peace and joy in the Holy Spirit. ¹⁸The one who thus serves Christ is acceptable to God and has human approval. ¹⁹Let us then pursue what makes for peace and for mutual upbuilding. ²⁰Do not, for the sake of food, destroy the work of God. Everything is indeed clean, but it is wrong for you to make others fall by what you eat; ²¹it is good not to eat meat or drink wine or do anything that makes your brother or sister*t* stumble.*y* ²²The faith that you have, have as your own conviction before God. Blessed are those who have no reason to condemn themselves because of what they approve. ²³But those who have doubts are condemned if they eat, because they do not act from faith;*z* for whatever does not proceed from faith*z* is sin.*a*

---

s Other ancient authorities read *for God*
t Gk *brother*
u Other ancient authorities read *of Christ*
v Or *confess*
w Other ancient authorities lack *to God*

x Gk *of a brother*
y Other ancient authorities add *or be upset or be weakened*
z Or *conviction*
a Other authorities, some ancient, add here 16.25–27

14:5 Once again Paul notes a common difference among Christians everywhere: calendar observance. Since he singles out *one day* as better than the others, he might well be referring to the Sabbath. Gentiles did not traditionally keep one regular day of rest aside from the other days of the week; their holidays were irregular, based on local celebrations. If the Sabbath is meant, then Paul is referring to Jews, proselytes (full converts to Judaism), sympathizers, and others who had adopted the Jewish practice. Josephus claims that by the end of the 1st century, Sabbath observance had been widely adopted (*Ag. Ap.* 2.282). It is also possible, in view of the next sentence, that some Christians had begun to single out Sunday, the day on which Christians met early to celebrate Jesus' resurrection, as a special day. **14:8** The practical implication of Paul's oft-repeated position that, in view of the coming of Christ, all of the "old" cultural issues are immaterial. See *2 Cor.* 5:17; *Gal.* 3:28; *Rom.* 10:12. **14:10** *judgment seat* Paul's word for *judgment seat* is *bēma*, the place where a Roman governor would hear cases (see *Acts* 12:21; 18:12, 16; *1 Cor.* 3:12–15.). The *bēma* in Corinth has been found by archaeologists. **14:11** *Isa.* 45:23. MT: "By Myself have I sworn, / [two lines omitted] To Me every knee shall bend, / Every tongue swear loyalty." LXX: "By myself I swear [two lines omitted], that every knee shall bow to me, and every tongue shall swear by God." **14:14** *nothing is unclean in itself* This apparently innocent statement reflects a radical position: Paul has laid aside the dietary laws that were part and parcel of Jewish culture (*Deut.* 14:3–21), laws that attracted considerable attention, often ridicule, from Gentiles in his day. See the words attributed to Jesus in *Mark* 7:19, and the note there. **unclean** The language of "clean" and "unclean" for food derives from the Jewish biblical tradition (*Deut.* 14:3–21) but was not a common way for Gentile vegetarians to describe food. What we may have in Rome, then, are differences among Jewish-Christians, between those who have been more influenced by Paul's understanding of Jesus' significance—such as Prisca and Aquila, Epaenetus, Andronicus and Junia, Urbanus, and Rufus (*Romans* 16)—and those who have not been so influenced. **14:20** *clean* See previous note. **14:21** Paul has not so far discussed wine. The use of wine (normally mixed with water) was general in Greco-Roman antiquity, and Jews were known for their use of it (Persius, *Satires* 5.179–84; Plutarch, *Convivial Questions* 4.6.2). Again, in both Jewish and Gentile circles, wine could be forfeited under special circumstances or for "philosophical" purposes (Plutarch, *Advice about Keeping Well* 132b–f).

Please Others, Not Yourselves

15 We who are strong ought to put up with the failings of the weak, and not to please ourselves. ²Each of us must please our neighbor for the good purpose of building up the neighbor. ³For Christ did not please himself; but, as it is written, "The insults of those who insult you have fallen on me." ⁴For whatever was written in former days was written for our instruction, so that by steadfastness and by the encouragement of the scriptures we might have hope. ⁵May the God of steadfastness and encouragement grant you to live in harmony with one another, in accordance with Christ Jesus, ⁶so that together you may with one voice glorify the God and Father of our Lord Jesus Christ.

The Gospel for Jews and Gentiles Alike

⁷Welcome one another, therefore, just as Christ has welcomed you, for the glory of God. ⁸For I tell you that Christ has become a servant of the circumcised on behalf of the truth of God in order that he might confirm the promises given to the patriarchs, ⁹and in order that the Gentiles might glorify God for his mercy. As it is written,

"Therefore I will confess[b] you among the
Gentiles,
and sing praises to your name";
¹⁰and again he says,

"Rejoice, O Gentiles, with his people";
¹¹and again,
"Praise the Lord, all you Gentiles,
and let all the peoples praise him";
¹²and again Isaiah says,
"The root of Jesse shall come,
the one who rises to rule the Gentiles;
in him the Gentiles shall hope."
¹³May the God of hope fill you with all joy and peace in believing, so that you may abound in hope by the power of the Holy Spirit.

Paul's Reason for Writing So Boldly

¹⁴I myself feel confident about you, my brothers and sisters,[c] that you yourselves are full of goodness, filled with all knowledge, and able to instruct one another. ¹⁵Nevertheless on some points I have written to you rather boldly by way of reminder, because of the grace given me by God ¹⁶to be a minister of Christ Jesus to the Gentiles in the priestly service of the gospel of God, so that the offering of the Gentiles may be acceptable, sanctified by the Holy Spirit. ¹⁷In Christ Jesus, then, I have reason to boast of my work for God. ¹⁸For I will not venture to speak of anything except what Christ has accomplished[d] through me to win obedience from the Gentiles, by word and deed, ¹⁹by the power of signs and wonders, by the power of the Spirit of God,[e] so that from Jerusalem and as far

---

b Or *thank*

c Gk *brothers*

d Gk *speak of those things that Christ has not accomplished*

e Other ancient authorities read *of the Spirit* or *of the Holy Spirit*

15:1–7 This reads as a summary statement of the general exhortation to get along in spite of religiously grounded lifestyle differences. Paul's main concern, however, is to apply this general principle of toleration to the issue at hand: the acceptance of his Gentile mission. He now turns to this application. **15:1** See 14:14, 20. In the Corinthian correspondence, by contrast, Paul consistently takes the position of the "weak" over against the strong (see *1 Cor.* 1:25, 27; 2:3; 4:10–13; 8:7–13; 10:19–22; *2 Cor.* 10:10). **15:3** *Ps.* 69:9 (MT 69:10; LXX 68:9). Paul's Gk agrees exactly with the LXX. **15:4** Paul's characteristic position. See *1 Cor.* 9:9–10; 10:11; *Rom.* 4:23–24; 10:6. **15:9** Paul here reverts to the theme of the letter: salvation for the Jews, yes, but equally for the Gentiles. See 1:3–5, 16; 3:9, 21–22, 29–30. **written** Although Paul has insisted that all Christians welcome all other Christians, the following four proof texts all relate to the inclusion of Gentiles, as does what follows them. It seems to be the welcoming of *Gentiles* through his ministry that is Paul's ultimate concern. **your name** *Ps.* 18:49 (MT 18:50; LXX 17:49). Paul's Gk agrees exactly with the LXX. The Gk and Hebrew words for "Gentiles" cited in these biblical texts have the sense of "nations [of the world]," not individual non-Jews. Paul has applied them, however, to the individual Gentiles who have accepted his gospel. **15:10** *Deut.* 32:43. MT: "O nations, acclaim His people! / For He'll avenge the blood of His servants, / wreak vengeance on his foes." LXX (32:43b) reads exactly like Paul. Paul depends here on the LXX translation, which already had the tendency to facilitate Jewish-Gentile relations, since it was produced for Jews living in the Diaspora. **15:11** *Ps.* 117:1. LXX (116:1), which follows the MT: "Praise the Lord, all you Gentiles [nations]; praise him all you peoples." **15:12** *Isa.* 11:10. MT: "In that day, / The stock of Jesse that has remained standing / Shall become a standard to peoples — / Nations shall seek his counsel / And his abode shall be honored." The LXX reads exactly like Paul, but with the insertion of "in that day" in the first clause. **15:14** See 1:12. Note again Paul's unusual admission—in sharp contrast to his other letters—of the readers' independence from him. **15:16** **priestly service** Paul evokes the historic mission of Israel to be a "kingdom of priests, a holy nation" in the world (*Exod.* 19:4–6) and implies that his mission to the Gentiles fulfills this mandate. See 1:1, 5. **offering of the Gentiles** Does Paul mean "the offering that consists of the Gentiles" or "the offering [of money] *from* the Gentiles"? The latter is supported by what follows (15:25–26), but Paul may have both senses in view here. **15:17** Paul now begins to conclude the presentation, which he began in 1:16, of his gospel ("special announcement") for Gentiles and its implications for Judaism. **15:19** **around** The region in question describes a large arc, from Judea through northwestern Greece.

around as Illyricum I have fully proclaimed the good news*f* of Christ. 20Thus I make it my ambition to proclaim the good news,*f* not where Christ has already been named, so that I do not build on someone else's foundation, 21but as it is written,

> "Those who have never been told of him shall see,
> and those who have never heard of him shall
> understand."

Paul's Plan to Visit Rome

22This is the reason that I have so often been hindered from coming to you. 23But now, with no further place for me in these regions, I desire, as I have for many years, to come to you 24when I go to Spain. For I do hope to see you on my journey and to be sent on by you, once I have enjoyed your company for a little while. 25At present, however, I am going to Jerusalem in a ministry to the saints; 26for Macedonia and Achaia have been pleased to share their resources with the poor among the saints at Jerusalem. 27They were pleased to do this, and indeed they owe it to them; for if the Gentiles have come to share in their spiritual blessings, they ought also to be of ser-vice to them in material things. 28So, when I have completed this, and have delivered to them what has been collected,*g* I will set out by way of you to Spain; 29and I know that when I come to you, I will come in the fullness of the blessing*h* of Christ.

30I appeal to you, brothers and sisters,*i* by our Lord Jesus Christ and by the love of the Spirit, to join me in earnest prayer to God on my behalf, 31that I may be rescued from the unbelievers in Judea, and that my ministry*j* to Jerusalem may be acceptable to the saints, 32so that by God's will I may come to you with joy and be refreshed in your company. 33The God of peace be with all of you.*k* Amen.

Personal Greetings

16I commend to you our sister Phoebe, a deacon*l* of the church at Cenchreae, 2so that you may welcome her in the Lord as is fitting for the saints, and help her in whatever she may require from you, for she has been a benefactor of many and of myself as well.

3Greet Prisca and Aquila, who work with me in Christ Jesus, 4and who risked their necks for my life,

---

f Or *gospel*

g Gk *have sealed to them this fruit*
h Other ancient authorities add *of the gospel*
i Gk *brothers*
j Other ancient authorities read *my bringing of a gift*
k One ancient authority adds 16.25–27 here
l Or *minister*

15:20 See *1 Cor.* 3:10–15; *2 Cor.* 10:13–18, where Paul complains about those who have built on his foundation. **15:21** *Isa.* 52:15. MT: "For they [the nations] shall see what has not been told them, / Shall behold what they have never heard." The LXX reads exactly like Paul. The "of him" in the LXX and Paul refers to the Servant of the Lord, the subject of the passage in *Isaiah.* **15:24** See 1:13–15. Since the Roman church does not fall within Paul's Gentile mission area but belongs to someone else, he will visit only in passing. **15:26** The major collection in which Paul has been engaged for years (*1 Cor.* 16:1–4; *2 Corinthians* 8–9; perhaps *Gal.* 2:10) is finally ready, and he will soon leave Corinth for Jerusalem with it. Note that (a) Paul does not even hint at a contribution from the Romans to this offering *from the Gentiles,* and (b) he does not mention any contribution from Galatia, although the Galatians had been early contributors (*1 Cor.* 16:1–2). Point (a) may confirm that the Roman Christians are Jewish. Point (b) may indicate that the rupture between Paul and the Galatians (see *Gal.* 4:15–20) finally removed them from his circle. **15:31** *the unbelievers* Or "the disobedient," possibly including Christian Jews who have difficulty with Paul's kind of Gentile mission, as the second half of the verse suggests (see also *Acts* 21:20–21). But since Paul uses the Gk term elsewhere in *Romans* (2:8; 10:21; 11:30, 31) to refer to those who do not believe at all, in this verse he is probably referring to anticipated problems from both non-Christian (*the unbelievers* [or "the disobedient"]) and Christian (*the saints*) Judeans. **16:1–27** Some scholars think that the unusual character of ch. 16, with its long list of greetings, comes from another letter. There is no manuscript evidence for this, although one manuscript inserts the doxology of 16:25–27 before the *Amen* at 15:33. The interpretation of *Romans* proposed here (see introduction to *Romans*) finds great value in ch. 16 with its long list of greetings. **16:1** Paul apparently writes from Corinth, for which Cenchreae was a neighboring port. Phoebe will apparently bring his letter to Rome. There was no postal service for nongovernmental business in Paul's day; one had to send mail through traveling friends and acquaintances. **16:3** This long list of greetings, mentioning twenty-eight individuals, is unparalleled in Paul's letters. It seems that he has an urgent need to consolidate his connections with this group and to extend them as far as possible. *Prisca and Aquila* Christian Jews (*Acts* 18:2) who worked with Paul in his Gentile mission. This husband and wife both have Latin names, unlike most others in the list, even though they (or he?) came from provincial Pontus (*Acts* 18:2). Since they were able to travel extensively, and sometimes hosted churches in their house, they were likely freeborn (not slaves) and comfortable relative to the majority. They reportedly worked with leather or linen in the manufacture of tents and awnings for private use (*Acts* 18:3). Paul's unusual mention of the wife's name first (contrast *Acts*) might suggest that she had more of a leadership role. According to *Acts* 18:2, the couple were among the Jews expelled from Rome by Claudius (see introduction). By the time Paul writes to Rome, they have obviously found a way to return. *work with me* See *1 Cor.* 16:19. While they were in Ephesus, according to *Acts*, the couple provided accommodation for Paul—a fellow tentmaker or leatherworker (*Acts* 18:3)—and a meeting place (probably very

to whom not only I give thanks, but also all the churches of the Gentiles. ⁵Greet also the church in their house. Greet my beloved Epaenetus, who was the first convert^m in Asia for Christ. ⁶Greet Mary, who has worked very hard among you. ⁷Greet Andronicus and Junia,^n my relatives^o who were in prison with me; they are prominent among the apostles, and they were in Christ before I was. ⁸Greet Ampliatus, my beloved in the Lord. ⁹Greet Urbanus, our co-worker in Christ, and my beloved Stachys. ¹⁰Greet Apelles, who is approved in Christ. Greet those who belong to the family of Aristobulus. ¹¹Greet my relative^p Herodion. Greet those in the Lord who belong to the family of Narcissus. ¹²Greet those workers in the Lord, Tryphaena and Tryphosa. Greet the beloved Persis, who has worked hard in the Lord. ¹³Greet Rufus, chosen in the Lord; and greet his mother—a mother to me also. ¹⁴Greet Asyncritus, Phlegon,

---

m Gk *first fruits*
n Or *Junias*; other ancient authorities read *Julia*
o Or *compatriots*

p Or *compatriot*

---

small) for some Christians. It is easy to see why this couple, Jewish Christians who had worked so closely with Paul, would be first on his list of greetings. Apparently, he wishes that all Jewish Christians in Rome would follow their example of acceptance and cooperation with his mission. **16:4 *all the churches of the Gentiles*** Paul does not hesitate to speak for all Gentile churches, of which he is the apostle (15:16–18), apparently to the exclusion of the Romans. Although Paul does not use the word for "church" *(ekklēsia)* elsewhere in Romans, he will use it five times in this chapter, of his own followers and associates' groups. He shows the same kind of reserve as he does with the term *euangelion* ("gospel"); see note to 6:17. **16:5 *house*** Throughout at least the first few Christian generations, most Christians met in the homes of their more prosperous (though generally still far from affluent) members. ***Epaenetus, who was the first convert in Asia*** Evidently one of the many non-Romans now living in Rome, about whom Roman intellectuals complained. That he is mentioned second and is known to Paul suggests that he, like Prisca and Aquila, has been influenced by, quite likely converted through, Paul's ministry. Asia was the westernmost province of Anatolia (Turkey), of which the capital was Ephesus. **16:6 *Mary*** Some Gk manuscripts have Maria, others Mariam, representing the Hebrew Miriam. But the form *Maria,* which is widely attested on inscriptions from Roman and Italian Jews, can be the feminine form of the Latin family name *Marius.* **16:7 *Andronicus and Junia*** Probably husband and wife although the second name has often been read as a masculine Junias. Since the feminine Junia is common in inscriptions but the closest masculine forms are Junius, Junio, and Junianus, we should probably read "Junia" (feminine) as translated here. In any case, the pairing of these names suggests a couple. ***relatives*** Not literally. The same Gk word is used in 16:11, 21; it is part of the familial vocabulary used throughout this passage, e.g., "mother," "brother," "beloved." Although some scholars have argued that it means "fellow-Jews" (so that persons not so designated are Gentiles), the word does not mean "fellow nationals" but "relatives," quite in keeping with these other forms of familial affection. ***apostles*** It is unclear whether Paul regards them as apostles or means that they are well known *to* the other apostles. Given the enormous prestige that attaches to the term "apostle" elsewhere in Paul (e.g., *1 Cor.* 9:1–2), the latter seems more likely. If they were themselves prominent apostles, it would be strange for Paul to mention them so incidentally. ***before I was*** This seems to mark Andronicus and Junia as Jewish Christians, since Paul's was apparently the first mission to Gentiles who remained Gentiles (*Gal.* 2:7–9). If they were Christians even before Paul—and thus very soon after Jesus' death and resurrection—then (a) they were likely converted elsewhere and came to Rome later, and (b) it is understandable why they would be well known to the first apostles. **16:8 *Ampliatus*** This is a widely attested Latin third name *(cognomen),* but this person does not otherwise appear in the early Christian texts. **16:9 *Urbanus*** This is a widely attested Latin third name *(cognomen),* although the bearer is otherwise unknown. That he is one of the few called a fellow-worker of Paul indicates that (a) he, too, has been outside Rome for some period, (b) he has some limited means for independent travel, and probably (c) he has accepted Paul's gospel to some extent. ***Stachys*** This name does not appear widely in ancient inscriptions and literature. In only three of the eleven instances, it is known to have belonged to slaves or former slaves. **16:10 *Apelles*** Apparently named after a famous painter (see Pliny, *Natural History* 35.79). About half the contemporary instances of this name are known to have belonged to slaves or former slaves. ***family of Aristobulus*** The Gk does not specify "family"; it would more naturally refer to the larger household—including the slaves, freedmen, and perhaps female family members of Aristobulus. The man himself was probably not a Christian, since he is not greeted. His Gk name was rare in Rome but was common among Herod the Great's descendants, who had close ties to Rome. He may have been a member of the Herodian family, which had brought slaves from the East. The Christians in this household may have formed their own house-church group. **16:11 *relative Herodion*** Not a literal relative; see note to 16:7. The name is not otherwise attested in Rome and may indicate a freed slave from the Herodian family. ***family of Narcissus*** See the note to "Aristobulus" in 16:10. *Those in the Lord* of Narcissus's household would be the Christian subgroup among his domestics. Narcissus himself appears to be a wealthy household-owner, not necessarily a believer himself. **16:12 *Tryphaena and Tryphosa*** About half the instances of these names found in the ancient documentation are known to have belonged to slaves or former slaves. ***Persis*** An ethnic name meaning "Persian," possibly reflecting slave origins. **16:13 *Rufus*** An extremely common Latin *cognomen* ("Red"), though the bearer is otherwise unknown. That Rufus's mother has hosted Paul or otherwise helped him suggests that (a) the family is free, not slave, (b) it has traveled somewhat, and (c) it, too, has been influenced by Paul's gospel. *Mark* 15:21 mentions a Rufus apparently known to the author, and Rome has often been proposed as the place where *Mark* was written.

Hermes, Patrobas, Hermas, and the brothers and sisters*q* who are with them. [15]Greet Philologus, Julia, Nereus and his sister, and Olympas, and all the saints who are with them. [16]Greet one another with a holy kiss. All the churches of Christ greet you.

Final Instructions

[17]I urge you, brothers and sisters,*q* to keep an eye on those who cause dissensions and offenses, in opposition to the teaching that you have learned; avoid them. [18]For such people do not serve our Lord Christ, but their own appetites,*r* and by smooth talk and flattery they deceive the hearts of the simple-minded. [19]For while your obedience is known to all, so that I rejoice over you, I want you to be wise in what is good and guileless in what is evil. [20]The God of peace will shortly crush Satan under your feet. The grace of our Lord Jesus Christ be with you.*s*

---

q Gk *brothers*
r Gk *their own belly*
s Other ancient authorities lack this sentence

[21]Timothy, my co-worker, greets you; so do Lucius and Jason and Sosipater, my relatives.*t*
[22]I Tertius, the writer of this letter, greet you in the Lord.*u*
[23]Gaius, who is host to me and to the whole church, greets you. Erastus, the city treasurer, and our brother Quartus, greet you.*v*

Final Doxology

[25]Now to God*w* who is able to strengthen you according to my gospel and the proclamation of Jesus Christ, according to the revelation of the mystery that was kept secret for long ages [26]but is now disclosed, and through the prophetic writings is made known to all the Gentiles, according to the command of the eternal God, to bring about the obedience of faith— [27]to the only wise God, through Jesus Christ, to whom*x* be the glory forever! Amen.*y*

---

t Or *compatriots*
u Or *I Tertius, writing this letter in the Lord, greet you*
v Other ancient authorities add verse 24, *The grace of our Lord Jesus Christ be with all of you. Amen.*
w Gk *the one*
x Other ancient authorities lack *to whom.* The verse then reads, *to the only wise God be the glory through Jesus Christ forever. Amen.*
y Other ancient authorities lack 16.25–27 or include it after 14.23 or 15.33; others put verse 24 after verse 27

16:14 These names are all Gk. They may well be slaves or freedmen, since many Greeks came to Rome as slaves, but we cannot be sure. **16:15** *Philologus* ("lover of language") could be a Greek teacher. *Nereus* and *Olympas* are also Gk names, possibly of slaves or freedmen. *Julia* is the family *(gens)* name of the Julio-Claudian dynasty. The bearer was most likely a former slave of the imperial family, who took the name when she was freed. **16:16** Is there a connection between this greeting from *all the churches* and Paul's withholding of the term "church" from the Roman Christian community (except for the group at Prisca's house)? He may have wished to reserve the special terms *euangelion* ("gospel") and *ekklēsia* ("church") for his own Gentile groups. **16:17** See 6:17. Again Paul fails to call what the Romans believe "gospel." **16:20** *feet* One of the very few eschatological notes in this long letter. See 2:16; 13:11–12. **16:21** *relatives* See 16:7, 11 and notes. **16:22** *the writer of this letter* Paul ordinarily dictated his letters to a scribe. Sometimes he appended a greeting in his own hand (see *1 Cor.* 16:21; *Gal.* 6:11 [*Col.* 4:18; *2 Thess.* 3:17]). **16:23** *Gaius . . . Erastus* Both names confirm that Paul is writing from Corinth (see 16:1). Gaius is named as a prominent member of the Corinthian church in *1 Cor.* 1:14. In 1929 and 1947, archaeologists found fragments of an inscription at Corinth, from Paul's period, indicating that one Erastus had paved the city square at his own expense in return for his "aedileship." The office of aedile was a high civic honor: Two were elected annually in each major city. Since the Erastus of *Rom.* 16:24 is described as a civic official ("steward" or *treasurer* of the city), he may well have been the Erastus of the inscription, but the difference in title suggests that he had not yet been elected aedile when Paul stayed with him. **16:25–27** Although the best manuscripts include these verses here, a number of others either omit them altogether or locate them elsewhere in *Romans* (after 14:23 or 15:33). Such a blessing of God *(doxology)* is not found at the end of Paul's other letters.

EARLY

CHRISTIAN

READER

LETTERS ATTRIBUTED TO PAUL

THE QUESTION OF PSEUDONYMITY

ALL OF THE LETTERS in this section—*2 Thessalonians, Colossians, Ephesians,* and the Pastoral Epistles *(1 Timothy, 2 Timothy, Titus)*—were accepted into the NT because they were thought to have been written by Paul. At least the first three had apparently circulated with Paul's letters from the earliest period. Since F. C. Baur's analysis of Paul in the nineteenth century, however, scholars have become keenly aware of the tensions between these letters and Paul's other writings. Everyone today acknowledges the disparities in characteristic vocabulary, sentence structure, and ideas. What scholars debate is whether these disparities are best explained by the changed circumstances of Paul's own life or by difference of authorship. Even many conservative scholars entertain the possibility that at least a couple of these letters were written not by Paul himself but by Christians who admired him and perhaps even represented his "school of thought."

There is, of course, much more of interest in these letters than the question of authorship. No matter who wrote them, they present rare and valuable insight into aspects of early Christianity. Each letter is rich in special themes and topics. We shall discuss these larger issues in the specific introduction to each text. Here we restrict ourselves to the basic problem: What if Paul did not write one or more of the letters attributed to him? Why would another early Christian writer impersonate Paul? All the disputed letters claim to be written by Paul, some of them emphatically: "I, Paul, write this greeting with my own hand. This is the mark in every letter of mine; it is the way I write" (*2 Thess.* 3:17; see *Col.* 4:18). Several of them include Paul's detailed travel plans, personal requests, and greetings (*Col.* 4:7–17; *2 Tim.* 4:9–22). Were, then, some other early Christians so bold that they could shamelessly impersonate the apostle in this way?

Reasons for Pseudonymity

The question of pseudonymity (taking a "false name") needs to be viewed, first, in a larger context. Writing under a pseudonym was an old and widespread practice in the Greco-Roman world generally, as also in Jewish circles. It quickly became popular among Christians too. There is a modern convention of pseudonymity, by which famous writers occasionally *create* a false "pen name" in order to disguise their own identity for some reason. Famous examples are George Eliot and Mark Twain. But that is quite different from the ancient practice, in which an inconspicuous writer assumed the name of someone who was already famous. We have numerous writings falsely attributed to Homer, Pythagoras, Demosthenes, Isocrates, Plato, Aristotle, Cicero, Virgil, Ovid, and Seneca; to Enoch, Moses, Joshua, Solomon, and Ezra; to Peter, James, Paul (e.g., *3 Corinthians*), Thomas, Nicodemus, and Clement. In most of these cases, the unknown writer brazenly claims to be the famous person whose name he has adopted.

Occasionally, perhaps, pseudonymity among the literate classes of the Greco-Roman world was motivated simply by the desire to sell more books through association with a famous name. But income from books was not usually significant in a world in which there was no mass printing: few people wrote to make a living from the proceeds. More typically, students involved in rhetorical exercises in school attempted to imitate their targeted author as closely as possible in order to develop their writing skills. Over time, some of the better student works became confused with those of the famous author. The phenomenon of pseudonymity was particularly widespread among students of some great figure, such as a philosopher. Such students might (innocently?) try to co-opt the founder's support for their own ideas by actually putting them in his mouth. We see this obviously with Plato's portrait of his teacher Socrates, though he does not write formally under Socrates's name.

But the most widespread motive for assuming someone else's name, whether in Greco-Roman, Jewish, or Christian culture, was a deep conviction that a classical, more glorious era or golden age had long since passed. Therefore, any writing from the present time was automatically relegated to a secondary, derivative status—unless the new writing could be successfully attributed to one of the great authors of bygone days.

Perhaps one reason why we do not see this kind of pseudonymity today is that we do not venerate the past as the ancients did. Since the Enlightenment, Western society has tended rather to value the new, the creative, the progressive. If the ancients preferred what was old and established, we tend to equate the "new" with the "improved." So, whereas an ancient author was willing to disguise his or her personality behind some revered figure in order to publicize his own ideas, the modern writer can gain little by this technique. On the contrary, he or she usually tries to win over an audience by exposing the *deficiencies* of earlier writers who had been accepted as authorities.

Pseudonymity in Jewish and Christian Circles

The ancient rationale for pseudonymity took on particular nuances in various cultural contexts. For example, in some ancient Jewish circles we find the notion that the spirit of prophecy had been withdrawn from Israel in the Persian period (fourth century B.C.E.; see Josephus, *Ag. Ap.* 1.41). Therefore, any later books that wished to convey a prophetic (often "apocalyptic") message would have been relegated to ignominy had their authors simply declared their real names: "I am Avi and I think that the world is about to end." It helped the prestige of such works to associate them with revered or mysterious figures from Israel's distant past—Enoch, Moses, Solomon, or Ezra. Further, in order to gain credence for their predictions of imminent salvation, the apocalyptic writers often employed a technique known today as "prophecy after the fact" (in Latin, *vaticinium ex eventu*): They *recounted* centuries of Jewish history as if *predicting* it long before it happened, back in the alleged author's time. For this purpose too they had to present themselves as inspired figures from the past.

In Christian circles, the second and third centuries saw a wide diversity of belief about what "Christianity" really meant—from Christian Judaism on the one extreme through apocalypticism and "early catholicism" to so-called gnosticism on the other side. Most of the opposing groups recognized in principle the founding authority of the apostles. Each group claimed, however, that its own interpretation of Christianity was original and "apostolic." The problem was that the genuine writings of the apostolic period allowed considerable room for interpretation. The author of *2 Peter* (3:16) complains about those who "twist" the writings of Paul and others to support their views. One of the best ways to clarify what Paul or Peter or James *really* meant was to produce another document, in his name and if possible in his style, associating one's chosen apostle with the views of one's own party.

The Moral Problem

It is sometimes suggested that the ancient practice of writing in the name of another person, because it seemed necessary or innocent, was not considered morally offensive at the time. This conclusion should be resisted. All the evidence we possess, meager though it is, indicates that if such forgeries were discovered, they would be repudiated. In the Jewish pseudepigrapha ("falsely attributed writings"), for example, the writers frequently anticipate the objection: "If this work was written by Moses (or Daniel or Enoch or Ezra), then why has it only now appeared?" The common refrain in this literature is that God (or an angel) had instructed the seer to seal up the revealed book and hide it until the events described in it should come to pass. The implication is that the long-hidden book has fortunately now been discovered—and look at what it says! The ancient seer had accurately forecast the events of the reader's own day. Apparently, the author of such a document is not playing a game but really wants to convince the reader that his composition is ancient. If his true identity were known, his work would be disdained. But the deceit was transparent enough to the Jewish sages, and so the pseudepigrapha, although accepted and read by the masses, were excluded from the Jewish canon.

Similarly, in Christian circles, obvious frauds were immediately repudiated. The "Muratorian Canon," a list of authoritative Christian writings that is usually dated to the late second century but may come from the fourth, specifically mentions two letters attributed to Paul that were known forgeries. Once they had been exposed as forgeries, they were rejected by the church. The theologian Tertullian (ca. 200) incidentally relates that a Christian presbyter from Asia Minor was removed from his post because he admitted to having composed the *Acts of Paul and Thecla*—"out of love for Paul" (*On Baptism* 17). And Eusebius tells about the second-century bishop of Antioch, Serapion, who was indignant when he determined that the *Gospel of Peter* was a forgery: "we receive both Peter and the other apostles as Christ, but the writings which falsely bear their names we reject" (*Eccl. hist.* 6.12).

So we should not conclude from the widespread practice of pseudonymity, or from its apparent innocence, that it was considered morally acceptable in antiquity. Even less plausible is the suggestion of some commentators that Christianity alone recognized the ethical shortcomings of this practice. Rather, we are faced with the perpetual conflict between moral precept and real human action. Writing under an apostle's name was condemned, *and* it did happen.

Weighing the Evidence

But is it clear that in the first century, such an important phase in Christian beginnings, pseudonymous letter-writing was already a possibility? Indeed it is. *2 Thessalonians* itself, whether written by Paul or not, indicates that at the time of its composition various writers were passing off their own letters as Paul's. The author tells his readers not to be disturbed "by letter purporting to be from us [literally "as if from us"], to the effect that the day of the Lord has come" (2:2). Evidently, there was *already* some controversy over the authenticity of letters claiming to be from Paul. This is confirmed by the closing note (*2 Thess.* 3:17), cited earlier, which insistently offers Paul's handwritten closing greeting as proof of his letter's genuineness. Ironically, that note itself raises a question about the letter, inasmuch as it demonstrates further the possibility of pseudonymity. Whether *2 Thessalonians* is authentic or not, it shows clearly that some Christians were writing letters in Paul's name during or very soon after his lifetime. It is worth noting that Paul's younger contemporary Josephus raises the prospect of forged letters several times in his account of his own life (*Life* 50, 177, 285). Therefore, historically interested students must keep an open mind to the possibility that any particular text is not by the alleged author.

This discussion of imitation and forgery is not intended as proof of the inauthenticity of *2 Thessalonians, Colossians, Ephesians,* or *1 Timothy, 2 Timothy,* and *Titus.* The evidence for each letter must be considered in its own right. The purpose of this introduction is only to face what is probably the biggest—though often unspoken—obstacle in the debate over authenticity. On the basis of modern analogies, a student might suppose that a letter's forthright claim to Pauline authorship itself creates a compelling case in favor of its authenticity, which could only be challenged by extraordinary evidence to the contrary, such as a new manuscript discovery. In view of the widespread phenomenon of pseudonymity in the ancient world, however, it is probably safer to allow that we cannot be certain of authorship *in advance* for any letter. Substantial tensions between different groups of letters may cast some doubt on their authorship. Should such tensions appear, it is best to allow them their full weight, rather than adopting heroic measures. If the differences cannot reasonably be seen as resulting from Paul's changes of circumstance and evolution of thought, then we should consider pseudonymity as a possibility. Remember: Paul's honor would not be at stake in such judgments, but only the honor of the anonymous person who committed the forgery. Why protect the forger's image?

Doubt about Paul's authorship is, of course, very far from certainty of non-Pauline authorship. To prove that someone else wrote the letters would require a major step beyond the recognition of problems with Paul's authorship. The letters in this group are those whose authenticity is less certain than that of the seven "undisputed letters" (*1 Thessalonians, 1 Corinthians, Philemon, Philippians, 2 Corinthians, Galatians,* and *Romans*). Few scholars would claim certain knowledge as to their authorship.

For Further Reading

Beker, J. Christiaan. *Heirs of Paul: Paul's Legacy in the New Testament and in the Church Today.* Minneapolis: Fortress, 1991.

Kiley, Mark. *Colossians as Pseudepigraphy.* Sheffield: JSOT Press, 1986.

Metzger, Bruce M. "Literary Forgeries and Canonical Pseudepigrapha." *Journal of Biblical Literature* 91 (1972): 3–14.

To the Holy and Faithful in Christ at Colossae

COLOSSIANS

Authorship, Themes, and Literary Features

The reader of *Colossians* is confronted with a world of ideas and language significantly different from that of Paul's undisputed letters. This new theological outlook must be explained as a result of either changes in Paul's own thinking or authorship by someone other than Paul.

In his undisputed writings, as we have seen, Paul's preaching is fundamentally apocalyptic. Especially in the earlier letters, his orientation is toward the future. "Salvation" is an urgently anticipated event, and means concretely the rescue of Jesus' followers from the wrath that is about to fall on the world (*1 Thess.* 1:9–10; 5:23; *Phil.* 3:20). In *1 Corinthians,* Paul takes issue with teachers who espouse a non-eschatological view, as if trust in Jesus brought ultimate knowledge, power, and wisdom immediately (*1 Cor.* 4:8–10; 3:18–20). Against such teaching, Paul repeatedly asserts there that the present age is a time of suffering and hardship for believers (*1 Cor.* 4:9–13), that this age will soon end (*1 Cor.* 7:26–31; 10:11), and that complete knowledge and wisdom are reserved for the future aeon (*1 Cor.* 13:8–12).

Colossians, however, presents a theology that is conspicuously like that of Paul's Corinthian opponents. It dwells almost exclusively on the present benefits of salvation, on the wisdom, power, and "riches of assured understanding and knowledge of God's mystery" (2:2) that Christians already possess by virtue of Jesus' *past* work in bringing salvation. *Colossians* claims that God "*has* rescued us from the power of darkness and transferred us into the kingdom of his beloved Son" (1:13) and that "you *have come* to fullness in him" (2:10).

This general reorientation is matched in particulars. Whereas the "kingdom of God" is still a future prospect in the undisputed letters (*1 Cor.* 6:9; 15:50; *Gal.* 5:21), here it is an accomplished reality (1:13). Whereas even Paul's latest undisputed letter puts the believer's "resurrection" with Christ in the future (*Rom.* 6:5, 8), *Colossians* seems to adopt Paul's Corinthian opponents' position that "you were buried with him in baptism, you were also raised with him through faith . . ." (2:12–13; 3:1). And whereas *1 Corinthians* 15 looks forward to the day when Christ will finally triumph over the powers of darkness (15:24–28), *Colossians* sees the decisive moment as already past: "[God] disarmed the rulers and authorities and made a public example of them, triumphing over them in [Christ]" (2:15). So the feeling of urgent hope that characterizes Paul's undisputed letters, which is captured in the Aramaic prayer *marana tha* (O Lord, come! [*1 Cor.* 16:22]), has almost completely dissolved in *Colossians.*

Now, it is true that Paul's later letters already began to discuss the present benefits of salvation and also that *Colossians,* in spite of its focus on the present, occasionally hints at a consummation in the indefinite future (1:11, 28; 2:17; 3:4, 24–25). But a profound change has taken place. In Paul's undisputed letters, the other world with which believers should be occupied is a future one; in *Colossians* it is present (thus accessible without delay) and spiritual. So the writer frequently invokes the platonic and (later) gnostic distinctions between shadow and substance (2:17), appearance and reality (2:23), visible and invisible (1:15–16), light and darkness (1:12–13), the world above and the world below (3:2).

In accord with these themes, *Colossians* is more mystical than Paul's undisputed letters. Christ appears here, in language reminiscent of the *tao* and *brahman* of Eastern philosophy, as the unifying principle of all things: "in him all things hold together" (1:17) and "in him the whole fullness of deity dwells bodily" (2:9). In place of the combative tone that prevails in Paul's other letters, *Colossians* presents the cosmic Christ as one who "reconciles" all dualities in himself (1:20, 22). In his undisputed letters Paul describes the church as Christ's "body," but that is obviously a metaphor with a practical moral (*1 Cor.* 12:12–31); *Colossians'* mystical portrayal of Christ as the head of the body and the reconciling "fullness" of all things (ontologically: in his being; 1:17–19) is new.

In brief, then, the case against the authenticity of *Colossians* lies in its peculiar language and theological perspective. The new outlook is not only unattested elsewhere in Paul; it also seems to agree with positions that Paul himself denounced. The letter seems to appropriate Paul for gnostic Christianity.

If Paul did not write *Colossians,* logical candidates for the role of author include Tychicus, Epaphras, Luke, Demas, and Archippus. All of these men receive strong endorsement from Paul at the end of the letter (4:7–17). We know little about them from other sources, though most of them are mentioned in Paul's greetings to Philemon (*Phlm.* 23), except Archippus, who is corecipient of the letter with Philemon (*Phlm.* 2). Archippus appears to be a leading Christian figure in western Asia Minor. Most intriguing is Demas, for *2 Tim.* 4:10 claims that this man abandoned Paul, "having fallen in love with this present world [or 'age']." Perhaps, then, he is among the substantial group of Christians, also mentioned in *2 Tim.* 2:17–18, who claim that "the resurrection has already taken place." Among Paul's Corinthian opponents, both views seem to have gone together: focus on the present benefits of salvation and denial of future resurrection (*1 Cor.* 4:8–13; 15:12). And the *Acts of Paul,* perhaps roughly contemporary with *2 Timothy* (second century), asserts that Demas saw the resurrection as already past (3:14). Since *Colossians* itself supports such views, with its emphasis on past resurrection and present benefits, it is a logical conclusion that one of this circle attempted to seize Paul's support by writing this letter in his name.

The case in favor of authenticity, by contrast, begins with the observation that *Colossians* claims to be written at the end of Paul's career. At the time of writing, the gospel is growing in "the whole world" (1:6) and "has been preached to every creature under heaven" (1:23). The seven undisputed letters, by contrast, all come from Paul's early ministry in the Eastern Mediterranean; but when he finished there he still looked forward to a mission in the West (*Rom.* 15:23–28). In view of its confidence that the gospel has been preached worldwide, therefore, *Colossians* should be assigned to a much later period in Paul's life if it is authentic. And this chronological distance might explain some of the peculiarities noted above. Since Paul's undisputed letters already evince a move away from apocalyptic toward "realized eschatology," why should *Colossians* not be interpreted as a final, extreme product of this development?

Other considerations favor authenticity: *Colossians* circulated with Paul's genuine letters from at least the middle of the second century, and was considered genuine by all of the church fathers who mentioned it; the document contains many personal references, which strike some readers as too casual to be literary inventions (4:7–17); it abounds with Pauline language and ideas, even if these are often used in a strange way; and if *Ephesians* is not Pauline, its author probably borrowed from *Colossians* thinking that this was a Pauline letter.

None of these observations is decisive, however, for there was plenty of time for *Colossians* to find a home among Paul's genuine letters even if it was not Pauline, and more or less artful personal references are common in later Christian literature that is universally considered forged (from the second to fifth centuries). Indeed, the personal remarks in *Colossians* appear to some readers excessive and forced— for example: in the author's reminder that Onesimus is "one of you" (4:9), that the readers have received instructions about Mark (4:10), and that some of his companions belong to "the circumcision" (4:11), which is a somewhat pejorative term to use in direct address.

Date and Setting

If Paul wrote *Colossians,* he wrote it for a Christian group that he did not personally establish; the "assembly" at Colossae was founded by his coworker Epaphras (1:6–9). Colossae lay beside the Lycus River, about twenty miles from Laodicea, in the Roman province of Asia. There is some reason to suppose that this area, anchored in the Asian capital Ephesus, which Paul made his base of operations, would be particularly supportive of Pauline Christianity. Although Paul allegedly writes from prison (4:10, 18), this cannot be either an early imprisonment like the one reflected in *Philippians* or the Roman imprisonment that resulted from his trip to Jerusalem (with the offering from his Gentile churches in the East). Because of its assumption that the gospel has been preached worldwide and because of its peculiar theology, if it is authentic *Colossians* must come from an even later imprisonment than that with which *Acts* closes, and thus from a period in Paul's life about which we can hardly even speculate.

Although *Acts* seems to end Paul's active career with his trip to Jerusalem and subsequent Roman imprisonment, it does not say that he died at that time. The silence of *Acts* can be plausibly explained in various ways even if he did die at that time. But it is also possible that he survived this Roman imprisonment and fulfilled his ambition to preach in the Western Mediterranean (see *Rom.* 15:24). *1 Clement*, which dates from about 90 C.E., asserts that he reached the "furthest limits of the West" before his death (*1 Clement* 5), though we cannot be sure whether the author writes from sure knowledge or infers this from Paul's plans in *Romans*. Eusebius's later claim (in the fourth century) that Paul survived his first Roman imprisonment and was beheaded during a second, also under Nero, is of uncertain origin but agrees with the notice in *1 Clement*.[1]

If Paul wrote *Colossians* during such a second Roman imprisonment, that might explain its many peculiarities. Perhaps, for example, a long career of suffering had led him to de-emphasize the imminence of Jesus' return and to stress rather the past work of Jesus and the present benefits of salvation. Perhaps his serious conflicts with Corinthian Christianity sowed seeds that eventually changed his perspective on some issues. Perhaps he mellowed with age and began to adopt a more conciliatory and also mystical tone. Perhaps his writing style changed considerably with age, for he now composes very long sentences piled up with repetitious nouns, possessives, and adjectives. Perhaps by this time, Christian Judaism was no longer a serious threat to communities within his circle, so it could be treated in such a vague and distant way.

Overview

One of the peculiarities of *Colossians* is the vagueness of purpose and outline. It opens with a greeting (1:1–2) and a thanksgiving (1:3–14) that are typical of Paul's, but then it becomes more of an essay than a letter. The author includes (or creates) a hymn to Christ (1:15–20) and then talks about the faith of the Colossians and himself (1:21–29). Chapter 2 continues the praise of Christ, but intersperses it with vague warnings about rival teachings. Chapter 3 proceeds from an opening statement about what Christ has accomplished to behavioral implications for the readers, which reflect the philosophers' lists of virtues and vices that were in common currency; it closes with exhortations to each category of the

---

[1] *Eccl. hist.* 2.22. Eusebius claims that "there is evidence" of Paul's release from the first Roman imprisonment and preaching in the West, but he cites only *2 Tim.* 4:16–17 (according to his interpretation) as proof. Since this letter itself is of uncertain authorship, it cannot serve as proof. Nevertheless, Eusebius may have had some tradition in the back of his mind.

ancient household: masters and slaves, husbands and wives, parents and children. Chapter 4 contains further general exhortations (4:2–6) and specific personal notices (4:7–17), followed by a closing greeting (4:18).

The Author's Opponents

Much scholarly discussion has dealt with the opponents of the author of *Colossians*. The letter does not combat the opposing party in the vivid style of Paul's undisputed letters—responding to personal criticisms, making pointed arguments on specific issues—and so it is harder to piece together their views. A simple mirror reading of *Colossians* (see the introduction to *Galatians*) produces a group of opponents who make plausible arguments (2:4); value philosophy and wisdom (2:8, 23); value circumcision and the law (2:11, 14); are concerned with matters of food and drink, festivals, new moons, and sabbaths (2:16); value self-abasement, worship of angels, and visions (2:18); support (merely human, says the author) regulations about tasting and handling certain things (2:21); and are generally ascetic (2:23). Putting all of these clues together, many scholars propose that the other teachers are ascetic and gnostic (because of the angels and visions), Christian-Jewish, syncretistic (combining elements of various traditions) teachers.

That description is less than helpful, and it also underestimates the role of rhetoric in the author's remarks about these opponents. For example, just because he insists that his readers not become involved in the "worship of angels," it does not mean that anyone was necessarily advocating worship of angels; indeed, it is a common polemical strategy to exaggerate one's opponents' position. Most of the clues above—sensitivity about food and drink, circumcision, and the Jewish calendar—would fit a group of Christian Jews. So would the reference to angels, for both Paul and the author of *Hebrews* criticize (Christian) Jews for their *alleged* reverence of angels (*Gal.* 3:19–20; 4:8–11; *Heb.* 1:4–2:9).

As for the opponents' "philosophical" overtones, we must remember that Jews in the Roman world, such as Philo, Josephus, and the author of *4 Maccabees*, saw Jewish culture as a philosophy. Indeed, when the author warns his readers not to embrace philosophy according to the "elemental spirits of the universe" (2:8, 20) he uses a phrase similar to that used by Paul in *Galatians* with reference to Christian Judaism (*Gal.* 4:9). *Colossians* perceives Judaism as a rigorous system of prohibitions (2:20–23) stemming from human tradition (2:8);[2] its portrayal of Christian faith, by contrast, is replete with images of treasure, riches, fullness, and life.

Either, then, *Colossians* is Paul's own, mature reflection on Christianity and final repudiation of Judaism or it represents someone's attempt to enlist Paul in favor of a knowledge- and wisdom-based Christianity, akin to gnosticism, but against Judaism.

---

[2]See the gospels' critique of Pharisaic (and Jewish) teaching as human "tradition," or "the precepts of men" (*Matt.* 15:6–8, interpreting *Isa.* 29:13).

For Further Reading

Barclay, John. *Colossians, Philemon.* Sheffield: Sheffield Academic Press, 1997.

Beker, J. Christiaan. *Heirs of Paul: Paul's Legacy in the New Testament and in the Church Today.* Minneapolis: Fortress, 1991.

Furnish. Victor Paul. "Colossians, Epistle to the." Pages 1090–96 in vol. 1 of *Anchor Bible Dictionary.* Edited by D. N. Freedman. 6 vols. New York: Doubleday, 1992.

Kiley, Mark. *Colossians as Pseudepigraphy.* Sheffield: JSOT Press, 1986.

THE LETTER OF PAUL
TO THE COLOSSIANS

Salutation

1 Paul, an apostle of Christ Jesus by the will of God, and Timothy our brother,

[2]To the saints and faithful brothers and sisters[a] in Christ in Colossae:

Grace to you and peace from God our Father.

Paul Thanks God for the Colossians

[3]In our prayers for you we always thank God, the Father of our Lord Jesus Christ, [4]for we have heard of your faith in Christ Jesus and of the love that you have for all the saints, [5]because of the hope laid up for you in heaven. You have heard of this hope before in the word of the truth, the gospel [6]that has come to you. Just as it is bearing fruit and growing in the whole world, so it has been bearing fruit among yourselves from the day you heard it and truly comprehended the grace of God. [7]This you learned from Epaphras, our beloved fellow servant.[b] He is a faithful minister of Christ on your[c] behalf, [8]and he has made known to us your love in the Spirit.

[9]For this reason, since the day we heard it, we have not ceased praying for you and asking that you may be filled with the knowledge of God's[d] will in all spiritual wisdom and understanding, [10]so that you may lead lives worthy of the Lord, fully pleasing to him, as you bear fruit in every good work and as you grow in the knowledge of God. [11]May you be made strong with all the strength that comes from his glorious power, and may you be prepared to endure everything with patience, while joyfully [12]giving thanks to the Father, who has enabled[e] you[f] to share in the inheritance of the saints in the light. [13]He has rescued us from the power of darkness and transferred us into the kingdom of his beloved Son, [14]in whom we have redemption, the forgiveness of sins.[g]

The Supremacy of Christ

[15]He is the image of the invisible God, the firstborn of all creation; [16]for in[h] him all things in heaven and on earth were created, things visible and invisible, whether thrones or dominions or rulers or powers—all things have been created through him and for him. [17]He himself is before all things, and in[h] him all things hold together. [18]He is the head of the body, the church; he is the beginning, the firstborn from the dead, so that he might come to have first place in everything. [19]For in him all the fullness of God was pleased to dwell, [20]and through him God was pleased to reconcile to himself all things,

---

a Gk brothers
b Gk slave
c Other ancient authorities read our
d Gk his

e Other ancient authorities read called
f Other ancient authorities read us
g Other ancient authorities add through his blood
h Or by

1:1–2 A typical Pauline letter opening. **1:4** Thus, Paul did not establish this Christian group; see 1:7. **1:5** *hope laid up for you in heaven* This hope for the future does not seem nearly as urgent as in Paul's other letters. **1:6** *the whole world* Presumably the Mediterranean basin. But even this interpretation would require that Paul's career had advanced considerably beyond *Romans;* see introduction to *Colossians.* **1:7** Thus, Epaphras, not Paul, founded the Colossian Christian community. If *Colossians* is genuine, it addresses the only group known to us that was not established by Paul but that he treated as his own. Roman Christianity, too, did not begin with Paul, but his letter to that group is much more restrained and distant. Perhaps his assumption of a leadership role in Colossae would not violate his principle of not building on another's foundation (*Rom.* 15:20) because Epaphras was part of his entourage (*Phlm.* 23). **1:9–11** Paul speaks of Christian faith in terms of wisdom, understanding, knowledge, and power elsewhere in his letters. Contrast *1 Corinthians* 1–4. **1:12** *saints in the light* Vivid contrast between the children of light and those of darkness was a basic feature of apocalyptic thinking; see *1 Thess.* 5:5 and the Dead Sea Scrolls (1QS; 1QM 1.1). **1:13** Note the past tenses of these verbs; contrast Paul's undisputed letters, in which rescue from the powers of the age is decidedly future (*1 Thess.* 1:9–10; *1 Cor.* 13:8–13; 15:24–25; *2 Cor.* 4:17; 5:2; *Gal.* 1:4). **1:14** *redemption* The purchasing of a slave's freedom. *forgiveness of sins* Paul does not elsewhere speak of the "forgiveness" of sins, but *Acts* (13:38) attributes such language to him. **1:15–17** Perhaps the author envisions Jesus, as some later Christian writers did, as the personification of wisdom (*Sophia*) or God's word (*Logos*), which was God's first creation. See *Proverbs* 8; *John* 1:1–18. **1:18** *head of the body* Paul compares the church to a human body in *1 Cor.* 12:12–31 and *Rom.* 12:4–8, but he does not develop this mystical idea, in which Christ is the real head of a spiritual body. See 1:24. *firstborn from the dead* By resurrection; see *1 Cor.* 15:20. **1:19** *fullness of God* "Fullness" becomes an important term and concept in 2d-century Valentinian (gnostic) Christianity. This mystical conception of fullness does not appear in Paul's undisputed letters but only in *Colossians* (see 2:9) and *Ephesians* (3:19; 4:13). **1:20** *blood of his cross* A phrase not found elsewhere in Paul, who does not speak much about Jesus' blood.

whether on earth or in heaven, by making peace through the blood of his cross.

²¹And you who were once estranged and hostile in mind, doing evil deeds, ²²he has now reconciled[i] in his fleshly body[j] through death, so as to present you holy and blameless and irreproachable before him— ²³provided that you continue securely established and steadfast in the faith, without shifting from the hope promised by the gospel that you heard, which has been proclaimed to every creature under heaven. I, Paul, became a servant of this gospel.

Paul's Interest in the Colossians

²⁴I am now rejoicing in my sufferings for your sake, and in my flesh I am completing what is lacking in Christ's afflictions for the sake of his body, that is, the church. ²⁵I became its servant according to God's commission that was given to me for you, to make the word of God fully known, ²⁶the mystery that has been hidden throughout the ages and generations but has now been revealed to his saints. ²⁷To them God chose to make known how great among the Gentiles are the riches of the glory of this mystery, which is Christ in you, the hope of glory. ²⁸It is he whom we proclaim, warning everyone and teaching everyone in all wisdom, so that we may present everyone mature in Christ. ²⁹For this I toil and

struggle with all the energy that he powerfully inspires within me.

2 For I want you to know how much I am struggling for you, and for those in Laodicea, and for all who have not seen me face to face. ²I want their hearts to be encouraged and united in love, so that they may have all the riches of assured understanding and have the knowledge of God's mystery, that is, Christ himself,[k] ³in whom are hidden all the treasures of wisdom and knowledge. ⁴I am saying this so that no one may deceive you with plausible arguments. ⁵For though I am absent in body, yet I am with you in spirit, and I rejoice to see your morale and the firmness of your faith in Christ.

Fullness of Life in Christ

⁶As you therefore have received Christ Jesus the Lord, continue to live your lives[l] in him, ⁷rooted and built up in him and established in the faith, just as you were taught, abounding in thanksgiving.

⁸See to it that no one takes you captive through philosophy and empty deceit, according to human tradition, according to the elemental spirits of the universe,[m] and not according to Christ. ⁹For in him the whole fullness of deity dwells bodily, ¹⁰and you have come to fullness in him, who is the head of every ruler and authority. ¹¹In him also you were circumcised with a spiritual circumcision,[n] by putting

---

i Other ancient authorities read *you have now been reconciled*
j Gk *in the body of his flesh*

k Other ancient authorities read *of the mystery of God, both of the Father and of Christ*
l Gk *to walk*
m Or *the rudiments of the world*
n Gk *a circumcision made without hands*

1:23 A sweeping statement for Paul, in view of *Rom.* 15:19–24. **1:24** Or "I am completing what is lacking in Christ's afflictions in my flesh for the sake of his body." Paul is saying either that he will somehow complete Christ's sufferings (a unique notion) or that he has so far not suffered as Christ did but is now completing what was lacking in this respect for the church's benefit. On the church as Christ's spiritual body, see 1:18. **1:26–27** The word "mystery" is disproportionately frequent and important in *Colossians* (see 2:2; 4:3) and *Ephesians* (1:9; 3:3, 4, 9; 5:32; 6:19). **1:28** *in all wisdom* Paul does not understand the gospel in terms of wisdom in his undisputed letters. His opponents at Corinth apparently do (see *1 Cor.* 1:12–2:16). *so that we may present everyone mature in Christ* Perhaps at Jesus' return, but the author does not spell this out in the way Paul typically does (*1 Thess.* 1:10; 2:19; 3:13; 5:23; *1 Cor.* 3:12–15; *2 Cor.* 5:10). **2:1** *Laodicea* Downriver about twenty miles from Colossae. They seem to be twin cities in the author's thinking (see 4:16). **2:2–3** Paul elsewhere suggests that Christians do not have assured knowledge and wisdom in their possession. See *1 Cor.* 13:9–12. **2:2** *mystery* See 1:26–27. **2:4** *plausible arguments* See note to 2:8. **2:5** *morale* Lit. "order." **2:8** *philosophy* This is the only occurrence of this word in 1st-century Christian literature, and its connotations are clearly negative. But philosophy in the ancient world was an extremely broad term, referring to any given discipline of life, so we can deduce little about the Colossian opponents from the author's use of this term. Ironically, from the middle of the 2d century, many later Christian writers would endeavor to portray Christianity as a philosophy. *according to human tradition* Ancient philosophical schools tended to see themselves as "traditions" (the same Greek word as here)—as groups devoted to the teaching of a founder from an earlier generation. The Jewish author Josephus saw Jewish culture as a philosophical tradition descended from Moses. Within Jewish circles, the Pharisees were most often credited with (or accused of) holding to special tradition from their own teachers, which their opponents considered merely human; Josephus, *Ant.* 13.297–298; 18.12–15; see *Mark* 7:1–15. *elemental spirits of the universe* Or "elements of the universe." In *Gal.* 4:3, 9, Paul uses this phrase to describe both his Gentile readers' former gods and the heavenly beings who, he says, supervise Judaism. Thus, the phrase refers broadly to the powers of this age who are opposed to Paul's gospel. If one does not follow Christ, one is subject to these elements, as the remainder of the verse confirms. **2:9** *fullness of deity* See 1:19. **2:11** Evidently a response to Jewish opponents.

off the body of the flesh in the circumcision of Christ; 12when you were buried with him in baptism, you were also raised with him through faith in the power of God, who raised him from the dead. 13And when you were dead in trespasses and the uncircumcision of your flesh, God*o* made you*p* alive together with him, when he forgave us all our trespasses, 14erasing the record that stood against us with its legal demands. He set this aside, nailing it to the cross. 15He disarmed*q* the rulers and authorities and made a public example of them, triumphing over them in it.

16Therefore do not let anyone condemn you in matters of food and drink or of observing festivals, new moons, or sabbaths. 17These are only a shadow of what is to come, but the substance belongs to Christ. 18Do not let anyone disqualify you, insisting on self-abasement and worship of angels, dwelling*r* on visions,*s* puffed up without cause by a human way of thinking,*t* 19and not holding fast to the head, from whom the whole body, nourished and held together by its ligaments and sinews, grows with a growth that is from God.

Warnings against False Teachers

20If with Christ you died to the elemental spirits of the universe,*u* why do you live as if you still belonged to the world? Why do you submit to regulations,

21"Do not handle, Do not taste, Do not touch"? 22All these regulations refer to things that perish with use; they are simply human commands and teachings. 23These have indeed an appearance of wisdom in promoting self-imposed piety, humility, and severe treatment of the body, but they are of no value in checking self-indulgence.*v*

The New Life in Christ

3 So if you have been raised with Christ, seek the things that are above, where Christ is, seated at the right hand of God. 2Set your minds on things that are above, not on things that are on earth, 3for you have died, and your life is hidden with Christ in God. 4When Christ who is your*w* life is revealed, then you also will be revealed with him in glory.

5Put to death, therefore, whatever in you is earthly: fornication, impurity, passion, evil desire, and greed (which is idolatry). 6On account of these the wrath of God is coming on those who are disobedient.*x* 7These are the ways you also once followed, when you were living that life.*y* 8But now you must get rid of all such things—anger, wrath, malice, slander, and abusive*z* language from your mouth. 9Do not lie to one another, seeing that you have stripped off the old self with its practices 10and have clothed yourselves with the new self, which is being renewed in knowledge according to the image of its creator.

---

o Gk he
p Other ancient authorities read made us; others, made
q Or divested himself of
r Other ancient authorities read not dwelling
s Meaning of Gk uncertain
t Gk by the mind of his flesh
u Or the rudiments of the world

v Or are of no value, serving only to indulge the flesh
w Other authorities read our
x Other ancient authorities lack on those who are disobedient (Gk the children of disobedience)
y Or living among such people
z Or filthy

2:12 Contrast *Rom.* 6:3–6, in which resurrection is still future. **uncircumcision of your flesh** Thus, Paul's readers were Gentiles. **2:14 erasing the record that stood against us with its legal demands** Or "erasing the subscription to the ordinances, which stood against us." The author seems to be speaking of the Torah. **2:15 Disarmed** and **triumphing over** might suggest to Paul's readers the actions of a victorious general in war who leads his captives through the streets in humiliation. The author may be writing after the failed Jewish revolt against Rome and linking the victorious Titus's triumph (with captured Judean leaders in tow) with Christ's victory over the heavenly powers that allegedly supervised Judaism (see note to 2:8). Contrast *1 Cor.* 15:24–28, according to which the subjection of all things under Christ is still future. **2:16** The Jewish calendar is apparently meant. See *Gal.* 4:10. **2:17** The shadow-substance metaphor was commonplace in Paul's world and had been since Plato. The image here matches closely Paul's routine connection between Judaism and the transient material world, on the one hand, and Christ and eternal spiritual truth on the other (*Phil.* 3:3–21; *Gal.* 3:2–5). **2:18 worship of angels** Christian authors sometimes implicitly equated Judaism with the worship of angels; see *Heb.* 1:4–2:2; 2:5; *Gal.* 3:19–20; 4:3, 9. **2:20** See note to 2:8. In this respect the author shares Paul's view of Christian experience as a completely new creation over against all former modes of life, effected through the believer's participation in Christ's death (see *2 Cor.* 5:17; *Gal.* 6:14–15). **2:21** The author seems to be referring to prohibited foods and, in view of his allusions to the Jewish calendar and circumcision, to Jewish dietary laws based in the Bible (*Deut.* 14:3–21 and parallels). **3:1** Paul does not elsewhere mention as past the believer's resurrection with Christ (see *1 Thess.* 4:13–18; *1 Cor.* 15; *Phil.* 3:1–11). **3:2** This continues the encouragement to shun the rival Christian-Jewish teachers and their views. **3:3** See note to 2:20. **3:4** The author holds out a future hope, similar to Paul's, of Jesus' return *in glory* (e.g., *1 Thess.* 4:13–18; *1 Cor.* 15:50–57) although it is not central to this work. **3:5–8** 1st-century moral philosophers commonly compiled such lists of vices (and virtues). See also *1 Cor.* 6:9–10; *Gal.* 5:19–21; *Rom.* 1:29–31. **3:9–10** Paul uses similar clothing language in *2 Cor.* 5:3–4; there he is looking to be reclothed mainly in the future, whereas this author puts it in the past.

[11]In that renewal[a] there is no longer Greek and Jew, circumcised and uncircumcised, barbarian, Scythian, slave and free; but Christ is all and in all!

[12]As God's chosen ones, holy and beloved, clothe yourselves with compassion, kindness, humility, meekness, and patience. [13]Bear with one another and, if anyone has a complaint against another, forgive each other; just as the Lord[b] has forgiven you, so you also must forgive. [14]Above all, clothe yourselves with love, which binds everything together in perfect harmony. [15]And let the peace of Christ rule in your hearts, to which indeed you were called in the one body. And be thankful. [16]Let the word of Christ[c] dwell in you richly; teach and admonish one another in all wisdom; and with gratitude in your hearts sing psalms, hymns, and spiritual songs to God.[d] [17]And whatever you do, in word or deed, do everything in the name of the Lord Jesus, giving thanks to God the Father through him.

Rules for Christian Households

[18]Wives, be subject to your husbands, as is fitting in the Lord. [19]Husbands, love your wives and never treat them harshly.

[20]Children, obey your parents in everything, for this is your acceptable duty in the Lord. [21]Fathers, do not provoke your children, or they may lose heart. [22]Slaves, obey your earthly masters[e] in everything, not only while being watched and in order to please them, but wholeheartedly, fearing the Lord.[e] [23]Whatever your task, put yourselves into it, as done for the Lord and not for your masters,[f] [24]since you know that from the Lord you will receive the inheritance as your reward; you serve[g] the Lord Christ. [25]For the wrongdoer will be paid back for whatever wrong has been done, and there is no partiality. [1]Masters, treat your slaves justly and fairly, for you know that you also have a Master in heaven.

Further Instructions

[2]Devote yourselves to prayer, keeping alert in it with thanksgiving. [3]At the same time pray for us as well that God will open to us a door for the word, that we may declare the mystery of Christ, for which I am in prison, [4]so that I may reveal it clearly, as I should.

[5]Conduct yourselves wisely toward outsiders, making the most of the time.[h] [6]Let your speech always be gracious, seasoned with salt, so that you may know how you ought to answer everyone.

Final Greetings and Benediction

[7]Tychicus will tell you all the news about me; he is a beloved brother, a faithful minister, and a fellow servant[i] in the Lord. [8]I have sent him to you for this very purpose, so that you may know how we are[j] and that he may encourage your hearts; [9]he is coming with Onesimus, the faithful and beloved brother, who is one of you. They will tell you about everything here.

[10]Aristarchus my fellow prisoner greets you, as does Mark the cousin of Barnabas, concerning whom

---

a Gk *its creator,* [11]*where*
b Other ancient authorities read *just as Christ*
c Other ancient authorities read *of God,* or *of the Lord*
d Other ancient authorities read *to the Lord*
e In Greek the same word is used for *master* and *Lord*

f Gk *not for men*
g Or *you are slaves of,* or *be slaves of*
h Or *opportunity*
i Gk *slave*
j Other authorities read *that I may know how you are*

3:11 *Greek and Jew* See Paul in *Gal.* 3:28. ***Scythian*** A surprising reference to a people who had faded from history several centuries earlier. These horse-riding nomads, based in the area north and east of the Black Sea, were famous for their brutality in combat. **3:12** 1st-century moral teachers commonly compiled such lists of virtues. **3:13** *forgive* See the Lord's Prayer, *Matt.* 6:14. **3:14** *perfect harmony* The Gk text does not explicitly mention harmony; the Gk word here, which is not found elsewhere in Paul, simply means "perfection." **3:16** See *1 Cor.* 14:26. **3:18–4:1** These instructions to each of the basic groups of the ancient household are widely paralleled in ancient philosophers' writings. See Seneca, *An Essay about Kindness* 3.38.2 (on children); Pliny the Younger, *Letters* 9.12 (on fathers) and 8.5.1–2 (on wives and husbands); and Seneca, *Letters* 47; Pliny the Younger, *Letters* 8.16 (on slaves and masters). Although Paul's advice is almost the same as that of many philosophers, he grounds it entirely in Christian principles rather than in laws of nature or other sources. **4:3** *mystery of Christ* A phrase not found elsewhere in Paul. See 1:26–27. **4:7** *Tychicus* A Gk name of the sort commonly given to slaves, meaning "of Fortune"; possibly a freedman. *Acts* 20:4 identifies a person of the same name as a companion of Paul's from Asia, where Colossae was situated. The name appears also in *Eph.* 6:21; *2 Tim.* 4:12; *Titus* 3:12. *minister* This is the same Gk word that Paul uses of himself in 1:7, 23, 25, where it is translated "servant." *fellow servant* Or "fellow slave." **4:9** Possibly the Onesimus of *Phlm.* 10. If so, and if *Colossians* was written by Paul, Philemon must have complied with Paul's implicit request for Onesimus's release into his service (see introduction to *Philemon*). *who is one of you* If this phrasing seems artificial, it may be that it is a device of the pseudonymous author. **4:10** *Aristarchus* A Jewish Christian (see 4:11). See note to *Phlm.* 24. *Mark the cousin of Barnabas* A Jewish Christian (see 4:11). According to *Acts* 15:37–40, Barnabas's desire to take John Mark (not identified there as his cousin) on the mission resulted in the former's separation from Paul. See note to *Phlm.* 24.

you have received instructions—if he comes to you, welcome him. [11]And Jesus who is called Justus greets you. These are the only ones of the circumcision among my co-workers for the kingdom of God, and they have been a comfort to me. [12]Epaphras, who is one of you, a servant[k] of Christ Jesus, greets you. He is always wrestling in his prayers on your behalf, so that you may stand mature and fully assured in everything that God wills. [13]For I testify for him that he has worked hard for you and for those in Laodicea and in Hierapolis. [14]Luke, the beloved physician, and Demas greet you. [15]Give my greetings to the brothers and sisters[l] in Laodicea, and to Nympha and the church in her house. [16]And when this letter has been read among you, have it read also in the church of the Laodiceans; and see that you read also the letter from Laodicea. [17]And say to Archippus, "See that you complete the task that you have received in the Lord."

[18]I, Paul, write this greeting with my own hand. Remember my chains. Grace be with you.[m]

---

k Gk slave

l Gk brothers
m Other ancient authorities add *Amen*

4:11 *Jesus who is called Justus* Jesus was a common Jewish name (Hebrew, "Joshua"; Aramaic, "Jeshua"); this man, mentioned only here, was distinguished by his Latin name, Justus, which meant "good citizen" or "law-abiding." Perhaps, then, his family had immigrated to Rome.   *the circumcision* That is, the Jews. The writer thus implies that the remainder of his entourage is Gentile, as are his readers, for it would be strange for Paul to call Jewish readers by this derisive term. **4:12** *Epaphras* See 1:7 and note.   **4:13** *Laodicea . . . Hierapolis* These towns formed a triangle with Colossae, about twenty to twenty-five miles apart.   **4:14** *Luke, the beloved physician* See note to *Phlm.* 24.   *Demas* See note to *Phlm.* 24. **4:15** *Nympha and the church in her house* Many manuscripts have "Nymphas and the church in his house," but this reading seems to result from the medieval copyists' difficulty in believing that a woman could hold such a leadership role. She must have possessed means because she had a house large enough to hold group meetings; that she held such a leadership role may indicate that she was a widow. It is not clear whether Nympha's assembly was in Laodicea or in Hierapolis. **4:17** *Archippus* See note to *Phlm.* 2.   **4:18** *my own hand* See *Gal.* 6:11; *Rom.* 16:22; *2 Thess.* 2:2; 3:17. The author implies that he (allegedly Paul) is appending this personal greeting to a letter actually written by a secretary. From an early date, forgeries existed under Paul's name; this letter might be one of them.

To the Holy and Faithful in Christ Jesus

EPHESIANS

Overview, Themes, and Purpose

The text traditionally known as *Ephesians* presents many fascinating problems, whether considered as a genuine letter of Paul's or as a forgery by one of his admirers after his death. It has a fairly straightforward outline. After the opening greetings, the author blesses God, then offers a thanksgiving before beginning the body of the letter (1:15–23). The body falls quite neatly into two sections: a theoretical part, which discusses some theological principles (2:1–4:16), and then a very long list of practical exhortations (4:17–6:20). The text closes with some brief personal remarks and a benediction (6:21–24).

Admittedly, the outline is complicated by one obvious irregularity: the author introduces a prayer and benediction at 3:14–21, which seem to close one section of the letter. But then he continues with the abstract theology, and turns to practical matters only in 4:17.

Similarly, the major themes of the letter are unmistakable, because the author likes to repeat them often in a short space. Many of these are similar to the leading ideas of *Colossians:* Thus, *Ephesians* is preoccupied with the past and present aspects of salvation. It declares that Christians have already been raised up to sit in "heavenly places" in Christ Jesus (2:1, 6, 8). The emphasis is squarely on what Christ *has* definitively accomplished (1:20–23; 3:11), and so any urgency of hope for Jesus' return is missing. As in *Colossians,* the author likes to describe his faith in terms of riches (1:7, 18; 2:4, 7; 3:8, 16), fullness (1:10, 23; 3:19; 4:13), and wisdom (1:8, 17; 3:10). And once again, Christ appears as the cosmic being who unites all dualities and opposites in himself (1:10; 2:14–15). The letter seems to quote a "gnostic" hymn, to the effect that Christ comes with truth to arouse those who are caught in a stupor (5:14). So *Ephesians* takes over, and even exaggerates, the mystical tendencies of *Colossians.*

But absent from *Ephesians* is *Colossians'* effort to deal with a specific threat in a particular church. In place of that, we might say, is an emphasis on the worldwide unity of Gentiles and Jews in Christ. In this text, the word "church" (*ekklēsia*) means always the entire Christian community, rather than a single assembly, as

Paul normally uses the term. The letter should not really be called *Ephesians* because that phrase does not appear in the earliest manuscripts and versions (see note to 1:1–2). The writer simply addresses "those who are also faithful in Christ Jesus" (1:1), and these faithful are later identified as Gentile converts (2:11). The text generously elaborates Paul's point that the categories of Jew and Gentile have no validity since the coming of Christ (2:11–3:13; see *Gal.* 3:28). And in the remarkably long section of practical exhortations, it insists that its readers must no longer live as Gentiles but rather observe some common principles with respect to personal morality, household relationships, and social behavior (4:17–6:20). It seems, then, that the document is a kind of circular to Gentile Christians everywhere, welcoming them into this new faith with its biblical roots, and setting forth some essential ethical guidelines. To say more about the work's unique features, date, or author's outlook brings us to the fundamental problem of its authenticity.

Literary Features and Authorship

If there is doubt about the authenticity of *Colossians* because of its "gnosticizing" theological outlook, doubt about *Ephesians* must be much greater. In addition to the problem that it seems to represent a non-Pauline outlook, *Ephesians* appears to be verbally dependent on Paul's other letters; it is written in a tortuous style not typical of Paul elsewhere; and it lacks any clear occasion or purpose.

Scholars long ago noted striking verbal parallels between *Ephesians* and other Pauline letters, but especially *Colossians*. The final two chapters of *Ephesians* are so close to *Colossians* that they suggest direct borrowing. Consider the examples in the table opposite.

The parallels between *Colossians* and *Ephesians*, therefore, are not confined to general themes. We find extensive agreements in the order of statements, in the precise choice of vocabulary, and even in sentence structure. Given the almost inexhaustible range of expression in Greek, we are forced to conclude that agreements such as these indicate literary dependence. That is, if two different authors had claimed to write these works, we would immediately accuse them of collusion.[1]

But is it possible that Paul plagiarized his own letter in this way? Possible, yes; likely, no. We should not, of course, suppose that he had a model letter (as on a computer disk), which he could manipulate for different audiences, or even a photocopier with which to keep records of his letters. Such extensive agreements have no precedent in Paul's undisputed letters. Given his ability to craft a uniquely appropriate letter for each new occasion—an ability that seems to have been widely recognized (*2 Cor.* 10:10)—it is more than a little strange that he would so slavishly have copied *Colossians*. Although it is conceivable that some kind of extenuating circumstances caused him to do so, the data seem more easily explained by the hypothesis that someone else, who wished to write a plausible "Pauline" letter,

---

[1]See the introduction to BIOGRAPHY, ANECDOTE, AND HISTORY.

PARALLELS BETWEEN *COLOSSIANS* AND *EPHESIANS*

COLOSSIANS

1:1–2
Paul, an apostle of Christ Jesus by the will of God....
To the saints and faithful brothers and sisters *in Christ* in Colossae: *Grace to you and peace from God our Father.*

2:19
from whom the whole body, nourished *and knit together by* its *ligaments* and sinews, grows with a *growth* that is from God.

3:16
sing psalms and hymns and spiritual songs to God. And whatever you do, in word or deed, do *everything in the name of the Lord Jesus, giving thanks to God the Father* through him.

3:18
Wives, be subject to your husbands, as is fitting in *the Lord.*

3:19
Husbands, love your wives, and never treat them harshly.

3:20
Children, obey your parents in everything, *for this is* your acceptable duty to the Lord.

3:21
Fathers, do not provoke your children, or they may lose heart.

3:22–24
Slaves, obey *your earthly masters in everything, not only while being watched, in order to please them, but in singleness of heart,* fearing the Lord. Whatever your task, put yourselves into it, *as* done for *the Lord and not for your masters, knowing that from the Lord* you *will receive* the inheritance as your reward.

4:1
Masters, treat your slaves justly and fairly, *for you know that* you also *have* a *Master in heaven.*

4:2–4
Devote yourselves to *prayer,* keeping alert in it with thanksgiving. At the same time *pray for* us *also that* God will *open* to us a door for the word, that we may declare *the mystery of* Christ, *for which I am* in prison, so *that I may* reveal it clearly, *as I must speak.*

4:7–8
Tychicus will tell everything about how I am; he is a dear brother, a faithful minister, and a fellow servant *in the Lord. I have sent him to you for this very purpose, so that you may know how we are and that he may encourage your hearts.*

EPHESIANS

1:1–2
Paul, an apostle of Christ Jesus by the will of God, To the saints who are also *faithful in Christ* Jesus: *Grace to you and peace from God our Father* and the Lord Jesus Christ.

4:16
from whom the whole body, joined *and knit together by* every *ligament* with which it is equipped . . . , promotes the body's *growth.* . . .

5:19–20
sing psalms and hymns and spiritual songs . . . *giving thanks to God the Father* at all times and for *everything in the name of our Lord Jesus* Christ.

5:22
Wives, be subject to your husbands, as you are to *the Lord.*

5:25
Husbands, love your wives, just as Christ loved the church . . .

6:1
Children, obey your parents in the Lord, *for this is* right.

6:4
Fathers, do not provoke your children to anger, but bring them up . . .

6:5–8
Slaves, obey *your earthly masters* with *fear* and trembling, *in singleness of heart,* as you obey Christ, *not only while being watched, and in order to please them, but* as slaves of Christ, doing the will of God from the heart. Render service with enthusiasm, *as* to *the Lord and not* to *men and women, knowing that* whatever good we do, we *will receive* the same again *from the Lord.*

6:9
Masters, do the same to them. Stop threatening them, *for you know that* both of you *have* the same *Master in heaven.* . . .

6:18–20
Pray in the Spirit at all times in every *prayer* and supplication. . . . *Pray also for* me, so *that* when I speak, a message may be given to me to make known with boldness *the mystery of* the gospel, *for which I am* an ambassador in chains. Pray *that I may* declare it boldly, *as I must speak.*

6:21–22
So that you also may know *how I am* and what I am doing, *Tychicus will tell you everything. He is a dear brother and a faithful minister in the Lord. I have sent him to you for this very purpose, so that you may know how we are and that he may encourage your hearts.*

borrowed heavily from Paul's recognized letters. He favored *Colossians* because it most closely reflected the vision he wished to put across.

This conclusion seems to be confirmed by the style of *Ephesians*. The letter is characterized by run-on sentences and verbosity, resulting in part from the multiplication of similar words (e.g., "a spirit of wisdom and of revelation in the knowledge of him"—1:17; "the immeasurable greatness of his power in us . . . according to the working of the strength of his might"—1:19; "far above all rule and authority and power and dominion"—1:21). The blessing (1:3–14) is a single sentence of more than two hundred words, and the thanksgiving (1:15–23) is another sentence: so chapter 1 consists of two sentences with a short greeting! Paul's undisputed letters reveal his capacity for a poetic turn of phrase, but his style is ordinarily direct and pithy. The sentences of *Ephesians* lose the reader in piles of repeated nouns and adjectives—though the NRSV translators have masked much of this in order to make the English version readable.

Although this letter takes over many Pauline phrases, it seems to use them in ways that are not typical of Paul's usage. For example, in *1 Cor.* 12:12–31 Paul borrows the common political metaphor of the body to illustrate the interdependence of Christians. In *Ephesians,* however, the author portrays the church as the body of Christ in a cosmic sense. It lives with Christ, its head, in the heavenly places (1:3; 2:6, 21–22; 4:15–16). Similarly, Paul speaks of the Holy Spirit as a "guarantee" (*2 Cor.* 5:5) of the coming new order; Ephesians uses the same term, but here the Spirit guarantees the current inheritance already enjoyed by Christians (1:14). Finally, Paul often speaks of himself as an apostle, but he knows that the issue is hotly debated. More often than not, he must defend his claim to apostleship (e.g., *1 Cor.* 9:1–2). For the writer of *Ephesians,* however, the issue of apostleship is long settled: the church is "built upon the foundation of the apostles and prophets" (2:20; see 3:5). Without parallel in Paul's undisputed letters, this phrase suggests a period when the first Christian generation is long gone and fondly remembered. The closest parallel is in *Revelation* (18:20), which seems to come from the end of the first century.

A final set of problems concerns the occasion and purpose of *Ephesians*. Unlike all of Paul's other letters, *Ephesians* omits any personal greetings at either the beginning or the end—except for the reference to Tychicus, which, as we have seen, matches *Colossians* verbatim. But if the letter has no addressees, to whom will Tychicus take it? The reference to Tychicus appears to be a token borrowing aimed at making what is essentially an essay appear more as a genuine letter.

Date and Relation to Other Early Christian Texts

Because there is nothing in *Ephesians* to indicate its intended audience, E. J. Goodspeed suggested that it was actually a covering letter written by the editor and publisher of Paul's letters to summarize Paul's theology and commend him to readers. Goodspeed supported this hypothesis with the observation that almost every second line of *Ephesians* recalls a passage from one of Paul's letters, especially *1 Thessalonians*, the Corinthian correspondence, and *Romans*. Compare, for example: the passage about the "armor of God" in *Eph.* 6:13–15 with the similar metaphor in *1 Thess.* 5:8; the discussion of the Holy Spirit as a "guarantee" (*Eph.* 1:13–14; 4:30) with *2 Cor.* 5:4–5; and the exhortation to "build up the body of Christ" (*Eph.* 4:11) with *1 Cor.* 12:4–31; 14:12. These parallels make *Ephesians* read like a porridge of Paulinisms.

Goodspeed's hypothesis is no longer widely accepted, because the writer of a covering letter would have had little to gain by passing himself off as Paul, and although *Ephesians* does pull in numerous tidbits from Paul's letters, it does not as a whole introduce or encapsulate his views very well. Nevertheless, it does seem most plausible to conclude with Goodspeed that *Ephesians* was written by someone familiar with Paul's writings, especially *Colossians,* and not by Paul himself. The writer appropriates Paul for a Christian vision that was rather different from Paul's own.

Taking all of this into account, a date in the second Christian generation, roughly 65 to 100 C.E., seems most likely. *Ephesians* must have been completed by 100 if we are correct that Ignatius, writing in first decade of the second century, knows the work (see the wording of his address to his *Ephesians*).

For Further Reading

Goodspeed, Edgar J. *The Meaning of Ephesians.* Chicago: University of Chicago Press, 1933.

Furnish, Victor Paul. "Ephesians, Epistle to the." Pages 535–42 in vol. 2 of *Anchor Bible Dictionary.* Edited by D. N. Freedman. 6 vols. New York: Doubleday, 1992.

Lincoln, A. T., and A. J. M. Wedderburn. *The Theology of the Later Pauline Letters.* Cambridge: Cambridge University Press, 1993.

THE LETTER OF PAUL
TO THE EPHESIANS

Salutation

1 Paul, an apostle of Christ Jesus by the will of God, To the saints who are in Ephesus and are faithful[a] in Christ Jesus:

2Grace to you and peace from God our Father and the Lord Jesus Christ.

Spiritual Blessings in Christ

3Blessed be the God and Father of our Lord Jesus Christ, who has blessed us in Christ with every spiritual blessing in the heavenly places, 4just as he chose us in Christ[b] before the foundation of the world to be holy and blameless before him in love. 5He destined us for adoption as his children through Jesus Christ, according to the good pleasure of his will, 6to the praise of his glorious grace that he freely bestowed on us in the Beloved. 7In him we have redemption through his blood, the forgiveness of our trespasses, according to the riches of his grace 8that he lavished on us. With all wisdom and insight 9he has made known to us the mystery of his will, according to his good pleasure that he set forth in Christ, 10as a plan for the fullness of time, to gather up all things in him, things in heaven and things on earth. 11In Christ we have also obtained an inheritance,[c] having been destined according to the purpose of him who accomplishes all things according to his counsel and will, 12so that we, who were the first to set our hope on Christ, might live for the praise of his glory. 13In him you also, when you had heard the word of truth, the gospel of your salvation, and had believed in him, were marked with the seal of the promised Holy Spirit; 14this[d] is the pledge of our inheritance toward redemption as God's own people, to the praise of his glory.

Paul's Prayer

15I have heard of your faith in the Lord Jesus and your love[e] toward all the saints, and for this reason 16I do not cease to give thanks for you as I remember you in my prayers. 17I pray that the God of our Lord Jesus Christ, the Father of glory, may give you a spirit of wisdom and revelation as you come to know him, 18so that, with the eyes of your heart enlightened, you may know what is the hope to which he has called you, what are the riches of his glorious inheritance among the saints, 19and what is the immeasurable greatness of his power for us who believe, according to the working of his great power.

a Other ancient authorities lack in Ephesus, reading saints who are also faithful
b Gk in him

c Or been made a heritage
d Other ancient authorities read who
e Other ancient authorities lack and your love

1:1–2 This greeting is extremely close to that of *Col.* 1:1–2. The three best manuscripts of *Ephesians* (𝔓46 from around 200 C.E., Sinaiticus and Vaticanus of the 4th century) lack the phrase *in Ephesus,* and it was unknown to 2d-century Christian leaders (Marcion and those who responded to him). There are strong reasons for doubting, therefore, that it was part of the original text. **1:3–14** This blessing is unusual in Paul's letters. Only *2 Corinthians* (1:3–7) has one, beginning with precisely the same words, and there it replaces the typical thanksgiving. *Ephesians* is peculiar because it includes a thanksgiving after the blessing (1:15–23)—almost as if the writer is combining various features of Paul's letters. The entire blessing is a single sentence of more than two hundred words in Gk (the NRSV translators have created many more sentences for ease of reading); it illustrates well the author's repetitive style. The blessing focuses on the past actions of Christ and the recent benefits of salvation, and features the themes of knowledge, wisdom, understanding, riches, and inheritance. Contrast Paul in, for example, *1 Cor.* 4:8–13. **1:3 in the heavenly places** This is a favorite expression of the author. It occurs five times throughout this brief letter (also 1:20; 2:6; 3:10; 6:12). Whereas Paul uses the word *epouranios,* "heavenly," only of the future when Jesus returns (*1 Cor.* 15:40–49; *Phil.* 2:10), this author speaks enthusiastically about believers' *present* installation "in the heavenlies." Thus Christians currently share the place that Christ enjoys, as his body (see 1:20; 2:6). **1:5 adoption as his children** See *Gal.* 4:4–7; *Rom.* 8:14–17. **1:7 redemption** This word, which means "a buying back" or "a ransom," is a favorite of the author's (1:14; 4:30). **riches** Another characteristic term in this text; 1:18; 2:7; 3:8, 16. See also *Phil.* 4:19; *Rom.* 9:23; 11:33. **1:8 wisdom** Paul celebrates the wisdom and knowledge of God (*Rom.* 11:33) but typically condemns mortals who claim to have it (*1 Cor.* 1:17–3:19 often; *2 Cor.* 1:12). He does not think that human knowledge can be complete until Jesus returns (*1 Cor.* 13:9–13). **1:13–14** The Holy Spirit as seal and pledge appears also in *2 Cor.* 1:22; 5:5, where what the Spirit guarantees is the coming new age. Here, however, it seems to be a guarantee of the current *inheritance* in riches already given. **1:15–16** The author uses Paul's typical Gk expression, "making memory" of a particular church in his prayers (*1 Thess.* 1:2; *Phil.* 1:3; *Phlm.* 4; *Rom.* 1:9). But here, strangely, no particular group is mentioned in the address. **1:18 riches** See note to 1:7.

20God*f* put this power to work in Christ when he raised him from the dead and seated him at his right hand in the heavenly places, 21far above all rule and authority and power and dominion, and above every name that is named, not only in this age but also in the age to come. 22And he has put all things under his feet and has made him the head over all things for the church, 23which is his body, the fullness of him who fills all in all.

From Death to Life

2 You were dead through the trespasses and sins 2in which you once lived, following the course of this world, following the ruler of the power of the air, the spirit that is now at work among those who are disobedient. 3All of us once lived among them in the passions of our flesh, following the desires of flesh and senses, and we were by nature children of wrath, like everyone else. 4But God, who is rich in mercy, out of the great love with which he loved us 5even when we were dead through our trespasses, made us alive together with Christ*g*—by grace you have been saved— 6and raised us up with him and seated us with him in the heavenly places in Christ Jesus, 7so that in the ages to come he might show the immeasurable riches of his grace in kindness toward us in Christ Jesus. 8For by grace you have been saved through faith, and this is not your own doing; it is the gift of God— 9not the result of works, so that no one may boast. 10For we are what he has made us, created in Christ Jesus for good works, which God prepared beforehand to be our way of life.

One in Christ

11So then, remember that at one time you Gentiles by birth,*h* called "the uncircumcision" by those who are called "the circumcision"—a physical circumcision made in the flesh by human hands— 12remember that you were at that time without Christ, being aliens from the commonwealth of Israel, and strangers to the covenants of promise, having no hope and without God in the world. 13But now in Christ Jesus you who once were far off were brought near by the blood of Christ. 14For he is our peace; in his flesh he has made both groups into one and has broken down the dividing wall, that is, the hostility between us. 15He has abolished the law with its commandments and ordinances, that he might create in himself one new humanity in place of the two, thus making peace, 16and might reconcile both groups to God in one body*i* through the cross, thus putting to death that hostility through it.*j* 17So he came and proclaimed peace to you who were far off and peace to those who were near; 18for through him both of us have access in one Spirit to the Father. 19So then you are no longer strangers and aliens, but you are citizens with the saints and also members of the household of God, 20built upon the foundation of the apostles and prophets, with Christ Jesus himself as the cornerstone.*k* 21In him the whole structure is joined together and grows into a holy temple in the Lord; 22in whom you also are built together spiritually*l* into a dwelling place for God.

---

f Gk *He*
g Other ancient authorities read *in Christ*

h Gk *in the flesh*
i Or *reconcile both of us in one body for God*
j Or *in him*, or *in himself*
k Or *keystone*
l Gk *in the Spirit*

1:20 *seated him at his right hand in the heavenly places* See 1:3; 2:6. **1:21** *the age to come* It is not clear how the age to come functions for this author, since, in *Ephesians*, Christians have already been given so much that, in Paul's writings, awaits the coming age. The author does not develop the thought. **1:22** *he has put all things under his feet* Contrast Paul, for whom the putting of all things under Christ's feet has yet to be accomplished, at "the end" (*1 Cor.* 15:24–28). **1:23** *which is his body, the fullness of him who fills all in all* This cosmic view of the church as Christ's spiritual body, of which he is the head, is unique and important to this author (2:21–22; 4:14–16). Paul had borrowed the conventional political image of a body to talk about different spiritual gifts in the church (*1 Cor.* 12:12–31), but this vision of the cosmic church is different. **2:1–2** The notion that sinners or unbelievers were enslaved to the devil was prominent in many Jewish and Christian groups; see, among the Dead Sea Scrolls, 1QS 3.20–4.27 and, in Paul, *2 Cor.* 4:4; *Gal.* 4:8–10. **2:5–6** All of this past-tense language *(made us alive, raised us up, seated us)* contrasts sharply with Paul's basic orientation toward future salvation. **2:7** *in the ages to come* What this author expects to happen in the age to come is unclear; see note to 1:21. **2:11–12** Thus, the intended readers were Gentiles. The author consistently places himself over against the Gentiles—as a Jew by birth. This fits with his claim to be Paul (1:1). **2:11** *called "the uncircumcision."* Lit. "the foreskin" (which is removed in circumcision). **2:13–16** This passage seems to capture faithfully Paul's view; see *Gal.* 3:19–29, especially 28. **2:18** *both of us* That is, Jews and Gentiles. See note to 2:11–12. **2:20** *built upon the foundation of the apostles and prophets* This language, which casually assumes that the apostles were a fixed and well-known group, contrasts sharply with the constant battles in Paul's day concerning the foundation of the church (*1 Cor.* 3:10–15) and membership among the apostles (e.g., *1 Cor.* 9:1–2; 15:9–10; *2 Cor.* 11:13; *Gal.* 1:1). *Prophets* here are Christian prophets (see *1 Cor.* 12:10; 14:1; *Matt.* 23:34; *Did.* 11.3–12; 13.1–7).

Paul's Ministry to the Gentiles

3 This is the reason that I Paul am a prisoner for[m] Christ Jesus for the sake of you Gentiles— 2for surely you have already heard of the commission of God's grace that was given me for you, 3and how the mystery was made known to me by revelation, as I wrote above in a few words, 4a reading of which will enable you to perceive my understanding of the mystery of Christ. 5In former generations this mystery[n] was not made known to humankind, as it has now been revealed to his holy apostles and prophets by the Spirit: 6that is, the Gentiles have become fellow heirs, members of the same body, and sharers in the promise in Christ Jesus through the gospel.

7Of this gospel I have become a servant according to the gift of God's grace that was given me by the working of his power. 8Although I am the very least of all the saints, this grace was given to me to bring to the Gentiles the news of the boundless riches of Christ, 9and to make everyone see[o] what is the plan of the mystery hidden for ages in[p] God who created all things; 10so that through the church the wisdom of God in its rich variety might now be made known to the rulers and authorities in the heavenly places. 11This was in accordance with the eternal purpose that he has carried out in Christ Jesus our Lord, 12in whom we have access to God in boldness and confidence through faith in him.[q] 13I pray therefore that you[r] may not lose heart over my sufferings for you; they are your glory.

Prayer for the Readers

14For this reason I bow my knees before the Father,[s] 15from whom every family[t] in heaven and on earth takes its name. 16I pray that, according to the riches of his glory, he may grant that you may be strengthened in your inner being with power through his Spirit, 17and that Christ may dwell in your hearts through faith, as you are being rooted and grounded in love. 18I pray that you may have the power to comprehend, with all the saints, what is the breadth and length and height and depth, 19and to know the love of Christ that surpasses knowledge, so that you may be filled with all the fullness of God.

20Now to him who by the power at work within us is able to accomplish abundantly far more than all we can ask or imagine, 21to him be glory in the church and in Christ Jesus to all generations, forever and ever. Amen.

Unity in the Body of Christ

4 I therefore, the prisoner in the Lord, beg you to lead a life worthy of the calling to which you have been called, 2with all humility and gentleness, with patience, bearing with one another in love, 3making every effort to maintain the unity of the Spirit in the bond of peace. 4There is one body and one Spirit, just as you were called to the one hope of your calling, 5one Lord, one faith, one baptism, 6one God and Father of all, who is above all and through all and in all.

7But each of us was given grace according to the measure of Christ's gift. 8Therefore it is said,

"When he ascended on high he made captivity itself a captive;
    he gave gifts to his people."

---

m Or of
n Gk it
o Other ancient authorities read to bring to light
p Or by
q Or the faith of him
r Or I

s Other ancient authorities add of our Lord Jesus Christ
t Gk fatherhood

3:1–7 A single sentence in the Gk, illustrating the author's run-on style. **3:1–4** Although the imprisonment theme is found in other Pauline letters (*Phil.* 1:7), the author here writes as a very distant figure who must explain himself to his audience as if for the first time. He has to explain to them that he was called to be their apostle, and he must tell them for the first time his basic understanding of *the mystery of Christ.* Concerning Paul's call to the Gentiles, see *Gal.* 1:13–17. **3:1 his holy apostles and prophets** See note to 2:20. **3:8 I am the very least of all the saints** See *1 Cor.* 15:9. **3:10** This responsibility of the church to teach supernatural powers in the heavenly places contrasts with Paul's observations about the strictly terrestrial reach of his local communities (e.g., *1 Thess.* 1:8). On *heavenly places,* see note to 1:3. **3:16** See *2 Cor.* 4:16. **3:18–19** See Paul in *Rom.* 8:38–39. **3:20** Paul writes similar doxologies in *Gal.* 1:5; *Rom.* 16:25–27. This one completes the theoretical part of the essay in preparation for the ethical instructions of *Ephesians* 4–6. **4:1 the prisoner in the Lord** See note to 3:1–4. **4:4–6** These lines recall *1 Cor.* 12:12–13; 15:28. **4:7–13** This discussion of gifts given to the church recalls *1 Cor.* 12:4–11 although the Gk word for *gifts* is different and the author here traces Christ's giving of these gifts to a fulfillment of scripture. **4:8** *Ps.* 68:18. The psalmist speaks of God's glory on Mount Zion although the surrounding nations abuse Israel's God and king. MT (68:19): "You went up to the heights, / having taken captives, / having received tribute of men, / even of those who rebel / against the Lord God's abiding there." LXX (67:18): "When you ascended on high you made captivity itself a captive; you received gifts for people, for indeed they were rebellious that you should live among them."

9(When it says, "He ascended," what does it mean but that he had also descended[u] into the lower parts of the earth? 10He who descended is the same one who ascended far above all the heavens, so that he might fill all things.) 11The gifts he gave were that some would be apostles, some prophets, some evangelists, some pastors and teachers, 12to equip the saints for the work of ministry, for building up the body of Christ, 13until all of us come to the unity of the faith and of the knowledge of the Son of God, to maturity, to the measure of the full stature of Christ. 14We must no longer be children, tossed to and fro and blown about by every wind of doctrine, by people's trickery, by their craftiness in deceitful scheming. 15But speaking the truth in love, we must grow up in every way into him who is the head, into Christ, 16from whom the whole body, joined and knit together by every ligament with which it is equipped, as each part is working properly, promotes the body's growth in building itself up in love.

The Old Life and the New

17Now this I affirm and insist on in the Lord: you must no longer live as the Gentiles live, in the futility of their minds. 18They are darkened in their understanding, alienated from the life of God because of their ignorance and hardness of heart. 19They have lost all sensitivity and have abandoned themselves to licentiousness, greedy to practice every kind of impurity. 20That is not the way you learned Christ! 21For surely you have heard about him and were taught in him, as truth is in Jesus. 22You were taught to put away your former way of life, your old self, corrupt and deluded by its lusts, 23and to be renewed in the spirit of your minds, 24and to clothe yourselves with the new self, created according to the likeness of God in true righteousness and holiness.

Rules for the New Life

25So then, putting away falsehood, let all of us speak the truth to our neighbors, for we are members of one another. 26Be angry but do not sin; do not let the sun go down on your anger, 27and do not make room for the devil. 28Thieves must give up stealing; rather let them labor and work honestly with their own hands, so as to have something to share with the needy. 29Let no evil talk come out of your mouths, but only what is useful for building up,[v] as there is need, so that your words may give grace to those who hear. 30And do not grieve the Holy Spirit of God, with which you were marked with a seal for the day of redemption. 31Put away from you all bitterness and wrath and anger and wrangling and slander, together with all malice, 32and be kind to one another, tenderhearted, forgiving one another, as God in Christ has forgiven you.[w] 5 1Therefore be imitators of God, as beloved children, 2and live in love, as Christ loved us[x] and gave himself up for us, a fragrant offering and sacrifice to God.

Renounce Pagan Ways

3But fornication and impurity of any kind, or greed, must not even be mentioned among you, as is proper among saints. 4Entirely out of place is obscene, silly, and vulgar talk; but instead, let there be thanksgiving. 5Be sure of this, that no fornicator or impure person, or one who is greedy (that is, an idolater), has any inheritance in the kingdom of Christ and of God.

6Let no one deceive you with empty words, for because of these things the wrath of God comes on those who are disobedient. 7Therefore do not be associated with them. 8For once you were darkness, but now in the Lord you are light. Live as children of light— 9for the fruit of the light is found in all that is good and right and true. 10Try to find out what is pleasing to the Lord. 11Take no part in the unfruitful works of darkness, but instead expose them. 12For it is shameful even to mention what such people do secretly; 13but everything exposed by the light becomes

---

u Other ancient authorities add *first*

v Other ancient authorities read *building up faith*
w Other ancient authorities read *us*
x Other ancient authorities read *you*

4:9–10 The author takes this verse from the psalms as a statement about Christ's death and resurrection and adds an intervening visit to the underworld (see also *1 Pet.* 3:19 and *Gos. Pet.* 8.41). This visit, known as the harrowing of hell, became important in later Christian thinking. The ascending is no longer to a mountaintop but into heaven. These verses are in parentheses because they digress from the author's original point, the gifts given by Christ. **4:11–13** This recalls *1 Cor.* 12:28, where the list also begins with apostles and prophets. **4:14** This recalls *1 Cor.* 3:1–4. **4:15–16** The author develops his characteristic theme of the church as Christ's cosmic body, of which Christ is the head. See note to 1:23. The wording seems to be taken from *Col.* 2:19 (see introduction to *Ephesians*). **4:17–19** See note to 2:11–12. **4:30** See note to 1:13–14. **5:1** The imitation of God's virtue was a common theme in ancient writing; see Josephus, *Ant.* 1.23; *Matt.* 5:48. **5:5** This recalls *1 Cor.* 6:9–11. For the Jewish accusation that idolatry leads to sexual and other sin, see *Wis.* 14:12; *Rom.* 1:23–24. **5:8–14** This recalls *1 Thess.* 5:4–5. The language of light and darkness, representing the righteous and the unrighteous, has numerous parallels in antiquity. See, for example, 1QM 1.1, 3, 7, 9, 10–11; 1QS 1.9–10; 2.16; 3.13, 21.

visible, [14]for everything that becomes visible is light. Therefore it says,

> "Sleeper, awake!
> Rise from the dead,
> and Christ will shine on you."

[15]Be careful then how you live, not as unwise people but as wise, [16]making the most of the time, because the days are evil. [17]So do not be foolish, but understand what the will of the Lord is. [18]Do not get drunk with wine, for that is debauchery; but be filled with the Spirit, [19]as you sing psalms and hymns and spiritual songs among yourselves, singing and making melody to the Lord in your hearts, [20]giving thanks to God the Father at all times and for everything in the name of our Lord Jesus Christ.

The Christian Household

[21]Be subject to one another out of reverence for Christ.

[22]Wives, be subject to your husbands as you are to the Lord. [23]For the husband is the head of the wife just as Christ is the head of the church, the body of which he is the Savior. [24]Just as the church is subject to Christ, so also wives ought to be, in everything, to their husbands.

[25]Husbands, love your wives, just as Christ loved the church and gave himself up for her, [26]in order to make her holy by cleansing her with the washing of water by the word, [27]so as to present the church to himself in splendor, without a spot or wrinkle or anything of the kind—yes, so that she may be holy and without blemish. [28]In the same way, husbands should love their wives as they do their own bodies. He who loves his wife loves himself. [29]For no one ever hates his own body, but he nourishes and tenderly cares for it, just as Christ does for the church,

[30]because we are members of his body.[y] [31]"For this reason a man will leave his father and mother and be joined to his wife, and the two will become one flesh." [32]This is a great mystery, and I am applying it to Christ and the church. [33]Each of you, however, should love his wife as himself, and a wife should respect her husband.

Children and Parents

6Children, obey your parents in the Lord,[z] for this is right. [2]"Honor your father and mother"—this is the first commandment with a promise: [3]"so that it may be well with you and you may live long on the earth."

[4]And, fathers, do not provoke your children to anger, but bring them up in the discipline and instruction of the Lord.

Slaves and Masters

[5]Slaves, obey your earthly masters with fear and trembling, in singleness of heart, as you obey Christ; [6]not only while being watched, and in order to please them, but as slaves of Christ, doing the will of God from the heart. [7]Render service with enthusiasm, as to the Lord and not to men and women, [8]knowing that whatever good we do, we will receive the same again from the Lord, whether we are slaves or free.

[9]And, masters, do the same to them. Stop threatening them, for you know that both of you have the same Master in heaven, and with him there is no partiality.

The Whole Armor of God

[10]Finally, be strong in the Lord and in the strength of his power. [11]Put on the whole armor of God, so

---

y Other ancient authorities add *of his flesh and of his bones*
z Other ancient authorities lack *in the Lord*

5:14 Evidently, the author is quoting some kind of poem, the origins of which can no longer be traced. The idea expressed, that Christians should rise from stupor to see the light of Christ and that this amounts to a spiritual resurrection *from the dead* in the present, is one that Paul's gnosticizing opponents in Corinth seem to have espoused (*1 Cor.* 4:8–13; 15:12). **5:19–20** This wording is very similar to *Col.* 3:16 (see introduction to *Ephesians*). **5:22–24** This recalls *Col.* 3:18 and *1 Cor.* 11:3. Only in *Ephesians,* however, is Christ made the head of the church (see note to 1:23). **5:25–33** It is noteworthy that the author needs or chooses to say much more, with argument, about the need for husbands to love their wives than about the need for wives to love their husbands. Ancient patriarchal society did not generally assume mutuality in husband-wife relationships; the husband had by far the greater legal and social power. **5:25** See *Col.* 3:19. **5:27** This recalls *1 Thess.* 5:23. **5:28–33** From *Gen.* 2:24, which was quoted by Jesus to support monogamy (*Matt.* 19:5), the author make his case for loving one's wife: since the text says that husband and wife become "one flesh," it would be absurd for a husband to mistreat his wife. **6:1** This recalls *Col.* 3:20. **6:2–3** The author paraphrases the fourth commandment, according to the version in *Deut.* 5:16, which includes the phrase "it may go well with you." See also *Exod.* 20:12, which is similar but lacks this phrase. It is, the author notes, the first commandment—indeed the only one—with an explicit reward attached to it. **6:4** This recalls *Col.* 3:21. **6:5** This section on slaves and masters, which assumes that many Christians were fairly comfortable by the time the author wrote, is close to *Col.* 3:22–4:1. Various philosophers of the period also called for the humane treatment of slaves. **6:9 with him there is no partiality** See Paul in *Gal.* 3:28—"there is no longer slave or free" in Christ. **6:10–17 the whole armor of God** This discussion of the armor of God recalls and develops considerably *1 Thess.* 5:8. The image has a solid background in biblical and later Jewish literature; see *Isa.* 11:5; 49:2; especially *Wis.* 5:17–20.

that you may be able to stand against the wiles of the devil. ¹²For our[a] struggle is not against enemies of blood and flesh, but against the rulers, against the authorities, against the cosmic powers of this present darkness, against the spiritual forces of evil in the heavenly places. ¹³Therefore take up the whole armor of God, so that you may be able to withstand on that evil day, and having done everything, to stand firm. ¹⁴Stand therefore, and fasten the belt of truth around your waist, and put on the breastplate of righteousness. ¹⁵As shoes for your feet put on whatever will make you ready to proclaim the gospel of peace. ¹⁶With all of these,[b] take the shield of faith, with which you will be able to quench all the flaming arrows of the evil one. ¹⁷Take the helmet of salvation, and the sword of the Spirit, which is the word of God.

¹⁸Pray in the Spirit at all times in every prayer and supplication. To that end keep alert and always persevere in supplication for all the saints. ¹⁹Pray also for me, so that when I speak, a message may be given to me to make known with boldness the mystery of the gospel,[c] ²⁰for which I am an ambassador in chains. Pray that I may declare it boldly, as I must speak.

Personal Matters and Benediction

²¹So that you also may know how I am and what I am doing, Tychicus will tell you everything. He is a dear brother and a faithful minister in the Lord. ²²I am sending him to you for this very purpose, to let you know how we are, and to encourage your hearts.

²³Peace be to the whole community,[d] and love with faith, from God the Father and the Lord Jesus Christ. ²⁴Grace be with all who have an undying love for our Lord Jesus Christ.[e]

---

a Other ancient authorities read *your*
b Or *In all circumstances*

c Other ancient authorities lack *of the gospel*
d Gk *to the brothers*
e Other ancient authorities add *Amen*

6:18–20 These lines are similar to *Col.* 4:2–4. **6:21–22** These verses reproduce almost exactly *Col.* 4:7–8. *Ephesians* gives no other personal details; the text here gives the impression that the author, seeking to give his creation some personal connection, has fallen back on those of another text.

Further to the Assembly of the Thessalonians

2 THESSALONIANS

Overview and Themes

Second Thessalonians is a concise letter expressing an intense apocalyptic vision. It opens with the author's assurance of Jesus' imminent return: he will come in judgment, with flaming fire, and wreak vengeance on unbelievers and the church's enemies while rewarding the faithful (1:5–12). This passage presents the most vivid portrayal of coming judgment in the Pauline corpus.

Evidently, some people in the assembly to whom the letter is addressed have surmised that the "Day of the Lord" has come (2:1–2). The author's primary concern in the letter is to disabuse them of this notion. To that end he "reminds" them of the apocalyptic timetable that must work itself out before the end (2:3–12). Namely: there will first come a "rebellion" and a "lawless one"; and "what is now restraining" the lawless one must be removed so that the latter can be revealed and destroyed by Jesus. All of this abstract discussion seems intended, practically, to undermine the position of those who are living in idleness because they think that the day of the Lord has come (3:6–15).

Authorship, Literary Features, Date, Purpose

Because there is much scholarly dispute about whether this letter was written by Paul, our customary categories of analysis are best combined here in the context of the authenticity question.

Paradoxically, the case against Pauline authorship rests on both the close similarities and the striking differences between *2 Thessalonians* and Paul's other letters. On the one hand, *2 Thessalonians* reproduces the form and vocabulary of *1 Thessalonians* to an uncanny degree. It has a double thanksgiving (1:3–5; 2:13–15; see *1 Thess.* 1:2–10; 2:13–3:10), the second of which is followed by a benediction (2:16–17; see *1 Thess.* 3:11–13); after that come exhortations introduced by the word "finally" (3:1–15; see *1 Thess.* 4:1–5:22) and a second benediction (3:16; see *1 Thess.* 5:23–24). But since the format of *1 Thessalonians* is itself peculiar, determined by its unique purpose and the flow of Paul's thought at that time, it is all the more peculiar that *2 Thessalonians* should reproduce its format so closely.

Even the opening salutation of *2 Thessalonians* (1:1–2) is enough to create an initial feeling of unusual similarity. It begins with the identical Greek words of *1 Thess.* 1:1: "Paul and Silvanus and Timothy to the assembly of the Thessalonians in God the Father and the Lord Jesus Christ." Were the two letters written so close in time that Paul had exactly the same entourage at his side, even though none of his other letters begins just this way? Possibly. But the problem is then magnified because *2 Thess.* 1:1–2 repeats the phrase "God our Father and the Lord Jesus Christ" in a way that seems unnecessary. Paul does not do this elsewhere. He typically includes this phrase after his standard "grace and peace" wish, following the identification of the audience (see *1 Cor.* 1:3; *Phil.* 1:2; *Phlm.* 3; *2 Cor.* 1:2; *Gal.* 1:3; *Rom.* 1:7). But in *1 Thessalonians* (1:1) alone he places it after the identification of the church. In *2 Thessalonians*, however, the author *both* follows *1 Thessalonians* in appending this phrase to the audience identifier *and* follows Paul's more common practice in appending it to the grace and peace wish. From the resulting awkwardness, many scholars conclude that another writer has artificially combined Paul's usual opening with that of *1 Thessalonians*.

Given Paul's demonstrable versatility in composing letters elsewhere, it seems odd that he should mimic his own style in this case. Even particular phrases from *1 Thessalonians* such as "worked night and day, so that we might not burden any of you" (2:9), "We appeal to you, brothers and sisters" (5:12), and "Beloved, pray for us" (5:25), turn up in *2 Thessalonians* (3:8; 2:1; 3:1). Within the letter itself, the author uses the identical formula for both thanksgivings ("We must always give thanks to God for you, brothers and sisters"; 1:3; 2:13). Given the brevity of the letter, this repeated verbal agreement contributes to the sense of artificiality. The question is whether such close agreement is better explained by supposing that Paul copied his own format rigidly or by positing a later Christian's imitation of Paul's style.

More significant than the similarities between *1* and *2 Thessalonians*, however, are the obvious *differences* of content and vocabulary. First, the eschatological picture offered by *2 Thessalonians* apparently conflicts with Paul's vision in *1 Thessalonians*. There, Paul had to respond to pressing questions about when Jesus would return (*1 Thess.* 5:1). He declared that, as he had already told them during his founding visit (from which he had recently come), no one knew when Jesus would return; he would come "like a thief in the night" (5:2). How, then, can Paul now say in *2 Thessalonians* that, as he told them when he was with them (!), certain specific events must take place before Jesus' return (*2 Thess.* 2:3–5)? If he had discussed the "lawless one" and the "rebellion" when he had made his recent (founding) visit to the Thessalonians, why does he make no mention of these in *1 Thessalonians* 5 (which responds directly to the question "When will the end come?")?

Some scholars point out that Jesus' own apocalyptic speeches in the gospels (e.g., *Mark* 13) reflect a similar tension between "thief-in-the-night" and "signs-before-the-end" language. They deny, therefore, that Paul's two scenarios are mutually exclusive. But this parallel does not really solve the problem. For *Mark*'s Jesus delineates the signs before the end in response to the question "When will the end be?" (*Mark* 13:4). But when Paul is asked a similar question (see *1 Thess.* 5:1) he responds without any reference to "signs." Indeed, nowhere else in Paul's letters does he indicate any knowledge of such a clear, unfulfilled apocalyptic timetable. So the question remains: If both *1* and *2 Thessalonians* are authentic, what did Paul say to the Thessalonians "when he was with them"?

Another proposed solution to the problem is the hypothesis that Paul wrote *2 Thessalonians* before *1 Thessalonians*. (Recall that the NT arrangement and labeling of the books is historically arbitrary). According to this argument, the Thessalonians have perhaps understood the attempt of the emperor Gaius (Caligula) to erect his statue in the temple in 38/39 C.E. as the expected desecration of the temple (2:4). Counting three and a half years from that date, according to the timetable of *Dan.* 12:11–12, they now think that the day of the Lord has arrived. Paul writes *2 Thessalonians* in part to deny this identification (since Gaius's attempt was unsuccessful). The lack of reference to the apocalyptic timetable in *1 Thessalonians* would then make sense because the issue had already been discussed thoroughly.

The chief problem with this view is fitting in *2 Thessalonians* between Paul's founding visit to Thessalonica and the writing of *1 Thessalonians,* for *1 Thessalonians* gives every indication of being the first letter that Paul wrote to the Thessalonian church. See the introduction to *1 Thessalonians* there and *1 Thess.* 2:1–2, 17–3:6. The problem is compounded by the implication in *2 Thess.* 2:15 that the church already has at least one previous letter from Paul. And finally, the author of *2 Thessalonians* has to *remind* his readers about the signs before the end, as something that they had allegedly forgotten (2:5). Therefore, it is hard to imagine that their belief that the day of the Lord had come was motivated by the perceived fulfillment of a sign for which they were watching.

Several indicators in *2 Thessalonians* point to a date much later than *1 Thessalonians*. For example, Paul's (earlier) teachings are twice referred to here as "traditions" (*2 Thess.* 2:15; 3:6). The word means literally "something handed down." But Paul does not elsewhere refer to his own teachings as "traditions." In rare cases he does refer to something received from the apostles before him as "tradition" (*1 Cor.* 11:23; 15:3), but in general he is very concerned to show that his announcement (gospel) comes directly from God, without human mediation (*Gal.* 1:1, 11–2:10). Indeed, it is the very nontraditional character of his preaching that so frequently lands him in trouble with other Christian teachers. These references to Paul's founding instructions as "traditions," therefore, may betray the (later) author's own community situation, in which Paul's teachings were already traditional.

Moreover, *2 Thessalonians* presupposes that Paul is already an established, well-known letter-writer. The author signs off with his autograph, which, he says, is the mark of "every letter of mine" (3:17), and this suggests that someone is already imitating his letters. It may even be that the Thessalonians have received a forged letter "as if from us" (2:2). But if people are trying to mimic his letters, this indicates that Paul has an established reputation and recognized style. The cumulative effect of these data is to distance *2 Thessalonians* from *1 Thessalonians,* which comes without doubt from the earliest phase of Paul's mission in Greece.

It is not easy, however, to imagine a later date in Paul's career at which he might have sent *2 Thessalonians,* for we have traced in his other letters a fairly steady movement away from fervent apocalypticism toward a more "realized eschatology"; he develops a greater appreciation of the present benefits of salvation and of life in this world. His last letter, for example, suggests that God has "consigned all men to disobedience so that he might have mercy upon all" (*Rom.* 11:32).[1] How, then, to explain Paul's reversion to the black-and-white, us-and-them outlook of *2 Thessalonians,* which calls down "eternal destruction" on those who reject the gospel?

It seems best to suppose that Paul did not write *2 Thessalonians,* although that conclusion is itself not without difficulties, such as the bold statement in 3:17. Perhaps the author was an admirer of Paul's who was concerned about the movement in some church[2] toward a radically realized eschatology. So he penned a fictional letter in Paul's name, asserting both that the end had not yet come and that when it did come it would be unmistakable. Nevertheless, he included a timetable to watch for, in order to postpone the end indefinitely.

Relation to Other Early Christian Texts

If this proposal seems likely, then we have in *2 Thessalonians* a third kind of effort to appropriate Paul for a particular Christian view. Over against the protognosticism of *Colossians* and *Ephesians,* and the structured "early catholicism" of the pastoral letters (*1–2 Timothy* and *Titus*), this author wants to reassert an early-Pauline apocalyptic hope. All three streams of Paulinism would flourish in various second- to fourth-century Christian contexts. All three would claim support from Paul.

This letter has the strongest affinities, as we have seen, to Paul's *1 Thessalonians.* But it draws its energy and images from a large reservoir of apocalyptic thinking and writing in both Jewish and early Christian circles. The notion of an eschatological timetable against which one might count down toward the end is well established in *1 Enoch, Daniel,* the *Testament of Moses,* and other apocalyptic writings. After the destruction of Jerusalem in 70 C.E., this line of thought was developed further in the Jewish books of *4 Ezra* and *2 Baruch,* and the Christian *Revelation.*

For Further Reading

Hughes, Frank Witt. *Early Christian Rhetoric and 2 Thessalonians.* Sheffield: JSOT Press, 1989.

Jewett, Robert K. *The Thessalonian Correspondence.* Philadelphia: Fortress, 1986.

Krentz, Edgar M. "Thessalonians, First and Second Epistles to the." Pages 515–23 in vol. 6 of *Anchor Bible Dictionary.* Edited by D. N. Freedman. 6 vols. New York: Doubleday, 1992.

---

[1]If *Colossians* is Pauline, it documents an even further step away from apocalypticism, with its pervasive themes of reconciliation and peace.

[2]If the letter is a forgery, there is no need to assume that it was actually sent to Thessalonica. That might be a fictional address suggested by the forger's chosen model, *1 Thessalonians.*

THE SECOND LETTER OF PAUL
TO THE THESSALONIANS

Salutation

1 Paul, Silvanus, and Timothy,
To the church of the Thessalonians in God our[a] Father and the Lord Jesus Christ:
²Grace to you and peace from God our Father and the Lord Jesus Christ.

Thanksgiving

³We must always give thanks to God for you, brothers and sisters,[b] as is right, because your faith is growing abundantly, and the love of everyone of you for one another is increasing. ⁴Therefore we ourselves boast of you among the churches of God for your steadfastness and faith during all your persecutions and the afflictions that you are enduring.

The Judgment at Christ's Coming

⁵This is evidence of the righteous judgment of God, and is intended to make you worthy of the kingdom of God, for which you are also suffering. ⁶For it is indeed just of God to repay with affliction those who afflict you, ⁷and to give relief to the afflicted as well as to us, when the Lord Jesus is revealed from heaven with his mighty angels ⁸in flam-

ing fire, inflicting vengeance on those who do not know God and on those who do not obey the gospel of our Lord Jesus. ⁹These will suffer the punishment of eternal destruction, separated from the presence of the Lord and from the glory of his might, ¹⁰when he comes to be glorified by his saints and to be marveled at on that day among all who have believed, because our testimony to you was believed. ¹¹To this end we always pray for you, asking that our God will make you worthy of his call and will fulfill by his power every good resolve and work of faith, ¹²so that the name of our Lord Jesus may be glorified in you, and you in him, according to the grace of our God and the Lord Jesus Christ.

The Man of Lawlessness

2 As to the coming of our Lord Jesus Christ and our being gathered together to him, we beg you, brothers and sisters,[b] ²not to be quickly shaken in mind or alarmed, either by spirit or by word or by letter, as though from us, to the effect that the day of the Lord is already here. ³Let no one deceive you in any way; for that day will not come unless the rebellion comes first and the lawless one[c] is revealed, the one destined for destruction.[d] ⁴He opposes and exalts

---

a Other ancient authorities read *the*
b Gk *brothers*

c Gk *the man of lawlessness*; other ancient authorities read *the man of sin*
d Gk *the son of destruction*

1:1 This duplicates exactly *1 Thess.* 1:1. See note there. **1:2** This greeting is typical of Paul (see *1 Cor.* 1:3; *Phil.* 1:2; *Phlm.* 4; *2 Cor.* 1:2; *Gal.* 1:3; *Rom.* 1:7), but in the light of the preceding address, it seems repetitive. **1:3** *We must always give thanks to God for you, brothers and sisters . . . because* The writer will use the identical phrase to introduce his 2d thanksgiving in 2:13. **1:5–10** Paul nowhere else dwells at such length on the fate of unbelievers, although he does say in passing that they are perishing (*1 Cor.* 1:18) or will face wrath (*1 Thess.* 1:10). See also 2:9–12, which still further develops this thread. The theme of God's justice, which will cause all present status assignments to be reversed, is, however, basic to prophetic and apocalyptic thinking (*Isa.* 14–17; 40:4, 23; 41:11–20; *Ezek.* 17:2–24; 27–32; *1 Enoch* 1.5–9; 62.9–12; *Wis.* 3:1–13). **2:1** *As to* This is not the same Gk phrase as appears in *1 Thess.* 4:9, 13; 5:1; *1 Cor.* 7:1, 25; 8:1; 10:1; 12:1; 16:1, 12, where Paul responds to questions raised beforehand by his readers. It seems that the author has turned to this issue without invitation. *our being gathered together to him* Presumably in the air, recalling *1 Thess.* 4:17. **2:2** *by letter, as though from us* This might mean that the author is denouncing spiritual utterances and a forged Pauline letter asserting that the day of the Lord has come. But since the possibility of a letter seems almost an afterthought, he may be saying, in effect, "No matter where you might get the idea that the day of the Lord has already come—whether from a spiritual utterance, a prophetic word, or even in a letter from us (as if we should say such a thing)—do not believe it!" Nevertheless, in 3:17 he will make an issue of the genuineness of this letter, which strikes many interpreters as protesting too much. At least it indicates that the authenticity of Pauline letters was already an issue at the time of writing. **2:3** *the rebellion* The Gk *apostasia* could also mean a "falling away" of the faithful. See *Matt.* 24:10–12, which, speaking about the end of the age, says, "Then many will fall away [a different Gk word but possibly the same idea]. . . . Because of the increase of lawlessness [the same word as in *lawless one*, lit. 'man of lawlessness,' here], the love of many will grow cold." **2:4** This language recalls *Dan.* 11:31, 36–37. Originally the passage described the actions of Antiochus IV (Epiphanes), the Seleucid king who tried to outlaw Judaism and desecrated the temple in Jerusalem by erecting altars to foreign gods and offering unclean sacrifices. But in 1st-century and later Judaism and Christianity, the prophecies of Daniel were often taken as applying to the current time. See *Mark* 13:14;

himself above every so-called god or object of worship, so that he takes his seat in the temple of God, declaring himself to be God. 5Do you not remember that I told you these things when I was still with you? 6And you know what is now restraining him, so that he may be revealed when his time comes. 7For the mystery of lawlessness is already at work, but only until the one who now restrains it is removed. 8And then the lawless one will be revealed, whom the Lord Jesus*e* will destroy*f* with the breath of his mouth, annihilating him by the manifestation of his coming. 9The coming of the lawless one is apparent in the working of Satan, who uses all power, signs, lying wonders, 10and every kind of wicked deception for those who are perishing, because they refused to love the truth and so be saved. 11For this reason God sends them a powerful delusion, leading them to believe what is false, 12so that all who have not believed the truth but took pleasure in unrighteousness will be condemned.

Chosen for Salvation

13But we must always give thanks to God for you, brothers and sisters*g* beloved by the Lord, because God chose you as the first fruits*h* for salvation through sanctification by the Spirit and through belief in the truth. 14For this purpose he called you through our proclamation of the good news,*i* so that you may obtain the glory of our Lord Jesus Christ. 15So then, brothers and sisters,*g* stand firm and hold fast to the traditions that you were taught by us, either by word of mouth or by our letter.

16Now may our Lord Jesus Christ himself and God our Father, who loved us and through grace gave us eternal comfort and good hope, 17comfort your hearts and strengthen them in every good work and word.

Request for Prayer

3 Finally, brothers and sisters,*g* pray for us, so that the word of the Lord may spread rapidly and be glorified everywhere, just as it is among you, 2and that we may be rescued from wicked and evil people; for not all have faith. 3But the Lord is faithful; he will strengthen you and guard you from the evil one.*j* 4And we have confidence in the Lord concerning you, that you are doing and will go on doing

---

e Other ancient authorities lack *Jesus*
f Other ancient authorities read *consume*
g Gk *brothers*

h Other ancient authorities read *from the beginning*
i Or *through our gospel*
j Or *from evil*

Josephus, *Ant.* 10.210. If *2 Thessalonians* were written after 70, the lawless one could be the Roman general Titus, who entered the temple, or a personification of the Romans, or many other figures. The original meaning is lost to us so far. **2:5 *Do you not remember . . . when I was still with you?*** Since the author needs to remind the readers of this timetable, it is unlikely that they thought the end had come because they considered the timetable fulfilled. See introduction to *2 Thessalonians*. If the letter is a forgery, then the author is not in fact reminding readers but taking the opportunity to tell them for the first time. **2:6 *what is now restraining him*** So this restrainer has, in effect, temporarily suspended the apocalyptic countdown, which will resume only when it (or he) is out of the way. Although the Greek participle here for *restraining* is in the neuter grammatical gender, and so has often been identified by commentators as the Holy Spirit (also neuter), the writer may have some concrete historical force or person in mind. In 2:7, he will use the masculine form for "restraining." Some who consider the letter authentic have identified the restrainer with the relatively benign emperor Claudius (41–54 C.E.). We cannot yet, however, attain any degree of certainty in this matter. **2:8 *will destroy with the breath of his mouth*** See *Job* 4:9; *Isa.* 11:4; *Rev.* 19:15. **2:9–10** Compare the activities of the "angel of darkness" described in 1QS 3.22–23. **2:13** This second thanksgiving serves to sharpen the contrast between the perishing and the saved. **2:15 *hold fast to the traditions that you were taught by us*** See also 3:6. Paul does not elsewhere characterize his own teaching as "tradition," although he uses the word of things handed down from Jesus' earlier students; see *1 Cor.* 11:23; 15:3. For himself, Paul claims to preach a unique gospel for Gentiles (*Gal.* 1:11–17), and it is precisely the nontraditional nature of his gospel that places him at odds with other Christian teachers. In calling Paul's teachings *traditions,* therefore, the writer may be betraying his own situation, in which Paul's teachings have themselves been handed down over time. ***by our letter*** At least one of Paul's letters is well known to the readers. But *1 Thessalonians,* which talks about Paul's recent visit and the future hope, does not contain much that could be called tradition in Paul's day. The Gk phrase need not refer to a single letter (*letter* is singular, but so is "word"), and this entire sentence about traditions associated with Paul's letters may reflect the author's later vantage point. **2:16–17** The first of two benedictions in this letter; see also 3:16. **3:1 *Finally, brothers and sisters, pray for us*** Recalling *1 Thess.* 4:1; 5:25. ***the word of the Lord*** This phrase appears in Paul's letters only in *1 Thessalonians* (twice: 1:8; 4:15). ***be glorified*** Paul typically speaks of glorifying God (*1 Cor.* 6:20; *2 Cor.* 9:13; *Gal.* 1:24; *Rom.* 1:21; 15:6, 9) but not "the word of the Lord." **3:2 *that we may be rescued from wicked and evil people*** See *1 Thess.* 1:9, which speaks of Jesus, "who rescues us from the coming wrath." ***for not all have faith*** Lit. "faith [or 'the faith'] is not in [or 'with' or 'of'] everyone." Although Paul uses the word "faith" dozens of times, this usage of "the faith" as something that can be in others or not is unparalleled. **3:4 *the things that we command*** In Paul's other letters, he uses the verb *parangellō* ("command" or "instruct") sparingly (*1 Thess.* 4:11; *1 Cor.* 7:10; 11:17). His only use of the noun *parangelia* for "command" is in *1 Thess.* 4:2. But this brief letter (*2 Thessalonians*) uses the verb four times (3:4, 6, 10, 12). The author

the things that we command. [5]May the Lord direct your hearts to the love of God and to the steadfastness of Christ.

Warning against Idleness

[6]Now we command you, beloved,[k] in the name of our Lord Jesus Christ, to keep away from believers who are[l] living in idleness and not according to the tradition that they[m] received from us. [7]For you yourselves know how you ought to imitate us; we were not idle when we were with you, [8]and we did not eat anyone's bread without paying for it; but with toil and labor we worked night and day, so that we might not burden any of you. [9]This was not because we do not have that right, but in order to give you an example to imitate. [10]For even when we were with you, we gave you this command: Anyone unwilling to work should not eat. [11]For we hear that some of you are living in idleness, mere busybodies, not doing any work. [12]Now such persons we command and exhort in the Lord Jesus Christ to do their work quietly and to earn their own living. [13]Brothers and sisters,[n] do not be weary in doing what is right.

[14]Take note of those who do not obey what we say in this letter; have nothing to do with them, so that they may be ashamed. [15]Do not regard them as enemies, but warn them as believers.[o]

Final Greetings and Benediction

[16]Now may the Lord of peace himself give you peace at all times in all ways. The Lord be with all of you.

[17]I, Paul, write this greeting with my own hand. This is the mark in every letter of mine; it is the way I write. [18]The grace of our Lord Jesus Christ be with all of you.[p]

---

k Gk *brothers*
l Gk *from every brother who is*
m Other ancient authorities read *you*

n Gk *Brothers*
o Gk *a brother*
p Other ancient authorities add *Amen*

---

seems very concerned to maintain an authority traceable to Paul, as is the author of *1 Timothy* (1:3, 5, 18; 4:11; 5:7; 6:13, 17). The concepts of tradition and command go together well in a post-Pauline context. **3:6** *we command you* See note to 3:4. **believers who are living in idleness** In *1 Thess.* 5:14 Paul said simply "to admonish the idlers," with no elaboration. The Gk word used there for "idlers" occurs (*ataktos*, in its noun, verb, or adjectival forms) in these early Christian texts only there and three times here in *2 Thessalonians* (3:6, 7, 11). The word group carries the root idea of "undisciplined," but in the context here it particularly suggests those who do not wish to work (3:8, 10, 11, 12). This perceived idleness could result from principle (e.g., if the Day of the Lord has come, why bother working?). But the writer might well be developing a safe topic from *1 Thessalonians* simply in order to lend Pauline credibility to the letter. **the tradition that they received from us** See note to 2:15. **3:7** *For you yourselves know* This letter formula, to refer to something already conveyed in a previous meeting or letter, occurs elsewhere in Paul only in *1 Thessalonians* (three times, 2:1; 3:3; 5:2). **imitate us** The theme of imitation is prominent in Paul's early letters: *1 Thess.* 1:6; 2:14; *1 Cor.* 4:16; 11:1; *Phil.* 3:17. **3:8** Much of this sentence is a verbatim parallel to *1 Thess.* 2:9. **3:9** On Paul's right to be supported, which he voluntarily waives, see also *1 Cor.* 9:4–18; *2 Cor.* 11:7–15; but see also *Phil.* 4:15. **an example to imitate** See note to 3:7. **3:17** Paul typically dictated his letters to a stenographer, or amanuensis (*Rom.* 16:22), and added a greeting in his own hand (*1 Cor.* 16:21; *Phlm.* 19; *Gal.* 6:11). The author's language here, however, is unparalleled; it seems to be defensive, suggesting that the authenticity of Pauline letters was already an issue at the time of writing. See also 2:2.

The Pastoral Letters

TITUS ✠ 1 TIMOTHY ✠ 2 TIMOTHY

The Pastoral Corpus

Most of the letters attributed to Paul were sent to city churches (Corinth, Rome, Thessalonica, Philippi, Colossae, Ephesus, Laodicea[1]) or to larger ethnic areas or provinces (Galatians). But four Pauline letters were addressed to individuals. Three of these generally have been grouped together, and from the middle of the eighteenth century have been known as the Pastoral Letters. These letters were so named because they were addressed to associates of Paul[2] (Timothy and Titus) who were functioning as "pastors."[3]

These three letters are linked by identical concerns regarding church office, Christian behavior, and sound teaching. Equally striking is their stylistic unity, so much so that these letters have become a test case for a number of literary and linguistic arguments used in determining the authenticity of documents.

Setting

The picture the letters paint is of apostolic delegates engaged in defending the Pauline position against "false" doctrine, accomplishing this largely through the establishment and regulation of church offices and duties. According to the letters,

---

[1]Such a letter is mentioned in *Col.* 4:16. In the second century, someone passed off a compilation of Pauline material as the letter to the *Laodiceans*. If *Colossians* is itself the work of a pseudonymous author, as many contend, a letter to the *Laodiceans* may be part of that author's fiction.

[2]Two of the Pastoral Letters are addressed to Timothy, one to Titus. Both men figure prominently as Paul's close associates. Their specific role is difficult to determine, since they (according to the Pastoral Letters themselves) were responsible for setting up offices in the church. They appear in some way to be above or apart from the offices they establish. Some scholars have argued that they function like monarchical bishops, similar to what we find in the Ignatian letters.

[3]The word *pastor* is used occasionally in our literature to translate the Gk word *poimēn*, which is normally translated *shepherd*. Leaders in the early church were sometimes called shepherds, though never in the Pastoral Letters themselves (*Eph.* 4:11). In *Acts* 20:28, *1 Pet.* 2:25 and 5:2, the term *pastor* or the related verb is used of bishops, though it is not clear whether the term *bishop* is to be taken as a technical term for a special office or to be translated merely as *overseer* or, in the verb form, as *overseeing*, describing function rather than formal office.

Paul was away[4] and needed to call various matters to the attention of Timothy and Titus by means of letters. These letters, in turn, not only instructed Paul's associates but functioned as the very tool by which the instructions could be carried out, serving as Paul's authoritative voice and calling the full Christian assembly to obedience. The letters could have served in this way whether they were the work of Paul or a later pseudonymous author in the Pauline tradition.

The first letter addressed to Timothy and the one addressed to Titus reflect situations in which close associates of Paul are called on to defend "true" doctrine and to instruct church leaders and the wider membership in matters of general behavior. Further, the qualifications and duties of those who hold positions of authority in the hierarchy of the church are common themes. No doubt, the themes go together: credible leadership and a properly instructed membership, protected from the threat of "heresy,"[5] which involves both bad teaching and morally flawed teachers.

The second letter to Timothy is somewhat different, having all the appearances of a final testament, containing Paul's dying requests and directions. Even here, however, many of the concerns are identical with those expressed in the other two Pastoral Letters.

The question of "setting" is related to the question of the date of the documents. If the Pastorals are pseudonymous (see "authorship"), as is widely thought, the letters are set in the context of a struggle to defend and maintain the pseudonymous author's particular theological position by appealing to Pauline authority sometime after the death of Paul. If authentic, then Paul is defending his own position against serious challenge. In neither case do we know anything else about the conflict; these letters are our only witness.

Overview

The letter to Titus appears first in the *Reader,* in accord with what appears to have been an early order for the Pastoral letter collection.[6] The longer preface of *Titus* is thought by some to have served as a preface to the entire collection.

The second letter to Timothy is placed at the end of the collection, since Paul's approaching death is a key topic. This is the natural position for Paul's "last words,"

---

[4]*First Timothy* 1:3 mentions that Paul had gone to Macedonia (a Roman province); *Titus* 3:12 states that Paul was wintering in Nicopolis, a seaport on the western coast of Achaia (Greece); *2 Tim.* 4:16 suggests that Paul was in Rome.

[5]Many scholars are uncomfortable using such terms as *heresy, orthodoxy, truth, error,* etc. to identify groups or positions within the early church. These labels, they contend, obscure the rich variety of belief that was tolerated initially. Further, they argue, by using such terminology, we basically side with the winning party and accept the winner's assessment of right and wrong, to the disadvantage of the others.

[6] This order occurs in a canonical list dating possibly from the second century, the so-called Muratorian Canon. The same order is reflected in Ambrosiaster's fourth-century Latin commentary on the Pauline letters. Some argue that the Muratorian Canon is itself from the fourth century.

whether the letters are from Paul or from a later Paulinist. The more familiar canonical order *(1 Timothy, 2 Timothy, Titus)* is thought to have been determined by length, from longest to shortest.

Themes and Issues

In the fight with beliefs that the author judged unacceptable, he put forward a detailed structure of church hierarchy, in which credible individuals were appointed to recognizable positions. These officeholders not only had general duties for the care of the church, they were also to guard against these "heretical" positions that the author had dismissed. Thus these letters have come to be a major focus of study for understanding the development of church office and the process of self-definition by which one stream of the early church evaluated and rejected alternative forms of Christian belief and practice.

The primary insight into the development of church office is that the terms *presbyters* and *bishops* seem to be used largely as synonyms.[7] Later, a clear distinction was to be made, with individual bishops set off from and having authority over the body of presbyters. A comparison of the duties and character traits of the elders mentioned in *Titus* (1:5–9) and the bishops of *1 Timothy* (3:1–7) will show the long list of parallels.

Authorship

In scholarly circles, the authenticity of the Pastoral Letters has received the roughest ride of the letters attributed to Paul. About the only thing agreed on is that the three letters likely came from the same hand. Everything else has produced sharp debate. The following is only a sketch of some of the issues that have occupied scholars for the last two hundred years.

Although the opening of each letter specifies that it is from Paul, the majority of scholars have challenged that attribution on stylistic, historical, ecclesiastical, and theological grounds. The arguments are complicated and detailed; they cannot be considered in more than outline form here. It can be said though (whatever the conclusion about authorship) that these letters do stand clearly in a Pauline tradition, and probably a *centrist* Pauline tradition. Some scholars have even argued that, though the letters as they now stand are not compositions of Paul, genuine Pauline fragments or notes are preserved within them.[8]

In the last two hundred years, the most effective argument against Paul's authorship of the Pastorals has emphasized the differences in style and vocabulary.

---

[7] In *Titus* 1:5, 7, the terms are most clearly used as synonyms.

[8] One theory posits three genuine Pauline fragments, which were themselves fragmented further by the author of the Pastorals as he incorporated them into his letter: (1) *Titus* 3:12–15; (2) *2 Tim.* 4:9–15, 20, 21a, 22b; and (3) *2 Tim.* 1:16–18; 3:10, 11, 4:1, 2a, 5b–8, 16–19; 21b–22a.

Many features are pointed to: the richer or more literary vocabulary of the Pastoral Letters; the use of different synonyms (where the Pastorals employ a different word than Paul used in the undisputed letters for the same concept); and the number of words unique to each document (called improperly *hapax legomena*). More recently, computers have been used to determine the frequency or pattern of specific words,[9] or to determine whether authors had an average sentence length consistent throughout their writings that might serve as a fingerprint (or voiceprint) useful in identifying the works of an author.

Those who defend Pauline authorship for the Pastorals usually dismiss these observations about style as insignificant. Some have argued that as a person ages, style will change, so that letters written toward the end of Paul's life (as they assume the Pastorals were) could be expected to show stylistic variation from an earlier pattern. Others have argued that prison confinement may have affected Paul's style,[10] perhaps by requiring the use of an amanuensis (or secretary), so that the letter reflected the scribe's style but the apostle's thought. Still others have argued that a change in theme may account for some of the stylistic differences. But none of these explanations has reversed the fairly widespread conclusion in scholarly circles that the Pastoral Letters did not come from Paul.

Although the linguistic arguments still dominate much of the debate over authorship, other issues are thought to offer at least as substantial a base for deciding the question. Some scholars point out that various historical or biographical details from the Pastoral Letters do not seem to fit with what we know about Paul from the accounts of his activities in the book of *Acts* or from the glimpses we can get of Paul's itinerary from his own letters.[11]

Other scholars have emphasized the different ecclesiology (church structure and order) in the Pastorals from the order found in Paul's churches during his life. They argue that whereas Paul spoke of apostles, prophets, and teachers, and seems to have promoted a charismatic leadership, the author of the Pastorals spoke of bishops, presbyters, and deacons, which reflects an institutionalization of leadership against charismatic tendencies. But some caution must be used in specifying a uniform structure in the Pauline communities.[12]

---

[9]Lack of care has marked some of the computer investigations, though it is generally accepted that the identification of common words that people use almost unconsciously are useful indicators of an author's distinctive style. In English, we could examine words such as *and, now, yet, but, again, thus,* etc. These words should remain largely unaffected by content, which might affect other vocabulary. Similar words are examined in Gk.

[10]The case can be made only for *2 Timothy,* where a number of comments are made about trial and imprisonment (1:8, 16; 2:9; 4:6; 16).

[11]The problem with this argument is that the *Acts* account is itself difficult to fit into Paul's movements as reflected in his letters, which provide only minimal details useful for reconstructing Paul's itinerary. Further, though the Pastorals are not illuminated by the itinerary of Paul in *Acts,* the differences between the two are not so great as to make common authorship entirely impossible.

[12]Paul's clearest statement on the topic is found in *1 Cor.* 12:28, but it is difficult to argue that Paul was deeply committed to this structure. A different structure (with bishops and deacons) seems to

Another difference between the Pastorals and the undisputed Pauline letters is the theology. Even here scholars argue whether the distance in theological perspective is a matter of development (in which case the letters could still be attributed to Paul), or a matter of discontinuity or dissimilarity (in which case the letters are better attributed to another author). Of particular concern is the way the author speaks of *the faith* or *sound teaching* as fixed elements to be protected and transmitted, an attitude, it is argued, that is foreign to the creative period of the earliest Christians and equally foreign to Paul's own creative genius. Most scholars are sufficiently impressed by the difference in theological perspective to conclude that the Pastorals were not written by Paul, though it is impossible to deny that they at least stand in the Pauline tradition. Paul is clearly the hero of both the writer and the recipients, and the author is relying on the strength of Paul's authority to gain his letters a hearing.

Date

The dating of the letters is problematic too. The Pastorals are usually taken as a group and assumed to have been written over a short period of time—whether by Paul or by someone else. Scholars who argue for the authenticity of these letters usually place them late in Paul's career, shortly before his death, because *2 Timothy* reflects a period toward the end of Paul's life (in prison and expecting death: *2 Tim.* 4:6–8), and *Titus* and *1 Timothy* are judged to come from the same period.

But most scholars conclude that the Pastorals are pseudonymous and relate to the end of Paul's life only as fiction. The question of the date, then, is focused on when a Paulinist may have been interested in providing a fresh "word of Paul" for a new and troubling situation.

If we take western Asia Minor to be the setting of the Pastorals, the comments in the letters regarding church office may help us determine the date. The Ignatian letters, written to the same area and dealing with similar concerns about church office, seem to reflect a more developed structure. Though both Ignatius and the author of the Pastorals mention bishops, elders, and deacons as the primary church leaders, in the Pastorals the bishops do not seem to be set off clearly from the presbytery (or body of elders), as they are in the Ignatian material. In the Pastorals, the term *bishop* seems to be used almost as a synonym for *elder* or *presbyter*, suggesting an earlier period than the Ignatian letters, perhaps somewhere in the 90s or early 100s.

---

have been in place in the church at Philippi, yet Paul, the founder of that church, mentioned the structure without so much as even "raising his eyebrows" (*Phil.* 1:1). Further, churches or writers within the Pauline orbit promoted various kinds of structures (*Eph.* 4:11–12, and the Pastoral Letters themselves). In fact, no Pauline apologist in the second generation of the church comes to the defense of any Pauline structure of church order. So it appears that no view of church structure had gained normative status in the Pauline communities, and the comment in *1 Corinthians* need not be taken as the *locus classicus* for Paul's view of church office.

Some scholars have contended that not all second-century Christians knew the Pastorals as Paul's writings. They are missing from Marcion's canon (ca. 140 C.E.). But this omission may reflect Marcion's hostility to the Pastorals rather than an ignorance of their existence. They are also missing from the Chester Beatty Papyrus ($\mathfrak{P}^{46}$), a third-century Egyptian manuscript of Paul's letters. But since that manuscript is not complete, not everyone is convinced that it did not originally contain the Pastorals.

Audience

The letters are addressed to Timothy and Titus, colleagues of Paul.[13] But the content of the three letters clearly indicates that the instructions were intended for a wider audience,[14] addressing every member of the Christian assembly. That would indicate the Christians of Ephesus (*1 Tim.* 1:3; *2 Tim.* 1:18; 4:12) and Crete (*Titus* 1:5), if the letters are authentic.

Even if the letters are pseudonymous, as is more widely thought, the greetings to Timothy in Ephesus and Titus in Crete still provide some clue about the audience. Such notes about location must have been at least of some interest to the initial audience. This holds true even if the references to locale are merely part of the pseudonymous author's attempt to give an air of authenticity to the letters.[15] Further, the letters must have been addressed to a circle in which Timothy and Titus were fondly remembered, and in which Paul himself (the putative author of these letters) would have been viewed as a primary authority. So an audience firmly within the Pauline circle is required, and western Asia Minor is as likely a region as any.

The Opponents

All three letters battle common opponents. Scholars have long debated the identification of this "other side" in the Pastorals without much success or consensus. The description of the enemy is sufficiently detailed to show that the author has specific opponents in mind; it is not specific enough, however, for us to identify

---

[13]According to *1 Tim.* 1:3, Paul had recently left Ephesus for Macedonia and had placed Timothy in charge in Ephesus. It is not explicitly stated where Timothy was when *2 Timothy* was written, though given the number of things said about Asia (1:15–18; 4:12–13; 19–21), the author clearly places him in that area, and probably in Ephesus, for Onesiphorus is tied to Ephesus (*2 Tim.* 1:16–18), and Timothy is expected to greet Onesiphorus's household (4:19). Titus is on Crete (*Titus* 1:5), which is close enough to western Asia Minor to have had some contact with churches there, and perhaps to have been under the influence of the church leaders in the area.

[14]This observation is less certain for *2 Timothy*, which has a more personal and perhaps private character than the other two letters. For example, instructions for various offices in the church are missing. If the letters are pseudonymous, such a tone becomes more a literary device than a clue to the nature of the document and the relation of author to recipient.

[15]Although we know nothing of a Pauline mission to Crete, we cannot rule out such a mission, either by Paul himself or an associate—perhaps even Titus. This places the writings in the general area of Paul's main mission, and at the center if the Ephesian connection is emphasized.

these opponents. We should not assume that our inability to identify the opponents reflects a similar difficulty for the original readers. They, no doubt, were able to point to individuals or groups familiar to them, since these letters clearly were intended to be an effective response to undesirable beliefs and practices.

Many have argued that the opponents confronted in the Pastoral Letters were gnostics of some kind, who emphasized initiation into secret knowledge through which the individual could attain liberation from the bondage of the material world.[16] During the early part of the second century, elaborate gnostic systems were beginning to develop, but it is a matter of scholarly debate how much earlier such developed systems can be found.

Some scholars see in gnosticism a system that grew out of Christianity. The other more dominant group sees gnosticism as a religion initially independent of Christianity, and contemporary with the beginnings of the church. Part of the disagreement stems from gnosticism's use of religious terms that a variety of groups might comfortably have employed;[17] part of the disagreement stems from the numerous and varied forms within gnosticism and Christianity. The Pastorals may confront some such system, but it is unlikely that any particular gnostic system can be identified as the object of the Pastorals' attack. The polemic of the Pastorals is simply not specific enough to assist much in identifying the opponents.

All that can be said with certainty is that the author does not seem to be concerned with the kind of judaizing confronted by Paul (e.g., in *Galatians*), though the opponents in the Pastorals do seem to have some judaizing traits, and questions about the law do play some role.[18] Some argue that to expect to discover exactly who these opponents were may be a little too optimistic. It may even be that references to opponents have been included simply to give a "Pauline flavor" to the Pastorals.

The dismissal of the opponents and the call to approved order and behavior is supported by an appeal to cherished tradition. Yet, the detail of some of the instructions suggests that they are being presented for the first time in such a full and orderly way.

---

[16]Gnostic tendencies are suggested by references to ascetic behavior (*1 Tim.* 4:3), myths (*1 Tim.* 1:4; 4:7; *2 Tim.* 4:4), a particular view of the resurrection (*2 Tim.* 2:18), and the striking phrase "what is falsely called knowledge" (*1 Tim.* 6:20). Perhaps the reference to *genealogies* should be included too (*Titus* 3:9; *1 Tim.* 1:4). But the details are vague and puzzling, making any reconstruction of the beliefs of the opponents highly speculative.

[17]There is a developed and distinctive gnostic jargon in the second century. Such jargon is not shared with other Christian texts. Many scholars consider a more general language to be largely *gnostic,* and this kind of language appears in a wider range of early Christian literature (the *Gospel of John,* for example). But terms that gnostics might conveniently use are not necessarily terms they have exclusive right to.

[18]Judaizing tendencies are suggested by the author's references to *those of the circumcision* (*Titus* 1:10), *Jewish myths* (*Titus* 1:14), *quarrels about the law* (*Titus* 3:9), *teachers of the law* and a discourse on the purpose of the law (*1 Tim.* 1:7–11).

Relation to Other Early Christian Writings

Although much has been made of the striking differences between the Pastoral Letters and the other letters of Paul, when everything is considered the Pastorals share more with the Pauline materials than with any other document or corpus. Perhaps that similarity is owing to a pseudonymous author's conscious attempt to make his own compositions appear to be genuinely Pauline. If so, he was successful, since the letters appear to have been widely and early accepted as Pauline. Indeed, there are more than 450 quotations or allusions to the Pastorals in the surviving second-century literature alone. Some scholars contend that both Ignatius and Clement of Rome knew the Pastorals; somewhat more certain is Polycarp's knowledge of the letters.

Value for the Study of the Early Church

Most scholars place the Pastorals somewhere in the line of development of the Pauline tradition after Paul's death. By dating the Pastorals in this postapostolic period, they believe that they can make better sense of the new concerns that seem now to affect the Pauline communities. For example, the particular kind of struggle with Judaism that is central in some of Paul's writings is missing from the Pastorals.[19] Also gone is the urgent apocalyptic expectation that had marked Paul's writings. These issues have been replaced by a concern for church structure and order, individual behavior,[20] and respect for the tradition.

The cluster of features found in the Pastorals can be found within a wide spectrum of Christian thinking in the second generation of the church. This new tendency, characterized by a move away from charismatic and informal structures to institutionalized and formal ones, has often been labeled "early catholicism." But there is considerable disagreement regarding how marked or uniform that tendency was, and whether it marked a positive or negative change for the early church.

---

[19]That does not mean that the issue of Torah was absent from the Pastorals or that the issue is always present in the authentic Pauline letters. In fact, Torah is central to the debate in the Pastorals (*1 Tim.* 1:7–10; *Titus* 1:10, 14; 3:9). The problem is that the arguments and issues seem different, or at least more obscured. The debate is whether the perspective on Torah is so different from Paul's perspective to require a different author.

[20]The concern about behavior is reflected in the use of household or domestic codes (*Titus* 2:2–10; *1 Tim.* 5:1–2; 6:1–2), and by catalogues of virtues (*1 Tim.* 3:2–7) and vices (*Titus* 1:5–9) found scattered throughout these letters. Similar codes (German *Haustafeln*) existed in the Hellenistic literature of the day. Some scholars have argued that the use of such codes points to the "house church" structure that characterized most early Christian communities. The evidence from a wide variety of sources seems to point to the use of homes or "household" as the primary unit for regular corporate worship of the young churches, with several, and perhaps even many, such units within each city.

Comparing the Three Pastoral Letters

Titus and *1 Timothy*

The *Letter to Titus* shares much with *1 Timothy*. Indeed, one wonders why an author would have bothered to write the second letter. Surely either one could have served his purposes.[21] Almost everything of a substantial nature in one is mentioned in the other also. There are, of course, some differences in detail, but the differences are not striking; they clearly come from the same mind focused on the same set of problems. Some differences stem from the more detailed presentation that the author provides in *1 Timothy*, a letter that is twice as long as *Titus*. As well, in *1 Timothy* the author has a few special concerns: the duties of the deacons and a more detailed analysis of the position of women, especially widows. He also includes a discussion about wealth and contentment in his closing remarks (6:6–10, 17–19).

The most significant difference between the two letters is that *1 Timothy* is richer in what appear to be autobiographical musings, offering a number of personal and private details of Paul and Timothy's lives. *Titus* is more skeletal: the author addresses the pressing issues briefly and clearly. One might say that *1 Timothy* is a more detailed version of *Titus*, with biographical nostalgia providing a bit of color.

1 Timothy and *2 Timothy*

Biographical details in *1 Timothy* are scattered throughout the letter. In this, it resembles more closely the structure of *2 Timothy* but not of *Titus*, where personal notes are kept to the opening and closing comments. To what extent biographical information can be treated as reliable information about Paul and his associates is debated.

2 Timothy

The second letter addressed to Timothy, though sharing much of the language and worldview of the other two Pastorals, is distinctive. It lacks the interest in church office that is characteristic of the other two. Further, it is more heavily biographical and personal.

Twenty-three people (associates, friends, and even enemies) are mentioned by name. This compares to two people named in the longer *1 Timothy* and four people in *Titus*. Further, Paul is presented as a prisoner in this letter (1:8; 4:16–18), but that is not the case in the other two (*1 Tim.* 3:14–15; *Titus* 3:12). Indeed, the tone of the letter and its prison context in Rome (where Paul was to die) make the letter function almost as Paul's "last words."[22]

---

[21]One might argue that the second letter was especially tailored for churches in a particular locale, such as the island of Crete (*Titus* 1:1–16). Yet the two passages that mention Crete (1:5, 12) really add nothing to the overall argument. The same problem exists for the mention of Ephesus in *1 Timothy*.

[22]As a last will and testament, it is similar to *2 Peter*.

Most of the people mentioned by name in the Pastoral Letters as Paul's associates are not mentioned by Paul in his undisputed letters; nor are they mentioned in the portrayal of his mission provided in *Acts*. This has been taken by many to be evidence that the Pastorals were not written by Paul: people supposedly associated with Paul do not appear in Paul's real world as we know it from other evidence.

No convincing explanation of the identity of these characters has been offered: whether fictional creations, or contemporaries of the pseudonymous author, or otherwise unknown contemporaries of Paul. Some investigators can make so little sense of such personal material in the work of a pseudonymous author that they have concluded these passages must reflect genuine Pauline fragments from now lost authentic correspondence.

For Further Reading

Dibelius, Martin, and Hans Conzelmann. *The Pastoral Epistles.* Translated by Philip Buttolph and Adela Yarbro [Collins]. Hermeneia. Philadelphia: Fortress Press, 1972.

Fee, Gordon D. *1 and 2 Timothy, Titus.* New International Biblical Commentary. Peabody, Mass.: Hendrickson, 1988.

Hanson, A. T. *The Pastoral Epistles.* New Century Bible Commentary. Grand Rapids: Eerdmans, 1982.

Harrison, P. N. *The Problem of the Pastoral Epistles.* London: Oxford University Press, 1921.

Kelly, J. N. D. *The Pastoral Epistles.* Black's New Testament Commentary. London: A & C Black, 1960. Repr., Peabody, Mass.: Hendrickson, 1993.

Newman, Kenneth J. *The Authenticity of the Pauline Epistles in the Light of Stylostatistical Analysis.* Atlanta: Scholars Press, 1990.

THE LETTER OF PAUL
TO TITUS

Salutation

1 Paul, a servant*a* of God and an apostle of Jesus Christ, for the sake of the faith of God's elect and the knowledge of the truth that is in accordance with godliness, ²in the hope of eternal life that God, who never lies, promised before the ages began— ³in due time he revealed his word through the proclamation with which I have been entrusted by the command of God our Savior,

⁴To Titus, my loyal child in the faith we share:

Grace*b* and peace from God the Father and Christ Jesus our Savior.

Titus in Crete

⁵I left you behind in Crete for this reason, so that you should put in order what remained to be done, and should appoint elders in every town, as I directed you: ⁶someone who is blameless, married only once,*c* whose children are believers, not accused of debauchery and not rebellious. ⁷For a bishop,*d* as God's steward, must be blameless; he must not be arrogant or quick-tempered or addicted to wine or violent or greedy for gain; ⁸but he must be hospitable, a lover of goodness, prudent, upright, devout, and self-controlled. ⁹He must have a firm grasp of the word that is trustworthy in accordance with the teaching, so that he may be able both to preach with sound doctrine and to refute those who contradict it.

¹⁰There are also many rebellious people, idle talkers and deceivers, especially those of the circumcision; ¹¹they must be silenced, since they are upsetting whole families by teaching for sordid gain what it is

---

a Gk *slave*
b Other ancient authorities read *Grace, mercy,*

c Gk *husband of one wife*
d Or *an overseer*

1:1 *God our Savior* This phrase is used five times in the Pastorals (*Titus* 1:1, 3; 2:10; 3:4; *1 Tim.* 2:3; see also *1 Tim.* 4:10 and *Jude* 25) but never in the other letters attributed to Paul; the word "savior" (*sōtēr*) is used only once in the undisputed Paulines (*Phil.* 3:20) but ten times in the Pastorals (also once in *Eph.* 5:23). The imperial cult and Hellenistic mystery cults frequently used the titles "savior" and "lord" (*kyrios*) for their deity, as did Hellenistic Judaism when speaking of God (e.g., in the writings of Philo of Alexandria). **1:3** *with which I have been entrusted* 2 *Tim.* 1:11. **1:4** *loyal child* Lit. "legitimate child." In our literature, the phrase occurs elsewhere only in the description of Timothy (*1 Tim.* 1:4, 18; *2 Tim.* 1:2; 2:1). This is one of the shared features that suggest all the Pastoral Letters were written by the same author. Indeed, the entire opening parallels the opening of *1 Timothy* (1:1–2). Paul's own view may have informed the author at this point (see *1 Cor.* 4:17 and *Phil.* 2:22, both in reference to Timothy). **1:5** There is no record of Paul's being on Crete except for a brief stay on his way to Rome as a prisoner. Certainly the author's presentation of a Pauline mission to Crete is not in itself implausible. The island was within easy reach of western Asia Minor, the center of Paul's mission. This does not help us in determining the historical accuracy of the account here, however, for a pseudonymous author could have had a fine sense of the historically probable. The only other reference to Crete in our literature is in *Acts* 27, reporting Paul's brief stop there as a prisoner. *should appoint elders* The author seems to be using the words "elder" and "bishop" as synonyms. In his attempt to justify the criteria he is prescribing for *elders* (1:5), he says: "For a bishop, as God's steward, must be blameless" (1:7). Further, the criteria parallel those listed for bishops in *1 Tim.* 3:1–7. **1:6** *married only once* Lit. "husband of one wife." The phrase occurs elsewhere in the Pastorals (*1 Tim.* 3:2, 12; *1 Tim.* 5:9). There has been considerable debate about the meaning, with the following options suggested: (a) against divorce, (b) against polygamy, (c) against remarriage after the death of the wife, or (d) against unfaithfulness in marriage. The NRSV translators have opted for the third possibility. Both Christian and pagan authors sometimes idealized those who did not remarry after the death of their spouse (*1 Tim.* 3:2, 12; 5:9; Seneca, *On Marriage* 72–77). **1:9** *sound doctrine* This verse seems to speak of a core of received teaching or doctrine by which current teaching was to be judged. In this, many scholars see evidence for a second-generation composition, where the teacher's duty was to preserve what had been handed on. Other passages in the Pastorals are judged to reflect this same attitude (*Titus* 1:13; 2:1, 2; *1 Tim.* 1:3, 10–11; 6:3; 20; *2 Tim.* 1:13–14; 2:2; 3:14–15; 4:1–3). Compare, too, passages identified as "faithful sayings," which may suggest the development of tradition (*See* 3:8). **1:10** *those of the circumcision* Scholars have found it difficult to identify the opponents targeted in the Pastorals from the details provided. Terms such as *rebellious people, idle talkers,* and *deceivers* are largely without content and are drawn from a stock of polemical terms that could be applied at random to the opponent of choice. The tag *those of the circumcision* is a little more specific. It probably refers to Christians who are Jews or who are promoting Jewish practices in the churches. **1:11** *whole families* The Pastorals' striking emphasis on the family unit is not paralleled in the other literature of our collection. Compare the treatment in *1 Clem.* 1.14 to that of the Pastorals (*Titus* 1:11; 2:5; 3:12, 15; 5:4, 8, 14; *2 Tim.* 1:16; 3:6; 4:19). *sordid gain* See *1 Tim.* 6:5.

not right to teach. [12]It was one of them, their very own prophet, who said,

"Cretans are always liars, vicious brutes, lazy gluttons."

[13]That testimony is true. For this reason rebuke them sharply, so that they may become sound in the faith, [14]not paying attention to Jewish myths or to commandments of those who reject the truth. [15]To the pure all things are pure, but to the corrupt and unbelieving nothing is pure. Their very minds and consciences are corrupted. [16]They profess to know God, but they deny him by their actions. They are detestable, disobedient, unfit for any good work.

Teach Sound Doctrine

2 But as for you, teach what is consistent with sound doctrine. [2]Tell the older men to be temperate, serious, prudent, and sound in faith, in love, and in endurance.

[3]Likewise, tell the older women to be reverent in behavior, not to be slanderers or slaves to drink; they are to teach what is good, [4]so that they may encourage the young women to love their husbands, to love their children, [5]to be self-controlled, chaste, good managers of the household, kind, being submissive to their husbands, so that the word of God may not be discredited.

[6]Likewise, urge the younger men to be self-controlled. [7]Show yourself in all respects a model of good works, and in your teaching show integrity, gravity, [8]and sound speech that cannot be censured; then any opponent will be put to shame, having nothing evil to say of us.

[9]Tell slaves to be submissive to their masters and to give satisfaction in every respect; they are not to talk back, [10]not to pilfer, but to show complete and perfect fidelity, so that in everything they may be an ornament to the doctrine of God our Savior.

[11]For the grace of God has appeared, bringing salvation to all,[e] [12]training us to renounce impiety and worldly passions, and in the present age to live lives that are self-controlled, upright, and godly, [13]while we wait for the blessed hope and the manifestation of the glory of our great God and Savior,[f] Jesus Christ. [14]He it is who gave himself for us that he might redeem us from all iniquity and purify for himself a people of his own who are zealous for good deeds.

---

e Or has appeared to all, bringing salvation
f Or of the great God and our Savior

1:12 lazy gluttons The quotation was thought to have been made by Epimenides about seven hundred years earlier. The slur apparently stuck and is mentioned by various writers (Callimachus, *Hymn to Zeus* 8; Lucian, *Lovers of Lies* 3). The use of this phrase is not proof that the author of the Pastorals was familiar with any more than this brief quotation. **1:14 Jewish myths** It is not clear what is intended by *myths* or the "genealogies" mentioned with myths in other passages. Perhaps they were the epic stories and genealogies of Jewish scripture (*Titus* 3:9; *1 Tim.* 1:4; 4:7; *2 Tim.* 4:4; see *1 Tim.* 1:4). **1:15 all things are pure** *1 Tim.* 4:3–5; *Mark* 7:19; *Rom.* 14:20. The opponents may have been ascetic; the evidence for this is clearer in *1 Timothy*. In *Titus*, a few comments suggest that the opposite tendency marked at least some of the Christians— "lazy gluttons" (1:12) and "slaves to drink" (2:3). Even in *1 Timothy*, where asceticism perhaps was a problem, the author nonetheless encourages temperance (3:3, 8, 11) **2:2 older men** This word is a cognate of the word translated "elders" in 1:5. Although the words can mean the same thing, the two groups should be distinguished here. Separate instructions have been provided for each (1:6–9; 2:1), and the instructions for *older* men (2:2) are linked with instructions for "younger" men (2:6–8), a group that did not constitute a formal office. Those called "elders" were leaders in some identifiable way, it seems; the others were simply the older men in the congregation. The word translated "elder" (Gk *presbyteros*) became the technical term for a church office. See *1 Tim.* 5:1. **2:3 the older women** The words in verses 2 and 3 translated here as *older men* and *older women* are slightly different from the words used elsewhere by the author of the Pastorals. See 2:2. It is unlikely that this verse can serve as evidence of an order of women elders, since this body is linked with a male counterpart in the previous verse, which was itself distinguished from a formal body of "elders." **2:5 managers of the household** *1 Tim.* 3:12; 5:14. See 1:11. **submissive to their husbands** *1 Cor.* 11:3; *Eph.* 5:22, 24; *Col.* 3:18; *1 Pet.* 3:1; Plutarch, *Advice to Bride and Groom* 33. **2:7 good works** This phrase (in either a singular or plural form) is characteristic of the Pastoral Letters (*Titus* 1:16; 3:1, 8, 14; *1 Tim.* 2:10; 5:10, 25; 6:18; *2 Tim.* 2:21; 3:17). It does not occur in the other Paulines except in *Eph.* 2:10. Some have argued that this is proof of the non-Pauline authorship of the Pastorals, where the author has fallen into a moralizing interest that was foreign to Paul. **2:9 slaves** Modern readers have frequently condemned the early Christian acceptance of slavery. Many in ancient Mediterranean society feared the possibility of a slave revolt, a fear that does not shape modern thinking (*1 Tim.* 6:1–2; *1 Cor.* 7:21–24; *Col.* 3:22–4:1; *Eph.* 6:5–9; *1 Pet.* 2:18–21; *Barn.* 19.7; Ign. *Pol.* 4.3; *1 Clement* 61). **2:11–14** Some scholars argue that this is a liturgical fragment. **2:13 manifestation** Gk *epiphaneian*, referring to the second coming of Christ. Paul always uses *parousia;* the author of the Pastorals always uses *epiphaneia*. Such a difference in choice of synonyms has been used as evidence that Paul was not the author of the Pastorals. See *1 Tim.* 6:14; *2 Tim.* 1:10; 4:1, 8. The verb form is used in *Titus* 2:11 and 3:4, translated in the NRSV as "appeared." The language of the Pastorals here is similar to that used in the imperial cult. **our great God** This is a bold statement about the divine status of Jesus and, as such, is rare in the earliest Christian texts (*John* 20:28; *Heb.* 1:8), but in Ignatius's writings (Ign. *Eph.* 1.2; Ign. *Rom.* 1.2, 7; 3.8), such language is routine; see Ign. *Eph.* salutation. **2:14 redeem** See *1 Tim.* 2:6. There is probably an allusion here to similar statements in the Jewish scriptures (*Ps.* 130:8; *Ezek.* 37:23; *Deut.* 14:2).

15Declare these things; exhort and reprove with all authority.g Let no one look down on you.

Maintain Good Deeds

3 Remind them to be subject to rulers and authorities, to be obedient, to be ready for every good work, 2to speak evil of no one, to avoid quarreling, to be gentle, and to show every courtesy to everyone. 3For we ourselves were once foolish, disobedient, led astray, slaves to various passions and pleasures, passing our days in malice and envy, despicable, hating one another. 4But when the goodness and loving kindness of God our Savior appeared, 5he saved us, not because of any works of righteousness that we had done, but according to his mercy, through the waterh of rebirth and renewal by the Holy Spirit. 6This Spirit he poured out on us richly through Jesus Christ our Savior, 7so that, having been justified by his grace, we might become heirs according to the hope of eternal life. 8The saying is sure.

I desire that you insist on these things, so that those who have come to believe in God may be careful to devote themselves to good works; these things are excellent and profitable to everyone. 9But avoid stupid controversies, genealogies, dissensions, and quarrels about the law, for they are unprofitable and worthless. 10After a first and second admonition, have nothing more to do with anyone who causes divisions, 11since you know that such a person is perverted and sinful, being self-condemned.

Final Messages and Benediction

12When I send Artemas to you, or Tychicus, do your best to come to me at Nicopolis, for I have decided to spend the winter there. 13Make every effort to send Zenas the lawyer and Apollos on their way, and see that they lack nothing. 14And let people learn to devote themselves to good works in order to meet urgent needs, so that they may not be unproductive.

15All who are with me send greetings to you. Greet those who love us in the faith.

Grace be with all of you.i

---

g Gk *commandment*
h Gk *washing*

i Other ancient authorities add *Amen*

2:15 *Let no one look down on you* 1 Tim. 4:12. **3:1** *subject to rulers and authorities* See 1 Tim. 2:2. **3:3** *slaves to various passions* The image of being a slave to passions was popular in moralistic writing of the period (Seneca, *Letters* 47.17). **3:4–7** Some scholars argue that this is a liturgical fragment or hymn. **3:7** *justified by his grace* Rom. 3:24. **3:8** *The saying is sure* The *saying* probably refers to the whole passage (from 3:4), which may have been a liturgical piece. The phrase "The saying is sure" is used five times in the Pastoral Letters (here; *1 Tim.* 1:15; 3:1; 4:9; *2 Tim.* 2:11) but is not found in the writings of Paul. Various theories have been put forward about the meaning of the phrase. Some have argued that it identifies liturgical material; others, proverbial material; others, community material; yet others, propheticlike material. No description seems to do justice to the character of all the sayings. The phrase itself is common in Greek literature. See similar comments in *Rev.* 21:5; 22:6. *devote themselves to good works* This may mean "work at honorable occupations." Later Christians were forbidden, if they could avoid it, from taking jobs as actors, painters, and even teachers, since each of these jobs brought one into closer contact with the pagan gods in some way. Reflection on the worth of certain occupations can also be found in Roman authors (Seneca, *Letters* 88). **3:9** *stupid controversies, genealogies, dissensions, and quarrels about the law* See 1:14; *1 Tim.* 1:4. **3:12–13** Neither Artemas nor Zenas is mentioned elsewhere in our literature, but Tychicus is a regular character in the literature (*Acts* 20:4; *Col.* 4:7; *Eph.* 6:21; *2 Tim.* 4:12). He was sent to Ephesus, according to *2 Tim.* 4:12. See the introduction to the Pastorals for a discussion of personal names. *Nicopolis* The name, given to several cities, means "City of Victory." The reference here is probably to the Nicopolis on the western coast of Achaia (modern Greece). *winter there* Travel in the winter was not undertaken without good reason. The seas were too dangerous for ships; the roads offered much more difficult travel than the water even in the best weather, and with mountain passes on some of the routes, winter travel could be brutal (*2 Tim.* 4:21; *Mark* 13:18; *Acts* 27:12; *1 Cor.* 16:6). The Roman historian Livy reports on various people who made special provision to winter in particular cities (*Annals* 33.38; 37.45; 38.27.9).

THE FIRST LETTER OF PAUL
TO TIMOTHY

Salutation

1 Paul, an apostle of Christ Jesus by the command of God our Savior and of Christ Jesus our hope, [2]To Timothy, my loyal child in the faith:

Grace, mercy, and peace from God the Father and Christ Jesus our Lord.

Warning against False Teachers

[3]I urge you, as I did when I was on my way to Macedonia, to remain in Ephesus so that you may instruct certain people not to teach any different doctrine, [4]and not to occupy themselves with myths and endless genealogies that promote speculations rather than the divine training[a] that is known by faith. [5]But the aim of such instruction is love that comes from a pure heart, a good conscience, and sincere faith. [6]Some people have deviated from these and turned to meaningless talk, [7]desiring to be teachers of the law, without understanding either what they are saying or the things about which they make assertions.

[8]Now we know that the law is good, if one uses it legitimately. [9]This means understanding that the law is laid down not for the innocent but for the lawless and disobedient, for the godless and sinful, for the

---

a Or plan

1:1 God our Savior See *Titus* 1:1. **1:2 Timothy** Timothy was a close associate of Paul. His name occurs in the salutations of six of the Pauline letters *(2 Corinthians, Philippians, Colossians, 1 Thessalonians, 2 Thessalonians,* and *Philemon)* and in the closing of another *(Rom.* 16:21). **loyal child** Lit. "legitimate child." See *Titus* 1:4. **Grace, mercy, and peace** The phrase also occurs in the opening of *2 Timothy* but nowhere else in the letters attributed to Paul. All the other letters are introduced by the phrase "Grace to you and peace" (as in *Titus* 1:4). Many scholars believe that the change of greeting in the Pastorals marks these letters as pseudonymous; others argue that another author would never have tampered with the typical Pauline signature. "Peace" was a common Jewish greeting. **God the Father and Christ Jesus our Lord** The phrase also occurs in *2 Tim.* 1:2 but not elsewhere in the letters attributed to Paul. The common Pauline expression is, "from God our Father and the Lord Jesus Christ" (missing from only *Colossians* and *1 Thessalonians*). *Titus* is different from all these. The significance of this difference in *1 Timothy* for determining authorship is debated (see previous note). **1:3** In the Gk this sentence is incomplete—a grammatical error called anacoluthon, found frequently in Paul's writings. **remain in Ephesus** Acts 20:1–4 has an account of Paul's travel from Ephesus to Macedonia. But there Timothy seems to have been part of the entourage, linking up with it after having gone in advance to Macedonia from Ephesus *(Acts* 19:22). On grounds such as this, some scholars have argued that the Pastoral Letters are inaccurate in historical detail and therefore unlikely to be the work of Paul, who surely would have recalled his travels more accurately. Other scholars have countered by questioning how completely *Acts* narrates Paul's itinerary; still others have dismissed the itineraries in both *Acts* and the Pastoral Letters as fictions. To avoid a conflict with *Acts,* one would have to suppose that Paul was released from the Roman imprisonment described in *Acts,* after which he might have made this trip. **teach any different doctrine** Gk *heterodidaskalein.* This is a compound word possibly coined by the author. It is picked up later by others with an interest in the problem of heresy (Ign. *Pol.* 3.1). **1:4 myths and endless genealogies** The concern is unclear, but the phrase is clearly negative and could have such a connotation in secular literature also (Plato, *Timeaus* 22; Polybius, *Histories* 9.2.1). *Genealogies* here could refer to some fanciful use of the genealogies of the MT, such as in *Jubilees* or later Jewish gnostic systems. Indeed, Irenaeus, the late-2d-century defender against heresy, begins his massive work against gnosticism by speaking of its proponents' "lying words and vain genealogies," quoting this very passage from *1 Timothy.* We cannot, however, assume that Irenaeus and the author of the Pastorals (writing many decades earlier) were addressing the same teaching *(Titus* 1:14; 3:9; 6:4, 20; *2 Tim.* 2:14, 16–17, 23). *speculations* Translated from a compound Gk noun that occurs here for the first time (for a simple form, see *1 Tim.* 6:4; *2 Tim.* 2:23; *Titus* 3:9; note that *Acts* 15:17 and *Heb.* 12:17 use the compound in a verb form). The Pastoral Letters have a higher proportion of rare words than do the Pauline Epistles, and this difference has become one of the bases for questioning Pauline authorship. A word that occurs only once in all of Greek literature can present difficulties for translators. Since there are no other passages to examine, the translator must try to determine the possible range of meaning of the word solely from that one context. Fortunately, when such words are compounds, meaning is relatively easy to determine because we know the meaning of the words that make up the compound. **divine training** Other authorities read "plan." The difference in the Gk is slight: *oikodomēn (training)* and *oikonomian* ("plan"). **1:5 conscience** This word, which became popular in the 1st century in Hellenistic thought, is used thirteen times by Paul and six times by the author of the Pastorals. **1:7 teachers of the law** Lit. "law teachers," a compound word in Gk. Scholars disagree about the meaning of the phrase here. Some argue that they were much like the judaizers who frequently challenged Paul. Others think they were gnostics who employed the Jewish scriptures in novel ways. In either case, the concept of the law is on the author's mind, for he uses some form of this word five times in this short section (1:7–9). **1:8 the law is good** Rom. 7:12, 16. **1:9** Such catalogs of vices were commonplace in the ethical literature of the day. They are a mark of the Pastoral Letters (*1 Tim.* 6:4–5;

unholy and profane, for those who kill their father or mother, for murderers, [10]fornicators, sodomites, slave traders, liars, perjurers, and whatever else is contrary to the sound teaching [11]that conforms to the glorious gospel of the blessed God, which he entrusted to me.

Gratitude for Mercy

[12]I am grateful to Christ Jesus our Lord, who has strengthened me, because he judged me faithful and appointed me to his service, [13]even though I was formerly a blasphemer, a persecutor, and a man of violence. But I received mercy because I had acted ignorantly in unbelief, [14]and the grace of our Lord overflowed for me with the faith and love that are in Christ Jesus. [15]The saying is sure and worthy of full acceptance, that Christ Jesus came into the world to save sinners—of whom I am the foremost. [16]But for that very reason I received mercy, so that in me, as the foremost, Jesus Christ might display the utmost patience, making me an example to those who would

come to believe in him for eternal life. [17]To the King of the ages, immortal, invisible, the only God, be honor and glory forever and ever.[b] Amen.

[18]I am giving you these instructions, Timothy, my child, in accordance with the prophecies made earlier about you, so that by following them you may fight the good fight, [19]having faith and a good conscience. By rejecting conscience, certain persons have suffered shipwreck in the faith; [20]among them are Hymenaeus and Alexander, whom I have turned over to Satan, so that they may learn not to blaspheme.

Instructions concerning Prayer

2 First of all, then, I urge that supplications, prayers, intercessions, and thanksgivings be made for everyone, [2]for kings and all who are in high positions, so that we may lead a quiet and peaceable life in all godliness and dignity. [3]This is right and is acceptable in

---

b Gk *to the ages of the ages*

---

2 Tim. 3:2–5; *Titus* 3:3) and the Pauline writings (*Rom.* 1:28–32; *1 Cor.* 6:9–10; *Gal.* 5:19–21). The list here parallels the Decalogue. See also 1QS 3.1.15. **1:10** *sodomites* Or "male homosexuals." The Gk word used here is found only here and in *1 Cor.* 6:10 in our literature; it is also used in Polycarp, *To the Philippians* 5.3. *sound teaching* Lit. "healthy teaching." The phrase occurs in all three Pastoral Letters (*2 Tim.* 4:3; *Titus* 2:1) but nowhere else in our literature. **1:11** *the blessed God* Gk *makarios*. Only here and in 6:15 is the epithet "blessed" used of God in our literature. It is a Gk description (used, e.g., in Homer) that Hellenistic Judaism borrowed. Another synonym for "blessed" (*eulogētos*) is more frequently used in the Paulines. *which he entrusted to me* This is one of numerous biographical reflections about Paul's conversion and call in *1 Timothy* (1:12–17; 2:7; see *Gal.* 2:7). **1:12** *I am grateful* Gk *charin echō*. The phrase is used elsewhere in the Pastorals in *2 Tim.* 1:3. It is not used in the undisputed Paulines; Paul uses *eucharistō* (eight times). The use of different synonyms is seen by many as evidence that Paul did not write the Pastorals. *to his service* Gk *diakonian*, a cognate of the word translated "deacon," which will become a technical term for an official position in the church's hierarchy. **1:13** Paul's first contact with the Christian movement was as a fierce persecutor (*Gal.* 1:13; *Acts* 8:3; 9:1–2; 26:9–12). **1:15** *The saying is sure* See *Titus* 3:8. *I am the foremost* *1 Cor.* 15:9; *Eph.* 3:8. Some scholars contend that this comment reveals the hand of a forger—not of Paul. Paul is described as the foremost of sinners whereas in *1 Cor.* 15:9 Paul described himself as "the least of the apostles." This kind of argument impresses scholars differently. Do we have evidence here for similarity of thought (the sense of being unworthy) or dissimilarity (all apostles contrasted with all sinners)? See *Eph.* 3:8, where the phrase "least of all saints" is used. **1:18** The author speaks of Timothy's calling and encourages him to *fight the good fight*. This is another of the biographical reflections about Timothy in the letter (see also 4:14; 6:12, 20). In 6:12 the same ideas are linked—Timothy's call and the need to fight a good fight. The shorter *2 Timothy* contains even more personal references to Timothy. *my child* See *Titus* 1:4. *fight the good fight* Christian authors often used military language to describe the Christian life (see Ign. *Pol.* 6.2). The idiom was popular in philosophical writings of the time to portray rigorous moral life and the philosophical life (see Seneca, *Letters* 18.6; 48.10; 53.12; 56.9), and it was stock language of the Qumran community. **1:19** *shipwreck.* See *Jas.* 3:4. **1:20** *Hymenaeus and Alexander* Nothing is known about these men. Alexander is too common a name in a Hellenistic world still dominated by Alexander the Great's influence to link this individual to any other Alexander mentioned in early Christian literature (e.g., *Acts* 19:33–34 or *2 Tim.* 4:14–15). Hymenaeus is mentioned again in *2 Tim.* 2:17, where we learn that he was charged with having a defective belief about the resurrection. *turned over to Satan* The phrase is used by Paul in *1 Cor.* 5:5. **2:1** The author uses four different words for prayerlike activity. It is impossible to specify what differences the author had in mind; more than likely, the list is intended more for its overall impact than for precision in specifying modes of prayer or petitions. **2:2** This reflects one view of the relationship of the Christian to the state (*Titus* 3:1; *Rom.* 13:1–7; *1 Pet.* 2:13–17). Jewish temple prayers included a daily or twice-daily sacrifice for the Roman emperor in the 1st century (Josephus, *J.W.* 2.197, 409; *1 Clem.* 60.4–61.1). In 66 C.E., the leaders of the revolt against Roman rule stopped this sacrifice—basically a declaration of war, leading finally to the destruction of the temple itself and the end of sacrifices by the year 70. *lead a quiet and peaceable life* *1 Thess.* 4:11–12. *godliness* Gk *eusebeia*. The cognates of this word, frequently translated "religious," occur thirteen times in the Pastorals, but not once in the other letters attributed to Paul. Some scholars contend that Paul would have used a word such as "righteousness" where the author of the Pastorals uses the word "godliness."

the sight of God our Savior, 4who desires everyone to be saved and to come to the knowledge of the truth. 5For

there is one God;
    there is also one mediator between God and
        humankind,
    Christ Jesus, himself human,
6   who gave himself a ransom for all
—this was attested at the right time. 7For this I was appointed a herald and an apostle (I am telling the truth,c I am not lying), a teacher of the Gentiles in faith and truth.

8I desire, then, that in every place the men should pray, lifting up holy hands without anger or argument; 9also that the women should dress themselves modestly and decently in suitable clothing, not with their hair braided, or with gold, pearls, or expensive clothes, 10but with good works, as is proper for women who profess reverence for God. 11Let a womand learn in silence with full submission. 12I permit no womand to teach or to have authority over a man;e she is to keep silent. 13For Adam was formed first, then Eve; 14and Adam was not deceived, but the woman was deceived and became a transgressor. 15Yet she will be saved through childbearing, provided they continue in faith and love and holiness, with modesty.

Qualifications of Bishops

3 The saying is sure:f whoever aspires to the office of bishopg desires a noble task. 2Now a bishoph must be above reproach, married only once,i temperate, sensible, respectable, hospitable, an apt teacher, 3not

---

c Other ancient authorities add *in Christ*

d Or *wife*

e Or *her husband*

f Some interpreters place these words at the end of the previous paragraph. Other ancient authorities read *The saying is commonly accepted*

g Or *overseer*

h Or *an overseer*

i Gk *the husband of one wife*

2:5 there is one God This is the primary Jewish confession (*Deut.* 6:4–9). It is thought that this passage was part of an early Christian hymn, and for this reason the translators have marked it off clearly in the English text although such formatting was not used in the Gk manuscripts. Other possible fragments of hymns can be found in 3:16 and *2 Tim.* 2:11–13 in the Pastorals. **mediator** The word is used only once in the Pastorals. In the other Paulines, it is used only in *Gal.* 3:19–20, where it refers negatively to the covenant of the Jews. **2:6 ransom** Gk *antilytron.* This may be a reflection on a word of Jesus in *Mark* 10:45, where the cognate *lytron* was used. The verb form "to redeem" (*lytroumai*) is found in *Titus* 2:14. In the other Pauline Letters, the compound word *apolytrōsis* is used (*Rom.* 3:24; 8:23; *Col.* 1:14; *Eph.* 1:7, 14; 4:30). **this was attested at the right time** Lit. "the witness in his own time." Grammatically, this is a difficult phrase, and translators often set it off from the first part of the sentence. The phrase occurs again in 6:15 and in *Titus* 1:3. **2:7 herald** This description of Paul is found only here and in *2 Tim.* 1:11 in the Pauline literature. **teacher of the Gentiles** The theme of the Pauline mission to the Gentiles is mentioned frequently in the literature (*Gal.* 1:16; 2:1–10; *Rom.* 1:13–14; 11:13; 15:16, 18; *Eph.* 3:7–8; *Acts* 9:15; 13:46–47; 22:21; 26:17; 28:28). **I am not lying** *Rom.* 9:1; *2 Cor.* 11:31. **2:8 pray, lifting up holy hands** This describes the typical position for prayer in the ancient Mediterranean world; one would stand with hands raised and the palms toward the sky. Pagan, Jewish, and Christian art from the period illustrates the common position for prayer (Seneca, *Letters* 41.1). **2:9 dress themselves modestly.** *1 Pet.* 3:3–5. There is nothing particularly Christian about these injunctions, for Greek moralists expressed the same concerns about such overadornment, which implied to many sexual unfaithfulness (*Sentences of Sextus* 235, 513; Juvenal, *Satires* 6). Modesty was considered the mark of a good woman. **hair braided** *1 Pet.* 3:3. Such a style was fashionable and can be seen in various art forms from the period. **2:11–12** *1 Cor.* 14:34–35. This passage has been used as the basis for refusing ordination to women. Actually, women played a fairly active role in the early church, and formal ordination even of men was probably not a regular practice in the earliest period (*Titus* 2:5; *Col.* 3:18; *Eph.* 5:22; *1 Pet.* 3:1; contrast these with *Acts* 18:26). Plutarch offers a similar comment on the silence of women (*Advice to Bride and Groom* 26.30–32). **2:13 Eve** *Gen.* 2:18–23; 3:13; *2 Cor.* 11:3; *Barn.* 12.5. **2:14 woman was deceived** *Gen.* 3:1–6; *1 Cor.* 11:3–12; *Sir.* 25:24. **2:15 saved through childbearing** It is not clear what exactly is intended here; pain in childbirth was the primary element of the curse on the woman in the *Genesis* story (*Gen.* 3:16). **3:1 The saying is sure** See *Titus* 3:8. **office of bishop** Or "office of overseer." The phrase is a translation of the Gk *episkopēs.* In the passage, the author discusses the roles of bishops and deacons. Presbyters are mentioned later (4:14; 5:17–19); they seem to be indistinguishable from bishops, and the two terms are used interchangeably in *Titus* 1:5–7, where a similar list of virtues is specified (also *Acts* 20:17). Some believe that the Pastorals reflect a situation in which one member of the presbytery (or council of elders) is beginning to assume a chief position, but it not clear that the author uses the term "office of bishop" in such a restricted way. **3:2** The list of qualifications is general and similar to non-Christian lists of virtues found in the ancient world; indeed, one might say that it is a list of universal virtues—Mediterranean or oriental, ancient or modern. **married only once** Lit. "the husband of one wife." See *Titus* 1:6. **temperate** Perhaps meaning "self-controlled," since drunkenness is dealt with below (3:3, 11; *Titus* 2:2). The word is used nowhere else in our literature. **hospitable** See 5:10; *1 Pet.* 4:9; *1 Clem.* 11.1; *Did.* 11.5; 12.1–5. **3:3 drunkard** The word is used only here and in *Titus* 1:7 in our literature (see *1 Tim.* 3:8; *1 Cor.* 11:21).

a drunkard, not violent but gentle, not quarrelsome, and not a lover of money. 4He must manage his own household well, keeping his children submissive and respectful in every way— 5for if someone does not know how to manage his own household, how can he take care of God's church? 6He must not be a recent convert, or he may be puffed up with conceit and fall into the condemnation of the devil. 7Moreover, he must be well thought of by outsiders, so that he may not fall into disgrace and the snare of the devil.

Qualifications of Deacons

8Deacons likewise must be serious, not double-tongued, not indulging in much wine, not greedy for money; 9they must hold fast to the mystery of the faith with a clear conscience. 10And let them first be tested; then, if they prove themselves blameless, let them serve as deacons. 11Women[j] likewise must be serious, not slanderers, but temperate, faithful in all things. 12Let deacons be married only once,[k] and let them manage their children and their households well; 13for those who serve well as deacons gain a good standing for themselves and great boldness in the faith that is in Christ Jesus.

The Mystery of Our Religion

14I hope to come to you soon, but I am writing these instructions to you so that, 15if I am delayed, you may know how one ought to behave in the household of God, which is the church of the living God, the pillar and bulwark of the truth. 16Without any doubt, the mystery of our religion is great:

He[l] was revealed in flesh,
  vindicated[m] in spirit,[n]
    seen by angels,
proclaimed among Gentiles,
  believed in throughout the world,
    taken up in glory.

False Asceticism

4 Now the Spirit expressly says that in later[o] times some will renounce the faith by paying attention to deceitful spirits and teachings of demons, 2through the hypocrisy of liars whose consciences are seared with a hot iron. 3They forbid marriage and demand abstinence from foods, which God created to be received with thanksgiving by those who believe and know the truth. 4For everything created by God is good, and nothing is to be rejected, provided it is received with thanksgiving; 5for it is sanctified by God's word and by prayer.

A Good Minister of Jesus Christ

6If you put these instructions before the brothers and sisters,[p] you will be a good servant[q] of Christ Jesus, nourished on the words of the faith and of the sound teaching that you have followed. 7Have nothing to do with profane myths and old wives' tales. Train yourself in godliness, 8for, while physical training is of some value, godliness is valuable in every

j Or *Their wives,* or *Women deacons*
k Gk *be husbands of one wife*

l Gk *Who;* other ancient authorities read *God;* others, *Which*
m Or *justified*
n Or *by the Spirit*
o Or *the last*
p Gk *brothers*
q Or *deacon*

3:6 ***recent convert*** Gk *neophyton* (see English "neophyte"). **3:7** See 5:14; 6:1; *Titus* 2:5–10; *1 Cor.* 10:32; 14:15–17; *Phil.* 2:15; *Col.* 4:5; *1 Thess.* 4:12; 6:1. **3:8** ***deacons*** Lit. "servants." Deacons are not mentioned in *Titus.* At this time, the term could have been used as a technical term for an office, though the more general meaning of "servant" was by far the more common. See notes to *1 Tim.* 1:12; Ign. *Smyrn.* 10.1. **3:11** ***women*** Or "their wives" or "women deacons." It is an open and much debated question whether the author means the wives of the deacons, or women who are deaconesses, or women generally. The Gk simply reads "women." See *Rom.* 16:1. **3:12** ***married only once*** See *Titus* 1:6. **3:14** This note about Paul's travel plans does not help us place this letter into Paul's career as we know it from his letters or from the accounts in *Acts.* **3:15** ***bulwark*** This is the first occurrence of the Gk word in Gk literature. It perhaps could be translated "foundation." **3:16** This passage appears to have been part of an early Christian hymn. In it are the themes of incarnation and perhaps preexistence *(revealed in the flesh),* resurrection *(vindicated in spirit),* and ascension *(taken up in glory).* ***religion*** This is a favorite word of the author; it does not occur in the undisputed Pauline letters. The general sense of the word is "piety," and in some places in the Pastorals it is translated as "godliness" (see *Titus* 2:2). ***He*** Lit. "who." Some manuscripts read "God." The Gk abbreviation for "God" and the word "who," when written in uppercase letters (as the earliest manuscripts would have been), are only slightly different (Θ and O), similar to the difference between our uppercase O and Q—one small line, which could easily lead to a scribal error. Either reading makes sense in the passage. **4:1** ***in later times*** *2 Tim.* 3:1; *2 Pet.* 3:3; *Jude* 18; see *1 Pet.* 1:5. ***teachings of demons*** *2 Tim.* 3:1; *Acts* 20:30; *Mark* 13:22; *2 Thess.* 2:3, 10–12. **4:3** Many scholars think these comments point to a group of opponents involved in some form of ascetic gnosticism. The author seems more concerned about restrictions on food than restrictions on marriage. The primary issue regarding food in the 1st-century church was meat sacrificed to idols, but it is not clear that such is the issue here. Compare the attitude expressed in *Did.* 10.3. **4:7** ***myths and old wives' tales*** See *Titus* 1:14. Lucian, a Greek writer of the 2d century, offered this same kind of dismissal of an opponent's position (*Lover of Lies* 9).

way, holding promise for both the present life and the life to come. [9]The saying is sure and worthy of full acceptance. [10]For to this end we toil and struggle,[r] because we have our hope set on the living God, who is the Savior of all people, especially of those who believe.

[11]These are the things you must insist on and teach. [12]Let no one despise your youth, but set the believers an example in speech and conduct, in love, in faith, in purity. [13]Until I arrive, give attention to the public reading of scripture,[s] to exhorting, to teaching. [14]Do not neglect the gift that is in you, which was given to you through prophecy with the laying on of hands by the council of elders.[t] [15]Put these things into practice, devote yourself to them, so that all may see your progress. [16]Pay close attention to yourself and to your teaching; continue in these things, for in doing this you will save both yourself and your hearers.

Duties toward Believers

5 Do not speak harshly to an older man,[u] but speak to him as to a father, to younger men as brothers, [2]to older women as mothers, to younger women as sisters—with absolute purity.

[3]Honor widows who are really widows. [4]If a widow has children or grandchildren, they should first learn their religious duty to their own family and make some repayment to their parents; for this is pleasing in God's sight. [5]The real widow, left alone, has set her hope on God and continues in supplications and prayers night and day; [6]but the widow[v] who lives for pleasure is dead even while she lives. [7]Give these commands as well, so that they may be above reproach. [8]And whoever does not provide for relatives, and especially for family members, has denied the faith and is worse than an unbeliever.

[9]Let a widow be put on the list if she is not less than sixty years old and has been married only once;[w] [10]she must be well attested for her good works, as one who has brought up children, shown hospitality, washed the saints' feet, helped the afflicted, and devoted herself to doing good in every way. [11]But refuse to put younger widows on the list; for when their sensual desires alienate them from Christ, they want to marry, [12]and so they incur condemnation for having violated their first pledge. [13]Besides that, they

---

r Other ancient authorities read *suffer reproach*
s Gk *to the reading*
t Gk *by the presbytery*
u Or *an elder, or a presbyter*

v Gk *she*
w Gk *the wife of one husband*

4:9 *The saying is sure* See *Titus* 3:8. Usually this phrase introduces the saying; here, however, and in *Titus* 3:8 it probably follows the saying. **4:12** *despise your youth* *2 Tim.* 1:6–7. Ignatius encounters a similar problem in the church at Magnesia (Ign. *Magn.* 3.1). Some scholars argue that this comment shows the hand of an author attempting to imitate Paul's letters (*1 Cor.* 16:11). **4:13** *reading of scripture* Almost certainly a reference to the reading of scripture in the church assembly, a feature borrowed from the Jewish synagogue service. The reading would have involved passages of the LXX even in the Christian assemblies, with a particularly heavy use of the prophets. **4:14** *laying on of hands* This phrase may refer to some kind of formal ordination. The exact nature of, and source for, this ordination ritual are disputed. See *1 Tim.* 3:11; 5:22; *2 Tim.* 1:6. **5:1** *an older man* Or "an elder" or "a presbyter." Whether to translate it as "presbyter" (in terms of a formal office) or as *older man* (descriptive merely of age) is a matter of interpretation. The range of possible meanings in Gk is similar to the range presented by the English word "elder." Probably it should be treated as a reference to age rather than to office here, since all the other groups discussed in this passage seem to be defined by age and the reference to *older man* is followed immediately by a reference to *younger men,* which does not refer to an office. Use of the Gk word in other passages of the Pastorals may imply the formal office, as in *Titus* 1:5. **5:3** *honor* This probably indicates financial support, as it does in 5:17. But it can mean simply honor, as in 6:1. *who are really widows* By the author's time, the church seems to have an established system of support for its widows (see *Acts* 6:1; 9:39, 41). The instructions about widows are extensive in *1 Timothy,* taking up most of *1 Timothy* 5, yet it is difficult to determine the function and the position of the widows from the comments made there. Later, widows were clearly a distinct order in the church, with support and responsibilities, but most of the comments about widows in the early literature reflect simply a general concern for the welfare of such people rather than official duties (*Jas.* 1:27; *1 Clem.* 8.4; Ign. *Smyrn.* 6.2; 13.1; Ign. *Pol.* 4.1; Polycarp, *To the Philippians* 4.3; 6.1; *Barn.* 20.2). The concern for widows was deeply rooted in the Jewish heritage that Christians brought to their movement. **5:6** *dead even while she lives* *Rev.* 3:1; Philo, *On Flight and Finding* 55. **5:9** *put on the list* Gk *katalegesthō* (from which we get the English word "catalog"). Two meanings are possible. It might imply a formal list, or it might mean merely a general recognition of a widow's need for, and right to, assistance—something considerably less formal. **5:10** *washed the saints' feet* It is not clear whether the reference is to a formal practice in the church or is used figuratively to indicate humble work in the church. Augustine (*Letters* 55.33) makes the first clear reference to foot washing as a ritual practice in the church. It had been an expression of hospitality and welcome in the Middle East (*John* 13:17). **5:12** *violated their first pledge* Lit. "set aside their first faith." This is ambiguous. It need not mean something as formal as a violation of a vow of celibacy taken upon joining the order of widows. Such a view probably draws too much from a later, more developed situation. **5:13** *gossips* The Gk word is used only in *3 John* 10 elsewhere in our literature.

learn to be idle, gadding about from house to house; and they are not merely idle, but also gossips and busybodies, saying what they should not say. 14So I would have younger widows marry, bear children, and manage their households, so as to give the adversary no occasion to revile us. 15For some have already turned away to follow Satan. 16If any believing woman[x] has relatives who are really widows, let her assist them; let the church not be burdened, so that it can assist those who are real widows.

17Let the elders who rule well be considered worthy of double honor,[y] especially those who labor in preaching and teaching; 18for the scripture says, "You shall not muzzle an ox while it is treading out the grain," and, "The laborer deserves to be paid." 19Never accept any accusation against an elder except on the evidence of two or three witnesses. 20As for those who persist in sin, rebuke them in the presence of all, so that the rest also may stand in fear. 21In the presence of God and of Christ Jesus and of the elect angels, I warn you to keep these instructions without prejudice, doing nothing on the basis of partiality. 22Do not ordain[z] anyone hastily, and do not participate in the sins of others; keep yourself pure.

23No longer drink only water, but take a little wine for the sake of your stomach and your frequent ailments.

24The sins of some people are conspicuous and precede them to judgment, while the sins of others follow them there. 25So also good works are conspicuous; and even when they are not, they cannot remain hidden.

6Let all who are under the yoke of slavery regard their masters as worthy of all honor, so that the name of God and the teaching may not be blasphemed. 2Those who have believing masters must not be disrespectful to them on the ground that they are members of the church;[a] rather they must serve them all the more, since those who benefit by their service are believers and beloved.[b]

False Teaching and True Riches

Teach and urge these duties. 3Whoever teaches otherwise and does not agree with the sound words of our Lord Jesus Christ and the teaching that is in accordance with godliness, 4is conceited, understanding nothing, and has a morbid craving for controversy and for disputes about words. From these come envy, dissension, slander, base suspicions, 5and wrangling among those who are depraved in mind and bereft of the truth, imagining that godliness is a means of gain.[c] 6Of course, there is great gain in godliness combined with contentment; 7for we brought nothing into the world, so that[d] we can take nothing out of it; 8but if we have food and clothing, we will be content with these. 9But those who want to be rich fall into temptation and are trapped by many senseless and harmful desires that plunge people into ruin and destruction. 10For the love of money is a root of all kinds of evil, and in their eagerness to be rich

---

x Other ancient authorities read *believing man or woman*; others, *believing man*

y Or *compensation*

z Gk *Do not lay hands on*

a Gk *are brothers*

b Or *since they are believers and beloved, who devote themselves to good deeds*

c Other ancient authorities add *Withdraw yourself from such people*

d Other ancient authorities read *world-it is certain that*

5:14 have younger widows marry Contrast this with the position of the opponents in 4:3, who forbid marriage. **5:17** It is not clear why these instructions are placed here rather than in *1 Timothy* 3 with the instructions for bishops and deacons. It could be that the author moves from financial support for widows to financial support for elders (5:18), a topic that was not broached when the duties of church officers were addressed earlier. **5:1 deserves to be paid** The first passage is from *Deut.* 25:4, and it is quoted by Paul in *1 Cor.* 9:9. The second passage is a word of Jesus from Q material (*Matt.* 10:10; *Luke* 10:7). **5:22 do not ordain** Lit. "Do not lay hands on." Two interpretations are offered for this caution: (a) it refers to ordination (as the translators have read it), or (b) it refers to the reception of a member who had been excommunicated. **5:23** Wine was considered to have medicinal value in the ancient world. Seneca says that doctors tell their patients to make use of wine as a "restorative" (*Letters* 78.5). Here in *1 Timothy* this comment seems oddly placed and even breaks the flow of thought from 5:22 to 5:24 (both of which speak of the "sins of others"). It may be related to the position of the opponents, who had an ascetic view regarding food (4:3–5). **6:1** Instructions to slaves are offered elsewhere in early Christian literature (see *Titus* 2:9; *1 Cor.* 7:21–24; *Col.* 3:22–24; *Eph.* 6:5–8). **worthy of all honor** See *Titus* 2:9. **6:4 disputes about words** See *1 Tim.* 1:4. **6:6–10** In a letter that has spent considerable time on the duties of leaders, the author concludes with an attack on riches (6:9–10), then, after a final *Amen*, adds a postscript about riches (6:17–19). It appears that some people had profited financially from their connection with the church—perhaps from positions of leadership. The author rejects from leadership anyone who is a lover of money (*1 Tim.* 3:3, 8; *2 Tim.* 3:2). This was a major theme in Polycarp's *To the Philippians* (a document not included in our collection). Hellenistic philosophers were themselves aware of the trap of financial greed awaiting leaders and teachers (Seneca, *Letters* 56.10). They were aware also of the problem of wealth generally (Seneca, *Letters* 2.6; 18.1–15), as were Christian writers (*Luke* 16:14; *Heb.* 13:5; *Did.* 15.1). Philosophers also praised the value of contentment (Seneca, *Letters* 78.11–27); Christian authors had similar ideas (*Mark* 6:8–10; *Phil.* 4:11; *Heb.* 13:5; *1 Clem.* 2.1).

some have wandered away from the faith and pierced themselves with many pains.

The Good Fight of Faith

[11]But as for you, man of God, shun all this; pursue righteousness, godliness, faith, love, endurance, gentleness. [12]Fight the good fight of the faith; take hold of the eternal life, to which you were called and for which you made[e] the good confession in the presence of many witnesses. [13]In the presence of God, who gives life to all things, and of Christ Jesus, who in his testimony before Pontius Pilate made the good confession, I charge you [14]to keep the commandment without spot or blame until the manifestation of our Lord Jesus Christ, [15]which he will bring about at the right time—he who is the blessed and only Sovereign, the King of kings and Lord of lords. [16]It is he alone who has immortality and dwells in unapproachable light, whom no one has ever seen or can see; to him be honor and eternal dominion. Amen.

[17]As for those who in the present age are rich, command them not to be haughty, or to set their hopes on the uncertainty of riches, but rather on God who richly provides us with everything for our enjoyment. [18]They are to do good, to be rich in good works, generous, and ready to share, [19]thus storing up for themselves the treasure of a good foundation for the future, so that they may take hold of the life that really is life.

Personal Instructions and Benediction

[20]Timothy, guard what has been entrusted to you. Avoid the profane chatter and contradictions of what is falsely called knowledge; [21]by professing it some have missed the mark as regards the faith.

Grace be with you.[f]

---

e Gk confessed

f The Greek word for you here is plural; in other ancient authorities it is singular. Other ancient authorities add Amen

6:12 As the author closes his letter, he links Timothy's calling to the need to fight a good fight, just as he had at the opening of his letter (see 1:18). **6:13** *Pontius Pilate* Besides here, the gospels, and *Acts*, Pilate, the Roman governor of Judea when Jesus was executed, is mentioned only in the writings of Ignatius in our collection (Ign. *Magn.* 11.3; Ign. *Trall.* 8.8; Ign. *Smyrn.* 1.13). He receives more attention in later documents, such as the *Acts of Pilate*. **6:20 what has been entrusted to you** See 1:18; see also *2 Tim.* 1:14. **profane chatter and contradictions** See 1:4; see also *2 Tim.* 2:16. **falsely called knowledge** The Gk here for *knowledge* is *gnōsis*. Some scholars have tried to use this comment to date the Pastoral Letters near the middle of the 2d century, in the context of the church's struggle with developed gnosticism, in particular with Marcion.

THE SECOND LETTER OF PAUL
TO TIMOTHY

Salutation

1 Paul, an apostle of Christ Jesus by the will of God, for the sake of the promise of life that is in Christ Jesus,

[2] To Timothy, my beloved child:

Grace, mercy, and peace from God the Father and Christ Jesus our Lord.

Thanksgiving and Encouragement

[3] I am grateful to God—whom I worship with a clear conscience, as my ancestors did—when I remember you constantly in my prayers night and day. [4] Recalling your tears, I long to see you so that I may be filled with joy. [5] I am reminded of your sincere faith, a faith that lived first in your grandmother Lois and your mother Eunice and now, I am sure, lives in you. [6] For this reason I remind you to rekindle the gift of God that is within you through the laying on of my hands; [7] for God did not give us a spirit of cowardice, but rather a spirit of power and of love and of self-discipline.

[8] Do not be ashamed, then, of the testimony about our Lord or of me his prisoner, but join with me in suffering for the gospel, relying on the power of God, [9] who saved us and called us with a holy calling, not according to our works but according to his own purpose and grace. This grace was given to us in Christ Jesus before the ages began, [10] but it has now been revealed through the appearing of our Savior Christ Jesus, who abolished death and brought life and immortality to light through the gospel. [11] For this gospel I was appointed a herald and an apostle and a teacher,[a] [12] and for this reason I suffer as I do. But I am not ashamed, for I know the one in whom I have put my trust, and I am sure that he is able to guard until that day what I have entrusted to him.[b] [13] Hold to the standard of sound teaching that you have heard from me, in the faith and love that are in Christ Jesus. [14] Guard the good treasure entrusted to you, with the help of the Holy Spirit living in us.

[15] You are aware that all who are in Asia have turned away from me, including Phygelus and Hermogenes. [16] May the Lord grant mercy to the household of Onesiphorus, because he often refreshed me and was not ashamed of my chain; [17] when he arrived in Rome, he eagerly[c] searched for me and found me [18]—may the Lord grant that he will find mercy from the Lord on that day! And you know very well how much service he rendered in Ephesus.

---

a Other ancient authorities add *of the Gentiles*
b Or *what has been entrusted to me*
c Or *promptly*

1:2 *grace, mercy, and peace* See *1 Tim.* 1:2. **1:5** *Lois and your mother Eunice* Acts 16:1. This is the first of many personal notes about Timothy in this letter. See note to *1 Tim.* 1:18. **1:6** *laying on of my hands* *1 Tim.* 4:14. See *1 Tim.* 5:22. **1:8** *Do not be ashamed* Rom. 1:16. The Gk word for "ashamed" occurs only five times in all the letters attributed to Paul, including three times in the introduction of this letter (1:8, 12, 16). When a word comes to an author's mind, it may be used a few times before it is discarded, rarely to be picked up again. Recognition of this prevents us from concluding, on the basis of word frequencies alone, that Paul did not write this letter. **1:9** *before the ages began* Rom. 16:25. **1:10–11** This may be a liturgical fragment. **1:11** See *1 Tim.* 2:7. **1:15** This statement is puzzling, since Asia was the center of the Pauline mission. Some scholars take this as evidence that the Pastorals were written after the death of Paul, when there may have been a loss of Pauline influence in Asia Minor—perhaps even a loss that the pseudonymous author of the Pastorals was attempting to reverse by writing these very letters. But compare the comment in the closing of this letter (4:16), where a similar statement is made. There it is connected specifically to Paul's trial. It is not clear that more than this is intended. *Phygelus and Hermogenes* These individuals are otherwise unknown. *2 Timothy* is marked by the passing mention of twelve people, otherwise unmentioned in our literature. **1:16–17** According to these comments, Paul was a prisoner in Rome. Paul did not reach Rome until after his arrest in Jerusalem, according to the account in *Acts,* and this fits well enough into his travel plans as they can be constructed from his letters (*Rom.* 1:10–15; 15:18–29). We know almost nothing about this imprisonment (*Acts* 28:16, 31–32). The reference to imprisonment in Rome places the letter in the final period of Paul's life, even if this setting is a literary fiction. **1:16** *Onesiphorus* Onesiphorus is also mentioned in 4:19. He appears to have been a person of some substance, with a residence in Ephesus and perhaps business connections in Rome. He is presented here as "refreshing" Paul—that is to say, providing financial support. **1:18** Nothing is known about Onesiphorus, but Paul's connection to Ephesus is well established. The city served as his major center of mission in the mid-50s, and after his death it seems to have remained a center of Pauline thought for some time, as the Pastoral Letters themselves and *Acts* bear witness. Some scholars argue that Paul's influence waned considerably in the 2d century.

A Good Soldier of Christ Jesus

2 You then, my child, be strong in the grace that is in Christ Jesus; ²and what you have heard from me through many witnesses entrust to faithful people who will be able to teach others as well. ³Share in suffering like a good soldier of Christ Jesus. ⁴No one serving in the army gets entangled in everyday affairs; the soldier's aim is to please the enlisting officer. ⁵And in the case of an athlete, no one is crowned without competing according to the rules. ⁶It is the farmer who does the work who ought to have the first share of the crops. ⁷Think over what I say, for the Lord will give you understanding in all things.

⁸Remember Jesus Christ, raised from the dead, a descendant of David—that is my gospel, ⁹for which I suffer hardship, even to the point of being chained like a criminal. But the word of God is not chained. ¹⁰Therefore I endure everything for the sake of the elect, so that they may also obtain the salvation that is in Christ Jesus, with eternal glory. ¹¹The saying is sure:

If we have died with him, we will also live with
    him;
¹² if we endure, we will also reign with him;
if we deny him, he will also deny us;
¹³ if we are faithless, he remains faithful—
for he cannot deny himself.

A Worker Approved by God

¹⁴Remind them of this, and warn them before God*d* that they are to avoid wrangling over words, which does no good but only ruins those who are listening. ¹⁵Do your best to present yourself to God as one approved by him, a worker who has no need to be ashamed, rightly explaining the word of truth. ¹⁶Avoid profane chatter, for it will lead people into more and more impiety, ¹⁷and their talk will spread like gangrene. Among them are Hymenaeus and Philetus, ¹⁸who have swerved from the truth by claiming that the resurrection has already taken place. They are upsetting the faith of some. ¹⁹But God's firm foundation stands, bearing this inscription: "The Lord knows those who are his," and, "Let everyone who calls on the name of the Lord turn away from wickedness."

²⁰In a large house there are utensils not only of gold and silver but also of wood and clay, some for special use, some for ordinary. ²¹All who cleanse themselves of the things I have mentioned*e* will become special utensils, dedicated and useful to the owner of the house, ready for every good work. ²²Shun youthful passions and pursue righteousness, faith, love, and peace, along with those who call on the Lord from a pure heart. ²³Have nothing to do with stupid and senseless controversies; you know that they breed quarrels. ²⁴And the Lord's servant*f* must not be quarrelsome but kindly to everyone, an apt teacher, patient, ²⁵correcting opponents with gentleness. God may perhaps grant that they will repent and come to know the truth, ²⁶and that they may escape from the snare of the devil, having been held captive by him to do his will.*g*

Godlessness in the Last Days

3 You must understand this, that in the last days distressing times will come. ²For people will be

---

d Other ancient authorities read *the Lord*

e Gk *of these things*
f Gk *slave*
g Or *by him, to do his* (that is, God's) *will*

2:1 my child See *Titus* 1:4. **2:4** This is perhaps the earliest reference to a full-time paid position in the early church. The daily rigor of the Roman soldier is described by Josephus, *J.W.* 3.71, 107; Vegetius, *A Book about Military Affairs* 1.1; see also *1 Clem.* 37.2. **2:8 a descendant of David** *Rom.* 1:3; *Rev.* 22:16; *Did.* 9.2; Ign. *Eph.* 18.2; 20.2; Ign. *Trall.* 9.1; Ign. *Rom.* 7.3; Ign. *Smyrn.* 1.1; *Barn.* 12.10. The idea is found throughout the gospels and *Acts*. **my gospel** *Rom.* 1:3–4. **2:11 The saying is sure** The following seems to be an early Christian hymn. See *Titus* 3:8; *Rom.* 6:1–11. **2:12** *Matt.* 25:41–46. **2:14 wrangling over words** The author has various ways of indicating the fruitlessness of debate with opponents: "profane chatter" (2:16); "their talk will spread like gangrene" (2:17); "stupid and senseless controversies" (2:23). The author does not confront his opponents head-on, as Paul usually does in *Galatians* and *Romans*. **2:16 profane chatter** Lit. "empty sounds." *1 Tim.* 6:20. **2:17** Hymenaeus is mentioned in *1 Tim.* 1:20; Philetus is mentioned only here. **2:18 the resurrection has already taken place** A somewhat different controversy about the resurrection of the dead is found in *1 Cor.* 15:12–52. Such controversies are also found in the 2d century: Polycarp, *To the Philippians* 7.3; *Acts of Paul and Thecla* 14; and in various gnostic and anti-gnostic writings. **2:19** This verse shows the influence of different passages from the Jewish scriptures: *God's firm foundation stands* (*Isa.* 28:16); *the Lord knows who are his* (*Num.* 16:5); and *Let everyone who calls . . .* (thought to be a composite from *Isa.* 52:11 and *Lev.* 24:16). **2:20** *Rom.* 9:19–24. The focus is different, but the images are similar. **2:22 youthful passions** *1 Tim.* 4:12. **2:23 stupid and senseless controversies** See 2:14. **3:1 last days** *1 Tim.* 4:1. See *1 Pet.* 1:5. A "vice list" follows this comment about the last days. It was a feature of popular thinking that evil would increase more and more in the final days of this present era; apocalyptic thought in Judaism developed this idea most dramatically. Even the Hellenistic philosophers talked of an earlier golden age—the discourse often revealing much of what they thought about the corruption and decline of the present age (Seneca, *Letters* 90.35–46).

lovers of themselves, lovers of money, boasters, arrogant, abusive, disobedient to their parents, ungrateful, unholy, ³inhuman, implacable, slanderers, profligates, brutes, haters of good, ⁴treacherous, reckless, swollen with conceit, lovers of pleasure rather than lovers of God, ⁵holding to the outward form of godliness but denying its power. Avoid them! ⁶For among them are those who make their way into households and captivate silly women, overwhelmed by their sins and swayed by all kinds of desires, ⁷who are always being instructed and can never arrive at a knowledge of the truth. ⁸As Jannes and Jambres opposed Moses, so these people, of corrupt mind and counterfeit faith, also oppose the truth. ⁹But they will not make much progress, because, as in the case of those two men,*h* their folly will become plain to everyone.

Paul's Charge to Timothy

¹⁰Now you have observed my teaching, my conduct, my aim in life, my faith, my patience, my love, my steadfastness, ¹¹my persecutions and suffering the things that happened to me in Antioch, Iconium, and Lystra. What persecutions I endured! Yet the Lord rescued me from all of them. ¹²Indeed, all who want to live a godly life in Christ Jesus will be persecuted. ¹³But wicked people and impostors will go from bad to worse, deceiving others and being deceived. ¹⁴But as for you, continue in what you have learned and firmly believed, knowing from whom you learned it, ¹⁵and how from childhood you have known the sacred writings that are able to instruct

you for salvation through faith in Christ Jesus. ¹⁶All scripture is inspired by God and is*i* useful for teaching, for reproof, for correction, and for training in righteousness, ¹⁷so that everyone who belongs to God may be proficient, equipped for every good work.

4 In the presence of God and of Christ Jesus, who is to judge the living and the dead, and in view of his appearing and his kingdom, I solemnly urge you: ²proclaim the message; be persistent whether the time is favorable or unfavorable; convince, rebuke, and encourage, with the utmost patience in teaching. ³For the time is coming when people will not put up with sound doctrine, but having itching ears, they will accumulate for themselves teachers to suit their own desires, ⁴and will turn away from listening to the truth and wander away to myths. ⁵As for you, always be sober, endure suffering, do the work of an evangelist, carry out your ministry fully.

⁶As for me, I am already being poured out as a libation, and the time of my departure has come. ⁷I have fought the good fight, I have finished the race, I have kept the faith. ⁸From now on there is reserved for me the crown of righteousness, which the Lord, the righteous judge, will give me on that day, and not only to me but also to all who have longed for his appearing.

Personal Instructions

⁹Do your best to come to me soon, ¹⁰for Demas, in love with this present world, has deserted me and gone to Thessalonica; Crescens has gone to Galatia,*j*

---

h Gk lacks *two men*

i Or *Every scripture inspired by God is also*
j Other ancient authorities read *Gaul*

3:6 *households* See *Titus* 1:11. *silly women* Lit. "little women," certainly not intended as a compliment. **3:8** The report of the conflict between Moses and Egyptian magicians is recorded in *Exod.* 7:11–12, but no names of the opponents are supplied there. By the first century, the names of Jannes and Jambres had been given to the magicians in Jewish, Christian, and even pagan literature. The oldest reference to the names is in the Dead Sea Scrolls, CD 5.18–19. There is even a document titled *Jannes and Jambres*, the date of which is uncertain. Even Pliny knows their names (*Natural History* 30.2.11). **3:11** Stories of Paul's difficulties in these three cites are recorded in *Acts* 13:13–14:28. **3:14** *from childhood* See 1:5. **4:10** *Demas* From here to the end of the letter, the author mentions seventeen friends, associates, and less favored contacts of Paul (others were mentioned earlier in the letter). It is difficult to understand why an author other than Paul would have referred to such a range of individuals. Some scholars argue that it was done to give the letter a look of authenticity; others contend that the author has incorporated fragments of genuine Pauline notes. Many of the characters are mentioned nowhere else in our literature (Crescens, Carpus, Eubulus, Pudens, Linus, and Claudia). Some are mentioned briefly elsewhere, but with a changed relationship to Paul: Demas is spoken of in two other places, both times without criticism (*Col.* 4:14; *Phlm.* 24), yet he is criticized here; Mark is mentioned with disfavor elsewhere (*Acts* 15:36–39), yet with favor here, and in other places without comment (*Col.* 4:10; *Phlm.* 24) but with a positive tone. Luke is mentioned with Demas in two other places (*Col.* 4:14; *Phlm.* 24). Tychicus is mentioned in three other places (*Col.* 4:7; *Eph.* 6:21; *Titus* 3:12); Prisca and Aquila are mentioned often (*Acts* 18:2, 18; *Rom.* 16:3; *1 Cor.* 16:19); Onesiphorus is mentioned earlier in the letter (1:16–18); and Alexander, a common name, is perhaps mentioned elsewhere (see *1 Tim.* 1:20; *Acts* 19:33). A number of these individuals are incorporated into the apocryphal literature of the 2d century. *Galatia* Other ancient authorities read "Gaul" (modern-day France). The ethnic Galatians were from Gaul originally. In Gk the difference is slighter, with manuscripts reading "Galatian," "Gallian," or "Galilaian." *Dalmatia* Dalmatia (or Illyricum) bordered the eastern shores of the Sea of Adria, roughly corresponding to the modern Albania and the former Yugoslavian territories. We know little about early Christian activity in this area although Paul hints at some work there (*Rom.* 15:19). Titus seems to have been one of the key

Titus to Dalmatia. [11]Only Luke is with me. Get Mark and bring him with you, for he is useful in my ministry. [12]I have sent Tychicus to Ephesus. [13]When you come, bring the cloak that I left with Carpus at Troas, also the books, and above all the parchments. [14]Alexander the coppersmith did me great harm; the Lord will pay him back for his deeds. [15]You also must beware of him, for he strongly opposed our message.

[16]At my first defense no one came to my support, but all deserted me. May it not be counted against them! [17]But the Lord stood by me and gave me strength, so that through me the message might be fully proclaimed and all the Gentiles might hear it. So I was rescued from the lion's mouth. [18]The Lord will rescue me from every evil attack and save me for his heavenly kingdom. To him be the glory forever and ever. Amen.

Final Greetings and Benediction

[19]Greet Prisca and Aquila, and the household of Onesiphorus. [20]Erastus remained in Corinth; Trophimus I left ill in Miletus. [21]Do your best to come before winter. Eubulus sends greetings to you, as do Pudens and Linus and Claudia and all the brothers and sisters.[k]

[22]The Lord be with your spirit. Grace be with you.[l]

---

k Gk *all the brothers*
l The Greek word for *you* here is plural. Other ancient authorities add *Amen*

---

associates of Paul. Apart from the Pastoral Letters, however, he is mentioned only in *2 Corinthians* (eight times) and in *Galatians*. If the Pastoral Letters are pseudonymous, then one might conclude that Titus was, in fact, remembered as a leading associate of Paul; this would make the author's choice of Timothy and Titus as key players in his pseudonymous works a logical one. **4:13 *parchments*** It is uncertain what is meant by the parchments. There are several options: special documents, blank parchment, scrolls of the Jewish scriptures. **4:17 *from the lion's mouth*** Roman citizens were generally spared death in the arena, where the animal and gladiator fights were held. If this text is alluding to these methods of execution, then its author does not consider Paul a Roman citizen, since people of that status, when convicted of a capital offense, were beheaded (see *Acts* 22:22–29). But perhaps the phrase *from the lion's mouth* simply echoes *Ps.* 22:21 and means nothing more specific than deliverance from persecution. **4:21 *winter*** See *Titus* 3:12.

EARLY

CHRISTIAN

READER

LETTERS ASSOCIATED WITH PETER

THE PETRINE TRADITIONS

PETER FIGURES PROMINENTLY as a leading member of the inner circle of Jesus' disciples in both the synoptic and the Johannine accounts. Yet only about 2 percent of the pages of accepted early Christian writings are attributed to Peter—two short letters—and the authenticity of both of these has been widely questioned. Indeed, in contrast to the center stage Peter occupies in the stories about Jesus and in the events of the first year of the church in Jerusalem as recorded in *Acts,* other characters came to dominate the postresurrection church. James,[1] a brother of Jesus, assumed leadership of the mother-church in Jerusalem, and Paul, whose writings tower over much of early Christian literature, took the initiative in the Gentile mission. In both cases, the new leaders played no role in Jesus' career: James had not been a disciple of Jesus, and Paul, in his first appearance, was a violent persecutor of the new faith.

The Historical Peter

But Peter's importance in the developing church is not to be dismissed. There is ample material from which to sketch a portrait of the "historical Peter." According to Paul, who is often credited with the success of the early Christian mission, Peter played a prominent role. Paul recognized Peter as a leader of the church in Jerusalem at the beginning, and he counted Peter as a leading apostle years later as the church was beginning to develop a Gentile mission (*Gal.* 1:18–19; 2:6–10). Further, Paul's references to Cephas (a nickname for Peter)[2] in *1 Corinthians*[3] demonstrates Peter's continuing influential role in key areas of Paul's mission. Thus Paul's testimony shows that Peter was active and known at least by name—and perhaps by face—in a wide area of the early Christian mission at least twenty-five years beyond what we might have concluded from reference merely to the gospels and *Acts.*

---

[1]See the section "The Letter of James."

[2]The word "Cephas" is the Aramaic equivalent for the Gk "Peter." This is a nickname, perhaps something like our modern "Rocky." Peter's given name was Simon, or Simeon (see authorship discussion in the introduction to *2 Peter*).

[3]Mentioned four times: 1:12; 3:22; 9:5; 15:5.

Further evidence of Peter's continuing influence is reflected in the two letters known as *1 Peter* and *2 Peter*. Either Peter was the writer of these letters, with influence over most of Asia Minor, the area to which the letters are addressed, or he was of impressive enough stature in the communities' consciousness that he became the authority for a corpus of pseudonymous writings toward the end of the first century.

Even *Acts* itself, which highlights the role of Peter only in the first year after the crucifixion of Jesus, shows the continuing importance of Peter much later in the century. If *Acts* was written toward the end of the first century, then memories of Peter had been kept alive in the tradition. The author has to acknowledge Peter's strategic role in the development of the early church.

A similarly prominent role for Peter is demonstrated in the *Gospel of John*. Peter's prominence here is particularly surprising, since the Beloved Disciple,[4] not Peter, was the person of note in the Johannine circle. Yet, in Johannine literature, written in the late first century, Peter was recognized as a leader of the post-resurrection church. The prominent role of Peter in documents preserved by a *Petrine* community would be easy to understand; the prominent role of Peter in documents from a non-Petrine community is more puzzling, and points to the continuing significance of Peter in the late-first-century church.

Further, Peter's key role in the gospel accounts attests not just to his position as a member of the inner circle of Jesus' disciples but also to his stature in the later first-century church. Form and redaction criticism suggest that the gospels reflect, in part, the interests of the communities that preserved the stories—communities from the middle and late decades of the first century. Both *John* and the Synoptics feature Peter. Since these are generally considered to be independent traditions, Peter's continuing importance is well established by the gospel tradition.

Peter in Tradition

Finally, though only two documents are attributed to Peter in the collection that came to be known as the New Testament, Peter figures significantly in a rich literary tradition in the second century. Writings appeared under his name, such as the *Apocalypse of Peter, Gospel of Peter, Acts of Peter,* and *Preaching of Peter,* as well as various gnostic writings in which Peter figured in some way.

Thus Peter, though perhaps without leaving one written word of his own, looms large over the developing church, and whatever the exact nature of his activity and leadership, becomes linked in tradition as bishop of the church in the capital of the empire, and in that role served as the apostolic witness for all of Western Christianity.

---

[4]See introduction to *John*.

For Further Reading

Brown, Raymond E., Karl P. Donfried, and John Reumann, eds. *Peter in the New Testament: A Collaborative Assessment by Protestant and Roman Catholic Scholars.* New York: Paulist, 1979.

Cullmann, Oscar. *Peter: Disciple—Apostle—Martyr.* 2d ed. Translated by Floyd V. Filson. London: SCM, 1962.

Perkins, Pheme. *Peter: Apostle for the Whole Church.* Columbia, S.C.: University of South Carolina Press, 1994. Repr., Minneapolis: Fortress, 2000.

To the Chosen Ones Dispersed in Asia Minor

1 PETER

Setting

The document purports to be a letter, reflecting the features that letters were expected to have. In spite of the letterlike appearance of *1 Peter*, the core is much more like a sermon.

The author is particularly sensitive to the persecution and suffering faced by the audience. Although the audience is specified, covering the main Roman provinces of what is today western and central Turkey, we cannot identify with certainty the particular period of persecution to which this letter was responding. Both *Revelation* (mid-90s) and Pliny's letter to the emperor Trajan, written about fifteen years later, suggest that some persecution of Christians did take place in that same general area. We can be no more specific than that.

Overview

Like *James* in some ways, *1 Peter* addresses a variety of themes, not always in a clear structure. Frequently a theme is picked up, addressed briefly, and set aside to be returned to later. Unlike *James*, however, a more unifying theme of suffering and trials on account of belief in Jesus helps to tie the whole work together. Moreover, in the midst of these trials, hope awaits the faithful in the final reckoning.

In addition to the theme of suffering and trial set against the assurance of salvation, *1 Peter* consists of numerous ethical injunctions of a general sort, along with more specific injunctions about submission to civil authority (2:12–17) and special instructions for slaves (2:18–20), wives (3:1–6), husbands (3:7), and elders (1–4), and a short statement to the young (5:5).

Purpose

Four general descriptions of the literary character of *1 Peter* have been proposed. Some scholars argue that *1 Peter* was not a letter at all, but an Easter baptismal liturgy,[1] around which the literary structure of a letter has been added. This, they believe, accounts for the references to the passion[2] of Jesus in 1:3, 23; 3:20–21, since baptisms frequently were conducted at Easter (or the Jewish Passover), the time of year when Jesus had been crucified. The moral instructions could fit the context of baptism, as could the comments contrasting the previous life of sin with the Christian life.

Other scholars conclude that the references to the passion of Jesus in *1 Peter* focus attention on Christian suffering generally, rather than specifically on the suffering of Jesus. These scholars place the composition of the letter during a period of persecution, though the exact occasion has been difficult to establish.

Still others call attention to the general character of admonition throughout the letter. They conclude that it applies not to baptism or specific persecution but to the situation regularly experienced by any Christian in a society that found the Christian message offensive, silly, or suspicious.

Finally, some argue that the exhortations are directed especially at recent converts, but without a specific baptismal service or concrete persecution in mind. The themes of both baptism (by which converts were initiated into the Christian movement) and persecution (which often resulted from their conversion) could, then, have a meaningful place in a document of general exhortation to recent converts, without either item necessarily being the primary focus of the letter. But this hypothesis may not be able to account for the instructions that are more general and practical, and which probably are reasonably seen as directed to the whole community. Indeed, some of the instructions are addressed to the leaders of the churches—not to recent converts at all.

Themes and Issues

First Peter lacks any overarching structure tying all the parts together into a grand scheme, but smaller structures stress practical Christian living in the midst of persecution. The author encourages Christians to do good in spite of being

---

[1]Easter became the customary time for Christian baptism. As many as three years of instruction were required before an individual fully joined the community. This transition brought the right to participate in the Eucharist. The earliest evidence for the Easter baptismal practice is, however, from the early third century (Tertullian, *Exhortation to Chastity* 7.3; and Hippolytus, *The Apostolic Tradition* 20), so this is unreliable witness to the practice of the first-century church; indeed, it is unreliable witness to the *uniform* practice even of the third-century church. One must be cautious about reading later liturgical practice back into the practice of the first century (see Paul Bradshaw, *The Search for the Origins of Christian Worship* [London: SPCK, 1992]). For example, the developing Easter baptismal liturgy may have been shaped under the influence of a document such as *1 Peter*, without *1 Peter* itself having been written for such an occasion.

[2]The term *passion* describes the sufferings and death of Jesus. Easter, the time of the death of Jesus, was connected in early Christian tradition with the Jewish Passover, which celebrated the Hebrew exodus. At the time of the exodus, the death of a lamb was central to the saving of the Hebrew first-born children and the liberation of the Hebrews from slavery in Egypt. The Christian church picked up on many of those themes in their Easter celebrations, but in no uniform or routine way.

wrongfully treated. He repeatedly sets Jesus forward as the example. Jesus, though he committed no sin (2:22), was nevertheless mistreated, condemned, and killed. In the midst of injustice, Jesus remained silent, waiting for God, the one who judges justly (2:23). So Christians ought also to conduct their lives, knowing that such suffering will be brief, and salvation will be sure (1:6).

Audience

The letter addresses "the exiles of the Dispersion" (or Diaspora), which might identify groups of Jewish Christians. But there is nothing else that suggests a Jewish audience, and the term "Dispersion" (used for Jews who lived outside of Palestine) seems to have been used as well for Gentile Christian communities. Gentiles might have considered themselves as citizens of heaven, aliens in the present world. The author employs the word with that metaphorical sense in 2:10–11, where he encourages them, as "God's people," who are aliens and exiles, to "abstain from the desires of the flesh that wage war against the soul."

Some think the address reveals more. The Greek terms translated as "aliens" and "exiles" might identify those who were resident aliens and visiting strangers in the Roman world. Such would not have enjoyed the rights guaranteed to citizens of the cities where they lived. Today, we think of citizenship involving rights within a nation; in the Roman empire, basic citizenship rights were extended by individual cities, though Roman law qualified what city councils could do. At a time when the Roman peace allowed for considerable mobility, many residents of major cities in the empire—especially those in provinces addressed by the author of *1 Peter*—would have been disadvantaged by their lack of citizenship rights. Peter's audience may have consisted of such noncitizen residents. (A modern parallel might be a church in which most of the people had "green cards" or "landed immigrant" status.) If we could establish that this was the make-up of the churches addressed by this letter, we might have a key to understanding their suffering.

The letter addresses churches across most of Asia Minor.[3] Named are the provinces of Pontus, Galatia, Cappadocia, Asia, and Bithynia. Only the small areas of Lycia, Pamphylia, and Cilicia are unnamed. It is difficult to identify a particular theological group—Pauline, judaizing, gnosticizing—to which this letter might have been directed. Although the theology of the letter has affinities to the Pauline tradition (which may have been dominant in at least some of the areas addressed

---

[3]Asia Minor was a general term for what is now the regions of western and central Turkey, or what was earlier called Anatolia (i.e., the place where the sun came up, from the Greek perspective). This area included several Roman provinces, the number and borders of which were redrawn from time to time. The term *Asia* was used for one of these provinces, on the Aegean coast of western Turkey. It was perhaps the most prosperous area of the Roman Empire. The other provinces in the address of *1 Peter* were more remote and backward.

by this letter), this author and the authors in the Pauline tradition all shared a wider theological perspective.

Authorship

In the first letter attributed to Peter, the author identifies himself as Peter, an apostle of Jesus Christ (1:1), and as an elder (5:1). The intention of such language is to ascribe the document to Jesus' famous disciple Peter. Two other features of this document imply that Peter the apostle was its author. The closing of the letter mentions Silvanus and Mark as contemporaries (5:12–13), and the letter appears to have been written from Rome (called Babylon by some early Christians).[4] Other statements in early Christian tradition associate Peter with Rome[5] and identify Mark as Peter's assistant.[6] Thus the references to Rome and Mark in this letter would strengthen the case that this letter was from the apostle Peter.

But scholars have called for caution here. For one thing, these somewhat later traditions about Peter's association with Rome and with Mark are not necessarily independent data, useful for reconstructing the "historical Peter." We really know almost nothing about Peter's missionary career, except for hints in Paul's letters that it was extensive. It could be that the references to Rome and Mark in *1 Peter* are themselves the bases for the later linkages between Peter, Mark, and Rome.

Yet it must be admitted that the tradition about Peter's connection to Rome is fairly early, and his association with Mark is not unlikely. That observation, of course, does not settle the question of authorship. Such remarks may be merely coloring used by a pseudonymous author to give *1 Peter* a Petrine look.

Many scholars have questioned Peter's authorship of this letter because of its polished literary Greek. Such linguistic skill, they contend, is convincing evidence against the likelihood that a Galilean fisherman (which is the portrait of Peter presented in the gospels) wrote the work. But other scholars have contended that Jews in the area of Galilee (a heavily Gentile and Greek area)[7] normally would have been bilingual.

---

[4]Both Jews and Christians identified Rome with Babylon. The association occurs here and in the *Apocalypse* (14:8; 16:19; 17:5; 18:2–21); and elsewhere in Jewish pseudepigraphical literature of this period (*Sib. Or.* 5.143, 159; *2 Bar.* 11.1; 67.7; and *4 Ezra* 3.1–31). All this literature is generally dated after 70 C.E., the year of the destruction of Jerusalem and the temple by the Romans, and the capture and enslavement of large numbers of Jews. The last time that such a fate had befallen the Jews was about 650 years previously, when the Babylonians were the victorious enemy. The link between Babylon and Rome would have been an obvious one—with Jerusalem smoldering in ruins, its population deported to slavery, and its temple and priesthood gone.

[5]Peter is mentioned in a letter written from the church at Rome in the last decade of the first century (*1 Clem.* 5.4) and in a letter to the church at Rome written by Ignatius ten or fifteen years later (Ign. *Rom.* 4.3), though without explicit comment as to Peter's whereabouts.

[6]The information comes from Papias, who was bishop of Hieropolis (a city near Colossae and Laodicea in the province of Asia) in the early part of the second century. Although his writings have not survived, passages from them have been preserved in the works of Irenaeus (late second century) and Eusebius (early fourth century). The reference to Mark and Peter is in Eusebius, *Eccl. hist.* 3.39.

[7]The large cities and most of the prominent towns in Galilee were Greek. Although some Jews had always lived there, the region was opened to wide-scale Jewish settlement only under the Hasmoneans

But the real problem is not that the letter is written in Greek; rather, it is that the letter is written in exceptionally good Greek, probably requiring a particular kind of educational background unavailable to Peter. Paul, whose educational background may have been above average, does not write such refined Greek.

The use of a coauthor or secretary (amanuensis) may need to be factored into questions about the literary level of documents, where the question of literary ability would shift then from the named author to the scribe. The author does state that Silvanus (whoever he was)[8] was involved with this letter (5:12).[9] Perhaps the less skill an author had with Greek language, the more likely a competent assistant would have been employed. If that is the case, Peter's linguistic skills become irrelevant to the question of authorship.

Date

Dating the letter depends upon two main issues. The first is the question of authorship. If Peter the apostle was the author, an early date is required, not later than the early 60s, when he was martyred. If Peter is not the author, then clues to the date must be found in the content. Most telling is the church structure reflected in the letter. The author knew of, and approved, offices that were coming to be established widely in the church. He called himself an elder (*presbyteros;* 5:1). Although he recognized Jesus as the Chief Shepherd (5:4) and Overseer (*episkopos,* meaning bishop), he noted the role of elders as shepherds themselves, and he termed them overseers. He used the words elder (or presbyter) and bishop (overseer or *episkopos*) as synonyms, as they commonly were used in Christian literature prior to the second century and, in many areas, even later.

But in the regions to which *1 Peter* was addressed, churches distinguished between the terms early. *Bishop* denoted the primary leader of the church, an office distinct from the council of elders. This evolution appears earliest in the letters of Ignatius. The structure in *1 Peter* seems to be less developed than that. This may be

---

after 104–103 B.C.E., when Aristobulus I conquered it. Four decades later it was again under foreign control, this time by the Romans. The various Rome-appointed puppets of the Herodian dynasty served as good Hellenistic rulers, even building *Greek* cities in Galilee. Furthermore, one must keep in mind just how small the area of Galilee was, covering little more than a twenty-five-mile square. The Jewish element in Galilee had neither the population nor the isolation that could have prevented influence from the dominant Greek culture. Jewish life in Galilee was almost certainly bilingual.

[8]Silas (also called Silvanus) is mentioned several times in the early Christian literature, usually in association with Paul (*Acts* 15:22–18:5; *2 Cor.* 1:19; *1 Thess.* 1:1; *2 Thess.* 1:1). His level of literacy is unknown—unless, of course, he was responsible for the wording and style of *1 Peter,* the content being approved by Peter by the addition of his signature. If, on the other hand, the work is pseudonymous, then the mention of Silas would seem to be part of the attempt to disguise the real facts of the composition, though why Silas was chosen, rather than someone else, is unclear. As for Mark, he was clearly an important assistant in various early missions (*Acts* 12:12–15:39; *Col.* 4:10; *2 Tim.* 4:11; *Phlm.* 24).

[9]The Gk reads with as much ambiguity as does the English translation "through Silvanus." Some scholars argue that this means little more than that Silvanus carried the letter; others argue he was the secretary, with wide freedom to put the message in his own words.

reason enough to set the latest possible date for the composition of *1 Peter* around the year 100 C.E.

The only other clues to the date of the document are the concrete references to persecution. Two persecutions occurred in the general region (see setting). Unfortunately, the details of these persecutions are too sketchy to tie the problems in *1 Peter* to adverse conditions mentioned in other documents.

Relation to Other Early Christian Literature

This letter has more parallels with first-century Christian literature than any other document in the *Reader,* and numerous literary affinities have been uncovered between *1 Peter* and the letters of Paul, the synoptic tradition, and the letter of James. Further, *1 Peter* shares images or themes with pseudepigraphical material, particularly *1 Enoch,* and the author is fully at home in the world of the Septuagint, quoting two dozen times from that corpus.

Apart from the gospels and Paul's writings, this letter is the most widely attested of our writings in the patristic literature; and documents as early as *1 Clement* and Polycarp's *Letter to the Philippians* contain echoes of it, though it is not cited by name until the writings of Irenaeus in the latter part of the second century (*Haer.* 4.9.2, 16.5; 5.7.2).

Value for the Study of Early Christianity

Possibly the hints of liturgical elements in *1 Peter* are of greatest value for the study of early Christianity, largely because many of the early writings lack indications of such developments or influences. One problem, however, is that experts do not agree about the extent of liturgical material in *1 Peter,* and even if consensus existed, we would not be able to determine how widely known such materials were.

The letter also offers tantalizing clues about the sociological context of the Christian movement, and this topic has recently come to the forefront in studies of *1 Peter.*

Finally, there will always be the problem of determining exactly which theological community the letter best reflects. Given what we know of Peter from Paul's letters (especially *Galatians* 2), it is surprising how "Pauline" the theology of the letter is. *Second Peter* has a similarly surprising Pauline connection (*2 Pet.* 3:15–17). While *1 Peter* probably cannot provide insight into a distinctively Petrine theology or mission, we should not lightly dismiss the association with Peter. Such association reflects at least the continuing respect with which this leader was held by some elements of the Christian church.

For Further Reading

Davids, Peter H. *1 Peter.* New International Commentary on the New Testament. Grand Rapids: Eerdmans, 1990.

Elliott, J. H. *A Home for the Homeless: A Sociological Exegesis of 1 Peter, Its Setting and Strategy.* Philadelphia: Fortress, 1981.

Kelly, J. N. D. *A Commentary on the Epistles of Peter and of Jude.* New York: Harper & Row, 1969. Repr., Peabody, Mass.: Hendrickson, 1993.

Reicke, Bo. *The Epistles of James, Peter, and Jude.* Anchor Bible 37. Garden City, N.Y.: Doubleday, 1964.

Selwyn, E. G. *The First Epistle of Peter.* London, Macmillan, 1946.

THE FIRST LETTER OF
PETER

Salutation

1 Peter, an apostle of Jesus Christ,
To the exiles of the Dispersion in Pontus, Galatia, Cappadocia, Asia, and Bithynia, ²who have been chosen and destined by God the Father and sanctified by the Spirit to be obedient to Jesus Christ and to be sprinkled with his blood:

May grace and peace be yours in abundance.

A Living Hope

³Blessed be the God and Father of our Lord Jesus Christ! By his great mercy he has given us a new birth into a living hope through the resurrection of Jesus Christ from the dead, ⁴and into an inheritance that is imperishable, undefiled, and unfading, kept in heaven for you, ⁵who are being protected by the power of God through faith for a salvation ready to be revealed in the last time. ⁶In this you rejoice,*a* even if now for a little while you have had to suffer various trials, ⁷so that the genuineness of your faith—being more precious than gold that, though perishable, is tested by fire—may be found to result in praise and glory and honor when Jesus Christ is revealed. ⁸Although you have not seen*b* him, you love him; and even though you do not see him now, you believe in him and rejoice with an indescribable and glorious joy, ⁹for you are receiving the outcome of your faith, the salvation of your souls.

¹⁰Concerning this salvation, the prophets who prophesied of the grace that was to be yours made careful search and inquiry, ¹¹inquiring about the person or time that the Spirit of Christ within them indicated when it testified in advance to the sufferings destined for Christ and the subsequent glory. ¹²It was revealed to them that they were serving not themselves but you, in regard to the things that have now been announced to you through those who brought you good news by the Holy Spirit sent from heaven—things into which angels long to look!

---

a Or *Rejoice in this*

b Other ancient authorities read *known*

1:1 Compare the phrase "aliens and exiles" in 2:11 and the word "exile" in 1:17. These ideas often have been taken as an allegory of the Christian's exile in the world, as the author seems to suggest in 2:10–11. Perhaps there is a double meaning here, since the terms could also indicate a particular status in Greco-Roman society: that of "resident alien" or "visiting stranger," a position between a full citizen and a foreigner (see introduction to *1 Peter*). **Dispersion** The Gk word is *diaspora*. Christian writers took over the language of the Jews in describing their present existence as one of exile, dispersion, and alienation. For Jews, it meant displacement (whether voluntary or forced) from their Palestinian roots. For Christians, it meant life in the present age, contrasted with the age to come (1:17; 2:11; *Jas.* 1:1). **Bithynia** Most of Asia Minor is included here (roughly western and central Turkey). Only the small provinces on the southern coast (Lycia, Pamphylia, and Cilicia) are omitted. Bithynia and Pontus at this time formed a joint province. The separation of the two districts in this address is puzzling; some scholars think that it indicates the circular route the carrier was to take. Much of the area addressed is outside the more urbanized centers of the Pauline mission. **1:2** *grace and peace be yours in abundance* This greeting, which is found also in *2 Pet.* 1:2 and *Jude* 2, differs slightly from the greeting in the Pauline letters. Still, it is closer to the Pauline form than to more common forms of literary greetings of the time. **1:3** *new birth* Similar, but not identical, language is used in *John* 3 to describe the Christian life. The idea of being reborn was not exclusively Christian; it was an occasional feature of religious aspirations in the Greco-Roman world. Parallels with the mystery religions are often drawn, but the extent and direction of the exchange of ideas is debated. **1:5** *in the last times* Early Christians frequently understood that they lived in the last days or at the end of time (1:20; *2 Pet.* 3:3; *Acts* 2:17; *1 Tim.* 4:1; *2 Tim.* 3:1; *Heb.* 1:2; Ign. *Eph.* 11.1; Ign. *Magn.* 6.1; *Barn.* 4.9; 16.5; *Did.* 16.3). **1:6** *trials Jas.* 1:2. The situation is unclear, but the distress Christians were facing is a dominant theme of this letter. We know of two occasions of organized persecutions in the area (see introduction to *1 Peter*). **1:8** See note *b* above. The manuscript variants *(seen* and *known)* are similar in Gk—*eidotes* ("know") and *idontes* ("see"). Both make sense in the passage and both have extensive manuscript support. **1:12** This is typical of the way in which early Christians used the Bible. They concentrated on the prophets and argued that the predictions of the prophets were fulfilled in Jesus. This approach continued in Christian dialogue with Jews for several centuries. Even the apologists (defenders) of the church in the early centuries argued from biblical prophecies in their exchanges with Greek philosophy. *Matthew* and Justin's *Dialogue with Trypho* (from the mid-2d century) illustrate this approach. *Gospel of Thomas* 52 takes a slightly different attitude. *they were serving* The Gk word for *serving* is the verb form of the noun *diakonos* ("deacon"), a term for one of the early offices in the church's hierarchy. *good news* Or "gospel." This is a compound word in Gk. Either the noun or the verb form ("to evangelize") is used in almost every early Christian document—the most surprising exceptions being *John* and the Johannine letters. Christian use of the word may derive from *Isa.* 40:9 or from Roman imperial propaganda about "good news" generated by Augustus.

A Call to Holy Living

[13]Therefore prepare your minds for action;[c] discipline yourselves; set all your hope on the grace that Jesus Christ will bring you when he is revealed. [14]Like obedient children, do not be conformed to the desires that you formerly had in ignorance. [15]Instead, as he who called you is holy, be holy yourselves in all your conduct; [16]for it is written, "You shall be holy, for I am holy."

[17]If you invoke as Father the one who judges all people impartially according to their deeds, live in reverent fear during the time of your exile. [18]You know that you were ransomed from the futile ways inherited from your ancestors, not with perishable things like silver or gold, [19]but with the precious blood of Christ, like that of a lamb without defect or blemish. [20]He was destined before the foundation of the world, but was revealed at the end of the ages for your sake. [21]Through him you have come to trust in God, who raised him from the dead and gave him glory, so that your faith and hope are set on God.

[22]Now that you have purified your souls by your obedience to the truth[d] so that you have genuine mutual love, love one another deeply[e] from the heart.[f] [23]You have been born anew, not of perishable but of imperishable seed, through the living and enduring word of God.[g] [24]For

"All flesh is like grass
   and all its glory like the flower of grass.
The grass withers,
   and the flower falls,
[25] but the word of the Lord endures forever."

That word is the good news that was announced to you.

The Living Stone and a Chosen People

2 Rid yourselves, therefore, of all malice, and all guile, insincerity, envy, and all slander. [2]Like newborn infants, long for the pure, spiritual milk, so that by it you may grow into salvation— [3]if indeed you have tasted that the Lord is good.

[4]Come to him, a living stone, though rejected by mortals yet chosen and precious in God's sight, and [5]like living stones, let yourselves be built[h] into a spiritual house, to be a holy priesthood, to offer spiritual sacrifices acceptable to God through Jesus Christ. [6]For it stands in scripture:

"See, I am laying in Zion a stone,
   a cornerstone chosen and precious;
and whoever believes in him[i] will not be put to
   shame."

[7]To you then who believe, he is precious; but for those who do not believe,

"The stone that the builders rejected
   has become the very head of the corner,"
[8]and

"A stone that makes them stumble,
   and a rock that makes them fall."

They stumble because they disobey the word, as they were destined to do.

[9]But you are a chosen race, a royal priesthood, a holy nation, God's own people,[j] in order that you may proclaim the mighty acts of him who called you out of darkness into his marvelous light.

[10] Once you were not a people,
   but now you are God's people;
once you had not received mercy,
   but now you have received mercy.

---

c Gk *gird up the loins of your mind*
d Other ancient authorities add *through the Spirit*
e Or *constantly*
f Other ancient authorities read *a pure heart*
g Or *through the word of the living and enduring God*

h Or *you yourselves are being built*
i Or *it*
j Gk *a people for his possession*

1:14 The description of the readers as those who were *in ignorance* and whose ancestors had passed on futile ways (1:18) points to a Gentile rather than a Jewish audience. The point is more clearly made in 4:3–4. **1:15** *Rom.* 12:2. **1:16** *Lev.* 11:44; 19:2. **1:19** Jesus is referred to as a lamb in many of the early Christian texts (*Mark* 14:12; *Luke* 22:7; *John* 1:29, 36; *Acts* 8:32; *1 Cor.* 5:7, *Barn.* 5.5; *1 Clem.* 16.21), and it is the favorite expression for Jesus in the *Apocalypse,* where it is used thirty times. The image could come from the Passover lamb or the lamb of *Isaiah* 53, both of which the church early fused into a portrait of Jesus. **1:23–24** Two different Gk words are translated by the English *word* in these verses. **1:25** *Isa.* 40:6–9. The quotation follows the LXX (see *Jas.* 1:10–11). **2:1** *Ps.* 34:8. **2:3** *Jas.* 1:21. **2:5** See note *h* above. Regular Gk verbs have more than seven hundred different forms. In a few cases, two different forms are spelled the same. This is particularly true for some forms of the second person plural. Usually the translator must make a decision from the context on which form the author meant—in this case, the imperative or the indicative. *into a spiritual house* Ign. *Eph.* 9.3. **2:6–8** The author brings together three biblical passages linked by the word *stone,* which was one of the images used by early Christians for Jesus (2:6 from *Isa.* 28:16 [following the LXX, which reads "chief" and "shame"; the MT lacks "chief" and reads "fear" rather than "shame"]; 2:7 from *Ps.* 118:22.; 2:8 from *Isa.* 8:14). For similar treatments, see *Mark* 12:10; *Matt.* 21:42–44; *Luke* 20:17–18; *Acts* 4:11; *Rom.* 9:32–33; *Eph.* 2:20; *Barn.* 6.7–17. **2:6** *Zion* Jerusalem, or the heavenly city of God. **2:9** *Exod.* 19:6. **2:10** *Hos.* 1:9; 2:23. A similar combining of themes is found in *Rom.* 9:25–26, 32–33.

Live as Servants of God

[11]Beloved, I urge you as aliens and exiles to abstain from the desires of the flesh that wage war against the soul. [12]Conduct yourselves honorably among the Gentiles, so that, though they malign you as evildoers, they may see your honorable deeds and glorify God when he comes to judge.[k]

[13]For the Lord's sake accept the authority of every human institution,[l] whether of the emperor as supreme, [14]or of governors, as sent by him to punish those who do wrong and to praise those who do right. [15]For it is God's will that by doing right you should silence the ignorance of the foolish. [16]As servants[m] of God, live as free people, yet do not use your freedom as a pretext for evil. [17]Honor everyone. Love the family of believers.[n] Fear God. Honor the emperor.

The Example of Christ's Suffering

[18]Slaves, accept the authority of your masters with all deference, not only those who are kind and gentle but also those who are harsh. [19]For it is a credit to you if, being aware of God, you endure pain while suffering unjustly. [20]If you endure when you are beaten for doing wrong, what credit is that? But if you endure when you do right and suffer for it, you have God's approval. [21]For to this you have been called, because Christ also suffered for you, leaving you an example, so that you should follow in his steps.

[22] "He committed no sin,
and no deceit was found in his mouth."

[23]When he was abused, he did not return abuse; when he suffered, he did not threaten; but he entrusted himself to the one who judges justly. [24]He himself bore our sins in his body on the cross,[o] so that, free from sins, we might live for righteousness; by his wounds[p] you have been healed. [25]For you were going astray like sheep, but now you have returned to the shepherd and guardian of your souls.

Wives and Husbands

3 Wives, in the same way, accept the authority of your husbands, so that, even if some of them do

---

k Gk *God on the day of visitation*
l Or *every institution ordained for human beings*
m Gk *slaves*
n Gk *Love the brotherhood*

o Or *carried up our sins in his body to the tree*
p Gk *bruise*

2:11 This comment introduces an extended household code (2:13–3:7), a popular literary device used to specify acceptable and expected behavior of various groups. Christian writers often set their own moral injunctions in this framework (*Eph.* 5:21–6:9; *Col.* 3:18–4:1; *Jas.* 4:1). **2:17** *Honor everyone* This is set within the theme of the proper attitude to civil authority (2:13–17). The command to *honor everyone* could just as well be translated "honor everyone in authority" in this context, without doing violence to the intent. For a similar handling of this theme, see *Rom.* 13:1–7; *1 Tim.* 2:1–2. **Honor the emperor** At least part of the region addressed by *1 Peter* faced an invigorated imperial cult; temples were built to Emperors Domitian, Trajan, and Hadrian in the late 1st and early 2d centuries. The *Apocalypse* seems to be set in a context of persecution stemming from the refusal of Christians to sacrifice to the emperor. Compare what is said about Rome (or its code name, "Babylon") in the *Apocalypse* with the positive, though cautious, instructions about honoring the emperor in *1 Peter.* Whether this is a matter of difference in fundamental perspective or a difference in circumstances is uncertain. Certainly the author of *1 Peter* would not have encouraged sacrificing to the emperor. His theme of suffering as a Christian (4:16) is too prominent for this kind of accommodation to the imperial will. Whatever the author meant by *honor the emperor,* the readers must have known that it did not mean to sacrifice to him. **2:18** *slaves* Lit. "household servants." Gk has various words to describe particular aspects of slavery. Similar instructions to slaves are given in *Eph.* 6:5–8; *Col.* 3:22–25; *1 Tim.* 6:1–2; *Titus* 2:9–10; Ign. *Pol.* 4.1–3; *Did.* 4.10–11. Slaves had little protection. In the early 2d century, Emperor Hadrian brought in legislation that provided some protection from the most serious abuses, and other prominent figures called for more reasonable treatment of slaves (Seneca, *Letters* 47). **2:20** The author frequently mentions those who suffer unjustly (3:14, 16–17). **2:21** Local churches that faced persecution and martyrdom frequently appealed to the sufferings of Christ. The letters of Ignatius are especially shaped by this concern, and the theme is repeated often in *1 Peter* (4:1, 12–13). **2:22** *Isa.* 53:9. This may have been part of an early Christian hymn. The quotation follows the LXX, which reads "sin" rather than "injustice" (or "violence," as the NRSV renders the Hebrew). **2:22–25** Much of the language in this paragraph is influenced by *Isaiah* 53, which was a favorite among early Christians as they tried to make sense of the sufferings and death of Jesus. The author portrays Jesus as a lamb (1:19) and a shepherd; the latter image came to be applied to some early Christian leaders (*John* 10:1–18; *1 Pet.* 5:2–4). **guardian** Gk *episkopos.* This word also could be translated "bishop" or "overseer." The technical sense of this term ("bishop"), indicating a key church office, is lost in the NRSV translation here, and this illustrates a key problem in the debate over the development of church office. Many of the words that became technical terms initially had merely a descriptive sense of function or status. In this case, *episkopos* could mean "bishop" (technical term) or "guardian" or "overseer" (a mere description of function). The question is, at what time did the merely descriptive word take on a technical sense? **3:1–6** Similar instructions to women or wives are found in *Col.* 3:18; *Eph.* 5:22–24; *Titus* 2:4–5; *1 Clem.* 1.3; Ign. *Pol.* 5.1; Polycarp, *To the Philadelphians* 4.3. The Roman historian Livy was particularly concerned about disregard for the authority of the husband (*History of Rome* 34.2.1, 2, 8–11, 14), and Juvenal, in his *Satires,* written about the

not obey the word, they may be won over without a word by their wives' conduct, [2]when they see the purity and reverence of your lives. [3]Do not adorn yourselves outwardly by braiding your hair, and by wearing gold ornaments or fine clothing; [4]rather, let your adornment be the inner self with the lasting beauty of a gentle and quiet spirit, which is very precious in God's sight. [5]It was in this way long ago that the holy women who hoped in God used to adorn themselves by accepting the authority of their husbands. [6]Thus Sarah obeyed Abraham and called him lord. You have become her daughters as long as you do what is good and never let fears alarm you.

[7]Husbands, in the same way, show consideration for your wives in your life together, paying honor to the woman as the weaker sex,[q] since they too are also heirs of the gracious gift of life—so that nothing may hinder your prayers.

Suffering for Doing Right

[8]Finally, all of you, have unity of spirit, sympathy, love for one another, a tender heart, and a humble mind. [9]Do not repay evil for evil or abuse for abuse; but, on the contrary, repay with a blessing. It is for this that you were called—that you might inherit a blessing. [10]For

"Those who desire life
　　and desire to see good days,
let them keep their tongues from evil
　　and their lips from speaking deceit;
[11]　let them turn away from evil and do good;
　　let them seek peace and pursue it.
[12]　For the eyes of the Lord are on the righteous,
　　and his ears are open to their prayer.
But the face of the Lord is against those who do
　　evil."

[13]Now who will harm you if you are eager to do what is good? [14]But even if you do suffer for doing

what is right, you are blessed. Do not fear what they fear,[r] and do not be intimidated, [15]but in your hearts sanctify Christ as Lord. Always be ready to make your defense to anyone who demands from you an accounting for the hope that is in you; [16]yet do it with gentleness and reverence.[s] Keep your conscience clear, so that, when you are maligned, those who abuse you for your good conduct in Christ may be put to shame. [17]For it is better to suffer for doing good, if suffering should be God's will, than to suffer for doing evil. [18]For Christ also suffered[t] for sins once for all, the righteous for the unrighteous, in order to bring you[u] to God. He was put to death in the flesh, but made alive in the spirit, [19]in which also he went and made a proclamation to the spirits in prison, [20]who in former times did not obey, when God waited patiently in the days of Noah, during the building of the ark, in which a few, that is, eight persons, were saved through water. [21]And baptism, which this prefigured, now saves you—not as a removal of dirt from the body, but as an appeal to God for[v] a good conscience, through the resurrection of Jesus Christ, [22]who has gone into heaven and is at the right hand of God, with angels, authorities, and powers made subject to him.

Good Stewards of God's Grace

4 Since therefore Christ suffered in the flesh,[w] arm yourselves also with the same intention (for whoever has suffered in the flesh has finished with sin), [2]so as to live for the rest of your earthly life[x] no longer by human desires but by the will of God. [3]You have already spent enough time in doing what the Gentiles like to do, living in licentiousness, passions, drunkenness, revels, carousing, and lawless idolatry. [4]They are surprised that you no longer join them in the same excesses of dissipation, and so they blaspheme.[y] [5]But they will have to give an accounting to him who

---

q Gk vessel

r Gk their fear
s Or respect
t Other ancient authorities read died
u Other ancient authorities read us
v Or a pledge to God from
w Other ancient authorities add for us; others, for you
x Gk rest of the time in the flesh
y Or they malign you

---

time of 1 Peter, contrasts the chastity that was born of poverty to the immoral behavior and adornments brought on by wealth (6.286–295, 298–300). **3:3** *braiding your hair* 1 Tim. 2:9. **3:6** Gen. 18:12. **3:7** Similar instructions to husbands are found in Col. 3:19; Eph. 5:25–28. *weaker sex* Gk word translated here as *sex* means "vessel." In what way the wife is weaker is not specified, but clearly it is not considered a disadvantage carried over into the final state, according to the comment following. The claim that women were weaker was common (Musonius Rufus, *Fragment* 12; *Gospel of Thomas* 114). **3:8–9** See 2:23; Luke 6:28; Rom. 12:16–17. **3:12** Ps. 34:12–16. **3:13** Rom. 13:3. **3:18** See note t above. In Gk, the difference between *suffered* and *died* is slight: *epathen* and *apethanen*. **3:19** *the spirits in prison* This is a much disputed comment. It became the basis for the belief that Jesus had descended into hell between his death and resurrection to preach to the dead (4:6), who sometimes were connected with the sons of God in the story of Noah (see Eph. 4:9; Gen. 6:1–4; 1 En. 10.4–6). **3:20** Noah and the flood story are found in *Genesis* 6–9.

stands ready to judge the living and the dead. [6]For this is the reason the gospel was proclaimed even to the dead, so that, though they had been judged in the flesh as everyone is judged, they might live in the spirit as God does.

[7]The end of all things is near;[z] therefore be serious and discipline yourselves for the sake of your prayers. [8]Above all, maintain constant love for one another, for love covers a multitude of sins. [9]Be hospitable to one another without complaining. [10]Like good stewards of the manifold grace of God, serve one another with whatever gift each of you has received. [11]Whoever speaks must do so as one speaking the very words of God; whoever serves must do so with the strength that God supplies, so that God may be glorified in all things through Jesus Christ. To him belong the glory and the power forever and ever. Amen.

Suffering as a Christian

[12]Beloved, do not be surprised at the fiery ordeal that is taking place among you to test you, as though something strange were happening to you. [13]But rejoice insofar as you are sharing Christ's sufferings, so that you may also be glad and shout for joy when his glory is revealed. [14]If you are reviled for the name of Christ, you are blessed, because the spirit of glory,[a] which is the Spirit of God, is resting on you.[b] [15]But let none of you suffer as a murderer, a thief, a criminal, or even as a mischief maker. [16]Yet if any of you

suffers as a Christian, do not consider it a disgrace, but glorify God because you bear this name. [17]For the time has come for judgment to begin with the household of God; if it begins with us, what will be the end for those who do not obey the gospel of God? [18]And

"If it is hard for the righteous to be saved,
what will become of the ungodly and the sinners?"

[19]Therefore, let those suffering in accordance with God's will entrust themselves to a faithful Creator, while continuing to do good.

Tending the Flock of God

5 Now as an elder myself and a witness of the sufferings of Christ, as well as one who shares in the glory to be revealed, I exhort the elders among you [2]to tend the flock of God that is in your charge, exercising the oversight,[c] not under compulsion but willingly, as God would have you do it[d]—not for sordid gain but eagerly. [3]Do not lord it over those in your charge, but be examples to the flock. [4]And when the chief shepherd appears, you will win the crown of glory that never fades away. [5]In the same way, you who are younger must accept the authority of the elders.[e] And all of you must clothe yourselves with humility in your dealings with one another, for

"God opposes the proud,
but gives grace to the humble."

---

z Or *is at hand*
a Other ancient authorities add *and of power*
b Other ancient authorities add *On their part he is blasphemed, but on your part he is glorified*

c Other ancient authorities lack *exercising the oversight*
d Other ancient authorities lack *as God would have you do it*
e Or *of those who are older*

4:9 The theme of hospitality appears often in early Christian writing. Note particularly *2 and 3 John* and the *Didache,* and the instruction to church leaders in the Pastoral Letters (*1 Tim.* 5:10; also *Rom.* 12:13; *Heb.* 13:2). **4:10 *serve*** The Gk word is from the same root as that for "deacon," as also in 4:11. **4:11 *Amen*** According to many scholars, the material from 1:3 to this point was originally a separate baptismal homily, later incorporated as the substantial element of the letter we now have. But there is no manuscript evidence for such source theories, and no examples of other letters built around a homily exist. A similar doxology appears in 5:11. **4:12** At this point the author seems to repeat many of the concerns he expressed in the earlier part of the letter: *ordeal* (4:12) is the same Gk word as that translated "trial" in 1:6 (both are described as *fiery* [4:12; 1:7]); the Christian is to rejoice in persecution (4:13; 1:6) and to share in Christ's sufferings (4:13; 2:21; 4:1). **4:14** *Matt.* 5:11; *Luke* 6:22. ***for the name of Christ*** See 4:16; *Acts* 11:26. Around 111 C.E., Pliny the Younger asked the emperor Trajan whether "the name" alone is sufficient ground for punishment of Christians. A few decades later, Christian apologists argued that Christians should not be persecuted for "the name" itself but only for immoral activities. **4:18** *Prov.* 11:31, The text here follows the LXX; the MT reads "If the righteous on earth get their deserts, How much more the wicked man and the sinner." **5:1 *a witness to the sufferings of Christ*** Many scholars see in this comment an attempt by a pseudonymous author to link the letter to Peter. **5:2 *tend the flock*** These two words in Gk come from the same root, as does the word "chief shepherd" in 5:4. One might translate it "shepherd the sheep." ***oversight*** The Gk word is based on the same root as the word *episkopos*, which can be translated "bishop." The idea of shepherding and overseeing are linked here, in 2:12, and *Acts* 20:28. It is difficult to determine from the use of these terms the precise stage of development of church office (see also Ign. *Phld.* 2.1). **5:5** See note *e* above. It is not clear whether a formal office is intended here. The Gk word *presbyteros* could refer simply to the older men in the group or to a formal group of elders known as presbyters. The translator must decide the issue on the basis of context. Note how a similar problem of translation is handled in a different way in 2:25. ***God opposes . . .*** LXX *Prov.* 3:34. The LXX is followed, as it is in *Jas.* 4:6. See *Isa.* 57:15; *Ps.* 138:6.

⁶Humble yourselves therefore under the mighty hand of God, so that he may exalt you in due time. ⁷Cast all your anxiety on him, because he cares for you. ⁸Discipline yourselves, keep alert.ᶠ Like a roaring lion your adversary the devil prowls around, looking for someone to devour. ⁹Resist him, steadfast in your faith, for you know that your brothers and sistersᵍ in all the world are undergoing the same kinds of suffering. ¹⁰And after you have suffered for a little while, the God of all grace, who has called you to his eternal glory in Christ, will himself restore, support, strengthen, and establish you. ¹¹To him be the power forever and ever. Amen.

Final Greetings and Benediction

¹²Through Silvanus, whom I consider a faithful brother, I have written this short letter to encourage you and to testify that this is the true grace of God. Stand fast in it. ¹³Your sister churchʰ in Babylon, chosen together with you, sends you greetings; and so does my son Mark. ¹⁴Greet one another with a kiss of love.

Peace to all of you who are in Christ.ⁱ

---

f Or *be vigilant*
g Gk *your brotherhood*

h Gk *She who is*
i Other ancient authorities add *Amen*

5:6 *Jas.* 4:10. **5:9** For a similar linking of the themes of humility and resisting the devil, see *Jas.* 4:6–7. **5:12** *Silvanus* Possibly Silas, an associate of Paul, who may have served as secretary. **5:13** *Babylon* Cryptic for Rome, an indication of the home of the author or a device to tie the letter to Peter, which would suggest that traditions about Peter's final residence in Rome developed early. See also *Rev.* 17:5. *Mark* See *Acts* 12:12–17; 15:37–39; *Col.* 4:9; *2 Tim.* 4:11; *Phlm.* 24. In the early 2d century, Papias, the bishop of Hierapolis, linked *Mark* with Peter (see introduction to *1 Peter*).

To Those Beloved and Called

JUDE

Setting and Date

A letter this short,[1] focused intensely on one general theme, filled largely with examples from its sacred traditions, can be particularly difficult to situate. Some argue that it is one of the earliest Christian documents and one of the few from the Palestinian church, which would make it a rare and significant document indeed.[2] Others see it as a part of the later vast Christian pseudepigraphical literature that the second-century church produced. They take the author's reflection on an earlier apostolic period (discussed below) as evidence for a second-generation Christian document.

If the author of *2 Peter* copied *Jude*, then *Jude* must have been written prior to *2 Peter*, but since *2 Peter* is itself difficult to date, this observation provides no useful *terminus ad quem* ("date before which"). If the traditional attribution of authorship is accepted, then *Jude* must have been written fairly early, but we know nothing about Jude (a brother of Jesus) that would help us date it more precisely. Other than the letter itself, we have little to indicate that Jude played any role in the early Christian church. Eusebius records a report by Hegesippus that the grandsons of Jude were church leaders during the reigns of Domitian and Trajan (*Eccl. hist.* 3.19–20). That report may suggest that Jude was a leader too, but it does not say that; in fact, according to the story, the grandsons became leaders not because they were descendants of Jude or relatives of Jesus, but because they were faithful in face of probable martyrdom. That does sound a little pietistic on Eusebius's part. The family connection surely contributed much to the credibility these individuals had, though that is not to dismiss their reputation for piety.

---

[1]Only *Philemon, 2 John,* and *3 John* are shorter.

[2]Evidence of a Palestinian setting includes the author's routine use of the Hebrew Bible rather than the LXX, and his fondness for popular Jewish apocalyptic writings, a perspective that seems to have colored Jesus and the earliest Palestinian church.

Authorship

The author is identified as Jude, a brother of James. That description would generally not be very helpful, given how common both of those names were. But the pairing of the names James and Jude provides the key to the identity of the author. Jesus had brothers named James and Jude,[3] and there is little doubt that the attribution of this letter to Jude the brother of James was intended to imply that Jude, the brother of Jesus, was the author.[4]

It is not particularly problematic that a brother of Jesus should identify himself as a brother of James rather than a brother of Jesus. He has identified himself as the *servant* of Jesus. After that, his relationship to James may serve as an adequate identification, because James (the brother of both Jesus and Jude) had become a prominent leader of the church.

Thus the early church and most modern scholars have agreed that *Jude* 1 attributes the letter to Jude, the brother of Jesus, but as we have seen with some other texts, attribution to a famous person should not be accepted without further inquiry. Many scholars think that this is another case of pseudonymous Christian literature, attributed by a second- or third-generation author to a respected first-generation figure. They emphasize any features of the letter that show traces of development or indicate distance from the first generation. If a late date can be established, it becomes easy to reject a first-generation individual as author.[5]

For example, the author seems to look back on an earlier age of the church. He appeals to his readers to *contend for the faith which was once delivered to the saints* (3). Further, he speaks of *the predictions of the apostles* that pointed to the last days, which the author identified with his own time (17–18). Many scholars judge these as marks of a later period and therefore dismiss the attribution of authorship to Jude, the brother of Jesus.

Yet a case can be made that the author was at least Palestinian, for his biblical references agree with the Hebrew Bible rather than the Septuagint, and he was more familiar than any other early Christian writer with the Jewish literature that seems to have emanated mainly from Palestine. These observations have led some scholars to accept the traditional ascription of authorship.

---

[3] Called Judas (not Iscariot) in the gospels. Jude is a shortened form of that name.

[4] There are a number of references in the early Christian literature to the "brothers" of Jesus (*Mark* 3:31; *Matt.* 12:46; *Mark* 6:3; *Matt.* 13:55; *John* 7:3–10; *Acts* 1:14; *1 Cor.* 9:5; *Gal.* 1:19). In the Roman Catholic tradition these brothers are understood to be such not in the restricted sense (offspring of the same parents) but in a looser sense (half-brothers or close relatives).

[5] The traditional authorship of several early Christian documents has been challenged on the basis of their second-generation perspective (*Ephesians* and *2 Peter*, in particular, in addition to *Jude*). But the matter of the changing perspective in a second-generation community needs closer study.

Overview and Purpose

The author spares no time getting to his point. After a few brief words of epistolary politeness and with an unmistakable urgency, he states his purpose: certain *intruders have stolen in* among his readers (4), and they must guard against this danger by contending *for the faith once for all entrusted to the saints* (3). Then follows a list of the most notorious reprobates in biblical history. The author links the present intruders with those degenerate characters, and promises the same kind of judgment that befell them (13–16).

Themes and Issues

This brief document is primarily a plea for cautious moral behavior, in opposition to the looser ethic espoused by the intruders. But the identification of these opponents seems beyond the grasp of the modern investigator. Some scholars have argued that they were proto-gnostic antinomians,[6] but others disagree. We really know too little about the opponents to attempt much of a description other than to say that, from the author's perspective, they had libertine tendencies. It may even be that the opponents were merely straw men, put forward to draw the lines more clearly between correct and incorrect behavior. This hypothesis is worth some consideration, especially since the letter lacks a specific address: It is written to those who are called, who are beloved in God the Father and kept safe for Jesus Christ. In any case, the tone against the opponents is extremely sharp.

The opponents are set in the company of the most despicable characters of biblical history. Cain, Balaam, and Korah (11), brutal Egyptian slave-masters (5), fallen angels (6), and evil Sodom and Gomorrah (7) all make the list. As if this name-calling were not enough, the author blasts away at his opponents with such a torrent of abuse that his letter becomes almost an exemplar for polemical writing. The opponents are called ungodly persons (4), blemishes, waterless clouds, fruitless trees, wild waves, wandering stars (12–13), grumblers, malcontents, loud-mouthed boasters, and scoffers (16). The author takes morality seriously. His readers could not have missed that point.

Relation to Other Early Christian Literature

The imagery is drawn from a wide range of Jewish literature. A number of examples are drawn from the Bible (5, 7, 11). Other Jewish literature was used too (6, 9, 14–15). The *Testament of Moses* provides the details regarding Michael and the body of Moses (v. 9); *1 Enoch*, which is quoted by the author, provides the scene of judgment. Yet, though the author is clearly at home in apocalyptic literature, and

---

[6]Second-century gnostics came in two stripes. Some were libertine; others were rigorously ascetic. Antinomian (i.e. "anti-law" or libertine) proto-gnostics would have been forerunners of the libertine gnostics.

though apocalyptic language surfaces frequently (6–7, 13–15, 18, 23–24), the apocalyptic tone of *Jude* seems absorbed by the letter's moralizing.

Value for the Study of Early Christianity

If the document could be located in a Palestinian context, the letter would be of particular importance. Almost all of the earliest Christian literature comes from outside of Palestine, the birthplace of the Christian movement. If it could be established that *Jude* was Palestinian, that could give us a look at early Christianity much closer to its source.

But even if we could establish that *Jude* was Palestinian, it would be difficult to determine how representative it was of early Palestinian Christianity. Indeed, the letter itself witnesses to two forms: that of the author and that of the intruders, who could have been as Palestinian as the author himself.

For Further Reading

Bauckham, R. J. "Jude: An Account of Research," in *Aufsteig und Niedergang der römischen Welt: Geschichte und Kultur Roms im Spiegel der neueren Forschung.* 25.5:3791–3826. Part 2, *Principat* 25.5. New York: de Gruyter, 1988.

Kelly, J. N. D. *A Commentary on the Epistles of Peter and Jude.* New York: Harper & Row, 1969.

Neyrey, Jerome H. *2 Peter, Jude.* Anchor Bible 37c. Garden City, N.Y.: Doubleday. 1993.

THE LETTER OF
JUDE

Salutation

[1]Jude,[a] a servant[b] of Jesus Christ and brother of James,

To those who are called, who are beloved[c] in[d] God the Father and kept safe for[d] Jesus Christ:

[2]May mercy, peace, and love be yours in abundance.

Occasion of the Letter

[3]Beloved, while eagerly preparing to write to you about the salvation we share, I find it necessary to write and appeal to you to contend for the faith that was once for all entrusted to the saints. [4]For certain intruders have stolen in among you, people who long ago were designated for this condemnation as ungodly, who pervert the grace of our God into licentiousness and deny our only Master and Lord, Jesus Christ.[e]

Judgment on False Teachers

[5]Now I desire to remind you, though you are fully informed, that the Lord, who once for all saved[f] a people out of the land of Egypt, afterward destroyed those who did not believe. [6]And the angels who did not keep their own position, but left their proper dwelling, he has kept in eternal chains in deepest darkness for the judgment of the great Day. [7]Likewise, Sodom and Gomorrah and the surrounding cities, which, in the same manner as they, indulged in sexual immorality and pursued unnatural lust,[g] serve as an example by undergoing a punishment of eternal fire.

[8]Yet in the same way these dreamers also defile the flesh, reject authority, and slander the glorious ones.[h] [9]But when the archangel Michael contended with the devil and disputed about the body of Moses, he did not dare to bring a condemnation of slander[i] against him, but said, "The Lord rebuke you!" [10]But these people slander whatever they do not understand, and they are destroyed by those things that, like irrational animals, they know by instinct. [11]Woe to them! For they go the way of Cain, and abandon themselves to Balaam's error for the sake of gain, and perish in Korah's rebellion. [12]These are blemishes[j] on your love-feasts, while they feast with you without fear, feeding themselves.[k] They are waterless

a Gk Judas
b Gk slave
c Other ancient authorities read sanctified
d Or by
e Or the only Master and our Lord Jesus Christ
f Other ancient authorities read though you were once for all fully informed, that Jesus (or Joshua) who saved

g Gk went after other flesh
h Or angels; Gk glories
i Or condemnation for blasphemy
j Or reefs
k Or without fear. They are shepherds who care only for themselves

1 beloved Other ancient authorities read "sanctified." The difference is minor in Gk; *beloved* is *ēgapēmenois;* "sanctified" is *hēgiasmenois.* **2** This is slightly different from the openings of other Christian letters in this collection. Paul's letters typically mention grace and peace, as do the letters of *Peter* and the *Apocalypse* (1:7). *Jude* finds parallels in *1 and 2 Timothy* and in *2 John.* See Ign. *Smyrn.* 12.2. **3** There is a marked urgency in the tone. The author had planned a different kind of letter. He goes immediately to the point of the "intruders," as he calls them. Other authors warned of intruders (*2 Pet.* 2:1; *Gal.* 2:4; *2 Tim.* 3:6). **5** *Numbers* 13–14. According to the Bible, the Israelites, after being freed from Egyptian slavery, came quickly to the borders of Palestine, a land God promised to Abraham. But after spying out the land, most of the spies reported that the Israelites were not strong enough to defeat the inhabitants. When the Israelites hesitated, God condemned them to forty years of wandering in the desert, until a new generation would be ready to possess the land. **6** In the *Genesis* flood story, it is said that the sons of God began to marry the daughters of men, a union that produced giants (*Gen.* 6:1–2). Many commentators came to understand the term "sons of God" as a reference to angels. The theme is developed in *1 Enoch* 6–19. **7** Again the author turns to the book of *Genesis,* which provides a detailed story about the destruction of Sodom and Gomorrah (*Gen.* 18:16–19:29). **8 the glorious ones** Or "angels"; lit. "glories." This has presented a puzzle for translators and commentators. If the parallel holds with v. 9, these must be evil powers of some kind. **9** The author is probably using material from the *Testament of Moses,* although this passage does not appear in any extant manuscript. We know from comments by patristic writers such as Clement, Origen, and Didymus that this was the source of *Jude's* story. **11** These are three classic examples of evil or disobedience (Cain, *Gen.* 4:8–16; Balaam, *Num.* 22:1–24:25; Korah, *Num.* 16:1–40). **12–13** The "intruders" are judged to be empty, self-serving, and dangerous. **12 love-feasts** Or "agapes." Early Christians had a special meal called the *agape,* which seems to have been originally connected to the Eucharist. **waterless clouds** *Prov.* 25:14; *2 Pet.* 2:17. **feeding themselves** See note *k* on the next page. The Gk verb has the same root as the word for "shepherds," as Christian ministers were sometimes called (see "pastor," which is from *pastor,* the Latin word for "herdsman"). This may hint at the status of the intruders as recognized clergy, but we cannot determine the exact office they held. Perhaps they were itinerant ministers.

clouds carried along by the winds; autumn trees without fruit, twice dead, uprooted; [13]wild waves of the sea, casting up the foam of their own shame; wandering stars, for whom the deepest darkness has been reserved forever.

[14]It was also about these that Enoch, in the seventh generation from Adam, prophesied, saying, "See, the Lord is coming[l] with ten thousands of his holy ones, [15]to execute judgment on all, and to convict everyone of all the deeds of ungodliness that they have committed in such an ungodly way, and of all the harsh things that ungodly sinners have spoken against him." [16]These are grumblers and malcontents; they indulge their own lusts; they are bombastic in speech, flattering people to their own advantage.

Warnings and Exhortations

[17]But you, beloved, must remember the predictions of the apostles of our Lord Jesus Christ; [18]for they said to you, "In the last time there will be scoffers, indulging their own ungodly lusts." [19]It is these worldly people, devoid of the Spirit, who are causing divisions. [20]But you, beloved, build yourselves up on your most holy faith; pray in the Holy Spirit; [21]keep yourselves in the love of God; look forward to the mercy of our Lord Jesus Christ that leads to[m] eternal life. [22]And have mercy on some who are wavering; [23]save others by snatching them out of the fire; and have mercy on still others with fear, hating even the tunic defiled by their bodies.[n]

Benediction

[24]Now to him who is able to keep you from falling, and to make you stand without blemish in the presence of his glory with rejoicing, [25]to the only God our Savior, through Jesus Christ our Lord, be glory, majesty, power, and authority, before all time and now and forever. Amen.

---

l Gk came
m Gk Christ to

n Gk *by the flesh*. The Greek text of verses 22–23 is uncertain at several points

---

autumn trees without fruit Autumn was the time for the fruit harvest (see APPENDIX C). **13** *waves of the sea* Isa. 57:20. **14–15** The author quotes from *1 En.* 1:9, a source for his comments in 1:6 also. **17–18** Not a direct quote, but it is at least the essence of what such people would have said (*Matt.* 24:11, 24; *Acts* 20:29–30; *2 Tim.* 4:3; *2 Pet.* 2:1; *1 John* 4:1).

To Those Who Have Received a Precious Faith

2 PETER

Authorship and Date

The author identifies himself as Simeon Peter (or Simon Peter, according to some manuscripts). He further describes himself as an apostle and an eyewitness to the transfiguration of Jesus (1:16–18) and speaks of the nature of his own approaching death as something revealed to him by Jesus (1:14). These clues point to Peter, the disciple, as the author. This identification is strengthened by the author's statement that this letter was his second (3:1). The reference is apparently to *1 Peter,* which also bore Peter's name as author.

But, almost from the day this so-called second letter of Peter appeared, some people have disputed its authenticity. Evidence from the third and fourth centuries (Origen, Eusebius, and Jerome) shows suspicion about its authorship. Modern scholars have confirmed the grounds for suspicion. The styles of *1 Peter* and *2 Peter* are different and features of the letter suggest a late date. (1) The author seems to equate Paul's letters with "scripture" and may have known them in a collection, rather than as individual documents, which is how they would have at first circulated (3:15–16). (2) The founders of the church apparently were dead by this time (3:4). (3) The hints of concern over the delay of Christ's return (3:3–4) date it somewhat late, and if that concern was being expressed by a group of libertine gnostics, as some think, it would date *2 Peter* well into the second century. (4) Finally, *2 Peter* is not explicitly mentioned by any church father until Origen (mid-third century).

If the traditional attribution of authorship could be maintained, then the letter would be dated after *1 Peter,* and shortly before Peter's death, which was clearly on the author's mind (1:14–15). But, as we have seen, traditional authorship has long been widely disputed. Perhaps the references to Paul's letters and to the death of the apostles are sufficient grounds for dating the document no earlier than the late first century. Some still argue for a date as late as 150 C.E., which would make this document the latest of all those that came to be part of the collection called the New Testament.

Purpose

The author presents his writing as a reminder (1:12; 3:1–2), made necessary by troublemakers in the community whose views about the second coming of Jesus would lead to moral failure (3:3–10). But it is more than a reminder. It is a stinging attack on these troublemakers who deny the *parousia* (second coming).

The opponents apparently have been quite convincing, or at least the author senses that they are a deadly threat, for he levels at them (ch. 2) a most fierce and venomous attack. Readers are assured that the judgment of God will come on the erring individuals just as surely as it came on the leading reprobates of the past: angels who sinned, the ungodly of Noah's day, and the inhabitants of Sodom and Gomorrah. And to the reader the author offers this caution: since you are forewarned, beware lest you be carried away with the error of the lawless and lose your own stability (3:17).

Experts debate the identy of the opponents. The most popular view is that they were gnostics of some sort, but most of the invective is general enough to be applied to any group that met with disapproval. Even the various comments that seem to point to a libertine lifestyle could be mere stock polemical vilification, without much substance for identifying the opponents.

Setting

The letter presents itself explicitly as the "last words" of the apostle Peter (1:13–15), written to counter those who were mocking the Christian belief that Jesus would return and the world would be judged.

But questions of date and authorship place the self-claim of the letter under serious suspicion. Most scholars now think that someone other than Peter wrote this document. They take it as evidence of a post-apostolic church, supposing that it does not offer reliable information about Peter's activities or theology. Consequently, they look for a later setting for the letter in which its major theme makes sense (see Purpose above).

Overview

The most noticeable feature of the structure is the incorporation of most of the letter of *Jude* into the middle of *2 Peter* (2:1–3:4). In *2 Peter*'s opening, clear association with Peter is made. After the insertion of material from *Jude*, the apocalyptic tone is continued with reference to the coming judgment and the day of the Lord.

Themes and Issues

The letter is filled with polemic and apologetic. The delay of the *parousia* had shaken some and soured others. The author calls for confidence in God, and reminds his readers that God works according to his own time frame, and on that level nothing had been delayed or derailed.

The readers have their choice: being duped by those who deny the *parousia*, or holding steadily to the traditions they had received. The author leaves no doubt that the consequences of the wrong decision will be immeasurable.

Audience

The audience may be the same as that addressed by *1 Peter*, since this document claims to be a second letter to them (3:1), thus placing it in the area of western and central Turkey. At the time of *2 Peter*, this region was divided into a number of Roman provinces, listed in the address of *1 Peter* (1:1). But calling this the second letter could have been merely the device of a pseudonymous author.

The audience does seem to respect the Pauline letters, though certain interpretations of these letters concern the author (*2 Pet.* 3:15–17). This, too, could reasonably place the letter in the general area of the address of *1 Peter*, since prominent parts of that locale were important in Paul's mission.

Relation to Other Early Christian Literature

The author effectively uses apocalyptic imagery; some of it comes from incorporating a large section of the letter of *Jude*, though the author of *2 Peter* contributes far more material of apocalyptic tone than he has received from *Jude*. Further, this author is more circumspect than the author of *Jude* in his borrowing of material from apocalyptic works. For example, he modifies the passage about Michael and the body of Moses (*Jude* 9 = *2 Pet.* 2:11) and omits entirely the quotation from *1 Enoch* (*Jude* 14). The extensive material shared by *Jude* and *2 Peter* indicates a kind of literary dependency. In all likelihood *2 Peter* copied from *Jude*, rather than the other way around.

Value for the Study of Early Christianity

This document may give us a first-hand glimpse of a church adjusting to a situation in which its original apocalyptic perspective had to be modified. However much the author might protest, his defense of the apocalyptic position here actually involved modifying the position and distancing it from more urgent apocalyptic speculation. The question remains, however, whether this adjustment was minor (a retouching of apocalyptic hopes in light of the delay of the *parousia*) or major (an adjustment to a world in which the apocalyptic perspective would have seemed irrelevant or implausible).

For Further Reading

Bauckham, R. J. "2 Peter: An Account of Research," in *Aufsteig und Niedergang der römischen Welt: Geschichte und Kultur Roms im Spiegel der neueren Forschung.* 25.5:3713–3752. Part 2, *Principat* 25.5. New York: de Gruyter, 1988.

Fornberg, Tord. *An Early Church in a Pluralistic Society: A Study of 2 Peter.* Coniectanea biblica New Testament. Translated by Jean Gray. Lund: Gleerup, 1977.

Käsemann, Ernst. "An Apologia for Primitive Christian Eschatology." Pages 169–95 in *Essays on New Testament Themes.* Studies in Biblical Theology 41. London: SCM, 1964.

Kelly, J. N. D. *A Commentary on the Epistles of Peter and Jude.* New York: Harper & Row, 1969.

Neyrey, Jerome H. *2 Peter, Jude.* Anchor Bible 37c. Garden City, N.Y.: Doubleday. 1993.

THE SECOND LETTER OF PETER

Salutation

1 Simeon[a] Peter, a servant[b] and apostle of Jesus Christ,

To those who have received a faith as precious as ours through the righteousness of our God and Savior Jesus Christ:[c]

[2]May grace and peace be yours in abundance in the knowledge of God and of Jesus our Lord.

The Christian's Call and Election

[3]His divine power has given us everything needed for life and godliness, through the knowledge of him who called us by[d] his own glory and goodness. [4]Thus he has given us, through these things, his precious and very great promises, so that through them you may escape from the corruption that is in the world because of lust, and may become participants of the divine nature. [5]For this very reason, you must make every effort to support your faith with goodness, and goodness with knowledge, [6]and knowledge with self-control, and self-control with endurance, and endurance with godliness, [7]and godliness with mutual[e] affection, and mutual[e] affection with love. [8]For if these things are yours and are increasing among you, they keep you from being ineffective and unfruitful in the knowledge of our Lord Jesus Christ. [9]For anyone who lacks these things is nearsighted and blind, and is forgetful of the cleansing of past sins. [10]Therefore, brothers and sisters,[f] be all the more eager to confirm your call and election, for if you do this, you will never stumble. [11]For in this way, entry into the eternal kingdom of our Lord and Savior Jesus Christ will be richly provided for you.

[12]Therefore I intend to keep on reminding you of these things, though you know them already and are established in the truth that has come to you. [13]I think it right, as long as I am in this body,[g] to refresh your memory, [14]since I know that my death[h] will come soon, as indeed our Lord Jesus Christ has made clear to me. [15]And I will make every effort so that after my departure you may be able at any time to recall these things.

Eyewitnesses of Christ's Glory

[16]For we did not follow cleverly devised myths when we made known to you the power and coming of our Lord Jesus Christ, but we had been eyewitnesses of his majesty. [17]For he received honor and glory from God the Father when that voice was conveyed to him by the Majestic Glory, saying, "This is my Son, my Beloved,[i] with whom I am well pleased." [18]We ourselves heard this voice come from heaven, while we were with him on the holy mountain.

[19]So we have the prophetic message more fully confirmed. You will do well to be attentive to this as to a lamp shining in a dark place, until the day dawns and the morning star rises in your hearts. [20]First of all you must understand this, that no prophecy of scripture is a matter of one's own interpretation, [21]because no prophecy ever came by human will, but men and women moved by the Holy Spirit spoke from God.[j]

---

a Other ancient authorities read *Simon*
b Gk *slave*
c Or *of our God and the Savior Jesus Christ*
d Other ancient authorities read *through*
e Gk *brotherly*
f Gk *brothers*

g Gk *tent*
h Gk *the putting off of my tent*
i Other ancient authorities read *my beloved Son*
j Other ancient authorities read *but moved by the Holy Spirit saints of God spoke*

1:2 *grace and peace* See note to *1 Pet.* 1:2. **1:3** *godliness* The author uses a form of this root five times (1:3, 6, 7; 2:9; 3:11). This root is used elsewhere in our literature only in *Acts*, the Pastorals, and *1 Clement* (see note to *1 Tim.* 2:2). **1:4** *lust* Gk *epithymia.* The author uses this word or a cognate four times (2:10, 18; 3:3). It is the primary word for "passions," which Greek philosophy generally saw as the negative side of the human psyche. **1:9** *cleansing of past sins* Probably a reference to baptism. **1:10** There is considerable textual variation at this point. **1:13–14** *John* 21:18–19 contains an account of Jesus telling Peter about the nature of his death. That story may not be in the author's mind here, but he certainly presents the letter as Peter's last will. **1:16–18** *1 Pet.* 5:1. The letter presents itself as the work of Peter the apostle, an eyewitness of Jesus' life. In 1:17, the author refers to a story involving Peter that is in the Jesus tradition (*Mark* 9:2–13; *Matt.* 17:1–13; *Luke* 9:28–36). Some scholars think that this reference to the incident reveals the hand of a pseudonymous author who overplayed the Petrine connection. **1:19** *prophetic message* See note to *1 Pet.* 1:12. *morning star Rev.* 22:16.

False Prophets and Their Punishment

2 But false prophets also arose among the people, just as there will be false teachers among you, who will secretly bring in destructive opinions. They will even deny the Master who bought them—bringing swift destruction on themselves. [2]Even so, many will follow their licentious ways, and because of these teachers[k] the way of truth will be maligned. [3]And in their greed they will exploit you with deceptive words. Their condemnation, pronounced against them long ago, has not been idle, and their destruction is not asleep.

[4]For if God did not spare the angels when they sinned, but cast them into hell[l] and committed them to chains[m] of deepest darkness to be kept until the judgment; [5]and if he did not spare the ancient world, even though he saved Noah, a herald of righteousness, with seven others, when he brought a flood on a world of the ungodly; [6]and if by turning the cities of Sodom and Gomorrah to ashes he condemned them to extinction[n] and made them an example of what is coming to the ungodly;[o] [7]and if he rescued Lot, a righteous man greatly distressed by the licentiousness of the lawless [8](for that righteous man, living among them day after day, was tormented in his righteous soul by their lawless deeds that he saw and heard), [9]then the Lord knows how to rescue the godly from trial, and to keep the unrighteous under punishment until the day of judgment [10]—especially those who indulge their flesh in depraved lust, and who despise authority.

Bold and willful, they are not afraid to slander the glorious ones,[p] [11]whereas angels, though greater in might and power, do not bring against them a slanderous judgment from the Lord.[q] [12]These people, however, are like irrational animals, mere creatures of instinct, born to be caught and killed. They slander what they do not understand, and when those creatures are destroyed,[r] they also will be destroyed, [13]suffering[s] the penalty for doing wrong. They count it a pleasure to revel in the daytime. They are blots and blemishes, reveling in their dissipation[t] while they feast with you. [14]They have eyes full of adultery, insatiable for sin. They entice unsteady souls. They have hearts trained in greed. Accursed children! [15]They have left the straight road and have gone astray, following the road of Balaam son of Bosor,[u] who loved the wages of doing wrong, [16]but was rebuked for his own transgression; a speechless donkey spoke with a human voice and restrained the prophet's madness.

[17]These are waterless springs and mists driven by a storm; for them the deepest darkness has been re-

---

k Gk because of them
l Gk Tartaros
m Other ancient authorities read pits
n Other ancient authorities lack to extinction
o Other ancient authorities read an example to those who were to be ungodly

p Or angels; Gk glories
q Other ancient authorities read before the Lord; others lack the phrase
r Gk in their destruction
s Other ancient authorities read receiving
t Other ancient authorities read love feasts
u Other ancient authorities read Beor

2:1–3:4 The middle 3d of 2 Peter is heavily dependent on Jude, using most of the material from Jude 4–18 and in much the same order. See the section following on the parallels between Jude and 2 Peter. **2:1–3** Here and elsewhere in this letter, the description of opponents uses stock polemical language, which tells us nothing about the opponents. **2:1** Compare Acts 20:30, where the author has Paul issue a similar warning about false teachers. **2:4** The author must have in mind the "sons of God" in Gen. 6:1–4 (Jude 6; 1 Pet. 3:19–20). **hell** Gk tartaros. In Greek mythology this word refers to the dreadful pit in which Zeus imprisoned the Titans. Hence it is specifically a place of punishment, as opposed to the more generalized concept of Hades, a dreary, shadowy underworld to which the dead in general are consigned. **chains** Other ancient authorities read "pits." In Gk the difference is slight: "chains" is seirais; "pits" is sirois. The translators have opted for chains because the parallel passage in Jude (v. 6), from which the author of 2 Peter is thought to have copied, uses another word for "chains" (desmois), which is not subject to the same confusion. The assumption is that an author borrowing from another work more likely would have used another synonym than a completely new image. **2:5** Genesis 7. The author provides the number of persons saved in the flood, as does the author of 1 Peter (3:20). **2:6–8** Jude 7. The detailed story appears in Gen. 18:16–19:29. Jude does not mention Lot but speaks only of the destruction of Sodom and Gomorrah. See also 1 Clem. 10.6; 11.1. **2:10** **glorious ones** See note p above and note to Jude 8. **2:11** The parallel passage in Jude 10 is more detailed, drawing from the Testament of Moses, a text that the author of 2 Peter may have intentionally avoided quoting. **2:13** **suffering** See note s above. In the Gk, suffering is the compound word adikoumenoi; "receiving" is the simple word komioumenoi. The variants provide a good example of the work of text critics (scholars who try to reconstruct the original text). The translators of the NRSV have chosen suffering because a cognate of this word appears two words later (adikoumenoi misthon adikias), but other translators favor "receiving," since a tired scribe could have carelessly combined the words komioumenoi and adikias to get adikoumenoi. **in their dissipation** See note t above. In Gk the difference between these variants is slight: dissipation is apatais; "love feasts" is agapais. In uppercase Gk letters, the letters p and g are similar (Π, Γ); so with t and p (Τ, Π). The parallel passage in Jude 12, from which the author is thought to have copied, reads "love feasts." Some think that the author provides a pun on the word "love feasts" here. **2:15** Jude 11. The story is told in Numbers 22–24. **2:17** **waterless springs** Jude 12 reads "waterless clouds."

served. ¹⁸For they speak bombastic nonsense, and with licentious desires of the flesh they entice people who have just*v* escaped from those who live in error. ¹⁹They promise them freedom, but they themselves are slaves of corruption; for people are slaves to whatever masters them. ²⁰For if, after they have escaped the defilements of the world through the knowledge of our Lord and Savior Jesus Christ, they are again entangled in them and overpowered, the last state has become worse for them than the first. ²¹For it would have been better for them never to have known the way of righteousness than, after knowing it, to turn back from the holy commandment that was passed on to them. ²²It has happened to them according to the true proverb,

"The dog turns back to its own vomit,"
and,
"The sow is washed only to wallow in the mud."

The Promise of the Lord's Coming

3 This is now, beloved, the second letter I am writing to you; in them I am trying to arouse your sincere intention by reminding you ²that you should remember the words spoken in the past by the holy prophets, and the commandment of the Lord and Savior spoken through your apostles. ³First of all you must understand this, that in the last days scoffers will come, scoffing and indulging their own lusts ⁴and saying, "Where is the promise of his coming? For ever since our ancestors died,*w* all things continue as they were from the beginning of creation!" ⁵They deliberately ignore this fact, that by the word of God heavens existed long ago and an earth was formed out of water and by means of water, ⁶through which the world of that time was deluged with water and perished. ⁷But by the same word the present heavens and earth have

been reserved for fire, being kept until the day of judgment and destruction of the godless.

⁸But do not ignore this one fact, beloved, that with the Lord one day is like a thousand years, and a thousand years are like one day. ⁹The Lord is not slow about his promise, as some think of slowness, but is patient with you,*x* not wanting any to perish, but all to come to repentance. ¹⁰But the day of the Lord will come like a thief, and then the heavens will pass away with a loud noise, and the elements will be dissolved with fire, and the earth and everything that is done on it will be disclosed.*y*

¹¹Since all these things are to be dissolved in this way, what sort of persons ought you to be in leading lives of holiness and godliness, ¹²waiting for and hastening*z* the coming of the day of God, because of which the heavens will be set ablaze and dissolved, and the elements will melt with fire? ¹³But, in accordance with his promise, we wait for new heavens and a new earth, where righteousness is at home.

Final Exhortation and Doxology

¹⁴Therefore, beloved, while you are waiting for these things, strive to be found by him at peace, without spot or blemish; ¹⁵and regard the patience of our Lord as salvation. So also our beloved brother Paul wrote to you according to the wisdom given him, ¹⁶speaking of this as he does in all his letters. There are some things in them hard to understand, which the ignorant and unstable twist to their own destruction, as they do the other scriptures. ¹⁷You therefore, beloved, since you are forewarned, beware that you are not carried away with the error of the lawless and lose your own stability. ¹⁸But grow in the grace and knowledge of our Lord and Savior Jesus Christ. To him be the glory both now and to the day of eternity. Amen.*a*

---

v Other ancient authorities read *actually*
w Gk *our fathers fell asleep*

x Other ancient authorities read *on your account*
y Other ancient authorities read *will be burned up*
z Or *earnestly desiring*
a Other ancient authorities lack *Amen*

2:19 Seneca, a Stoic philosopher, denounced enslavement to passions (*Letters* 47.17). **2:20** *Matt.* 12:43–45. **2:22** *Prov.* 26:11. **3:2** **holy prophets** Some scholars believe this is a reference to prophets in the early church rather than to the Hebrew prophets of the Bible. *Eph.* 3:5. **3:4** **his coming** Gk *parousia,* the technical term for the second coming of Jesus. **ancestors died** Lit. "our fathers fell asleep." Many scholars believe that this is a reference to the first Christian generation, which was already dead. This would make the traditional attribution of authorship difficult to defend. Apocalyptic thought saw creation as on the verge of collapse; it was neither stable nor unchanged. Against any who would claim the contrary (perhaps the position of the opponents), the author pointed to the destruction of the world by a flood in Noah's time, serving as a warning of a new destruction ready to burst upon the world. **3:8** *Ps.* 90:4. **3:9** *Ezek.* 33:11. **3:10** **like a thief** The image of the end coming as a thief is common in early Christianity (*Matt.* 24:43; *Luke* 12:39; *2 Thess.* 2:5; *Rev.* 3:3; 16:15). **dissolved with fire** Fire was often connected to judgment in the writings of the Jewish scripture and the early church. **3:13** **new earth** *Rev.* 21:1, 27. **3:14** **without spot or blemish** *1 Pet.* 1:19. **3:16** **in all his letters** This comment is usually taken to indicate that a collection of Paul's letters had already been made by the time of the composition of *2 Peter,* and thus to provide another argument against the traditional attribution of authorship. **the other scriptures** Paul's letters seem to be equated with scripture. Assuming that it took some time for this attitude to develop, many scholars find here another clue that *2 Peter* comes from the 2d generation of the church or later.

EARLY

CHRISTIAN

READER

BIOGRAPHY, ANECDOTE, AND HISTORY

PORTRAITS OF JESUS AND THE FIRST CHRISTIANS

Anyone who attempts to understand the earliest Christian texts from a historical point of view must soon face the special challenges posed by the gospels and *Acts*. Because these texts tell the story of Jesus' life and the church's first generation, respectively, and the NT places them first in its arrangement, it takes a great deal of mental discipline to remember that they are actually products of the second and third generations of Jesus' followers (say, 65 to 120 C.E.). This general introduction to the gospels and *Acts* will discuss the basic questions: Where did these writings come from? And how are they related to the events they describe? In the process, we shall sketch out the main lines of current thinking about the gospels and *Acts*. More specific introductions will accompany each document in turn.

Origin of the Gospels

First, the gospels are *anonymous texts*. Unlike the letters of Paul, which repeatedly name their author, the traditional gospels and *Acts* nowhere claim that they were written by Matthew, Mark, Luke, or John. Ancient writers were generally careful to introduce their works in the opening lines of the text itself, and to mention their own names if they wished these to be known. Although the gospels contain titles and, in one case, even a prologue (*Luke* 1:1–14), none of them mentions its author. The *Fourth Gospel* comes closest, when it identifies the source of much of its material (though not the final author, apparently) as the "student whom Jesus loved" (*John* 21:20–24). But it is unclear from the story itself who this beloved student is supposed to have been.[1]

Why, then, do we call the gospels by their traditional names? As the manuscripts of the gospels and *Acts* were copied and recopied through the centuries, Christian copyists added names to the tops of the scrolls in standardized formats—*According to Matthew* [or *Mark* or *Luke* or *John*]"—on the basis of growing oral traditions

---

[1] The only male character identified as the special object of Jesus' love is Lazarus (11:3, 5). Since the Lazarus episode is pivotal to the gospel, perhaps the author implies that the source is Lazarus?

about their authorship. Modern scholarship has demonstrated, however, that those oral traditions were wrong in many ways.

It is not entirely clear how the oral traditions about the gospels' authors came into being. The first witness known to us is a man named Papias, bishop of Hierapolis, who flourished in the middle of the second century; at least, we have the fourth-century church historian Eusebius's claims about what Papias said in five lost volumes. According to Eusebius, Papias "was a man of very little intelligence, as is clear from his books" (*Eccl. hist.* 3.39.13), and Eusebius complains that people have given too much credence to Papias's work. Nevertheless, Papias claimed to report what he had heard from some seniors who were alleged to have associated with the original apostles, and Eusebius repeats some of these traditions with approval. Papias asserted that an associate of Peter's named Mark wrote down all that he could remember of Peter's teaching (in Rome) concerning Jesus. Since Peter related single items from Jesus' life as the occasion demanded, this Mark ended up composing a haphazard account of individual items from Jesus' life ("not in order"). Papias also claimed that a certain Matthew "arranged the sayings [of Jesus] in the Hebrew dialect, and each person interpreted them as well as possible" (3.39.16). Papias may have written more on these subjects, but that is the extent of Eusebius's report on him.

By the end of the second century, however, the bishop of Lyons, Irenaeus, could confidently state that only four of the many gospels then in circulation were authoritative because only these were traceable to an apostle's authority. Possibly from Papias and Marcion earlier in the century, he had learned a tradition that *Luke* and *Acts* were written by a physician associate of Paul's named Luke; a version of this tradition held that when Paul refers to "my gospel," he is talking about the written text of *Luke* (Eusebius, *Eccl. hist.* 3.4.7; 6.25.6). Finally, another second-century tradition known to Irenaeus held that *John* was written by the apostle of that name (*Against Heresies* 3.1.1). Thus the four canonical gospels appeared to represent *independent apostolic testimony* about Jesus' life. This position was occasionally challenged, as when the fifth-century scholar Augustine noticed close parallels between *Matthew* and *Mark* and so argued that the briefer *Mark* was an abridgment of *Matthew*. But after Augustine the notion that all four gospels were independent and apostolic remained the standard view until the rise of historical study in the eighteenth century.

Eighteenth-century European scholars, energized by the rise of scientific thinking and a philosophy of free inquiry, undertook a massive reappraisal of all ancient traditions, especially those that had led to the establishment of the Christian West. In this mood, it did not take them long to realize that the traditional attributions of authorship for the gospels and *Acts* were built on sand. In the first place, the evidence of the gospels and *Acts* does not support the ancient claims. *Matthew,* for example, is by no means a collection of Jesus' sayings in Hebrew, to be interpreted at will; it is a coherent account of Jesus' life written *in Greek,* and (we may add) it shows many signs of being an original Greek production: quotations of the Greek Bible and use of typically Greek vocabulary and word plays. *Mark* is not a hap-hazard collection of items about Jesus such as Mark might have recalled from Pe-ter's preaching in Rome as Papias claimed, but a story with a thematic arrangement of materials, driven by a clear plot. Far from featuring Peter, it rather belittles him. (Indeed, *Matthew* treats Peter much more favorably.) The gospel of *Luke* can hardly be attributed to Paul's influence, since Paul did not know Jesus in Galilee, where most of the action takes place. And this gospel places Jesus so squarely within Juda-ism that it would be hard to square with Paul's views; and *Acts* too presents a Paul who is hard to reconcile with the person that he reveals in his own letters (see the introduction to Paul). When Paul speaks of "my gospel" in his letters, he plainly re-fers to his preaching, not to a document (*Gal.* 1:11; 2:2, 14; *Rom.* 2:16; 15:16; 16:25). Finally: How did *John* end up so entirely different from the other three, as such a "spiritualized" gospel, if it was simply another eyewitness report?

But the fundamental objection to the traditional view came from the discovery by these eighteenth-century scholars that the first three gospels are related in some way. Thus, no matter who wrote them, they are not independent accounts of Jesus' life. One of the first to recognize this fact was J. J. Griesbach, who, in 1774, pub-lished a *synopsis* of the gospels. He seems to have been the first to apply the adjective "synoptic" to the first three gospels, on the ground that they could easily be read or seen *(-optic)* together *(syn-).*

What Griesbach meant was that, if one lays out the texts of the first three gos-pels side by side, one notices a vast number of striking similarities, both in general and in particular. In general, they share much the same content and in much the same order. If independent authors were writing biographies of an individual, we should expect them to focus on different elements of the subject's life. But the synoptists agree on ignoring virtually all the expected details about Jesus' appear-ance, education, childhood friends and influences, job training, and entertain-ments. They all focus rather on the period of his life beginning with his immersion by John the Baptist. From that point on, they include the same select kinds of ma-terial—parables, proverbs, cures, controversies—and they all give a large amount of space to Jesus' arrest and trial.

To be more specific, *Matthew* has about 1069 verses, *Mark* about 662, and *Luke* about 1150—"about" because different manuscripts include slightly different material. Now, roughly 523 verses of *Matthew*, nearly half of the gospel, are closely parallel to 609 verses of *Mark*, so that 92 percent of the shorter gospel is represented also in *Matthew*. About 357 verses of *Mark* (53 percent) are closely parallel to 325 verses (28 percent) of *Luke* and an additional 95 have more distant counterparts there. Moreover, of the ma-terial that is in *Matthew* and *Luke* but without parallel in *Mark*, about 171 verses in *Matthew* (16 percent) are extremely close to 151 verses (13 percent) of *Luke*, and an ad-ditional 90 verses of *Matthew* (8.5 percent) parallel 94 verses of *Luke* (8 percent) more distantly. So the *content* of these three gospels is remarkably similar: a mere 4.5 percent of Mark, 29 percent of *Matthew*, and 43 percent of *Luke* have no close parallel in one of the others. Consider the following chart.

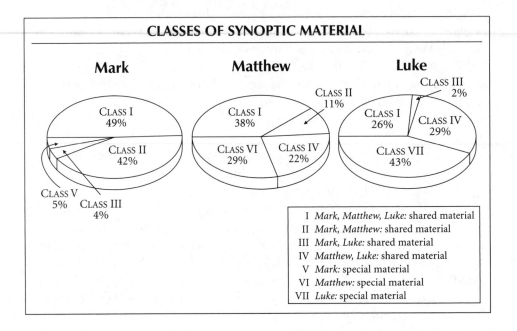

CLASSES OF SYNOPTIC MATERIAL

Mark — Class I 49%, Class II 42%, Class V 5%, Class III 4%

Matthew — Class I 38%, Class II 11%, Class IV 22%, Class VI 29%

Luke — Class I 26%, Class III 2%, Class IV 29%, Class VII 43%

I *Mark, Matthew, Luke:* shared material
II *Mark, Matthew:* shared material
III *Mark, Luke:* shared material
IV *Matthew, Luke:* shared material
V *Mark:* special material
VI *Matthew:* special material
VII *Luke:* special material

The really impressive thing is that, although most of the synoptic stories about Jesus do not carry within them any chronological indicators, and so could be placed in various locations, the Synoptics agree in following basically the same order in the material they share. The *Gospel of John* takes quite an independent course, for example by locating Jesus' cleansing of the temple early in his career (2:14–22), so it is striking that the Synoptics agree so closely in placing this incident at precisely the same point in a complex of events near the end of Jesus' life (*Mark* 11:15–17). From Jesus' baptism onward, in fact, the first three gospel authors tend to place the same events in the same sequence. In Jesus' various controversies with Jewish leaders (*Mark* 2:1–3:6), there is nothing to require that one story should be told before another, since the authors merely say that an incident occurred "one sabbath" or the like. But all three synoptists place these five stories in the same order, and that order is *Mark's*. That is, with only one exception, either *Matthew* or *Luke* agrees with *Mark's* order; often, all three agree in order.

When we move from such macro-analysis of the first three gospels to micro-analysis, we find that not only do the Synoptics follow a similar order for their shared material, but they also use similar sentence structure and Greek vocabulary within their common material. Here, verbatim agreement is about 50 percent. This fact requires that there was *some kind of literary relationship* among them—some kind of borrowing.

We can see the principle clearly enough in English. If we asked several people to write short accounts of their summer walk in the country, they might understandably use some common images (e.g., grass, sky, sun, air), but we would expect their stories to be quite different. One might say, "I felt great. What a day! The birds were singing away, you could smell the grass, and the sky was really blue—no clouds in sight." Another might report, "Overwhelmed by the tranquillity of nature, I felt as if the eternal azure sky were pouring its energy into my soul. A brilliant red cardinal lightly crossed my path, tacitly advising me that I was a welcome guest in his home." A third person: "It was nice out, for sure. Great day for a canoe trip or a baseball game." But if two reporters ended up with the same words in the same order, even if they added or omitted a word here or there, then we would be forced to conclude that their reports were connected in some way. This is the principle behind determinations of plagiarism. And these are just the kinds of agreements that we find among the Synoptic Gospels.

The easiest way to visualize the issue is to take a synopsis and compare parallel episodes. Some synopses include *John* in a fourth column or row. Comparing *John* is useful because it shows how differently an independent author (or someone determined to go his own way even if he had knowledge of the Synoptics) might write a gospel. Thus, when the Synoptics are being compared the *John* column is usually empty; elsewhere, it is full and the synoptic columns are empty, because there is very little verbal agreement between *John* and the synoptic tradition. Any substantial set of parallel passages will suffice to illustrate the literary relationship. Here are a few examples, chosen more or less at random.[2] Bold type highlights close agreements. (In some cases the English translation suggests agreements that are not present in the Greek; in other cases, the Greek agrees more closely than the English suggests.)

The extensive agreements within these passages are obvious. Although we might imagine that relatively short sayings of John the Baptist and Jesus could be remembered easily (as in examples 1 and 3), remember that this agreement is in the Greek text of the gospels, whereas John and Jesus appear to have spoken Aramaic (and perhaps Hebrew) most of the time. Anyone who has ever undertaken to translate something, or has read various translations of the same thing, knows that each translation will be unique because different languages open up numerous possibilities. But here the *Greek* texts agree, so we have to assume some kind of relationship at the *literary* level.

---

[2]Here are some further examples, with references to the section numbers in two of the most popular synopses included (T = B. Throckmorton; A = K. Aland).

For all three gospels compare: *Matt.* 9:1–8/*Mark* 2:1–12/*Luke* 5:17–26 (T 52; A 43); *Matt.* 9:9–13/*Mark* 2:13–17/*Luke* 5:27–32 (T 53; A 44); *Matt.* 9:14–27/*Mark* 2:18–22/*Luke* 5:33–39 (T 54; A 45); *Matt.* 13:1–23/*Mark* 4:1–20/*Luke* 8:4–18 (T 90–93; A 122–24); *Matt.* 8:18–9:26/*Mark* 4:35–5:43/*Luke* 8:22–56 (T 105–107; A 136–138); *Matt.* 22:23–33/*Mark* 12:18–27/*Luke* 20:27–40 (T 207; A 281).

For *Matthew* and *Mark:* *Matt.* 4:18–22/*Mark* 1:16–20 (T 11; A 21); *Matt.* 14:22–15:39/*Mark* 6:45–8:10 (T 113–18; A 147–48, 150–53); *Matt.* 24:32–33/*Mark* 13:28–29 (T 220; A 293); *Matt.* 17:1–8; *Mark* 9:2–8 (T 124; A 161).

Example 1: John the Baptist and Jesus

Matthew 3:11–12

11 "I baptize you with water for repentance, but one who is more powerful than I is coming after me;

I am not worthy to carry his sandals.

He will baptize you with the Holy Spirit and fire.

12 His winnowing fork is in his hand, and he will clear his threshing floor and will gather his wheat into the granary; but the chaff he will burn with unquenchable fire."

Mark 1:7–8

7 He proclaimed, "The one who is more powerful than I is coming after me;

I am not worthy to stoop down and untie the thong of his sandals.

8 I have baptized you with water; but he will baptize you with the Holy Spirit."

Luke 3:16–17

16 John answered all of them by saying, "I baptize you with water; but one who is more powerful than I is coming;

I am not worthy to untie the thong of his sandals.

He will baptize you with the Holy Spirit and fire.

17 His winnowing fork is in his hand, to clear his threshing floor and to gather the wheat into his granary; but the chaff he will burn with unquenchable fire."

Example 2: Jesus Calls His First Students

Matthew 4:18–22

18 As he walked by the Sea of Galilee, he saw two brothers, Simon, who is called Peter, and Andrew his brother, casting a net into the sea—for they were fishermen.
19 And he said to them, "Follow me, and I will make you fish for people."
20 Immediately they left their nets and followed him.
21 As he went from there, he saw two other brothers, James son of Zebedee and his brother John, in the boat with their father Zebedee, mending their nets, and he called them.
22 Immediately they left the boat and their father, and followed him.

Mark 1:16–20

16 As Jesus passed along the Sea of Galilee, he saw Simon and his brother Andrew casting a net into the sea—for they were fishermen.
17 And Jesus said to them, "Follow me and I will make you fish for people."
18 And immediately they left their nets and followed him.
19 As he went a little farther, he saw James son of Zebedee and his brother John, who were in their boat mending the nets.
20 Immediately he called them; and they left their father Zebedee in the boat with the hired men, and followed him.

Example 3: A Leper Cured

Matthew 8:2–4

2 and there was a leper who came to him and knelt before him, saying,

"Lord, if you choose, you can make me clean."

3 He stretched out his hand and touched him, saying, "I do choose. Be made clean!" Immediately his leprosy was cleansed.

Mark 1:40–45

40 A leper came to him begging him, and kneeling he said to him,

"If you choose, you can make me clean."

41 Moved with pity, Jesus stretched out his hand and touched him, and said to him, "I do choose. Be made clean!" 42 Immediately the leprosy left him, and he was made clean.

Luke 5:12–16

12 Once, when he was in one of the cities, there was a man covered with leprosy. When he saw Jesus, he bowed with his face to the ground and begged him,

"Lord, if you choose, you can make me clean."

13 Then Jesus stretched out his hand, touched him, and said, "I do choose. Be made clean." Immediately the leprosy left him.

4 **Then** Jesus said to him, **"See that you say nothing to anyone; but**

go, show yourself to the priest, and offer the gift that Moses commanded, as a testimony to them."

43 After sternly warning him he sent him away at once, 44 saying to him, **"See that you say nothing to anyone; but**

go, show yourself to the priest, and offer for your cleansing what Moses commanded, as a testimony to them."

45 **But** he went out and began to proclaim it freely, and to spread **the word.**

14 **And** he ordered **him to tell no one.**

"Go," he said, "and **show yourself to the priest, and, as Moses commanded, make an offering for your cleansing, for a testimony to them."**

15 **But** now more than ever **the word** about Jesus spread abroad.

Example 4: **Healing the Paralytic**

Matthew 9:2–6

2 **And just then** some people were **carrying a paralyzed man** lying **on a bed.**

When Jesus saw their faith, he said to the paralytic, "Take heart, son; your sins are forgiven."

3 Then **some of the scribes** said to themselves, **"This man is blaspheming."**

4 But Jesus, perceiving their thoughts, said, "Why do you think evil **in your hearts?**

5 For **which is easier, to say, 'Your sins are forgiven,' or to say, 'Stand up and walk'?**

Mark 2:3–11

3 Then some people came, **bringing to him a paralyzed man,** carried by four of them.

4 **And when they could not bring him to Jesus because of the crowd,** they removed the roof above him; and after having dug through it, they let down the mat on which the paralytic lay.

5 **When Jesus saw their faith,** he said **to the paralytic, "Son, your sins are forgiven."**

6 Now **some of the scribes** were sitting there, **questioning** in their hearts, 7 "Why does **this fellow** speak in this way? It is **blasphemy! Who can forgive sins but God** alone?" 8 At once **Jesus perceived** in his spirit **that they were discussing these questions** among themselves; and he said to **them, "Why do you raise such questions in your hearts?**

9 **Which is easier, to say** to the paralytic, **'Your sins are forgiven,' or to say, 'Stand up** and take your mat **and walk'?**

Luke 5:18–24

18 **Just then** some men came, **carrying** a paralyzed man **on a bed.** They were trying to bring him in and lay him before Jesus;

19 but finding **no way to bring him in because of the crowd,** they went up on the roof and let him down with his bed through the tiles into the middle of the crowd in front of Jesus.

20 **When he saw their faith, he said,** "Friend, **your sins are forgiven you."**

21 Then the scribes and the Pharisees began **to question,** "Who is **this** who is speaking **blasphemies? Who can forgive sins but God** alone?"

22 When Jesus perceived their questionings, he answered them, **"Why do you raise** such **questions in your hearts?**

23 **Which is easier, to say, 'Your sins are forgiven you,' or to say, 'Stand up and walk'?**

6 But so that you may know that the Son of Man has authority on earth to forgive sins"—he then said to the paralytic—"Stand up, take your bed and go to your home."

10 But so that you may know that the Son of Man has authority on earth to forgive sins"—he said to the paralytic—11 "I say to you, stand up, take your mat and go to your home."

24 But so that you may know that the Son of Man has authority on earth to forgive sins"—he said to the one who was paralyzed—"I say to you, stand up and take your bed and go to your home."

Example 5: Plucking Grain on the Sabbath

Matthew 12:1–8

1 At that time **Jesus** went **through the grainfields on the sabbath; his disciples** were hungry, and **they began to pluck heads of grain and to eat.**

2 When the Pharisees saw it, they said to him, "**Look,** your disciples **are doing what is not lawful** to do **on the sabbath.**"

3 **He said to them, "Have you not read what David did when he and his companions were hungry?**

4 **He entered the house of God and ate the bread of the Presence, which it** was **not lawful for** him or **his companions to eat, but** only **for the priests.**

5 Or have you not read in the law that on the sabbath the priests in the temple break the sabbath and yet are guiltless?

6 I tell you, something greater than the temple is here.

7 But if you had known what this means, 'I desire mercy and not sacrifice,' you would not have condemned the guiltless.

8 For **the Son of Man is lord of the sabbath.**"

Mark 2:23–28

23 **One sabbath** he **was going through the grainfields;** and as they made their way **his disciples began to pluck heads of grain.**

24 The Pharisees said to him, "**Look, why are** they **doing what is not lawful on the sabbath?**"

25 And **he said to them, "Have you never read what David did when he and his companions were hungry** and in need of food?

26 **He entered the house of God,** when Abiathar was high priest, **and ate the bread of the Presence, which it is not lawful for any but the priests to eat, and he gave some to his companions.**"

27 Then he said to them, "The sabbath was made for humankind, and not humankind for the sabbath;

28 so **the Son of Man is lord** even **of the sabbath.**"

Luke 6:1–5

6:1 **One sabbath** while **Jesus was going through the grainfields, his disciples plucked** some **heads of grain,** rubbed them in their hands, **and ate** them.

2 But some of the Pharisees said, "**Why are** you **doing what is not lawful on the sabbath?**"

3 Jesus answered, "**Have you not read what David did when he and his companions were hungry?**

4 **He entered the house of God** and took **and ate the bread of the Presence, which it is not lawful for any but the priests to eat, and gave some to his companions?**"

5 Then he said to them, "**The Son of Man is lord of the sabbath.**"

Example 6: A Woman with a Hemorrhage Cured

Matthew 9:20–22

20 Then suddenly **a woman** who had been suffering from hemorrhages **for twelve years**

came up behind him and touched the fringe of his cloak,

21 **for she said** to herself, "If I only touch his cloak, I will be made well."

22 Jesus turned, and seeing her **he said,** "Take heart, **daughter; your faith has made you well."** And instantly the woman was made well.

Mark 5:25–34

25 **Now there was a woman who had been suffering from hemorrhages for twelve years.**

26 **She** had endured much under many **physicians,** and **had spent all that she had;** and she was no better, but rather grew worse.

27 She had heard about Jesus, and **came up behind him** in the crowd **and touched his cloak,**

28 **for she said, "If I but touch his clothes, I will be made well."**

29 Immediately her hemorrhage **stopped;** and she felt in her body that she was healed of her disease.

30 Immediately **aware that power had gone forth** from him, Jesus turned about in the crowd and said, **"Who touched my** clothes?"
31 And his disciples said to him, "You see **the crowd pressing in on you;** how can you say, 'Who touched me?'"
32 He looked all around to see who had done it.

33 But **the woman,** knowing what had happened to her, **came** in fear and **trembling, fell down before him,** and told him the whole truth.

34 **He said to her, "Daughter, your faith has made you well;** go **in peace,** and be healed of your disease."

Luke 8:43–48

43 **Now there was a woman who had been suffering from hemorrhages for twelve years;**

and **though she had spent all she had** on **physicians,** no one could cure her.

44 **She came up behind him and touched the fringe of his clothes,**

and immediately her hemorrhage **stopped.**

45 Then Jesus asked, **"Who touched me?"**
When all denied it, Peter said, "Master, **the crowds** surround you and **press in on you."**

46 But Jesus said, "Someone touched me; for **I noticed that power had gone out** from me."
47 When **the woman** saw that she could not remain hidden, **she came trembling; and falling down before him,** she declared in the presence of all the people why she had touched him, and how she had been immediately healed.

48 **He said to her, "Daughter, your faith has made you well;** go **in peace."**

What proves this conclusively is that the agreement extends far beyond the sayings of Jesus and the Baptist, to the *narrative framework supplied by the authors*. In example 2, *Matthew* and *Mark* agree in their sentence constructions and use of verb forms such as participles ("as Jesus passed . . . ," "casting a net into the sea—for they were fishermen"). Near the end of example 4, we even have the three authors simultaneously interrupting Jesus' words, breaking his sentence, with their common editorial statement, "he said to the paralytic." And example 6 is taken from the same place in all three gospels: nested within another story in which Jesus is on his way to cure a dying girl (or raise a dead girl, as in *Matthew*).

Now, the basic historical question is simple: Is it more likely that these writers independently agreed in their word choices and sentence constructions, or that there was some borrowing among them? According to the ordinary principles of common sense and historical research described above, we are forced to conclude that there is *some kind of literary relationship* among the first three gospels.

But what kind? Who used whom? It would be most convenient, of course, if we could apply some simple tests, for example: the longer or more detailed text is the earlier one, because borrowers tend to simplify and abbreviate their sources. Unfortunately, such tests are completely unreliable. Studies have shown that in the later Christian gospel tradition—in the production of gospels attributed to Philip, Nicodemus, James, and Thomas in the second to fifth centuries, and in the recopying of earlier gospel manuscripts—the tendencies of the borrowers are not reducible to simple rules. Sometimes later versions add detail; sometimes they omit it. Or again, some scholars have proposed that, since early Christianity obviously moved from a Jewish environment to the larger Gentile world, texts that most clearly reflect Jesus' Jewish environment are more likely to be original, and those that replace Jewish themes with Greek and Roman are later. Although this principle, which would put *Matthew* first, might seem reasonable at first glance, it cannot be trusted because we know from other evidence that some very late Christian texts took a "judaizing" turn.

Alas, there is no universal agreement today, among those scholars who know these texts intimately, on the appropriate criteria for determining the direction of dependence. Everyone agrees with the commonsense proposition that the text most likely to be original is the one that, if original, best explains the later emergence of the others. For example, to argue for the order *Matthew, Mark,* and *Luke,* one would need to show how the text of *Mark* is more easily explained as an alteration of *Matthew* than vice versa. But the amount of evidence is enormous: every word and phrase of the 2,881 verses in the Synoptics, multiplied by the number of possible relationships to be analyzed for each case. And the criteria for determining who came first seem quite subjective. All of this is complicated further by the fact that our earliest complete manuscripts of the gospels (Sinaiticus and Vaticanus) come from the middle of the fourth century, more than two hundred and fifty years after they were composed. The frequent recopying between their time of composition and our earliest manuscripts means that we can never be certain that a given word or phrase in our hypothetically reconstructed text was even there in the original! Although in the face of these circumstances we should perhaps abandon the synoptic problem as insoluble, it has proven far too tantalizing and too important for historical reasons to be left in abeyance.

Most scholars, not all, have narrowed the options by reaching a degree of consensus on the question of criteria. They have concurred that the earliest text is likely to be the one that causes the most problems—literary and theological—and that later texts (the borrowers) would be expected to consistently remove such problems. The reasoning here is that people who borrow other people's material do so because it is useful to them. Borrowers will, therefore, often preserve their sources intact. When they make deliberate alterations, it will be in order to "improve" them in some way—to make them more suited to the author's present needs. Since it is hard to understand why borrowers would deliberately destroy or render unclear what their source has already said well, scholars have concluded: In a case of two texts (A and B), where the differences between them *consistently* show B "improving" A, or adapting A to a plausible context, B has used A as a source. Scholars have made the task easier for themselves by (most often) resorting to comparisons of only two texts at a time—*Matthew/Mark, Mark/Luke, Matthew/Luke.* Perhaps it has seemed an impossible mental challenge to hold all triangular and quadrilateral possibilities—What if Mark used *Matthew* and *Luke* together?—in one's head for each comparison.

With such qualifications, most scholars today have concluded that such a consistent relationship exists between *Matthew* and *Mark* and between *Luke* and *Mark.* Namely, *Matthew* and *Luke* both improve the often awkward language, style, story line, and theology of *Mark.* Thus in example 1, *Mark* exhibits its tendency to use the adverb "immediately" far too often—a tendency that becomes clearer if one reads the following sections in the synopsis. In the second occurrence here, it might seem odd that Jesus should call James and John "immediately." *Matthew,* while retaining both occurrences of the word, shifts the second so that James and John *immediately follow* Jesus when they are called. This appears to make better sense. One might argue as well that *Matthew*'s story is clearer because it tells the reader up front about the family relationships among the characters, whereas in *Mark* these are afterthoughts (note especially Zebedee). In example 5, the author of *Mark* errs when he places David's action during the high priesthood of Abiathar (*1 Sam.* 21:1–6). It seems easier to believe that the authors of *Matthew* and *Luke* saw this error and omitted this phrase than to believe that the author of *Mark* deliberately introduced the error when copying sources that did not have it. *Matthew* and *Luke* also seem to exhibit a more elevated view of Jesus here when they make him, as Son of Man, to be the only Lord of the Sabbath. *Mark,* by contrast, undercuts any special status in the term Son of Man by making all humanity masters of the sabbath ("the sabbath was made for humankind"). Finally, *Mark*'s story of the woman with the hemorrhage (example 6) presents what might appear to be a slightly embarrassing picture of Jesus: He has power oozing out of his clothing, which someone can steal without his knowledge. He looks around helplessly and is ridiculed by his students for doing so. Both *Matthew* and *Luke* clean this story, abbreviating it in the process. *Matthew* omits the entire scene of Jesus' looking about and simply has the woman's cure follow on Jesus' confident pronouncement. *Luke* follows *Mark* more closely, but omits several redundancies and at least has Peter address Jesus with respect: "Master . . ."

If these judgments appear too subjective, another line of evidence might prove more compelling. In several cases, namely, the authors of *Matthew* and *Luke* seem to betray their knowledge of *Mark* by preserving language and forms that make good sense only in *Mark*. For example, we have noted that *Mark* tends to embed or "nest" one story within another: When the woman with the hemorrhage interrupts Jesus on his way to cure Jairus's dying daughter, this is typical of *Mark*. But in *Mark*, the interruption creates dramatic tension, for the delay results in the girl's death (*Mark* 5:35). Strangely, the parallel in *Matthew* preserves the nesting of these two stories even though there the girl is dead from the outset (*Matt.* 9:18), so that the dramatic tension is dissipated. Perhaps *Matthew*'s point is to suggest that the man's faith was heroic, inasmuch as he invited Jesus when his daughter was already dead. But since the technique of nesting is characteristic of *Mark*, it seems that *Matthew* has betrayed its source by preserving the nesting without purpose.

Matthew offers a number of other examples of what seem to be Markan vestiges. In *Matt.* 20:20, the mother of James and John asks that her sons be able to sit at places of honor in Jesus' kingdom (*Matt.* 20:20). Curiously, although Jesus first responds to her with appropriate singular verbs ("What do you [singular] want?"), he then switches to the plural, "You [plural] do not know what you [plural] are asking" (20:22). This part of the passage parallels *Mark* (10:38) precisely, but in *Mark* it makes much better sense because there the brothers themselves make the request (10:35). It appears that the author of *Matthew* has tried to soften *Mark*'s portrayal of the disciples as crassly self-interested, but he has nonetheless preserved a vestige of his source. Again, when *Mark*'s Jesus forthrightly challenges the Jewish scribes' alleged view that "the Christ" must be a descendant of David's line (*Mark* 12:35–37), the reader has no problem because this work understands Jesus Christ much as Paul did—as the Son of God (1:1) who brings "a new teaching" that makes a radical break with Judaism (1:27; 7:19). Even though a few of the Jewish characters in *Mark* hail Jesus Son of David, the author nowhere endorses this title, and it may well be that the passage in view is meant to reject it. In *Matthew*, however, the author positively celebrates Jesus' identity as Son of David, in keeping with his gospel's overwhelmingly Jewish atmosphere (see *Matt.* 1:1, 6, 17, 20). Why, then, does he parallel *Mark*'s challenge to the Christ's descent from David? In *Matthew*'s version, to be sure, this story is no longer a direct challenge to the Jewish leadership, and the author uses it to illustrate Jesus' brilliance in interpreting the Bible (*Matt.* 22:46). But the internal logic of the story—that the Messiah is not Son of David—is at odds with *Matthew*'s overall presentation. It is easier to imagine that the author of *Mark* was the first to write this passage down, since it fits his narrative so well, and that the author of *Matthew,* preserving *Mark* wherever possible, tried to adapt the passage—with only partial success—than to imagine that such a problematic passage in *Matthew* just happened to fit the plan of *Mark* so well. The episode concerning David's son, then, appears to be a vestige of *Mark* in *Matthew.*

One finds the same phenomenon in *Luke,* where the author has the people of Nazareth refer to Jesus' deeds in Capernaum (*Luke* 4:23) *before* he introduces Capernaum as a place of Jesus' activity (4:31); this may well result from his reading of *Mark,* in which Jesus had moved to Capernaum much earlier (*Mark* 1:21). And *Luke* 8:40–56 also preserves the nested stories of *Mark* 5:21–43, even though this author does not typically use the same device. So we seem to have telltale remnants of *Mark* in both *Matthew* and *Luke.*

On the basis of thousands of comparisons such as these, scholars have concluded that *Matthew* and *Luke* depend upon *Mark* as a major source. That explains both their generally common order in material they share with *Mark* and much of their extensive agreement in diction.

Now, if *Matthew* and *Luke* used *Mark,* that still leaves to be explained the material shared by *Matthew* and *Luke* that does not come from *Mark.* Recall that this shared material comprises 171 verses of *Matthew* (16 percent) that very closely resemble 151 verses in *Luke* (13 percent) and an additional 90 verses in *Matthew* (8.5 percent) that more loosely parallel 94 verses in *Luke* (8 percent). In some cases, the agreement between *Matthew* and *Luke* is more or less verbatim, as in Jesus' lament over Jerusalem (*Matt.* 23:37–39/*Luke* 13:34–35) or in his saying about anxiety (*Matt.* 6:25–33/*Luke* 12:22–31). By contrast, the Lord's Prayer and the Beatitudes appear quite differently in the two books, and in some cases one cannot be sure if it is even the same story that is being retold. Almost all of this non-Markan shared material, significantly, consists of *sayings* attributed to John the Baptist and Jesus.

If, for the moment, we discount wild-card intermediate sources, we are left with three main possibilities for this common sayings material: either *Matthew* used *Luke,* or *Luke* used *Matthew,* or *Matthew* and *Luke* independently used another source or group of sources. In this case, however, it is difficult to argue that the author of one text knew the other. First, the shared material almost always turns up in completely different places in the two works. One can see this quickly by looking at *Matthew's* Sermon on the Mount in a synopsis. Most of the sayings in *Matthew* 5–7 are closely paralleled in *Luke,* but the reader notices that the Lukan passages equivalent to *Matthew* come from a wide variety of places. Luke does not even have a Sermon on the Mount, but rather places the Beatitudes within a short speech on a low "level place" (*Luke* 6:17)! Note also the cases just mentioned: In *Matthew* Jesus' lament over Jerusalem occurs during the last week of his life, in the courtyard of the Jerusalem temple, while *Luke* has Jesus still in Galilee. Although *Matthew* makes the Lord's Prayer part of the Sermon on the Mount, *Luke* has Jesus give it in response to his students' question: How shall we pray? So, although the sayings often look identical in *Matthew* and *Luke*, there is very little agreement in placement. Second, there is no consistent relationship of "improvement": Both *Matthew* and *Luke* are relatively well written; at some points *Matthew*'s version of a saying appears to be the earlier one, whereas at other times *Luke*'s appears earlier. Third, although both *Matthew* and *Luke* include stories of Jesus' ancestry and birth, and of his resurrection appearances, these non-Markan stories are completely different from each other. A glance at a synopsis shows that they have hardly a word in common. Therefore, to believe that *Matthew* used *Luke* or *Luke* used *Matthew*, one would need to suppose that the author, while following *Mark*'s order and wording closely, ruthlessly exploded the other source's narrative, completely ignoring its birth and resurrection stories, and *its* treatment of *Mark*—so that *Mark*'s wording is always the basis when all three gospels share material—and all this *while* often borrowing the exact wording of the other gospel's sayings material.

Since it strains belief to imagine such an author, most scholars have concluded that the non-Markan material shared by *Matthew* and *Luke* must come from another source. This would be a collection, or collections, of Jesus' sayings that lacked much narrative arrangement. Thus, the authors of *Matthew* and *Luke* were able to draw upon individual sayings, which they could then place where they wished. When German scholars first reached this conclusion, in the late nineteenth century, they called the lost sayings source "Q," either because that is the first letter of the German word for "source" *(Quelle)* or because they had identified another source, P, behind *Mark*. In any case, the name Q has remained with us as the label for this lost, hypothetical collection of Jesus' sayings. Although some scholars originally scoffed at the notion of a "gospel" consisting solely of Jesus' sayings, the Q hypothesis was given a powerful boost with the discovery of the full *Gospel of Thomas* in 1945 at Nag Hammadi. This is indeed a gospel, with a claim to composition roughly in the period of the other early gospels (see the introduction to the *Gospel of Thomas*), but it consists exclusively of a short prologue and 114 sayings.

The Q hypothesis does not enjoy the same level of consensus as the hypothesis that *Mark* was used by *Matthew* and *Luke*. For reasons that we shall presently consider, a few scholars who accept Markan priority remain convinced that *Luke* derives from *Matthew* (or vice versa). However, in recent years a number of scholars have taken the Q hypothesis quite a bit further. Positing that a single written source underlies the shared *Matthew/Luke* material, they have first tried to reconstruct the exact content and limits of Q, then to read it as an interpretation of Jesus in its own right, then to reconstruct the early Christian community or communities for which Q was produced. Unfortunately, each link in this logical chain is contingent upon the preceding link. Since every one of the links is more or less vigorously contested, any proposal about the Q community, no matter how compelling it might be were we to grant all of the other premises, will always be highly speculative because it depends upon uncertain premises.

The main problem with the "Two-Document Hypothesis," as the majority view is known, is that almost every block of material shared by all three Synoptic Gospels contains agreements between *Matthew* and *Luke* against *Mark*. Yet according to the theory, *Matthew* and *Luke* are supposed to be *independently* using *Mark* at these points. Example 1 above is an obvious case: *Matthew* and *Luke* must be following *Mark*'s account of Jesus' baptism, according to the hypothesis, because of the pivotal location of the story in all three narratives and the fact that *Luke* describes the Baptist's words ("one more powerful than I is coming . . . not worthy to untie the thong of his sandals") almost precisely as *Mark* does, but quite differently from *Matthew*. And yet, we see much more compelling agreements between *Matthew* and *Luke* against *Mark*, in their whole arrangement of the passage, and in the addition of "and fire" to Holy Spirit, along with the saying about the winnowing fork. In example 2, while following *Mark*, according to the Two-Document Hypothesis, *Matthew* and *Luke* independently agree on inserting "Lord" into the man's request. Example 4 has several such agreements against *Mark*: the paralytic is brought on *a bed*; Jesus' response to the scribes omits any reference to taking up one's *mat*; and Jesus finally tells the paralytic to take up his *bed* (not *mat*, as in

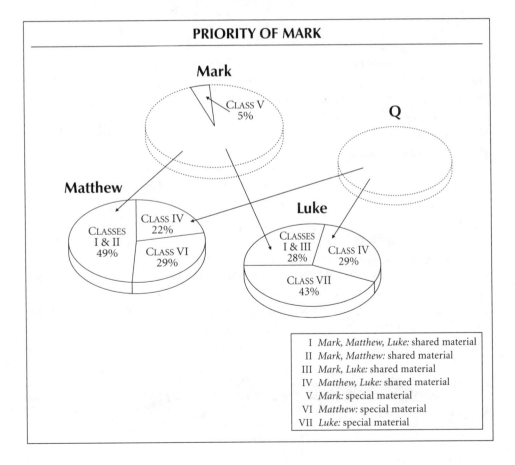

PRIORITY OF MARK

Mark

CLASS V
5%

Q

Matthew

CLASSES
I & II
49%

CLASS IV
22%

CLASS VI
29%

Luke

CLASSES
I & III
28%

CLASS IV
29%

CLASS VII
43%

I *Mark, Matthew, Luke:* shared material
II *Mark, Matthew:* shared material
III *Mark, Luke:* shared material
IV *Matthew, Luke:* shared material
V *Mark:* special material
VI *Matthew:* special material
VII *Luke:* special material

Mark) and go home. In example 5, *Matthew* and *Luke* agree in omitting both *Mark*'s references to David's companions being in need of food and its (incorrect) claim that Abiathar was high priest at the time; they also omit *Mark*'s saying that the sabbath was made for humankind. And then in example 6, even though we mainly see the typical independence of *Matthew* and *Luke* over against *Mark*, it is striking that both of the later gospels have the woman touching "the fringe" of Jesus' clothes. So how did *Matthew* and *Luke* come to agree so extensively, in both what they include and what they omit, in passages that they supposedly took independently from *Mark*?[3]

Another difficulty with the Two-Document Hypothesis is posed by the occurrence of typically "Matthean" expressions in *Luke*. A clear example of this phenomenon occurs in *Matt.* 8:11–12/*Luke* 13:28–29. In *Matthew*, Jesus says that "the heirs of the kingdom will be thrown into the outer darkness, where there will be weeping and gnashing of teeth." This saying features *Matthew*'s customary language: only in *Matthew* are the Jews called "heirs of the kingdom" (see 13:38 and the parallel construction in 21:43); only in *Matthew* does Jesus speak of "outer darkness" (22:13; 25:30); and the phrase "weeping and gnashing of teeth" is characteristic of *Matthew* alone (13:42, 50; 22:13; 24:51; 25:30). It is odd, then, that *Luke* happens to use the phrase "weeping and gnashing of teeth" once, in the parallel passage. If *Matthew* and *Luke* were independently written, as the common theory holds, this agreement could only be explained if Q had the phrase "weeping and gnashing of teeth" and the author of *Matthew*, having seen it there, liked it so much that he used it often in other contexts. But, leaving other considerations aside, this is harder to believe than the simpler view that the author of *Luke* knew *Matthew* and in this one case preserved its language. Indeed, a few other examples (more complex to demonstrate in English) have been discovered.

In view of these data, the two main alternatives to the Two-Document Hypothesis hold that *Luke* must have used *Matthew*. *Luke* is put later because no one has found vestiges of *Luke* in *Matthew*, and in *Luke* 1:1–4 the author acknowledges having consulted several other gospels. Griesbach's own hypothesis, still maintained by a significant minority of scholars, now often called the "two-gospel hypothesis," was that *Luke* used *Matthew*, and then *Mark* used both of these.

This hypothesis is rejected by the majority because of the criteria discussed above, which require that *Mark* was the earliest of the gospels. To be sure, the Griesbach hypothesis does not face the problem of explaining *Luke*'s handling of *Matthew* in a radically different way from its treatment of *Mark*, because *Mark* is understood here to be the *latest* gospel, attempting to reconcile the other two. But then this hypothesis makes

---

[3]Further examples: *Matt.* 3:11–12/*Mark* 1:7–8/*Luke* 3:15–18 (T 4; A 16); *Matt.* 4:1–11/*Mark* 1:12–13/*Luke* 4:1–13 (T 8; A 20); *Matt.* 8:1–4/*Mark* 1:40–45/*Luke* 5:12–16 (T 45; A 42); *Matt.* 9:1–8/*Mark* 2:1–12/*Luke* 5:17–26 (T 52; A 43); *Matt.* 12:22–30; 9:32–34/*Mark* 3:22–27/*Luke* 11:14–23 (T 85–86; A 117); *Matt.* 14:13–21/*Mark* 6:32–44/*Luke* 9:10–17 (T 112; A 146); *Matt.* 13:31–32/*Mark* 4:30–32/*Luke* 13:18–19 (T 97, 164; A 209).

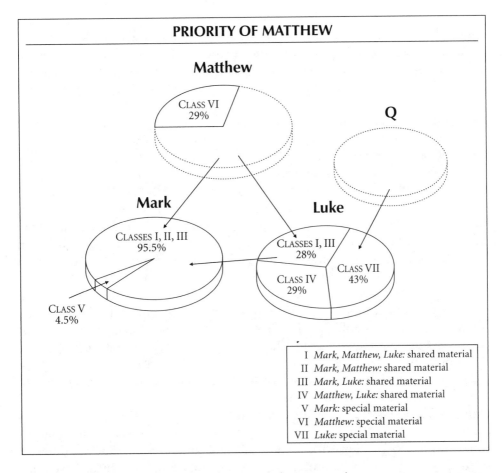

PRIORITY OF MATTHEW

Matthew

CLASS VI
29%

Q

Mark

Luke

CLASSES I, II, III
95.5%

CLASSES I, III
28%

CLASS VII
43%

CLASS IV
29%

CLASS V
4.5%

I *Mark, Matthew, Luke:* shared material
II *Mark, Matthew:* shared material
III *Mark, Luke:* shared material
IV *Matthew, Luke:* shared material
V *Mark:* special material
VI *Matthew:* special material
VII *Luke:* special material

the author of *Mark* out to be a bit of a strange character: going to extreme measures to reconcile *Matthew* and *Luke* where they disagree, with the resulting crabbed prose, and then, where *Matthew* and *Luke* agree most closely and his job should have been easiest (in the sayings of Jesus and John), omitting their material altogether! Another significant minority of scholars, based mainly in the United Kingdom, accepts the priority of *Mark* but proposes that *Luke* used *Matthew* directly for their other shared material. This proposal, however, runs up against the objections to direct *Matthew-Luke* borrowing raised above, the most significant of which is the difference between *Luke's* treatment of *Matthew* and its treatment of *Mark*.

Proponents of the Two-Document Hypothesis have addressed the problems emphasized by this alternative scholarship, though the adequacy of their solutions remains a point of contention. For example they observe that agreements between *Matthew* and *Luke* are relatively few, in contrast to the many thousands of cases in which *Matthew* and *Luke* go different ways in relation to *Mark*. Also, many of the "minor agreements" between *Matthew* and *Luke* against *Mark*—the small agreements of added or omitted wording—can be explained as sheer coincidence, resulting from the similar motives of the later authors. If *Matthew* and *Luke* both disagreed with *Mark*'s portrayal of Jesus' family and students, considered its presentation of Jesus troubling in places, and set out to remove its grammatical barbarisms and historical errors, it stands to reason that they would occasionally agree in their revisions. For example, it is not hard to see why they would agree in correcting *Mark*'s opening quotation from *Isaiah* (actually, from *Malachi* and *Isaiah*) or in dropping the reference to the high priesthood of Abiathar in example 5 above.

It is much harder to explain the more extensive agreements between *Matthew* and *Luke* against *Mark* in some passages (as in example 1). For these, the Two-Document Hypothesis usually resorts to the proposal that *Mark* and Q *each* had its own version of such episodes as Jesus' baptism and temptation (*Matt.* 4:1–11; *Mark* 1:12–13; *Luke* 4:1–13) or the Pharisees' accusation that he served Beelzebul (*Mark* 3:22–27/*Matt.* 9:32–34; 12:22–30/ *Luke* 11:11–23). *Matthew* and *Luke*, therefore, were faced in these cases with reconciling two different accounts. One problem with this solution is that *Mark*/Q parallels are proposed only for those cases in which *Matthew* and *Luke* agree against *Mark* (and thus follow Q). But this means that in every single case of *Mark*/Q overlap, they both independently favored Q and spliced their sources together in the same way. To make the overlap hypothesis more probable, we should imagine that the lost Q included many more overlaps with *Mark* than these, and that in other cases only *Matthew* or *Luke* followed Q, or both preferred *Mark*'s arrangement. But if we multiplied the *Mark*/Q overlaps by three or four times the number required by the *Matthew*/*Luke* agreements, to account for these other kinds of adaptation, Q would be a rather different animal from the simple "sayings collection" that gave rise to the Two-Document Hypothesis. Other solutions that have been proposed raise the possibility of multiple editions: perhaps the authors of *Matthew* and *Luke* knew a *Mark* that was different from ours and included many of the agreements that we find in them against *Mark*. The problem here is simply a lack of evidence.

What shall we conclude? The whole problem of synoptic relations is complicated by the fact that we do not possess the original texts. We must base our analysis on manuscripts of the gospels that date from the fourth century. We have a few brief text portions from before that time, to be sure, but not enough to build much of a case with. Between the composition of the original gospels and the copying or our earliest versions, we must reckon with about two hundred and fifty years of transmission. That is more than enough time for small changes that would thwart any simple solution to the synoptic problem. But since we do not know where those changes occurred, the problem may be insoluble in its details.

In the *Reader*, we shall assume for argument's sake that *Mark* was the first of the known gospels to be written. This position seems to explain the main evidence most adequately, and it is favored by the vast majority of those who know the evidence well. The Q hypothesis is less secure, especially in all of its parts: that Q was a single written document that represented a coherent presentation of Jesus. Although we shall occasionally use Q as a code for the shared sayings material in *Matthew* and *Luke*, we shall not argue for a particular reconstruction of this hypothetical document.

Oral Traditions behind the Gospels

Once the source question was considered settled, scholars began to probe behind the earliest written gospels—*Mark,* Q, and the material unique to *Matthew* and *Luke*—in order to figure out where the gospel writers got their material. Clarifying the literary relationships among the gospels still left open the question: But where did they find their information on Jesus? And how did it get from its point of origin to the author who wrote it down in a gospel?

A striking feature of the gospels in comparison with most modern biographies is their episodic character: their stringing together of a relatively few short episodes with simple connective devices. In *Mark,* for example, the characters keep changing. The tax collector, the paralytic, the woman with the hemorrhage, Jairus, the Gerasene demoniac, and many others appear only in the stories in which they star; they are never mentioned again.[4] The author makes extensive use of such phrases as "and immediately," "one sabbath," "in those days," and "again" (e.g., 1:9, 12, 21, 29, 40; 3:20; 4:1) to connect these brief episodes. Even when *Mark* includes some geographical notice, such as "having entered Capernaum," the reader has no clear picture of any historical outline. Moreover, the distinct episodes are often joined together in a thematic, rather than chronological, order (e.g., a series of undated conflict stories in 2:1–3:6, or representative parables in 4:1–34). The same general looseness of construction is visible throughout *Matthew* and *Luke. Thomas* and the hypothetical Q, for their parts, lack a sequential framework altogether. This absence of a distinct story line suggests that the gospel writers crafted their works out of individual, undated stories about Jesus that had been floating around in early Christian circles, but that they did not know a uniform story of Jesus' life.

A few stories may have been collected on the basis of themes before the gospel writers' time (e.g., the various items constituting the trial narrative, the parables, conflict and miracle stories), but the connective devices used by the author of *Mark* to weld these blocks of material into his gospel match his style elsewhere. This makes it look as if *Mark* was the first gospel to provide a coherent narrative. This conclusion has led scholars to hope that they might isolate pregospel units from the text of *Mark* (as well as from the non-Markan sections of *Matthew* and *Luke*) and then explore how these units were used in the "oral tradition" of the young church, before they were committed to writing.

That might seem like an impossible task. Even if the gospel writers used oral traditions in the first century, those traditions have been embedded in the written gospel texts for some nineteen hundred years. How can one analyze oral traditions that have long since ceased to be oral? In the study of the Pentateuch (*Genesis* to *Deuteronomy*), scholars of the late nineteenth century had achieved some success in applying folklore studies to ancient Israelite oral traditions. Although the period of

---

[4]Contrast *John,* which has many long speeches developing a single theme, and in which characters such as Lazarus or Nicodemus reappear in different contexts.

oral transmission would be much shorter in the case of early Christianity—thirty to seventy years instead of several centuries—they were hopeful that the same kind of principles could be applied to the gospels. Between 1919 and 1921, three German scholars, Karl Ludwig Schmidt, Martin Dibelius, and Rudolf Bultmann, published ground-breaking studies of early Christian oral tradition. These scholars differed somewhat in their terminology and procedure, but they shared at least four hypotheses.

Pericope

First, they concluded from the episodic character of the gospels that it was possible to separate the traditional oral units or "pericopes" from their present settings in the gospel narratives. Like a piece of sculpture made from car tires and soda bottles, the gospels have often left the form of the traditional material clearly visible. A synopsis illustrates this phenomenon well, for (after the birth narratives of *Matthew* and *Luke*) it breaks up the gospel material into its constituent parts. We have seen hints of artificial construction in *Mark*. The same observations are generally true of *Luke* and *Matthew*: *Matthew* artificially constructs the Sermon on the Mount by providing an opening and closing notice for the many distinct short sayings of chapters 5 to 7 (5:1; 7:28). *Matthew*'s editorial seams do not hide the fact, which is confirmed by *Luke*'s arrangement, that the Sermon is really a collection of distinct proverbs, prayers, and admonitions. In general, then, it seems possible to isolate original pericopes from their present framework in the gospels.

Form

Having identified these short units out of which the Synoptics are constructed (contrast *John*), the above-named scholars observed that most of these units fell into a small number of categories. If we were to write out each short episode on a separate file card and then spread all of the cards on a desk, we would discover that we could group all of the cards into just a few categories. While the Synoptics do not include much information about Jesus' youth, education, job training, friends, appearance, family, entertainments, and so on, they do contain several examples of a few distinct "forms" of material. On the one side are Jesus' *sayings,* for example: parables, proverbs, woes, admonitions, authoritative sayings, and the Lord's Prayer. The sayings often contain little contextual information, other than what has been supplied by the gospel author to fit them into his story ("one Sabbath" or "having entered Capernaum"). On the other side are Jesus' *actions,* such as his baptism by John, his transfiguration, stories of his wonder-working (nature miracles, cures, exorcisms, resuscitation of the dead), his triumphal entry, and the narrative of his arrest, trial, and death, which is constructed out of numerous short pieces. One of the most common forms of material in the gospels, however, is a mixture of story and saying. Called the "pronouncement story," apophthegm, paradigm, or chreia, this is a brief situation that ends with a wise saying from Jesus, for example: "being asked by the Pharisees when the kingdom was coming he replied . . ." (*Luke*

17:20–21). Two of the main kinds of *chreiai* (plural) are those in which Jesus responds to his disciples, and those in which he responds to adversaries—the "conflict stories" of *Mark* (2:1–3:6 and 11:11–12:40). So it turns out that the gospels are constructed out of a few typical and fairly fixed forms, or kinds of material.

Once they had classified the gospel material in this manner, these scholars proceeded to compare all examples of each particular form. What they found was a remarkable uniformity within each type. For example, Bultmann observed that the "controversy story" usually begins with an action of Jesus, which causes an opponent's objection, which is followed in turn by Jesus' response—often with a scripture citation or a counterquestion. Or again, healing stories typically state the nature and the gravity of the complaint, then describe an exchange between Jesus and the sick person or a representative, then mention the healing word or touch, as well as the faith of the sick person, and finally relate the effect of the cure. These common features appeared to indicate that the gospel stories had been streamlined, so to speak, for easier recollection and use in the early church. They were not simply events remembered from Jesus' career and recounted with the individual peculiarity that one would normally expect.

Because these scholars contended that analysis of the oral tradition depended on the identification of such typical forms of gospel material, they called their work "form criticism." The label does not describe their main goal, which was simply to study the gospel traditions in their oral phase, but only the tool that was used to facilitate their analysis.

Function

Their ability to classify the gospel material in typical categories seemed to prove the form critics' assumption that this material still bears the marks of its oral prehistory. Now they were able to go a step further. They concluded from the relatively small number of forms and from the typical structure of each form, that the young church preserved only what was germane to its needs. Consequently, understanding the material of the gospels required understanding how each form was connected to some ongoing need or function in the church's life. These scholars used the German term *Sitz im Leben,* or "setting in life," to describe such a function.

We already know, from our examination of Paul's letters, what some of the church's main concerns were throughout its first generation. This was the period during which the oral traditions about Jesus were circulating before being committed to writing. Externally, the young church was facing opposition from some Gentile townspeople and courts (e.g., in Thessalonica). Paul's style of missionary work among the Gentiles was having considerable success, although some Gentile Christians were choosing to embrace Judaism through circumcision and participation in Jewish communal life (*Philippians* 3; *2 Corinthians* 10–13; *Galatians*). Tensions between Christians and non-Christian Jews were apparently serious (as the death of Jesus' brother James suggests). Internally, there was already considerable diversity among the followers of Jesus: Some Christians were committed to Judaism; Paul proclaimed a gospel for Gentiles that emphasized the imminence of Jesus' return; and some Christians appear to have valued Jesus primarily as a teacher of wisdom. So questions of authority, leadership, and legitimacy were very much in the air. Still, the various Christian communities shared some common needs. They had to develop instructional material for their members, prayers, hymns, and recitations for worship (also for baptism and the eucharist), and directives for problem-solving, and for resolving disputes over leadership, or for establishing common ethical standards. Especially for Christians who had no background in Jewish law, this involved admonitions to be faithful and to endure in the face of persecution from outsiders, and responses to theological problems, such as the apparent delay of Jesus' return.

Paul's letters make little use of Jesus' sayings, but they do furnish clues about how oral traditions functioned in the earliest church. He cites Jesus' sayings, for example, to illuminate the issue of marriage and divorce (*1 Cor.* 7:10), to defend his right—freely relinquished—to financial support (*1 Cor.* 9:14), and to recall the basis for the Christian celebration of the Lord's Supper (11:23–26). These examples, few though they are, suggest typical contexts in which items recalled from Jesus' life could function: for ethical instruction and the Eucharist.

Now the form critics believed that each and every form, or kind of material about Jesus, could be tied to such a typical situation in the early church's life *(Sitz im Leben)*. For example, the stories of Jesus' controversies with Jewish leaders (*Mark* 2:1–3:6; 7:1–23) would have been cited by the Christians in their own disputes with non-Christian Jews. Jesus' discussions with his students must have provided some guidance for the church in matters of ethics (*Matt.* 5–7; 19:1–12), church order (*Matt.* 5:23–26; 18:15–20), and worship (*Matt.* 6:9–15). And Jesus' miracle stories were doubtless used in the church's missionary preaching, to demonstrate Jesus' divine power. Thus, every form that survived to be included in the written gospels at the end of the first century must have fulfilled some such ongoing function in early Christian life.

Origin

The form critics' most controversial proposal, and the one with which the label "form criticism" is often associated, followed logically from the others, namely: any pericope that presupposes conditions that only existed in the church's life must have come into being within the first-generation church and not in Jesus' lifetime. All of the gospel material has been shaped by its use in the church, they said, but some pericopes actually show signs of having *originated* in the church's preaching. How could this have happened? First, the ordinary processes of oral transmission would allow for some embellishment over time. Second, the peculiar circumstances of the young church, which continued to communicate with the risen Jesus in prayer and prophecy (see *1 Cor.* 14:3–5), might have rendered it difficult to distinguish between what Jesus had said while he walked around Galilee and what the church understood the risen Lord to say to them after his resurrection. The form critics differed among themselves about the extent of such embellishments and post-resurrection sayings in the gospels.

An example of probable embellishment is the interpretation of the parable of the sower (*Mark* 4:13–20), which seems to match the conditions of the church's life better than those of Jesus' career. (a) Several phrases in the interpretation use language that is well established for the early church but hard to understand in Jesus' situation, e.g., "the word" for the gospel. (b) Further, tribulation and persecution "on account of the word" do not seem to have been the experience of Jesus' followers during his lifetime, for the Synoptics give Jesus a large following in Galilee before his final trip to Jerusalem. Yet the interpretation cites persecution and apostasy (falling away) from Christian faith as commonplace occurrences that should be understood by the hearers. (c) Jesus' other parables (with one exception in *Matthew*) do not have interpretations appended, because parables are themselves intended as illustrations, so interpretations are superfluous. (d) The interpretation turns the parable into an *allegory*, a form that is uncharacteristic of Jesus' teaching but would have obvious sermonic value in the young church. (e) The *Gospel of Thomas* preserves a simple version of the parable of the sower that lacks any interpretation (saying 9), confirming that the parable could circulate on its own without an interpretation. And (f) the basic idea of the parable is as clear as the ideas of other parables about seeds and leaven, without any interpretation.

All this suggests (proof is beyond the historian's reach) that the interpretation is a secondary accretion to the parable. It is easier to understand as an addition from the early church than as a saying of Jesus. Thus, as Jesus' parable of the sower was used in the church's preaching, preachers naturally applied it to specific situations in the lives of their hearers. One such interpretation began to circulate with the parable and its origin was soon forgotten. The author of *Mark* unwittingly attributed both parable and its interpretation to Jesus.

In addition to this natural "snowball" effect in oral traditions, the early Christians' special circumstances might have given rise to the incorporation of new Jesus material into their sources after Jesus' death. Namely, the young church considered itself to be in ongoing communication with Jesus, through prayer and "prophecy," after his resurrection (*Acts* 9:5–16; 10:10–16). Paul, for one, seems to have had little inclination to distinguish words of the risen Christ from those of Jesus of Nazareth. He claimed to speak with the resurrected Jesus and even quoted him (*1 Cor.* 9:14; *1 Thess.* 4:15; *2 Cor.* 12:8–9). The author of *John*, in particular, seems to feel little constraint in presenting the exalted Christ as the historical figure Jesus. So the form critics asked whether the Synoptic Gospels might not also have incorporated a few sayings of the risen Jesus, revealed to the church through Christian prophets, into their accounts of Jesus' life.

A possible example of the phenomenon is *Matt.* 18:15–20, where Jesus of Nazareth is said to give clear instructions about behavior in the "church," as if his hearers should understand what "the church" is. But other indications suggest that the church was not yet envisioned by Jesus' followers before his death and resurrection, and the Greek word for church does not appear in any other early gospel. Further, *Matthew*'s Jesus closes this section by saying, "Where two or three are gathered in my name, there I am in the midst of them." Note the present tense—not "I *will be* in the midst of them." This statement of consolation, as indeed the whole discussion of church discipline here, has struck many interpreters as more appropriate to the risen Christ in communication with his followers than to Jesus of Nazareth as he walked around Galilee. What would it have meant for him to say these things then? What would his hearers have understood? Other possible sayings of the risen Jesus are detailed predictions of persecutions in the synagogues (e.g., *Matt.* 10:17–20) and the remark in *Matt.* 23:10—"you have one master, the Christ!" Public allegiance to Jesus as Messiah/Christ does not seem to fit the situation of Jesus' followers before his death, when his messianic identity was at best ambiguous (*Mark* 8:27–30; *Matt.* 16:20). The Synoptics do not make it a public issue before Jesus' trial.

These, then, were the distinctive insights and proposals of the form critics. Their approach provided the basis of much study of the gospels for a generation, perhaps forty years. Although many of their particular suggestions have since been overturned as unlikely, their most basic proposal, that the gospels depend on material already shaped to a degree by the young church's experience, is generally accepted.

In recent years, scholars have tried to base their understanding of what happened to the Jesus tradition before the gospels on more demonstrable tendencies in other literature of the period. Ancient education placed a heavy emphasis on the recollection and manipulation of famous sayings. Students of rhetoric, as a way of developing their skills, were required to take sayings *(chreiai)* attributed to eminent figures and recast them in various grammatical formulations, argue opposite positions, draw out logical consequences, extract a moral, and so on. Such worked-over sayings appear, for example, in Plutarch's *Parallel Lives* and Diogenes Laertius's *Lives of Eminent Philosophers*. Often, two or three (or more) different versions of the same tradition—an incident concerning Diogenes the Cynic or Alexander the Great—circulated just as we find in the gospels. Even though few Christians of our period would have had the opportunity for the kind of advanced education that required these exercises (for students fourteen and older), and many would have lacked formal education altogether, the rhetorical tradition of reinterpreting sayings apparently pervaded Greco-Roman society at all levels.

These more recent investigations have confirmed the likelihood that oral traditions about Jesus would have been pliable before they were committed to writing, and that Christian teachers would have felt free to adapt them to various situations. The ancients did not share (or understand) our post-Enlightenment concern with precise accounts of the past. We have an intriguing example in Flavius Josephus, the first-century Jewish author who insists that he is not changing anything when he represents for Greek-speaking Gentiles the stories of the Bible, but who immediately proceeds without flinching to retell the stories in completely new ways, making all sorts of rhetorical adaptations. Recent study of the gospels has made scholars reluctant to pursue the form critics' rigid idea of "form" and to relate each form to a single prescribed function in the church's life. The Jesus tradition did not function as mechanically as the form critics imagined.

Whereas, then, the church and Western tradition had innocently assumed a direct connection between the gospel stories and Jesus' actual life-story, form criticism severed that connection by drawing attention to something that was real but not obvious within the texts: the underlying experience of the church, through which these stories were preserved. The form critics did not spend much time discussing either the gospels as integrated stories or the historical Jesus, but their focus on the mediating activity of the church had negative implications for both pursuits. On the one hand, the gospel writers were seen as more or less artfully cutting and pasting church traditions for desired effect. On the other hand, the young church's interest in only a few features of Jesus' life, which they then stereotyped, seemed to make recovery of Jesus' actual career impossible. Although some remained optimistic about the value of the gospels for gaining access to Jesus' life, the dominant mood resulting from this study was one of skepticism. Rudolf Bultmann's influential *History of the Synoptic Tradition* (German 1921; English 1963) attributed the bulk of the gospel material to the creative influence of the church in its contact with the risen Jesus. In the 1950s, about thirty years after form criticism arrived on the scene, a new generation of scholars reacted to its effects on both the literary and the historical sides of the ledger.

Searching for the Jesus of History

Some of Bultmann's own students began to ask whether their teacher's preoccupation with the church's creative role had not led him to overstate, or perhaps misstate, the problem of the historical Jesus. They accepted that a "life of Jesus" could no longer be written in the old style, by excerpting passages from the gospels. There was no basic framework on which to hang a connected narrative of Jesus' life. Nor could one identify influences on Jesus' thinking or chart crises that might have changed his outlook. A proper biography of Jesus was not possible. But then again, by the middle of this century, historians in other fields had largely given up the definition of history as a comprehensive account of "cause and effect" in someone's life. Given the limitations of our knowledge and the pervasive problem of human bias, historians had redirected their attention to encountering persons from the past by understanding something of their *goals* or aims. In these terms, recovery of the historical Jesus would not require any sequential account of his life, but only sound insight into central aspects of his outlook. It would be enough to figure out "what he was about." If even that much could be done successfully, then the form critics' complete exclusion of historical-Jesus questions might have been extreme.

Could it be done successfully? Could we devise techniques to help us penetrate the church's oral transmission of traditions about Jesus, to reach events or sayings that were probably authentic? The efforts of Bultmann's students in this area, though they intersected with general historical considerations, were closely tied up with theological concerns then current in Germany. Their successors have brought the enterprise more into the historiographical mainstream. All that we can do here is show how particular techniques of historical-Jesus research fit within a broader framework.

The basic problem of history is that human actions from the past are no longer directly accessible. This is true for all cases: Socrates, Hannibal, Cleopatra, Nero, John the Baptist, Mary, Jesus of Nazareth, and even a Winston Churchill or John F. Kennedy. The actor is gone, and we are left with only traces of his or her existence. This means that the past is not a given; it does not now exist anywhere *except in the minds of historians,* in the constructions that they create to explain the traces that have survived. And since all historical reconstruction is hypothetical—arising from someone's intelligent attempt to explain the surviving evidence—history actually changes from one generation to the next. A Polish proverb wryly observes, "Only the future is certain; the past is always changing." What really happened does not change, of course, but our explanations of what happened, which pass for "history," must change as we discover new information and learn new ways of looking at old evidence. For example, until recently, a majority of experts favored the hypothesis that the inhabitants of Qumran, who wrote and copied the Dead Sea Scrolls, were the sectarian "Essenes" described by Josephus and other ancient writers. That was the "history" confidently given by authorized tour guides. But in recent years quite a few scholars have abandoned that view in favor of other hypotheses that they consider more adequate to the evidence. If they are right, then the "history" will have to be changed. Even though the past itself cannot change, our perception of it is in constant flux.

This does not mean that history is arbitrary. Many basic hypotheses about the ancient world from a century ago remain viable today. If we can come up with a hypothesis that explains an array of independent evidence more adequately than any other, then we may have hit upon one aspect of what really did happen, and our hypothesis might be around for a long time.

A probable hypothesis is one that most convincingly explains, to the satisfaction of those who know the evidence intimately, how all the surviving traces came into being. The most valuable support for any hypothesis, of course, is the conjunction of two or more lines of independent evidence. A second witness who agrees independently with the first witness shows that the item in question was not merely a part of the first witness's interpretive construction; it must go back to an earlier reality. In the case of Jesus, then, agreements among Paul's letters, *Mark, Q,* and *Thomas* (if it is independent), or at least between any two of these earlier sources, would provide useful starting points. This line of evidence is called "multiple attestation."

But such conjunctions are relatively rare and show only that a tradition is older than a particular writer; they could not prove that it goes back to Jesus' life. Moreover, a later author *(Matthew, Luke or John)* may well have better information than a predecessor on some point or other. They are all still close enough to the events that they can correct an earlier writer. It seems, indeed, that the author of *Luke-Acts* intends to correct, in some measure, earlier accounts of Christian origins (*Luke* 1:1–4). Thus we need a method of evaluating traditions beyond simply counting agreements.

An important tool for historical purposes is a witness's "incidental" or "unintentional" testimony. Imagine any historical evidence (say, the gospels) as prepared statements of witnesses summoned to a courtroom. It is an unavoidable human tendency to structure the data that we see around us in meaningful ways, to interpret it according to our conscious and unconscious predispositions. Because everyone recognizes that human bias is unavoidable, lawyers are given the opportunity to "cross-examine" witnesses, to uncover things that might have lingered in the witnesses' memory but were not part of their prepared interpretations of events. We cannot cross-examine our sources in the same way, of course, because the authors are not around to speak with us, but we can scrutinize the early Christian texts for hints of events that they did not intend to tell us about.

Finding such slips is admittedly easier in Paul's letters, which were dictated quickly to deal with crises, than in narratives such as the gospels. For example, after insisting that he has baptized *none* of the Corinthians except Crispus and Gaius, Paul suddenly remembers that he did also baptize the household of Stephanas, and perhaps others too; now he cannot remember (*1 Cor.* 1:14–16). This was apparently not something that he intended to say, for it undercuts his original point. It therefore becomes all the more valuable evidence that he did indeed baptize several people in Corinth. Another example is Paul's admission that he had to go to Jerusalem to secure approval for his work, even while he insists that the status of the Jerusalem apostles means nothing to him (*Gal.* 2:2, 6), and that he went up only because of a revelation (*Gal.* 2:1). We may take confidence, then, in the conclusion that he did go to Jerusalem to meet with the "pillars" on the Gentile question. He did not invent a story that he evidently feels a need to explain.

Acts also offers several interesting cases of unintentional evidence, such as its report of accusations about Paul's apostasy from Judaism, which are immediately repudiated by the author (*Acts* 21:21, 28). We may be sure that the author did not create these accusations for literary purposes, because they stand in some tension with his presentation of harmony within the early church on the Gentile issue. Moreover, Paul's own letters confirm (independently, in *Galatians*) that his fidelity to Judaism was a live issue during his lifetime. All of this suggests that, in spite of *Acts*'s quick dismissal of the charges against Paul as baseless, its author knew that these charges were seriously held by some of Paul's Christian and non-Christian opponents.

It is more difficult to locate unintentional evidence in the gospels, simply because the authors' intentions are not as clear. They leave all sorts of loose ends. But we cannot tell what is incidental to an author's purpose until we clarify what that purpose is; we cannot read between the lines until we know where the lines are. Matters seem a bit easier with *John* because *John's* main themes are so forcefully stated from the beginning. For example, John takes a good deal of trouble to clarify the Baptist's status in relation to Jesus, culminating in the self-effacing line, "He must increase; I must decrease" (*John* 3:30). But John also has a good deal of information about Jesus' relationship with the Baptist that is not found in the Synoptics, including the claim that the two preachers baptized alongside each other (*John* 3:22; 4:1). This claim was probably not invented by the author, for he then insists that Jesus did not really baptize (4:2; did he forget about 3:22?). Since the whole matter appears to cause him some discomfort, we may conclude that he knew a tradition to the effect that Jesus immersed people alongside John.

Many scholars have concluded that the whole problem of Jesus' relationship to the Baptist provides one of the most helpful starting points in the quest to recover Jesus' aims. To begin with, it seems beyond reasonable doubt that Jesus was immersed by John the Baptist because: (a) Jesus' connection with John appears in three apparently independent sources: *Mark,* the non-Markan sayings material common to *Matthew* and *Luke* (Q), and *John.* (b) Moreover, the Christian writers all seem to have had a problem with Jesus' baptism, whether the theological problem of Jesus' receiving a baptism for forgiveness, or simply the problem of John's status in relationship to Jesus. John the Baptist was apparently an eminent Jewish preacher in his own right, with his own students, as Josephus (*Ant.* 18.116–119) also indicates. If Jesus had been immersed by him, then we would expect exactly the sort of problems that we find in our sources. His submission to John's baptism might imply that Jesus was John's student, a conclusion that would pose problems for the young church.

Accordingly, each gospel in its own way addresses the problem of John's status, whether by citing a word of Jesus dismissing any objection to the baptism *(Matthew),* by omitting an actual baptismal episode *(John),* by including a story of prenatal connections that sorted out the question of status in advance *(Luke),* or simply by repeated and emphatic assurances of John's preparatory and subordinate role *(Mark* and *John).* The combination of multiple attestation and evidence contrary to the interests of the church (= unintentional evidence) here produces an overwhelming probability that Jesus was immersed by John. It is much harder to imagine that early Christians invented the story than that they were handed the story as the starting-point of Jesus' career and struggled to put an appropriate spin on it.

We may go further. If Jesus was immersed by John, then he sympathized with John's message. Therefore, if we can recover something of John's message (which happens to be summarized independently in Josephus, *Mark,* Q, *John,* and *Luke),* then we shall have learned a little bit more about one important influence on Jesus' thinking. To be sure, we still face the further problem that the sources do not converge perfectly on what John taught, so we need an explanatory hypothesis there too. But in principle, we can infer something about Jesus from his association with John.

To summarize: We can hope to learn a few things about the historical Jesus' life by applying common historical techniques to the special case of the gospel material, with due regard for its oral prehistory. Negatively, most would agree with the form critics that whatever in the gospels presupposes post-resurrection church conditions, for example, a conscious mission to Gentiles, or Jesus' forthright abandonment of Jewish dietary and Sabbath law, cannot go back to Jesus of Nazareth. Positively, we may say that whatever contradicts the young church's observable tendencies did not come from the church, and may reflect an aspect of Jesus' life. This principle, a variation of which is sometimes called "discontinuity" or "dissimilarity" in the scholarly literature, holds for both sayings and events of Jesus' life.

Some scholars have extended this principle to suggest that aspects of Jesus' life that seem to run counter to first-century Judaism—e.g., his eating with sinners, loving enemies, prohibition of divorce—have an inherent claim to authenticity because conventional Jewish teachings—insistence on obedience to the law, encouragement of sacrifice, avoiding contact with Gentiles—might have been unconsciously foisted upon Jesus by the earliest Jewish church. Therefore, unusual or non-Jewish traditions would not have been invented. The problem here is that we still know little about the varieties of Judaism current in Jesus' day and, the more we discover, the less reason we have to think that Jesus was unique in his Jewishness. For example, the *Damascus Document* from Qumran forbids divorce as Jesus did, and it even cites the same biblical proof text (CD 4.22). It would be hazardous to speak of Jesus' unique teaching, when we really mean that we so far know of no parallel in Jewish circles.

Even the principle of favoring what runs counter to the "tendencies of early Christians" runs aground on our ignorance of the range of early Christian viewpoints. A saying that appears in only one gospel, such as *Luke*'s "the kingdom of God is within you" (*Luke* 17:21), might be thought to run counter to the general stress of "early Christian eschatology" on Jesus' imminent return. But then, it might also reflect the author's peculiar outlook, or even a one-time situation created by the author for narrative effect. Paul's letters show that Christianity went in several different directions from the start. This knowledge forces us to be cautious about what we think is contrary to "Christian" interests.

Moreover, pursuing dissimilar traits, even if we could be sure of reasonable success, would turn up only what was *peculiar* about Jesus—what was not mainstream in Judaism and what the church did not adopt. But the great figures of history often seem to have achieved greatness not through eccentricity but by encapsulating and articulating the deepest hopes of their age. Perhaps Jesus too acquired a following because his claims resonated with the latent hopes of many people. He sounded *right*, not peculiar. So even if we could be sure that Jesus prohibited divorce and remarriage because this was an odd prohibition for a first-century Jew, we might have found only a tangential and unimportant aspect of his teaching. It is inherently likely that much of what he said became basic to Christian teaching, though we do not know in advance which parts. Looking only at what seems "non-Christian" or "non-Jewish" in the gospels will give us a skewed picture of Jesus.

An interesting case is provided by *Luke*'s presentation of Jesus as a kind of philosopher. *Luke* accommodates Jesus to the model of a countercultural preacher, constantly harassing the rich and complacent in his call for admission of social outcasts, and he dies a martyr in the manner of Socrates. Although the author of *Luke* has made this portrait forceful and thematic (see the introduction to *Luke-Acts*), several important notices of Jesus' countercultural behavior were already present in pre-Lukan stories about Jesus; he did not then invent his picture out of whole cloth. Similarly, although *Luke* makes a theme out of Jesus' adherence to Jewish law, pre-Lukan tradition already contained adequate clues that Jesus did live as an observant Jew. Since it is demonstrable that some basic features of Jesus' life were carried forward and developed by second-generation Christian writers, we cannot build an image of him exclusively on the basis of "strange" or incidental items.

Other proposed indices of historical plausibility must be mentioned, even though none of them on its own can recreate for us the historical Jesus. First, any saying attributed to Jesus that seems to depend on Greek constructions, and cannot be retrojected into a Semitic language (Aramaic or Hebrew) without massive loss, is difficult to attribute to Jesus himself—on the common assumption that Jesus ordinarily spoke Aramaic. But this common assumption may be unwarranted, since Greek was so widely spoken throughout the region. Second, the gospels' claims of paranormal events, such as Jesus' walking on the water or his cures of the sick, although they are no longer dismissed out of hand on the basis of scientific "laws," must still be judged by the same criteria that we apply to similar claims in other literature of the time. It was quite common in the ancient world to claim that great figures of the time were able to perform remarkable feats. Third, archaeological discoveries (e.g., of average "house" styles and sizes in Jesus' native Galilee) and well-established social norms in ancient Mediterranean culture (e.g., how meals were typically eaten by various classes) might offer some help in evaluating the general plausibility of episodes in the gospels. Fourth, descriptions of public figures such as Pontius Pilate, Herod Antipas, and the high priests in other literature, though these should not be treated as "facts," can serve as something of a check on the gospels. Finally, an understanding of how people tended to persuade readers in the first century, of the role of literary features such as genealogies or exorcism stories, might help as well.

In short, although we can imagine principles for historical-Jesus research that correspond to broad historical considerations, it is not easy to implement them in any given case. The number of variables is huge. An important scholarly debate continues, for example, on the question: Was Jesus primarily a forward-looking prophetic figure, expecting the kingdom of God to erupt at any moment, or did he mean to stress that the kingdom had arrived already, or that it was potentially present now? The gospels contain statements of both kinds, and some scholars have taken the diplomatic course of arguing that for Jesus the kingdom was "both now and not yet." But others find the inner logic of the two kinds of statements mutually exclusive: the forward-looking Jesus counsels expectant watchfulness, while the other Jesus rejects such waiting and watching in favor of action here and now.

Those who see Jesus as a forward-looking prophet point out that John the Baptist had a strong orientation to the future, as did Paul and most other early Christians, so Jesus could not have been all that different. Since he spoke of the imminent "kingdom of God" without explaining what he meant, he must have meant by this expression what other Jews of his time and place understood by it. Some suggest that the opposite view, called "realized (= present) eschatology," which is evident in isolated notices of *Matthew* and *Luke*, results from the authors' peculiar tendencies at their time of writing. Jesus had not returned by the end of the first century and so these Christian writers began to come to terms with living in the world.

Those who think that Jesus was mainly concerned with the present, however, turn these arguments on their head. If the "present-reality" sayings do not fit the main outlook of the church, and are only incidental in the gospels, then it is likelier that they originate with Jesus; it is the futurist material that can more easily be explained as serving the church's interests (as a consequence of Jesus' unexpected death, resurrection, and expected return in glory). They also cite the parables, which seem to represent Jesus' authentic teaching style (independent sources agree), for some of these at least suggest that the kingdom will gradually grow through individual "realization." Further, this school frequently draws upon the *Gospel of Thomas* and a hypothetical early stratum of Q for the support of multiple attestation.

Not every issue is so hotly debated. One widely accepted hypothesis of historical-Jesus scholarship is that Jesus lived his life as a committed Jew, did not envision a world mission to Gentiles, and did not intend a break with Judaism. This may already sound like old hat to some readers, but it is a relatively recent conclusion of historical scholarship. It is not obvious from reading Paul's letters, *Mark, Thomas,* or *John,* all of which assume that Judaism and Christianity are divorced. The single most important factor in deciding the issue is the career of Paul. Plainly, Paul's effort to establish a Torah-free mission among the Gentiles brought him into serious conflict with the Jerusalem apostles, especially with Jesus' closest associate (Peter) and his brother (James). These developments are difficult to understand if Jesus himself had plainly endorsed the Gentile mission and the abrogation of Jewish law. It is easiest to suppose that gospel material asserting such actions on Jesus' part (e.g., *Mark* 7:19) was itself influenced by the intervening activity of the church. Moreover, even where a gospel's ultimate tendency is to overturn the law, as in *Mark* (7:19), we find incidental notes that point in the opposite direction (e.g., *Mark* 2:25; 3:4; 12:26, 29).

An essential point to remember in evaluating historical-Jesus hypotheses is that the "burden of proof" does not lie either with those who doubt a particular episode in the gospels or with those who defend it. Our basic position today is one of *not knowing* what really happened, and so the burden of proof lies with anyone who wishes to make a compelling explanation of the evidence.

The Gospels as Compositions

On the literary side, too, scholars reacted to the perceived barrenness of form criticism by asking whether each gospel writer did not have a more coherent vision of things than the form-critics' scissors-and-paste model would suggest. Even if the gospel stories could not be assumed to reflect unalloyed recollections of Jesus' life, surely the stories themselves were worthy of careful analysis *as stories* from a particular time and place. Reacting against a criticism that had exploded the texts into mere collections of disparate units, these scholars called for a new kind of gospel analysis, one that dealt with the narratives as we have them and not exclusively with their constituent parts. This new analysis was first styled "redaction criticism" because it concentrated on the work of the final editor or *Redaktor* (German) of each gospel.

The earliest efforts of the redaction critics—W. Marxsen, H. Conzelmann, W. Trilling, G. Bornkamm, G. Barth, and H. J. Held in the 1950s—were still largely preoccupied with the analysis of written sources. By looking at *Matthew*'s use of *Mark,* they argued, one could see how the later evangelist worked out his own agenda. A later author's views would be most apparent in his modifications of material. For example, *Matthew*'s omission of *Mark*'s statement that Jesus abrogated the dietary laws fits with *Matthew*'s general insistence on Torah observance (*Matt.* 5:17–21); it is understandable as editorial activity. The strength of this procedure was (and is) that it seemed to offer visible proof of theories about the evangelists' intentions. Its weakness, however, was its inability to handle such anomalies as an author's verbatim reproduction or only trivial rearrangement of his sources, and seemingly conflicting editorial tendencies in the later work. Preoccupation with the use of sources prevents the reader from appreciating the narrative as a whole. Even where *Luke* seems to agree almost exactly with *Mark* in a particular pericope, for example, the Lukan context gives a different meaning to that common pericope. Moreover, since the source-critical foundation of this work was itself only hypothetical, any theories built upon it faced an immediate reduction in probability. Such theories have little persuasive power for those who reject the Two-Document or Q hypotheses.

In view of these weaknesses, other scholars recommended that we begin the analysis of a gospel as a whole composition, as its first readers were expected to do. Redaction criticism should be more "vertical" than "horizontal," they said; some preferred to call this enterprise "composition criticism." Their point was that one must interpret any text first of all within its own parameters, with the clues that it offers about its meaning. Each writer must be trusted to convey his own meaning.

Many refinements of this story-based approach have since emerged. Narrative (or narratological), reader-response, and rhetorical criticism were first honed in the study of nonbiblical literature. Rhetorical criticism applies knowledge about ancient techniques of persuasion, acquired from handbooks and actual examples of Greco-Roman storytelling, to the Christian texts. Each kind or genre of ancient writing had its own prescribed format. Most required a clear beginning, middle, and end. Standard devices (called *topoi*) include genealogies, shipwreck stories, humorous anecdotes, trickster stories, or stories of virtue overcoming desire. Knowing which elements of a story are such commonplace "set pieces" helps the modern reader to recover the situation of the first readers.

Narratological and reader-response modes of literary criticism have been developed largely for the study of modern poetry and novel. They teach us to unpack the many components of a narrative, including plot and character. Literary critics urge us, first, not to confuse the real author of a text and its real flesh-and-blood readers, who are unknown to us, with the author and readers "implied" by the narrative itself, since authors necessarily role-play when they write stories. They rightly insist that language is too versatile and symbolic to be tied to any single construction of an author's "intention." They require that we read stories "closely" for what is said and what is not said. What devices does the author use to advance the plot and subplots? What surprises the reader? We also learn from literary criticism to distinguish between flat, or two-dimensional, characters who play a static role in a story (representing good or evil, moralizing, worrying, encouraging) and dynamic, round, or three-dimensional figures who are capable of introspection and change as real people. But what we conclude from a text about an author's or audience's outlook may have little relation to the historical author. Authors often adopt a pose for writing that reflects only their ideal self or another persona. That is why we are sometimes disappointed to meet our favorite authors in the flesh!

In reading texts such as letters and memos these distinctions are admittedly of limited use. It would be unwise for a professor to leave a dean's memo unanswered on the grounds that he or she had no assurance that the real author intended what the implied author said. In Paul's letters, too, we are positively invited into a particular historical situation from the distant past, and we justifiably assume a secure link between the real Paul and the author that we meet in the letters. But in more creative genres, including the gospel narratives, these distinctions help to make us aware of the many levels of meaning in texts, and they prevent us from hastily associating a literary theme with some real person's "theology."

For reasons of space, the following introductions and notes to the gospels do not consistently distinguish between real and implied authors and audiences. When we speak of author and audience, we usually mean the author and audience implied by the narrative, since we have no other access to the real author and audience. It would be too severe to insist that, because we cannot be *sure* of an exact correspondence between implied and real, we ought to abandon all attempts to imagine real authors and audiences.

Meanings Other than the Intended Sense

So far we have been identifying a gospel's "meaning" with the point that its author was consciously trying to make. In recent years, however, many critics—including some of the rhetorical and reader-response critics mentioned already—have challenged the assumption that the meaning of a text is restricted or even tied to its author's intention. Developments in linguistic, anthropological, sociological, literary, and rhetorical theory have generated modes of interpretation that seek to discover other meanings in the gospel narratives.

The different senses of "meaning" are apparent in our everyday speech. If, when you are trying to explain to me the formula $E = MC^2$, I say, "I do not know what you mean," then I am talking about your failure to communicate your *intention*. But if I say, "Opera has no meaning for me," I am talking about something else. It is not that I fail to understand the intention of the performers, but rather that the production does not resonate with my life experience. Westerners, and especially academics, often like to think that life is really about ideas, even that we conduct our lives according to a consistent idea; accordingly, we want to know the ideas that writers from other cultures have tried to convey. We sometimes fail to realize that, even for us, pure rationality plays a relatively small role in our lives—in the food we eat, the clothes we wear, in our entertainments and romances. We are conditioned by social processes beyond our control, and in our daily exchanges with others we regularly resort to nonrational forms, such as the enjoyment of humor, food, and drink. Some modes of gospel interpretation insist that these other dimensions of meaning—intuitive, poetic, unconscious—provide a more worthwhile goal for the reader.

The variety of such approaches defies brief summarization. It might help to subdivide them into (a) strategies for uncovering a single demonstrable (or refutable) truth and (b) strategies for cataloging the many "truths" that emerge from reading. Under the former head, structuralist interpretation holds that an author is constrained by linguistic and cultural patterns that he or she does not recognize, and it seeks to uncover these "deep structures" in texts. Relationships of power and submission, for example, might be demonstrable in an author's unconscious arrangement of words symbolizing those categories. Though different in many ways, and markedly theological in its aim, canonical criticism also treats an author's work as part of a much larger whole of which he or she was unaware; it deals with the functions of the gospels in their settings within the canon, both "New" and "Old" Testaments.

Other commentators would abandon as futile not only the quest to know what an author intended but also any effort to recover such global, demonstrable truths that the authors might have unwittingly served. They would say that all meaning is *constructed* by readers, whether those readers think of themselves as historians or literary critics or theologians. If a single intended meaning ever existed, it is irrelevant and irrecoverable now. There is no longer an *object to be known*. Rather, meaning is imparted by the reader as much as by the author. And the importance of texts does not derive from their original contexts, but from their subsequent appropriations. Just as the works of Shakespeare or Goethe can be read without any knowledge of the authors' historical situations, so can the gospels. These avenues of interpretation therefore focus on the transactions between reader and text, not on an illusory "objective sense."

These approaches prepare us to enjoy and experience the gospels as well as to understand them. To the extent that such readings require the abandonment of historical analysis, however, they are difficult to apply to the gospels and *Acts*. We cannot escape historical concerns, for we are reading English translations of twentieth-century Greek texts (*Thomas* survives in Coptic) that attempt to recreate first-century documents according to historical principles, from thousands of ancient and medieval manuscripts. And these texts mention such historical figures as Herod the Great and his family, Pilate, and John the Baptist. They assume that the reader shares many cultural assumptions. Therefore, we cannot easily read the gospels as if they were English-language compositions of the recent past. To read them responsibly requires constant attention to what a particular Greek word might have connoted in the first century. This process necessarily involves us in a kind of historical thinking, even if we wish to read the gospels purely for enjoyment.

Insights from Social History

Just as Paul's letters have been the object of social-historical questioning in recent years, so have the gospels and *Acts*. The effect is somewhat different here, admittedly, because the gospels do not give us as direct access to a living community with concrete situations. Still, social-historical study of the gospels can, as we have seen, help suggest plausible models for situations in Jesus' career, or support hypotheses about Jesus' aims. And social history can also help to refine composition-critical approaches to the gospels by exploring the social implications of a text's language and story.

An example of sociologically sensitive questioning concerns the names given to Jesus in the gospels. Until recently, the names given to Jesus by friend and foe alike within these texts were understood as primarily theological titles or slurs. If Jesus was charged with being possessed by Beelzebul, scholars looked for other examples of the name Beelzebul to understand the *idea* involved, to connect the label with some articulated theology or demonology current in ancient Judaism. Social-historical analysis, however, looks at how such labels would *function* in group contexts—among the first-century Mediterranean readers of the gospels. Scholars often find it helpful to use "models" of social deviance or witchcraft or shamanism, which have been shaped and tested for other cultures, as a way of gaining access to the (otherwise irrecoverable) specific situation of gospel author and readers. They ask, in this case, about the social effect of labeling someone "demon-possessed." In a society very different from ours, and preoccupied with personal honor and shame, what would it mean to be called demon-possessed or a blasphemer—not theologically, but in social terms?

Or again, *Luke* often refers to Jesus as "Lord." Older scholarship assumed that this was a theological title, evoking Jesus' relationship to God—who is often called the "Lord" in the Bible. But the Greek term was widely used in the first century to denote masters of households, revered teachers, and even the emperor. Social history asks about the social impact of such word on its first-century hearers, in addition to the idea that it expresses.

In its quest to uncover dynamics of real human relationships behind a text's superficial story of famous figures—usually men—social-historical analysis has been energized by feminist historiography. Because almost all of our texts were written by men, and the situations described in ancient literature mainly concern men's affairs, recovering the lost voices of women involves extremely careful analysis. It requires attention to plausible social relations in the episodes described in the gospels. *Luke-Acts* gives the most explicit attention to the roles of women. One might ask, then, how *Luke*'s claims that Jesus was sponsored by wealthy women (8:1), or that prominent women God-fearers acted for and against the young church, would have resonated with *Luke*'s readers? What social conditions are in view here? When Jesus "reclines" at dinner with a prominent leader and is greeted by a woman who anoints his feet, what social taboos and relationships come into play? In texts that do not feature women, where would women have been expected to fit in behind the scenes—say, in the burial of the dead or in preparation of dinners? What differences would class and status make to a woman's behavior? This kind of social awareness can only improve our efforts to recapture the first readers' situation.

What Is a Gospel?

As the focus of gospel interpretation shifted to the complete work of an individual author, it became more and more urgent to answer the question: But what exactly is a gospel? The question does not concern the name "gospel," because none of the texts we know as gospels calls itself by that label. Recall from the introduction to the *Reader* that the English word *gospel* represents the Greek *euangelion*, "announcement," which Paul used as a technical term for his declaration of Jesus' death, resurrection, and imminent return. *Mark* (1:1) claims only to be about the *origin* of this announcement; it does not call itself a gospel. Although we adopt the term for the gospels out of convenience, we should remember that the issue in defining a gospel is not about the name but about the form. What kind of story is this that we see in the Synoptics and *John*?

This question is important for understanding a document's intention. Just as we interpret a poem or a song very differently from a lecture, we need to know what to look for in the gospels. Recall that the discovery of the genre of Paul's writings— as real, lively letters responding to passing historical situations—has fundamentally changed the way we read them. In the same way, it is important to know where the Christian "gospel" genre fits in the world of ancient literature because different genres had different rhetorical constraints. The question of genre might even challenge our search for an author's intention, for if the gospels were deliberately produced as one of the "creative writing" genres, then perhaps one ought not to seek a single intention in them, any more than one seeks the "intention" of a painting or sculpture. Perhaps they were meant to be enjoyed and savored, not "understood" as theoretical statements.

Since the gospels of the NT all describe a portion of Jesus' life ending with his death and resurrection, and two of them begin the story with his birth, early readers commonly assumed that they were more or less biographical. The many "lives" of Jesus that appeared in the eighteenth and nineteenth centuries treated the gospels as if they were biographies; they sought to isolate a reasonable (= believable by modern readers) core from the gospels' basic framework. This approach was dealt devastating blows, however, by a succession of scholars who, in one way or another, demonstrated that the gospel framework is itself artificial. In the mid-nineteenth century D. F. Strauss argued that the gospels cannot simply be salvaged for biographical purposes, since they reflect a world that is wholly "mythopoeic"—one that already *interprets* Jesus' significance in relation to ancient views of the universe. This approach was developed on the theological side by Martin Kähler, who insisted that the gospels give us only the Christ of salvation history, not a recoverable Jesus of everyday human history. On the literary-historical side, William Wrede followed with his argument that even the earliest gospel, *Mark,* is not naive and artless—as Jesus' would-be biographers had hoped—but it is already an elaborate theological statement, shaping its account of Jesus' career so as to help with theological problems in the early church. And all these insights were absorbed into the analysis of Bultmann and the form critics, which seemed to exclude any biographical use of the gospels. If the gospels were essentially collections of a few forms of material from the church's preaching, then they provided no basis for biography.

Classifying the genre of the gospels has only been complicated by the Q hypothesis and the gradual incorporation of the *Gospel of Thomas* into the early gospel collection alongside the NT texts (see the introduction to *Thomas*). Thomas does not provide a shred of "narrative" or biographical outline, but comprises 114 sayings attributed to Jesus. Yet more than half of those sayings are so similar to material in the other gospels that this document cannot be dismissed as belonging to another genre. The other gospels also include significant stretches of sayings material without narrative, and the hypothetical sayings gospel Q would also support the conclusion that any description of "gospel" must take into account both narrative and sayings-based portraits.

If the gospels are not biographies, what are they? The form critics left a powerful legacy in their insistence that the gospels were both "faith-writings" and "folk [not upper-class] literature." But these observations did not greatly help to locate the gospels within an ancient literary context, for we lacked solid parallels of other faith documents from the masses. Some have discovered correspondences between the Christian texts and *encomia* (singular *encomium*), which recounted the great sayings and deeds of a divine or quasi-divine figure, or the deeds of an emperor (notably, Augustus). Others have looked to Jewish parallels such as the "sayings of the fathers" transmitted with the Mishnah *(Pirqe Avot),* or those biblical prophetic books that include biographical material along with the prophets' sayings and actions. Still others have thought that the gospel genre was a Christian innovation traceable to the author of *Mark,* who, it was suggested on the basis of *Mark* 1:1, first applied the word "gospel" to a written text. (But we have suggested that the author does not use the word quite that way. See the introduction to *Mark.*)

What we need in any discussion of genre is a secure entry point, a criterion. That control material may be provided by the prologue to *Luke* and *Acts* (*Luke* 1:1–4; see *Acts* 1:1–2). As we shall see in the introduction to that two-volume set, the author borrows the formal language of Hellenistic historiography. In so doing, he presents his own work as historical or biographical. He promises to write about "the events fulfilled among us" (*Luke* 1:1), and the first volume contains "what Jesus began to do and teach" (*Acts* 1:1). Most important, the author cites earlier efforts by "many" others at the same sort of writing, even if they have not matched his quality (*Luke* 1:1). Yet we are fairly sure that *Luke's* sources included *Mark,* other narratives (for infancy and trial sections, perhaps also the journey to Jerusalem), and at least one sayings collection. This author, therefore, seemed to think that all of this material fell within the broad confines of history and biography. Perhaps, then, we should take this early identification as a starting point.

To think of the gospels and *Acts* as historical or biographical, however, we need to leave aside all modern connotations of those words. Ancient biography was extremely diverse. The closest parallels to the gospels and *Acts* are the *Lives of Eminent Philosophers* by Diogenes Laertius (early third century C.E.); Plutarch's famous *Parallel Lives* (early second century C.E.); and Flavius Josephus's autobiography (late first century C.E.). One might also consider Suetonius's *Lives of the Caesars* (early second century C.E.). Like the gospels, these texts do not provide comprehensive narratives in the modern sense of biography. Josephus briefly comments on his genealogy and childhood, then focuses almost exclusively on a five-month period in his career. Note too that Josephus's *Life* is part of his lengthy history, the *Jewish Antiquities.* Thus, "life-writing" and history were closely allied genres. This is confirmed by Plutarch, who plainly thinks of his biographical work as a kind of historical writing (e.g., *Theseus* 1.1–3), and Suetonius, who writes history by means of biography. Diogenes' *Lives* draws upon earlier biographies and, like them, presents the careers of great philosophers largely through the combination of narrative and *chreiai;* the latter include proverbs, answers to hard questions, and responses to difficult situations. All of these attempts at biography are, then, episodic and utterly lacking in proportion—rather like the gospels.

To say that the Christian gospels have a historical or biographical character does not imply anything about their accuracy; the description refers only to genre. Even in the most deliberate histories of the period, one finds fantastic stories, terrifying omens, supernatural births, cures, and exorcisms. No modern historian would simply accept the accounts given by an author as more than one interpretation of stories that had been passed down in that author's sources. Among the non-Christian historians and biographers, as among the Christian authors, one must always distinguish between more and less careful, more and less plausible, craftsmen.

Given the wide diversity of quality, style, and format in Greco-Roman history and biography, the diversity among the Christian gospels, and the author of *Luke*'s explicit claims for himself and his predecessors, there seems to be no good reason to doubt that the gospels and *Acts* fall within the broad category of ancient biographical/historical writing. That the parallels are not exact should not trouble us any more than the absence of precise parallels for, say, Josephus's autobiography.

Historical Context: Dates, Authors, Audiences, and Occasions

Ideally, we would like to know who wrote the gospels, where, to whom, and why—though if we did know these things, a lot of the excitement of gospel study would be removed. Fortunately, there is no immediate danger of our knowing so much; we are still in the exploratory stage. Highest probability, among these issues, attaches to the dating question. Most scholars agree on a date range of about a half-century for all of the texts considered here, thus between 60 and 120 C.E., and in fact most would date the gospels toward the middle of that range: 70 to 100. So we find in the gospels and *Acts* the major surviving texts of the second Christian generation.

The case for locating each document within a specific historical context and date range will be considered in the separate introductions. Here, we shall point out only that none of the gospels dates itself by an unambiguous means. The external evidence for the gospels' existence is not helpful. They are first known in the mid-second century (for *John*, an Egyptian fragment is known dating from 125–150 C.E.), but they likely circulated several decades before that time, since they seem to have acquired some status by the time they are first mentioned. The text of a gospel itself provides internal clues about its historical circumstances. Paul's letters contain many such clues because he writes as one participant in a dialogue. But the gospels and *Acts* have no reason to send greetings, discuss the community's past, or mention travel plans. Thus internal evidence in the gospels about their circumstances of composition is incidental, extremely ambiguous, and vague, such as the special attention given to one region (e.g., Galilee or Syria) or one person (e.g., Peter in *Matthew*). A kind of negative evidence is easier to find, though. For example, *Mark* and *Luke* were probably not written in Palestine or Syria: *Mark* because it makes basic errors about Palestinian geography, history, and culture, and *Luke* because it makes assumptions that were only valid in other Mediterranean locations.

The deficiencies in internal and external evidence mean that certainty about the gospel writers' circumstances will probably elude us for a long time, but they also encourage us to look for other ways of approaching the issue. Perhaps the single most promising tool is to ask a legal question: Who stands to benefit *(cui bono?)* from this portrait of Jesus? Applying this principle requires that we first reach a compelling interpretation of the gospel as a whole, and that is the hard part. The gospels have so much material, and preserve so many disparate traditions, that different readers end up with diverse interpretations.

But in theory at least, if we could propose a reading of a gospel's main points that explained the data more convincingly than any other reading, then we could proceed to the easy part: deciding where this viewpoint fit in the range of early Christian experience. To date, no interpretation of any gospel (or *Acts*) has won such universal approval that we might proceed with confidence to such historical location. *John* arguably has the clearest set of themes, but even there the task of location is difficult. Still, we are usually dealing with two or three main options, not a complete lack of clues. These options will be considered in each of the introductions. In any case, the challenge of locating the gospels historically is a profitable experience in itself.

For Further Reading

Aland, K., ed. *Synopsis of the Four Gospels: Greek-English Edition of the Synopsis Quattuor Evangelium.* 10th ed. Stuttgart: German Bible Society, 1993.

Barr, Alan. *A Diagram of Synoptic Relationships.* Edinburgh: T&T Clark, 1976.

Bultmann, Rudolf. *The History of the Synoptic Tradition.* Translated by John Marsh. New York: Harper & Row, 1963.

Crossan, John Dominic. *Jesus: A Revolutionary Biography.* San Francisco: HarperSanFrancisco, 1993.

———. *Sayings Parallels: A Workbook for the Jesus Tradition.* Philadelphia: Fortress, 1986.

Fredriksen, Paula. *From Jesus to Christ: The Origins of the New Testament Images of Jesus.* New Haven: Yale University Press, 1988.

Kloppenborg, John S. *Excavating Q: The History and Setting of the Sayings Gospel.* Minneapolis: Fortress, 2000.

Koester, H. *Ancient Christian Gospels: Their History and Development.* Philadelphia: Trinity, 1990.

Malina, Bruce J., and Richard Rohrbaugh. *Social Science Commentary on the Synoptic Gospels.* Minneapolis: Fortress, 1992.

Sanders, E. P. *The Historical Figure of Jesus.* London: Penguin, 1993.

Sanders, E. P., and Margaret Davies. *Studying the Synoptic Gospels.* Philadelphia: Trinity, 1989.

Streeter, B. H. *The Four Gospels: A Study of Origins.* New York: Macmillan, 1925.

Throckmorton, B. H., Jr., ed. *Gospel Parallels: A Comparison of the Synoptic Gospels.* Nashville: Nelson, 1992.

The Origin of the Gospel

MARK

PERHAPS THE HARDEST LESSON for anyone reading early Christian literature is to distinguish among the gospels, especially the three Synoptics. They often seem to sound the same, and they contain extensive agreements. If we can free ourselves of the ingrained tradition that lumps all the stories together, however, we shall see that even very similar stories can be retold with markedly different effect, depending upon their context and manner of presentation. Even with the earliest known written gospel, *Mark,* we can see that the author has a decided perspective.

One motive behind the search for the earliest gospel was a quest for "simple historical truth." Many nineteenth-century scholars were concerned above all to recover a reasonable form of Christianity, one that would not conflict with the scientific developments they saw all around them. In *Mark* they found a gospel that displayed no knowledge of the scientifically problematic virgin birth and did not recount Jesus' resurrection appearances (i.e., *Mark* 16:9–20 was missing from the best manuscripts). *Mark* also appeared stylistically awkward, with its overuse of "and" and "immediately," and theologically naive. Jesus curses a fig tree for barrenness although "it was not the season for figs" (11:12–14); and when a woman touches his clothes to receive a cure, he does not know who stole this power from him (5:30–31).

Whereas literary critics and theologians might find *Mark* the least attractive gospel because of this awkwardness, it seemed to offer the historian pristine material, unaffected by the more overt theological agendas of *Matthew* or *Luke. Mark's* miracle stories, it was thought, could be explained away as unsophisticated interpretations of natural events. Jesus' "walking on the water," for example, might have been no more than a stroll on a hidden sandbar, which a primitive mind innocently misunderstood. Biographies of Jesus' life based on such rationalistic reinterpretations of *Mark* proliferated in the nineteenth century.

This enthusiasm for *Mark's* "raw data" took a severe blow, however, with the publication of William Wrede's *The Messianic Secret in the Gospels* in 1901. This study was concerned with the theme—present in all the Synoptic Gospels but first set out in *Mark*—of Jesus' secret identity. From the beginning of *Mark*, the reader is told that whenever Jesus' true status was recognized, whether by evil spirits or disciples, Jesus commanded that the insight be kept secret (*Mark* 1:25, 34, 44; 3:12; 5:43; 7:36; 8:30). And he appears to have had a secret doctrine, exclusively for his inner group of disciples, in contrast to his public teaching for the masses (4:10–12, 33–34). The disciples were instructed to keep their special knowledge secret until after Jesus' resurrection (9:9).

What to make of all this? Wrede argued that the technique of the "secret" was *Mark*'s solution to a glaring problem in the early church. The problem was that, although the church steadfastly believed that Jesus was Messiah and Son of God, his reported sayings did not make this claim; he himself preferred to speak of the kingdom of God. How could these two facts be reconciled? *Mark*'s solution was to claim that Jesus' failure to bring his messianic status into the open during his lifetime was deliberate. He signaled his identity only to his small inner circle and commanded that it be kept secret; that is why it only came to light with his resurrection from the dead.

Although details of Wrede's hypothesis have often been challenged, his work swiftly ended the practice of treating *Mark* as naive history. It was now clear that this author, like any other, had a point to make. He selected, arranged, and created his material in order to serve his literary purposes. Wrede's treatment of *Mark* as theological history has been more than confirmed by the rise of redaction criticism and literary studies of *Mark* in more recent years.

Date

Most scholars consider *Mark* the earliest surviving gospel, on the view that it served as a source for *Matthew* and *Luke*. But can we locate its time of composition more precisely in relation to events in the non-Christian world? Because the text is anonymous (in contrast to Paul's letters), we cannot appeal to the author's birth and death dates. We must find clues about the date within the text itself. Various factors indicate a date range between about 65 and 80 C.E.—a generation or more after Jesus' death.

Mark seems to have been removed from the events of Jesus' life, for the main body of this work strings together isolated stories about Jesus that the author or a predecessor has shaped into thematic groups (see below). Between Jesus' encounter with John the Baptist and his last few days in Jerusalem, his life story is told by means of a few exemplary episodes: some conflicts, some teaching (including parables), some miracles, more conflicts, and so on. These are grouped according to theme much more than chronology, and the author suggests that they are examples only (e.g., 4:33). He makes some effort to supply chronological links in order to move the story along, but many of these links are vague, for example: "and," "then," or "again" (1:21, 40; 3:1, 13; 4:1; 7:1, 31), "one sabbath" (2:23), and "in those days" (8:1). They can be easily removed to reveal an underlying collection of fairly streamlined, stereotyped episodes. If these episodes had already been processed through a period of oral transmission—to the extent that the author could no longer distinguish Jesus' parable of the sower from its Christian interpretation (4:13–20; see the introduction to the gospels)—then a substantial amount of time has passed since Jesus' death.

Other considerations confirm that Jesus' death (about 30 C.E.) lies a generation or more in the past. For example, the author either anticipates the destruction of Jerusalem, which occurred in 70 C.E., or reflects back upon it. The complete rupture of the temple curtain, which was critical to the temple's sanctity, at the moment of Jesus' death (15:38) seems to reflect a Christian interpretation of the temple's destruction. The parable of the wicked tenants (12:1–12, esp. 12:9) and the apocalyptic discourse (13:2, 14) provide further examples. Still, *Mark*'s Jesus does not betray the kind of elaborate Christian interpretation of Jerusalem's destruction that one finds in *Luke* 19:41–44. On the basis of ordinary historical criteria (i.e., leaving aside the possibility of divine intervention, which would create its own problems in the case of *Mark*), one might imagine the author writing these things shortly before the destruction of the temple—perhaps after the outset of the conflict with Rome—or soon after it.

Another kind of date indicator is *Mark*'s notice that Simon of Cyrene, who carried Jesus' cross, was "the father of Alexander and Rufus" (15:21). A natural (though not certain) inference is that Alexander and Rufus are adults known to *Mark*'s readers; the father Simon, however, is unknown to them and may have died. Apparently, *Mark* mentions Alexander and Rufus in order to verify the source of the Simon story, in effect: "Alexander and Rufus, whom you all know, say that their father, a man named Simon, carried Jesus' cross!" Both *Matthew* (27:32) and *Luke* (23:26) omit the sons' names, presumably because they would mean nothing to readers outside *Mark*'s group, even though they include the story about Simon. Although we must reckon with a number of variables—whether the reference to the sons is a purely literary invention, whether Simon fathered the boys before or after Jesus' crucifixion, the sons' ages at the time of *Mark*'s composition—the story works best on the rationale given above if *Mark* was composed between, say, 55 and 80.

Moreover, *Mark* has an urgent eschatological tone (e.g., 13:29–37). It claims that some of Jesus' own students (9:1), or possibly *Mark*'s first readers (13:30), will not die before they see the kingdom of God. *Matthew* and *Luke-Acts* both take over these references, but they include much other material pertaining to the establishment of the church that mitigates the urgency of the future hope.

Finally, to the extent that we can successfully date *Matthew* and *Luke* between 80 and 100 C.E. on other grounds, and argue that they used *Mark* as a source, we should place *Mark* before 80. All things considered, a date range of 65 to 80 C.E. seems most plausible.

Authorship and Audience

Mark provides numerous clues that both author and audience were unfamiliar with Judean geography and culture, and even Jewish scripture. This becomes apparent early, when the author attributes to *Isaiah* a composite passage from *Isaiah* and *Malachi* (1:2). Soon afterward, he misrepresents a biblical story (2:25–26). The geography is particularly confusing and vague. Jesus' repeated crossings of the "sea" (actually, a lake) of Galilee land him in unlikely places such as Gerasa (5:1), and he takes baffling routes (7:24, 31). Before the trial of Jesus in Jerusalem, the reader is seldom sure where the story is taking place. *Matthew* and *Luke* typically change *Mark*'s geography to clarify matters. Nor does the author seem to know basic political facts, for example that Herod Antipas was a tetrarch rather than a king (6:14), or that Herodias was Antipas's mother-in-law, not wife (6:17); again, *Matthew* and *Luke* usually make the necessary corrections. Finally, the author likes to sprinkle the Greek narrative with Aramaic phrases—perhaps to add local color and to lend an air of mystery (5:41; 7:34)—but he must explain even the simplest Aramaic constructions such as "bar-Timaeus" ("son of Timaeus," 10:46). He expects no knowledge of Aramaic or of what he claims are standard Jewish customs (7:2–4).

This book appears to have been written, then, for Gentile Christians living somewhere in the Greek-speaking (eastern) Mediterranean. Although Eusebius associates it with Rome, he does so for unlikely reasons. *Mark*'s explanation of Greek currency by reference to a Roman standard (12:42) might support that conclusion; however, in *Matthew* (5:26; 10:29; 20:9), Roman currency is also the standard. Any significant center in the eastern Mediterranean outside of Syria-Palestine seems a plausible location.

Literary Features

Mark is one of the most impressive literary paradoxes in the early Christian corpus because, while it is filled with awkward and confusing language, it reflects a good deal of studied arrangement and thoughtful phrasing.

The book's literary shortcomings are apparent everywhere: a highly repetitive sentence structure that links together endless clauses with the conjunction "and"; repetitious and inappropriate use of "immediately" to enliven the narrative; scenic incongruities (4:10, 13; 5:9–12); flat, two-dimensional characters (12:13, 18); and vague statements that cry out for clarification (5:21; 6:32, 40–48; 9:30; 10:1). *Matthew* and *Luke* routinely smooth out these rough features of *Mark*.

At the same time, the author has apparently tried to create a rich, multilayered narrative. One can see this in the overall structure of the work, according to which the dramatic center falls about half-way through the story with Peter's confession (8:27–9:8). We have already noted his arrangement of distinct stories according to theme or type, rather than strict chronology. Further, he cleverly situates one story next to a contrasting episode in order to highlight a theme (e.g., 9:33–41), and he is particularly fond of enclosing or nesting one story inside another (3:19–35; 5:21–35; 6:7–30; 11:12–20). This can create a powerful dramatic effect, as when Jesus, on his way to cure a girl on the point of death, is detained so long by a woman with a hemorrhage that the girl dies in the meantime (5:21–35). The entire narrative of *Mark* is somewhat "ironic," because the Christian reader knows a great deal that is hidden from the characters in the story—both Jesus' opponents and his own students. This irony comes to the fore in several places (e.g., 15:39).

Overview, Themes, and Issues

As a rule of thumb, one should pay careful attention to the opening lines of ancient works, for they frequently announce the themes to be developed. In the case of *Mark*, the first verse is a title. This book will deal with "the origin of the announcement [NRSV 'beginning of the gospel']." The term "announcement" (Gk *euangelion*) is familiar to us from Paul's letters, where it refers to his proclamation of Jesus' saving death, resurrection, and imminent return. Apparently this book, then, sets out to describe the *background* to those saving events, how things began in Jesus' lifetime. If "announcement" or gospel was a term of special significance for Paul's communities (see the introduction to *Romans*), then we must ask whether *Mark* presents a characteristically Pauline perspective. We shall suggest here that it does.

Mark's title (1:1) also announces Jesus' identity as "Christ" and "Son of God," both of which were terms well known in Paul's communities. The unfolding of Jesus' identity, plainly known to author and readers from the start, will become a major part of the subsequent narrative.

The first chapter establishes at least four themes that will continue throughout the book: (a) Jesus is identified repeatedly as Son of God (1:1, 11, 24). (b) He is credited with extraordinary authority and as superior to the Baptist (1:7), by virtue of his embodiment of the Holy Spirit (1:10, 12), his ability to summon students at will (1:17), and his power over the spirit world (1:22, 27, 34, 39). (c) Still, he commands secrecy about his identity (1:25, 34, 44). It will not be an issue in the public arena for some time. (d) Jesus is completely at odds with his Jewish environment.

As soon as he has been immersed by John and has called his first students, Jesus heads ("immediately") to a synagogue. There, in the synagogue, he confronts evil spirits (1:22, 39) with his unique authority—not found among the Jewish teachers (1:21–22). Indeed, the writer emphasizes that Jesus brings a "new teaching" (1:27). In the shared world of author and reader, the Jews are outsiders. *Mark*'s Jesus speaks of "their synagogues" (1:39) and commands the cured leper to show himself to the priest as a testimony to "them" (1:44). So Jesus comes into a Jewish world, to be sure, but that world is at best incidental, at worst inimical, to his divine mission.

Chapter 1, then, sets the stage for 2:1–3:6, in which Jesus repeatedly runs into direct conflict with the Jewish leaders. They, of course, do not know what the audience knows about his identity. So when he begins to exercise his authority and his new teaching—forgiving sins, eating with sinners, and violating the Sabbath—the opposition of the Jewish leadership quickly builds to lethal proportions: At this early point in the story, they set out to kill him (3:6). *Mark*'s Jesus stands in serious tension with the Jewish leaders from the beginning, and this tension moves the plot quickly forward.

In the next section of the story (3:7–4:34), *Mark* makes several important distinctions. In general, this section features Jesus' typical teaching but, in light of the opposition from Jewish leaders, *Mark* sharply distinguishes a public from a private teaching. Jesus selects twelve students from the rest (3:13–19) and directs a special teaching toward them, while conceding that the Jewish masses will not understand him (4:11–12). Most important, *Mark* stresses that even Jesus' own family—his mother, brothers, and sisters—do not understand him at all. At first, they think that he is crazy (3:21). They are mentioned alongside the Jewish leaders who think that he is possessed by the devil (3:22). These Jewish leaders, by rejecting Jesus, commit an eternally unpardonable sin. When his family arrives to take him home, according to *Mark,* Jesus forthrightly rebuffs them, claiming that his family consists rather of those who "do the will of God" (3:31–35). Having a blood relationship to Jesus is no claim on the truth. For *Mark's* readers in the first century, when family connections with Jesus were still a live issue in leadership disputes, this must have seemed a pointed statement.

It is not only the Jewish leaders and his family who fail to understand Jesus, however. The reader also begins to wonder about his inner group of students. As early as 4:13 Jesus criticizes them for not understanding the deep meaning of his parables, and at 4:40 he chastises them for their lack of trust. After he miraculously calms a storm, they are still wondering, "Who then is this?" (4:41).

Chapters 4:35 through 6 recount a series of exemplary miracles, including exorcisms, cures, the resuscitation of a girl who has died, and nature miracles such as the feeding of the five thousand and Jesus' walking on the water. In the midst of recounting these feats, which should be sufficient proof of Jesus' identity, the author drives home his earlier points: Jesus' fellow Jews, his own students, the people of his hometown, and his flesh-and-blood family, in their different ways and degrees, reject him. The critical passage is 6:1–6. After performing remarkable cures elsewhere, he returns to his home, where he offends those who know his family, the members of which are spelled out by name. They include James and Jude, who have by the time of *Mark's* writing become leading figures in some Christian circles. Jesus reflects on the singular lack of prophetic honor that he finds "in his own country, and among his own kin (or family), and in his own house" (6:4). As for his students, although Jesus enables them to perform cures of their own (6:12–13), they remain completely obtuse after his feeding of the crowds, and after he walked on the water, their "heart was hardened" (6:52). For readers who know that Jesus' brother James, his closest disciples (e.g., Peter), and their followers are influential figures in Jerusalem Christianity, this remark would presumably have challenged their authority.

In 7:1–8:26 *Mark* presents further conflicts between Jesus and the Jews (e.g., 7:1–23; 8:11–15) and a contrasting visit to Gentile territories (7:24–8:10), where he is warmly received. In the important story of 7:1–23, *Mark* has Jesus plainly cancel-ing the biblical laws about unclean food (*Deut.* 14:1–21). Since those laws were fun-damental to Judaism, this passage represents a decisive break with the whole Jewish tradition of observing Moses' instructions from Mount Sinai. In this block, Jesus also criticizes his students at length for their lack of understanding and hardness of heart (8:15–21). The author includes a second miraculous feeding, of four thou-sand people. Because this story comes soon after the feeding of the five thousand, and grows out of very similar circumstances, the reader is driven to despair over Jesus' students when they ask, "How can one feed these people with bread here in the desert?" (8:4).

When reading ancient Greek plays and epics or the works of an author such as Josephus, one should pay particular attention to the center of the work, for authors tended to make the literary center also the thematic focus. In *Mark,* the section 8:27 to 9:10 provides such a core. This is signaled by *Mark's* reversion to the basic issue of Jesus' identity, which Jesus raises with the leading question to his disciples, "Who do people say that I am?" (8:27). This paves the way for Peter's confession that he is "Christ" (8:29). But Jesus' response to Peter is at first enigmatic as he develops the conflict theme with a new intensity, telling his disciples that "the son of man" must suffer and be killed by the Jewish authorities, then rise again (8:31). When Peter ob-jects to this, Jesus responds to him, "Get behind me, Satan! For you are not on the side of God, but of men" (8:33).

At this point, a new element of apocalyptic urgency breaks in: Jesus begins to speak of the coming of the son of man in glory, after his death and resurrection (8:38). And he promises that some of those present will not die before they witness the coming of God's kingdom (9:1). At this pivotal moment in the narrative, Jesus' identity as son of God is resoundingly affirmed by a heavenly voice (9:7). But the disciples are characteristically perplexed and Peter mutters something that reveals his lack of understanding (9:6). It is a puzzle that, at the same time as the author emphasizes the disciples' incomprehension, he has Jesus command them to secrecy about what they have seen (9:9). Could they have said anything if they had wanted to? Did they understand? In this case, *Mark* gives the secrecy theme an intriguing twist: they are not to disclose what they have seen until after his resurrection (9:9).

Barely halfway through the story, Jesus' teaching and healing career is now largely over. From now on, Jesus will be absorbed with the coming crisis in Jeru-salem and with his students' relationships. After criticizing them again for their spiritual deficiency (9:18–29), he repeats his prediction concerning his death, and still they fail to understand (9:30–32). In response to his dramatic announcement, they can only debate which of them is the greatest (9:34)! Jesus insists that merit does not come from mere association with him, but from dedication to service (9:35–37). By way of illustration, he then welcomes a man who is not one of "the Twelve" but is effectively curing people in Jesus' name (9:38–41). (What signifi-cance might this episode have at *Mark's* time of composition? Would Paul have been understood as such a person?) Jesus also welcomes children whom his disciples have tried to send away (10:13–14). After describing at length the hardships and suffering that await those who would follow him—the forsaking of all goods and normal social ties for "the gospel" (10:17–31)—Jesus again predicts his forthcoming death and resurrection, but yet again the disciples respond by debating which of them has the highest status (10:32–45).

When Martin Kähler called *Mark* "a passion story with an extended introduction," he rightly identified *Mark*'s preoccupation with Jesus' conflict, arrest, and crucifixion. The plot to kill Jesus was established early (3:6). After providing a few examples of teaching, cures, and further conflict, *Mark* now moves quickly to the climax; chapters 11 to 16 are devoted to the final week of Jesus' life. A series of intense conflicts between Jesus and the Jewish leaders in chapters 11 and 12 turns on the basic question of his unique authority. Although he enters the city in triumph as Israel's king (11:1–11), he symbolically curses the unproductive fig tree: "May no one ever eat fruit from you again" (11:14), indicating Israel's unbelief and rejection by God. When he then causes a major disturbance in the temple, claiming that it has been debased by its leadership, the Jewish leaders confirm the plot to kill him (11:18), challenging his authority (11:27–33). The symbolism of the barren fig tree is developed in the parable of the wicked tenants, who refuse to turn over the fruit of the vineyard to its rightful owner, and even kill the owner's son when he comes to collect it; the owner destroys them and gives the vineyard to others (12:1–12). This parable, told against the Jewish leaders (12:12), fits well with Paul's presentation of Israel's status in *Romans* 9–11. The rest of chapter 12 harshly criticizes various groups of Jewish leaders.

In chapter 13, the author picks up the apocalyptic themes that have appeared incidentally since the pivotal section (8:27–9:10) in a dramatic speech of Jesus that deals with the brief period between his coming death and the end of the age. Jesus predicts the destruction of the temple (13:1–8), horrific persecution—including synagogue beatings and appearances of his followers before "governors and kings" for the sake of "the gospel," the dissolution of families (13:9–13), and standard, end-time Jewish apocalyptic signs (13:14–37). He stresses, however, that this time will be short (13:20) and that his hearers will find salvation if they endure (13:13, 30). The closing exhortation to "watch" recalls Paul's appeal in *1 Thess.* 5:12–22.

Chapters 14–15 deal with the last two days of Jesus' life. With the help of the traitor Judas Iscariot, *Mark*'s Jewish leaders arrest and try him, disregarding any notion of due process because of their deep animosity. They deliberately seek out false witnesses (14:55–58). When they finally force Jesus to admit that he is the son of God, they accuse him of blasphemy, spit on him and beat him (14:59–65). Once they have decided on Jesus' fate, they manipulate the Roman governor, portrayed as a shrewd judge of human character who sees through their envy (15:10), to have him crucified.

If the Jews have now succeeded in their plot, what about Jesus' family and students? Do they finally redeem themselves in *Mark*'s trial narrative? Apparently not.

One of the students present throughout his teaching and cures, Judas, immediately betrays him for money (14:10–11). Jesus claims that *all* his students will quickly fall away (14:27). Although Peter and others object to this charge, that is exactly what they do. While Jesus prays in his spiritual agony, they repeatedly fall asleep (14:37, 40–41), unable to stay alert even one hour with Jesus. At the critical moment all of them desert him (14:50). Peter, who was most vocal in claiming loyalty to Jesus, is singled out for special narrative treatment. He denies knowing Jesus, not once but three times; when he realizes what he has done, he breaks down crying (14:66–72). That is the last we hear of the disciples in the story. They are not rehabilitated.

Neither are the women who were close to Jesus, including his mother. Mary ("the mother of James the younger and Joses," 15:40) watches the crucifixion from a distance and joins with other women in buying spices to prepare Jesus' body for burial (15:47; 16:1). Mary's actions at the time of Jesus' death represent common familial obligations and do not necessarily suggest that she has come to follow Jesus. Unaware of Jesus' promised resurrection, she expects to ask someone to roll the stone away for her (16:3). So she is surprised when she finds the stone rolled away and Jesus gone (16:4–6). *Mark* ends with the notice that she and the others "fled from the tomb; for trembling and astonishment had come upon them; and they said nothing to anyone, for they were afraid" (16:8).

Importance and Relation to Other Texts

Let us now try to locate *Mark* along the spectrum of early Christian views that we have begun to develop on the basis of Paul's letters. It appears from Paul's letters that he championed a kind of Christianity that was rejected by various other Christians. He rejected these other views as if they presented "another Jesus" and a "different gospel altogether" (*Gal.* 1:6), and many non-Pauline Christians disavowed his mission too. Issues in those early disputes included: the whole relationship of Christianity to Jewish culture and tradition; the status of Jesus' original students (including Peter/Cephas), Jesus' brothers James and Jude, and those accredited by them; the significance of Jesus' death, resurrection, and imminent return as instruments of salvation (Paul)—in relation to Jesus' roles as Jewish Messiah and wisdom teacher; and the related question, whether Christian salvation issued primarily in present wisdom or a secure afterlife.

If we read *Mark* against this background, we discover a text that extends Paul's "announcement" or "gospel" into a comprehensive story. In this account, Jesus' mission is fulfilled in his saving death, resurrection, and imminent return in glory. He comes into a Jewish world that rejects him from the start, failing to understand his "new teaching" and unique authority. He abrogates Jewish law by his own authority, and finds his best reception among Gentiles. The last word on Jesus' identity is given to a Roman centurion: "Truly this man was God's son" (15:39). Jesus' own mother and brothers—his famous brother James is mentioned three times—are part and parcel of the unresponsive Jewish environment. Although Jesus tries hard to create a faithful, inner core of students who will understand him, they consistently fail because they lack spiritual perception. While they are consumed with claims to special status, other true followers of Jesus are faithfully doing his work.

Mark appears, then, as a kind of Pauline interpretation of Jesus. Jesus represents something radically new. His coming marks the end of Jewish culture. It also involves suffering and turmoil for his elect ones now, in the brief interim before his return, but glory afterward.

Notwithstanding all of the studies that have elucidated *Mark*'s literary and theological concerns, most scholars still concede that the earliest gospel is the least perfectly edited of those that have survived. It seems to leave more loose ends—in terms of story line, literary style, and theological coherence—than the others. Nevertheless, this clumsiness can no longer be mistaken for naive reporting.

For Further Reading

Anderson, Janice Capel, and Stephen D. Moore. *Mark and Method: New Approaches in Biblical Studies*. Minneapolis: Fortress, 1992.

Best, Ernest. *Mark: The Gospel as Story*. Edinburgh: T&T Clark, 1983.

Collins, Adela Yarbro. "Mark and His Readers: The Son of God among Jews." *Harvard Theological Review* 92 (1999): 393–408.

———. "Mark and His Readers: The Son of God among Greeks and Romans." *Harvard Theological Review* 93 (2000): 85–100.

Hooker, Morna D. *The Message of Mark*. London: Epworth, 1983.

Kelber, Werner H. *Mark's Story of Jesus*. Philadelphia: Fortress, 1979.

Mack, Burton L. *A Myth of Innocence: Mark and Christian Origins*. Philadelphia: Fortress, 1988.

Marxsen, Willi. *Mark the Evangelist*. Nashville: Abingdon, 1969.

Rhoads, David, and Donald Michie. *Mark as Story*. Philadelphia: Fortress, 1982.

Telford, William, ed. *The Interpretation of Mark*. Philadelphia: Fortress, 1985.

Weeden, Theodore J., Jr. *Mark: Traditions in Conflict*. Philadelphia: Fortress, 1971.

THE GOSPEL ACCORDING TO
MARK

The Proclamation of John the Baptist

1 The beginning of the good news*a* of Jesus Christ, the Son of God.*b*

2 As it is written in the prophet Isaiah,*c*
"See, I am sending my messenger ahead of you,*d*
    who will prepare your way;
3 the voice of one crying out in the wilderness:
    'Prepare the way of the Lord,
        make his paths straight,'"

4 John the baptizer appeared*e* in the wilderness, proclaiming a baptism of repentance for the forgiveness of sins. 5 And people from the whole Judean countryside and all the people of Jerusalem were going out to him, and were baptized by him in the river Jordan, confessing their sins. 6 Now John was clothed with camel's hair, with a leather belt around his waist, and he ate locusts and wild honey. 7 He proclaimed, "The one who is more powerful than I is coming after me; I am not worthy to stoop down and untie the thong of his sandals. 8 I have baptized you with*f* water; but he will baptize you with*f* the Holy Spirit."

---

a Or *gospel*
b Other ancient authorities lack *the Son of God*
c Other ancient authorities read *in the prophets*
d Gk *before your face*
e Other ancient authorities read *John was baptizing*

f Or *in*

1:1 *The beginning of the good news of Jesus Christ, the Son of God* This is not an opening sentence but a title for the work. The title that appears in modern Bibles, "The Gospel according to Mark," is not an original part of the text. It was added by the church fathers. Although we have come to know the first four documents of the NT as "gospels," the author of *Mark* is the only one to use this term in relation to his writing. But even he does not call the text itself a gospel. His readers already know the *good news,* or "gospel" ("announcement"; *euangelion*), of Jesus' saving death, resurrection, and return; he will now explain to them how this good news came about—its beginning in Jesus' life and deeds. As often in Paul's writings, *Christ* appears here as a proper name rather than as the title "Messiah"; this may suggest a chiefly non-Jewish audience. **1:2** *Isaiah* The quotation is actually a composite of *Mal.* 3:1 (paraphrased) and LXX *Isa.* 40:3. *Matt.* 3:3 and *Luke* 3:4 both correct *Mark* by omitting the words from *Malachi.* Numerous church fathers and copyists tried to correct *Mark*'s text by emending it to read "written in the prophets" instead of *in the prophet Isaiah. See . . . your way* This part of the quotation paraphrases *Mal.* 3:1. Thus, whereas *Malachi* has God threatening imminent judgment and sending a herald before God arrives, *Mark* has God promising to send a herald before Jesus. **1:3** *Isa.* 40:3. Only the LXX, the Gk translation of the Jewish scripture, which *Mark* follows here, has a voice crying in the wilderness; it drops the parallelism found in the Hebrew poetry of *Isaiah.* The Hebrew version ("Clear in the desert a road for the Lord!") was important for some other Jewish groups of Jesus' time, notably those behind the Dead Sea Scrolls (1QS 7.15), who literally retreated to the desert, as John did. **1:4** *the baptizer* Only *Mark* uses this title for John (see 6:14, 24), who was better known as "the Baptist," as *Mark* also calls him elsewhere. In Jewish circles, John was remembered as a famous preacher in his own right, not as an associate of Jesus. See Josephus, *Ant.* 18.116–119. *baptism of repentance for the forgiveness of sins* This is a dense formulation: "immersion of rethinking, for [or 'leading to'] the forgiveness of failures." Evidently, several of these peculiar terms were already familiar, with technical Christian senses, to *Mark*'s readers. "Rethinking" or "change of mind" (repentance) was also a common theme among moral philosophers of the day. **1:5** *people from* Not in the Gk. *confessing their sins* Or "acknowledging their failures." **1:6** For Jewish readers, John's dress and diet would have recalled the fiery biblical prophets who announced God's impending judgment; they, too, wore uncomfortable hairy shirts and belts of skin (*2 Kgs.* 1:8; *Zech.* 13:4). Elijah presents the closest parallel to John; this is significant because Jesus will later claim that John was Elijah (*Mark* 9:11–13). Biblically illiterate Gentile readers might have understood John as a devoted philosopher who practiced the simplicity that he taught (see Josephus, *Life* 11). **1:7** Given that John was remembered as a famous preacher in his own right (see note to 1:4), he may not have preached mainly about Jesus (*Acts* 19:2–4). Instead he probably preached about broader themes of coming judgment and was later made to focus on Jesus by the author of *Mark* and other early Christians. Untying the sandal thongs of a guest in preparation for foot washing—entailing the humiliation of stooping and handling dirty feet—was something that a household slave would do. *Mark*'s portrayal of John's extreme self-effacement here might be an attempt to win an endorsement of Christianity from the famous preacher, or it might reflect competition between John's and Jesus' followers at the time of *Mark*'s composition. **1:8** *Matt.* 3:11–12 and *Luke* 3:16–17—hence Q?—have John contrasting his immersion in water with a coming immersion in the fire of judgment. The sense is this: If you have trouble with an immersion in water now, wait until the immersion in fire arrives! *Mark*'s version has an entirely different sense; it predicts the Christian reception of a holy Spirit at a later date and suggests a connection between this and water immersion. This connection was a widespread Christian expectation. See *Acts* 2:38; 10:44–48; 19:5–6.

The Baptism of Jesus

9In those days Jesus came from Nazareth of Galilee and was baptized by John in the Jordan. 10And just as he was coming up out of the water, he saw the heavens torn apart and the Spirit descending like a dove on him. 11And a voice came from heaven, "You are my Son, the Beloved;*g* with you I am well pleased."

The Temptation of Jesus

12And the Spirit immediately drove him out into the wilderness. 13He was in the wilderness forty days, tempted by Satan; and he was with the wild beasts; and the angels waited on him.

The Beginning of the Galilean Ministry

14Now after John was arrested, Jesus came to Galilee, proclaiming the good news*h* of God,*i* 15and saying,

"The time is fulfilled, and the kingdom of God has come near;*j* repent, and believe in the good news."*h*

Jesus Calls the First Disciples

16As Jesus passed along the Sea of Galilee, he saw Simon and his brother Andrew casting a net into the sea—for they were fishermen. 17And Jesus said to them, "Follow me and I will make you fish for people." 18And immediately they left their nets and followed him. 19As he went a little farther, he saw James son of Zebedee and his brother John, who were in their boat mending the nets. 20Immediately he called them; and they left their father Zebedee in the boat with the hired men, and followed him.

The Man with an Unclean Spirit

21They went to Capernaum; and when the sabbath came, he entered the synagogue and taught.

g Or *my beloved Son*
h Or *gospel*
i Other ancient authorities read *of the kingdom*

j Or *is at hand*

1:9 Nazareth was an obscure agricultural village of fewer than five hundred inhabitants; it lay, however, just four miles southeast of Sepphoris, a leading city of Galilee (along with Tiberias, which was built in 20 C.E.). Several independent gospel traditions trace Jesus' family to Nazareth. In coming to John, Jesus moved from one administrative district to another: from the jurisdiction of the ethnarch Herod Antipas, son of King Herod the Great, to Judea, which was governed directly by the Romans since 6 C.E. and whose governor prefect was Pontius Pilate. **1:11** The heavenly voice recalls both *Ps.* 2:7 ("you are my son; today I have given you birth," addressed to the king of Israel) and *Isa.* 42:1 ("my chosen one, in whom I delight" [MT], speaking of God's Suffering Servant). But the parallels are probably not close enough to require that the author means to combine divine-sonship and Suffering Servant themes here. **1:13** The numbers four and four hundred were significant in the Bible; note especially that Moses, too, spent forty days fasting in the presence of God and in the wilderness while he received the laws (*Exod.* 34:28). The Gk word for *tempted* could suggest either testing, in the sense of proving, or an effort to seduce or draw away. **1:14** *after John was arrested* The author's failure to explain anything about John's arrest at this point (he describes it in 6:17) seems to have impressed the author of *Luke*, who includes a brief elaboration here (Luke 3:19). Jesus begins his mission only after John's arrest. Perhaps he worked with John up to that point. See *John* 3:22–4:4. *Jesus came to Galilee* See 1:9. *good news of God* The author promised in the title to relate the origins of the good news. He takes a major step forward now by having Jesus proclaim the good news, but he has not yet defined it—unless it is that "the kingdom of God has come near" (1:15). **1:15** *kingdom of God* In Hebrew and Jesus' native Aramaic, the phrase would mean something closer to "reign [or 'rule' or 'sovereignty'] of God" (see *Ps.* 93:1; 96:10; 97:1; 99:1); it is not a certain geographical kingdom but God's rule that is about to begin. The hoped-for reign of God is especially prominent in *Isaiah* 40–55, where it is indeed the "good tidings" or "good news" to be proclaimed (40:9; 52:7). **1:16** *Sea of Galilee* A lake, known locally as the Sea of Kinneret or the Lake of Gennesaret, within the Jordan River valley. *Luke* (e.g., 5:1, 2; 8:22) corrects *Mark* by using the latter name. Today the lake is about 12.5 miles long (north-south) and 7 miles wide. It sits about fifteen miles from Jesus' village, Nazareth. *Simon and his brother Andrew* The author will later note (3:16) that Jesus gave Simon the name Peter (Gk *petros*, "stone" or "rock"). In Jesus' native Aramaic, this name was *Kefa* (Cephas), and Simon was known to the later church mainly as Peter or Cephas: *1 Cor.* 9:5; *Gal.* 1:18; 2:9. *Matt.* 16:13–20 connects the nickname with Jesus' saying that Simon would be the rock upon which the church was to be built, but the author of *Mark* seems not to know this tradition (see the parallel story in *Mark* 8:27–30). *John* preserves a different story altogether: Andrew was a student of John the Baptist's who, after discovering Jesus, introduced his brother Simon to him; Jesus gave Simon the name Cephas at their first meeting (*John* 1:41–42). *John* also claims that the brothers were from Bethsaida (1:44), whereas *Mark* makes Capernaum their hometown (1:21, 29). **1:19** James and John also became leading figures in the early church. James was executed by the Judean king Agrippa I (r. 41–44 C.E.; see *Acts* 12:2–3). John went on to become one of the three "pillars" based in Jerusalem—along with Jesus' brother James and Simon Peter (*Gal.* 2:9). **1:21** *Capernaum* Means "village of Nahum." It was located near the north end of Lake Gennesar (Sea of Galilee), a day's walk (about twenty-one miles as the crow flies) from Nazareth. *entered the synagogue* The author does not explain the basis on which Jesus might have addressed the synagogue membership—as an acknowledged teacher, as a lay reader of the scriptures, or as the uniquely powerful Son of God who simply did what he chose to do. The context (1:22) might suggest the last option. *Luke* 4:16–21 has Jesus—after sitting down—give a brief addendum to the scripture he read while standing. Extensive remains of a substantial

22They were astounded at his teaching, for he taught them as one having authority, and not as the scribes. 23Just then there was in their synagogue a man with an unclean spirit, 24and he cried out, "What have you to do with us, Jesus of Nazareth? Have you come to destroy us? I know who you are, the Holy One of God." 25But Jesus rebuked him, saying, "Be silent, and come out of him!" 26And the unclean spirit, convulsing him and crying with a loud voice, came out of him. 27They were all amazed, and they kept on asking one another, "What is this? A new teaching—with authority! He[k] commands even the unclean spirits, and they obey him." 28At once his fame began to spread throughout the surrounding region of Galilee.

Jesus Heals Many at Simon's House

29As soon as they[l] left the synagogue, they entered the house of Simon and Andrew, with James and John. 30Now Simon's mother-in-law was in bed with a fever, and they told him about her at once. 31He came and took her by the hand and lifted her up. Then the fever left her, and she began to serve them.

32That evening, at sundown, they brought to him all who were sick or possessed with demons. 33And the whole city was gathered around the door. 34And he cured many who were sick with various diseases, and cast out many demons; and he would not permit the demons to speak, because they knew him.

A Preaching Tour in Galilee

35In the morning, while it was still very dark, he got up and went out to a deserted place, and there he prayed. 36And Simon and his companions hunted for him. 37When they found him, they said to him, "Everyone is searching for you." 38He answered, "Let us go on to the neighboring towns, so that I may proclaim the message there also; for that is what I came out to do." 39And he went throughout Galilee, proclaiming the message in their synagogues and casting out demons.

Jesus Cleanses a Leper

40A leper[m] came to him begging him, and kneeling[n] he said to him, "If you choose, you can make

---

k Or *A new teaching! With authority he*
l Other ancient authorities read *he*

m The terms *leper* and *leprosy* can refer to several diseases
n Other ancient authorities lack *kneeling*

4th- or 5th-century synagogue have been found at Capernaum; the 1st-century synagogue apparently stood on the same site. According to *Luke* 7:1–5, the synagogue at Capernaum was built by a centurion who was friendly toward the Jews. **1:22 *the scribes*** A group defined not by doctrine and regimen, such as the Pharisees, Sadducees, and Essenes, but by occupation—copying, studying, and teaching sacred texts. Every faction, including the priests and the groups mentioned above, would have needed its own scribes. This author does not provide a clear picture of the scribes he writes about; they are leading teachers of the laws, sometimes linked with the Pharisees (2:16; 7:1, 5; 12:38), more often with the Jerusalem temple authorities (3:22; 8:31; 10:33; 11:18, 27; 14:1, 43, 53; 15:1, 31). **1:23 *Just then*** Lit. "And immediately." This is *Mark*'s characteristic connector. ***their*** Here it could simply mean the people of Capernaum, or it might reflect the time of the author, when it would be understood by his readers as the Jews. See 1:39. ***a man with an unclean spirit*** That Jesus begins his fateful battle with the evil spirits in the synagogue may reflect *Mark*'s narrative interests. Spirit possession was understood throughout the ancient Mediterranean to be the cause of much sickness and evil (see 3:10–11; see 1QS 3.22–24). Such possession was most evident in mental illnesses in which the afflicted spoke or acted in strange ways (with inappropriate emotion, volume, or tone), for it seemed that some other being had taken over their mind or breath. Epilepsy, muteness, deafness, blindness, and spinal disorders are attributed to demonic activity in the gospels, and the gospels typically speak of Jesus' cures and exorcisms in the same breath, even asserting that he cast the demons out of those who were brought to him sick (1:32–34). Various groups and teachers—Greek, Persian, Jewish, Christian—claimed to have the most effective cures for such problems. See Josephus, *Ant.* 8.41–44; Philostratus, *Vit. Apoll.* 4.20. Less common and more desirable was possession by a good (clean, holy) spirit, which could also co-opt one's voice for its purposes; see *1 Cor.* 12:7–8; 14:2, 14, 23. **1:24 *with us*** This one unclean spirit speaks on behalf of his entire class. ***I know who you are*** The author here creates the conditions for a cosmic battle acted out on the human stage—a scenario familiar to the ancient reader (see Homer's *Iliad* and *Odyssey*). Jesus Son of God is taking on the evil spirits, who realize immediately that their days are numbered. **1:25 *Be silent*** The author here initiates the theme of Jesus' secret identity, which can only be revealed after his resurrection from the dead. See 8:27–30; 9:9. **1:27 *A new teaching—with authority*** Much like Paul, this author presents Jesus' arrival as something essentially new, in radical conflict with existing Judaism. ***commands even the unclean spirits*** Jesus' powers of exorcism are credentials of his divine origin. Interestingly, the Jewish author Josephus makes the same kind of claim for Judaism: its unique powers testify to its divine charter (*Ant.* 8.41–44). A problem is that elsewhere the author concedes that the ability to work cures was not seen by others as irrefutable evidence of divine origin; see 3:2; see *Matt.* 12:27. **1:29 *As soon as*** Lit. "And immediately." This is *Mark*'s characteristic connector. **1:31 *she began to serve them*** Although modern readers might expect the men to take care of her, since she has just recovered from illness, the author's point seems to be that because she was immediately able to resume the role expected of a woman in his day, the cure must have been completely effective. **1:32** Notice the close connection between sickness and spirit possession; see note to 1:23. **1:39 *their*** See note to 1:23. **1:40 *leper*** The Gk word here, *lepros,* can refer to someone afflicted with any number of skin diseases, such as eczema, psoriasis, and seborrhea. What we know as leprosy today does not match biblical descriptions (e.g.,

me clean." [41]Moved with pity,[o] Jesus[p] stretched out his hand and touched him, and said to him, "I do choose. Be made clean!" [42]Immediately the leprosy[q] left him, and he was made clean. [43]After sternly warning him he sent him away at once, [44]saying to him, "See that you say nothing to anyone; but go, show yourself to the priest, and offer for your cleansing what Moses commanded, as a testimony to them." [45]But he went out and began to proclaim it freely, and to spread the word, so that Jesus[p] could no longer go into a town openly, but stayed out in the country; and people came to him from every quarter.

Jesus Heals a Paralytic

2 When he returned to Capernaum after some days, it was reported that he was at home. [2]So many gathered around that there was no longer room for them, not even in front of the door; and he was speaking the word to them. [3]Then some people[r] came, bringing to him a paralyzed man, carried by four of them. [4]And when they could not bring him to Jesus because of the crowd, they removed the roof above him; and after having dug through it, they let down the mat on which the paralytic lay. [5]When Jesus saw their faith, he said to the paralytic, "Son, your sins are forgiven." [6]Now some of the scribes were sitting there, questioning in their hearts, [7]"Why does this fellow speak in this way? It is blasphemy! Who can forgive sins but God alone?" [8]At once Jesus perceived in his spirit that they were discussing these questions among themselves; and he said to them, "Why do you raise such questions in your hearts? [9]Which is easier, to say to the paralytic, 'Your sins are forgiven,' or to say, 'Stand up and take your mat and walk'? [10]But so that you may know that the Son of Man has authority on earth to forgive sins"—he said to the paralytic— [11]"I say to you, stand up, take your mat and go to your home." [12]And he stood up, and immediately took the mat and went out before all of them; so that they were all amazed and glorified God, saying, "We have never seen anything like this!"

Jesus Calls Levi

[13]Jesus[s] went out again beside the sea; the whole crowd gathered around him, and he taught them.

o Other ancient authorities read *anger*
p Gk *he*
q The terms *leper* and *leprosy* can refer to several diseases
r Gk *they*

s Gk *He*

Lev. 13:1–59) of the ailment that has traditionally been translated as "leprosy" in English Bibles. Ancient Gk writers usually called the disease we know as leprosy *elephantiasis*. These lesser skin diseases caused considerable fear: the houses of those suspected of carrying the disease were quarantined; those determined to be afflicted were required to live outside the community borders; and those claiming to be cured were not admitted back to full communal participation until they had undergone examination by priests and a weeklong series of purifications. See *Lev.* 14:1–32. **1:41** Jesus thus breaks the strong taboo against contact with "lepers." **1:44** See notes to 1:25 and 1:40. **2:1–12** The healing of the paralytic is the first of five controversy stories that the author has strung together (2:1–3:6). They conclude with a plot hatched by certain leading Jews to kill Jesus (3:6). Thus Jesus' death at the hands of religious and political adversaries is anticipated early (according to *Mark*); this is the "beginning of the good news" (1:1). **2:1** *at home* Although the author does not expressly state it, the reader should probably understand that Jesus has quietly moved from Nazareth to Capernaum (1:9, 24). **2:2** Given the size of ordinary houses in ancient Capernaum (perhaps fifteen by twenty feet) and their arrangement in connected blocks, this observation would not necessarily indicate a large crowd. Nevertheless, the author envisions a huge crowd (1:33). **2:4** *having dug through it* The author supposes that the roof was made in common Palestinian style, with wooden beams covered by packed mud. These were solid enough to walk on; the archaeology of Capernaum has turned up stairs leading to household roofs. *Luke* 5:19 presents a different picture, of a tiled roof. **2:6** *scribes* See note to 1:22. **2:7** *blasphemy* The Gk word used here is quite elastic in meaning: almost any kind of unseemly speech about another person, an insult, was blasphemy. See also 14:64. But Jesus does not commit blasphemy in the technical sense of (at least later) Jewish law, which understood the crime exclusively as pronouncing the sacred name of God (*m. Sanhedrin* 7:5). This was punishable by death. It could not have been an offense, however, either to forgive sins or to call oneself God's son, since we have parallels for both in mainstream Jewish literature of the time; see *Wis.* 2:13, 18 and note to 2:10. **2:9** That is, the supernatural cure proves Jesus' divine origin and ability to forgive sins. **2:10** *Son of Man* A much-debated phrase that reads awkwardly in Gk ("the son of the man"); it appears to be drawn from Hebrew and Aramaic usage. The author of *Mark* assumes that it is some kind of honorific title (esp. 8:38; 15:62), and scholars also used to think, on the basis of *Dan.* 7:13 and post-Christian passages in *1 Enoch*, that Jews of Jesus' time commonly recognized a heavenly and/or messianic figure with the title "Son of Man." But study of parallel Semitic phrases has shown that elsewhere the phrase typically means "humanity," "a human being," or "I." Even here, Jesus' meaning (as distinct from *Mark's*) might well have been that human beings have the ability to forgive sins. Jewish literature of the period, such as the fragmentary *Prayer of Nabonidus* among the Dead Sea Scrolls (4QprNab ar), shows Jews declaring sins forgiven.

¹⁴As he was walking along, he saw Levi son of Alphaeus sitting at the tax booth, and he said to him, "Follow me." And he got up and followed him.

¹⁵And as he sat at dinner[t] in Levi's[u] house, many tax collectors and sinners were also sitting[v] with Jesus and his disciples—for there were many who followed him. ¹⁶When the scribes of[w] the Pharisees saw that he was eating with sinners and tax collectors, they said to his disciples, "Why does he eat[x] with tax collectors and sinners?" ¹⁷When Jesus heard this, he said to them, "Those who are well have no need of a physician, but those who are sick; I have come to call not the righteous but sinners."

The Question about Fasting

¹⁸Now John's disciples and the Pharisees were fasting; and people[y] came and said to him, "Why do John's disciples and the disciples of the Pharisees fast, but your disciples do not fast?" ¹⁹Jesus said to them, "The wedding guests cannot fast while the bridegroom is with them, can they? As long as they have the bridegroom with them, they cannot fast. ²⁰The days will come when the bridegroom is taken away from them, and then they will fast on that day.

²¹"No one sews a piece of unshrunk cloth on an old cloak; otherwise, the patch pulls away from it, the new from the old, and a worse tear is made. ²²And no

---

t Gk *reclined*
u Gk *his*
v Gk *reclining*
w Other ancient authorities read *and*
x Other ancient authorities add *and drink*

y Gk *they*

2:14 *Levi* Although he is the fifth student called—and with the same language as were Simon, Andrew, James, and John—this Levi will not appear among the twelve apostles named in 3:14–19. The author of *Matthew* seems to have noticed this, for he gives the tax collector a name that does appear in *Mark*'s apostle list, namely, Matthew (*Matt.* 9:9). **tax booth** Since he seems to be staffing a one-person tax booth, Levi appears to be imagined by the author as a collector of tolls on goods in transit—an important component of the comprehensive Roman taxation system. Capernaum was within the tetrarchy of Herod Antipas but close to the border of Philip's region, so it would have been a likely spot for such a booth. **2:15** *sat at dinner* People in the ancient Mediterranean did not sit at a table to eat. The Gk verb means "to recline," as on a couch—leaning on the left elbow and holding food (from a small central table) with the right hand. Poorer people typically sat on stools to eat, with no tables. *Levi's* Lit. "his." Since the tax collector has left to follow Jesus, one might suppose that Jesus' house was meant. *Luke* 5:29 clarifies the issue by having Levi put on a feast in his house. **tax collectors and sinners** Jesus and his contemporaries were subject to a wide variety of taxes, including personal and land taxes, tolls on transported goods, and tithes ("tenths") for the upkeep of the hereditary priesthood. In Galilee the personal and land taxes were collected by agents of Herod Antipas, in Judea by officials of the Roman prefect; taxes on transported goods and food production were probably farmed out to wealthy businessmen. *Tax collectors*, therefore, might be these wealthy individuals, supervisors of various ranks in the Roman (and, in Galilee, the Herodian) tax structure, or the actual collectors. Tax collection jobs were commonly despised because of their associations with violence, corruption, and abuse; because of Roman oppression, since much of the money went to pay tribute to Rome; and because of the burdensome scale of taxation. *Tax collectors and sinners* was an easy association. It was characteristic of Jesus' career, according to all sources, that he deliberately chose to associate with such social misfits. **2:16** *the scribes of the Pharisees* See note to 1:22. The Pharisees were the most popular of the Jewish schools known to us. They seem to have combined a concern for devotion to God's laws with a humane and manageable system of observance. Alongside scripture, they gave some authority to the living tradition passed along by their teachers (Josephus, *Ant.* 13.297–298; 18.12–15). They seem to have had a particular concern with the Bible's teaching about purity, and they may even have supposed that all Jews should emulate the special requirements of the priesthood. In contrast with the Sadducees but in keeping with common views, they accepted the notion of an afterlife with rewards and punishments. Little else is known about the Pharisees; the gospels are primary sources, along with the writings of Josephus and early rabbinic literature. **2:17** In Jesus' day, philosophy was often viewed as medicine for sick souls; the philosophical lecture hall was a hospital. See *Luke* 4:23; Epictetus, *Discourses* 3.23.30. The sentiment expressed here, that philosopher-physicians should go where the *sick* are, was current: see Diogenes Laertius, *Lives of the Eminent Philosophers* 2.70; 6.6. **2:18** *John's disciples* This observation about the continuation of John's students as a group after his arrest and about the differences of practice between them and Jesus' followers is one of many clues that John's career was independent of Jesus'; see *Mark* 6:29; *Matt.* 11:2; *Acts* 19:1–6; Josephus, *Ant.* 18.116–119. We should probably not imagine that the historical John saw his role primarily as paving the way for Jesus. See note to 1:7. *Pharisees were fasting* Only one day of the Jewish year was prescribed as a fast day in the Bible: the Day of Atonement (Yom Kippur), on the 10th day of the new year in the fall; *Lev.* 16:29. Fasts could be called at any other time, however, for purposes such as mourning or repentance. By the 1st century, it seems likely that many Jewish groups, including the Pharisees, had adopted more routine fast days; see *Did.* 8.1. **2:18–20** Within a generation or two of Jesus' life, many Christian groups had indeed adopted routine fasts; *Matt.* 6:16–18; *Did.* 8.1. The author of *Mark* perhaps knew this situation already. **2:19** *the bridegroom is with them* For Jesus as the groom of the church, see *2 Cor.* 11:2; *Eph.* 5:23–25; *John* 3:29; *Rev.* 19:7. **2:21–22** *Mark*'s point seems to be that Jesus' teaching, which is radically new (1:27), cannot be accommodated to the old established Jewish forms. Contrast the parallel passage in *Luke* 5:36–39, which favors the old.

one puts new wine into old wineskins; otherwise, the wine will burst the skins, and the wine is lost, and so are the skins; but one puts new wine into fresh wineskins."[z]

Pronouncement about the Sabbath

²³One sabbath he was going through the grainfields; and as they made their way his disciples began to pluck heads of grain. ²⁴The Pharisees said to him, "Look, why are they doing what is not lawful on the sabbath?" ²⁵And he said to them, "Have you never read what David did when he and his companions were hungry and in need of food? ²⁶He entered the house of God, when Abiathar was high priest, and ate the bread of the Presence, which it is not lawful for any but the priests to eat, and he gave some to his companions." ²⁷Then he said to them, "The sabbath was made for humankind, and not humankind for the sabbath; ²⁸so the Son of Man is lord even of the sabbath."

---

[z] Other ancient authorities lack *but one puts new wine into fresh wineskins*

The Man with a Withered Hand

3 Again he entered the synagogue, and a man was there who had a withered hand. ²They watched him to see whether he would cure him on the sabbath, so that they might accuse him. ³And he said to the man who had the withered hand, "Come forward." ⁴Then he said to them, "Is it lawful to do good or to do harm on the sabbath, to save life or to kill?" But they were silent. ⁵He looked around at them with anger; he was grieved at their hardness of heart and said to the man, "Stretch out your hand." He stretched it out, and his hand was restored. ⁶The Pharisees went out and immediately conspired with the Herodians against him, how to destroy him.

A Multitude at the Seaside

⁷Jesus departed with his disciples to the sea, and a great multitude from Galilee followed him; ⁸hearing all that he was doing, they came to him in great numbers from Judea, Jerusalem, Idumea, beyond the Jordan, and the region around Tyre and Sidon. ⁹He told his disciples to have a boat ready for him because of the crowd, so that they would not crush

---

2:23–24 Although harvesting one's fields was prohibited on the sabbath rest day (*Exod.* 34:21), Jewish groups of Jesus' day differed about the definition of such work. The practice described here was not an offense against the law but perhaps indicates a difference between Pharisees and other groups. **2:25–26** Actually, David ate the bread of the Presence before he became king, when Ahimelech was high priest (*1 Sam.* 21:1–6). Abiathar was high priest later, when David was king (*2 Sam.* 15:35). Both *Matthew* and *Luke,* while agreeing substantially with *Mark*'s story, omit the reference to Abiathar. **2:27–28** In the Markan and Lukan parallels, Jesus says that only the Son of Man is Lord of the Sabbath. *Mark* combines this exalted idea of Jesus' unique authority as Son of Man with the common observation (in Jewish literature) that the Sabbath was made for the benefit of humanity. This rather awkward combination of ideas supports the argument of many scholars (based largely on Jesus' underlying Aramaic) that the phrase "Son of Man" originally meant "I" or "humanity." See note to 2:10. **3:2** *They watched* The observers seem to be a vague amalgam of those attending this synagogue, the Pharisees and Herodians in general (3:6), and perhaps the scribes who have been present all along (2:6, 16). The author's vagueness creates a sense that Jesus was opposed by the Jewish people and their leaders as a whole, although it seems from other sources that the various groups did not easily cooperate with each other. *accuse him* The issue is not whether Jesus can heal but whether he does so on the Sabbath. This confirms that cures and exorcisms were by no means unique to Jesus and his followers (see 3:22–27; *Matt.* 12:27). **3:4** In later rabbinic Judaism, and no doubt already in Jesus' day, it was a clearly established principle that saving a life took precedence over Sabbath restrictions. Still, respecting the divine commandment to observe a day of rest meant that anything that could be done on another day, even "doing good," was to be avoided on the Sabbath. **3:6** This observation concludes the block of five controversy stories that began in 2:1. Thus, according to *Mark,* right at the beginning of his public career Jesus came into lethal conflict with the vaguely defined Jewish authorities—Pharisees, Herodians, scribes, synagogue leaders—because of disagreements about Sabbath observance and the right to forgive sins. This is historically problematic, since the offenses listed were matters of dispute among Jews of Jesus' day and, in any case, not grounds for capital punishment. *Mark*'s Jesus was committed to Sabbath observance; he simply debated, as others did, the proper definition of this observance. *Matthew* includes the same conflict stories but postpones them to a much later point in Jesus' career (*Matthew* 12). *Luke* omits this plot altogether, since *Luke*'s Jesus gets along fairly well with the Pharisees. *the Herodians* Their identity is unclear. They could be officials of Herod Antipas, in whose territory Jesus mainly worked, political partisans of his government, or connected to the family of the deceased King Herod in some other way. The author of *Matthew* may already have shared our ignorance, for he usually omits this name from his narrative (or substitutes another; *Matt.* 12:14; *Mark* 8:15 par. *Matt.* 16:6). He preserves it only once: *Mark* 12:13 par. *Matt.* 22:15. *Luke* does not mention the Herodians. **3:8** *Tyre and Sidon* These two coastal cities, two days' journey from Lake Gennesar, were already old and famous in Jesus' day. They had been major trading centers from the 2d millennium B.C.E., then capitals of the Phoenicians, who had built Carthage, Rome's old enemy. Jesus' attracting Gentile hearers from these cities to Galilee would have been remarkable; *Matt.* 4:25 substitutes the nearby Gentile cities of the Decapolis. In *Mark* 7:24, Jesus will later visit Tyre and Sidon to a warm reception.

him; [10]for he had cured many, so that all who had diseases pressed upon him to touch him. [11]Whenever the unclean spirits saw him, they fell down before him and shouted, "You are the Son of God!" [12]But he sternly ordered them not to make him known.

Jesus Appoints the Twelve

[13]He went up the mountain and called to him those whom he wanted, and they came to him. [14]And he appointed twelve, whom he also named apostles,[a] to be with him, and to be sent out to proclaim the message, [15]and to have authority to cast out demons. [16]So he appointed the twelve:[b] Simon (to whom he gave the name Peter); [17]James son of Zebedee and John the brother of James (to whom he gave the name Boanerges, that is, Sons of Thunder); [18]and Andrew, and Philip, and Bartholomew, and Matthew, and Thomas, and James son of Alphaeus, and Thaddaeus, and Simon the Cananaean, [19]and Judas Iscariot, who betrayed him.

Jesus and Beelzebul

Then he went home; [20]and the crowd came together again, so that they could not even eat. [21]When his family heard it, they went out to restrain him, for people were saying, "He has gone out of his mind."

[22]And the scribes who came down from Jerusalem said, "He has Beelzebul, and by the ruler of the demons he casts out demons." [23]And he called them to him, and spoke to them in parables, "How can Satan cast out Satan? [24]If a kingdom is divided against itself, that kingdom cannot stand. [25]And if a house is divided against itself, that house will not be able to stand. [26]And if Satan has risen up against himself and is divided, he cannot stand, but his end has come. [27]But no one can enter a strong man's house and plunder his property without first tying up the strong man; then indeed the house can be plundered.

[28]"Truly I tell you, people will be forgiven for their sins and whatever blasphemies they utter; [29]but whoever blasphemes against the Holy Spirit can never have forgiveness, but is guilty of an eternal sin"— [30]for they had said, "He has an unclean spirit."

The True Kindred of Jesus

[31]Then his mother and his brothers came; and standing outside, they sent to him and called him. [32]A crowd was sitting around him; and they said to him, "Your mother and your brothers and sisters[c] are outside, asking for you." [33]And he replied, "Who are my mother and my brothers?" [34]And looking at those who sat around him, he said, "Here are my mother and my brothers! [35]Whoever does the will of God is my brother and sister and mother."

---

a Other ancient authorities lack *whom he also named apostles*
b Other ancient authorities lack *So he appointed the twelve*

c Other ancient authorities lack *and sisters*

3:10–11 Notice the close connection between cures and exorcisms, on the assumption that illness is often caused by evil spirits. See note to 1:23. **3:12** See 1:25, 34. **3:14** *proclaim the message* This entire phrase translates one Gk verb; *the message* is not explicit in the Gk. **3:16–19** *Matt.* 10:1–4 has the same list of apostles' names (but see note to *Mark* 2:14). *Luke* 6:14–16 substitutes a second Judas, the "son of James," for *Mark's* Thaddeus and calls Simon a Zealot instead of a Cananaean. **3:16** *Simon . . . Peter* This is *Mark's* only reference about Simon's change of name; from now on, the author will refer to him as Peter (except in 14:37, where he quotes Jesus' direct address to "Simon"). **3:17** *Boanerges* It remains unclear how the author constructed this Gk word from the Aramaic or Hebrew words meaning *Sons of Thunder. Matthew* and *Luke,* characteristically, omit this strange term. **3:19** *Iscariot* Some kind of identifier, but the meaning is unclear; "man from Kerioth," "scoundrel," and "knife-wielding assassin" have been proposed. *who betrayed him* The author's introduction of this note here without explanation seems to suggest that his first readers already knew a version of the betrayal story; *1 Cor.* 11:23; *Mark* 14:43–50. *he went home* Evidently in Capernaum, not Nazareth; see 2:1 and note. **3:21** More literally: "And his folks, when they had heard, went out to restrain [or 'seize'] him, for they said, 'He has gone crazy.'" The Gk suggests that it was his family who questioned Jesus' sanity. This is one of the few sentences in *Mark* omitted by both *Matthew* and *Luke,* which seems to confirm that the authors of those gospels found it troublesome. It fits *Mark* well because the author wishes to dissociate Jesus from his family (e.g., James) and students (e.g., Peter) who assumed leadership of the church after Jesus' death. But *Matthew* and *Luke* offer much more favorable pictures of Jesus' family and students, beginning with the birth narratives and the angelic appearances to Jesus' parents. The authors of those texts could not reasonably claim that Jesus' family thought him crazy. Jesus' family members will be named only in 6:3: four brothers, his mother Mary, and unnamed sisters. **3:22** Thus the author ranges Jesus' family immediately alongside the Jerusalem scribes: both fail to understand Jesus, thinking that he is out of his mind. *Beelzebul* One of many names for the archdemon. Other names are Satan (3:23), Mastema, Beliar, and the devil. **3:28–30** It seems that *Mark* is presenting either the Jews as a whole or the Jewish leaders as guilty of an eternal, unforgivable sin. **3:28** *Truly I tell you* All of the gospels have Jesus using the Aramaic phrase "*Amen,* I tell you"; the NRSV translates *Amen* as "Truly." It was normal in Jewish circles for someone to say *Amen*—an expression of complete assent—in response to someone else's statement, and this practice was taken over by the Greek-speaking Christian churches (see *1 Cor.* 14:16). It seems to have been a characteristic of Jesus' speech that he expressed *Amen* of his own statements. **3:31** This return to Jesus' family after reference to other groups is typical of *Mark's* "sandwich," or A-B-A, technique: one story (B) is nested inside another (A). See, e.g., 5:21–35; 6:7–30; 11:12–20.

The Parable of the Sower

4 Again he began to teach beside the sea. Such a very large crowd gathered around him that he got into a boat on the sea and sat there, while the whole crowd was beside the sea on the land. ²He began to teach them many things in parables, and in his teaching he said to them: ³"Listen! A sower went out to sow. ⁴And as he sowed, some seed fell on the path, and the birds came and ate it up. ⁵Other seed fell on rocky ground, where it did not have much soil, and it sprang up quickly, since it had no depth of soil. ⁶And when the sun rose, it was scorched; and since it had no root, it withered away. ⁷Other seed fell among thorns, and the thorns grew up and choked it, and it yielded no grain. ⁸Other seed fell into good soil and brought forth grain, growing up and increasing and yielding thirty and sixty and a hundredfold." ⁹And he said, "Let anyone with ears to hear listen!"

The Purpose of the Parables

¹⁰When he was alone, those who were around him along with the twelve asked him about the parables. ¹¹And he said to them, "To you has been given the secret[d] of the kingdom of God, but for those outside, everything comes in parables; ¹²in order that

'they may indeed look, but not perceive,
     and may indeed listen, but not understand;
   so that they may not turn again and be
       forgiven.'"

¹³And he said to them, "Do you not understand this parable? Then how will you understand all the parables? ¹⁴The sower sows the word. ¹⁵These are the ones on the path where the word is sown: when they hear, Satan immediately comes and takes away the word that is sown in them. ¹⁶And these are the ones sown on rocky ground: when they hear the word, they immediately receive it with joy. ¹⁷But they have no root, and endure only for a while; then, when trouble or persecution arises on account of the word, immediately they fall away.[e] ¹⁸And others are those sown among the thorns: these are the ones who hear the word, ¹⁹but the cares of the world, and the lure of wealth, and the desire for other things come in and choke the word, and it yields nothing. ²⁰And these are the ones sown on the good soil: they hear the word and accept it and bear fruit, thirty and sixty and a hundredfold."

A Lamp under a Bushel Basket

²¹He said to them, "Is a lamp brought in to be put under the bushel basket, or under the bed, and not

---

d mystery

e Or stumble

4:1 the sea The Sea of Galilee (Lake Gennesar); see note to 1:16. **4:2** The author now offers three or four examples of Jesus' teaching, thus continuing his thematic arrangement of Jesus' career. Because he sees Jesus' significance primarily in his saving death, resurrection, and return—as does Paul—he is not much interested in Jesus as teacher. *Matthew* and *Luke* give much greater scope to Jesus' teaching and also value Jesus' Jewish environment more highly. **4:3–9** The parable of the sower is offered as the best example of Jesus' teaching in parables. It was famous in early Christianity and is found not only in the synoptic parallels but also in *Gospel of Thomas* 9 and *1 Clem.* 24.5—with no interpretation needed. Indeed, the image of teaching as disseminating seed on soil of varying degrees of fertility was common among philosophers of the period; see Plutarch, *Education of Children* 4.2.B–E. **4:10** A problematic sentence because Jesus is supposed to be offshore in a boat (4:1, see 4:35–36). *Matthew* removes the awkwardness by stating that the disciples came to Jesus to ask about the parable (13:10). *Luke* solves the problem by placing the entire scene on dry land (8:1–19). **4:11** The author here first indicates that Jesus' students were given a secret teaching. **4:12 in order that** This use of parables to obstruct understanding seems peculiar. The author of *Matthew* rejects *Mark* at this point, insisting that parables were given in order to facilitate understanding (13:34–35) because the outsiders could not otherwise understand (13:13). This quotation is from *Isa.* 6:9–10, as *Matt.* 13:14–15 clarifies: The image of ears that do not hear, however, also occurs in Greek literature: Aeschylus, *Prometheus Bound* 445. **4:13** An awkward sequence. Only one parable has so far been told, but Jesus' students are said to have asked about the parables in general (4:10). And now Jesus responds as if they had asked only about this parable; it is he who makes the connection with other parables. *Matthew* solves the problem by making the students' question and Jesus' answer relate to parables in general (13:10–13). *Luke* has both question and answer relate to this parable only (8:9–11). **4:14–20** It seems likely that this interpretation of the parable originated in the early church's preaching, because Jesus' parables do not normally carry interpretations, being themselves aids to interpretation. Furthermore, the parable stands alone, without interpretation, in the *Gospel of Thomas*, and the interpretation here in *Mark* seems to presuppose conditions that existed only in the early church, not during Jesus' career. **4:14 the word** A term used commonly in early Christianity to denote the announcement of Jesus' saving death, resurrection, and return (*1 Thess.* 1:6), but not otherwise used by Jesus himself. **4:15–18** These verses presuppose the conditions of early Christianity in which people fall away from the faith (*Heb.* 6:4–8; 10:26–31; Pliny, *Letters* 10.96). **4:16–17 persecution arises on account of the word** This scenario apparently was possible, and so these words would have been meaningful, only after Jesus' death. **4:18** The author of *Hebrews* uses the same imagery, of thistle-producing ground, to describe apostates from Christian faith (6:7–8). **4:19** For an example, see *2 Tim.* 4:10. **4:21–32** The author seems to have strung together various sayings of Jesus from different occasions to illustrate his characteristic way of speaking.

on the lampstand? 22For there is nothing hidden, except to be disclosed; nor is anything secret, except to come to light. 23Let anyone with ears to hear listen!" 24And he said to them, "Pay attention to what you hear; the measure you give will be the measure you get, and still more will be given you. 25For to those who have, more will be given; and from those who have nothing, even what they have will be taken away."

The Parable of the Growing Seed

26He also said, "The kingdom of God is as if someone would scatter seed on the ground, 27and would sleep and rise night and day, and the seed would sprout and grow, he does not know how. 28The earth produces of itself, first the stalk, then the head, then the full grain in the head. 29But when the grain is ripe, at once he goes in with his sickle, because the harvest has come."

The Parable of the Mustard Seed

30He also said, "With what can we compare the kingdom of God, or what parable will we use for it? 31It is like a mustard seed, which, when sown upon the ground, is the smallest of all the seeds on earth; 32yet when it is sown it grows up and becomes the greatest of all shrubs, and puts forth large branches, so that the birds of the air can make nests in its shade."

The Use of Parables

33With many such parables he spoke the word to them, as they were able to hear it; 34he did not speak to them except in parables, but he explained everything in private to his disciples.

Jesus Stills a Storm

35On that day, when evening had come, he said to them, "Let us go across to the other side." 36And leaving the crowd behind, they took him with them in the boat, just as he was. Other boats were with him. 37A great windstorm arose, and the waves beat into the boat, so that the boat was already being swamped. 38But he was in the stern, asleep on the cushion; and they woke him up and said to him, "Teacher, do you not care that we are perishing?" 39He woke up and rebuked the wind, and said to the sea, "Peace! Be still!" Then the wind ceased, and there was a dead calm. 40He said to them, "Why are you afraid? Have you still no faith?" 41And they were filled with great awe and said to one another, "Who then is this, that even the wind and the sea obey him?"

Jesus Heals the Gerasene Demoniac

5 They came to the other side of the sea, to the country of the Gerasenes.*f* 2And when he had stepped out of the boat, immediately a man out of the tombs with an unclean spirit met him. 3He lived among the tombs; and no one could restrain him any more, even with a chain; 4for he had often been restrained with shackles and chains, but the chains he wrenched apart, and the shackles he broke in pieces; and no one had the strength to subdue him. 5Night and day among the tombs and on the mountains he was always howling and bruising himself with stones. 6When he saw Jesus from a distance, he ran and bowed down before him; 7and he shouted at the top of his voice, "What have you to do with me, Jesus, Son of the Most High God? I adjure you by God, do not torment me." 8For he had said to him, "Come out of the man, you unclean spirit!" 9Then Jesus*g* asked him, "What is your name?" He replied, "My name is Legion;

---

f Other ancient authorities read *Gergesenes*; others, *Gadarenes*
g Gk *he*

4:26–32 These two parables of the kingdom of God present it as something that grows gradually from small beginnings. This image does not seem to fit well with *Mark*'s more prominent presentation of the kingdom as something that will arrive suddenly with Jesus' return (1:15; 9:1; 13; 14:25, 62). **4:30–32** The mustard seed (*brassica nigra*) is an annual herb that grows to a height between two and six feet. Since leaves grow out from the base of the stem, it makes some sense that birds find shade in the plant. See note at *Matt*. 13:31–32. **4:35** *other side* See note to 5:1. **4:40** It is perhaps an indictment of Jesus' students that he points out their fear even after he has calmed the storm. *Matt*. 8:25–27 rearranges the passage so that they are, understandably, afraid only before Jesus calms the storm. **5:1** *Mark*'s geography is as confusing to us as it was to ancient readers. *The other side* of the lake presumably indicates a point to the east or southeast, across the lake from Capernaum. But Gerasa was about thirty-five miles southeast of the lake. Even though these Greek cities of the "Decapolis" had large territories around them, Gerasa (Jerash) was too far away for this to make sense. *Matt*. 8:28 changes the place to Gadara, which is more plausible. Later copyists of *Mark* proposed Gergesa; no such place has yet been identified. **5:2** *immediately Mark*'s characteristic adverb is omitted by *Matthew* and *Luke*. *with an unclean spirit* See note to 1:23. The connection with mental illness is obvious here; see 5:15. **5:7** See 1:24. Throughout *Mark*, the spirits know Jesus' identity as Son of God and see him as the one who is about to bring their doom. **5:9** *Legion* A Roman army division, typically numbering about 5,300 soldiers, in ten cohorts of six centuries each (80 men in most centuries, five centuries of 160 in the

for we are many." [10]He begged him earnestly not to send them out of the country. [11]Now there on the hillside a great herd of swine was feeding; [12]and the unclean spirits[h] begged him, "Send us into the swine; let us enter them." [13]So he gave them permission. And the unclean spirits came out and entered the swine; and the herd, numbering about two thousand, rushed down the steep bank into the sea, and were drowned in the sea.

[14]The swineherds ran off and told it in the city and in the country. Then people came to see what it was that had happened. [15]They came to Jesus and saw the demoniac sitting there, clothed and in his right mind, the very man who had had the legion; and they were afraid. [16]Those who had seen what had happened to the demoniac and to the swine reported it. [17]Then they began to beg Jesus[i] to leave their neighborhood. [18]As he was getting into the boat, the man who had been possessed by demons begged him that he might be with him. [19]But Jesus[j] refused, and said to him, "Go home to your friends, and tell them how much the Lord has done for you, and what mercy he has shown you." [20]And he went away and began to proclaim in the Decapolis how much Jesus had done for him; and everyone was amazed.

A Girl Restored to Life and a Woman Healed

[21]When Jesus had crossed again in the boat[k] to the other side, a great crowd gathered around him; and he was by the sea. [22]Then one of the leaders of the synagogue named Jairus came and, when he saw him, fell at his feet [23]and begged him repeatedly, "My little daughter is at the point of death. Come and lay your hands on her, so that she may be made well, and live." [24]So he went with him.

And a large crowd followed him and pressed in on him. [25]Now there was a woman who had been suffering from hemorrhages for twelve years. [26]She had endured much under many physicians, and had spent all that she had; and she was no better, but rather grew worse. [27]She had heard about Jesus, and came up behind him in the crowd and touched his cloak, [28]for she said, "If I but touch his clothes, I will be made well." [29]Immediately her hemorrhage stopped; and she felt in her body that she was healed of her disease. [30]Immediately aware that power had gone forth from him, Jesus turned about in the crowd and said, "Who touched my clothes?" [31]And his disciples said to him, "You see the crowd pressing in on you; how can you say, 'Who touched me?'" [32]He looked all around to see who had done it. [33]But the woman, knowing what had happened to her, came in fear and trembling, fell down before him, and told him the whole truth. [34]He said to her, "Daughter, your faith has made you well; go in peace, and be healed of your disease."

---

h Gk *they*
i Gk *him*
j Gk *he*

k Other ancient authorities lack *in the boat*

---

privileged 1st cohort). The use of the term out of context perhaps suggests the common awareness of Roman military presence throughout the Mediterranean, such that any large number might be called a legion. **5:10** Here and in 5:12 the personal pronouns seem confused. Both *Matt.* 8:28–32 and *Luke* 8:28–31 eliminate the confusion, though in different ways. **5:12** According to the Bible and Jewish tradition, pigs were ritually unclean (*Deut.* 14:8). **5:13** The author assumes that Jesus is still by the lake; but see note to 5:1. **5:20** *Decapolis* Both Gerasa and Gadara were part of the Decapolis, or "ten-city area." These were self-governing Gentile cities east of the Jordan River, except for Scythopolis. They were organized according to Greek political principles and largely free from Roman intervention. Nevertheless, they belonged to the Roman province of Syria. Pliny the Elder (*Nat.* 5.74), writing in the 70s, notes that different authors include different cities in this group, and that there were not always ten. **5:21** *the other side* Presumably Capernaum, from which Jesus had departed to Gerasa. **5:22** *one of the leaders of the synagogue* Lit. "one of the synagogue leaders." The Gk term need not suggest that there was a single synagogue in question. The author may simply be suggesting that Jairus was "one of those Jewish synagogue presidents." *Jairus* The Hebrew name *Ya'ir* was common at the time. **5:25** Since the child has been portrayed as on the point of the death, the woman's interruption of Jesus adds tension to the story: Will Jesus make it to the girl in time? This menstrual flow would have rendered the woman ritually impure (*Lev.* 15:25–33)—a condition that excluded her and those who touched her from participation in the temple service in Jerusalem. Many Jews of the time aspired to live their entire lives under the constraints of temple-related purity, and so the woman's condition would have entailed a degree of social exclusion as well as physical discomfort. It is uncertain how much of this *Mark*'s Gentile readers would have understood, but the image of a man having this kind of close encounter with a sick woman might have occasioned surprise. **5:26** Perhaps the author of *Mark* has in mind the Bible's implicit condemnation of turning to physicians rather than to God for cures (*2 Chr.* 16:12–13). 1st-century physicians were unlicensed and mainly of low social standing; fees were high, cure rates low. Ridicule of physicians was common. Martial remarks that former physicians who were now undertakers or gladiators were doing essentially the same work (*Epigrams* 1.47; 8.74; see Pliny, *Natural History* 29.8.16–18). **5:27–31** The woman is able to get a cure from Jesus without his knowing, simply by virtue of the power that flows out from him. He realizes only that some power has left him. *Matthew* rearranges the story to make Jesus' word precede the cure (9:22).

35While he was still speaking, some people came from the leader's house to say, "Your daughter is dead. Why trouble the teacher any further?" 36But overhearing[l] what they said, Jesus said to the leader of the synagogue, "Do not fear, only believe." 37He allowed no one to follow him except Peter, James, and John, the brother of James. 38When they came to the house of the leader of the synagogue, he saw a commotion, people weeping and wailing loudly. 39When he had entered, he said to them, "Why do you make a commotion and weep? The child is not dead but sleeping." 40And they laughed at him. Then he put them all outside, and took the child's father and mother and those who were with him, and went in where the child was. 41He took her by the hand and said to her, "Talitha cum," which means, "Little girl, get up!" 42And immediately the girl got up and began to walk about (she was twelve years of age). At this they were overcome with amazement. 43He strictly ordered them that no one should know this, and told them to give her something to eat.

The Rejection of Jesus at Nazareth

6 He left that place and came to his hometown, and his disciples followed him. 2On the sabbath he began to teach in the synagogue, and many who heard him were astounded. They said, "Where did this man get all this? What is this wisdom that has been given to him? What deeds of power are being done by his hands! 3Is not this the carpenter, the son of Mary[m] and brother of James and Joses and Judas and Simon, and are not his sisters here with us?" And they took offense[n] at him. 4Then Jesus said to them, "Prophets are not without honor, except in their hometown, and among their own kin, and in their own house." 5And he could do no deed of power there, except that he laid his hands on a few sick people and cured them. 6And he was amazed at their unbelief.

The Mission of the Twelve

Then he went about among the villages teaching. 7He called the twelve and began to send them out two by two, and gave them authority over the unclean spirits. 8He ordered them to take nothing for their journey except a staff; no bread, no bag, no money in their belts; 9but to wear sandals and not to put on two tunics. 10He said to them, "Wherever you enter a house, stay there until you leave the place. 11If any place will not welcome you and they refuse to hear you, as you leave, shake off the dust that is on your feet as a testimony against them." 12So they went out and proclaimed that all should repent. 13They cast out many demons, and anointed with oil many who were sick and cured them.

---

l Or *ignoring;* other ancient authorities read *hearing*

m Other ancient authorities read *son of the carpenter and of Mary*
n Or *stumbled*

5:35 *Your daughter is dead* Tension reaches its height as Jesus, finally released from the woman, finds that the girl has died in the meantime. See note to 3:31. **5:37** *Peter and James and John* This is an inner circle of apostles that we will meet again in several important contexts, notably 9:2; 14:33 but also 10:28–41; 13:3. These are three of the four students 1st called by Jesus (1:16–20). Strangely, the 4th, Andrew, appears among the inner circle only in 13:3. The James in question here met an early death under King Agrippa (41–44 C.E.; Josephus, *Ant.* 20.200–202; *Acts* 12:1–3), while Peter and John, along with Jesus' brother James, remained recognized "pillars" of the Jerusalem church through the first Christian generation (*Gal.* 2:9). **5:41** Since *Mark*'s readers do not appear to speak Aramaic, it is difficult to see why the author includes these strange-sounding words (see also 7:34). We know, however, from the Gk magical papyri that many Gk speakers of the time were captivated by Hebrew/Aramaic phrases (or corruptions thereof), apparently believing that these ancient languages possessed effective powers. *Matt.* 9:25 and *Luke* 8:54 omit the Aramaic phrase. **5:43** The author continues his theme of secrecy; see note to 1:25, but see also 5:19. **6:1** *hometown* The Gk word's root meaning conveys the idea of ancestral home or place; presumably Nazareth, since Jesus' family members are known there. **6:2** *to teach* See 1:21; Jesus appears in *Mark* as freely teaching in the synagogue. **6:3** *carpenter* The Gk word *(tektōn)* refers to any kind of construction worker. Given Jesus' Galilean environment, it is possible that he worked in stone more than wood—perhaps on some of the major building projects in nearby Sepphoris. Note the absence of Joseph, whom *Mark* nowhere mentions. Both *Matthew* (13:55) and *Luke* (4:22) know Joseph from their infancy stories and so make Jesus his (*Matthew:* "the carpenter's") son. *And they took offense Luke* 4:16–30 has a much fuller tradition concerning Jesus' rejection at Nazareth. **6:4** This pivotal statement encapsulates *Mark*'s view of Jesus' relationship to his family and to Judaism—his ancestral home, his blood relatives, and his household (mother, brothers, and sisters). **6:5** *And he could do no . . . there* The author of *Matthew* (13:58) substitutes "And he did not do many might works there." **6:6–13** This is one of the most troublesome passages for the Two-Document Hypothesis because *Matt.* 10:1–14 and *Luke* 9:1–6 often agree with each other against *Mark* in their parallel versions. For the general problem, see introduction to BIOGRAPHY, ANECDOTE, AND HISTORY. **6:7** *two by two Matthew* and *Luke* omit this detail. *unclean spirits* See note to 1:23. **6:8** *except a staff Luke* 9:3 excludes the staff. **6:9** *to wear sandals Matt.* 10:10 excludes sandals. **6:10–11** See *Did.* 11.4–6; 12.1–2. **6:12** Thus the apostles extend Jesus' own mission (see 1:15). Since Jesus has not given any instructions about preaching, this comes as a bit of a surprise to the reader. Both *Matthew* (10:7) and *Luke* (9:2) introduce such a directive earlier in the narrative. **6:13** Olive oil was widely used in Jesus' world. It was important not only for cooking, bathing, and lighting, but also in religious ritual (*Exod.*

The Death of John the Baptist

14King Herod heard of it, for Jesus'[o] name had become known. Some were[p] saying, "John the baptizer has been raised from the dead; and for this reason these powers are at work in him." 15But others said, "It is Elijah." And others said, "It is a prophet, like one of the prophets of old." 16But when Herod heard of it, he said, "John, whom I beheaded, has been raised."

17For Herod himself had sent men who arrested John, bound him, and put him in prison on account of Herodias, his brother Philip's wife, because Herod[q] had married her. 18For John had been telling Herod, "It is not lawful for you to have your brother's wife." 19And Herodias had a grudge against him, and wanted to kill him. But she could not, 20for Herod feared John, knowing that he was a righteous and holy man, and he protected him. When he heard him, he was greatly perplexed;[r] and yet he liked to listen to him. 21But an opportunity came when Herod on his birthday gave a banquet for his courtiers and officers and for the leaders of Galilee. 22When his daughter Herodias[s] came in and danced, she pleased Herod and his guests; and the king said to the girl, "Ask me for whatever you wish, and I will give it." 23And he solemnly swore to her, "Whatever you ask me, I will give you, even half of my kingdom." 24She went out and said to her mother, "What should I ask for?" She replied, "The head of John the baptizer." 25Immediately she rushed back to the king and requested, "I want you to give me at once the head of John the Baptist on a platter." 26The king was deeply grieved; yet out of regard for his oaths and for the guests, he did not want to refuse her. 27Immediately the king sent a soldier of the guard with orders to bring John's[o] head. He went and beheaded him in the prison, 28brought his head on a platter, and gave it to the girl. Then the girl gave it to her mother. 29When his disciples heard about it, they came and took his body, and laid it in a tomb.

o Gk *his*
p Other ancient authorities read *He was*
q Gk *he*
r Other ancient authorities read *he did many things*
s Other ancient authorities read *the daughter of Herodias herself*

30:23–35; *1 Sam.* 10:1), as a perfume (*Song* 1:3), in burial preparations (*Luke* 23:56), as a valuable gift, and probably in popular cures and remedies (see *Jer.* 8:22: the "balm in Gilead"). It quickly became a practice of the early church to use oil in prayers for the sick (*Jas.* 5:14). *Mark*'s readers are familiar with the practice. Jesus himself could have initiated the practice, or *Mark* may have read early Christian practice back to Jesus' time. **6:14** ***King Herod*** Actually, Herod Antipas, son of King Herod. Antipas was not king but tetrarch ("quarter-ruler") of Galilee and Perea—only a portion of his father's kingdom. *Matthew* corrects *Mark* at first (*Matt.* 14:1) but then defaults to the language of its source (14:9). ***John the baptizer*** See note to 1:4. **6:15** The same three options concerning Jesus' identity will be offered in response to Jesus' direct question, a little later in the narrative, "Who do people say that I am?" (8:28). ***Elijah*** Some Jews of Jesus' time expected Elijah to return at the end of time because he had not died but ascended directly to heaven and because the Bible itself anticipated his return (*2 Kgs.* 2:10–12; *Mal.* 4:5–6; *Sir.* 48:1–14). Later in the narrative, Jesus will claim that John the Baptist was the returned Elijah (9:4, 11–13; see 8:28). **6:17** ***put him in prison*** The author finally explains his passing reference in 1:14. ***Herodias, his brother Philip's wife*** Philip was Antipas's brother and also a tetrarch—of regions to the north and northeast of Judea (see *Luke* 3:1)—but Herodias was not Philip's wife. She was the wife of another brother named Herod. Herodias's daughter Salome, the one who dances according to this story, was Philip's wife. See Josephus, *Ant.* 18.136. **6:18–20** According to Josephus, *Ant.* 18.118–119, Antipas imprisoned John because he feared his great popularity with the people and suspected that it would lead to sedition in unstable political times. *Mark*'s reason, that John had criticized the tetrarch's private marital arrangements, does not contradict Josephus's claim; such criticism might have made John's popularity seem especially threatening. But Josephus insists that Antipas himself, not his wife, had trouble with John. **6:20** ***protected him . . . liked to listen to him*** It is difficult to understand how the tetrarch, if he was indeed disturbed by John's popularity and stung by John's criticism of his marriage (see previous note), could have shown such favor to John. The authors of *Matthew* and *Luke* were apparently aware of the problem. *Matthew* claims, rather, that Herod "wanted to put him to death" (14:5). *Luke,* which seems to have had special information about Herod (*Luke* 8:3; *Acts* 13:1) and which implicates him as a consistent enemy of Jesus (13:31; 23:9–11), omits *Mark*'s story altogether. **6:21** The story suggests that the banquet was held at Antipas's capital in Galilee, Tiberias, since only Galilean officials are present. The story assumes (6:27–28) that the banquet and the prison where John was held were close to each other. Josephus, however, locates John's death at the fortress Machaerus, across the Jordan River in Perea (Josephus, *Ant.* 18.119). **6:22** ***his daughter Herodias*** The Gk text is uncertain here. If this is what it says, it is extremely confusing because *Mark* has already indicated that Antipas's *wife* was named Herodias and no daughter of Herod named Herodias is otherwise known. Many later manuscripts of *Mark,* as well as *Matt.* 14:6, say plainly that it was the daughter *of* Herodias who danced. ***danced*** It is odd that a noblewoman such as Salome, wife of the tetrarch Philip, or even a daughter of Antipas, would dance for the entertainment of the tetrarch and his male friends. Such provocative dancing was ordinarily the task of slave girls. **6:23** Herod Antipas did not have a kingdom to give away. Notice *Matthew*'s adjustment of the language (14:7). **6:25** ***Immediately*** *Mark*'s characteristic connective adverb. **6:29** ***his disciples*** Another indicator that John's students continued as an independent group. See note to 2:18.

Feeding the Five Thousand

³⁰The apostles gathered around Jesus, and told him all that they had done and taught. ³¹He said to them, "Come away to a deserted place all by yourselves and rest a while." For many were coming and going, and they had no leisure even to eat. ³²And they went away in the boat to a deserted place by themselves. ³³Now many saw them going and recognized them, and they hurried there on foot from all the towns and arrived ahead of them. ³⁴As he went ashore, he saw a great crowd; and he had compassion for them, because they were like sheep without a shepherd; and he began to teach them many things. ³⁵When it grew late, his disciples came to him and said, "This is a deserted place, and the hour is now very late; ³⁶send them away so that they may go into the surrounding country and villages and buy something for themselves to eat." ³⁷But he answered them, "You give them something to eat." They said to him, "Are we to go and buy two hundred denarii*t* worth of bread, and give it to them to eat?" ³⁸And he said to them, "How many loaves have you? Go and see." When they had found out, they said, "Five, and two fish." ³⁹Then he ordered them to get all the people to sit down in groups on the green grass. ⁴⁰So they sat down in groups of hundreds and of fifties. ⁴¹Taking the five loaves and the two fish, he looked up to heaven, and blessed and broke the loaves, and gave them to his disciples to set before the people; and he divided the two fish among them all. ⁴²And all ate and were filled; ⁴³and they took up twelve baskets full of broken pieces and of the fish. ⁴⁴Those who had eaten the loaves numbered five thousand men.

Jesus Walks on the Water

⁴⁵Immediately he made his disciples get into the boat and go on ahead to the other side, to Bethsaida, while he dismissed the crowd. ⁴⁶After saying farewell to them, he went up on the mountain to pray.

⁴⁷When evening came, the boat was out on the sea, and he was alone on the land. ⁴⁸When he saw that they were straining at the oars against an adverse wind, he came towards them early in the morning, walking on the sea. He intended to pass them by. ⁴⁹But when they saw him walking on the sea, they thought it was a ghost and cried out; ⁵⁰for they all saw him and were terrified. But immediately he spoke to them and said, "Take heart, it is I; do not be afraid." ⁵¹Then he got into the boat with them and the wind ceased. And they were utterly astounded, ⁵²for they did not understand about the loaves, but their hearts were hardened.

---

t The denarius was the usual day's wage for a laborer

6:30 The author resumes a story begun in 6:7; see note to 3:31. **6:32** The reader has no clear picture of the destination, somewhere on the shore of the Sea of Galilee (Lake Gennesar). In one of its few parallels with the synoptic tradition, *John* (6:1) specifies that the feeding of the 5,000 occurred on "the other side" of the lake, which is as vague as *Mark*. *Luke* 9:10 supplies Bethsaida, where the Jordan River enters the lake from the north. But the author of *Mark* will later claim that after the feeding Jesus and his students moved to Bethsaida, on "the other side" of the lake (6:45); this suggests that the feeding occurred at the southern end of the lake. **6:34** *teach them many things* *Mark* typically refers to many teachings without describing them (1:39; 4:33–34; 6:30), in contrast to *Matthew* and *Luke*. **6:36** Common people typically ate only one or two meals per day; by this time of day, they would be in real need of their main meal. **6:37** *two hundred denarii worth* Close to a year's income for most people of Jesus' time and place; therefore, an impossible amount of bread and money for his students to produce. **6:40** *in groups of hundreds and of fifties* Perhaps an awkward way of saying "fifty groups of a hundred" or "a hundred groups of fifty" (i.e., five thousand; see 6:44). The author of *Luke* understands the latter (9:14), whereas *Matthew* omits the numbers. Given the parallels to the miraculous provision of food for the Israelites when they were starving in a deserted locale (*Exodus* 16–17), the author may well have in mind Moses' practice of dividing the Israelites into such groups (*Exod.* 18:21, 25). Following Moses, the authors of the Dead Sea Scrolls also divided themselves into groups of "thousands, hundreds, fifties, and tens" (e.g., CD 13.1). **6:41** *blessed and broke the loaves* *Mark's* ambiguous Gk could mean either that Jesus blessed God, then broke the loaves (*Matt.* 14:19), or that he blessed the loaves and broke them (*Luke* 9:16). **6:44** *five thousand men* *Mark's* identification of 5,000 males might suggest either that women and children were also present (*Matt.* 14:21) or that it was an all-male gathering (*Luke* 9:14). **6:45** *Bethsaida* See note to 6:32. Bethsaida was a fishing village to the east of the Jordan River, where it flows into Lake Gennesar. The tetrarch Philip founded the city of Julias at roughly the same location, which also marked the gateway from Galilee (governed by Antipas) to his territory. Since the more elite authors refer to Julias at this site (Pliny, *Nat.* 5.71; Ptolemy, *Geog.* 5.14.4; Josephus, *Life* 398), it seems that the fishing village coexisted with the city to the north. Jesus' career took him close to Julias as to Sepphoris and Tiberias, but he avoided these cities. **6:46** *the mountain* The identity of the mountain is unclear. It is very hilly around Bethsaida. **6:48** *He intended to pass them by* A peculiar sentence, as if walking on the water were simply Jesus' normal mode of transportation. The preceding statement, which implies that Jesus set out to help them, makes the remark even odder. *Matt.* 9:25, though following *Mark* closely in this story, omits both statements. **6:51** *the wind ceased* See 4:39. **6:52** It is strange that Jesus' students' hearts should be hardened after he has fed the five thousand and twice calmed the stormy lake, but it accords with *Mark's* literary aims. See introduction to *Mark*. Contrast *Matt.* 14:33.

Healing the Sick in Gennesaret

53When they had crossed over, they came to land at Gennesaret and moored the boat. 54When they got out of the boat, people at once recognized him, 55and rushed about that whole region and began to bring the sick on mats to wherever they heard he was. 56And wherever he went, into villages or cities or farms, they laid the sick in the marketplaces, and begged him that they might touch even the fringe of his cloak; and all who touched it were healed.

The Tradition of the Elders

7Now when the Pharisees and some of the scribes who had come from Jerusalem gathered around him, 2they noticed that some of his disciples were eating with defiled hands, that is, without washing them. 3(For the Pharisees, and all the Jews, do not eat unless they thoroughly wash their hands,u thus observing the tradition of the elders; 4and they do not eat anything from the market unless they wash it;v and there

are also many other traditions that they observe, the washing of cups, pots, and bronze kettles.w) 5So the Pharisees and the scribes asked him, "Why do your disciples not livex according to the tradition of the elders, but eat with defiled hands?" 6He said to them, "Isaiah prophesied rightly about you hypocrites, as it is written,

'This people honors me with their lips,
but their hearts are far from me;
7 in vain do they worship me,
teaching human precepts as doctrines.'

8You abandon the commandment of God and hold to human tradition."

9Then he said to them, "You have a fine way of rejecting the commandment of God in order to keep your tradition! 10For Moses said, 'Honor your father and your mother'; and, 'Whoever speaks evil of father or mother must surely die.' 11But you say that if anyone tells father or mother, 'Whatever support you might have had from me is Corban' (that is, an offer-

---

u Meaning of Gk uncertain
v Other ancient authorities read *and when they come from the marketplace, they do not eat unless they purify themselves*

w Other ancient authorities add *and beds*
x Gk *walk*

6:53 *at Gennesaret* Only here and in the Matthean parallel (14:34) do early Christian texts mention such a place. It is a puzzle because the author had indicated that Jesus' students were bound for Bethsaida (6:45) and because a town of Gennesaret is unknown. The Gennesaret plain occupied an area of about 3.5 by 1.5 miles on the northwest shore of the lake. The author's knowledge of Galilean geography is suspect. **6:56** *in the marketplaces* Greek cities typically had a central area including courts, temples, gymnasium, and *agora* or marketplace. This corresponded to the *forum* of Roman cities. *the fringe of his cloak* Jewish men were required to wear fringes on the corners of their garments, with a blue cord at each corner (*Num.* 15:37–41). See 5:27–28, where the woman with the hemorrhage touched Jesus' clothes to receive a cure. See also *Acts* 5:15; 19:12, where Peter's shadow and handkerchiefs or aprons that have touched Paul's skin convey healing power. **7:1** *Pharisees* See note to 2:16. *scribes . . . from Jerusalem* See notes to 1:22 and 3:22. **7:2–3** That the author needs to explain Jewish customs, while speaking of the Jews in the third person, appears to indicate that his first readers were Gentiles. **7:2** *eating* Lit. "eating the loaves [of bread]." The author may be using a Semitic expression that simply means "eating." *without washing them* Our awareness of germs and dirt was unknown to the ancient world; the issue here is ritual purity— the state of wholeness that would allow one to participate in the temple service, where God's presence was localized. Although the Bible itself says little about washing hands, and only in specific contexts (*Lev.* 15:11), *Mark* here confirms that a body of tradition about routine hand-washing before meals—to extend ritual purity to all of life—was developing among some groups in the 1st century. See *m. Yadayim.* **7:3** *the Pharisees, and all the Jews* See note to 2:16. Although all indications are that the Pharisees were the most popular group of Jesus' day and that their program was largely adopted by the masses (Josephus, *Ant.* 13.297–298; 18.12–15), the author seems to exaggerate when he attributes their traditions to *all* Jews. *thoroughly wash their hands* Lit. "wash their hands with a fist": perhaps with cupped hands or as far as the wrist. *the tradition of the elders* A quasi-technical term for the extrabiblical living tradition recognized by the Pharisees as authoritative. See Josephus, *Ant.* 13.297–298; 18.12–15; *m. Avot* 1–2; *Gal.* 1:14. **7:4** *the washing of cups, pots, and bronze kettles* See Mishnah, *Kelim.* By the 1st century, the Pharisees had evidently extended the biblical laws about priestly and temple-related purity to all of life. **7:5** The assumption beneath this question seems to be that observance of the Pharisees' special tradition was the norm among nonpriestly groups. There were at least a few exceptions to this principle: the Essenes, the circles of the Dead Sea Scrolls, the Sadducees, and nonobservant Jews. Jesus and his students were another nonconformist group. **7:6–7** *Isa.* 29:13. MT: "Because that people has approached [Me] with its mouth / And honored Me with its lips, / But has kept its heart far from Me, / And its worship of Me has been / A commandment of men, learned by rote." LXX: "This people honor me with their lips, but their hearts are far from me; in vain do they worship me, teaching human precepts and doctrines." The early Christians had a particular fondness for *Isaiah*, especially its accusations of Israel's stubbornness and its references to God's Suffering Servant. Whether the author of *Mark* knew the biblical scrolls firsthand or only an anthology of such quotations is an open question. **7:8–9** Jesus' rejection of the Pharisees' tradition as human, in contrast to the divinely inspired biblical laws, was similar to the Sadducees' critique of that tradition (Josephus, *Ant.* 13.297–298; 18.12–15). **7:10** *Exod.* 20:12 par. *Deut.* 5:16; *Exod.* 21:17 par. *Lev.* 20:9.

ing to God*y*)— ¹²then you no longer permit doing anything for a father or mother, ¹³thus making void the word of God through your tradition that you have handed on. And you do many things like this."

¹⁴Then he called the crowd again and said to them, "Listen to me, all of you, and understand: ¹⁵there is nothing outside a person that by going in can defile, but the things that come out are what defile."*z*

¹⁷When he had left the crowd and entered the house, his disciples asked him about the parable. ¹⁸He said to them, "Then do you also fail to understand? Do you not see that whatever goes into a person from outside cannot defile, ¹⁹since it enters, not the heart but the stomach, and goes out into the sewer?" (Thus he declared all foods clean.) ²⁰And he said, "It is what comes out of a person that defiles. ²¹For it is from within, from the human heart, that evil intentions come: fornication, theft, murder,

²²adultery, avarice, wickedness, deceit, licentiousness, envy, slander, pride, folly. ²³All these evil things come from within, and they defile a person."

The Syrophoenician Woman's Faith

²⁴From there he set out and went away to the region of Tyre.*a* He entered a house and did not want anyone to know he was there. Yet he could not escape notice, ²⁵but a woman whose little daughter had an unclean spirit immediately heard about him, and she came and bowed down at his feet. ²⁶Now the woman was a Gentile, of Syrophoenician origin. She begged him to cast the demon out of her daughter. ²⁷He said to her, "Let the children be fed first, for it is not fair to take the children's food and throw it to the dogs." ²⁸But she answered him, "Sir,*b* even the dogs under the table eat the children's crumbs." ²⁹Then he said to her, "For saying that, you may go—the demon has

---

y Gk lacks *to God*
z Other ancient authorities add verse 16, "*Let anyone with ears to hear listen.*"

a Other ancient authorities add *and Sidon*
b Or *Lord;* other ancient authorities prefix *Yes*

7:12 The Hebrew word *corban* means literally "what is brought near" and signifies in the Bible all sacrifices and offerings in the temple. The charge seems to be that the Pharisees encouraged people to avoid obligations to their parents by having them dedicate offerings to the temple instead. But although some individuals may have tried to avoid parental support through pious offerings, everything we see in postbiblical Judaism suggests that most Jews would have seen this as a flagrant violation of the Torah. Even *Matthew,* which intensifies *Mark's* anti-Pharisaic polemic, removes *Mark's* assertion that an offering to the temple prevented one from honoring one's parents (*Matt.* 15:5). **7:15–23** This section is only tangentially related to what precedes. There Jesus rejected the Pharisees' special tradition as a human creation. Here he is in dialogue with biblical laws, observed by Jews around the Roman world, concerning suitable food; the divine commandments explicitly declare unclean several varieties of bird, seafood, and land animal (*Deut.* 14:1–21). Jesus' reported words do not necessarily reject these laws. His formulation "there is nothing outside a person that by going in can defile, but the things that come out are what defile" is a typically Semitic construction whose approximate meaning is that what comes out of a person is *much more important* than what goes in. Compare the prophets' call for "mercy, *not* sacrifice" (*Hos.* 6:6), which was not an appeal to end divinely mandated sacrifice but an insistence that mercy was more urgent and that only sacrifice in conjunction with mercy was acceptable. **7:18 fail to understand** The author continues his portrayal of Jesus' students as largely uncomprehending in spite of their special teaching and time with Jesus; they tend to hold on to the customary views. **7:19 he declared all foods clean** The author understands Jesus' statement "there is nothing outside that . . . can defile" in an absolute way, rather than in the relative sense typical of Semitic speech (see note to 7:15–23). This is by no means a necessary deduction, and it was not followed by *Matthew,* which retains Jesus' words, but drops *Mark's* interpretation and also presents Jesus as requiring scrupulous observance of Moses' laws (15:17–18; see 5:17–21). If Jesus had so forthrightly overturned the dietary laws—a significant part of the Torah and a hallmark of Judaism—it would be difficult to explain why Jesus' closest associates remained adamant in their refusal to violate the dietary laws after his death (see *Gal.* 2:11–14; *Acts* 10–11). In the controversies that ensued, as far as we know, no one cited the precedent of Jesus himself. It appears, then, the author of *Mark* has read back into Jesus' lifetime the practices of his own Gentile community. **7:21–22** This is a vice list, typically used by 1st-century moral philosophers; it was often paralleled by a list of virtues. Hellenistic Jewish authors and Paul also used such catalogues (*Wis.* 7:23–23; 14:25–26; *Gal.* 5:19–24; *Rom.* 1:29–31). **7:24 From there . . . to the region of Tyre** *Mark's* geography continues to be vague: the last reference had Jesus in "Gennesaret" (6:53). To reach the coastal region of Tyre, in what is now Lebanon, would have required the better part of a two-day journey. This will be Jesus' 2d foray into the Gentile territories neighboring Jewish regions; first he went into the Decapolis to the east (5:1–20). **did not want anyone to know** The theme of secrecy was established early in *Mark* (see note to 1:25). But it is not clear whether Jesus' concern for privacy and anonymity here (see 5:43; 7:36) has the same motive as his command to the unclean spirits (1:25) or his students (8:30; 9:9)—not to reveal his divine identity. One might understand the concern for anonymity in simply practical terms, because of the pressures of the crowds (2:2; 3:20; 4:36; 6:31, 53–56). **7:25 an unclean spirit** See note to 1:23. **bowed down at his feet** A posture of humble supplication. **7:26** In this story, Jesus seems to stress that his turning to Gentiles was reluctant: he tried hard to reach his fellow Jews and took over the slander of Gentiles as "dogs" (*1 Sam.* 17:43; *Phil.* 3:2), but many Jews would not listen; the Gentiles, on the other hand, were receptive. Jesus' career thus matches the later experience of the church (see *Rom.* 11:7–24; *Acts* 28:25–28). **a Gentile** Lit. "a Greek."

left your daughter." [30]So she went home, found the child lying on the bed, and the demon gone.

Jesus Cures a Deaf Man

[31]Then he returned from the region of Tyre, and went by way of Sidon towards the Sea of Galilee, in the region of the Decapolis. [32]They brought to him a deaf man who had an impediment in his speech; and they begged him to lay his hand on him. [33]He took him aside in private, away from the crowd, and put his fingers into his ears, and he spat and touched his tongue. [34]Then looking up to heaven, he sighed and said to him, "Ephphatha," that is, "Be opened." [35]And immediately his ears were opened, his tongue was released, and he spoke plainly. [36]Then Jesus[c] ordered them to tell no one; but the more he ordered them, the more zealously they proclaimed it. [37]They were astounded beyond measure, saying, "He has done everything well; he even makes the deaf to hear and the mute to speak."

Feeding the Four Thousand

8 In those days when there was again a great crowd without anything to eat, he called his disciples and said to them, [2]"I have compassion for the crowd, because they have been with me now for three days and have nothing to eat. [3]If I send them away hungry to their homes, they will faint on the way—and some of them have come from a great distance." [4]His disciples

replied, "How can one feed these people with bread here in the desert?" [5]He asked them, "How many loaves do you have?" They said, "Seven." [6]Then he ordered the crowd to sit down on the ground; and he took the seven loaves, and after giving thanks he broke them and gave them to his disciples to distribute; and they distributed them to the crowd. [7]They had also a few small fish; and after blessing them, he ordered that these too should be distributed. [8]They ate and were filled; and they took up the broken pieces left over, seven baskets full. [9]Now there were about four thousand people. And he sent them away. [10]And immediately he got into the boat with his disciples and went to the district of Dalmanutha.[d]

The Demand for a Sign

[11]The Pharisees came and began to argue with him, asking him for a sign from heaven, to test him. [12]And he sighed deeply in his spirit and said, "Why does this generation ask for a sign? Truly I tell you, no sign will be given to this generation." [13]And he left them, and getting into the boat again, he went across to the other side.

The Yeast of the Pharisees and of Herod

[14]Now the disciples[e] had forgotten to bring any bread; and they had only one loaf with them in the boat. [15]And he cautioned them, saying, "Watch out—beware of the yeast of the Pharisees and the

---

c Gk he

d Other ancient authorities read Mageda or Magdala
e Gk they

7:31 This route seems confused because Jesus travels a long way north (to Sidon) to go southeast (to the Sea of Galilee). Mark's identification of the Sea of Galilee by means of the Decapolis may say something about his audience: as non-Jews, they knew where the Decapolis was, but not the lake. Matt. 15:29 omits both problematic references. **7:32–33** The use of touch and spittle is not typical of Jesus' cures in the gospels but does resemble others' cures in Jesus' day (see Tacitus, Hist. 4.81; Suetonius, Vesp. 7.8). **7:34** As in 5:41 (see note), the author cites an Aramaic phrase used by Jesus in a cure—not simply as a matter of record (since his readers do not know Aramaic, and so he must translate), but for some other reason. **7:36** The author continues the theme of secrecy (see note to 1:25; also 5:43; 7:24). **8:1–10** This 2d feeding story is peculiar because, although it closely parallels the story recently told in 6:30–44, even in precise phrases (Jesus had compassion, asked, "How many loaves do you have?" commanded the crowds to sit, blessed and distributed the food; they took up several baskets of leftovers), it does not acknowledge the earlier episode but begins as if this were the 1st time this happened. One important effect of the story, then, and possibly the author's reason for including it, is to make Jesus' students appear truly unbelieving: they have already seen a precisely parallel situation, and yet they still cannot imagine how they might provide food for the crowds (8:4; see 8:14–21). **8:1** *In those days* This typically vague Markan connector has a biblical ring. It confirms that the author is stringing together stories in thematic, rather than chronological, order. **8:3** *from a great distance* It is unclear where this story takes place; see note to 7:31. **8:10** *Dalmanutha* The uncertain chronology continues: this place does not appear elsewhere in the gospels, and its location is unknown. Matthew substitutes the equally obscure Magadan (15:39). **8:12** *no sign will be given* Curiously, in Matthew's two parallels to this saying (12:39; 16:4) and in the Lukan parallel (11:29), Jesus allows that only the "sign of Jonah" will be given. **8:13** Since we do not know which part of the lake Jesus began from in 7:31 or where Dalmanutha is (8:10), we are uncertain about the meaning of this move to "the other side." Nevertheless, Jesus will eventually come to Bethsaida, on the northern tip of the lake (8:22; see 6:45). **8:14–21** The gist of this story confirms that the author's main reason for including two feeding stories was to expose the incomprehension of Jesus' students. **8:15** *the yeast of the Pharisees and the yeast of Herod* A puzzling combination and completely enigmatic. Herod would be Antipas, then tetrarch of Galilee and Perea, who had reluctantly—according to Mark—executed John the Baptist (6:14–29). It was the Pharisees and "Herodians" (some manuscripts read

yeast of Herod."*f* 16They said to one another, "It is because we have no bread." 17And becoming aware of it, Jesus said to them, "Why are you talking about having no bread? Do you still not perceive or understand? Are your hearts hardened? 18Do you have eyes, and fail to see? Do you have ears, and fail to hear? And do you not remember? 19When I broke the five loaves for the five thousand, how many baskets full of broken pieces did you collect?" They said to him, "Twelve." 20"And the seven for the four thousand, how many baskets full of broken pieces did you collect?" And they said to him, "Seven." 21Then he said to them, "Do you not yet understand?"

Jesus Cures a Blind Man at Bethsaida

22They came to Bethsaida. Some people*g* brought a blind man to him and begged him to touch him. 23He took the blind man by the hand and led him out of the village; and when he had put saliva on his eyes and laid his hands on him, he asked him, "Can you see anything?" 24And the man*h* looked up and said, "I can see people, but they look like trees, walking." 25Then Jesus*h* laid his hands on his eyes again; and he looked intently and his sight was restored, and he saw everything clearly. 26Then he sent him away to his home, saying, "Do not even go into the village."*i*

Peter's Declaration about Jesus

27Jesus went on with his disciples to the villages of Caesarea Philippi; and on the way he asked his disciples, "Who do people say that I am?" 28And they answered him, "John the Baptist; and others, Elijah; and still others, one of the prophets." 29He asked them, "But who do you say that I am?" Peter answered him, "You are the Messiah."*j* 30And he sternly ordered them not to tell anyone about him.

Jesus Foretells His Death and Resurrection

31Then he began to teach them that the Son of Man must undergo great suffering, and be rejected by the elders, the chief priests, and the scribes, and be

---

f Other ancient authorities read *the Herodians*
g Gk *They*
h Gk *he*

i Other ancient authorities add *or tell anyone in the village*
j Or *the Christ*

"Herodians" instead of "Herod" here as well) who first hatched the lethal plot against Jesus in 3:6. *Matthew* substitutes Sadducees for Herod and explains that the teaching of these two groups is the yeast to be avoided (16:6–12). *Luke* omits the reference to Herod and explains that the hypocrisy of the Pharisees is the yeast (12:1). In commanding his followers to avoid the yeast of the Pharisees, *Mark*'s Jesus makes a pointed barb because the Pharisees might have been the most zealous about avoiding yeast at Passover (see *Exod.* 13:3–10). **8:17–18** Jesus' questions to his students paraphrase *Isa.* 6:9–10, concerning Israel's stubbornness—a favorite passage among early Christian writers (*Rom.* 11:8; *Acts* 28:26–27) and one already employed in *Mark* 4:11–12. See also *Jer.* 5:21; *Ezek.* 12:12. *Mark*'s association of Jesus' students with stubborn Israel may suit his purposes in showing the disciples' inability to understand Jesus. **8:22** *Bethsaida* See 7:31; 8:10. **8:22–26** Once again (see 7:32–37), Jesus uses both saliva and the touch of hands to effect his cure—untypical of him in the gospels but typical of other healers in his day. This is one of the few Markan episodes not paralleled in either *Matthew* or *Luke*. **8:26** The secrecy theme continues; see note to 7:24. **8:27** *Caesarea Philippi* About twenty-five miles (a good day's walk) north of Bethsaida, in the tetrarchy of Philip (as was Bethsaida). This was an ancient site of great religious significance to the non-Jewish population. At the foot of majestic Mount Hermon, it hosted a cave and spring devoted to the god Pan; it was thus first known as Paneas. First King Herod and then his son Philip dedicated it to Caesar Augustus, giving it the honorary name Caesarea. The designation Philippi ("belonging to Philip") attached itself for a time in the 1st century to distinguish this from several other towns named Caesarea. It is surely no coincidence that this place of great spiritual significance provides the setting for Peter's confession and, apparently, for Jesus' transfiguration in *Mark*. **8:28** These three popular opinions are familiar to the reader from 6:14–15. **8:29** *you say* The *you* is plural: Jesus asks all of his students. *the Messiah* Although the author likes to use Hebrew or Aramaic terms in certain contexts (5:41; 7:34), he chooses the Gk term *christos* rather than transliterating *meshiach*. Presumably, his Pauline Gentile Christian audience is familiar with the Gk title. This confession, which falls roughly in the center of the work, is pivotal to the plot. From now on, Jesus' tone will change; he will immediately begin to anticipate his trial and death (8:31; 9:31; 10:33). **8:30** The secrecy motif continues; see notes to 1:25 and 7:24. It is unclear whether *Mark*'s Jesus is mainly concerned to preserve himself from the crowds (as in 7:24), or from the authorities (9:30–31), or whether there is some theological principle involved in his secrecy (see notes to 1:25 and 9:9). **8:31** Jesus' career has entered a new and dark phase: The plot hatched against him in 3:6 will quickly be realized. *Son of Man* See notes to 2:10, 27–28. *the elders, the chief priests* This is the first mention of these groups in *Mark* (not counting the "tradition of the elders" in 7:3, 5); it was the Pharisees, Herodians, and scribes who devised the plot to kill Jesus in 2:1–3:6. But since the scribes continue as a common element, since the Pharisees and Herodians will indeed appear in the Jerusalem controversies (12:13), and since this author is uncertain about real conditions in Palestine (see introduction to *Mark*), it seems more likely that he means to lump all of these Jewish groups together—along with the Sadducees (12:18)— as Jesus' opponents than that he understands significant differences in their relationships to Jesus. *Luke* will make these distinctions clearer. It is unclear to what extent "elders" was a technical term. Greek readers would naturally understand it as

killed, and after three days rise again. ³²He said all this quite openly. And Peter took him aside and began to rebuke him. ³³But turning and looking at his disciples, he rebuked Peter and said, "Get behind me, Satan! For you are setting your mind not on divine things but on human things."

³⁴He called the crowd with his disciples, and said to them, "If any want to become my followers, let them deny themselves and take up their cross and follow me. ³⁵For those who want to save their life will lose it, and those who lose their life for my sake, and for the sake of the gospel,ᵏ will save it. ³⁶For what will it profit them to gain the whole world and forfeit their life? ³⁷Indeed, what can they give in return for their life? ³⁸Those who are ashamed of me and of my wordsˡ in this adulterous and sinful generation, of them the Son of Man will also be ashamed when he comes in the glory of his Father with the holy angels."

9 And he said to them, "Truly I tell you, there are some standing here who will not taste death until they see that the kingdom of God has come withᵐ power."

The Transfiguration

²Six days later, Jesus took with him Peter and James and John, and led them up a high mountain apart, by themselves. And he was transfigured before them, ³and his clothes became dazzling white, such as no oneⁿ on earth could bleach them. ⁴And there appeared to them Elijah with Moses, who were talking with Jesus. ⁵Then Peter said to Jesus, "Rabbi, it is good for us to be here; let us make three dwellings,ᵒ one for you, one for Moses, and one for Elijah." ⁶He did not know what to say, for they were terrified. ⁷Then a cloud overshadowed them, and from the cloud there came a voice, "This is my Son, the Beloved;ᵖ listen to him!" ⁸Suddenly when they looked

k Other ancient authorities read *lose their life for the sake of the gospel*

l Other ancient authorities read *and of mine*

m Or *in*
n Gk *no fuller*
o Or *tents*
p Or *my beloved Son*

the dignified group from which the governing council came (Gk *gerousia* and Latin *senatus* both mean "council of elders"). Scholars tend to see this group as distinct from the hereditary aristocracy of the priesthood, which appears separately. Jewish priesthood was not a voluntary occupation but a hereditary caste; the chief priests were simply the leading families—wealthier and more prominent—within this caste, allegedly descended from the tribe of Levi through Aaron. **8:32–33** Since Jesus predicted his future clearly and forcefully (8:32), Peter's rebuke appears completely out of line—a continuation of the Markan pattern that Jesus' students simply do not understand his divine mission. Jesus' criticism of Peter is devastating and unqualified. *Luke-Acts,* which gives a fundamental role to the apostles and to Peter in particular, omits this exchange while otherwise following *Mark* (*Luke* 9:22–23). *Matthew,* which also favors Peter, retains this material from its source but tones it down in several striking ways (16:21–23); most important, it includes this passage only after Jesus has highly praised Peter and designated him the "rock" upon which the church should be built (16:16–19). **8:35** *sake of the gospel* Another place (see 1:1; 4:13–20; 13:10) in which the author seems to assume his own church context—in which Christians are suffering for their trust in, and proclamation of, Jesus' saving death and resurrection (the *gospel,* or "announcement")—rather than Jesus' context, in which the disciples do not understand such things. Both *Matt.* 16:25 and *Luke* 9:24 omit this clause while otherwise following *Mark.* **8:38** *Son of Man* See notes to 2:10, 27–28. The reader might have expected "I" here. The use of "son of man" instead supports the theory that the historical Jesus sometimes used this phrase with such meaning. As it stands, however, *Mark's* Jesus appears to expect another figure called the Son of Man. **9:1** The author's readers, like Paul and many of his followers, expected Jesus' return within the lifetime of at least some of Jesus' contemporaries (see *1 Thess.* 1:9–10; 4:13–5:11; *1 Cor.* 15:51; 16:22). **9:2** *Peter and James and John* See note to 5:37. *a high mountain* Perhaps one of the mountains that rise from behind Caesarea Philippi (8:27) to Mount Hermon, which reaches a height in excess of 6,600 ft. *transfigured* The Latin-based English word "trans-figure" closely represents the Gk ("meta-morphose"); his form or appearance was changed. **9:4** *Elijah with Moses* Elijah and Moses were two important figures in speculations of Jesus' day about the end times, for it was commonly believed that both had gone to heaven without dying. On Elijah, see *2 Kgs.* 2:10–12; *Mal.* 4:5–6; *Sir.* 48:1–14. Although the Bible asserts that Moses died (*Deut.* 34:5), its admission that no one knew the location of his grave (*Deut.* 34:6), and its promise of another true prophet like him (*Deut.* 18:15), fueled speculation that he had not really died (see *Assumption of Moses;* Josephus, *Ant.* 4.325–326). **9:5** *Rabbi* The title did not yet have its later connotation of ordination but meant something like "master," in the ancient sense of "revered teacher." It seems odd that *Mark* should have Jesus' students use this form of address only from this point (10:51; 11:21; 14:45). Perhaps the author intends to lend some local color. In the parallels, *Luke* either omits the term or uses a Gk substitute; *Matthew* omits the term in most instances, leaving the address only on the lips of the despicable traitor Judas (26:25, 49). **9:6** Any attempt to try to determine Peter's meaning (e.g., that he meant that the autumn Feast of Booths was approaching) seems pointless, since the author plainly dismisses his words as irrelevant. **9:7** Here, roughly halfway through the book, the author confirms Jesus' identity in a close parallel to the heavenly voice at his immersion by John (1:11). But now the voice addresses the witnesses rather than Jesus.

around, they saw no one with them any more, but only Jesus.

The Coming of Elijah

9As they were coming down the mountain, he ordered them to tell no one about what they had seen, until after the Son of Man had risen from the dead. 10So they kept the matter to themselves, questioning what this rising from the dead could mean. 11Then they asked him, "Why do the scribes say that Elijah must come first?" 12He said to them, "Elijah is indeed coming first to restore all things. How then is it written about the Son of Man, that he is to go through many sufferings and be treated with contempt? 13But I tell you that Elijah has come, and they did to him whatever they pleased, as it is written about him."

The Healing of a Boy with a Spirit

14When they came to the disciples, they saw a great crowd around them, and some scribes arguing with them. 15When the whole crowd saw him, they were immediately overcome with awe, and they ran forward to greet him. 16He asked them, "What are you arguing about with them?" 17Someone from the crowd answered him, "Teacher, I brought you my son; he has a spirit that makes him unable to speak; 18and whenever it seizes him, it dashes him down; and he foams and grinds his teeth and becomes rigid; and I asked your disciples to cast it out, but they could not do so." 19He answered them, "You faithless generation, how much longer must I be among you? How much longer must I put up with you? Bring him to

me." 20And they brought the boy*q* to him. When the spirit saw him, immediately it convulsed the boy,*q* and he fell on the ground and rolled about, foaming at the mouth. 21Jesus*r* asked the father, "How long has this been happening to him?" And he said, "From childhood. 22It has often cast him into the fire and into the water, to destroy him; but if you are able to do anything, have pity on us and help us." 23Jesus said to him, "If you are able!—All things can be done for the one who believes." 24Immediately the father of the child cried out,*s* "I believe; help my unbelief!" 25When Jesus saw that a crowd came running together, he rebuked the unclean spirit, saying to it, "You spirit that keeps this boy from speaking and hearing, I command you, come out of him, and never enter him again!" 26After crying out and convulsing him terribly, it came out, and the boy was like a corpse, so that most of them said, "He is dead." 27But Jesus took him by the hand and lifted him up, and he was able to stand. 28When he had entered the house, his disciples asked him privately, "Why could we not cast it out?" 29He said to them, "This kind can come out only through prayer."*t*

Jesus Again Foretells His Death and Resurrection

30They went on from there and passed through Galilee. He did not want anyone to know it; 31for he

---

q Gk *him*
r Gk *He*
s Other ancient authorities add *with tears*
t Other ancient authorities add *and fasting*

9:9 This sentence offers the clearest clue about a deeper reason for Jesus' secrecy in *Mark*: the disciples' expression of his divine character was not silenced merely in order to protect him from crowds and from harm (see note to 7:24). The common theory holds that the author wished to explain to readers why the early church's belief in Jesus as dying and rising Savior was so poorly attested in Jesus' own teaching, which talks about God in parables (4:34). The answer given is that Jesus knew that his students understood his identity, but commanded them to keep it secret until after his resurrection. See notes to 1:25; 7:24. **Son of Man** See notes to 2:10, 27–28; 8:31. **9:10** The author continues to drive home his criticism of Jesus' students: Jesus had already plainly predicted his death and resurrection in 8:31. **this rising from the dead** The Gk does not say *this* but suggests, rather, that Jesus' students had trouble with the entire notion of resurrection. This is puzzling even in *Mark*, where it appears that only the Sadducees doubt resurrection (12:18). *Matthew* and *Luke* omit this observation. **9:11** See *Mal.* 4:5–6; *Sir.* 48:10. The Bible does not say that Elijah would come before the Messiah; rather, Elijah appears as a quasi-messianic figure in his own right, who prepares for the Day of the Lord (i.e., God). In the Dead Sea Scrolls and other apocalyptic literature, we see a variety of messianic figures expected, with different scenarios envisaged. The idea that Elijah would anoint the royal Messiah was one of the many current scenarios. **9:12** **written about the Son of Man** Nothing in the Bible talks about the suffering of the Son of Man. Possibly the author is taking the liberty of associating this title with the Suffering Servant passages of *Isaiah*, such as *Isaiah* 53. For Son of Man, see notes to 2:10, 27–28. **9:13** A clear reference to John the Baptist, as *Matt.* 11:14 and *Luke* 1:17 make explicit. Interestingly, the Baptist of *John* (1:21) forthrightly rejects the identification with Elijah. **9:14–29** This unusually long story is essentially a further indictment of Jesus' students—their faithlessness (9:19) and lack of prayer (9:29), which produce incompetence (9:18). They do not authentically represent Jesus; he merely tolerates them as long as he must (9:19). **9:17–18** The disease sounds like epilepsy, which is what *Matt.* 17:15 calls it. For the perceived relation between sickness and spirit possession in antiquity, see note to 1:23. **9:30** **from there** *Mark*'s geography continues to be vague. The last definite indicator was Caesarea Philippi in 8:27; the high mountain in 9:2 may be Mount Hermon, from which Jesus and his students have descended (9:9). **He did not want anyone to know it** See notes to 1:25; 7:24; 9:9; also 8:30. **9:31–32** This second prediction of Jesus' death and resurrection, following quickly on the first (8:31), both heightens the narrative tension and exposes further Jesus' students' dullness. They still do not understand despite having been told plainly and repeatedly (see also 9:9–10).

was teaching his disciples, saying to them, "The Son of Man is to be betrayed into human hands, and they will kill him, and three days after being killed, he will rise again." 32But they did not understand what he was saying and were afraid to ask him.

Who Is the Greatest?

33Then they came to Capernaum; and when he was in the house he asked them, "What were you arguing about on the way?" 34But they were silent, for on the way they had argued with one another who was the greatest. 35He sat down, called the twelve, and said to them, "Whoever wants to be first must be last of all and servant of all." 36Then he took a little child and put it among them; and taking it in his arms, he said to them, 37"Whoever welcomes one such child in my name welcomes me, and whoever welcomes me welcomes not me but the one who sent me."

Another Exorcist

38John said to him, "Teacher, we saw someone[u] casting out demons in your name, and we tried to stop him, because he was not following us." 39But Jesus said, "Do not stop him; for no one who does a deed of power in my name will be able soon afterward to speak evil of me. 40Whoever is not against us is for us. 41For truly I tell you, whoever gives you a cup of water to drink because you bear the name of Christ will by no means lose the reward.

---

u Other ancient authorities add who does not follow us

Temptations to Sin

42"If any of you put a stumbling block before one of these little ones who believe in me,[v] it would be better for you if a great millstone were hung around your neck and you were thrown into the sea. 43If your hand causes you to stumble, cut it off; it is better for you to enter life maimed than to have two hands and to go to hell,[w] to the unquenchable fire.[x] 45And if your foot causes you to stumble, cut it off; it is better for you to enter life lame than to have two feet and to be thrown into hell.[w, x] 47And if your eye causes you to stumble, tear it out; it is better for you to enter the kingdom of God with one eye than to have two eyes and to be thrown into hell,[w] 48where their worm never dies, and the fire is never quenched.

49"For everyone will be salted with fire.[y] 50Salt is good; but if salt has lost its saltiness, how can you season it?[z] Have salt in yourselves, and be at peace with one another."

Teaching about Divorce

10He left that place and went to the region of Judea and[a] beyond the Jordan. And crowds again gathered around him; and, as was his custom, he again taught them.

2Some Pharisees came, and to test him they asked, "Is it lawful for a man to divorce his wife?" 3He answered them, "What did Moses command you?"

---

v Other ancient authorities lack in me
w Gk Gehenna
x Verses 44 and 46 (which are identical with verse 48) are lacking in the best ancient authorities
y Other ancient authorities either add or substitute and every sacrifice will be salted with salt
z Or how can you restore its saltiness?
a Other ancient authorities lack and

9:33 *Capernaum . . . in the house* Mark's Jesus appears to have moved his home from Nazareth to Capernaum; see 2:1. **9:33–37** Jesus' students' argument concerning which one is greatest further exposes their insensitivity to Jesus' aims. It prepares for the following story (9:38–41), by way of contrast, and also for a more serious debate about greatness in 10:35–45. **9:38–41** This story contrasts neatly with the preceding one: while Jesus' official students argue about which one is greatest and completely fail to understand his aims, another who is not one of them is actually doing Jesus' work. In the context in which Mark was written, one wonders whether Paul and his associates—those with no credentials from having been with Jesus, but preaching his gospel nonetheless—might have been viewed as such people. **9:41** *bear the name of Christ* Again the author assumes a situation that existed at his time of writing, not in the life of Jesus, since Jesus evidently was not known as Christ until after his resurrection. **9:42–50** The author returns to the *little ones* after a brief detour, continuing his A-B-A pattern. See note to 3:31. He then strings together six miscellaneous sayings of Jesus, which are connected only by catchwords: stumbling (9:43–48), fire (9:48), and salt (9:49–50). **9:43** *hell* Lit. "Gehenna," taken from the name of the valley to the south and east of Jerusalem. Originally a place of child sacrifice for the non-Israelite nations, the name came to be associated in Jewish apocalyptic expectation with the place of fiery punishment for the Gentiles. **9:44** Because this verse, identical to 9:48, is missing from the best manuscripts of Mark, it was not likely part of the original text. **9:46** Missing from the best manuscripts of Mark; identical to 9:48. **10:1** *that place* Capernaum (9:33). *Judea and beyond the Jordan* This is Jesus' first southward turn in Mark; he begins his fateful trip toward Jerusalem. *Beyond the Jordan* was Perea, part of the tetrarch Antipas's territory in addition to Galilee. These are large and distinct regions; Mark's geography continues to be vague. **10:2** Jewish scripture permits divorce and remarriage, except remarriage to one's former wife if her second husband divorces her or dies (*Deut.* 24:1–4), and most Jews have always accepted this. In the 1st century, there was not even a

4They said, "Moses allowed a man to write a certificate of dismissal and to divorce her." 5But Jesus said to them, "Because of your hardness of heart he wrote this commandment for you. 6But from the beginning of creation, 'God made them male and female.' 7For this reason a man shall leave his father and mother and be joined to his wife,*b* 8and the two shall become one flesh.' So they are no longer two, but one flesh. 9Therefore what God has joined together, let no one separate."

10Then in the house the disciples asked him again about this matter. 11He said to them, "Whoever divorces his wife and marries another commits adultery against her; 12and if she divorces her husband and marries another, she commits adultery."

Jesus Blesses Little Children

13People were bringing little children to him in order that he might touch them; and the disciples spoke sternly to them. 14But when Jesus saw this, he was indignant and said to them, "Let the little children come to me; do not stop them; for it is to such as these that the kingdom of God belongs. 15Truly I tell you, whoever does not receive the kingdom of God as a little child will never enter it." 16And he took them up in his arms, laid his hands on them, and blessed them.

The Rich Man

17As he was setting out on a journey, a man ran up and knelt before him, and asked him, "Good Teacher, what must I do to inherit eternal life?" 18Jesus said to him, "Why do you call me good? No one is good but God alone. 19You know the commandments: 'You shall not murder; You shall not commit adultery; You shall not steal; You shall not bear false witness; You shall not defraud; Honor your father and mother.'" 20He said to him, "Teacher, I have kept all these since my youth." 21Jesus, looking at him, loved him and said, "You lack one thing; go, sell what you own, and give the money*c* to the poor, and you will have treasure in heaven; then come, follow me." 22When he heard this, he was shocked and went away grieving, for he had many possessions.

23Then Jesus looked around and said to his disciples, "How hard it will be for those who have wealth to enter the kingdom of God!" 24And the disciples were perplexed at these words. But Jesus said to them again, "Children, how hard it is*d* to enter the kingdom of God! 25It is easier for a camel to go through the eye of a needle than for someone who is rich to enter the kingdom of God." 26They were greatly astounded and said to one another,*e* "Then who can be saved?" 27Jesus looked at them and said, "For mortals it is impossible, but not for God; for God all things are possible."

28Peter began to say to him, "Look, we have left everything and followed you." 29Jesus said, "Truly I tell you, there is no one who has left house or brothers or sisters or mother or father or children or fields, for my sake and for the sake of the good news,*f* 30who will not receive a hundredfold now in this age—

---

b Other ancient authorities lack *and be joined to his wife*

c Gk lacks *the money*
d Other ancient authorities add *for those who trust in riches*
e Other ancient authorities read *to him*
f Or *gospel*

---

prohibition of polygamy in Judaism, but the Roman practice of monogamy had a strong influence. The Pharisees debated among themselves the appropriate conditions for divorce, in particular the meaning of *Deut.* 24:1: "finds something objectionable about her." See the note to *Matt.* 19:3. Whether the author knew about this internal debate is uncertain. **10:4** See *Deut.* 24:1–4. **10:6** *Gen.* 1:27. **10:7–9** *Gen.* 2:24. The same argument, with the same scriptural proof, is used in the Dead Sea Scrolls' CD 4.23. **10:10** *in the house* Jesus' house in Capernaum; see 9:33. **10:11–12** This blanket prohibition of remarriage after divorce is qualified in the Matthean parallel (19:9) to take account of an unfaithful spouse. **10:13** *the disciples spoke sternly* Jesus' students continue to mistake his aims. **10:14–15** See *Gospel of Thomas* 22. **10:17** *As he was setting out on a journey* Mark's chronological and geographical connectors remain vague. *inherit eternal life* The English obscures the root senses of the Gk words: "receive a lot [or 'a place'] in agelong life." The notion of agelong life—namely, in the age to come—only became prominent in Jewish literature from about the 3d century B.C.E.; see *Dan.* 12:2. **10:17–18** *God alone* This statement, inasmuch as Jesus appears to dissociate himself sharply from God, creates a theological problem. *Matthew* (19:16) changes the wording slightly in order to soften Jesus' response. **10:19** A rearrangement and paraphrase of the human-to-human (as distinct from the human-divine) commandments in *Deut.* 5:16–20; see *Exod.* 20:12–16. **10:24** *Matt.* 19:23 and *Luke* 18:24 omit this critical observation about relinquishing wealth. **10:26** Both the astonished response (see previous note) and the question of Jesus' students are puzzling. The vast majority of the population was poor, so excluding the few rich would still leave many who could be saved. *Luke* 18:26 once again omits the implied criticism of the disciples, but *Matt.* 19:24 retains Mark's language here. **10:29** *for the sake of the good news* That is, for the sake of the gospel: another indicator of Mark's setting in the early church (if *good news* here means the proclamation of Jesus' saving death and resurrection). See notes to 1:1; 8:35. *who has left* In *1 Cor.* 9:5 Paul claims that the apostles, Cephas/Peter, and Jesus' brothers all took wives with them on their missions. **10:30** *now in this age* Presumably, the author has in view Jesus' claim that one's real family is not physical (3:33–35); thus, one can have in the church countless homes, parents, and houses, brothers and sisters, mothers and children, and fields with persecutions—and in the age to come eternal life. 31But many who are first will be last, and the last will be first."

A Third Time Jesus Foretells His Death and Resurrection

32They were on the road, going up to Jerusalem, and Jesus was walking ahead of them; they were amazed, and those who followed were afraid. He took the twelve aside again and began to tell them what was to happen to him, 33saying, "See, we are going up to Jerusalem, and the Son of Man will be handed over to the chief priests and the scribes, and they will condemn him to death; then they will hand him over to the Gentiles; 34they will mock him, and spit upon him, and flog him, and kill him; and after three days he will rise again."

The Request of James and John

35James and John, the sons of Zebedee, came forward to him and said to him, "Teacher, we want you to do for us whatever we ask of you." 36And he said to them, "What is it you want me to do for you?" 37And they said to him, "Grant us to sit, one at your right hand and one at your left, in your glory." 38But Jesus said to them, "You do not know what you are asking. Are you able to drink the cup that I drink, or be baptized with the baptism that I am baptized with?" 39They replied, "We are able." Then Jesus said to them, "The cup that I drink you will drink; and with the baptism with which I am baptized, you will be baptized; 40but to sit at my right hand or at my left is not mine to grant, but it is for those for whom it has been prepared."

41When the ten heard this, they began to be angry with James and John. 42So Jesus called them and said to them, "You know that among the Gentiles those whom they recognize as their rulers lord it over them, and their great ones are tyrants over them. 43But it is not so among you; but whoever wishes to become great among you must be your servant, 44and whoever wishes to be first among you must be slave of all. 45For the Son of Man came not to be served but to serve, and to give his life a ransom for many."

The Healing of Blind Bartimaeus

46They came to Jericho. As he and his disciples and a large crowd were leaving Jericho, Bartimaeus son of Timaeus, a blind beggar, was sitting by the roadside. 47When he heard that it was Jesus of Nazareth, he began to shout out and say, "Jesus, Son of David, have mercy on me!" 48Many sternly ordered him to be quiet, but he cried out even more loudly, "Son of David, have mercy on me!" 49Jesus stood still and said, "Call him here." And they called the blind man, saying to him, "Take heart; get up, he is calling you." 50So throwing off his cloak, he sprang up and came to Jesus. 51Then Jesus said to him, "What do you want me to do for you?" The blind man said to him, "My teacher,g let me see again." 52Jesus said to him, "Go; your faith has made you well." Immediately he regained his sight and followed him on the way.

Jesus' Triumphal Entry into Jerusalem

11 When they were approaching Jerusalem, at Bethphage and Bethany, near the Mount of Olives, he sent two of his disciples 2and said to them,

---

g Aramaic *Rabbouni*

siblings (see *Rom.* 16:7–16). Nevertheless, the obvious sense of concrete rewards *in this age* may have seemed troublesome to others: *Matt.* 19:28–29 places all such rewards in the age to come; *Luke* 18:30 is vaguer about the nature of reward in this age. **10:31 *in the age to come eternal life*** Or "in the coming age, agelong life." See note to 10:17. **10:32** Jesus' third and final prediction of his coming trial, death, and resurrection; see 8:31; 9:31. These predictions have kept the momentum of the narrative moving from Peter's first recognition of Jesus' identity (8:29) to Jesus' final approach to Jerusalem here. He approaches Jerusalem from the north and east (see 10:46). **10:33–34** Both the specification of *the Gentiles* and the references to abuse reflect a progressive clarity in the predictions. **10:35–45** Another lengthy exposure of the students' misunderstanding of Jesus' mission as of their preoccupation with questions of their own status and benefits as his apostles—a developing theme in *Mark* (9:33–41; 10:28). See *2 Cor.* 3:1; 5:12; 10:17–18; 11:5; *Gal.* 1:8; 2:6, 9. Perhaps it was embarrassment felt by the author of *Matthew* over this request from two of Jesus' students that led him to attribute it to their mother instead (*Matt.* 20:20). A mother could be forgiven for such a request for her sons. **10:38 *the cup*** For suffering as draining a cup, see Aeschylus, *Prometheus Bound* 367. **10:45 *Son of Man*** See notes to 2:10, 27–28. **10:46 *They came to Jericho*** Jesus continues to approach Jerusalem from the north and east, heading south along the Jordan River valley. ***leaving Jericho*** Contrast *Luke* 18:35, which places the Bartimaeus story on the road to Jericho. ***Bartimaeus son of Timaeus*** That the author must explain bar-Timaeus as "son of Timaeus" confirms that he does not expect his readers to know easy Aramaic. See 5:41; 7:34. **10:47–48 *Son of David*** The only passage in which Jesus is addressed as Son of David in *Mark*. Since the author does not present a Davidic genealogy for Jesus (contrast *Matthew* and *Luke*) and since he will shortly present an argument for the non-Davidic lineage of the Messiah (12:35–37), it is not clear that he actually considers Jesus Davidic. Possibly, Bartimaeus is presented as using typical Jewish categories (see 11:10; *Psalms of Solomon* 17) even though they are insignificant for the author. **11:1 *at Bethphage and Bethany, near the Mount of Olives*** Jesus has now moved in from the Jordan River valley (see 10:45) to approach Jerusalem from the east. The location of both places is uncertain, but it seems

"Go into the village ahead of you, and immediately as you enter it, you will find tied there a colt that has never been ridden; untie it and bring it. ³If anyone says to you, 'Why are you doing this?' just say this, 'The Lord needs it and will send it back here immediately.'" ⁴They went away and found a colt tied near a door, outside in the street. As they were untying it, ⁵some of the bystanders said to them, "What are you doing, untying the colt?" ⁶They told them what Jesus had said; and they allowed them to take it. ⁷Then they brought the colt to Jesus and threw their cloaks on it; and he sat on it. ⁸Many people spread their cloaks on the road, and others spread leafy branches that they had cut in the fields. ⁹Then those who went ahead and those who followed were shouting,

"Hosanna!
Blessed is the one who comes in the name of the Lord!
¹⁰ Blessed is the coming kingdom of our ancestor David!
Hosanna in the highest heaven!"

¹¹Then he entered Jerusalem and went into the temple; and when he had looked around at everything, as it was already late, he went out to Bethany with the twelve.

Jesus Curses the Fig Tree

¹²On the following day, when they came from Bethany, he was hungry. ¹³Seeing in the distance a fig tree in leaf, he went to see whether perhaps he would find anything on it. When he came to it, he found nothing but leaves, for it was not the season for figs. ¹⁴He said to it, "May no one ever eat fruit from you again." And his disciples heard it.

Jesus Cleanses the Temple

¹⁵Then they came to Jerusalem. And he entered the temple and began to drive out those who were selling and those who were buying in the temple, and he overturned the tables of the money changers and the seats of those who sold doves; ¹⁶and he would not allow anyone to carry anything through the temple. ¹⁷He was teaching and saying, "Is it not written,

'My house shall be called a house of prayer for all the nations'?
But you have made it a den of robbers."

¹⁸And when the chief priests and the scribes heard it, they kept looking for a way to kill him; for they were afraid of him, because the whole crowd was

likely that Bethany was about two miles east of Jerusalem, with the Mount of Olives between; Jesus will make Bethany a sort of base for his final days in Jerusalem around Passover time. It was common for pilgrims to stay in nearby towns during feasts because the city itself was overcrowded. Bethphage, mentioned only here and in the parallels, probably lay between Bethany and the Mount of Olives. The Mount of Olives stands immediately to the east of Jerusalem and overlooks the city. **11:9–10 *Hosannah!*** This author and other Christian writers after him use the biblical Hebrew phrase *hoshi'ah na*—meaning "Please, save!"—as if it were a term of praise (see *Did.* 10.6). *Luke* 19:38 omits the phrase. The combination "Hosanna" and "Blessed is the one who comes" is found in the Hebrew Bible (*Ps.* 118:25–26) but not in the Gk version (LXX 117:25–26), which properly translates "Hosanna" as "Save us now." This suggests that the author was not using the LXX firsthand, that instead he and other Christian authors used a preexisting anthology of suitable biblical passages. See note to 7:6–7. **11:10 *the coming kingdom of our ancestor David*** Jewish literature from Jesus' time displays a wide range of expectations about the future. One basic hope, grounded in the Bible itself, envisioned a restoration of the kingdom of David, which many viewed as a golden age (*2 Sam.* 7:10–16; *Isa.* 9:7; 11:1; *Psalms of Solomon* 17). **11:11** This brief visit—Jesus' first in Jerusalem as far as we know from this text—prepares him for his actions the next day (11:15). See note to 11:1. **11:13–21** The author once again nests one story (cleansing the temple) inside another (cursing the fig tree). See note to 3:31. They are related because Israel is often compared by the biblical prophets to a barren fig tree (*Jer.* 8:13; *Hos.* 9:10). **11:13 *not the season for figs*** Although the author may have had theological reasons for saying this (e.g., it was not Israel's time to trust Christ; *Rom.* 11:11–26), it reads strangely because Jesus' cursing of the tree then appears groundless and arbitrary. *Matt.* 21:9 omits this observation. *Luke* omits the entire story in favor of a parable about a fruitless fig tree (13:6–9). **11:15–16** Since Jews came from all over the world for the pilgrimage feasts, such as Passover (14:1), money changers and sellers of animals were necessary in the temple area. Money had to be changed because the only currency that could be used in the temple was that of Tyre; sacrificial animals had to be sold because pilgrims could not easily bring them from faraway places. Doves (pigeons, especially the smaller varieties) were in special demand because, in addition to being the specified victims for certain kinds of sacrifice (*Lev.* 12:6; 15:14, 30; *Num.* 6:10), they could also substitute for larger animals when the person making the sacrifice could not afford the specified victim (*Lev.* 5:7; 12:8; 14:21–22). Archaeologists have turned up about a thousand underground dove-raising installations in ancient Palestine, most of them along the coastal plain; it was an important industry. It seems that the money changers and animal sellers set up in the royal portico built by Herod the Great—the huge, triple-aisled, covered promenade at the south entrance to the Temple Mount, where pilgrims normally entered. **11:17** *Isa.* 56:7. The phrase *for all the nations* supports *Mark*'s Gentile interests. *Matt.* 21:13 and *Luke* 19:46 omit it. **den of robbers** An allusion to *Jer.* 7:11. Josephus often uses the term "robbers" to characterize those who have polluted the temple, in his view (e.g., *J.W.* 2.228–229); he may well have derived the term from this passage in *Jeremiah*. **11:18** Just as Jesus ran into immediate and lethal conflict with Jewish leaders in Galilee at the beginning of his public career (2:1–3:6), so now in Jerusalem the leaders quickly set out to kill him. With the first narrative appearance of the chief priests and scribes, the reader is alerted that the predictions of 8:31, 9:31, and 10:32 are soon to be fulfilled. The observation that Jesus' large following was spellbound by his teaching. [19]And when evening came, Jesus and his disciples[h] went out of the city.

The Lesson from the Withered Fig Tree

[20]In the morning as they passed by, they saw the fig tree withered away to its roots. [21]Then Peter remembered and said to him, "Rabbi, look! The fig tree that you cursed has withered." [22]Jesus answered them, "Have[i] faith in God. [23]Truly I tell you, if you say to this mountain, 'Be taken up and thrown into the sea,' and if you do not doubt in your heart, but believe that what you say will come to pass, it will be done for you. [24]So I tell you, whatever you ask for in prayer, believe that you have received[j] it, and it will be yours.

[25]"Whenever you stand praying, forgive, if you have anything against anyone; so that your Father in heaven may also forgive you your trespasses."[k]

Jesus' Authority Is Questioned

[27]Again they came to Jerusalem. As he was walking in the temple, the chief priests, the scribes, and the elders came to him [28]and said, "By what authority are you doing these things? Who gave you this authority to do them?" [29]Jesus said to them, "I will ask you one question; answer me, and I will tell you by what authority I do these things. [30]Did the baptism of John come from heaven, or was it of human origin? Answer me." [31]They argued with one another, "If we say, 'From heaven,' he will say, 'Why then did you not believe him?' [32]But shall we say, 'Of human origin'?"—they were afraid of the crowd, for all regarded John as truly a prophet. [33]So they answered Jesus, "We do not know." And Jesus said to them, "Neither will I tell you by what authority I am doing these things."

The Parable of the Wicked Tenants

12 Then he began to speak to them in parables. "A man planted a vineyard, put a fence around it, dug a pit for the wine press, and built a watchtower; then he leased it to tenants and went to another country. [2]When the season came, he sent a slave to the tenants to collect from them his share of the produce of the vineyard. [3]But they seized him, and beat him, and sent him away empty-handed. [4]And again he sent another slave to them; this one they beat over the head and insulted. [5]Then he sent another, and that one they killed. And so it was with many others; some they beat, and others they killed. [6]He had still one other, a beloved son. Finally he sent him to them, saying, 'They will respect my son.' [7]But those tenants said to one another, 'This is the heir; come, let us kill him, and the inheritance will be ours.' [8]So they seized him, killed him, and threw him out of the vineyard. [9]What then will the owner of the vineyard do? He will come and destroy the tenants and give the vineyard to others. [10]Have you not read this scripture:

'The stone that the builders rejected
    has become the cornerstone;[l]
[11] this was the Lord's doing,
    and it is amazing in our eyes'?"

[12]When they realized that he had told this parable against them, they wanted to arrest him, but they feared the crowd. So they left him and went away.

---

h Gk *they;* other ancient authorities read *he*
i Other ancient authorities read *"If you have*
j Other ancient authorities read *are receiving*
k Other ancient authorities add verse 26, *"But if you do not forgive, neither will your Father in heaven forgive your trespasses."*

l Or *keystone*

---

the cause for concern makes historical sense inasmuch as feast times in Jerusalem made the Roman and Jewish authorities particularly sensitive to troublemakers (Josephus, e.g., *J.W.* 2.42–43, 224, 232, 255), although *Mark* has not yet indicated that it was a feast time (see 14:1). **11:19 went out of the city** Probably to Bethany; see 11:11 and note to 11:1. **11:20–24** The author's inclusion of the temple cleansing within the fig tree story suggests a theological relation; the author, however, does not draw it out. The lesson of the fig tree appears to be that one can perform similar or greater marvels with sufficient faith. **11:25** This appears to be an individual saying, which the author connects with 11:24 on the strength of the common theme of prayer. See note to 9:42–50. **11:27 the chief priests, the scribes, and the elders** See note to 11:18. **11:32** That John had a large and devoted following is confirmed by Josephus, *Ant.* 18.116–119. **12:1–12** This parable is actually an allegory, since it does not merely illustrate a single point but also has each item in the story stand for something else (e.g., the wicked tenants are the Jewish leaders; the vineyard is perhaps the covenant; the messengers are the prophets; the son is Jesus). For a simpler version of the parable, which lacks all reference to the destruction of Jerusalem as punishment for the Jews' rejection of Jesus, see *Gospel of Thomas* 65–66. **12:1** The point of these details seems to be that the vineyard owner had put a lot of work into the place; the revenue was rightfully his. **12:6 a beloved son** The reader can have no doubt that this son represents Jesus in view of 1:1, 11; 9:7. **12:9 give the vineyard to others** Jesus thus anticipates the success of the largely Pauline mission to the Gentiles in the first generation; see note to 7:26. **12:10–11** *Ps.* 118:22 (LXX 117:22). See note to *Matt.* 21:42.

The Question about Paying Taxes

13Then they sent to him some Pharisees and some Herodians to trap him in what he said. 14And they came and said to him, "Teacher, we know that you are sincere, and show deference to no one; for you do not regard people with partiality, but teach the way of God in accordance with truth. Is it lawful to pay taxes to the emperor, or not? 15Should we pay them, or should we not?" But knowing their hypocrisy, he said to them, "Why are you putting me to the test? Bring me a denarius and let me see it." 16And they brought one. Then he said to them, "Whose head is this, and whose title?" They answered, "The emperor's." 17Jesus said to them, "Give to the emperor the things that are the emperor's, and to God the things that are God's." And they were utterly amazed at him.

The Question about the Resurrection

18Some Sadducees, who say there is no resurrection, came to him and asked him a question, saying, 19"Teacher, Moses wrote for us that if a man's brother dies, leaving a wife but no child, the man*m* shall marry the widow and raise up children for his brother. 20There were seven brothers; the first married and, when he died, left no children; 21and the second married her and died, leaving no children; and the third likewise; 22none of the seven left chil-

dren. Last of all the woman herself died. 23In the resurrection*n* whose wife will she be? For the seven had married her."

24Jesus said to them, "Is not this the reason you are wrong, that you know neither the scriptures nor the power of God? 25For when they rise from the dead, they neither marry nor are given in marriage, but are like angels in heaven. 26And as for the dead being raised, have you not read in the book of Moses, in the story about the bush, how God said to him, 'I am the God of Abraham, the God of Isaac, and the God of Jacob'? 27He is God not of the dead, but of the living; you are quite wrong."

The First Commandment

28One of the scribes came near and heard them disputing with one another, and seeing that he answered them well, he asked him, "Which commandment is the first of all?" 29Jesus answered, "The first is, 'Hear, O Israel: the Lord our God, the Lord is one; 30you shall love the Lord your God with all your heart, and with all your soul, and with all your mind, and with all your strength.' 31The second is this, 'You shall love your neighbor as yourself.' There is no other commandment greater than these." 32Then the scribe said to him, "You are right, Teacher; you have truly said that 'he is one, and besides him there is no

---

m Gk *his brother*

n Other ancient authorities add *when they rise*

12:13 **they sent** This confirms that in this author's view, the Pharisees and Herodians, who had long ago determined to kill Jesus (3:6), were closely connected with the Jerusalem leadership. See note to 8:31. **12:14–15** Since 6 C.E., when Judea had been formally annexed to the Roman Empire as a province, taxation had become a major issue; a violent tax revolt had occurred in that year, led by a Galilean (or Gaulanite) named Judas. The issues were both the amount of taxation (burdensome even when the Jews had governed themselves under client rulers) and, just as important, the subservience to Rome that it demonstrated. See Josephus, *Ant.* 18.4–10. **12:15** **denarius** This was a fairly large silver coin, struck in one of the major cities of the empire, not locally produced. Local coins were usually for small denominations and lacked human or animal images (*Exod.* 20:4). The emperor whose image appeared on the coin was probably Tiberius (ruled 14–37 C.E.). **12:18** According to Josephus (*Ant.* 13.297–298; 18.16), the Sadducees rejected every teaching that was not in the laws of Moses. Since everyone who wished to put biblical law into practice necessarily had to bring some kind of interpretative framework to it, this means that the Sadducees repudiated the postbiblical tradition accepted by the Pharisees; they were unconscious of the nonbiblical elements in their own viewpoint. Their deliberate repudiation of nonbiblical teaching led them to reject, among other things, the notion of resurrection; it is not taught in the Torah. **12:19–23** *Deut.* 25:5. The practice was known as levirate marriage. The Sadducees argue in effect that their devoted adherence to the laws of Moses precludes a belief in resurrection. **12:25** See Paul's description of the resurrection body (a "spiritual" body) in *1 Cor.* 15:35–50. *Luke* 24:39 reflects a different view. **12:26–27** The story and citation are from *Exod.* 3:6, slightly compressed. Jesus' argument seems to run as follows: since (a) God is the God of the living only (major premise) and since (b) God claimed to be the God of the patriarchs after they had died—in Moses' day (minor premise); therefore, (c) the patriarchs must still have been living (or awaiting new life?) after their death; hence, there is resurrection. Jesus must argue from the Torah of Moses because this is all that the Sadducees will accept (Josephus, *Ant.* 13.297–298). **12:28** Once again, the author assumes a close connection among all of the Jewish groups; here the scribes, previously linked with the Pharisees, take the side of the Sadducees although it appears from Josephus (*Ant.* 13.297–298) and rabbinic literature (also *Acts* 23:6–7) that these groups had serious differences. **12:29–30** *Deut.* 6:4. This is the foundation of the Shema (Hebrew for "Hear!"), the biblical declaration recited twice daily by observant Jews. **12:31** *Lev.* 19:18. **12:32** **You are right** As far as we know, no Jew would have disputed Jesus' identification of these two commandments as central to the Torah. The eminent Hillel is said to have summarized the entire Torah in the golden rule (*b. Shabbat* 31a). The distinction between commandments dealing with human-divine relations and those dealing with relations among humans is also standard in rabbinic Judaism.

other'; [33]and 'to love him with all the heart, and with all the understanding, and with all the strength,' and 'to love one's neighbor as oneself,'—this is much more important than all whole burnt offerings and sacrifices." [34]When Jesus saw that he answered wisely, he said to him, "You are not far from the kingdom of God." After that no one dared to ask him any question.

The Question about David's Son

[35]While Jesus was teaching in the temple, he said, "How can the scribes say that the Messiah[o] is the son of David? [36]David himself, by the Holy Spirit, declared,

'The Lord said to my Lord,
"Sit at my right hand,
       until I put your enemies under your feet."'
[37]David himself calls him Lord; so how can he be his son?" And the large crowd was listening to him with delight.

Jesus Denounces the Scribes

[38]As he taught, he said, "Beware of the scribes, who like to walk around in long robes, and to be greeted with respect in the marketplaces, [39]and to

---

o Or the Christ

have the best seats in the synagogues and places of honor at banquets! [40]They devour widows' houses and for the sake of appearance say long prayers. They will receive the greater condemnation."

The Widow's Offering

[41]He sat down opposite the treasury, and watched the crowd putting money into the treasury. Many rich people put in large sums. [42]A poor widow came and put in two small copper coins, which are worth a penny. [43]Then he called his disciples and said to them, "Truly I tell you, this poor widow has put in more than all those who are contributing to the treasury. [44]For all of them have contributed out of their abundance; but she out of her poverty has put in everything she had, all she had to live on."

The Destruction of the Temple Foretold

13 As he came out of the temple, one of his disciples said to him, "Look, Teacher, what large stones and what large buildings!" [2]Then Jesus asked him, "Do you see these great buildings? Not one stone will be left here upon another; all will be thrown down."

[3]When he was sitting on the Mount of Olives opposite the temple, Peter, James, John, and Andrew

---

12:33 *more important than all whole burnt offerings and sacrifices* It was a standard position in the prophets and in later rabbinic Judaism that prayer, obedience, and the intention of the heart took precedence over sacrifices. See *Hos.* 6:6. But perhaps *Mark* means more—that the entire Jewish temple regimen is unnecessary. **12:35–37** *Mark*'s Jesus essentially challenges the scribal view that the Messiah would be a descendant of David. See note to 10:47–48. He argues from *Ps.* 110:1 (LXX 109:1). The psalmist was extolling the Israelite king (perhaps at his inauguration), as the rest of the psalm makes clear; the king was "my lord" from the psalmist's point of view. *Mark*'s Jesus attributes the psalm to David, as if it were a prophecy concerning the Messiah ("my lord"). Since David allegedly calls the future Messiah "my lord," he cannot be the Messiah's father. *Mark* goes to great lengths to argue that the Messiah was not a descendant of David, while *Matthew* and *Luke* were keen to demonstrate Jesus' Davidic ancestry (*Matt.* 1:2–17; *Luke* 3:31; see *Rom.* 1:4). **12:36** *Ps.* 110:1. **12:38** The author may have included this criticism of the scribes here, although it could have been inserted at many points in the narrative, because the two preceding blocks of material concern scribes. See note to 9:42–50. **12:41** *the treasury* The temple accepted all sorts of gifts, in addition to the mandatory half-shekel tax collected from Jews all around the world; like other temples in the ancient world, it also served as a bank for holding savings (on the often disproved theory that in time of war armies would respect the sanctity of a temple). **12:42** *two small copper coins, which are worth a penny* Lit. "two *lepta*, which are a *quadrans*." The *lepton* (plural *lepta*) was a tiny, locally minted copper coin. The *quadrans* was a Roman coin, worth one-sixtieth of a denarius (a generous daily wage for a laborer), so the *lepton* was worth little indeed. That the author must explain the *lepton* is another clue that his audience did not know Palestinian conditions (see introduction to *Mark*). **13:1** Herod the Great had carried out such extensive renovations of the second postexilic temple that it could justifiably be called the "third temple" (after Solomon's and the one built by the returning Babylonian exiles). He created a massive artificial platform grounded in bedrock for the various courtyards of the temple, monumental porticos and staircases, and magnificent buildings. Some of the foundation stones of the retaining wall for the platform remain to this day; the largest weigh about four hundred metric tons, and they are so perfectly cut that they require no mortar to hold them together. The renovation process was still going on in Jesus' day, although Herod had long since died. See Josephus's descriptions in *J.W.* 5.184–229; *Ant.* 15.380–402. It must have seemed to an observer, as it did to Josephus and even the conquering general Titus (according to Josephus, *J.W.* 6.409–413), that Jerusalem and its temple could withstand almost anything. **13:2** *Mark*'s Jesus predicts the destruction of the temple, which occurred in 70 C.E. (about forty years after Jesus' death) after a four-year war with the Romans. Given that *Mark* was written at least about the time of the temple's destruction and that this event was well known throughout the rest of the world, it seems more likely that the early church developed Jesus' criticisms of temple practice into a full-scale prediction. **13:3** *Mount of Olives* This high hill immediately to the east of Jerusalem, which continues into Mount Scopus in the northeast, affords an excellent view of the east side of the Temple Mount.

asked him privately, 4"Tell us, when will this be, and what will be the sign that all these things are about to be accomplished?" 5Then Jesus began to say to them, "Beware that no one leads you astray. 6Many will come in my name and say, 'I am he!'*p* and they will lead many astray. 7When you hear of wars and rumors of wars, do not be alarmed; this must take place, but the end is still to come. 8For nation will rise against nation, and kingdom against kingdom; there will be earthquakes in various places; there will be famines. This is but the beginning of the birth pangs.

Persecution Foretold

9"As for yourselves, beware; for they will hand you over to councils; and you will be beaten in synagogues; and you will stand before governors and kings because of me, as a testimony to them. 10And the good news*q* must first be proclaimed to all nations. 11When they bring you to trial and hand you over, do not worry beforehand about what you are to say; but say whatever is given you at that time, for it is not you who speak, but the Holy Spirit. 12Brother will betray brother to death, and a father his child, and children will rise against parents and have them put to death; 13and you will be hated by all because of my name. But the one who endures to the end will be saved.

The Desolating Sacrilege

14"But when you see the desolating sacrilege set up where it ought not to be (let the reader understand), then those in Judea must flee to the mountains; 15the one on the housetop must not go down or enter the house to take anything away; 16the one in the field must not turn back to get a coat. 17Woe to those who are pregnant and to those who are nursing infants in those days! 18Pray that it may not be in winter. 19For in those days there will be suffering, such as has not been from the beginning of the creation that God created until now, no, and never will be. 20And if the Lord had not cut short those days, no one would be saved; but for the sake of the elect, whom he chose, he has cut short those days. 21And if anyone says to you at that time, 'Look! Here is the Messiah!'*r* or 'Look! There he is!'—do not believe it. 22False messiahs*s* and false prophets will appear and produce signs and omens, to lead astray, if possible, the elect. 23But be alert; I have already told you everything.

The Coming of the Son of Man

24"But in those days, after that suffering,
  the sun will be darkened,
      and the moon will not give its light,
25 and the stars will be falling from heaven,
      and the powers in the heavens will be shaken.

---

p Gk *I am*
q Gk *gospel*

r Or *the Christ*
s Or *christs*

13:4 *Peter, James, John, and Andrew* Jesus' first four students (1:16–20), who form a sort of inner circle; see note to 5:37. **13:4–37** This "little apocalypse" is central to *Mark*'s outlook; it mirrors Paul's view that the end of the age, marked by Jesus' return and the arrival of the new age, is imminent. See 1 *Thess.* 1:9–10; 4:13–5:11; *1 Cor.* 7:26–31. **13:6** The 1st century saw many charismatic leaders who thought themselves to be, or were thought by others to be, the awaited Anointed One (Messiah); see Josephus, *J.W.* 2.42–43, 224, 232, 255. See also *Did.* 16.3. **13:8** Famines were common in the eastern Mediterranean, especially in Judea, which suffered a particularly devastating drought in 46–47 C.E. (*Acts* 11:29–30; Josephus, *Ant.* 20.51–53). Famine also accompanied the destruction of Jerusalem in 70 (*J.W.* 5.424–438, 571; 6.193–213). Earthquakes were not as well known, though they are typical symbols of apocalyptic terror; the volcanic eruption of Mount Vesuvius, which destroyed Pompeii in 79 C.E., became widely known (although it may have occurred after the composition of *Mark*). **13:9** All of these things happened to Paul, according to his letters (*2 Cor.* 11:23–27) and *Acts* (23–26). Trials before a king could be predicated of those living in the times and regions of Agrippa I (e.g., James, the brother of John; *Acts* 12:1–2) and II, but of few other Christians in the Roman world. **13:10** Compare Paul's claim that he has fully preached the gospel in the eastern Mediterranean (*Rom.* 15:19); see also *Col.* 1:6, 23. **13:11** *not you who speak, but the Holy Spirit* See note to 1:23. **13:12** The conditions described were typical of dread scenarios in ancient writing, going back to Hesiod's (8th century B.C.E.) description of the present evil age in his *Works and Days* 170–195. **13:13** *endures to the end* The hope that salvation would come at the end of this specific period, to those who have remained blameless, is characteristic of Paul's early gospel (*1 Thess.* 1:10; 5:23). *Mark*'s first readers expected the end to come very soon (9:1; 13:30). **13:14** *desolating sacrilege* The term is from *Daniel* (as *Matt.* 24:15 elaborates), an extremely popular book among apocalyptic groups such as the circles of the Dead Sea Scrolls and some early Christians. The original reference (*Dan.* 9:27; 11:31; 12:11; *1 Macc.* 1:54) was to the pagan altar set up by the Seleucid King Antiochus IV in the Jerusalem temple; this was one cause of the Maccabean revolt (167–164 B.C.E.). In the 1st century, many Jews had reinterpreted *Daniel* to refer to events of their own time, such that the Romans (rather than the Seleucids) should be the final world empire before the dawn of the new age. See Josephus, *Ant.* 10.266–281; *2 Thess.* 2:4. **13:21–22** According to Josephus, a considerable range of popular leaders, both militants and visionaries, emerged during the decades preceding the revolt of 66–74 C.E. See *J.W.* 2.42–43, 224, 232, 255. **13:24–25** This language is typical of Jewish apocalyptic; see *Testament of Moses* 10.4–6; *Sibylline Oracles* 8.170–212. Its source may well be *Joel* 2:31, which is cited in *Acts* 2:20. See *Isa.* 13:10; 34:4. This scenario also recalls the heavenly warfare resulting from the clash between the Titans and the Olympians, in Hesiod, *Theogony* 685–715.

[26]Then they will see 'the Son of Man coming in clouds' with great power and glory. [27]Then he will send out the angels, and gather his elect from the four winds, from the ends of the earth to the ends of heaven.

The Lesson of the Fig Tree

[28]"From the fig tree learn its lesson: as soon as its branch becomes tender and puts forth its leaves, you know that summer is near. [29]So also, when you see these things taking place, you know that he[t] is near, at the very gates. [30]Truly I tell you, this generation will not pass away until all these things have taken place. [31]Heaven and earth will pass away, but my words will not pass away.

The Necessity for Watchfulness

[32]"But about that day or hour no one knows, neither the angels in heaven, nor the Son, but only the Father. [33]Beware, keep alert;[u] for you do not know when the time will come. [34]It is like a man going on a journey, when he leaves home and puts his slaves in charge, each with his work, and commands the doorkeeper to be on the watch. [35]Therefore, keep awake—for you do not know when the master of the house will come, in the evening, or at midnight, or at cockcrow, or at dawn, [36]or else he may find you asleep when he comes suddenly. [37]And what I say to you I say to all: Keep awake."

The Plot to Kill Jesus

14 It was two days before the Passover and the festival of Unleavened Bread. The chief priests and the scribes were looking for a way to arrest Jesus[v] by stealth and kill him; [2]for they said, "Not during the festival, or there may be a riot among the people."

The Anointing at Bethany

[3]While he was at Bethany in the house of Simon the leper,[w] as he sat at the table, a woman came with an alabaster jar of very costly ointment of nard, and she broke open the jar and poured the ointment on his head. [4]But some were there who said to one another in anger, "Why was the ointment wasted in this way? [5]For this ointment could have been sold for more than three hundred denarii,[x] and the money given to the poor." And they scolded her. [6]But Jesus said, "Let her alone; why do you trouble her? She has performed a good service for me. [7]For you always have the poor with you, and you can show kindness to them whenever you wish; but you will not always have me. [8]She has done what she could; she has anointed my body beforehand for its burial. [9]Truly I tell you, wherever the good news[y] is proclaimed in the whole world, what she has done will be told in remembrance of her."

Judas Agrees to Betray Jesus

[10]Then Judas Iscariot, who was one of the twelve, went to the chief priests in order to betray him to them. [11]When they heard it, they were greatly pleased, and promised to give him money. So he began to look for an opportunity to betray him.

The Passover with the Disciples

[12]On the first day of Unleavened Bread, when the Passover lamb is sacrificed, his disciples said to him, "Where do you want us to go and make the prepara-

---

t Or it
u Other ancient authorities add *and pray*
v Gk *him*

w The terms *leper* and *leprosy* can refer to several diseases
x The denarius was the usual day's wage for a laborer
y Or *gospel*

13:26 The reference is to *Dan.* 7:13: a human figure (lit. "one like a son of man," in contrast to the animal figures preceding) ascends to heaven in triumph over Israel's enemies; this represents Israel. *Mark*'s Jesus envisions this Son of Man (Jesus himself) *descending* from heaven in glory at the end of age. **13:30** See 9:1; the end of the age is imminent. **13:32–37** See *1 Thess.* 5:1–4. The time of Jesus' return in glory was a major concern to the young church. **14:1** Although the Feast of Unleavened Bread may have originated independently of Passover traditions, by Jesus' time they were celebrated together as a weeklong feast; see *Luke* 22:1. They commemorated the deliverance of the Israelites from slavery in Egypt under Moses; see *Exod.* 12–13. **the chief priests and the scribes** See 11:18. **14:2 may be a riot** On the dangers of rioting at feast times, see Josephus, *J.W.* 2.42–43, 224, 232, 255. **14:3 Simon** Oddly, *Luke* 7:36–50 locates this story in the home of an unnamed Pharisee, whereas *John* 12:1–8 puts it in the home of Mary, Martha, and Lazarus. **the leper** See note to 1:40. **sat at the table** Better: "reclined [for a meal]." See note to 2:15. **nard** This root-based perfume had to be imported from Nepal. It was therefore rare in 1st-century Judea and expensive (14:5). **14:4 some were there who said** *John* 12:4 attributes this statement to Judas Iscariot; *Luke* 7:39 introduces a different kind of criticism from the Pharisee host. **14:5 three hundred denarii** About one year's wages for a day laborer. **14:10 Judas Iscariot** See 3:19 and note. If we can deduce anything from the positioning of episodes here, Judas's motive would have been his disdain for Jesus' willingness to have expensive ointment used in this manner. Indeed, according to *John* 12:4, it was Judas who criticized the woman's action. **14:12 when the Passover lamb is sacrificed** The feast itself ran from Nisan 15 to Nisan 21; on the day before the feast (Nisan 14), the sacrificial lambs were slaughtered (see APPENDIX C). See *Num.* 28:16–25; *Deut.* 16:1–8.

tions for you to eat the Passover?" 13So he sent two of his disciples, saying to them, "Go into the city, and a man carrying a jar of water will meet you; follow him, 14and wherever he enters, say to the owner of the house, 'The Teacher asks, Where is my guest room where I may eat the Passover with my disciples?' 15He will show you a large room upstairs, furnished and ready. Make preparations for us there." 16So the disciples set out and went to the city, and found everything as he had told them; and they prepared the Passover meal.

17When it was evening, he came with the twelve. 18And when they had taken their places and were eating, Jesus said, "Truly I tell you, one of you will betray me, one who is eating with me." 19They began to be distressed and to say to him one after another, "Surely, not I?" 20He said to them, "It is one of the twelve, one who is dipping bread*z* into the bowl*a* with me. 21For the Son of Man goes as it is written of him, but woe to that one by whom the Son of Man is betrayed! It would have been better for that one not to have been born."

The Institution of the Lord's Supper

22While they were eating, he took a loaf of bread, and after blessing it he broke it, gave it to them, and said, "Take; this is my body." 23Then he took a cup, and after giving thanks he gave it to them, and all of them drank from it. 24He said to them, "This is my blood of the*b* covenant, which is poured out for many. 25Truly I tell you, I will never again drink of the fruit of the vine until that day when I drink it new in the kingdom of God."

Peter's Denial Foretold

26When they had sung the hymn, they went out to the Mount of Olives. 27And Jesus said to them, "You will all become deserters; for it is written,

'I will strike the shepherd,
    and the sheep will be scattered.'

28But after I am raised up, I will go before you to Galilee." 29Peter said to him, "Even though all become deserters, I will not." 30Jesus said to him, "Truly I tell you, this day, this very night, before the cock crows twice, you will deny me three times." 31But he said vehemently, "Even though I must die with you, I will not deny you." And all of them said the same.

Jesus Prays in Gethsemane

32They went to a place called Gethsemane; and he said to his disciples, "Sit here while I pray." 33He took with him Peter and James and John, and began to be distressed and agitated. 34And he said to them, "I am deeply grieved, even to death; remain here, and keep awake." 35And going a little farther, he threw himself on the ground and prayed that, if it were possible, the hour might pass from him. 36He said, "Abba,*c* Father, for you all things are possible; remove this cup from me; yet, not what I want, but what you want." 37He came and found them sleeping; and he said to Peter, "Simon, are you asleep? Could you not keep awake one hour? 38Keep awake and pray that you may not come into the time of trial;*d* the spirit indeed is willing, but the flesh is weak." 39And again he went away and prayed, saying the same words. 40And once more he came and found them sleeping, for their eyes were very heavy; and they did not know what to say to him. 41He came a third time and said to them, "Are you still sleeping and taking your rest? Enough! The hour has come; the Son of Man is betrayed into the hands of sinners. 42Get up, let us be going. See, my betrayer is at hand."

The Betrayal and Arrest of Jesus

43Immediately, while he was still speaking, Judas, one of the twelve, arrived; and with him there was a

---

z Gk lacks *bread*
a Other ancient authorities read *same bowl*
b Other ancient authorities add *new*

c Aramaic for *Father*
d Or *into temptation*

14:17 *When it was evening* The Jewish day began at sundown (see *Gen.* 1:5). Thus, evening ushered in Nisan 15, the beginning of the feast. *taken their places* Better: "reclined." See note to 2:15. **14:21** *Son of Man* Scripture nowhere describes the suffering of a Son of Man, so it is unclear what *Mark* means here. See notes to 2:10, 27–28; 13:26. **14:22–24** The earliest version of the Last Supper story, with the eucharistic words that have become part of the Christian tradition of Communion, is in Paul's letters, *1 Cor.* 11:23–26. *Mark* differs in several respects. *Matt.* 26:26–29 basically follows *Mark*, whereas *Luke* 22:15–20 incorporates much of the wording from Paul's version. **14:25** *kingdom of God* See note to 4:26–32. **14:26** *sung the hymn* The Gk—a single word meaning "they hymned"—does not suggest that a particular hymn was in view. **14:27** A loose paraphrase of *Zech.* 13:7: "Strike down the shepherd, / And let the flock scatter." **14:28** See 16:7. **14:32** *Gethsemane* A garden on the western slope of the Mount of Olives, immediately east of Jerusalem. **14:33** *Peter and James and John* See notes to 5:37; 13:4. **14:36** *Abba* Characteristically (see 5:41; 7:34), this author injects an Aramaic term (for "Father"), one that was already commonly used in prayer in some Greek-speaking churches of the eastern Mediterranean (*Gal.* 4:6; *Rom.* 8:15). *Matt.* 26:39 and *Luke* 22:42, typically, omit it. *this cup* For the cup as an image of suffering, see note to 10:38. **14:38** *Simon* See note to 3:16. **14:41** *Son of Man* See notes to 2:10, 27–28. **14:43** *the chief priests, the scribes, and the elders* See note to 11:18.

crowd with swords and clubs, from the chief priests, the scribes, and the elders. ⁴⁴Now the betrayer had given them a sign, saying, "The one I will kiss is the man; arrest him and lead him away under guard." ⁴⁵So when he came, he went up to him at once and said, "Rabbi!" and kissed him. ⁴⁶Then they laid hands on him and arrested him. ⁴⁷But one of those who stood near drew his sword and struck the slave of the high priest, cutting off his ear. ⁴⁸Then Jesus said to them, "Have you come out with swords and clubs to arrest me as though I were a bandit? ⁴⁹Day after day I was with you in the temple teaching, and you did not arrest me. But let the scriptures be fulfilled." ⁵⁰All of them deserted him and fled.

⁵¹A certain young man was following him, wearing nothing but a linen cloth. They caught hold of him, ⁵²but he left the linen cloth and ran off naked.

Jesus before the Council

⁵³They took Jesus to the high priest; and all the chief priests, the elders, and the scribes were as-sembled. ⁵⁴Peter had followed him at a distance, right into the courtyard of the high priest; and he was sitting with the guards, warming himself at the fire. ⁵⁵Now the chief priests and the whole council were looking for testimony against Jesus to put him to death; but they found none. ⁵⁶For many gave false testimony against him, and their testimony did not agree. ⁵⁷Some stood up and gave false testimony against him, saying, ⁵⁸"We heard him say, 'I will destroy this temple that is made with hands, and in three days I will build another, not made with hands.'" ⁵⁹But even on this point their testimony did not agree. ⁶⁰Then the high priest stood up before them and asked Jesus, "Have you no answer? What is it that they testify against you?" ⁶¹But he was silent and did not answer. Again the high priest asked him, "Are you the Messiah,ᵉ the Son of the Blessed One?"

---

e Or the Christ

14:45 Rabbi See note to 9:5. **14:47** *Matt.* 26:51–54, *Luke* 22:50–51, and *John* 18:10–11 all have Jesus rebuking the one who drew the sword, even healing the ear *(Luke)*. **14:49 let the scriptures be fulfilled** It is unclear which scripture is meant. **14:50** This is the last we see of Jesus' students except Peter. **14:51–52** This story is peculiar because it does not seem to support the following narrative except for providing the linen cloth of 15:46 and the young man of 16:5. It is one of the few passages in *Mark* that is not picked up in either *Matthew* or *Luke*. In 1958, Morton Smith discovered a transcription of a letter from Clement of Alexandria (ca. 200 C.E.) that indicates that there was a secret gospel of Mark, in addition to the well-known *Mark*, circulating in Alexandria. In one of the two fragments from this gospel quoted by Clement, Jesus raises a young man from the dead. This happens between *Mark* 10:34 and 10:35. The young man then goes to visit Jesus dressed only in a linen cloth and spends the night with him. Some scholars argue that *Mark* 14:51–52 was part of a connected series of secret additions to *Mark* in the 2d century. See also *Mark* 16:5, where a young man is at the empty tomb. **14:53 the high priest** Since the return from exile (late 6th and 5th centuries B.C.E.), in the absence of monarchy, the high priest had been the effective ruler of the Jewish nation as leader of the high court. He was chosen from a small circle of elite priestly families. At the time of Jesus' trial, the high priest was Joseph Caiaphas (18–37 C.E.; see *Matt.* 26:57; Josephus, *Ant.* 18.35, 95). **the chief priests, the elders, and the scribes** See note to 11:18. **14:54** This observation creates one of *Mark*'s typical A-B-A structures (see notes to 3:31; 9:42–50); the narrative will return to Peter by the fire after the trial of Jesus before the high priest. **14:55–65** The entire trial of Jesus is most irregular from the standpoint of Jewish criminal law as it was codified in *m. San.* 4:1; 7:5. According to this law, (a) the Jewish council could not try capital cases at night or on the eve of a festival (this trial is both); (b) trial and sentence could not take place at the same meeting; (c) the council met in its own hall, not in the high priest's house; (d) someone had to speak in defense of the accused at the trial; (e) only uttering the divine name (YHWH)—not calling oneself Messiah or even Son of God—was blasphemy; and (f) the high priest was the one person who was not permitted to rip his clothes. Although the Mishnah was not published until the early 3d century C.E., such legal principles are not usually susceptible to rapid change, and we may suppose that most of them were in place in the 1st century. This seems confirmed by the fact that *Luke* 22:63–71 removes many of *Mark*'s difficulties in its version of the trial. **14:55 the whole council** Gk *synedrion:* "meeting, assembly, congress." According to *m. Sanh.,* the Great Council in Jerusalem numbered seventy-one members. Capital cases required twenty-three judges. It is not clear, however, that the council here matched the composition specified in the Mishnah. Josephus presents the chief priests and leading Pharisees as the core of the leading council (*J.W.* 2.411). Some scholars doubt whether there was a *standing* council under Roman rule. **14:58** This charge functions on at least two levels. On the surface, since Jesus has nowhere said any such thing in the preceding narrative and it is introduced as a lie, it appears obviously untrue. But the Christian reader knows that the part about building a temple not made with hands, to replace the standing center of Judaism, has been ironically fulfilled in Jesus' resurrection. *Luke* removes this entire charge from the trial narrative, postponing it to Stephen's trial in *Acts* (6:14); the author can then elaborate considerably on the temple not made with hands (*Acts* 7:47–50). **14:61 Messiah, the Son of the Blessed One** *Mark* uses the Gk term *christos;* see note to 8:29. At last Jesus' identity, announced in the title of *Mark* (1:1) and confirmed at several points in the narrative (1:15; 8:29; 9:7), becomes the fatal issue in his long-developing conflict with the Jewish religious leaders.

62Jesus said, "I am; and

'you will see the Son of Man
seated at the right hand of the Power,'
and 'coming with the clouds of heaven.'"

63Then the high priest tore his clothes and said, "Why do we still need witnesses? 64You have heard his blasphemy! What is your decision?" All of them condemned him as deserving death. 65Some began to spit on him, to blindfold him, and to strike him, saying to him, "Prophesy!" The guards also took him over and beat him.

Peter Denies Jesus

66While Peter was below in the courtyard, one of the servant-girls of the high priest came by. 67When she saw Peter warming himself, she stared at him and said, "You also were with Jesus, the man from Nazareth." 68But he denied it, saying, "I do not know or understand what you are talking about." And he went out into the forecourt.f Then the cock crowed.g 69And the servant-girl, on seeing him, began again to say to the bystanders, "This man is one of them." 70But again he denied it. Then after a little while the bystanders again said to Peter, "Certainly you are one of them; for you are a Galilean." 71But he began to curse, and he swore an oath, "I do not know this man you are talking about." 72At that moment the cock crowed for the second time. Then Peter remembered that Jesus had said to him, "Before the cock crows twice, you will deny me three times." And he broke down and wept.

Jesus before Pilate

15 As soon as it was morning, the chief priests held a consultation with the elders and scribes and the whole council. They bound Jesus, led him away, and handed him over to Pilate. 2Pilate asked him, "Are you the King of the Jews?" He answered him, "You say so." 3Then the chief priests accused him of many things. 4Pilate asked him again, "Have you no answer? See how many charges they bring against you." 5But Jesus made no further reply, so that Pilate was amazed.

Pilate Hands Jesus over to Be Crucified

6Now at the festival he used to release a prisoner for them, anyone for whom they asked. 7Now a man called Barabbas was in prison with the rebels who had committed murder during the insurrection. 8So the crowd came and began to ask Pilate to do for them according to his custom. 9Then he answered them, "Do you want me to release for you the King of the Jews?" 10For he realized that it was out of jealousy that the chief priests had handed him over. 11But the chief priests stirred up the crowd to have him release Barabbas for them instead. 12Pilate spoke to them again, "Then what do you wish me to doh with the man you calli the King of the Jews?" 13They shouted back, "Crucify him!" 14Pilate asked them, "Why, what evil has he done?" But they shouted all the more, "Crucify him!" 15So Pilate, wishing to satisfy the crowd, released Barabbas for them; and after flogging Jesus, he handed him over to be crucified.

---

f Or gateway
g Other ancient authorities lack Then the cock crowed

h Other ancient authorities read what should I do
i Other ancient authorities lack the man you call

14:62 A reference to *Dan.* 7:13; but see note to 13:26. **14:65** That the judges would personally abuse Jesus confirms *Mark*'s presentation of the trial as a mockery of justice. *Luke* 22:63–65 removes this scene, transferring all such abuse to the guards. **14:66–72** Peter strenuously denied that he would ever desert Jesus; now his denial is singled out for detailed elaboration. Peter's breakdown, weeping, is the last we see of him in the story. Each of the four gospels gives a different portrayal of Peter's three questioners. **15:1** *Pilate* Pontius Pilate, prefect of Judea from 26 to 36 C.E. (see *Matt.* 27:1). **15:2** *King of the Jews* Apparently, the author and his readers see this term as roughly equivalent (from a Roman's perspective) to the term "Messiah" in the trial before the Sanhedrin (15:61). Claiming to be either Messiah or Son of God was not a capital offense in Judaism, but claiming to be *King of the Jews* might create serious problems at feast times in Jerusalem if one had much of a following. *You say so* The meaning of this answer has been much debated. *Luke* 23:3–4 seems to take it as a negative reply, but parallels in other literature have been found for both affirmative and negative senses. Even here the accusation quickly gets buried in a mass of other vague charges. But it is the charge of political insurrection (being *King of the Jews*) that Pilate will order written on Jesus' cross (*Mark* 15:26). **15:6** This alleged custom, the *privilegium paschale,* is unknown outside the gospels. See *Matt.* 27:15. **15:7** *Barabbas* A peculiar Aramaic name, "son of the father." See notes on *John* 18:40; *Matt.* 27:16. *the insurrection* We do not know from other literature of an insurrection in Judea at the time of Jesus' death, but such events were apparently common enough. Given the author's (and presumably the readers') lack of knowledge of things Judean, it seems unlikely that they knew precisely which insurrection was meant. **15:13** *Crucify him* Crucifixion was well known to all readers in the Roman Empire, since it was the common punishment for slaves and provincials (not Roman citizens) guilty of serious crimes. It entailed hanging the convicted person from a crossbeam attached to an upright post, with ropes and/or spikes through the wrists and heels. The victim died, after a couple of days of humiliating suffering, from asphyxiation. **15:15** It was customary for the Romans to have a provincial criminal flogged before being led to crucifixion.

The Soldiers Mock Jesus

16Then the soldiers led him into the courtyard of the palace (that is, the governor's headquarters*j*); and they called together the whole cohort. 17And they clothed him in a purple cloak; and after twisting some thorns into a crown, they put it on him. 18And they began saluting him, "Hail, King of the Jews!" 19They struck his head with a reed, spat upon him, and knelt down in homage to him. 20After mocking him, they stripped him of the purple cloak and put his own clothes on him. Then they led him out to crucify him.

The Crucifixion of Jesus

21They compelled a passer-by, who was coming in from the country, to carry his cross; it was Simon of Cyrene, the father of Alexander and Rufus. 22Then they brought Jesus*k* to the place called Golgotha (which means the place of a skull). 23And they offered him wine mixed with myrrh; but he did not take it. 24And they crucified him, and divided his clothes among them, casting lots to decide what each should take.

25It was nine o'clock in the morning when they crucified him. 26The inscription of the charge against him read, "The King of the Jews." 27And with him they crucified two bandits, one on his right and one on his left.*l*And he was counted among the lawless.

29Those who passed by derided*m* him, shaking their heads and saying, "Aha! You who would destroy the temple and build it in three days, 30save yourself, and come down from the cross!" 31In the same way the chief priests, along with the scribes, were also mocking him among themselves and saying, "He saved others; he cannot save himself. 32Let the Messiah,*n* the King of Israel, come down from the cross now, so that we may see and believe." Those who were crucified with him also taunted him.

The Death of Jesus

33When it was noon, darkness came over the whole land*o* until three in the afternoon. 34At three o'clock Jesus cried out with a loud voice, "Eloi, Eloi, lema sabachthani?" which means, "My God, my God, why have you forsaken me?"*p* 35When some of the bystanders heard it, they said, "Listen, he is calling for Elijah." 36And someone ran, filled a sponge with sour wine, put it on a stick, and gave it to him to drink, saying, "Wait, let us see whether Elijah will come to take him down." 37Then Jesus gave a loud cry and breathed his last. 38And the curtain of the temple was torn in two, from top to bottom. 39Now when the centurion, who stood facing him, saw that in this way he*q* breathed his last, he said, "Truly this man was God's Son!"*r*

---

j Gk the praetorium
k Gk him
l Other ancient authorities add verse 28, *And the scripture was fulfilled that says, "And he was counted among the lawless."*

m Or *blasphemed*
n Or *the Christ*
o Or *earth*
p Other ancient authorities read *made me a reproach*
q Other ancient authorities add *cried out and*
r Or *a son of God*

15:16 The author is hinting that the former palace of Herod the Great served as the Roman governor's residence in Jerusalem. This palace was located on the west side of Jerusalem, near the present Jaffa Gate. The Roman governor ordinarily resided, however, in Caesarea Maritima. **15:21** Accused criminals might be required to carry the crossbeam of the cross to the place of execution; see note to 15:13. See *John* 19:17, according to which Jesus carried his own cross. Evidently, *Mark's* readers were expected to know Alexander and Rufus; these two Christians perhaps supplied the author with the story. Since the readers of *Matthew* and *Luke* had no idea who Alexander and Rufus were, however, those authors drop their names while otherwise retaining the story about Simon of Cyrene (*Matt.* 27:32; *Luke* 23:26). **15:22** *Golgotha* In this case, the author seems to include an Aramaic place-name for local color, though perhaps also because of the site's significance; see 5:41; 7:34; 14:36; 15:7. *Luke*, characteristically, drops the Aramaic (23:33). **15:23** *wine mixed with myrrh* A sedative. Myrrh was produced from tree resin in East Africa and imported to Judea. It had many uses, such as in incense and perfume. **15:24** See *Ps.* 22:18. The entire crucifixion scene contains many evocations of *Psalm* 22. **15:25** *nine o'clock in the morning* Lit. "the third hour" (past sunrise, roughly 6:00–7:00 A.M.). Contrast *John* 19:14, which claims that at about the sixth hour (noon), Jesus was still with Pilate. Moreover, whereas the Synoptics have Jesus eat the Passover meal with his disciples (*Mark* 14:12–14), *John* 19:14, 31 claims that he was crucified on Nisan 14, the day of Preparation. **15:29** *You who would destroy the temple* See 14:58. *shaking their heads* See *Ps.* 22:7. **15:30–32** These taunts recall those of the wicked toward the righteous in *Wis.* 2:16–20. **15:33** See note to 15:25. **15:34** A quotation of *Ps.* 22:1, but in Aramaic rather than in biblical Hebrew (contrast *Matt.* 27:46). On the author's interest in Aramaic expressions, see notes to 5:41; 7:34; 14:36; 15:7. **15:35–36** Because none of the languages spoken in this period and region had an English J sound, Eloi or Eli would sound vaguely like Elijah, but only someone who did not speak Aramaic or Hebrew (such as the author and his readers) would confuse the two. On Elijah, see note to 6:15; 9:4, 11. **15:38** *the curtain of the temple* Presumably, the curtain that separated the "holy place" from the holy of holies (*Exod.* 26:31–35), where the presence of God was localized over the mercy seat in the temple. The complete destruction of this curtain at the moment of Jesus' death supports *Mark's* narrative themes with respect to Judaism. **15:39** Because this centurion was in Jerusalem, in the Roman province of Judea, he likely either belonged to the auxiliary forces stationed in Jerusalem itself or came with the prefect into Jerusalem from Caesarea for the fes-

⁴⁰There were also women looking on from a distance; among them were Mary Magdalene, and Mary the mother of James the younger and of Joses, and Salome. ⁴¹These used to follow him and provided for him when he was in Galilee; and there were many other women who had come up with him to Jerusalem.

The Burial of Jesus

⁴²When evening had come, and since it was the day of Preparation, that is, the day before the sabbath, ⁴³Joseph of Arimathea, a respected member of the council, who was also himself waiting expectantly for the kingdom of God, went boldly to Pilate and asked for the body of Jesus. ⁴⁴Then Pilate wondered if he were already dead; and summoning the centurion, he asked him whether he had been dead for some time. ⁴⁵When he learned from the centurion that he was dead, he granted the body to Joseph. ⁴⁶Then Joseph*ˢ* bought a linen cloth, and taking down the body,*ᵗ* wrapped it in the linen cloth, and laid it in a tomb that had been hewn out of the rock. He then rolled a stone against the door of the tomb. ⁴⁷Mary Magdalene and Mary the mother of Joses saw where the body*ᵗ* was laid.

The Resurrection of Jesus

16 When the sabbath was over, Mary Magdalene, and Mary the mother of James, and Salome bought spices, so that they might go and anoint him. ²And very early on the first day of the week, when the sun had risen, they went to the tomb. ³They had been saying to one another, "Who will roll away the stone for us from the entrance to the tomb?" ⁴When they looked up, they saw that the stone, which was very large, had already been rolled back. ⁵As they entered the tomb, they saw a young man, dressed in a white robe, sitting on the right side; and they were alarmed. ⁶But he said to them, "Do not be alarmed; you are looking for Jesus of Nazareth, who was crucified. He has been raised; he is not here. Look, there is the place they laid him. ⁷But go, tell his disciples and Peter that he is going ahead of you to Galilee; there you will see him, just as he told you." ⁸So they went out and fled from the tomb, for terror and amazement had seized them; and they said nothing to anyone, for they were afraid.*ᵘ*

---

s Gk *he*
t Gk *it*

u Some of the most ancient authorities bring the book to a close at the end of verse 8. One authority concludes the book with the shorter ending; others include the shorter ending and then continue with verses 9–20. In most authorities verses 9–20 follow immediately after verse 8, though in some of these authorities the passage is marked as being doubtful.

---

tival; he would not have belonged to the Roman legions, which were stationed north, in Syria. A centurion was a prestigious officer in the army, commanding a century of about 80 men, possibly 160 (in the first cohort). The centurion's remark here is ironic because it operates at two levels. He might plausibly have said such a thing in a noncommittal way, offering some praise of Jesus as innocent and saintly. Indeed, *Luke*'s version (23:47) has the centurion say instead, "Certainly this man was innocent." But the author and readers of *Mark* can also see this as the climax of the work: after the Jewish leaders have rejected Jesus and the temple has been symbolically destroyed, without hesitation a Gentile reasserts Jesus' identity (see 1:1, 11; 9:7). **15:40–41** It is remarkable that the author introduces these women, who played a large role in Jesus' support network, only here. **15:40** *Mary Magdalene* Mentioned here for the 1st time in *Mark*. See *Luke* 8:2, where she appears as one of the women who consistently supported Jesus' ministry. ***Mary the mother of James the younger and of Joses*** Since James and Joses are the named as brothers of Jesus in 6:3, this Mary appears to be Jesus' mother, as *John* 19:25 plainly says. (Although *Mark* and *John* seem largely independent, they have some striking parallels; in particular, their stories of Jesus' arrest, trial, and crucifixion appear to come from the same source.) See also *Luke* 24:10; *Acts* 1:14; and their notes. *Mark* seemingly hesitates to call Mary Jesus' mother (see 3:32–35). Alternatively, since both Mary and James were extremely common names in Jesus' world, this might be an otherwise unknown Mary. *Salome* Unknown, but the parallel in *Matt.* 27:56 has "the mother of the sons of Zebedee" in her place. **15:42** Therefore, not the same "day of Preparation" as mentioned in *John* 19:31, which was the day of Preparation for Passover (Nisan 14). According to *Mark* 14:12, the day of Preparation for Passover was already past. This is Friday, the day of preparing for Sabbath. **15:43–47** *Joseph of Arimathea* Arimathea is probably to be identified with a Jewish town, known as Ramah or Rathamin (*1 Sam.* 1:1, 19), near the northern edge of Judea proper (before Samaria), northwest of Jerusalem. That he was a member of the (presumably Jerusalem) council is puzzling, in view of the trial just reported (14:64, "All of them condemned him"). Accordingly, *Matt.* 27:54 omits the claim that he was a member of the council; *Luke* 23:51 takes the only other approach, explaining that Joseph had not consented to their decision. Burial of corpses before sundown, even those of enemies, was required by Jewish law (*Deut.* 21:23). Still, upon touching the corpse, Joseph would have been rendered ritually impure and hence unable to visit the temple for the remainder of the holiday (*Num.* 19:10–13). **15:47** See note to 15:40. **16:1** *anoint him* That is, prepare the body for burial with a wrapping of spices such as myrrh. Burial preparations were typically part of women's domestic responsibilities. **16:8** *Mark* seems to end abruptly and uncomfortably, with the failure of the women around Jesus, including his mother, and following upon the failure of his dearest students, including Peter. The best explanation, perhaps, is that the author's negative portrayal of Jesus' closest associates and family was a fundamental part of his interpretation of (Pauline) Christianity, that

THE SHORTER ENDING OF MARK

[[And all that had been commanded them they told briefly to those around Peter. And afterward Jesus himself sent out through them, from east to west, the sacred and imperishable proclamation of eternal salvation.[v]]]

THE LONGER ENDING OF MARK

Jesus Appears to Mary Magdalene

9[[Now after he rose early on the first day of the week, he appeared first to Mary Magdalene, from whom he had cast out seven demons. 10She went out and told those who had been with him, while they were mourning and weeping. 11But when they heard that he was alive and had been seen by her, they would not believe it.

Jesus Appears to Two Disciples

12After this he appeared in another form to two of them, as they were walking into the country. 13And they went back and told the rest, but they did not believe them.

Jesus Commissions the Disciples

14Later he appeared to the eleven themselves as they were sitting at the table; and he upbraided them for their lack of faith and stubbornness, because they had not believed those who saw him after he had risen.[w] 15And he said to them, "Go into all the world and proclaim the good news[x] to the whole creation. 16The one who believes and is baptized will be saved; but the one who does not believe will be condemned. 17And these signs will accompany those who believe: by using my name they will cast out demons; they will speak in new tongues; 18they will pick up snakes in their hands,[y] and if they drink any deadly thing, it will not hurt them; they will lay their hands on the sick, and they will recover."

The Ascension of Jesus

19So then the Lord Jesus, after he had spoken to them, was taken up into heaven and sat down at the right hand of God. 20And they went out and proclaimed the good news everywhere, while the Lord worked with them and confirmed the message by the signs that accompanied it.[z]]]

---

v Other ancient authorities add *Amen*

w Other ancient authorities add, in whole or in part, *And they excused themselves, saying, "This age of lawlessness and unbelief is under Satan, who does not allow the truth and power of God to prevail over the unclean things of the spirits. Therefore reveal your righteousness now"—thus they spoke to Christ. And Christ replied to them, "The term of years of Satan's power has been fulfilled, but other terrible things draw near. And for those who have sinned I was handed over to death, that they may return to the truth and sin no more, that they may inherit the spiritual and imperishable glory of righteousness that is in heaven."*

x Or *gospel*

y Other ancient authorities lack *in their hands*

z Other ancient authorities add *Amen*

---

such connections do not offer any advantage. But hardly anyone found this abrupt ending satisfactory. *Matt.* 28 and *Luke* 24 both change it into a resounding finale that reflects well upon the apostles. Even later copyists of *Mark* itself, although they left intact most of the gospel, saw fit to add material to this ending in order to render it more palatable. The two fuller endings given here (*Mark* 16:8b; 9–19) do not appear in the most reliable (earliest) manuscripts of *Mark* and are almost certainly inauthentic.

The Book of the Genesis of Jesus the Messiah

MATTHEW

I N THE INTRODUCTION TO *MARK* we saw that each "gospel"—as tradition has come to call each of these narratives—has a distinctive outlook, style, vocabulary, and set of themes. *Matthew* provides a fascinating study because, although it uses *Mark* as its main source (92 percent of *Mark* is reproduced somewhere in *Matthew*), it creates from the same stories and sayings a strikingly different portrait of Jesus and of what it means to be his follower.

Overview

The author of *Matthew* creates this new impression in various ways: by supplying a new beginning (chs. 1–2) and ending (ch. 28); by adding considerable material not found in *Mark,* though much of it is paralleled in *Luke* and *Thomas* (from Q, according to the common hypothesis); and by making innumerable subtle adjustments to *Mark*'s language.

The new atmosphere becomes obvious in the opening title: "the Book of the Genesis [as the Greek says] of Jesus the Messiah, son of David, son of Abraham" (1:1). All of these words immediately conjure up biblical images. "Book of the genesis" recalls *Gen.* 2:4; 5:1 (LXX). Abraham was the founder of the Jewish nation, called by God to inhabit the land of Israel with his descendants (*Genesis* 12). David was Israel's greatest king, and the ideal for all future government (*2 Samuel* 5–7).

An elaborate genealogy (1:2–17), taken from the Bible for the earlier generations, and using the exile to Babylon as a chronological marker, then demonstrates Jesus' classically Jewish pedigree. Next comes a birth story (1:18–23) permeated with biblical overtones: angelic appearances in dreams, scriptures fulfilled on every hand, and biblical-sounding people and places. Jesus appears here as a new Moses and a new Israel, who survives the slaughter of innocent children by a wicked king (2:16–18; see *Exod.* 1:15–2:10) and then emerges from Egypt as "God's Son" (2:13–15). This new material sets a scene very different from *Mark*'s, for Jesus now stands in complete continuity with Israel's past and hopes.

It is not until the third chapter that *Matthew* begins to intersect with *Mark,* but the new beginning has already set up different expectations for *Matthew*'s readers.

Matthew follows *Mark* fairly closely through many of the initiation events (chs. 3–4: Jesus' immersion by John, temptation, call of the first students), but omits Jesus' prototypical conflict in the synagogue, where *Mark* had credited him with a radical "new teaching" (*Mark* 1:23–28). And the author postpones until the ninth chapter even the beginning of serious controversies between the Jewish leaders and Jesus. Whereas *Mark* had set in motion a plot to kill Jesus right at the outset (*Mark* 3:6), *Matthew* will come to that plot only in the twelfth chapter (12:14)—approaching the mid-point of the gospel. The net effect of these changes is to portray Jesus as successful and comfortable in his native Jewish world for the early part of his career (4:23; 9:35)—that is, until particular groups of authorities (scribes and Pharisees) intervene and cause him trouble. Jesus is not, therefore, fundamentally opposed to either Judaism or the Torah of Moses.

Nevertheless, lethal opposition to Jesus surely develops among these leaders. In chapters 11–12 they reject him as they rejected John the Baptist (the author notes at length) and plot to kill him (12:14), accusing him of being in league with the devil. After several further demonstrations of his effective power and a major confrontation with the Pharisees, Jesus begins to tell his students about his coming death and resurrection in Jerusalem (16:21; 17:22–23) at the hands of the authorities. But through all of this, *Matthew* maintains a sense of Jesus' original belonging in Judaism by having the crowds, as distinct from the leaders, continue to welcome him (17:14). When he finally enters Jerusalem, the crowds recognize and praise him (21:11), and the crowds' support becomes a major problem for the authorities who wish to kill him (21:46). In the end, however, the leaders win over the "whole people" in their clamor for his crucifixion, and so the guilt for Jesus' death passes to the whole nation and its descendants (27:25). So what was mainly an in-house Jewish controversy between the Messiah Jesus and the "blind" and "stubborn" leaders becomes a conflict between Jews as a whole and Christians.

The story ends, as it began, very differently from *Mark*'s. At the same time as Jesus begins to predict his death, not coincidentally he confidently prepares for the establishment of "my church"—a word that turns up only in *Matthew*. The church will be founded squarely upon Jesus' original students, led by Peter (the Rock; 16:16–18; 18:18–20), who are trustworthy reporters of his teaching (26:20). Although they falter at the moment of testing, according to Jesus' prediction (26:31, 40, 69–75), after his resurrection they join him in his triumph and he gives them his final charge (28:16–20).

Overlaid on this story, and reflecting the author's concern to create a basic manual for the new church, are several large blocks of Jesus' teaching. These occupy chapters 5–7, 10, 13, 18, and 23–25, creating the impression that the author has positioned them deliberately, even symmetrically (5–7 matching 23–25), throughout the story. This impression is confirmed by the author's use of a formula at the end of each discourse: "And when Jesus had finished saying these things" (7:28; 11:1; 13:53; 19:1; 26:1). The first of the great speeches is the famous Sermon on the

Mount (chs. 5–7), covering a wide range of behavioral norms for Jesus' followers. The second is a set of instructions for his missionaries (ch. 10). The third is a collection of exemplary parables—some given to the crowds by the lake, other given to his students in his house (ch. 13). The fourth comprises a set of specific instructions for "church" life, particularly with respect to sin and forgiveness (ch. 18). The final discourse includes both seven woes directed at the scribes and Pharisees (ch. 23) and an extensive apocalyptic discourse given to Jesus' students on the Mount of Olives, in which he describes the coming judgment upon the world (chs. 24–25). So the speeches become increasingly narrow in their focus, as they also change their tone from the "happy" sayings of the beatitudes ("Blessed are . . . ") to Jesus' dark warnings about impending doom.

The neatness and symmetry of the five-speech scenario has invited many proposals about the author's aims. *Matthew* has Jesus emulate the five books of Moses; each narrative section (chs. 3–4, 8–9, 11–12, 14–17, 19–22) is somehow tied to the speech that follows it, so that the entire gospel consists of five "volumes" plus introduction and conclusion; the author creates from these five speeches a "concentric" pattern that highlights the central speech (ch. 13, on parables); and so on. While these are all helpful proposals, we should not minimize the discomfiting fact that the fifth "speech" (chs. 23–25) actually appears in the story as two different discourses. Chapter 23, with its seven woes, is a highly stylized attack on the scribes and Pharisees in the temple area, continuing Jesus' earlier debate with them (22:41). Chapters 24–25 come after a significant break and in response to his students' question about the end of the age. He responds while sitting on the Mount of Olives (24:1–3). The location, audience, content, and tone of this speech make it quite different from that of chapter 23.

Literary Features

Perhaps the best response to this inconvenient fact is to see it as the author's way of telling us not to impose any single interpretive system on his book. Everywhere we look, in fact, the work reveals multiple layers, which defy simple or rigid constructions. The author is an artist and a master of evocation. He seems comfortable with a great deal of ambiguity.

For example, the birth narratives lead us to see Jesus as a new Moses, since he survives the slaughter of innocent children by a wicked king, just as Moses did. And so, when Jesus ascends a mountain in 5:1, we immediately think of Mount Sinai, where Moses received the Torah from God. But this parallel is confounded by the fact that whereas Moses had to bring God's teaching down to deliver it, Jesus actually sits on the mountain and teaches in the manner of a rabbi. Perhaps the mountain imagery here, as in the transfiguration story, draws more from common assumptions in prophetic and apocalyptic literature about mountains as places for encountering God. And although Jesus can appear as a substitute Moses in *Matthew,* reinterpreting *God*'s intentions in non-Mosaic ways (19:7–9), elsewhere he speaks as a respectful interpreter of Moses and he fully expects Moses' commandments to continue (5:17–48; 23:2–3). Thus, although *Matthew's* Jesus *evokes* the figure of Moses in some ways, the reader cannot place too rigid a set of expectations upon the meaning of "new Moses." Jesus is also a new Solomon and a new Jonah (12:41–42), even a new temple (12:6), but none of these images is fully developed either.

That *Matthew* can be read on so many levels, many of which seem to be loose threads, suggests a literary playfulness on the author's part. This applies also to his individual words, phrases, and larger structures. Recall the title of the work (1:1): "the Book of the Genesis." That word *genesis* has many connotations that all apply here: birth (1:18), genealogy (1:2), beginning (chs. 1–4), and the biblical book of *Genesis* (*Gen.* 2:4; 5:1). It is impossible to translate such a word with one English equivalent because the author does not mean one thing exclusively. In 19:28, the author has Jesus refer to the new age as "again being" or "rebirth" *(palingenesia)*—a term popular in Stoic philosophy to describe the rebirth of the cosmos after the great fiery reversion of all things. Any single translation of such a rich term is too narrow and misleading. Or again, *Matthew's* many references to the curing of blindness and deafness have both an obvious physical meaning but also a link with the prophetic book of *Isaiah,* a major theme of which is the blindness and deafness of Israel (e.g., 11:3–6). And when the text speaks of "little ones" it appears to slide, in the same passage, from actual children to new members of the Christian group (18:2–6, 10). The author seems deliberately to use language that works at several levels.

The same can be said of the entire structure of the work. Some scholars have imagined that the five-speech format must be most central to the author's intentions, while others have pointed out a different kind of formulaic division. In 4:17, after the initiation events of Jesus' life, the author uses the phrase "From that time Jesus began . . ." to introduce Jesus' teaching and healing career. In 16:21, the same phrase marks the transition to Jesus' anticipation of death and resurrection in Jerusalem. Can one say that this three-part division of the story is more central than the five- (or six-) speech structure? No. It is part of the author's art to have all of these things going on simultaneously.

Other noteworthy patterns further illustrate the book's literary playfulness. This author seems to delight in repetition and (near) symmetry. Most obvious is his taste for formulas that can be repeated. We have noted his speech-ending formulas and the transition markers at 4:17 and 16:21. Others are found in the birth narrative (chs. 1–2). After the formulaic genealogy (*x* was the father of *y; y* was the father of *z*), it contains three dream sequences, all of which follow a clear pattern: "an angel of the Lord appeared to Joseph in a dream and said," command given by the angel, reason for the command, and Joseph "got up" and complied with the command (1:20–21; 2:13–14, 19–21). Another prominent formula occurs throughout the book, fourteen times, after Jesus fulfills some scriptural hope: "this happened to fulfill what was spoken by [the prophet]" (e.g., 1:22; 2:17). Some sixty-one times the author uses the biblical phrase "Look" or "Behold" (Gk *idou*) when he is describing events. This helps maintain an aura of biblical mystery around the story; often the NRSV leaves these words untranslated in English. A particularly impressive Matthean formula is Jesus' refrain about being cast into "outer darkness, where there is weeping and gnashing of teeth" (8:12; 13:42, 50; 22:13; 24:51; 25:30). All of this repetition creates a sense of stability and control. The author is not simply patching together stories, but dexterously conveys a message that permeates the whole work.

Another kind of repetition appears in *Matthew*'s many duplications and pairs. The reader often has the feeling that some story or saying sounds familiar, and that is because it has already appeared in the earlier narrative. *Matthew* not only takes over the two miraculous feedings from *Mark*, but also has two cures of blind men (9:27–31; 20:29–34), two cures of deaf-mutes and the related charges that Jesus is possessed by the devil (9:32–34; 12:22–24), and two requests for a sign (12:38–42; 16:1–4). Jesus' sayings about divorce (5:31–32; 19:3–9), coming persecution (10:17–22; 24:9–13), and receiving the kingdom as a child (18:1–3; 19:13–15) likewise reappear in similar forms.

Not only are these episodes duplicated but, most remarkably, the author often doubles the number of characters within a story. For example, in each of his two accounts of curing the blind, he has two blind men instead of *Mark*'s lone Bartimaeus (9:27; 20:30). He similarly has two demon-possessed men in Gadara (8:28) instead of *Mark*'s one (in Gerasa), and even two animals for Jesus to ride—a difficult image—into Jerusalem (21:2–7).

When we search for a reason for this proliferation of episodes and characters, one answer seems to lie in the author's awareness of the Bible's principle that every case must be advanced on the strength of two or three witnesses, not one alone (*Deut.* 19:15). Since *Matthew* cites this principle for church life (18:16) and alters *Mark*'s story of Jesus' trial to have *two* false witnesses bring the charge against Jesus (26:60), it seems likely that the author has the requirement of two or three witness in mind throughout the book.

Still, that much of *Matthew*'s repetition stems from literary motives is suggested by the author's parallel practice of "inclusion." This occurs when a theme or principle is stated, another unit such as a parable follows, and then the author repeats the initial theme in order to tie in the intervening unit, which might otherwise have been open to different interpretations. For example, in 18:21 Peter asks Jesus how many times he should forgive, and Jesus answers (in effect, "a lot"). The reader might think that this episode has finished with the following parable of the servants, but the final sentence (18:35) applies that parable directly to the problem of forgiveness. Again, Jesus ends his discussion of future reward for his students with the remark that many of the last will be first, and the first, last (19:30). That unit seems to have ended. Then he tells a parable about vineyard workers who are hired at different times but receive the same wage (20:1–15), which he closes with a repetition of the line in 19:30 (20:16). Since the parables by themselves are open to many different applications (as the parallels in *Thomas* often show), we see in this technique of "inclusion" the author's concern to shape the parable's meaning in one direction. See also 12:39–45; 21:25–32; 24:42–25:13.

One kind of repetitive wordplay in *Matthew* that has wide parallels in both biblical and Greek literature is called "chiasm." This is an arrangement of words or phrases that appears like the Greek capital letter X. That is, if we call one phrase "A" and another "B," the pattern is A, B, B, A. Thus 20:16:

A   the last
  B   will be first
  B′   and the first
A′   will be last

In other cases, the author switches more than two terms. For example, the title of the work calls Jesus Messiah, son of David, son of Abraham, and then the genealogy moves in reverse order from Abraham to David to the Messiah.

A   Jesus the Messiah (1:1)
  B   the son of David (1:1)
    C   the son of Abraham (1:1)
    C′   Abraham was the father (1:2)
  B′   And David was the father (1:6)
A′   Jesus was born, called the Messiah (1:16)

Or again, if it is correct that the author intended five main speeches, the first (A, chs. 5–7) and last (A′, chs. 23–25) are symmetrical in length, and the middle speech (C, ch. 13), which has no match, is featured. Since these inversions of more than two items no longer fit the X image, it is better to call this a "concentric" pattern; this label works with any number of items repeated in reverse order.

Of the many patterns used by the author of *Matthew*, the other one that we shall mention here has to do with numbers. More than any other gospel writer, this one seems alert to the power of numbers. Remember that ancient Western languages did not have separate character sets for letters and numbers. In Greek, Latin, and Hebrew one counted with letters, each of which had a numerical value. This situation understandably gave rise to all sorts of reflection on the numerical values of words and names (see *Rev.* 13:18). In *Matthew*, multiples of three and seven seem to carry particular weight. Jesus' genealogy is divided into three blocks of fourteen generations, the author says (1:17)—even though the arithmetic does not work. This corresponds to the fourteen fulfillment citations sprinkled throughout the work. The author's interest in the number fourteen has suggested to some scholars the he derived it from the numerical value of the name "David" (Hebrew: *DWD*, 4 + 6 + 4). Jesus faces three tests in the desert (4:3–11), and gives nine beatitudes (5:3–11), six antitheses (5:21–48), seven parables (ch. 13), and seven woes against the Pharisees (ch. 23). Once again, it seems counterproductive to press any of these too far. Seven denotes completion or fullness (as in seven days), and that fits with *Matthew*'s pronounced "fulfillment theme." But these numbers are more suggestive than logically conclusive.

Distinctive Themes

Because of the author's highly allusive style, it is impossible to identify more than a few of *Matthew*'s most characteristic themes here.

Of these, the first might be called "continuity and fulfillment." The reader's sense that the author and his first readers lived in a world filled with Jewish imagery and assumptions, a world most unlike *Mark*'s, comes to expression clearly in Jesus' first major speech. There, Jesus takes pointed issue with anyone who would suppose that he has come to abolish "the law and the prophets"—Jewish scripture (5:17). For he has come not to abolish but to *fulfill* them. Whatever this fulfillment means, it does not mean that the Torah is now dispensable (contrast Paul and *Mark*). Rather, whereas the Torah had prohibited murder, adultery, and disproportionate revenge, *Matthew*'s Jesus goes *further* and forbids anger, lust, and the demand for simple justice (5:21–48). Like the authors of the Dead Sea Scrolls (in this respect), he requires of his followers a much higher standard of Torah observance than was normal (5:20)—setting a fence around the Torah, as it were, so that one would never even come close to violating its minimal requirements. The minimal standard of Torah is not itself negotiable.

Throughout the subsequent narrative, *Matthew*'s Jesus assumes the validity of Jewish categories. In passages peculiar to *Matthew,* he addresses himself exclusively to "the lost sheep of the house of Israel," not Gentiles (15:24), and he demands that his students do the same (10:5–6). Indeed, he labels those who are outsiders to the community of readers "Gentiles" (6:7, 32; 10:5; 18:17). He accepts temple sacrifice (5:24) and also tithing for the Jewish priesthood (23:23). While following *Mark* closely, the author nevertheless rejects *Mark*'s claim that Jesus' concern about what comes out a person, rather than what goes in, implies the abolition of the Jewish dietary laws (*Mark* 7:19). He is determined that Jesus' followers should observe the Torah of Moses, and even has Jesus advocating deference to the Pharisees to the extent that they teach Moses' laws (23:2–3).

In keeping with his stated requirement of Torah observance, the author expects his readers to appreciate (on some level) both biblical history and Jewish customs. Fourteen times throughout the narrative, he pauses to say that Jesus' action "fulfilled" some scriptural passage. He corrects one of *Mark*'s scriptural citations (*Mark* 1:2–3; *Matt.* 3:3; 11:10). He omits *Mark*'s explanation of Jewish hand-washing customs (*Mark* 7:3–4; *Matt.* 15:2) and of the relationship between Passover and the Feast of Unleavened Bread (*Mark* 14:12; *Matt.* 26:17), and even introduces without explanation references to Jewish clothing (fringes and prayer cases; 23:5) and the *didrachma* (temple tax; 17:24). He appears to expect a fair degree of Jewish and biblical knowledge from his intended readers. That expectation fits with the requirement that they scrupulously observe Torah, or be "righteous."

Matthew's use of the "righteousness" word group (also "righteous" and "be righteous") further reflects the book's continuity with Judaism. In Jewish scripture, righteousness essentially means fulfilling God's commandments, observing God's gracious gift, the Torah (*Gen.* 6:9; 15:6; 26:5; *Ps.* 5:12; 119:7). We have seen that in the first Christian generation Paul, reacting to claims that his Gentile converts should also be righteous in this way, argued that righteousness came solely through being "in Christ" and not through observance of Torah. But when the author of *Matthew* emphasizes the language of righteousness, he understands the word group in the typically Jewish, non-Pauline mode. This is his most characteristic way of describing the program of Jesus' followers: They *are* the righteous, who should seek a righteousness surpassing that of the scribes and Pharisees (by observing every word of the commandments). Although they will be persecuted on account of their righteousness, they will also shine like the sun because of it (1:19; 5:6, 10, 20; 6:33; 10:41; 13:43; 21:32; 25:46).

Another mechanism for connecting Jesus with the biblical-Jewish world in *Matthew* is the label Son of David. Every time it is used of Jesus, from the book's title (1:1) onward, it reminds the biblically knowledgeable reader of the prophet Nathan's promise to King David that the kingdom of his "son" would be established forever (*2 Sam.* 7:12–16). After the collapse of the Davidic monarchy (with the fall of Jerusalem and Judah in 586 B.C.E.), some prophets began to hope for a restoration of Davidic kingship (*Hag.* 2:20–23). By Jesus' day there was a vast array of hopes for national deliverance, but the dream of a Davidic king was still alive in some circles (*Psalms of Solomon* 17). Whereas *Mark* had used this title sparingly, mainly to *challenge* the notion that the Messiah should be a descendant of David (*Mark* 12:35–37), *Matthew* uses it often and deliberately: in the title and genealogy (1:17); in the angel's address to Jesus' father, Joseph (1:20); in Jesus' triumphal entry into Jerusalem (21:9); and on the lips of many different characters in the story (9:27; 12:23; 15:22; 20:30; 21:15). Most Christians seem to have been willing to call Jesus "Messiah" or "Christ," but *Matthew* presents that title largely in classical Jewish terms. Jesus is the awaited King of the Jews, the Son of David who has come to restore Israel.

Matthew's concern to locate Jesus squarely within Judaism should not, however, lead us to view this Jesus as simply another Jewish teacher among many. While stressing his continuity with Judaism, the author at the same time emphasizes his completely unique authority as Messiah and Son of God. In the birth narrative the angel announces that Jesus is born by divine agency (1:20), and the adult Jesus behaves with full knowledge of his origins and mission. He challenges the devil himself (4:1–11) and authoritatively interprets God's will, over against Moses (19:8), recognizing himself as someone greater than Solomon, Jonah (12:41–42), and the temple (12:6). Indeed, he knows himself to be the Son of God who alone can reveal his Father to the world (11:25–27). He accomplishes this revelation through the five lengthy discourses mentioned earlier, which cover a variety of topics for his followers.

It is this claim to unique authority that brings *Matthew*'s Messiah Jesus, in spite of his strong base in Judaism, into conflict with other Jewish leaders. The whole book of *Matthew* charts a rupture between Jesus and Judaism that transparently reflects a conflict between *Matthew*'s community and the Jews. In chapters 11–12, the Jewish leaders begin to break ranks with the "crowds," who recognize Jesus as the awaited Son of David (12:23–24; 21:9–11, 46). For his part, Jesus is relentlessly critical of the scribes, Pharisees, and Sadducees, especially the first two groups, whom he castigates in harsh terms (15:13–14; 23:13, 15, 16, 23, 25, 27, 29). At times, his critique of the leaders seems to spill over into a general repudiation of the whole Jewish people or "this generation" (11:16–19; 12:39–42, 45; 15:8), and at the trial scene *Matthew* finally brings people and leaders together in a forceful condemnation of Jesus (27:25). But one of *Matthew*'s characteristic terms for these leaders, "the hypocrites," taken together with its recurring reference to "their" or "your" synagogues (apparently as distinct from the readers'; 4:23; 6:2; 9:35; 10:17; 12:9; 13:54; 23:34) and the author's overriding concern to remain within Judaism (above), suggests that this is an in-house critique—from one group to another within the broad spectrum of Judaism. So we have the paradox that, while the author and readers of *Matthew* seem fully at home with the Jewish world, they see themselves in deep conflict with Judaism as a whole. They are at once insiders and outsiders.

An important piece of this puzzle seems to lie in *Matthew*'s openness to Gentiles and critique of Jewish ancestry. This two-sided appeal begins almost imperceptibly in Jesus' genealogy, which introduces four Gentile women (Tamar, Rahab, Ruth, and Uriah's wife, Bathsheba). These women are not necessary to the all-male, biblical-style genealogy, and the reader naturally wonders why they are there. It is at least clear that they were people who *came into* the heritage of Israel from outside. Soon afterward we meet the Magi, astrologers from Mesopotamia (2:1), who have also *come in* to share the blessings of Israel's Messiah. John the Baptist then criticizes the Jewish leaders' pride in ancestry from Abraham, on the ground that God can create descendants of Abraham at will (3:8–9). When Jesus makes his home in Capernaum, the author selects for citation a biblical passage calling this region "Galilee of *the Gentiles*" (4:15). In one of his first cures, Jesus heals the servant of a Gentile soldier and remarks, having said that he has not found such faith in Israel, that "many will come from east and west and will eat with Abraham, Isaac, and Jacob in the kingdom of heaven" (8:10–11). At the same time, the "heirs of the kingdom" will be expelled to the place of outer darkness (8:12). Precisely the same theme of Gentile inclusion and the expulsion of historic Israel continues through the parables of the wicked tenants and the wedding banquet (21:33–22:14), and reaches a climax in the final words of the gospel, which send Jesus' students to "all the Gentiles [or 'nations']" (28:16–20).

Matthew's critique of Jewish ancestry comes through most forcefully in 23:29–36, where Jesus accuses the scribes and Pharisees of being the heirs of those who killed the prophets. The remarkable thing here is that, although the author admits that the Jewish leaders completely disavow their ancestors' rejection of the prophets (23:30), he still has Jesus insist that their very admission of ancestry is itself, and inescapably, blameworthy (23:31–33). His generation of Jews will have to pay for *all* of the crimes committed by Israel throughout history (23:34–35). This is quite different from saying simply that the Pharisees prove their ancestry by their (allegedly wicked) deeds, *consenting* to the (alleged) murders of their fathers, as the parallel in *Luke* (11:48) has it. In this revealing passage, though the author might not wish to stand by the point in general, *Matthew*'s Jesus indicts the Jews' ancestry itself, irrespective of the Pharisees' actions.

This combination in *Matthew* of emphatic commitment to Israel's Torah and heritage, on the one hand, and equally emphatic repudiation of Israel on the other, with a concomitant enthusiasm for Gentiles' coming into salvation, has led to much scholarly debate about the author and audience. Were they Gentiles or Jews? We shall return to the question below, after discussing three other related themes in *Matthew*.

First, although the author and characters in the story present Jesus as Son of David, Jesus more often calls himself Son of Man—a title familiar from *Mark*, but used much more frequently in *Matthew*. This was not, as far as we can tell, a phrase used in pre-Christian Judaism to refer to a powerful heavenly being. In *Dan.* 7:13, the passage most often cited as a source, it simply refers to a "humanlike figure" seen in a vision. The author of *Matthew*, however, has Jesus talk often about the "coming of the Son of Man in glory," on the clouds of heaven with many angels, to save the righteous and punish the wicked (13:36–43; 24:29–31; 25:31). Indeed, as the book progresses, the theme of impending judgment from the Son of Man becomes increasingly prominent, and the threat of being cast into "outer darkness," increasingly vivid. Those who are cast out from salvation will be "cut in pieces" (24:51) and tortured (18:34); they will have their city burned (22:7) and will face the age-long fire prepared for the devil (25:41). Thus *Matthew* takes over not only the biblical prophetic heritage but also, from some contemporary Jewish circles, a dark apocalyptic tone.

One of the most important bases for the Son of Man's judgment is the reception of Jesus' missionaries, those sent out to bring people into salvation. The second major speech (ch. 10) is devoted to the theme of mission. Although the speech is set in Jesus' lifetime, the language shows that it is really a manual for later missionaries, since it predicts fierce persecution, appearances before governors and kings, and the coming of the Son of Man before the mission concludes—none of which applied to Jesus' lifetime (10:17, 23). This speech shows that the author has a deep concern with the reception of missionaries, for he threatens dire judgment for those who rebuff them (10:40–42). Apparently, those expected to mistreat the missionaries are Jews (10:17). Later in the narrative, one of Jesus' strongest woes against the scribes and Pharisees is pronounced because they allegedly mistreat his missionaries (23:33–37). These missionaries may be included among the messengers sent by the vineyard-owner to collect his rent (21:35), whose mistreatment will be avenged by the "miserable death" of the wicked tenants (21:40). Most striking is the lengthy scene in 25:31–46, where all the nations are to be judged by the Son of Man according to the way in which they have treated Jesus' missionaries. The "great commission" in 28:16–20 seals this important theme for the author.

Finally, we noted that *Matthew* appears somewhat as the Messiah's manual for his church, and that one of its discourses is devoted to church life. A fundamental change in *Matthew* over against *Mark* is the way in which this church's foundation is understood. Whereas *Mark* had consistently denigrated both Jesus' original students and his family members, who happened to have played leading roles in the Jerusalem church before *Mark* was written, *Matthew* unmistakably supports both Jesus' students and his family. The author simply omits many of *Mark*'s more cutting remarks about these groups (*Mark* 3:21) and alters a great deal of other material to present them in a better light. When Jesus walks on the water, his students are no longer dumbfounded and hard-hearted (*Mark* 6:52), but worship him as Son of God (*Matt.* 14:33). James and John no longer grasp after status in Jesus' kingdom (*Mark* 10:35); it is their mother who, as mothers are inclined to do, looks out for their interests (*Matt.* 20:20). Peter, an acknowledged leader of non-Pauline first-generation Christianity (*1 Cor.* 9:5; *Gal.* 1:18; 2:8; *Acts* 1–12), appears in a particularly glowing light, for Jesus makes him the Rock on which the church will be established (16:16–18). But all of Jesus' students receive the authority to act in Jesus' stead (18:18–20), as his trustworthy interpreters (28:20). This support for the Jerusalem church leadership fits with the work's Jewish, Torah-observant ethos. Jesus' final words in the gospel (28:20) show that he expects his followers to observe *everything* he has taught his students, including full Torah observance.

Church life in *Matthew* appears quite severe and ascetic. *Matthew*'s Jesus twice advocates the removal of body parts as preferable to facing the fire of hell (5:29; 18:8–9). Forgiveness should be unlimited (18:21–35), but those who fall away from the faith will face the same judgment as the hypocrites (24:26–51). The community aims at an extremely high standard of moral purity, namely, perfection (5:48). This kind of zeal rivals that of those who produced the Dead Sea Scrolls, though there is less discussion in *Matthew* of particular commandments.

Author and Audience

Since we know nothing reliable about the author or his situation from outside sources, we must reconstruct the conditions of writing from the text itself. The themes we have just considered, however, seem to point in different directions.

On the one hand, we have an author who is not only comfortable within the world of Bible and Judaism, but zealous for it. He presents Jesus as demanding full and scrupulous compliance with God's commandments in the Torah. Such compliance would presumably begin with circumcision for males, the mark of Jewish male identity (*Gen.* 17:9–14), and would continue through the dietary laws and general ordering of life in a Jewish community. Thus, the church fathers believed that *Matthew* had been originally written in Hebrew "for believers of Jewish origin."[1] And it seems that that the *Gospel of the Hebrews,* used by the Jewish-Christian Ebionites, was a paraphrase of *Matthew.* On the other hand, the Jewish Christians of antiquity could not accept *Matthew's* gospel as it stood; that is why their own gospel was a paraphrase of it.[2] One reason for this was that they rejected *Matthew's* claim that Jesus was literally God's Son, born of a virgin.[3] But they might also have noted *Matthew's* strong statements in favor of Gentile salvation and opposing Israel and Jewish ancestry. Was the author a Jew or a Gentile, and for whom did he write?

Before confronting that question, we need to consider another side to the problem. Although the author vociferously supports Israel's heritage and laws, it is a legitimate question how well he knows the scriptures, Jewish customs, or conditions in Judea. He does correct one of *Mark's* scripture citations (*Mark* 1:2–3; see *Matt.* 3:3; 11:10), but then he makes several obvious errors of his own. For example, he misunderstands the poetic repetition of *Zech.* 9:9 as if it required Israel's king to ride on two animals, a colt *and* a donkey, and he even rewrites *Mark's* story so that this happens (21:1–11). He claims that the death of Judas fulfills scripture from *Jeremiah* (*Matt.* 27:9), but the passage he cites is actually a paraphrase of *Zech.* 11:13. Other alleged fulfillment passages have no known parallel in the Bible (*Matt.* 2:23; 26:54–56), and still others are given in forms that differ significantly from those known to us in the Hebrew Bible and Septuagint (LXX): 4:15–16; 8:17; 12:18–21.

Of course, one must always reckon with the possibilities that the author's Bible read differently from ours (the text was in constant flux) and that he deliberately altered a reading to reinterpret it, but some of these differences appear to be outright mistakes. Although the author tries to clean up some of *Mark's* geographical improbabilities (*Mark* 5:1/*Matt.* 8:28; *Mark* 7:31/*Matt.* 15:29), he still leaves a great deal of vagueness and difficulty, as in his claim that Jesus went to "Judea beyond the Jordan" (19:1). He improbably creates a close association between Pharisees and Sadducees (3:7; 16:6–12; 22:34). And although he introduces some Jewish customs, his reference to "broad phylacteries" (23:5) is puzzling. He also takes over *Mark's* problems concerning the nighttime trial of Jesus on the first day of a major holiday—problems corrected somewhat by *Luke* and *John* (see notes to *Mark* 14:53–65).

---

[1]Origen, *Commentary on Matthew,* cited in Eusebius, *Eccl. hist.* 6.25.
[2]Eusebius claims that *Matthew* was a particular object of scorn for the Ebionites (*Eccl. hist.* 6.17).
[3]See Eusebius, *Eccl. hist.* 3.27; 6.17.

We have, then, the paradox of a Christian writer who is extremely zealous for the Torah, Israel's heritage, and things Jewish, but who has an uncertain grasp of them. At the same time, he repudiates the natural heirs to this heritage ("children of the kingdom") and shuns Jewish ancestry, while making much of the Gentiles' *coming in* to share the blessings of Israel's Messiah.

Two broad kinds of interpretation, with many fine distinctions, dominate the scholarly field today. According to one view, *Matthew* was written for an observant Christian-Jewish community that saw itself as a faithful remnant of the Jews—those few who had responded to the revelation of Israel's Messiah. This faithful remnant warmly accepted the Gentile mission, which was well under way by the time the book was written. Perhaps in keeping with Paul's "remnant" idea (*Rom.* 11:1–5), these Jews who had accepted Jesus saw the salvation of Gentiles as part of God's plan to discipline the bulk of Jews (*Rom.* 11:11–12, 23–26). The opposite view is that, in its present form, *Matthew* is a work by and for Gentile Christians: it seeks to justify Gentile salvation on the ground that the Jews as a body rejected their Messiah. Adherents to this hypothesis often attribute *Matthew*'s Jewish character to its special (non-Markan) sources. The writer perhaps drew on earlier material that showed Jesus' original orientation to the Jews in order to emphasize that Israel had lost its chance and now deserved punishment.

But a third alternative deserves consideration. We know from Paul's letters that other Christian teachers were trying to persuade his Gentile converts to embrace Judaism as part and parcel of their acceptance of Jesus. And we have reason to think that these "judaizing" teachers, who claimed the warrant of Jesus and his original students, were quite successful (*Gal.* 3:1–5; 4:9–10, 21; 5:2–4; 6:12–13). They were able to persuade people that following the Messiah Jesus necessarily involved the adoption of his own biblical tradition. Only such followers of Jesus were the "genuine article." They often became extremely devoted to Jewish customs. The phenomenon was still well known to Ignatius of Antioch (*Magnesians* 8–11; *Philadelphians* 6, 8–9). It is plausible to imagine, therefore, that the author and community of *Matthew* were products of the non-Pauline (judaizing) mission to Gentiles. That would explain well the peculiar features of *Matthew* discussed above. The author embraces Judaism and the Torah with the zeal of a convert, though it is not his native tradition. He disparages native Jews, while exulting in the conversion of Gentiles from east and west, among whom he finds his own roots. Missionary activities occupy a central place in his thinking. This new kind of Christian Judaism, avidly seeking converts, might understandably have aroused the ire of more mainstream Jews,[4] and their efforts to stop the new group would have appeared to *Matthew*'s community as persecution.

---

[4]Possible reasons: The Jewish leadership wanted to distance itself from the popular leader whom the Romans had crucified. Some native Jews were involved in this new movement and their fellow-Jews felt obligated to keep them from error. The new group tended to portray other Jews in a bad light, which seemed like defamation when Jews around the world were already extremely vulnerable (after the war with Rome).

If this hypothesis is correct, we have in *Matthew* the unique written product of a *centripetal* mission to Gentiles in Christianity—the one that invited Gentiles to come into Israel. Contrast Paul's *centrifugal* mission, which *went out* to meet Gentiles where they were and required no real movement toward Judaism. In that case, it would be no coincidence that the author's favorite biblical books, *Isaiah* and *Zechariah*, both look forward to such a mission:

> Many peoples shall come and say,
> "Come,
> let us go up to the mountain of the LORD,
> to the house of the God of Jacob;
> that he may teach us his ways
> and that we may walk in his paths." (*Isa.* 2:3)

> Many peoples and strong nations shall come
> to seek the LORD of hosts in Jerusalem,
> and to entreat the favor of the LORD.
> Thus says the LORD of hosts:
> In those days ten men from nations of every language
> shall take hold of a Jew,
> grasping his garment and saying,
> "Let us go with you,
> for we have heard that God is with you." (*Zech.* 8:22–23)

Date and Location

If the dominant theory of gospel origins is correct (see the introduction to the gospels), then the church fathers of the second and third centuries were incorrect in their supposition that *Matthew* was the first gospel, written by a student of Jesus in Hebrew or Aramaic. Since all of the Synoptic Gospels are anonymous, it seems that the Fathers' view was itself a guess, based on oral traditions known to them. Perhaps it was connected in some way to this gospel's identification of Matthew rather than Levi (see *Mark* 2:14) as Jesus' tax-collector disciple (*Matt.* 9:9). But the widely accepted theory that *Matthew* used *Mark* as its main source excludes the possibility that this was a firsthand account, and, if *Matthew*'s changes to *Mark* can best be explained on the basis of literary considerations and additional sources, it is also unlikely that *Matthew* is an eyewitness account.

Even if we were to disregard the Two-Document Hypothesis, there is compelling evidence within the gospel of a date somewhat after 70 C.E., for the author evidently knew about the Roman destruction of the Jewish temple in that year. In 22:1–14, *Matthew*'s Jesus tells the parable of the wedding feast, in which a king invited guests to a wedding banquet for his son. But when the guests excused themselves and killed his messengers, he "sent his troops, destroyed those murderers, and burned their city" (22:7). This parable seems to be a transparent allegory: the Jews will reject Jesus (the king's son) and kill his missionaries; God (the king) will punish them by destroying their city with fire. Elsewhere, Jesus plainly predicts the destruction of the temple (24:2, 15), and one of his sayings assumes that it already lies "desolate" as punishment for the Jews' rejection of Jesus and his missionaries (23:37–39).

It should be stressed that this kind of analysis does not presuppose the impossibility of Jesus' actually having predicted the temple's destruction in his lifetime. It is rather a question of historical probability. For example, both *Luke* (14:16–24) and *Thomas* (64) include the parable of the banquet, but without the references to either the guests' killing of the messengers or the king's destruction of their city by fire. In the other gospels, it simply illustrates a point about showing hospitality to the socially powerless. The extreme violence in *Matthew*'s version seems out of place. The historian's question is, therefore, simple: Is it more likely that Jesus actually gave *Matthew*'s version, predicting the rejection of his missionaries and the consequent destruction of Jerusalem, but that the parable was trimmed of these references by *Luke* and *Thomas,* or that Jesus gave the "simpler" version, which was elaborated by *Matthew* in light of the temple's destruction? Since we have numerous examples of "prophecy after the fact" in ancient Jewish and Christian (and other) literature, since the author of *Matthew* had a much more obvious motive for making the application than the others had for removing it, and since *Matthew*'s application appears to strain the internal logic of the story, most scholars incline toward the latter option. This would date *Matthew* far enough after 70 for the author to have reflected on the implications of Jerusalem's destruction.

That date would fit with the many clues in the gospel that the "church" is well established (above), and also with the common view that *Matthew* used *Mark* as its main source—which should probably favor a date after 80 C.E.

We should not place *Matthew* later than 100 C.E., however, because from the early second century Matthean formulations of the virgin birth, the Lord's Prayer, and other material are picked up by other Christian writers, in particular Ignatius (*Polycarp* 2; see *Matt.* 10:16; *Smyrnaeans* 1). It could be that Ignatius cites oral or partially written traditions, which would not require that *Matthew* was already a complete gospel, but most people who know the evidence think that *Matthew* was known as a coherent text by the early second century. So we may take the rough date range of 80 to 100 C.E. as the likeliest.

The location of the author and first readers is uncertain. Many scholars favor Antioch in Syria, the third-largest city in the Roman empire. This proposal has much to commend it. Ignatius of Antioch seems to know *Matthew* by the year 100 or so, quite soon after it must have been written. Ignatius is also familiar with the conditions assumed in *Matthew*—judaizing trends among Gentiles, Jewish/Gentile conflicts. And Antioch is a likely place for a community such as *Matthew*'s to have been in conflict with a large body of other Jews. But these considerations by no means exclude other regions, for example in Asia Minor.

For Further Reading

Bornkamm, Günther, Gerhard Barth, and Heinz Joachim Held. *Tradition and Interpretation in Matthew.* Philadelphia: Westminster, 1963.

Clarke, Howard W. *The Gospel of Matthew and Its Readers: A Historical Introduction to the First Gospel.* Bloomington, Ind.: Indiana University Press, 2003.

Cope, O. Lamar. *Matthew: A Scribe Trained for the Kingdom of Heaven.* Washington, D.C.: Catholic Biblical Association, 1976.

Cousland, J. R. C. *The Crowds in the Gospel of Matthew.* Leiden: Brill, 2002.

Davies, W. D. *The Setting of the Sermon on the Mount.* Cambridge: Cambridge University Press, 1964.

Donaldson, Terence L. *Jesus on the Mountain: A Study in Matthean Theology.* Sheffield: JSOT Press, 1985.

Kingsbury, Jack Dean. *Matthew as Story.* Philadelphia: Fortress, 1988.

Malina, Bruce J., and Jerome H. Neyrey. *Calling Jesus Names: The Social Value of Labels in Matthew.* Sonoma: Polebridge, 1988.

Przybylski, Benno. *Righteousness in Matthew and His World of Thought.* Cambridge: Cambridge University Press, 1980.

Stanton, Graham, ed. *The Interpretation of Matthew.* Philadelphia: Fortress, 1983.

THE GOSPEL ACCORDING TO
MATTHEW

The Genealogy of Jesus the Messiah

1 An account of the genealogy*a* of Jesus the Messiah,*b* the son of David, the son of Abraham.

²Abraham was the father of Isaac, and Isaac the father of Jacob, and Jacob the father of Judah and his brothers, ³and Judah the father of Perez and Zerah by Tamar, and Perez the father of Hezron, and Hezron the father of Aram, ⁴and Aram the father of Aminadab, and Aminadab the father of Nahshon, and Nahshon the father of Salmon, ⁵and Salmon the father of Boaz by Rahab, and Boaz the father of Obed by Ruth, and Obed the father of Jesse, ⁶and Jesse the father of King David.

And David was the father of Solomon by the wife of Uriah, ⁷and Solomon the father of Rehoboam, and Rehoboam the father of Abijah, and Abijah the father of Asaph,*c* ⁸and Asaph*c* the father of Jehoshaphat, and Jehoshaphat the father of Joram, and Joram the father of Uzziah, ⁹and Uzziah the father of Jotham, and Jotham the father of Ahaz, and Ahaz the father of Hezekiah, ¹⁰and Hezekiah the father of Manasseh, and Manasseh the father of Amos,*d* and Amos*d* the father of Josiah, ¹¹and Josiah the father of Jechoniah and his brothers, at the time of the deportation to Babylon.

¹²And after the deportation to Babylon: Jechoniah was the father of Salathiel, and Salathiel the father of Zerubbabel, ¹³and Zerubbabel the father of Abiud, and Abiud the father of Eliakim, and Eliakim the father of Azor, ¹⁴and Azor the father of Zadok, and

---

a Or *birth*
b Or *Jesus Christ*

c Other ancient authorities read *Asa*
d Other ancient authorities read *Amon*

1:1 Like *Mark* 1:1, this is an incomplete sentence (lacking a verb) because it is a title, indicating how the author sees his entire work. Unlike the author of *Mark,* he wishes to present Jesus as deeply rooted in Jewish tradition. At the outset he introduces one of the multilevel wordplays that will come to characterize his gospel. Here, *an account of the genealogy* is more literally "book of the genesis," which recalls *Gen.* 2:4; 5:1. And "genesis" can mean origin, beginning, creation, birth, or genealogy. Though translated *genealogy* here, the same word is rendered "birth" in 1:18. The sequence Messiah, David, Abraham sets up a concentric pattern because the coming genealogy is divided into three blocks, from Abraham to David to Jesus the Messiah. **the Messiah** The Gk *christos* is simply a translation of the Hebrew term *mashiaḥ* (Messiah), which means "anointed (one)." Although Paul and some Greco-Roman authors came to use the word as if it were Jesus' given name, *Matthew* retains its original sense as a title. So the NRSV rightly translates *Jesus the Messiah* (see 1:17), rather than "Jesus Christ." **1:2–6** This portion of the genealogy is drawn straight from the Bible (see *Ruth* 4:18–22; *1 Chr.* 2:1–15, with the addition of Abraham and Isaac at the beginning). But the Bible itself telescopes the four-hundred-year stay in Egypt into about three generations: Perez and Hezron were the son and grandson respectively of Judah, who went into Egypt with Jacob's sons about 1700 B.C.E. (if the narrative has a historical core; *Gen.* 46:12–13); Nahshon the son of Amminadab came out of Egypt with Moses about 1280 B.C.E. (*Lev.* 1:7). But that leaves only Ram (or Aram), father of Amminadab and son of Hezron, to bridge the intervening three hundred (or more) years. **1:5 by Rahab** Evidently, Rahab the prostitute of Jericho, who assisted the Israelites led by Joshua in conquering her city (*Joshua* 2; 6). Although the Bible does not identify her as the wife of Salmon and mother of Boaz, it does say that Salmon was Boaz's father. Since the prostitute of Jericho is the only Rahab mentioned in the Bible, since she became popular in later Jewish and Christian writing as a hero of faith and a convert to Judaism (see *Heb.* 11:31; *Jas.* 2:25)—a wife to Joshua in rabbinic tradition—and since the other three women mentioned in the genealogy are all well-known biblical figures, we might have expected the author to add "not the famous Rahab" if he had meant another person. If the author meant this Rahab, he creates a historical difficulty, since she lived several generations before Boaz's time; in the biblical story, the long period of the Judges intervenes. But he is apparently repeating or creating a tradition that this Rahab was the mother of Boaz. **1:6–11** This portion of the genealogy simply enumerates the kings of Judah from David to the Babylonian exile as described in *1–2 Kings*. Note, however, that the genealogist of *Matthew* (a) telescopes the four generations from Joram/Jehoram to Uzziah/Azariah (*2 Kgs.* 8:25; 11:1; 12:1; 14:1; 15:1) into one and (b) confuses Jeconiah/Jehoiachin with either his father Jehoiakim or his uncle Jehoahaz (*2 Kgs.* 23:30–31, 34–36; 24:6–8; *1 Chr.* 3:15–16), thus skipping another generation. **1:6 the wife of Uriah** Bathsheba, wife of David's Hittite general (*2 Sam.* 11). David had the general killed in order to sleep with Bathsheba, who later became his wife. **1:11 the deportation to Babylon** Commonly called the exile. The Babylonian King Nebuchadrezzar finally destroyed Jerusalem in 586 B.C.E. after a series of measures against the city. The Judean leaders exiled to Babylonia were released beginning in 538 B.C.E., however, when the Persian king Cyrus triumphed over the Babylonian Empire. **1:12–16** After Zerubbabel, the genealogist departs from the latest biblical source (*1 Chr.* 3:19ff.); the remaining names, down to Joseph, are otherwise unknown. Although *Luke* also offers a genealogy of Jesus, *Luke* 3:23–27 gives an entirely different list for the period from Zerubbabel to Joseph. Even Joseph's father is identified there as Heli rather than Jacob.

Zadok the father of Achim, and Achim the father of Eliud, ¹⁵and Eliud the father of Eleazar, and Eleazar the father of Matthan, and Matthan the father of Jacob, ¹⁶and Jacob the father of Joseph the husband of Mary, of whom Jesus was born, who is called the Messiah.ᵉ

¹⁷So all the generations from Abraham to David are fourteen generations; and from David to the deportation to Babylon, fourteen generations; and from the deportation to Babylon to the Messiah,ᵉ fourteen generations.

The Birth of Jesus the Messiah

¹⁸Now the birth of Jesus the Messiahᶠtook place in this way. When his mother Mary had been engaged to Joseph, but before they lived together, she was found to be with child from the Holy Spirit. ¹⁹Her husband Joseph, being a righteous man and unwilling to expose her to public disgrace, planned to dismiss her quietly. ²⁰But just when he had resolved to do this, an angel of the Lord appeared to him in a dream and said, "Joseph, son of David, do not be afraid to take Mary as your wife, for the child conceived in her is from the Holy Spirit. ²¹She will bear a son, and you are to name him Jesus, for he will save his people from their sins." ²²All this took place to fulfill what had been spoken by the Lord through the prophet:

²³   "Look, the virgin shall conceive and bear a son,
       and they shall name him Emmanuel,"

which means, "God is with us." ²⁴When Joseph awoke from sleep, he did as the angel of the Lord commanded him; he took her as his wife, ²⁵but had no

---

ᵉ Or *the Christ*
ᶠ Or *Jesus Christ*

1:16 *the father of Joseph the husband of Mary, of whom Jesus was born* The author goes to some lengths to insist that Jesus was not Joseph's child; see 1:18–20. But if Jesus was not Joseph's son, how was Jesus, then, related to David and Abraham? Perhaps the author takes over a genealogy from a community that did not think of Jesus as born of a virgin. See the next note.   **1:17** Unless one counts in different ways for the three periods, only the middle period comprises fourteen generations; the first and third yield thirteen each. This suggests that the author of *Matthew* did not create the genealogy (otherwise he would have made the numbers fit better) but, rather, found it ready-made. See the previous note.   **birth** Gk *genesis*. See note to 1:1.   **1:18** *engaged* Engagement in this context means the period of betrothal (normally about one year) preceding marriage. In ancient Judaism, women were commonly betrothed by arrangement of their fathers at the age of twelve; after the age of twelve and a half, a woman could not be betrothed without her consent. This betrothal meant more than modern engagement but less than marriage. Although the marriage was not yet consummated, infidelity during this period was considered adultery, and the abrogation of betrothal required formal divorce.   **1:19** *a righteous man* The adjective "righteous" and the noun "righteousness" are important to this author (see introduction to *Matthew*). This passage is the 1st clue that for him righteousness means both faithfulness to other human beings and faithfulness to God, both of which are achieved through observance of God's commandments. See note to 5:20 and contrast Paul's notion of righteousness by faith alone (*Gal.* 2:16; 3:8, 11, 24; 5:5; *Rom.* 3:26, 28; 5:1; see *Jas.* 2:21–22).   **unwilling to expose her to public disgrace** That is, Joseph was unwilling to accuse her of adultery, which might carry the death penalty (*Deut.* 22:13–21) or at least massive public shame.   **1:20–25** The 1st of three formulaic dream appearances in the birth narrative (see introduction to *Matthew*). In each case an angel of the Lord appears to Joseph in a dream; the angel issues a command to him; the angel provides a rationale for the command; Joseph gets up and obeys the angel's command; and a (cited) scripture is fulfilled. The other dreams are in 2:13–15, 19–23.   **1:20** *from the Holy Spirit* The Gk lacks the definite article. We might read "[a] holy spirit"—a common phrase in the Bible and Jewish literature—without the connotations of later Christian (4th-century) trinitarian theology.   **1:21** *name him Jesus, for he will save* The Gk name *Iēsous* is a transliteration of the common Hebrew name Yeshuᶜa, which is an abbreviation of Yehoshuᶜa (= Joshua), meaning "the Lord helps." *Matthew*, however, follows the popular etymology that derived the name from the Hebrew root "to save."   **1:22–23** *Isa.* 7:14. The 1st of many scripture citations in *Matthew*, each of which is introduced with a similar fulfillment formula. Showing that Jesus fulfills scripture supports the author's claim that Jesus is the Messiah, the culmination of Israel's hope. MT: "Look, the young woman is with child and about to give birth to a son. Let her name him Immanuel." LXX: "Look, the virgin shall conceive [different verb from *Matthew*] and bear a son, and you [singular] shall name him Emmanuel." The passage refers to a ("the" in the Bible) young woman known to both Isaiah and King Ahaz (late 8th century B.C.E.). The sign in question is not a miraculous birth, since the woman is not described as a virgin. Rather, the expected son's infancy will serve as a chronological marker: before he is capable of distinguishing good from evil (i.e., very soon), God will have delivered King Ahaz from his enemies (*Isa.* 7:15–16). That the LXX chose to render the Hebrew for "maiden" with the more specific Gk word for "virgin" is no great surprise, since in antiquity an unmarried woman was assumed to be a virgin. Although it is not clear in the Hebrew whether the woman is already or soon will be pregnant, the Gk translator (LXX) chose a future verb for the conception; this choice may have disposed him to describe the woman as (presently) a virgin. *Matthew*'s point depends on the Gk translation, but the author has even altered this to make his story fit better with scripture by substituting *they shall name him* for "you [Ahaz] will name him." The author has wrenched the verse out of its historical context in a manner that was common among Jewish and Christian interpreters of the period.   **1:25** *until she had borne a son* Remarkably, this is all that *Matthew* says about Jesus' birth itself.

marital relations with her until she had borne a son;[g] and he named him Jesus.

The Visit of the Wise Men

2 In the time of King Herod, after Jesus was born in Bethlehem of Judea, wise men[h] from the East came to Jerusalem, [2]asking, "Where is the child who has been born king of the Jews? For we observed his star at its rising,[i] and have come to pay him homage." [3]When King Herod heard this, he was frightened, and all Jerusalem with him; [4]and calling together all the chief priests and scribes of the people, he inquired of them where the Messiah[j] was to be born. [5]They told him, "In Bethlehem of Judea; for so it has been written by the prophet:

[6]   'And you, Bethlehem, in the land of Judah,
        are by no means least among the rulers of
            Judah;
     for from you shall come a ruler
        who is to shepherd[k] my people Israel.'"

[7]Then Herod secretly called for the wise men[h] and learned from them the exact time when the star had appeared. [8]Then he sent them to Bethlehem, saying,

"Go and search diligently for the child; and when you have found him, bring me word so that I may also go and pay him homage." [9]When they had heard the king, they set out; and there, ahead of them, went the star that they had seen at its rising,[i] until it stopped over the place where the child was. [10]When they saw that the star had stopped,[l] they were overwhelmed with joy. [11]On entering the house, they saw the child with Mary his mother; and they knelt down and paid him homage. Then, opening their treasure chests, they offered him gifts of gold, frankincense, and myrrh. [12]And having been warned in a dream not to return to Herod, they left for their own country by another road.

The Escape to Egypt

[13]Now after they had left, an angel of the Lord appeared to Joseph in a dream and said, "Get up, take the child and his mother, and flee to Egypt, and remain there until I tell you; for Herod is about to search for the child, to destroy him." [14]Then Joseph[m] got up, took the child and his mother by night, and went to Egypt, [15]and remained there until the death

---

g Other ancient authorities read *her firstborn son*
h Or *astrologers*; Gk *magi*
i Or *in the East*
j Or *the Christ*
k Or *rule*

l Gk *saw the star*
m Gk *he*

2:1 **King Herod** Herod the Great, a client of the Romans, effectively ruled Judea only from 37 B.C.E., although he was appointed king three years earlier, until his death in 4 B.C.E. **after Jesus was born in Bethlehem** Once again (see 1:25), this is a remarkably spare reference to Jesus' birth, which the author nowhere describes. The author assumes that Jesus' family was from Bethlehem (see 2:11, 23). **of Judea** The author apparently needs to explain Palestinian geography to the reader, at least regarding smaller towns (see 2:23). **wise men** Gk *magoi*. This term and its Latin parallel, *magi*, refer to practitioners of astrology and magic (hence the English word; see *Acts* 13:6, 8), especially those among the Chaldeans of Babylon and Persia. In describing these *magoi* from the east who watch the stars, the author means not wise men in general but Persian astrologers. **2:3** **frightened** King Herod was a famous figure in Judean history. Out of fear for the security of his throne, he had several of his sons, a wife, and other relatives killed. His fear at the Messiah's birth seems plausible, for there is some reason to think that Herod was viewed as a Messiah by some Jews. That "all" the people of Jerusalem would share this fear, instead of joy, at the prospect of the Messiah's birth is puzzling on the historical level. **2:4** **chief priests and scribes** See notes to *Mark* 8:31; 1:22. **where the Messiah was to be born** Perhaps a slur on Herod: the "king of the Jews" does not know anything about scripture. Herod was notorious in later Jewish recollection for his ignorance of, and disregard for, Jewish tradition. See Josephus, *Ant.* 15.267; 16.150–159, 179–187. **2:5–6** This should probably be counted as *Matthew*'s 2d fulfillment citation even though it is part of the narrative and not introduced editorially; see 1:22. The passage cited is based upon *Mic.* 5:1 (LXX 5:2), perhaps under the influence of *2 Sam.* 5:2. **2:7** From 2:16 it appears that they gave him a date of about two years previous. **2:9–10** How close to the earth would a star need to be to identify a single dwelling? Although numerous efforts have been made in our time to identify this star with some kind of astronomical phenomenon, the details of *Matthew*'s story simply presuppose an ancient worldview. **2:11** **On entering the house** The author is unaware of *Luke*'s birth narrative (2:1–7), according to which Jesus was born in a manger when his parents were visiting Bethlehem. Here Mary and Joseph live in a house in Bethlehem; see 2:1, 23. **gold, frankincense, and myrrh** The combination of a precious metal and two imported spices enhances the exotic atmosphere created by the arrival of the astrologers. **2:13–15** The 2d formulaic dream vision of the birth narrative; see note to 1:20–25. **2:14** **took the child and his mother by night, and went to Egypt** A trip of at least 150 miles (a week's travel) through the coastal Greek cities and the edge of the Nabatean kingdom; twice that time and distance to the more central parts of the province of Egypt. **2:15** **the death of Herod** 4 B.C.E. *Hos.* 11:1. *Matthew*'s 3rd fulfillment citation; see 1:22. The reference is based on a pun on *my son*. In Hosea it refers to Israel, which was in a sense formed, or defined as a nation, through the exodus from Egypt (see *Exod.* 4:22–23). *Matthew*, of course, links it to Jesus.

of Herod. This was to fulfill what had been spoken by the Lord through the prophet, "Out of Egypt I have called my son."

The Massacre of the Infants

[16]When Herod saw that he had been tricked by the wise men,[n] he was infuriated, and he sent and killed all the children in and around Bethlehem who were two years old or under, according to the time that he had learned from the wise men.[n] [17]Then was fulfilled what had been spoken through the prophet Jeremiah:

[18] "A voice was heard in Ramah,
> wailing and loud lamentation,
> Rachel weeping for her children;
> she refused to be consoled,
>> because they are no more."

The Return from Egypt

[19]When Herod died, an angel of the Lord suddenly appeared in a dream to Joseph in Egypt and said,

[20]"Get up, take the child and his mother, and go to the land of Israel, for those who were seeking the child's life are dead." [21]Then Joseph[o] got up, took the child and his mother, and went to the land of Israel. [22]But when he heard that Archelaus was ruling over Judea in place of his father Herod, he was afraid to go there. And after being warned in a dream, he went away to the district of Galilee. [23]There he made his home in a town called Nazareth, so that what had been spoken through the prophets might be fulfilled, "He will be called a Nazorean."

The Proclamation of John the Baptist

3 In those days John the Baptist appeared in the wilderness of Judea, proclaiming, [2]"Repent, for the kingdom of heaven has come near."[p] [3]This is the one of whom the prophet Isaiah spoke when he said,

> "The voice of one crying out in the wilderness:
> 'Prepare the way of the Lord,
>> make his paths straight.'"

[4]Now John wore clothing of camel's hair with a leather belt around his waist, and his food was locusts

---

n Or *astrologers*; Gk *magi*

o Gk *he*
p Or *is at hand*

2:16 *killed all the children* Although this episode fits Herod's character as far as we know it, it is strange that such a heinous crime finds no mention in Josephus, who pulls out all the stops to expose Herod's wickedness. *two years old or under* See 2:7: the magi did not arrive promptly at Jesus' birth. The author envisions Bethlehem as the permanent home of Mary and Joseph; he does not know *Luke's* version (2:21, 39), according to which they returned to Nazareth after little more than a week in Bethlehem. **2:17–18** *Matthew's* 4th fulfillment citation; see 1:22. *Jer.* 31:15. MT: "A cry is heard in Ramah— / Wailing, bitter weeping— / Rachel weeping for her children. She refuses to be comforted / For her children, who are gone." LXX (38:15): "A voice of dirge was heard in Rama, of weeping and of lamentation, Rachel refused to stop weeping loudly for her sons, because they are no more." **2:19–21** The 3d formulaic dream vision in the birth narrative; see note to 1:20–25. **2:19** *When Herod died* 4 B.C.E. **2:22** *Archelaus was ruling over Judea* Herod's son by Malthace, one of several wives. Archelaus contended in Rome for Herod's entire kingdom but was given only Judea, Idumea, and Samaria, over which he presided as ethnarch (ruler of a nation or people), since his territory was the heartland of the Jews. He ruled from 4 B.C.E. to 6 C.E. His removal for incompetence in 6 C.E. marked the end of native rule in Judea; the region was annexed to Rome as a province and was assigned a Roman governor. Twenty years after Archelaus's removal, Pontius Pilate arrived as governor. **2:23** *made his home in a town called Nazareth* Unlike the author of *Luke*, this author supposes that Jesus' family 1st moved to Nazareth in Galilee when they were unable to return home to Bethlehem in Judea; see 2:11. *Matthew's* 5th fulfillment citation; see 1:22. There is, however, no such statement in either the MT or the LXX. The main scholarly guesses about *Matthew's* meaning are: (a) He is making a pun on the Hebrew *netser* ("branch" from David's line) in *Isa.* 11:1. (b) He is quoting an ancient prophetic text that is no longer known to us. (c) He is not intending to cite any specific text. (d) He wants to connect Jesus' hometown, Nazareth, with Jesus' status as "the holy one of God" by means of a pun—that Jesus was raised as a Nazirite devoted to God's service (see *Isa.* 4:3; *Judg.* 16:17). All these proposals face major difficulties if pressed. Given the author's penchant for puns, we should consider that he is simply having fun with words here, perhaps even deliberately confounding logical inquiry. In later Judaism, Christians in general were known as *notsrim.* **3:1** *In those days* A biblical phrase that serves here as a segue from Jesus' infancy to his adult life. At this point the author takes up *Mark* as his chief narrative source, although he also has access to a great deal of sayings material (from Q?) that is not found in *Mark.* **3:2** Thus *Matthew's* Baptist proclaims the same message as Jesus will later (4:17); contrast *Mark* 1:4. *Kingdom of heaven* is a characteristic phrase of this author; it occurs thirty-three times in *Matthew,* but nowhere else in the 1st-century Christian texts. The most likely explanation—the author wished to avoid using the name of God and so substituted the euphemism "heaven"—is problematic because *Matthew* also includes "kingdom of God" three times (12:28; 21:34, 43). Concerning "kingdom" as "reign" or "rule" in Jesus' native Aramaic speech, see note to *Mark* 1:14. **3:3** *Isa.* 40:3. *Matthew's* 6th fulfillment citation; see 1:22. *Matthew* here corrects the scripture citation in *Mark* 1:2. Only the Gk translation of Jewish scripture, which *Matthew* follows here, has a voice crying in the wilderness; it misses the parallelism found in the Hebrew poetry of *Isaiah.* See note to *Mark* 1:2. **3:4–5** These verses invert *Mark* 1:5–6. See note to *Mark* 1:6 concerning John's dress and appearance.

and wild honey. 5Then the people of Jerusalem and all Judea were going out to him, and all the region along the Jordan, 6and they were baptized by him in the river Jordan, confessing their sins.

7But when he saw many Pharisees and Sadducees coming for baptism, he said to them, "You brood of vipers! Who warned you to flee from the wrath to come? 8Bear fruit worthy of repentance. 9Do not presume to say to yourselves, 'We have Abraham as our ancestor'; for I tell you, God is able from these stones to raise up children to Abraham. 10Even now the ax is lying at the root of the trees; every tree therefore that does not bear good fruit is cut down and thrown into the fire.

11"I baptize you with*q* water for repentance, but one who is more powerful than I is coming after me; I am not worthy to carry his sandals. He will baptize you with*q* the Holy Spirit and fire. 12His winnowing fork is in his hand, and he will clear his threshing floor and will gather his wheat into the granary; but the chaff he will burn with unquenchable fire."

The Baptism of Jesus

13Then Jesus came from Galilee to John at the Jordan, to be baptized by him. 14John would have prevented him, saying, "I need to be baptized by you, and do you come to me?" 15But Jesus answered him, "Let it be so now; for it is proper for us in this way to fulfill all righteousness." Then he consented. 16And when Jesus had been baptized, just as he came up from the water, suddenly the heavens were opened to him and he saw the Spirit of God descending like a dove and alighting on him. 17And a voice from heaven said, "This is my Son, the Beloved,*r* with whom I am well pleased."

---

q Or *in*

r Or *my beloved Son*

3:7–10 The first significant agreement between *Matthew* and *Luke* (3:7–9) in non-Markan material; thus, important evidence for Q (see introduction to BIOGRAPHY, ANECDOTE, AND HISTORY). **3:7 *Pharisees and Sadducees*** The first reference to these important groups in *Matthew*; see notes to *Mark* 2:16; 12:18. Only *Matthew* groups the Pharisees and Sadducees together in this way (see 16:1, 6, 11–12). This seems a peculiar combination, since the Pharisees and Sadducees were notoriously opposed to each other (*Acts* 23:6–9; Josephus, *Ant.* 13.297–298). Contrast *Luke* 3:7, in which John addresses precisely the same speech to "the crowds." ***brood of vipers*** It is typical of *Matthew* to label the Pharisees poisonous snakes and to lay this image alongside that of the unfruitful tree; see 12:34; 23:33; see 15:13–14. The image here is of snakes escaping oncoming brush fires; see 3:12. **3:8** *Matthew* here agrees with Josephus's presentation of John the Baptist (*Ant.* 18.116–119), according to which he required a demonstrated change of life *before* he permitted immersion. ***Bear fruit*** The image of the fruitful (and unfruitful) tree is well established in the prophets and later Jewish literature (*Jer.* 8:13; *Hos.* 9:10; see *Gal.* 5:22–23; *John* 15:1–6); *Matthew* uses it extensively (7:15–20; 12:33; 15:13; 21:19, 43). **3:9** The Bible restricts Israel's promises to the descendants of Abraham through Isaac and Jacob, from whom the twelve tribes sprang (renamed Israel—*Gen.* 32:28). Thus, Ishmael and Esau, for example, though sons of Abraham, were not part of the Israelite line. Nevertheless "descended from Abraham" was convenient shorthand for "ethnic Jew" because God had made the chief promises for Israel to Abraham (*Gen.* 12:2–3; 15:1–21; 22:15–18). Descent from Abraham was a source of national pride (*4 Macc.* 6:17, 22). In the 1st century, some Jews believed that Gentiles could (perhaps should) become children of Abraham through conversion to Judaism and, in the case of males, circumcision (*Gen.* 17:1–14). The issue of descent from Abraham loomed large in the early church's rhetoric. Some Christians insisted that physical connection with Judaism was necessary for all, while others argued that spiritual descent from Abraham was adequate or even preferable (*Gal.* 3:6–29; *Rom.* 4:1–25; 9:6–18; *John* 8:39–59; *Barnabas* 9–14). **3:10 *bear good fruit*** See note to 3:8. **3:11–12** The emphasis on fire in John's preaching is absent from *Matthew*'s source, *Mark*. Evidently, the author of *Matthew* had another source concerning the Baptist (Q?), which he conflated with *Mark*'s account and which presented John as warning about coming fire. John's message would, then, have been something like this: "Be immersed in water now, showing your repentance, or you will soon be immersed in fire!" See *Ezek.* 15:2–8; *Sib. Or.* 4.162–186. If Q is closer to what John actually taught, then *Mark* has already spiritualized this message by erasing John's fire and making his prediction hopeful—of the coming Holy Spirit. Faced with somewhat conflicting portraits, the author of *Matthew* has combined them. This is another close parallel to *Luke* not found in *Mark*. **3:11 *winnowing fork . . . threshing floor . . . chaff*** *Matthew* uses images from ancient grain-processing practices: tossing the grain in the air so that the light and useless chaff would be blown away by the wind, leaving only the heavier wheat to be gathered from the floor. But here the chaff will be burned. **3:14–15** *Matthew* answers a problem in the early church, namely: the status of John the Baptist in relation to Jesus. It was undeniable that John had immersed Jesus, but this raised the obvious questions whether Jesus was John's student and whether Jesus needed an immersion for repentance. Different gospel writers deal with the issue in different ways; it is most prominent in *John* (1:15, 19–27, 30, 37; 3:27–20). Here we see *Matthew*'s solution, which the author edits into his use of *Mark*: to have John explicitly challenge the propriety of his immersing Jesus. **3:15 *righteousness*** See notes to 1:19; 5:20. **3:17** *Matthew* changes *Mark*'s direct address ("you are"), perhaps for theological reasons: did not Jesus already know that he was God's son? In doing so, however, the text loses a suggestive parallel with *Ps.* 2:7. One still hears an echo of *Isa.* 42:1, however. See note to *Mark* 1:11.

The Temptation of Jesus

4 Then Jesus was led up by the Spirit into the wilderness to be tempted by the devil. ²He fasted forty days and forty nights, and afterwards he was famished. ³The tempter came and said to him, "If you are the Son of God, command these stones to become loaves of bread." ⁴But he answered, "It is written,

'One does not live by bread alone,
    but by every word that comes
       from the mouth of God.'"

⁵Then the devil took him to the holy city and placed him on the pinnacle of the temple, ⁶saying to him, "If you are the Son of God, throw yourself down; for it is written,

'He will command his angels concerning you,'
    and 'On their hands they will bear you up,
so that you will not dash your foot against a
       stone.'"

⁷Jesus said to him, "Again it is written, 'Do not put the Lord your God to the test.'"

⁸Again, the devil took him to a very high mountain and showed him all the kingdoms of the world and their splendor; ⁹and he said to him, "All these I will give you, if you will fall down and worship me." ¹⁰Jesus said to him, "Away with you, Satan! for it is written,

'Worship the Lord your God,
    and serve only him.'"

¹¹Then the devil left him, and suddenly angels came and waited on him.

Jesus Begins His Ministry in Galilee

¹²Now when Jesus[s] heard that John had been arrested, he withdrew to Galilee. ¹³He left Nazareth and made his home in Capernaum by the sea, in the territory of Zebulun and Naphtali, ¹⁴so that what had been spoken through the prophet Isaiah might be fulfilled:

¹⁵ "Land of Zebulun, land of Naphtali,
    on the road by the sea, across the Jordan,
       Galilee of the Gentiles—
¹⁶ the people who sat in darkness
    have seen a great light,
and for those who sat in the region and shadow
       of death
light has dawned."

¹⁷From that time Jesus began to proclaim, "Repent, for the kingdom of heaven has come near."[t]

Jesus Calls the First Disciples

¹⁸As he walked by the Sea of Galilee, he saw two brothers, Simon, who is called Peter, and Andrew his brother, casting a net into the sea—for they were fishermen. ¹⁹And he said to them, "Follow me, and I will make you fish for people." ²⁰Immediately they left their nets and followed him. ²¹As he went from there, he saw two other brothers, James son of Zebedee and his brother John, in the boat with their father Zebedee, mending their nets, and he called them. ²²Immediately they left the boat and their father, and followed him.

Jesus Ministers to Crowds of People

²³Jesus[u] went throughout Galilee, teaching in their synagogues and proclaiming the good news[v] of the kingdom and curing every disease and every sickness among the people. ²⁴So his fame spread throughout all Syria, and they brought to him all the sick, those

---

s Gk *he*

t Or *is at hand*
u Gk *He*
v Gk *gospel*

4:1–11 Although *Matthew* incorporates *Mark*'s brief temptation story (see esp. 1:11), *Matthew*'s own version is much fuller, and this is paralleled in *Luke* 4:1–13. In the fuller version, significantly, *Matthew*'s Jesus resorts to scripture, indeed the presentation of the Torah in *Deuteronomy*, to dismiss the devil's three temptations. See note to *Mark* 1:13. **4:4** *Deut.* 8:3. **4:6** *Ps.* 91:11–12 (LXX 90:11–12). **4:7** *Deut.* 6:16. **4:10** *Deut.* 6:13. **4:12** See note to *Mark* 1:14; *Matthew* follows *Mark* in postponing an account of John's imprisonment (*Matt.* 11:2; 14:3). **4:13 made his home in Capernaum** This text makes explicit what *Mark* had left vague (see *Mark* 1:21; 2:1). Capernaum was a fishing village at the northern end of the Sea of Galilee (Chinnereth), about twenty-one miles from Nazareth. **by the sea** Actually a lake; see note to *Mark* 1:16. **4:14 in the territory of Zebulun and Naphtali** Two of the twelve tribes of Israel, given the land of Canaan by God according to the biblical story; see *Joshua* 13–19. Since Capernaum probably falls squarely in Naphtali's region, the author apparently makes this statement so that he can cite the following scripture as fulfilled. **4:15** Based upon *Isa.* 8:23–9:1 (LXX 9:1–2). *Matthew*'s 7th fulfillment citation. **4:17 From that time Jesus began to proclaim** This phrase marks a major turning point in the story: Jesus has completed his initiation events and begun his public career. See the similar phrase at 16:21, another dramatic transition. **Repent** Thus Jesus proclaims the same message as John (3:2). **4:18–22** The author follows *Mark* closely. See *Mark* 1:16–20 with notes. **4:23–25** The first of *Matthew*'s major summaries, much fuller than the parallel in *Mark* 1:39. See *Matt.* 8:16; 9:35; 14:35–36; 15:29–31. The author uses these summaries in part to emphasize Jesus' great success in both Jewish and Gentile areas. There is no hint of opposition at this point, although we are well into the narrative. The summaries also help to sustain the air of repetition and formulaic structure that pervades *Matthew* (see introduction to *Matthew*).

who were afflicted with various diseases and pains, demoniacs, epileptics, and paralytics, and he cured them. 25And great crowds followed him from Galilee, the Decapolis, Jerusalem, Judea, and from beyond the Jordan.

The Beatitudes

5When Jesus[w] saw the crowds, he went up the mountain; and after he sat down, his disciples came to him. 2Then he began to speak, and taught them, saying:

3"Blessed are the poor in spirit, for theirs is the kingdom of heaven.

4"Blessed are those who mourn, for they will be comforted.

5"Blessed are the meek, for they will inherit the earth.

6"Blessed are those who hunger and thirst for righteousness, for they will be filled.

7"Blessed are the merciful, for they will receive mercy.

8"Blessed are the pure in heart, for they will see God.

9"Blessed are the peacemakers, for they will be called children of God.

10"Blessed are those who are persecuted for righteousness' sake, for theirs is the kingdom of heaven.

11"Blessed are you when people revile you and persecute you and utter all kinds of evil against you falsely[x] on my account. 12Rejoice and be glad, for your reward is great in heaven, for in the same way they persecuted the prophets who were before you.

Salt and Light

13"You are the salt of the earth; but if salt has lost its taste, how can its saltiness be restored? It is no longer good for anything, but is thrown out and trampled under foot.

14"You are the light of the world. A city built on a hill cannot be hid. 15No one after lighting a lamp puts it under the bushel basket, but on the lampstand, and it gives light to all in the house. 16In the same way, let your light shine before others, so that they may see your good works and give glory to your Father in heaven.

The Law and the Prophets

17"Do not think that I have come to abolish the law or the prophets; I have come not to abolish but to

---

w Gk he

x Other ancient authorities lack *falsely*

5:1 the crowds See 4:25: the author envisions massive crowds. **went up the mountain** It is unclear which mountain is meant. In view of *Matthew*'s sustained Moses imagery (see the birth narrative above), the author likely wishes to compare Jesus with Moses, who also brought divine teaching from a mountain (Sinai). Mountains have great significance in ancient Jewish and Near Eastern texts as places of connection between heaven and earth. Remarkably, *Luke* 6:17 reports that a similar speech took place in a low, level place. **sat down** A typical posture for a rabbinic teacher. **his disciples** At this point in the story, Jesus has only four students (4:18–22). Only in 10:1, apparently, will he select twelve; the author, however, may be intending there to catch up on the story by listing the twelve *after* they have been chosen. **5:2** *Matthew*'s phrasing, "he opened his mouth and taught them, saying," is typical of Semitic languages although it sounds redundant in both Gk and English. **5:3–12** *Matthew*'s famous Beatitudes (from the Latin for "blessed"). *Luke* (6:20b–23) has only four, coupled with four woes. All of them stress the theme, common in prophetic and apocalyptic literature, of eschatological reversal: The present state of things will be completely inverted when the new age (or aeon) breaks in (*Isa.* 14–17; 40:4, 23; 41:11–20; *Ezek.* 17:2–24; 27–32; *Wis.* 3:1–13). **5:3 poor in spirit** The phrase is striking because (a) the parallels in *Luke* 6:20 and *Gospel of Thomas* 54 say simply "the poor"; (b) Paul occasionally calls some of the Jerusalem Christians "the poor" (*Gal.* 2:10; *Rom.* 15:26); and (c) a 2d-century (and later) group of Christians was known as the Ebionites, from the Hebrew for "the poor," and some of them explained their name as meaning "poor in spirit." **kingdom of heaven** See note to 3:2. **5:6 for righteousness** See notes to 1:19; 5:20. *Luke* 6:21 and *Gospel of Thomas* 69 have Jesus speak of physical hunger. **5:10 for righteousness' sake** See notes to 1:19; 5:20. See *Gospel of Thomas* 68–69. **5:11 people revile you** Since the people in question [the Gk says simply "they"] mistreated the prophets, *Matthew*'s Jesus seems to have in mind the Jews; see 10:17; 21:33–46; 23:29–36. The author and his readers appear to be in serious conflict with the (mainstream?) Jewish community. **5:13–16** Versions of the salt and light sayings are found in *Mark* 4:21, 9:49–50, *Luke* 14:34–35, 8:16, and *Gos. Thom.* 33:2; 24:3. Distinctive to *Matthew* is Jesus' direct address to his students at the beginning of each saying: "You are . . ." The two sayings offer several examples of the agreement between *Matthew* and *Luke* against *Mark;* this creates difficulties for the hypothesis that the two later gospels are independent. See introduction to BIOGRAPHY, ANECDOTE, AND HISTORY. **5:17–20** This distinctive passage seems programmatic for *Matthew*'s understanding of Jesus. Unlike Paul, or the authors of *Mark, Luke, John,* or *Thomas,* the author of *Matthew* assumed and insisted upon full commitment to the laws of Moses. This forces the question whether the author and his community were themselves Jewish, or rather Gentiles who had adopted a Jewish way of life in some measure. See introduction to *Matthew.* **5:17 Do not think** The phrasing could suggest, along with 5:19, that the author knows of some who think that Jesus came to abolish the law. **the law or the prophets** The later rabbis divided the biblical books into three groups: Torah (or law), prophets, and writings. The state of the biblical canon in the 1st century is uncertain. *Matthew*'s phrase here (see 7:12; 11:13; 23:40) might suggest that only the 1st

fulfill. [18]For truly I tell you, until heaven and earth pass away, not one letter,[y] not one stroke of a letter, will pass from the law until all is accomplished. [19]Therefore, whoever breaks[z] one of the least of these commandments, and teaches others to do the same, will be called least in the kingdom of heaven; but whoever does them and teaches them will be called great in the kingdom of heaven. [20]For I tell you, unless your righteousness exceeds that of the scribes and Pharisees, you will never enter the kingdom of heaven.

Concerning Anger

[21]"You have heard that it was said to those of ancient times, 'You shall not murder'; and 'whoever murders shall be liable to judgment.' [22]But I say to you that if you are angry with a brother or sister,[a] you will be liable to judgment; and if you insult[b] a brother or sister,[c] you will be liable to the council; and if you say, 'You fool,' you will be liable to the hell[d] of fire. [23]So when you are offering your gift at the altar, if you remember that your brother or sister[e] has something against you, [24]leave your gift there before the altar and go; first be reconciled to your brother or sister,[e] and then come and offer your gift. [25]Come to terms quickly with your accuser while you are on the way to court[f] with him, or your accuser may hand you over to the judge, and the judge to the guard, and you will be thrown into prison. [26]Truly I tell you, you will never get out until you have paid the last penny.

Concerning Adultery

[27]"You have heard that it was said, 'You shall not commit adultery.' [28]But I say to you that everyone who looks at a woman with lust has already committed adultery with her in his heart. [29]If your right eye

---

y Gk *one iota*
z Or *annuls*
a Gk *a brother*; other ancient authorities add *without cause*
b Gk *say Raca to* (an obscure term of abuse)
c Gk *a brother*

d Gk *Gehenna*
e Gk *your brother*
f Gk lacks *to court*

---

two sections of the Bible were so far recognized, but it might also be a kind of shorthand way of referring to the three-part Bible. **to fulfill** This is programmatic for *Matthew*, which frequently pauses to demonstrate (by citation) Jesus' fulfillment of Jewish scripture. *Matthew*'s Jesus thus stands in continuity with Israel's heritage. **5:18** A somewhat confusing sentence because of the double *until*, unless the accomplishment of all things is meant to develop further the "passing away of heaven and earth." The author is emphatic about the importance of the law. The Gk reads "iota" (the smallest letter, *yodh* in Hebrew) for *one letter*, and "little horn" (the tiny projections on letters in Hebrew and Aramaic calligraphy) for *one stroke of a letter*. **truly, I tell you** According to all of the gospels, Jesus characteristically used the Aramaic word ʾ*amēn* (here: *truly*) of his own sayings; see note to *Mark* 3:28. **5:20 righteousness** This is the most important passage for understanding *Matthew*'s characteristic righteousness theme. See note to 1:19. The context implies that the author understands righteousness in a typically biblical-Jewish way: as observance of the divine commandments concerning both human-human and human-divine relationships. The author assumes that Pharisees and scribes aim at such righteousness; Jesus' followers are to surpass them. This requirement reminds one of the religious circles that produced the Dead Sea Scrolls; they saw the Pharisees as insufficiently stringent in their observance of the Torah. **scribes and Pharisees** See notes to *Mark* 1:22; 2:16. **5:21–48** Jesus' "sermon" now turns to a series of six so-called antitheses, or contrasts between what *you have heard* and what *Matthew*'s Jesus teaches. Each of the six opening propositions derives in some way from the Torah of Moses, although we must note the nuances (below). Jesus responds, but his responses are not disagreements with the Torah of Moses, since (a) 5:17–20 has just required rigorous observance of the Torah and (b) Jesus' responses do not in fact call for departure from the laws. Thus, like the later rabbis and the authors of some of the Dead Sea Scrolls, Jesus demands that his followers do more than the minimum required by the Torah. **5:21** *Exod.* 20:13; *Deut.* 5:17. **5:22 liable to the council** A peculiar remark, since the council (Gk *synedrion*) appears elsewhere in *Matthew* and the other gospels only as the Jerusalem court (10:17; 26:59). Perhaps *Matthew*'s Jesus, as the Jewish Messiah, assumes the prerogative of declaring how the court will try cases in the future. **hell** Lit. "Gehenna," the name of the valley to the southeast of Jerusalem in which the Canaanites had practiced child sacrifice by burning. By the time of Jesus, Jewish literature had identified the name with the place of punishment for the wicked (*1 En.* 27.1–2; 90.26; *4 Ezra* 7.26–36). **5:23 offering your gift at the altar** That is, presenting a sacrifice at the temple. Since *Matthew* was written after the temple's destruction, we may ask whether the author includes this simply in order to reflect conditions in Jesus' lifetime or whether the author and his community expect the rebuilding of the temple, as many Jews did. *Did.* 14.1–2 transposes this principle of prior forgiveness to participation in the Christian Eucharist. **your brother or sister** This familial language was typical of the early Christians (*1 Thess.* 1:4; 2:1; *1 Cor.* 1:10; 7:15; *Rom.* 1:13; *Heb.* 3:1; 10:19; *Jas.* 1:2, 19; *1 John* 2:9–11). **5:25–26** A debtor's imprisonment, the result of a judge's decision, was an ancient practice. Prisoners (and their families) would be forced to perform hard labor until the debt was discharged or they died (*2 Kgs.* 4:1; *Neh.* 5:5). See 18:30 and *Did.* 1.5. **5:26 the last penny** Lit. "the last *quadrans*," the smallest Roman coin. *Luke* (12:59) has *lepton*—the smallest Greek coin in circulation, half the value of the *quadrans*—for the same saying. **5:27** *Exod.* 20:14; *Deut.* 5:18. **5:28–30** Along with *Matt.* 19:12, which refers to those who have made themselves eunuchs for the kingdom of heaven, this passage suggests that *Matthew*'s

causes you to sin, tear it out and throw it away; it is better for you to lose one of your members than for your whole body to be thrown into hell.*g* 30And if your right hand causes you to sin, cut it off and throw it away; it is better for you to lose one of your members than for your whole body to go into hell.*g*

Concerning Divorce

31"It was also said, 'Whoever divorces his wife, let him give her a certificate of divorce.' 32But I say to you that anyone who divorces his wife, except on the ground of unchastity, causes her to commit adultery; and whoever marries a divorced woman commits adultery.

Concerning Oaths

33"Again, you have heard that it was said to those of ancient times, 'You shall not swear falsely, but carry out the vows you have made to the Lord.' 34But I say to you, Do not swear at all, either by heaven, for it is the throne of God, 35or by the earth, for it is his footstool, or by Jerusalem, for it is the city of the great King. 36And do not swear by your head, for you cannot make one hair white or black. 37Let your word be 'Yes, Yes' or 'No, No'; anything more than this comes from the evil one.*h*

Concerning Retaliation

38"You have heard that it was said, 'An eye for an eye and a tooth for a tooth.' 39But I say to you, Do not

resist an evildoer. But if anyone strikes you on the right cheek, turn the other also; 40and if anyone wants to sue you and take your coat, give your cloak as well; 41and if anyone forces you to go one mile, go also the second mile. 42Give to everyone who begs from you, and do not refuse anyone who wants to borrow from you.

Love for Enemies

43"You have heard that it was said, 'You shall love your neighbor and hate your enemy.' 44But I say to you, Love your enemies and pray for those who persecute you, 45so that you may be children of your Father in heaven; for he makes his sun rise on the evil and on the good, and sends rain on the righteous and on the unrighteous. 46For if you love those who love you, what reward do you have? Do not even the tax collectors do the same? 47And if you greet only your brothers and sisters,*i* what more are you doing than others? Do not even the Gentiles do the same? 48Be perfect, therefore, as your heavenly Father is perfect.

Concerning Almsgiving

6"Beware of practicing your piety before others in order to be seen by them; for then you have no reward from your Father in heaven.

2"So whenever you give alms, do not sound a

---

g Gk *Gehenna*
h Or *evil*

i Gk *your brothers*

---

community practiced (or at least admired) an extreme asceticism. Origen, a prominent church leader of the 3d century, castrated himself for the sake of the kingdom. Later he joined the Palestinian community. **5:31** A paraphrase of *Deut.* 24:1. **5:32** In contrast to *Mark* 10:1–12, *Matthew* has Jesus permitting divorce on the basis of the wife's unfaithfulness. The alleged faithlessness of women was a common theme in ancient writings. See Josephus, *J.W.* 2.121. **5:33** A conflation and paraphrase of *Lev.* 19:12; *Num.* 30:2; *Deut.* 23:21. See CD 9.1–12; 15.1–4; 16.1–13. **5:34–35** The images of throne, footstool, and the city of the great king are biblical (*Isa.* 66:1; *Ps.* 48:1–2). This language helps to keep *Matthew's* Jesus wholly within the stream of biblical tradition. **5:34 Do not swear at all** The prohibition of oaths was found in other radical Jewish groups of the time, such as Josephus's Essenes (*J.W.* 2.135). See also *Jas.* 5:12, which may have arisen from Jewish-Christian circles. But *Matt.* 23:16–22 seems to recognize oaths. **5:38** *Exod.* 21:24; *Lev.* 24:20; *Deut.* 19:21. These passages do not concern personal ethics but civil and criminal law in Israel, establishing the principle of precise retribution: The community's judges will assign a penalty commensurate with the crime. The principle is as much restrictive (no more than an eye for an eye—to prevent personal vendettas) as it is prescriptive (the community must exact retribution). *Matthew's* Jesus lays down a radical agenda for his community: One should not exercise any right to fairness. **5:39–41** The conditions specified here reflect common occurrences in a land occupied by foreign armies, and so familiar to all Judeans of the time: forced labor and billeting, as well as random violence. See *Luke* 3:14 and *Did.* 1.4. **5:42** See *Did.* 1.4–5; *Gospel of Thomas* 95. **5:43** Unlike the previous five statements of what *you have heard*, this one does not present any biblical passage. The Torah commands love of one's neighbor (*Lev.* 19:18) but not hatred of one's enemies. Indeed, *Prov.* 25:21–22 recommends treating enemies with kindness, as *Matthew's* Jesus does. Josephus also stresses the Jews' humane treatment of enemies (*Ag. Ap.* 2.212). See *Did.* 1.3. **5:47** This distinction between *brothers and sisters* (see note to 5:23), on the one hand, and *Gentiles,* on the other (*Luke* 6:33–34 has "sinners"), suggests that *Matthew's* community sees itself as closely connected with Judaism. See *Did.* 1.3. **5:48** To emulate or participate in God's virtue was a goal of other Jewish groups at the time (Josephus, *Ant.* 1.23). In the parallel passage (*Luke* 6:36), Jesus counsels mercy rather than perfection. **6:2–8** *Matthew's* Jesus issues instructions for his followers in contrast to *the hypocrites . . . in the synagogues,* on the one hand, and *the Gentiles,* on the other. This seems to situate the community as a radical group within Jewish circles.

trumpet before you, as the hypocrites do in the synagogues and in the streets, so that they may be praised by others. Truly I tell you, they have received their reward. ³But when you give alms, do not let your left hand know what your right hand is doing, ⁴so that your alms may be done in secret; and your Father who sees in secret will reward you.ʲ

Concerning Prayer

⁵"And whenever you pray, do not be like the hypocrites; for they love to stand and pray in the synagogues and at the street corners, so that they may be seen by others. Truly I tell you, they have received their reward. ⁶But whenever you pray, go into your room and shut the door and pray to your Father who is in secret; and your Father who sees in secret will reward you.ʲ

⁷"When you are praying, do not heap up empty phrases as the Gentiles do; for they think that they will be heard because of their many words. ⁸Do not be like them, for your Father knows what you need before you ask him.

⁹"Pray then in this way:
Our Father in heaven,
    hallowed be your name.
    ¹⁰Your kingdom come.
Your will be done,
    on earth as it is in heaven.
    ¹¹Give us this day our daily bread.ᵏ
    ¹²And forgive us our debts,
    as we also have forgiven our debtors.

¹³And do not bring us to the time of trial,ˡ
    but rescue us from the evil one.ᵐ
¹⁴For if you forgive others their trespasses, your heavenly Father will also forgive you; ¹⁵but if you do not forgive others, neither will your Father forgive your trespasses.

Concerning Fasting

¹⁶"And whenever you fast, do not look dismal, like the hypocrites, for they disfigure their faces so as to show others that they are fasting. Truly I tell you, they have received their reward. ¹⁷But when you fast, put oil on your head and wash your face, ¹⁸so that your fasting may be seen not by others but by your Father who is in secret; and your Father who sees in secret will reward you.ⁿ

Concerning Treasures

¹⁹"Do not store up for yourselves treasures on earth, where moth and rustᵒ consume and where thieves break in and steal; ²⁰but store up for yourselves treasures in heaven, where neither moth nor rustᵒ consumes and where thieves do not break in and steal. ²¹For where your treasure is, there your heart will be also.

The Sound Eye

²²"The eye is the lamp of the body. So, if your eye is healthy, your whole body will be full of light; ²³but if your eye is unhealthy, your whole body will be full of darkness. If then the light in you is darkness, how great is the darkness!

---

j Other ancient authorities add *openly*
k Or *our bread for tomorrow*
l Or *us into temptation*
m Or *from evil;* other ancient authorities add, in some form, *For the kingdom and the power and the glory are yours forever. Amen.*

n Other ancient authorities add *openly*
o Gk *eating*

6:2 hypocrites . . . in the synagogues The Gk word from which "hypocrite" derives was commonly used of an actor, someone who put on a mask to play a role. Consistently in *Matthew,* the hypocrites are the Jewish leaders, in particular the Pharisees (15:7; 23:2–3, 13, 23, 25, 27, 29). The author's preoccupation with these figures suggests that his own circle is close to the Jewish community. **6:3** See *Did.* 62.2. **6:5** See the charges against the scribes and Pharisees in 23:5–7. **6:9–13** *Matthew's* version of the Lord's Prayer is more famous than the shorter parallel in *Luke* 11:2–4, and it has taken an important place in subsequent Christian liturgy. By the time of the *Didache,* it was already established as a prayer to be said three times each day (*Did.* 8.2). It resembles a Jewish prayer that may have already been current in Jesus' day. **6:9 hallowed** Made or kept holy, set aside for special use. **6:10 Your kingdom come** See 3:2; 4:17. Jesus and his followers expect the kingdom of God (heaven) at any moment. **6:11 daily bread** The Gk is uncertain but may well mean "the bread of tomorrow." **6:13 the time of trial** Trial or testing (the same word in Gk) by the evil one (Satan, the devil) is precisely what Jesus has already endured in the story (4:1–11). This aspect of the prayer comes up again in *Matthew* when Jesus advises his sleeping students in Gethsemane to pray that they not come to the time of trial (26:41). **6:14–15** See *1 Clem.* 13.2. **6:16 whenever you fast** Although the Bible prescribes only one set fast day per year (*Lev.* 16:29), fasts were called at other times, and groups such as the Pharisees appear to have established further routine fasts. See notes to *Mark* 2:18; *Did.* 8.1. **6:17 put oil on your head** In the eastern Mediterranean, olive oil was commonly used in personal grooming. **6:19–20** See *Gos. Thom.* 76:2. **6:22–34** These three sayings, about light, serving two masters, and anxiety concerning money, provide important evidence for the hypothesis of a lost sayings collection (Q). *Luke* has remarkably close verbal parallels but in three different locations (11:34; 16:13; 12:22), which suggests that each author took the same sayings and located them in his work in a distinctive way. **6:22–23** See *Gospel of Thomas* 24.

Serving Two Masters

24"No one can serve two masters; for a slave will either hate the one and love the other, or be devoted to the one and despise the other. You cannot serve God and wealth.*p*

Do Not Worry

25"Therefore I tell you, do not worry about your life, what you will eat or what you will drink,*q* or about your body, what you will wear. Is not life more than food, and the body more than clothing? 26Look at the birds of the air; they neither sow nor reap nor gather into barns, and yet your heavenly Father feeds them. Are you not of more value than they? 27And can any of you by worrying add a single hour to your span of life?*r* 28And why do you worry about clothing? Consider the lilies of the field, how they grow; they neither toil nor spin, 29yet I tell you, even Solomon in all his glory was not clothed like one of these. 30But if God so clothes the grass of the field, which is alive today and tomorrow is thrown into the oven, will he not much more clothe you—you of little faith? 31Therefore do not worry, saying, 'What will we eat?' or 'What will we drink?' or 'What will we wear?' 32For it is the Gentiles who strive for all these things; and indeed your heavenly Father knows that you need all these things. 33But strive first for the kingdom of God*s* and his*t* righteousness, and all these things will be given to you as well.

34"So do not worry about tomorrow, for tomorrow will bring worries of its own. Today's trouble is enough for today.

Judging Others

7"Do not judge, so that you may not be judged. 2For with the judgment you make you will be judged, and the measure you give will be the measure you get. 3Why do you see the speck in your neighbor's*u* eye, but do not notice the log in your own eye? 4Or how can you say to your neighbor,*v* 'Let me take the speck out of your eye,' while the log is in your own eye? 5You hypocrite, first take the log out of your own eye, and then you will see clearly to take the speck out of your neighbor's*u* eye.

Profaning the Holy

6"Do not give what is holy to dogs; and do not throw your pearls before swine, or they will trample them under foot and turn and maul you.

Ask, Search, Knock

7"Ask, and it will be given you; search, and you will find; knock, and the door will be opened for you. 8For everyone who asks receives, and everyone who searches finds, and for everyone who knocks, the door will be opened. 9Is there anyone among you who, if your child asks for bread, will give a stone? 10Or if the child asks for a fish, will give a snake? 11If you then, who are evil, know how to give good gifts to your children, how much more will your Father in heaven give good things to those who ask him!

The Golden Rule

12"In everything do to others as you would have them do to you; for this is the law and the prophets.

---

p Gk *mammon*
q Other ancient authorities lack *or what you will drink*
r Or *add one cubit to your height*
s Other ancient authorities lack *of God*
t Or *its*

u Gk *brother's*
v Gk *brother*

6:24 *wealth* Curiously, both *Matthew* and *Luke* 16:13 preserve here an Aramaic word for wealth. Perhaps some Aramaic-speaking Jews personified mammon as a demon of wealth. See *Gos. Thom.* 47:2. **6:25–34** See *Luke* 12:22–32; *Gospel of Thomas* 36. **6:29** *Solomon* The author expects the reader's familiarity with the famous and enormously wealthy King Solomon of the Bible. See *1 Kgs.* 10:4–7. **6:32** *the Gentiles* Once again, the author calls outsiders Gentiles, suggesting that his own readers are Jews; see 5:47; 6:2–8; 18:17. **6:33** *kingdom of God* A rare departure from *Matthew*'s characteristic "kingdom of heaven." See note to 3:2. *his righteousness* An important theme in *Matthew*; see notes to 1:19; 5:20. On *his* (God's) righteousness as something to be desired, see 5:48 and note. **7:1–5** Another case in which *Matthew* and *Luke* (6:37–42) agree somewhat in changing *Mark* (4:24). Both append a prohibition of judgment and a saying about specks and logs to *Mark*'s saying about recompense. This coincidence is a problem for the hypothesis that they acted independently. **7:1–2** See *1 Clem.* 13.2. **7:3–5** *Gospel of Thomas* 26. **7:6** See *Gospel of Thomas* 26; *Did.* 9.5. Dogs and swine are both significant from a Jewish perspective. Gentiles are sometimes called dogs (*1 Sam.* 17:43; *Phil.* 3:2), and pigs are unclean animals (*Deut.* 14:8). **7:7–11** The form of argument from the lesser to the greater (*a fortiori* in Western logic; *qal vaḥomer* in Hebrew) was common in rabbinic analysis. *Matthew*'s Jesus uses it often; see 12:6, 41, 42. **7:7–8** A widely reported saying. See *Luke* 11:9–10 (from Q?); *John* 14:13; 15:7, 16; 16:23, 26; *Gospel of Thomas* 2; 92; 94. **7:12** This is the so-called golden rule, which is paralleled in many ancient religious traditions, including Judaism (*Luke* 6:31; *Did.* 1.2; *Gos. Thom.* 6:3). Jesus' summary of the entire "law and prophets" (see 22:36–40 and note to 5:17) in this way is also characteristically Jewish (Hillel, *b. Shab.* 31a). Such a summary of the Torah does not suggest in *Matthew* or in rabbinic literature, as it does for Paul (*Gal.* 5:14; 6:2), that those who follow the single principle are thereby excused from other obligations to the Torah.

The Narrow Gate

13"Enter through the narrow gate; for the gate is wide and the road is easy[w] that leads to destruction, and there are many who take it. 14For the gate is narrow and the road is hard that leads to life, and there are few who find it.

A Tree and Its Fruit

15"Beware of false prophets, who come to you in sheep's clothing but inwardly are ravenous wolves. 16You will know them by their fruits. Are grapes gathered from thorns, or figs from thistles? 17In the same way, every good tree bears good fruit, but the bad tree bears bad fruit. 18A good tree cannot bear bad fruit, nor can a bad tree bear good fruit. 19Every tree that does not bear good fruit is cut down and thrown into the fire. 20Thus you will know them by their fruits.

Concerning Self-Deception

21"Not everyone who says to me, 'Lord, Lord,' will enter the kingdom of heaven, but only the one who does the will of my Father in heaven. 22On that day many will say to me, 'Lord, Lord, did we not prophesy in your name, and cast out demons in your name, and do many deeds of power in your name?' 23Then I will declare to them, 'I never knew you; go away from me, you evildoers.'

Hearers and Doers

24"Everyone then who hears these words of mine and acts on them will be like a wise man who built his house on rock. 25The rain fell, the floods came, and the winds blew and beat on that house, but it did not fall, because it had been founded on rock. 26And everyone who hears these words of mine and does not act on them will be like a foolish man who built his house on sand. 27The rain fell, and the floods came, and the winds blew and beat against that house, and it fell—and great was its fall!"

28Now when Jesus had finished saying these things, the crowds were astounded at his teaching, 29for he taught them as one having authority, and not as their scribes.

Jesus Cleanses a Leper

8 When Jesus[x] had come down from the mountain, great crowds followed him; 2and there was a leper[y] who came to him and knelt before him, saying, "Lord, if you choose, you can make me clean." 3He stretched out his hand and touched him, saying, "I do choose. Be made clean!" Immediately his leprosy[y] was cleansed. 4Then Jesus said to him, "See that you say nothing to anyone; but go, show yourself to the priest, and offer the gift that Moses commanded, as a testimony to them."

Jesus Heals a Centurion's Servant

5When he entered Capernaum, a centurion came to him, appealing to him 6and saying, "Lord, my ser-

---

w Other ancient authorities read *for the road is wide and easy*

x Gk *he*

y The terms *leper* and *leprosy* can refer to several diseases

---

7:15 *Matthew* will use the image again; see 10:16. **7:16–20** Trees bearing fruit, good and bad, is a common image in *Matthew*; see 3:8–10; 12:33–35; note to 3:8. See *Gospel of Thomas* 45; Ign. *Eph.* 14.2. **7:23** *Luke* 13:25–27 (see 6:46) has what seems to be a variant of this saying, although it reads quite differently. **7:24–27** *Luke* 6:47–49 has a close but shorter parallel. **7:28** *Now when Jesus had finished saying these things* *Matthew*'s formulaic phrase for closing Jesus' five major speeches. See 11:1; 13:53; 19:1; 26:1. **7:29** *Matthew*'s almost precise verbal parallel with *Mark* 1:22 (as the author now returns to the Markan narrative outline) is all the more remarkable because of the completely different context and sense. In *Matthew* there is no hint yet of the cosmic battle with the spirits that precedes this observation by the crowds in *Mark*. Taken together with Jesus' accusations against the "hypocrites" in the preceding sermon and John the Baptist's description of the Pharisees and Sadducees, this saying places Jesus in a slowly developing in-house conflict with the Jewish leadership. **8:1** *down from the mountain* See 5:1. **8:2–4** *Matthew* follows *Mark* 1:40–44 quite closely. The passage is a problem for the hypothesis that *Matthew* and *Luke* were independent, however, because they agree against *Mark* in several additions, omissions, and cases of rephrasing. **8:2** *A leper* See note to *Mark* 1:40. **8:5–13** The story is fascinating both for its role in *Matthew*'s narrative and for its transmission history. *Matthew* here continues its emphasis, established already in the genealogy and birth story, of Gentiles' coming into salvation. The story is one of the few synoptic traditions represented in *John* (4:46–54). Although it should be a candidate for inclusion in the hypothetical Q because it is material common to *Luke* (7:1–10) and *Matthew* but not *Mark,* it is a problem for the Q hypothesis because it is narrative and not sayings material. **8:5** *Capernaum* See notes to 4:13, 14. *centurion* Since this officer was stationed in the territory of Herod Antipas, he was presumably part of the tetrarch's mercenary forces, not the Roman army or its auxiliaries. The title "centurion" reflects the common practice of such armies to imitate the Roman organization. A centurion was in charge of a century—usually about eighty men—and enjoyed much prestige. Still, from the perspective of the local Jews, such foreign soldiers were usually hated and feared. Notice that *Luke* 7:4–5 provides a reason why Jesus should help the centurion. **8:6** *my servant* The Gk word can also mean "son" or "child"; the slave in 8:9 is not necessarily the one who is sick. *Luke* 7:2 has "slave"; *John* 4:46 has "son."

vant is lying at home paralyzed, in terrible distress." ⁷And he said to him, "I will come and cure him." ⁸The centurion answered, "Lord, I am not worthy to have you come under my roof; but only speak the word, and my servant will be healed. ⁹For I also am a man under authority, with soldiers under me; and I say to one, 'Go,' and he goes, and to another, 'Come,' and he comes, and to my slave, 'Do this,' and the slave does it." ¹⁰When Jesus heard him, he was amazed and said to those who followed him, "Truly I tell you, in no one^z in Israel have I found such faith. ¹¹I tell you, many will come from east and west and will eat with Abraham and Isaac and Jacob in the kingdom of heaven, ¹²while the heirs of the kingdom will be thrown into the outer darkness, where there will be weeping and gnashing of teeth." ¹³And to the centurion Jesus said, "Go; let it be done for you according to your faith." And the servant was healed in that hour.

Jesus Heals Many at Peter's House

¹⁴When Jesus entered Peter's house, he saw his mother-in-law lying in bed with a fever; ¹⁵he touched her hand, and the fever left her, and she got up and began to serve him. ¹⁶That evening they brought to him many who were possessed with demons; and he cast out the spirits with a word, and cured all who were sick. ¹⁷This was to fulfill what had been spoken through the prophet Isaiah, "He took our infirmities and bore our diseases."

Would-Be Followers of Jesus

¹⁸Now when Jesus saw great crowds around him, he gave orders to go over to the other side. ¹⁹A scribe then approached and said, "Teacher, I will follow you wherever you go." ²⁰And Jesus said to him, "Foxes have holes, and birds of the air have nests; but the Son of Man has nowhere to lay his head." ²¹Another of his disciples said to him, "Lord, first let me go and bury my father." ²²But Jesus said to him, "Follow me, and let the dead bury their own dead."

Jesus Stills the Storm

²³And when he got into the boat, his disciples followed him. ²⁴A windstorm arose on the sea, so great that the boat was being swamped by the waves; but he was asleep. ²⁵And they went and woke him up,

---

z Other ancient authorities read *Truly I tell you, not even*

8:11–12 This moral or lesson seems to be strategically placed and thus important for the author. The image of people flowing in from other nations to join the patriarchs recalls the prophetic hope (*Isa.* 2:2–3; *Zech.* 8:20–23), and it was a common enough vision among Jews of Jesus' day (Josephus, *Ag. Ap.* 2.209–210). It also matches *Matthew*'s emphasis on Gentile salvation. All of this suggests that *Matthew* envisages Gentiles coming into salvation by becoming Jews as well as followers of Jesus. The heirs of the kingdom who are excluded are the native Jews who fail to accept Jesus (see 20:1–16; 21:33–44; 22:2–14; *2 Esd.* 1:33–38). **8:12 *weeping and gnashing of teeth*** This is a characteristic expression of *Matthew*'s Jesus (see 13:42, 50; 22:13; 24:51; 25:30). Interestingly, *Luke* has one occurrence of this expression, in its rough parallel to this passage (13:28). This parallel presents something of a problem for the common view that *Matthew* and *Luke* were independently written, since one plausible explanation is that the author of *Luke* learned the saying from *Matthew*. **8:14 *Peter's house*** See notes to *Mark* 1:16, 29. **8:15 *serve him*** *Mark* 1:31 and *Luke* 4:39 have "served them." **8:16–17** A Matthean summary. See note to 4:23–25. **8:17** *Matthew*'s 8th fulfillment citation (see note to 1:22–23). *Isa.* 53:5. Neither the MT nor the LXX has the language of sickness that makes the passage relevant for *Matthew*. **8:18 *the other side*** Across the lake somewhere from Capernaum (see 8:5). **8:19–22** These radical demands upon would-be followers of Jesus have a close verbal parallel in *Luke* 9:57–62, although *Luke* includes a 3d example; according to the most common theory, therefore, they come from Q. See *Gospel of Thomas* 86. **8:19 *scribe*** See note to *Mark* 1:22. Note *Matthew*'s positive disposition toward at least some scribes, especially in the reference to the scribe trained for the kingdom of heaven (13:52). **8:20 *Son of Man*** The 1st of thirty-one occurrences of this much debated title in *Matthew*. See notes to *Mark* 2:10, 27–28. Here, although the author treats it as a title, the phrase could also mean "I." **8:21 *Another of his disciples*** As far as the reader knows, Jesus has so far called four students. Only in 10:1–4 will the Twelve be named. This passage seems to suggest that Jesus is in the process of calling more students. **8:21–22** Jesus' dismissal of this request would have seemed radical indeed in the 1st century, for in the ancient world generally burying one's family members was considered an inescapable obligation. See Sophocles, *Antigone* 40–50. **8:23 *got into the boat*** The geography becomes a little confusing, probably under *Mark*'s influence. In 8:18 Jesus crossed to the "other side" of the lake from Capernaum in the north (see 8:5). It seems from 8:28 that he is now going to Gadara, on "the other side." Gadara was indeed on the other side of the lake from Capernaum, but about six miles of hard walking inland. Where was Jesus, then, between Capernaum and Gadara on "the other side"? **8:24–27** *Matthew* follows *Mark* 4:37–41 fairly closely, abbreviating the story and slightly improving the image of Jesus' students. They ask him respectfully to save them (rather than wondering scornfully whether he cares about them); they marvel at his accomplishment (rather than fearing him); and they ask only what sort of man he might be (rather than who he is). The passage creates problems for the theory that *Matthew* and *Luke* independently used *Mark* because *Matthew* and *Luke* agree against *Mark* in the phrase *they went*, the exclamation *we are perishing*, and the concluding note that the students *were amazed*. **8:24 *A windstorm arose*** The NRSV neglects to translate *Matthew*'s characteristic "Look!" (or "Behold!"), a biblical phrase that evokes an air of sacred mystery.

saying, "Lord, save us! We are perishing!" 26And he said to them, "Why are you afraid, you of little faith?" Then he got up and rebuked the winds and the sea; and there was a dead calm. 27They were amazed, saying, "What sort of man is this, that even the winds and the sea obey him?"

Jesus Heals the Gadarene Demoniacs

28When he came to the other side, to the country of the Gadarenes,*a* two demoniacs coming out of the tombs met him. They were so fierce that no one could pass that way. 29Suddenly they shouted, "What have you to do with us, Son of God? Have you come here to torment us before the time?" 30Now a large herd of swine was feeding at some distance from them. 31The demons begged him, "If you cast us out, send us into the herd of swine." 32And he said to them, "Go!" So they came out and entered the swine; and suddenly, the whole herd rushed down the steep bank into the sea and perished in the water. 33The swineherds ran off, and on going into the town, they told the whole story about what had happened to the demoniacs. 34Then the whole town came out to meet Jesus; and when they saw him, they begged him to leave their 9 neighborhood. 1And after getting into a boat he crossed the sea and came to his own town.

Jesus Heals a Paralytic

2And just then some people were carrying a paralyzed man lying on a bed. When Jesus saw their faith, he said to the paralytic, "Take heart, son; your sins are forgiven." 3Then some of the scribes said to themselves, "This man is blaspheming." 4But Jesus, perceiving their thoughts, said, "Why do you think evil in your hearts? 5For which is easier, to say, 'Your sins are forgiven,' or to say, 'Stand up and walk'? 6But so that you may know that the Son of Man has authority on earth to forgive sins"—he then said to the paralytic—"Stand up, take your bed and go to your home." 7And he stood up and went to his home. 8When the crowds saw it, they were filled with awe, and they glorified God, who had given such authority to human beings.

The Call of Matthew

9As Jesus was walking along, he saw a man called Matthew sitting at the tax booth; and he said to him, "Follow me." And he got up and followed him.

10And as he sat at dinner*b* in the house, many tax collectors and sinners came and were sitting*c* with him and his disciples. 11When the Pharisees saw this, they said to his disciples, "Why does your teacher

---

a Other ancient authorities read *Gergesenes;* others, *Gerasenes*

b Gk *reclined*
c Gk *were reclining*

8:28–34 *Matthew* considerably abbreviates the story found in *Mark* 5:1–20. **8:28 the other side** See note to 8:23. **the country of the Gadarenes** Gadara was an important city of the Greek Decapolis (the "ten cities") east of the Jordan and south of the Sea of Galilee (Lake Gennesar). A famous cultural center, it had produced world-renowned philosophers and writers. It is noteworthy that the Jesus tradition should associate the site only with demonic possession. The author of *Matthew* perhaps realized that *Mark's* Gerasa (*Mark* 5:1) was altogether too far from the lake for the pigs to run into it (*Matt.* 8:32), and so proposed the similar-sounding Gadarene region. Each Greek city had a "country" (*chōra*) around it, comprising numerous villages. Although Gadara itself was six miles from the lake, its territory reached at least that far (Josephus, *Life* 42). **two demoniacs** One of *Matthew's* peculiar changes to *Mark's* story is the substitution of two demon-possessed men. This fits with *Matthew's* general preference for pairs (see 20:29–34; 21:2–7), which might in part be explained by a concern to have "two or three witnesses" for proof, as the Torah requires in criminal cases (*Deut.* 19:15). **9:1–8** Jesus' first significant conflict with the scribes, who accuse him of blasphemy—the charge on which he will finally be condemned by the Jewish court (26:65). *Matthew* considerably abbreviates the story in *Mark* 2:1–12, partly by omitting *Mark's* claim that the men carrying the paralytic lowered him through the roof, partly by omitting the scribes' assertion that only God can forgive sins. Yet the author seems to think it obvious that claiming to forgive sins amounts to blasphemy (9:3). **9:1 he crossed the sea and came to his own town** That is, Capernaum (see 4:13). **9:2 lying on a bed** *Matthew* and *Luke* 5:18 agree against *Mark* 2:3 in supplying this note—a problem for the hypothesis that they were independent. **blaspheming** See note to *Mark* 2:7. **9:4 in your hearts** *Matthew's* source (*Mark* 2:6) had spelled out that the scribes questioned in their hearts. **9:6 Son of Man** The second occurrence of this term in *Matthew*; see note to *Mark* 2:10. Although the author treats it as an honorific title for Jesus, the phrase might well mean "human being" here, especially in view of 9:8: God has given such authority to human beings. **bed** Another agreement with *Luke* (5:24) against *Mark* (2:11: "mat"); see note to 9:2. **9:8 to human beings** See note to 9:6. **9:9–13** *Matthew* continues to follow *Mark* 2. Aside from abbreviation and simplification of the language, *Matthew's* most striking change is the alteration of the tax collector's name from Levi son of Alphaeus (*Mark* 2:14) to Matthew. The author may simply have considered it more sensible to use a name that would turn up among the Twelve (*Mark* 3:16–19; *Matt.* 10:2–4). This distinctive feature may have been one factor in the church fathers' connection of this anonymous story with Matthew. **9:9 tax booth** See note to *Mark* 2:14. **9:10 sat at dinner** That is, reclined on couches in Mediterranean fashion. See note to *Mark* 2:15. **the house** Presumably, this is Jesus' house, since the tax collector has followed Jesus (see 9:28). *Matthew* preserves *Mark's* (2:15) vagueness, but see *Luke* 5:29, which puts the feast in Levi's house. **many tax collectors and sinners** See note to *Mark* 2:15. **9:11 the Pharisees** An alteration of *Mark's* puzzling "scribes of the Pharisees." See note to *Mark* 2:16.

eat with tax collectors and sinners?" 12But when he heard this, he said, "Those who are well have no need of a physician, but those who are sick. 13Go and learn what this means, 'I desire mercy, not sacrifice.' For I have come to call not the righteous but sinners."

The Question about Fasting

14Then the disciples of John came to him, saying, "Why do we and the Pharisees fast often,*d* but your disciples do not fast?" 15And Jesus said to them, "The wedding guests cannot mourn as long as the bridegroom is with them, can they? The days will come when the bridegroom is taken away from them, and then they will fast. 16No one sews a piece of unshrunk cloth on an old cloak, for the patch pulls away from the cloak, and a worse tear is made. 17Neither is new wine put into old wineskins; otherwise, the skins burst, and the wine is spilled, and the skins are destroyed; but new wine is put into fresh wineskins, and so both are preserved."

A Girl Restored to Life and a Woman Healed

18While he was saying these things to them, suddenly a leader of the synagogue*e* came in and knelt before him, saying, "My daughter has just died; but come and lay your hand on her, and she will live." 19And Jesus got up and followed him, with his disciples. 20Then suddenly a woman who had been suffering from hemorrhages for twelve years came up behind him and touched the fringe of his cloak, 21for she said to herself, "If I only touch his cloak, I will be made well." 22Jesus turned, and seeing her he said, "Take heart, daughter; your faith has made you well." And instantly the woman was made well.

---

d Other ancient authorities lack *often*

e Gk lacks *of the synagogue*

9:12 A common image among moral philosophers of the time; see note to *Mark* 2:17. **9:13** *I desire mercy, not sacrifice* A quotation of *Hos.* 6:6, much the same in the MT and the LXX, which occurs again at *Matt.* 12:7. *Hosea* continues with a parallel phrase, "the knowledge of God rather than burnt offerings." The 8th-century B.C.E. prophet of the northern kingdom (Israel) was condemning his nation's continued routine of sacrifice in the midst of rampant idolatry and political machination. *Matthew*, for its part, typically presents the Jewish leadership of the 1st century as perpetuating a system that loses sight of real human needs (12:9–11, 33–37; 13:13–15; 15:4–14; 16:6–12; 21:12–13; 23:2–36) at a time when Judea/Galilee was in difficult straits. The critique was shared by many other groups. Neither *Hosea*'s nor Jesus' words necessarily reject the sacrificial system, for Semitic languages commonly used the formulation "A, *not* B" to mean "A, *much more than* B." See note to *Mark* 7:15–23. Elsewhere *Matthew* both assumes the validity of temple sacrifice (5:23–24) and predicts the destruction of the temple (24:1–28). **9:14** *the disciples of John* One of many clues in the gospels that the Baptist's following continued intact and separate from Jesus'. See note to *Mark* 2:18. *Matthew* follows *Mark* 2:18 but has John's own students, rather than outside observers, pose the question. *Luke* 5:33 has the Pharisees at the preceding banquet pose the question. *fast often* See notes to 6:16 and *Mark* 2:18. **9:15** Although the image of the bridegroom is here taken over from *Mark* 2:18–20, *Matthew* alone will introduce a later parable about a wedding feast in which Jesus is again the bridegroom. The image of God as the groom of Israel was common in the biblical prophets (e.g., throughout *Hosea*), and Jesus appears as a groom to his bride, the church, in 2 *Cor.* 11:2; *Eph.* 5:23–25; *John* 3:29; *Rev.* 19:7. *then they will fast* See *Did.* 8.1: some Christian groups did adopt routine fasts after Jesus' death and resurrection. **9:16–17** See *Mark* 2:21–22 and note. *Matthew* seems to take over *Mark*'s point that old forms cannot accommodate something new (see *Gos. Thom.* 47:4). But contrast *Luke* 5:36–39. Is Jesus' message as new in *Matthew* as in *Mark*? See *Matt.* 13:52. **9:18–26** *Matthew* considerably abbreviates two nested stories from *Mark* 5:21–43. At the same time, the author makes several important changes. Most significantly, it was the author of *Mark* who had a reason to nest the stories, because the fact that the girl was "at the point of death" (*Mark* 5:23) makes the story suspenseful: the woman with the hemorrhage impedes Jesus' progress toward the girl, who dies in the meantime (*Mark* 5:35). In *Matthew*, since the girl is already dead (9:18), the dramatic reason for nesting the stories seems to have disappeared; yet the author follows his source. **9:18** *a leader of the synagogue* A peculiar translation, since the Gk text says nothing about the synagogue; indeed, the author deliberately chooses not to use *Mark*'s "leader of the synagogue," possibly because of *Matthew*'s general hostility to "their synagogues" (6:2, 5; 10:17; 12:9–14; 23:6, 34), or possibly because in Jewish areas there was little distinction between synagogue and community leaders. The Gk in *Matthew* says simply "a leader." *has just died* See *Mark* 5:23: "at the point of death." On the one hand, *Matthew*'s version makes the man's faith more heroic, since he believes from the outset that Jesus can raise the dead. On the other hand, the dramatic reason for enclosing the story of the woman with the hemorrhages within this story is gone. **9:19** *with his disciples* An addition to *Mark*, possibly indicating the elevated stature of Jesus' students in *Matthew*. **9:20** *suddenly* NRSV translation of *Matthew*'s biblical-sounding "Look" or "Behold." This translation often omits the word altogether, although it is important for creating atmosphere within the text; see note to 8:24. *suffering from hemorrhages for twelve years* See *Lev.* 15:25–33 and note to *Mark* 5:25. *fringe of his cloak* Jewish men were required to wear four corner tassels on their clothes; see note to *Mark* 6:56. *Luke*'s agreement (8:44) with *Matthew* in inserting this phrase where it was lacking in *Mark* poses a problem for the common theory that *Matthew* and *Luke* were independently written. **9:22** A major change to *Mark* 5:28–34, for now Jesus is in complete control and the woman is cured only in response to his deliberate word. This change allows the author to omit much of the Markan story.

23When Jesus came to the leader's house and saw the flute players and the crowd making a commotion, 24he said, "Go away; for the girl is not dead but sleeping." And they laughed at him. 25But when the crowd had been put outside, he went in and took her by the hand, and the girl got up. 26And the report of this spread throughout that district.

Jesus Heals Two Blind Men

27As Jesus went on from there, two blind men followed him, crying loudly, "Have mercy on us, Son of David!" 28When he entered the house, the blind men came to him; and Jesus said to them, "Do you believe that I am able to do this?" They said to him, "Yes, Lord." 29Then he touched their eyes and said, "According to your faith let it be done to you." 30And their eyes were opened. Then Jesus sternly ordered them, "See that no one knows of this." 31But they went away and spread the news about him throughout that district.

Jesus Heals One Who Was Mute

32After they had gone away, a demoniac who was mute was brought to him. 33And when the demon had been cast out, the one who had been mute spoke; and the crowds were amazed and said, "Never has anything like this been seen in Israel." 34But the Pharisees said, "By the ruler of the demons he casts out the demons."*f*

The Harvest Is Great, the Laborers Few

35Then Jesus went about all the cities and villages, teaching in their synagogues, and proclaiming the good news of the kingdom, and curing every disease and every sickness. 36When he saw the crowds, he had compassion for them, because they were harassed and helpless, like sheep without a shepherd. 37Then he said to his disciples, "The harvest is plentiful, but the laborers are few; 38therefore ask the Lord of the harvest to send out laborers into his harvest."

The Twelve Apostles

10 Then Jesus*g* summoned his twelve disciples and gave them authority over unclean spirits, to cast them out, and to cure every disease and every sickness. 2These are the names of the twelve apostles: first, Simon, also known as Peter, and his brother Andrew; James son of Zebedee, and his brother John; 3Philip and Bartholomew; Thomas and Matthew the tax collector; James son of Alphaeus, and Thaddaeus;*h*

---

f Other ancient authorities lack this verse
g Gk *he*
h Other ancient authorities read *Lebbaeus* or *Lebbaeus called Thaddaeus*

9:23–26 *Matthew* greatly abbreviates *Mark* 5:35–43. This text omits the news of the girl's death (since she has been dead from the outset); the note that Jesus took only Peter, James, John, and the child's parents with him (perhaps because of *Matthew's* general diminution of *Mark's* messianic-secret theme [see *Mark* 13:3/*Matt.* 24:3] or its critique of the leading disciples); Jesus' words in raising the dead child, including his Aramaic phrase; and his final command of secrecy. **9:27–31** The first of two similar stories in *Matthew* (see 20:29–34), each of which involves two blind men—an illustration of *Matthew's* preference for pairs and repetition (see note to 8:28). **9:27 Have mercy . . .** This appeal is identical to that of the blind men in 20:30. **Son of David** The 1st occurrence of this phrase since the birth narrative, when Jesus was plainly shown to be the awaited, anointed descendant of David, the "Messiah." In both *Matthew* and *Luke,* this title is much more positively integrated into the text than in *Mark* (see note to *Mark* 10:47–48). **9:28 the house** Presumably Jesus' house in Capernaum; see 9:10. **Do you believe** Or "Do you trust?" **9:30** It is puzzling that *Matthew* introduces the secrecy motif (commonly found in *Mark*) here, in material peculiar to this gospel, while omitting it elsewhere (e.g., 9:26). **9:32–34** Another passage that will be closely paralleled later in the narrative (12:22–24), illustrating *Matthew's* fondness for repetition; see note to 9:27–31. *Mark* (3:22) parallels only the accusation of demon possession; *Luke* (11:14–15), however, also has this charge follow on Jesus' exorcism of a demon of muteness. On the perceived relationship between sickness and demon possession in antiquity, see notes to *Mark* 1:23; 9:17–18. **9:34 the ruler of the demons** In Jewish literature of the time, the devil is given many names, for example, Satan, Mastema, Belial, Beelzebul (or Beelzebub); see 12:24. **9:35** One of *Matthew's* summaries, which contribute to the narrative sense of repetition and formulaic structure. See note to 4:23–25. **9:36–37** *Matthew* combines sayings here that occur in quite different places in *Mark* (*Matt.* 9:36 par. *Mark* 6:34) and *Luke* (*Matt.* 9:37 par. *Luke* 10:2—from Q?). See *John* 4:35 and *Gospel of Thomas* 73. With these words, the author sets up the following discourse for Christian missionaries, one of *Matthew's* major concerns (see introduction to *Matthew*). **10:1 summoned his twelve disciples** Although this is the 1st time the reader hears of the Twelve, the language here might suggest that the group has been intact for some time and the author is only now getting around to listing the members. The preceding narrative has given some indications that Jesus has been assembling a group of students (8:18–22; 9:9). **unclean spirits** On the relationship between sickness and spirit possession, see note to *Mark* 1:23. **10:2–4** *Matthew* follows *Mark's* list of names; *Luke* 6:13–16, however, substitutes "Judas the son of James" for Thaddaeus. **10:2 Simon, also known as Peter** Although the author will not describe Simon's renaming until 16:18, he does not hesitate to use before that point the name familiar to his readers (see 4:18; 8:14); he never calls him Simon without qualification. Contrast *Mark* 1:16, 29, 30, 36; 14:37. **10:3 Matthew the tax collector** Only *Matthew* can supply this information because the author has changed *Mark's* Levi to Matthew; see 9:9 and note to 9:9–13.

⁴Simon the Cananaean, and Judas Iscariot, the one who betrayed him.

The Mission of the Twelve

⁵These twelve Jesus sent out with the following instructions: "Go nowhere among the Gentiles, and enter no town of the Samaritans, ⁶but go rather to the lost sheep of the house of Israel. ⁷As you go, proclaim the good news, 'The kingdom of heaven has come near.'ⁱ ⁸Cure the sick, raise the dead, cleanse the lepers,ʲ cast out demons. You received without payment; give without payment. ⁹Take no gold, or silver, or copper in your belts, ¹⁰no bag for your journey, or two tunics, or sandals, or a staff; for laborers deserve their food. ¹¹Whatever town or village you enter, find out who in it is worthy, and stay there until you leave. ¹²As you enter the house, greet it. ¹³If the house is worthy, let your peace come upon it; but if it is not worthy, let your peace return to you. ¹⁴If anyone will not welcome you or listen to your words, shake off

_____

i Or *is at hand*
j The terms *leper* and *leprosy* can refer to several diseases

the dust from your feet as you leave that house or town. ¹⁵Truly I tell you, it will be more tolerable for the land of Sodom and Gomorrah on the day of judgment than for that town.

Coming Persecutions

¹⁶"See, I am sending you out like sheep into the midst of wolves; so be wise as serpents and innocent as doves. ¹⁷Beware of them, for they will hand you over to councils and flog you in their synagogues; ¹⁸and you will be dragged before governors and kings because of me, as a testimony to them and the Gentiles. ¹⁹When they hand you over, do not worry about how you are to speak or what you are to say; for what you are to say will be given to you at that time; ²⁰for it is not you who speak, but the Spirit of your Father speaking through you. ²¹Brother will betray brother to death, and a father his child, and children will rise against parents and have them put to death; ²²and you will be hated by all because of my name. But the one who endures to the end will be saved. ²³When they persecute you in one town, flee to the next; for truly I tell you, you will not have gone through all the towns of Israel before the Son of Man comes.

10:4 *Judas Iscariot, the one who betrayed him* The author assumes the reader's familiarity with some key aspects of the later story (see *1 Cor.* 11:23); see note to *Mark* 3:19. **10:5–11:1** Jesus' 2d major discourse in *Matthew*—after the Sermon on the Mount (*Matt.* 5–7)—is a missionary address. It has some parallels with *Mark*'s apocalyptic discourse (*Mark* 13) and with *Luke*'s presentation of Jesus' general admonitions to followers (*Luke* 12:2–9, 51–53), but the parts that are peculiar to *Matthew* in 10:5–15, together with *Matthew*'s arrangement of the text, give it an entirely new force. One of the speech's puzzling properties is its inclusion, in a speech directed toward a particular mission among Jewish areas during Jesus' lifetime (10:5–12), of predictions of appearances before "governors and kings" (10:18) and the claim that they would not have gone through the towns of Israel before the Son of Man comes (10:23)—conditions that were obviously unfulfilled at the time of *Matthew*'s composition. **10:5–6** These verses are peculiar to *Matthew* and provide striking evidence of the Jewish atmosphere of the work. See introduction to *Matthew*. **10:5** *nowhere among the Gentiles* Or "into the path [or road] of the Gentiles [or nations]." The areas around Judea and Galilee were dotted with Greek cities: the Decapolis to the east and the Greek coastal cities to the west. Interestingly, in view of this command and 15:24, Jesus himself has gone to a Decapolis city—Gadara—in 8:28. *Samaritans* There were old and serious tensions between the Samaritans and Jews of Jesus' time; see Josephus, *J.W.* 2.232–235; *Ant.* 10.288–291; 11.114. **10:6** *to the lost sheep of the house of Israel* In 15:24, also without parallel in the other gospels, Jesus claims that he has the same mission. **10:7** Thus Jesus' students carry on the same message as John the Baptist (3:2) and Jesus himself (4:17) have borne. **10:8** See *Gos. Thom.* 14:2. *raise the dead* Only in *Matthew* do Jesus' students receive this instruction. *give without payment* But see *Did.* 13.1–7. **10:10** *or sandals* Only *Matthew*'s Jesus prohibits sandals; *Mark* 6:9 explicitly allows them. *Luke* 10:4 prohibits them, however, in the sending out of the "seventy." *or a staff* *Matthew* agrees with *Luke* 9:3 against *Mark* 6:8. This agreement is a problem for the theory that *Matthew* and *Luke* were independently written. **10:13** Wishing peace upon a house, or withholding the wish, seems to have an almost magical sense: that wish or its absence will produce consequences. **10:14** *shake off the dust from your feet* In *Luke-Acts*, the parallel instruction (*Luke* 9:5; 10:11) is shown to be fulfilled in the early church's missions (*Acts* 13:51). **10:15** *Sodom and Gomorrah* Extremely sinful cities of the Bible (*Gen.* 19:1–26; see the modern term "sodomy"), remembered as prototypes of wickedness in later literature (e.g., *Jude* 7); see 11:23. **10:16** *sheep into the midst of wolves* Recall the same image in 7:15. *wise as serpents and innocent as doves* See *Gos. Thom.* 39:2; Ign. *Pol.* 2.2. *innocent* Or "without guile or sophistication," "artless." **10:17–25** In using *Mark*, the author of *Matthew* has chosen to include some of his source's apocalyptic discourse (*Mark* 13) here in the mission instructions to the Twelve, and some of it in *Matthew*'s own apocalyptic discourse (24:9–14). **10:17–18** See note to Mark 13:9. **10:18** *to them and the Gentiles* Only in *Matthew*; the author envisions the church's mission to Gentiles. **10:19–20** See note to Mark 13:11. **10:21** See note to Mark 13:12. **10:23** A puzzling verse, since the apostles' mission had long been completed by the author's time of writing and the Son of Man had not come. According to some scholars, the best explanation is that Jesus must have said some such thing, for the author would not have created such a problem. Alternatively, the author witnessed an unfinished mission, accompanied by opposition, to *the towns of Israel* in his own time and expected the Son of Man to come before it was over. *Son of Man* See notes to 8:20; 9:6; *Mark* 2:10. Here the phrase seems clearly to be an honorific title for a heavenly being.

24"A disciple is not above the teacher, nor a slave above the master; 25it is enough for the disciple to be like the teacher, and the slave like the master. If they have called the master of the house Beelzebul, how much more will they malign those of his household!

Whom to Fear

26"So have no fear of them; for nothing is covered up that will not be uncovered, and nothing secret that will not become known. 27What I say to you in the dark, tell in the light; and what you hear whispered, proclaim from the housetops. 28Do not fear those who kill the body but cannot kill the soul; rather fear him who can destroy both soul and body in hell.*k* 29Are not two sparrows sold for a penny? Yet not one of them will fall to the ground apart from your Father. 30And even the hairs of your head are all counted. 31So do not be afraid; you are of more value than many sparrows.

32"Everyone therefore who acknowledges me before others, I also will acknowledge before my Father in heaven; 33but whoever denies me before others, I also will deny before my Father in heaven.

Not Peace, but a Sword

34"Do not think that I have come to bring peace to the earth; I have not come to bring peace, but a sword.

35 For I have come to set a man against his father,
and a daughter against her mother,
and a daughter-in-law against her mother-in-law;
36 and one's foes will be members of one's own household.

37Whoever loves father or mother more than me is not worthy of me; and whoever loves son or daughter more than me is not worthy of me; 38and whoever does not take up the cross and follow me is not worthy of me. 39Those who find their life will lose it, and those who lose their life for my sake will find it.

Rewards

40"Whoever welcomes you welcomes me, and whoever welcomes me welcomes the one who sent me. 41Whoever welcomes a prophet in the name of a prophet will receive a prophet's reward; and whoever welcomes a righteous person in the name of a righteous person will receive the reward of the righteous; 42and whoever gives even a cup of cold water to one of these little ones in the name of a disciple—truly I tell you, none of these will lose their reward."

11 Now when Jesus had finished instructing his twelve disciples, he went on from there to teach and proclaim his message in their cities.

---

k Gk *Gehenna*

10:24 See *John* 13:16; 15:20. ***the teacher ... the master*** Gk has a possessive ("his") in each case. Likewise the next verse. **10:25** ***If they have called the master of the house Beelzebul*** Recall 9:34 although the name Beelzebul has not yet been used in *Matthew*; see 12:24. **10:26–33** This section is paralleled only in *Luke* 12:2–9; it thus comes from Q according to the common hypothesis. **10:26** See *Gos. Thom.* 5:2; 6:4. **10:27** *Matthew* has much the same sense here as *Gos. Thom.* 33:1, but contrast the otherwise close parallel in *Luke* 12:3, which warns that things uttered secretly will be proclaimed publicly. **10:28** Fearlessness in the face of death was a virtue widely admired among philosophers; it was considered the acid test of a philosophy's power. Jews and Christians were admired by some for their contempt of death (Epictetus, *Dissertations* 3.26.37–39; *4 Macc.* 6.1–35; Josephus, *Ag. Ap.* 2.232–235; *Diognetus* 7). **10:29** See 6:26, where a similar point was made. ***a penny*** Here the Roman *as,* not the same as the penny (*quadrans*) in 5:26. The former was reckoned at four times the weight of the latter. **10:32** ***I also will acknowledge*** The Lukan parallel (12:8; see *Mark* 8:38) has "the Son of Man" instead of *Matthew*'s I. See note to *Mark* 2:10. **10:34–37** See *Gospel of Thomas* 16. These are among the most stridently counter-cultural of Jesus' sayings in *Matthew*. His followers will be nonconformists who reject even some of the most basic conventional (e.g., family) values. Here Jesus sounds much like the Cynic philosopher, disdained by and disdaining the world. The reference is apparently to cases in which one member of a family converts to Christian faith and faces hostility from other family members—a common problem in early Christianity (*1 Cor.* 7:12–16). **10:37** See *Gospel of Thomas* 101; 55:2. **10:38** See 16:24 (note *Matthew*'s tendency to repetition; the saying is also duplicated in *Luke* 9:23; 14:27); *Gos. Thom.* 55:2. **10:39** See *Matt.* 16:25; *Mark* 8:35; *John* 12:25. **10:40** See *John* 13:20; Ign. *Eph.* 6.1; *Did.* 11.4. **10:41** This saying is found only in *Matthew*. ***a prophet*** Presumably, a Christian prophet. See 23:34; *1 Cor.* 12:28; *Didache* 11–13. Whereas some 1st-century Jews believed that prophecy in its authoritative sense had ended with the biblical period (Josephus, *Ag. Ap.* 1.40–41) although it was still possible to communicate with God and perhaps to see into the future, other Jews and some Christians were willing to recognize prophets in their own day (Josephus, *J.W.* 6.285). ***a righteous person*** Righteousness, in the sense of complete devotion to the divine commandments, is an important theme for *Matthew;* its readership seems to see itself as the righteous. See notes to 1:19; 5:20, 48; 6:33. **10:42** ***these little ones*** In the context here in *Matthew*, where no little ones have been mentioned, the meaning is unclear. Perhaps the author betrays his recollection of *Mark* 9:37, which speaks of receiving children. But note that in 18:2–6, 10 the author slides back and forth between discussing children and (apparently) new converts to Christianity with the label "little ones." **11:1** ***Now when Jesus had finished*** Thus the author closes Jesus' second major speech with a standard formula; see note to 7:28. ***in their cities*** A vague and puzzling phrase, since Galilee did not have many cities in the proper sense. Presumably *their* refers to the Jews.

Messengers from John the Baptist

²When John heard in prison what the Messiah^l was doing, he sent word by his^m disciples ³and said to him, "Are you the one who is to come, or are we to wait for another?" ⁴Jesus answered them, "Go and tell John what you hear and see: ⁵the blind receive their sight, the lame walk, the lepers^n are cleansed, the deaf hear, the dead are raised, and the poor have good news brought to them. ⁶And blessed is anyone who takes no offense at me."

Jesus Praises John the Baptist

⁷As they went away, Jesus began to speak to the crowds about John: "What did you go out into the wilderness to look at? A reed shaken by the wind? ⁸What then did you go out to see? Someone^o dressed in soft robes? Look, those who wear soft robes are in royal palaces. ⁹What then did you go out to see? A prophet?^p Yes, I tell you, and more than a prophet. ¹⁰This is the one about whom it is written,

'See, I am sending my messenger ahead of you,
who will prepare your way before you.'

¹¹Truly I tell you, among those born of women no one has arisen greater than John the Baptist; yet the least in the kingdom of heaven is greater than he. ¹²From the days of John the Baptist until now the kingdom of heaven has suffered violence,^q and the violent take it by force. ¹³For all the prophets and

---

l Or the Christ
m Other ancient authorities read two of his
n The terms leper and leprosy can refer to several diseases

o Or Why then did you go out? To see someone
p Other ancient authorities read Why then did you go out? To see a prophet?
q Or has been coming violently

11:2–19 This material on John the Baptist is found only in *Matthew* and *Luke* 7:18–35; according to the common hypothesis, it thus comes from Q, which must have had a considerable interest in John (see the Q material in *Luke* 3:7–17). Some sayings have parallels in *Thomas*. **11:2 When John heard in prison** John's arrest was mentioned incidentally in 4:12; his imprisonment and execution will be described in 14:3–12. According to Josephus, *Ant.* 18.119, John was arrested and executed at Herod Antipas's fortress of Machaerus in Perea, not in Galilee. **the Messiah** *Matthew* typically uses the Gk *christos* with its full titular meaning, not simply as a name for Jesus; see note to 1:1. **his disciples** Another indicator that John the Baptist, as a teacher independent of Jesus, retained his own circle of students. See *Acts* 19:1–6; Josephus, *Ant.* 18.116–119; note to *Mark* 1:7. **11:3 the one who is to come** In *Matt.* 3:11 John had spoken of a coming one, and here he picks up the same wording. But his question is a puzzle in the story of *Matthew*. Earlier, John had plainly recognized Jesus' status (3:14) and had even witnessed God's public declaration of Jesus' identity (3:17). In view of this background and 11:6—an admonition not to take offense at Jesus—perhaps the author of *Matthew* understands the Baptist's question as the beginning of his doubt about Jesus' identity, perhaps because Jesus is not fulfilling some classical messianic role. But the internal logic of the passage suggests that it originally reflected the beginning of John's trust in Jesus: news of Jesus' miracles prompts John's interest, and Jesus answers his question by allowing John's students to see for themselves (11:4–5). If the miracles had been the cause of doubt, Jesus' allowing the students to see them firsthand would not help. So it seems plausible that this passage, which *Matthew* picks up from another source, recalled John's original interest in Jesus whereas the gospel authors have made him a firm supporter and herald from the beginning. **11:5** Jesus' answer alludes to the promises of *Isa.* 35:5–6 (also 29:18; 42:7) although in *Isaiah* the cure of the blind and deaf is largely metaphorical—referring to formerly blind and deaf Israel (*Isa.* 6:9–10; 30:9–10; 42:18–20; 43:8). In *Matthew*'s story, Jesus' answer recalls several earlier passages; see 4:23–24; 8:16; 9:35; 10:8. **11:7 into the wilderness** Recalling 3:1, 5. **11:7–8** Some of the coins of Herod Antipas pictured reeds—in deference to the Jewish custom of avoiding animal or human images. *Shaken by the wind* here, along with v. 8, provides a devastating critique, from the moral philosopher's point of view, of the tetrarch who killed John: the one who has the ostensible power is really empty of substance, in contrast to John the "prophet," who has no external power but is inwardly strong. See the parallel in *Gospel of Thomas* 78. **11:9 A prophet** See note to 10:41. **11:10** A citation of *Mal.* 3:1, correcting *Mark* 1:2. MT: "Behold, I am sending my messenger before Me, and the Lord whom you seek shall come to His temple suddenly." LXX: "See, I am sending my messenger, and he shall survey the way before me, and the Lord whom you seek shall come to his temple suddenly." Curiously, although the MT and the LXX agree that the messenger comes before "me" (the Lord God), *Mark* and *Matthew/Luke* (Q?) agree almost perfectly on a different Gk version of the saying, which has the messenger come before "you" (Jesus). Perhaps the Christian version, designed to fit the connection between John the Baptist and Jesus, circulated in a collection of such proof texts. **11:11** See *Gospel of Thomas* 46. A problematic passage, since it appears to place John outside the kingdom of heaven. Perhaps the saying arose or was remembered in the context of competition between John's and Jesus' followers. See 11:13 and *John* 1:6–8, 19–23; 3:23–30. **11:12 the kingdom of heaven has suffered violence, and the violent take it by force** A notoriously puzzling remark, appearing only in *Matthew*. It may reflect a conflict in ancient Judaism between those who thought that they should work (and fight, if necessary) to establish God's kingdom—involving the overthrow of Israel's oppressors—and those who insisted upon waiting for God to intervene. In that case, *Matthew*'s Jesus would stand on the side of *Daniel* (11:14, 33–35) and Josephus (*J.W.* 2.345–405; 5.362–419) in rejecting militant action. **11:13** The phrase "the law and the prophets" signified Jewish scripture; see note to 5:17. Contrast the Lukan parallel (16:16), which says that the law and prophets were until John, suggesting that their period has ended with him. *Matthew* includes John with the law and prophets in a period of looking forward to the Messiah: John was the last

the law prophesied until John came; [14]and if you are willing to accept it, he is Elijah who is to come. [15]Let anyone with ears[r] listen!

[16]"But to what will I compare this generation? It is like children sitting in the marketplaces and calling to one another,

[17] 'We played the flute for you, and you did not dance;
    we wailed, and you did not mourn.'

[18]For John came neither eating nor drinking, and they say, 'He has a demon'; [19]the Son of Man came eating and drinking, and they say, 'Look, a glutton and a drunkard, a friend of tax collectors and sinners!' Yet wisdom is vindicated by her deeds."[s]

Woes to Unrepentant Cities

[20]Then he began to reproach the cities in which most of his deeds of power had been done, because

they did not repent. [21]"Woe to you, Chorazin! Woe to you, Bethsaida! For if the deeds of power done in you had been done in Tyre and Sidon, they would have repented long ago in sackcloth and ashes. [22]But I tell you, on the day of judgment it will be more tolerable for Tyre and Sidon than for you.

[23]And you, Capernaum,
    will you be exalted to heaven?
    No, you will be brought down to Hades.

For if the deeds of power done in you had been done in Sodom, it would have remained until this day. [24]But I tell you that on the day of judgment it will be more tolerable for the land of Sodom than for you."

Jesus Thanks His Father

[25]At that time Jesus said, "I thank[t] you, Father, Lord of heaven and earth, because you have hidden these things from the wise and the intelligent and

---

r Other ancient authorities add *to hear*
s Other ancient authorities read *children*

t Or *praise*

---

of the classical prophets. *Matthew*'s formulation seems to allow for an easier continuity between the world of scripture and Jesus' mission. **11:14 *he is Elijah who is to come*** According to *Mal.* 4:5–6 (MT 3:23–24), Elijah, who had not died but had been summoned directly to heaven (*2 Kgs.* 2:10–12), would return before the Day of the Lord (the day of God's intervention and judgment) to help improve matters so that God would not need to bring catastrophic punishment. This hope was remembered in some later Jewish literature (*Sir.* 48:1–10) and became a customary part of rabbinic Jewish hope. According to *John* 1:21, the Baptist rejects the title of Elijah. **11:15 *Let anyone with ears listen*** This saying of Jesus, which may derive in part from *Isaiah*'s constant critique of Israel's deafness, turns up in many different contexts, especially those featuring Jesus' secret teaching to his students; see 13:9, 43; see *Mark* 4:23; *Luke* 14:35; *Gos. Thom.* 8:2; 21:5; 24:2; 63:2; 65:2; 96:2; *Rev.* 2:7, 11, 17; 3:6, 13, 22; 13:9. John the Baptist's identity as Elijah is something that only the attuned hearer will understand. **11:16–19** In other words, you behaved as a self-directed individual, following your own will rather than that of the crowd. Jesus' criticism of mob rule as childish recalls Plato's Socrates, who fell victim to majority vote. Jesus then illustrates the point by noting that he and John practiced very different lifestyles yet both were condemned by *this generation*. Thus, the crowd favors not any particular, principled way of life but only conformity. **11:16 *the marketplaces*** The agora was a common feature of Greek cities: see note to *Mark* 6:56. **11:17 *the flute*** Or, simply, "the pipe." **11:18** New information. The reader has not yet been told of such a charge against John although it seems from 9:14 that John and his students fasted, perhaps routinely. **11:19 *Son of Man*** See notes to 8:20; 9:6; 10:23, 32; *Mark* 2:10. Here the phrase means "I." *a glutton and a drunkard* This is a revealing charge. Unlike the ascetic John the Baptist, Jesus seems characteristically to have feasted and celebrated with socially questionable people. *wisdom is vindicated by her deeds* The parallel in *Luke* 7:35 has "by all her children." In both cases, the point seems to be the same as that in the saying "A tree is known by its fruit"; see 3:8–10; 7:16–20; 12:33. The author may be personifying wisdom here—a common theme in Jewish literature since *Proverbs* 8— and seeing Jesus as this Wisdom (see 23:34 in comparison with *Luke* 11:49—from Q?). **11:20–22** It is strange that the bulk of Jesus' powerful deeds should have been done in these cities, since *Matthew* does not otherwise mention them. **11:21 *Chorazin*** A midsized town in the hills about two miles north of Capernaum, in the territory of Herod Antipas— easily within Jesus' range. It does not appear elsewhere in the early Christian texts outside the Lukan parallel (*Luke* 10:13). The archaeological finds discovered there so far come from the 2d century and later. *Bethsaida* Appears in *John* 1:44 as the home of Simon Peter and Andrew, but see *Mark* 1:16 (with its note), 29. Although only three miles from Capernaum, it was in the territory of Philip. *Tyre and Sidon ... sackcloth and ashes* Two famous ancient cities—already two thousand years old by Jesus' time—on the Phoenician coast, about twenty-five miles apart. Although biblical Israel and Judah long enjoyed fruitful cooperation with these cities, they were remembered as great cities doomed by divine judgment (*Isa.* 23:1–18; *Ezek.* 28:11–24). *Matthew*'s Jesus will eventually visit Tyre and Sidon (15:21) and receive a favorable response. **11:23 *Capernaum*** Unlike the other cities mentioned, this was Jesus' base; see 4:13–14. *will you be exalted to heaven?* Confirmation that Jesus or the author has in mind the woes against the cities in *Isa.* 14:12–13; *Ezek.* 28:2. *Hades* Although *Matthew* typically uses the Aramaic name Gehenna for hell, the place of punishment (5:22, 29, 30; 10:28; 18:9; 23:15), the author here adopts the common Gk term for the place of the dead (not a place of punishment). The word is shared by *Luke* 10:15 in the parallel and turns up again at *Matt.* 16:18. *Sodom* See note to 10:15. **11:25–27** This saying, which is paralleled in *Luke* (and so from Q?), is remarkable in the Synoptic Gospels because it sounds like the Jesus of *John* (3:31–36; 13:3) and, to some extent, of *Thomas* (4; 22; 37; 61:3). Jesus displays a keen awareness of his heavenly mission from the Father and identifies a group of

have revealed them to infants; ²⁶yes, Father, for such was your gracious will.^u ²⁷All things have been handed over to me by my Father; and no one knows the Son except the Father, and no one knows the Father except the Son and anyone to whom the Son chooses to reveal him.

²⁸"Come to me, all you that are weary and are carrying heavy burdens, and I will give you rest. ²⁹Take my yoke upon you, and learn from me; for I am gentle and humble in heart, and you will find rest for your souls. ³⁰For my yoke is easy, and my burden is light."

Plucking Grain on the Sabbath

12 At that time Jesus went through the grainfields on the sabbath; his disciples were hungry, and they began to pluck heads of grain and to eat. ²When the Pharisees saw it, they said to him, "Look, your disciples are doing what is not lawful to do on the sabbath." ³He said to them, "Have you not read what David did when he and his companions were hungry? ⁴He entered the house of God and ate the bread of the Presence, which it was not lawful for him or his companions to eat, but only for the priests. ⁵Or have you not read in the law that on the sabbath the priests in the temple break the sabbath and yet are guiltless? ⁶I tell you, something greater than the temple is here. ⁷But if you had known what this means, 'I desire mercy and not sacrifice,' you would not have condemned the guiltless. ⁸For the Son of Man is lord of the sabbath."

The Man with a Withered Hand

⁹He left that place and entered their synagogue; ¹⁰a man was there with a withered hand, and they asked him, "Is it lawful to cure on the sabbath?" so that they might accuse him. ¹¹He said to them, "Suppose one of you has only one sheep and it falls into a pit on the sabbath; will you not lay hold of it and lift it out? ¹²How much more valuable is a human being than a sheep! So it is lawful to do good on the sabbath." ¹³Then he said to the man, "Stretch out your hand." He stretched it out, and it was restored, as sound as the other. ¹⁴But the Pharisees went out and conspired against him, how to destroy him.

God's Chosen Servant

¹⁵When Jesus became aware of this, he departed. Many crowds^v followed him, and he cured all of

---

u Or *for so it was well-pleasing in your sight*   *v* Other ancient authorities lack *crowds*

infants to whom his teaching is given. This passage prevents us from distinguishing too sharply between a Johannine and a synoptic sayings tradition; *Thomas* and the hypothetical Q provide further evidence of links. **11:28–30** A yoke was used to join two oxen around the neck so that they would pull a plow in unison. Later rabbis spoke of the "yoke of Torah"—commitment to living one's life in step with the commandments—as a joy. It is not clear whether *Matthew's* Jesus assumes knowledge of the image, in which case he would be in some competition with the early rabbis. **12:1–14** After a considerable hiatus (9:17), the author returns to the final two controversy stories of *Mark* 2:1–3:6, which result in the plot to kill Jesus (*Mark* 3:6 par. *Matt.* 12:14). This long delay has allowed him to embed Jesus in a biblical-Jewish environment as Israel's Messiah. The plot to kill him comes about only gradually, after Jesus experiences much initial success. But now Jesus' rejection by various groups of Jewish leaders, who represent Israel in general, will become clear. Although the command to keep the Sabbath holy was clear in the Bible (*Exod.* 20:8–11; *Deut.* 5:12–15), it was unclear what constituted forbidden work; the issue was widely discussed by Jewish teachers of Jesus' time and later. **12:1–4, 8** *Matthew* follows *Mark* 2:23–28 (see notes there) although it also agrees with *Luke* 6:1–5 against *Mark* on several points (verb of saying in 12:2, omission in 12:3, omission of Abiathar in 12:4, omission of the general statement about the Sabbath in 12:8)—a problem for the common theory that *Matthew* and *Luke* were independently written. **12:1** *At that time . . . on the sabbath* This is an awkward combination of chronological indicators, instead of "one sabbath" at *Mark* 2:23. **12:4** *Matthew* omits *Mark's* incorrect reference to the high priesthood of Abiathar (see note to *Mark* 2:25–26). **12:5** Presumably a reference to the fact that the priests work on the Sabbath, since sacrifices must be offered then (*Num.* 28:9–10). Having established that some Jews are exempt from ordinary Sabbath constraints, *Matthew's* Jesus may be implying that he, too, is a guiltless exception. **12:6** *greater than the temple* *Matthew's* Jesus argues from the lesser to the greater, *a fortiori*: if the priests could have special Sabbath provisions, so can Jesus, since he (or the reign of God that he announces) is much greater than the temple regime. See note to 7:7–11. But this assumes recognition of Jesus' special status. See "greater than Jonah" and "greater than Solomon" in 12:41–42. **12:7** *Matthew* repeats the allusion to *Hos.* 6:6. See 9:13 and note. **12:8** The author uses "Son of Man" as an exalted title, indicating Jesus' unique status. But he leaves out the preceding saying in *Mark* (2:27) that the Sabbath was made for humanity. This might suggest a different sense for "Son of Man." See note to *Mark* 2:10. **12:9–14** *Matthew* basically follows *Mark* 3:1–6, but the author abbreviates much and adds the illustration of the sheep in the pit (12:11–12). A similar illustration turns up in *Luke* in a different context (14:5; see 13:15). **12:9** The last geographical indicator had said simply that Jesus was "in their cities" (11:1), presumably in Galilee, from which he proceeded to "the grainfields" (12:1). **12:14** The tenor of the narrative begins to change dramatically now that the Pharisees' plot has been hatched. *Matthew* omits *Mark's* problematic Herodians (*Mark* 3:6) from the plot. **12:15** *he departed* Another vague geographical indicator. It is clear neither where he departed from nor where he went. The Markan source (3:7–12) has Jesus depart to the lake, where great crowds from Judea, Galilee, Idumea, Perea, and the coastal Phoenician cities follow him. *he cured all of them* One of *Matthew's* shorter summary statements; see 4:23–25.

them, 16and he ordered them not to make him known. 17This was to fulfill what had been spoken through the prophet Isaiah:

18 "Here is my servant, whom I have chosen,
    my beloved, with whom my soul is well pleased.
I will put my Spirit upon him,
    and he will proclaim justice to the Gentiles.
19 He will not wrangle or cry aloud,
    nor will anyone hear his voice in the streets.
20 He will not break a bruised reed
    or quench a smoldering wick
until he brings justice to victory.
    21And in his name the Gentiles will hope."

Jesus and Beelzebul

22Then they brought to him a demoniac who was blind and mute; and he cured him, so that the one who had been mute could speak and see. 23All the crowds were amazed and said, "Can this be the Son of David?" 24But when the Pharisees heard it, they said, "It is only by Beelzebul, the ruler of the demons, that this fellow casts out the demons." 25He knew what they were thinking and said to them, "Every kingdom divided against itself is laid waste, and no city or house divided against itself will stand. 26If Satan casts out Satan, he is divided against himself; how then will his kingdom stand? 27If I cast out demons by Beelzebul, by whom do your own exorcistsw cast them

w Gk sons

out? Therefore they will be your judges. 28But if it is by the Spirit of God that I cast out demons, then the kingdom of God has come to you. 29Or how can one enter a strong man's house and plunder his property, without first tying up the strong man? Then indeed the house can be plundered. 30Whoever is not with me is against me, and whoever does not gather with me scatters. 31Therefore I tell you, people will be forgiven for every sin and blasphemy, but blasphemy against the Spirit will not be forgiven. 32Whoever speaks a word against the Son of Man will be forgiven, but whoever speaks against the Holy Spirit will not be forgiven, either in this age or in the age to come.

A Tree and Its Fruit

33"Either make the tree good, and its fruit good; or make the tree bad, and its fruit bad; for the tree is known by its fruit. 34You brood of vipers! How can you speak good things, when you are evil? For out of the abundance of the heart the mouth speaks. 35The good person brings good things out of a good treasure, and the evil person brings evil things out of an evil treasure. 36I tell you, on the day of judgment you will have to give an account for every careless word you utter; 37for by your words you will be justified, and by your words you will be condemned."

The Sign of Jonah

38Then some of the scribes and Pharisees said to him, "Teacher, we wish to see a sign from you."

12:16 The secrecy theme is not as prominent in Matthew as in Mark, and this reference to it is taken over from the source: Mark 3:11–12 has Jesus issue this command to the unclean spirits cast out of the sick and possessed. 12:17–21 The 9th fulfillment citation in Matthew, after a break; see 8:17 and note to 1:22–23. The passage is an abbreviation of Isa. 42:1–4 (note the author's strong interest in Isaiah), which presents Israel as God's chosen servant among the nations; see Exod. 19:5–6. 12:22–50 The remainder of the chapter strings together various sayings of Jesus, sprinkled in among three episodes. All have to do with the growing conflict between Jesus and the Jewish leaders. But as this conflict opens up, the crowds remain on the side of Jesus—hopefully wondering whether he is indeed the Son of David (12:23; see 1:1). 12:22–24 A doublet of the story in 9:32–34, except that this demon causes both blindness and dumbness. See note to Mark 1:23. 12:23 All the crowds . . . Son of David An important title in Matthew, in contrast to Mark; see 1:1 and note to 9:27. In Matthew, the crowds remain open to Jesus, recognizing him as Son of David (21:9–11, 46), even as the Pharisees and scribes become increasingly antagonistic. 12:24 Beelzebul See note to 9:34. 12:26 how then will his kingdom stand? From here to 12:30, Matthew often agrees with Luke 11:18–23 against Mark. This is a problem for the common theory that Matthew and Luke were independently written. 12:27 your own exorcists An admission, somewhat inimical to Christian claims concerning Jesus' uniqueness, that other Jewish exorcists were able to expel demons. See Mark 9:38; Acts 19:13; Josephus, Ant. 8.41–44; 4QprNab ar. 12:28 the kingdom of God has come to you The past tense of the verb (note the parallel in Luke 11:20) is striking in view of the general Christian expectation of the kingdom as a future event (1 Cor. 6:9; 15:50; Matt. 25:34; 26:29). 12:29 Gospel of Thomas 35 gives this saying by itself, as an observation (without critique) about life. 12:30 In Mark 9:40, which Matthew omits, Jesus had made the opposite claim; Luke (9:50; 11:23) has both. 12:31–32 It is not clear in Matthew what is meant by the unpardonable blasphemy against the Holy Spirit. Whereas Mark had plainly accused the Jewish leaders, and perhaps Jesus' family, of this sin because they said that Jesus had an unclean spirit (3:30), Matthew both omits this editorial remark and adds the specific exemption that speaking against the Son of Man can be forgiven (12:32). The material that intervenes in Matthew between the Jewish leaders' accusation and this statement (contrast Mark 3:22–30) further serves to obfuscate the issue. See also Gospel of Thomas 44 and Did. 11.7. 12:33–37 See notes to 3:8; 11:19. The theme of good and bad fruit is prominent in Matthew. 12:34 brood of vipers A favorite expression in Matthew; see 3:7; 23:33. 12:38–42 This passage has a parallel in Mark 8:11–12, but there Jesus makes no mention of Jonah. A closer parallel is Luke 11:29–32, which suggests Q material according to the common theory. An even closer parallel comes later in Matthew itself (16:1–4); this is one of the text's many doublets. 12:38 scribes and Pharisees See notes to Mark 1:22; 2:16.

³⁹But he answered them, "An evil and adulterous generation asks for a sign, but no sign will be given to it except the sign of the prophet Jonah. ⁴⁰For just as Jonah was three days and three nights in the belly of the sea monster, so for three days and three nights the Son of Man will be in the heart of the earth. ⁴¹The people of Nineveh will rise up at the judgment with this generation and condemn it, because they repented at the proclamation of Jonah, and see, something greater than Jonah is here! ⁴²The queen of the South will rise up at the judgment with this generation and condemn it, because she came from the ends of the earth to listen to the wisdom of Solomon, and see, something greater than Solomon is here!

The Return of the Unclean Spirit

⁴³"When the unclean spirit has gone out of a person, it wanders through waterless regions looking for a resting place, but it finds none. ⁴⁴Then it says, 'I will return to my house from which I came.' When it comes, it finds it empty, swept, and put in order. ⁴⁵Then it goes and brings along seven other spirits more evil than itself, and they enter and live there; and the last state of that person is worse than the first. So will it be also with this evil generation."

The True Kindred of Jesus

⁴⁶While he was still speaking to the crowds, his mother and his brothers were standing outside, wanting to speak to him. ⁴⁷Someone told him, "Look, your mother and your brothers are standing outside, wanting to speak to you."^x ⁴⁸But to the one who had told him this, Jesus^y replied, "Who is my mother, and who are my brothers?" ⁴⁹And pointing to his disciples, he said, "Here are my mother and my brothers! ⁵⁰For whoever does the will of my Father in heaven is my brother and sister and mother."

The Parable of the Sower

13 That same day Jesus went out of the house and sat beside the sea. ²Such great crowds gathered around him that he got into a boat and sat there, while the whole crowd stood on the beach. ³And he told them many things in parables, saying: "Listen! A sower went out to sow. ⁴And as he sowed, some seeds fell on the path, and the birds came and ate them up. ⁵Other seeds fell on rocky ground, where they did not have much soil, and they sprang up quickly, since

---

x Other ancient authorities lack verse 47
y Gk *he*

12:39–41 Jesus refers to the famous story told in the biblical book of *Jonah:* the prophet from Israel reluctantly visits the Assyrian city of Nineveh after causing a storm because of his desire to escape the mission and then being delivered to his destination by a great fish; the Ninevites repent. Here Jesus will become a Jonah figure by lying in the earth for three days (actually, Friday afternoon to Sunday morning, two nights; see 27:57–28:1). **12:40** *Son of Man* See notes to 8:20 and *Mark* 2:10. **12:41** *greater than Jonah* See "greater than the temple" in 12:6. **12:42** The reference is to *1 Kgs.* 10:1–13 and *2 Chr.* 9:1–12, which tell of the Queen of Sheba's visit to King Solomon. Solomon's peerless wisdom was much discussed in later Jewish literature, and many books of secret wisdom (e.g., formulas for cures and exorcisms, moral exhortation) were attributed to him; see Josephus, *Ant.* 8.41–44. **12:43–45** This passage seems unrelated to what has gone before, but it is connected by the final sentence, concerning *this evil generation.* The world of Jesus and his contemporaries was filled with good and evil spirits; every small village visited by Jesus had many who were oppressed by evil spirits. In a way that is not entirely clear, Jesus applies this observation about individual spirit possession (perhaps in connection with the people in 12:22) to his entire generation of fellow Jews. The extremely close verbal parallel in *Luke* 11:24–26 requires some kind of literary dependence—the shared source Q according to the common theory. **12:46–49** This episode is taken over from *Mark* 3:31–35, but the author of *Matthew* considerably softens the critique of Jesus' family. (a) He omits the earlier statement in *Mark* (3:20–21) that Jesus' family set out to pick him up because they thought that he was crazy. (b) The family consequently does not come to get him (contrast *Mark* 3:31). In *Matthew* they happen to come by and ask to speak with him; it is not a critical moment. Therefore, Jesus' momentary snub of them in order to make the point about his true family does not carry the same weight as in *Mark.* *Matthew*'s readers also have already learned that Joseph and Mary know Jesus' identity (1:20–21; 2:11). Note, too, that *Matthew*'s Jesus plainly identifies his students as his real family (12:49)—a great improvement in their status over *Mark.* **12:46** *standing outside* Although the story has not placed Jesus anywhere in particular (see 12:9, 15), 13:1 seems to presuppose that he is now in his house in Capernaum; see 9:10, 28. **13:1–53** *Matthew* continues to follow *Mark* very closely, from Jesus' rejection to his exemplary parables. This is the third of Jesus' five major speeches in *Matthew* and therefore the central one, coming about halfway through the book. It seems likely, then, that these parables about the kingdom (or reign) of God are in some way decisive for *Matthew*'s image of Jesus. *Matthew* presents seven parables; four of them are not found in either *Mark* or *Luke,* and one is found in *Luke* but not *Mark.* All of *Matthew*'s parables are represented in *Thomas.* Of the seven, the 1st three emphasize the gradual growth of God's kingdom—as seeds, yeast, or grain—and are given to the crowds. The final three (along with the interpretation of the weeds parable) are given privately to Jesus' students, within his house. Although they concern more the disposition of the one who seeks God's kingdom, the parable of the net thrown into the sea is like that of the weeds. **13:1** *out of the house* Presumably his house in Capernaum (see 9:10, 28), although the text has not clearly placed him there; see 12:9, 15, 46. **13:3–9** *Matthew* follows *Mark* 4:3–9 closely; see note there. Simple parallels to the parable, without the allegorical interpretation found in the Synoptics, occur in *Gospel of Thomas* 9 and *1 Clem.* 24.5.

they had no depth of soil. [6]But when the sun rose, they were scorched; and since they had no root, they withered away. [7]Other seeds fell among thorns, and the thorns grew up and choked them. [8]Other seeds fell on good soil and brought forth grain, some a hundredfold, some sixty, some thirty. [9]Let anyone with ears[z] listen!"

The Purpose of the Parables

[10]Then the disciples came and asked him, "Why do you speak to them in parables?" [11]He answered, "To you it has been given to know the secrets[a] of the kingdom of heaven, but to them it has not been given. [12]For to those who have, more will be given, and they will have an abundance; but from those who have nothing, even what they have will be taken away. [13]The reason I speak to them in parables is that 'seeing they do not perceive, and hearing they do not listen, nor do they understand.' [14]With them indeed is fulfilled the prophecy of Isaiah that says:

'You will indeed listen, but never understand,
    and you will indeed look, but never perceive.
[15] For this people's heart has grown dull,
        and their ears are hard of hearing,
            and they have shut their eyes;
        so that they might not look with their
            eyes,
        and listen with their ears,
    and understand with their heart and turn—
        and I would heal them.'
[16]But blessed are your eyes, for they see, and your ears, for they hear. [17]Truly I tell you, many prophets and righteous people longed to see what you see, but did not see it, and to hear what you hear, but did not hear it.

The Parable of the Sower Explained

[18]"Hear then the parable of the sower. [19]When anyone hears the word of the kingdom and does not understand it, the evil one comes and snatches away what is sown in the heart; this is what was sown on the path. [20]As for what was sown on rocky ground, this is the one who hears the word and immediately receives it with joy; [21]yet such a person has no root, but endures only for a while, and when trouble or persecution arises on account of the word, that person immediately falls away.[b] [22]As for what was sown among thorns, this is the one who hears the word, but the cares of the world and the lure of wealth choke the word, and it yields nothing. [23]But as for what was sown on good soil, this is the one who hears the word and understands it, who indeed bears fruit and yields, in one case a hundredfold, in another sixty, and in another thirty."

The Parable of Weeds among the Wheat

[24]He put before them another parable: "The kingdom of heaven may be compared to someone who sowed good seed in his field; [25]but while everybody was asleep, an enemy came and sowed weeds among the wheat, and then went away. [26]So when the plants came up and bore grain, then the weeds appeared as well. [27]And the slaves of the householder came and said to him, 'Master, did you not sow good seed in your field? Where, then, did these weeds come from?' [28]He answered, 'An enemy has done this.' The slaves said to him, 'Then do you want us to go and gather them?' [29]But he replied, 'No; for in gathering the weeds you would uproot the wheat along with them. [30]Let both of them grow together until the harvest;

---

z Other ancient authorities add to hear
a Or mysteries

b Gk stumbles

13:9 See note to 11:15. **13:10–13** The students' question and Jesus' response make much more sense in *Matthew* than in *Mark,* where they ask vaguely about "the parables" and Jesus strangely criticizes them for not understanding *this* parable (*Mark* 4:10, 13). Here, as soon as Jesus has given the first of his exemplary parables to the crowds, the students ask why he uses parables, and Jesus answers them respectfully. **13:11** See *Gos. Thom.* 62:1. Jesus' students, the future leaders of the church (e.g., 16:18), are positively valued in *Matthew:* They have been entrusted with the truth about the kingdom. Contrast *Mark,* where, although Jesus tries to impart secret teaching to his students, they fail to understand anything. **13:12** The author pulls this sentence ahead from his Markan source (4:25), thinking perhaps that it was more relevant here in reference to those who have and have not the secrets of the kingdom. See 25:29; *Luke* 19:26; *Gospel of Thomas* 41. **13:13 The reason . . . is that** A significant alteration of *Mark* 4:12, which had Jesus speak in parables so that his hearers would not understand. In *Matthew,* parables are instruments of disclosure; see 13:34–35. **seeing . . . understand** A paraphrase of *Isa.* 6:9–10, which the author is about to quote. **13:14–15** *Matthew*'s 10th fulfillment citation (see 12:17–21 and note to 1:22–23). *Isa.* 6:9–10 was a very popular passage in the early church because it spoke of Israel's stubbornness, a theme that seemed easily applicable to the Jews' general refusal to accept Jesus. See *Rom.* 11:8; *Acts* 28:26–27. *Matthew* has a particular fondness for passages from *Isaiah.* The LXX is as *Matthew,* except for a shift in the pronoun "their" in the 2d part. **13:16–17** Thus, according to *Matthew,* Jesus and his students fulfill the hope of the prophets for a restored and faithful Israel. **13:18–23** Follows *Mark* 4:14–20 closely; see notes there. The passage agrees in several respects with *Luke* 8:11–15 against *Mark,* however, and this poses problems for the common view that *Matthew* and *Luke* were independently written. **13:24–30** This parable is found only in *Matthew* and *Gospel of Thomas* 57. See the interpretation in 13:36–43. **13:30** The image of saving the wheat and burning the weeds (or chaff) picks up a theme established early in *Matthew* (3:8–12).

and at harvest time I will tell the reapers, Collect the weeds first and bind them in bundles to be burned, but gather the wheat into my barn.'"

The Parable of the Mustard Seed

31He put before them another parable: "The kingdom of heaven is like a mustard seed that someone took and sowed in his field; 32it is the smallest of all the seeds, but when it has grown it is the greatest of shrubs and becomes a tree, so that the birds of the air come and make nests in its branches."

The Parable of the Yeast

33He told them another parable: "The kingdom of heaven is like yeast that a woman took and mixed in with*c* three measures of flour until all of it was leavened."

The Use of Parables

34Jesus told the crowds all these things in parables; without a parable he told them nothing. 35This was to fulfill what had been spoken through the prophet:*d*
"I will open my mouth to speak in parables;
    I will proclaim what has been hidden from
      the foundation of the world."*e*

Jesus Explains the Parable of the Weeds

36Then he left the crowds and went into the house. And his disciples approached him, saying, "Explain to us the parable of the weeds of the field." 37He answered, "The one who sows the good seed is the Son of Man; 38the field is the world, and the good seed are the children of the kingdom; the weeds are the children of the evil one, 39and the enemy who sowed them is the devil; the harvest is the end of the age, and the reapers are angels. 40Just as the weeds are collected and burned up with fire, so will it be at the end of the age. 41The Son of Man will send his angels, and they will collect out of his kingdom all causes of sin and all evildoers, 42and they will throw them into the furnace of fire, where there will be weeping and gnashing of teeth. 43Then the righteous will shine like the sun in the kingdom of their Father. Let anyone with ears*f* listen!

Three Parables

44"The kingdom of heaven is like treasure hidden in a field, which someone found and hid; then in his joy he goes and sells all that he has and buys that field.

45"Again, the kingdom of heaven is like a merchant in search of fine pearls; 46on finding one pearl of great value, he went and sold all that he had and bought it.

47"Again, the kingdom of heaven is like a net that was thrown into the sea and caught fish of every kind; 48when it was full, they drew it ashore, sat down, and put the good into baskets but threw out the bad. 49So it will be at the end of the age. The angels will come out and separate the evil from the righteous 50and throw them into the furnace of fire, where there will be weeping and gnashing of teeth.

Treasures New and Old

51"Have you understood all this?" They answered, "Yes." 52And he said to them, "Therefore every scribe who has been trained for the kingdom of heaven is like the master of a household who brings out of his

---

c Gk *hid in*
d Other ancient authorities read *the prophet Isaiah*
e Other ancient authorities lack *of the world*

f Other ancient authorities add *to hear*

13:31–32 The parable is presumably taken from *Mark* 4:30–32 (see note there concerning the plant), but *Matthew* agrees with *Luke* 13:18–19 against *Mark* in several ways—for example, in the claim that the seed becomes a tree in which birds make nests. This agreement is a problem for the theory that *Matthew* and *Luke* used *Mark* independently. *Gospel of Thomas* 20:1–2 is closer to *Mark*. **13:35** *Matthew's* 11th fulfillment citation (see 13:14–15 and note to 1:22–23) paraphrases *Ps.* 78:2 (LXX 77:2). **13:36–43** This is the only parable in the synoptic tradition, except that of the sower, for which the disciples request (and receive) an allegorical interpretation. *Gospel of Thomas* 57 has the parable without any such interpretation. The interpretation has a strong eschatological orientation, which matches closely *Matthew's* image of the Son of Man coming in glory with his angels to judge the world (see 16:27–28; 24:30–31; 25:31; 26:64). In view of this correspondence and the fact that a noneschatological version of the parable appears in *Thomas*, it seems likely that the author of *Matthew* has molded the parable to fit his presentation. **13:36 *went into the house*** Jesus thus returns to his house in Capernaum from the lake's shore (13:1). **13:42 *weeping and gnashing of teeth*** A favorite expression in *Matthew*; see note to 8:12. **13:43 *righteous will shine*** See *Dan.* 12:3. On the righteous in *Matthew*, see notes to 1:19; 5:20, 48; 6:33; 10:41. ***anyone with ears*** See note to 11:15. **13:44** See *Gospel of Thomas* 109. **13:45–46** See *Gos. Thom.* 76:1. **13:47–50** See *Gos. Thom.* 8:1. *Thomas*, however, lacks the distinctly Matthean application to the end of the age (*Matt.* 13:49–50), which raises the question whether the original parable might also have lacked this application. **13:50 *weeping and gnashing of teeth*** See note to 8:12. **13:51–52** This passage, peculiar to *Matthew*, has suggested to some that the author is describing either himself or the ideal Christian—a learned Jew who has accepted Jesus as Messiah.

treasure what is new and what is old." [53]When Jesus had finished these parables, he left that place.

The Rejection of Jesus at Nazareth

[54]He came to his hometown and began to teach the people[g] in their synagogue, so that they were astounded and said, "Where did this man get this wisdom and these deeds of power? [55]Is not this the carpenter's son? Is not his mother called Mary? And are not his brothers James and Joseph and Simon and Judas? [56]And are not all his sisters with us? Where then did this man get all this?" [57]And they took offense at him. But Jesus said to them, "Prophets are not without honor except in their own country and in their own house." [58]And he did not do many deeds of power there, because of their unbelief.

The Death of John the Baptist

14 At that time Herod the ruler[h] heard reports about Jesus; [2]and he said to his servants, "This is John the Baptist; he has been raised from the dead, and for this reason these powers are at work in him." [3]For Herod had arrested John, bound him, and put him in prison on account of Herodias, his brother Philip's wife,[i] [4]because John had been telling him, "It is not lawful for you to have her." [5]Though Herod[j] wanted to put him to death, he feared the crowd, because they regarded him as a prophet. [6]But when Herod's birthday came, the daughter of Herodias danced before the company, and she pleased Herod [7]so much that he promised on oath to grant her whatever she might ask. [8]Prompted by her mother, she said, "Give me the head of John the Baptist here on a platter." [9]The king was grieved, yet out of regard for his oaths and for the guests, he commanded it to be given; [10]he sent and had John beheaded in the prison. [11]The head was brought on a platter and given to the girl, who brought it to her mother. [12]His disciples came and took the body and buried it; then they went and told Jesus.

Feeding the Five Thousand

[13]Now when Jesus heard this, he withdrew from there in a boat to a deserted place by himself. But when the crowds heard it, they followed him on foot from the towns. [14]When he went ashore, he saw a

---

g Gk *them*
h Gk *tetrarch*

i Other ancient authorities read *his brother's wife*
j Gk *he*

13:53 When Jesus had finished these parables So ends the 3d of the five major discourses; see 7:28 and 11:1. **that place** Jesus' house (13:36). **13:54 his hometown** Presumably Nazareth, the place of Jesus' childhood, not Capernaum, his current place of residence (4:13). **13:55 the carpenter's son** Although following *Mark* 6:1–6 closely, the author makes Jesus the builder's son, in part because he has introduced Joseph into the narrative (1:18–2:23) and needs to make a place for him here; *Mark* nowhere mentions Joseph. **13:56** At least some of Jesus' brothers (James and Jude) were former leaders of the church by the time of *Matthew*'s composition. See the letters that bear their names, *Acts* 12:17; 15:13, and the introduction to *Thomas*. **13:57** See *John* 4:44; *Gospel of Thomas* 31. **13:58** *Matthew* adjusts *Mark*'s comment (6:6) that Jesus *could not* perform deeds of power there. **14:1–12** Like *Mark*, *Matthew* uses Antipas's speculation about Jesus to introduce the story of John the Baptist's arrest, long after his arrest was first mentioned (4:12; see 11:2). *Mark*'s account (6:14–29) brims with historical problems; see notes there. *Matthew*'s version is a drastic abbreviation that incidentally removes many of *Mark*'s difficulties. *Luke*, the author of which may have known people in Antipas's court (*Luke* 8:3; *Acts* 13:1), omits the story altogether. **14:1 Herod the ruler** The Gk correctly reads "Herod the tetrarch," referring to Herod Antipas, son of King Herod the Great, who received a portion of his father's kingdom—principally Galilee and Perea—not as a kingdom but as a territory. A correction of *Mark*'s King Herod (*Mark* 6:14), but see 14:9. **14:3 Herodias, his brother Philip's wife** See notes to *Mark* 6:17, 18–20. **14:5 Herod wanted to put him to death** *Mark* attributed this motive to Herodias only (6:19) and had Herod Antipas hoping to save John (6:20, 26). In making this change, *Matthew* creates an inconsistency with 14:9, which is borrowed from *Mark* with little change. **14:7 whatever she might ask** A correction of *Mark*'s "half of my kingdom" (6:23), since Antipas did not have a kingdom. **14:9 The king was grieved** Doubly problematic: (a) Antipas was not a king but a tetrarch (see 14:1), and (b) the author has already said that Antipas wished to kill John (14:5). By mentioning Antipas's remorse, *Matthew* may want the reader to understand that he did not wish to kill John just because of the popular outcry, since John was highly regarded by many (see 21:26; Josephus, *Ant.* 18.116–119). **14:10 beheaded in the prison** Josephus, *Ant.* 18.119, locates John's death in Antipas's fortress of Machaerus, east of the Jordan River in Perea, which was part of Antipas's territory along with Galilee. **14:12** This sentence confirms the independence of John the Baptist and his students from Jesus' circles. But *Matthew* adds to *Mark* the statement that John's students notified Jesus (see 11:2). **14:13** *Matthew* thus deepens the relationship between Jesus and John. **withdrew from there in a boat** This is another geographical puzzle. "There" seems to indicate Jesus' home town or native place (Gk, *patris*), which is where he was last located (13:54–57). This should mean Nazareth (2:23; 4:13), as in the Markan parallel (*Mark* 6:1–6). But one cannot leave Nazareth in a boat, since it is about fifteen miles from the lake. It appears that, in changing around *Mark*'s order (see *Mark* 6:6b), the author of *Matthew* has lost the geographical thread. **to a deserted place** Somewhere, evidently, on the Sea of Galilee (Lake Gennesar). *Matthew* carries over *Mark*'s vagueness. *Luke* 9:10 supplies Bethsaida, but this cannot work for *Mark*, which has Jesus go to Bethsaida from this place (6:45). See note to *Mark* 6:32, *Matthew*'s source.

great crowd; and he had compassion for them and cured their sick. 15When it was evening, the disciples came to him and said, "This is a deserted place, and the hour is now late; send the crowds away so that they may go into the villages and buy food for themselves." 16Jesus said to them, "They need not go away; you give them something to eat." 17They replied, "We have nothing here but five loaves and two fish." 18And he said, "Bring them here to me." 19Then he ordered the crowds to sit down on the grass. Taking the five loaves and the two fish, he looked up to heaven, and blessed and broke the loaves, and gave them to the disciples, and the disciples gave them to the crowds. 20And all ate and were filled; and they took up what was left over of the broken pieces, twelve baskets full. 21And those who ate were about five thousand men, besides women and children.

Jesus Walks on the Water

22Immediately he made the disciples get into the boat and go on ahead to the other side, while he dismissed the crowds. 23And after he had dismissed the crowds, he went up the mountain by himself to pray. When evening came, he was there alone, 24but by this time the boat, battered by the waves, was far from the land,*k* for the wind was against them. 25And early in the morning he came walking toward them on the sea. 26But when the disciples saw him walking on the sea, they were terrified, saying, "It is a ghost!"

And they cried out in fear. 27But immediately Jesus spoke to them and said, "Take heart, it is I; do not be afraid."

28Peter answered him, "Lord, if it is you, command me to come to you on the water." 29He said, "Come." So Peter got out of the boat, started walking on the water, and came toward Jesus. 30But when he noticed the strong wind,*l* he became frightened, and beginning to sink, he cried out, "Lord, save me!" 31Jesus immediately reached out his hand and caught him, saying to him, "You of little faith, why did you doubt?" 32When they got into the boat, the wind ceased. 33And those in the boat worshiped him, saying, "Truly you are the Son of God."

Jesus Heals the Sick in Gennesaret

34When they had crossed over, they came to land at Gennesaret. 35After the people of that place recognized him, they sent word throughout the region and brought all who were sick to him, 36and begged him that they might touch even the fringe of his cloak; and all who touched it were healed.

The Tradition of the Elders

15 Then Pharisees and scribes came to Jesus from Jerusalem and said, 2"Why do your disciples break the tradition of the elders? For they do not wash their hands before they eat." 3He answered

---

k Other ancient authorities read *was out on the sea*   *l* Other ancient authorities read *the wind*

14:15–21 *Matthew*'s story of the feeding of the five thousand characteristically abbreviates *Mark*'s (6:32–44). The author thereby omits the disciples' somewhat impudent response to Jesus (*Mark* 6:37–38) and so maintains an air of dignity around them. **14:19 blessed and broke the loaves** In contrast to *Mark* 6:41, the Gk of *Matthew* suggests that Jesus did not bless the loaves; presumably, he blessed God, which would have been more in keeping with Jewish custom. **14:20 besides women and children** *Matthew*'s elaboration of *Mark*'s comment (6:44) that there were five thousand males. **14:22–33** *Matthew* continues to follow but abbreviate *Mark*. This passage is longer than the Markan parallel (6:45–42), however, because the author introduces an entirely new ending. According to this ending, Peter walks on the water and then the disciples worship Jesus. This recasting affords an entirely new complexion to *Mark*'s story, which ended with the disciples' hardness of heart and lack of comprehension. **14:22 the other side** *Mark* 6:45 identifies Bethsaida, but the author of *Matthew* seems uncertain about the destination (see note to 14:1). **14:25 early in the morning** Lit. "in the fourth watch of the night," roughly between 3:00 and 6:00 A.M. **the sea** The Sea of Galilee (Lake Gennesar). **14:28–33** The story of Peter's walking on the water and the disciples' adoration of Jesus is peculiar to *Matthew*. It fits with this text's high esteem of the disciples and especially of Peter (see 16:18–20). **14:33 Truly you are the Son of God** Jesus' students are therefore trustworthy associates who recognize his identity early in the narrative. **14:34–36** *Matthew*'s dependence upon *Mark* 6:53–56 for this summary description seems clear. Note, for example, the phrase *even the fringe of his cloak* in 14:36; see note to *Mark* 6:56. **14:34 Gennesaret** *Matthew* takes over the curious reference from *Mark* 6:53; see note there. **15:1–20** *Matthew* continues to follow *Mark* (7:1–23), generally abbreviating this story of Jesus' conflict with the Pharisees but also adding a section to it. In the narrative of *Matthew*, Jesus' conflict with the Pharisees, as a subgroup of Judaism, is heightened in preparation for the stinging indictments of *Matthew* 23. Unlike *Mark* (see 7:3), *Matthew* does not present this so much as a conflict with Jews in general and so leaves more space for Jesus to maintain his roots with Jewish tradition. **15:2** See notes to *Mark* 7:2–5. Although the Pharisees seem to have been the dominant group in Jewish society, Jesus' followers were not alone in dissenting from their views. The Sadducees (Josephus, *Ant.* 13.297–298), Essenes (*Ant.* 18.18–20), and authors of the DSS (4Q169), as well as Josephus himself (*Ant.* 1.110), appear to have distanced themselves from the Pharisees. **15:3** See note to *Mark* 7:8–9; the Sadducees likewise rejected the Pharisees' living tradition as not part of God's commandments:

them, "And why do you break the commandment of God for the sake of your tradition? [4]For God said,[m] 'Honor your father and your mother,' and, 'Whoever speaks evil of father or mother must surely die.' [5]But you say that whoever tells father or mother, 'Whatever support you might have had from me is given to God,'[n] then that person need not honor the father.[o] [6]So, for the sake of your tradition, you make void the word[p] of God. [7]You hypocrites! Isaiah prophesied rightly about you when he said:

[8] 'This people honors me with their lips,
      but their hearts are far from me;
[9] in vain do they worship me,
      teaching human precepts as doctrines.' "

Things That Defile

[10]Then he called the crowd to him and said to them, "Listen and understand: [11]it is not what goes into the mouth that defiles a person, but it is what comes out of the mouth that defiles." [12]Then the disciples approached and said to him, "Do you know that the Pharisees took offense when they heard what you said?" [13]He answered, "Every plant that my heavenly Father has not planted will be uprooted. [14]Let them alone; they are blind guides of the blind.[q] And if one blind person guides another, both will fall into a pit." [15]But Peter said to him, "Explain this parable to us." [16]Then he said, "Are you also still without

understanding? [17]Do you not see that whatever goes into the mouth enters the stomach, and goes out into the sewer? [18]But what comes out of the mouth proceeds from the heart, and this is what defiles. [19]For out of the heart come evil intentions, murder, adultery, fornication, theft, false witness, slander. [20]These are what defile a person, but to eat with unwashed hands does not defile."

The Canaanite Woman's Faith

[21]Jesus left that place and went away to the district of Tyre and Sidon. [22]Just then a Canaanite woman from that region came out and started shouting, "Have mercy on me, Lord, Son of David; my daughter is tormented by a demon." [23]But he did not answer her at all. And his disciples came and urged him, saying, "Send her away, for she keeps shouting after us." [24]He answered, "I was sent only to the lost sheep of the house of Israel." [25]But she came and knelt before him, saying, "Lord, help me." [26]He answered, "It is not fair to take the children's food and throw it to the dogs." [27]She said, "Yes, Lord, yet even the dogs eat the crumbs that fall from their masters' table." [28]Then Jesus answered her, "Woman, great is your faith! Let it be done for you as you wish." And her daughter was healed instantly.

Jesus Cures Many People

[29]After Jesus had left that place, he passed along the Sea of Galilee, and he went up the mountain, where he sat down. [30]Great crowds came to him, bringing with them the lame, the maimed, the blind,

---

m Other ancient authorities read *commanded, saying*
n Or *is an offering*
o Other ancient authorities add *or the mother*
p Other ancient authorities read *law;* others, *commandment*
q Other ancient authorities lack *of the blind*

15:4–6 See notes to *Mark* 7:10–12. Most Jews (and Pharisees), as far as we can tell from surviving sources, would have agreed with Jesus' critique of such a practice. **15:4** *Exod.* 20:12 par. *Deut.* 5:16; *Exod.* 21:17 par. *Lev.* 20:9. **15:5** *Matthew* softens *Mark*'s remarkable claim (7:12) that the Pharisees prevented people from supporting their parents after making a gift to God. **15:7–9** *Matthew* follows *Mark*'s citation of *Isa.* 29:13; this fits nicely with *Matthew*'s general fondness for *Isaiah*. **15:11** *Matthew* softens *Mark*'s claim (7:15) that nothing that enters a person's mouth can defile, presumably in light of the biblical laws concerning food (*Deut.* 14:1–21; see *Matt.* 5:17–20). See note to *Mark* 7:15–23. The author of *Matthew* might well have understood Jesus' words in this vein: what comes out of the mouth is much more important than what goes in. See *Gos. Thom.* 14:3. **15:12–14** *Matthew* introduces new material to sharpen its critique of the Pharisees. **15:13** See *Gospel of Thomas* 40; Ign. *Trall.* 11.1; *Phld.* 3.1. **15:14 blind guides** A common image in *Matthew* (23:16, 19, 24, 26), no doubt derivative of *Isaiah*'s critique of Israel's blindness (see note to 13:14–15). See *Luke* 6:39; John 9:41; *Gospel of Thomas* 34; also Plutarch, *Galba* 1.4. **15:15 this parable** Presumably, in view of Jesus' response, the saying about what goes in (15:11)—following *Mark* 7:17. **15:16 you also** The *you* is plural, taken over from *Mark* 7:18. **15:17** *Matthew* omits, presumably because of a concern for the commandments (5:17–20), *Mark*'s comment (7:19) that Jesus declared all foods clean. **15:21–28** Jesus mentioned the ancient coastal cities of Tyre and Sidon in 11:15, claiming that they would have repented if they had seen his works performed. Now he visits these Gentile areas. *Matthew* 15:24–30 continues to follow *Mark*. **15:22 a Canaanite woman** *Matthew* uses the old biblical term for people of the region; contrast *Mark* 7:26. This helps to preserve the aura of sacred tradition. **15:22–24** In *Matthew*, the woman's annoying actions and Canaanite ancestry—all of which make her a poor candidate for help—only throw into sharper relief her remarkable trust (15:28). **15:22 Son of David** See notes to 9:27; 12:23. An important title for *Matthew*. **15:24** See 10:5–6 and notes there. This is characteristic of *Matthew*'s pronounced Jewish atmosphere. **15:25–28** See note to *Mark* 7:26. Jesus' admission of Gentiles to salvation is not automatic but a direct response to their faith. See 8:5–13. **15:29–31** One of *Matthew*'s typical summaries. See 4:23–25 and note. *Matthew* omits *Mark*'s example (7:32–36) of a saliva-based cure here—also in *Mark* 8:22–26. **15:29 went up the mountain, where he sat down** See 5:1 and note.

the mute, and many others. They put them at his feet, and he cured them, ³¹so that the crowd was amazed when they saw the mute speaking, the maimed whole, the lame walking, and the blind seeing. And they praised the God of Israel.

Feeding the Four Thousand

³²Then Jesus called his disciples to him and said, "I have compassion for the crowd, because they have been with me now for three days and have nothing to eat; and I do not want to send them away hungry, for they might faint on the way." ³³The disciples said to him, "Where are we to get enough bread in the desert to feed so great a crowd?" ³⁴Jesus asked them, "How many loaves have you?" They said, "Seven, and a few small fish." ³⁵Then ordering the crowd to sit down on the ground, ³⁶he took the seven loaves and the fish; and after giving thanks he broke them and gave them to the disciples, and the disciples gave them to the crowds. ³⁷And all of them ate and were filled; and they took up the broken pieces left over, seven baskets full. ³⁸Those who had eaten were four thousand men, besides women and children. ³⁹After sending away the crowds, he got into the boat and went to the region of Magadan.ʳ

The Demand for a Sign

16 The Pharisees and Sadducees came, and to test Jesusˢ they asked him to show them a sign from heaven. ²He answered them, "When it is evening, you say, 'It will be fair weather, for the sky is red.' ³And in the morning, 'It will be stormy today, for the sky is red and threatening.' You know how to interpret the appearance of the sky, but you cannot interpret the signs of the times.ᵗ ⁴An evil and adulterous generation asks for a sign, but no sign will be given to it except the sign of Jonah." Then he left them and went away.

The Yeast of the Pharisees and Sadducees

⁵When the disciples reached the other side, they had forgotten to bring any bread. ⁶Jesus said to them, "Watch out, and beware of the yeast of the Pharisees and Sadducees." ⁷They said to one another, "It is because we have brought no bread." ⁸And becoming aware of it, Jesus said, "You of little faith, why are you talking about having no bread? ⁹Do you still not perceive? Do you not remember the five loaves for the five thousand, and how many baskets you gathered? ¹⁰Or the seven loaves for the four thousand, and how many baskets you gathered? ¹¹How could you fail to perceive that I was not speaking about bread? Beware of the yeast of the Pharisees and Sadducees!" ¹²Then they understood that he had not told them to beware of the yeast of bread, but of the teaching of the Pharisees and Sadducees.

---

r Other ancient authorities read *Magdala* or *Magdalan*
s Gk *him*

t Other ancient authorities lack ²*When it is . . . of the times*

15:32–39 It is unlikely that this author includes the 2d feeding story for the same reason as the author of *Mark* (8:1–10)—to stress the disciples' lack of understanding—since *Matthew* does not support this image of the disciples. Finding the second story in his source, the author perhaps included it in part because it fit his predilection for pairs and duplicates (see introduction to *Matthew*). **15:38 *four thousand men, besides women and children*** Curiously, *Matthew* here changes *Mark*'s explicit statement that the total number of people was four thousand. Since *Matthew* has assimilated the story to that of the feeding of the five thousand (14:21), it appears that the second story was included to provide a duplicate (see previous note). **15:39 *Magadan*** *Mark* 8:10 says Dalmanutha, which is otherwise unattested. Perhaps the author of *Matthew* preferred this place because he knew it; unfortunately, we do not. **16:1–4** Another Matthean doublet, this time recalling 12:38–39. *Matthew* continues to follow *Mark* (which lacked the earlier sign request). **16:1 *Pharisees and Sadducees*** Only *Matthew* presents these two groups in such close collusion; see note to 3:7. The source, *Mark* 8:11, has Pharisees alone. **16:2–3** This saying is not found in *Matthew*'s main source, *Mark*. Similar sayings are given, however, in *Luke* 12:54–56 and *Gos. Thom.* 91:2. Jesus' audience would have watched the sky in preparation for either agriculture (in the Galilean villages) or fishing (by the lake). **16:4 *the sign of Jonah*** Already explained in the note to 12:39–41. **16:5–12** *Matthew* continues to follow *Mark*, making slight but significant adjustments. Whereas *Mark* seems to place this scene in the boat (8:13) between Dalmanutha (8:10) and Bethsaida (8:22), *Matthew* places it on land, on *the other side* (16:5) of the lake from Magadan (15:39). *Matthew* changes *Mark*'s Pharisees and Herod to *Pharisees and Sadducees*, indicting the most prominent Jewish leadership groups together. While maintaining some of the criticism of Jesus' students that he found in his source, the author omits Jesus' sharper words (*Mark* 8:17–18), comparing the students to hard-hearted, blind, and deaf Israel (see *Mark* 4:12). He also changes *Mark*'s ending, so that the story concludes with the disciples' understanding (16:12) rather than with their failure to understand (*Mark* 8:21). **16:12 *the teaching of the Pharisees and Sadducees*** The Pharisees and Sadducees espoused quite different teachings and were vigorously opposed to each other for this reason (Josephus, *Ant.* 13.297–298; 18.12–17; *Acts* 23:6–10). *Matthew* seems somewhat inconsistent. On the one hand, it denounces the Pharisees' teaching (see also 15:3–14). On the other hand, it endorses their teaching and criticizes only their behavior (23:2–3). *Luke* 12:1 identifies the yeast of the Pharisees as their hypocrisy, not their teaching.

Peter's Declaration about Jesus

¹³Now when Jesus came into the district of Caesarea Philippi, he asked his disciples, "Who do people say that the Son of Man is?" ¹⁴And they said, "Some say John the Baptist, but others Elijah, and still others Jeremiah or one of the prophets." ¹⁵He said to them, "But who do you say that I am?" ¹⁶Simon Peter answered, "You are the Messiah,ᵘ the Son of the living God." ¹⁷And Jesus answered him, "Blessed are you, Simon son of Jonah! For flesh and blood has not revealed this to you, but my Father in heaven. ¹⁸And I tell you, you are Peter,ᵛ and on this rockʷ I will build my church, and the gates of Hades will not prevail against it. ¹⁹I will give you the keys of the kingdom of heaven, and whatever you bind on earth will be bound in heaven, and whatever you loose on earth will be loosed in heaven." ²⁰Then he sternly ordered the disciples not to tell anyone that he wasˣ the Messiah.ʸ

Jesus Foretells His Death and Resurrection

²¹From that time on, Jesus began to show his disciples that he must go to Jerusalem and undergo great suffering at the hands of the elders and chief priests and scribes, and be killed, and on the third day be raised. ²²And Peter took him aside and began to rebuke him, saying, "God forbid it, Lord! This must never happen to you." ²³But he turned and said to Peter, "Get behind me, Satan! You are a stumbling block to me; for you are setting your mind not on divine things but on human things."

---

u Or *the Christ*
v Gk *Petros*
w Gk *petra*

x Other ancient authorities add *Jesus*
y Or *the Christ*

16:13–20 *Matthew* continues to follow *Mark*'s outline, although omitting the healing of the blind man with the use of saliva (*Mark* 8:22–26). *Matthew* earlier omitted a similar (saliva-mediated) cure from *Mark* 7:32–36. *Matthew*'s principal addition to *Mark* is Jesus' famous positive response to Peter's confession of Jesus' identity (16:17–19). This changes the scene entirely, especially the reader's impression of Peter and the disciples. **16:13 Caesarea Philippi** See note to *Mark* 8:27. **the Son of Man is** A peculiar formulation, in place of "I am" (*Mark* 8:27; *Luke* 9:18). Although *Matthew* often uses the term "Son of Man" as a special title (see note to 13:36–43), the usage here supports one of the more common meanings of the phrase—"I." See note to *Mark* 2:10. **16:14** See notes to *Mark* 6:14–15. *Matthew*, curiously, adds Jeremiah as an example of the prophets. The prophet figure in Jewish and early Christian eschatology was more commonly the prophet like Moses anticipated in *Deut.* 18:15. *Jeremiah* is mentioned by name only in *Matthew*, twice in the fulfillment citations (2:17; 27:9), although one of these actually fits *Zechariah* more closely. Jeremiah was famous for being the weeping prophet who allegedly wrote *Lamentations* and for counseling the submission of Judah to the Babylonian powers—seen as God's agents to punish Judah for its sins. Josephus, a contemporary of the author of *Matthew*, was also partial to *Jeremiah* (*J.W.* 5.391–393). **16:16 the Messiah, the Son of the living God** For *Messiah*, see note to *Mark* 8:29. The rest is *Matthew*'s addition, connecting messiahship to divine sonship (see 3:17); the disciples fully understand Jesus' identity. "Living God" occurs again at 26:63, in the high priest's question to Jesus. An expression common in the Bible and later Judaism—to distinguish the God of Israel from idols of wood and stone (*1 Kgs.* 18:20–40; *Wis.* 15:1; *1 Thess.* 1:9–10)—it was particularly appropriate in Caesarea Philippi, a center of Gentile worship (see note to *Mark* 8:27). **16:17 Simon son of Jonah** *Matthew* uses the Aramaic name *bar-Yona*, perhaps as a prelude to the following change of names. According to *John* 1:42, Simon's father was named John. In view of the author's taste for wordplay, he may well mean to link Simon with Jesus as Jonah (12:38–41; 16:4). **my Father in heaven** Jesus recalls his mission from heaven (see 11:27). This response of Jesus is entirely different from that given in *Mark* 8:30. **16:18 Peter** Gk *petros*, meaning "rock" (compare "Rocky") or "stone." The Aramaic equivalent was *Kefa* (Cephas); see *1 Cor.* 9:5; *Gal.* 2:9. As far as we know, this peculiar Gk name was not used outside Christian circles. **on this rock I will build** Rock here in the Gk is the feminine form *petra*, presumably because the feminine tended to signify a slab of rock or rock in general, rather than a particular stone (*petros*) and thus more suitable as a foundation (see 7:24–25); Simon, however, could hardly carry the feminine form of the name. This ringing authorization of Peter's leadership among the early Christians fits with *Matthew*'s presentation of Jesus' students as trustworthy, over against *Mark*'s. We know from *Gal.* 2:9 that Peter/Cephas was widely considered a "pillar" of the church, along with Jesus' brother James and the disciple John. Peter's leadership is also attested in *1 Cor.* 9:5; *Acts* 1:15; 2:14–41; 5:1–11; *1 Clement* 5. **my church** This saying and 18:17 are the only ones in the gospels that mention the church, which came into existence only after Jesus' death and resurrection. See note to 18:17. **gates of Hades** See note to 11:23. **16:19** Authority "to bind and loose" was a common expression in Near Eastern antiquity for complete civil authority—to imprison and release (Josephus, *J.W.* 1.111). *Matthew* uses it metaphorically. In 18:18, the same power will be given to the church as a whole; see *John* 20:23. **16:20** *Matthew* reverts to its source, *Mark* 8:30, but clarifies what Jesus' students should not tell. **16:21** See note to *Mark* 8:31. **From that time on** The 2d occurrence of this phrase (see 4:17). It seems to mark a major dramatic transition, as did the first. Having finished the period, begun in 4:17, of proclaiming the kingdom of heaven, Jesus now mainly looks ahead to his saving death and resurrection. In the narrative, Jesus will predict his fate on three subsequent occasions before the end actually comes (17:22–23; 20:18–19; 26:2). **16:22–23** *Matthew* preserves Peter's rebuke of Jesus and Jesus' response from *Mark* 8:32–33 but lowers the tension in several ways: by placing it within the context of Jesus' high praise for Peter; by omitting the claim that Jesus spoke "quite openly," which made Peter look particularly dense; by explaining the na-

The Cross and Self-Denial

24Then Jesus told his disciples, "If any want to become my followers, let them deny themselves and take up their cross and follow me. 25For those who want to save their life will lose it, and those who lose their life for my sake will find it. 26For what will it profit them if they gain the whole world but forfeit their life? Or what will they give in return for their life?

27"For the Son of Man is to come with his angels in the glory of his Father, and then he will repay everyone for what has been done. 28Truly I tell you, there are some standing here who will not taste death before they see the Son of Man coming in his kingdom."

The Transfiguration

17 Six days later, Jesus took with him Peter and James and his brother John and led them up a high mountain, by themselves. 2And he was transfigured before them, and his face shone like the sun, and his clothes became dazzling white. 3Suddenly there appeared to them Moses and Elijah, talking with him. 4Then Peter said to Jesus, "Lord, it is good for us to be here; if you wish, I*z* will make three dwellings*a* here, one for you, one for Moses, and one for Elijah." 5While he was still speaking, suddenly a bright cloud overshadowed them, and from the cloud a voice said,

"This is my Son, the Beloved;*b* with him I am well pleased; listen to him!" 6When the disciples heard this, they fell to the ground and were overcome by fear. 7But Jesus came and touched them, saying, "Get up and do not be afraid." 8And when they looked up, they saw no one except Jesus himself alone.

9As they were coming down the mountain, Jesus ordered them, "Tell no one about the vision until after the Son of Man has been raised from the dead." 10And the disciples asked him, "Why, then, do the scribes say that Elijah must come first?" 11He replied, "Elijah is indeed coming and will restore all things; 12but I tell you that Elijah has already come, and they did not recognize him, but they did to him whatever they pleased. So also the Son of Man is about to suffer at their hands." 13Then the disciples understood that he was speaking to them about John the Baptist.

Jesus Cures a Boy with a Demon

14When they came to the crowd, a man came to him, knelt before him, 15and said, "Lord, have mercy on my son, for he is an epileptic and he suffers terribly; he often falls into the fire and often into the water. 16And I brought him to your disciples, but they could not cure him." 17Jesus answered, "You faithless and perverse generation, how much longer must I be with you? How much longer must I put up with you? Bring him here to me." 18And Jesus

---

z Other ancient authorities read *we*
a Or *tents*

b Or *my beloved Son*

---

ture of Peter's objection; and by removing the word "rebuke" from its description of Jesus' words. Jesus still criticizes Peter sharply, but in context Peter's misunderstanding is redeemable. **16:24–28** *Matthew* takes over this series of loosely related sayings, in order and often verbatim, from *Mark* 8:34–9:1. **16:27** A recurring theme in *Matthew*. See note to 13:36–43. **16:28** Following the saying about the coming of the kingdom in *Mark* 9:1, but featuring the Son of Man (see 10:23; also note to 13:36–43). Like *Mark*, *Matthew* expects Jesus' return within the lifetime of the first readers; see 24:34. **17:1–9** *Matthew* continues to follow *Mark* (9:2–10; see notes there) very closely, even with the opening connective, *Six days later*. The author's changes to his source are mainly calculated to change the style, elevate the theological tone, and enhance the image of Jesus' students. **17:1** *a high mountain* Possibly the range leading up to Mount Hermon, the highest mountain in the region (about 6,700 ft.), which rises above Caesarea Philippi. **17:2** *his face shone like the sun* *Matthew*'s addition. *dazzling white* Lit. "white as light," replacing *Mark*'s (9:3) comparison with a human cleaner's abilities. **17:3** *Moses and Elijah* See note to *Mark* 9:4. **17:4** *Matthew* omits *Mark*'s remark that Peter did not know what to say. Peter, rather, begins to fulfill the leadership role assigned to him in 16:18–19; see also 17:24 and 18:21. **17:5** *with him I am well pleased* *Matthew*'s addition, to match the words of the divine voice at Jesus' immersion (3:17). **17:6–7** The disciples' understandable response and Jesus' compassionate words to them take the place of *Mark*'s presentation of their complete confusion, even about the notion of resurrection (8:10). **17:10–13** *Matthew* follows *Mark* 9:11–13 closely, postponing the apparently misplaced line about the Son of Man's suffering (*Mark* 9:12) and adding that the disciples understood Jesus to identify Elijah with John the Baptist. Unlike *Mark*, *Matthew* has already made this identification; see 11:14–15 and notes there concerning the Elijah figure. **17:14–21** *Matthew* drastically abbreviates *Mark* 9:14–29. *Luke* 9:37–43 gives a similarly abbreviated version—in the same places and ways—which would be remarkable if *Matthew* and *Luke* were independently written, as the common theory holds. **17:14** *When they came to the crowd* No crowd has been mentioned recently; rather, Jesus had left the larger group of students to go up the mountain with Peter, James, and John (17:1). Presumably, they are still in the region of Caesarea Philippi (16:13) or en route back to Galilee (17:22). **17:15** *an epileptic* *Matthew* alters *Mark*'s description (9:17–18) of possession by a spirit. See note to *Mark* 1:23. **17:17** Jesus' criticism of his students is taken over from *Mark* 9:19, and even intensified with the word *perverse*. The same change in the same place in *Luke* (9:41) is a problem for the theory that *Matthew* and *Luke* were independently written.

rebuked the demon,[c] and it[d] came out of him, and the boy was cured instantly. [19]Then the disciples came to Jesus privately and said, "Why could we not cast it out?" [20]He said to them, "Because of your little faith. For truly I tell you, if you have faith the size of a[e] mustard seed, you will say to this mountain, 'Move from here to there,' and it will move; and nothing will be impossible for you."[f]

Jesus Again Foretells His Death and Resurrection

[22]As they were gathering[g] in Galilee, Jesus said to them, "The Son of Man is going to be betrayed into human hands, [23]and they will kill him, and on the third day he will be raised." And they were greatly distressed.

Jesus and the Temple Tax

[24]When they reached Capernaum, the collectors of the temple tax[h] came to Peter and said, "Does your teacher not pay the temple tax?"[h] [25]He said, "Yes, he does." And when he came home, Jesus spoke of it first, asking, "What do you think, Simon? From whom do kings of the earth take toll or tribute? From their children or from others?" [26]When Peter[i] said, "From others," Jesus said to him, "Then the children are free. [27]However, so that we do not give offense to them, go to the sea and cast a hook; take the first fish that comes up; and when you open its mouth, you will find a coin;[j] take that and give it to them for you and me."

True Greatness

18 At that time the disciples came to Jesus and asked, "Who is the greatest in the kingdom of heaven?" [2]He called a child, whom he put among them, [3]and said, "Truly I tell you, unless you change and become like children, you will never enter the kingdom of heaven. [4]Whoever becomes humble like this child is the greatest in the kingdom of heaven. [5]Whoever welcomes one such child in my name welcomes me.

Temptations to Sin

[6]"If any of you put a stumbling block before one of these little ones who believe in me, it would be better for you if a great millstone were fastened around your neck and you were drowned in the depth of the sea. [7]Woe to the world because of stumbling blocks! Occasions for stumbling are bound to come, but woe to the one by whom the stumbling block comes!

---

c Gk it or him
d Gk the demon
e Gk faith as a grain of
f Other ancient authorities add verse 21, But this kind does not come out except by prayer and fasting.
g Other ancient authorities read living
h Gk didrachma
i Gk he

j Gk stater; the stater was worth two didrachmas

17:20 This saying about the mustard seed is not in *Mark* but is paralleled in *Luke* 17:6. Presumably, the author of *Matthew* knew the saying from another source (Q?) and felt that it fit well here. **17:22–23** The second prediction of Jesus' death and resurrection in *Matthew;* see 16:21. **17:22 *gathering in Galilee*** Having returned from Caesarea Philippi (16:13). **17:24–27** The author of *Matthew* splices this story, which is found nowhere else in the ancient gospels, into the narrative outline adopted from *Mark;* he borrows the setting of Capernaum from the next story in *Mark* (9:33). The issue is Jesus' attitude toward the annual tax, of half a shekel or a Greek *didrachma* (two *drachmas*), paid by Jews over the age of twenty around the world for the upkeep of the temple in Jerusalem. See *Exod.* 30:11–16; Josephus, *J.W.* 7.218; *Ant.* 18.312. The tax was apparently collected in late winter (Adar—February/March) of each year (*m. Sheqalim* 1:1, 3). *Matthew*'s Jesus responds here in a way that matches the rest of the gospel, where he appears as greater than the temple, Moses, and Solomon—indeed, as son of God (12:6). He does not finally object to paying the tax, but it is a triviality, since he is the Son of the One who inhabits the temple. Peter continues to act out the leadership role given to him in 16:18–19; see 17:4; 18:21. **17:24 *temple tax*** Lit. "didrachma." See previous note. **17:27 *a coin*** Lit. "stater," a Greek coin worth one shekel or two didrachmas (four drachmas), therefore enough for two. **18:1–19:1** This is the 4th of Jesus' five major discourses in *Matthew*. It covers a variety of themes but is often called the church or ecclesiastical discourse because of its prescriptions for life in the church (18:15–20). **18:1–5** *Matthew* reverts to the Markan narrative (9:33–37) but significantly alters this discussion about greatness to improve the image of Jesus' students. They no longer argue among themselves about which of them is greatest but, rather, ask Jesus who is greatest in the kingdom of heaven. Therefore, Jesus' saying about becoming like a child is not a direct criticism. This saying *Matthew* borrows from a later section of *Mark* (10:15); it has a rough parallel in *Gospel of Thomas* 22. **18:6–9** *Matthew* has omitted *Mark*'s story (9:38–41) about the unfamiliar exorcist, which was nested in a discussion of children and "little ones" (see note to *Mark* 9:42–50). *Matthew* here continues the theme without a break. As in *Mark*, the author strings together several distinct sayings according to the catchwords *stumbling* and *little ones*. **18:6 *little ones who believe in me*** This language seems to flag the author's double meaning: little ones can be both children and new believers. **18:7** *Matthew*'s addition to *Mark*, paralleled in *Luke* 17:1 (from Q?).

8"If your hand or your foot causes you to stumble, cut it off and throw it away; it is better for you to enter life maimed or lame than to have two hands or two feet and to be thrown into the eternal fire. 9And if your eye causes you to stumble, tear it out and throw it away; it is better for you to enter life with one eye than to have two eyes and to be thrown into the hell*k* of fire.

The Parable of the Lost Sheep

10"Take care that you do not despise one of these little ones; for, I tell you, in heaven their angels continually see the face of my Father in heaven.*l* 12What do you think? If a shepherd has a hundred sheep, and one of them has gone astray, does he not leave the ninety-nine on the mountains and go in search of the one that went astray? 13And if he finds it, truly I tell you, he rejoices over it more than over the ninety-nine that never went astray. 14So it is not the will of your*m* Father in heaven that one of these little ones should be lost.

Reproving Another Who Sins

15"If another member of the church*n* sins against you,*o* go and point out the fault when the two of you are alone. If the member listens to you, you have re-

gained that one.*p* 16But if you are not listened to, take one or two others along with you, so that every word may be confirmed by the evidence of two or three witnesses. 17If the member refuses to listen to them, tell it to the church; and if the offender refuses to listen even to the church, let such a one be to you as a Gentile and a tax collector. 18Truly I tell you, whatever you bind on earth will be bound in heaven, and whatever you loose on earth will be loosed in heaven. 19Again, truly I tell you, if two of you agree on earth about anything you ask, it will be done for you by my Father in heaven. 20For where two or three are gathered in my name, I am there among them."

Forgiveness

21Then Peter came and said to him, "Lord, if another member of the church*q* sins against me, how often should I forgive? As many as seven times?" 22Jesus said to him, "Not seven times, but, I tell you, seventy-seven*r* times.

The Parable of the Unforgiving Servant

23"For this reason the kingdom of heaven may be compared to a king who wished to settle accounts with his slaves. 24When he began the reckoning, one who owed him ten thousand talents*s* was brought to

---

k Gk *Gehenna*

l Other ancient authorities add verse 11, *For the Son of Man came to save the lost.*

m Other ancient authorities read *my*

n Gk *If your brother*

o Other ancient authorities lack *against you*

p Gk *the brother*

q Gk *if my brother*

r Or *seventy times seven*

s A talent was worth more than fifteen years' wages of a laborer

---

18:8–9 Following *Mark* 9:43–47 leads the author to create a doublet of *Matt.* 5:28–30—quite likely intentional, in view of the prominence of doublets in *Matthew*. **18:10** A saying found only in *Matthew*. The concept of angels' representing human beings before God is not developed elsewhere in the earliest Christian literature. **18:12–14** This parable, found also in *Luke* 15:3–7 with a different application and in *Gospel of Thomas* 107, is linked to the context by the final sentence about the *little ones*, a characteristic Matthean inclusion (see 18:35; 20:16). **18:15–20** These instructions for "church" behavior are unique to *Matthew*. Given that the church did not exist in Jesus' day, and that his students seemed so entirely surprised by his resurrection and the sequel (*1 Cor.* 15:3–8; *Mark* 16 par. *Matt.* 28 par. *Luke* 24 par. *John* 20–21), is it more likely that Jesus gave these instructions, and they were simply remembered and reported here, or that the resurrected Jesus communicated them to his church—perhaps through prayer and prophecy (*1 Cor.* 14:3–25)? **18:15** *another member of the church* The Gk uses the word for "brother," which (along with "sister") was the common term for designating fellow members of the early church. The Gk does not mention "church" here. **18:16** *evidence of two or three witnesses* The author alludes to *Deut.* 19:15, which excludes legal testimony from one witness alone. It is plausible that this legal principle plays a role in the author's preference for pairs (see introduction to *Matthew*). **18:17** *a Gentile and a tax collector* This saying seems to reflect the Jewish perspective of both author and readers. But this need not mean that they were native Jews, because Paul speaks to his Gentile converts of a time when they "were Gentiles." **18:18–20** This authority was already given to Peter in 16:19—another Matthean duplication. On binding and loosing, see note to the earlier passage; it typically refers to governmental authority. (In *John* 20:23 Jesus gives similar authority to his students after his resurrection.) Here Jesus gives small disciplinary committees the authority to act in his stead, much as Paul did (*1 Cor.* 5:3–5; *2 Cor.* 2:5–11). **18:19–20** See Ign. *Eph.* 5.2; *Gospel of Thomas* 30. The context is one of church discipline (see previous note). **18:21–22** The parallel in *Luke* (17:4) mentions only seven times. In any case, the number typically suggests comprehensiveness. **18:21** *Peter came and said* Peter acts in a positive way, as leader of Jesus' students, fulfilling the role given him in 16:18–19; see 17:4, 24. **18:23–35** This parable about the kingdom of heaven (perhaps meaning now the church) is found only in *Matthew*. It is applied to its context—the importance of forgiveness—by its final sentence. **18:24** *ten thousand talents* Even a single talent (= 6,000 drachmas, a Greek value) would be an unimaginable figure for a slave to owe. Heads of state,

him; 25and, as he could not pay, his lord ordered him to be sold, together with his wife and children and all his possessions, and payment to be made. 26So the slave fell on his knees before him, saying, 'Have patience with me, and I will pay you everything.' 27And out of pity for him, the lord of that slave released him and forgave him the debt. 28But that same slave, as he went out, came upon one of his fellow slaves who owed him a hundred denarii;*t* and seizing him by the throat, he said, 'Pay what you owe.' 29Then his fellow slave fell down and pleaded with him, 'Have patience with me, and I will pay you.' 30But he refused; then he went and threw him into prison until he would pay the debt. 31When his fellow slaves saw what had happened, they were greatly distressed, and they went and reported to their lord all that had taken place. 32Then his lord summoned him and said to him, 'You wicked slave! I forgave you all that debt because you pleaded with me. 33Should you not have had mercy on your fellow slave, as I had mercy on you?' 34And in anger his lord handed him over to be tortured until he would pay his entire debt. 35So my heavenly Father will also do to every one of you, if you do not forgive your brother or sister*u* from your heart."

Teaching about Divorce

19 When Jesus had finished saying these things, he left Galilee and went to the region of Judea beyond the Jordan. 2Large crowds followed him, and he cured them there.

3Some Pharisees came to him, and to test him they asked, "Is it lawful for a man to divorce his wife for any cause?" 4He answered, "Have you not read that the one who made them at the beginning 'made them male and female,' 5and said, 'For this reason a man shall leave his father and mother and be joined to his wife, and the two shall become one flesh'? 6So they are no longer two, but one flesh. Therefore what God has joined together, let no one separate." 7They said to him, "Why then did Moses command us to give a certificate of dismissal and to divorce her?" 8He said to them, "It was because you were so hardhearted that Moses allowed you to divorce your wives, but from the beginning it was not so. 9And I say to you, whoever divorces his wife, except for unchastity, and marries another commits adultery."*v*

10His disciples said to him, "If such is the case of a man with his wife, it is better not to marry." 11But he

---

t The denarius was the usual day's wage for a laborer
u Gk brother

v Other ancient authorities read *except on the ground of unchastity, causes her to commit adultery;* others add at the end of the verse *and he who marries a divorced woman commits adultery*

---

with national treasuries at their disposal, might deal in hundreds of talents (*2 Macc.* 4:8). The author's Gk expression, "myriad [ten thousand] talents," is not precise but conjures up the picture of a vast and impossible fortune. **18:28 a hundred denarii** A desirable sum of money, perhaps one third of a year's wages for the ordinary laborer (*Matt.* 20:2). Legionary soldiers earned 225 denarii per year at the beginning of the 1st century, 300 per year from the end of the century. The denarius was a Roman unit of currency. **18:29** This slave behaves and speaks exactly as the first (18:26), except that he promises to repay everything, which is plausible in view of the small amount owed. **18:30 threw him into prison** See note to 5:25–26. **18:35** This sentence connects the parable with the original issue of forgiveness, a characteristic Matthean inclusion (see note to 18:12–14). **19:1 When Jesus had finished saying** So ends the fourth of Jesus' major speeches in *Matthew*, with the standard formula (see 7:28; 11:1; 13:53). *Matthew* begins to follow *Mark* (10:1) again, after leaving it at 18:9. **the region of Judea beyond the Jordan** Jesus begins his fateful journey southward toward Jerusalem, foreseen in 16:21; 17:22–23. But *Matthew's* language does not suit Jesus' time: Perea *beyond the Jordan* was not part of Judea but was another part of Herod Antipas's territory in addition to Galilee. Perhaps the author uses *Judea* in its greater, historical sense; or perhaps he is uncritically adopting the language of *Mark* 10:1 although the best manuscripts of that passage do not contain the error. It is also plausible that the author assumes the boundaries of his own time, when Perea was an integrated part of Judea. **19:3–9** *Matthew* follows *Mark* 10:2–12 closely, with some rearrangement. But this is also more or less a doublet of 5:31–32 (on *Matthew's* pairs, see introduction to *Matthew*). The question of divorce was a live one in Jewish circles of Jesus' day. **19:3 to divorce his wife for any cause** Scripture plainly permits divorce (*Deut.* 24:1–4). Rabbinic literature compiled after Jesus' time reveals internal debates about the grounds for divorce, especially about the interpretation of *Deut.* 24:1: "he finds something objectionable about her." See the Mishnah tractates *Ketubbot* and *Gittin*, especially *Gittin* 9:10. Jesus is invited by the Pharisees, who debated these issues, to discuss his view of the grounds for divorce, not simply whether divorce should be permitted, as in *Mark* 10:2. **19:4** Partial quotation of a line from the creation story, *Gen.* 1:27. The Dead Sea Scrolls use the same verse to prohibit divorce and remarriage (CD 4.20–22). **19:5** Quoting further from the creation story, *Gen.* 2:24. **19:6–9** Jesus' prohibition of divorce, paralleled in the Dead Sea Scrolls (above), became standard in early Christianity (*1 Cor.* 7:10–11). **19:7** See *Deut.* 24:1. **19:8** *Matthew's* Jesus does more than simply interpret Moses; he claims to have special insight into the divine motives behind Moses' legislation. This befits his status as Son of God (11:26–27; 12:6–7). **19:9 except for unchastity** *Matthew's* exception is not found in the parallels *Mark* 10:11 and *Luke* 16:18, but it matches *Matt.* 5:31–32. **19:10–12** This passage is peculiar to *Matthew*, and it fits with the extreme asceticism suggested in 5:27–30; 18:6–9. **19:10 better not to marry** So also Paul, *1 Cor.* 7:6–7, 25–35.

said to them, "Not everyone can accept this teaching, but only those to whom it is given. ¹²For there are eunuchs who have been so from birth, and there are eunuchs who have been made eunuchs by others, and there are eunuchs who have made themselves eunuchs for the sake of the kingdom of heaven. Let anyone accept this who can."

Jesus Blesses Little Children

¹³Then little children were being brought to him in order that he might lay his hands on them and pray. The disciples spoke sternly to those who brought them; ¹⁴but Jesus said, "Let the little children come to me, and do not stop them; for it is to such as these that the kingdom of heaven belongs." ¹⁵And he laid his hands on them and went on his way.

The Rich Young Man

¹⁶Then someone came to him and said, "Teacher, what good deed must I do to have eternal life?" ¹⁷And he said to him, "Why do you ask me about what is good? There is only one who is good. If you wish to enter into life, keep the commandments." ¹⁸He said to him, "Which ones?" And Jesus said, "You shall not murder; You shall not commit adultery; You shall not steal; You shall not bear false witness; ¹⁹Honor

your father and mother; also, You shall love your neighbor as yourself." ²⁰The young man said to him, "I have kept all these;ʷ what do I still lack?" ²¹Jesus said to him, "If you wish to be perfect, go, sell your possessions, and give the moneyˣ to the poor, and you will have treasure in heaven; then come, follow me." ²²When the young man heard this word, he went away grieving, for he had many possessions.

²³Then Jesus said to his disciples, "Truly I tell you, it will be hard for a rich person to enter the kingdom of heaven. ²⁴Again I tell you, it is easier for a camel to go through the eye of a needle than for someone who is rich to enter the kingdom of God." ²⁵When the disciples heard this, they were greatly astounded and said, "Then who can be saved?" ²⁶But Jesus looked at them and said, "For mortals it is impossible, but for God all things are possible."

²⁷Then Peter said in reply, "Look, we have left everything and followed you. What then will we have?" ²⁸Jesus said to them, "Truly I tell you, at the renewal of all things, when the Son of Man is seated on the throne of his glory, you who have followed me will also sit on twelve thrones, judging the twelve tribes of Israel. ²⁹And everyone who has left houses

---

w Other ancient authorities add *from my youth*
x Gk lacks *the money*

19:12 made themselves eunuchs for the sake of the kingdom of heaven See note to 5:28–30. **19:13–15** See notes to *Mark* 10:13–16. In *Matthew*, this seems to be a doublet of 18:1–3, reprising the theme of the little ones. The implicit critique of Jesus' students is, in the context of *Matthew*, mild and reversible. See *Gospel of Thomas* 22. **19:16–22** *Matthew* follows *Mark* 10:17–22, with a few significant changes. **19:16 what good deed** An adjustment of *Mark*'s "Good teacher, what must I do?" Since Jesus is not addressed as "good," his response here in *Matthew* does not distinguish him from God as sharply as *Mark* 10:18 seemed to: "Why do you call me good? No one is good but God alone." **eternal life** Or agelong life; see note to *Mark* 10:17. **19:17 ask me about what is good** Jesus' reply is adjusted from *Mark* 10:18 (see note there) to match the new question in *Matthew*. **There is only one who is good** This part of the answer does not match the question Jesus is asked in *Matthew*. It seems to betray *Matthew*'s reliance on *Mark* 10:18, where Jesus responds to being addressed as "good." **19:18 Which ones?** Although it is commonly imagined that Moses received only ten commandments on Mount Sinai, according to *Exod.* 20:22ff. these ten were merely the first of many. Later rabbis counted 613 commandments in the Torah. **19:18–19** The list of commandments largely follows that in *Mark* 10:19, which paraphrases and rearranges the human-to-human (not human-to-divine) commandments of *Deut.* 5:16–20 and *Exod.* 20:12–16. *Matthew*, however, substitutes *Lev.* 19:18 (love of neighbor), a favorite text of Jesus and the early Christians (*Gal.* 5:14; *Rom.* 13:9; *Mark* 12:31; *Matt.* 5:43; 22:39; *Luke* 10:27; *Jas.* 2:8), for *Mark*'s prohibition of fraud, which is not explicit in the Bible. The addition of this commandment makes this passage a parallel with 22:38–39. *Luke* 18:18 also omits the prohibition of fraud. **19:20 young man** Only *Matthew* (also in 19:22) makes the qualification, "young." **19:21 perfect** In *Matthew*'s version only; see 5:48. **19:23–26** *Matthew* continues to follow *Mark* (10:23–31), abbreviating somewhat. *Luke* abbreviates in very similar ways, a problem for the common theory that these two texts were independently written. **19:24 Again** The author betrays his use of *Mark* 10:24, which has Jesus repeat the saying; here Jesus moves directly to the analogy without such repetition. **camel . . . through the eye of a needle** An image so absurd as to drive home the point. See 23:24. **kingdom of God** This is the only case in which the author of *Matthew* takes over this phrase from *Mark*, without changing it to "kingdom of heaven." **19:27–30** *Matthew* continues to follow *Mark* (10:28–31) but adds 19:28. This addition pointedly validates the disciples, removing the ongoing sense in *Mark* that they are out of touch with Jesus. **19:28 at the renewal of all things** Curiously, *Matthew* uses a word *(palingenesia)* that was common in Stoic philosophy for the "rebirth" of the cosmos. **Son of Man is seated on the throne of his glory** This is a typically Matthean scenario; see 13:36–43 and note. **twelve tribes of Israel** *Matthew* strongly reinforces the biblical/Jewish tone of the work. In reality, the twelve tribes had long since disappeared; they played an important role in speculations about the future. See *1 Cor.* 6:2; *Rev.* 3:21; 7:4–8; 1QM 1.1; *Testaments of the Twelve Patriarchs*. **19:29** *Matthew* and *Luke* (18:30) both omit *Mark*'s claim (10:30), which may have seemed bizarre, that the faithful would receive hundreds of houses and family members in this age.

or brothers or sisters or father or mother or children or fields, for my name's sake, will receive a hundred-fold,[y] and will inherit eternal life. [30]But many who are first will be last, and the last will be first.

The Laborers in the Vineyard

20 "For the kingdom of heaven is like a landowner who went out early in the morning to hire laborers for his vineyard. [2]After agreeing with the laborers for the usual daily wage,[z] he sent them into his vineyard. [3]When he went out about nine o'clock, he saw others standing idle in the marketplace; [4]and he said to them, 'You also go into the vineyard, and I will pay you whatever is right.' So they went. [5]When he went out again about noon and about three o'clock, he did the same. [6]And about five o'clock he went out and found others standing around; and he said to them, 'Why are you standing here idle all day?' [7]They said to him, 'Because no one has hired us.' He said to them, 'You also go into the vineyard.' [8]When evening came, the owner of the vineyard said to his manager, 'Call the laborers and give them their pay, beginning with the last and then going to the first.' [9]When those hired about five o'clock came, each of them received the usual daily wage.[z] [10]Now when the first came, they thought they would receive more; but each of them also received the usual daily wage.[z] [11]And when they received it, they grumbled against the landowner, [12]saying, 'These last worked only one hour, and you have made them equal to us who have borne the burden of the day and the scorching heat.' [13]But he replied to one of them, 'Friend, I am doing you no wrong; did you not agree with me for the usual daily wage?[z] [14]Take what belongs to you and go; I choose to give to this last the same as I give to you. [15]Am I not allowed to do what I choose with what belongs to me? Or are you envious because I am generous?'[a] [16]So the last will be first, and the first will be last."[b]

A Third Time Jesus Foretells His Death and Resurrection

[17]While Jesus was going up to Jerusalem, he took the twelve disciples aside by themselves, and said to them on the way, [18]"See, we are going up to Jerusalem, and the Son of Man will be handed over to the chief priests and scribes, and they will condemn him to death; [19]then they will hand him over to the Gentiles to be mocked and flogged and crucified; and on the third day he will be raised."

The Request of the Mother of James and John

[20]Then the mother of the sons of Zebedee came to him with her sons, and kneeling before him, she asked a favor of him. [21]And he said to her, "What do you want?" She said to him, "Declare that these two sons of mine will sit, one at your right hand and one at your left, in your kingdom." [22]But Jesus answered, "You do not know what you are asking. Are you able to drink the cup that I am about to drink?"[c] They said to him, "We are able." [23]He said to them, "You will indeed drink my cup, but to sit at my right hand

---

y Other ancient authorities read *manifold*
z Gk *a denarius*

a Gk *is your eye evil because I am good?*
b Other ancient authorities add *for many are called but few are chosen*
c Other ancient authorities add *or to be baptized with the baptism that I am baptized with?*

19:30 A succinct statement of the eschatological reversal announced by prophets and seers; see also 20:16; Luke 13:30; *Gos. Thom.* 4:2. See note to 5:3–12. **20:1–16** A parable of the kingdom, peculiar to *Matthew*, illustrating the preceding statement (19:30), which will be repeated at the end (20:16). This inclusion is characteristic of *Matthew* (see note to 18:12–14). Here the kingdom is decidedly in the future, since the point concerns future rewards. Presumably, the latecomers to salvation are Gentile converts to (Jewish?) Christianity. See 21:41, where the vineyard is also the context; 22:10. **20:2 the usual daily wage** Lit. "a denarius," apparently a generous daily wage for a casual laborer. Legionary soldiers were paid 225 denarii per year in the early part of the 1st century. **20:3 about nine o'clock** That is, the 3d hour after the landlord first went out (20:1). Timekeeping in the ancient Mediterranean world was inexact; people divided the daylight hours, which varied with the seasons, into twelve hours. **the marketplace** The *agora*; see note to *Mark* 6:56. **20:5 about noon and about three o'clock** About the 6th and 9th hours, respectively, after sunup. **20:6 about five o'clock** The 11th hour after sunup; by definition the final hour of the usable workday outside. **idle all day** It seems, from a variety of clues, that Galilee and Judea of the mid-1st century and later faced massive unemployment—in part as a result of the gradual completion of Herod the Great's temple complex. **20:16** *Matthew* creates an inclusion by repeating the line that preceded the parable (19:30). **20:17–19** *Matthew* returns to parallel *Mark* (10:32–34) with Jesus' third prediction of his trial, death, and resurrection (see 16:21; 17:22–23). **20:20–28** *Matthew*'s adaptation of *Mark* 10:35–45 considerably improves the image of James and John by having their mother ask about their future status. A mother's concern for her sons is perhaps forgivable. **20:20 the mother of the sons of Zebedee** This awkward construction seems to result from the author's light adaptation of *Mark* 10:35. In *Mark*, it is James and John who ask. **20:22 what you are asking** The author betrays his use of *Mark* because Jesus answers James and John as in *Mark*: the *you* is plural. In Matthew, however, the brothers have not asked anything. For the cup as an image of suffering, see 26:39 and Aeschylus, *Prometheus Bound* 377.

and at my left, this is not mine to grant, but it is for those for whom it has been prepared by my Father."

24When the ten heard it, they were angry with the two brothers. 25But Jesus called them to him and said, "You know that the rulers of the Gentiles lord it over them, and their great ones are tyrants over them. 26It will not be so among you; but whoever wishes to be great among you must be your servant, 27and whoever wishes to be first among you must be your slave; 28just as the Son of Man came not to be served but to serve, and to give his life a ransom for many."

Jesus Heals Two Blind Men

29As they were leaving Jericho, a large crowd followed him. 30There were two blind men sitting by the roadside. When they heard that Jesus was passing by, they shouted, "Lord,*d* have mercy on us, Son of David!" 31The crowd sternly ordered them to be quiet; but they shouted even more loudly, "Have mercy on us, Lord, Son of David!" 32Jesus stood still and called them, saying, "What do you want me to do for you?" 33They said to him, "Lord, let our eyes be opened." 34Moved with compassion, Jesus touched their eyes. Immediately they regained their sight and followed him.

Jesus' Triumphal Entry into Jerusalem

21 When they had come near Jerusalem and had reached Bethphage, at the Mount of Olives, Jesus sent two disciples, 2saying to them, "Go into the village ahead of you, and immediately you will find a donkey tied, and a colt with her; untie them and bring them to me. 3If anyone says anything to you, just say this, 'The Lord needs them.' And he will send them immediately.*e*" 4This took place to fulfill what had been spoken through the prophet, saying,

5   "Tell the daughter of Zion,
   Look, your king is coming to you,
      humble, and mounted on a donkey,
         and on a colt, the foal of a donkey."
6The disciples went and did as Jesus had directed them; 7they brought the donkey and the colt, and put their cloaks on them, and he sat on them. 8A very large crowd*f* spread their cloaks on the road, and others cut branches from the trees and spread them on the road. 9The crowds that went ahead of him and that followed were shouting,
   "Hosanna to the Son of David!
      Blessed is the one who comes in the name of
         the Lord!
   Hosanna in the highest heaven!"

---

d Other ancient authorities lack *Lord*

e Or *'The Lord needs them and will send them back immediately.'*
f Or *Most of the crowd*

20:24–28 *Matthew* follows *Mark* 10:41–45 almost verbatim. **20:29–34** *Matthew* continues to follow and abbreviate *Mark* (10:46–52). In *Matthew*, however, this story forms a doublet with the similar account in 9:27–31. And characteristically (see introduction to *Matthew*), *Matthew* introduces a pair of blind men rather than the single Bartimaeus of *Mark*. **20:29 leaving Jericho** The geography continues to be confusing, although *Matthew* removes the awkwardness of *Mark's* language (10:46). The last we heard, Jesus had gone to "Judea beyond the Jordan" (19:1). Now he is on this side of the Jordan (the one closest Jerusalem) and is already leaving Jericho, although the story has not mentioned Jericho before. Jericho, a very old city even in Jesus' day, sits just west of the Jordan River, about seven miles north of the Dead Sea. Although situated in the Judean desert, it was fed by an oasis. **20:30 two blind men** *Matthew* cannot take over *Mark's* name, Bartimaeus, since there are now two men; note the two blind men of 9:27–31 and the two demoniacs of 8:28. **Son of David** An important title for *Matthew*: see 1:1 and notes to 9:27; 12:23. **20:32–34** *Matthew* follows *Mark* almost verbatim but changes the pronouns to suit the story with two blind men. **21:1–9** *Matthew* continues to follow *Mark* (11:1–10) closely, slightly abbreviating the story, but also adds a characteristic fulfillment citation (21:4) and has Jesus ride two animals instead of one—a remarkable extension of the author's taste for pairs (see introduction to *Matthew*). **21:1 Bethphage, at the Mount of Olives** Having left Jericho (20:29), Jesus approaches Jerusalem from the east. Bethphage's precise location is uncertain; see note to *Mark* 11:1. **two disciples** This feature of *Mark's* story was already well suited to *Matthew's* literary tendency to create pairs (see introduction to *Matthew*). **21:2** The author dramatically alters *Mark* 11:2 to speak of both a colt and an ass. It appears that he adapts the story to fit the fulfillment citation (21:4). **21:4–5** *Matthew's* 12th fulfillment citation (see 13:35 and note to 1:22–23), taken from *Zech.* 9:9. The LXX's Gk translation rather woodenly supplies an "and" before "a young colt," although the Hebrew idiom implies only one animal (the translator probably knew this). The Bible routinely uses poetic repetition (synonymous parallelism) to express a single image or idea. The author of *Matthew* has re-created the story by having Jesus ride two animals so that the passage will be obviously fulfilled. *Matthew's* version of this saying may be influenced in its first two lines by *Isa.* 62:11 ("Tell the daughter of Zion, Look, your savior . . ."). **21:7 he sat on them** This awkward image was apparently created by the author's determination to have Jesus fulfill scripture; see note to 21:4–5. **21:9 Hosanna . . . the highest heaven!** *Matthew* condenses *Mark* 11:9–10 by placing a reference to David after the *Hosanna*. The author thereby exaggerates *Mark's* use of *Hosanna* as a term of praise in spite of its meaning "Please save!" The passage draws from *Ps.* 118:25–26 (LXX 117:25–26), which may have been used when the king of Judah entered the city in procession. See notes to *Mark* 11:9–10.

[10]When he entered Jerusalem, the whole city was in turmoil, asking, "Who is this?" [11]The crowds were saying, "This is the prophet Jesus from Nazareth in Galilee."

Jesus Cleanses the Temple

[12]Then Jesus entered the temple[g] and drove out all who were selling and buying in the temple, and he overturned the tables of the money changers and the seats of those who sold doves. [13]He said to them, "It is written,

'My house shall be called a house of prayer';
    but you are making it a den of robbers."

[14]The blind and the lame came to him in the temple, and he cured them. [15]But when the chief priests and the scribes saw the amazing things that he did, and heard[h] the children crying out in the temple, "Hosanna to the Son of David," they became angry [16]and said to him, "Do you hear what these are saying?" Jesus said to them, "Yes; have you never read,

'Out of the mouths of infants and nursing babies
    you have prepared praise for yourself'?"

g Other ancient authorities add *of God*
h Gk lacks *heard*

[17]He left them, went out of the city to Bethany, and spent the night there.

Jesus Curses the Fig Tree

[18]In the morning, when he returned to the city, he was hungry. [19]And seeing a fig tree by the side of the road, he went to it and found nothing at all on it but leaves. Then he said to it, "May no fruit ever come from you again!" And the fig tree withered at once. [20]When the disciples saw it, they were amazed, saying, "How did the fig tree wither at once?" [21]Jesus answered them, "Truly I tell you, if you have faith and do not doubt, not only will you do what has been done to the fig tree, but even if you say to this mountain, 'Be lifted up and thrown into the sea,' it will be done. [22]Whatever you ask for in prayer with faith, you will receive."

The Authority of Jesus Questioned

[23]When he entered the temple, the chief priests and the elders of the people came to him as he was teaching, and said, "By what authority are you doing these things, and who gave you this authority?" [24]Jesus said to them, "I will also ask you one

21:10–17 The author of *Matthew* alters the story from *Mark* to make Jesus' first visit to Jerusalem a much more significant affair. Whereas *Mark* 11:11 had Jesus pay a very brief, uneventful, and anticlimactic visit after the triumphal entry—postponing until the following day Jesus' cleansing of the temple (11:15–17)—*Matthew* combines all of this and more in the single visit that follows Jesus' grand entry. **21:10** An appropriate response if Jesus' entry was as grand as *Matthew* describes. According to Josephus and the gospels, messianic pretenders and popular leaders abounded in Jesus' day (Josephus, *J.W.* 2.253–263): their presence in Jerusalem near the time of a feast (*Matt.* 26:2)—when trouble often developed (e.g., *J.W.* 2.42–43, 224, 232, 255)—would certainly have attracted such attention. **21:11 the prophet Jesus from Nazareth in Galilee** *Matthew*'s statement has an air of historical plausibility. "Prophet" was not this author's preferred title for Jesus (the Son of David, Son of God, Messiah, Son of Man), since it could be applied to many others as well. But it is the kind of label that other people might have given to Jesus. Although some Jews thought that prophets had long ceased to exist, others recognized true prophets in their own day. See note to 10:41. **21:12** See note to *Mark* 11:15–16. Money changing and animal selling were necessary so that Jews could fulfill their obligations at feast times. They were conducted in the portico that pilgrims 1st encountered on entering the temple precincts from the south, some distance from the inner courts and the sanctuary itself. Whether *Matthew*'s Jesus (or the historical Jesus) was disagreeing with this entire system or with some particular abuse in it is debated. See note to *Mark* 11:15–16. *Matthew* omits *Mark*'s difficult statement (11:16) that Jesus even prevented movement in the temple area. **21:13** *Matthew*'s Jesus cites *Isa.* 56:7. *Matthew*, though following *Mark* 11:17, curiously omits the phrase "for all the nations" from the end of the verse. The phrase *a den of robbers* recalls *Jer.* 7:11. See note to *Mark* 11:17. Just as *Matthew* postpones the Pharisees' plot to kill Jesus, which *Mark* had placed at the outset of his career (2:1–3:6), so also the author omits *Mark*'s claim (11:18) that Jesus' actions in the temple led the Jerusalem authorities to plan his immediate death. **21:14–17** The author adds this unparalleled passage to the story taken from *Mark,* perhaps in part so that he could cite the scripture in 21:16. **21:15 Hosanna to the Son of David** See note to 21:9. **21:16 Out of the mouths of infants . . .** *Ps.* 8:2. **21:17 Bethany** The first reference to this town in *Matthew.* Its location is not completely certain, but the likeliest spot is on the other side of the Mount of Olives, about two miles east of Jerusalem. This town becomes a base for Jesus' final days in Jerusalem. See 26:6 and note to *Mark* 11:1. **21:18–22** The author continues to follow *Mark* but removes his source's nesting of stories by having the fig tree wither immediately after being cursed (contrast *Mark* 11:12–14, 20–24). One reason for this change is that *Matthew* has already used *Mark*'s intervening story, the cleansing of the temple. Another reason might be to heighten the effect of Jesus' curse. Since the fig tree was a common image for Israel in the prophets (*Jer.* 8:13; *Hos.* 9:10), there can be little doubt that the author understands this encounter with the barren fig tree as highly symbolic. **21:19** The author omits *Mark*'s observation that it was not the season for figs (11:13), which would seem to make Jesus' anger misplaced. **21:20** The author of *Matthew,* as of *Mark,* chooses not to draw out whatever symbolic meaning the cursing might have had, but uses it simply as an example of the power of faith. **21:21 *say to this mountain*** See *1 Cor.* 13:2, where Paul seems to know this saying of Jesus. **21:22** See 7:7–11. **21:23–27** *Matthew* continues to follow *Mark* (11:27–33) quite closely. In *Matthew,* however, the use of John the Baptist has greater force because he has

question; if you tell me the answer, then I will also tell you by what authority I do these things. 25Did the baptism of John come from heaven, or was it of human origin?" And they argued with one another, "If we say, 'From heaven,' he will say to us, 'Why then did you not believe him?' 26But if we say, 'Of human origin,' we are afraid of the crowd; for all regard John as a prophet." 27So they answered Jesus, "We do not know." And he said to them, "Neither will I tell you by what authority I am doing these things.

The Parable of the Two Sons

28"What do you think? A man had two sons; he went to the first and said, 'Son, go and work in the vineyard today.' 29He answered, 'I will not'; but later he changed his mind and went. 30The father*i* went to the second and said the same; and he answered, 'I go, sir'; but he did not go. 31Which of the two did the will of his father?" They said, "The first." Jesus said to them, "Truly I tell you, the tax collectors and the prostitutes are going into the kingdom of God ahead of you. 32For John came to you in the way of righteousness and you did not believe him, but the tax collectors and the prostitutes believed him; and even after you saw it, you did not change your minds and believe him.

The Parable of the Wicked Tenants

33"Listen to another parable. There was a landowner who planted a vineyard, put a fence around it,

dug a wine press in it, and built a watchtower. Then he leased it to tenants and went to another country. 34When the harvest time had come, he sent his slaves to the tenants to collect his produce. 35But the tenants seized his slaves and beat one, killed another, and stoned another. 36Again he sent other slaves, more than the first; and they treated them in the same way. 37Finally he sent his son to them, saying, 'They will respect my son.' 38But when the tenants saw the son, they said to themselves, 'This is the heir; come, let us kill him and get his inheritance.' 39So they seized him, threw him out of the vineyard, and killed him. 40Now when the owner of the vineyard comes, what will he do to those tenants?" 41They said to him, "He will put those wretches to a miserable death, and lease the vineyard to other tenants who will give him the produce at the harvest time."

42Jesus said to them, "Have you never read in the scriptures:

'The stone that the builders rejected
     has become the cornerstone;*j*
this was the Lord's doing,
     and it is amazing in our eyes'?
43Therefore I tell you, the kingdom of God will be taken away from you and given to a people that produces the fruits of the kingdom.*k* 44The one who falls on this stone will be broken to pieces; and it will crush anyone on whom it falls."*l*

45When the chief priests and the Pharisees heard his parables, they realized that he was speaking about

---

i Gk *He*

j Or *keystone*
k Gk *the fruits of it*
l Other ancient authorities lack verse 44

---

played a much larger role in the narrative and his alleged rejection by "this generation" has already been exposed (11:16–18). **21:26** See note to *Mark* 11:32. **21:28–32** This illustration of true obedience to God, contrasting with hypocrisy (see 23:2–3), is peculiar to *Matthew*. The author ties it to its context by its final sentence, the application to John. This is a characteristic Matthean inclusion; see 18:35; 20:16 and introduction to *Matthew*. **21:31 the tax collectors and the prostitutes** In *Matthew* Jesus has typically associated with such individuals, considered outcasts according to conventional morality (9:10–11; 10:3; 11:19). On tax collectors, see notes to *Mark* 2:14–15. **21:33–46** *Matthew* continues to follow *Mark* (12:1–12; see notes there) closely. The main difference is that whereas *Mark* has a long series of individual servants sent to collect the rent, *Matthew* has two missions of several servants each. Perhaps this arises from the author's concern for pairs and two or three witnesses; see introduction to *Matthew*. In the simpler version of *Gospel of Thomas* 65–66, the parable does not envisage the destruction of the bad tenants (who seem to represent Jerusalem). **21:33 parable** This is really an allegory, since the various characters in the story obviously represent other people (see 21:45). **21:41 They said to him** This question from the audience is only in *Matthew*, where it seems to mean that Jesus has the chief priests and elders, who have become engrossed in the story, effectively condemning themselves (see 21:23, 24, 28, 31–32). This recalls the technique of Nathan the prophet when he used a parable to force King David to condemn himself (*2 Sam.* 12:1–7). **wretches to a miserable death** *Matthew* intensifies the punishment envisaged, perhaps with a view to the destruction of Jerusalem in 70 C.E. (see 22:7), which had apparently already occurred by the time of writing. **other tenants** Evidently the Gentiles. **21:42** *Ps.* 118:22 (LXX 117:22). This was a favorite passage among early Christians. After Jesus' death (rejection by builders) and resurrection (becoming the cornerstone), the application seemed obvious; see *Acts* 4:11; *1 Pet.* 2:7. This scripture is also cited in connection with the parable in *Gospel of Thomas* 65–66. **21:43** Only *Matthew* drives home the point of Gentile salvation. **21:44** Paralleled in *Luke* 20:18 (from Q?). This strange passage sounds as if it is meant to have some biblical resonances; *Isa.* 8:14 is a likely candidate. **21:45 the chief priests and the Pharisees** Remarkably, *Matthew* deviates from its source by introducing Pharisees here in Jerusalem. The author assumes that they are a standing part of the Jewish leadership everywhere, along with the Sadducees (see 22:15, 23, 34, 41); contrast *Luke*, which leaves the Pharisees at the triumphal entry

them. [46]They wanted to arrest him, but they feared the crowds, because they regarded him as a prophet.

The Parable of the Wedding Banquet

22 Once more Jesus spoke to them in parables, saying: [2]"The kingdom of heaven may be compared to a king who gave a wedding banquet for his son. [3]He sent his slaves to call those who had been invited to the wedding banquet, but they would not come. [4]Again he sent other slaves, saying, 'Tell those who have been invited: Look, I have prepared my dinner, my oxen and my fat calves have been slaughtered, and everything is ready; come to the wedding banquet.' [5]But they made light of it and went away, one to his farm, another to his business, [6]while the rest seized his slaves, mistreated them, and killed them. [7]The king was enraged. He sent his troops, destroyed those murderers, and burned their city. [8]Then he said to his slaves, 'The wedding is ready, but those invited were not worthy. [9]Go therefore into the main streets, and invite everyone you find to the wedding banquet.' [10]Those slaves went out into the streets and gathered all whom they found, both good and bad; so the wedding hall was filled with guests.

[11]"But when the king came in to see the guests, he noticed a man there who was not wearing a wedding robe, [12]and he said to him, 'Friend, how did you get in here without a wedding robe?' And he was speechless. [13]Then the king said to the attendants, 'Bind him hand and foot, and throw him into the outer darkness, where there will be weeping and gnashing of teeth.' [14]For many are called, but few are chosen."

The Question about Paying Taxes

[15]Then the Pharisees went and plotted to entrap him in what he said. [16]So they sent their disciples to him, along with the Herodians, saying, "Teacher, we know that you are sincere, and teach the way of God in accordance with truth, and show deference to no one; for you do not regard people with partiality. [17]Tell us, then, what you think. Is it lawful to pay taxes to the emperor, or not?" [18]But Jesus, aware of their malice, said, "Why are you putting me to the test, you hypocrites? [19]Show me the coin used for the tax." And they brought him a denarius. [20]Then he said to them, "Whose head is this, and whose title?" [21]They answered, "The emperor's." Then he said to them, "Give therefore to the emperor the things that are the emperor's, and to God the things that are God's." [22]When they heard this, they were amazed; and they left him and went away.

The Question about the Resurrection

[23]The same day some Sadducees came to him, saying there is no resurrection;[m] and they asked him a

---

m Other ancient authorities read *who say that there is no resurrection*

(19:39; 20:19). It is historically unlikely, in view of the information in Josephus and hints elsewhere, that the Pharisees as a group had any official role in government. **21:46** This assessment recalls the same fear expressed in 21:26. The leaders did not want to say anything about John because the people regarded him as a prophet. Thus the author drives a sharp wedge—which was implied, but not as clearly, in the earlier narrative—between the Jewish leaders and the people as a whole. Indeed, in 21:11 the crowds had declared Jesus to be a prophet. **22:1–10** The author departs briefly from *Mark* to include this parable of the feast, which is paralleled in *Luke* 14:15–24 (which sets it long before Jesus' entry into Jerusalem) and in *Gos. Thom.* 64:1. In both of these parallels, however, it is a genuine parable, making a general point about open table fellowship and lacking the allegorical references to the king, his son, the wedding, and the severe punishment (through a burned city!) of those who excused themselves. **22:2 *a king*** Part of *Matthew*'s allegorization (the king is God); the parallels speak only of a man. **wedding banquet for his son** Another allegorization peculiar to *Matthew*: Jesus is the son of the king, also the bridegroom of the church (see notes to 9:15; 25:1–13). **22:7** This punishment, which is out of all proportion to the crime of declining an invitation, seems to make sense only as an allusion to the destruction of Jerusalem in 70 C.E.—as God's punishment of the Jews for having declined to accept Jesus as Messiah and Savior. **22:11–14** The precise point of this addition, found only in *Matthew,* is perplexing. Presumably, the saying has something to do with the necessity of proper preparation through the right (*Matthew*'s) kind of Christian faith and practice. **22:13 *outer darkness . . . weeping and gnashing of teeth*** Typical Matthean language; see note to 8:12. **22:14** See *Barn.* 4.14. **22:15–40** With the following three stories, *Matthew* begins to follow *Mark* again. But *Matthew*'s author links the stories in a way that *Mark*'s had not, by presenting the Pharisees and Sadducees as more obviously in collusion (22:34). Their cooperation supports *Matthew*'s unique partnering of Pharisees and Sadducees earlier in the narrative (see notes to 3:7; 16:1, 5–12). On the historical problems, see note to 21:45. **22:15–22** Roman taxation (in addition to the many taxes—tithes—to be paid according to Jewish law, although it is uncertain how many people could manage all of the tithes) had been an extremely sensitive issue since the annexation of Judea as a Roman province in 6 C.E. See Josephus, *Ant.* 18.4–10, and note to *Mark* 12:14–15. The malice of the question (22:18) lies in its determination to make Jesus offend either the Romans or the Jews. **22:16 *the Herodians*** The author takes over this designation, the meaning of which has eluded scholars, from *Mark* 12:13; see note to *Mark* 3:6. **22:19–20** This *denarius* would not be a local coin but one struck in one of the large imperial mints; authorities in Judea and Galilee (whether Jewish or Roman) respected the Jewish prohibition of human images (*Exod.* 20:4). See note to *Mark* 12:15. **22:23–33** The issue of resurrection was important to the Sadducees because, although most Jews accepted the notion, the Sadducees rejected it. This may have been a function of their principled rejection of everything that was not laid out in the laws of Moses (Josephus, *Ant.* 13.197–198), for resurrection and afterlife are not taught there. See notes to *Mark* 12:18–27.

question, saying, 24"Teacher, Moses said, 'If a man dies childless, his brother shall marry the widow, and raise up children for his brother.' 25Now there were seven brothers among us; the first married, and died childless, leaving the widow to his brother. 26The second did the same, so also the third, down to the seventh. 27Last of all, the woman herself died. 28In the resurrection, then, whose wife of the seven will she be? For all of them had married her."

29Jesus answered them, "You are wrong, because you know neither the scriptures nor the power of God. 30For in the resurrection they neither marry nor are given in marriage, but are like angels[n] in heaven. 31And as for the resurrection of the dead, have you not read what was said to you by God, 32'I am the God of Abraham, the God of Isaac, and the God of Jacob'? He is God not of the dead, but of the living." 33And when the crowd heard it, they were astounded at his teaching.

The Greatest Commandment

34When the Pharisees heard that he had silenced the Sadducees, they gathered together, 35and one of them, a lawyer, asked him a question to test him.

36"Teacher, which commandment in the law is the greatest?" 37He said to him, " 'You shall love the Lord your God with all your heart, and with all your soul, and with all your mind.' 38This is the greatest and first commandment. 39And a second is like it: 'You shall love your neighbor as yourself.' 40On these two commandments hang all the law and the prophets."

The Question about David's Son

41Now while the Pharisees were gathered together, Jesus asked them this question: 42"What do you think of the Messiah?[o] Whose son is he?" They said to him, "The son of David." 43He said to them, "How is it then that David by the Spirit[p] calls him Lord, saying,

44 'The Lord said to my Lord,
    "Sit at my right hand,
        until I put your enemies under your feet" '?
45If David thus calls him Lord, how can he be his son?" 46No one was able to give him an answer, nor from that day did anyone dare to ask him any more questions.

Jesus Denounces Scribes and Pharisees

23 Then Jesus said to the crowds and to his disciples, 2"The scribes and the Pharisees sit on

---

n Other ancient authorities add *of God*

o Or *Christ*
p Gk *in spirit*

22:24 The practice of levirate marriage is mandated in *Deut.* 25:5. See note to *Mark* 12:18–23. **22:30** *like angels in heaven* See Paul's description of the spiritual resurrection body in *1 Cor.* 15:35–50. **22:31–33** Jesus draws upon *Exod.* 3:6, where Moses encounters God at the burning bush. It is important that he use the books of Moses to prove his case, since the Sadducees trust only these. See note to *Mark* 12:26–27. **22:34–40** The question of the greatest commandment was also current in Judaism of the time. Hillel is said to have summarized the whole law in the golden rule (*b. Shabbat* 31a). Perhaps because *Matthew* makes this an exchange with a Pharisaic lawyer rather than a scribe (*Mark* 12:28), the author omits the scribe's response and Jesus' positive assessment. See notes to *Mark* 12:28–33. **22:34** *Matthew* makes the collusion between Pharisees and Sadducees clearer than *Mark* had. **22:37** *Deut.* 6:4. This was the foundation of the Shema, a confession made twice a day by observant Jews and a central part of the Jewish liturgy. *Matthew*'s Jesus omits the 1st part (contrast *Mark* 12:29), perhaps because it is not strictly a commandment. **22:39** *Lev.* 19:18. **22:41–45** This passage, about the relationship of the Messiah to David, is perplexing if taken at face value. In *Mark* 12:35–37, the parallel plainly challenged the notion that the Messiah should be a descendant of David. But *Mark* does not have any great investment in Jesus as Son of David. Because *Matthew* has such an investment (see 1:1 and notes to 9:27; 12:23), it is odd that this author should intensify the controversy by having Jesus initiate the pointed question *"Whose son is he?"* The main possibilities seem to be (a) that the author has unwittingly taken over a passage that conflicts with his larger themes or (b) that he wishes to display Jesus' rhetorical abilities: Jesus could even prove, if he wished, that the Messiah was not a descendant of David (although, of course, he is). **22:44–46** Jesus argues from *Ps.* 110:1 (LXX 109:1). See note to *Mark* 12:35–37. **23:1–39** The author now abruptly departs from *Mark*, which has only a brief reference about Jesus' critique of the scribes (12:37–40), to mount a sustained attack on the alleged hypocrisy of the scribes and Pharisees. This takes the form of seven woes in the 2d person (*"Woe to you"*); Jesus continues to address the scribes and Pharisees with whom he has been in conversation in *Matthew* 22. These woes often recall scattered statements made earlier in the narrative. Much of this material is paralleled in *Luke* 11 and so is commonly traced to Q. In *Luke*, the context is different: Jesus denounces the lawyers and Pharisees while eating in a Pharisee's home, long before his trip to Jerusalem. It would be easier for scholarship on *Matthew* if this speech could be considered of one piece with *Matthew* 24–25, to form Jesus' fifth and final major discourse (see introduction to *Matthew*). It is somewhat inconvenient, however, that *Matthew* 23 has a focused theme and style quite different from those of *Matthew* 24–25, that it occurs in a different place and for a different audience, and that there is a clear break between *Matthew* 23 and 24 (24:1–2). **23:1** *to the crowds and to his disciples* *Matthew* emphasizes the wedge between the Jewish leaders, who reject him, and the crowds, who are receptive to him (see note to 21:46). **23:2–3** In preparation for the seven woes, Jesus accuses the scribes and Pharisees of classic hypocrisy: they do not practice what they teach, although their teaching is admirable in itself. Accord between word and deed was the acid test of true philosophy in Jesus' day; it was much discussed (Seneca, *Epistles*

Moses' seat; [3]therefore, do whatever they teach you and follow it; but do not do as they do, for they do not practice what they teach. [4]They tie up heavy burdens, hard to bear,[q] and lay them on the shoulders of others; but they themselves are unwilling to lift a finger to move them. [5]They do all their deeds to be seen by others; for they make their phylacteries broad and their fringes long. [6]They love to have the place of honor at banquets and the best seats in the synagogues, [7]and to be greeted with respect in the marketplaces, and to have people call them rabbi. [8]But you are not to be called rabbi, for you have one teacher, and you are all students.[r] [9]And call no one your father on earth, for you have one Father—the one in heaven. [10]Nor are you to be called instructors, for you have one instructor, the Messiah.[s] [11]The greatest among you will be your servant. [12]All who exalt themselves will be humbled, and all who humble themselves will be exalted.

[13]"But woe to you, scribes and Pharisees, hypocrites! For you lock people out of the kingdom of heaven. For you do not go in yourselves, and when others are going in, you stop them.[t] [15]Woe to you, scribes and Pharisees, hypocrites! For you cross sea and land to make a single convert, and you make the new convert twice as much a child of hell[u] as yourselves.

[16]"Woe to you, blind guides, who say, 'Whoever swears by the sanctuary is bound by nothing, but whoever swears by the gold of the sanctuary is bound

---

q Other ancient authorities lack *hard to bear*
r Gk *brothers*

s Or *the Christ*
t Other authorities add here (or after verse 12) verse 14, *Woe to you, scribes and Pharisees, hypocrites! For you devour widows' houses and for the sake of appearance you make long prayers; therefore you will receive the greater condemnation.*
u Gk *Gehenna*

20.2; Dio of Prusa, *Discourses* 70.3; Plutarch, *Stoic Self-Contradictions* 1; Epictetus, *Discourses* 3.26.8–23). This incidental endorsement of the Pharisees' teaching, however, stands in some tension with earlier segments, which condemned it (15:14; 16:12). **23:2** *sit on Moses' seat* At least for the moment, *Matthew*'s Jesus acknowledges their authority as legitimate interpreters of Moses' laws. This agrees with Josephus's claim that the Pharisees were recognized and widely followed experts in the laws (*J.W.* 1.110; 2.161; *Ant.* 17.41; 18.12–15). It is debated whether the phrase might have a more literal meaning: the president's seat in the synagogue, such as archaeologists turned up in the 2d- or 3d-century synagogue of Chorazin. See 23:6. **23:3** *whatever they teach . . . follow it* An emphatic command, used again of Jesus' own teaching in 28:20. **23:4–12** Before he begins the woes, *Matthew*'s Jesus provides examples of the alleged hypocrisy and gives instructions about behavior that would preclude such pitfalls among his own followers. **23:4** See *Luke* 11:46. **23:5** *phylacteries* Tefillin, worn by male Jews at prayer in observance of *Deut.* 6:8; 11:18, were small leather cases containing sections from the Torah in minute writing (*Exod.* 13:1–10, 11–16). These were tied to the forehead and left forearm with leather straps. Tefillin have been discovered at Qumran. The English word "phylactery" transliterates the Gk term "protection device," which suggests that Greek observers and/or some Jews viewed these objects as amulets to ward off evil powers. The Aramaic term *tefillin* means "prayers" or perhaps "separation markers." *fringes* These are the corner tassels, or *tsitsith*, worn by Jewish males in observance of *Num.* 15:37–41; see *Matt.* 14:36 and note to *Mark* 6:56. **23:6–7** Here *Matthew* follows *Mark* 12:38–39. **23:7–8** In later (rabbinic) Judaism, "rabbi" would come to designate an ordained teacher who had gone through a recognized program of study and accreditation. But it is doubtful that the word (lit. "my great one"; thus chief, lord, sir, master) was such a proper title in the 1st century; it was simply a term of respect for a socially significant person. *Matthew*'s debate with contemporary Judaism is evidenced by the author's singular dislike for this word. Although his major source has people address Jesus as rabbi (*Mark* 9:5; 10:51; 11:21), he systematically removes it from their lips except in the case of Judas Iscariot (26:25, 49)—a telling exception. **23:11** Recalling 20:26–28; see *John* 13:12–15. **23:12** A classic statement of eschatological reversal in the tradition of the prophets; see note to 5:3–12; also 19:30; *Luke* 18:14. Whereas the hope for such reversal was typically held in the face of political oppression by Israel's enemies, *Matthew*'s Jesus makes it a personal issue for Jewish leaders. **23:13** A widely paralleled accusation; see *Luke* 11:52; *Gos. Thom.* 39:1; 102. **23:15** A fascinating claim, unique in *Matthew* and among the other early Christian texts. Although there is considerable evidence that Judaism in Jesus' time attracted converts (Tacitus, *Histories* 5.5; Juvenal, *Satires* 5.14.96–106; Epictetus, *Discourses* 2.9.20) and that at least some individual Jews encouraged these conversions (Josephus, *Ant.* 20.17–96), this is the only passage that identifies Pharisees as missionaries. The reference may be to proselytizing *within* Jewish circles—to attract members to the Pharisaic party. The author himself may be a convert to *Christian* Judaism or may serve a group composed of such people and so be sensitive to this issue (see introduction to *Matthew*). In any case, the charge shows that *Matthew*'s Jesus is not challenging an inconsequential opponent; the Pharisees had considerable influence. **23:16–22** This sounds much like an in-house Jewish debate, such as the Mishnah posits of the Pharisees and Sadducees, who likewise accused each other of inconsistency in their prescriptions (e.g., *m. Yad.* 4:6–7). Oaths were a matter of much discussion (see CD 9.1–12; 15.1–4; 16.1–13). They were forbidden by the Essenes for the same reason that Jesus gave in 5:33–37 (Josephus, *J.W.* 2.135). The Mishnah contains a tractate concerning vows (*Nedarim*—forbidding certain things to be used) and one concerning oaths (*Shevu'ot*—forbidding the swearer to do a certain thing). Strangely, *Matthew*'s Jesus here seems to enter the debate about oaths whereas he had earlier prohibited them (5:34). **23:16** *blind guides* See 15:14. The label carries a particular sting in *Matthew* because of the author's

by the oath.' [17]You blind fools! For which is greater, the gold or the sanctuary that has made the gold sacred? [18]And you say, 'Whoever swears by the altar is bound by nothing, but whoever swears by the gift that is on the altar is bound by the oath.' [19]How blind you are! For which is greater, the gift or the altar that makes the gift sacred? [20]So whoever swears by the altar, swears by it and by everything on it; [21]and whoever swears by the sanctuary, swears by it and by the one who dwells in it; [22]and whoever swears by heaven, swears by the throne of God and by the one who is seated upon it.

[23]"Woe to you, scribes and Pharisees, hypocrites! For you tithe mint, dill, and cummin, and have neglected the weightier matters of the law: justice and mercy and faith. It is these you ought to have practiced without neglecting the others. [24]You blind guides! You strain out a gnat but swallow a camel!

[25]"Woe to you, scribes and Pharisees, hypocrites! For you clean the outside of the cup and of the plate, but inside they are full of greed and self-indulgence. [26]You blind Pharisee! First clean the inside of the cup,[v] so that the outside also may become clean.

[27]"Woe to you, scribes and Pharisees, hypocrites! For you are like whitewashed tombs, which on the outside look beautiful, but inside they are full of bones of the dead and of all kinds of filth. [28]So you also on the outside look righteous to others, but inside you are full of hypocrisy and lawlessness.

[29]"Woe to you, scribes and Pharisees, hypocrites! For you build the tombs of the prophets and decorate the graves of the righteous, [30]and you say, 'If we had lived in the days of our ancestors, we would not have taken part with them in shedding the blood of the prophets.' [31]Thus you testify against yourselves that you are descendants of those who murdered the prophets. [32]Fill up, then, the measure of your ancestors. [33]You snakes, you brood of vipers! How can you escape being sentenced to hell?[w] [34]Therefore I send you prophets, sages, and scribes, some of whom you will kill and crucify, and some you will flog in your synagogues and pursue from town to town, [35]so that

---

v Other ancient authorities add *and of the plate*
w Gk *Gehenna*

---

constant resort to *Isaiah,* which accuses Israel of blindness and deafness (e.g., *Isa.* 6:9–10); see notes to 11:5, 15; 13:14–15; 15:14. **23:23–24** See *Luke* 11:42. Tithing ("giving a tenth of") produce was commanded in the Bible for the support of the Levites and priests (*Lev.* 27:30–33; *Num.* 18:8–32; *Deut.* 14:22–29), and the Mishnah contains several tractates clarifying the matter (*Demai, Ma'aserot, Ma'aser Sheni*). Some Christians later transposed the practice into support for Christian clergy (*Did.* 13.3–7). *Matthew's* Jesus does not challenge the practice (see 23:23, "without neglecting the others") but, as the prophets and Pharisees would also have done, calls for attention to basic issues of justice and mercy (see *Hos.* 6:6). He chooses some of the smallest herbs to make his point. **23:24** *swallow a camel* Once again, *Matthew's* Jesus uses the camel—the largest animal commonly seen—to create an absurd image; see 19:24. **23:25–26** Jesus' charge resonates with deep sensitivities in the Gk-speaking world to the contrast between outward impression, or *seeming,* and really *being;* see note to 23:2–3. See *Luke* 11:39–41; *Gospel of Thomas* 89. On washing cups and plates, see *Mark* 7:4, which was omitted by the author of *Matthew* in the parallel passage (15:1–20). **23:27–28** It seems likely from this note that Jews of Jesus' time painted tombs white so that people could avoid "corpse uncleanness"—the impurity associated with corpses that would temporarily prevent one from visiting the temple (*Num.* 19:11–20). *Luke* 11:44 makes a different point from the parallel saying: the Pharisees are ineffective, like unmarked tombs that people walk over unwittingly. **23:32** This 7th woe seems unfair: the Pharisees disavow the reported deeds of their ancestors, but *Matthew's* Jesus takes their very admission of ancestry as proof of guilt by association. See the parallel in *Luke* 11:47–48. Nevertheless, early Christians popularized the notion that Jews were killers of the prophets (see *1 Thess.* 2:14–16; *Acts* 7:52; *Heb.* 11:36–38). This view helped the Christians understand their own perception of persecution (see 23:34). **23:33–36** Part justification (23:35), part application (23:34) of what Jesus has just said: Christian prophets will suffer the alleged historical fate of the classical prophets. **23:33** This recalls the Baptist's charge in 3:7, which seems to confirm that the author still has in mind John's comments about Jewish ancestry (3:8 par. 23:29–32). **hell** Lit. Gehenna (see note to 5:22; 11:15). **23:34–36** This saying closely parallels *2 Esd.* 1:32, a Christian work (the first part is also known as *5 Ezra*) of the 2d century or later. **23:34** *I send you* The parallel in *Luke* 11:49–51 has the "wisdom of God" as sender. Jesus' unabashed assumption of authority here fits with *Matthew's* entire presentation (see 5:21–48; 11:25–30; 12:6, 41–42; 17:24–27). **prophets** Christian prophets (*1 Cor.* 12:28; 14:5; *Luke* 11:49; *Eph.* 2:20; 3:6; *Did.* 10.7–13.7) of the author's own time, whom he places in a continuous line with the old biblical prophets. **sages, and scribes** The parallel in *Luke* (11:49) has "apostles." *Sages* is puzzling because *Matthew* has used the word only in a negative sense before (11:25), but the Hebrew equivalent of "sage" was a common term for a revered teacher in later Judaism. The notion of Christian *scribes* in *Matthew's* circles is particularly intriguing in light of the "scribe . . . trained for the kingdom" in 13:52. **kill . . . pursue** The intense conflict between *Matthew's* Christians and the Jewish leaders is assumed by numerous other Christian texts of the period (e.g., *2 Cor.* 11:23–28; *Acts* 3–28). See the similar predictions in 10:17–18. **23:35–36** The author plainly intends to summarize all of the alleged murders by the Jews' ancestors reported in the Bible. Cain and Abel were the sons of Adam and Eve (*Gen.* 4:1–16); Cain's murder of his brother was the 1st homicide in the story. It is unclear why this murder should be charged to Jesus' generation. The Bible mentions about thirty men with the name

upon you may come all the righteous blood shed on earth, from the blood of righteous Abel to the blood of Zechariah son of Barachiah, whom you murdered between the sanctuary and the altar. ³⁶Truly I tell you, all this will come upon this generation.

The Lament over Jerusalem

³⁷"Jerusalem, Jerusalem, the city that kills the prophets and stones those who are sent to it! How often have I desired to gather your children together as a hen gathers her brood under her wings, and you were not willing! ³⁸See, your house is left to you, desolate.ˣ ³⁹For I tell you, you will not see me again until you say, 'Blessed is the one who comes in the name of the Lord.'"

The Destruction of the Temple Foretold

24 As Jesus came out of the temple and was going away, his disciples came to point out to him the buildings of the temple. ²Then he asked them, "You see all these, do you not? Truly I tell you, not one stone will be left here upon another; all will be thrown down."

Signs of the End of the Age

³When he was sitting on the Mount of Olives, the disciples came to him privately, saying, "Tell us, when will this be, and what will be the sign of your coming and of the end of the age?" ⁴Jesus answered them, "Beware that no one leads you astray. ⁵For many will come in my name, saying, 'I am the Messiah!'ʸ and they will lead many astray. ⁶And you will hear of wars and rumors of wars; see that you are not alarmed; for this must take place, but the end is not yet. ⁷For nation will rise against nation, and kingdom against kingdom, and there will be faminesᶻ and earthquakes in various places: ⁸all this is but the beginning of the birth pangs.

---

x Other ancient authorities lack *desolate*

y Or *the Christ*
z Other ancient authorities add *and pestilences*

Zechariah. The description of this man's death, however, identifies him as the priest and son of Jehoiada (not Barachiah), killed by order of King Joash of Judah for his prophecies against the king (*2 Chr.* 24:20–22). The author of *2 Chronicles,* and therefore subsequent Jewish tradition (Josephus, *Ant.* 9.168–169), condemned Joash for this crime. *Matthew's* identification of this Zechariah as the son of Barachiah—absent from the parallel in *Luke* 11:51 (from Q?)—is a mistake resulting from the identification of him with the prophet who wrote the book *Zechariah* (*Zech.* 1:1). That both *Matthew* and *Luke* should have Jesus assume that the Bible extends from *Genesis* to *2 Chronicles* indicates that at least some Jews in Jesus' day recognized a complete Bible in the same arrangement as the later rabbinic Bible: Torah, prophets, and writings, ending with *2 Chronicles.* This arrangement differs dramatically from the standard arrangement in the LXX, which influenced the Christian OT. **23:36 *all this will come upon this generation*** This dire prediction of catastrophe in recompense for all the crimes committed in biblical history is most easily understood with reference to the destruction of Jerusalem in 70 (see also 23:38), which Christians understood as divine punishment for the Jews' rejection of Jesus (see 21:33–44; 22:7). **23:37–39** Jesus' lament summarizes what he has just said: the killing of prophets old and new, his efforts to reach Jerusalem rebuffed, divine punishment in the form of the temple's destruction. The saying is paralleled almost verbatim in *Luke* 13:34–35, long before Jesus has reached Jerusalem. See *2 Esd.* 1:30–33. **23:37** Given that this is Jesus' first reported trip to Jerusalem and only his 2d day in the city, it is difficult to make sense of his *often* having tried to reach Jerusalem in the past with prophets and messengers except as a saying of the resurrected Jesus to the church through the Spirit. **23:38** The temple was often known as God's "house" in Jerusalem, since God was believed to inhabit it (*2 Sam.* 7:5, 11). The reference is to the temple's destruction in 70 C.E. as punishment of the Jews for their failure to respond to Jesus (see 21:33–44; 22:7; 23:36). **23:39** The quotation is from *Ps.* 118:26, which the crowds recited as Jesus entered Jerusalem the day before (21:9). The text subtly indicts the scribes and Pharisees for having failed to join in the crowd's welcome—along with a threat they shall welcome Jesus when he comes in glory (26:64; see note to 13:36–43). **24:1–25:46** Jesus' final (fifth? see note to 23:1–39) speech in *Matthew* returns to follow *Mark* (ch. 13). More strictly, one might put the beginning of the speech at 24:3 or 4, once Jesus has moved over to the Mount of Olives. The author fills out his source material from *Mark* with three lengthy parables about coming judgment, a saying about watchfulness and the flood, and the gripping scene of the judgment of nations (or Gentiles). Much of this non-Markan material is paralleled in *Luke* and *Thomas* and so may come from Q. **24:1** The temple had been rebuilt by Herod the Great on a grand scale (Josephus, *Ant.* 15.308–402), and the renovations were still being completed in Jesus' day. The whole complex was magnificent, set on a massive raised platform. See note to *Mark* 13:1. **24:2** Another prediction of Jerusalem's destruction (see 21:41; 22:7; 23:36, 38), but this one is taken over from *Mark* 13:2. **24:3 *the Mount of Olives*** The high hill immediately to the east of Jerusalem; it affords an excellent overview of the Temple Mount and the east side of Jerusalem. ***disciples came to him privately*** *Matthew* takes this over from *Mark* (13:3), where Jesus' secret teaching is a developed theme (see *Mark* 4:10–12). It is not clear that *Matthew* has much stake in this privacy; the author substitutes *disciples* for *Mark's* inner circle. ***of your coming and of the end of the age*** *Matthew* has spoken often of Jesus' (the Son of Man's) coming in glory and judgment; see note to 13:36–43. **24:5 *saying, "I am the Messiah."*** The 1st century saw many charismatic leaders who either thought themselves to be or were thought by others to be the awaited Anointed One (Messiah); see Josephus, *J.W.* 2.42–43, 224, 232, 255. See also *Did.* 16.3. **24:6–7** See note to *Mark* 13:8.

Persecutions Foretold

9"Then they will hand you over to be tortured and will put you to death, and you will be hated by all nations because of my name. 10Then many will fall away,[a] and they will betray one another and hate one another. 11And many false prophets will arise and lead many astray. 12And because of the increase of lawlessness, the love of many will grow cold. 13But the one who endures to the end will be saved. 14And this good news[b] of the kingdom will be proclaimed throughout the world, as a testimony to all the nations; and then the end will come.

The Desolating Sacrilege

15"So when you see the desolating sacrilege standing in the holy place, as was spoken of by the prophet Daniel (let the reader understand), 16then those in Judea must flee to the mountains; 17the one on the housetop must not go down to take what is in the house; 18the one in the field must not turn back to get a coat. 19Woe to those who are pregnant and to those who are nursing infants in those days! 20Pray that your flight may not be in winter or on a sabbath. 21For at that time there will be great suffering, such as has not been from the beginning of the world until now, no, and never will be. 22And if those days had not been cut short, no one would be saved; but for the sake of the elect those days will be cut short. 23Then if anyone says to you, 'Look! Here is the Messiah!'[c] or 'There he is!'—do not believe it. 24For

false messiahs[d] and false prophets will appear and produce great signs and omens, to lead astray, if possible, even the elect. 25Take note, I have told you beforehand. 26So, if they say to you, 'Look! He is in the wilderness,' do not go out. If they say, 'Look! He is in the inner rooms,' do not believe it. 27For as the lightning comes from the east and flashes as far as the west, so will be the coming of the Son of Man. 28Wherever the corpse is, there the vultures will gather.

The Coming of the Son of Man

29"Immediately after the suffering of those days
the sun will be darkened,
    and the moon will not give its light;
the stars will fall from heaven,
    and the powers of heaven will be shaken.
30Then the sign of the Son of Man will appear in heaven, and then all the tribes of the earth will mourn, and they will see 'the Son of Man coming on the clouds of heaven' with power and great glory. 31And he will send out his angels with a loud trumpet call, and they will gather his elect from the four winds, from one end of heaven to the other.

The Lesson of the Fig Tree

32"From the fig tree learn its lesson: as soon as its branch becomes tender and puts forth its leaves, you know that summer is near. 33So also, when you see all these things, you know that he[e] is near, at the very gates. 34Truly I tell you, this generation will not pass

---

a Or *stumble*
b Or *gospel*
c Or *the Christ*

d Or *christs*
e Or *it*

24:9 See *10:17–19. Matthew* has transferred some of *Mark*'s apocalyptic speech (13:9–12) to the earlier missionary speech. **24:10–13** *Matthew* develops more fully than *Mark* the apostasy or falling away of new Christians, which was a significant problem. See 13:19–22; *Heb.* 6:4–8; 10:26–31; Pliny the Younger, *Letters* 10.96. **24:15** The reference is to a pagan altar set up over the altar of the Jerusalem temple by the Seleucid King Antiochus IV in the 4th decade of the 2d century B.C.E.; see *Dan.* 9:27; 11:31; 12:11 (see *1 Macc.* 1:54). *Daniel* was an influential book in the 1st century, as many groups looked forward to some kind of intervention from God to rescue them from perceived oppression. They reinterpreted the book's judgments upon the Seleucids as judgments on the Romans. See note to *Mark* 13:14. **24:20** *on a sabbath* In an effort to implement the Bible's rather vague strictures against work on the Sabbath (*Exod.* 20:8–11; *Deut.* 5:12–15), later Jews developed traditions about the distance one should travel and what one should carry on that day (almost nothing; *Jer.* 17:21–22). The Sabbath distance assumed in rabbinic literature of the 2d century and later, possibly representing the 1st-century Pharisees' view, was two thousand cubits (one thousand yards, nearly one kilometer, or more than half a mile); *m. Eruvin* 4:3; 5:7. Other Jewish groups were stricter, permitting only one thousand cubits—less than half a kilometer and one-third of a mile; CD 10.14–12.5. Only *Matthew* includes this note about the Sabbath, as an addition to *Mark* 13:18. This suggests that *Matthew*'s readers were expected to maintain Jewish law rigorously; see 5:17–20; 23:24. **24:24–26** See notes to 24:5 and *Did.* 16.3. **24:27** The glorious coming of the Son of Man is a central theme in *Matthew*; see note to 13:36–43. This saying is paralleled in *Luke* 17:24. **24:28** The precise relevance of this saying here is unclear, unless it means simply that when the Son of Man comes, it will be obvious (but why *corpse* and *vultures*?). The parallel saying in *Luke* 17:37 makes a little more sense, inasmuch as Jesus is responding to the question "Where?" **24:29** This is standard apocalyptic imagery; see *Testament of Moses* 10.4–6; *Sib. Or.* 8.170–212; *Did.* 16.6. **24:30** An allusion to *Dan.* 7:13, where a figure like a human being, representing victorious Israel, ascends to heaven on a cloud to meet God. See Jesus' answer to the high priest in *Matt.* 26:64. *Matthew* follows *Mark* in expecting the *Son of Man* (now a mysterious person of great power) to *descend* from heaven at the end of the age. **24:31** See note to 13:36–43; also *1 Thess.* 4:16. **24:32–36** *Matthew* follows *Mark* 13:28–32 closely. The imminence of the end (24:33–34), within the lifetime of the first readers, is a common expectation in both works; see 10:23; 16:28.

away until all these things have taken place. [35]Heaven and earth will pass away, but my words will not pass away.

The Necessity for Watchfulness

[36]"But about that day and hour no one knows, neither the angels of heaven, nor the Son,[f] but only the Father. [37]For as the days of Noah were, so will be the coming of the Son of Man. [38]For as in those days before the flood they were eating and drinking, marrying and giving in marriage, until the day Noah entered the ark, [39]and they knew nothing until the flood came and swept them all away, so too will be the coming of the Son of Man. [40]Then two will be in the field; one will be taken and one will be left. [41]Two women will be grinding meal together; one will be taken and one will be left. [42]Keep awake therefore, for you do not know on what day[g] your Lord is coming. [43]But understand this: if the owner of the house had known in what part of the night the thief was coming, he would have stayed awake and would not have let his house be broken into. [44]Therefore you also must be ready, for the Son of Man is coming at an unexpected hour.

The Faithful or the Unfaithful Slave

[45]"Who then is the faithful and wise slave, whom his master has put in charge of his household, to give the other slaves[h] their allowance of food at the proper time? [46]Blessed is that slave whom his master will find at work when he arrives. [47]Truly I tell you, he will put that one in charge of all his possessions. [48]But if that wicked slave says to himself, 'My master is delayed,' [49]and he begins to beat his fellow slaves, and eats and drinks with drunkards, [50]the master of that slave will come on a day when he does not expect him and at an hour that he does not know. [51]He will cut him in pieces[i] and put him with the hypocrites, where there will be weeping and gnashing of teeth.

The Parable of the Ten Bridesmaids

25 "Then the kingdom of heaven will be like this. Ten bridesmaids[j] took their lamps and went to meet the bridegroom.[k] [2]Five of them were foolish, and five were wise. [3]When the foolish took their lamps, they took no oil with them; [4]but the wise took flasks of oil with their lamps. [5]As the bridegroom was delayed, all of them became drowsy and slept. [6]But at midnight there was a shout, 'Look! Here is the bridegroom! Come out to meet him.' [7]Then all those bridesmaids[j] got up and trimmed their lamps. [8]The foolish said to the wise, 'Give us some of your oil, for our lamps are going out.' [9]But the wise replied, 'No! there will not be enough for you and for us; you had better go to the dealers and buy some for yourselves.' [10]And while they went to buy it, the bridegroom came, and those who were ready went with him into the wedding banquet; and the door was shut. [11]Later

---

f Other ancient authorities lack *nor the Son*
g Other ancient authorities read *at what hour*
h Gk *to give them*

i Or *cut him off*
j Gk *virgins*
k Other ancient authorities add *and the bride*

24:37–39 The famous story of the flood and Noah's rescue is in *Genesis* 6–8. *Matthew* departs from *Mark* here, but there is a parallel in *Luke* 17:26–27. **24:40–41** It is often assumed (in light of Paul's scenario; see *1 Thess.* 1:10; 4:16–17) that those taken are the evacuated believers who are caught up in the air; those left must face the wrath of God. But in the close parallel in *Gos. Thom.* 61:1, the one left is the one who survives; to be taken is to die. **24:42–44** See *Luke* 12:39–40. Watching for the Lord's return as for a thief in the night is a common image in early Christian texts; see *1 Thess.* 5:2–4; *Rev.* 3:3; 16:15; *2 Pet.* 3:10. Even *Thomas*, which does not develop the theme of Jesus' return, uses the image of the householder who guards against the thief to illustrate protecting oneself from the world (21:3; 103). This parallel reminds us that Jesus' original saying need not have had the eschatological application that others placed upon it. **24:42** Since this challenge will be repeated in 25:13, after the parable of the bridesmaids, *Matthew* has created another inclusion (see introduction to *Matthew*). **24:45–51** Jesus' words here (as in the parallel *Luke* 12:41–46) slide into a parable without Jesus' making a formal introduction. This seems to warn those leading the church not to be either lax or tyrannical, or they will suffer the same fate as the *hypocrites* (see next note). **24:51** *cut him in pieces* Another of *Matthew*'s grisly images (see 18:34; 22:7; 24:28, although this one is shared by *Luke* 12:46) and an overreaction in the simple terms of the story. The Gk verb means "to cut [something or someone] in two." **with the hypocrites, where there will be weeping and gnashing of teeth** The *hypocrites* have been clearly identified in *Matthew* as the Jewish leaders; see 6:2, 5, 16; 15:7; 22:18; 23:13, 14, 15. See *Did.* 8.1. They are the sons of the kingdom consigned to the place of weeping and teeth gnashing; see 8:12; 22:13. **25:1–13** This parable, illustrating the need for constant vigilance, is found only in *Matthew*. The main point is that the delay of Jesus' return should not make Christians less prepared for it (25:5): the foolish bridesmaids are those who fail to take enough oil for the duration. The delay of Jesus' return posed a significant problem even in the first Christian generation; see *1 Thess.* 5:1–12; *Luke* 19:11; somewhat later, *2 Pet.* 3:3–10. This parable fits the early Christian situation well. The image of Jesus as the bridegroom of the church was common; see note to 9:14–15; 22:2. **25:1** This statement, recalling 24:42, creates a typically Matthean inclusion, tying in the parable to Jesus' teaching; see introduction to *Matthew*. **25:10–11** The closed door and the refusal of entry have a partial parallel in *Luke* 12:42–46.

the other bridesmaids*l* came also, saying, 'Lord, lord, open to us.' 12But he replied, 'Truly I tell you, I do not know you.' 13Keep awake therefore, for you know neither the day nor the hour.*m*

The Parable of the Talents

14"For it is as if a man, going on a journey, summoned his slaves and entrusted his property to them; 15to one he gave five talents,*n* to another two, to another one, to each according to his ability. Then he went away. 16The one who had received the five talents went off at once and traded with them, and made five more talents. 17In the same way, the one who had the two talents made two more talents. 18But the one who had received the one talent went off and dug a hole in the ground and hid his master's money. 19After a long time the master of those slaves came and settled accounts with them. 20Then the one who had received the five talents came forward, bringing five more talents, saying, 'Master, you handed over to me five talents; see, I have made five more talents.' 21His master said to him, 'Well done, good and trustworthy slave; you have been trustworthy in a few things, I will put you in charge of many things; enter into the joy of your master.' 22And the one with the two talents also came forward, saying, 'Master, you handed over to me two talents; see, I have made two more talents.' 23His master said to him, 'Well done, good and trustworthy slave; you have been trustworthy in a few things, I will put you in charge of many things; enter into the joy of your master.' 24Then the one who had received the one talent also came forward, saying, 'Master, I knew that you were a harsh man, reaping where you did not sow, and gathering where you did not scatter seed; 25so I was afraid, and I went and hid your talent in the ground. Here you have what is yours.' 26But his master replied, 'You wicked and lazy slave! You knew, did you, that I reap where I did not sow, and gather where I did not scatter? 27Then you ought to have invested my money with the bankers, and on my return I would have received what was my own with interest. 28So take the talent from him, and give it to the one with the ten talents. 29For to all those who have, more will be given, and they will have an abundance; but from those who have nothing, even what they have will be taken away. 30As for this worthless slave, throw him into the outer darkness, where there will be weeping and gnashing of teeth.'

The Judgment of the Nations

31"When the Son of Man comes in his glory, and all the angels with him, then he will sit on the throne of his glory. 32All the nations will be gathered before him, and he will separate people one from another as a shepherd separates the sheep from the goats, 33and he will put the sheep at his right hand and the goats at the left. 34Then the king will say to those at his right hand, 'Come, you that are blessed by my Father, inherit the kingdom prepared for you from the foundation of the world; 35for I was hungry and you gave me food, I was thirsty and you gave me something to drink, I was a stranger and you welcomed me, 36I was naked and you gave me clothing, I was sick and you took care of me, I was in prison and you visited me.' 37Then the righteous will answer him, 'Lord, when was it that we saw you hungry and gave you food, or thirsty and gave you something to drink? 38And when was it that we saw you a stranger and welcomed you, or naked and gave you clothing? 39And when was it that we saw you sick or in prison and visited you?' 40And the king will answer them, 'Truly I tell you, just as you did it to one of the least of these who are members of my family,*o* you did it to me.' 41Then he will say to those at his left hand, 'You that are accursed, depart from me into the eternal fire prepared for the devil and his angels; 42for I was hungry and you gave me no food, I was thirsty and you gave me nothing to drink, 43I was a stranger and you did not welcome me, naked and you did not give me

---

l Gk *virgins*
m Other ancient authorities add *in which the Son of Man is coming*
n A talent was worth more than fifteen years' wages of a laborer

o Gk *these my brothers*

25:14–30 *Matthew*'s parable of the talents illustrates the need for continued effort before the property owner's return. **25:15** *talents* A talent was worth about 6,000 drachmas or denarii: a vast sum of money for the average person. See note to 18:24. **25:29** A widely reported saying of Jesus. See 13:12; also *Mark* 4:25; *Luke* 8:18; *Gospel of Thomas* 41. **25:30** A characteristically Matthean ending, making clear the application to the terrifying events about to happen. See 8:12; 22:13; 24:51. Once again the unfaithful Christians share the same fate as the "hypocrites." **25:31–46** This lengthy passage, entirely unique to *Matthew*, fully develops earlier hints about the Son of Man's coming in glory, a central theme in this work; see note to 13:36–43. It also explains clearly what was suggested in 10:11–15, 40–42 about the reward and punishment of those who support or reject the Christian missionaries. Perhaps the main point, in this context, is to encourage these missionaries not to waver in their zeal, in the knowledge that those who mistreat them will suffer the consequences. **25:37** *the righteous* An important term for *Matthew*; see notes to 1:19; 5:20, 48; 6:33; 10:41; 13:43. **25:40** *members of my family* See 12:46–50: those who do "the will of my Father."

clothing, sick and in prison and you did not visit me.' [44]Then they also will answer, 'Lord, when was it that we saw you hungry or thirsty or a stranger or naked or sick or in prison, and did not take care of you?' [45]Then he will answer them, 'Truly I tell you, just as you did not do it to one of the least of these, you did not do it to me.' [46]And these will go away into eternal punishment, but the righteous into eternal life."

The Plot to Kill Jesus

26 When Jesus had finished saying all these things, he said to his disciples, [2]"You know that after two days the Passover is coming, and the Son of Man will be handed over to be crucified."

[3]Then the chief priests and the elders of the people gathered in the palace of the high priest, who was called Caiaphas, [4]and they conspired to arrest Jesus by stealth and kill him. [5]But they said, "Not during the festival, or there may be a riot among the people."

The Anointing at Bethany

[6]Now while Jesus was at Bethany in the house of Simon the leper,[p] [7]a woman came to him with an alabaster jar of very costly ointment, and she poured it on his head as he sat at the table. [8]But when the disciples saw it, they were angry and said, "Why this waste? [9]For this ointment could have been sold for a large sum, and the money given to the poor." [10]But Jesus, aware of this, said to them, "Why do you trouble the woman? She has performed a good service for me. [11]For you always have the poor with you, but you will not always have me. [12]By pouring this ointment on my body she has prepared me for burial. [13]Truly I tell you, wherever this good news[q] is proclaimed in the whole world, what she has done will be told in remembrance of her."

Judas Agrees to Betray Jesus

[14]Then one of the twelve, who was called Judas Iscariot, went to the chief priests [15]and said, "What will you give me if I betray him to you?" They paid him thirty pieces of silver. [16]And from that moment he began to look for an opportunity to betray him.

The Passover with the Disciples

[17]On the first day of Unleavened Bread the disciples came to Jesus, saying, "Where do you want us to make the preparations for you to eat the Passover?" [18]He said, "Go into the city to a certain man, and say to him, 'The Teacher says, My time is near; I will keep the Passover at your house with my disciples.'" [19]So the disciples did as Jesus had directed them, and they prepared the Passover meal.

---

p The terms *leper* and *leprosy* can refer to several diseases

q Or *gospel*

25:46 eternal More literally, "of an age," or "agelong." **26:1** This is the formulaic ending to Jesus' final major speech in *Matthew;* see 7:28; 11:1; 13:53; 19:1. **26:1–27:61** For its account of Jesus' arrest, trial, and death, *Matthew* will once again follow *Mark* (chs. 14–15) closely, with the exception of the story of Judas's suicide (27:3–10), which is peculiar to *Matthew.* The author evidently has no other sources. **26:2** The first notice to the reader that Jesus had come to Jerusalem (21:10–11) just four days before Passover. This might be a significant factor in understanding the earlier response of the Jewish leaders, given that the three major feasts, when Jews came to Jerusalem from around the world, were notoriously sensitive times; see 26:5 and Josephus, *J.W.* 2.42–43, 224, 232, 255; 6.423. Passover was the feast that celebrated the liberation of Israel from Egypt in the exodus; the English name comes from the story that God "passed over" the homes of the Hebrews while punishing the Egyptians (*Exodus* 12–13). **Son of Man** Jesus now begins to fulfill the predictions he has repeatedly made about the suffering of the Son of Man in Jerusalem; see 16:21; 17:22–23; 20:17–19. On the phrase, see note to *Mark* 2:10. **26:3 the high priest, who was called Caiaphas** See 26:57. Joseph Caiaphas was high priest from 18 to 36/37 C.E., covering the entirety of Pilate's term as governor (26–36); see Josephus, *Ant.* 18.35, 95. Elsewhere there is confusion about the identity of the serving high priest: *Mark* does not name him; *Luke* and *John* inconsistently suggest Annas (*Luke* 3:2; *Acts* 4:6; *John* 18:12–24). **26:5 may be a riot** See note to 26:2. **26:6–13** *Matthew* follows *Mark* 14:3–9 closely; see notes there. Both authors assume, without saying so explicitly, that Jesus retreats to Bethany from the crowded Jerusalem in the evenings. See note to 21:17. **26:6 in the house of Simon the leper** Contrast *Luke* 7:36–50 and *John* 12:1–8, which locate the same story in different places. On leprosy and what it would mean for Jesus to be in this home, see note to *Mark* 1:40. **26:8 the disciples** *Mark* does not identify the critics, so unexpectedly *Matthew* is more critical of the disciples here than *Mark. John* 12:4 attributes the criticism to Judas Iscariot, which would perhaps explain Judas's decision to betray Jesus, which follows here immediately (26:14–16). **26:11 you will not always have me** Though taken over from *Mark,* this remark fits *Matthew's* portrayal of Jesus as acutely conscious of his unique status; see 11:25–30; 17:24–27. **26:14–16** On Judas's possible motives (in the story), see note to 26:8. **26:15 thirty pieces of silver** Given his earlier practice (21:1–11) and his failure to identify the denomination of currency involved, it is likely that the author introduces this detail, which is missing from his Markan source, in order to prepare for a fulfillment of scripture (27:9). **26:17** *Matthew* omits *Mark's* explanation that this was the day on which Passover animals were sacrificed, perhaps because the author expected his readers, who observed Jewish law (5:17–20), to know this. The day was Nisan 14, the evening following which would begin the Passover proper with the special meal (*Num.* 28:16–25; *Deut.* 16:1–8).

20When it was evening, he took his place with the twelve;*r* 21and while they were eating, he said, "Truly I tell you, one of you will betray me." 22And they became greatly distressed and began to say to him one after another, "Surely not I, Lord?" 23He answered, "The one who has dipped his hand into the bowl with me will betray me. 24The Son of Man goes as it is written of him, but woe to that one by whom the Son of Man is betrayed! It would have been better for that one not to have been born." 25Judas, who betrayed him, said, "Surely not I, Rabbi?" He replied, "You have said so."

The Institution of the Lord's Supper

26While they were eating, Jesus took a loaf of bread, and after blessing it he broke it, gave it to the disciples, and said, "Take, eat; this is my body." 27Then he took a cup, and after giving thanks he gave it to them, saying, "Drink from it, all of you; 28for this is my blood of the*s* covenant, which is poured out for many for the forgiveness of sins. 29I tell you, I will never again drink of this fruit of the vine until that day when I drink it new with you in my Father's kingdom."

30When they had sung the hymn, they went out to the Mount of Olives.

Peter's Denial Foretold

31Then Jesus said to them, "You will all become deserters because of me this night; for it is written,

'I will strike the shepherd,
    and the sheep of the flock will be scattered.'
32But after I am raised up, I will go ahead of you to Galilee." 33Peter said to him, "Though all become deserters because of you, I will never desert you." 34Jesus said to him, "Truly I tell you, this very night, before the cock crows, you will deny me three times." 35Peter said to him, "Even though I must die with you, I will not deny you." And so said all the disciples.

Jesus Prays in Gethsemane

36Then Jesus went with them to a place called Gethsemane; and he said to his disciples, "Sit here while I go over there and pray." 37He took with him Peter and the two sons of Zebedee, and began to be grieved and agitated. 38Then he said to them, "I am deeply grieved, even to death; remain here, and stay awake with me." 39And going a little farther, he threw himself on the ground and prayed, "My Father, if it is possible, let this cup pass from me; yet not what I want but what you want." 40Then he came to the disciples and found them sleeping; and he said to Peter, "So, could you not stay awake with me one hour? 41Stay awake and pray that you may not come into the time of trial;*t* the spirit indeed is willing, but the flesh is weak." 42Again he went away for the second time and prayed, "My Father, if this cannot pass unless I drink it, your will be done." 43Again he came and found them sleeping, for their eyes were heavy. 44So leaving them again, he went away and prayed for the third time, saying the same words. 45Then he came to the disciples and said to them, "Are you still sleeping and taking your rest? See, the hour is at hand, and the Son of Man is betrayed into the hands of sinners. 46Get up, let us be going. See, my betrayer is at hand."

The Betrayal and Arrest of Jesus

47While he was still speaking, Judas, one of the twelve, arrived; with him was a large crowd with swords and clubs, from the chief priests and the elders of the people. 48Now the betrayer had given them a sign, saying, "The one I will kiss is the man; arrest him." 49At once he came up to Jesus and said, "Greetings, Rabbi!" and kissed him. 50Jesus said to him, "Friend, do what you are here to do." Then they came and laid hands on Jesus and arrested him. 51Suddenly, one of those with Jesus put his hand on his sword, drew it, and struck the slave of the high

---

r Other ancient authorities add *disciples*
s Other ancient authorities add *new*

t Or *into temptation*

26:20 When it was evening The Jewish day, and hence Nisan 15, the first day of Unleavened Bread, began at sundown. **he took his place** Lit. "reclined [on a couch]" to eat in Mediterranean style. See note to *Mark* 2:15. **26:25 You have said so** This is the same response that Jesus will give to the high priest's question about being the Son of God (26:64) and (in a different tense) to Pilate's question "Are you the king of the Jews?" (27:11). It seems to be a circumlocution for a positive answer in *Matthew;* in *Luke* 23:3–4, this response is taken to be innocuous. **26:26–29** *Matthew* closely follows *Mark's* (14:22–25) version of the Last Supper although different traditions were current (see *1 Cor.* 11:23–26; *Luke* 22:15–20). **26:30 sung the hymn** The Gk—a single word meaning "they hymned"—does not suggest that a particular hymn was in view. **26:31** A loose paraphrase of *Zech.* 13:7 "Strike down the shepherd, / And let the flock scatter." The MT and the LXX agree. **26:32** See 28:7, 10. **26:36 Gethsemane** A garden on the western slope of the Mount of Olives, immediately east of Jerusalem. **the two sons of Zebedee** *Matthew* also changed *Mark's* "James and John" in this way at 20:20. **26:39 this cup** For the cup as an image of suffering, see 20:22 and Aeschylus, *Prometheus Bound* 377. **26:42 My Father** *Matthew* omits *Mark's* (14:36) Aramaic term, *abba*. **26:47** *Matthew* omits "scribes" from *Mark's* (14:43) list of officials. **26:49 Rabbi** Given Jesus' instructions in 23:8, this form of address seems a pointed attack by the author.

priest, cutting off his ear. [52]Then Jesus said to him, "Put your sword back into its place; for all who take the sword will perish by the sword. [53]Do you think that I cannot appeal to my Father, and he will at once send me more than twelve legions of angels? [54]But how then would the scriptures be fulfilled, which say it must happen in this way?" [55]At that hour Jesus said to the crowds, "Have you come out with swords and clubs to arrest me as though I were a bandit? Day after day I sat in the temple teaching, and you did not arrest me. [56]But all this has taken place, so that the scriptures of the prophets may be fulfilled." Then all the disciples deserted him and fled.

Jesus before the High Priest

[57]Those who had arrested Jesus took him to Caiaphas the high priest, in whose house the scribes and the elders had gathered. [58]But Peter was following him at a distance, as far as the courtyard of the high priest; and going inside, he sat with the guards in order to see how this would end. [59]Now the chief priests and the whole council were looking for false testimony against Jesus so that they might put him to death, [60]but they found none, though many false witnesses came forward. At last two came forward [61]and said, "This fellow said, 'I am able to destroy the temple of God and to build it in three days.'" [62]The high priest stood up and said, "Have you no answer? What is it that they testify against you?" [63]But Jesus was silent. Then the high priest said to him, "I put you under oath before the living God, tell us if you are the Messiah,[u] the Son of God." [64]Jesus said to him, "You have said so. But I tell you,

From now on you will see the Son of Man
    seated at the right hand of Power
    and coming on the clouds of heaven."

[65]Then the high priest tore his clothes and said, "He has blasphemed! Why do we still need witnesses? You have now heard his blasphemy. [66]What is your verdict?" They answered, "He deserves death." [67]Then they spat in his face and struck him; and some slapped him, [68]saying, "Prophesy to us, you Messiah![u] Who is it that struck you?"

Peter's Denial of Jesus

[69]Now Peter was sitting outside in the courtyard. A servant-girl came to him and said, "You also were with Jesus the Galilean." [70]But he denied it before all of them, saying, "I do not know what you are talking about." [71]When he went out to the porch, another servant-girl saw him, and she said to the bystanders, "This man was with Jesus of Nazareth."[v] [72]Again he denied it with an oath, "I do not know the man." [73]After a little while the bystanders came up and said to Peter, "Certainly you are also one of them, for your accent betrays you." [74]Then he began to curse, and he swore an oath, "I do not know the man!" At that moment the cock crowed. [75]Then Peter remembered what Jesus had said: "Before the cock crows, you will deny me three times." And he went out and wept bitterly.

Jesus Brought before Pilate

27 When morning came, all the chief priests and the elders of the people conferred together against Jesus in order to bring about his death. [2]They

---

u Or Christ   v Gk the Nazorean

26:52–54 *Matthew* adds to *Mark*'s story this criticism; see *Luke* 22:51 and *John* 18:11. **26:53** *twelve legions* A legion consisted of about 5,300 men. In the eastern Mediterranean, it seems to have been an obvious metaphor for large numbers (see *Mark* 5:9). **26:54** *the scriptures be fulfilled . . . must happen in this way.* Although the theme of fulfillment is clearly important for this author (see introduction to *Matthew*), it is unclear which scriptures he has in mind that might speak of a betrayal and arrest. See 26:56. **26:56** *so that the scriptures of the prophets may be fulfilled* This is the 13th of *Matthew*'s fulfillment formulas, but the author declines to cite the scripture in question. See 26:54. It is likely that he simply took this over from *Mark* 14:49 without knowing which scripture *Mark* referred to, for the author would surely have cited the passage had he known it. He thus betrays his use of *Mark* as a source. **26:57–68** This account of the trial before the council, in the high priest's house, follows closely *Mark* 14:53–65. See notes there, especially concerning the many historical problems with this trial. **26:57** *Caiaphas the high priest* Only *Matthew* correctly identifies the current high priest. See note to 26:3. **26:60** *two came forward Matthew*'s adjustment of *Mark*'s "some" (14:57) may result from the author's preference for pairs and keen awareness of the law requiring two witnesses (see note to 18:16). **26:63** Although the charge is introduced as a lie, because Jesus has said no such thing, the Christian reader also knows that it has a deeper meaning, with respect to Jesus' death and resurrection; see note to *Mark* 14:58. Jesus' identity, plainly disclosed to his students earlier (16:16; 17:5) and known to the Christian reader throughout, finally becomes the critical issue in his confrontation with the Jewish leaders. **26:64** A reference to *Dan.* 7:13; but see note to 24:30. **26:65–66** See note to *Mark* 14:55–65. **26:67–68** *Matthew* follows *Mark*'s presentation of the trial as a complete mockery of ordinary justice. **26:69–75** *Matthew*'s story of Peter's denial follows *Mark*'s (14:66–72) closely, except that the author makes the 2d questioner (*Matt.* 26:71) another servant-girl, rather than the same person as the first questioner.

bound him, led him away, and handed him over to Pilate the governor.

The Suicide of Judas

³When Judas, his betrayer, saw that Jesusʷ was condemned, he repented and brought back the thirty pieces of silver to the chief priests and the elders. ⁴He said, "I have sinned by betraying innocentˣ blood." But they said, "What is that to us? See to it yourself." ⁵Throwing down the pieces of silver in the temple, he departed; and he went and hanged himself. ⁶But the chief priests, taking the pieces of silver, said, "It is not lawful to put them into the treasury, since they are blood money." ⁷After conferring together, they used them to buy the potter's field as a place to bury foreigners. ⁸For this reason that field has been called the Field of Blood to this day. ⁹Then was fulfilled what had been spoken through the prophet Jeremiah,ʸ "And they tookᶻ the thirty pieces of silver, the price of the one on whom a price had been set,ᵃ on whom some of the people of Israel had set a price, ¹⁰and they gaveᵇ them for the potter's field, as the Lord commanded me."

Pilate Questions Jesus

¹¹Now Jesus stood before the governor; and the governor asked him, "Are you the King of the Jews?" Jesus said, "You say so." ¹²But when he was accused by the chief priests and elders, he did not answer. ¹³Then Pilate said to him, "Do you not hear how many accusations they make against you?" ¹⁴But he gave him no answer, not even to a single charge, so that the governor was greatly amazed.

Barabbas or Jesus?

¹⁵Now at the festival the governor was accustomed to release a prisoner for the crowd, anyone whom they wanted. ¹⁶At that time they had a notorious prisoner, called Jesusᶜ Barabbas. ¹⁷So after they had gathered, Pilate said to them, "Whom do you want me to release for you, Jesusᶜ Barabbas or Jesus who is called the Messiah?"ᵈ ¹⁸For he realized that it was out of jealousy that they had handed him over. ¹⁹While he was sitting on the judgment seat, his wife sent word to him, "Have nothing to do with that innocent man, for today I have suffered a great deal because of a dream about him." ²⁰Now the chief priests and the elders persuaded the crowds to ask for Barabbas and to have Jesus killed. ²¹The governor again said to them, "Which of the two do you want me to release for you?" And they said, "Barabbas." ²²Pilate said to them, "Then what should I do with Jesus who is called the Messiah?"ᵈ All of them said, "Let him be crucified!" ²³Then he asked, "Why, what evil has he done?" But they shouted all the more, "Let him be crucified!"

Pilate Hands Jesus over to Be Crucified

²⁴So when Pilate saw that he could do nothing, but rather that a riot was beginning, he took some water and washed his hands before the crowd, saying, "I

---

w Gk *he*
x Other ancient authorities read *righteous*
y Other ancient authorities read *Zechariah* or *Isaiah*
z Or *I took*
a Or *the price of the precious One*
b Other ancient authorities read *I gave*

c Other ancient authorities lack *Jesus*
d Or *the Christ*

27:2 ***Pilate the governor*** Pontius Pilate was prefect of Judea from 26 to 36 C.E. Although *Matthew* follows *Mark* in portraying him as a weak pawn in the hands of the Jewish leaders, this picture is hard to reconcile with either the general situation of Roman governors in Judea or the particular evidence for Pilate in other sources. See *Mark* 15:1. **27:3–10** This story of Judas's death is unique to *Matthew*. *Luke-Acts* has an entirely different story (*Acts* 1:16–20). There Judas buys a field with his reward money and dies unrepentant. **27:9–10** *Matthew*'s 14th and final fulfillment citation (see note to 1:22–23) resembles *Zech.* 11:12–13 most closely. MT: "So they weighed out my wages, thirty shekels of silver—the noble sum that I was worth in their estimation. The Lord said to me, 'Deposit it in the treasury.' And I took the thirty shekels and deposited it in the treasury in the House of the Lord." LXX: "And they weighed for my price thirty pieces of silver. And the Lord said to me, 'Drop them into the furnace, and I will see if it is good metal, as I was tested for their sakes.' And I took the thirty pieces of silver, and cast them into the furnace in the house of the Lord." The identification of *Jeremiah* as the source is a mistake, although *Matthew*'s references to a potter's field possibly come from *Jer.* 32:6–15 (see 18:2–3). **27:11** Apparently, the author and his readers see this term as roughly equivalent (from a Roman's perspective) to the term "messiah" in the trial before the Jewish council (26:63). Claiming to be either Messiah or Son of God was not a capital offense in Judaism, but claiming to be king of the Jews might create serious problems, if one had much of a following, at feast times in Jerusalem. Apparently, an affirmative answer; see note to 26:25; 26:64. **27:15** On the custom, alleged here, of releasing a prisoner each Passover, see the note to *Mark* 15:6. **27:16** ***Barabbas*** is a peculiar Aramaic name, for it means "son of a [or 'the'] father." *Jesus* is *Matthew*'s addition to *Mark*, presumably to intensify the drama of the people's choice; see 27:17. Jesus, a form of Joshua, was an extremely common name in 1st-century Judaism. **27:19** This story of Pilate's wife's dream is peculiar to *Matthew*. It became the basis for her elevation to sainthood in eastern Christianity. **27:22** ***crucified.*** See the note to *Mark* 15:13. **27:24** ***washed his hands*** Pilate's famous action, found only in Matthew, is in fact a biblical, not Roman, custom for declaring one's innocence (*Deut.* 21:6–7; *Ps.* 26:6; 73:13).

am innocent of this man's blood;[e] see to it yourselves." [25]Then the people as a whole answered, "His
blood be on us and on our children!" [26]So he released
Barabbas for them; and after flogging Jesus, he handed
him over to be crucified.

The Soldiers Mock Jesus

[27]Then the soldiers of the governor took Jesus into
the governor's headquarters,[f] and they gathered the
whole cohort around him. [28]They stripped him and
put a scarlet robe on him, [29]and after twisting some
thorns into a crown, they put it on his head. They put
a reed in his right hand and knelt before him and
mocked him, saying, "Hail, King of the Jews!" [30]They
spat on him, and took the reed and struck him on the
head. [31]After mocking him, they stripped him of the
robe and put his own clothes on him. Then they led
him away to crucify him.

The Crucifixion of Jesus

[32]As they went out, they came upon a man from
Cyrene named Simon; they compelled this man to
carry his cross. [33]And when they came to a place
called Golgotha (which means Place of a Skull),
[34]they offered him wine to drink, mixed with gall;
but when he tasted it, he would not drink it. [35]And
when they had crucified him, they divided his clothes
among themselves by casting lots;[g] [36]then they sat

down there and kept watch over him. [37]Over his head
they put the charge against him, which read, "This is
Jesus, the King of the Jews."

[38]Then two bandits were crucified with him, one
on his right and one on his left. [39]Those who passed
by derided[h] him, shaking their heads [40]and saying,
"You who would destroy the temple and build it in
three days, save yourself! If you are the Son of God,
come down from the cross." [41]In the same way the
chief priests also, along with the scribes and elders,
were mocking him, saying, [42]"He saved others; he
cannot save himself.[i] He is the King of Israel; let him
come down from the cross now, and we will believe
in him. [43]He trusts in God; let God deliver him now,
if he wants to; for he said, 'I am God's Son.'" [44]The
bandits who were crucified with him also taunted
him in the same way.

The Death of Jesus

[45]From noon on, darkness came over the whole
land[j] until three in the afternoon. [46]And about three
o'clock Jesus cried with a loud voice, "Eli, Eli, lema
sabachthani?" that is, "My God, my God, why have
you forsaken me?" [47]When some of the bystanders
heard it, they said, "This man is calling for Elijah."
[48]At once one of them ran and got a sponge, filled it
with sour wine, put it on a stick, and gave it to him to
drink. [49]But the others said, "Wait, let us see whether
Elijah will come to save him."[k] [50]Then Jesus cried

---

e Other ancient authorities read *this righteous blood*, or *this righ-*
teous man's blood

f Gk *the praetorium*

g Other ancient authorities add *in order that what had been spo-*
ken through the prophet might be fulfilled, "They divided my clothes
among themselves, and for my clothing they cast lots."

h Or *blasphemed*

i Or *is he unable to save himself?*

j Or *earth*

k Other ancient authorities add *And another took a spear and*
pierced his side, and out came water and blood.

27:25 At this critical moment in the narrative, the author seems to break down the distinction, which he had so sharply
maintained earlier, between the Jewish leaders and the crowds unless we are to understand that the people, as a whole, spoke
this way only under the influence of their leaders. This alleged willing acceptance of blood guilt for all future generations has
had terrible consequences for the Jewish people in the Christian West. **27:27** *governor's headquarters* The governor ordinarily lived in Caesarea, by the coast, and came to Jerusalem only for festivals. His residence while in Jerusalem may have
been the fortress Antonia, which overlooked the northwest corner of the Temple Mount. But *Mark* 15:16 suggests that it was
the "palace"—the former home of Herod the Great in western Jerusalem. *the whole cohort* A cohort, theoretically one-
tenth of a legion, consisted of six centuries (80 men each, therefore 480 in total). One auxiliary cohort was quartered in Jerusalem, in the fortress Antonia, but the governor also brought supplementary troops from Caesarea for the main festivals. It is
not clear which soldiers are in view here. **27:32–34** *Matthew* follows *Mark* 15:20–21 but omits the names of Simon's sons,
perhaps because they were known only to *Mark's* readers. **27:34** *wine to drink, mixed with gall* By changing *Mark's*
"wine mixed with myrrh" (15:23) and by introducing the observation that Jesus first tasted the drink before refusing
it, Matthew seems to suggest that the guards were trying to poison Jesus. Gall was a bitter and poisonous herb. **27:35** See *Ps.*
22:18. The entire crucifixion scene contains many evocations of *Psalm* 22. **27:39** *shaking their heads* See *Ps.* 22:7.
27:40 *would destroy the temple* See the false charge against Jesus in 26:61. **27:41–43** These taunts recall those of the
wicked toward the righteous in *Wis.* 2:16–20. **27:45** *Matthew* has omitted *Mark's* observation (15:25) that Jesus was
crucified about the 3d hour of the day (near 9:00 A.M.; see note to 20:3), possibly because there seemed insufficient
time before that for the meeting of the council, the trial before Pilate, the mocking, the walk, and the crucifixion itself.
27:46 Jesus' cry (from *Mark* 15:34; see note there) is preserved in Aramaic—characteristic of *Mark* but not typical of *Matthew.*
It recalls *Ps.* 22:1. **27:47** *calling for Elijah* See note to *Mark* 15:35–36.

again with a loud voice and breathed his last.[l] [51]At that moment the curtain of the temple was torn in two, from top to bottom. The earth shook, and the rocks were split. [52]The tombs also were opened, and many bodies of the saints who had fallen asleep were raised. [53]After his resurrection they came out of the tombs and entered the holy city and appeared to many. [54]Now when the centurion and those with him, who were keeping watch over Jesus, saw the earthquake and what took place, they were terrified and said, "Truly this man was God's Son!"[m]

[55]Many women were also there, looking on from a distance; they had followed Jesus from Galilee and had provided for him. [56]Among them were Mary Magdalene, and Mary the mother of James and Joseph, and the mother of the sons of Zebedee.

The Burial of Jesus

[57]When it was evening, there came a rich man from Arimathea, named Joseph, who was also a disciple of Jesus. [58]He went to Pilate and asked for the body of Jesus; then Pilate ordered it to be given to him. [59]So Joseph took the body and wrapped it in a clean linen cloth [60]and laid it in his own new tomb, which he had hewn in the rock. He then rolled a great stone to the door of the tomb and went away. [61]Mary Magdalene and the other Mary were there, sitting opposite the tomb.

The Guard at the Tomb

[62]The next day, that is, after the day of Preparation, the chief priests and the Pharisees gathered before Pilate [63]and said, "Sir, we remember what that impostor said while he was still alive, 'After three days I will rise again.' [64]Therefore command the tomb to be made secure until the third day; otherwise his disciples may go and steal him away, and tell the people, 'He has been raised from the dead,' and the last deception would be worse than the first." [65]Pilate said to them, "You have a guard[n] of soldiers; go, make it as secure as you can."[o] [66]So they went with the guard and made the tomb secure by sealing the stone.

The Resurrection of Jesus

28 [1]After the sabbath, as the first day of the week was dawning, Mary Magdalene and the other

---

l Or *gave up his spirit*
m Or *a son of God*

n Or *Take a guard*
o Gk *you know how*

27:51 See note to *Mark* 15:38. **27:52–53** This remarkable story occurs only in *Matthew*. The qualification that although the tombs were opened at Jesus' death, the saints did not leave until after his resurrection suggests that the author created the story to embellish his interpretation of Jesus' saving death. **27:54** See note to *Mark* 15:39. **27:56** *Matthew* follows *Mark* 15:41 but identifies the 2d Mary as the mother of James and Joseph rather than James the younger (or smaller) and Joses. In *Mark,* the woman in question appears to be Jesus' mother because there James and Joses are the 1st-named brothers of Jesus (see *Mark* 6:3); in *Matthew* similarly, these brothers are named James and Joseph (13:55). It is odd that the author would refer to Jesus' mother so indirectly, but he similarly declines to call the mother of the sons of Zebedee the wife of Zebedee (20:20). *Sons of Zebedee* is *Matthew*'s preferred way of referring to the other James and John (10:2; 26:37), and their mother is familiar from a recent story (20:20); *Matthew* substitutes her name for *Mark*'s Salome. **27:57–61** *Matthew* considerably abbreviates *Mark*'s story of Jesus' burial, altering it significantly. Joseph is no longer a member of the council— probably because of the foregoing story, in which the court made a vocal and unanimous decision for Jesus' death (26:59, 66–67; 27:25). He is a rich man, as the author might have inferred from the fact that he had his own new tomb built from rock, and Jesus' student. Jewish law required the burial of corpses before sundown on the day of death (*Deut.* 21:23). Still, Joseph would have contracted corpse impurity, which would remain with him for seven days and thus prevent him from visiting the temple for the remainder of the festival (*Num.* 19:10–13). **27:57** *When it was evening* That is, the beginning of Nisan 16, the 2d day of Passover, also a Sabbath and so Friday evening. **27:61** *the other Mary* See note to 27:56. **27:62–66** The story of the placing of the guard is unique to *Matthew*. One of its purposes seems to be to emphasize that nothing short of a miraculous resurrection could have freed Jesus' body from the tomb (27:65–66). But the story itself undercuts this point because (a) the resurrection took place *before* the stone was rolled away (28:2–6) and (b) the rumor still developed among the Jews of the late 1st century that Jesus' body was stolen while the guards slept (28:15). Another purpose was simply to show the lengths to which the Jewish leaders went (in futility, thwarting the plan of God) to prevent Jesus from accomplishing his mission. Then, when they knew the truth, they deliberately chose to ignore it. The introduction of this story changes *Mark*'s account in several ways: the women can no longer expect simply to go and anoint Jesus' body (*Mark* 16:1); they cannot naively wonder who will help them move the stone (*Mark* 16:3); and it would be an anticlimax if the stone were already removed when they arrived (*Mark* 16:4). **27:62** *The next day, that is, after the day of Preparation* Thus, not the next day after the Friday evening just mentioned (27:57), which would technically be Saturday evening or Sunday, but the daylight period following the day of Jesus' death. A confusing formulation, since *Matthew* has not yet mentioned the day of Preparation itself. And if it is the day after the day of Preparation for Sabbath (see 28:1), then it *is* the Sabbath—which would have been easier to say. But *Mark*'s parallel narrative has earlier mentioned the day of Sabbath preparation (15:42). Since the author seems to have this in mind, he betrays his use of *Mark* as a source. **28:1** *first day of the week* Thus, Sunday. *the other Mary* See note to 27:56.

Mary went to see the tomb. ²And suddenly there was a great earthquake; for an angel of the Lord, descending from heaven, came and rolled back the stone and sat on it. ³His appearance was like lightning, and his clothing white as snow. ⁴For fear of him the guards shook and became like dead men. ⁵But the angel said to the women, "Do not be afraid; I know that you are looking for Jesus who was crucified. ⁶He is not here; for he has been raised, as he said. Come, see the place where he*p* lay. ⁷Then go quickly and tell his disciples, 'He has been raised from the dead,*q* and indeed he is going ahead of you to Galilee; there you will see him.' This is my message for you." ⁸So they left the tomb quickly with fear and great joy, and ran to tell his disciples. ⁹Suddenly Jesus met them and said, "Greetings!" And they came to him, took hold of his feet, and worshiped him. ¹⁰Then Jesus said to them, "Do not be afraid; go and tell my brothers to go to Galilee; there they will see me."

The Report of the Guard

¹¹While they were going, some of the guard went into the city and told the chief priests everything that had happened. ¹²After the priests*r* had assembled with the elders, they devised a plan to give a large sum of money to the soldiers, ¹³telling them, "You must say, 'His disciples came by night and stole him away while we were asleep.' ¹⁴If this comes to the governor's ears, we will satisfy him and keep you out of trouble." ¹⁵So they took the money and did as they were directed. And this story is still told among the Jews to this day.

The Commissioning of the Disciples

¹⁶Now the eleven disciples went to Galilee, to the mountain to which Jesus had directed them. ¹⁷When they saw him, they worshiped him; but some doubted. ¹⁸And Jesus came and said to them, "All authority in heaven and on earth has been given to me. ¹⁹Go therefore and make disciples of all nations, baptizing them in the name of the Father and of the Son and of the Holy Spirit, ²⁰and teaching them to obey everything that I have commanded you. And remember, I am with you always, to the end of the age."*s*

---

p Other ancient authorities read *the Lord*
q Other ancient authorities lack *from the dead*

r Gk *they*
s Other ancient authorities add *Amen*

---

went to see the tomb Because of the guard, *Mark's* claims that the women had bought spices and intended to anoint Jesus' body (*Mark* 16:1) and that they wondered who might help them move the stone (16:3) are no longer plausible. The women come simply to see the tomb. **28:6 been raised, as he said** See 16:21; 17:22–23. **28:7 going ahead of you to Galilee** See 26:32. Contrast the story in *Luke-Acts,* where Jesus' students are pointedly instructed to stay in Jerusalem, the site of all Jesus' postresurrection appearances (*Luke* 24:6, 13–49; esp. 27:18, 47; *Acts* 1:4). **28:8** Here *Matthew* radically alters the final sentence of *Mark* (16:8) and adds a confirming sequel: rather than falling silent from fear, the women tell Jesus' students with great joy. **28:10 go to Galilee** See note to 28:7. This will be fulfilled in 28:16–20. **28:11–15** This story completes *Matthew's* portrayal of the Jewish leaders: although they plainly knew the truth of Jesus' resurrection, they deliberately chose to ignore it, buying off the soldiers to create another rumor. Thus, according to this author, the reason that most Jews do not accept Jesus in his own day is that their leaders have deceived them. **28:16–20** This "great commission," as it is known, is unique to *Matthew*. It reflects the author's great concern with Christian missionaries (see 9:36–10:42; 22:9; 25:31–46). **28:19 Father . . . Son and . . . Holy Spirit** Although this formulation happens to sound like the Christian Trinity, this doctrine was fully developed only in the 4th century, after long and vigorous debate within the churches. The earliest Christian texts do not articulate such a developed theology—one divine essence in three persons. The author of *Matthew* knows God as Father and Jesus as Son but does not work out the relationship between them or between them and the Holy Spirit. **28:20** This final reminder reflects the book's fundamental concern with Jesus' teaching, in five (or six) major discourses and elsewhere. It seems to imply that all of Jesus' reported teachings are applicable to Christian life and mission. This is different from *Luke-Acts,* where the author tells an evolving story: what Jesus said before his death and resurrection has become transformed by these new circumstances.

An Orderly Account for Theophilus

LUKE ✢ ACTS

THE AUTHOR TRADITIONALLY KNOWN AS LUKE was the only gospel writer to continue his story through the first Christian generation. Because it is the only early account of that period in existence, the book of *Acts* has decisively shaped all subsequent understanding of the church's origins. But the NT arrangement, which places *John* before *Acts*, obscures the fact that *Acts* was intended as a sequel to the author's own gospel (see *Acts* 1:1). This introduction suggests that *Luke-Acts* tells a single coherent story, which becomes clear only if the two volumes are read together.

The Prologue to Luke-Acts

In trying to understand the author's aims, we cannot go far wrong if we begin at the beginning, where the writer intended his readers to begin. Uniquely among the gospels, *Luke* begins with a prologue, in which the author sets out briefly his situation and purpose. Such prologues were an expected part of historical and other kinds of writing in the Greco-Roman tradition. Because books were written on rolls they offered no space for indexes, and potential readers had no efficient way of skimming the work to see what it was about. The prologue was intended both to inform the potential reader about the subject and to show its importance. Where such a prologue exists, therefore, we should always examine it carefully for clues about the author's purpose.

Predictably, as successive authors tried to outdo each other in writing an appealing preface, they began to sound more and more like each other. By the end of the first century, almost any historical preface reflects these typical features: the unparalleled importance of the subject; the unique qualifications of the author to write on the subject; the author's strenuous efforts to be scrupulously accurate or "precise," by using where possible the reports of eyewitnesses; the defects of all previous work on the subject; and, if appropriate, a gesture of thanks toward the sponsor or patron of the work. In a multivolume collection such as Flavius Josephus's *Jewish War, Jewish Antiquities,* and *Against Apion,* it was also customary in the later volumes to refer back to what had been attempted in the earlier parts. Like a good salesman, an effective writer had to employ these standard devices in such a creative way that the reader would not see them as the same old thing.

Although the preface to *Luke-Acts* is a model of conciseness, it contains the essential features of the Hellenistic prologue:

> Since many have undertaken to set down an orderly account of the events that have been fulfilled among us, just as they were handed on to us by those who from the beginning were eyewitnesses and servants of the word, I too decided, after investigating everything carefully from the very first, to write an orderly account for you, most excellent Theophilus, so that you may know the truth concerning the things about which you have been instructed. (*Luke* 1:1–4)

The author begins by referring to previous treatments of his subject. Admittedly, he does not dismiss those earlier accounts in the way that many historians did, but it is not difficult to see that he finds them seriously defective. If he considered them reliable, then the logic of the prologue would make no sense. We expect him to say: "since many have already written about this, there is *no need* for me to do so." Originality was and is the most basic justification for any writer; if it has already been done, one does not need to do it again. But the author bases his eagerness to write on the fact that "many"—often a slightly pejorative term in Greek—have already done so. This can only mean that he sees much room for improvement.

Such a reading is confirmed by what follows. First, the verb translated "undertaken," which is peculiar to this author among early Christian writers, might better be translated "taken it upon themselves." In its other occurrences, it has the sense of presumptuous or misguided effort, as when the hapless Jewish exorcists "take it upon themselves" to cast out devils in Jesus' name (*Acts* 19:13), or some Jews try ineffectively to kill Paul (9:29). Second, in verses 3 and 4 the author makes it clear that he will offer something that the others have not provided: he has researched everything "with precision" from the beginning (translated "carefully" above, but a standard term in historical prologues), and he is going to provide the "truth." The word rendered "truth" is *asphaleia,* and it more literally means "sure ground" or "certainty." Notice that the three occurrences of the related adjective in *Acts* (21:34; 22:30; 25:26) all concern the problem of sorting out the reliable ground in the midst of conflicting claims. That is also the sense in the prologue. The author says, in effect: "you have read many competing accounts; now I shall set the record straight." Although his criticism is restrained, he regards his story as superior to its predecessors.

How will it be superior? Verses 1 and 2 describe the work of the previous authors. They and the present writer share the same basic task: to "write up an account of the events fulfilled among us" on the basis of evidence handed down by eyewitnesses and by people who have been active in this teaching ("the word"). What this writer hopes will distinguish his account from the others comes in verses 3 and 4. He has researched everything from the start and so he (alone) is in a position to write "precisely" and "in order." Although claims to precision were standard among history-writers, the adverb "in an orderly manner" (Gk *kathexēs*) is distinctive and important for this author.

Overview: In Order

The NRSV translation given above obscures the point by using the English phrase "orderly account" for both the earlier gospels (v. 1) and the writer's own work (v. 3). But the Greek is different in the two cases, and only the latter passage has this word, which stresses a proper *sequence,* where events are told one after the other in correct order. The word appears five times in *Luke-Acts,* but in no other gospel. The author evidently thinks that an orderly progression will be the hallmark of his narrative.

A careful reading of *Luke-Acts* shows that we could hardly have come up with a better term to describe these books. First, the mere fact that the author bothers to include a history of the church after Jesus' resurrection means that he alone can reserve many of his major points for the second volume. For example, we have seen that *Mark* and *John* place Jesus in dire conflict with the Jewish authorities right from the beginning and, in their different ways, relativize Jesus' own Jewishness. In *Luke-Acts,* however, Jesus operates comfortably within the Jewish world throughout the entire gospel, attending temple and synagogue, consorting in a friendly manner with leading Jewish figures, and debating with other teachers the correct interpretation of Sabbath law. In the end, it is only a small group of Jerusalem leaders who have him killed. For *Luke,* the serious conflict with Judaism begins only with the events immediately before Jesus' death. It then builds in stages: at first, Christian leaders are told simply to refrain from teaching in the name of their recently crucified leader; over time, it is the Christians' criticisms of the Jerusalem temple, dietary and other laws, and of the Jewish people, as well as their dealings with Gentiles, that bring the conflict to a head.

It may be, then, that the author found other gospels inadequate in part because they read too much of the church's own situation back into Jesus' own lifetime, and thus ignored what he understood to be the proper development of Christian origins. Whether that guess is accurate or not, *Luke*'s author has a pronounced concern to lay things out "in order."

He is a master of scene. We observe this first in the abrupt shift at *Luke* 1:5, from the businesslike historical prologue to the scene in the Jerusalem temple where the priest Zechariah receives the divine promise of John the Baptist's birth. It is as if the master storyteller had said, "Come with me to a faraway place long ago." He sets the stage with authentic "period language"—with the "courses" of priests fulfilling their scheduled duties in the temple, and the various pieces of temple furniture. Most remarkably, he even adjusts his sentence structure and vocabulary to create an old-fashioned "biblical" atmosphere—with angelic appearances and actors spontaneously breaking into poetic verse. (People do not speak like that in the rest of *Luke-Acts.*) Throughout the gospel, he adopts the antiquated, Hebrew-tinged Greek of the Septuagint to help create atmosphere.

The detailed story of John the Baptist's birth hooks the reader in, by raising an immediate question: "I thought that this was an account of Jesus and his followers. Why is he talking about the famous preacher John the Baptist?" The answer comes as a surprise: "Did you know that the two men were blood relatives?"

Luke's birth narratives also establish expectations for the story. Jesus is the Messiah, the anointed one hoped for by Israel, the descendant of David and (in this sense, at least) Son of God, who will indeed restore Israel's glory and defeat its enemies (*Luke* 1:32–33, 69–70). These themes create a sense of curiosity that remains with the reader throughout the two volumes, and actually increases with each new turn: If he is the Messiah who will deliver Israel, why does he not say so clearly? Why does John doubt? Why do his disciples not understand? Why does he devote his energies to social relations and the welfare of individuals? Why must he suffer and die? When will he in fact restore Israel? Why are so many of his followers Gentiles, who do not live as Jews? Why is he ultimately rejected by most Jews? In other words, the birth story establishes the conditions for irony. The reader knows in advance what the characters do not know. At the same time, the reader is in a perpetual state of questioning.

In *Luke* 3:1, the author abruptly shifts by mentioning Roman and Jewish political figures of the more recent past. We step out of the sublime world of biblical poetry, suffused with peace and hope, to the jarring reality of Herod's family and of a Pontius Pilate. This is still remote history from the author's perspective, but we are beginning the approach to everyday reality. It is within this mundane world—among the sick, the sinners, and the poor—that Jesus appears with his message of hope and promise. Most readers agree that the episode in the synagogue at Nazareth, in which Jesus reads from *Isaiah* 61 and applies the passage to himself (*Luke* 4:16–30), becomes a keynote for the whole gospel. Jesus is an anointed prophet, who comes mainly for the sick, the poor, and the foreigner. It is an illuminating exercise to read that passage carefully and to identify the various themes that will turn up again in the remainder of the story.

This is still a stable world, and Jesus continues to live as a fully observant Jew. He attends synagogue faithfully and gets along well with most people, though he occasionally upsets some. Most important, he is recognized by all as a teacher with a certain dignity and social status. His students and others address him, only in *Luke*, with a Greek term that means "chief" or "master" or "overseer" (*epistatēs*). On three separate occasions (only in *Luke*) he is invited to dine with Pharisees, who appear as recognized leaders of the people, and he "reclines" with them—a term that suggests the kind of meal eaten by the privileged. Although he forthrightly criticizes the behavior of these popular leaders, they still befriend him and even warn him to flee from Herod Antipas (*Luke* 13:31).

Unlike *Mark* and *John*, where a strong sense of foreboding dominates the story from the start, the author uses the extended travel narrative in *Luke* (9:51–19:10) to delay Jesus' intense conflict with authorities until the arrival in Jerusalem. Throughout this period Jesus continues to advocate his message of peace and consolation for the downtrodden; the word "peace" occurs thirteen times in *Luke,* once in *Mark,* three times in *Matthew.* To be sure, the very fact that Jesus is now headed for Jerusalem (after 9:51) introduces a note of tension, and he occasionally refers to coming disturbances (12:49–53). But by and large, he continues as a provocative and effective teacher, and no plot is hatched against him. Significantly, again in contrast to other gospels, the Pharisees do not appear as Jesus' opponents at this point. They are simply the ineffective "righteous," who do not appear to need his message for the poor. They are the ones, like the older brother of the prodigal son, who have always enjoyed God's bounty (*Luke* 15:29–31). Indeed, *Luke* implies that they have the capacity within themselves, if they are willing, to begin to bring in the kingdom of God (*Luke* 17:20–21).

When Jesus finally arrives at Jerusalem, however, the situation quickly becomes ugly. The benign Pharisees disappear, after being typically (but not lethally) scandalized at his failure to rebuke his followers for praising him as he enters the city (*Luke* 19:39). Once in the city, however, Jesus disrupts the temple, expelling the merchants and teaching his provocative message. This arouses the ire of the temple-based leadership. Immediately these leaders plot to kill him (19:47). They send in spies to monitor his activities and collect evidence for charges (20:20), and they hire Judas to help them seize Jesus in private (22:1–4). For his part, Jesus vehemently denounces these leaders and repeatedly predicts the destruction of Jerusalem (19:41–44; 21:5, 20–24). In this context, he deliberately retracts his earlier instructions about carrying purse, bag, and sandals (9:35; 10:4). Now he tells his students to take all of these things, and also to carry swords (22:35–38). Soon after, he is arrested, beaten and mocked, paraded before Herod Antipas (who has long wished to try him), bitterly rejected by the Jerusalem leaders (who perversely allow that they would rather have a murderous rebel released than Jesus), and finally executed. This intense suffering and conflict, though vividly described, occupies a relatively short section of the book (chs. 19 to 23).

With *Luke*'s detailed account of Jesus' resurrection and appearances, the story recaptures an air of serenity and hope. The risen Jesus says "Peace to you" as he consoles his followers (24:36), and he begins to prepare for the sequel. His resurrection does not mark a *return* to normal, however, for the story has taken a decisive new turn. The short period after Jesus' resurrection is very busy as he imparts new information to his followers. Although he has spoken of his future suffering on three previous occasions, *Luke*'s author made it clear then that Jesus' students did not understand him, for his words were "hidden" (9:45; 18:34). And although the birth narrative has already announced that Jesus is the awaited Messiah, his messianic status is at best ambiguous in the main narrative of *Luke.* Now, however, the risen Jesus begins very clearly to explain that "it was necessary" according to scripture for the Messiah to suffer, die, and rise again. He opens his students' minds to see that all scripture—Moses, the prophets, and the psalms—points to this conclusion (24:26–27, 44–47). He further tells them that, now that they know these things and have become witnesses to his resurrection, they must begin to preach repentance and forgiveness of sins in his name, starting in Jerusalem—after they have been equipped with the power of the Holy Spirit (24:47–49).

Note that the answer to the question "Is Jesus the Messiah?" was what distinguished Christians, whether Jewish or Gentile, from non-Christian Jews. And we learn from the second-century *Dialogue with Trypho,* by the Christian writer Justin Martyr, that this debate turned partly on the issue of the Messiah's suffering and death. Justin and other Christians thought that the Messiah's suffering was in keeping with scripture; Trypho and other non-Christian Jews did not accept the claim. In *Luke* 24 our author shows that he is already keenly aware of this debate. *Luke's* Jesus shows his followers the scriptures that refer to his suffering, death, and resurrection. But *Luke* withholds these critical passages from the reader, thereby creating further suspense, until they can be appropriately introduced "in order"—in *Acts.*

This flurry of post-resurrection activity in *Luke* 24 sets the stage for the second volume, which begins with a new set of assumptions. Jesus clearly is the Messiah and Son of God, who has proven his divine mission by being raised from the dead and by showing himself alive to credible witnesses through a period of forty days— therefore, beyond all question. References to Jesus in *Acts* consistently maintain this two-stage scenario: he was a righteous teacher, healer, and prophet, whom God raised from the dead and thereby declared him to be Messiah (*Acts* 2:36; 10:38; 13:27–31). The days of ambiguity are now over. Now people must repent and trust in Jesus for forgiveness of sins, for outside of him there is no salvation (*Acts* 4:11). From now on, the scriptures proving that the Messiah had to suffer— which turn out to include various psalms, *Deut.* 18:15, and *Isaiah* 53—will be abundantly cited whenever Christians speak to Jews. Only in this new environment are Jesus' followers called the "church" (beginning with *Acts* 5:11; contrast *Matt.* 18:15–17), and *Acts* also notes the first moment at which they were called "Christians" (11:26). Once again, the author is concerned to relate developments in their proper sequence.

Within the narrative of *Acts* itself, one notices several major turning points. Some of these are anticipated by the risen Jesus' keynote address in *Acts* 1:8: the apostles will be his witnesses in Jerusalem, Judea, Samaria, and the extreme ends of the earth (from the perspective of the ancient reader). Chapters 1–7, accordingly, present the preaching of the apostles in Jerusalem, until the persecution that erupts in response to Stephen's activity and execution. Chapters 8–12 outline missionary efforts by those dispersed from Jerusalem because of the persecution, such as Philip in Samaria, and by the apostles themselves, who somehow had managed to stay in the city. An important episode here is Peter's reluctant mission to the Gentile Cornelius, which brings Peter under the scrutiny of the other apostles. The episode is important because Peter and the other apostles are now convinced, against their initial judgment, that salvation through Jesus—with the accompanying gift of the Holy Spirit—has been extended to Gentiles. With this shift, God unilaterally declares the Jewish dietary laws, based on biblical commandments, null and void. God has now made clean what was formerly unclean (10:14; 11:9). (Contrast *Mark*, which attributes this declaration to Jesus of Nazareth; 7:19.) This monumental change is necessary to allow Jews like Peter, Barnabas, and Paul to move freely in Gentile homes and regions. The section also describes the founding of the church at Antioch in Syria—a church that will become second only to Jerusalem in importance by the end of the first century—by those who had been driven from Jerusalem (11:19).

The remainder of the book (chs. 13–28) portrays the exploits of the recent convert Paul (who had worked for a time in Antioch), as he and associates take their mission to faraway lands, if not quite the "ends of the earth." The story ends with Paul in the world capital, Rome.

A central development in the latter half of *Acts* is the movement of Christianity from a Jewish to a largely Gentile constituency. This change is not the result of someone's whim, *Luke* stresses, but results from painstaking and repeated experience. When Paul sets out on his missionary journeys, he routinely heads straight for the Jewish synagogue of a given town, in order to demonstrate to his fellow-Jews that it was necessary for the Messiah to die and, arguing back from that, that Jesus is the Messiah. Although some Jews believe what he says, others oppose Paul vehemently; they even pursue him from town to town. Jews from Asia Minor will eventually come to Jerusalem to ensure his arrest. He finds a much better reception among Gentiles, including the "God-fearers" or Gentile adherents of the synagogue. This unexpected result, contrary to his original intention, leads him ultimately to forsake the unbelieving Jews in favor of the Gentiles (13:51; 18:6; 28:23–28).

In the course of describing the growing mission to the Gentiles, the author indicates his view that for them as much as for Jews, Jesus' death and resurrection have changed everything. Before Jesus, God allowed Gentiles to go their own way (14:17–18) and overlooked their sins (17:30), but now he commands everyone everywhere to repent and trust Jesus (17:31).

By chapter 15, the positive response of Gentiles to Christian preaching has raised yet another question. Should Gentiles be circumcised and thus become Jews in order to be followers of the Jewish Messiah? Can they be saved otherwise (15:1)? The resolution of this issue is a major problem because circumcision is the most basic defining characteristic of a male Jew, originating in God's instruction to Abraham (*Gen.* 17:9–14). Yet under divine direction the apostles decide that, since the Holy Spirit has been given to Gentile believers (15:8, 12), God has obviously accepted them without circumcision. Therefore, circumcision is unnecessary, but Gentiles must observe God's requirements to abstain from idolatry, sexual immorality, strangled meat, and blood (15:20). It is in keeping with *Luke*'s well-ordered narrative that now, in the wake of this big decision, Paul and Silas revisit their Gentile converts to pass along the Jerusalem council's decision (16:4). In spite of this solution for Gentiles, however, *Luke* continues to stress that Jewish Christians steadfastly maintained their observance, with temple and synagogue attendance, purifications, festival celebration, and even special vows—notwithstanding Peter's telling observation about the burden of keeping the laws (15:10–11, 19).

In short, this author has admirably fulfilled his promise to recount events "in order," though it is another matter to decide whether the narrative is historically accurate. Much more than any other gospel, *Luke-Acts* tells a dynamic story, one that is constantly evolving in order to present a plausible account of Christian origins. This author seems already to have sensed and responded to some of the same historical problems in other gospels, especially the difference between the Jesus of Nazareth and the risen Christ, that eventually confront modern scholars. It is this concern for plausible sequence that allows him to claim the status of *asphaleia,* or "sure ground," for his narratives.

But *Luke*'s virtues also make it more difficult for the interpreter to determine its main points. In a more static narrative, such as *John,* main points are introduced at the beginning and regularly repeated. In *Luke-Acts,* however, one risks attributing to the author a position that he may have stated clearly in one passage, but only as appropriate to a bygone time and place. For example, does *Luke*'s author still think that the Pharisees at his time of writing are righteous, and that they have the capacity, if they would use it, to establish the kingdom (*Luke* 17:21)? Should Jesus' followers leave their families (*Luke* 14:26) and sell all of their possessions (*Luke* 18:22; *Acts* 2:45)? Or should they carry swords (*Luke* 22:36)? Or is it wise, when fired from one's job, to bilk the owner out of money (*Luke* 16:1–9)? Do all human beings really live and move in God (*Acts* 17:28)? Given the many substantial twists in the narrative, it seems that each of these items is tied to a particular scene and period. Some of them, indeed, may have been introduced largely for rhetorical effect. It would be hazardous to trace any of them to a fixed "theology" of the author.

In view of these constant shifts, it is important to notice where the story ends, in *Acts* 28. What we find there is a programmatic statement: the Jews have proven stubborn and unresponsive, so "this salvation" has gone out to the Gentiles (28:25–28). Indeed, for some time now, the author has, without qualification, quietly begun to speak of "the Jews" as opponents of the Christians (12:3, 11; 14:4–5), even while insisting that many Jews believed (13:43; 14:4). By the end of *Acts* the reader has come to associate the term "Jew" with unbelief and opposition. This ending point of conflict is where *Mark* and *John* begin Jesus' story, but *Luke*'s author is careful to postpone the hardened opposition until the end of the first Christian generation. The reader of *Luke-Acts* knows that it was not always so. Although Judaism and Christianity now seem to be distinct, and Christians do not live as Jews, that separation occurred over a long period of time and after many particular incidents. Indeed, one might suppose that the author's main point is nothing other than the *gradual development of Christianity from Jewish roots.*

Christian Teaching as Necessary Obedience

Critical to this gradual development is the idea of simple obedience to divine revelation. From a Jewish perspective, Christianity seemed arbitrary. How, Jews asked, can Christians claim any stake in Israel's heritage when they do not live as Jews, according to biblical commandments? And how can Christians revere as Messiah this man who was recently executed in Judea? One of the author's apparent motives in charting the sequence of events that established Christianity is to show that Christians are not perverse; they simply *obey* what has been definitively revealed. They have no choice, and cannot do otherwise.

This emphasis comes through first in *Luke*'s attention to "proof," "evidence," and "witness." From the beginning, Jesus never simply teaches but always couples his talk with actions that prove his divine calling. His signs and wonders are therefore his divine *accreditation,* unquestionable proof that the Holy Spirit is working through him. Similarly, *Luke*'s author goes to great lengths to demonstrate that Jesus' resurrection was tested by many people and in many ways over a period of forty days, so that now the apostles are credible witnesses. As Peter and John complain to the Jewish council, it does no good to tell them to stop teaching in Jesus' name; they must obey God and report what they have seen and heard (*Acts* 4:19–20). They cannot resist God.

The same point is made in *Luke*'s pivotal accounts of Peter's visit to Cornelius and of Paul's conversion. Peter insists that he has never eaten Gentile food; if it were his choice, he would not go to Gentiles. But it is not his choice, and he is driven by divine command to visit Cornelius. When he is subsequently challenged, the other apostles concede that they too cannot resist God's obvious decision.

In Saul (Paul), *Luke*'s author finds the most compelling example of the unwilling recruit, a vigorous representative of non-Christian Judaism, who so opposes the church that he seeks to root it out—men, women, and children. Plainly, one could not accuse him of arbitrarily conjuring up an aberrant religion! (In fact, Paul was so accused, in Jewish Christian circles, for a long time afterward.) Paul becomes a leading Christian figure in Acts only because he cannot do otherwise. The risen Jesus confronts him on the road to Damascus, blinds him, and compels him to stop resisting. Significantly, *Luke*'s author tells the story of Paul's conversion on three separate occasions. The story is featured, apparently, because it demonstrates that Paul "was not disobedient to the heavenly vision" (*Acts* 26:19). What reasonable person could accuse him of being perverse? It turns out, then, that the words of the Pharisee Gamaliel to his fellow councilors in the Sanhedrin have great significance for the author's whole project: If this way of thinking or acting has a human origin, it will be destroyed. But if it is from God, you ought not oppose them, lest you be found to be God-fighters (*Acts* 5:38–39).

If Christians are simply those people who have accepted the unavoidable fact of salvation through Jesus, then *Luke* also has a reasonable response to the otherwise troubling question: If you people are right that Jesus is the Messiah, then why have the majority of Jews not accepted your claim? How can your position be so compelling and obvious if they all reject it? *Luke's* answer is astute. The author says, in effect, that most people are complacent and unwilling to change; since Jesus' coming involves one of the major turning points in the history of salvation, most Jews naturally oppose it. This was not always the case, for when Jesus walked the villages of Galilee he attracted masses of the poor and sick eager for his message. But by the end of *Acts,* when the cosmic implications of Jesus' mission have become manifest, Jewish opposition has ossified.

That *Luke's* author sees Jewish opposition as a predictable social phenomenon is indicated in various passages. In the gospel, Jesus observes that no prophet finds a reception in his home country (*Luke* 4:24), and comments on Israel's alleged history of killing prophets (11:47–48; 13:33–35). The temple leaders ridicule the notion that Jesus could be either a prophet or Messiah (*Luke* 2:63–71; 23:35): administrators never look kindly on prophets! In *Luke-Acts,* both Jesus and Stephen request divine forgiveness for their killers, who act in ignorance (*Luke* 23:34—according to some manuscripts; *Acts* 7:60). Peter also asserts that Jesus was killed in ignorance (*Acts* 3:17). The point is developed in what might otherwise appear as a rambling speech by Stephen (*Acts* 7). Why does Stephen, who is about to be stoned, go into such detail about minor aspects of Moses' career? The answer seems to be that Moses, like Jesus, faced constant rejection by his contemporaries, not only at the beginning, when his credentials might have been unknown, but also long after he had proven his divine call with irrefutable miracles (*Acts* 7:23–43). Moses' experience, preserved in Jewish scripture itself, illustrates the problem of rejection faced by Jesus' followers.

Finally, *Luke's* author finds in *Isa.* 6:9–10 a scathing indictment of Israel's complacency and he closes his work with it (*Acts* 28:26–27). Although Jewish opposition is an obvious fact, and no doubt a thorn in the flesh of early Christians, the author tries to show that it is understandable, and so does not cast doubt on the truth of Christian claims.

Other Themes

In such a long and richly textured narrative as *Luke-Acts,* the number of subordinate themes already discovered defies even simple listing; many more will be uncovered by new readers. The following might at least help to alert the reader to the many levels on which the story operates.

Roles of Women

In contrast to the other gospels, *Luke-Acts* features women from beginning to end. Its lengthy stories of John the Baptist's and Jesus' births are told largely in relation to the pious and faithful mothers, Elisabeth and Mary. The fathers are background figures at best. Zechariah's claim to fame is his lack of trust in the angel's words, and Joseph could be played by an "extra." Only *Luke* specifies that Jesus' ministry was underwritten by a group of women from Galilee, at least some of whom had significant resources (*Luke* 8:2–3). It is these women from Galilee who see Jesus' burial place (*Luke* 23:55) and first discover the resurrection (*Luke* 24:1–10). At 11:31, *Luke*'s Jesus predicts that the Queen of Sheba will stand in judgment over the *males* of "this generation" because she was zealous for the truth and they are not. Interestingly, *Luke* transfers the charge of adultery from a remarried woman to her new husband (*Luke* 16:18; see *Mark* 10:12), and specially mentions strained relations between mothers-in-law and daughters-in-law (*Luke* 12:53). *Luke*'s gospel has at least six unique episodes that focus on women: the raising of the widow's son (7:11–17); Jesus' acceptance of the sinful woman scorned by the Pharisee (7:36–50); Jesus' encounter with Martha and Mary, in which he approves of Mary's eagerness to learn (10:38–42); the cure of a crippled woman (13:10–17); the parable of the woman's lost coin (15:8–10); and the parable of the persistent widow (18:1–8). When these are added to the common tradition of stories about women (e.g., the woman with the hemorrhage, the widow's mite), the effect is to create an air of mutuality between male and female that is rare in ancient literature.

The same emphasis continues throughout *Acts*. The women from Galilee are still present when Jesus' followers receive the Holy Spirit (*Acts* 1:14). *Luke* repeatedly draws attention to influential women God-fearers, who can either hurt or help the Christian missionaries (13:50; 16:13; 17:1). And the author often mentions couples rather than men alone: Ananias and Sapphira, Prisca and Aquila (note that the woman's name appears first), Felix and Drusilla, Agrippa and Berenice (brother and sister). In addition to the several women who play obvious supporting roles—Tabitha/Dorcas, Lydia, and Philip's prophetic daughters—the author slips in many casual references to women (8:3, 12; 9:2; 17:12, 34), which strengthen the sense of mutuality already noted.

Luke's attention to women is all the more intriguing because we have reason to believe that women constituted a large proportion of the converts to both Judaism and Christianity (and to some other Mediterranean religious groups). Christians will be ridiculed by the second-century philosopher Celsus for having attracted mainly women and the uneducated poor. He means to say that Christians are gullible. One might suppose that *Luke*'s emphasis reflects the author's desire to tell a plausible story, that he merely recounts the way things were in the early church. But Josephus, to take a counterexample, only acknowledges the numbers of women converts in incidental notes; he does not highlight their roles in his story. *Luke*, by contrast, stresses women's roles where there is no apparent constraint to do so. We must wonder how the audience was expected to receive such a presentation.

Jerusalem, the Temple, and Jewish Tradition

Both the gospel and *Acts* chart geographical progressions, and in both cases Jerusalem functions as a kind of magnet. Both stories begin in Jerusalem (*Luke* 1–2; *Acts* 1–7) and, although the characters move away in the interim, the climactic sections occur in Jerusalem once again (*Luke* 19–23; *Acts* 21–24). In the gospel, much of Jesus' career is presented as a fateful progression toward Jerusalem (9:51; 13:31–34; 17:11), and in *Acts* Jerusalem is constantly present in the background as the home of Christianity and the apostles. The most important location within the city is the world-famous Jewish temple, and most of the activity in Jerusalem takes place in or near the temple precincts.

In keeping with its unambiguous location of Christian origins in Jerusalem is *Luke-Acts'* pervasive emphasis on Jewish history and culture. Jesus' parents are devout Jews who fulfill all of their obligations according to the law. Jesus himself regularly participates in synagogue life. Long after Jesus' resurrection his followers can be found in the temple at the regular time of sacrifice. Even Paul's established custom was to attend synagogue on the Sabbath. Thus Christianity emerges from the heart of Jewish tradition and stands within the orb of Jewish culture. *Luke* repeatedly claims that Roman authorities are incompetent to judge Christians, for the Christian problem is an internal Jewish affair. Accordingly, the speeches of *Acts* tend to preface their introduction of Jesus with a short history of the nation, and copious citation of scripture. Although Christian teaching is new, the author implies, it is only the latest chapter in the age-old story of God's dealings with his people. Indeed, *Luke's* Paul claims that he has said nothing that was not already said about the Messiah by the prophets (*Acts* 26:22–23). The term "the People" is very important in *Luke-Acts:* Throughout the gospel and much of *Acts*, it refers to the Jews, who are open to be drawn to Christianity if they can escape the influence of their leaders, but in the middle of *Acts* (15:14), in the face of growing Jewish resistance, we begin to see the recognition that God has condescended to accept a "people" from the Gentiles. The Jews as a people have ultimately chosen to resist God's work (*Acts* 28:26).

Apostolic Supervision, Peace, and Harmony

Corresponding to the centrality of Jerusalem is *Luke's* emphasis on the role of the apostles as guarantors of Christian legitimacy. This theme begins almost imperceptibly in the gospel, where Jesus chooses twelve men from among his many students and calls them by the name "apostles" (*Luke* 6:13). That incident may have been common to *Mark* (3:14, in some manuscripts) but only *Luke* builds directly on it. This author alone refers to this group several times by their special name. Most important, *Acts* opens by describing the problem caused by Judas's defection from the group of apostles (*Acts* 1:12–26). We learn here that apostleship is an "office" and that there must be twelve members, so Judas must be replaced. We also learn the necessary (but not sufficient) qualifications for the office: One must have been with Jesus from his immersion by John until his ascension. Once a replacement has been named, the apostles assume a critical role in the story. Only they provide credible witness to the cornerstone of Christian preaching, Jesus' bodily resurrection. And only they—the central committee—can authorize innovations such as the Samaritan and Antiochene missions, the mission to Gentiles, and the waiving of circumcision. It is striking that the author of *Luke*, in spite of his obvious admiration for Paul, does not consider him an apostle.[1]

An unmistakable air of peace and harmony pervades *Luke-Acts*, partly as a result of the apostles' supervisory activity in *Acts*. We have noted the importance of the word "peace" to *Luke*. The author also uses various phrases to stress that Jesus' followers were "in one accord" or "of one mind." He admits that problems arose within the young church—a dispute between two groups of widows, controversy over Peter's visit to Gentiles, disagreement about circumcision for Gentiles—but he claims that these were quickly and amicably settled by the apostles. The reader might compare Paul's letters, written during the period in question, to determine whether *Luke* has imagined more harmony than actually existed. By choosing to include Paul's prediction of coming strife and internal division after his death (*Acts* 20:29–31), the author seems to reflect a nostalgia for the time of the apostles and perhaps an oblique admission that the church of his own day is not nearly so unified.

Roman Authorities and Christianity

In contrast to the Jewish opposition that begins with Jesus' death and grows throughout the book of *Acts*, the Roman authorities appear quite consistently tolerant of this Jewish teacher and his followers. This does not mean that *Luke-Acts* flatters them; rather, it takes an appropriately realistic tone. It notes both Pilate's savagery (*Luke* 13:1) and the proconsul Gallio's complete lack of interest in Jewish affairs (*Acts* 18:14–17). Still, in the face of Jewish accusations *Luke's* Pilate protests four times that he finds no cause of death in Jesus. In *Acts*, the blame for Jesus' death is shifted entirely to the Jewish leaders. When Paul visits Cyprus, we seem to have a kind of model episode. He finds the Roman governor of the island intelligent and open to Christian teaching, in spite of the scheming of his Jewish magician advisor, whom Paul calls a "son of the devil." And when Paul himself becomes the target of a Jewish plot, it is again the Roman military that rescues him. There we are told not only that the Roman governors find no cause of death in him, but also—a datum that is not hinted at in Paul's letters—that he himself enjoys the prized Roman citizenship.

Christianity as a Philosophical School

The final theme to be mentioned here is not as obvious as the others on the literary level, but it would have been clear to first-century readers. *Luke* presents Jesus and his students in terms reminiscent of philosophical schools. Jesus appears as the founder of a new philosophical tradition within ancient Jewish culture, which already included other such schools. In the first century, philosophy involved much

---

[1] *Acts* 14:4, 14 do admittedly use the Greek term *apostolos* of Barnabas and Paul. But it seems, given the incidental nature of these references and the author's stress on the formal role of apostles, that he is using the word here in its wider sense of "emissary" or "missionary."

more than the merely abstract reasoning that we commonly associate with philosophers today. Embracing philosophy required conversion to a particular discipline of life, and it affected one's whole lifestyle, from diet to dress to manner of speech, which is why it was often rejected by aristocratic Romans as unbecoming for men of affairs. Philosophers of all stripes—Stoic, Cynic, Epicurean, Platonist, Pythagorean, and others—were associated with an extremely simple lifestyle, free of life's cares. They were also often considered obnoxious people, who put a premium on free, uninhibited speech, even before rulers. This reputation fit Socrates' description of the philosopher as a "gadfly," always challenging and provoking society's leaders. Philosophical "schools" were not buildings, but international groups of students dedicated to preserving and living out the teachings of the deceased founder.

To be sure, *Luke* does not call Jesus a "philosopher" in so many words. But consider the following data. The prologue indicates *Luke's* concern with what has been "handed down" from Jesus' contemporaries—a technical term for the transmission of school teachings. Jesus appears as a "teacher" who, in spite of his humble origins, is recognized and consulted by other teachers. Jesus' message focuses on the poor, and he requires that his own followers leave their homes and sell their goods. He demands this ascetic behavior in order that they might be effective "salt"—a metaphor, like that of Socrates' gadfly, that emphasizes their countercultural role (Plato, *Apology* 8 [31]). He is free in his criticism of local leaders, who are represented most consistently by the Pharisees. The main point of his critique is that the Pharisees are ineffective—hypocrites, lovers of money, irrelevant logic-choppers, concerned with outward appearance and not reality. Like the notorious "sophists" among Greek and Hellenistic philosophers, they are paid time-servers, who complacently preserve the way things are. They have no "bite" whatsoever, and are utterly ineffective in the face of people's real needs.

Luke's Jesus and his students are not like the Pharisees because they bring effective teaching, which is always accompanied by deeds. Notice that *Luke* almost always speaks of Jesus' words and deeds together, a combination that would preserve Jesus from the philosopher's biggest pitfall, hypocrisy. A non-Christian contemporary of *Luke's*, Epictetus, complained bitterly about philosophers unworthy of the name, who delighted merely in abstract reasoning. He insisted that true philosophy was a cure for the soul, which required that the "sick" person first realize his sickness and then seek help (*Discourses* 2.9; 19; 3.21.30–38). It is precisely this contrast that we see in *Luke-Acts,* for Jesus is a "physician"; his words and those of his followers pierce to the heart of the hearer and bring about a "change of mind"—the Greek word favored by *Luke* that is usually translated "repentance." Jesus, like Socrates in many respects, is brought to trial for having caused an upheaval in the society of his day.

In *Acts* the philosophical overtones become more explicit. We see there the early Christian community sharing all things in common, like the famous Pythagoreans or the Jewish Essenes; Christians routinely speaking out before crowds and authorities with perfect freedom—*Luke* uses the same Greek word group here that philosophers used to describe this virtue; Paul comparing Christian teaching to a philosophy in his speech in Athens; and, most important, several passages that place the Christians alongside the Pharisees and Sadducees as another Jewish "philosophical school." The Greek word used in *Acts (hairesis)* was a technical term for philosophical schools in the first century. Although the Christian belief in resurrection attracts the derision of some Athenian philosophers, *Luke* stresses that one of the major recognized Jewish schools, that of the Pharisees, already accepts resurrection. Indeed, the Christians share many ideas with the Pharisees—also belief in spirits and angels—which is perhaps why so many Pharisees become Christians and why the Pharisee Paul can live as a Christian in good conscience. But in contrast to all other Jewish schools, again, the Christians' teaching is effective. Unlike the hapless sons of the Jewish high priest, who are scornfully ignored by the evil spirits (*Acts* 19:12–20), Jesus' followers wield undeniable power through the Holy Spirit to cure and cast out devils. Paul is a model of Christian effectiveness when he saves all of his shipmates from drowning because of his complete composure and farsightedness under stress; these were the essential marks of a true philosopher.

Obviously, many of *Luke*'s categories—prophet, Holy Spirit, Messiah, scripture—do not fit the typical language of the Greek philosophical schools. The author plants Christian origins firmly within the sphere of Jewish culture. Yet a contemporary Jewish author, Flavius Josephus, also uses biblical and Jewish categories (e.g., Jewish priesthood) in his argument that Jewish culture as a whole represents a philosophical tradition comparable to the Greek, and that it contains within it various schools corresponding to the major Greek schools. A good example of this transferability of categories is in the theme of divine retribution. Josephus makes much of his claim that the Jewish God inevitably rewards righteousness and punishes wickedness. This involvement in human affairs shows that the Jewish philosophy articulated by Moses is effective and compelling. *Luke* similarly stresses the theme of divine retribution in his demonstration of Christianity's effective power. Although readers with a background in the Bible might be inclined to say, "Of course, Josephus is adapting the outlook of *Deuteronomy* 28, with its blessings and cursings," we must realize that the theme of "justice" *(dikē)* was also basic to Greek thinking. Therefore the use of Jewish categories in *Luke* would not have prevented its readers from understanding Jesus' school in philosophical terms.

Having mentioned Josephus in this context, we should note further that *Luke*'s portrayal of the church as a philosophical school within Jewish culture, alongside the Pharisees and Sadducees, seems to require that he and his readers thought of Jewish culture in philosophical terms to begin with. But since the only Jewish author we know to have made such a sustained argument about the Pharisees and Sadducees was Josephus, we must ask also whether the author of *Luke-Acts* knew of

Josephus's work. This issue is made more intriguing by many particular coincidences of language between the two authors, in addition to the overall similarity of their projects.

Literary Features

The sheer size of this two-part narrative allows the author to employ an array of storytelling techniques to maintain the reader's interest. These tried and true devices were used by even the most sober historians of the day. Space does not permit a full discussion, but we may indicate some features to watch for.

Language Appropriate to Scene

One of the author's most useful techniques is his adaptation of language to the scene at hand. He does not advertise these changes, and many of them are not obvious in English translation, but he varies his vocabulary, sentence structure, and even dialect with each new environment. We have already observed the abrupt shift from the historian's prologue to the serene world of "biblical" antiquity, with angels and heavenly choirs, at *Luke* 1:5. Like the modern moviemaker who deliberately used black-and-white film to evoke bygone days, *Luke* employs the old-fashioned sentence structure of the Bible throughout *Luke,* but then modernizes it significantly when he begins *Acts.* Similarly, he uses Hebrew names for weights and measures in *Luke,* appropriately to the scene, but abandons them in *Acts.* He calls Paul by his Hebrew name, Saul, while the story is set in Syria/Palestine, but quietly shifts to the Greek *Paulos* when Paul leaves on his missionary journeys (*Acts* 13:9). His care to call Roman and Jewish officials by their correct titles, to have them speak as such officials might plausibly speak, and to describe particular regions of the Eastern Mediterranean accurately, is famous. The vivid shipwreck story of *Acts* 27, which is filled with nautical terms for particular ropes and sails and ship features, is a striking example of the author's art.

Editorial Summaries and Speeches

It was customary for Hellenistic historians to make extensive use of summaries and speeches to help convey their main points. These devices served much the same purpose: They interrupted the narrative so that the author could reflect on some pertinent issue related to the events that had just occurred. Summaries were the most direct way to do that, and the author employs them at several strategic points. But they had to be short if they were not to stifle the flow of the story. Speeches placed in the mouths of the leading characters, by contrast, could be quite long, elaborating several important themes, without departing from the scene. Authors were obliged to make their speeches appropriate to the speaker and the scene, but no one expected precision in this area. Because speeches were created for each occasion by the author (see Thucydides, *Peloponnesian War* 1.22.1), they gave him an opportunity to shape the narrative quite directly.

In the gospel, interestingly enough, *Luke*'s author does not take *Matthew*'s route of welding Jesus' short sayings into a few long speeches. He prefers to keep the speeches relatively short and representative of Jesus' behavior in specific situations. Perhaps partly under the influence of his sources, he presents Jesus as a teacher who speaks briefly on a wide range of issues. In *Acts,* formal speeches become common and, like the speeches of other works in the author's day, they carry the author's own stamp more visibly. One third of the book consists of some twenty-four speeches, and these share many structural similarities—most obviously (in Gk) the direct opening address, "Men, *x*," where *x* serves to further identify the audience (1:1, 16; 2:14; 3:17; 5:35; 7:2; 13:16; 15:7; 17:22). We invite the reader to compare the speeches of *Acts,* with an eye on the Greek if possible, and to assess the degree to which they reflect the author's voice versus that of the speaker's (compare for example, Paul's letters).

Doublets and Parallels

Luke frequently, but again without advertisement, suggests parallels between Jesus' story and that of his followers. We have seen some of these already: the centrality of Jerusalem, and the roles of Jewish and Roman authorities in the trials of the main characters. But the author also uses the *Acts* quietly to complete the story begun in the gospel. For example, Jesus' warning about false Messiahs (*Luke* 21:8) is fulfilled in Gamaliel's observation about such figures (*Acts* 5:35–39). Jesus' prediction of persecution and suffering for his followers, including their punishment in synagogues and appearance before kings (*Luke* 21:12–15), is fulfilled in *Acts* (3–4; 7; 12:1–5; 26). Invulnerability to snakebite, promised in the gospel (*Luke* 10:19), is enjoyed by Paul in *Acts* (28:3–5). Even Jesus' instruction about how to respond to unreceptive towns (*Luke* 9:5; 10:11) is followed by the later Christian missionaries (*Acts* 13:51). The careful reader will note many similar kinds of stories—raising the dead; encounters with Samaritans, Roman centurions, and exorcists other than Jesus' followers—linking the two halves of the story.

Irony, Pathos, Deceit, Sarcasm, and Humor

A whole range of storytelling techniques employed by *Luke*'s author should be mentioned because they are not always obvious to the modern English reader. Ancient historians did not share our scruples about distinguishing rigidly between entertainment and history. Historians were supposed to use dramatic techniques with restraint, to be sure, but it was understood that stories would be read only if they offered some prospect of "delight." To appreciate the author's efforts in this area, it helps to know a bit about the reputations of his characters; see the notes to *Acts* 24:25–26; 26:2–3. But most of his techniques will emerge from a careful reading of the story itself.

Not to be missed are *Luke*'s insights into human nature. We can almost hear the prodigal's older brother pouting about his lack of fair reward (*Luke* 15:29). The manager (or steward) who is terminated by his wealthy employer wonders what he will do: "I am not strong enough to dig, and I ashamed to beg" (*Luke* 16:3). When the Philippian magistrates discover that they have unwittingly imprisoned and beaten Roman citizens, Paul and Silas, they beg the pair to leave town quietly (*Acts* 16:39). The Roman tribune in Jerusalem, exceedingly embarrassed to find, when he is about to have his prisoner flogged, that Paul was a Roman citizen, later writes to the governor that he was quick to rescue Paul from the Jews because he had *already* learned of Paul's citizenship (*Acts* 23:27)! And when Paul's storm-tossed ship is on the verge of sinking, it is he who draws the centurion's attention to the sailors' plan to escape—on the pretext of lowering a lifeboat to drop anchor (*Acts* 27:30–31). The author's astute observations on human nature make him an unusually good storyteller.

Historical Circumstances: Date, Author, Audience, and Occasion

It is one thing to describe the contours of this fascinating story, but another to determine the historical situation that inspired the author to write. Who was this person whom tradition has called "Luke"? When did his work appear? Did he (possibly she) write mainly for Christians or non-Christians, for Jews, Gentiles, or God-fearers? Because of its size and style, *Luke-Acts* offers more tantalizing clues about these issues than the other gospels, but in the end they are still insufficient to establish anything near certainty. We are once again reduced to speculation about whose interests would be best served by this narrative.

Only the rough date of *Luke-Acts* can be settled with probability. It was written toward the end of the first century, or in the early second. Several independent factors point to such a date: (a) the author's knowledge of several (he says "many") existing gospels, including *Mark,* which seems to date itself to at least the 60s or 70s; (b) his detailed knowledge of the Roman destruction of Jerusalem in 70 C.E., and his interpretation of that event as divine punishment for the Jewish rejection of Jesus (*Luke* 19:41–44; 21:20–24); (c) his presentation of the apostles' time as a bygone golden age of harmony, in contrast to the author's own situation of serious division (see *Acts* 20:29–30); and (d) the possibility that he knew the *Jewish Antiquities* of Josephus, which was completed in 93/94 C.E. *Luke-Acts* could not have been written much later than 120 C.E., however, because it was well known to Marcion no later than 140.

From the late second century, at least, Christian tradition attributed the gospel to a physician and companion of Paul, named Luke, who is mentioned in *Col.* 4:14 (see *Phlm.* 24; *2 Tim.* 4:11). Some commentators at the beginning of the twentieth century supposed that they could even find traces of the physician's touch in *Luke*'s emphasis on words of "healing" and its vivid vocabulary for body parts. And the so-called "we" passages (*Acts* 16:10–17; 20:5–15; 21:8–18; 27:1–28:16) seemed to confirm that the author was Paul's companion for several sea journeys.

It is, of course, possible that the author was a companion of Paul's, but the arguments are insecure. The same second-century Christians who made the identification were evidently wrong about other attributions of texts (such as to *Mark* and *Matthew*); it appears that they were guessing. The "medical" vocabulary in *Luke* is of a piece with all of the other specialized vocabulary that this expert narrator uses, but it does not make him a physician any more than it makes him a sailor or a philosopher. He was, without doubt, an educated and creative writer. The emphasis on "healing" is basic to his presentation of Jesus' effectiveness; it need not reflect the author's profession. And the "we" passages, strangely, appear and disappear without explanation. Although they do suggest that their author accompanied Paul on some sea journeys (only), that unstated implication might itself be part of *Luke's* narrative craft, or it might result from the author's use of someone's travel diaries; we cannot be sure with such an artful writer. If the author of *Luke-Acts* had accompanied Paul, we might have hoped for a clear statement to that effect, since eyewitness presence was considered the greatest virtue of historians, and the author stresses his credentials where he can (*Luke* 1:3–4).

It is tempting to deduce something about the author's identity and location from his narrative emphases: the "we" passages; the importance attributed to Antioch—or any of the other locales featured from time to time (Ephesus, Corinth, Rome); the author's consistent concern for women; and his emphasis on "God-fearers" or righteous Gentiles. It does seem clear that the author and audience are somewhat removed from Judea, since he regularly explains Palestinian geography, assumes that the hot wind is from the south (rather than from the east, as in Judea or Galilee; *Luke* 12:55), and supposes that roofs are tiled. Perhaps, then, the author was a God-fearer in Ephesus or Rome, perhaps a woman. We have no way of confirming such speculations.

We know equally little about *Luke's* audience. Both volumes are addressed to one Theophilus, described as "most excellent" or "most noble" (*Luke* 1:3; *Acts* 1:1). Theophilus appears in the place where one would expect a writer to acknowledge his literary patron—someone who had encouraged the work and perhaps provided materials or a stipend. His name, literally "friend of God," tells us little. It could be the name of a freed slave (freedman), but it is also attested for members of the Jewish and Greek elite (Josephus, *Ant.* 17.78; 18.123; *Ag. Ap.* 2.116). The address "most excellent" was commonly, but not exclusively, used for the Roman lower nobility, the "equestrian" order, and within the story itself *Luke* uses it only of the equestrian governors Felix and Festus. This might suggest that Theophilus was a man of some means, who had expressed an interest in Christianity. Perhaps he had achieved rank in Roman society, so that the author could use him as a broker of the church's interests—someone who would defend the Christian cause in his circles and before his own patrons. The author says that Theophilus has already been "instructed" somewhat, and he will provide "sure ground" for him. But does this mean that he was an interested outsider, or an eager recent convert, or a Christian who had become disenchanted—perhaps in part by the many conflicting interpretations mentioned? In truth, we cannot even be sure (though it seems likely) that Theophilus was a real person, and not another literary creation of the author.

If it is hard to figure out who Theophilus was, it is more difficult to establish *Luke*'s wider intended audience. Acknowledgment of a patron was a literary formality, but the author usually had a larger audience in view. A basic question is whether the text was written mainly for Christians or non-Christians. The problem here is that many of the defensive (or "apologetic") emphases of the work—the church's deep roots in Judaism, opposition from Jews, friendliness toward Rome—could be aimed at both insiders and outsiders. The main problems with Christianity from an outsider's perspective—its ambiguous social status, novelty, separation from Judaism, reverence for a condemned criminal, reputation for immorality, and consequent vulnerability to discipline by the authorities—were no doubt the very things that also gave Christians themselves cause for concern, and led some of them ultimately to abandon the faith. We know from several contemporary Christian texts, as well as Pliny's letter to Trajan, that defection ("apostasy") was a continuing problem for Christians. *Luke*'s author highlights the issue when he has Paul routinely exhorting converts to remain in the faith. So we cannot conclude from *Luke*'s defensive posture that it was written mainly for outsiders. In view of considerable evidence that Christians did not yet have a foothold in higher social circles, especially at Rome, it seems most likely that *Luke-Acts* would have found most of its readers among Christians.

If so, then these Christian readers must have been deeply interested in the church's relationship to Judaism. The author expects them to be helped by his charting of the gradual separation of Christianity from Judaism, of God's unilateral abrogation of the dietary laws, and of the general relaxation of the law for Gentiles. They are evidently Gentiles who share *Luke*'s perspective (by the end of *Acts*) that the Jews as a people had rejected Christianity. They should be reassured by his insistence that non-Christian Judaism is utterly ineffective; that the church is the real heir of Jewish culture—rejected by Jews only because of its fearless submission to God's undeniable recent revelation; that Jesus really is the Messiah hoped for in Israel's classical texts; and that Roman authorities have never found any sound basis for hostility toward the group. The theme of Jewish resistance and Roman support would, of course, take on a special resonance after the failed Jewish revolt of 66–73 C.E., in the aftermath of which the Jews' reputation as opponents of the Roman peace was entrenched in many minds (Tacitus, *Hist.* 5.4). The audience must be fairly sophisticated to appreciate the author's remarkable efforts; they must have some idea of Israelite history and prophecy, and of biblical language.

It may be that this history was intended merely to provide faithful Christians with an answer when they were challenged concerning the origins of their "way." But we usually assume that early Christians wrote lengthy works such as this for more immediate reasons, not merely for leisurely self-expression or posterity. As we have noted, *Luke-Acts* claims that many Christians were themselves tempted to abandon their faith in difficult times. If *Luke*'s anticipated readers included such potential apostates, his elaborate argument makes the best sense if we suppose that they felt some attraction to Judaism, perhaps a form of Christian Judaism, as a more secure home than Gentile Christianity. Why would *Luke* make such an enormous effort to show the historic legitimacy of Christianity and its superiority to other Jewish schools if its readers had already written off Judaism as obsolete? We know from other sources that Judaism continued to attract a conspicuous number of adherents and converts throughout the period in which *Luke* was writing, and some Gentile Christians also found the more established culture attractive. This possible historical context may or may not be rendered probable, but it illustrates how little we know about the conditions in which this influential two-volume work appeared.

For Further Reading

Darr, John A. *On Character Building: The Reader and the Rhetoric of Characterization in Luke-Acts.* Louisville: Westminster John Knox, 1992.

Hemer, Colin J. *The Book of Acts in the Setting of Hellenistic History.* Winona Lake, Ind.: Eisenbrauns, 1990.

Hengel, Martin. *Acts and the History of Earliest Christianity.* Translated by John Bowden. Philadelphia; Fortress, 1979.

Keck, Leander E., and J. Louis Martyn, eds. *Studies in Luke-Acts.* Philadelphia: Fortress, 1980.

Mason, Steve. *Josephus and the New Testament.* 2d ed. Peabody, Mass.: Hendrickson, 2003.

Sanders, Jack T. *The Jews in Luke-Acts.* Philadelphia: Fortress, 1987.

Tannehill, Robert C. *The Narrative Unity of Luke-Acts: A Literary Interpretation.* 2 vols. Philadelphia: Fortress, 1986.

Tyson, Joseph B. *Luke, Judaism, and the Scholars: Critical Approaches to Luke-Acts.* Columbia: University of South Carolina Press, 1999.

Winter, Bruce, ed. *The Book of Acts in Its First Century Setting.* 5 vols. Grand Rapids: Eerdmans, 1993–2003.

THE GOSPEL ACCORDING TO LUKE

Dedication to Theophilus

1 Since many have undertaken to set down an orderly account of the events that have been fulfilled among us, [2] just as they were handed on to us by those who from the beginning were eyewitnesses and servants of the word, [3] I too decided, after investigating everything carefully from the very first,[a] to write an orderly account for you, most excellent Theophilus, [4] so that you may know the truth concerning the things about which you have been instructed.

a Or *for a long time*

The Birth of John the Baptist Foretold

[5] In the days of King Herod of Judea, there was a priest named Zechariah, who belonged to the priestly order of Abijah. His wife was a descendant of Aaron, and her name was Elizabeth. [6] Both of them were righteous before God, living blamelessly according to all the commandments and regulations of the Lord. [7] But they had no children, because Elizabeth was barren, and both were getting on in years.

[8] Once when he was serving as priest before God and his section was on duty, [9] he was chosen by lot, according to the custom of the priesthood, to enter

---

1:1 undertaken Or "taken it upon themselves," pejoratively. The Gk word occurs again in *Acts* 9:29; 19:13. **set down an orderly account** Or "write up a narrative." This is not the same Gk phrase as in 1:3; only there does the word for "orderly" explicitly appear. **1:2 handed on** In both Greco-Roman philosophical schools and Jewish rabbinical circles, this could be a technical term for the passing down of tradition. **eyewitnesses and servants** These two categories may correspond to the source material of the two volumes—*eyewitnesses* of Jesus' life in *Luke* and *servants* of the word in *Acts*. The author does not seem to include himself among these. **the word** Or "teaching," "doctrine." Gk *logos*, a term often used by early Christians to denote the substance of their faith; see *1 Thess.* 1:6; *Acts* 6:4; 8:4. **1:3 I too decided** The author evidently considered existing accounts inadequate. **carefully** Or "precisely." This is a common term in Gk historical prefaces. It is not certain whether the adverb should go with *investigating* or with *to write.* **to write an orderly account for you** Or "to write for you in order." The author mentions precision and orderliness only here, speaking of his own work. The word for *in order* appears only in *Luke-Acts* in the NT; note the sense in *Acts* 3:24 ("after him"); 11:4 ("step by step"); 18:23 ("from place to place"). The author presents this as a distinctive feature of his work. **most excellent** Or "noblest." Commonly, but not necessarily, an address for Roman knights (members of the equestrian order, ranking below senators), used thus elsewhere in this work; *Acts* 23:26; 24:3; 26:25. **Theophilus** Lit. "friend of God." See *Acts* 1:1. Nothing further is known about this person. Several men named Theophilus held high hereditary social positions in Judea (Josephus, *Ant.* 17.8; 18.123; see *Ag. Ap.* 1.216). Apparently the man is in a position of some influence. In the absence of post-Enlightenment ideals about equality, influence in ancient Mediterranean society depended largely upon networks of patrons and clients. An ancient reader would immediately recognize Theophilus as some kind of patron for the author. It is possible that, lacking a real patron, the author has created this figure as a literary device, perhaps even ironically, to match the kind of patron elite writers had, such as Josephus enjoyed in Epaphroditus (*Ant.* 1.8). But we have no good reason to doubt that he was a real person. **1:4 truth** Gk *asphaleia*: sure ground, security; *not* truth in any abstract sense. In *Acts* 21:34; 22:30; 25:26 the corresponding adjective is used when an interested outsider is unable to discern the truth amid competing claims. This suggests that the author presents his account of Jesus as more reliable than its competitors. **been instructed** Theophilus has *been instructed* already about Christian origins. When the Gk verb used here appears later (*Acts* 18:25; 21:21, 24), it has the sense of preliminary instruction yet to be confirmed, qualified, or disputed. Its use here *may* suggest that the author does not see Theophilus as a firm believer. He could be an interested outsider, a new believer, or someone who is contemplating a departure from the Christian movement. **1:5 In the days of King Herod** Herod ruled Judea from 37 (though appointed in 40) to 4 B.C.E. The wording here confirms that *Luke's* readers lived considerably later than Herod's time. **order of Abijah** See *1 Chr.* 24:10. There were too many priests to serve in the temple at once. (*Ezra* 2:36–39 par. *Neh.* 7:39–42 claims that more than four thousand returned from the Babylonian exile; a Gentile writer about 300 B.C.E. [Hecataeus in Josephus, *Ag. Ap.* 1.188] put the number of priests at fifteen hundred.) According to *1 Chr.* 24:7–18, the priesthood was therefore divided into twenty-four courses, each of which took care of temple duties for one week. This rotating service supplemented the core of full-time temple-based priests. **a descendant of Aaron** Thus, from a high-priestly family in theory, though in practice only a few families were eligible for service. The author assumes some knowledge of the Bible among his readers. Jewish priesthood was hereditary, and the lineage of priests was a matter of special concern (*Lev.* 21:2–23; Josephus, *Ag. Ap.* 1.30–36). *Luke's* point seems to be that Zechariah and his wife were as righteous as could be (see 1:6). **1:7** See Abraham and Sarah (*Genesis* 15–22); Elkanah and Hannah (*1 Sam.* 1–2). **1:9** According to later rabbinic literature, each of the twenty-four priestly courses was subdivided into smaller groups and served only one or two days of the duty week (*y. Ta'an.* 68a). Before the

the sanctuary of the Lord and offer incense. ¹⁰Now at the time of the incense offering, the whole assembly of the people was praying outside. ¹¹Then there appeared to him an angel of the Lord, standing at the right side of the altar of incense. ¹²When Zechariah saw him, he was terrified; and fear overwhelmed him. ¹³But the angel said to him, "Do not be afraid, Zechariah, for your prayer has been heard. Your wife Elizabeth will bear you a son, and you will name him John. ¹⁴You will have joy and gladness, and many will rejoice at his birth, ¹⁵for he will be great in the sight of the Lord. He must never drink wine or strong drink; even before his birth he will be filled with the Holy Spirit. ¹⁶He will turn many of the people of Israel to the Lord their God. ¹⁷With the spirit and power of Elijah he will go before him, to turn the hearts of parents to their children, and the disobedient to the wisdom of the righteous, to make ready a people prepared for the Lord." ¹⁸Zechariah said to the angel, "How will I know that this is so? For I am an old man, and my wife is getting on in years." ¹⁹The angel replied, "I am Gabriel. I stand in the presence of God, and I have been sent to speak to you and to bring you this good news. ²⁰But now, because you did not believe my words, which will be fulfilled in their time, you will become mute, unable to speak, until the day these things occur."

²¹Meanwhile the people were waiting for Zechariah, and wondered at his delay in the sanctuary. ²²When he did come out, he could not speak to them, and they realized that he had seen a vision in the sanctuary. He kept motioning to them and remained unable to speak. ²³When his time of service was ended, he went to his home.

²⁴After those days his wife Elizabeth conceived, and for five months she remained in seclusion. She said, ²⁵"This is what the Lord has done for me when he looked favorably on me and took away the disgrace I have endured among my people."

The Birth of Jesus Foretold

²⁶In the sixth month the angel Gabriel was sent by God to a town in Galilee called Nazareth, ²⁷to a virgin engaged to a man whose name was Joseph, of the house of David. The virgin's name was Mary. ²⁸And he came to her and said, "Greetings, favored one! The Lord is with you."[b] ²⁹But she was much perplexed by his words and pondered what sort of greeting this might be. ³⁰The angel said to her, "Do not be afraid, Mary, for you have found favor with God. ³¹And now, you will conceive in your womb and bear a son, and you will name him Jesus. ³²He will be great, and will be called the Son of the Most High, and the Lord God will give to him the throne of his ancestor David. ³³He will reign over the house of Jacob forever, and of his kingdom there will be no end." ³⁴Mary said to the angel, "How can this be, since I am a virgin?"[c] ³⁵The angel said to her, "The Holy Spirit will come upon you, and the power of the Most High will overshadow you; therefore the child to be born[d] will be holy; he will be called Son of God. ³⁶And now, your relative Elizabeth in her old age has also conceived a son; and this is the sixth month for her who was said to be barren. ³⁷For nothing will be impossible with God." ³⁸Then Mary said, "Here am I, the servant of the Lord; let it be with me according to your word." Then the angel departed from her.

---

b Other ancient authorities add *Blessed are you among women*
c Gk *I do not know a man*
d Other ancient authorities add *of you*

---

morning daily sacrifice, visiting officiants were chosen by lot, and the others did not officiate. Three priests prepared the incense offering, though only one remained in the Holy Place for the actual offering (*m. Tamid* 6:1–3). **1:10** *the time of the incense offering* Either before daybreak or before the 9th hour (about 3:00 P.M.). *the whole...people* The entire nation was reportedly divided into twenty-four courses matching those of the priests, but for practical reasons each course sent only a representative delegation to the temple (*m. Ta'an.* 4:2). **1:15** See the prescriptions for the Nazirite in *Num.* 6:1–4. **1:17** *Elijah...turn the hearts* See *Mal.* 4:5–6; *Sir.* 48:10; *Matt.* 11:14. In *John* 1:21 the Baptist denies that he is Elijah. *a people prepared for the Lord* See *Mal.* 3:1; *Isa.* 40:3. **1:19** *Gabriel* Early Jewish literature speculated freely about angels and demons. Several archangels are named, such as Raphael and Uriel, but the most famous are Gabriel and Michael, who already appear in the biblical book of *Daniel* (*Dan.* 8:16; 9:21; 10:21; 12:1). **1:23** *time of service was ended* That is, at the end of the week. **1:25** It was considered a blessing to have children (*Deut.* 28:4); to be childless was a social and religious liability. **1:27** On betrothal, see the note to *Matt.* 1:18. *Luke's* readers would probably assume that Mary was a girl of twelve to fourteen, the normal age of marriage for girls in the ancient Mediterranean world. Joseph would be assumed to be somewhat older, perhaps in his mid-twenties. **1:31** The wording recalls *Isa.* 7:14. If the author expected his readers to make the connection, they must have either known the Bible very well or possessed a collection of Christian proof texts such as this one. **1:33** These statements recall various aspects of Israel's hope for an anointed son of David, a Messiah (Hebrew for "anointed") who was a "son of God" in the same way that the king of Israel was said to be God's son: he would assume David's throne, deal with Israel's oppressors, and install a kingdom of righteousness; see *Ps.* 2:7; *2 Sam.* 7:14; *Isa.* 9:6–7; *Song* 17. *Luke* makes it clear that Jesus is the fulfillment of this ancient hope. **1:36** Thus, *Luke* has two parallel miraculous births: Mary was a virgin when she bore Jesus, and Elizabeth was well beyond childbearing age when she bore John.

Mary Visits Elizabeth

³⁹In those days Mary set out and went with haste to a Judean town in the hill country, ⁴⁰where she entered the house of Zechariah and greeted Elizabeth. ⁴¹When Elizabeth heard Mary's greeting, the child leaped in her womb. And Elizabeth was filled with the Holy Spirit ⁴²and exclaimed with a loud cry, "Blessed are you among women, and blessed is the fruit of your womb. ⁴³And why has this happened to me, that the mother of my Lord comes to me? ⁴⁴For as soon as I heard the sound of your greeting, the child in my womb leaped for joy. ⁴⁵And blessed is she who believed that there would be*e* a fulfillment of what was spoken to her by the Lord."

Mary's Song of Praise

⁴⁶And Mary*f* said,

"My soul magnifies the Lord,
⁴⁷   and my spirit rejoices in God my Savior,
⁴⁸ for he has looked with favor on the lowliness of his servant.
      Surely, from now on all generations will call me blessed;
⁴⁹ for the Mighty One has done great things for me, and holy is his name.
⁵⁰ His mercy is for those who fear him from generation to generation.
⁵¹ He has shown strength with his arm; he has scattered the proud in the thoughts of their hearts.
⁵² He has brought down the powerful from their thrones, and lifted up the lowly;
⁵³ he has filled the hungry with good things, and sent the rich away empty.
⁵⁴ He has helped his servant Israel, in remembrance of his mercy,
⁵⁵ according to the promise he made to our ancestors, to Abraham and to his descendants forever."

⁵⁶And Mary remained with her about three months and then returned to her home.

The Birth of John the Baptist

⁵⁷Now the time came for Elizabeth to give birth, and she bore a son. ⁵⁸Her neighbors and relatives heard that the Lord had shown his great mercy to her, and they rejoiced with her.

⁵⁹On the eighth day they came to circumcise the child, and they were going to name him Zechariah after his father. ⁶⁰But his mother said, "No; he is to be called John." ⁶¹They said to her, "None of your relatives has this name." ⁶²Then they began motioning to his father to find out what name he wanted to give him. ⁶³He asked for a writing tablet and wrote, "His name is John." And all of them were amazed. ⁶⁴Immediately his mouth was opened and his tongue freed, and he began to speak, praising God. ⁶⁵Fear came over all their neighbors, and all these things were talked about throughout the entire hill country of Judea. ⁶⁶All who heard them pondered them and said, "What then will this child become?" For, indeed, the hand of the Lord was with him.

Zechariah's Prophecy

⁶⁷Then his father Zechariah was filled with the Holy Spirit and spoke this prophecy:

⁶⁸ "Blessed be the Lord God of Israel,
      for he has looked favorably on his people and redeemed them.
⁶⁹ He has raised up a mighty savior*g* for us in the house of his servant David,
⁷⁰ as he spoke through the mouth of his holy prophets from of old,
⁷¹   that we would be saved from our enemies and from the hand of all who hate us.
⁷² Thus he has shown the mercy promised to our ancestors, and has remembered his holy covenant,
⁷³ the oath that he swore to our ancestor Abraham, to grant us ⁷⁴that we, being rescued from the hands of our enemies, might serve him without fear,
⁷⁵in holiness and righteousness before him all our days.
⁷⁶ And you, child, will be called the prophet of the Most High; for you will go before the Lord to prepare his ways,
⁷⁷ to give knowledge of salvation to his people by the forgiveness of their sins.

---

e Or *believed, for there will be*
f Other ancient authorities read *Elizabeth*

g Gk *a horn of salvation*

1:46 Mary's song, later known as the Magnificat, draws heavily from Hannah's song in *1 Sam.* 2:1–10. **1:53** These lines anticipate the prominent *Luke-Acts* themes of reversal and of the mission to the poor. See 6:21–25. **1:55** The focus of *Luke-Acts* will gradually shift from *Abraham and . . . his descendants* to the Gentile world (see *Acts* 1:6; 18:6). **1:59** See *Gen.* 17:12. **1:63** Because writing material was scarce and expensive, reusable wax tablets were commonly employed for notes. **1:69** *a mighty savior* Lit. "a horn of salvation." The horn was a symbol of power; see *Ps.* 18:1; 92:10. **1:74** Notice the traditional messianic hopes here (see note to 1:33); *Luke* has not yet assimilated them to the Christian idea of Jesus' messiahship.

78 By the tender mercy of our God,
>the dawn from on high will break upon[h] us,

79 to give light to those who sit in darkness and in
>the shadow of death,
>to guide our feet into the way of peace."

80The child grew and became strong in spirit, and he was in the wilderness until the day he appeared publicly to Israel.

The Birth of Jesus

2 In those days a decree went out from Emperor Augustus that all the world should be registered. 2This was the first registration and was taken while Quirinius was governor of Syria. 3All went to their own towns to be registered. 4Joseph also went from the town of Nazareth in Galilee to Judea, to the city of David called Bethlehem, because he was descended from the house and family of David. 5He went to be registered with Mary, to whom he was engaged and who was expecting a child. 6While they were there, the time came for her to deliver her child. 7And she gave birth to her firstborn son and wrapped him in bands of cloth, and laid him in a manger, because there was no place for them in the inn.

The Shepherds and the Angels

8In that region there were shepherds living in the fields, keeping watch over their flock by night. 9Then an angel of the Lord stood before them, and the glory of the Lord shone around them, and they were terrified. 10But the angel said to them, "Do not be afraid; for see—I am bringing you good news of great joy

for all the people: 11to you is born this day in the city of David a Savior, who is the Messiah,[i] the Lord. 12This will be a sign for you: you will find a child wrapped in bands of cloth and lying in a manger." 13And suddenly there was with the angel a multitude of the heavenly host,[j] praising God and saying,

14 "Glory to God in the highest heaven,
>and on earth peace among those whom he
>favors!"[k]

15When the angels had left them and gone into heaven, the shepherds said to one another, "Let us go now to Bethlehem and see this thing that has taken place, which the Lord has made known to us." 16So they went with haste and found Mary and Joseph, and the child lying in the manger. 17When they saw this, they made known what had been told them about this child; 18and all who heard it were amazed at what the shepherds told them. 19But Mary treasured all these words and pondered them in her heart. 20The shepherds returned, glorifying and praising God for all they had heard and seen, as it had been told them.

Jesus Is Named

21After eight days had passed, it was time to circumcise the child; and he was called Jesus, the name given by the angel before he was conceived in the womb.

Jesus Is Presented in the Temple

22When the time came for their purification according to the law of Moses, they brought him up to

---

h Other ancient authorities read *has broken upon*

i Or *the Christ*
j Gk *army*
k Other ancient authorities read *peace, goodwill among people*

1:80 See 2:52. **2:1–3** This account is historically problematic because (a) Quirinius was apparently not governor of Syria during the reign of Herod the Great (died 4 B.C.E.), but only from 6 C.E.; (b) according to Josephus, *Ant.* 18.1–2, there was indeed an assessment of property under Quirinius, but only in 6 C.E., when Judea was annexed to the Roman province of Syria; (c) this assessment was not decreed for the entire world but was confined to Syria and Judea; and (d) it did not involve the return to one's tribal home, which would have been both pointless from an administrative point of view (because land ownership could not easily be verified) and practically impossible (because of the disappearance of many old towns, the difficulty of deciding which ancestor's home to visit, the expense and risk of travel, and the sheer chaos created by tens of millions of people on the move). Such an event could not easily have escaped the notice of other contemporary writers. **2:1** *Augustus* The title assumed by Octavian, who ruled as emperor *(princeps)* from 27 B.C.E. to 14 C.E. **2:4** Contrast *Matt.* 2:1–23, according to which Joseph and Mary were from Bethlehem and later moved to Nazareth. The author of *Luke* must not have expected his readers to know much about Palestinian geography, since he repeats that Nazareth is in Galilee (see 1:26) and also specifies that Bethlehem is in Judea. **2:7** *firstborn son* According to the Synoptics (*Mark* 3:31–35; 6:3; *Luke* 8:19–21), Jesus had several siblings. His brother James would become a major figure in the 1st-generation church. *the inn* Although it is possible that Bethlehem had an "inn"—a small hostel for travelers, the Gk word *(katalyma)* means only "lodging" or "billet." If one had family or friends in a town, ancient hospitality would require accommodation with them. **2:11** See notes to 1:33, 74; Jesus is for *Luke* the Messiah of Israel's classical hope, the anointed descendant of King David. **2:14** *heaven* The translators supply this word. *those whom he favors* Lit. "among those of favor [or 'goodwill']." If God's favor is meant, then this passage continues *Luke*'s initial emphasis on Israel (see 1:55). **2:19** See 2:51. **2:21** *time to circumcise* See 1:59 and its note. *name given* See 1:31. **2:22** See *Lev.* 12:1–8.

Jerusalem to present him to the Lord [23](as it is written in the law of the Lord, "Every firstborn male shall be designated as holy to the Lord"), [24]and they offered a sacrifice according to what is stated in the law of the Lord, "a pair of turtledoves or two young pigeons."

[25]Now there was a man in Jerusalem whose name was Simeon;[l] this man was righteous and devout, looking forward to the consolation of Israel, and the Holy Spirit rested on him. [26]It had been revealed to him by the Holy Spirit that he would not see death before he had seen the Lord's Messiah.[m] [27]Guided by the Spirit, Simeon[n] came into the temple; and when the parents brought in the child Jesus, to do for him what was customary under the law, [28]Simeon[o] took him in his arms and praised God, saying,

[29]   "Master, now you are dismissing your servant[p]
       in peace,
       according to your word;
[30]   for my eyes have seen your salvation,
[31]   which you have prepared in the presence of
       all peoples,
[32]   a light for revelation to the Gentiles
       and for glory to your people Israel."

[33]And the child's father and mother were amazed at what was being said about him. [34]Then Simeon[l] blessed them and said to his mother Mary, "This child is destined for the falling and the rising of many in Israel, and to be a sign that will be opposed [35]so that the inner thoughts of many will be revealed—and a sword will pierce your own soul too."

[36]There was also a prophet, Anna[q] the daughter of Phanuel, of the tribe of Asher. She was of a great age, having lived with her husband seven years after her marriage, [37]then as a widow to the age of eighty-four. She never left the temple but worshiped there with fasting and prayer night and day. [38]At that moment she came, and began to praise God and to speak about the child[r] to all who were looking for the redemption of Jerusalem.

The Return to Nazareth

[39]When they had finished everything required by the law of the Lord, they returned to Galilee, to their own town of Nazareth. [40]The child grew and became strong, filled with wisdom; and the favor of God was upon him.

The Boy Jesus in the Temple

[41]Now every year his parents went to Jerusalem for the festival of the Passover. [42]And when he was twelve years old, they went up as usual for the festival. [43]When the festival was ended and they started to return, the boy Jesus stayed behind in Jerusalem, but his parents did not know it. [44]Assuming that he was in the group of travelers, they went a day's journey. Then they started to look for him among their relatives and friends. [45]When they did not find him, they returned to Jerusalem to search for him. [46]After three days they found him in the temple, sitting among the teachers, listening to them and asking them questions. [47]And all who heard him were amazed at his understanding and his answers. [48]When his parents[s] saw him they were astonished; and his mother said to him, "Child, why have you treated us like this? Look, your father and I have been searching for you in great anxiety." [49]He said to them, "Why were you searching for me? Did you not know that I must be in my Father's house?"[t] [50]But they did not understand what he said to them. [51]Then he went down with them and came to Nazareth, and was obedient to them. His mother treasured all these things in her heart.

[52]And Jesus increased in wisdom and in years,[u] and in divine and human favor.

---

l Gk *Symeon*
m Or *the Lord's Christ*
n Gk *In the Spirit, he*
o Gk *he*
p Gk *slave*
q Gk *Hanna*

r Gk *him*
s Gk *they*
t Or *be about my Father's interests?*
u Or *in stature*

2:23 A conflation of phrases from *Exod.* 13:2, 12, 15. Firstborn sons were "redeemed," or bought back, from God by an offering. Note *Luke's* continued emphasis on Jesus' total observance of the law. **2:24** *a pair of turtledoves or two young pigeons Lev.* 12:8 prescribes this offering for those who cannot afford a lamb. *Luke's* implication, that Jesus' family was poor, like the vast majority of the population, would perhaps be clear enough even to those without much biblical knowledge, since animal sacrifice was widely practiced in the ancient world. **2:32** *Luke* begins to hint of Jesus' significance for Gentiles at this point in the narrative. **2:33** *child's father* That is, Joseph; but see 3:23. **2:34–35** A preview of the coming story. **2:36** *Asher* See *Gen.* 30:13; 49:20. *Luke* continues to evoke ancient, authentic Israelite culture, but it is doubtful that ancient tribal lines were still clear in the 1st century. **2:38** *the redemption of Jerusalem* That is, the rescue of the holy city from foreign domination. Note again the classically Jewish themes. **2:39** Contrast *Matt.* 2:23. **2:41** See *Exod.* 12:1–51. **2:47** This story of a precocious youth is typical of the biographies of great men—emperors and philosophers (Iamblichus, *Life of Pythagoras* 8–10), even the historian Josephus (*Life* 7–12)—in the Roman period. **2:50** An example of irony: the reader knows clearly what is still opaque to the characters, that Jesus is the son of God. **2:51** See 2:19. **2:52** See 1:80.

The Proclamation of John the Baptist

3 In the fifteenth year of the reign of Emperor Tiberius, when Pontius Pilate was governor of Judea, and Herod was ruler[v] of Galilee, and his brother Philip ruler[v] of the region of Ituraea and Trachonitis, and Lysanias ruler[v] of Abilene, 2during the high priesthood of Annas and Caiaphas, the word of God came to John son of Zechariah in the wilderness. 3He went into all the region around the Jordan, proclaiming a baptism of repentance for the forgiveness of sins, 4as it is written in the book of the words of the prophet Isaiah,

"The voice of one crying out in the wilderness:
'Prepare the way of the Lord,
    make his paths straight.
5 Every valley shall be filled,
    and every mountain and hill shall be made
      low,
and the crooked shall be made straight,
    and the rough ways made smooth;
6 and all flesh shall see the salvation of God.'"

7John said to the crowds that came out to be baptized by him, "You brood of vipers! Who warned you to flee from the wrath to come? 8Bear fruits worthy of repentance. Do not begin to say to yourselves, 'We have Abraham as our ancestor'; for I tell you, God is able from these stones to raise up children to Abraham. 9Even now the ax is lying at the root of the trees; every tree therefore that does not bear good fruit is cut down and thrown into the fire."

10And the crowds asked him, "What then should we do?" 11In reply he said to them, "Whoever has two coats must share with anyone who has none; and whoever has food must do likewise." 12Even tax collectors came to be baptized, and they asked him, "Teacher, what should we do?" 13He said to them, "Collect no more than the amount prescribed for you." 14Soldiers also asked him, "And we, what should we do?" He said to them, "Do not extort money from anyone by threats or false accusation, and be satisfied with your wages."

15As the people were filled with expectation, and all were questioning in their hearts concerning John, whether he might be the Messiah,[w] 16John answered all of them by saying, "I baptize you with water; but one who is more powerful than I is coming; I am not worthy to untie the thong of his sandals. He will baptize you with[x] the Holy Spirit and fire. 17His winnowing fork is in his hand, to clear his threshing floor and to gather the wheat into his granary; but the chaff he will burn with unquenchable fire."

18So, with many other exhortations, he proclaimed the good news to the people. 19But Herod the ruler,[v] who had been rebuked by him because of Herodias, his brother's wife, and because of all the evil things that Herod had done, 20added to them all by shutting up John in prison.

The Baptism of Jesus

21Now when all the people were baptized, and when Jesus also had been baptized and was praying,

---

v Gk *tetrarch*

w Or *the Christ*
x Or *in*

3:1 *Tiberius* He became emperor in 14 C.E., when he was fifty-six; his 15th year in office would be 28–29 C.E. **Pilate was governor** That is, 26–36 C.E. **Herod was ruler of Galilee** That is, Herod Antipas, son of Herod the Great; "tetrarch" (as the Gk of *Luke* correctly says) of Galilee and Perea from 4 B.C.E. to 39 C.E. **Philip** Another son of Herod the Great, tetrarch over the named regions from 4 B.C.E. to 34 C.E. **Lysanias** Family connection uncertain, but mentioned by Josephus (*Ant.* 18.237; see 19.275) as tetrarch of this region (in what is now Lebanon) at roughly the same time as Philip. Perhaps the author of *Luke* knew these passages in Josephus. **3:2** *during the high priesthood of Annas and Caiaphas* A difficult phrase, since only one high priest could serve at a time. Although a former high priest retained the honorary title (as do some former government officials today), he would not be called high priest for official purposes. Evidently, the author thought that Annas was serving as high priest during this period (see *Acts* 4:6). *Matt.* 26:3, 57, however, says it was Caiaphas. According to Josephus (*Ant.* 18.26, 34–35, 95), Annas was high priest 6–15 C.E. and Caiaphas 18–36/37 C.E., the period in question. Perhaps an early copyist inserted *and Caiaphas* here to help *Luke* agree with *Matthew* or Josephus. Note the apparent confusion over the identity of the high priest in *John* 18:13–14, 19–24; see 11:49. **John son of Zechariah** That is, John the Baptist; see 1:80. **3:4–6** *Isa.* 40:3–5. LXX reads like *Luke* (missing the initial parallelism of the MT), except for the following in italic: "'make straight the paths *of our God* . . . ; . . . and *all* the crooked shall be made straight, and the rough ways made *plains. And the glory of the Lord shall appear,* and all flesh shall see the salvation of God,' *for the Lord has spoken.*" **3:7** *John said* Like all of the Gk verbs of saying in 3:7–14, this could also be translated "used to say" or "would say." *Luke* is thus describing typical situations from this bygone period, not necessarily particular speeches. **3:10–14** These examples of John's preaching are unique to *Luke*. **3:15** The author knows of a problem with the Baptist's status in early Christianity. See *John* 1:19–23; 3:28–31. It appears that some of John's own followers considered him a messianic figure, for they persevered as a distinct group long after the rise of Christianity (see *Acts* 19:1–6). **3:19** *Luke-Acts* gives a consistently negative picture of Herod Antipas (see *Luke* 13:31–32; 23:8–12; *Acts* 4:27), in sharp contrast to *Mark* (6:19–20, 26). Perhaps the author had some special information about the tetrarch (*Luke* 8:3; *Acts* 13:1). His omission of *Mark*'s account of the Baptist's death (*Mark* 6:14–29) may be attributed to this difference.

the heaven was opened, ²²and the Holy Spirit descended upon him in bodily form like a dove. And a voice came from heaven, "You are my Son, the Beloved;ʸ with you I am well pleased."ᶻ

The Ancestors of Jesus

²³Jesus was about thirty years old when he began his work. He was the son (as was thought) of Joseph son of Heli, ²⁴son of Matthat, son of Levi, son of Melchi, son of Jannai, son of Joseph, ²⁵son of Mattathias, son of Amos, son of Nahum, son of Esli, son of Naggai, ²⁶son of Maath, son of Mattathias, son of Semein, son of Josech, son of Joda, ²⁷son of Joanan, son of Rhesa, son of Zerubbabel, son of Shealtiel,ᵃ son of Neri, ²⁸son of Melchi, son of Addi, son of Cosam, son of Elmadam, son of Er, ²⁹son of Joshua, son of Eliezer, son of Jorim, son of Matthat, son of Levi, ³⁰son of Simeon, son of Judah, son of Joseph, son of Jonam, son of Eliakim, ³¹son of Melea, son of Menna, son of Mattatha, son of Nathan, son of David, ³²son of Jesse, son of Obed, son of Boaz, son of Sala,ᵇ son of Nahshon, ³³son of Amminadab, son of Admin, son of Arni,ᶜ son of Hezron, son of Perez, son of Judah, ³⁴son of Jacob, son of Isaac, son of Abraham, son of Terah, son of Nahor, ³⁵son of Serug, son of Reu, son of Peleg, son of Eber, son of Shelah, ³⁶son of Cainan, son of Arphaxad, son of Shem, son of Noah, son of Lamech, ³⁷son of Methuselah, son of Enoch, son of Jared, son of Mahalaleel, son of Cainan, ³⁸son of Enos, son of Seth, son of Adam, son of God.

The Temptation of Jesus

4 Jesus, full of the Holy Spirit, returned from the Jordan and was led by the Spirit in the wilderness, ²where for forty days he was tempted by the devil. He ate nothing at all during those days, and when they were over, he was famished. ³The devil said to him, "If you are the Son of God, command this stone to become a loaf of bread." ⁴Jesus answered him, "It is written, 'One does not live by bread alone.'"

⁵Then the devilᵈ led him up and showed him in an instant all the kingdoms of the world. ⁶And the devilᵈ said to him, "To you I will give their glory and all this authority; for it has been given over to me, and I give it to anyone I please. ⁷If you, then, will worship me, it will all be yours." ⁸Jesus answered him, "It is written,

'Worship the Lord your God,
      and serve only him.'"

⁹Then the devilᵈ took him to Jerusalem, and placed him on the pinnacle of the temple, saying to him, "If you are the Son of God, throw yourself down from here, ¹⁰for it is written,

'He will command his angels concerning you,
      to protect you,'

---

y Or *my beloved Son*
z Other ancient authorities read *You are my Son, today I have begotten you*
a Gk *Salathiel*
b Other ancient authorities read *Salmon*
c Other ancient authorities read *Amminadab, son of Aram;* others vary widely

d Gk *he*

3:22 *my Son* The first part of the saying echoes *Ps.* 2:7, which is addressed to the king of Israel. Although *Luke* agrees here with common synoptic tradition, the allusion also supports *Luke*'s special connection between divine sonship and anointed kingship (see 1:32, 69; 2:11). *well pleased* This language vaguely parallels the servant of the Lord (Israel, according to the LXX) of *Isa.* 42:1. **3:23** *his work* Phrase supplied by the translators. **3:27** *Zerubbabel* This is the first name after Joseph that agrees with *Matthew*'s genealogy and the first that is mentioned in the Hebrew Bible (*1 Chr.* 1:19–24). *Matthew* has eleven generations between Zerubbabel and Jesus; *Luke* has twenty. *Neri* Although *Matthew* and *Luke* agree on Zerubbabel and Shealtiel, they disagree again from Shealtiel's father to David. Neri is otherwise unknown. *Matthew*'s claim that Jeconiah was Shealtiel's father (*Matt.* 1:12) is supported by *1 Chr.* 3:17. The rest of these names disagree because, whereas *Matthew* traces Jesus' Davidic lineage through the kings of Judah beginning with Solomon (thus following the lists in *1–2 Kings*), *Luke* traces it through nonruling relatives of the kings. *Luke* has twenty-two generations from David to Zerubbabel following this line, whereas *Matthew* has fourteen, and the Hebrew Bible itself has seventeen. **3:31** *Nathan* *Matt.* 1:6 traces the line through David's more famous son, Solomon. **3:31–34** *David . . . son of Abraham* From David back to Abraham, *Luke* more or less agrees with *Matthew* and the Hebrew Bible (*1 Chr.* 1:28–2:15; *Ruth* 4:18–22), except that both *Matthew* and *Luke* must follow a gap in the biblical record for the names of the generations between Perez, who went down into Egypt with Jacob (*Gen.* 46:12), and Hezron, who was among those who came out in the exodus four hundred years later. Also, *Luke*'s Admin and Arni take the place of biblical (and Matthean) Aram (or Ram). **3:34–38** *son of Terah . . . Adam* Only *Luke* includes names from Abraham to creation; these agree with *1 Chr.* 1:27 except for Cainan. Whereas *Matthew*'s emphasis on Jesus' descent from Abraham through David highlights Jesus' Jewishness, *Luke*'s tracing back of seventy generations to Adam suggests a connection with the whole human race. **4:4** *Deut.* 8:3. **4:6** Several Jewish writings of the period reflect the belief that Satan (for whom various other names were used) had been permitted to run the world until the allotted time of judgment. See *1 Enoch* 16; 1QS 3.23; *2 Cor.* 4:4. **4:8** *Deut.* 6:13; both the MT and the LXX have "fear" or "revere" where *Luke* says *worship*. **4:10–11** *Ps.* 91:11–12.

[11]and

> 'On their hands they will bear you up,
>> so that you will not dash your foot against a stone.'"

[12]Jesus answered him, "It is said, 'Do not put the Lord your God to the test.'" [13]When the devil had finished every test, he departed from him until an opportune time.

The Beginning of the Galilean Ministry

[14]Then Jesus, filled with the power of the Spirit, returned to Galilee, and a report about him spread through all the surrounding country. [15]He began to teach in their synagogues and was praised by everyone.

The Rejection of Jesus at Nazareth

[16]When he came to Nazareth, where he had been brought up, he went to the synagogue on the sabbath day, as was his custom. He stood up to read, [17]and the scroll of the prophet Isaiah was given to him. He unrolled the scroll and found the place where it was written:

[18] "The Spirit of the Lord is upon me,
> because he has anointed me
>> to bring good news to the poor.
> He has sent me to proclaim release to the captives
> and recovery of sight to the blind,
>> to let the oppressed go free,
[19] to proclaim the year of the Lord's favor."

[20]And he rolled up the scroll, gave it back to the attendant, and sat down. The eyes of all in the synagogue were fixed on him. [21]Then he began to say to them, "Today this scripture has been fulfilled in your hearing." [22]All spoke well of him and were amazed at the gracious words that came from his mouth. They said, "Is not this Joseph's son?" [23]He said to them, "Doubtless you will quote to me this proverb, 'Doctor, cure yourself!' And you will say, 'Do here also in your hometown the things that we have heard you did at Capernaum.'" [24]And he said, "Truly I tell you, no prophet is accepted in the prophet's hometown. [25]But the truth is, there were many widows in Israel in the time of Elijah, when the heaven was shut up three years and six months, and there was a severe famine over all the land; [26]yet Elijah was sent to none of them except to a widow at Zarephath in Sidon. [27]There were also many lepers[e] in Israel in the time of the prophet Elisha, and none of them was cleansed except Naaman the Syrian." [28]When they heard this, all in the synagogue were filled with rage. [29]They got up, drove him out of the town, and led him to the brow of the hill on which their town was built, so that they might hurl him off the cliff. [30]But he passed through the midst of them and went on his way.

The Man with an Unclean Spirit

[31]He went down to Capernaum, a city in Galilee, and was teaching them on the sabbath. [32]They were astounded at his teaching, because he spoke with authority. [33]In the synagogue there was a man who had the spirit of an unclean demon, and he cried out with a loud voice, [34]"Let us alone! What have you to do with us, Jesus of Nazareth? Have you come to destroy us? I know who you are, the Holy One of God." [35]But Jesus rebuked him, saying, "Be silent, and come out of him!" When the demon had thrown him down before them, he came out of him without having done him any harm. [36]They were all amazed and kept saying to one another, "What kind of utterance is this? For with authority and power he commands the unclean spirits, and out they come!" [37]And a

---

e The terms *leper* and *leprosy* can refer to several diseases

---

4:12 *Deut.* 6:16. **4:13 until an opportune time** Only *Luke* mentions the prospect of further testing. Satan will reenter the narrative in 22:3. **4:16–30** Although *Mark* and *Matthew* also mention a rejection in Nazareth, only *Luke* describes the following scene. Coming as early as it does (contrast *Mark* 6:1–6; *Matt.* 13:53–58), it appears to be programmatic for his gospel. Some themes in this section will appear later in *Luke-Acts.* **4:18–19** *Isa.* 61:1–2. *Luke* follows the LXX here except that the LXX reads "to heal the broken-hearted" after *the poor;* it lacks *to let the oppressed go free* (but see *Isa.* 58:6); and it has "declare" for *proclaim.* The MT agrees with the LXX except that the MT has "Lord God" in the first line and "liberation to the imprisoned" instead of *recovery of sight to the blind.* **4:23 what you did at Capernaum** The author of *Luke* seems to betray his use of sources here. In *Mark* and *Matthew,* the rejection at Nazareth comes long after Jesus has preached in Capernaum, so the reference to Capernaum would make sense on their chronology. In *Luke,* however, Jesus has not yet gone to Capernaum in the story; when he does so, the author will mention it as a new place—"a city in Galilee" (4:31). **4:24 in the prophet's hometown** Lit. "in his ancestral home." But Jesus has so far been honored (4:22) in Nazareth, and he seems to bring the ensuing conflict on himself without the people's provocation. **4:25–27** These stories are from *1 Kgs.* 17:1–16 and *2 Kgs.* 5:1–14. **4:26 Zarephath in Sidon** Sidon was already an old and famous city in the 1st century, the former capital of the Phoenicians, who founded Carthage, the old enemy of Rome. See 6:17, where Jesus' audience will quickly include Gentile Sidonians. **4:31 Capernaum, a city in Galilee** See notes to *Mark* 1:21; 2:1–4. Capernaum was a fishing village on the northern end of the Sea of Galilee (Lake Gennesar), about twenty-one miles from Nazareth. **teaching them on the sabbath** *Luke's* Jesus has some status as a teacher in the synagogues. *Luke* returns here to *Mark's* order (*Mark* 1).

report about him began to reach every place in the region.

Healings at Simon's House

38After leaving the synagogue he entered Simon's house. Now Simon's mother-in-law was suffering from a high fever, and they asked him about her. 39Then he stood over her and rebuked the fever, and it left her. Immediately she got up and began to serve them.

40As the sun was setting, all those who had any who were sick with various kinds of diseases brought them to him; and he laid his hands on each of them and cured them. 41Demons also came out of many, shouting, "You are the Son of God!" But he rebuked them and would not allow them to speak, because they knew that he was the Messiah.*f*

Jesus Preaches in the Synagogues

42At daybreak he departed and went into a deserted place. And the crowds were looking for him; and when they reached him, they wanted to prevent him from leaving them. 43But he said to them, "I must proclaim the good news of the kingdom of God to the other cities also; for I was sent for this purpose." 44So he continued proclaiming the message in the synagogues of Judea.*g*

Jesus Calls the First Disciples

5 Once while Jesus*h* was standing beside the lake of Gennesaret, and the crowd was pressing in on him to hear the word of God, 2he saw two boats there at the shore of the lake; the fishermen had gone out of them and were washing their nets. 3He got into one of the boats, the one belonging to Simon, and asked him to put out a little way from the shore. Then he sat down and taught the crowds from the boat. 4When he had finished speaking, he said to Simon, "Put out into the deep water and let down your nets for a catch." 5Simon answered, "Master, we have worked all night long but have caught nothing. Yet if you say so, I will let down the nets." 6When they had done this, they caught so many fish that their nets were beginning to break. 7So they signaled their partners in the other boat to come and help them. And they came and filled both boats, so that they began to sink. 8But when Simon Peter saw it, he fell down at Jesus' knees, saying, "Go away from me, Lord, for I am a sinful man!" 9For he and all who were with him were amazed at the catch of fish that they had taken; 10and so also were James and John, sons of Zebedee, who were partners with Simon. Then Jesus said to Simon, "Do not be afraid; from now on you will be catching people." 11When they had brought their boats to shore, they left everything and followed him.

Jesus Cleanses a Leper

12Once, when he was in one of the cities, there was a man covered with leprosy.*i* When he saw Jesus, he bowed with his face to the ground and begged him, "Lord, if you choose, you can make me clean." 13Then Jesus*h* stretched out his hand, touched him, and said, "I do choose. Be made clean." Immediately the leprosy*i* left him. 14And he ordered him to tell no one. "Go," he said, "and show yourself to the priest, and, as Moses commanded, make an offering for your cleansing, for a testimony to them." 15But now more than ever the word about Jesus*j* spread abroad; many crowds would gather to hear him and to be cured of their diseases. 16But he would withdraw to deserted places and pray.

---

f Or *the Christ*
g Other ancient authorities read *Galilee*
h Gk *he*

i The terms *leper* and *leprosy* can refer to several diseases
j Gk *him*

4:41 *Luke* has a fairly consistent connection between healing and exorcism; at that time, sickness was often attributed to the work of evil spirits (see note to *Mark* 1:23). **4:44 Judea** A puzzling remark because (a) the close parallels in *Mark* 1:39 and *Matt.* 4:23 have Galilee as the location; (b) the context here suggests continued preaching in Galilee (see next verse); and (c) *Luke* will make a great deal of Jesus' gradual and purposeful movement toward Judea after 9:51. The problem has been obvious to readers from the beginning: many later manuscripts of *Luke* have "synagogues of the Jews" or "synagogues of Galilee"—obvious attempts at correction. **5:1–11** The author uses a phrase, translated *once*, which recalls biblical language ("Now it was [or 'happened'] that"). The Gk is perhaps not quite as vague with respect to timing as the translation suggests. This story is unparalleled in *Mark* and *Matthew,* which have only brief accounts of how Jesus' students were first called. A similar story appears in *John,* but there it concerns the actions of Jesus after his resurrection (21:1–11). **5:8 Peter** *Luke* has not yet explained where this nickname comes from. Contrast *Mark* 3:16 and *John* 1:40–42. The reader must wait for *Luke* 6:14 (although the Christian reader may already know). **5:10** In the 2d century and later (perhaps earlier), the fish was a Christian symbol. The origins of the symbol are uncertain. **5:12 *While he was in one of the cities*** A vague connective, apparently used by the author to rejoin his Markan source (*Mark* 1:40) after the story of the miraculous fish catch. **leprosy** See note to *Mark* 1:40. **5:14** See *Lev.* 14:1–32. *Luke's* Jesus continues to work wholly within the world of Judaism.

Jesus Heals a Paralytic

17One day, while he was teaching, Pharisees and teachers of the law were sitting near by (they had come from every village of Galilee and Judea and from Jerusalem); and the power of the Lord was with him to heal.*k* 18Just then some men came, carrying a paralyzed man on a bed. They were trying to bring him in and lay him before Jesus;*l* 19but finding no way to bring him in because of the crowd, they went up on the roof and let him down with his bed through the tiles into the middle of the crowd*m* in front of Jesus. 20When he saw their faith, he said, "Friend,*n* your sins are forgiven you." 21Then the scribes and the Pharisees began to question, "Who is this who is speaking blasphemies? Who can forgive sins but God alone?" 22When Jesus perceived their questionings, he answered them, "Why do you raise such questions in your hearts? 23Which is easier, to say, 'Your sins are forgiven you,' or to say, 'Stand up and walk'? 24But so that you may know that the Son of Man has authority on earth to forgive sins"—he said to the one who was paralyzed—"I say to you, stand up and take your bed and go to your home." 25Immediately he stood up before them, took what he had been lying on, and went to his home, glorifying God. 26Amazement seized all of them, and they glorified God and were filled with awe, saying, "We have seen strange things today."

Jesus Calls Levi

27After this he went out and saw a tax collector named Levi, sitting at the tax booth; and he said to him, "Follow me." 28And he got up, left everything, and followed him.

29Then Levi gave a great banquet for him in his house; and there was a large crowd of tax collectors and others sitting at the table*o* with them. 30The Pharisees and their scribes were complaining to his disciples, saying, "Why do you eat and drink with tax collectors and sinners?" 31Jesus answered, "Those who are well have no need of a physician, but those who are sick; 32I have come to call not the righteous but sinners to repentance."

The Question about Fasting

33Then they said to him, "John's disciples, like the disciples of the Pharisees, frequently fast and pray, but your disciples eat and drink." 34Jesus said to them, "You cannot make wedding guests fast while the bridegroom is with them, can you? 35The days will come when the bridegroom will be taken away from them, and then they will fast in those days." 36He also told them a parable: "No one tears a piece from a new garment and sews it on an old garment; otherwise the new will be torn, and the piece from the new will not match the old. 37And no one puts new wine into old wineskins; otherwise the new wine will burst the skins and will be spilled, and the skins will be destroyed. 38But new wine must be put into fresh wineskins. 39And no one after drinking old wine desires new wine, but says, 'The old is good.'"*p*

The Question about the Sabbath

6One sabbath*q* while Jesus*r* was going through the grainfields, his disciples plucked some heads of grain, rubbed them in their hands, and ate them. 2But some of the Pharisees said, "Why are you doing what is not lawful*s* on the sabbath?" 3Jesus answered,

---

k Other ancient authorities read *was present to heal them*
l Gk *him*
m Gk *into the midst*
n Gk *Man*

o Gk *reclining*
p Other ancient authorities read *better;* others lack verse 39
q Other ancient authorities read *On the second first sabbath*
r Gk *he*
s Other ancient authorities add *to do*

5:17 Pharisees and teachers of the law The first reference to these groups in *Luke* although the Pharisees play an important role in the story of *Luke-Acts.* The first few times he mentions the Pharisees, the author couples them with *teachers of the law* or "scribes" (5:21, 30). These pairs might be intended to help explain who the Pharisees were, for the coupling becomes increasingly sporadic (6:7; 7:30), then disappears altogether in the latter half of *Luke* and *Acts.* On the Pharisees, see note to *Mark* 2:16. **the power of the Lord was with him to heal** Only in *Luke;* see 24:19; *Acts* 2:22; 10:38. **5:19 tiles** *Luke* changes *Mark*'s "removed the roof," suggesting again that *Luke*'s readers are distant from the rural Palestinian situation. The author is thinking of the tiled roofs of urban homes, not the clay or thatched roofs of a Galilean village. **5:20–21** On the question of forgiveness of sins as blasphemy, see notes to *Mark* 2:7, 10. Jesus will forgive sins again in *Luke* 7:48. Forgiveness of sins is a characteristic theme of *Luke-Acts.* **5:27 Levi** Matthew, according to *Matthew.* **5:29–39** Only in *Luke,* this banquet initiates a theme of large festive meals. **5:29 sitting at the table** Lit. "reclining." See note to 7:36. **5:31** See note to *Mark* 2:17. **5:33–39** Unlike *Matthew* and *Mark, Luke* places this scene within the preceding context—the great feast at Levi's house. *Matthew* and *Mark* make it a new scene. See *Gospel of Thomas* 47, 104. **5:33** Thus, again in *Luke,* Jesus appears as a recognized teacher comparable to others. **5:39** This conclusion is only in *Luke.* Contrast the author's source, *Mark* 2:22, where the author emphasizes that Jesus' teaching is entirely new and therefore bound to break the old forms. It suits *Luke*'s perspective, however, to stress the ancient roots of Jesus' mission. **6:1 One sabbath** Again the connection is vague and thematic only. **6:2 not lawful on the sabbath** The divine law forbids "work" on the Sabbath (*Exod.* 20:8–11),

"Have you not read what David did when he and his companions were hungry? [4]He entered the house of God and took and ate the bread of the Presence, which it is not lawful for any but the priests to eat, and gave some to his companions?" [5]Then he said to them, "The Son of Man is lord of the sabbath."

The Man with a Withered Hand

[6]On another sabbath he entered the synagogue and taught, and there was a man there whose right hand was withered. [7]The scribes and the Pharisees watched him to see whether he would cure on the sabbath, so that they might find an accusation against him. [8]Even though he knew what they were thinking, he said to the man who had the withered hand, "Come and stand here." He got up and stood there. [9]Then Jesus said to them, "I ask you, is it lawful to do good or to do harm on the sabbath, to save life or to destroy it?" [10]After looking around at all of them, he said to him, "Stretch out your hand." He did so, and his hand was restored. [11]But they were filled with fury and discussed with one another what they might do to Jesus.

Jesus Chooses the Twelve Apostles

[12]Now during those days he went out to the mountain to pray; and he spent the night in prayer to God. [13]And when day came, he called his disciples and chose twelve of them, whom he also named apostles: [14]Simon, whom he named Peter, and his brother Andrew, and James, and John, and Philip, and Bartholomew, [15]and Matthew, and Thomas, and James son of Alphaeus, and Simon, who was called the Zealot, [16]and Judas son of James, and Judas Iscariot, who became a traitor.

Jesus Teaches and Heals

[17]He came down with them and stood on a level place, with a great crowd of his disciples and a great multitude of people from all Judea, Jerusalem, and the coast of Tyre and Sidon. [18]They had come to hear him and to be healed of their diseases; and those who were troubled with unclean spirits were cured. [19]And all in the crowd were trying to touch him, for power came out from him and healed all of them.

Blessings and Woes

[20]Then he looked up at his disciples and said:
"Blessed are you who are poor,
　　for yours is the kingdom of God.
[21] "Blessed are you who are hungry now,
　　for you will be filled.
"Blessed are you who weep now,
　　for you will laugh.
[22]"Blessed are you when people hate you, and when they exclude you, revile you, and defame you[t] on account of the Son of Man. [23]Rejoice in that day and leap for joy, for surely your reward is great in heaven; for that is what their ancestors did to the prophets.
[24] "But woe to you who are rich,
　　for you have received your consolation.

_____

t Gk *cast out your name as evil*

but it was not always clear what constituted work. Jewish teachers had to clarify the matter, and there was some disagreement in Jesus' day. He does not challenge the law itself but uses a scriptural example to show his interpretation of the law. Note the irony in the story: The stunning fact that Jesus has the power to effect a cure, which should say something about his status, is ignored by leaders who focus on mundane legal debate. **6:3–4** The story is told in *1 Sam.* 21:1–6. **6:5** *Son of Man* See notes to *Mark* 2:10, 27–28. **6:6** *and taught* Only *Luke* emphasizes Jesus' teaching role here; see *Mark* 3:1; *Matt.* 12:9. **6:9** Again, the debate in *Luke* is not about whether one should observe the law (one must do so) but about what the law means. See note to 6:2. **6:11** *do to Jesus* Or "do with Jesus." Contrast *Mark* 3:6 and *Matt.* 12:14, which have the Pharisees now beginning to plot Jesus' death. *Luke*'s milder conclusion portrays Jesus as someone who angers the more mainstream and complacent teachers but who will continue to work within the framework of Jewish leadership. **6:12** *during those days* Another vague Lukan bridge between different sources and stories. **6:13** Only *Luke* here distinguishes between *disciples* (students) in general and the *apostles;* the office of apostle will become extremely important in *Acts* (1:15–26). **6:14** *Simon, whom he named Peter* See note to 5:8. *Luke* gives no explanation of Peter's new name; contrast *Matt.* 16:18. **6:15** *Simon, who was called the Zealot* See *Acts* 1:13; *Mark* 3:18 and *Matt.* 10:3 call him Simon the Cananaean. **6:16** *Judas son of James* Instead of the Thaddeus in *Mark* 3:18 and *Matt.* 10:3. *Judas Iscariot* That is, the one who became a traitor. See 22:3, 21; *Acts* 1:16–19. **6:17** *a level place* Curiously, much of what follows is placed by *Matthew* in its Sermon on the Mount (5:1–7:28). *the coast of Tyre and Sidon* Thus, *Luke*'s Jesus quickly attracts Gentile hearers from quite a distance; see note to *Mark* 3:8. This reference fulfills the expectation created in 4:26 that he would reach out to these cities. Tyre was famous throughout the world as a trade center and former sister city of Sidon, the old Phoenician capital. **6:20** *you who are poor* See also *Gospel of Thomas* 54, but *Matt.* 5:3 has "poor in spirit" and speaks of such people in the third person. **6:21** *you who are hungry now* See *Gos. Thom.* 69:2, but *Matt.* 5:6 has "hunger and thirst for righteousness." *you who weep now . . .* This promise of happiness has no parallel in the earliest Christian literature. **6:22–23** See *Gospel of Thomas* 68–69; *Matt.* 5:11–12. The persecutors in question seem to be the Jews, in view of the reference to their ancestors' persecution of the prophets. **6:24–26** These four woes are found only in *Luke*.

25 "Woe to you who are full now,
　　for you will be hungry.
"Woe to you who are laughing now,
　　for you will mourn and weep.
26"Woe to you when all speak well of you, for that is what their ancestors did to the false prophets.

Love for Enemies

27 "But I say to you that listen, Love your enemies, do good to those who hate you, 28bless those who curse you, pray for those who abuse you. 29If anyone strikes you on the cheek, offer the other also; and from anyone who takes away your coat do not withhold even your shirt. 30Give to everyone who begs from you; and if anyone takes away your goods, do not ask for them again. 31Do to others as you would have them do to you.

32"If you love those who love you, what credit is that to you? For even sinners love those who love them. 33If you do good to those who do good to you, what credit is that to you? For even sinners do the same. 34If you lend to those from whom you hope to receive, what credit is that to you? Even sinners lend to sinners, to receive as much again. 35But love your enemies, do good, and lend, expecting nothing in return.*u* Your reward will be great, and you will be children of the Most High; for he is kind to the ungrateful and the wicked. 36Be merciful, just as your Father is merciful.

Judging Others

37"Do not judge, and you will not be judged; do not condemn, and you will not be condemned. Forgive, and you will be forgiven; 38give, and it will be given to you. A good measure, pressed down, shaken together, running over, will be put into your lap; for the measure you give will be the measure you get back."

39He also told them a parable: "Can a blind person guide a blind person? Will not both fall into a pit?

40A disciple is not above the teacher, but everyone who is fully qualified will be like the teacher. 41Why do you see the speck in your neighbor's*v* eye, but do not notice the log in your own eye? 42Or how can you say to your neighbor,*w* 'Friend,*w* let me take out the speck in your eye,' when you yourself do not see the log in your own eye? You hypocrite, first take the log out of your own eye, and then you will see clearly to take the speck out of your neighbor's*v* eye.

A Tree and Its Fruit

43"No good tree bears bad fruit, nor again does a bad tree bear good fruit; 44for each tree is known by its own fruit. Figs are not gathered from thorns, nor are grapes picked from a bramble bush. 45The good person out of the good treasure of the heart produces good, and the evil person out of evil treasure produces evil; for it is out of the abundance of the heart that the mouth speaks.

The Two Foundations

46"Why do you call me 'Lord, Lord,' and do not do what I tell you? 47I will show you what someone is like who comes to me, hears my words, and acts on them. 48That one is like a man building a house, who dug deeply and laid the foundation on rock; when a flood arose, the river burst against that house but could not shake it, because it had been well built.*x* 49But the one who hears and does not act is like a man who built a house on the ground without a foundation. When the river burst against it, immediately it fell, and great was the ruin of that house."

Jesus Heals a Centurion's Servant

7 After Jesus*y* had finished all his sayings in the hearing of the people, he entered Capernaum. 2A centurion there had a slave whom he valued highly,

---

u Other ancient authorities read *despairing of no one*

v Gk *brother's*
w Gk *brother*
x Other ancient authorities read *founded upon the rock*
y Gk *he*

6:29–36 See *Matt.* 5:38–48; *Gospel of Thomas* 95. **6:31** The famous golden rule is found, in slightly different forms, in many religious traditions, including Judaism (see *b. Shabbat* 31a). See *Matt.* 7:12; *Did.* 1.2; *Gos. Thom.* 6:3. **6:37** See *Mark* 4:24–25; *Matt.* 7:1–2. **6:38** Although this saying is found only in *Luke,* the principle of abundant reward for acts of kindness was common in rabbinic literature. **6:39** See *Matt.* 15:14, where this saying is applied to the Pharisees, and *Gospel of Thomas* 34. **6:40** See *Matt.* 10:24–25; *John* 13:16. Only *Luke* shapes this saying to encourage a student's growth to parity with the teacher. This supports the atmosphere of teaching and learning, as in a philosophical school, in *Luke* (see introduction to *Luke-Acts*). **6:41–42** See *Matt.* 7:3–5; *Gospel of Thomas* 26. **6:43–44** See *Matt.* 7:16; *Gos. Thom.* 45; 43:3. **6:45** See *Matt.* 12:34–35. **6:46–49** See *Matt.* 7:21–27. **7:1–10** One of the few stories in the Synoptics, outside the Passion Narrative, with a close parallel in *John* (4:46–54). See *Matt.* 8:5–10. **7:1** *Capernaum* Jesus' base of operations; see 4:31–41. **7:2** *a centurion* See notes to *Mark* 15:39; *Matt.* 8:5. A prestigious officer in charge of a century (about eighty men) in either the Roman legions or the provincial auxiliary forces. Since this man was stationed in or near Capernaum, he would have been employed in the mainly foreign mercenary army of Herod Antipas, the tetrarch.

and who was ill and close to death. ³When he heard about Jesus, he sent some Jewish elders to him, asking him to come and heal his slave. ⁴When they came to Jesus, they appealed to him earnestly, saying, "He is worthy of having you do this for him, ⁵for he loves our people, and it is he who built our synagogue for us." ⁶And Jesus went with them, but when he was not far from the house, the centurion sent friends to say to him, "Lord, do not trouble yourself, for I am not worthy to have you come under my roof; ⁷therefore I did not presume to come to you. But only speak the word, and let my servant be healed. ⁸For I also am a man set under authority, with soldiers under me; and I say to one, 'Go,' and he goes, and to another, 'Come,' and he comes, and to my slave, 'Do this,' and the slave does it." ⁹When Jesus heard this he was amazed at him, and turning to the crowd that followed him, he said, "I tell you, not even in Israel have I found such faith." ¹⁰When those who had been sent returned to the house, they found the slave in good health.

Jesus Raises the Widow's Son at Nain

¹¹Soon afterwards*ᶻ* he went to a town called Nain, and his disciples and a large crowd went with him.

¹²As he approached the gate of the town, a man who had died was being carried out. He was his mother's only son, and she was a widow; and with her was a large crowd from the town. ¹³When the Lord saw her, he had compassion for her and said to her, "Do not weep." ¹⁴Then he came forward and touched the bier, and the bearers stood still. And he said, "Young man, I say to you, rise!" ¹⁵The dead man sat up and began to speak, and Jesus*ᵃ* gave him to his mother. ¹⁶Fear seized all of them; and they glorified God, saying, "A great prophet has risen among us!" and "God has looked favorably on his people!" ¹⁷This word about him spread throughout Judea and all the surrounding country.

Messengers from John the Baptist

¹⁸The disciples of John reported all these things to him. So John summoned two of his disciples ¹⁹and sent them to the Lord to ask, "Are you the one who is to come, or are we to wait for another?" ²⁰When the men had come to him, they said, "John the Baptist has sent us to you to ask, 'Are you the one who is to come, or are we to wait for another?'" ²¹Jesus*ᵇ* had just then cured many people of diseases, plagues, and evil spirits, and had given sight to many who were blind. ²²And he answered them, "Go and tell John

---

z Other ancient authorities read *Next day*

a Gk *he*
b Gk *He*

7:5 This justification, missing from the parallel accounts, meets the inevitable animosity of people subject to a foreign military officer. Perhaps it does more, in *Luke*'s scheme, by presenting the local Jewish leaders as Jesus' friendly colleagues at this point; see 13:31. **7:9** *not even in Israel have I found such faith* This statement anticipates *Acts*, in which the apostles will turn decisively from the Jews to the Gentiles (*Acts* 18:6). Interestingly, a devout centurion also serves as a watershed figure there (10:1–43). **7:11** *Soon afterwards* Another vague Lukan connective, apparently used to join stories from different sources. This story of resurrection has no parallel in other Christian texts. *a town called Nain* A small village nearly ten miles southeast of Nazareth. **7:12** Ancient readers would understand this as a catastrophe, for most women depended completely upon men—their husbands, brothers, and sons—for protection and support. This story develops *Luke*'s pronounced interest in Jesus' concern for women (see introduction to *Luke-Acts*). **7:13** *the Lord* An unexpected title for the narrator to use of Jesus, since the text has previously spoken only of God as the Lord (4:18–19; 5:17) and the author is in general concerned to delay the Christian understanding of Jesus until its proper time, in *Acts* (see introduction to *Luke-Acts*). The narrator will continue this usage from time to time, however, especially in material that is not parallel with *Mark* (e.g., 7:19; 10:1; 11:39; 12:42). He may assume a Christian readership that shares his devotion to Jesus as supreme Lord, or he may simply take over the language of a non-Markan source without alteration. Some scholars argue that this language was characteristic of "Proto-Luke"—an initial version of this gospel written without the benefit of *Mark*. **7:17** A plausible reaction within popular Jewish circles, though not the author's own Christian view of Jesus. **7:18–35** See *Matt.* 11:2–19 and notes. According to the common view, this extensive non-Markan material on John the Baptist comes from Q; a couple of sayings are paralleled in *Thomas*. In *Matthew*'s parallel, John's question comes in an entirely different setting: Jesus' students have been exercising their delegated missionary powers (10:1–5), and Jesus himself has been teaching (11:1). *Luke* does not remind the reader, as *Matt.* 11:2 does, that John is now in prison (see *Luke* 3:20). And *Luke* will omit the account of John's death in *Mark* 6:14–29. But Jesus' words in *Luke* 7:24 seem to assume that John is no longer active. **7:19** The question is surprising here because John is supposed to have recognized Jesus already in the womb (1:41) and witnessed the heavenly voice at the baptism (3:22). Perhaps this episode, which circulated freely in pregospel church tradition, originally reflected the Baptist's initial interest in Jesus—before the infancy stories had developed. That the historical John did not finally teach his followers that Jesus was the coming one seems implied by *Acts* 19:1–6. **7:21** *Jesus had just then cured* Lit. "In that hour he cured." **7:22** Jesus' answer alludes to the promises of *Isa.* 35:5–6 (also 29:18; 42:7), although in *Isaiah* the cure of the blind and the deaf is largely a metaphorical reference to formerly blind and deaf Israel (6:9–10; 30:9–10; 42:18–20; 43:8). In *Luke-Acts* too

what you have seen and heard: the blind receive their sight, the lame walk, the lepers^c are cleansed, the deaf hear, the dead are raised, the poor have good news brought to them. 23And blessed is anyone who takes no offense at me."

24When John's messengers had gone, Jesus^d began to speak to the crowds about John:^e "What did you go out into the wilderness to look at? A reed shaken by the wind? 25What then did you go out to see? Someone^f dressed in soft robes? Look, those who put on fine clothing and live in luxury are in royal palaces. 26What then did you go out to see? A prophet? Yes, I tell you, and more than a prophet. 27This is the one about whom it is written,

'See, I am sending my messenger ahead of you,
who will prepare your way before you.'
28I tell you, among those born of women no one is greater than John; yet the least in the kingdom of God is greater than he." 29(And all the people who heard this, including the tax collectors, acknowledged the justice of God,^g because they had been baptized with

John's baptism. 30But by refusing to be baptized by him, the Pharisees and the lawyers rejected God's purpose for themselves.)

31"To what then will I compare the people of this generation, and what are they like? 32They are like children sitting in the marketplace and calling to one another,

'We played the flute for you, and you did not dance;
we wailed, and you did not weep.'
33For John the Baptist has come eating no bread and drinking no wine, and you say, 'He has a demon'; 34the Son of Man has come eating and drinking, and you say, 'Look, a glutton and a drunkard, a friend of tax collectors and sinners!' 35Nevertheless, wisdom is vindicated by all her children."

A Sinful Woman Forgiven

36One of the Pharisees asked Jesus^e to eat with him, and he went into the Pharisee's house and took his place at the table. 37And a woman in the city, who was a sinner, having learned that he was eating in the Pharisee's house, brought an alabaster jar of ointment. 38She stood behind him at his feet, weeping, and began to bathe his feet with her tears and to dry them with her hair. Then she continued kissing his

---

c The terms *leper* and *leprosy* can refer to several diseases
d Gk *he*
e Gk *him*
f Or *Why then did you go out? To see someone*
g Or *praised God*

---

this slide into a metaphorical sense will become important, especially in *Acts,* where the Jews are often accused of hardhearted resistance to Jesus (*Acts* 9:9; 13:6–11; 28:26–28; also 7:39–53). **7:24–25** See *Gospel of Thomas* 78. Both of these word pictures ridicule Herod Antipas, who had John executed. Some of the tetrarch's coins, which were free of human or animal images, pictured reeds. *Luke's* Jesus draws a sharp contrast, common among moral philosophers of that time, between a man who has all of the external power one could desire but is internally weak and one who is externally powerless but inwardly unconquerable. The author will create the same contrast when he describes Jesus' confrontation of the Jerusalem authorities (*Luke* 20–23). **7:27** *Mal.* 3:1 (correcting *Mark* 1:2, which attributes the quotation to *Isaiah*). LXX: "See, I am sending out my messenger, and he shall survey the way before me, and the Lord whom you seek shall come to his temple suddenly." Curiously, although the MT and the LXX agree that the messenger comes before "me" (the Lord God), *Mark, Luke,* and *Luke's* parallel in *Matthew* (11:10) (Q?) agree almost perfectly on a different Gk version of the saying, which has the messenger come before *you* (Jesus). Perhaps the Christian version, designed to fit the connection between John the Baptist and Jesus, circulated in a collection of such proof texts. **7:28** See *Gospel of Thomas* 46. See note to *Matt.* 11:11. **7:29–30** This editorial note, contrasting the repentant sinner and the self-righteous, unrepentant Pharisee, is unique to *Luke;* it is part of a theme in this gospel (see 15:11–32; 18:9–14). See notes to *Matt.* 11:16–19. **7:34** *eating and drinking* Note the many banquet scenes in *Luke* (5:29, 33; 7:36; 11:37; 14:1, 7) and the contrast between Jesus and John in 5:33. **7:36–50** See *John* 12:1–8. The gospels contain three similar stories of Jesus' being anointed by a woman. *Mark* 14:3–9 has the anointing in Bethany, two days before Jesus' final Passover, and in the home of "Simon the leper." *John* 12:1–8 has a different version of the same tradition: six days before the Passover, in the home of Mary, Martha, and Lazarus. In both of these cases, the complaint is that the ointment could have been sold for three hundred denarii and the money given to the poor. In both cases, Jesus responds, "You always have the poor with you, but you do not always have me." *Luke's* story is somewhat different, since the issue is the character of the woman who does the anointing. Yet the host is still named Simon (although now he is a Pharisee), and the author of *Luke,* when he comes to *Mark's* later story (*Mark* 14:3–9), omits it. Given *Luke's* pronounced concern for the poor, Jesus' words about the poor in *Mark* and *John* might not be appropriate here. Perhaps, then, it was the author of *Luke,* rather than one of his sources, who adapted *Mark's* story to contrast the repentant sinner with the complacent Pharisee (see *Luke* 18:9–14). **7:36** *to eat with him* Only in *Luke* does Jesus eat with Pharisees (see also 11:37; 14:1). Although *Luke* continues the standard gospel portrayal of the Pharisees as hypocrites (12:1; see 16:14), Jesus' frequent dining with them must indicate—at least at this stage in the story—some degree of mutual tolerance (see 13:31–32; *Acts* 5:17, 33–40). *took his place at the table* Lit. "reclined." The Gk does not mention a table. The scene portrays the diners reclining to eat on couches; participants lay, as many as three to a couch, leaning on their left elbows while taking food with their right hands from a small central table. Poorer families could not afford homes with dining rooms and so ate sitting on stools. The author thus assumes that the Pharisees had some status, with homes large enough for such meals.

feet and anointing them with the ointment. [39]Now when the Pharisee who had invited him saw it, he said to himself, "If this man were a prophet, he would have known who and what kind of woman this is who is touching him—that she is a sinner." [40]Jesus spoke up and said to him, "Simon, I have something to say to you." "Teacher," he replied, "Speak." [41]"A certain creditor had two debtors; one owed five hundred denarii,[h] and the other fifty. [42]When they could not pay, he canceled the debts for both of them. Now which of them will love him more?" [43]Simon answered, "I suppose the one for whom he canceled the greater debt." And Jesus[i] said to him, "You have judged rightly." [44]Then turning toward the woman, he said to Simon, "Do you see this woman? I entered your house; you gave me no water for my feet, but she has bathed my feet with her tears and dried them with her hair. [45]You gave me no kiss, but from the time I came in she has not stopped kissing my feet. [46]You did not anoint my head with oil, but she has anointed my feet with ointment. [47]Therefore, I tell you, her sins, which were many, have been forgiven; hence she has shown great love. But the one to whom little is forgiven, loves little." [48]Then he said to her, "Your sins are forgiven." [49]But those who were at the table with him began to say among themselves, "Who is this who even forgives sins?" [50]And he said to the woman, "Your faith has saved you; go in peace."

Some Women Accompany Jesus

[8] Soon afterwards he went on through cities and villages, proclaiming and bringing the good news of the kingdom of God. The twelve were with him, [2]as well as some women who had been cured of evil spirits and infirmities: Mary, called Magdalene, from whom seven demons had gone out, [3]and Joanna, the wife of Herod's steward Chuza, and Susanna, and many others, who provided for them[j] out of their resources.

The Parable of the Sower

[4]When a great crowd gathered and people from town after town came to him, he said in a parable: [5]"A sower went out to sow his seed; and as he sowed, some fell on the path and was trampled on, and the birds of the air ate it up. [6]Some fell on the rock; and as it grew up, it withered for lack of moisture. [7]Some fell among thorns, and the thorns grew with it and choked it. [8]Some fell into good soil, and when it grew, it produced a hundredfold." As he said this, he called out, "Let anyone with ears to hear listen!"

The Purpose of the Parables

[9]Then his disciples asked him what this parable meant. [10]He said, "To you it has been given to know the secrets[k] of the kingdom of God; but to others I speak[l] in parables, so that
'looking they may not perceive,
     and listening they may not understand.'

The Parable of the Sower Explained

[11]"Now the parable is this: The seed is the word of God. [12]The ones on the path are those who have heard; then the devil comes and takes away the word from their hearts, so that they may not believe and be saved. [13]The ones on the rock are those who, when they hear the word, receive it with joy. But these have

---

h The denarius was the usual day's wage for a laborer
i Gk he

j Other ancient authorities read him
k Or mysteries
l Gk lacks I speak

7:40 Teacher The Pharisee, himself a teacher, recognizes Jesus as another teacher and is willing to learn from him. Contrast the Pharisees of *Mark* and *Luke*. **7:41 denarii** One denarius (plural *denarii*) was a generous wage for a daily laborer (*Matt.* 20:2). In the early 1st century, legionary soldiers earned 225 denarii per year, which rose to 300 denarii in the 80s. **7:49 even forgives sins** See 5:20–21, where Jesus forgave the sins of the paralytic. Jesus scandalizes his hosts. **8:2–3** Note again *Luke*'s special interest in women (see 7:11–17; 13:10–17; 23:37). **8:3 Joanna** Possibly one of the author's special sources about Herod the tetrarch, accounting in part for his animosity toward this ruler (3:19–20; 13:31–32; 23:6–12). See also Menaen in *Acts* 13:1. **provided for them** Although these women do not play a featured role, they remain constantly in the background (23:55; *Acts* 1:14), and it is significant that only *Luke*, with its interest in women (see note to 8:2–3) mentions them here. But this claim fits with *Matt.* 27:56, which also (incidentally) seems to suggest that a group of women had funded Jesus' career. **8:4–8** See *Gospel of Thomas* 9 and notes to *Mark* 4:1–9. **8:9** Before *Luke*'s Jesus answers this question (8:11), he comments on parables in general (8:10) although his students have not asked about parables in general. According to *Mark* 4:10 and *Matt.* 13:10, however, the students do ask about parables generally. **8:10** An allusion to *Isa.* 6:9–10, with the *looking* and *listening* in reverse order (following *Mark* 4:12). *Matt.* 13:13, in the parallel, quotes *Isaiah* almost exactly (LXX), altering the sense significantly. **8:11–15** It may have been the author's concern for proper sequence that led him to make several changes to *Mark*'s version of this allegory if he found it unsuited to the conditions of Jesus' life. For example, he changes "the word" to *the word of God* (8:11), an expression used elsewhere by Jesus (5:1; 8:21; 11:28); he changes *Mark*'s "trouble or persecution . . . on account of the word" to a more general *a time of testing* (8:13); and he removes the apocalyptic tone from *Mark*'s "cares of the world [or 'the age']" by substituting *cares . . . and pleasures of life* (8:14).

no root; they believe only for a while and in a time of testing fall away. [14]As for what fell among the thorns, these are the ones who hear; but as they go on their way, they are choked by the cares and riches and pleasures of life, and their fruit does not mature. [15]But as for that in the good soil, these are the ones who, when they hear the word, hold it fast in an honest and good heart, and bear fruit with patient endurance.

A Lamp under a Jar

[16]"No one after lighting a lamp hides it under a jar, or puts it under a bed, but puts it on a lampstand, so that those who enter may see the light. [17]For nothing is hidden that will not be disclosed, nor is anything secret that will not become known and come to light. [18]Then pay attention to how you listen; for to those who have, more will be given; and from those who do not have, even what they seem to have will be taken away."

The True Kindred of Jesus

[19]Then his mother and his brothers came to him, but they could not reach him because of the crowd. [20]And he was told, "Your mother and your brothers are standing outside, wanting to see you." [21]But he said to them, "My mother and my brothers are those who hear the word of God and do it."

Jesus Calms a Storm

[22]One day he got into a boat with his disciples, and he said to them, "Let us go across to the other side of the lake." So they put out, [23]and while they were sailing he fell asleep. A windstorm swept down on the lake, and the boat was filling with water, and they were in danger. [24]They went to him and woke him up, shouting, "Master, Master, we are perishing!" And he woke up and rebuked the wind and the raging waves; they ceased, and there was a calm. [25]He said to them, "Where is your faith?" They were afraid and amazed, and said to one another, "Who then is this, that he commands even the winds and the water, and they obey him?"

Jesus Heals the Gerasene Demoniac

[26]Then they arrived at the country of the Gerasenes,[m] which is opposite Galilee. [27]As he stepped out on land, a man of the city who had demons met him. For a long time he had worn[n] no clothes, and he did not live in a house but in the tombs. [28]When he saw Jesus, he fell down before him and shouted at the top of his voice, "What have you to do with me, Jesus, Son of the Most High God? I beg you, do not torment me"— [29]for Jesus[o] had commanded the unclean spirit to come out of the man. (For many times it had seized him; he was kept under guard and bound with chains and shackles, but he would break the bonds and be driven by the demon into the wilds.) [30]Jesus then asked him, "What is your name?" He said, "Legion"; for many demons had entered him. [31]They begged him not to order them to go back into the abyss.

[32]Now there on the hillside a large herd of swine was feeding; and the demons[p] begged Jesus[q] to let them enter these. So he gave them permission. [33]Then the demons came out of the man and entered the swine, and the herd rushed down the steep bank into the lake and was drowned.

[34]When the swineherds saw what had happened, they ran off and told it in the city and in the country. [35]Then people came out to see what had happened, and when they came to Jesus, they found the man from whom the demons had gone sitting at the feet of Jesus, clothed and in his right mind. And they were afraid. [36]Those who had seen it told them how the one who had been possessed by demons had been healed. [37]Then all the people of the surrounding country of the Gerasenes[r] asked Jesus[q] to leave them; for they were seized with great fear. So he got into the boat and returned. [38]The man from whom the demons had gone begged that he might be with

---

m Other ancient authorities read *Gadarenes*; others, *Gergesenes*
n Other ancient authorities read *a man of the city who had had demons for a long time met him. He wore*
o Gk *he*
p Gk *they*
q Gk *him*
r Other ancient authorities read *Gadarenes*; others, *Gergesenes*

8:16 See *Matt.* 5:15.   **8:17** See *Matt.* 10:26.   **8:18** *to those who have* The Gk is singular: "to the one who has." See *Mark* 4:25; *Matt.* 13:12; *Gospel of Thomas* 41.   **8:19–20** Like *Matt.* 12:46–50, this passage removes the sharp critique of Jesus' immediate family that one finds in *Mark* 3:20–21, 31–35. Still, the radical nature of Jesus' call to sever family ties for his work remains; see note to 14:25–33.   **8:22–25** See *Mark* 4:35–37; *Matt.* 8:23–27.   **8:26–39** See *Mark* 5:1–20; *Matt.* 8:28–34. **8:26** *Gerasenes* So also *Mark* 5:1. *Matt.* 8:28 has "Gadarenes." Some later manuscripts of *Luke* read "Gadarenes" here, others "Gergesenes." Gerasa was thirty miles from the Sea of Galilee (Chinnereth); Gadara was at least six miles; Gergesa is unknown. **8:27** *who had demons* Demonic possession was common in antiquity; in both the Jewish and the pagan worlds it was held to account for much physical and mental illness. Other literature indicates that exorcism was a common form of healing, in which Jews and other Easterners were often considered adept (see Josephus, *Ant.* 8.44–49). Christian literature presents Jesus as the exorcist par excellence, but it concedes incidentally that other exorcists were around (see *Luke* 9:49–50; 11:19; *Acts* 19:13). **8:30** *Legion* See note to *Mark* 5:9.

him; but Jesus[s] sent him away, saying, [39]"Return to your home, and declare how much God has done for you." So he went away, proclaiming throughout the city how much Jesus had done for him.

A Girl Restored to Life and a Woman Healed

[40]Now when Jesus returned, the crowd welcomed him, for they were all waiting for him. [41]Just then there came a man named Jairus, a leader of the synagogue. He fell at Jesus' feet and begged him to come to his house, [42]for he had an only daughter, about twelve years old, who was dying.

As he went, the crowds pressed in on him. [43]Now there was a woman who had been suffering from hemorrhages for twelve years; and though she had spent all she had on physicians,[t] no one could cure her. [44]She came up behind him and touched the fringe of his clothes, and immediately her hemorrhage stopped. [45]Then Jesus asked, "Who touched me?" When all denied it, Peter[u] said, "Master, the crowds surround you and press in on you." [46]But Jesus said, "Someone touched me; for I noticed that power had gone out from me." [47]When the woman saw that she could not remain hidden, she came trembling; and falling down before him, she declared in the presence of all the people why she had touched him, and how she had been immediately healed. [48]He said to her, "Daughter, your faith has made you well; go in peace."

[49]While he was still speaking, someone came from the leader's house to say, "Your daughter is dead; do not trouble the teacher any longer." [50]When Jesus heard this, he replied, "Do not fear. Only believe, and she will be saved." [51]When he came to the house, he did not allow anyone to enter with him, except Peter, John, and James, and the child's father and mother. [52]They were all weeping and wailing for her; but he said, "Do not weep; for she is not dead but sleeping." [53]And they laughed at him, knowing that she was dead. [54]But he took her by the hand and called out, "Child, get up!" [55]Her spirit returned, and she got up at once. Then he directed them to give her something to eat. [56]Her parents were astounded; but he ordered them to tell no one what had happened.

The Mission of the Twelve

9 Then Jesus[s] called the twelve together and gave them power and authority over all demons and to cure diseases, [2]and he sent them out to proclaim the kingdom of God and to heal. [3]He said to them, "Take nothing for your journey, no staff, nor bag, nor bread, nor money—not even an extra tunic. [4]Whatever house you enter, stay there, and leave from there. [5]Wherever they do not welcome you, as you are leaving that town shake the dust off your feet as a testimony against them." [6]They departed and went through the villages, bringing the good news and curing diseases everywhere.

Herod's Perplexity

[7]Now Herod the ruler[v] heard about all that had taken place, and he was perplexed, because it was said by some that John had been raised from the dead, [8]by some that Elijah had appeared, and by others that one of the ancient prophets had arisen.

---

s Gk *he*
t Other ancient authorities lack *and had spent all she had on physicians*
u Other ancient authorities add *and those who were with him*

v Gk *tetrarch*

8:40–56 *Luke* here takes over *Mark*'s nested stories (*Mark* 5:21–46)—a literary characteristic of *Mark* (see introduction to that text) but not of *Luke*, which betrays this use of sources. See *Matt.* 9:18–26. **8:40** The geography is vague, but the author enhances the story line by having the crowds who had been with Jesus on the northern shore of the lake eagerly awaiting him while he is far away in Gerasa. **8:41** *Jairus, a leader of the synagogue* The Gk word *archisynagōgos* is widely attested in inscriptions throughout the Roman Empire. It refers to the synagogue president, whose responsibilities appear to have been mainly concerned with maintaining the physical structure and the financial stability and general order of synagogue life. He therefore had to be a relatively prosperous person. **8:43** *she had spent all she had on physicians* If this phrase belongs in *Luke* (see note u above), this was a woman of some means, for few people could afford the services of a physician in antiquity. *no one could cure her* See note to *Mark* 5:26. **8:46** On Jesus' healing power, see *Acts* 19:12. **8:49** *Luke* preserves the dramatic tension of *Mark*'s story: Jesus' delay with the woman has resulted in the death of the child. Contrast *Matt.* 9:18. **8:54** *Luke* omits Jesus' Aramaic words (*Mark* 5:41), perhaps in order to avoid any connotations of magic. **9:1–6** See *Mark* 6:6–13; *Matt.* 10:1, 7–11, 14. **9:3** These would all be necessary items for the ancient traveler. Jesus here requires radical poverty; his students will appear as the most virtuous and rugged of philosophers. *Luke*'s agreement with *Matt.* 10:10 against *Mark* 6:8 in excluding even a staff is a problem for the common view that *Matthew* and *Luke* are independent. **9:5** See *Acts* 13:51; 18:6, where Christian missionaries actually do this. **9:7–9** See *Mark* 6:14–16; *Matt.* 14:1–2; and notes. Herod Antipas speaks in *Luke* as a hard-nosed administrator, rejecting out of hand others' suggestions of resurrection. Contrast *Mark* 6:16, where Herod himself thinks that John has been raised. *Luke*'s omission of *Mark*'s story of the Baptist's death at this point may well result from the author's general disagreement with *Mark* about Herod's character. **9:7** *ruler* Lit. "tetrarch," Herod Antipas's proper title; *Luke* thus corrects the "King Herod" of *Mark* 6:14.

⁹Herod said, "John I beheaded; but who is this about whom I hear such things?" And he tried to see him.

Feeding the Five Thousand

¹⁰On their return the apostles told Jesusʷ all they had done. He took them with him and withdrew privately to a city called Bethsaida. ¹¹When the crowds found out about it, they followed him; and he welcomed them, and spoke to them about the kingdom of God, and healed those who needed to be cured.

¹²The day was drawing to a close, and the twelve came to him and said, "Send the crowd away, so that they may go into the surrounding villages and countryside, to lodge and get provisions; for we are here in a deserted place." ¹³But he said to them, "You give them something to eat." They said, "We have no more than five loaves and two fish—unless we are to go and buy food for all these people." ¹⁴For there were about five thousand men. And he said to his disciples, "Make them sit down in groups of about fifty each." ¹⁵They did so and made them all sit down. ¹⁶And taking the five loaves and the two fish, he looked up to heaven, and blessed and broke them, and gave them to the disciples to set before the crowd. ¹⁷And all ate and were filled. What was left over was gathered up, twelve baskets of broken pieces.

Peter's Declaration about Jesus

¹⁸Once when Jesusˣ was praying alone, with only the disciples near him, he asked them, "Who do the crowds say that I am?" ¹⁹They answered, "John the Baptist; but others, Elijah; and still others, that one of the ancient prophets has arisen." ²⁰He said

to them, "But who do you say that I am?" Peter answered, "The Messiahʸ of God."

Jesus Foretells His Death and Resurrection

²¹He sternly ordered and commanded them not to tell anyone, ²²saying, "The Son of Man must undergo great suffering, and be rejected by the elders, chief priests, and scribes, and be killed, and on the third day be raised."

²³Then he said to them all, "If any want to become my followers, let them deny themselves and take up their cross daily and follow me. ²⁴For those who want to save their life will lose it, and those who lose their life for my sake will save it. ²⁵What does it profit them if they gain the whole world, but lose or forfeit themselves? ²⁶Those who are ashamed of me and of my words, of them the Son of Man will be ashamed when he comes in his glory and the glory of the Father and of the holy angels. ²⁷But truly I tell you, there are some standing here who will not taste death before they see the kingdom of God."

The Transfiguration

²⁸Now about eight days after these sayings Jesusˣ took with him Peter and John and James, and went up on the mountain to pray. ²⁹And while he was praying, the appearance of his face changed, and his clothes became dazzling white. ³⁰Suddenly they saw two men, Moses and Elijah, talking to him. ³¹They appeared in glory and were speaking of his departure, which he was about to accomplish at Jerusalem. ³²Now Peter and his companions were weighed down with sleep; but since they had stayed awake,ᶻ they saw

---

w Gk *him*
x Gk *he*

y Or *The Christ*
z Or *but when they were fully awake*

9:9 ***And he tried to see him*** The author thus prepares for Herod's trial of Jesus, which is only in *Luke* (23:8). **9:10** ***a city called Bethsaida*** The author once again assumes his readers' ignorance of Palestinian geography. He continues to follow *Mark* (6:30–31). **9:11–17** See *Mark* 6:32–44; *Matt.* 14:13–21; *John* 6:1–15; and notes. **9:14** The author of *Luke,* following *Mark* 6:44, seems to think that this was a male-only group. Contrast *Matt.* 14:21. **9:18–22** See *Mark* 8:27–33; *Matt.* 16:13–23. Peter's confession of Jesus' identity and his prediction of coming suffering comes much earlier in *Luke* than in the parallel stories. One effect of this is to show that Peter and the apostles were in tune with Jesus from the beginning. **9:18** ***Once*** This vague editorial bridge allows the author to rejoin his Markan source, which he has abandoned for most of *Mark* 7 and 8: Jesus' walking on the water, various cures, Jesus' cure of a Gentile woman's daughter after protesting about giving children's bread to "dogs," Jesus' forthright denunciation of the Pharisees, and the feeding of the four thousand. **9:19** Only *Luke* qualifies this (see 9:8). **9:22** *Luke* omits Peter's strong objection and Jesus' rebuke of him as "Satan" in *Mark* 8:32–33. **9:23–27** See *Mark* 8:34–9:1; *Matt.* 16:24–28; *John* 12:25; and notes. **9:23** ***take up their cross daily*** A vivid image of convicts on their way to crucifixion, beaten and ridiculed; crosses could often be seen outside any city of the eastern Mediterranean in Jesus' day. **9:28–36** See *Mark* 9:2–10; *Matt.* 17:1–9; and notes. **9:28** ***about eight days after*** One of the few clear chronological connectives in *Luke.* Remarkably, however, it contradicts *Mark*'s and *Matthew*'s explicit statement that the transfiguration took place six days after the earlier sayings. ***the mountain*** Apparently, *Luke*'s readers do not know which mountain he has in mind, since the author has had to explain other geographical references and he gives no hint about the exact location of Jesus' recent activity. **9:31** ***his departure . . . at Jerusalem*** This statement about what was discussed appears only in *Luke,* recalling Jesus' earlier prediction (9:22) and preparing for the decisive move toward Jerusalem in 9:51. *Luke*'s speaking of Jesus' *departure,* or "exit" (Gk *exodos*), rather than death accords with his ascension story.

his glory and the two men who stood with him. [33]Just as they were leaving him, Peter said to Jesus, "Master, it is good for us to be here; let us make three dwellings,[a] one for you, one for Moses, and one for Elijah"—not knowing what he said. [34]While he was saying this, a cloud came and overshadowed them; and they were terrified as they entered the cloud. [35]Then from the cloud came a voice that said, "This is my Son, my Chosen;[b] listen to him!" [36]When the voice had spoken, Jesus was found alone. And they kept silent and in those days told no one any of the things they had seen.

Jesus Heals a Boy with a Demon

[37]On the next day, when they had come down from the mountain, a great crowd met him. [38]Just then a man from the crowd shouted, "Teacher, I beg you to look at my son; he is my only child. [39]Suddenly a spirit seizes him, and all at once he[c] shrieks. It convulses him until he foams at the mouth; it mauls him and will scarcely leave him. [40]I begged your disciples to cast it out, but they could not." [41]Jesus answered, "You faithless and perverse generation, how much longer must I be with you and bear with you? Bring your son here." [42]While he was coming, the demon dashed him to the ground in convulsions. But Jesus rebuked the unclean spirit, healed the boy, and gave him back to his father. [43]And all were astounded at the greatness of God.

Jesus Again Foretells His Death

While everyone was amazed at all that he was doing, he said to his disciples, [44]"Let these words sink into your ears: The Son of Man is going to be be-trayed into human hands." [45]But they did not understand this saying; its meaning was concealed from them, so that they could not perceive it. And they were afraid to ask him about this saying.

True Greatness

[46]An argument arose among them as to which one of them was the greatest. [47]But Jesus, aware of their inner thoughts, took a little child and put it by his side, [48]and said to them, "Whoever welcomes this child in my name welcomes me, and whoever welcomes me welcomes the one who sent me; for the least among all of you is the greatest."

Another Exorcist

[49]John answered, "Master, we saw someone casting out demons in your name, and we tried to stop him, because he does not follow with us." [50]But Jesus said to him, "Do not stop him; for whoever is not against you is for you."

A Samaritan Village Refuses to Receive Jesus

[51]When the days drew near for him to be taken up, he set his face to go to Jerusalem. [52]And he sent messengers ahead of him. On their way they entered a village of the Samaritans to make ready for him; [53]but they did not receive him, because his face was set toward Jerusalem. [54]When his disciples James and John saw it, they said, "Lord, do you want us to command fire to come down from heaven and consume them?"[d] [55]But he turned and rebuked them. [56]Then[e] they went on to another village.

---

a Or *tents*
b Other ancient authorities read *my Beloved*
c Or *it*

d Other ancient authorities add *as Elijah did*
e Other ancient authorities read *rebuked them, and said, "You do not know what spirit you are of,* [56]*for the Son of Man has not come to destroy the lives of human beings but to save them." Then*

9:35 As at Jesus' baptism, the voice recalls *Ps.* 2:7 and *Isa.* 42:1. **9:36** *in those days told no one* Only in *Luke.* Perhaps a suggestion that the apostles subsequently related this experience. **9:37–43** See *Mark* 9:14–32; *Matt.* 17:14–23. **9:39** Epilepsy, as *Matthew* identifies this ailment (17:15), was an obvious candidate for attribution to invading spirits. **9:41** *and perverse Luke* agrees with *Matt.* 17:17 against *Mark* 9:19 here—a problem for the hypothesis that these two texts were independently written. **9:42** *rebuked the unclean spirit, healed the boy* Notice the close connection between healing and exorcism. **9:44–45** Jesus' second prediction of his death in *Luke.* In contrast to its source, *Mark* 9:32, *Luke* seems to imply that God prevented the apostles from understanding Jesus' words at this point; they do not appear blameworthy. **9:46–48** See *Mark* 9:33–37; *Matt.* 18:1–5. **9:49–50** See *Mark* 9:38–41. It appears from the many magical papyri that have survived from antiquity that exorcists would use any words or names that offered promise of success. Semitic phrases were popular. **9:51** *to be taken up* See note to 9:31. *he set his face to go to Jerusalem* This is a relatively early point in the gospel for Jesus to begin to move toward Jerusalem. Contrast *Mark* and *Matthew*, where the movement toward Jerusalem comes late and quickly. We see here *Luke*'s concern to ground Jesus' career and Christian origins in the famous city. Jesus will, however, still be in the northern territory of Herod Antipas in 13:31 and will not leave Galilee until 17:11. From here until 18:15, coincidentally, *Luke* will make very little use of *Mark*, preferring material that is either common with *Matthew* or unique. **9:52–53** According to Josephus (*Ant.* 20.118–124), there were serious ongoing tensions between Samaritans and Galileans who passed through Samaria en route to and from Jerusalem.

Would-Be Followers of Jesus

57As they were going along the road, someone said to him, "I will follow you wherever you go." 58And Jesus said to him, "Foxes have holes, and birds of the air have nests; but the Son of Man has nowhere to lay his head." 59To another he said, "Follow me." But he said, "Lord, first let me go and bury my father." 60But Jesus*f* said to him, "Let the dead bury their own dead; but as for you, go and proclaim the kingdom of God." 61Another said, "I will follow you, Lord; but let me first say farewell to those at my home." 62Jesus said to him, "No one who puts a hand to the plow and looks back is fit for the kingdom of God."

The Mission of the Seventy

10 After this the Lord appointed seventy*g* others and sent them on ahead of him in pairs to every town and place where he himself intended to go. 2He said to them, "The harvest is plentiful, but the laborers are few; therefore ask the Lord of the harvest to send out laborers into his harvest. 3Go on your way. See, I am sending you out like lambs into the midst of wolves. 4Carry no purse, no bag, no sandals; and greet no one on the road. 5Whatever house you enter, first say, 'Peace to this house!' 6And if anyone is there who shares in peace, your peace will rest on that person; but if not, it will return to you. 7Remain in the same house, eating and drinking whatever they provide, for the laborer deserves to be paid. Do not move about from house to house. 8Whenever you enter a town and its people welcome you, eat what is set before you; 9cure the sick who are there, and say to them, 'The kingdom of God has come near to you.'*h* 10But whenever you enter a town and they do not welcome you, go out into its streets and say, 11'Even the dust of your town that clings to our feet, we wipe off in protest against you. Yet know this: the kingdom of God has come near.'*i* 12I tell you, on that day it will be more tolerable for Sodom than for that town.

Woes to Unrepentant Cities

13"Woe to you, Chorazin! Woe to you, Bethsaida! For if the deeds of power done in you had been done in Tyre and Sidon, they would have repented long ago, sitting in sackcloth and ashes. 14But at the judgment it will be more tolerable for Tyre and Sidon than for you. 15And you, Capernaum,

will you be exalted to heaven?

No, you will be brought down to Hades.

16"Whoever listens to you listens to me, and whoever rejects you rejects me, and whoever rejects me rejects the one who sent me."

The Return of the Seventy

17The seventy*g* returned with joy, saying, "Lord, in your name even the demons submit to us!" 18He said to them, "I watched Satan fall from heaven like a flash of lightning. 19See, I have given you authority

---

f Gk *he*
g Other ancient authorities read *seventy-two*

h Or *is at hand for you*
i Or *is at hand*

9:57–62 Together, these three exchanges present Jesus as a social radical, not unlike a Cynic philosopher, who demands the repudiation of normal social conventions. Burial of one's parents, for example, was generally considered the most basic social duty. See *Matt.* 8:18–22; *Gospel of Thomas* 86.   **10:1** The sending of the seventy as an advance team to prepare for Jesus' arrival in various places is unique to *Luke.* But much of what follows is paralleled in *Matthew*'s version of the missionary instructions to the Twelve (*Matt.* 10:7–16).   **10:2** See *Matt.* 9:37–38; *John* 4:35; *Gospel of Thomas* 73, and note the different contexts for this saying.   **10:3–11** See *Matt.* 10:16, 9–10a, 10b, 7–8, 14–15; *Did.* 11.4–6; *Gospel of Thomas* 39, 14; and notes.   **10:10–11** See *Acts* 13:51; 18:6, where the Christian missionaries will actually do this; see *Luke* 9:5, where Jesus gave the same command to his apostles.   **10:12** *Sodom* The city whose name lingers in the English term "sodomy"; see *Gen.* 19:1–26; *Jude* 7. The biblical story features Sodom alone, although the entire "land of Sodom and Gomorrah" (*Matt.* 10:15) is punished; this may be the reason the author omits Gomorrah, unlike the parallel in *Matthew.*   **10:13–15** See *Matt.* 11:20–24 and notes.   **10:13** *Chorazin* About two miles north of Capernaum; it appears only in the Matthean parallel to this passage (*Matt.* 11:21) although the saying assumes that Jesus taught there.   *Bethsaida* Although only three miles east of Capernaum, it was in the territory of Philip, not of Herod Antipas. *John* 1:44 claims that it was the home of Peter and Andrew, but *Mark* 1:16, 29 (see note to 1:16) give this role to Capernaum.   *Tyre and Sidon* Two famous ancient cities— already two thousand years old by Jesus' time—on the Phoenician coast, about twenty-five miles apart. Although biblical Israel and Judah long enjoyed fruitful cooperation with these cities, they were denounced in the prophets as great cities doomed by divine judgment (*Isa.* 23:1–18; *Ezek.* 28:11–24). Earlier in *Luke,* Jesus has mentioned Sidon favorably (4:26), and he has attracted followers from both Tyre and Sidon (6:17). This may be the basis of his claim that these Gentile cities would repent more easily than the Jewish Galilean towns mentioned. In *Mark* 7:24 Jesus goes to Tyre and Sidon, but *Luke* omits this passage.   **10:15** *Hades* In Greek literature, Hades is not a place of punishment but simply the place of the dead, like the early biblical *Sheol.*   **10:16** See *Matt.* 10:40; *John* 13:20.   **10:17–18** Only in *Luke.* It was commonly felt in Jesus' day that Satan, or the prince of demons, had been allowed by God to control the world for a time (*1 Enoch* 6–10; *1 Cor.* 15:24–28; *2 Cor.* 4:4). Jesus announces the end of that time.   **10:19** A similar saying is attributed to the risen Jesus in the long ending of *Mark* (16:18), which is not part of the original gospel. This power over snakes is realized by *Luke*'s Paul in *Acts* 28:3–5.

to tread on snakes and scorpions, and over all the power of the enemy; and nothing will hurt you. [20]Nevertheless, do not rejoice at this, that the spirits submit to you, but rejoice that your names are written in heaven."

Jesus Rejoices

[21]At that same hour Jesus[j] rejoiced in the Holy Spirit[k] and said, "I thank[l] you, Father, Lord of heaven and earth, because you have hidden these things from the wise and the intelligent and have revealed them to infants; yes, Father, for such was your gracious will.[m] [22]All things have been handed over to me by my Father; and no one knows who the Son is except the Father, or who the Father is except the Son and anyone to whom the Son chooses to reveal him."

[23]Then turning to the disciples, Jesus[j] said to them privately, "Blessed are the eyes that see what you see! [24]For I tell you that many prophets and kings desired to see what you see, but did not see it, and to hear what you hear, but did not hear it."

The Parable of the Good Samaritan

[25]Just then a lawyer stood up to test Jesus.[n] "Teacher," he said, "what must I do to inherit eternal life?" [26]He said to him, "What is written in the law? What do you read there?" [27]He answered, "You shall love the Lord your God with all your heart, and with all your soul, and with all your strength, and with all your mind; and your neighbor as yourself." [28]And he said to him, "You have given the right answer; do this, and you will live."

[29]But wanting to justify himself, he asked Jesus, "And who is my neighbor?" [30]Jesus replied, "A man was going down from Jerusalem to Jericho, and fell into the hands of robbers, who stripped him, beat him, and went away, leaving him half dead. [31]Now by chance a priest was going down that road; and when he saw him, he passed by on the other side. [32]So likewise a Levite, when he came to the place and saw him, passed by on the other side. [33]But a Samaritan while traveling came near him; and when he saw him, he was moved with pity. [34]He went to him and bandaged his wounds, having poured oil and wine on them. Then he put him on his own animal, brought him to an inn, and took care of him. [35]The next day he took out two denarii,[o] gave them to the innkeeper, and said, 'Take care of him; and when I come back, I will repay you whatever more you spend.' [36]Which of these three, do you think, was a neighbor to the man

---

j Gk he
k Other authorities read in the spirit
l Or praise
m Or for so it was well-pleasing in your sight
n Gk him

o The denarius was the usual day's wage for a laborer

10:20 *written in heaven* The image of a book of life, in which the names of the faithful were inscribed, was common in apocalyptic thinking; see *Rev.* 3:5; 20:12. **10:21–22** See *Matt.* 11:25–27; *John* 3:35; 7:29; 10:15; 17:2, 25. Although this bold self-referential saying (from Q?) is typical of *John's* portrait of Jesus, it is without real parallel in the synoptic tradition. **10:22** See *1 Cor.* 15:27–28, where Paul derives the subjection of all things to the risen Christ from the application of *Ps.* 8:4 to Jesus. **10:23–24** See *Matt.* 13:16–17; *Gospel of Thomas* 38. **10:25–28** See *Mark* 12:38–44 (one of the few Markan passages in the middle section of *Luke*); *Matt.* 22:34–40. **10:25** *a lawyer* Lawyers were introduced as companions of the Pharisees, or perhaps in explanation of who the Pharisees were, in 7:30. The term "lawyer"—meaning here an expert in the Jewish Torah—is favored by *Luke;* it appears only once in *Matthew* and not at all in *Mark,* but seven times in *Luke.* *eternal life* Or "agelong life," life in the new age. **10:26–27** In *Mark* and *Matthew,* it is Jesus who answers the lawyer's (or scribe's) question by citing these verses. Perhaps *Luke's* emphasis on Jesus' recognized status as a teacher leads the author to put the lawyer, not Jesus, under examination. **10:27** *You shall love* Deut. 6:5. *Luke* follows *Mark* but has reversed the final two items. *and your neighbor as yourself* Lev. 19:18. *Luke* combines into one verse with a single verb what *Mark* and *Matthew* correctly present as two verses with two verbs. See *Mark* 12:31. **10:28** In *Mark,* it is the questioner who commends Jesus' answer. **10:29** The author of *Luke* thus joins the preceding episode with the parable of the good Samaritan, although they appear to have been separate items before he wrote (since only the former is in *Mark* and parables elsewhere are freestanding units). See the similar joining of distinct sayings in 5:32–33. **10:30–37** The parable of the good Samaritan is unique to *Luke.* It helps to develop *Luke's* characteristic emphases on forgiveness and reversal of status. **10:30** *going down* Jerusalem is in the hills; Jericho is in the Jordan River valley, about fifteen miles to the northeast. The ancient road between them was difficult. Ancient writers typically thought of "up" and "down" in relation to topography, not the points of the compass. **10:31** *a priest* One of the hereditary caste of priests, perhaps on his way to or from Jerusalem for his week of service in the temple. See notes to 1:5–10. **10:32** *a Levite* Levites were supposed to be the nonpriestly descendants of Levi, one of the twelve sons of Jacob/Israel. By Jesus' time, they had come to occupy a supporting role in the temple activities as musicians and attendants. See *Num.* 8:5–26; Josephus, *Ant.* 3.287. They were supported by the tithes of Israel—contributions of one-tenth of the people's income and produce. Levites in turn tithed to the priests. **10:33** *a Samaritan* See note to 9:52–53; the reader of *Luke* already knows of the strained relations between Judeans and Samaritans. The Samaritan would naturally be viewed as an enemy. It is unclear why a Samaritan might have been walking near Jerusalem, since the Samaritans had their own place of sacrifice. **10:35** *two denarii* See note to 7:41.

who fell into the hands of the robbers?" 37He said, "The one who showed him mercy." Jesus said to him, "Go and do likewise."

Jesus Visits Martha and Mary

38Now as they went on their way, he entered a certain village, where a woman named Martha welcomed him into her home. 39She had a sister named Mary, who sat at the Lord's feet and listened to what he was saying. 40But Martha was distracted by her many tasks; so she came to him and asked, "Lord, do you not care that my sister has left me to do all the work by myself? Tell her then to help me." 41But the Lord answered her, "Martha, Martha, you are worried and distracted by many things; 42there is need of only one thing.*p* Mary has chosen the better part, which will not be taken away from her."

The Lord's Prayer

11 He was praying in a certain place, and after he had finished, one of his disciples said to him, "Lord, teach us to pray, as John taught his disciples." 2He said to them, "When you pray, say:

Father,*q* hallowed be your name.
    Your kingdom come.*r*
3   Give us each day our daily bread.*s*
4   And forgive us our sins,
        for we ourselves forgive everyone
          indebted to us.
    And do not bring us to the time of trial."*t*

Perseverance in Prayer

5And he said to them, "Suppose one of you has a friend, and you go to him at midnight and say to him, 'Friend, lend me three loaves of bread; 6for a friend of mine has arrived, and I have nothing to set before him.' 7And he answers from within, 'Do not bother me; the door has already been locked, and my children are with me in bed; I cannot get up and give you anything.' 8I tell you, even though he will not get up and give him anything because he is his friend, at least because of his persistence he will get up and give him whatever he needs.

9"So I say to you, Ask, and it will be given you; search, and you will find; knock, and the door will be opened for you. 10For everyone who asks receives, and everyone who searches finds, and for everyone who knocks, the door will be opened. 11Is there anyone among you who, if your child asks for*u* a fish, will give a snake instead of a fish? 12Or if the child asks for an egg, will give a scorpion? 13If you then, who are evil, know how to give good gifts to your children, how much more will the heavenly Father give the Holy Spirit*v* to those who ask him!"

Jesus and Beelzebul

14Now he was casting out a demon that was mute; when the demon had gone out, the one who had been mute spoke, and the crowds were amazed. 15But some of them said, "He casts out demons by Beelzebul, the ruler of the demons." 16Others, to test him,

---

p Other ancient authorities read *few things are necessary, or only one*

q Other ancient authorities read *Our Father in heaven*

r A few ancient authorities read *Your Holy Spirit come upon us and cleanse us;* other ancient authorities add *Your will be done, on earth as in heaven*

s Or *our bread for tomorrow*

t Or *us into temptation.* Other ancient authorities add *but rescue us from the evil one* (or *from evil*)

u Other ancient authorities add *bread, will give a stone; or if your child asks for*

v Other ancient authorities read *the Father give the Holy Spirit from heaven*

10:38–42 Jesus appears as a countercultural teacher who invites women to be his students. **10:38–39** According to *John* 11:1–2, 18–19, Mary and Martha lived in Bethany with their brother Lazarus, a couple of miles east of Jerusalem. The author of *Luke* evidently does not know this location for their home, because in his story Jesus has not yet left Galilee (9:51; 13:31; 17:11). **10:39** *the Lord's* See note to 7:6. **10:40** *distracted by her many tasks* A lower-class woman's work was domestic, including not only cooking and cleaning but also visiting the market to buy and sell. **11:1–4** See *Matt.* 6:9–13 for the more famous version of the Lord's Prayer. Note the entirely different context there, as part of the Sermon on the Mount. **11:1** *as John taught his disciples* An interesting rationale, which incidentally confirms that the Baptist's students continued in their own ways (7:18–19, 33–34; *Acts* 19:1–6). In *Matthew,* Jesus freely provides this model prayer as part of his Sermon on the Mount. **11:5–8** This parable about the value of persistence is peculiar to *Luke.* **11:9–12** See *Matt.* 7:7–11; *John* 16:24; 14:13–14; *Gospel of Thomas* 2, 92, 94. *Matthew's* pairs are bread/stone and fish/serpent, thus overlapping with *Luke's.* Perhaps their shared source (Q) had all three items, including egg/scorpion: The author of *Matthew* chose the first two pairs, *Luke* the 2d two. **11:13** *Matthew* has "good things." *Luke* displays an ongoing interest in the Holy Spirit. **11:14–23** See *Mark* 3:22–27 (one of the few intersections with *Mark* in the large central part of *Luke*); *Matt.* 12:22–30; *John* 7:20; 10:20; 8:48, 52; *Gospel of Thomas* 35. **11:15** *Beelzebul, the ruler of the demons* One of several names for the chief devil: Jesus more commonly calls him Satan (see 11:18); other common names were Azazel, Mastema, and Belial. Various explanations of the name Beelzebul have been offered; most likely is the meaning "master of the house," which would make the following illustration of the strong man (10:21; see *Matt.* 12:29) a play on the name.

kept demanding from him a sign from heaven. [17]But he knew what they were thinking and said to them, "Every kingdom divided against itself becomes a desert, and house falls on house. [18]If Satan also is divided against himself, how will his kingdom stand? —for you say that I cast out the demons by Beelzebul. [19]Now if I cast out the demons by Beelzebul, by whom do your exorcists[w] cast them out? Therefore they will be your judges. [20]But if it is by the finger of God that I cast out the demons, then the kingdom of God has come to you. [21]When a strong man, fully armed, guards his castle, his property is safe. [22]But when one stronger than he attacks him and overpowers him, he takes away his armor in which he trusted and divides his plunder. [23]Whoever is not with me is against me, and whoever does not gather with me scatters.

The Return of the Unclean Spirit

[24]"When the unclean spirit has gone out of a person, it wanders through waterless regions looking for a resting place, but not finding any, it says, 'I will return to my house from which I came.' [25]When it comes, it finds it swept and put in order. [26]Then it goes and brings seven other spirits more evil than itself, and they enter and live there; and the last state of that person is worse than the first."

True Blessedness

[27]While he was saying this, a woman in the crowd raised her voice and said to him, "Blessed is the womb that bore you and the breasts that nursed you!" [28]But he said, "Blessed rather are those who hear the word of God and obey it!"

The Sign of Jonah

[29]When the crowds were increasing, he began to say, "This generation is an evil generation; it asks for a sign, but no sign will be given to it except the sign of Jonah. [30]For just as Jonah became a sign to the people of Nineveh, so the Son of Man will be to this generation. [31]The queen of the South will rise at the judgment with the people of this generation and condemn them, because she came from the ends of the earth to listen to the wisdom of Solomon, and see, something greater than Solomon is here! [32]The people of Nineveh will rise up at the judgment with this generation and condemn it, because they repented at the proclamation of Jonah, and see, something greater than Jonah is here!

The Light of the Body

[33]"No one after lighting a lamp puts it in a cellar,[x] but on the lampstand so that those who enter may see the light. [34]Your eye is the lamp of your body. If your eye is healthy, your whole body is full of light; but if it is not healthy, your body is full of darkness. [35]Therefore consider whether the light in you is not darkness. [36]If then your whole body is full of light, with no part of it in darkness, it will be as full of light as when a lamp gives you light with its rays."

Jesus Denounces Pharisees and Lawyers

[37]While he was speaking, a Pharisee invited him to dine with him; so he went in and took his place at the table. [38]The Pharisee was amazed to see that he did

---

w Gk *sons*

x Other ancient authorities add *or under the bushel basket*

11:19 *your exorcists* See notes to 8:27; 9:49–50. **11:20** *the kingdom of God has come to you* A key passage for the argument that the historical Jesus believed the kingdom to have decisively begun in some way. **11:21–22** This illustration seems to extend what has preceded and portrays Jesus as the stronger man. (*Gospel of Thomas* 35 understands it as merely a sober observation about life in general.) **11:23** Contrast 9:50. See *Matt.* 12:43–45 and notes. **11:24–26** See *Matt.* 12:43–45 and notes. **11:27–28** See *Gospel of Thomas* 79; *Luke* 8:19–21; 9:59–62; 12:49–53; 14:20–21, 26. Jesus appears as a social radical. **11:29–32** See *Mark* 8:11–12; *Matt.* 12:38–42. *Luke* omits the claim in *Mark* and *Matthew* that the Pharisees explicitly requested a sign. *Luke's* view of the Pharisees is markedly milder than that of the other gospels (see introduction to *Luke-Acts*). **11:30** See the biblical book of *Jonah* for the story. Luke's interpretation differs radically from Matthew's. See 11:32. **11:31** *The queen of the South* The queen of Sheba: *1 Kgs.* 10:1–10; *2 Chr.* 9:1–12. The Gk has "men" (males). Since the queen is a woman, and *Matthew's* parallel lacks the word "men," the contrast must be significant for *Luke.* The author is highlighting the salvation of both Gentiles and women. Male Jews are condemned here for failing to repent. **11:32** *The people* Lit. "men [males]." *they repented* See *Jonah* 3:8–10. **11:33** See *Mark* 4:21; *Matt.* 5:15; *Gospel of Thomas* 33. **11:34–36** See *Matt.* 6:22–23; *Gospel of Thomas* 24. **11:37** *Luke's* editorial bridge; the following story is not in *Matthew's* parallel. *to dine* The Gk word suggests an early meal, a luncheon. See note to 14:12. This is the second of Jesus' three meals with Pharisees in *Luke;* see 7:36–50; 14:1–24. *took his place at the table* Lit. "reclined." See note to 7:36. *Mark* 7:1–6 par. *Matt.* 15:1–2 **11:38** *that he did not first wash* Lit.: that he was not immersed (*baptizō*). It was customary to attend the (public) baths before going to a banquet, also for a slave to wash the guests' feet (see 7:44–46) and to provide water for the washing of hands. Pharisaic and later rabbinic society made the custom of hand-washing a religious requirement (see *Mark* 7:1–2). It is uncertain which of these "baptisms" Jesus omitted. His failure to wash evokes the behavior of Cynic philosophers, known as "doglike" for their unkempt appearance. The author may also be ironically echoing 7:30, where he noted that the Pharisees rejected John's baptism.

not first wash before dinner. ³⁹Then the Lord said to him, "Now you Pharisees clean the outside of the cup and of the dish, but inside you are full of greed and wickedness. ⁴⁰You fools! Did not the one who made the outside make the inside also? ⁴¹So give for alms those things that are within; and see, everything will be clean for you.

⁴²"But woe to you Pharisees! For you tithe mint and rue and herbs of all kinds, and neglect justice and the love of God; it is these you ought to have practiced, without neglecting the others. ⁴³Woe to you Pharisees! For you love to have the seat of honor in the synagogues and to be greeted with respect in the marketplaces. ⁴⁴Woe to you! For you are like unmarked graves, and people walk over them without realizing it."

⁴⁵One of the lawyers answered him, "Teacher, when you say these things, you insult us too." ⁴⁶And he said, "Woe also to you lawyers! For you load people with burdens hard to bear, and you yourselves do not lift a finger to ease them. ⁴⁷Woe to you! For you build the tombs of the prophets whom your ancestors killed. ⁴⁸So you are witnesses and approve of the deeds of your ancestors; for they killed them, and you build their tombs. ⁴⁹Therefore also the Wisdom of God said, 'I will send them prophets and apostles, some of whom they will kill and persecute,' ⁵⁰so that this generation may be charged with the blood of all the prophets shed since the foundation of the world, ⁵¹from the blood of Abel to the blood of Zechariah, who perished between the altar and the sanctuary. Yes, I tell you, it will be charged against this generation. ⁵²Woe to you lawyers! For you have taken away the key of knowledge; you did not enter yourselves, and you hindered those who were entering."

⁵³When he went outside, the scribes and the Pharisees began to be very hostile toward him and to cross-examine him about many things, ⁵⁴lying in wait for him, to catch him in something he might say.

A Warning against Hypocrisy

12Meanwhile, when the crowd gathered by the thousands, so that they trampled on one another, he began to speak first to his disciples, "Beware of the yeast of the Pharisees, that is, their hypocrisy. ²Nothing is covered up that will not be uncovered, and nothing secret that will not become known. ³Therefore whatever you have said in the dark will be heard in the light, and what you have whispered behind closed doors will be proclaimed from the housetops.

Exhortation to Fearless Confession

⁴"I tell you, my friends, do not fear those who kill the body, and after that can do nothing more. ⁵But I will warn you whom to fear: fear him who, after he has killed, has authority[y] to cast into hell.[z] Yes, I tell you, fear him! ⁶Are not five sparrows sold for two pennies? Yet not one of them is forgotten in God's sight. ⁷But even the hairs of your head are all counted. Do not be afraid; you are of more value than many sparrows.

⁸"And I tell you, everyone who acknowledges me before others, the Son of Man also will acknowledge

---

y Or *power*
z Gk *Gehenna*

11:39–41 See *Matt.* 23:25–26; *Gospel of Thomas* 89. **11:39** *the Lord* See note to 7:13. *outside . . . inside* See the Baptist's teaching about immersion in 3:7–8; Josephus, *Ant.* 18.116–117. **11:41** *everything will be clean for you* This does not evidently mean that *Luke*'s Jesus abolishes the Torah's prohibitions at this point; see *Acts* 10:1–33. **11:42** *tithe* Jews were required to set aside one-tenth (a *tithe*) of their produce for the maintenance of priests and Levites, who owned no land; *Lev.* 27:30. See *Matt.* 23:23. **11:43** See *Matt.* 23:6–7; also *Mark* 12:38–39. **11:44** Thus the Pharisees appear as ineffective and complacent representatives of the status quo. They offer no challenge to society as Jesus does. The similar saying in *Matt.* 23:27–28 makes the opposite point—that the Pharisees are like conspicuously whitewashed tombs. **11:45** *insult us too* The exact relationship between *Luke*'s "lawyers" and Pharisees is unclear. The author pairs the two groups also in 7:30; 11:53; 14:3. In 5:17 and *Acts* 5:34, he refers to certain Pharisees as "teachers of the law." Since the Pharisees were considered by many the most exact and astute teachers of the law (Josephus, *J.W.* 1.110), it makes sense that they would be known as legal experts. But the Torah was central to all Judaism, and every group may have had its lawyers. Here *Luke* implies that the two groups were not exactly the same. In view of 11:53, it seems "lawyer" is a synonym for "scribe." **11:46** See *Matt.* 23:4. **11:47–48** See *Matt.* 23:29–32. Building tombs for the ancient prophets was a noble task; *Luke*'s Jesus, as *Matthew*'s more explicitly, inverts the motive. **11:49–51** See *Matt.* 23:34–36. **11:49** *the Wisdom of God said* In the parallel (*Matt.* 23:34) it is Jesus who says these words (see *1 Cor.* 1:30; *John* 1:2–3; *Heb.* 1:19). **11:50–51** See note to *Matt.* 23:35–36. If *Luke*'s Jesus has in mind a general punishment of *this generation*, this is likely a reference to the fall of Jerusalem in 70 C.E. **11:52** See *Matt.* 23:13; *Gospel of Thomas* 39, 102. *key of knowledge* Only in *Luke* and *Thomas*: the notion that salvation involves *knowledge* supports *Luke*'s philosophical themes. **11:53–54** In spite of this growing hostility, Pharisees will help Jesus flee from Herod Antipas (13:31) and will invite him to dinner again (14:1). **12:1** See *Mark* 8:14–15; *Matt.* 16:5–6. *the thousands* Lit. "myriads" (one myriad = ten thousand). *Luke* gives the impression that Jesus' following grows steadily throughout his career. *yeast of the Pharisees . . . hypocrisy* Mark: "the yeast of the Pharisees and the yeast of Herod"; Matthew: "the yeast of the Pharisees and Sadducees," which is their teaching. **12:2–9** See *Matt.* 10:26–33; *Gospel of Thomas* 5, 6, 33. **12:8** *the Son of Man also will acknowledge* Matthew: "I also will acknowledge."

before the angels of God; [9]but whoever denies me before others will be denied before the angels of God. [10]And everyone who speaks a word against the Son of Man will be forgiven; but whoever blasphemes against the Holy Spirit will not be forgiven. [11]When they bring you before the synagogues, the rulers, and the authorities, do not worry about how[a] you are to defend yourselves or what you are to say; [12]for the Holy Spirit will teach you at that very hour what you ought to say."

The Parable of the Rich Fool

[13]Someone in the crowd said to him, "Teacher, tell my brother to divide the family inheritance with me." [14]But he said to him, "Friend, who set me to be a judge or arbitrator over you?" [15]And he said to them, "Take care! Be on your guard against all kinds of greed; for one's life does not consist in the abundance of possessions." [16]Then he told them a parable: "The land of a rich man produced abundantly. [17]And he thought to himself, 'What should I do, for I have no place to store my crops?' [18]Then he said, 'I will do this: I will pull down my barns and build larger ones, and there I will store all my grain and my goods. [19]And I will say to my soul, 'Soul, you have ample goods laid up for many years; relax, eat, drink, be merry.' [20]But God said to him, 'You fool! This very night your life is being demanded of you. And the things you have prepared, whose will they be?' [21]So it is with those who store up treasures for themselves but are not rich toward God."

Do Not Worry

[22]He said to his disciples, "Therefore I tell you, do not worry about your life, what you will eat, or about your body, what you will wear. [23]For life is more than food, and the body more than clothing. [24]Consider the ravens: they neither sow nor reap, they have nei-

ther storehouse nor barn, and yet God feeds them. Of how much more value are you than the birds! [25]And can any of you by worrying add a single hour to your span of life?[b] [26]If then you are not able to do so small a thing as that, why do you worry about the rest? [27]Consider the lilies, how they grow: they neither toil nor spin;[c] yet I tell you, even Solomon in all his glory was not clothed like one of these. [28]But if God so clothes the grass of the field, which is alive today and tomorrow is thrown into the oven, how much more will he clothe you—you of little faith! [29]And do not keep striving for what you are to eat and what you are to drink, and do not keep worrying. [30]For it is the nations of the world that strive after all these things, and your Father knows that you need them. [31]Instead, strive for his[d] kingdom, and these things will be given to you as well.

[32]"Do not be afraid, little flock, for it is your Father's good pleasure to give you the kingdom. [33]Sell your possessions, and give alms. Make purses for yourselves that do not wear out, an unfailing treasure in heaven, where no thief comes near and no moth destroys. [34]For where your treasure is, there your heart will be also.

Watchful Slaves

[35]"Be dressed for action and have your lamps lit; [36]be like those who are waiting for their master to return from the wedding banquet, so that they may open the door for him as soon as he comes and knocks. [37]Blessed are those slaves whom the master finds alert when he comes; truly I tell you, he will fasten his belt and have them sit down to eat, and he will come and serve them. [38]If he comes during the middle of the night, or near dawn, and finds them so, blessed are those slaves.

[39]"But know this: if the owner of the house had known at what hour the thief was coming, he[e] would

---

a Other ancient authorities add *or what*

b Or *add a cubit to your stature*
c Other ancient authorities read *Consider the lilies; they neither spin nor weave*
d Other ancient authorities read *God's*
e Other ancient authorities add *would have watched and*

12:10 See *Mark* 3:28–30; *Matt.* 12:31–32; *Gospel of Thomas* 44. *Mark* and *Matthew* place this saying immediately after Jesus is accused of being in league with Beelzebul—implying that this accusation by the Jewish leaders is an example of blaspheming against the Holy Spirit. They also make this an eternally unforgivable sin, an emphasis lacking in *Luke*. **12:11–12.** See Mark 13:11; *Matt.* 10:19–20; *John* 14:26; *Luke* 21:14–15. This passage is amply fulfilled among Jesus' followers in *Acts* (4:8, 29–31; 23:11). **12:13–15** See *Gospel of Thomas* 72. This episode and the next contribute to *Luke*'s critique of wealth. **12:13 Teacher** Jesus continues to appear in *Luke* as a respected and prominent Jewish teacher. **12:16–21** See *Gospel of Thomas* 63. **12:22–32** See *Matt.* 6:25–34; *Gospel of Thomas* 36. **12:30 the nations of the world** The parallel in *Matt.* 6:32 has simply "Gentiles," or "nations," in keeping with the thoroughly Jewish perspective of *Matthew*'s Jesus. *Luke*'s version of the phrase, in which Jesus does not simply speak of Gentiles as outsiders, might be understood to criticize rather the leaders of the nations or the political powers. **12:33–34** See *Matt.* 6:19–21; *Gospel of Thomas* 76. **12:35–48** See the loose parallels in *Mark* 13:33–37; *Matt.* 24:42–51; *Gospel of Thomas* 21, 103.

not have let his house be broken into. ⁴⁰You also must be ready, for the Son of Man is coming at an unexpected hour."

The Faithful or the Unfaithful Slave

⁴¹Peter said, "Lord, are you telling this parable for us or for everyone?" ⁴²And the Lord said, "Who then is the faithful and prudent manager whom his master will put in charge of his slaves, to give them their allowance of food at the proper time? ⁴³Blessed is that slave whom his master will find at work when he arrives. ⁴⁴Truly I tell you, he will put that one in charge of all his possessions. ⁴⁵But if that slave says to himself, 'My master is delayed in coming,' and if he begins to beat the other slaves, men and women, and to eat and drink and get drunk, ⁴⁶the master of that slave will come on a day when he does not expect him and at an hour that he does not know, and will cut him in pieces,ᶠ and put him with the unfaithful. ⁴⁷That slave who knew what his master wanted, but did not prepare himself or do what was wanted, will receive a severe beating. ⁴⁸But the one who did not know and did what deserved a beating will receive a light beating. From everyone to whom much has been given, much will be required; and from the one to whom much has been entrusted, even more will be demanded.

Jesus the Cause of Division

⁴⁹"I came to bring fire to the earth, and how I wish it were already kindled! ⁵⁰I have a baptism with which to be baptized, and what stress I am under until it is completed! ⁵¹Do you think that I have come to bring peace to the earth? No, I tell you, but rather division! ⁵²From now on five in one house-

hold will be divided, three against two and two against three; ⁵³they will be divided:

> father against son
> and son against father,
> mother against daughter
> and daughter against mother,
> mother-in-law against her daughter-in-law
> and daughter-in-law against mother-in-law."

Interpreting the Time

⁵⁴He also said to the crowds, "When you see a cloud rising in the west, you immediately say, 'It is going to rain'; and so it happens. ⁵⁵And when you see the south wind blowing, you say, 'There will be scorching heat'; and it happens. ⁵⁶You hypocrites! You know how to interpret the appearance of earth and sky, but why do you not know how to interpret the present time?

Settling with Your Opponent

⁵⁷"And why do you not judge for yourselves what is right? ⁵⁸Thus, when you go with your accuser before a magistrate, on the way make an effort to settle the case,ᵍ or you may be dragged before the judge, and the judge hand you over to the officer, and the officer throw you in prison. ⁵⁹I tell you, you will never get out until you have paid the very last penny."

Repent or Perish

13 At that very time there were some present who told him about the Galileans whose blood Pilate had mingled with their sacrifices. ²He asked them, "Do you think that because these Galileans suffered in this way they were worse sinners than all other Galileans? ³No, I tell you; but unless you repent,

---

ᶠ Or *cut him off*

ᵍ Gk *settle with him*

12:40 *at an unexpected hour* See Paul's remark in *1 Thess.* 5:2. **12:42 *the Lord*** See note to 7:13. **12:45 *My master is delayed in coming*** The perceived delay of Jesus' return was an acute problem for the earliest generations of Christians; *1 Thess.* 5:1–12; *Matt.* 25:1–13; *2 Pet.* 3:3–10. ***men and women*** Only *Luke* explicitly mentions women servants, in keeping with the author's special attention to women. **12:46 *cut him in pieces*** A shocking punishment by modern standards but perhaps not unthinkable in the ancient world, where physical punishment and violent death were common. **12:48 *a light beating*** *Luke* alone seems to suggest that ignorance of Jesus' claims might bring leniency from God. **12:49–53** See *Mark* 10:38; *Matt.* 10:34–46; *Gospel of Thomas* 10, 16, 82. *Luke* continues to emphasize Jesus' countercultural role, upsetting the status quo; see note to 11:27–28. **12:52 *five in one household*** The following scenario has two parents, a son and daughter, and the son's wife in one home—common enough, since a bride would normally go to live in the groom's house. All of the divisions specified are between the older and the younger generations (thus two against three). **12:54–56** See *Matt.* 16:2–3; *Gospel of Thomas* 91. **12:54 *said*** Or "would say," "used to say." **12:55 *south wind*** This saying seems to reflect the author's vantage point rather than Jesus', for the typical scorching desert wind in Palestine comes from the east. **12:57–59** See *Matt.* 5:25–26; *1 Cor.* 6:1–6. **12:59 *penny*** Gk *lepton,* the smallest unit of currency. **13:1–5** These episodes, valuable for the light they shed on Pontius Pilate's term as governor and current events in Judea, appear only in *Luke.* **13:1–2** This incident is otherwise unknown, but Pilate was involved in a famous attack on a group of Samaritans at Mount Gerizim (Josephus, *Ant.* 18.85–87). **13:3–4** The incident and the tower are otherwise unknown. Siloam was a valley to the southeast of Jerusalem, where Silwan is today. Like many of his time and place, *Luke*'s Jesus sees such events as instruments of divine retribution.

you will all perish as they did. ⁴Or those eighteen who were killed when the tower of Siloam fell on them—do you think that they were worse offenders than all the others living in Jerusalem? ⁵No, I tell you; but unless you repent, you will all perish just as they did."

The Parable of the Barren Fig Tree

⁶Then he told this parable: "A man had a fig tree planted in his vineyard; and he came looking for fruit on it and found none. ⁷So he said to the gardener, 'See here! For three years I have come looking for fruit on this fig tree, and still I find none. Cut it down! Why should it be wasting the soil?' ⁸He replied, 'Sir, let it alone for one more year, until I dig around it and put manure on it. ⁹If it bears fruit next year, well and good; but if not, you can cut it down.'"

Jesus Heals a Crippled Woman

¹⁰Now he was teaching in one of the synagogues on the sabbath. ¹¹And just then there appeared a woman with a spirit that had crippled her for eighteen years. She was bent over and was quite unable to stand up straight. ¹²When Jesus saw her, he called her over and said, "Woman, you are set free from your ailment." ¹³When he laid his hands on her, immediately she stood up straight and began praising God. ¹⁴But the leader of the synagogue, indignant because Jesus had cured on the sabbath, kept saying to the crowd, "There are six days on which work ought to be done; come on those days and be cured, and not on the sabbath day." ¹⁵But the Lord answered him and said, "You hypocrites! Does not each of you on the sabbath untie his ox or his donkey from the manger, and lead it away to give it water? ¹⁶And ought not

this woman, a daughter of Abraham whom Satan bound for eighteen long years, be set free from this bondage on the sabbath day?" ¹⁷When he said this, all his opponents were put to shame; and the entire crowd was rejoicing at all the wonderful things that he was doing.

The Parable of the Mustard Seed

¹⁸He said therefore, "What is the kingdom of God like? And to what should I compare it? ¹⁹It is like a mustard seed that someone took and sowed in the garden; it grew and became a tree, and the birds of the air made nests in its branches."

The Parable of the Yeast

²⁰And again he said, "To what should I compare the kingdom of God? ²¹It is like yeast that a woman took and mixed in with[h] three measures of flour until all of it was leavened."

The Narrow Door

²²Jesus[i] went through one town and village after another, teaching as he made his way to Jerusalem. ²³Someone asked him, "Lord, will only a few be saved?" He said to them, ²⁴"Strive to enter through the narrow door; for many, I tell you, will try to enter and will not be able. ²⁵When once the owner of the house has got up and shut the door, and you begin to stand outside and to knock at the door, saying, 'Lord, open to us,' then in reply he will say to you, 'I do not know where you come from.' ²⁶Then you will begin

---

h Gk *hid in*
i Gk *He*

13:6–9 This parable of the fig tree is not found in *Mark* or *Matthew*. They both claim, however, that Jesus himself cursed a fig tree for its failure to produce fruit (out of season!) and caused it to wither (*Mark* 11:12–14, 20–21 par. *Matt.* 21:18–19), and they both lack *Luke's* parable. Perhaps the author of *Luke*, finding the story of the cursing improbable or offensive, converted it into this parable.   **13:11–17** *a spirit that had crippled her* On the connection between spirit activity and disease, see note to 8:27.   **13:14** The leader is happy to have this teacher curing people in his synagogue. He is not fundamentally opposed to Jesus. (Contrast *Mark* 3:6.) Only the sabbath healing is a problem. See note to 6:2.   **13:15** Jesus does not challenge the principle of sabbath observance but, rather, debates what constitutes permissible work. See note to 6:2.   **the Lord** See note to 7:13.   *daughter of Abraham Luke's* Jesus, still firmly embedded in the Jewish world, gives a highly positive appraisal of descent from Abraham. The issue of physical Jewish ancestry would be much discussed in early Christianity; see *Gal.* 3:6–29; *Rom.* 4:1–25; *Luke* 3:8.   **13:18–19** See *Mark* 4:30–32; *Matt.* 13:31–32; *Gospel of Thomas* 20. The mustard plant is a shrub that normally grows to between two and six feet, with leaves growing out at the base of the stem. *Mark*, accordingly, has the birds making nests in its shade. In this passage there are several agreements between *Matthew* and *Luke* against *Mark*; this challenges the common hypothesis of their independence—unless there was both a Markan and a Q version of this saying.   **13:20–21** See *Matt.* 13:33; *Gospel of Thomas* 96.   **13:21** *measures* Gk *sata*, plural of *saton*, indicating an Aramaic dry measure of about fifteen liters—in keeping with *Luke's* concern for authentic atmosphere.   **13:22–24** See *Matt.* 7:13–14.   **13:24** *not be able* The image is of a walled city's gate, which creates a considerable bottleneck when many people are trying to enter with their bags. *Luke's* Jesus again advocates simplicity of life, for only those traveling without baggage will get through the narrow gate. See 18:25.   **13:25–27** See *Matt.* 7:22–23; 8:11–12.   **13:25** *I do not know . . . Luke's* Jesus attributes these words to *the owner of the house*, in parabolic form. In *Matt.* 7:21–23, however, *Matthew's* Jesus speaks of himself as future judge.   **13:26–28** Contrast *Matthew's* different application of these distinct sayings. *Luke* makes Jesus' fellow Jews the object of a warning. *Luke's* author anticipates Gentile salvation and Jewish exclusion (13:28)—which is indeed what gradually develops in *Acts* (see introduction to *Luke-Acts*).

to say, 'We ate and drank with you, and you taught in our streets.' 27But he will say, 'I do not know where you come from; go away from me, all you evildoers!' 28There will be weeping and gnashing of teeth when you see Abraham and Isaac and Jacob and all the prophets in the kingdom of God, and you yourselves thrown out. 29Then people will come from east and west, from north and south, and will eat in the kingdom of God. 30Indeed, some are last who will be first, and some are first who will be last."

The Lament over Jerusalem

31At that very hour some Pharisees came and said to him, "Get away from here, for Herod wants to kill you." 32He said to them, "Go and tell that fox for me,^{j} 'Listen, I am casting out demons and performing cures today and tomorrow, and on the third day I finish my work. 33Yet today, tomorrow, and the next day I must be on my way, because it is impossible for a prophet to be killed outside of Jerusalem.' 34Jerusalem, Jerusalem, the city that kills the prophets and stones those who are sent to it! How often have I desired to gather your children together as a hen gathers her brood under her wings, and you were not willing! 35See, your house is left to you. And I tell you, you will not see me until the time comes when^k you say, 'Blessed is the one who comes in the name of the Lord.'"

Jesus Heals the Man with Dropsy

14 On one occasion when Jesus^l was going to the house of a leader of the Pharisees to eat a meal on the sabbath, they were watching him closely. 2Just then, in front of him, there was a man who had dropsy. 3And Jesus asked the lawyers and Pharisees, "Is it lawful to cure people on the sabbath, or not?" 4But they were silent. So Jesus^l took him and healed him, and sent him away. 5Then he said to them, "If one of you has a child^m or an ox that has fallen into a well, will you not immediately pull it out on a sabbath day?" 6And they could not reply to this.

Humility and Hospitality

7When he noticed how the guests chose the places of honor, he told them a parable. 8"When you are invited by someone to a wedding banquet, do not sit down at the place of honor, in case someone more distinguished than you has been invited by your host; 9and the host who invited both of you may come and say to you, 'Give this person your place,' and then in disgrace you would start to take the lowest place. 10But when you are invited, go and sit down at the lowest place, so that when your host comes, he may say to you, 'Friend, move up higher'; then you will be honored in the presence of all who sit at the table with you. 11For all who exalt themselves will be humbled, and those who humble themselves will be exalted."

12He said also to the one who had invited him, "When you give a luncheon or a dinner, do not invite your friends or your brothers or your relatives or rich neighbors, in case they may invite you in return, and you would be repaid. 13But when you give a banquet, invite the poor, the crippled, the lame, and the blind. 14And you will be blessed, because they cannot repay you, for you will be repaid at the resurrection of the righteous."

---

j Gk lacks *for me*
k Other ancient authorities lack *the time comes when*
l Gk *he*

m Other ancient authorities read *a donkey*

13:30 See *Mark* 10:31; *Matt.* 19:30; *Gospel of Thomas* 4. **13:31–33** Once again the Pharisees appear (only in *Luke*) as Jesus' associates, even though he has criticized them severely; see 6:11; 7:36; 11:29, 37; 12:10. **13:32 *that fox*** Herod Antipas, the tetrarch of Galilee and Perea, consistently appears in *Luke* as Jesus' enemy; 3:19–20; 9:9; 13:31; 23:6–12. **13:33** See 9:51, where Jesus has "set his face" to go toward Jerusalem. It is remarkable that he has not yet left: See 17:11. **13:34–36** See *Matt.* 23:37–39 and notes. **13:35 *your house*** "House" was a common term for the Jerusalem temple, the dwelling place of God (see *Exod.* 25:8, 22; *2 Sam.* 7:2, 13). This saying seems to envision the destruction of the temple in 70 C.E.—either in Jesus' prediction or in the author's recollection. **13:36** In *Luke* this saying will be fulfilled in Jesus' triumphal entry into Jerusalem (19:38). Contrast *Matthew,* where the triumphal entry (21:1–11) has taken place before this saying (23:39); note *Matthew*'s "again" in 23:39. **14:1–24** Jesus' third major meal with Pharisees (see 7:36–50; 11:37–54) is, like the others, unique to this story. **14:1 *a leader of the Pharisees*** The phrase could mean either that he was a leader of the Pharisaic group or that he was a leader of the people and a Pharisee. The author assumes throughout, in any case, that the Pharisees were the prominent religious figures in Jesus' society. ***watching him closely*** See 11:54; the meals are taking on an increasingly hostile atmosphere. **14:5** The debate is not about whether to observe the Sabbath but about what constitutes violation of the Sabbath. See notes to 6:2; 13:14–15. **14:8 *the place of honor*** At all such ancient dinners, seating arrangements were crucial. On the couches arranged end-to-end, which usually held three diners each, the most honored position would usually be that closest to the host on the right; from there, guests were seated according to status. Those at the lower end could sometimes receive cheaper food and drink, and in smaller portions. See Plutarch, *Quaest. conv.* 1.2.1–5. **14:9** Such a removal would be extremely shameful in an ancient context. **14:12 *a luncheon*** See note to 11:37.

The Parable of the Great Dinner

[15]One of the dinner guests, on hearing this, said to him, "Blessed is anyone who will eat bread in the kingdom of God!" [16]Then Jesus[n] said to him, "Someone gave a great dinner and invited many. [17]At the time for the dinner he sent his slave to say to those who had been invited, 'Come; for everything is ready now.' [18]But they all alike began to make excuses. The first said to him, 'I have bought a piece of land, and I must go out and see it; please accept my regrets.' [19]Another said, 'I have bought five yoke of oxen, and I am going to try them out; please accept my regrets.' [20]Another said, 'I have just been married, and therefore I cannot come.' [21]So the slave returned and reported this to his master. Then the owner of the house became angry and said to his slave, 'Go out at once into the streets and lanes of the town and bring in the poor, the crippled, the blind, and the lame.' [22]And the slave said, 'Sir, what you ordered has been done, and there is still room.' [23]Then the master said to the slave, 'Go out into the roads and lanes, and compel people to come in, so that my house may be filled. [24]For I tell you,[o] none of those who were invited will taste my dinner.'"

The Cost of Discipleship

[25]Now large crowds were traveling with him; and he turned and said to them, [26]"Whoever comes to me and does not hate father and mother, wife and children, brothers and sisters, yes, and even life itself, cannot be my disciple. [27]Whoever does not carry the cross and follow me cannot be my disciple. [28]For which of you, intending to build a tower, does not first sit down and estimate the cost, to see whether he has enough to complete it? [29]Otherwise, when he has laid a foundation and is not able to finish, all who see it will begin to ridicule him, [30]saying, 'This fellow began to build and was not able to finish.' [31]Or what king, going out to wage war against another king, will not sit down first and consider whether he is able with ten thousand to oppose the one who comes against him with twenty thousand? [32]If he cannot, then, while the other is still far away, he sends a delegation and asks for the terms of peace. [33]So therefore, none of you can become my disciple if you do not give up all your possessions.

About Salt

[34]"Salt is good; but if salt has lost its taste, how can its saltiness be restored?[p] [35]It is fit neither for the soil nor for the manure pile; they throw it away. Let anyone with ears to hear listen!"

The Parable of the Lost Sheep

15 Now all the tax collectors and sinners were coming near to listen to him. [2]And the Pharisees and the scribes were grumbling and saying, "This fellow welcomes sinners and eats with them."

[3]So he told them this parable: [4]"Which one of you, having a hundred sheep and losing one of them, does not leave the ninety-nine in the wilderness and go after the one that is lost until he finds it? [5]When he has found it, he lays it on his shoulders and rejoices. [6]And when he comes home, he calls together his friends and neighbors, saying to them, 'Rejoice with me, for I have found my sheep that was lost.' [7]Just so, I tell you, there will be more joy in heaven over one sinner who repents than over ninety-nine righteous persons who need no repentance.

---

n Gk *he*
o The Greek word for *you* here is plural

p Or *how can it be used for seasoning?*

14:15–24 See *Matt.* 22:1–14; *Gospel of Thomas* 64. **14:16 *invited many*** It was customary to send out written dinner invitations, specifying the menu and planned entertainment. See Martial, *Epigrams* 5.78; 11.52. **14:25–33** See *Matt.* 10:37–38; *Gospel of Thomas* 55, 101. See also *Luke* 8:19–21; 9:59–62; 11:28; 12:49–53; 14:20–21; 18:29. Jesus' own followers, according to *Luke*, lived an extremely rigorous life apart from normal social obligations; *Luke*'s language is more severe than the parallel in *Matthew*. **14:33** See *Acts* 2:44–45; 4:32–37, where some Christians die because they fail to disclose all of their assets. *Acts*, however, assumes that Christians kept their houses and some amount of possessions. **14:34–35** See *Mark* 9:49–50; *Matt.* 5:13. Only *Luke* places the saying about salt here, stressing that the disciples' poverty and countercultural values are exactly what make them *salt*—something that is different from the ordinary. Note the agreements between *Matthew* and *Luke* against *Mark*—a problem for the common theory of their independence. **15:1–2** From a historical point of view, this complaint reflects not merely social snobbery but (a) the real fear of being contaminated by uncleanness affecting one's ability to participate in temple life, since sinners cannot be trusted to have made appropriate purifications, and (b) the conventional position that bad company corrupts good morals, as Paul also says (*1 Cor.* 15:33). It is not clear that the author means to criticize the Pharisees for this observation, since it is so easily understandable. The observation in 16:14 shows that all of the material between here and there, possibly also 16:16–31, is addressed in part to the Pharisees. This indicates how important it was for the author to define Jesus' mission in the context of the established Jewish teachers. **15:3–7** See *Matt.* 18:12–14; *Gospel of Thomas* 107. **15:7 *righteous persons who need no repentance*** One aspect of *Luke*'s view of the Pharisees; see 5:31.

The Parable of the Lost Coin

8"Or what woman having ten silver coins,*q* if she loses one of them, does not light a lamp, sweep the house, and search carefully until she finds it? 9When she has found it, she calls together her friends and neighbors, saying, 'Rejoice with me, for I have found the coin that I had lost.' 10Just so, I tell you, there is joy in the presence of the angels of God over one sinner who repents."

The Parable of the Prodigal and His Brother

11Then Jesus*r* said, "There was a man who had two sons. 12The younger of them said to his father, 'Father, give me the share of the property that will belong to me.' So he divided his property between them. 13A few days later the younger son gathered all he had and traveled to a distant country, and there he squandered his property in dissolute living. 14When he had spent everything, a severe famine took place throughout that country, and he began to be in need. 15So he went and hired himself out to one of the citizens of that country, who sent him to his fields to feed the pigs. 16He would gladly have filled himself with*s* the pods that the pigs were eating; and no one gave him anything. 17But when he came to himself he said, 'How many of my father's hired hands have bread enough and to spare, but here I am dying of hunger! 18I will get up and go to my father, and I will say to him, "Father, I have sinned against heaven and before you; 19I am no longer worthy to be called your son; treat me like one of your hired hands."' 20So he set off and went to his father. But while he was still far off, his father saw him and was filled with compassion; he ran and put his arms around him and kissed him. 21Then the son said to him, 'Father, I have sinned against heaven and before you; I am no longer worthy to be called your son.'*t* 22But the father said to his slaves, 'Quickly, bring out a robe—the best one—and put it on him; put a ring on his finger and sandals on his feet. 23And get the fatted calf and kill it, and let us eat and celebrate; 24for this son of mine was dead and is alive again; he was lost and is found!' And they began to celebrate.

25"Now his elder son was in the field; and when he came and approached the house, he heard music and dancing. 26He called one of the slaves and asked what was going on. 27He replied, 'Your brother has come, and your father has killed the fatted calf, because he has got him back safe and sound.' 28Then he became angry and refused to go in. His father came out and began to plead with him. 29But he answered his father, 'Listen! For all these years I have been working like a slave for you, and I have never disobeyed your command; yet you have never given me even a young goat so that I might celebrate with my friends. 30But when this son of yours came back, who has devoured your property with prostitutes, you killed the fatted calf for him!' 31Then the father*r* said to him, 'Son, you are always with me, and all that is mine is yours. 32But we had to celebrate and rejoice, because this brother of yours was dead and has come to life; he was lost and has been found.'"

The Parable of the Dishonest Manager

16 Then Jesus*r* said to the disciples, "There was a rich man who had a manager, and charges were brought to him that this man was squandering his property. 2So he summoned him and said to him, 'What is this that I hear about you? Give me an accounting of your management, because you cannot be my manager any longer.' 3Then the manager said to himself, 'What will I do, now that my master is taking the position away from me? I am not strong enough to dig, and I am ashamed to beg. 4I have decided what to do so that, when I am dismissed as manager, people may welcome me into their homes.' 5So, summoning his master's debtors one by one, he asked the first, 'How much do you owe my master?' 6He answered, 'A hundred jugs of olive oil.' He said to him, 'Take your bill, sit down quickly, and make it fifty.' 7Then he asked another, 'And how much do you owe?' He replied, 'A hundred containers of wheat.' He said to him, 'Take your bill and make it eighty.' 8And his master commended the dishonest

---

q Gk *drachmas*, each worth about a day's wage for a laborer
r Gk *he*
s Other ancient authorities read *filled his stomach with*
t Other ancient authorities add *treat me as one of your hired servants*

15:8–10 The parable of the lost coin is unique to *Luke*. **15:11–32** The parable of the prodigal son is unique to *Luke*. It plays an important role in defining Jesus' relationship to the Jewish leaders, who seem clearly represented by the older son; this is still part of Jesus' response to their criticism for associating with sinners (15:1–2). **15:11** *a man* This is the same Gk word as is usually rendered "person." **15:15** *to feed the pigs* Jewish abstinence from pork (*Deut.* 14:8) and pig farming was famous in the ancient world. This reference indicates that the son, now living in a Gentile country (15:13), was in desperate straits. **15:29** *I have never disobeyed your command* The older son appears to represent the righteous Pharisees, who are listening to Jesus' parable (15:1–2; 16:14). **16:1–9** The parable of the dishonest manager is unique to *Luke*. **16:1** *man* See note to 15:11. **16:3** *not strong enough ... ashamed* A characteristic touch of Lukan insight into human nature. **16:6** *jugs* Luke uses the Hebrew measure *bat*, perhaps for local color; one *bat* was at this time about four and a half gallons. **16:7** *containers* Luke uses the Hebrew measure *kor*; one kor was at this time about forty-five gallons.

manager because he had acted shrewdly; for the children of this age are more shrewd in dealing with their own generation than are the children of light. [9]And I tell you, make friends for yourselves by means of dishonest wealth[u] so that when it is gone, they may welcome you into the eternal homes.[v]

[10]"Whoever is faithful in a very little is faithful also in much; and whoever is dishonest in a very little is dishonest also in much. [11]If then you have not been faithful with the dishonest wealth,[u] who will entrust to you the true riches? [12]And if you have not been faithful with what belongs to another, who will give you what is your own? [13]No slave can serve two masters; for a slave will either hate the one and love the other, or be devoted to the one and despise the other. You cannot serve God and wealth."[u]

The Law and the Kingdom of God

[14]The Pharisees, who were lovers of money, heard all this, and they ridiculed him. [15]So he said to them, "You are those who justify yourselves in the sight of others; but God knows your hearts; for what is prized by human beings is an abomination in the sight of God.

[16]"The law and the prophets were in effect until John came; since then the good news of the kingdom of God is proclaimed, and everyone tries to enter it by force.[w] [17]But it is easier for heaven and earth to pass away, than for one stroke of a letter in the law to be dropped.

[18]"Anyone who divorces his wife and marries another commits adultery, and whoever marries a woman divorced from her husband commits adultery.

The Rich Man and Lazarus

[19]"There was a rich man who was dressed in purple and fine linen and who feasted sumptuously every day. [20]And at his gate lay a poor man named Lazarus, covered with sores, [21]who longed to satisfy his hunger with what fell from the rich man's table; even the dogs would come and lick his sores. [22]The poor man died and was carried away by the angels to be with Abraham.[x] The rich man also died and was buried. [23]In Hades, where he was being tormented, he looked up and saw Abraham far away with Lazarus by his side.[y] [24]He called out, 'Father Abraham, have mercy on me, and send Lazarus to dip the tip of his finger in water and cool my tongue; for I am in agony in these flames.' [25]But Abraham said, 'Child, remember that during your lifetime you received your good things, and Lazarus in like manner evil things; but now he is comforted here, and you are in agony. [26]Besides all this, between you and us a great chasm has been fixed, so that those who might want to pass from here to you cannot do so, and no one can cross from there to us.' [27]He said, 'Then, father, I beg you to send him to my father's house— [28]for I have five brothers—that he may warn them, so that they will not also come into this place of torment.' [29]Abraham replied, 'They have Moses and the prophets; they should listen to them.' [30]He said, 'No, father Abraham; but if someone goes to them from the dead, they will repent.' [31]He said to him, 'If they do not lis-

---

u Gk *mammon*
v Gk *tents*
w Or *everyone is strongly urged to enter it*

x Gk *to Abraham's bosom*
y Gk *in his bosom*

16:9 Does *Luke*'s Jesus really advocate involvement with dishonesty here? Although the story itself might be simply a sober observation on ordinary life, Jesus' final words and the master's approval seem to applaud the manager's actions. This advice pushes the limits of *Luke*'s overall portrait of Jesus' countercultural program. **16:13** See *Matt.* 6:24; *Gospel of Thomas* 47. **16:14** It was the Pharisees' criticism of Jesus' eating with sinners that led him to present these four parables (15:1–2). They are still listening. The accusation of being a money-grubber had a long history in debates among the Greek philosophical schools. The Pharisees appear as a Jewish version of the Greek Sophists—those who received payment of some kind for their teaching. Jesus' students, by contrast, are emphatically poor—like the Cynics. **16:15** Jesus' words intersect with the standard philosophical distinction, worked out in detail by Plato, between appearance and reality, or seeming and being. See Paul's use of this theme in *1 Cor.* 1–4 and *Gal.* 2:6. **16:16** See *Matt.* 11:12–13. **16:17** See *Matt.* 5:18. **16:18** See *Mark* 10:11–12; *Matt.* 19:9. **16:19–31** This story, unique to *Luke*, powerfully develops the theme of status reversal (see 4:18; 6:20–26). **16:29 *Moses and the prophets*** That is, the Jewish scripture, which was ordinarily characterized as the Torah, that is, the books of Moses *(Genesis* to *Deuteronomy);* the prophets; and, according to some 1st-century authors, a third section of miscellaneous writings (see 24:27, 44). It is unclear how fixed the Jewish canon of scripture was at the time of *Luke*'s composition. See Josephus, *Ag. Ap.* 1.29–45. **16:31** This observation is full of irony. On the surface level, the story is that the rich man's family should know how to live properly and compassionately by observing the Torah and the prophets, that even a resurrected preacher would not change their behavior. The irony is that the author and his readers are now engaged in preaching about a Savior who was raised from the dead and they believe that the Law and the Prophets clearly testify about him. To preserve the story line, the author does not introduce the Christian proof texts for Jesus' death and resurrection here; he will not even refer to them until after Jesus' resurrection (24:25–27), and he will cite them only in *Acts* (e.g., *Acts* 2:17–21, 25–28; 3:22).

ten to Moses and the prophets, neither will they be convinced even if someone rises from the dead.'"

Some Sayings of Jesus

17 Jesus[z] said to his disciples, "Occasions for stumbling are bound to come, but woe to anyone by whom they come! ²It would be better for you if a millstone were hung around your neck and you were thrown into the sea than for you to cause one of these little ones to stumble. ³Be on your guard! If another disciple[a] sins, you must rebuke the offender, and if there is repentance, you must forgive. ⁴And if the same person sins against you seven times a day, and turns back to you seven times and says, 'I repent,' you must forgive."

⁵The apostles said to the Lord, "Increase our faith!" ⁶The Lord replied, "If you had faith the size of a[b] mustard seed, you could say to this mulberry tree, 'Be uprooted and planted in the sea,' and it would obey you.

⁷"Who among you would say to your slave who has just come in from plowing or tending sheep in the field, 'Come here at once and take your place at the table'? ⁸Would you not rather say to him, 'Prepare supper for me, put on your apron and serve me while I eat and drink; later you may eat and drink'? ⁹Do you thank the slave for doing what was commanded? ¹⁰So you also, when you have done all that you were ordered to do, say, 'We are worthless slaves; we have done only what we ought to have done!'"

Jesus Cleanses Ten Lepers

¹¹On the way to Jerusalem Jesus[c] was going through the region between Samaria and Galilee. ¹²As he entered a village, ten lepers[d] approached him. Keeping their distance, ¹³they called out, saying, "Jesus, Master, have mercy on us!" ¹⁴When he saw them, he said to them, "Go and show yourselves to the priests." And as they went, they were made clean. ¹⁵Then one of them, when he saw that he was healed, turned back, praising God with a loud voice. ¹⁶He prostrated himself at Jesus'[e] feet and thanked him. And he was a Samaritan. ¹⁷Then Jesus asked, "Were not ten made clean? But the other nine, where are they? ¹⁸Was none of them found to return and give praise to God except this foreigner?" ¹⁹Then he said to him, "Get up and go on your way; your faith has made you well."

The Coming of the Kingdom

²⁰Once Jesus[c] was asked by the Pharisees when the kingdom of God was coming, and he answered, "The kingdom of God is not coming with things that can be observed; ²¹nor will they say, 'Look, here it is!' or 'There it is!' For, in fact, the kingdom of God is among[f] you."

---

z Gk *He*
a Gk *your brother*
b Gk *faith as a grain of*

c Gk *he*
d The terms *leper* and *leprosy* can refer to several diseases
e Gk *his*
f Or *within*

17:1–2 See *Mark* 9:42; *Matt.* 18:6–7. **17:2 these little ones** The identity of the *little ones* is uncertain. In the Markan parallel, Jesus has just singled out a child to illustrate a point about greatness (*Mark* 9:36–37), but in *Luke* that story occurred long ago (9:46–48) and so provides no context for this saying. In effect, the author of *Luke* has spliced in seven chapters of mostly non-Markan material between *Mark* 9:37 and *Mark* 9:42. *Luke* will again parallel *Mark* more consistently from *Luke* 18:15 onward (*Mark* 10:13). **17:3–4** See *Matt.* 18:15, 21–22. **17:5–6** See *Matt.* 17:19–21 and note to *Matt.* 17:20; *Gospel of Thomas* 48. **17:6 The Lord** See note to 7:13. **17:7–10** The inference is that his listeners were slave owners. It seems inappropriate for his students, but perhaps the Pharisees and others are still assumed to be listening (see 16:14; 17:20). **17:11** Jesus only now leaves Galilee, although the text has said long ago that he "set his face to go to Jerusalem" (9:51; see 13:33). See note to 9:51. The geography is confusing because the author has already implied that Jesus and his students entered Samaria (9:52–56). The region between Galilee and Samaria is the Great Plain of Esdraelon. If Jesus left Galilee at Xaloth or Dabaritta, he might well travel east along the plain toward the Jordan River valley, which he would follow down to Jericho (19:1). Although it was possible to reach Jerusalem more quickly by traveling due south through Samaria (Josephus, *Life* 269), that route was hazardous for pilgrims (see 9:52–56). **17:12–19** The story of the ten lepers is peculiar to *Luke*. **17:12 ten lepers** Not necessarily afflicted with leprosy as we know it. See note to *Mark* 1:40. **Keeping their distance** Those afflicted with such skin diseases, which were thought to convey pollution, were required to live outside the community and to call out "Unclean, unclean" when approached by others (*Lev.* 13:45–46). **17:14** As in 5:14, Jesus accepts the biblical requirement that only priests can pronounce a person clean of such diseases (*Lev.* 14:2–3). **17:16 a Samaritan** The author has a marked interest in Samaritans. See 10:29–37; *Acts* 8:4–14. **17:20–21** See *Gospel of Thomas* 3, 113. **17:20 asked by the Pharisees** Again *Luke's* Jesus appears as someone respected by the Pharisees, the most prominent teachers of his day—unless the question is meant as a trap, but this is not suggested by the context. See 7:36, 40; 11:37; 13:31; 14:1, 12. **things that can be observed** Lit. "observation." **17:21 among you** The preposition translated *among* here normally means "inside" or "within" a particular space or time: the potential for the kingdom lies within the Pharisees. This is a critical passage for the argument that the historical Jesus announced the present realization of the kingdom (as distinct from an exclusively or largely future kingdom). It is also a remarkable statement about *Luke's* Pharisees: *They* could have brought forth the kingdom in some way (but they did not).

22Then he said to the disciples, "The days are coming when you will long to see one of the days of the Son of Man, and you will not see it. 23They will say to you, 'Look there!' or 'Look here!' Do not go, do not set off in pursuit. 24For as the lightning flashes and lights up the sky from one side to the other, so will the Son of Man be in his day.*g* 25But first he must endure much suffering and be rejected by this generation. 26Just as it was in the days of Noah, so too it will be in the days of the Son of Man. 27They were eating and drinking, and marrying and being given in marriage, until the day Noah entered the ark, and the flood came and destroyed all of them. 28Likewise, just as it was in the days of Lot: they were eating and drinking, buying and selling, planting and building, 29but on the day that Lot left Sodom, it rained fire and sulfur from heaven and destroyed all of them 30—it will be like that on the day that the Son of Man is revealed. 31On that day, anyone on the housetop who has belongings in the house must not come down to take them away; and likewise anyone in the field must not turn back. 32Remember Lot's wife. 33Those who try to make their life secure will lose it, but those who lose their life will keep it. 34I tell you, on that night there will be two in one bed; one will be taken and the other left. 35There will be two women grinding meal together; one will be taken and the other left."*h* 37Then they asked him, "Where, Lord?" He said to them, "Where the corpse is, there the vultures will gather."

The Parable of the Widow and the Unjust Judge

18 Then Jesus*i* told them a parable about their need to pray always and not to lose heart. 2He said, "In a certain city there was a judge who neither feared God nor had respect for people. 3In that city there was a widow who kept coming to him and saying, 'Grant me justice against my opponent.' 4For a while he refused; but later he said to himself, 'Though I have no fear of God and no respect for anyone, 5yet because this widow keeps bothering me, I will grant her justice, so that she may not wear me out by continually coming.'*j* 6And the Lord said, "Listen to what the unjust judge says. 7And will not God grant justice to his chosen ones who cry to him day and night? Will he delay long in helping them? 8I tell you, he will quickly grant justice to them. And yet, when the Son of Man comes, will he find faith on earth?"

The Parable of the Pharisee and the Tax Collector

9He also told this parable to some who trusted in themselves that they were righteous and regarded others with contempt: 10"Two men went up to the temple to pray, one a Pharisee and the other a tax collector. 11The Pharisee, standing by himself, was praying thus, 'God, I thank you that I am not like other people: thieves, rogues, adulterers, or even like this tax collector. 12I fast twice a week; I give a tenth of all my income.' 13But the tax collector, standing far off, would not even look up to heaven, but was beating his breast and saying, 'God, be merciful to me, a sinner!' 14I tell you, this man went down to his home justified rather than the other; for all who exalt

---

g Other ancient authorities lack *in his day*

h Other ancient authorities add verse 36, "*Two will be in the field; one will be taken and the other left.*"

i Gk *he*

j Or *so that she may not finally come and slap me in the face*

17:22–23 See *Mark* 13:19–23; *Matt.* 24:23; *Gospel of Thomas* 113. **17:22** The Jesus of *Luke-Acts* seems to stress the indefinite postponement of Jesus' descent from heaven; see 19:11; *Acts* 1:6–8. Perhaps this portrayal might help the Christian readers of *Luke-Acts* understand the delay of Jesus' return. **17:23** See the note to *Mark* 13:21–22. **17:24–30** See *Matt.* 24:37–39. **17:26–27** See *Gen.* 6:5–8; 7:6–24. **17:28–29** *days of Lot* See *Gen.* 18:20–33; 19:24–25. The author assumes a fair amount of biblical knowledge from his readers. But even so, uninitiated readers can follow Jesus' point from the story itself, since the destruction of Sodom was already mentioned in 10:12. **17:31–32** See *Mark* 13:14–16; *Matt.* 24:17–18. **17:32** See *Gen.* 19:26. **17:33** See *Matt.* 10:39; *John* 12:25. **17:34–35** See *Matt.* 24:40–41; *Gospel of Thomas* 61. Evidently, in view of the analogies in the Bible and *Gospel of Thomas* 61, the one *left* should be understood as the one saved; the one *taken* dies. **17:37** See *Matt.* 24:28. Perhaps an allusion to the destroyed Jerusalem. See *Luke* 13:35. **18:1–8** This parable, which is unique to *Luke*, recalls a similar illustration, also found only in *Luke*, in 11:5–8. **18:6** *the Lord* See note to 7:13. **18:7** The argument is *a fortiori*, from a weak case (an unjust judge) to a strong one (God with his chosen ones). This form of argument was especially common in rabbinic literature; see also 11:13. **18:8** *Son of Man* See notes to *Mark* 2:10, 27–28. **18:9–14** This story appears only in *Luke*; it fits with the author's consistent contrast between self-satisfied Pharisees and sinners eager to repent. See 7:36–50 and note. **18:9** *Luke* does not isolate the Pharisees as sole targets; they seem representative of a common human condition. **18:12** *I fast twice a week* Such fasting was not required by the Torah, but it seems to have been customary by this time; see 5:33; *Did.* 8.1. *I give a tenth of all my income* See 11:42; tithing was required by the Torah (*Num.* 18:21–32; *Deut.* 14:22–29), but because the requirement could be extremely burdensome, in view of the many direct and indirect Roman taxes, many Jews simply could not afford to practice it. See Mishnah, *Demai*, which discusses produce that has not certainly been tithed. The Pharisee's boast stems from the recognition that only a few were scrupulous about tithes.

themselves will be humbled, but all who humble themselves will be exalted."

Jesus Blesses Little Children

[15]People were bringing even infants to him that he might touch them; and when the disciples saw it, they sternly ordered them not to do it. [16]But Jesus called for them and said, "Let the little children come to me, and do not stop them; for it is to such as these that the kingdom of God belongs. [17]Truly I tell you, whoever does not receive the kingdom of God as a little child will never enter it."

The Rich Ruler

[18]A certain ruler asked him, "Good Teacher, what must I do to inherit eternal life?" [19]Jesus said to him, "Why do you call me good? No one is good but God alone. [20]You know the commandments: 'You shall not commit adultery; You shall not murder; You shall not steal; You shall not bear false witness; Honor your father and mother.'" [21]He replied, "I have kept all these since my youth." [22]When Jesus heard this, he said to him, "There is still one thing lacking. Sell all that you own and distribute the money[k] to the poor, and you will have treasure in heaven; then come, follow me." [23]But when he heard this, he became sad; for he was very rich. [24]Jesus looked at him and said, "How hard it is for those who have wealth to enter the kingdom of God! [25]Indeed, it is easier for a camel to go through the eye of a needle than for someone who is rich to enter the kingdom of God."

[26]Those who heard it said, "Then who can be saved?" [27]He replied, "What is impossible for mortals is possible for God."

[28]Then Peter said, "Look, we have left our homes and followed you." [29]And he said to them, "Truly I tell you, there is no one who has left house or wife or brothers or parents or children, for the sake of the kingdom of God, [30]who will not get back very much more in this age, and in the age to come eternal life."

A Third Time Jesus Foretells His Death and Resurrection

[31]Then he took the twelve aside and said to them, "See, we are going up to Jerusalem, and everything that is written about the Son of Man by the prophets will be accomplished. [32]For he will be handed over to the Gentiles; and he will be mocked and insulted and spat upon. [33]After they have flogged him, they will kill him, and on the third day he will rise again." [34]But they understood nothing about all these things; in fact, what he said was hidden from them, and they did not grasp what was said.

Jesus Heals a Blind Beggar Near Jericho

[35]As he approached Jericho, a blind man was sitting by the roadside begging. [36]When he heard a crowd going by, he asked what was happening. [37]They told him, "Jesus of Nazareth[l] is passing by." [38]Then he shouted, "Jesus, Son of David, have mercy on me!" [39]Those who were in front sternly ordered him to be quiet; but he shouted even more loudly, "Son of David, have mercy on me!" [40]Jesus stood still and ordered the man to be brought to him; and when he came near, he asked him, [41]"What do you want me to do for you?" He said, "Lord, let me see again." [42]Jesus said to him, "Receive your sight; your faith has saved you." [43]Immediately he regained his sight and followed him, glorifying God; and all the people, when they saw it, praised God.

Jesus and Zacchaeus

19 He entered Jericho and was passing through it. [2]A man was there named Zacchaeus; he was a

---

k Gk lacks *the money*

l Gk *the Nazorean*

18:15–17 See *Mark* 10:13–16; *Matt.* 19:13–15; *Gospel of Thomas* 22. **18:15** *even infants Luke's* Jesus makes a point of reaching out to the socially marginalized—women, sinners, poor, and sick. In his adult world, small children were the least socially significant group. *Luke* alone claims that these were *infants*—the smallest children of all. **18:18–30** See *Mark* 10:17–31; *Matt.* 19:16–30. **18:18** *ruler* Or "leader." Only *Luke* so identifies him; *Matt.* 19:20 describes him as young—but the young were not normally leaders in Jewish society. **18:20** Five of the Ten Commandments (*Exod.* 20:2–14; *Deut.* 5:6–18), dealing with human relations, rearranged. **18:25** See note to 13:24. **18:29** *Luke's* Jesus assumes that his students have departed radically from social norms. See also 14:25–26, but see *1 Cor.* 9:5, where Paul indicates that the apostles generally, notably Peter (Cephas) and also Jesus' brothers, take their wives with them on their missions. **18:31–34** See *Mark* 10:32–34; *Matt.* 20:17–19. Jesus' 3d prediction of his death; see 9:21–22, 44–45. The author here and earlier points out that Jesus' students did not understand what he said. **18:35–43** See *Mark* 10:46–52; *Matt.* 20:29–34. **18:35** *approached Jericho* Jericho is an oasis town bordering on the Judean desert, in the Jordan River valley about fifteen miles northeast of Jerusalem. Although 9:51–56 suggested that Jesus was traveling inland, from Galilee to Judea through Samaria, this reference indicates that at some point he moved east to the river valley—a common approach to avoid Samaria. According to *Mark* 10:46 and *Matt.* 20:29, Jesus healed the blind man (*Matthew:* two men) on the way out of Jericho. **19:1–10** The famous story of Zacchaeus is found only in *Luke.* **19:2** *chief tax collector* Tax collectors were generally disliked by the common folk for the foreign domination that they represented, for the burden of the taxes, and sometimes for their methods of collection; chief tax collectors might be supremely despicable. See notes to *Mark* 2:14.

chief tax collector and was rich. ³He was trying to see who Jesus was, but on account of the crowd he could not, because he was short in stature. ⁴So he ran ahead and climbed a sycamore tree to see him, because he was going to pass that way. ⁵When Jesus came to the place, he looked up and said to him, "Zacchaeus, hurry and come down; for I must stay at your house today." ⁶So he hurried down and was happy to welcome him. ⁷All who saw it began to grumble and said, "He has gone to be the guest of one who is a sinner." ⁸Zacchaeus stood there and said to the Lord, "Look, half of my possessions, Lord, I will give to the poor; and if I have defrauded anyone of anything, I will pay back four times as much." ⁹Then Jesus said to him, "Today salvation has come to this house, because he too is a son of Abraham. ¹⁰For the Son of Man came to seek out and to save the lost."

The Parable of the Ten Pounds

¹¹As they were listening to this, he went on to tell a parable, because he was near Jerusalem, and because they supposed that the kingdom of God was to appear immediately. ¹²So he said, "A nobleman went to a distant country to get royal power for himself and then return. ¹³He summoned ten of his slaves, and gave them ten pounds,ᵐ and said to them, 'Do business with these until I come back.' ¹⁴But the citizens of his country hated him and sent a delegation after him, saying, 'We do not want this man to rule over us.' ¹⁵When he returned, having received royal power, he ordered these slaves, to whom he had given the money, to be summoned so that he might find out what they had gained by trading. ¹⁶The first came

---

ᵐ The mina, rendered here by *pound*, was about three months' wages for a laborer

forward and said, 'Lord, your pound has made ten more pounds.' ¹⁷He said to him, 'Well done, good slave! Because you have been trustworthy in a very small thing, take charge of ten cities.' ¹⁸Then the second came, saying, 'Lord, your pound has made five pounds.' ¹⁹He said to him, 'And you, rule over five cities.' ²⁰Then the other came, saying, 'Lord, here is your pound. I wrapped it up in a piece of cloth, ²¹for I was afraid of you, because you are a harsh man; you take what you did not deposit, and reap what you did not sow.' ²²He said to him, 'I will judge you by your own words, you wicked slave! You knew, did you, that I was a harsh man, taking what I did not deposit and reaping what I did not sow? ²³Why then did you not put my money into the bank? Then when I returned, I could have collected it with interest.' ²⁴He said to the bystanders, 'Take the pound from him and give it to the one who has ten pounds.' ²⁵(And they said to him, 'Lord, he has ten pounds!') ²⁶'I tell you, to all those who have, more will be given; but from those who have nothing, even what they have will be taken away. ²⁷But as for these enemies of mine who did not want me to be king over them—bring them here and slaughter them in my presence.'"

Jesus' Triumphal Entry into Jerusalem

²⁸After he had said this, he went on ahead, going up to Jerusalem.

²⁹When he had come near Bethphage and Bethany, at the place called the Mount of Olives, he sent two of the disciples, ³⁰saying, "Go into the village ahead of you, and as you enter it you will find tied there a colt that has never been ridden. Untie it and bring it here. ³¹If anyone asks you, 'Why are you untying it?' just say this, 'The Lord needs it.'" ³²So those who were sent departed and found it as he had told

---

19:9 At this stage in the developing story, salvation is still oriented toward the Jews, Abraham's descendants, even though the author has dropped numerous hints about Gentile salvation; see *Acts* 2:40; 4:12. **19:11 near Jerusalem** See 9:51; 13:33; 17:11. The plot has been steadily moving toward Jerusalem, and the author reminds the reader that it is approaching its consummation. Jesus' students apparently (mis)understood his trip to Jerusalem as preparatory to the inauguration of the kingdom. The author again, for his readers, emphasizes the indefinite postponement of the kingdom (see 12:45; 17:22; 18:7–8; *Acts* 1:6–8). **19:12–27** See *Matt.* 25:14–30. The parable of the ten pounds appears to illustrate in *Luke* the necessity of continuing to work diligently (in the Christian mission?) while the kingdom and Jesus' return are delayed (19:11), although the delay is not featured in the story itself. **19:12** In *Luke*'s day, it was necessary for rulers in alliance with the Roman Empire to receive their "client kingdoms" from the emperor in Rome. Jesus' illustration would call to mind the journeys to Rome made by Herod the Great, his sons, grandson, and great-grandson (Archelaus, Herod Antipas, Agrippa I, Agrippa II). **19:13 pounds** Lit. "minas," a unit of Greek currency worth one hundred Greek *drachmas* or Roman *denarii* (see *Matt.* 20:2). **19:14 sent a delegation** This happened in the case of Herod's son Archelaus, former ethnarch of Judea. See Josephus, *J.W.* 2.80–92. **19:28 going up to Jerusalem** See note to 19:11: the tension builds as the reader knows what awaits Jesus in Jerusalem. **19:29–40** See *Mark* 11:1–10; *Matt.* 21:1–9; *John* 12:12–19. **19:29 Bethphage and Bethany . . . Mount of Olives** Jesus has now moved in from the Jordan River valley (see 19:1) to approach Jerusalem from the east. The location of both towns is uncertain, though it seems likely that Bethany was about two miles east of Jerusalem, with the Mount of Olives between; Jesus will make Bethany a sort of base for his final days in Jerusalem around Passover time. Pilgrims often stayed in nearby towns during feasts because the city itself was overcrowded. Bethphage (mentioned only here and in the parallels) probably lay between Bethany and the Mount of Olives. The Mount of Olives rises immediately to the east of Jerusalem and overlooks the city. See 22:1.

them. ³³As they were untying the colt, its owners asked them, "Why are you untying the colt?" ³⁴They said, "The Lord needs it." ³⁵Then they brought it to Jesus; and after throwing their cloaks on the colt, they set Jesus on it. ³⁶As he rode along, people kept spreading their cloaks on the road. ³⁷As he was now approaching the path down from the Mount of Olives, the whole multitude of the disciples began to praise God joyfully with a loud voice for all the deeds of power that they had seen, ³⁸saying,

"Blessed is the king
> who comes in the name of the Lord!
Peace in heaven,
> and glory in the highest heaven!"

³⁹Some of the Pharisees in the crowd said to him, "Teacher, order your disciples to stop." ⁴⁰He answered, "I tell you, if these were silent, the stones would shout out."

Jesus Weeps over Jerusalem

⁴¹As he came near and saw the city, he wept over it, ⁴²saying, "If you, even you, had only recognized on this day the things that make for peace! But now they are hidden from your eyes. ⁴³Indeed, the days will come upon you, when your enemies will set up ramparts around you and surround you, and hem you in on every side. ⁴⁴They will crush you to the ground, you and your children within you, and they will not leave within you one stone upon another; because you did not recognize the time of your visitation from God."ⁿ

ⁿ Gk lacks *from God*

Jesus Cleanses the Temple

⁴⁵Then he entered the temple and began to drive out those who were selling things there; ⁴⁶and he said, "It is written,

'My house shall be a house of prayer';
> but you have made it a den of robbers."

⁴⁷Every day he was teaching in the temple. The chief priests, the scribes, and the leaders of the people kept looking for a way to kill him; ⁴⁸but they did not find anything they could do, for all the people were spellbound by what they heard.

The Authority of Jesus Questioned

20One day, as he was teaching the people in the temple and telling the good news, the chief priests and the scribes came with the elders ²and said to him, "Tell us, by what authority are you doing these things? Who is it who gave you this authority?" ³He answered them, "I will also ask you a question, and you tell me: ⁴Did the baptism of John come from heaven, or was it of human origin?" ⁵They discussed it with one another, saying, "If we say, 'From heaven,' he will say, 'Why did you not believe him?' ⁶But if we say, 'Of human origin,' all the people will stone us; for they are convinced that John was a prophet." ⁷So they answered that they did not know where it came from. ⁸Then Jesus said to them, "Neither will I tell you by what authority I am doing these things."

The Parable of the Wicked Tenants

⁹He began to tell the people this parable: "A man planted a vineyard, and leased it to tenants, and went to another country for a long time. ¹⁰When the

---

19:38 The 1st half of the saying recalls *Ps.* 118:26 (LXX 117:26), a blessing on one who enters the temple, although both the MT and the LXX omit the word "king": "Blessed is the one who comes in the name of the Lord!" This exclamation fulfills Jesus' promise in *Luke* 13:35. **19:39** Once again the Pharisees treat Jesus as a respected teacher, even if they are shocked by his behavior. This amicable request marks their final appearance in the gospel. **19:41–44** Unique to *Luke*. Because this prediction so accurately depicts the siege of Jerusalem in 68–70 C.E. (see Josephus, *Jewish War* 4–6) and because it closely reflects the developing Christian interpretation of the city's destruction as punishment of the Jews for their rejection of Jesus, scholars generally regard it as prediction after the fact—a common technique in Greek, Latin, Jewish, and later Christian literature. **19:45–46** See *Mark* 11:15–17; *Matt.* 21:10–17; *John* 2:13–17. *Luke* drastically abbreviates the story of the cleansing of the temple, toning it down by omitting reference to the overturning of tables and the prevention of movement (*Mark* 11:16). Perhaps the author considered these implausible; perhaps he was somewhat embarrassed that such actions should be attributed to Jesus, as he also seems concerned to stress that Christians are good citizens and no threat to the Roman authorities (23:4, 14–16; *Acts* 26:31–32). **19:45** *those who were selling things* See note to *Mark* 11:15–16. **19:46** *My house . . . of prayer* Isa. 56:7. *Luke* agrees with *Matthew* against *Mark* (and *Isaiah*) in dropping the phrase "for all the nations." *Luke* thus changes the issue from who can worship at the temple to what is appropriate behavior in the temple (prayer, not commerce). *a den of robbers* The phrase recalls *Jer.* 7:11. See note to *Mark* 11:17. **19:47–48** See *Mark* 11:18–19. Note the striking contrast between the Jerusalem leaders and the Pharisees. Whereas the Pharisees cordially associated with Jesus over a long period (in spite of being occasionally scandalized) and even warned him to flee from Herod Antipas's territory (13:31), the Jerusalem officials immediately set out to have him killed from their first encounter. Against *Mark*, *Luke* makes Jesus' daily teaching in the temple, not the cleansing incident, the focus of their wrath, and the author stresses the contrast between the leaders and *the people*. **20:1–8** See *Mark* 11:27–33; *Matt.* 21:23–37. **20:6** *the people will stone us* The contrast between Jerusalem leaders and the people is reinforced. **20:9–19** See *Mark* 12:1–12; *Matt.* 21:33–46; *Gospel of Thomas* 65; and notes.

season came, he sent a slave to the tenants in order that they might give him his share of the produce of the vineyard; but the tenants beat him and sent him away empty-handed. 11Next he sent another slave; that one also they beat and insulted and sent away empty-handed. 12And he sent still a third; this one also they wounded and threw out. 13Then the owner of the vineyard said, 'What shall I do? I will send my beloved son; perhaps they will respect him.' 14But when the tenants saw him, they discussed it among themselves and said, 'This is the heir; let us kill him so that the inheritance may be ours.' 15So they threw him out of the vineyard and killed him. What then will the owner of the vineyard do to them? 16He will come and destroy those tenants and give the vineyard to others." When they heard this, they said, "Heaven forbid!" 17But he looked at them and said, "What then does this text mean:

'The stone that the builders rejected
  has become the cornerstone'?o

18Everyone who falls on that stone will be broken to pieces; and it will crush anyone on whom it falls." 19When the scribes and chief priests realized that he had told this parable against them, they wanted to lay hands on him at that very hour, but they feared the people.

The Question about Paying Taxes

20So they watched him and sent spies who pretended to be honest, in order to trap him by what he said, so as to hand him over to the jurisdiction and authority of the governor. 21So they asked him,

"Teacher, we know that you are right in what you say and teach, and you show deference to no one, but teach the way of God in accordance with truth. 22Is it lawful for us to pay taxes to the emperor, or not?" 23But he perceived their craftiness and said to them, 24"Show me a denarius. Whose head and whose title does it bear?" They said, "The emperor's." 25He said to them, "Then give to the emperor the things that are the emperor's, and to God the things that are God's." 26And they were not able in the presence of the people to trap him by what he said; and being amazed by his answer, they became silent.

The Question about the Resurrection

27Some Sadducees, those who say there is no resurrection, came to him 28and asked him a question, "Teacher, Moses wrote for us that if a man's brother dies, leaving a wife but no children, the manp shall marry the widow and raise up children for his brother. 29Now there were seven brothers; the first married, and died childless; 30then the second 31and the third married her, and so in the same way all seven died childless. 32Finally the woman also died. 33In the resurrection, therefore, whose wife will the woman be? For the seven had married her."

34Jesus said to them, "Those who belong to this age marry and are given in marriage; 35but those who are considered worthy of a place in that age and in the resurrection from the dead neither marry nor are given in marriage. 36Indeed they cannot die anymore, because they are like angels and are children of God, being children of the resurrection. 37And the

---

o Or keystone

p Gk his brother

20:17 *Ps.* 118:22 (LXX 117:22). **20:18** According to the best manuscripts, *Matthew* agrees with *Luke* in including this line against *Mark*, which lacks it—a problem for the theory that *Matthew* and *Luke* were independently written. The main idea seems to be that the rejected stone has become a rock of offense or stumbling. See *Isa.* 8:14–15. Some early Christians developed the theme (*1 Pet.* 2:6–8). **20:19** *they feared the people* See 20:6. **20:20–26** See *Mark* 12:13–17; *Matt.* 22:15–22. Ever since 6 C.E., when Judea was directly annexed to the Roman Empire as a province, Roman taxation had been a major problem for the Jews; see Josephus, *Ant.* 18.4–10. **20:20** *they watched* That is, the chief priests and scribes. Contrast *Mark* and *Matthew*, which implicate the Pharisees in the effort to have Jesus killed. *so as to hand him over* The author seems to assume here what he later says explicitly: Roman governors typically knew and cared little about internal Jewish problems (see *Acts* 18:15; 23:29; 25:19; 26:3). To prosecute Jesus before the governor, the temple leaders would need a plausible charge related to disturbance of the peace. Interestingly, *Luke* does not have them cite the temple-cleansing incident, so briefly recounted in this gospel (19:45–46), as evidence for a charge. **20:21** This insincere summary, apparently calculated to please the people, would identify Jesus as a true philosopher—concerned with reality and not mere appearance, fearlessly devoted to the truth. **20:22** See note to *Mark* 12:14–15. **20:24** *a denarius* See notes to 7:41; *Mark* 12:15; and *Matt.* 20:2. **20:27–40** See *Mark* 12:18–27; *Matt.* 22:22–23. This is the first appearance of the Sadducees in *Luke-Acts* (contrast *Matthew*), which will later associate them closely with the temple-based leadership (see *Acts* 4:1; 5:17–18). They will play a significant role in *Acts,* but in the gospel they appear as flat, single-issue characters. **20:27** *Sadducees, those who say there is no resurrection* See note to *Mark* 12:18. No Sadducee writings have been discovered, but they appear to have had their base in the wealthier priestly aristocracy and to have rejected the living tradition of the Pharisees (Josephus, *Ant.* 13.297–298). They seem also to have rejected the notion of life after death along with other popular beliefs. **20:28** So-called levirate marriage. See *Deut.* 25:5–10. **20:37** See *Exod.* 3:6. *Luke's* Jesus paraphrases and explains the passage instead of quoting it (contrast *Mark* and *Matthew*). The net effect is a clearer treatment of *Luke's* view of two separate issues: the form in which the resurrected live, and whether there is resurrection.

fact that the dead are raised Moses himself showed, in the story about the bush, where he speaks of the Lord as the God of Abraham, the God of Isaac, and the God of Jacob. 38Now he is God not of the dead, but of the living; for to him all of them are alive." 39Then some of the scribes answered, "Teacher, you have spoken well." 40For they no longer dared to ask him another question.

The Question about David's Son

41Then he said to them, "How can they say that the Messiah*q* is David's son? 42For David himself says in the book of Psalms,

'The Lord said to my Lord,
    "Sit at my right hand,
43   until I make your enemies your footstool." '
44David thus calls him Lord; so how can he be his son?"

Jesus Denounces the Scribes

45In the hearing of all the people he said to the*r* disciples, 46"Beware of the scribes, who like to walk around in long robes, and love to be greeted with respect in the marketplaces, and to have the best seats in the synagogues and places of honor at banquets. 47They devour widows' houses and for the sake of appearance say long prayers. They will receive the greater condemnation."

The Widow's Offering

21 He looked up and saw rich people putting their gifts into the treasury; 2he also saw a poor widow put in two small copper coins. 3He said, "Truly I tell you, this poor widow has put in more than all of them; 4for all of them have contributed out of their abundance, but she out of her poverty has put in all she had to live on."

The Destruction of the Temple Foretold

5When some were speaking about the temple, how it was adorned with beautiful stones and gifts dedicated to God, he said, 6"As for these things that you see, the days will come when not one stone will be left upon another; all will be thrown down."

Signs and Persecutions

7They asked him, "Teacher, when will this be, and what will be the sign that this is about to take place?" 8And he said, "Beware that you are not led astray; for many will come in my name and say, 'I am he!'*s* and, 'The time is near!'*t* Do not go after them. 9"When you hear of wars and insurrections, do not be terrified; for these things must take place first, but the end will not follow immediately." 10Then he said to them, "Nation will rise against nation, and kingdom against kingdom; 11there will be great earthquakes, and in various places famines and plagues; and there will be dreadful portents and great signs from heaven.

12"But before all this occurs, they will arrest you and persecute you; they will hand you over to synagogues and prisons, and you will be brought before kings and governors because of my name. 13This will give you an opportunity to testify. 14So make up your minds not to prepare your defense in advance; 15for I will give you words*u* and a wisdom that none of your opponents will be able to withstand or contradict. 16You will be betrayed even by parents and brothers, by relatives and friends; and they will put some of you to death. 17You will be hated by all because of my name. 18But not a hair of your head will perish. 19By your endurance you will gain your souls.

The Destruction of Jerusalem Foretold

20"When you see Jerusalem surrounded by armies, then know that its desolation has come near.*v* 21Then

---

q Or *the Christ*
r Other ancient authorities read *his*

s Gk *I am*
t Or *at hand*
u Gk *a mouth*
v Or *is at hand*

20:39 Only in *Luke*, continuing the picture of Jesus as a respected teacher. **20:41–44** See *Mark* 12:35–37; *Matt.* 22:41–46. **20:41** *he said to them Luke*'s editorial bridge makes the Sadducees, rather than the people *(Mark)* or the Pharisees *(Matthew)*, the audience of Jesus' question. **20:42** *Sit at my right hand ... footstool Ps.* 110:1 (LXX 109:1). **20:44** See note to *Mark* 12:35–37. The point of this scriptural argument seems more suited to a Christian audience that held Jesus to be the Lord. See *Luke* 1:27, 32, 69; 2:4; 3:31; 18:38, 39. **20:45–47** See *Mark* 12:37–40; *Matt.* 23:1–13. **20:46** *places of honor at banquets* See 14:7–11. **21:1–4** See *Mark* 12:41–44. **21:2** *two small copper coins* Gk *lepta*. See note to 12:59. **21:5–28** See *Mark* 13:1–20; *Matt.* 24:1–22; *John* 16:2; 15:21; 14:26; and notes to *Mark* and *Matthew*. **21:12** See 12:11–12 (one of the few doublets in *Luke*) and note. Because of *Acts*, only the writer of *Luke* can anticipate the fulfillment of this prediction within the text *(Acts* 12:1–5; chs. 24–26). **21:18** But see the cases of Stephen *(Acts* 7:57–60) and James *(Acts* 12:1–5). **21:19** *gain your souls* Or "gain your lives." In the parallels *(Mark* 13:13; *Matt.* 24:13), the one who endures will "be saved." **21:20** *Jerusalem surrounded by armies* Only in *Luke*, which omits the mysterious "desolating sacrilege" of its source, *Mark* 13:14. See note to *Luke* 19:41–44.

those in Judea must flee to the mountains, and those inside the city must leave it, and those out in the country must not enter it; 22for these are days of vengeance, as a fulfillment of all that is written. 23Woe to those who are pregnant and to those who are nursing infants in those days! For there will be great distress on the earth and wrath against this people; 24they will fall by the edge of the sword and be taken away as captives among all nations; and Jerusalem will be trampled on by the Gentiles, until the times of the Gentiles are fulfilled.

The Coming of the Son of Man

25"There will be signs in the sun, the moon, and the stars, and on the earth distress among nations confused by the roaring of the sea and the waves. 26People will faint from fear and foreboding of what is coming upon the world, for the powers of the heavens will be shaken. 27Then they will see 'the Son of Man coming in a cloud' with power and great glory. 28Now when these things begin to take place, stand up and raise your heads, because your redemption is drawing near."

The Lesson of the Fig Tree

29Then he told them a parable: "Look at the fig tree and all the trees; 30as soon as they sprout leaves you can see for yourselves and know that summer is already near. 31So also, when you see these things taking place, you know that the kingdom of God is near. 32Truly I tell you, this generation will not pass away until all things have taken place. 33Heaven and earth will pass away, but my words will not pass away.

Exhortation to Watch

34"Be on guard so that your hearts are not weighed down with dissipation and drunkenness and the worries of this life, and that day catch you unexpectedly,

35like a trap. For it will come upon all who live on the face of the whole earth. 36Be alert at all times, praying that you may have the strength to escape all these things that will take place, and to stand before the Son of Man."

37Every day he was teaching in the temple, and at night he would go out and spend the night on the Mount of Olives, as it was called. 38And all the people would get up early in the morning to listen to him in the temple.

The Plot to Kill Jesus

22 Now the festival of Unleavened Bread, which is called the Passover, was near. 2The chief priests and the scribes were looking for a way to put Jesus[w] to death, for they were afraid of the people.

3Then Satan entered into Judas called Iscariot, who was one of the twelve; 4he went away and conferred with the chief priests and officers of the temple police about how he might betray him to them. 5They were greatly pleased and agreed to give him money. 6So he consented and began to look for an opportunity to betray him to them when no crowd was present.

The Preparation of the Passover

7Then came the day of Unleavened Bread, on which the Passover lamb had to be sacrificed. 8So Jesus[x] sent Peter and John, saying, "Go and prepare the Passover meal for us that we may eat it." 9They asked him, "Where do you want us to make preparations for it?" 10"Listen," he said to them, "when you have entered the city, a man carrying a jar of water will meet you; follow him into the house he enters 11and say to the owner of the house, 'The teacher

w Gk *him*
x Gk *he*

21:24 During the probable time of *Luke's* composition—the last decade or two of the 1st century—the subdued Jerusalem was indeed occupied by the Roman tenth legion *(Legio X Fretensis)*. Note again *Luke's* indefinite postponement of the end (see 19:11), in contrast to *Mark* 13:14–27, where the end of the age seems closely tied to the desecration of the temple. **21:25–26** See note to *Mark* 13:24–25. **21:27** The language is from *Dan.* 7:13, but there the humanlike figure "comes" from earth to heaven on the cloud. **21:29–33** See *Mark* 13:28–32; *Matt.* 24:32–36. **21:34** This forward-looking apocalyptic passage occurs only in *Luke*. See *1 Thess.* 5:3–8. **21:37** See note to 19:29. During the Passover feast (see 22:1), Jerusalem's population swelled with visiting pilgrims, so that accommodation outside the city was necessary for most. **21:38 all the people** Note *Luke's* consistent stress on Jesus' acceptance by all the people except the temple-based leadership. **22:1–2** See *Mark* 14:1–2; *Matt.* 26:1–5. The author omits the story of Jesus' anointing in Bethany *(Mark* 14:3–9) because he has already included it in 7:36–50, during Jesus' Galilean ministry. **22:2** As *Mark* explains more fully, the leaders could not simply arrest Jesus publicly because of his support among the people. *Luke* has already made the point (19:48; 20:6, 19, 26). **22:3–6** See *Mark* 14:10–11; *Matt.* 26:14–16. Only *Luke* places Judas's conspiracy immediately after the observation about the leaders' inability to find a way to arrest Jesus. By doing so and by adding the final clause *(when no crowd was present)*, it clarifies the nature of Judas's service: The authorities know who Jesus is, but they need to know where they can arrest him privately. In *Mark* and *Matthew*, by contrast, the betrayal involves a prearranged signal (a kiss) for *identifying* Jesus *(Mark* 14:44 par. *Matt.* 26:48). See *Luke* 22:48, where Jesus prevents the kiss. **22:7–14** See *Mark* 14:12–17; *Matt.* 26:17–20. **22:7** See note to *Mark* 14:12.

asks you, "Where is the guest room, where I may eat the Passover with my disciples?'" [12]He will show you a large room upstairs, already furnished. Make preparations for us there." [13]So they went and found everything as he had told them; and they prepared the Passover meal.

The Institution of the Lord's Supper

[14]When the hour came, he took his place at the table, and the apostles with him. [15]He said to them, "I have eagerly desired to eat this Passover with you before I suffer; [16]for I tell you, I will not eat it[y] until it is fulfilled in the kingdom of God." [17]Then he took a cup, and after giving thanks he said, "Take this and divide it among yourselves; [18]for I tell you that from now on I will not drink of the fruit of the vine until the kingdom of God comes." [19]Then he took a loaf of bread, and when he had given thanks, he broke it and gave it to them, saying, "This is my body, which is given for you. Do this in remembrance of me." [20]And he did the same with the cup after supper, saying, "This cup that is poured out for you is the new covenant in my blood.[z] [21]But see, the one who betrays me is with me, and his hand is on the table. [22]For the Son of Man is going as it has been determined, but woe to that one by whom he is betrayed!" [23]Then they began to ask one another, which one of them it could be who would do this.

The Dispute about Greatness

[24]A dispute also arose among them as to which one of them was to be regarded as the greatest. [25]But he said to them, "The kings of the Gentiles lord it over them; and those in authority over them are called benefactors. [26]But not so with you; rather the greatest among you must become like the youngest, and the leader like one who serves. [27]For who is greater, the one who is at the table or the one who serves? Is it not the one at the table? But I am among you as one who serves.

[28]"You are those who have stood by me in my trials; [29]and I confer on you, just as my Father has conferred on me, a kingdom, [30]so that you may eat and drink at my table in my kingdom, and you will sit on thrones judging the twelve tribes of Israel.

Jesus Predicts Peter's Denial

[31]"Simon, Simon, listen! Satan has demanded[a] to sift all of you like wheat, [32]but I have prayed for you that your own faith may not fail; and you, when once you have turned back, strengthen your brothers." [33]And he said to him, "Lord, I am ready to go with you to prison and to death!" [34]Jesus[b] said, "I tell you, Peter, the cock will not crow this day, until you have denied three times that you know me."

Purse, Bag, and Sword

[35]He said to them, "When I sent you out without a purse, bag, or sandals, did you lack anything?" They said, "No, not a thing." [36]He said to them, "But now, the one who has a purse must take it, and likewise a bag. And the one who has no sword must sell his cloak and buy one. [37]For I tell you, this scripture must be fulfilled in me, 'And he was counted among the lawless'; and indeed what is written about me is

---

y Other ancient authorities read *never eat it again*
z Other ancient authorities lack, in whole or in part, verses 19b–20 (*which is given . . . in my blood*)

a Or *has obtained permission*
b Gk *He*

22:14 When the hour came That is, the evening—when Passover (and the Jewish day) begins. **he took his place at the table** Better: "reclined." See note to 7:36. **22:15–18** This section is only in *Luke,* and it replaces a passage in *Mark* and *Matthew* that describes Jesus' sharing the meal with his students. The author of *Luke* apparently intends to convey that Jesus did not, in spite of his desire, partake in this last supper. *Luke*'s addition of the cup before the meal (as well as after; 22:20) conforms the Last Supper more closely to the common procedure for the Passover meal. **22:19–20** See *1 Cor.* 11:23–25; *Mark* 14:22–25; *Matt.* 26:26–29. **22:19 Do this in remembrance of me** Only in *Luke,* among the gospels, but paralleled in *1 Cor.* 11:24. The author accommodates the narrative to early Christian practice. **22:20** *Luke*'s language is also closer here to Paul's in *1 Cor.* 11:25 than to the other gospels. **22:21–23** See *Mark* 14:18–21; *Matt.* 26:21–25. **22:21 his hand is on the table** *Luke* assumes a single shared table (see 22:24), which would hold the food, but this does not mean that diners sat up to the table as modern Westerners do. See note to 7:36. In 16:21 likewise, *Luke* speaks of the "table" of the rich man. **22:24–27** See *Mark* 10:41–45; *Matt.* 20:24–28. *Luke* omits the more disturbing part of *Mark*'s story (10:35–40), in which two of the leading apostles (James and John) boldly jockey for power. **22:28–30** See *Matt.* 19:28. **22:29 as my Father has conferred on me, a kingdom** Only in *Luke.* Jesus for the first time speaks unequivocally of his kingdom, which the reader has known about since the birth narratives. See also 19:12. **22:31–32** Only in *Luke.* The author alternates freely, as here, between the names Simon and Peter (see 22:34). **22:33–34** See *Mark* 14:29–31; *Matt.* 26:33–35; *John* 13:36–38. Jesus' prediction is fulfilled in 22:54–62. **22:35–38** Only in *Luke.* **22:36** Thus *Luke*'s Jesus consciously modifies his earlier directions (9:3; 10:4), which were given under different circumstances. This passage illustrates the evolving character of *Luke*'s narrative. **22:37 And he was counted** *Isa.* 53:12. Through the bulk of the gospel, *Luke*'s Jesus has claimed only explicit fulfillment in himself of the hopeful predictions—of anointing and healing (*Isa.* 61:1 in *Luke* 4:18). Predictions of his death

being fulfilled." [38]They said, "Lord, look, here are two swords." He replied, "It is enough."

Jesus Prays on the Mount of Olives

[39]He came out and went, as was his custom, to the Mount of Olives; and the disciples followed him. [40]When he reached the place, he said to them, "Pray that you may not come into the time of trial." [c] [41]Then he withdrew from them about a stone's throw, knelt down, and prayed, [42]"Father, if you are willing, remove this cup from me; yet, not my will but yours be done." [[[43]Then an angel from heaven appeared to him and gave him strength. [44]In his anguish he prayed more earnestly, and his sweat became like great drops of blood falling down on the ground.]] [d] [45]When he got up from prayer, he came to the disciples and found them sleeping because of grief, [46]and he said to them, "Why are you sleeping? Get up and pray that you may not come into the time of trial." [c]

The Betrayal and Arrest of Jesus

[47]While he was still speaking, suddenly a crowd came, and the one called Judas, one of the twelve, was leading them. He approached Jesus to kiss him; [48]but Jesus said to him, "Judas, is it with a kiss that you are betraying the Son of Man?" [49]When those who were around him saw what was coming, they asked, "Lord, should we strike with the sword?" [50]Then one of them struck the slave of the high priest and cut off his right ear. [51]But Jesus said, "No more of this!" And he touched his ear and healed him. [52]Then Jesus said to the chief priests, the officers of the temple police, and the elders who had come for him, "Have you come out with swords and clubs as if I were a bandit? [53]When I was with you day after day in the temple, you did not lay hands on me. But this is your hour, and the power of darkness!"

Peter Denies Jesus

[54]Then they seized him and led him away, bringing him into the high priest's house. But Peter was following at a distance. [55]When they had kindled a fire in the middle of the courtyard and sat down together, Peter sat among them. [56]Then a servant-girl, seeing him in the firelight, stared at him and said, "This man also was with him." [57]But he denied it, saying, "Woman, I do not know him." [58]A little later someone else, on seeing him, said, "You also are one of them." But Peter said, "Man, I am not!" [59]Then about an hour later still another kept insisting, "Surely this man also was with him; for he is a Galilean." [60]But Peter said, "Man, I do not know what you are talking about!" At that moment, while he was still speaking, the cock crowed. [61]The Lord turned and looked at Peter. Then Peter remembered the word of the Lord, how he had said to him, "Before the cock crows today, you will deny me three times." [62]And he went out and wept bitterly.

The Mocking and Beating of Jesus

[63]Now the men who were holding Jesus began to mock him and beat him; [64]they also blindfolded him and kept asking him, "Prophesy! Who is it that struck you?" [65]They kept heaping many other insults on him.

Jesus before the Council

[66]When day came, the assembly of the elders of the people, both chief priests and scribes, gathered together, and they brought him to their council. [67]They said, "If you are the Messiah, [e] tell us." He replied, "If I tell you, you will not believe; [68]and if I question you, you will not answer. [69]But from now on the Son of Man will be seated at the right hand of the power of

---

c Or *into temptation*
d Other ancient authorities lack verses 43 and 44

e Or *the Christ*

---

and resurrection await fulfillment. Here *Luke* offers a brief glimpse at a key passage. *Isaiah* 53 was widely read by Christians as a blueprint of Jesus' career, and *Luke* will develop this point at the appropriate time (e.g., *Acts* 8:27–35). **22:39–46** See *Mark* 14:32–42; *Matt.* 26:36–46; *John* 18:1. The author considerably abbreviates this story, improving the image of the apostles by telescoping *Mark's* three episodes of their falling asleep into a single one. **22:45 because of grief** *Luke's* inclusion of this phrase makes the disciples' sleep more understandable than it appears in *Mark* 14:37. **22:47–53** See *Mark* 14:43–52; *Matt.* 26:47–56; *John* 18:2–12. **22:47–48** *Luke's* Jesus thus seems to prevent the kiss, but contrast *Mark* and *Matthew*. See note to 22:3–6. **22:51 healed him** Only in *Luke*. **22:52 a bandit** The Gk word often signified more than simple thievery; it was often applied to socially or politically motivated militancy, which might include banditry for the support of a rebel cause. See the charges against Jesus in 23:2–5. **22:54–71** See *Mark* 14:53–65; *Matt.* 26:57–68; *John* 18:13–24. **22:58 Man, I am not** But in *Mark* 14:69, Peter's second denial was prompted by a question from a maid (also *Matt.* 26:71). **22:61** See 22:34. **22:63** These are the guards in the high priest's house, not the members of the Jewish council as in *Mark* 14:65. In *Luke* (23:66) the council does not meet Jesus until the morning. **22:66 their council** Or "council chamber." Thus the author of *Luke* solves two major difficulties of *Mark's* account (see *Mark* 14:53–65 and notes). (a) He postpones the trial until the morning, in keeping with Jewish law, and (b) he properly moves the scene of the trial from the high priest's house to the council chamber.

God." [70]All of them asked, "Are you, then, the Son of God?" He said to them, "You say that I am." [71]Then they said, "What further testimony do we need? We have heard it ourselves from his own lips!"

Jesus before Pilate

23 Then the assembly rose as a body and brought Jesus[f] before Pilate. [2]They began to accuse him, saying, "We found this man perverting our nation, forbidding us to pay taxes to the emperor, and saying that he himself is the Messiah, a king."[g] [3]Then Pilate asked him, "Are you the king of the Jews?" He answered, "You say so." [4]Then Pilate said to the chief priests and the crowds, "I find no basis for an accusation against this man." [5]But they were insistent and said, "He stirs up the people by teaching throughout all Judea, from Galilee where he began even to this place."

Jesus before Herod

[6]When Pilate heard this, he asked whether the man was a Galilean. [7]And when he learned that he was under Herod's jurisdiction, he sent him off to Herod, who was himself in Jerusalem at that time. [8]When Herod saw Jesus, he was very glad, for he had been wanting to see him for a long time, because he had heard about him and was hoping to see him perform some sign. [9]He questioned him at some length, but Jesus[h] gave him no answer. [10]The chief priests and the scribes stood by, vehemently accusing him.

[11]Even Herod with his soldiers treated him with contempt and mocked him; then he put an elegant robe on him, and sent him back to Pilate. [12]That same day Herod and Pilate became friends with each other; before this they had been enemies.

Jesus Sentenced to Death

[13]Pilate then called together the chief priests, the leaders, and the people, [14]and said to them, "You brought me this man as one who was perverting the people; and here I have examined him in your presence and have not found this man guilty of any of your charges against him. [15]Neither has Herod, for he sent him back to us. Indeed, he has done nothing to deserve death. [16]I will therefore have him flogged and release him."[i]

[18]Then they all shouted out together, "Away with this fellow! Release Barabbas for us!" [19](This was a man who had been put in prison for an insurrection that had taken place in the city, and for murder.) [20]Pilate, wanting to release Jesus, addressed them again; [21]but they kept shouting, "Crucify, crucify him!" [22]A third time he said to them, "Why, what evil has he done? I have found in him no ground for the sentence of death; I will therefore have him flogged and then release him." [23]But they kept urgently demanding with loud shouts that he should be crucified; and their voices prevailed. [24]So Pilate gave his verdict that their demand should be granted. [25]He released the man

---

f Gk *him*
g Or *is an anointed king*
h Gk *he*

i Here, or after verse 19, other ancient authorities add verse 17, *Now he was obliged to release someone for them at the festival*

22:70 *Son of God* These leaders thus seem to use "Messiah" (see 22:67) and "Son of God" interchangeably, as *Luke* does elsewhere. See note to 1:33. *You say that I am* See note to *Mark* 15:2. Strangely, the council members take this reply as an admission of guilt (*Luke* 22:71), whereas Pilate will apparently interpret the identical reply, in the singular, as inoffensive (22:3). **23:1–5** See *Mark* 15:1–5; *Matt.* 27:11–14; *John* 18:28–38. **23:2** These three charges (only in *Luke*) are calculated to draw the attention of the Roman governor: being an instigator of trouble, challenging Roman taxation, and pretending to be a Jewish royal figure (when Rome had long since incorporated Judea under its control). When caught, such persons were summarily executed by governors of 1st-century Judea. The 2d charge, as the reader knows, is an outright lie (see 20:25); the last is a distortion, inasmuch as *Luke*'s Jesus has not paraded messianic claims. **23:3–4** See note to 22:70. **23:6–12** This story of the trial before Herod Antipas appears only in *Luke*. It may have come from the special sources that the author had for Antipas's affairs (8:3; *Acts* 13:1). **23:6–7** Herod Antipas was the tetrarch of Galilee (see note to 3:1). It accorded with developing Roman law that a man should be tried not only in the place of his crime but also, if convenient, in the place of his ordinary residence or domicile. Since the ruler of Galilee happened to be in Jerusalem according to *Luke*, such a second trial would have been most convenient. Nevertheless, none of the other gospel writers knows anything about this trial. It is difficult to imagine how they could have omitted it if they had known of it. The trial before Herod also ruins *Mark*'s chronology. *Luke* omits *Mark*'s claim (*Mark* 15:25) that Jesus was crucified at about 9:00 A.M. (the third hour). Since the trial before Herod—necessitating also a second trial before Pilate—would push the clock back somewhat, *Luke* 1st mentions the time (about noon, the 6th hour) in 23:44, when Jesus is already on the cross. **23:8** Read in the larger context of the gospel, Herod's wish to see Jesus is some cause for concern (9:9; 13:31; 23:11). **23:11** In *Mark* 15:17–18 Pilate's soldiers, not Herod's men, dress Jesus in robes and mock him. **23:14** *have not found this man guilty* See note to 23:22. **23:18–25** See *Mark* 15:6–15; *Matt.* 27:15–26; *John* 18:39–40; 19:16. **23:18–19** See notes to *Mark* 15:6–7. *Luke* omits *Mark*'s claim that Pilate had a custom of releasing one criminal each year at the crowd's request—which practice would contravene all known laws, including Jewish and Roman. He retains without explanation only *Mark*'s conclusion, that a man named Barabbas was released. **23:22** Only *Luke* emphasizes Pilate's assessment that Jesus was perfectly innocent as far as Roman law was concerned; *Luke*'s Pilate repeats his verdict three times here, having already pronounced it clearly in 23:4.

they asked for, the one who had been put in prison for insurrection and murder, and he handed Jesus over as they wished.

The Crucifixion of Jesus

26As they led him away, they seized a man, Simon of Cyrene, who was coming from the country, and they laid the cross on him, and made him carry it behind Jesus. 27A great number of the people followed him, and among them were women who were beating their breasts and wailing for him. 28But Jesus turned to them and said, "Daughters of Jerusalem, do not weep for me, but weep for yourselves and for your children. 29For the days are surely coming when they will say, 'Blessed are the barren, and the wombs that never bore, and the breasts that never nursed.' 30Then they will begin to say to the mountains, 'Fall on us'; and to the hills, 'Cover us.' 31For if they do this when the wood is green, what will happen when it is dry?"

32Two others also, who were criminals, were led away to be put to death with him. 33When they came to the place that is called The Skull, they crucified Jesus*j* there with the criminals, one on his right and one on his left. [[34Then Jesus said, "Father, forgive them; for they do not know what they are doing."]]*k* And they cast lots to divide his clothing. 35And the people stood by, watching; but the leaders scoffed at him, saying, "He saved others; let him save himself if he is the Messiah*l* of God, his chosen one!" 36The soldiers also mocked him, coming up and offering him sour wine, 37and saying, "If you are the King of the Jews, save yourself!" 38There was also an inscription over him,*m* "This is the King of the Jews."

39One of the criminals who were hanged there kept deriding*n* him and saying, "Are you not the Messiah?*o* Save yourself and us!" 40But the other rebuked him, saying, "Do you not fear God, since you are under the same sentence of condemnation? 41And we indeed have been condemned justly, for we are getting what we deserve for our deeds, but this man has done nothing wrong." 42Then he said, "Jesus, remember me when you come into*p* your kingdom." 43He replied, "Truly I tell you, today you will be with me in Paradise."

The Death of Jesus

44It was now about noon, and darkness came over the whole land*q* until three in the afternoon, 45while the sun's light failed;*r* and the curtain of the temple was torn in two. 46Then Jesus, crying with a loud voice, said, "Father, into your hands I commend my spirit." Having said this, he breathed his last. 47When the centurion saw what had taken place, he praised God and said, "Certainly this man was innocent."*s* 48And when all the crowds who had gathered there for this spectacle saw what had taken place, they returned home, beating their breasts. 49But all his acquaintances, including the women who had followed him from Galilee, stood at a distance, watching these things.

The Burial of Jesus

50Now there was a good and righteous man named Joseph, who, though a member of the council, 51had

---

j Gk *him*
k Other ancient authorities lack the sentence *Then Jesus . . . what they are doing*
l Or *the Christ*

m Other ancient authorities add *written in Greek and Latin and Hebrew* (that is, *Aramaic*)
n Or *blaspheming*
o Or *the Christ*
p Other ancient authorities read *in*
q Or *earth*
r Or *the sun was eclipsed;* other ancient authorities read *the sun was darkened*
s Or *righteous*

23:26–27 See *Mark* 15:20–21; *Matt.* 27:31–32; *John* 19:17. **23:26** See note to *Mark* 15:21. **23:27** *Luke* stresses both the popular support for Jesus and Jesus' special concern for women. This observation is unique to *Luke*. **23:28–31** See *Gospel of Thomas* 79. **23:31** Meaning uncertain. The image of green and dry trees obviously represents a contrast between life and death (and readiness for kindling). In the immediate and larger context, *Luke's* Jesus seems to be hinting at the contrast between Israel's bold present action, in having him executed in a time of relative prosperity, and its coming suffering, judgment, and barrenness as a result of this action (13:34–35; 19:41–44; see 3:9). Perhaps the author alludes to persecution of Christians in his later context. **23:32–38** See *Mark* 15:22–32; *Matt.* 27:33–43; *John* 19:17–18. **23:34** See also *Acts* 3:17. On the ignorance of the Jewish leaders, see introduction to *Luke-Acts*. **23:35** Once again *Luke* sharply contrasts the people with the leaders. **23:39–43** This uniquely Lukan exchange is typical of the author's insight into human personalities and motives. **23:43** *Paradise* The only reference to paradise in the gospels. Originally an Old Persian word for "garden," the term came to signify the "third heaven" and place of reward for the righteous in Jewish literature of Jesus' day. See *2 Cor.* 12:3; *2 En.* 8.1–3; *T. Levi* 18.11; *Rev.* 2:7. **23:44–49** See *Mark* 15:33–41; *Matt.* 27:45–56; *John* 19:28–30. **23:44** *about noon* See note to 23:6–7. **23:45** See note to *Mark* 15:38. **23:46** Only in *Luke*, replacing the cry of abandonment in *Mark* and *Matthew*. **23:47** *this man was innocent* Mark, *Luke's* source, credits the centurion with saying, "Truly this man was God's Son!" (*Mark* 15:39). **23:50–56** See *Mark* 15:42–47; *Matt.* 27:57–61. **23:50–51** The earlier narrative

not agreed to their plan and action. He came from the Jewish town of Arimathea, and he was waiting expectantly for the kingdom of God. 52This man went to Pilate and asked for the body of Jesus. 53Then he took it down, wrapped it in a linen cloth, and laid it in a rock-hewn tomb where no one had ever been laid. 54It was the day of Preparation, and the sabbath was beginning.*t* 55The women who had come with him from Galilee followed, and they saw the tomb and how his body was laid. 56Then they returned, and prepared spices and ointments.

On the sabbath they rested according to the commandment.

The Resurrection of Jesus

24 But on the first day of the week, at early dawn, they came to the tomb, taking the spices that they had prepared. 2They found the stone rolled away from the tomb, 3but when they went in, they did not find the body.*u* 4While they were perplexed about this, suddenly two men in dazzling clothes stood beside them. 5The women*v* were terrified and bowed their faces to the ground, but the men*w* said to them, "Why do you look for the living among the dead? He is not here, but has risen.*x* 6Remember how he told you, while he was still in Galilee, 7that the Son of Man must be handed over to sinners, and be crucified, and on the third day rise again." 8Then they remembered his words, 9and returning from the tomb, they told all this to the eleven and to all the rest. 10Now it was

Mary Magdalene, Joanna, Mary the mother of James, and the other women with them who told this to the apostles. 11But these words seemed to them an idle tale, and they did not believe them. 12But Peter got up and ran to the tomb; stooping and looking in, he saw the linen cloths by themselves; then he went home, amazed at what had happened.*y*

The Walk to Emmaus

13Now on that same day two of them were going to a village called Emmaus, about seven miles*z* from Jerusalem, 14and talking with each other about all these things that had happened. 15While they were talking and discussing, Jesus himself came near and went with them, 16but their eyes were kept from recognizing him. 17And he said to them, "What are you discussing with each other while you walk along?" They stood still, looking sad.*a* 18Then one of them, whose name was Cleopas, answered him, "Are you the only stranger in Jerusalem who does not know the things that have taken place there in these days?" 19He asked them, "What things?" They replied, "The things about Jesus of Nazareth,*b* who was a prophet mighty in deed and word before God and all the people, 20and how our chief priests and leaders handed him over to be condemned to death and crucified him. 21But we had hoped that he was the one to redeem Israel.*c* Yes, and besides all this, it is now the third day since these things took place. 22Moreover, some women of our group astounded us. They were at the tomb early this

---

t Gk *was dawning*
u Other ancient authorities add *of the Lord Jesus*
v Gk *They*
w Gk *but they*
x Other ancient authorities lack *He is not here, but has risen*

y Other ancient authorities lack verse 12
z Gk *sixty stadia;* other ancient authorities read *a hundred sixty stadia*
a Other ancient authorities read *walk along, looking sad?"*
b Other ancient authorities read *Jesus the Nazorean*
c Or *to set Israel free*

---

offers no clue that the council's decision had been less than unanimous. See 22:70–71; 23:1, 18. Apparently, the author feels forced to make such an explanation because he finds in his source, *Mark,* the puzzling claim that a member of the council buried Jesus. The author of *Matthew* resolves the problem by omitting any mention of Joseph's membership in the council and by making him instead Jesus' disciple. **23:54** Thus, Friday, when all preparations for the Sabbath were made; not the day of Preparation for Passover as in *John* 19:31. In *Luke* 22:13 the Passover meal was the last supper of Jesus' students. **23:55** *women who had come with him from Galilee* See 8:3. These were the women who funded his teaching. **23:56** *Exod.* 20:8–11. *Luke* continues to stress the absolute commitment of Jesus and his followers to the Torah of Moses. **24:1–9** See *Mark* 16:1–8; *Matt.* 28:1–8. **24:6** *he told you, while he was still in Galilee* See 9:22, 43; 18:31. *Mark* and *Matthew* instead have the angel(s) direct the women to tell the disciples to go to Galilee. The author of *Luke* cannot do this, since his story will remain set in Jerusalem through much of *Acts* (see *Luke* 24:13, 33, 47, 49, 52; *Acts* 1:8). **24:10** *Mary Magdalene, Joanna, Mary the mother of James, and the other women* The 1st two of these women were mentioned in 8:3, along with Susanna, as the women who supported Jesus' ministry. Apparently, the reader is supposed to understand that they have accompanied Jesus throughout (23:49, 55), although they have remained in the background. At the beginning of *Acts* (1:14), when Jesus' students are still in Jerusalem, Jesus' mother, Mary, will surprisingly appear among the Galilean women. This raises the question whether "Mary the mother of James" here is not meant to indicate Jesus' mother, who might have been known to the church as the mother of James because James was the effective head of the Jerusalem church (*Acts* 12:17; 15:13; 21:18; see *Gal.* 1:19; 2:9, 12). **24:19–20** This sentence neatly summarizes some key Lukan themes. **24:21** The author continues to build suspense: how can Jesus be the Messiah, Israel's Savior, if he has now been crucified? Although the reader knows well that Jesus is the Messiah, the full answer awaits the book of *Acts,* where the author argues in detail that Jesus' death and resurrection are an integral part of the scriptural hope.

morning, 23and when they did not find his body there, they came back and told us that they had indeed seen a vision of angels who said that he was alive. 24Some of those who were with us went to the tomb and found it just as the women had said; but they did not see him." 25Then he said to them, "Oh, how foolish you are, and how slow of heart to believe all that the prophets have declared! 26Was it not necessary that the Messiah*d* should suffer these things and then enter into his glory?" 27Then beginning with Moses and all the prophets, he interpreted to them the things about himself in all the scriptures.

28As they came near the village to which they were going, he walked ahead as if he were going on. 29But they urged him strongly, saying, "Stay with us, because it is almost evening and the day is now nearly over." So he went in to stay with them. 30When he was at the table with them, he took bread, blessed and broke it, and gave it to them. 31Then their eyes were opened, and they recognized him; and he vanished from their sight. 32They said to each other, "Were not our hearts burning within us*e* while he was talking to us on the road, while he was opening the scriptures to us?" 33That same hour they got up and returned to Jerusalem; and they found the eleven and their companions gathered together. 34They were saying, "The Lord has risen indeed, and he has appeared to Simon!" 35Then they told what had happened on the road, and how he had been made known to them in the breaking of the bread.

Jesus Appears to His Disciples

36While they were talking about this, Jesus himself stood among them and said to them, "Peace be with you."*f* 37They were startled and terrified, and thought that they were seeing a ghost. 38He said to them, "Why are you frightened, and why do doubts arise in your hearts? 39Look at my hands and my feet; see that it is I myself. Touch me and see; for a ghost does not have flesh and bones as you see that I have." 40And when he had said this, he showed them his hands and his feet.*g* 41While in their joy they were disbelieving and still wondering, he said to them, "Have you anything here to eat?" 42They gave him a piece of broiled fish, 43and he took it and ate in their presence.

44Then he said to them, "These are my words that I spoke to you while I was still with you—that everything written about me in the law of Moses, the prophets, and the psalms must be fulfilled." 45Then he opened their minds to understand the scriptures, 46and he said to them, "Thus it is written, that the Messiah*h* is to suffer and to rise from the dead on the third day, 47and that repentance and forgiveness of sins is to be proclaimed in his name to all nations,*i* beginning from Jerusalem. 48You are witnesses of these things. 49And see, I am sending upon you what my Father promised; so stay here in the city until you have been clothed with power from on high."

The Ascension of Jesus

50Then he led them out as far as Bethany, and, lifting up his hands, he blessed them. 51While he was blessing them, he withdrew from them and was carried up into heaven.*j* 52And they worshiped him, and*k* returned to Jerusalem with great joy; 53and they were continually in the temple blessing God.*l*

---

d Or *the Christ*
e Other ancient authorities lack *within us*
f Other ancient authorities lack *and said to them, "Peace be with you."*

---

g Other ancient authorities lack verse 40
h Or *the Christ*
i Or *nations. Beginning from Jerusalem you are witnesses*
j Other ancient authorities lack *and was carried up into heaven*
k Other ancient authorities lack *worshiped him, and*
l Other ancient authorities add *Amen*

24:27 *Moses and all the prophets* See note to 16:29. ***the things about himself in all the scriptures*** The author tantalizes the reader by insisting that the Messiah's death and resurrection are foreseen in scripture, without actually providing the proofs; they come only in *Acts*. **24:36** *Luke's* narrative thus recaptures the theme of peace, which pervaded the earlier narrative (see 1:79; 2:14, 29; 7:50; 8:48) before it was interrupted by the catastrophic events in Jerusalem (*Luke* 19–23). **24:37–39** See the earliest account of Jesus' resurrection, *1 Corinthians* 15, in which Paul insists that the resurrection body is "spiritual" (the Gk word is in same word group as that for "ghost") and not physical (15:44–50). **24:42–43** This demonstration of physicality is presumably one of the "many convincing proofs" of Jesus' resurrection that the author has in mind in *Acts* 1:3. **24:44 *the law of Moses, the prophets, and the psalms*** See note to 16:29. **24:45–46** That *Luke's* Jesus should devote so much attention to this theme immediately before his ascension indicates its centrality: the Messiah's suffering and resurrection are deeply rooted in scripture. **24:49** This directive is picked up as the starting point of *Acts* (see *Acts* 1:4, 8; 2:1–4, 16–21). **24:50 *Bethany*** On the far side of the Mount of Olives, just east of Jerusalem (see note to 19:29). See *Acts* 1:9–12. **24:53 *continually in the temple blessing God*** *Luke's* final words in the gospel stress the absolute devotion of Jesus' original followers to Jewish law and tradition: they did not abandon traditional Judaism arbitrarily.

THE ACTS OF THE APOSTLES

The Promise of the Holy Spirit

1 In the first book, Theophilus, I wrote about all that Jesus did and taught from the beginning ²until the day when he was taken up to heaven, after giving instructions through the Holy Spirit to the apostles whom he had chosen. ³After his suffering he presented himself alive to them by many convincing proofs, appearing to them during forty days and speaking about the kingdom of God. ⁴While staying*ª* with them, he ordered them not to leave Jerusalem, but to wait there for the promise of the Father. "This," he said, "is what you have heard from me; ⁵for John baptized with water, but you will be baptized with*ᵇ* the Holy Spirit not many days from now."

The Ascension of Jesus

⁶So when they had come together, they asked him, "Lord, is this the time when you will restore the kingdom to Israel?" ⁷He replied, "It is not for you to know the times or periods that the Father has set by his own authority. ⁸But you will receive power when the Holy Spirit has come upon you; and you will be my witnesses in Jerusalem, in all Judea and Samaria, and to the ends of the earth." ⁹When he had said this, as they were watching, he was lifted up, and a cloud took him out of their sight. ¹⁰While he was going and they were gazing up toward heaven, suddenly two men in white robes stood by them. ¹¹They said, "Men of Galilee, why do you stand looking up toward heaven? This Jesus, who has been taken up from you into heaven, will come in the same way as you saw him go into heaven."

Matthias Chosen to Replace Judas

¹²Then they returned to Jerusalem from the mount called Olivet, which is near Jerusalem, a sabbath

---

a Or *eating*
b Or *by*

1:1 *the first book* That is, the gospel now known as *Luke*. *Theophilus* The author's real or fictional patron, to whom the 1st volume was also dedicated; see note to *Luke* 1:3. *Jesus did and taught* This combination of word and action was the mark of the true philosopher. See Seneca, *Letters* 20.2; Lucian, *Menippus* 5; Epictetus, *Discourses* 2.9.17. **1:2** Referring to *Luke* 24. *the apostles whom he had chosen* Jesus' designation of twelve students as apostles (*Luke* 6:13–16; 9:10; 11:49; 17:5; 22:14; 24:10) is important to the development of the story, for these twelve, after the position of Judas has been filled (*Acts* 1:15–26), will become the authorized leaders of the young church (2:42–43; 4:33–35; 5:12, 18, 29; 6:2; 8:1, 14; 9:27; 11:1; 15:2, 4, 23; 16:4). **1:3** *many convincing proofs* This author seems most keenly aware that the extravagant nature of the claim that Jesus was raised needs support, whether for outsiders (17:32), the Christian faithful, or those on the threshold (the presumed readers of this book). The proofs referred to are the inspection of the empty tomb, the report of angels, Jesus' talking with Cleopas and his friend and breaking bread with them, and his eating broiled fish with the disciples (*Luke* 24:3, 4–7, 12, 15, 30, 41–43). *during forty days* New information for the reader of *Luke-Acts*. Forty was a number full of biblical resonances, often signifying a complete or exhaustive period (*Gen.* 8:6; *Exod.* 24:18; see *Luke* 4:2). *speaking about the kingdom of God* Curiously, *Luke* 24 omits any discussion of the kingdom of God, although this subject had dominated Jesus' teaching in *Luke* before Jesus' death. **1:4** *ordered them not to leave Jerusalem Luke* 24:49. **1:5** The coming "fire," which seems to have formed the heart of the Baptist's preaching (*Luke* 3:7–17), in contrast to the water of his immersion, has now been supplanted by the promise of the Holy Spirit. **1:6** *Luke* consistently asserts that Jesus will one day do what the Messiah was expected to do, namely, restore Israel's sovereignty and remove its enemies (see *Luke* 1:32–33, 69–74). In postponing all of this activity to Jesus' return in the indefinite future, the author set in motion an argument that later Christian apologists could exploit: Although Jesus did not fulfill common expectations of the Messiah when he died as a result of execution, he will return in power and glory to fulfill these hopes. **1:7** See *Mark* 13:32; the author of *Luke* omitted the claim in *Mark* that only the Father knows the time of the end (*Luke* 21:33), and even here in *Acts* he does not explicitly limit Jesus' knowledge as *Mark* had done. **1:8** This pronouncement is a keynote for the entire book. As the story unfolds, the gospel will spread from Jerusalem to Judea and Samaria (8:1), then to the Gentiles (10:1–11:1), then outside Palestine altogether (11:19), and ultimately to Rome (28:16). *Ends of the earth* Recalls *Isa.* 49:6, which the author cites in 13:47. *Luke* 24:50–51 simply said that Jesus was blessing his students while he was being taken up into heaven. **1:9** *lifted up, and a cloud took him* In the biblical and Jewish worlds, clouds were often seen as a means of heavenly transportation. *Dan.* 7:13; *1 Thess.* 4:17. **1:12** *from the mount called Olivet* That is, the Mount of Olives, the hill that rises from the Kidron valley, immediately to the east of Jerusalem; its summit overlooks the city. Curiously, *Luke* 24:50–51 had Jesus depart from Bethany, a village on the other side of the mountain. *a sabbath day's journey away* See note to *Matt.* 24:20. For most 1st-century Jews, apparently, the limit of Sabbath travel was one thousand yards (*m. Eruvin* 4:3; 5:7); for some, it was only five hundred yards (CD 10.14). The summit of the Mount of Olives would more or less meet this limit, but Bethany (*Luke* 24:50; two miles east of Jerusalem) would not. The author continues to stress that Jesus' students still faithfully observe the Jewish Torah.

day's journey away. [13]When they had entered the city, they went to the room upstairs where they were staying, Peter, and John, and James, and Andrew, Philip and Thomas, Bartholomew and Matthew, James son of Alphaeus, and Simon the Zealot, and Judas son of[c] James. [14]All these were constantly devoting themselves to prayer, together with certain women, including Mary the mother of Jesus, as well as his brothers.

[15]In those days Peter stood up among the believers[d] (together the crowd numbered about one hundred twenty persons) and said, [16]"Friends,[e] the scripture had to be fulfilled, which the Holy Spirit through David foretold concerning Judas, who became a guide for those who arrested Jesus— [17]for he was numbered among us and was allotted his share

in this ministry." [18](Now this man acquired a field with the reward of his wickedness; and falling headlong,[f] he burst open in the middle and all his bowels gushed out. [19]This became known to all the residents of Jerusalem, so that the field was called in their language Hakeldama, that is, Field of Blood.) [20]"For it is written in the book of Psalms,

'Let his homestead become desolate,
    and let there be no one to live in it';
and
'Let another take his position of overseer.'
[21]So one of the men who have accompanied us during all the time that the Lord Jesus went in and out among us, [22]beginning from the baptism of John until the day when he was taken up from us—one of these must become a witness with us to his resur-

---

c Or *the brother of*
d Gk *brothers*
e Gk *Men, brothers*

---

f Or *swelling up*

1:13 These are the twelve apostles of *Luke* 6:14–16, minus the traitor, Judas Iscariot (*Luke* 22:3–6). **1:14** The translation omits an important word in this sentence: the word meaning "in unanimity," which is part of the Gk phrase rendered "constantly devoting themselves to prayer" (see below). The Gk word for "in unanimity" occurs ten times in *Acts* but only once elsewhere in the earliest texts (*Rom.* 15:6; see LXX *Exod.* 19:8). The sublime unity of the early Christians is a characteristic theme of this author: 2:46; 4:24; 5:12; 7:57; 8:6; 12:20; 15:25; 18:12; 19:29. See also 2:1 ("all together"); 4:32. In the ancient world, which was profoundly influenced by Stoic aspirations, unity and harmony were recognized as indices of truth. Josephus claims that harmony was a particularly Jewish virtue (*J.W.* 6.17; *Ag. Ap.* 2.179–180). The author of *Luke-Acts* claims the same for the early Christians. ***constantly devoting themselves to prayer*** Presumably waiting for the fulfillment of Jesus' promise of the Spirit (*Luke* 24:49; *Acts* 1:4, 8). ***with certain women, including Mary the mother of Jesus*** The author features the role of women in Jesus' career; see *Luke* 1:26–62; 2:19, 36–38; 4:25–26; 7:11–17, 37–50; 8:2–3, 40–56; 10:38–42; 13:10–17, 20–21; 18:1–8; 21:1–4; 23:27–29, 49, 55; 24:10. Strangely, Jesus' mother was not mentioned as his companion, unless she is "Mary mother of James," referred to in *Luke* 24:10; see note there. ***as well as his brothers*** This puzzling reference raises the question of the role that Jesus' family played in the early church. Jesus' brothers are hardly mentioned even in *Mark*, a source for *Luke*; there they are named as James, Joses, Judas (Jude), and Simon (*Mark* 6:3; see *Matt.* 13:55), but they do not speak. They were apparently involved in the family effort—only related in *Mark*—to bring Jesus home for fear that he had gone mad (*Mark* 3:20–35). But *Luke* omits both that episode and the simple listing of the brothers' names, and so their appearance here comes as a surprise. The surprise is compounded by the fact that Jesus' brother James, at least, will assume a significant but unexplained role in the narrative (*Acts* 12:17; 15:13, 19; 21:18)—a role confirmed by other texts (*1 Cor.* 9:5; 15:7; *Gal.* 1:19; 2:9, 12; *James*; Josephus, *Ant.* 20.200–202). And Jesus' other brothers were well known to Paul (*1 Cor.* 9:5; see *Jude* 1; *Gospel of Thomas*, prologue), in the first Christian generation, as missionaries somewhat on the level of the apostles. It is noteworthy, then, that *Luke-Acts* should devote so much attention to the development of the apostles as a group and ignore Jesus' family, who played a central historical role. **1:16** ***Friends*** This translation obscures the author's typical form of address in the speeches of *Acts*: "men [i.e., males], X," where X can be "brothers" as here, or "Israelites" or "Jews" or "Galileans" (2:5, 14, 22, 29, 37; 3:12; 5:35; 7:2, 26; 13:15–16, 26; 15:7, 13; 19:35; 21:28; 22:1; 23:1, 6; 28:17). Angels use the same formula in 1:11 ("Men of Galilee," lit. "Men, Galileans"). **1:17** ***ministry*** The Gk word means simply "service." **1:18–19** Contrast the tradition about Judas's death recounted in *Matt.* 27:3–10. **1:20** ***Let his homestead ... live in it*** *Ps.* 69:25 (LXX 68:25). A curse upon the enemies of Israel. The author has taken the passage out of context and also made it refer to a single person. ***Let ... overseer*** *Ps.* 109:8 (LXX 108:8). Among further curses upon Israel's enemies. The LXX is translated here to match the NRSV translation of *Acts*, but in the context of *Psalm* 109, the Gk words could have several other meanings. **1:21–22** The author lays out his criteria for apostleship, criteria that would exclude Paul. Although he incidentally calls Paul and Barnabas apostles (14:4, 14), he seems to use the word in a nontechnical sense there, to mean "missionaries." Elsewhere they are not called apostles, and they do not have the official recognition of the Jerusalem apostles. Contrast Paul's letters: *1 Thess.* 1:1; *1 Cor.* 9:1; 15:9; *2 Cor.* 11:5–12:12; *Rom.* 1:1. **1:22** ***become a witness with us to his resurrection*** The fundamental role of an apostle in *Luke-Acts* is to serve as an authentic witness to Jesus' physical resurrection (proven during the forty-day period before his ascension), which forms the basis of the Christian preaching (see 1:2–3; 2:32; 3:15). This is the reason Paul cannot be counted an apostle in *Acts*, contrary to his own claim in his letters. In *Acts* (9:3–5), his encounter with the risen Jesus is quite different from that of the apostles who spoke and ate with Jesus during the definitive forty days.

rection." ²³So they proposed two, Joseph called Barsabbas, who was also known as Justus, and Matthias. ²⁴Then they prayed and said, "Lord, you know everyone's heart. Show us which one of these two you have chosen ²⁵to take the place[g] in this ministry and apostleship from which Judas turned aside to go to his own place." ²⁶And they cast lots for them, and the lot fell on Matthias; and he was added to the eleven apostles.

The Coming of the Holy Spirit

2 When the day of Pentecost had come, they were all together in one place. ²And suddenly from heaven there came a sound like the rush of a violent wind, and it filled the entire house where they were sitting. ³Divided tongues, as of fire, appeared among them, and a tongue rested on each of them. ⁴All of them were filled with the Holy Spirit and began to speak in other languages, as the Spirit gave them ability.

⁵Now there were devout Jews from every nation under heaven living in Jerusalem. ⁶And at this sound

---

g Other ancient authorities read *the share*

the crowd gathered and was bewildered, because each one heard them speaking in the native language of each. ⁷Amazed and astonished, they asked, "Are not all these who are speaking Galileans? ⁸And how is it that we hear, each of us, in our own native language? ⁹Parthians, Medes, Elamites, and residents of Mesopotamia, Judea and Cappadocia, Pontus and Asia, ¹⁰Phrygia and Pamphylia, Egypt and the parts of Libya belonging to Cyrene, and visitors from Rome, both Jews and proselytes, ¹¹Cretans and Arabs—in our own languages we hear them speaking about God's deeds of power." ¹²All were amazed and perplexed, saying to one another, "What does this mean?" ¹³But others sneered and said, "They are filled with new wine."

Peter Addresses the Crowd

¹⁴But Peter, standing with the eleven, raised his voice and addressed them, "Men of Judea and all who live in Jerusalem, let this be known to you, and listen to what I say. ¹⁵Indeed, these are not drunk, as you suppose, for it is only nine o'clock in the morning. ¹⁶No, this is what was spoken through the prophet Joel:

1:23 *Joseph called Barsabbas, who was also known as Justus* Otherwise unknown, although one Judas called Barsabbas ("son of Sabbas") turns up in 15:22 as a companion of Silas, Paul, and Barnabas, sent to Antioch with the apostle's letter. Joseph is a Hebrew name, Barsabbas is Aramaic, and Justus is Latin. *Matthias* Otherwise unknown. **1:26** That the author would dwell on this incident even though Matthias plays no role whatsoever in the following story indicates his concern for order and Christian government: it is important for the reader to know that there were twelve apostles again, even if most of them were insignificant. **2:1** *day of Pentecost* The 1st day of the late-spring Festival of Weeks (Shabuoth), which came seven weeks plus one day after Passover (*Lev.* 23:15–21). The exact date was a matter of controversy among different Jewish groups. The Gk from which the name Pentecost derives means "fiftieth [day]." Associated in Jewish tradition with the giving of the Torah through Moses at Mount Sinai (*Jub.* 1.1; 6.11), Pentecost was one of the three annual pilgrimage feasts; it accounts for the large number of Diaspora Jews in Jerusalem at the time (*Acts* 2:5). *all together in one place* Continuing the text's emphasis on harmony and unity; see note to 1:14. **2:2** *wind* In many ancient languages, the same word represents what English would distinguish as "wind" and "spirit." In the Gk here, the word for "wind" (*pnoē*) is related to the word for "spirit" (*pneuma*). *where they were sitting* See 1:13. **2:3** *Divided tongues* Or "distributed tongues." **2:4** *filled with the Holy Spirit* Being "full of [or 'filled with' or 'immersed with'] the Holy Spirit" is a recurrent theme in *Acts* (4:8, 31; 6:5; 7:55; 8:15–19; 10:44–46; 11:16, 24; 13:9; 19:6). *to speak in other languages* See also *1 Cor.* 12:10–13, 28, where "tongues" (the Gk word is the same as for "languages" here) is one among many signs of immersion in the Holy Spirit. **2:5** *living in Jerusalem* Presumably, some of them were living there temporarily, for the Feast of Weeks (2:1); see "visitors" in 2:10. **2:6–11** This understanding of glossolalia ("tongue speaking") as articulate speech in recognizable languages appears to be different from Paul, who understands tongues as speaking "mysteries in the Spirit," addressed to God (*1 Cor.* 14:2). **2:9** *Parthians, Medes, Elamites, and residents of Mesopotamia* Ethnic groups from regions to the east of Judea, mostly outside the Roman Empire. **2:9–10** *Judea and Cappadocia, Pontus and Asia, Phrygia and Pamphylia* Moving from Judea to the northwest, through what is now Turkey. The author omits Greece (Achaia and Macedonia), a significant region in the coming story; perhaps these regions, and likely the western Mediterranean, which is not mentioned at all, were not well represented in Jerusalem. **2:10** *Egypt and the parts of Libya belonging to Cyrene, and visitors from Rome* The author moves to the southern Mediterranean, then back north to the world capital, Rome. *proselytes* That is, converts to Judaism. The degree to which 1st-century Jews pursued missionary work among Gentiles, collectively or individually, is unclear. Nonetheless, considerable evidence indicates that Gentile conversion to Judaism was readily observable in Rome and the eastern Mediterranean. The audience in this story are Jews only, native and converted, because the gospel will go out to Gentiles only after much difficulty and direct intervention from God (10:9–43). **2:13–15** In Lucian (2d century C.E.), *Nigrinus* 5–6, a new convert to philosophy first compares his experience to drunkenness but then goes on to explain that his apparent delirium has good reason behind it. **2:15** *nine o'clock in the morning* Roughly. The 3d hour past sunrise. See note to *Mark* 15:25. **2:16–21** *Joel* 2:28–31. The date and context of this prophet, who predicted the restoration of Israel, are unknown. *Acts* agrees almost exactly with the LXX version of *Joel*, except for these changes: *Acts* reads *In the last*

17 'In the last days it will be, God declares,
    that I will pour out my Spirit upon all flesh,
       and your sons and your daughters shall
          prophesy,
    and your young men shall see visions,
      and your old men shall dream dreams.
18 Even upon my slaves, both men and women,
    in those days I will pour out my Spirit;
      and they shall prophesy.
19 And I will show portents in the heaven above
    and signs on the earth below,
      blood, and fire, and smoky mist.
20 The sun shall be turned to darkness
    and the moon to blood,
      before the coming of the Lord's great and
        glorious day.
21 Then everyone who calls on the name of the
    Lord shall be saved.'

22"You that are Israelites,[h] listen to what I have to say: Jesus of Nazareth,[i] a man attested to you by God with deeds of power, wonders, and signs that God did through him among you, as you yourselves know— 23this man, handed over to you according to the definite plan and foreknowledge of God, you crucified and killed by the hands of those outside the law. 24But God raised him up, having freed him from death,[j] because it was impossible for him to be held in its power. 25For David says concerning him,

'I saw the Lord always before me,
    for he is at my right hand so that I will not be
      shaken;
26 therefore my heart was glad, and my tongue
      rejoiced;
    moreover my flesh will live in hope.
27 For you will not abandon my soul to Hades,
    or let your Holy One experience corruption.
28 You have made known to me the ways of life;
    you will make me full of gladness with your
      presence.'

29"Fellow Israelites,[k] I may say to you confidently of our ancestor David that he both died and was buried, and his tomb is with us to this day. 30Since he was a prophet, he knew that God had sworn with an oath to him that he would put one of his descendants on his throne. 31Foreseeing this, David[l] spoke of the resurrection of the Messiah,[m] saying,

'He was not abandoned to Hades,
    nor did his flesh experience corruption.'

32This Jesus God raised up, and of that all of us are witnesses. 33Being therefore exalted at[n] the right hand of God, and having received from the Father the promise of the Holy Spirit, he has poured out this that you both see and hear. 34For David did not ascend into the heavens, but he himself says,

---

h Gk *Men, Israelites*
i Gk *the Nazorean*
j Gk *the pains of death*

k Gk *Men, brothers*
l Gk *he*
m Or *the Christ*
n Or *by*

---

instead of *Joel*'s concrete "after these things," and *Acts* omits *Joel*'s final sentence about being saved in Mount Zion and Jerusalem (these changes effectively transform a specific promise about Israel's restoration from current misery into a general promise about the end times); the lines about old men and young men are inverted; *and they shall prophesy* is added in 2:18; *above* and *below* are added to *heaven* and *earth*, respectively, in 2:19; *signs* is added in 2:19 to balance *portents* in the same verse ("signs and portents" is a characteristic Lukan phrase; *Acts* 2:22, 43; 4:30; 5:12; 6:8; 7:36; 14:3; 15:12). The MT (3:1–5) is substantively similar to the LXX, but several lines are transposed. **2:22–36** In the light of Jesus' resurrection, *Acts* develops this evolutionary portrait of Jesus with several proofs from scripture: He was first of all a man from Nazareth, who was chosen and anointed with the Holy Spirit by God (see *Luke* 24:19–20). Cruelly executed by the Jewish leaders, he was nonetheless rewarded and honored by God with resurrection and was thus made Messiah and Lord (2:36). He now deals with the world from this exalted state in heaven, from which he will return. See 3:13–15; 5:30; 10:38–42; 13:23–38; also Paul in *Phil.* 2:6–11; *Rom.* 1:4. Contrast the view, found in *John* 1:1–14, of Jesus as a preexistent heavenly being who returns to his former status after the resurrection. **2:22 *You that are Israelites*** See note to 1:16. ***wonders and signs*** See note to 2:16–21; the same Gk word is translated "portents" there and *wonders* here. Although the author did not use this phrase in *Luke*, he now attributes to Jesus the same evidence of divine favor as he attributes to the apostles. **2:23 *you crucified and killed*** Although, according to *Luke*, the Roman governor reluctantly ordered Jesus' execution (23:13–25), the author places the blame for it squarely on the Jewish leaders. See further *Acts* 2:36; 3:14; 4:10; 5:30. **2:25–28** *Ps.* 16:8–11. The author follows exactly the LXX (15:8–11), which mainly agrees with the MT. The psalmist is rejoicing that God has spared him from harm and death, whereas the author of *Luke-Acts* takes the psalm as proof of the Messiah's resurrection (*Acts* 2:29–31). He reasons that although the psalmist promised that God would not let him die, he died, and so the psalm could not have related to the psalmist's own life; he must have been writing about the Messiah. **2:27 *Hades*** The Gk equivalent of the biblical Sheol, the place of the dead—both good and bad—beneath the earth (*Num.* 16:31–35). **2:29 *Fellow Israelites*** See note to 1:16. **2:34–35** *Ps.* 110:1 (LXX 109:1). This became a favorite citation among early Christians because it fit the theme of Jesus' exaltation in heaven after his resurrection. It may even have helped to generate the common Christian belief that Jesus sat at God's right hand until all his enemies were conquered (see *1 Cor.* 15:24–28). Some circles used it to prove that the Messiah did not descend from David (*Mark* 12:35–37), but most Christian authors abandoned this view and claimed that Jesus was a descendant of David.

'The Lord said to my Lord,
"Sit at my right hand,
35   until I make your enemies your footstool."'
36Therefore let the entire house of Israel know with certainty that God has made him both Lord and Messiah,*o* this Jesus whom you crucified."

The First Converts

37Now when they heard this, they were cut to the heart and said to Peter and to the other apostles, "Brothers,*p* what should we do?" 38Peter said to them, "Repent, and be baptized every one of you in the name of Jesus Christ so that your sins may be forgiven; and you will receive the gift of the Holy Spirit. 39For the promise is for you, for your children, and for all who are far away, everyone whom the Lord our God calls to him." 40And he testified with many other arguments and exhorted them, saying, "Save yourselves from this corrupt generation." 41So those who welcomed his message were baptized, and that day about three thousand persons were added. 42They devoted themselves to the apostles' teaching and fellowship, to the breaking of bread and the prayers.

Life among the Believers

43Awe came upon everyone, because many wonders and signs were being done by the apostles. 44All who believed were together and had all things in common; 45they would sell their possessions and goods and distribute the proceeds*q* to all, as any had need. 46Day by day, as they spent much time together in the temple, they broke bread at home*r* and ate their food with glad and generous*s* hearts, 47praising God and having the goodwill of all the people. And day by day the Lord added to their number those who were being saved.

Peter Heals a Crippled Beggar

3 One day Peter and John were going up to the temple at the hour of prayer, at three o'clock in the afternoon. 2And a man lame from birth was being carried in. People would lay him daily at the gate of the temple called the Beautiful Gate so that he could ask for alms from those entering the temple. 3When he saw Peter and John about to go into the temple, he asked them for alms. 4Peter looked intently at him, as did John, and said, "Look at us." 5And he fixed his attention on them, expecting to receive something from them. 6But Peter said, "I have no silver or gold, but what I have I give you; in the name of Jesus Christ of Nazareth,*t* stand up and walk." 7And he took him by the right hand and raised him up; and immediately his feet and ankles were made strong. 8Jumping up, he stood and began to walk, and he entered the temple with them, walking and leaping and praising God. 9All the people saw him walking and praising God, 10and they recognized him as the one who used to sit and ask for alms at the Beautiful Gate of the temple; and they were filled with wonder and amazement at what had happened to him.

Peter Speaks in Solomon's Portico

11While he clung to Peter and John, all the people ran together to them in the portico called Solomon's Portico, utterly astonished. 12When Peter saw it, he addressed the people, "You Israelites,*u* why do you

---

o Or *Christ*
p Gk *Men, brothers*
q Gk *them*
r Or *from house to house*
s Or *sincere*

t Gk *the Nazorean*
u Gk *Men, Israelites*

2:36 The author seems to believe that, instead of reclaiming an earlier status after his resurrection, Jesus was first made God's son and Messiah at that time. See note to 2:22–36. **2:37** *cut to the heart* It was the mark of genuine philosophical preaching that it should "prick" or cut the heart of the hearers. See Lucian, *Nigrinus* 35; Epictetus, *Discourses* 3.23.37. **2:38** *sins may be forgiven* "Forgiveness of sins" is a characteristic phrase of this author: *Luke* 1:77; 3:3; 24:47; *Acts* 5:31; 10:43; 13:38; 26:18. **2:44–47** See the rules for new converts in 1QS 6.19–24; the descriptions of philosophers such as the Therapeutae in Philo, *On the Contemplative Life* 18–19, and of the Jewish Essenes in Philo, *Hypothetica* 11; Pliny, *Natural History* 5.73; Josephus, *J.W.* 2.119–161; *Ant.* 18.20–21. Greco-Roman readers were apparently as fascinated as modern readers by the practices of such disciplined groups, the model for which were the followers of Pythagoras. See note to 4:32–35. **3:1** *the hour of prayer, at three o'clock in the afternoon* This was the time at which the second daily offering of a one-year-old lamb (Hebrew, *tamid*) was sacrificed on the large altar at the temple. The continuing full participation of Jesus' students in temple life is important to the author because it shows their faithfulness to Judaism: They would change this only later, in the face of direct instruction from God. **3:2** *the Beautiful Gate* Not known in other literature. Josephus mentions one gate that surpassed the other nine in value; it was made of Corinthian bronze (*J.W.* 5.201) and was sometimes known as Nicanor's Gate (*m. Mid.* 2:3). Apparently, it was situated to the east of the temple proper. Each of the temple gates was about forty-five feet high and wide. **3:11** *Solomon's Portico* Josephus (*Ant.* 20.221–222) claims that the eastern portico edging the Temple Mount and containing two long aisles formed by three rows of columns remained from Solomon's time. **3:12** *You Israelites* See note to 1:16.

wonder at this, or why do you stare at us, as though by our own power or piety we had made him walk? 13The God of Abraham, the God of Isaac, and the God of Jacob, the God of our ancestors has glorified his servant*v* Jesus, whom you handed over and rejected in the presence of Pilate, though he had decided to release him. 14But you rejected the Holy and Righteous One and asked to have a murderer given to you, 15and you killed the Author of life, whom God raised from the dead. To this we are witnesses. 16And by faith in his name, his name itself has made this man strong, whom you see and know; and the faith that is through Jesus*w* has given him this perfect health in the presence of all of you.

17"And now, friends,*x* I know that you acted in ignorance, as did also your rulers. 18In this way God

fulfilled what he had foretold through all the prophets, that his Messiah*y* would suffer. 19Repent therefore, and turn to God so that your sins may be wiped out, 20so that times of refreshing may come from the presence of the Lord, and that he may send the Messiah*z* appointed for you, that is, Jesus, 21who must remain in heaven until the time of universal restoration that God announced long ago through his holy prophets. 22Moses said, 'The Lord your God will raise up for you from your own people*x* a prophet like me. You must listen to whatever he tells you. 23And it will be that everyone who does not listen to that prophet will be utterly rooted out of the people.' 24And all the prophets, as many as have spoken, from Samuel and those after him, also predicted these days. 25You are the descendants of the

---

v Or *child*
w Gk *him*
x Gk *brothers*

y Or *his Christ*
z Or *the Christ*

3:13–15 A characteristic statement of the author's view of Jesus: Jesus was a man whom God chose to make glorious (glorify) when he had been unjustly killed. See note to 2:22–36. **3:13** *God of Abraham . . . Isaac . . . Jacob* The author thus insists that trust in Jesus is wholly continuous with Jewish tradition: the same God has given a new and definitive revelation that must be accepted. This is typical of *Luke-Acts,* which tries to offer a solution in the fierce debates about the relationship between Christianity and Judaism—both within Christian circles and outside. The phrase here echoes *Exod.* 3:6, 15, an account of Moses' encounter with God at the burning bush. *he had decided to release him* So *Luke* 23:4, 16, 20, 22. **3:14–15** A forceful statement identifying the Jews (presumably through their leaders) as the sole culprits in Jesus' death; the Romans are considered completely innocent. See note to 2:23. **3:15** *the Author of life* A puzzling phrase in *Luke-Acts* if it means that Jesus was present at creation as some other Christians thought, because the text elsewhere seems to militate against that idea (see note to 2:22–36). Perhaps Peter refers to the *life* associated with Jesus' resurrection, which now becomes possible for the first time (2:28; 5:20; 11:18). The Gk word rendered "Author" here is translated "leader" in 5:31, and this sense may be preferable: He is the bringer of life. *we are witnesses* See note to 1:22. **3:17** The ignorance of the Jewish leaders is a continuing theme in *Luke-Acts* (*Luke* 23:34 [some manuscripts]; *Acts* 7:60; 13:27). **3:18** The author refers to biblical texts about suffering and subsequent reward or vindication, such as *Psalm* 16; 118:22; *Isaiah* 53. Early Christians appealed to these passages because they could be applied to Jesus' death and resurrection. The early chapters of *Acts* (2:25–28; 4:11; 8:32–33) cite many of them. The Bible says little about a coming Messiah, however, and nowhere suggests that such a person would suffer, die, and rise again. **3:21** Although the author envisions Jesus' eventual return from heaven, a great deal must happen before that time. *Luke-Acts* lacks, and actively discourages, the sense of Jesus' imminent return as found in, for example, Paul (*1 Thess.* 4:13–18) and *Mark* (9:2; 13:38). See *Luke* 12:35–48; 19:11; 21:19, 24; *Acts* 1:6. **3:22–23** *a prophet like me [Moses]* A conflation and rearrangement of *Deut.* 18:15, 18. Originally, the passage spoke of God's decision to mediate his presence to the Israelites through a prophet (or prophets) because God's direct contact was overwhelming (*Deut.* 18:16). The prophet like Moses seems to have been Joshua, his successor, who received some of the spirit that Moses had (*Num.* 27:18–19; *Deut.* 31:7–8; 34:9). Josephus (*Ant.* 4.165) claimed that Joshua succeeded Moses as prophet. But the promise of a prophet like Moses could remain unfulfilled in the popular imagination because (a) *Deuteronomy* ends by declaring there never was another prophet like Moses (34:10–12) and (b) the mysterious circumstances surrounding Moses' death and burial (*Deut.* 34:6) gave rise to the hope that he had not died but might come again (see *Luke* 9:30). Some Jews of Jesus' day, therefore, envisioned the Messiah as an anointed prophet instead of (or in addition to) a king like David. See 4QTest 5–9; 1QS 9.11; *John* 1:21. **3:22** *raise up* This wording easily served religious teachings of the early Christians. Although it originally meant simply that God would choose and train, or single out, a prophet from among the people, it fit perfectly with Jesus' resurrection from the dead. **3:23** Here the author significantly reworks *Deut.* 18:19. By changing the wording, he can argue that the Bible itself clearly mandates obedience to Jesus. Anyone who fails to accept Jesus will be cut off from *the people* of Israel. **3:24** *from Samuel* In some respects, he might be considered the first prophet: Except for the special cases of Moses and Joshua, he was the 1st one to write books, according to the tradition, and the 1st of the prophets linked with the period of Judean kings. Perhaps the author has in mind the famous prediction *2 Sam.* 7:14. **3:25** *You are the descendants* The passage recalls a promise made to Abraham in *Gen.* 12:3; 18:18; 22:18; 26:4 although this version does not agree verbatim with either the Hebrew or the Gk (LXX) versions of any of these verses. The main difference is *Acts'* use of *families* where *Genesis* has either "nations" (i.e., Gentiles) or "tribes." The original sense of the *Genesis* passages appears to have been that the very formation of Israel through Abraham's descendants,

prophets and of the covenant that God gave to your ancestors, saying to Abraham, 'And in your descendants all the families of the earth shall be blessed.' ²⁶When God raised up his servant,ᵃ he sent him first to you, to bless you by turning each of you from your wicked ways."

Peter and John before the Council

4 While Peter and Johnᵇ were speaking to the people, the priests, the captain of the temple, and the Sadducees came to them, ²much annoyed because they were teaching the people and proclaiming that in Jesus there is the resurrection of the dead. ³So they arrested them and put them in custody until the next day, for it was already evening. ⁴But many of those who heard the word believed; and they numbered about five thousand.

⁵The next day their rulers, elders, and scribes assembled in Jerusalem, ⁶with Annas the high priest, Caiaphas, John,ᶜ and Alexander, and all who were of the high-priestly family. ⁷When they had made the prisonersᵈ stand in their midst, they inquired, "By what power or by what name did you do this?" ⁸Then Peter, filled with the Holy Spirit, said to them, "Rulers of the people and elders, ⁹if we are questioned today because of a good deed done to someone who was sick and are asked how this man has been healed,

¹⁰let it be known to all of you, and to all the people of Israel, that this man is standing before you in good health by the name of Jesus Christ of Nazareth,ᵉ whom you crucified, whom God raised from the dead. ¹¹This Jesusᶠ is

> 'the stone that was rejected by you, the builders;
> it has become the cornerstone.'ᵍ

¹²There is salvation in no one else, for there is no other name under heaven given among mortals by which we must be saved."

¹³Now when they saw the boldness of Peter and John and realized that they were uneducated and ordinary men, they were amazed and recognized them as companions of Jesus. ¹⁴When they saw the man who had been cured standing beside them, they had nothing to say in opposition. ¹⁵So they ordered them to leave the council while they discussed the matter with one another. ¹⁶They said, "What will we do with them? For it is obvious to all who live in Jerusalem that a notable sign has been done through them; we cannot deny it. ¹⁷But to keep it from spreading further among the people, let us warn them to speak no more to anyone in this name." ¹⁸So they called them and ordered them not to speak or teach at all in the name of Jesus. ¹⁹But Peter and John answered them, "Whether it is right in God's sight to listen to you rather than to God, you must judge; ²⁰for we cannot keep from

---

a Or *child*
b Gk *While they*
c Other ancient authorities read *Jonathan*
d Gk *them*

e Gk *the Nazorean*
f Gk *This*
g Or *keystone*

---

the only people who would observe God's commands in the Torah, would bring benefit to the rest of the world (see *Exod.* 19:4–6). Paul makes much of these promises to Abraham, albeit in a different sense, in *Gal.* 3:8, 16. **3:26** This sentence recalls 1:8 and prepares for Peter's visit to Cornelius (*Acts* 10–11) and Paul's missionary journeys (*Acts* 13–28); the gospel goes first to Jews but then, although the apostles and Paul are extremely cautious, to Gentiles. **4:1** This reference recalls the atmosphere at the end of *Luke*: it was the Jerusalemite, temple-based authorities, including the Sadducees, who violently opposed Jesus and had him executed (*Luke* 19:47; 20:19, 27; 22:2, 52). As far as the reader knows, the Pharisees, who did not participate in Jesus' arrest, remained more or less friendly (*Luke* 7:36; 13:31; 14:1). See *Acts* 5:34; 15:5. **4:2** *annoyed because . . . resurrection of the dead* The author assumes that this temple-based group is largely Sadducean, and he has already explained that the Sadducees deny resurrection (*Luke* 20:27). The issue will become important again in *Acts* 23:6–8. By making the resurrection issue the cause of hostility, the author can firmly plant the Christians alongside the Pharisees and the mass of the people, who accept the idea. See Josephus, *Ant.* 18.12–17. **4:6** The author continues to claim that Annas was high priest during the period of Jesus' career, but it seems certain that Josephus and *Matthew* are right in saying that Caiaphas served as high priest from 18 to 36/37 C.E. See note to *Luke* 3:2. **4:10** *whom you crucified* Stressing Jewish leadership's exclusive responsibility (4:5) for Jesus' death; see note to 2:23. **4:11** The author recalls *Ps.* 118:22 (LXX 117:22), a favorite text among early Christians (see *Mark* 12:10). He applies the saying to the present by adding *you.* **4:13** This verse appears to suggest that the leaders grudgingly recognized Jesus as a good teacher. The ability to speak the truth fearlessly, even before those who held the power of life and death, was considered the surest mark of the genuine philosopher. This quality was often designated with the Gk word used here for *boldness;* for example, Dio Cassius, *History of Rome* 65.12.2. The term is used significantly in *Acts* 4:29, 31; 26:26; 28:31. **4:15** *the council* Or "council chamber." The council's place of assembly seems to have been beside the gymnasium on the west side of the Temple Mount (Josephus, *J.W.* 5.144; *m. Middot* 5:4). **4:17** *to speak no more . . . in this name* The issue of resurrection has now dropped out of the story; it seems that the council's real concern was with the propagation of teaching about Jesus—from their perspective, a troublesome criminal who had been duly executed. **4:19** Peter's response and the entire image here of the apostles being under divine compulsion to speak the truth no matter what the cost recall the famous portrayal of Socrates in Plato, *Apology* 17.29: "I will be persuaded by the god rather than by you" (see also 20.32).

speaking about what we have seen and heard." [21]After threatening them again, they let them go, finding no way to punish them because of the people, for all of them praised God for what had happened. [22]For the man on whom this sign of healing had been performed was more than forty years old.

The Believers Pray for Boldness

[23]After they were released, they went to their friends[h] and reported what the chief priests and the elders had said to them. [24]When they heard it, they raised their voices together to God and said, "Sovereign Lord, who made the heaven and the earth, the sea, and everything in them, [25]it is you who said by the Holy Spirit through our ancestor David, your servant:[i]

'Why did the Gentiles rage,
   and the peoples imagine vain things?
[26]   The kings of the earth took their stand,
      and the rulers have gathered together
         against the Lord and against his Messiah.'[j]

[27]For in this city, in fact, both Herod and Pontius Pilate, with the Gentiles and the peoples of Israel, gathered together against your holy servant[i] Jesus, whom you anointed, [28]to do whatever your hand and your plan had predestined to take place. [29]And now, Lord, look at their threats, and grant to your servants[k] to speak your word with all boldness, [30]while you stretch out your hand to heal, and signs and wonders are performed through the name of your holy servant[i] Jesus." [31]When they had prayed, the place in which they were gathered together was shaken; and they were all filled with the Holy Spirit and spoke the word of God with boldness.

The Believers Share Their Possessions

[32]Now the whole group of those who believed were of one heart and soul, and no one claimed private ownership of any possessions, but everything they owned was held in common. [33]With great power the apostles gave their testimony to the resurrection of the Lord Jesus, and great grace was upon them all. [34]There was not a needy person among them, for as many as owned lands or houses sold them and brought the proceeds of what was sold. [35]They laid it at the apostles' feet, and it was distributed to each as any had need. [36]There was a Levite, a native of Cyprus, Joseph, to whom the apostles gave the name Barnabas (which means "son of encouragement"). [37]He sold a field that belonged to him, then brought the money, and laid it at the apostles' feet.

Ananias and Sapphira

5 But a man named Ananias, with the consent of his wife Sapphira, sold a piece of property; [2]with his wife's knowledge, he kept back some of the proceeds, and brought only a part and laid it at the apostles' feet. [3]"Ananias," Peter asked, "why has Satan filled your heart to lie to the Holy Spirit and to keep back part of the proceeds of the land? [4]While it remained unsold, did it not remain your own? And after it was sold, were not the proceeds at your disposal? How is it that you have contrived this deed in your heart? You did not lie to us[l] but to God!" [5]Now when Ananias heard these words, he fell down and died. And great fear seized all who heard of it. [6]The young men came and wrapped up his body,[m] then carried him out and buried him.

---

h Gk *their own*
i Or *child*
j Or *his Christ*
k Gk *slaves*

l Gk *to men*
m Meaning of Gk uncertain

4:21 The author continues the tension between the people, who favor Jesus and his apostles, and the Jewish leaders, who, in spite of the means at their disposal, are impotent to stop this teaching. See also *Luke* 19:47–48; 20:19; 22:2, 6. **4:25–26** *Ps.* 2:1–2. The LXX reads exactly as *Acts*, except that (a) the word translated *Gentiles* here simply means non-Israelite "nations" in the Bible (see the following *peoples*), not individual non-Jews as here, and (b) the final English word *Messiah* (Gk *christos*) is in the LXX simply an adjective meaning "anointed one." It evidently referred to the current king of Israel, who had been anointed. **4:27** This application of the scripture to the trial of Jesus only works in *Luke-Acts*, which alone has a trial before Herod. In effect, this produces Gentile rulers "gathering together" against the Messiah (*Luke* 23:6–12; see *Matt.* 21:2–7). Curiously, in having the Gentile "rulers" plot thus (neither Antipas nor Pilate was a "king") against the Messiah, the author momentarily lays aside his position that the Jewish leaders were solely responsible for Jesus' death; see note to 2:23. **4:31** *boldness* See note to 4:13. **4:32–35** Again, the Christians of *Acts* behave as did the more rigorously ascetic groups of the Mediterranean world: Pythagoreans, Essenes, and those represented by some of the Dead Sea Scrolls. See note to 2:44–47. **4:32** *of one heart and soul* On the theme of unanimity in *Luke-Acts,* see note to 1:14. **4:36–37** This note both introduces Barnabas, an important figure later in the narrative (9:27; 13:2), and provides a foil for the improper actions of Ananias and Sapphira in the following paragraph. In his letters, Paul mentions Barnabas as a companion (*1 Cor.* 9:6; *Gal.* 2:1, 9, 13). **4:36** *Levite* See note to *Luke* 10:32. **5:1–11** This story clearly demonstrates the effective power of the Christians' God, but the space devoted to it suggests that the author also wishes to convey to his audience a lesson about financial disclosure.

7After an interval of about three hours his wife came in, not knowing what had happened. 8Peter said to her, "Tell me whether you and your husband sold the land for such and such a price." And she said, "Yes, that was the price." 9Then Peter said to her, "How is it that you have agreed together to put the Spirit of the Lord to the test? Look, the feet of those who have buried your husband are at the door, and they will carry you out." 10Immediately she fell down at his feet and died. When the young men came in they found her dead, so they carried her out and buried her beside her husband. 11And great fear seized the whole church and all who heard of these things.

The Apostles Heal Many

12Now many signs and wonders were done among the people through the apostles. And they were all together in Solomon's Portico. 13None of the rest dared to join them, but the people held them in high esteem. 14Yet more than ever believers were added to the Lord, great numbers of both men and women, 15so that they even carried out the sick into the streets, and laid them on cots and mats, in order that Peter's shadow might fall on some of them as he came by. 16A great number of people would also gather from the towns around Jerusalem, bringing the sick and those tormented by unclean spirits, and they were all cured.

The Apostles Are Persecuted

17Then the high priest took action; he and all who were with him (that is, the sect of the Sadducees), being filled with jealousy, 18arrested the apostles and put them in the public prison. 19But during the night an angel of the Lord opened the prison doors, brought them out, and said, 20"Go, stand in the temple and tell the people the whole message about this life."

21When they heard this, they entered the temple at daybreak and went on with their teaching.

When the high priest and those with him arrived, they called together the council and the whole body of the elders of Israel, and sent to the prison to have them brought. 22But when the temple police went there, they did not find them in the prison; so they returned and reported, 23"We found the prison securely locked and the guards standing at the doors, but when we opened them, we found no one inside." 24Now when the captain of the temple and the chief priests heard these words, they were perplexed about them, wondering what might be going on. 25Then someone arrived and announced, "Look, the men whom you put in prison are standing in the temple and teaching the people!" 26Then the captain went with the temple police and brought them, but without violence, for they were afraid of being stoned by the people.

27When they had brought them, they had them stand before the council. The high priest questioned them, 28saying, "We gave you strict orders not to teach in this name,[n] yet here you have filled Jerusalem with your teaching and you are determined to bring this man's blood on us." 29But Peter and the apostles answered, "We must obey God rather than any human authority.[o] 30The God of our ancestors raised up Jesus, whom you had killed by hanging him on a tree. 31God exalted him at his right hand as Leader and Savior that he might give repentance to Israel and forgiveness of sins. 32And we are witnesses to these things, and so is the Holy Spirit whom God has given to those who obey him."

33When they heard this, they were enraged and wanted to kill them. 34But a Pharisee in the council

---

n Other ancient authorities read *Did we not give you strict orders not to teach in this name?*
o Gk *than men*

5:12 signs and wonders See notes to 2:16–21, 22. **Solomon's Portico** See note to 3:11. **5:15** See also *Luke* 8:44 and *Acts* 19:11–12, where Jesus' clothes, or items that have touched Paul's skin, convey cures. **5:17** See notes to 4:1–2. **5:20 this life** See note to 3:15. **5:26** See note to 4:21. **5:28 determined to bring this man's blood on us** An interesting remark, since it reveals the author's keen awareness that he has attempted to remove the Roman governor from all blame in Jesus' death; see note to 2:23. **5:30 whom you had killed by hanging him on a tree** The strongest statement of Jewish guilt thus far because it sounds as if the Jews lynched Jesus whereas the author has plainly described a Roman crucifixion (*Luke* 23:25–49). **5:31** See note to 2:36. **at his right hand** See note to 2:34–35. **Leader** See note to 3:15. **forgiveness of sins** See note to 2:38. **5:32 we are witnesses** See note to 1:22. **5:34–40** Just as the author has continued to present the temple authorities as uniformly hostile to Jesus, so too he continues to present the Pharisees, who tend to speak for the people, as much more tolerant. See notes to 4:1–2. There are surprises here. The first is that a Pharisee should be a member of the council, since *Luke* 19:39 left the Pharisees outside Jerusalem. Perhaps the author failed to mention them in *Luke* so as to absolve them from complicity in Jesus' death. But *Acts* 23:4–6 confirms that the council included many Pharisees. The second is that the Pharisee's words win the day, since the Sadducean council has, to this point, been unanimously hostile. This might be best explained by the author's refrain that the temple authorities feared the people and that the people favored Jesus' students; if the Pharisees spoke for the people (5:34), they might be reluctantly heeded for this reason alone. See Josephus, *Ant.* 13.297–298. **5:34 a Pharisee in the council named Gamaliel** A prominent Jewish teacher known also from rabbinic literature (e.g., *m. Avot* 1:16). He was allegedly a member of the famous family of Hillel, whose members had a

named Gamaliel, a teacher of the law, respected by all the people, stood up and ordered the men to be put outside for a short time. [35]Then he said to them, "Fellow Israelites,[p] consider carefully what you propose to do to these men. [36]For some time ago Theudas rose up, claiming to be somebody, and a number of men, about four hundred, joined him; but he was killed, and all who followed him were dispersed and disappeared. [37]After him Judas the Galilean rose up at the time of the census and got people to follow him; he also perished, and all who followed him were scattered. [38]So in the present case, I tell you, keep away from these men and let them alone; because if this plan or this undertaking is of human origin, it will fail; [39]but if it is of God, you will not be able to overthrow them—in that case you may even be found fighting against God!"

They were convinced by him, [40]and when they had called in the apostles, they had them flogged. Then they ordered them not to speak in the name of Jesus, and let them go. [41]As they left the council, they rejoiced that they were considered worthy to suffer dishonor for the sake of the name. [42]And every day in the temple and at home[q] they did not cease to teach and proclaim Jesus as the Messiah.[r]

Seven Chosen to Serve

6 Now during those days, when the disciples were increasing in number, the Hellenists complained against the Hebrews because their widows were being neglected in the daily distribution of food. [2]And the twelve called together the whole community of the disciples and said, "It is not right that we should neglect the word of God in order to wait on tables.[s] [3]Therefore, friends,[t] select from among yourselves seven men of good standing, full of the Spirit and of wisdom, whom we may appoint to this task, [4]while we, for our part, will devote ourselves to prayer and to serving the word." [5]What they said pleased the whole community, and they chose Stephen, a man full of faith and the Holy Spirit, together with Philip, Prochorus, Nicanor, Timon, Parmenas, and Nicolaus, a proselyte of Antioch. [6]They had these men stand before the apostles, who prayed and laid their hands on them.

[7]The word of God continued to spread; the number of the disciples increased greatly in Jerusalem, and a great many of the priests became obedient to the faith.

p Gk *Men, Israelites*
q Or *from house to house*
r Or *the Christ*

s Or *keep accounts*
t Gk *brothers*

leading role in the council, and which was instrumental in the rabbinic consolidation of Judaism at Yavneh after the failed revolt of 66–74 C.E. **5:36** ***Theudas*** Josephus (*Ant.* 20.97–98) describes the activities of this messianic pretender. He took his followers out to the Jordan River, which he said he was going to part. But he was killed by the soldiers of the Roman governor, Cuspius Fadus, in about 45 C.E. This date, however, is after the supposed time of Gamaliel's speech, which is supposed to have happened in the months following Jesus' resurrection (about 30–33 C.E.). This is another clue that the author has created the speeches of his characters (see introduction to *Luke-Acts*). **5:37** ***After him Judas the Galilean*** Josephus describes in detail the activities of this man (*J.W.* 2.117–118; *Ant.* 18.3–10), whose children and grandchildren continued to lead the movement for revolt against Rome. But Judas's rebellion took place in 6 C.E., when Judea was annexed to the Roman Empire, and therefore somewhat before, not after, Theudas appeared. **5:41** ***left the council*** See note to 4:15. **6:1** One of several hints in this story that, in spite of the author's claims about complete accord among the early Christians (see note to 1:14), serious tensions emerged at times. ***Hellenists complained against the Hebrews*** These two labels have been the object of much scholarly discussion. They are usually taken to refer to Greek-speaking and Hebrew-speaking Jews, respectively, because Jerusalem was home to both native Judeans and Greek-speaking Jewish immigrants as well as long-term visitors. Since members of both groups became Christians, the linguistic division would have carried over into the church. ***the daily distribution of food*** See 4:32–35. **6:2** ***wait on tables*** The verb "to wait on" or "to serve" is, in the Gk, *diakonein,* from which emerges "deacon" (*diakonos: 1 Tim.* 3:8, 12; 4:6). The Gk word for "tables" can also mean "banks." The image, therefore, is not the modern one of serving food in a restaurant but that of seeing to the practical needs (food and/or money) of those lined up for help. **6:5** Since the complaint was lodged by the Gk speakers, it is noteworthy that all seven of the chosen men have Gk names. This episode mainly sets the stage for the stories of Stephen and Philip in the next few paragraphs, to which the author will quickly turn (6:8–8:40). Curiously, in those stories Stephen and Philip behave much as the apostles—preaching. They are not shown serving the practical needs of the community. The other five men do not appear elsewhere in *Acts* or other early Christian literature. ***a proselyte of Antioch*** See note to 2:10. Antioch was the capital of the province of Syria, somewhat north of Judea, and one of the three largest cities in the Roman empire. **6:6** ***laid their hands on them*** Laying on of hands was an old biblical custom for either conveying uncleanness and guilt to a sacrificial animal or conferring spiritual power on another person (*Num.* 27:23; *Deut.* 34:9). It persevered in both later Judaism and Christianity as a ritual for designating, or ordaining, authorized leaders (*1 Tim.* 4:14). **6:7** ***many of the priests became obedient*** A surprising observation, in view of the consistent hostility that the temple authorities of Jerusalem have shown, from the final chapters of *Luke* until now. These converted priests play no further role per se, although they would be included in *Acts* 21:20.

The Arrest of Stephen

8Stephen, full of grace and power, did great wonders and signs among the people. 9Then some of those who belonged to the synagogue of the Freedmen (as it was called), Cyrenians, Alexandrians, and others of those from Cilicia and Asia, stood up and argued with Stephen. 10But they could not withstand the wisdom and the Spirit[u] with which he spoke. 11Then they secretly instigated some men to say, "We have heard him speak blasphemous words against Moses and God." 12They stirred up the people as well as the elders and the scribes; then they suddenly confronted him, seized him, and brought him before the council. 13They set up false witnesses who said, "This man never stops saying things against this holy place and the law; 14for we have heard him say that this Jesus of Nazareth[v] will destroy this place and will change the customs that Moses handed on to us." 15And all who sat in the council looked intently at him, and they saw that his face was like the face of an angel.

Stephen's Speech to the Council

7Then the high priest asked him, "Are these things so?" 2And Stephen replied:

"Brothers[w] and fathers, listen to me. The God of glory appeared to our ancestor Abraham when he was in Mesopotamia, before he lived in Haran, 3and said to him, 'Leave your country and your relatives and go to the land that I will show you.' 4Then he left the country of the Chaldeans and settled in Haran. After his father died, God had him move from there to this country in which you are now living. 5He did not give him any of it as a heritage, not even a foot's length, but promised to give it to him as his possession and to his descendants after him, even though he had no child. 6And God spoke in these terms, that his descendants would be resident aliens in a country belonging to others, who would enslave them and mistreat them during four hundred years. 7'But I will judge the nation that they serve,' said God, 'and after that they shall come out and worship me in this place.' 8Then he gave him the covenant of circumcision. And so Abraham[x] became the father of Isaac and circumcised him on the eighth day; and Isaac became the father of Jacob, and Jacob of the twelve patriarchs.

9"The patriarchs, jealous of Joseph, sold him into Egypt; but God was with him, 10and rescued him from all his afflictions, and enabled him to win favor and to show wisdom when he stood before Pharaoh,

---

u Or *spirit*
v Gk *the Nazorean*

w Gk *Men, brothers*
x Gk *he*

6:8–7:60 The story of Stephen, renowned as "the first Christian martyr," accomplishes several things. For example, it shows that the committee chosen in 6:5 did much more than merely practical management. Also, Stephen embodies the innocent, selfless victim of lies and manipulation—an image that the author evokes for Jesus, the apostles, and the church as a whole. And Stephen's speech solidly grounds Christian belief about Jesus in biblical-Jewish history, asserting again that the Christians have simply followed God's will whereas the Jews have been the unfaithful ones. **6:8** *wonders and signs* See notes to 2:16–21, 22. **6:9** It is unclear how many synagogues the author envisions, but his language suggests two, since the Cilicians and Asians appear separately. A freedman was a former slave whose freedom had been bought or unilaterally granted by the master. The Gk word here for *Freedmen* is transliterated from the Latin *Libertini;* this suggests that the synagogue bore a Latin name and also that the members were former slaves of Romans living in Judea. A 1st-century inscription, written in Gk by one Theodotos, from a Jerusalem synagogue, confirms that some synagogues in the city catered to the needs of visitors and immigrants—even providing accommodation. The synagogue(s) in view here had members from some of the major centers of the eastern Mediterranean. **6:11–15** This trial is a major turning point in *Luke-Acts.* Until now, the author has sharply distinguished the people from the leaders, and the Pharisees from other leadership groups. Now, however, the people, too, turn against Stephen (6:11), and the reader knows that a Pharisee such as Gamaliel is among the members of the court trying Stephen (6:15). The persecution that arises from Stephen's death (8:1) will be a concerted effort of Pharisees and Sadducees, leaders and people. The entire trial recalls that of Jesus in *Luke* 22:66–23:25, which was also driven by lies. But the author of *Luke* omitted there *Mark's* story about the false witness and the temple accusation (*Mark* 14:57–58). The charges against Stephen come as a shock to the reader, since the author has made it very clear that just as Jesus scrupulously observed the Torah, so also did his students after his resurrection (*Acts* 2:1; 3:1); indeed, they will have a difficult time bringing themselves to abrogate the dietary laws (10:9–16; 11:2–10, 19). The charges appear, therefore, as complete fabrications by a bankrupt Jewish opposition. Note the similarity to accusations against Paul, current among both Christian and non-Christian Jews in 21:21, 28. **7:1–53** Stephen's answer to the charges is extremely circuitous, but he will eventually concede an element of truth in the claim that he and his master Jesus oppose the temple (7:44–48). Still, the writer stresses that the precise charges were mischievous (6:11, 13). Stephen's speech grounds Christian faith firmly in Israel's heritage, as a continuous development. See introduction to *Luke-Acts.* **7:2–16** See *Gen.* 12–50. **7:3** *Gen.* 12:1. *Acts* omits one clause but otherwise agrees with the LXX, which agrees substantially with the MT. **7:7** The 1st part matches LXX *Gen.* 15:14 exactly, and it agrees with the MT. The 2d part recalls *Exod.* 3:12.

king of Egypt, who appointed him ruler over Egypt and over all his household. [11]Now there came a famine throughout Egypt and Canaan, and great suffering, and our ancestors could find no food. [12]But when Jacob heard that there was grain in Egypt, he sent our ancestors there on their first visit. [13]On the second visit Joseph made himself known to his brothers, and Joseph's family became known to Pharaoh. [14]Then Joseph sent and invited his father Jacob and all his relatives to come to him, seventy-five in all; [15]so Jacob went down to Egypt. He himself died there as well as our ancestors, [16]and their bodies[y] were brought back to Shechem and laid in the tomb that Abraham had bought for a sum of silver from the sons of Hamor in Shechem.

[17]"But as the time drew near for the fulfillment of the promise that God had made to Abraham, our people in Egypt increased and multiplied [18]until another king who had not known Joseph ruled over Egypt. [19]He dealt craftily with our race and forced our ancestors to abandon their infants so that they would die. [20]At this time Moses was born, and he was beautiful before God. For three months he was brought up in his father's house; [21]and when he was abandoned, Pharaoh's daughter adopted him and brought him up as her own son. [22]So Moses was instructed in all the wisdom of the Egyptians and was powerful in his words and deeds.

[23]"When he was forty years old, it came into his heart to visit his relatives, the Israelites.[z] [24]When he saw one of them being wronged, he defended the oppressed man and avenged him by striking down the Egyptian. [25]He supposed that his kinsfolk would understand that God through him was rescuing them, but they did not understand. [26]The next day he came to some of them as they were quarreling and tried to reconcile them, saying, 'Men, you are brothers; why do you wrong each other?' [27]But the man who was wronging his neighbor pushed Moses[a] aside, saying, 'Who made you a ruler and a judge over us? [28]Do you want to kill me as you killed the Egyptian yesterday?' [29]When he heard this, Moses fled and became a resident alien in the land of Midian. There he became the father of two sons.

[30]"Now when forty years had passed, an angel appeared to him in the wilderness of Mount Sinai, in the flame of a burning bush. [31]When Moses saw it, he was amazed at the sight; and as he approached to look, there came the voice of the Lord: [32]'I am the God of your ancestors, the God of Abraham, Isaac, and Jacob.' Moses began to tremble and did not dare to look. [33]Then the Lord said to him, 'Take off the sandals from your feet, for the place where you are standing is holy ground. [34]I have surely seen the mistreatment of my people who are in Egypt and have heard their groaning, and I have come down to rescue them. Come now, I will send you to Egypt.'

[35]"It was this Moses whom they rejected when they said, 'Who made you a ruler and a judge?' and whom God now sent as both ruler and liberator through the angel who appeared to him in the bush. [36]He led them out, having performed wonders and signs in Egypt, at the Red Sea, and in the wilderness for forty years. [37]This is the Moses who said to the Israelites, 'God will raise up a prophet for you from your own people[b] as he raised me up.' [38]He is the one who was in the congregation in the wilderness with the angel who spoke to him at Mount Sinai, and with our ancestors; and he received living oracles to give to us. [39]Our ancestors were unwilling to obey him; instead, they pushed him aside, and in their hearts they turned back to Egypt, [40]saying to Aaron, 'Make gods for us who will lead the way for us; as for this Moses who led us out from the land of Egypt, we do not know what has happened to him.' [41]At that time they made a calf, offered a sacrifice to the idol, and reveled in the works of their hands. [42]But God turned away from them and handed them over to worship the host of heaven, as it is written in the book of the prophets:

'Did you offer to me slain victims and sacrifices
forty years in the wilderness, O house of
Israel?

43 No; you took along the tent of Moloch,
and the star of your god Rephan,
the images that you made to worship;
so I will remove you beyond Babylon.'

---

y Gk *they*
z Gk *his brothers, the sons of Israel*
a Gk *him*

b Gk *your brothers*

7:17–35 Stephen spends a disproportionately long time summarizing *Exodus* 1–3, probably to underscore the theme of rejection: No one would now doubt that Moses was sent by God. But when he 1st rose to the task, he faced massive opposition from the people. See especially 7:25, 27, 35. The quotations are from the burning-bush episode in *Exod.* 3:1–10. **7:36–43** The essential story is in *Exodus* 12–33. **7:37** Recalling *Acts* 3:22–23, which applies *Deut.* 18:15–19 to Jesus. **7:40** *Exod.* 32:1, repeated in 32:23. **7:42–43** *Amos* 5:25–27. *Acts* basically agrees with the LXX; the MT is quite different, especially for *Amos* 5:26–27.

44"Our ancestors had the tent of testimony in the wilderness, as God^c directed when he spoke to Moses, ordering him to make it according to the pattern he had seen. 45Our ancestors in turn brought it in with Joshua when they dispossessed the nations that God drove out before our ancestors. And it was there until the time of David, 46who found favor with God and asked that he might find a dwelling place for the house of Jacob.^d 47But it was Solomon who built a house for him. 48Yet the Most High does not dwell in houses made with human hands;^e as the prophet says,
49 'Heaven is my throne,
    and the earth is my footstool.
What kind of house will you build for me, says
        the Lord,
    or what is the place of my rest?
50 Did not my hand make all these things?'
51"You stiff-necked people, uncircumcised in heart and ears, you are forever opposing the Holy Spirit, just as your ancestors used to do. 52Which of the prophets did your ancestors not persecute? They killed those who foretold the coming of the Righteous One, and now you have become his betrayers and murderers. 53You are the ones that received the law as ordained by angels, and yet you have not kept it."

The Stoning of Stephen

54When they heard these things, they became enraged and ground their teeth at Stephen.^f 55But filled with the Holy Spirit, he gazed into heaven and saw the glory of God and Jesus standing at the right hand of God. 56"Look," he said, "I see the heavens opened and the Son of Man standing at the right hand of God!" 57But they covered their ears, and with a loud shout all rushed together against him. 58Then they dragged him out of the city and began to stone him; and the witnesses laid their coats at the feet of a young man named Saul. 59While they were stoning Stephen, he prayed, "Lord Jesus, receive my spirit." 60Then he knelt down and cried out in a loud voice, "Lord, do not hold this sin against them." When he had said this, he died.^g 8 1And Saul approved of their killing him.

Saul Persecutes the Church

That day a severe persecution began against the church in Jerusalem, and all except the apostles were

---

c Gk he
d Other ancient authorities read for the God of Jacob
e Gk with hands

f Gk him
g Gk fell asleep

7:44–47 This brief reference to the rest of the Pentateuch, *Joshua, 2 Samuel* (7:2), and *1 Kings* (ch. 6) finally begins to approach the issue of the temple, concerning which Stephen has been accused (6:13–14). **7:48–50** *Isa.* 66:1–2. The MT and the LXX agree substantially with *Acts,* except that the latter makes a question of the final verse whereas the others have a statement. Without further elaboration, Stephen suggests that there was something to the Christian critique of the temple. **7:51** Stephen's thoroughly biblical language is calculated to resonate with ancient critiques of Israel; see *Exod.* 33:3, 5; *Deut.* 10:16. **7:52** This alleged history of persecution recalls Jesus' words in *Luke* 11:47–51, directed against the "lawyers." It also continues the theme of exclusive Jewish responsibility for Jesus' death; see note to 2:23. **7:53** Although the Bible says nothing about it, some Jews of this period held that angels had been in attendance at the giving of the Torah at Sinai (see *Jub.* 1.29–2.1). This scenario was meant to heighten the grandeur of the event, as Stephen seems to assume here, but angelic mediation also provided a ready target for Christians who rejected the Torah; see *Gal.* 3:19–20; *Heb.* 2:2. **7:56** *Son of Man* The only passage outside the gospels and *Revelation* (1:13; 14:14) in which Jesus is called Son of Man—a term almost always placed on his own lips. The phrase recalls *Dan.* 7:13, which speaks of a humanlike figure ascending on the clouds to God's presence. *right hand of God* See note to 2:34–35. **7:57** The covering of the ears symbolizes the author's point about the Jewish leaders' "deafness" (see 28:26–27). **7:58** *began to stone him* Stoning was a common means of murder in the ancient Mediterranean and one of the four methods of execution prescribed by later rabbinic law, although the technique described differs from the one used in this scene (*m. Sanhedrin* 6). It is uncertain whether the Jewish court had the power to execute offenders at this time and whether the author intends to present Stephen's execution as a formal execution by the court or as murder. *a young man named Saul* Once again, the author uses one story to introduce a character who will become important later in the narrative (see 4:36; 6:5). This character is Paul. The switch of names will come in 13:9, when the Christian Saul begins his mission to Asia Minor and Greece (11:25, 30; 12:25; 13:1–2). The literary reason for the name change is obvious: Paul had both a Hebrew and a Gk name, and once he had embarked on his mission to the Greek world, he naturally used the Gk name. This is an example of the author's concern for realistic atmosphere. **7:59** *receive my spirit* These words recall Jesus' final appeal in *Luke* 23:46. **7:60** According to some fairly reliable manuscripts, Jesus had made a similar request for the forgiveness of his killers; *Luke* 23:34. **8:1–3** According to *Acts,* Stephen's death ignites a comprehensive effort to remove the Christians. They are no longer opposed simply by the temple leaders but by all leaders, such as the young Saul (who turns out to be a Pharisee trained by Gamaliel; 22:3). The Christians therefore have no refuge but, for the 1st time, must scatter. **8:1** *all except the apostles were scattered* This observation serves the following narrative well, for the dispersion of believers becomes the vehicle for the spread of the gospel (8:4–5; 11:19) while

scattered throughout the countryside of Judea and Samaria. [2]Devout men buried Stephen and made loud lamentation over him. [3]But Saul was ravaging the church by entering house after house; dragging off both men and women, he committed them to prison.

Philip Preaches in Samaria

[4]Now those who were scattered went from place to place, proclaiming the word. [5]Philip went down to the city[h] of Samaria and proclaimed the Messiah[i] to them. [6]The crowds with one accord listened eagerly to what was said by Philip, hearing and seeing the signs that he did, [7]for unclean spirits, crying with loud shrieks, came out of many who were possessed; and many others who were paralyzed or lame were cured. [8]So there was great joy in that city.

[9]Now a certain man named Simon had previously practiced magic in the city and amazed the people of Samaria, saying that he was someone great. [10]All of them, from the least to the greatest, listened to him eagerly, saying, "This man is the power of God that is called Great." [11]And they listened eagerly to him because for a long time he had amazed them with his magic. [12]But when they believed Philip, who was proclaiming the good news about the kingdom of God and the name of Jesus Christ, they were baptized, both men and women. [13]Even Simon himself believed. After being baptized, he stayed constantly with Philip and was amazed when he saw the signs and great miracles that took place.

[14]Now when the apostles at Jerusalem heard that Samaria had accepted the word of God, they sent Peter and John to them. [15]The two went down and prayed for them that they might receive the Holy Spirit [16](for as yet the Spirit had not come[j] upon any of them; they had only been baptized in the name of the Lord Jesus). [17]Then Peter and John[k] laid their hands on them, and they received the Holy Spirit. [18]Now when Simon saw that the Spirit was given through the laying on of the apostles' hands, he offered them money, [19]saying, "Give me also this power so that anyone on whom I lay my hands may receive the Holy Spirit." [20]But Peter said to him, "May your silver perish with you, because you thought you could obtain God's gift with money! [21]You have no part or share in this, for your heart is not right before God. [22]Repent therefore of this wickedness of yours, and pray to the Lord that, if possible, the intent of your heart may be forgiven you. [23]For I see that you are in the gall of bitterness and the chains of wickedness." [24]Simon answered, "Pray for me to the Lord, that nothing of what you[l] have said may happen to me."

[25]Now after Peter and John[m] had testified and spoken the word of the Lord, they returned to Jerusalem, proclaiming the good news to many villages of the Samaritans.

Philip and the Ethiopian Eunuch

[26]Then an angel of the Lord said to Philip, "Get up and go toward the south[n] to the road that goes down from Jerusalem to Gaza." (This is a wilderness road.)

---

h Other ancient authorities read *a city*
i Or *the Christ*

j Gk *fallen*
k Gk *they*
l The Greek word for *you* and the verb *pray* are plural
m Gk *after they*
n Or *go at noon*

---

the apostles' remaining in Jerusalem guarantees the stability of the church (e.g., 8:14; 9:27; 11:1–18, 22; 15:1–2). Nevertheless, the story seems peculiar from a historical point of view because, in any sort of persecution, the leaders of the offending group are usually the first to be arrested. **8:3** Saul's (Paul's) activities as persecutor of the church are further explained in 9:1–3 and then recalled in 22:4–5; 26:9–11. See Paul's own accounts in *1 Cor.* 15:9; *Gal.* 1:13, 22. **8:5–25** The mission to Samaria, about thirty-seven miles north of Jerusalem, begins to fulfill Jesus' command in 1:8. **8:5 *went down to the city of Samaria*** Ancient writers typically used "up" and "down" to refer to topography, not compass points, and one traditionally spoke of going up to or down from Jerusalem—the holy city on a hill—even though there were many higher hills around it. **8:9 *Simon had previously practiced magic*** Simon Magus (*magus* is Latin for "magician"), as he became known, was a popular figure in later church history and was regarded by some church fathers as the founder of all false teachings (Irenaeus, *Against Heresies* 1.23–27). He seems to have founded a sect in Samaria that combined quasi-biblical and Hellenistic ideas, and these may have grown into some forms of so-called "gnostic" teaching in the 2d century. ***saying that he was someone great*** The author has an ongoing interest in the dissonance between seeming or claiming and actually being; *Luke* 16:15; 18:9. ***the power of God that is called Great*** "Great Power" may be a sort of technical term from Simon's sect. **8:14** A clear example of the author's concern for church order: The official Jerusalem apostles must legitimize the Samaritan mission; see note to 8:1. **8:18–21** In the medieval church, Simon's name was borrowed for the practice of buying and selling church offices, called simony. **8:25** Between the city of Samaria and Jerusalem were many villages in the region of Samaria. **8:26–40** The story of the Ethiopian's conversion begins to set the stage for a full outreach to Gentiles (*Acts* 10–28) and a mission "to the ends of the earth" (1:8). Although *Acts* does not explicitly present this as a Gentile conversion (contrast 10:45; 11:1), it seems that the Ethiopian official is not Jewish. **8:26 *Gaza*** An ancient city (perhaps two thousand years old when *Acts* was written) near the coast, on the main north-south route from Asia and Syria to Africa.

27So he got up and went. Now there was an Ethiopian eunuch, a court official of the Candace, queen of the Ethiopians, in charge of her entire treasury. He had come to Jerusalem to worship 28and was returning home; seated in his chariot, he was reading the prophet Isaiah. 29Then the Spirit said to Philip, "Go over to this chariot and join it." 30So Philip ran up to it and heard him reading the prophet Isaiah. He asked, "Do you understand what you are reading?" 31He replied, "How can I, unless someone guides me?" And he invited Philip to get in and sit beside him. 32Now the passage of the scripture that he was reading was this:

"Like a sheep he was led to the slaughter,
    and like a lamb silent before its shearer,
      so he does not open his mouth.
33 In his humiliation justice was denied him.
    Who can describe his generation?
      For his life is taken away from the earth."

34The eunuch asked Philip, "About whom, may I ask you, does the prophet say this, about himself or about someone else?" 35Then Philip began to speak, and starting with this scripture, he proclaimed to him the good news about Jesus. 36As they were going along the road, they came to some water; and the eunuch said, "Look, here is water! What is to prevent me from being baptized?"*o* 38He commanded the chariot to stop, and both of them, Philip and the eunuch, went down into the water, and Philip*p* baptized him. 39When they came up out of the water, the Spirit of the Lord snatched Philip away; the eunuch saw him no more, and went on his way rejoicing. 40But Philip found himself at Azotus, and as he was passing through the region, he proclaimed the good news to all the towns until he came to Caesarea.

The Conversion of Saul

9 Meanwhile Saul, still breathing threats and murder against the disciples of the Lord, went to the high priest 2and asked him for letters to the synagogues at Damascus, so that if he found any who belonged to the Way, men or women, he might bring them bound to Jerusalem. 3Now as he was going along and approaching Damascus, suddenly a light from heaven flashed around him. 4He fell to the ground and heard a voice saying to him, "Saul, Saul,

---

o Other ancient authorities add all or most of verse 37, *And Philip said, "If you believe with all your heart, you may." And he replied, "I believe that Jesus Christ is the Son of God."*
p Gk *he*

Since the time of Alexander the Great, it had been a Greek city *(polis),* and it retained a good deal of internal political freedom even while it passed under Hasmonean, Herodian, and finally Roman control. **8:27** The Ethiopians, biblical "Cushites" located south of Egypt in what is now both Sudan and Ethiopia, were greatly respected in Greco-Roman literature as a handsome and brave people (see Herodotus, *History* 3.17–20; Josephus, *Ant.* 2.239–253). The queen of the kingdom of Meroë in this region held the title "Candace." Eunuchs were widely used for trusted positions. Ethiopians had been coming to Jerusalem for hundreds of years, for commercial and political reasons. They would be permitted to worship in the outer ("Gentile") court of the temple only. **8:32–33** *Isa.* 53:7–8. The LXX reads almost exactly as *Acts.* The MT is very similar, but it has "he was cut off from the land of the living" in the last quoted line. The LXX reading of this line—"his life is taken away [or 'up'] from the earth"—supports the narrative of *Acts* because it could be understood as a reference to Jesus' ascension (*Acts* 1:9 has a compound of the same verb). *Isaiah* 53, with its extended poem about humiliation, suffering, and vindication, was one of the most favored scriptural passages among early Christians because of the ease with which it could be applied to Jesus (see *Rom.* 10:16; *Matt.* 8:17; *Luke* 22:37; *John* 12:38; *1 Pet.* 2:22). Its original sense (in the context of *Isaiah* 44–66) concerned Israel, God's Suffering Servant. **8:39** *the Spirit of the Lord snatched Philip away* This story of spiritual transportation of a waking mortal is unparalleled in the early Christian texts. **8:40** *Azotus* Ancient Ashdod of the Philistines: a city near the Mediterranean coast, about twenty-two miles north of Gaza. It had a largely non-Jewish population although it had been under Jewish control (including Herod's kingdom), except for a few years, since the Hasmonean conquests. *Caesarea* About fifty-five miles north of Azotus, this port city was a showpiece of King Herod the Great (ruled 37–4 B.C.E.); he had entirely rebuilt it on the site of Strato's Tower. Since the annexation of Judea in 6 C.E., it headquartered the Roman governor and his cohort. **9:1–22** The story of Saul's conversion is very important to the author; he will retell the story at length in 22:3–16 and 26:9–21. It embodies the major theme of *Luke-Acts,* that acceptance of Jesus (together with the eventual mission to the Gentiles) was not a matter of whim or human fancy but an absolute, unavoidable necessity in obedience to God's irresistible revelation. **9:1** *still breathing threats and murder* See 8:3. *the high priest* This should be Caiaphas, but see notes to 4:6 and *Luke* 3:2. **9:2** *the synagogues at Damascus* Damascus lay in the Roman province of Syria, but through much of Paul's career, it was apparently administered by the neighboring Nabateans, based in Petra, east of the Jordan. It had a large Jewish community, perhaps numbering in the tens of thousands. The formal basis of the high priest's authority—especially the authority to extradite Christians to Jerusalem—is not clear. Nor is it clear why Saul should target Damascus, so far from Jerusalem, as a Christian center; the reader must assume that it had become a haven for Christian refugees from Jerusalem. Interestingly, one of the Dead Sea Scrolls describes the removal of another Jewish group to Damascus (CD 6.5–6). *any who belonged to the Way* Or "Path," "Road." It was common in popular philosophical circles to speak of a chosen life as a (or the) path or way. See Lucian, *Menippus* 4; Plutarch, *Superstition* 171E; see *Did.* 1.1ff. This is the author's characteristic designation of "Christians"—a title he claims was first used for them at Antioch (11:26).

why do you persecute me?" [5]He asked, "Who are you, Lord?" The reply came, "I am Jesus, whom you are persecuting. [6]But get up and enter the city, and you will be told what you are to do." [7]The men who were traveling with him stood speechless because they heard the voice but saw no one. [8]Saul got up from the ground, and though his eyes were open, he could see nothing; so they led him by the hand and brought him into Damascus. [9]For three days he was without sight, and neither ate nor drank.

[10]Now there was a disciple in Damascus named Ananias. The Lord said to him in a vision, "Ananias." He answered, "Here I am, Lord." [11]The Lord said to him, "Get up and go to the street called Straight, and at the house of Judas look for a man of Tarsus named Saul. At this moment he is praying, [12]and he has seen in a vision[q] a man named Ananias come in and lay his hands on him so that he might regain his sight." [13]But Ananias answered, "Lord, I have heard from many about this man, how much evil he has done to your saints in Jerusalem; [14]and here he has authority from the chief priests to bind all who invoke your name." [15]But the Lord said to him, "Go, for he is an instrument whom I have chosen to bring my name before Gentiles and kings and before the people of Israel; [16]I myself will show him how much he must suffer for the sake of my name." [17]So Ananias went and entered the house. He laid his hands on Saul[r] and said, "Brother Saul, the Lord Jesus, who ap-

peared to you on your way here, has sent me so that you may regain your sight and be filled with the Holy Spirit." [18]And immediately something like scales fell from his eyes, and his sight was restored. Then he got up and was baptized, [19]and after taking some food, he regained his strength.

Saul Preaches in Damascus

For several days he was with the disciples in Damascus, [20]and immediately he began to proclaim Jesus in the synagogues, saying, "He is the Son of God." [21]All who heard him were amazed and said, "Is not this the man who made havoc in Jerusalem among those who invoked this name? And has he not come here for the purpose of bringing them bound before the chief priests?" [22]Saul became increasingly more powerful and confounded the Jews who lived in Damascus by proving that Jesus[s] was the Messiah.[t]

Saul Escapes from the Jews

[23]After some time had passed, the Jews plotted to kill him, [24]but their plot became known to Saul. They were watching the gates day and night so that they might kill him; [25]but his disciples took him by night and let him down through an opening in the wall,[u] lowering him in a basket.

---

q Other ancient authorities lack *in a vision*
r Gk *him*

s Gk *that this*
t Or *the Christ*
u Gk *through the wall*

9:7 According to 22:9, those who were with Saul saw the light but heard nothing. **9:10** *Ananias* The common Hebrew name Hananiah. This person is unknown outside this story. **9:11** *the street called Straight* In this period, Damascus was built on a typical Roman grid pattern. Excavations of Damascus have revealed a main fifty-foot-wide colonnaded street running east-west; this may well be the street in question. *a man of Tarsus named Saul* The first indication that Saul was from the capital of the Roman province of Cilicia—a fact that will become important later (21:39). An extremely old city already in Paul's day (founded well before 2000 B.C.E.), Tarsus was a major center of trade, culture, and study (Strabo, *Geography* 14.5.131). Paul does not mention Tarsus in his letters. **9:15** *before Gentiles and kings* This prepares for the coming story of Paul's career, which will take him to the Gentiles (*Acts* 13 onward) and then before both King Agrippa II (25:23–26:32) and the Emperor Nero (25:11–12; chs. 27–28), who amounted to a king though was not considered so in Roman political theory. Curiously, the gospels claim that Jesus made the same prediction concerning his original students; *Mark* 13:9; *Matt.* 10:18. **9:22–24** Whereas the author has so far distinguished among various groups of Jewish leaders and between the leaders and the people, he will now speak much more routinely of "the Jews" as a body. In the story, this new language seems to stem from the trial of Stephen and the ensuing persecution, in which Jewish opposition was consolidated. Since some Jews will continue to accept Christian claims (17:4, 11–12; 18:8), the writer seems to mean only that the main period of Jewish conversion is over, so that from now on "the Jews" as a category represent hardened opposition. In the remainder of the story, as here, they characteristically plot to kill Christians as only the temple leaders had done before (12:1–3; 13:45, 50; 14:2, 5; 17:5–8; 18:17; 20:3; 21:31; 23:12), because they are too stubborn (the writer says) to accept the truth (19:9; 28:26–28). Nonetheless, Paul routinely visits the synagogue in his travels (13:14; 14:1; 17:2). **9:23** *After some time* Lit. "after sufficient days." The amount of time in view is not clear, but it seems not to fit Paul's own claim that he first visited Jerusalem three years after his conversion (*Gal.* 1:18), after a sojourn in Arabia that is not mentioned by *Acts*. **9:25** This episode provides one of the few clear parallels between *Acts'* account of Paul's life and his own letters: in *2 Cor.* 11:32–33, Paul notes that he fled Damascus, then controlled by the Nabatean king Aretas IV (died 39 C.E.), in a basket lowered down the wall.

Saul in Jerusalem

26When he had come to Jerusalem, he attempted to join the disciples; and they were all afraid of him, for they did not believe that he was a disciple. 27But Barnabas took him, brought him to the apostles, and described for them how on the road he had seen the Lord, who had spoken to him, and how in Damascus he had spoken boldly in the name of Jesus. 28So he went in and out among them in Jerusalem, speaking boldly in the name of the Lord. 29He spoke and argued with the Hellenists; but they were attempting to kill him. 30When the believers*v* learned of it, they brought him down to Caesarea and sent him off to Tarsus.

31Meanwhile the church throughout Judea, Galilee, and Samaria had peace and was built up. Living in the fear of the Lord and in the comfort of the Holy Spirit, it increased in numbers.

The Healing of Aeneas

32Now as Peter went here and there among all the believers,*w* he came down also to the saints living in Lydda. 33There he found a man named Aeneas, who had been bedridden for eight years, for he was paralyzed. 34Peter said to him, "Aeneas, Jesus Christ heals you; get up and make your bed!" And immediately he got up. 35And all the residents of Lydda and Sharon saw him and turned to the Lord.

Peter in Lydda and Joppa

36Now in Joppa there was a disciple whose name was Tabitha, which in Greek is Dorcas.*x* She was devoted to good works and acts of charity. 37At that time she became ill and died. When they had washed her, they laid her in a room upstairs. 38Since Lydda was near Joppa, the disciples, who heard that Peter was there, sent two men to him with the request, "Please come to us without delay." 39So Peter got up and went with them; and when he arrived, they took him to the room upstairs. All the widows stood beside him, weeping and showing tunics and other clothing that Dorcas had made while she was with them. 40Peter put all of them outside, and then he knelt down and prayed. He turned to the body and said, "Tabitha, get up." Then she opened her eyes, and seeing Peter, she sat up. 41He gave her his hand and helped her up. Then calling the saints and widows, he showed her to be alive. 42This became known throughout Joppa, and many believed in the Lord. 43Meanwhile he stayed in Joppa for some time with a certain Simon, a tanner.

Peter and Cornelius

10 In Caesarea there was a man named Cornelius, a centurion of the Italian Cohort, as it was called. 2He was a devout man who feared God with all his household; he gave alms generously to the people

---

v Gk *brothers*
w Gk *all of them*

x The name Tabitha in Aramaic and the name Dorcas in Greek mean *a gazelle*

9:27 The actions of Barnabas, who was introduced in 4:36, exemplify well the operation of social networks in the ancient Mediterranean: one usually needed an intermediary to facilitate a new contact; see Josephus, *Life* 16. **9:28** Paul claims, however, that his 1st visit to Jerusalem, three years after his conversion, was private; he insists that he went to see Peter only, although he also met Jesus' brother James (*Gal.* 1:18–19). **9:29** *the Hellenists* Presumably not the Christian Hellenists of 6:1 but other Gk-speaking Jews such as those who accused Stephen (6:9), but they were attempting to kill him. **9:30** *to Tarsus* Paul's home; see note to 9:11. **9:32** *Lydda* Hebrew name Lod, a small town situated on the coastal plain about ten miles from the Mediterranean, twenty-three miles west-northwest of Jerusalem. **9:33** *Aeneas* The name was famous in the 1st century from the heroic character of the Roman poet Virgil's *Aeneid*. **9:35** *Sharon* The plain on which Lydda was situated, the *shfela*. **9:36** *Joppa* Hebrew name, Yafo (Jaffa), an old Mediterranean port town, a little more than ten miles from Lydda and about twenty-eight miles west-northwest of Jerusalem (continuing on the road through Lydda). *Tabitha . . . Dorcas* Both names mean "gazelle." This woman is otherwise unknown. **9:43** *Simon, a tanner* Tanning hides was a notoriously unpleasant and smelly trade. Tanneries had to be located outside Jerusalem proper, and Rabbi Meir would give permission to wives of tanners to divorce them if they could no longer bear the smell (*m. Ketubbot* 7:10). Peter's decision to stay with a tanner was perhaps itself a symbolic move away from mainstream Judaism. Simon himself does not figure in the story. **10:1** *Cornelius, a centurion of the Italian Cohort* There were two kinds of cohorts: those that made up the Roman legions (composed of citizens) and auxiliary cohorts (mainly staffed by men from the provinces). Since there were no legions in Caesarea, this would be an auxiliary cohort. These regiments of five hundred to one thousand men were typically commanded by Romans. There is inscriptional evidence of an Italian Cohort in Syria from the late 60s onward, but it is unclear whether the author is correct in placing it in Caesarea at this time. Cornelius is a Latin family *(gens)* name. **10:2** *feared God* Acts often mentions "God-fearers," apparently Gentile adherents to Judaism who had not actually converted to Judaism through circumcision (for males) and perhaps baptism; see also 13:50; 14:1; 16:1; 17:4; 18:7. Although later rabbinic law does not specially recognize this group, since they remained Gentiles, we have no reason to doubt that they existed. *Acts* is generally precise in its evocation of life situations in the Roman Empire, even if it errs in recovering particular events and dates. Furthermore, Greek and Roman texts make it clear that Judaism appealed to many Gentiles (Tacitus, *Histories* 5.5; Epictetus, *Discourses* 2.9.20; Juvenal, *Satires* 5.14.96–106). And finally, a much discussed inscription from the

and prayed constantly to God. [3]One afternoon at about three o'clock he had a vision in which he clearly saw an angel of God coming in and saying to him, "Cornelius." [4]He stared at him in terror and said, "What is it, Lord?" He answered, "Your prayers and your alms have ascended as a memorial before God. [5]Now send men to Joppa for a certain Simon who is called Peter; [6]he is lodging with Simon, a tanner, whose house is by the seaside." [7]When the angel who spoke to him had left, he called two of his slaves and a devout soldier from the ranks of those who served him, [8]and after telling them everything, he sent them to Joppa.

[9]About noon the next day, as they were on their journey and approaching the city, Peter went up on the roof to pray. [10]He became hungry and wanted something to eat; and while it was being prepared, he fell into a trance. [11]He saw the heaven opened and something like a large sheet coming down, being lowered to the ground by its four corners. [12]In it were all kinds of four-footed creatures and reptiles and birds of the air. [13]Then he heard a voice saying, "Get up, Peter; kill and eat." [14]But Peter said, "By no means, Lord; for I have never eaten anything that is profane or unclean." [15]The voice said to him again, a second time, "What God has made clean, you must not call profane." [16]This happened three times, and the thing was suddenly taken up to heaven.

[17]Now while Peter was greatly puzzled about what to make of the vision that he had seen, suddenly the men sent by Cornelius appeared. They were asking for Simon's house and were standing by the gate. [18]They called out to ask whether Simon, who was called Peter, was staying there. [19]While Peter was still thinking about the vision, the Spirit said to him, "Look, three[y] men are searching for you. [20]Now get up, go down, and go with them without hesitation; for I have sent them." [21]So Peter went down to the men and said, "I am the one you are looking for; what is the reason for your coming?" [22]They answered, "Cornelius, a centurion, an upright and God-fearing man, who is well spoken of by the whole Jewish nation, was directed by a holy angel to send for you to come to his house and to hear what you have to say." [23]So Peter[z] invited them in and gave them lodging.

The next day he got up and went with them, and some of the believers[a] from Joppa accompanied him. [24]The following day they came to Caesarea. Cornelius was expecting them and had called together his relatives and close friends. [25]On Peter's arrival Cornelius met him, and falling at his feet, worshiped him. [26]But Peter made him get up, saying, "Stand up; I am only a mortal." [27]And as he talked with him, he went in and found that many had assembled; [28]and he said to them, "You yourselves know that it is unlawful for a Jew to associate with or to visit a Gentile; but God has shown me that I should not call anyone profane or unclean. [29]So when I was sent for, I came without objection. Now may I ask why you sent for me?"

[30]Cornelius replied, "Four days ago at this very hour, at three o'clock, I was praying in my house when suddenly a man in dazzling clothes stood before me. [31]He said, 'Cornelius, your prayer has been heard and your alms have been remembered before God. [32]Send therefore to Joppa and ask for Simon, who is called Peter; he is staying in the home of Simon, a tanner, by the sea.' [33]Therefore I sent for you immediately, and you have been kind enough to come. So now all of us are here in the presence of God to listen to all that the Lord has commanded you to say."

---

y One ancient authority reads *two*; others lack the word

z Gk *he*
a Gk *brothers*

synagogue in Aphrodisias, in Asia Minor (modern Turkey), appears to use the title "God-fearer" of people who were neither converts ("proselytes") nor native Jews. This story of the God-fearing centurion recalls *Luke* 7:1–10; it supports the author's continuing emphasis on the good relationship between Christianity and Roman officials of all ranks. **10:12–15** The Torah sets out dietary restrictions for Israel, which are summarized in *Deut.* 14:3–21. In Peter's vision, God definitively abrogates the dietary laws in order to free Peter to associate with Gentiles (see 11:3). Nevertheless, the author will continue to assert that Jews who became Christians remained fully observant of the Torah (21:20). Peter's extreme reluctance to countenance forbidden food conflicts with *Mark*'s claim (*Mark* 7:19) that Jesus had already abolished the dietary laws. No doubt this is one issue about which the author wishes to set the record straight by putting developments in their proper order (*Luke* 1:3). Peter's reluctance in this scene reinforces the theme of *Luke-Acts* that Jesus' students moved away from more mainstream Jewish practices only when God compelled them to do so. **10:22 *God-fearing man, who is well spoken of by the whole Jewish nation*** See the close parallel in *Luke* 7:5. Like the Ethiopian eunuch in 8:27, this early Gentile convert is well disposed to the Jewish nation. **10:25–26** Similarly in 14:11, Paul and Barnabas are worshiped as gods; their response is the same. These two episodes contrast with that of the Jewish king Agrippa, who was killed by God because he failed to correct those who worshiped him (12:22–23). **10:28 *it is unlawful for a Jew to associate with or to visit a Gentile*** A considerable exaggeration, especially as the Torah itself is concerned. Torah forbids only the consumption of "unclean" food routinely eaten by Gentiles (*Deuteronomy* 14). For the sake of their communal life, however, Jews tended to live in close colonies throughout the empire, and their refusal to participate in the routines of pagan life led to the perception that they were antisocial. The author may be playing up this perception here, to create a contrast with the newly outward-looking Christians.

Gentiles Hear the Good News

³⁴Then Peter began to speak to them: "I truly understand that God shows no partiality, ³⁵but in every nation anyone who fears him and does what is right is acceptable to him. ³⁶You know the message he sent to the people of Israel, preaching peace by Jesus Christ—he is Lord of all. ³⁷That message spread throughout Judea, beginning in Galilee after the baptism that John announced: ³⁸how God anointed Jesus of Nazareth with the Holy Spirit and with power; how he went about doing good and healing all who were oppressed by the devil, for God was with him. ³⁹We are witnesses to all that he did both in Judea and in Jerusalem. They put him to death by hanging him on a tree; ⁴⁰but God raised him on the third day and allowed him to appear, ⁴¹not to all the people but to us who were chosen by God as witnesses, and who ate and drank with him after he rose from the dead. ⁴²He commanded us to preach to the people and to testify that he is the one ordained by God as judge of the living and the dead. ⁴³All the prophets testify about him that everyone who believes in him receives forgiveness of sins through his name."

Gentiles Receive the Holy Spirit

⁴⁴While Peter was still speaking, the Holy Spirit fell upon all who heard the word. ⁴⁵The circumcised believers who had come with Peter were astounded that the gift of the Holy Spirit had been poured out even on the Gentiles, ⁴⁶for they heard them speaking in tongues and extolling God. Then Peter said, ⁴⁷"Can anyone withhold the water for baptizing these people who have received the Holy Spirit just as we have?" ⁴⁸So he ordered them to be baptized in the name of Jesus Christ. Then they invited him to stay for several days.

Peter's Report to the Church at Jerusalem

11 Now the apostles and the believers[b] who were in Judea heard that the Gentiles had also accepted the word of God. ²So when Peter went up to Jerusalem, the circumcised believers[c] criticized him, ³saying, "Why did you go to uncircumcised men and eat with them?" ⁴Then Peter began to explain it to them, step by step, saying, ⁵"I was in the city of Joppa praying, and in a trance I saw a vision. There was something like a large sheet coming down from heaven, being lowered by its four corners; and it came close to me. ⁶As I looked at it closely I saw four-footed animals, beasts of prey, reptiles, and birds of the air. ⁷I also heard a voice saying to me, 'Get up, Peter; kill and eat.' ⁸But I replied, 'By no means, Lord; for nothing profane or unclean has ever entered my mouth.' ⁹But a second time the voice answered from heaven, 'What God has made clean, you must not call profane.' ¹⁰This happened three times; then everything was pulled up again to heaven. ¹¹At that very moment three men, sent to me from Caesarea, arrived at the house where we were. ¹²The Spirit told me to go with them and not to make a distinction between them and us.[d] These six brothers also accompanied me, and we entered the man's house. ¹³He told us how he had seen the angel standing in his house and saying, 'Send to Joppa and bring Simon, who is called Peter; ¹⁴he will give you a message by which you and your entire household will be saved.' ¹⁵And as I began to speak, the Holy Spirit fell upon them just as it had upon us at the beginning. ¹⁶And I remembered the word of the Lord, how he had said, 'John baptized with water, but you will be baptized with the Holy

---

b Gk *brothers*
c Gk lacks *believers*
d Or *not to hesitate*

10:34 *God shows no partiality* This is, in fact, a standard position of the later rabbis: Gentiles who observe the basic commandments given to Noah (*Gen.* 9:1–7, but usually elaborated to seven: pursue justice, avoid blasphemy, idolatry, adultery, shedding blood, robbery, and eating blood or flesh cut from a living animal [*b. San.* 56a]) will find salvation. Philo and Josephus, the major Jewish writers of the 1st century, and many of their contemporaries also respected Gentiles who faithfully followed their own traditions. **10:38** Jesus appears again as a man chosen by God. See note to 2:22–36. **10:39** *hanging him on a tree* Jesus' death is again portrayed as if it had been a lynching by the Jews; no mention is made of the Roman trial or Roman cross. See 2:23; 3:13–15; 4:10; 5:30. **10:41** We see again the apostles' crucial role as witnesses to the resurrected body of Jesus; see also 1:2–3, 22; 2:32; 3:15; 5:32. **10:46** *for they heard them speaking in tongues* Thus their reception of the Spirit compares to that of the apostles themselves (2:4); there can be no question of an inferior gift, and so God evidently admits Gentiles to the community on the same basis as Jews. **11:2** *circumcised believers criticized him* That is, Jewish followers of Jesus, who until now (as far as the reader knows, but note the Ethiopian eunuch in 8:26–40) have constituted the church. Although *Acts* will claim that this conflict was quickly resolved and harmony restored (11:18), the same tension between observant Jewish Christians and those who take Jesus' message to Gentiles appears at several points in the subsequent narrative (15:1; 21:20–26). We know from other sources (*Philippians* 3; *2 Corinthians* 3; 10–13; *Galatians; Romans*) that the relationship between Gentile Christianity and Judaism was a major problem in the development of the young church. **11:3** *you go to uncircumcised men and eat with them* See note to 10:28. **11:16** Peter recalls 1:5, which was first fulfilled in 2:24. The author thus stresses the parallel between the Gentiles' reception of the Spirit and that of the apostles. This is incontrovertible proof that God has accepted the Gentiles (11:17).

Spirit.' [17]If then God gave them the same gift that he gave us when we believed in the Lord Jesus Christ, who was I that I could hinder God?" [18]When they heard this, they were silenced. And they praised God, saying, "Then God has given even to the Gentiles the repentance that leads to life."

The Church in Antioch

[19]Now those who were scattered because of the persecution that took place over Stephen traveled as far as Phoenicia, Cyprus, and Antioch, and they spoke the word to no one except Jews. [20]But among them were some men of Cyprus and Cyrene who, on coming to Antioch, spoke to the Hellenists[e] also, proclaiming the Lord Jesus. [21]The hand of the Lord was with them, and a great number became believers and turned to the Lord. [22]News of this came to the ears of the church in Jerusalem, and they sent Barnabas to Antioch. [23]When he came and saw the grace of God, he rejoiced, and he exhorted them all to remain faithful to the Lord with steadfast devotion; [24]for he was a good man, full of the Holy Spirit and of faith. And a great many people were brought to the Lord.

[25]Then Barnabas went to Tarsus to look for Saul, [26]and when he had found him, he brought him to Antioch. So it was that for an entire year they met with[f] the church and taught a great many people, and it was in Antioch that the disciples were first called "Christians."

[27]At that time prophets came down from Jerusalem to Antioch. [28]One of them named Agabus stood up and predicted by the Spirit that there would be a severe famine over all the world; and this took place during the reign of Claudius. [29]The disciples determined that according to their ability, each would send relief to the believers[g] living in Judea; [30]this they did, sending it to the elders by Barnabas and Saul.

James Killed and Peter Imprisoned

12 About that time King Herod laid violent hands upon some who belonged to the church. [2]He had James, the brother of John, killed with the sword. [3]After he saw that it pleased the Jews, he proceeded to arrest Peter also. (This was during the festival of Unleavened Bread.) [4]When he had seized him, he put him in prison and handed him over to four squads of soldiers to

---

e Other ancient authorities read *Greeks*

f Or *were guests of*
g Gk *brothers*

11:19 *those who were scattered because of the persecution that took place over Stephen* See 8:1, which first describes this persecution (from the Christian perspective). *Phoenicia, Cyprus, and Antioch* Phoenicia was the coastal region north of Judea, centered in ancient Tyre and Sidon. Although *Mark* 7:24 reported that Jesus journeyed there, the author of *Luke-Acts* postpones that mission for the Christians. Cyprus was the well-known island off the coast of Phoenicia. Antioch was a large city on the Orontes River, second or third in size to Rome (along with Alexandria), founded by the Seleucid kings nearly four centuries earlier. Now the capital of the Roman province of Syria, it oversaw the small province of Judea to its south. Cyprus and Antioch figure significantly in the subsequent narrative. *they spoke the word to no one except Jews* See the agreement that Paul mentions in *Gal.* 2:9. **11:20** *the Hellenists also* In context, this word must mean Gk-speaking Gentiles although earlier it meant Gk-speaking Jewish Christians (6:1) or Gk-speaking Jews (9:29). **11:22** Another example of the Jerusalem church's central administration of the entire church through the apostles; see note to 8:1. **11:25** Saul had departed for Tarsus in 9:30. **11:26** *first called "Christians."* The writer implies that the term was given by outsiders, as such names often are. His own preferred term is "followers of the Path (or 'Way')": see note to 9:2. **11:27** *came down from Jerusalem to Antioch* See note to 8:5. **11:28** *Agabus* This prophet reappears later in the text, when he warns Paul in Caesarea that imprisonment awaits him in Jerusalem (21:10–11). *during the reign of Claudius* Roman emperor 41–54 C.E. This reference indicates, perhaps surprisingly to the reader, that at least ten years have elapsed since the beginning of the story, for Jesus' death should be dated near 30 C.E. Judea was susceptible to famine, and Josephus reports a drought there between 45 and 48 (*Ant.* 20.51–53); it may also have affected Egypt, in the light of some papyri from there. **11:30** Thus Saul's second visit to Jerusalem was to bring famine relief, accompanying Barnabas. Paul claims, however, that his 2d visit to Jerusalem came seventeen years after his conversion, after he had been preaching to the Gentiles for many years, that it was motivated by a personal revelation from God (not the decision of the church at Antioch), and that he went in order to settle the issue of his mission to the Gentiles (*Gal.* 2:1–10). **12:1** *King Herod* King Agrippa I, 1st appointed king by his boyhood friend the emperor Gaius Caligula (37 C.E.) over the territory formerly governed by Philip the tetrarch (the Golan, Trachonitis, and Batanaea). His kingdom was extended by the Emperor Claudius to include all the territories that had belonged to his grandfather Herod the Great. His brief reign over this larger area (41–44 C.E.) created a hiatus in the direct Roman rule of Judea through prefects and procurators. **12:2** *James, the brother of John* These two brothers, the sons of Zebedee, were among the 1st students of Jesus (*Luke* 5:10). They appear to have had a certain eminence among the apostles (*Luke* 8:51; 9:28); presumably, this eminence in the young church has exposed them to risk in Jerusalem. **12:3** *it pleased the Jews* The author continues to harden his portrait of the Jews as a single group; see note to 9:22–24. *festival of Unleavened Bread* Or Passover, as the next verse makes clear. This is the annual festival mandated in the Torah (*Exod.* 12:37–43; 13:3–10) to celebrate Israel's deliverance from slavery in Egypt. It occurs in March or April.

guard him, intending to bring him out to the people after the Passover. [5]While Peter was kept in prison, the church prayed fervently to God for him.

Peter Delivered from Prison

[6]The very night before Herod was going to bring him out, Peter, bound with two chains, was sleeping between two soldiers, while guards in front of the door were keeping watch over the prison. [7]Suddenly an angel of the Lord appeared and a light shone in the cell. He tapped Peter on the side and woke him, saying, "Get up quickly." And the chains fell off his wrists. [8]The angel said to him, "Fasten your belt and put on your sandals." He did so. Then he said to him, "Wrap your cloak around you and follow me." [9]Peter[h] went out and followed him; he did not realize that what was happening with the angel's help was real; he thought he was seeing a vision. [10]After they had passed the first and the second guard, they came before the iron gate leading into the city. It opened for them of its own accord, and they went outside and walked along a lane, when suddenly the angel left him. [11]Then Peter came to himself and said, "Now I am sure that the Lord has sent his angel and rescued me from the hands of Herod and from all that the Jewish people were expecting."

[12]As soon as he realized this, he went to the house of Mary, the mother of John whose other name was Mark, where many had gathered and were praying. [13]When he knocked at the outer gate, a maid named Rhoda came to answer. [14]On recognizing Peter's voice, she was so overjoyed that, instead of opening the gate, she ran in and announced that Peter was standing at the gate. [15]They said to her, "You are out of your mind!" But she insisted that it was so. They said, "It is his angel." [16]Meanwhile Peter continued knocking; and when they opened the gate, they saw him and were amazed. [17]He motioned to them with his hand to be silent, and described for them how the Lord had brought him out of the prison. And he added, "Tell this to James and to the believers."[i] Then he left and went to another place.

[18]When morning came, there was no small commotion among the soldiers over what had become of Peter. [19]When Herod had searched for him and could not find him, he examined the guards and ordered them to be put to death. Then Peter[j] went down from Judea to Caesarea and stayed there.

The Death of Herod

[20]Now Herod was angry with the people of Tyre and Sidon. So they came to him in a body; and after winning over Blastus, the king's chamberlain, they asked for a reconciliation, because their country depended on the king's country for food. [21]On an appointed day Herod put on his royal robes, took his seat on the platform, and delivered a public address to them. [22]The people kept shouting, "The voice of a god, and not of a mortal!" [23]And immediately, because he had not given the glory to God, an angel of the Lord struck him down, and he was eaten by worms and died.

[24]But the word of God continued to advance and gain adherents. [25]Then after completing their mission

---

h Gk *He*

i Gk *brothers*
j Gk *he*

12:11 *all that the Jewish people were expecting* The Jewish people now represents a wall of opposition. See note to 9:22–24. **12:12** *Mary, the mother of John whose other name was Mark* Mary was an extremely common name in Jewish circles at the time. In keeping with the author's practice, he introduces John Mark here incidentally, before he plays his significant role in the story (12:25; 13:5, 13; 15:37–38). **12:13** *the outer gate* Mediterranean houses were typically built around central courtyards. Poorer families—the vast majority of the populace—had only one apartment in this complex, and the outer gate was shared by all. **12:17** *Tell this to James* Since Jesus' student James has already been killed (12:2), this is presumably Jesus' brother, whom Paul describes as one of the three "pillars" of the Jerusalem church (*Gal.* 1:19; 2:9, 12). His rise to a leading position in the church (see also 15:13, 19; 21:17) is not documented. See note to 1:14. This first, incidental reference to James is characteristic of the author inasmuch as it prepares the reader for James's later appearances. **12:19** *went down from Judea to Caesarea* Caesarea had been, and would be again, the headquarters for the Roman governors of Judea. Although Agrippa seems to have resided mainly in Jerusalem (Josephus, *Ant.* 19.331), Caesarea demanded his regular attention. **12:20–24** The story of Agrippa's death resembles in some respects the story told by Josephus, *Ant.* 19.343–352. In both, the king dies in Caesarea after being hailed as a god. But Josephus claims that this happened during games that the king had arranged in honor of the emperor. Josephus nowhere mentions Blastus, and the claims in *Acts* about the dependence of the people of Tyre and Sidon upon the king is puzzling, since they lived in the powerful Roman province of Syria. **12:21** *put on his royal robes* According to Josephus (see previous note), Agrippa's robe was woven entirely of silver thread, and it was the sun's reflection off this material at daybreak that created the impression of a god. **12:23** *because he had not given the glory to God* The author implicitly contrasts this Jewish king with Peter (10:25–26) and Paul (14:11), who were quick to reject worship. **12:24** The author characteristically contrasts the futile efforts of the ostensibly powerful with the success of the ostensibly powerless.

Barnabas and Saul returned to[k] Jerusalem and brought with them John, whose other name was Mark.

Barnabas and Saul Commissioned

13 Now in the church at Antioch there were prophets and teachers: Barnabas, Simeon who was called Niger, Lucius of Cyrene, Manaen a member of the court of Herod the ruler,[l] and Saul. ²While they were worshiping the Lord and fasting, the Holy Spirit said, "Set apart for me Barnabas and Saul for the work to which I have called them." ³Then after fasting and praying they laid their hands on them and sent them off.

The Apostles Preach in Cyprus

⁴So, being sent out by the Holy Spirit, they went down to Seleucia; and from there they sailed to Cyprus. ⁵When they arrived at Salamis, they pro-claimed the word of God in the synagogues of the Jews. And they had John also to assist them. ⁶When they had gone through the whole island as far as Paphos, they met a certain magician, a Jewish false prophet, named Bar-Jesus. ⁷He was with the procon-sul, Sergius Paulus, an intelligent man, who sum-moned Barnabas and Saul and wanted to hear the word of God. ⁸But the magician Elymas (for that is the translation of his name) opposed them and tried to turn the proconsul away from the faith. ⁹But Saul, also known as Paul, filled with the Holy Spirit, looked intently at him ¹⁰and said, "You son of the devil, you enemy of all righteousness, full of all de-ceit and villainy, will you not stop making crooked the straight paths of the Lord? ¹¹And now listen— the hand of the Lord is against you, and you will be blind for a while, unable to see the sun." Immediately mist and darkness came over him, and he went about groping for someone to lead him by the hand. ¹²When the proconsul saw what had happened, he believed, for he was astonished at the teaching about the Lord.

---

k Other ancient authorities read *from*
l Gk *tetrarch*

12:25 *returned to Jerusalem* A puzzling statement, since 11:29 left Barnabas and Saul on a mission to Jerusalem; they should, then, be returning from (not to) Jerusalem now, to their base in Antioch. The next sentence will, indeed, locate them in Antioch, and they seem to have brought John Mark from (not to) Jerusalem. Although the best manuscripts have *to Jeru-salem*, others have "from Jerusalem" or "to Antioch," indicating that the Christian copyists had as much difficulty with this as modern readers. *brought with them John, whose other name was Mark* Since John's home has already been located in Jerusalem (12:12), this is further evidence that Barnabas and Saul are returning from Jerusalem to Antioch. **13:1** *in the church at Antioch* A strong indication that 12:25 should read "from Jerusalem" and/or "to Antioch." *Barnabas* First in-troduced as an honest man in 4:36, he was the one who introduced Saul to the Jerusalem apostles (9:27) and was then sent to lead the church at Antioch (11:22); for help with this task, he enlisted Saul (11:25). The two men have taken the famine relief to Jerusalem and returned to Antioch (11:30; 12:25). *Simeon who was called Niger* Simeon (Hebrew *Shim᷾on*) was an extremely common name; he does not appear elsewhere in the early Christian texts. *Lucius of Cyrene* Paul mentions a Lucius in *Rom.* 16:21. *Manaen a member of the court of Herod the ruler* The Hebrew name is Menachem. A courtier of Herod "the tetrarch," as the Gk says, therefore of Herod Antipas, tetrarch of Galilee and Perea during Jesus' lifetime. Since Antipas was removed in 39 C.E. but the story has already covered the reign of Agrippa I in 41–44 C.E., either the author has made another chronological error (see, e.g., notes to *Luke* 3:2; *Acts* 4:6; 5:37) or he means that Menachem was formerly in the tetrarch's court. Interestingly, *Luke-Acts* reveals much special information about Herod Antipas (see *Luke* 8:3; 23:6–12). **13:2–4** Not quite halfway through the book, this episode provides a major turning point. The remainder of the story will be devoted to the career of the missionary hero (but not apostle in the author's sense) Saul/Paul. The apostles more or less fade from the scene even though Paul's letters indicate that they, too, traveled around the eastern Mediterranean on missions (*1 Cor.* 9:5). **13:4** *Seleucia* The port near Antioch, at the mouth of the Orontes River, which empties into the Mediterranean. *Cyprus* This island province off the coast of Syria was reportedly the home of Barnabas (4:36). **13:5** *Salamis* A city on the east coast of the island of Cyprus, 130 miles by sea from Seleucia. *in the synagogues of the Jews* Even after the mission to the Gentiles has received a distinct divine mandate, according to this author, Barnabas and Saul reach out first and foremost to Jews. It is only when they are flatly rejected by the Jews that they will necessarily turn to Gentiles (13:46; 18:6). The author continues his argument, therefore, that the mission to Gentiles was not the result of human whim but rather was an unavoidable development created by God in spite of the intentions of the Jerusalem church. But according to Paul, he was called from the outset to preach to Gentiles, and he did so (*Gal.* 1:16; 2:2, 8–9). *John* Presumably, the John Mark of 12:25. **13:6** *Paphos* At the western extremity of Cyprus. *Bar-Jesus* Aramaic for "son of Jesus"—a common Jewish name. **13:7–8** The contrast here between the intelligent and just Roman governor and the corrupt Jew who intends to thwart Christianity (see 13:10) epitomizes these themes in *Luke-Acts*. **13:7** *the proconsul, Sergius Paulus* A high-ranking offi-cial, former consul in Rome, now governor of this senatorial province. Two or three inscriptions have been found in other places with names that approximate his, but no certain identification has yet been made. **13:8** *the magician Elymas (for that is the translation of his name)* Although this puzzling statement seems to say that Bar-Jesus means Elymas, this is not the case; it must mean, rather, that some Aramaic word represented by "Elymas" (not a Gk word but a transliteration) means "magician." **13:9** *Saul, also known as Paul* The 1st time that Paul is identified by his more famous Gk name. See note to 7:58. **13:11** *blind for a while* Blindness is undoubtedly symbolic of the person's spiritual state; see 9:8; 28:27.

Paul and Barnabas in Antioch of Pisidia

13Then Paul and his companions set sail from Paphos and came to Perga in Pamphylia. John, however, left them and returned to Jerusalem; 14but they went on from Perga and came to Antioch in Pisidia. And on the sabbath day they went into the synagogue and sat down. 15After the reading of the law and the prophets, the officials of the synagogue sent them a message, saying, "Brothers, if you have any word of exhortation for the people, give it." 16So Paul stood up and with a gesture began to speak:

"You Israelites,*m* and others who fear God, listen. 17The God of this people Israel chose our ancestors and made the people great during their stay in the land of Egypt, and with uplifted arm he led them out of it. 18For about forty years he put up with*n* them in the wilderness. 19After he had destroyed seven nations in the land of Canaan, he gave them their land as an inheritance 20for about four hundred fifty years. After that he gave them judges until the time of the prophet Samuel. 21Then they asked for a king; and God gave them Saul son of Kish, a man of the tribe of Benjamin, who reigned for forty years. 22When he had removed him, he made David their king. In his testimony about him he said, 'I have found David, son of Jesse, to be a man after my heart, who will carry out all my wishes.' 23Of this man's posterity God has brought to Israel a Savior, Jesus, as

he promised; 24before his coming John had already proclaimed a baptism of repentance to all the people of Israel. 25And as John was finishing his work, he said, 'What do you suppose that I am? I am not he. No, but one is coming after me; I am not worthy to untie the thong of the sandals*o* on his feet.'

26"My brothers, you descendants of Abraham's family, and others who fear God, to us*p* the message of this salvation has been sent. 27Because the residents of Jerusalem and their leaders did not recognize him or understand the words of the prophets that are read every sabbath, they fulfilled those words by condemning him. 28Even though they found no cause for a sentence of death, they asked Pilate to have him killed. 29When they had carried out everything that was written about him, they took him down from the tree and laid him in a tomb. 30But God raised him from the dead; 31and for many days he appeared to those who came up with him from Galilee to Jerusalem, and they are now his witnesses to the people. 32And we bring you the good news that what God promised to our ancestors 33he has fulfilled for us, their children, by raising Jesus; as also it is written in the second psalm,

'You are my Son;
    today I have begotten you.'

34As to his raising him from the dead, no more to return to corruption, he has spoken in this way,

---

m Gk *Men, Israelites*
n Other ancient authorities read *cared for*

o Gk *untie the sandals*
p Other ancient authorities read *you*

13:13 *Perga in Pamphylia* The district of Pamphylia (a southern coastal section of Asia Minor [Turkey]) was first joined to each of the three major provinces around it—Cilicia, Asia, and Galatia—before Claudius joined it with neighboring Lycia to form a separate province in 43 C.E., the situation that obtains in our story time. Perga was a wealthy and beautiful city about seven miles inland from the Mediterranean. *John, however, left them and returned to Jerusalem* Speculation about John's reasons are as abundant as they are futile. His departure has further consequences in the story, however (15:37–38). **13:14** *Antioch in Pisidia* About eighty miles north of Perga. Pisidia was not a province but a mountainous district within southern Galatia. Antioch was actually in Phrygia, not Pisidia, at this time; the phrasing in some manuscripts suggests "Antioch facing Pisidia." *went into the synagogue* See note to 13:5. **13:16–41** Paul's speech in Pisidian Antioch seems to be intended by the author as a model of Paul's speeches to Jews because, although Paul will visit many more synagogues in the coming chapters, the author does not give such a detailed speech again. In both form (opening address, rehearsal of Israel's history, with Christian revelation included at the end) and specific mode of argument (choice of scriptures and lessons from them), Paul's speech closely resembles Peter's (*Acts* 2) and, to some extent, Stephen's (*Acts* 7). This reflects the author's literary creativity; these are not stenographic reports of real speeches. Still, the author makes some effort to suit the speech to the speaker—for example, here, in 13:39, with references to the characteristic Pauline language of faith and freedom from the law of Moses. **13:16** *You Israelites* See note to 1:16. Paul opens his speech as everyone else in *Acts* does. **13:17–22** Paul moves quickly from *Exodus* through *2 Samuel*. **13:22** *I have found David . . .* The author conflates *1 Sam.* 13:14; 16:1, 12–13. **13:25** The fact that this only loosely corresponds to what is reported in *Luke* 3:16 indicates that the author is not concerned with verbal accuracy. **13:26** *others who fear God* See note to 10:2. The group seems to have included both Jews and Gentile adherents, but see 13:43. **13:27** The ignorance of the Jewish leaders is a prominent theme in *Luke-Acts*. See note to 3:17. **13:28** On Jewish responsibility for Jesus' death in *Luke-Acts*, see note to 2:23. **13:29** *and laid him in a tomb* A curious note, since *Luke* 23:50 gave this role to Nicodemus, a "good and righteous" man. **13:31** *for many days he appeared* According to 1:3, forty days. *they are now his witnesses* See note to 1:22. **13:33** *in the second psalm* That is, *Ps.* 2:7, a favorite verse of the early Christians; see *Heb.* 1:5; 5:5. Although it originally spoke of the coronation of the Israelite king, it suited Christians who declared that Jesus had been made God's son through his resurrection. See notes to 2:36; *Rom.* 1:4. **13:34** *Isa.* 55:3. MT: "And I will make with you [repentant Israel] an everlasting covenant, / the enduring loyalty promised to David." LXX: "And I will make with you an age-long [or 'eternal'] covenant, the holy promises made to David."

'I will give you the holy promises made to David.'

[35]Therefore he has also said in another psalm,

'You will not let your Holy One experience corruption.'

[36]For David, after he had served the purpose of God in his own generation, died,[q] was laid beside his ancestors, and experienced corruption; [37]but he whom God raised up experienced no corruption. [38]Let it be known to you therefore, my brothers, that through this man forgiveness of sins is proclaimed to you; [39]by this Jesus[r] everyone who believes is set free from all those sins[s] from which you could not be freed by the law of Moses. [40]Beware, therefore, that what the prophets said does not happen to you:

[41] 'Look, you scoffers!

Be amazed and perish,

for in your days I am doing a work,

a work that you will never believe, even if someone tells you.'"

[42]As Paul and Barnabas[t] were going out, the people urged them to speak about these things again the next sabbath. [43]When the meeting of the synagogue broke up, many Jews and devout converts to Judaism followed Paul and Barnabas, who spoke to them and urged them to continue in the grace of God.

[44]The next sabbath almost the whole city gathered to hear the word of the Lord.[u] [45]But when the Jews saw the crowds, they were filled with jealousy; and blaspheming, they contradicted what was spoken by Paul. [46]Then both Paul and Barnabas spoke out boldly, saying, "It was necessary that the word of God should be spoken first to you. Since you reject it and judge yourselves to be unworthy of eternal life, we are now turning to the Gentiles. [47]For so the Lord has commanded us, saying,

'I have set you to be a light for the Gentiles,

so that you may bring salvation to the ends of the earth.'"

[48]When the Gentiles heard this, they were glad and praised the word of the Lord; and as many as had been destined for eternal life became believers. [49]Thus the word of the Lord spread throughout the region. [50]But the Jews incited the devout women of high standing and the leading men of the city, and stirred up persecution against Paul and Barnabas, and drove them out of their region. [51]So they shook the dust off their feet in protest against them, and went to Iconium. [52]And the disciples were filled with joy and with the Holy Spirit.

Paul and Barnabas in Iconium

14 The same thing occurred in Iconium, where Paul and Barnabas[v] went into the Jewish synagogue and spoke in such a way that a great number of both Jews and Greeks became believers. [2]But the unbelieving Jews stirred up the Gentiles and poisoned their minds against the brothers. [3]So they remained for a long time, speaking boldly for the Lord, who testified to the word of his grace by granting signs and wonders to be done through them. [4]But the residents of the city were divided; some sided with the Jews, and some with the

---

q Gk *fell asleep*
r Gk *this*
s Gk *all*
t Gk *they*
u Other ancient authorities read *God*

v Gk *they*

13:35–36 From *Ps.* 16:10 (LXX 15:10). See note to 2:25–28, where Peter cites the same passage and draws the same point from it. **13:38 forgiveness of sins** See note to 2:38. **13:39** One of the few places in which the author seems to capture Pauline-sounding language: faith leading to freedom from sin, and the ineffectiveness of the law of Moses (e.g., *Gal.* 2:21; 3:21). **13:41** *Hab.* 1:5. *Acts* reads very closely to the LXX. The MT begins instead, "Look among the nations." **13:43 many Jews and devout converts** How or whether the God-fearers of 13:26 fit into this description is unclear. **13:44** Neighboring Gentiles appear to have regularly visited synagogues. **13:45 filled with jealousy** This charge is perhaps the most frequent rhetorical accusation in antiquity against one's opponents: Success breeds jealousy. See also 17:5. **blaspheming** The word probably means here simply "speaking ill"—a common usage. **13:46–52** This sharp contrast between outspoken Jewish opposition and warm Gentile acceptance is characteristic of *Acts;* see 13:4–12; 18:6; 28:25–28. **13:47** *Isa.* 49:6. God speaks to Israel. **13:51 shook the dust off their feet** They thus comply with Jesus' instructions in *Luke* 9:5; 10:11. See also *Acts* 18:6. **13:52 to Iconium** Well over two thousand years old by Paul's time, this large and wealthy city in the Roman province of Galatia sat on a high plateau about eighty miles east of Pisidian Antioch. **14:1** See note to 13:5. **Greeks became believers** If the reader is to understand that these *Greeks* were in the synagogue, then they would be the God-fearers mentioned earlier (10:2; 13:26), that is, Gentile adherents of Judaism. **14:2** A characteristic scenario in *Acts;* see notes to 13:7–8, 46–52. **14:3 signs and wonders** See notes to 2:16–21, 22. **14:4** Although Barnabas and Paul are Jews, this sharp division reflects the author's developing perspective: "the Jews" have now become a solid wall of opposition to Christianity. **apostles** This title for Barnabas and Paul comes as a surprise in view of the author's deliberate efforts to specify who the apostles were, namely, men chosen from among Jesus' original students, who had also been present during his forty-day period of post-resurrection appearances (*Luke* 6:13–16; *Acts* 1:21–26). Paul and Barnabas are obviously not "apostles" in the proper sense of the word for this author. But "apostle" means literally "one who has been sent" or "missionary," and these

apostles. 5And when an attempt was made by both Gentiles and Jews, with their rulers, to mistreat them and to stone them, 6the apostles[w] learned of it and fled to Lystra and Derbe, cities of Lycaonia, and to the surrounding country; 7and there they continued proclaiming the good news.

Paul and Barnabas in Lystra and Derbe

8In Lystra there was a man sitting who could not use his feet and had never walked, for he had been crippled from birth. 9He listened to Paul as he was speaking. And Paul, looking at him intently and seeing that he had faith to be healed, 10said in a loud voice, "Stand upright on your feet." And the man[x] sprang up and began to walk. 11When the crowds saw what Paul had done, they shouted in the Lycaonian language, "The gods have come down to us in human form!" 12Barnabas they called Zeus, and Paul they called Hermes, because he was the chief speaker. 13The priest of Zeus, whose temple was just outside the city,[y] brought oxen and garlands to the gates; he and the crowds wanted to offer sacrifice. 14When the apostles Barnabas and Paul heard of it, they tore their clothes and rushed out into the crowd, shouting, 15"Friends,[z] why are you doing this? We are mortals just like you, and we bring you good news, that you should turn from these worthless things to the living God, who made the heaven and the earth and the sea and all that is in them. 16In past generations he allowed all the nations to follow their own ways; 17yet he has not left himself without a witness in doing good—giving you rains from heaven and fruitful seasons, and filling you with food and your hearts with joy." 18Even with these words, they scarcely restrained the crowds from offering sacrifice to them.

19But Jews came there from Antioch and Iconium and won over the crowds. Then they stoned Paul and dragged him out of the city, supposing that he was dead. 20But when the disciples surrounded him, he got up and went into the city. The next day he went on with Barnabas to Derbe.

The Return to Antioch in Syria

21After they had proclaimed the good news to that city and had made many disciples, they returned to Lystra, then on to Iconium and Antioch. 22There they strengthened the souls of the disciples and encouraged them to continue in the faith, saying, "It is through many persecutions that we must enter the kingdom of God." 23And after they had appointed elders for them in each church, with prayer and fasting they entrusted them to the Lord in whom they had come to believe.

24Then they passed through Pisidia and came to Pamphylia. 25When they had spoken the word in Perga, they went down to Attalia. 26From there they sailed back to Antioch, where they had been commended to the grace of God for the work[a] that they

---

w Gk *they*
x Gk *he*
y Or *The priest of Zeus-Outside-the-City*
z Gk *Men*

a Or *committed in the grace of God to the work*

---

men fit that description. That the author speaks of them as apostles only in this short passage (again in 14:14) may indicate that one of his other sources used "apostle" in this broader way. Or perhaps the author himself slipped into the looser usage. **14:6 *fled to Lystra and Derbe, cities of Lycaonia*** Moving south from Iconium at roughly twenty-five-mile intervals, close to the main north-south road. Lycaonia was the southern district of the province of Galatia, though not part of Galatia proper—the region of the ethnic Gauls who had migrated to Asia Minor centuries earlier. Lystra, situated on a low hill, was a midsized market town founded as a Roman colony in 26 B.C.E. by the Emperor Augustus; it preserved the use of Latin and some Roman forms of government. Nevertheless, because of its isolated location, it quickly assimilated Lycaonian language and customs as well. Relatively little is known about Derbe, and its location was in doubt until recently; coins found there indicate that it had a special connection with the Emperor Claudius. **14:12** Zeus was the revered chief of the Olympian gods, and Hermes was his energetic messenger—always moving and changing. This popular identification suggests that, at least in the author's mind, Barnabas was an older, perhaps bearded man at the time and Paul seemed young and energetic. **14:13** The old Greek religious tradition was so pervasive that its Olympian gods were identified by other nations with their own and so took on local personalities. This happened even in Rome, where Zeus was identified with Jupiter; his wife, Hera, with Juno; and so forth. In Lystra, Zeus was called Zeus Ampelites ("of the grapevine"). The garlands were placed upon the oxen as ornamentation before they were sacrificed to Zeus. **14:14–15** Contrast King Agrippa, who failed to reject worship and was punished with death (12:20–23). **14:14 *the apostles Barnabas and Paul*** See note to 14:4. **14:16** An illuminating discussion. The author believes that both Gentiles and Jews were free to follow other paths before Jesus' resurrection, but now that he has been raised, everything has changed. See also 17:30–31. **14:19 *Jews . . . from Antioch and Iconium*** See note to 9:22–24. **14:20 *to Derbe*** See note to 14:4. **14:24–26** Having made a rough clockwise circle in southern Asia Minor (Turkey), they retrace their steps all the way back to Syrian Antioch, from where the church originally sent them (13:2–4). On the return trip, however, they stop briefly in Attalia and omit Cyprus. **14:24 *appointed elders for them in each church*** This observation reflects the author's ongoing concern, evident since his discussion of Judas's replacement as apostle (1:15–26), for proper church order. **14:25 *Attalia*** The port for Perga, which is seven miles upriver from the coast. This stop would be necessary preparation for a sea voyage, and there is no hint that Paul and Barnabas preached here.

had completed. [27]When they arrived, they called the church together and related all that God had done with them, and how he had opened a door of faith for the Gentiles. [28]And they stayed there with the disciples for some time.

The Council at Jerusalem

15 Then certain individuals came down from Judea and were teaching the brothers, "Unless you are circumcised according to the custom of Moses, you cannot be saved." [2]And after Paul and Barnabas had no small dissension and debate with them, Paul and Barnabas and some of the others were appointed to go up to Jerusalem to discuss this question with the apostles and the elders. [3]So they were sent on their way by the church, and as they passed through both Phoenicia and Samaria, they reported the conversion of the Gentiles, and brought great joy to all the believers.[b] [4]When they came to Jerusalem, they were welcomed by the church and the apostles and the elders, and they reported all that God had done with them. [5]But some believers who belonged to the sect of the Pharisees stood up and said, "It is necessary for them to be circumcised and ordered to keep the law of Moses."

[6]The apostles and the elders met together to consider this matter. [7]After there had been much debate, Peter stood up and said to them, "My brothers,[c] you know that in the early days God made a choice among you, that I should be the one through whom

the Gentiles would hear the message of the good news and become believers. [8]And God, who knows the human heart, testified to them by giving them the Holy Spirit, just as he did to us; [9]and in cleansing their hearts by faith he has made no distinction between them and us. [10]Now therefore why are you putting God to the test by placing on the neck of the disciples a yoke that neither our ancestors nor we have been able to bear? [11]On the contrary, we believe that we will be saved through the grace of the Lord Jesus, just as they will."

[12]The whole assembly kept silence, and listened to Barnabas and Paul as they told of all the signs and wonders that God had done through them among the Gentiles. [13]After they finished speaking, James replied, "My brothers,[c] listen to me. [14]Simeon has related how God first looked favorably on the Gentiles, to take from among them a people for his name. [15]This agrees with the words of the prophets, as it is written,

[16] 'After this I will return,
    and I will rebuild the dwelling of David, which
       has fallen;
      from its ruins I will rebuild it,
        and I will set it up,
[17] so that all other peoples may seek the Lord—
      even all the Gentiles over whom my name
       has been called.
        Thus says the Lord, who has been making
         these things
        [18]known from long ago.'[d]

---

b Gk brothers
c Gk Men, brothers

d Other ancient authorities read things. [18]Known to God from of old are all his works.'

14:28 *for some time* The Gk phrase, lit. "not a little time," suggests a rather long time.   **15:1–4** We see again the author's concern for a centralized, authorized leadership, based in the apostles, that can manage such significant problems. See 1:15–26; 2:42; 4:35, 37; 5:2; 6:2; 8:1, 14; 9:27; 11:1, 18.   **15:1** These men—identified as Christian Pharisees in 15:5—are not presented as claiming that only Jews will be saved. The traditional rabbinic-Jewish position held that the righteous of all nations will be saved; see note to 10:34. Philo and Josephus took similar views. (Some Jewish texts from the period give the impression of extreme animosity toward Gentiles, but these documents emerge from circles that saw themselves under heavy oppression; it is difficult to know what they really thought of Gentiles.) At issue here, it seems, is the assumption of certain Christian Jews that a Gentile who sought salvation through Jesus the Messiah was thereby implicated in the Jewish covenant, since Jesus' messiahship could be understood only in terms of Israel's history. If, therefore, such Gentiles wished to follow Jesus as Messiah, they must also join themselves to Israel and its covenant with God. This also seems to have been the issue for the judaizers known from Paul's letters (*Gal.* 1:7; 2:14; 4:10, 21; 5:2; 6:12–13), where they are linked in some way with Peter (*Gal.* 2:14) and James (*Gal.* 2:12).   **15:2** *go up to Jerusalem* See note to 8:5.   **15:3** *Phoenicia and Samaria* Locations of earlier missionary activity, and therefore home to many Christians. See notes to 8:5; 11:19.   **15:5** *the sect of the Pharisees* Or better "the school of the Pharisees." The Gk word *hairesis* was commonly used of philosophical schools, and Josephus describes the Pharisees, Sadducees, and Essenes in just these terms (*J.W.* 1.162–166; *Ant.* 13.171–173; 18.12–20).   **15:7** Peter refers back to the events in *Acts* 10. Curiously, according to Paul, it was Paul who was called to the Gentiles, whereas Peter was to go to the Jews (*Gal.* 1:16; 2:2, 9), and it was Peter who compelled Gentiles to become Jews (*Gal.* 2:14).   **15:10** The author seems to betray his own perspective here, for it seems unlikely that the historical Peter (in light of *Gal.* 2:14) found it impossible to bear either circumcision in particular or Torah observance in general.   **15:11** This is Paul's argument against Peter in *Gal.* 2:11–21.   **15:13** *James replied* As 12:17 suggested, Jesus' brother James has quietly assumed a leading role in the young church. See notes to 12:17; 21:18.   **15:14** *Simeon* For local color, this Jerusalemite uses the closest Gk transliteration of the Hebrew *Shim^con.*   **15:16–18** Amos 9:11–12.

¹⁹Therefore I have reached the decision that we should not trouble those Gentiles who are turning to God, ²⁰but we should write to them to abstain only from things polluted by idols and from fornication and from whatever has been strangled*ᵉ* and from blood. ²¹For in every city, for generations past, Moses has had those who proclaim him, for he has been read aloud every sabbath in the synagogues."

The Council's Letter to Gentile Believers

²²Then the apostles and the elders, with the consent of the whole church, decided to choose men from among their members*ᶠ* and to send them to Antioch with Paul and Barnabas. They sent Judas called Barsabbas, and Silas, leaders among the brothers, ²³with the following letter: "The brothers, both the apostles and the elders, to the believers*ᵍ* of Gentile origin in Antioch and Syria and Cilicia, greetings. ²⁴Since we have heard that certain persons who have gone out from us, though with no instructions from us, have said things to disturb you and have unsettled your minds,*ʰ* ²⁵we have decided unanimously to choose representatives*ⁱ* and send them to you, along with our beloved Barnabas and Paul, ²⁶who have risked their lives for the sake of our Lord Jesus Christ. ²⁷We have therefore sent Judas and Silas, who themselves will tell you the same things by word of mouth. ²⁸For it has seemed good to the Holy Spirit and to us to impose on you no further burden than these essentials: ²⁹that you abstain from what has been sacrificed to idols and from blood and from

what is strangled*ʲ* and from fornication. If you keep yourselves from these, you will do well. Farewell."

³⁰So they were sent off and went down to Antioch. When they gathered the congregation together, they delivered the letter. ³¹When its members*ᵏ* read it, they rejoiced at the exhortation. ³²Judas and Silas, who were themselves prophets, said much to encourage and strengthen the believers.*ᵍ* ³³After they had been there for some time, they were sent off in peace by the believers*ᵍ* to those who had sent them.*ˡ* ³⁵But Paul and Barnabas remained in Antioch, and there, with many others, they taught and proclaimed the word of the Lord.

Paul and Barnabas Separate

³⁶After some days Paul said to Barnabas, "Come, let us return and visit the believers*ᵍ* in every city where we proclaimed the word of the Lord and see how they are doing." ³⁷Barnabas wanted to take with them John called Mark. ³⁸But Paul decided not to take with them one who had deserted them in Pamphylia and had not accompanied them in the work. ³⁹The disagreement became so sharp that they parted company; Barnabas took Mark with him and sailed away to Cyprus. ⁴⁰But Paul chose Silas and set out, the believers*ᵍ* commending him to the grace of the Lord. ⁴¹He went through Syria and Cilicia, strengthening the churches.

Timothy Joins Paul and Silas

16 Paul*ᵐ* went on also to Derbe and to Lystra, where there was a disciple named Timothy, the

---

e Other ancient authorities lack *and from whatever has been strangled*
f Gk *from among them*
g Gk *brothers*
h Other ancient authorities add *saying, 'You must be circumcised and keep the law,'*
i Gk *men*

j Other ancient authorities lack *and from what is strangled*
k Gk *When they*
l Other ancient authorities add verse 34, *But it seemed good to Silas to remain there*
m Gk *He*

15:19 *I have reached the decision* James therefore has the power to preside over the apostles. See note to 15:13. **15:20** These four prohibitions are basic to Judaism; see *Gen.* 9:4; *Exod.* 20:3, 4, 14. They represent the spirit, at least, of the seven "Noachide Laws" that the later rabbis considered mandatory for Gentiles (see note to 10:34). Paul, however, claims that no conditions were placed on the Gentile mission by the Jerusalem church, except that he should "remember the poor" (*Gal.* 2:10). **15:22 *Judas called Barsabbas*** Not otherwise known, but see note to 1:23. ***Silas*** The author characteristically introduces here a man who will become important in the following narrative (15:40–18:5). A variant of the name is Silvanus; a man by this name appears in Paul's company in his letters (*1 Thess.* 1:1; *2 Cor.* 1:19). **15:24** This recollection of the judaizing movement that gave Paul such trouble leaves open many historical questions. In particular, how was it related to the Jerusalem leaders? Although *Acts* pointedly distances James and the apostles from it, the author has them concede that it went out "from us," and Paul's letters drop several clues that the people involved have a very high, impressive status: *2 Cor.* 11:5–12:11; *Gal.* 1:8; 2:12, 14; 5:10; 6:12–13. **15:36–41** Thus begins Paul's second missionary tour, according to the presentation of *Acts*. In Paul's own letters, however, he does not make such trips out from Syria and Judea but, rather, is based in the mission cities, such as Ephesus, and hardly ever visits Syria and Judea (e.g., *Gal.* 1:11–2:10). **15:37–38** See 12:12, 25; 13:13. **15:39** Cyprus was Barnabas's home; 4:36. **15:41 *Cilicia*** According to the author, this was Paul's home, for it was the province of which Tarsus was the capital; see note to 9:11. Cilicia consisted of mostly rugged mountains in the west, and it was famous as the home of pirates who harassed shipping in the eastern Mediterranean before Augustus removed the problem. In the east, however, was the fertile plain on which Tarsus was situated. **16:1** Timothy will become a regular companion of Paul from now on; see 17:14–15; 18:5; 19:22; 20:4. He also appears in Paul's letters as his

son of a Jewish woman who was a believer; but his father was a Greek. [2]He was well spoken of by the believers[n] in Lystra and Iconium. [3]Paul wanted Timothy to accompany him; and he took him and had him circumcised because of the Jews who were in those places, for they all knew that his father was a Greek. [4]As they went from town to town, they delivered to them for observance the decisions that had been reached by the apostles and elders who were in Jerusalem. [5]So the churches were strengthened in the faith and increased in numbers daily.

Paul's Vision of the Man of Macedonia

[6]They went through the region of Phrygia and Galatia, having been forbidden by the Holy Spirit to speak the word in Asia. [7]When they had come opposite Mysia, they attempted to go into Bithynia, but the Spirit of Jesus did not allow them; [8]so, passing by Mysia, they went down to Troas. [9]During the night Paul had a vision: there stood a man of Macedonia pleading with him and saying, "Come over to Macedonia and help us." [10]When he had seen the vision, we immediately tried to cross over to Macedonia, being convinced that God had called us to proclaim the good news to them.

The Conversion of Lydia

[11]We set sail from Troas and took a straight course to Samothrace, the following day to Neapolis, [12]and from there to Philippi, which is a leading city of the district[o] of Macedonia and a Roman colony. We remained in this city for some days. [13]On the sabbath day we went outside the gate by the river, where we supposed there was a place of prayer; and we sat down and spoke to the women who had gathered there. [14]A certain woman named Lydia, a worshiper of God, was listening to us; she was from the city of Thyatira and a dealer in purple cloth. The Lord

---

n Gk brothers

o Other authorities read *a city of the first district*

---

closest aide; *1 Thess.* 1:1 (alongside Silvanus/Silas); 3:2; *1 Cor.* 4:17; 16:10; *Phlm.* 1; *Rom.* 16:21. Although, in later rabbinic Judaism, Jewish ancestry was determined solely by the mother, this passage indicates that this was not yet so in the 1st century (see 16:3). **16:3 had him circumcised because of the Jews** Circumcision was required of all male Jews (*Gen.* 17:9–14). But circumcision of an adult was no trivial business, and so the author's Paul must have been extremely concerned to make Timothy a Jew. The step is curious, since the council had already decided that Gentiles should be under no such obligation (15:5–21). And Paul himself was proud that he did not yield to pressure to circumcise his Gentile companion Titus even in Jerusalem (*Gal.* 2:3). The author's motive is not clear. **16:6–8** They travel northward through central Asia Minor (Turkey) and then westward, but avoiding the heart of the province of Asia along the west coast (to the south of them). Mysia was a coastal region in the northwestern part of the province of Asia, but the author distinguishes between it and Asia proper. Paul, Barnabas, and Timothy plan to go from Mysia northeast to the northernmost province, Bithynia-Pontus, situated along the Black Sea. Prevented from doing so, they turn west to Troas, on the coast. **16:8 Troas** Ten miles south of, and named for, the site of ancient Troy, important in Homer's *Iliad* and *Odyssey* and in Virgil's *Aeneid*. Troas, a large and famous transportation hub, was especially dear to the Romans because of the old legend, retold by Virgil, that Trojan expatriates had founded Rome. The Emperor Augustus had made the city a Roman colony. **16:9** The Roman province of Macedonia comprised the northern part of the Greek mainland. **16:10 we immediately tried** The beginning of the "we" passages of *Acts.* Traditionally these have been taken as proof that the author was a companion of Paul. But since in that case he ought to have explained this change to the reader, other explanations are at least as likely, for example, that he is drawing on a source written by one of Paul's companions or that he is employing a literary fiction—by no means beyond the repertoire of a Hellenistic historian. The "we" passages come and go without explanation through the remainder of *Acts*: 16:10–24; 20:5–15; 21:1–18; 27:1–28:16. **16:11 Samothrace** A small island in the Aegean, with a five-thousand-foot mountain. *Neapolis* This was a common name in the empire, meaning "new city." But this Neapolis was the port for the large Roman colony of Philippi. Established already by the 5th century B.C.E., it marked the beginning of the major highway toward Rome, the Egnatian Way, which went west through Philippi and Thessalonica. **16:12** See introduction to *Philippians.* Philippi was a large Roman colony on the east-west highway. **16:13 a place of prayer** The author uses the common Gk word for a Diaspora synagogue: "prayer [place]." Neither this word nor "synagogue" requires a building, and it seems that this was a routine outdoor meeting of women for worship in the Jewish tradition. The Jewish ritual of immersion (a strict necessity only for participating in the life of the Jerusalem temple but practiced by many Jews even in remote places) requires running water, and this might have been a reason for the location near water. **spoke to the women** These women could be Jews, proselytes, or Gentile sympathizers (see next note). Some passages in Josephus and other authors imply that Judaism proved especially attractive to Gentile women (e.g., *J.W.* 2.560). There may not have been enough male Jews (ten, according to custom) in Philippi to establish a regular synagogue. Perhaps some of these women should be understood as wives of the Romans (and Roman descendants) who lived in Philippi. That Paul met these women with his associates in the countryside on a regular basis (see 16:16) and accepted an invitation to stay at the house of one (16:15) would have been considered scandalous. The author continues to show interest in the role of women in the life of the church (see note to *Luke* 8:2–3). **16:14** Thyatira, in the province of Asia, was famous for its production of purple dye. Purple was a rare and expensive commodity, usually worn only by nobility and royalty. Lydia therefore seems to have been a woman of considerable means—a conclusion confirmed by the fact that she had a "household" (i.e., domestic workers) and was able to host the

opened her heart to listen eagerly to what was said by Paul. 15When she and her household were baptized, she urged us, saying, "If you have judged me to be faithful to the Lord, come and stay at my home." And she prevailed upon us.

Paul and Silas in Prison

16One day, as we were going to the place of prayer, we met a slave-girl who had a spirit of divination and brought her owners a great deal of money by fortune-telling. 17While she followed Paul and us, she would cry out, "These men are slaves of the Most High God, who proclaim to you*p* a way of salvation." 18She kept doing this for many days. But Paul, very much annoyed, turned and said to the spirit, "I order you in the name of Jesus Christ to come out of her." And it came out that very hour.

19But when her owners saw that their hope of making money was gone, they seized Paul and Silas and dragged them into the marketplace before the authorities. 20When they had brought them before the magistrates, they said, "These men are disturbing our city; they are Jews 21and are advocating customs that are not lawful for us as Romans to adopt or observe." 22The crowd joined in attacking them, and the magistrates had them stripped of their clothing and ordered them to be beaten with rods. 23After they had given them a severe flogging, they threw them into prison and ordered the jailer to keep them securely. 24Following these instructions, he put them in the innermost cell and fastened their feet in the stocks.

25About midnight Paul and Silas were praying and singing hymns to God, and the prisoners were listening to them. 26Suddenly there was an earthquake, so violent that the foundations of the prison were shaken; and immediately all the doors were opened and everyone's chains were unfastened. 27When the jailer woke up and saw the prison doors wide open, he drew his sword and was about to kill himself, since he supposed that the prisoners had escaped. 28But Paul shouted in a loud voice, "Do not harm yourself, for we are all here." 29The jailer*q* called for lights, and rushing in, he fell down trembling before Paul and Silas. 30Then he brought them outside and said, "Sirs, what must I do to be saved?" 31They answered, "Believe on the Lord Jesus, and you will be saved, you and your household." 32They spoke the word of the Lord*r* to him and to all who were in his house. 33At the same hour of the night he took them and washed their wounds; then he and his entire family were baptized without delay. 34He brought them up into the house and set food before them; and he and his entire household rejoiced that he had become a believer in God.

35When morning came, the magistrates sent the police, saying, "Let those men go." 36And the jailer reported the message to Paul, saying, "The magistrates sent word to let you go; therefore come out now and go in peace." 37But Paul replied, "They have beaten us in public, uncondemned, men who are Roman citizens, and have thrown us into prison; and now are they going to discharge us in secret? Certainly not! Let them come and take us out themselves." 38The police reported these words to the magistrates, and they were afraid when they heard that they were Roman citizens; 39so they came and apologized to them. And they took them out and asked them to leave the city. 40After leaving the prison they went to Lydia's home; and when they had seen and encouraged the brothers and sisters*s* there, they departed.

---

p Other ancient authorities read *to us*

q Gk *He*
r Other ancient authorities read *word of God*
s Gk *brothers*

Christian group in her house (16:15). That she was a *worshiper of God* suggests, in light of the way the same Gk term is used in 17:4, that she was a Gentile God-fearer; see notes to 10:2, 22. **16:16–18** Although Jesus performed countless exorcisms from the beginning of his career, this is the first reported in *Acts*. See 19:12–16. **16:19** *into the marketplace* That is, into the agora, equivalent to the forum in a Roman city. See note to *Mark* 6:56. **16:20–21** The Romans' words echo Tacitus's complaint that the Jews take people away from Roman customs (*Histories* 5.5). This passage appears to suggest that Jewish outreach to Gentiles was a familiar phenomenon. To identify them as Jews is enough to explain the charge that they propagate foreign traditions. See note to 2:10. **16:20** *magistrates* The author properly uses the common Gk equivalent *(stratēgos)* of the Latin term *(duumvir)* for the leaders of a Roman colony. **16:23–24** The precautions taken in imprisoning Paul and Silas, which set the backdrop for their miraculous release, recall those taken for Peter in 12:4–6. **16:37–39** Roman citizens enjoyed a completely different legal standing from that of provincials. Provincials were subject to the whims of governors and local authorities. Only citizens had to be treated with dignity: They could not lawfully be executed by governors (but see Josephus, *J.W.* 2.308), and they always had the right to appeal to Rome. This is the 1st reference to Paul's Roman citizenship, which will become an important issue later in the narrative, for it will allow him to appeal to Caesar and thus travel to Rome (22:24–29; 25:10–12). It is somewhat surprising that Paul himself (in the letters) does not mention Roman citizenship among his credentials. **16:40** *went to Lydia's home* See 16:15. Her home has now evidently become the Christian church. *encouraged the brothers and sisters* Paul claims that the Philippian Christians subsidized his further preaching

The Uproar in Thessalonica

17 After Paul and Silas[t] had passed through Amphipolis and Apollonia, they came to Thessalonica, where there was a synagogue of the Jews. [2]And Paul went in, as was his custom, and on three sabbath days argued with them from the scriptures, [3]explaining and proving that it was necessary for the Messiah[u] to suffer and to rise from the dead, and saying, "This is the Messiah,[u] Jesus whom I am proclaiming to you." [4]Some of them were persuaded and joined Paul and Silas, as did a great many of the devout Greeks and not a few of the leading women. [5]But the Jews became jealous, and with the help of some ruffians in the marketplaces they formed a mob and set the city in an uproar. While they were searching for Paul and Silas to bring them out to the assembly, they attacked Jason's house. [6]When they could not find them, they dragged Jason and some believers[v] before the city authorities,[w] shouting, "These people who have been turning the world upside down have come here also, [7]and Jason has entertained them as guests. They are all acting contrary to the decrees of the emperor, saying that there is another king named Jesus." [8]The people and the city officials were disturbed when they heard this, [9]and after they had taken bail from Jason and the others, they let them go.

Paul and Silas in Beroea

[10]That very night the believers[v] sent Paul and Silas off to Beroea; and when they arrived, they went to the Jewish synagogue. [11]These Jews were more receptive than those in Thessalonica, for they welcomed the message very eagerly and examined the scriptures every day to see whether these things were so. [12]Many of them therefore believed, including not a few Greek women and men of high standing. [13]But when the Jews of Thessalonica learned that the word of God had been proclaimed by Paul in Beroea as well, they came there too, to stir up and incite the crowds. [14]Then the believers[v] immediately sent Paul away to the coast, but Silas and Timothy remained behind. [15]Those who conducted Paul brought him as far as Athens; and after receiving instructions to have Silas and Timothy join him as soon as possible, they left him.

---

t Gk *they*
u Or *the Christ*
v Gk *brothers*
w Gk *politarchs*

Paul in Athens

[16]While Paul was waiting for them in Athens, he was deeply distressed to see that the city was full of

in Thessalonica and elsewhere (*Phil.* 4:15–16). **17:1** Paul and Silas advance westward along the Egnatian Way (see note to 16:11). The writer seems to imply that the towns before Thessalonica had no synagogue. Thessalonica was the capital of the province of Macedonia, and it had a protected harbor and connected with highways in two directions. See introduction to *1 Thessalonians.* **17:2** *as was his custom* See 13:4, 14; 14:1; 16:13. **17:3** *it was necessary for the Messiah to suffer and to rise* The writer knows well that Christian claims about Jesus' death and resurrection were fundamental obstacles to Jewish acceptance of his messiahship; the issue could become difficult for Christian readers as well. Much of *Acts* is devoted to proving (as the author thinks) from scripture that the Messiah should suffer, die, and rise; see 2:23–36; 4:11; 13:16–41. **17:4** *devout Greeks* Or God-fearers, Gentiles who attended the synagogue; see note to 10:2. *the leading women* On the appeal of Judaism to women, see note to 16:13. **17:5** Jewish jealousy of the Christians' success, allegedly a reason for their relentless hostility, is a stock theme in *Acts.* See note to 13:45. *Jason's house* Strangely, the author mentions this Jason as if he were familiar, although he has not introduced him; we learn quickly that he hosted Paul and his companions (17:7). In *Rom.* 16:21, Paul includes a Jason (a Gk name) among his colleagues in Corinth; this might well be the same person. **17:7** *acting contrary to the decrees of the emperor* The author has the Jews, who are allegedly motivated by jealousy, concoct a political charge in order to have the Christians silenced. See the trial of Jesus (*Luke* 23:2). The charge of disloyalty to the state quickly became a significant one for the Christians of Asia Minor and perhaps Greece, who refused to offer obeisance to the emperor by offering a pinch of incense before his statue; Pliny the Younger, *Letters* 10.96. **17:10** *to Beroea* That is, they continued nearly fifty miles along the Egnatian Way to this scenic town. Its location near natural springs and its abundance of streams suggest that this town suits the story as a place of refreshment for Paul, Silas, and Timothy. *went to the Jewish synagogue* See note to 17:4. **17:11–12** This reminds the reader that the author uses the phrase "the Jews" as if the Jews represented a solid wall of opposition to Christianity, although the author fully knows that some Jews accepted Christianity. See note to 9:22–24. **17:12** *Greek women and men of high standing* See notes to 17:4. **17:14–15** Contrast *1 Thess.* 3:16, according to which Timothy accompanied Paul to Athens and then was sent back to Thessalonica. **17:15** *Athens* A very long trip—nearly two hundred miles south of Beroea by land. But the author implies (17:14: "to the coast") that Paul traveled by ship. Athens had come to great prominence in the 5th century B.C.E. As a city-state, it had developed an idea of full democracy (from *dēmos* ["people"]; *kratos* ["rule"]) and had achieved both military and cultural fame. It left a remarkable legacy to the West in history, philosophy, tragedy, comedy, rhetoric, poetry, architecture, sculpture, and other art forms. By the 1st century C.E., it had long since lost this prominence, but the home of Socrates and Plato remained the center of Greek philosophy. **17:16** *full of idols* That is, statues representing the city gods, particularly Athena but also Zeus, Hephaestus, Poseidon, and Dionysus among others.

idols. ¹⁷So he argued in the synagogue with the Jews and the devout persons, and also in the marketplace^x every day with those who happened to be there. ¹⁸Also some Epicurean and Stoic philosophers debated with him. Some said, "What does this babbler want to say?" Others said, "He seems to be a proclaimer of foreign divinities." (This was because he was telling the good news about Jesus and the resurrection.) ¹⁹So they took him and brought him to the Areopagus and asked him, "May we know what this new teaching is that you are presenting? ²⁰It sounds rather strange to us, so we would like to know what it means." ²¹Now all the Athenians and the foreigners living there would spend their time in nothing but telling or hearing something new.

²²Then Paul stood in front of the Areopagus and said, "Athenians, I see how extremely religious you are in every way. ²³For as I went through the city and looked carefully at the objects of your worship, I found among them an altar with the inscription, 'To an unknown god.' What therefore you worship as unknown, this I proclaim to you. ²⁴The God who made the world and everything in it, he who is Lord of heaven and earth, does not live in shrines made by human hands, ²⁵nor is he served by human hands, as though he needed anything, since he himself gives to all mortals life and breath and all things. ²⁶From one ancestor^y he made all nations to inhabit the whole earth, and he allotted the times of their existence and the boundaries of the places where they would live, ²⁷so that they would search for God^z and perhaps grope for him and find him—though indeed he is not far from each one of us. ²⁸For 'In him we live and move and have our being'; as even some of your own poets have said,

'For we too are his offspring.'

²⁹Since we are God's offspring, we ought not to think that the deity is like gold, or silver, or stone, an image formed by the art and imagination of mortals. ³⁰While God has overlooked the times of human ignorance, now he commands all people everywhere to repent, ³¹because he has fixed a day on which he will have the world judged in righteousness by a man whom he has appointed, and of this he has given assurance to all by raising him from the dead."

³²When they heard of the resurrection of the dead, some scoffed; but others said, "We will hear you again about this." ³³At that point Paul left them.

---

x Or *civic center*; Gk *agora*

y Gk *From one;* other ancient authorities read *From one blood*
z Other ancient authorities read *the Lord*

17:17 *in the synagogue* Presumably not because the Jews endorsed the idols but because according to *Acts* it was Paul's habit to begin preaching in the synagogues (13:5, 14, 43, 46; 14:1–2; 17:1–2). ***and the devout persons*** Or God-fearers; see note to 10:2. ***the marketplace*** The Athenian agora, which was surrounded by porticos *(stoas)*, shrines, temples, and shops, has been uncovered by archaeologists. **17:18** Stoicism, founded by the Cypriot immigrant Zeno in the 3d century B.C.E. and taking its name from the Painted Stoa (a colonnade) by the agora at Athens, was the most popular philosophy of the day. It postulated the harmony of all nature, which was empowered by a world soul *(logos),* represented by fire. Epicureanism, founded in Athens by Epicurus of Samos in the early 3d century B.C.E., took an atomistic view of human nature, put a premium on seeking happiness in this life through simplicity and the renunciation of encumbrances, believed that the entire human being dissolved at death, and denied the influence of the gods on the world. Paul's interaction with these groups emphasizes that the author, ahead of his time (see Justin Martyr and Athenagoras in the mid- to late 2d century), imagines Christianity as a kind of philosophy. ***because he was telling the good news . . . the resurrection*** When Greek philosophers spoke of the afterlife at all, they envisioned it only for the soul/spirit, which was to be released from the physical body. Resurrection, the recovery of a decayed body, seemed to them a repugnant idea. See note to *1 Cor.* 15:35. **17:19 *brought him to the Areopagus*** Areopagus probably means "hill of Ares," in honor of the Greek god of war (see the Roman Mars). This small hillock, about one hundred and forty feet below the summit of the Acropolis, was the original meeting place of the Athenian council. But in Paul's day the council ordinarily met below, in the agora. In the 1st century, an aristocratic group governed the affairs of the city. It is unclear whether the author means to imply that Paul was literally taken up the hill; later in this context he seems to use "Areopagus" of the council rather than the rocky mound (17:22). **17:22–31** Paul's speech before the Areopagus council balances the example of his typical speech before a Jewish synagogue given in 13:16–43. This is the kind of speech that he reportedly gave to Gentiles. The author fulfills the historiographical requirement of suiting the speech to the character and scene (Thucydides 1.22.1). For example, he replaces scripture citations with quotations of Greek writers. At the same time, the speech repeats many of the author's characteristic themes: God is Lord of the entire creation; God's dwelling is not made with hands (see 7:44–50); before Jesus' resurrection, people followed their own traditions, but they must now all repent and follow the new revelation from God (see 14:16); Jesus was a man chosen or appointed by God (see 2:22–36 and note); Jesus' resurrection is the irrefutable proof of the new revelation (see 1:3; *Luke* 24). **17:22 *stood in front of the Areopagus*** See note to 17:19. ***Athenians*** Lit. "Men, Athenians"; see note to 1:16. **17:26 *From one ancestor he made all nations*** See *Gen.* 2:15–25; 10:1–32. **17:28 *In him we live . . .*** Often thought to have been written by the 6th-century B.C.E. Greek philosopher Epimenides in a lost work. ***For we too are his offspring*** From Aratus (mid-3d century B.C.E.), *Phaenomena* 5. This poetic work considered the stars and the myths concerning them. But see also the first paragraph of the *Hymn to Zeus* by Cleanthes, the second head of the Stoic school. **17:32 *some scoffed*** See note to 17:18.

[34]But some of them joined him and became believers, including Dionysius the Areopagite and a woman named Damaris, and others with them.

Paul in Corinth

18 After this Paul[a] left Athens and went to Corinth. [2]There he found a Jew named Aquila, a native of Pontus, who had recently come from Italy with his wife Priscilla, because Claudius had ordered all Jews to leave Rome. Paul[b] went to see them, [3]and, because he was of the same trade, he stayed with them, and they worked together—by trade they were tentmakers. [4]Every sabbath he would argue in the synagogue and would try to convince Jews and Greeks.

[5]When Silas and Timothy arrived from Macedonia, Paul was occupied with proclaiming the word,[c] testifying to the Jews that the Messiah[d] was Jesus.

[6]When they opposed and reviled him, in protest he shook the dust from his clothes[e] and said to them, "Your blood be on your own heads! I am innocent. From now on I will go to the Gentiles." [7]Then he left the synagogue[f] and went to the house of a man named Titius[g] Justus, a worshiper of God; his house was next door to the synagogue. [8]Crispus, the official of the synagogue, became a believer in the Lord, together with all his household; and many of the Corinthians who heard Paul became believers and were baptized. [9]One night the Lord said to Paul in a vision, "Do not be afraid, but speak and do not be silent; [10]for I am with you, and no one will lay a hand on you to harm you, for there are many in this city who are my people." [11]He stayed there a year and six months, teaching the word of God among them.

[12]But when Gallio was proconsul of Achaia, the Jews made a united attack on Paul and brought him

---

a Gk *he*
b Gk *He*
c Gk *with the word*
d Or *the Christ*

e Gk *reviled him, he shook out his clothes*
f Gk *left there*
g Other ancient authorities read *Titus*

17:34 Dionysius the Areopagite An Athenian name meaning "of [the god] Dionysus." He was allegedly a member of the Areopagus council—perhaps confirming that Paul stood before the council rather than the hill. According to later Christian tradition, this man became the first bishop of Athens (Eusebius, *Eccl. hist.* 3.4.11; 4.23.3). **Damaris** Although the name is otherwise unattested, this reference shows the author's continuing concern to include women. See note to 16:13. **18:1 Corinth** Nearly fifty miles from Athens, on the isthmus between the Aegean and Ionian/Adriatic seas. A major center of transportation, trade, and commerce, still being rebuilt through the 1st century; see introduction to *1 Corinthians.* **18:2 Aquila . . . with his wife Priscilla** This couple is mentioned among Paul's more important companions in *1 Cor.* 16:19 (where they are with Paul in Ephesus) and *Rom.* 16:3 (where they are in Rome). **native of Pontus** See note to 16:6–8. Pontus, on the Black Sea, formed with Bithynia the northern-most province of what is now Turkey. **Claudius had ordered all Jews to leave Rome** This reference raises a famous historical problem. The 3d-century historian Dio Cassius (*History of Rome* 60.6.6) insists that Claudius, though bothered by the growth of the Jews in Rome, did not expel them, because of their numbers, but only forbade them to assemble. Suetonius (early 2d century) has only the militant Jews expelled (*Claudius* 25.4), and this would fit the typical Roman practice of exemplary punishment. It would have been virtually impossible to expel the tens of thousands of Jews from Rome when they were fully integrated into social networks. Such an expulsion should have left a trace in Josephus or Tacitus, who had good reason to mention it, but they are silent. *All* may be the author's characteristic exaggeration; see note to *Luke* 2:1–3. **18:3 tentmakers** The Gk word could as easily mean "leather-worker"—a skill in high demand for awnings to protect homes and people from the burning Mediterranean sun. Paul's home region, however, was also famous for a kind of wool-based cloth. In any case, the home of Aquila and Priscilla would likely be a small apartment above or behind their shop. **18:4** Both the synagogue visit by Paul and the claim that one would find both Jews and Greeks there are typical in *Acts;* see 13:43–44; 14:1; 17:4. **18:5 When Silas and Timothy arrived** They had remained for a while in Beroea, according to 17:14–15. **18:6** The same thing has already happened in Pisidian Antioch (13:44–51), in fulfillment of Jesus' directive (*Luke* 9:5; 10:11). Even so, Paul will go to the synagogue and speak to Jews when he can (18:8, 19; 28:17). **18:7 Titius Justus, a worshiper of God** Apparently a God-fearer; see note to 10:2. This man with a Latin name is not mentioned elsewhere in early Christian literature. Although there seems to have been a large Jewish community in Corinth (Philo, *On the Embassy to Gaius* 281), we have no remains of it from this period despite the extensive archaeological digging in the city. Archaeologists have discovered part of an inscription, from perhaps the 4th century C.E., that appears to have read "synagogue of the Hebrews." **18:8 Crispus, the official of the synagogue** The widely attested Gk term *archisynagōgos* refers to a synagogue president, a relatively wealthy individual who oversaw the business side of community life. See note to *Luke* 8:41. (The author will shortly claim that Sosthenes had this position; see 18:17.) Paul mentions Crispus in his second letter to Corinth (*1 Cor.* 1:14) as one of the few people he personally baptized. **18:12–17** This episode is introduced in an abrupt way after the author has appeared to conclude his discussion of Corinth. It also assumes that a Sosthenes was president of the synagogue, although the author has just given this role to Crispus. The author evidently intends this story to be read as one piece with what precedes (18:1–11), and so perhaps implies that Crispus, after being removed as synagogue president because of his conversion, was replaced. But the abrupt introduction and reference to Sosthenes might also indicate that the author is using a different source about Paul's activities in Corinth, which he prefers to keep intact rather than fit it into the earlier story. If so, this trial before Gallio might not have occurred in

before the tribunal. ¹³They said, "This man is persuading people to worship God in ways that are contrary to the law." ¹⁴Just as Paul was about to speak, Gallio said to the Jews, "If it were a matter of crime or serious villainy, I would be justified in accepting the complaint of you Jews; ¹⁵but since it is a matter of questions about words and names and your own law, see to it yourselves; I do not wish to be a judge of these matters." ¹⁶And he dismissed them from the tribunal. ¹⁷Then all of them*ʰ* seized Sosthenes, the official of the synagogue, and beat him in front of the tribunal. But Gallio paid no attention to any of these things.

Paul's Return to Antioch

¹⁸After staying there for a considerable time, Paul said farewell to the believers*ⁱ* and sailed for Syria, accompanied by Priscilla and Aquila. At Cenchreae he had his hair cut, for he was under a vow. ¹⁹When they reached Ephesus, he left them there, but first he himself went into the synagogue and had a discussion with the Jews. ²⁰When they asked him to stay longer, he declined; ²¹but on taking leave of them, he said, "I*ʲ* will return to you, if God wills." Then he set sail from Ephesus.

²²When he had landed at Caesarea, he went up to Jerusalem*ᵏ* and greeted the church, and then went down to Antioch. ²³After spending some time there he departed and went from place to place through the region of Galatia*ˡ* and Phrygia, strengthening all the disciples.

Ministry of Apollos

²⁴Now there came to Ephesus a Jew named Apollos, a native of Alexandria. He was an eloquent man, well-versed in the scriptures. ²⁵He had been instructed in the Way of the Lord; and he spoke with burning enthusiasm and taught accurately the things concerning

---

h Other ancient authorities read *all the Greeks*
i Gk *brothers*

j Other ancient authorities read *I must at all costs keep the approaching festival in Jerusalem, but I*
k Gk *went up*
l Gk *the Galatian region*

---

the same visit to Corinth as described in 18:1–11. This is an important issue because Gallio can be identified as L. Iunius Gallio, brother to the philosopher Seneca. Fragments of an inscription from Delphi indicate that Gallio was proconsul of Achaia (i.e., governor of this senatorial province, of which Corinth was capital) from late in 50 C.E. to perhaps early in 52. Scholars often conclude that the visit described here must have occurred during this period. But even if the author is correct that Paul appeared before Gallio, this story may have been spliced in from a separate visit to Corinth. **18:12 the tribunal** Gk *bēma*, a standard feature of the agora; it has been uncovered at Corinth. It was a large platform of stone such as marble, where the governor would hear cases. The same term appears in 12:21; 25:6. Paul uses the word in reference to the judgment seat of Christ in letters written to or from Corinth (*2 Cor.* 5:10; *Rom.* 14:10). **18:14–15** The author uses restraint in preventing his main character, Paul, from speaking. Instead, he lends authenticity to the narrative by letting Gallio speak in a perfectly fitting way—as a jaded Roman aristocrat fed up with foreigners such as Jews. See 16:20. **18:17** See notes to 18:8 and 18:12–17. Gallio's inaction is not typical of the behavior of Roman officials in *Luke-Acts,* for they are generally favorable to Jesus and the church. But the author does not make much of this episode, and the main issue seems to be plausibility: Gallio acts as would a Roman official under such circumstances. **18:18** *After staying there for a considerable time* This observation seems redundant after 18:11; this provides further evidence that 18:12–17 comes from another period. *sailed for Syria* He is returning to Antioch (15:35–36). So ends Paul's second missionary journey, according to *Acts.* *Cenchreae* The eastern port town of the Corinthian isthmus, facing toward Syria, more than six hundred miles to the east. *had his hair cut, for he was under a vow* A bit confusing, since the only biblical vow involving hair, the Nazirite vow, specifies that the hair not be cut until the end, when it was to be shaved by a priest at the temple in Jerusalem and added to the sacrificial fire (*Num.* 6:1–21). Perhaps this was not a vow according to Jewish law, or it reflects a postbiblical custom, or the author is confused. **18:19** *Ephesus* This world-famous capital of the province of Asia housed one of the Seven Wonders of the World: the temple to the local goddess Artemis (the Greek name) or Diana (the Roman name). It appears from Paul's letters that Ephesus was a sort of base for him, the place from which he corresponded with Achaia (Corinth) and Macedonia (Philippi). *went into the synagogue* See notes to 17:4 and 18:6. **18:20–21** This passage sets the stage for Paul's later visit to Ephesus (19:1–20:1) on his third missionary tour. **18:22** *landed at Caesarea* See note to 12:19. The trip from Ephesus to Caesarea by boat would have taken several weeks. *greeted the church* Why Paul should have greeted the church at Caesarea, and why he should have landed at Caesarea when he was headed for Antioch, are unclear. It seems, therefore, that the author means the church of Jerusalem, from which one would "go down" to Antioch. *went down to Antioch* Paul's base (in *Acts*) and destination; see 18:18. **18:23** So begins, rather abruptly, Paul's third and final missionary journey in *Acts,* which begins when he revisits the newly established churches of south-central Asia Minor. **18:24** Apollos plays an important role in *1 Corinthians.* He has visited the church there after Paul established it and has built on Paul's foundation in a way that does not entirely please Paul. Paul seems to take issue with his intellectual and rhetorical abilities (*1 Cor.* 1:12, 17, 19–23; 2:1–5; 3:4; 3:10–15, 18–19; 4:6). Alexandria, capital of the Roman province of Egypt, was a renowned center of Jewish (and later Christian) philosophy, home of Philo. **18:25** A somewhat confusing sentence. The word "instructed" is the same as that used of Theophilus, the patron of *Luke-Acts* (*Luke* 1:4), who does not yet seem to have a perfect understanding

Jesus, though he knew only the baptism of John. 26He began to speak boldly in the synagogue; but when Priscilla and Aquila heard him, they took him aside and explained the Way of God to him more accurately. 27And when he wished to cross over to Achaia, the believers*m* encouraged him and wrote to the disciples to welcome him. On his arrival he greatly helped those who through grace had become believers, 28for he powerfully refuted the Jews in public, showing by the scriptures that the Messiah*n* is Jesus.

Paul in Ephesus

19 While Apollos was in Corinth, Paul passed through the interior regions and came to Ephesus, where he found some disciples. 2He said to them, "Did you receive the Holy Spirit when you became believers?" They replied, "No, we have not even heard that there is a Holy Spirit." 3Then he said, "Into what then were you baptized?" They answered, "Into John's baptism." 4Paul said, "John baptized with the baptism of repentance, telling the people to believe in the one who was to come after him, that is, in Jesus." 5On hearing this, they were baptized in the name of the Lord Jesus. 6When Paul had laid his hands on them, the Holy Spirit came upon them, and they spoke in tongues and prophesied— 7altogether there were about twelve of them.

8He entered the synagogue and for three months spoke out boldly, and argued persuasively about the kingdom of God. 9When some stubbornly refused to believe and spoke evil of the Way before the congregation, he left them, taking the disciples with him, and argued daily in the lecture hall of Tyrannus.*o* 10This continued for two years, so that all the residents of Asia, both Jews and Greeks, heard the word of the Lord.

The Sons of Sceva

11God did extraordinary miracles through Paul, 12so that when the handkerchiefs or aprons that had touched his skin were brought to the sick, their diseases left them, and the evil spirits came out of them. 13Then some itinerant Jewish exorcists tried to use the name of the Lord Jesus over those who had evil spirits, saying, "I adjure you by the Jesus whom Paul proclaims." 14Seven sons of a Jewish high priest named Sceva were doing this. 15But the evil spirit said to them in reply, "Jesus I know, and Paul I know; but who are you?" 16Then the man with the evil spirit leaped on them, mastered them all, and so overpowered them that they fled out of the house naked and wounded. 17When this became known to all residents of Ephesus, both Jews and Greeks, everyone was awestruck; and the name of the Lord Jesus was praised. 18Also many of those who became be-

---

m Gk brothers
n Or the Christ

o Other ancient authorities read *of a certain Tyrannus, from eleven o'clock in the morning to four in the afternoon*

---

of the author's Christian vision. Apollos's knowing only the baptism of John confirms that the Baptist's movement flourished outside of Judea and outside of Christian circles (see 19:2–6), but it is hard to square with the claims that he taught "precisely" the things concerning Jesus, or that he still needed to be taught "more accurately" (18:26). Perhaps the confusion results from the author's awareness that Paul was not happy with Apollos's teaching. **18:26 *Priscilla and Aquila heard him*** These Jewish Christians, then, continue to attend synagogue. Paul had left them in Ephesus when he departed for Judea and Syria (18:19). ***more accurately*** See note to 18:25. **18:27 *Achaia*** The large southern province of Greece, of which Corinth was the capital. Apollos indeed seems to have made quite an impression there: see note to 18:24. **19:1–7** In view of the author's portrayal of the Baptist as one who recognized Jesus' messiahship from the start, indeed was related to him, and then predicted the outpouring of the Holy Spirit (*Luke* 1:44; 3:16; *Acts* 1:5; 11:16), the reader is shocked to learn that the Baptist's students (who continue long after his death, outside of Judea) know nothing of a "holy spirit" or of Jesus' messiahship. Unless this passage can be explained on the basis of knowledge shared by author and reader but lost to us, it serves as strong incidental evidence that the Baptist's recognition and support of Jesus have been significantly overstated in the gospels. **19:7** Compare the experiences of the apostles and the first Gentile converts in 2:4 and 10:44. **19:8 *entered the synagogue*** See notes to 17:4 and 18:6. **19:9** This movement from a hostile Jewish setting to a welcoming Gentile context is typical of Paul in *Acts* (13:46; 18:6). Typical also is the allegation of Jewish stubbornness; see note to 9:22–24. ***the lecture hall of Tyrannus*** By speaking in such a lecture hall (Gk *scholē*, from which derives "school") over a two-year period, the Paul of *Acts* appears as a philosopher. See Epictetus, *Discourses* 3.23.30. Tyrannus, meaning "tyrant" or "usurper" or "illegitimate despot," was a peculiar name to be given by one's parents. Even though another case has been found on an inscription, we must wonder whether this was a nickname given by students. **19:10 *all the residents of Asia*** Plainly an exaggeration; see note to 18:2. **19:11** This kind of cure by energized material appears elsewhere in *Luke-Acts*. See 5:15 and note. **19:13** This humorous story seems to be a polemical attack upon the Christians' Jewish competitors for their alleged ineffectiveness. Although we have a more or less complete record of Jewish high priests in Josephus, no Sceva appears, and it is difficult to understand why he or his sons would be casting out devils in Ephesus. The "seven sons" is a literary convention. Writing about the same time as this author, Josephus claims that the Jews were uniquely effective exorcists (*Ant.* 8.44–49). In *Luke* 11:19 the author indirectly acknowledged that Jewish exorcists were capable.

lievers confessed and disclosed their practices. ¹⁹A number of those who practiced magic collected their books and burned them publicly; when the value of these books*ᵖ* was calculated, it was found to come to fifty thousand silver coins. ²⁰So the word of the Lord grew mightily and prevailed.

The Riot in Ephesus

²¹Now after these things had been accomplished, Paul resolved in the Spirit to go through Macedonia and Achaia, and then to go on to Jerusalem. He said, "After I have gone there, I must also see Rome." ²²So he sent two of his helpers, Timothy and Erastus, to Macedonia, while he himself stayed for some time longer in Asia.

²³About that time no little disturbance broke out concerning the Way. ²⁴A man named Demetrius, a silversmith who made silver shrines of Artemis, brought no little business to the artisans. ²⁵These he gathered together, with the workers of the same trade, and said, "Men, you know that we get our wealth from this business. ²⁶You also see and hear that not only in Ephesus but in almost the whole of Asia this Paul has persuaded and drawn away a considerable number of people by saying that gods made with hands are not gods. ²⁷And there is danger not only that this trade of ours may come into disrepute but also that the temple of the great goddess Artemis will be scorned, and she will be deprived of her majesty that brought all Asia and the world to worship her."

²⁸When they heard this, they were enraged and shouted, "Great is Artemis of the Ephesians!" ²⁹The city was filled with the confusion; and people*q* rushed together to the theater, dragging with them Gaius and Aristarchus, Macedonians who were Paul's travel companions. ³⁰Paul wished to go into the crowd, but the disciples would not let him; ³¹even some officials of the province of Asia,*ʳ* who were friendly to him, sent him a message urging him not to venture into the theater. ³²Meanwhile, some were shouting one thing, some another; for the assembly was in confusion, and most of them did not know why they had come together. ³³Some of the crowd gave instructions to Alexander, whom the Jews had pushed forward. And Alexander motioned for silence and tried to make a defense before the people. ³⁴But when they recognized that he was a Jew, for about two hours all of them shouted in unison, "Great is Artemis of the Ephesians!" ³⁵But when the town clerk had quieted the crowd, he said, "Citizens of Ephesus, who is there that does not know that the city of the Ephesians is the temple keeper of the great Artemis and of the

---

p Gk *them*

q Gk *they*
r Gk *some of the Asiarchs*

19:21–22 These travel plans of Paul fit with those he mentions in his letters from Ephesus (*1 Cor.* 16:3–6; *2 Cor.* 1:15–16), except that the second plan called for an initial visit to Achaia. Writing to the Romans from Corinth, he mentions his hope to visit them (*Rom.* 1:11–15; 15:22–29). **19:22** In Paul's letters, this stay in Ephesus would apparently coincide with a period in which he came into serious conflict with the Corinthians and sent Titus with a letter to help remedy the situation (*2 Cor.* 2:1–13; 7:5–16). *Erastus* An Erastus is mentioned in *Rom.* 16:23 as a companion of Paul in Corinth. He is said to hold a civic office in this city *(city treasurer)*. He is conceivably the person mentioned on an inscription, found in Corinth, that says that a certain Erastus with the office of aedile (not the same as the office mentioned in *Romans*) paid for a section of pavement at his own expense. Such an official would be a person of considerable means. *2 Tim.* 4:20 also connects Erastus with Timothy and Corinth. **19:23–41** The issue in the Ephesian riots—that adoption of Christianity kills the market for traditional religious goods and therefore a large part of the economy—has an interesting parallel in the letter of Pliny the Younger, governor of nearby Bithynia-Pontus not much later than the writing of *Acts*, to the Emperor Trajan. Pliny notes that the success of Christianity in the region has caused a severe drop in the sale of sacrificial animals (*Letters* 10.96). Ephesus was famous for its temple to Artemis, the largest in the Greek world, and the revenue from both locals' and tourists' purchases of small statues would have been considerable. The author of *Acts* continues to write in a basically plausible way, about reactions that various groups might understandably have had to the new faith. **19:24** *Artemis* One of the twelve Olympian gods, twin sister to Apollo. Although she is usually portrayed as a virgin hunter and protector of women in childbirth, at Ephesus she was also equated with a local fertility goddess. Archaeology has discovered some small statues of Artemis with numerous breasts or perhaps eggs. Terra-cotta shrines have also been found, but no silver ones. Artemis had come to be identified with the Roman goddess Diana. **19:29** *Gaius and Aristarchus, Macedonians* It is unclear whether this Gaius, with a common Latin name, is the same as the one mentioned in Paul's letters as one of the first converts in Corinth and one of the few baptized by Paul; *1 Cor.* 1:14; *Rom.* 6:23. But it would be odd for the Corinthian convert to be called a Macedonian here. A Gaius is also mentioned in *3 John* 1 as an elder, perhaps in Asia Minor. Aristarchus appears later in this narrative, where he is said to be from Thessalonica in Macedonia (20:4; 27:2), and a man of this name also appears as a companion of Paul in *Phlm.* 24 and *Col.* 4:10. **19:33–34** The role of Alexander the Jew in this story is unclear. Since *the Jews* put him forward, one might imagine that he intended to bring charges against the Christians, but his attempt to *make a defense* seems to be the action of a Christian Jew. **19:35** *the town clerk* The Gk word is simply what the author uses elsewhere for "scribe." *the statue that fell from heaven* Or simply "what fell from heaven [or 'Zeus']." We have no other record of such an object for Ephesian Artemis, but several other cults in the region protected meteorites as sacred objects.

statue that fell from heaven?[s] [36]Since these things cannot be denied, you ought to be quiet and do nothing rash. [37]You have brought these men here who are neither temple robbers nor blasphemers of our[t] goddess. [38]If therefore Demetrius and the artisans with him have a complaint against anyone, the courts are open, and there are proconsuls; let them bring charges there against one another. [39]If there is anything further[u] you want to know, it must be settled in the regular assembly. [40]For we are in danger of being charged with rioting today, since there is no cause that we can give to justify this commotion." [41]When he had said this, he dismissed the assembly.

Paul Goes to Macedonia and Greece

20 After the uproar had ceased, Paul sent for the disciples; and after encouraging them and saying farewell, he left for Macedonia. [2]When he had gone through those regions and had given the believers[v] much encouragement, he came to Greece, [3]where he stayed for three months. He was about to set sail for Syria when a plot was made against him by the Jews, and so he decided to return through Macedonia. [4]He was accompanied by Sopater son of

---

s Meaning of Gk uncertain
t Other ancient authorities read *your*
u Other ancient authorities read *about other matters*
v Gk *given them*

Pyrrhus from Beroea, by Aristarchus and Secundus from Thessalonica, by Gaius from Derbe, and by Timothy, as well as by Tychicus and Trophimus from Asia. [5]They went ahead and were waiting for us in Troas; [6]but we sailed from Philippi after the days of Unleavened Bread, and in five days we joined them in Troas, where we stayed for seven days.

Paul's Farewell Visit to Troas

[7]On the first day of the week, when we met to break bread, Paul was holding a discussion with them; since he intended to leave the next day, he continued speaking until midnight. [8]There were many lamps in the room upstairs where we were meeting. [9]A young man named Eutychus, who was sitting in the window, began to sink off into a deep sleep while Paul talked still longer. Overcome by sleep, he fell to the ground three floors below and was picked up dead. [10]But Paul went down, and bending over him took him in his arms, and said, "Do not be alarmed, for his life is in him." [11]Then Paul went upstairs, and after he had broken bread and eaten, he continued to converse with them until dawn; then he left. [12]Meanwhile they had taken the boy away alive and were not a little comforted.

The Voyage from Troas to Miletus

[13]We went ahead to the ship and set sail for Assos, intending to take Paul on board there; for he had

---

19:38 *there are proconsuls* Asia, like Cyprus (13:7) and Achaia (18:12), was a senatorial province. **20:2** *to Greece* The only occurrence of this word (Gk *Hellas*) in this author. It is odd that he should use it, in contrast to Macedonia, to denote southern Greece (Achaia). Elsewhere the word tends to have a looser sense than either Macedonia or Achaia, and it would normally include the northern province. **20:3** *a plot was made against him by the Jews* A theme in *Acts;* see note to 9:22–24. **20:4** *Sopater son of Pyrrhus from Beroea* Rom. 16:21 includes a Sosipater among Paul's companions at Corinth near the end of his career; this may well be the same person. Presumably, he was converted during Paul's visit to Beroea (17:10–15). The name given here and that of the father do not appear elsewhere in the early Christian texts. *Aristarchus and Secundus from Thessalonica* Aristarchus was introduced in 19:29 as a companion of Paul; see note there. The Latin-named Secundus appears only here. *Gaius from Derbe* Apparently not the Gaius recently introduced with Aristarchus (19:29; see note), because that man was called a Macedonian whereas Derbe was in Asia Minor. *Timothy* From Lystra, according to 16:1, where he was introduced; see note. According to Paul's letters, he was one of Paul's most trusted aides. *Tychicus and Trophimus from Asia* Tychicus appears only here in *Acts* but four times in Pauline letters of doubtful authenticity (*Col.* 4:7; *Eph.* 6:21 [which may well be plagiarized from the *Colossians* passage]; *2 Tim.* 4:12; *Titus* 3:12). Trophimus appears later in the narrative, where he is identified as an Ephesian (21:29), and again in *2 Tim.* 4:20. **20:5** *waiting for us in Troas* On Troas, see note to 16:8. The "we" passages resume here after a break since 16:25. **20:6** *after the days of Unleavened Bread* That is, Passover, in March/April; see note to 12:3. This might suggest that Philippi was home to a significant Jewish community, but see note to 16:13. Paul's companions appear to be Gentiles, and so they do not celebrate the Passover, but the case of Timothy is puzzling, for he is a circumcised Jew (20:4; see 16:3). **20:7–12** This story is noteworthy for several reasons: It incidentally portrays Paul as a long-winded and less-than-riveting speaker (see *1 Cor.* 2:1–4; *2 Cor.* 10:10), and it is unclear whether Paul actually does anything miraculous. The author evidently wishes to convey that Paul raised the boy from the dead by bending over him in the manner of Elijah and Elisha (*1 Kgs.* 17:21; *2 Kgs.* 4:34–35). But he does not clarify whether Paul simply observes that the boy is not dead or pronounces him alive, although he had been dead (20:10). This vagueness may be simple honesty on the author's part: he does not wish to claim too much. **20:7** *On the first day of the week, when we met to break bread* This is the Christians' regular Sunday celebration of Jesus' resurrection, established quite early (*1 Cor.* 16:2). At first, it included an actual meal together (*1 Cor.* 11:18–22); only later was the ritual of the communion/Eucharist made separate. It may well be that the author begins this day according to Jewish calculation, at dusk on Saturday. **20:9** *Eutychus* This person, who appears only in this story, had a fitting name (common among slaves and freedmen): "good fortune." **20:13** *Assos* A port city about twenty miles south of Troas.

made this arrangement, intending to go by land himself. 14When he met us in Assos, we took him on board and went to Mitylene. 15We sailed from there, and on the following day we arrived opposite Chios. The next day we touched at Samos, andʷ the day after that we came to Miletus. 16For Paul had decided to sail past Ephesus, so that he might not have to spend time in Asia; he was eager to be in Jerusalem, if possible, on the day of Pentecost.

Paul Speaks to the Ephesian Elders

17From Miletus he sent a message to Ephesus, asking the elders of the church to meet him. 18When they came to him, he said to them:

"You yourselves know how I lived among you the entire time from the first day that I set foot in Asia, 19serving the Lord with all humility and with tears, enduring the trials that came to me through the plots of the Jews. 20I did not shrink from doing anything helpful, proclaiming the message to you and teaching you publicly and from house to house, 21as I testified to both Jews and Greeks about repentance toward God and faith toward our Lord Jesus. 22And now, as a captive to the Spirit,ˣ I am on my way to Jerusalem, not knowing what will happen to me there, 23except that the Holy Spirit testifies to me in every city that imprisonment and persecutions are waiting

for me. 24But I do not count my life of any value to myself, if only I may finish my course and the ministry that I received from the Lord Jesus, to testify to the good news of God's grace.

25"And now I know that none of you, among whom I have gone about proclaiming the kingdom, will ever see my face again. 26Therefore I declare to you this day that I am not responsible for the blood of any of you, 27for I did not shrink from declaring to you the whole purpose of God. 28Keep watch over yourselves and over all the flock, of which the Holy Spirit has made you overseers, to shepherd the church of Godʸ that he obtained with the blood of his own Son.ᶻ 29I know that after I have gone, savage wolves will come in among you, not sparing the flock. 30Some even from your own group will come distorting the truth in order to entice the disciples to follow them. 31Therefore be alert, remembering that for three years I did not cease night or day to warn everyone with tears. 32And now I commend you to God and to the message of his grace, a message that is able to build you up and to give you the inheritance among all who are sanctified. 33I coveted no one's silver or gold or clothing. 34You know for yourselves that I worked with my own hands to support myself and my companions. 35In all this I have given you an example that by such work we must support the weak, remembering the words of the Lord Jesus, for

---

w Other ancient authorities add *after remaining at Trogyllium*
x Or *And now, bound in the spirit*

y Other ancient authorities read *of the Lord*
z Or *with his own blood;* Gk *with the blood of his Own*

20:14 *Mitylene* A city on the east side of the island of Lesbos, off the coast of the province of Asia; home of the famous poets Alcaeus and Sappho, and a popular resort for Roman aristocrats. **20:15** *Chios . . . Samos* Two significant islands on the sea route down the west coast of the province of Asia. *Miletus* An ancient site already in Paul's day and a major trade center. Though now five miles inland, it was a port in Paul's day. **20:16** *in Jerusalem . . . day of Pentecost* See note to 2:1. Pentecost came seven weeks after Passover, which Paul just celebrated (20:5–6). It is a noteworthy insight into ancient travel that it was going to be a challenge to reach Jerusalem within six weeks of ship travel from the province of Asia. This reference comes as a surprise, since Paul planned to return to Syria (20:3). Curiously, the author makes no clear mention of the major collection that, according to Paul's letters, provided the motive for his final trip to Jerusalem (see *Rom.* 15:25–33). Perhaps 24:17 contains some vague reminiscence of this collection. **20:17** It was a thirty-mile trip south for these elders. **20:18–35** Paul's farewell speech to the Ephesian elders has a much broader reach than the specific audience, as did his speeches in the synagogue of Antioch (13:16–43) and Athens (17:22–31). It recalls the many deathbed speeches, or oral wills (testaments), in Jewish literature, in which the character predicts the future and issues warnings about it. See the *Testaments of the Twelve Patriarchs* and *Mark* 13 par. *Matt.* 24–25. The speech contains many Paul-like phrases and themes: the opening *You yourselves know;* the insistence on his humility, suffering, and giving; his desire to finish his course; that he did not cease, night or day; that he worked with his own hands. Most of these expressions are found, for example, in *1 Thess.* 2:1–12. The speech suits Paul's character while it also serves the author's narrative. **20:19** *the plots of the Jews* A characteristic theme; see note to 9:22–24. **20:22–25** The 1st hint, so far unexplained, that Jerusalem will bring serious problems for Paul; it is confirmed in 21:10–12. He had planned to go back to Syria (20:3), then without explanation decided to visit Jerusalem for the celebration of Pentecost (20:16). **20:26** *not responsible for the blood of any of you* See also 18:6. **20:28** *overseers* The Gk word *episkopoi* is elsewhere translated "bishops." Thus this author, like the author of the Pastorals (*Titus* 1:5–7), equates "elder" (20:17) and "bishop." *the blood of his own Son* The Gk lacks the word *Son*, so the passage can also read either "with his own blood" or "with the blood of his own [one]." The former reading would anticipate Ignatius of Antioch, who speaks of the "blood of God" (*Ephesians* 1). Paul talks about Jesus' blood sacrifice mainly in *Romans*, which has a Jewish-Christian ethos (*Rom.* 3:25; 5:9). This is not a prominent image in his letters. **20:29** See Jesus' words in *Luke* 10:3. **20:35** *the words of the Lord Jesus* Although this is among the most frequently quoted sayings of Jesus, it does not appear in any gospel. This should remind us that the written texts were still secondary to oral traditions about Jesus' life at the author's time of writing.

he himself said, 'It is more blessed to give than to receive.'"

³⁶When he had finished speaking, he knelt down with them all and prayed. ³⁷There was much weeping among them all; they embraced Paul and kissed him, ³⁸grieving especially because of what he had said, that they would not see him again. Then they brought him to the ship.

Paul's Journey to Jerusalem

21 When we had parted from them and set sail, we came by a straight course to Cos, and the next day to Rhodes, and from there to Patara.ᵃ ²When we found a ship bound for Phoenicia, we went on board and set sail. ³We came in sight of Cyprus; and leaving it on our left, we sailed to Syria and landed at Tyre, because the ship was to unload its cargo there. ⁴We looked up the disciples and stayed there for seven days. Through the Spirit they told Paul not to go on to Jerusalem. ⁵When our days there were ended, we left and proceeded on our journey; and all of them, with wives and children, escorted us outside the city. There we knelt down on the beach and prayed ⁶and said farewell to one another. Then we went on board the ship, and they returned home.

⁷When we had finishedᵇ the voyage from Tyre, we arrived at Ptolemais; and we greeted the believersᶜ and stayed with them for one day. ⁸The next day we left and came to Caesarea; and we went into the house of Philip the evangelist, one of the seven, and stayed with him. ⁹He had four unmarried daughtersᵈ who had the gift of prophecy. ¹⁰While we were staying there for several days, a prophet named Agabus

---

a Other ancient authorities add *and Myra*
b Or *continued*
c Gk *brothers*
d Gk *four daughters, virgins,*

came down from Judea. ¹¹He came to us and took Paul's belt, bound his own feet and hands with it, and said, "Thus says the Holy Spirit, 'This is the way the Jews in Jerusalem will bind the man who owns this belt and will hand him over to the Gentiles.'" ¹²When we heard this, we and the people there urged him not to go up to Jerusalem. ¹³Then Paul answered, "What are you doing, weeping and breaking my heart? For I am ready not only to be bound but even to die in Jerusalem for the name of the Lord Jesus." ¹⁴Since he would not be persuaded, we remained silent except to say, "The Lord's will be done."

¹⁵After these days we got ready and started to go up to Jerusalem. ¹⁶Some of the disciples from Caesarea also came along and brought us to the house of Mnason of Cyprus, an early disciple, with whom we were to stay.

Paul Visits James at Jerusalem

¹⁷When we arrived in Jerusalem, the brothers welcomed us warmly. ¹⁸The next day Paul went with us to visit James; and all the elders were present. ¹⁹After greeting them, he related one by one the things that God had done among the Gentiles through his ministry. ²⁰When they heard it, they praised God. Then they said to him, "You see, brother, how many thousands of believers there are among the Jews, and they are all zealous for the law. ²¹They have been told about you that you teach all the Jews living among the Gentiles to forsake Moses, and that you tell them not to circumcise their children or observe the customs. ²²What then is to be done? They will certainly hear that you have come. ²³So do what we tell you. We have four men who are under a vow. ²⁴Join these men, go through the rite of purification with them, and pay for the shaving of their heads. Thus all will know that there is nothing in what they have been told about you, but that you yourself observe and

---

21:1 *Cos...Rhodes...Patara* Continuing the line of movement southward through the Aegean Sea to the Mediterranean. The first two places are significant islands en route. A ship might have sailed directly from Rhodes to the east, but it appears (21:2) that this particular ship was ending its journey in Patara, a city on the southwest point of Asia Minor. **21:4 *We looked up*** Or "We sought out." **21:7 *Ptolemais*** About twenty-seven miles south of Tyre and thirty-five miles north of Caesarea—a likely place to break the journey. Traveling by foot, one could usually cover about twenty to thirty miles, depending upon the terrain. **21:8 *Philip the evangelist, one of the seven*** See 6:1–4 and 8:4–40, which left Philip in Caesarea. **21:9** The daughters' gift does not play a role in the narrative. Perhaps the author mentions it as a sign of Philip's virtue. **21:10 *a prophet named Agabus*** This is the 2d time that this prophet has come from Jerusalem to a place where Paul is; see 11:27–28. **21:12** See the roles of Jews and Gentiles in Jesus' trial (*Luke* 23). **21:14 *The Lord's will be done*** See Jesus' words before his arrest (*Luke* 22:42). **21:16 *Mnason of Cyprus*** Not otherwise known. **21:18** Once again we see that Jesus' brother James has quietly become the leader of the Jerusalem church, in spite of the author's emphasis on the apostles. See notes to 12:17; 15:13, 19. **21:20–22** The only passage in *Acts* that comes close to reflecting the seriousness of the internal Christian dispute between Paul and the Jewish Christians who denounced him. Paul's letters provide abundant evidence of the conflict (*Phil.* 3; *2 Corinthians* 3, 10–13; *Galatians*). But here Paul is accused not of failing to have Gentiles adopt Judaism (as in his letters) but of leading Jews away from their tradition. This indeed is a reasonable inference from his letters, which announce that the regime of Torah has ended (*Gal.* 3:19–29). **21:23–24** Here (in contrast to 18:18) the issue is clearly the Nazirite vow prescribed in *Num.* 6:1–21. The men are already observing the vow and, at the end, will need to have their heads shaved and offer sacrifice at the temple. Paul will join them for the remainder of the vow and then pay their expenses.

guard the law. 25But as for the Gentiles who have become believers, we have sent a letter with our judgment that they should abstain from what has been sacrificed to idols and from blood and from what is strangled*e* and from fornication." 26Then Paul took the men, and the next day, having purified himself, he entered the temple with them, making public the completion of the days of purification when the sacrifice would be made for each of them.

Paul Arrested in the Temple

27When the seven days were almost completed, the Jews from Asia, who had seen him in the temple, stirred up the whole crowd. They seized him, 28shouting, "Fellow Israelites, help! This is the man who is teaching everyone everywhere against our people, our law, and this place; more than that, he has actually brought Greeks into the temple and has defiled this holy place." 29For they had previously seen Trophimus the Ephesian with him in the city, and they supposed that Paul had brought him into the temple. 30Then all the city was aroused, and the people rushed together. They seized Paul and dragged him out of the temple, and immediately the doors were shut. 31While they were trying to kill him, word came to the tribune of the cohort that all Jerusalem was in an uproar. 32Immediately he took soldiers and centurions and ran down to them. When they saw the tribune and the soldiers, they stopped beating Paul. 33Then the tribune came, arrested him, and ordered him to be bound with two chains; he inquired who he was and what he had done. 34Some in the crowd shouted one thing, some another; and as he could not learn the facts because of the uproar, he ordered him to be brought into the barracks. 35When Paul*f* came to the steps, the violence of the mob was so great that he had to be carried by the soldiers. 36The crowd that followed kept shouting, "Away with him!"

Paul Defends Himself

37Just as Paul was about to be brought into the barracks, he said to the tribune, "May I say something to you?" The tribune*g* replied, "Do you know Greek? 38Then you are not the Egyptian who recently stirred up a revolt and led the four thousand assassins out into the wilderness?" 39Paul replied, "I am a Jew, from Tarsus in Cilicia, a citizen of an important city; I beg you, let me speak to the people." 40When he had given him permission, Paul stood on the steps and motioned to the people for silence; and when there was a great hush, he addressed them in the Hebrew*h* language, saying:

---

e Other ancient authorities lack *and from what is strangled*

f Gk *he*
g Gk *He*
h That is, *Aramaic*

21:25 See 15:20, 29. This is a reminder to the reader, more than to Paul, that the Christianity of *Acts* is fundamentally Jewish; Paul himself is fully observant, and even Gentile Christians must observe some minimal prohibitions. There is no willful deviance here, the author is stressing, from Jewish law and tradition.   **the Jews from Asia** Presumably, these Jews have come for Pentecost as Paul did, although the author does not tell us whether Paul made it in time for the holiday (see 19:16). **21:28** *Fellow Israelites* See note to 1:16.   **teaching everyone everywhere against our people, our law, and this place** Although the author presents these charges as nonsensical, in view of his strenuous efforts to show Paul's fidelity to Judaism, the reader of Paul's letters *(Philippians* 3; *Galatians; Romans)* might well deduce that he considered Judaism without Christ no longer viable.   **brought Greeks into the temple** Foreigners were permitted in the outer court of the temple. But between there and the inner court was a half-wall partition with thirteen signs, posted at regular intervals, indicating that any Gentile passing that point would be responsible for his or her own death. These signs are known from both literature (Josephus, *J.W.* 5.194; *Ant.* 15.417) and archaeology (two of the tablets have been found). The serious but mistaken charge that Paul had brought a Gentile into the main temple area, and so defiled it, is presented as the main cause of his arrest.   **21:30** *immediately the doors were shut* The gates were ordinarily closed in the evening, but this was no simple task, since the ten double gates each measured forty-five feet by forty-five feet. The gate made of Corinthian bronze (possibly the Beautiful Gate of 3:2) allegedly required twenty men or more to close (Josephus, *J.W.* 6.293).   **21:31** *the tribune of the cohort* For *cohort,* see note to 10:1. It is unclear whether this was the regular Jerusalem cohort or the one that came in from Caesarea with the governor, Felix, for major festivals such as Pentecost. The tribune was probably the commanding officer of this auxiliary cohort of five hundred or one thousand men.   **21:32** *took soldiers and centurions* The centurions were the officers, each commanding a century of eighty to one hundred men. It is plausible that the Roman authorities would intervene simply to prevent riots, and it is characteristic of this author to present them as differing from the Jews in finding Christianity nonthreatening (*Luke* 23:1–26; *Acts* 13:4–12; 17:12–16).   **21:38** *the Egyptian who recently stirred up a revolt* Josephus (*J.W.* 2.261; *Ant.* 20.167–172) describes this messianic pretender, who came to Jerusalem about 54 C.E. He is said to have promised his hundreds or thousands of followers that, at his command from the Mount of Olives, the walls of Jerusalem would collapse. But before he could demonstrate this feat, the soldiers of the procurator, Felix, dispersed or killed his followers. He escaped.   **led the four thousand assassins out into the wilderness** The Gk word for "assassin" here is transliterated from the Latin *sicarius,* "dagger-man." Josephus, however, distinguishes sharply between the visionary Egyptian and the militant Sicarii, political rebels who used to follow their opponents into large urban crowds so that they could stab them with impunity (*J.W.* 2.254–257; *Ant.* 20.164–165).   **21:40** *in the Hebrew language* Aramaic is usually assumed (see footnote *h*) because there is considerable other evidence—including Jesus' transliterated sayings in the gospels—that Aramaic was the

22

"Brothers and fathers, listen to the defense that I now make before you."

²When they heard him addressing them in Hebrew,*i* they became even more quiet. Then he said:

³"I am a Jew, born in Tarsus in Cilicia, but brought up in this city at the feet of Gamaliel, educated strictly according to our ancestral law, being zealous for God, just as all of you are today. ⁴I persecuted this Way up to the point of death by binding both men and women and putting them in prison, ⁵as the high priest and the whole council of elders can testify about me. From them I also received letters to the brothers in Damascus, and I went there in order to bind those who were there and to bring them back to Jerusalem for punishment.

Paul Tells of His Conversion

⁶"While I was on my way and approaching Damascus, about noon a great light from heaven suddenly shone about me. ⁷I fell to the ground and heard a voice saying to me, 'Saul, Saul, why are you persecuting me?' ⁸I answered, 'Who are you, Lord?' Then he said to me, 'I am Jesus of Nazareth*j* whom you are persecuting.' ⁹Now those who were with me saw the light but did not hear the voice of the one who was speaking to me. ¹⁰I asked, 'What am I to do, Lord?' The Lord said to me, 'Get up and go to Damascus; there you will be told everything that has been assigned to you to do.' ¹¹Since I could not see because of the brightness of that light, those who were with me took my hand and led me to Damascus.

¹²"A certain Ananias, who was a devout man according to the law and well spoken of by all the Jews living there, ¹³came to me; and standing beside me, he said, 'Brother Saul, regain your sight!' In that very hour I regained my sight and saw him. ¹⁴Then he said, 'The God of our ancestors has chosen you to know his will, to see the Righteous One and to hear his own voice; ¹⁵for you will be his witness to all the world of what you have seen and heard. ¹⁶And now why do you delay? Get up, be baptized, and have your sins washed away, calling on his name.'

Paul Sent to the Gentiles

¹⁷"After I had returned to Jerusalem and while I was praying in the temple, I fell into a trance ¹⁸and saw Jesus*k* saying to me, 'Hurry and get out of Jerusalem quickly, because they will not accept your testimony about me.' ¹⁹And I said, 'Lord, they themselves know that in every synagogue I imprisoned and beat those who believed in you. ²⁰And while the blood of your witness Stephen was shed, I myself was standing by, approving and keeping the coats of those who killed him.' ²¹Then he said to me, 'Go, for I will send you far away to the Gentiles.'"

Paul and the Roman Tribune

²²Up to this point they listened to him, but then they shouted, "Away with such a fellow from the earth! For he should not be allowed to live." ²³And while they were shouting, throwing off their cloaks, and tossing dust into the air, ²⁴the tribune directed that he was to be brought into the barracks, and ordered him to be examined by flogging, to find out the reason for this outcry against him. ²⁵But when they had tied him up with thongs,*l* Paul said to the centurion who was standing by, "Is it legal for you to flog a Roman citizen who is uncondemned?" ²⁶When the centurion heard that, he went to the tribune and said to him, "What are you about to do? This man is a Roman citizen." ²⁷The tribune came and asked Paul,*k* "Tell me, are you a Roman citizen?" And he said, "Yes." ²⁸The tribune answered, "It cost me a large sum of money to get my citizenship." Paul said, "But I was born a citizen." ²⁹Immediately those who were

---

i That is, *Aramaic*
j Gk *the Nazorean*

k Gk *him*
l Or *up for the lashes*

---

common language in 1st-century Judea. But Hebrew, the language of the Bible and culture, was certainly known by many, and it is not impossible that the writer does mean Hebrew. This possibility is enhanced by the observation that Paul's speaking Hebrew quickly attracted the attention of his hearers (22:2)—as would something unusual. **22:3** Paul claims an education from a leading and respected Pharisee; see note to 5:34. **22:4–5** See 8:3; 9:1–2. **22:6–16** Essentially a recollection of 9:3–19, but with some new information. **22:9** Contrast 9:7, which says that his companions "heard the voice but saw no one." **22:14–16** Ananias's words were not reported earlier. **22:17–21** Paul's conversation with the risen Jesus was not reported earlier. It has the effect of exposing the stubbornness of the Jews. Paul thinks that because he was one of them and with the best possible credentials—he was known to have vigorously persecuted the Christians—they would listen to him. But the risen Jesus knowingly discounts this possibility and sends him to Gentiles. **22:21** This statement of Paul in *Acts* matches his own letters, where he is conscious of being called to reach Gentiles (*Gal.* 1:16). In the narrative of *Acts*, however, Paul routinely goes first to the Jews, only turning to Gentiles when the Jews reject him (13:5, 14, 44; 14:1–2; 16:13; 17:2–5). **22:25 to flog a Roman citizen** See note to 16:37–39.

about to examine him drew back from him; and the tribune also was afraid, for he realized that Paul was a Roman citizen and that he had bound him.

Paul before the Council

30Since he wanted to find out what Paul[m] was being accused of by the Jews, the next day he released him and ordered the chief priests and the entire council to meet. He brought Paul down and had him stand before them.

23 While Paul was looking intently at the council he said, "Brothers,[n] up to this day I have lived my life with a clear conscience before God." 2Then the high priest Ananias ordered those standing near him to strike him on the mouth. 3At this Paul said to him, "God will strike you, you whitewashed wall! Are you sitting there to judge me according to the law, and yet in violation of the law you order me to be struck?" 4Those standing nearby said, "Do you dare to insult God's high priest?" 5And Paul said, "I did not realize, brothers, that he was high priest; for it is written, 'You shall not speak evil of a leader of your people.'"

6When Paul noticed that some were Sadducees and others were Pharisees, he called out in the council, "Brothers, I am a Pharisee, a son of Pharisees. I am on trial concerning the hope of the resurrection[o] of the dead." 7When he said this, a dissension began between the Pharisees and the Sadducees, and the assembly was divided. 8(The Sadducees say that there is

---

m Gk *he*
n Gk *Men, brothers*
o Gk *concerning hope and resurrection*

no resurrection, or angel, or spirit; but the Pharisees acknowledge all three.) 9Then a great clamor arose, and certain scribes of the Pharisees' group stood up and contended, "We find nothing wrong with this man. What if a spirit or an angel has spoken to him?" 10When the dissension became violent, the tribune, fearing that they would tear Paul to pieces, ordered the soldiers to go down, take him by force, and bring him into the barracks.

11That night the Lord stood near him and said, "Keep up your courage! For just as you have testified for me in Jerusalem, so you must bear witness also in Rome."

The Plot to Kill Paul

12In the morning the Jews joined in a conspiracy and bound themselves by an oath neither to eat nor drink until they had killed Paul. 13There were more than forty who joined in this conspiracy. 14They went to the chief priests and elders and said, "We have strictly bound ourselves by an oath to taste no food until we have killed Paul. 15Now then, you and the council must notify the tribune to bring him down to you, on the pretext that you want to make a more thorough examination of his case. And we are ready to do away with him before he arrives."

16Now the son of Paul's sister heard about the ambush; so he went and gained entrance to the barracks and told Paul. 17Paul called one of the centurions and said, "Take this young man to the tribune, for he has something to report to him." 18So he took him, brought him to the tribune, and said, "The prisoner Paul called me and asked me to bring this young man to you; he has something to tell you." 19The tribune

---

22:30 *the chief priests and the entire council* That is, the Jewish high court—traditionally called the Sanhedrin. See also Jesus' trial before this body in *Luke* 22:66–23:1. **23:1–5** The story of Paul's exchange with the high priest may be humorously intended. In view of the probably hierarchical seating plan in the council and general ancient concerns about status, it is difficult to imagine that Paul would not have known which person was the high priest. It is perhaps easier to read his comments as sarcastic: After declaring his honest view of the high priest, he pretends to retract his remark because of the formal requirement of the Torah. The sarcasm continues in 23:6–10. **23:2 *the high priest Ananias*** According to Josephus, Ananias (the Hebrew name is Hananiah) the son of Nebedaeus was high priest in 47–59 C.E. (*J.W.* 2.243, 409–442; *Ant.* 20.103, 131). The fact that Felix is now near the end of his term as governor (52–59/60 C.E.; see *Acts* 23:24; 24:27) puts Paul's arrest somewhere in the mid- to late 50s. This roughly accords with his letters, which seem to require a seventeen-year span from his conversion (in the mid-30s) to his writing of *Galatians* (*Gal.* 1:18; 2:1), followed by some further activity and letter writing. **23:5** *Exod.* 22:28 (MT 22:27). **23:6–12** This appears to be another humorous story. Paul is not really on trial for being a Pharisee, but the author has him use his resourcefulness in order to save himself—like Homer's *Odysseus*. The author pokes fun at the Jewish leaders, alleging that they could be so obsessed with their own doctrinal differences that they overlook the simple matter at hand. They go so far as to welcome Paul as one of them. **23:8** According to Josephus (*Ant.* 13.297–298; 18.16–17), the Sadducees rejected everything not found in the books of Moses, including the hope for a future life. Their rejection of angels, mentioned by no other source, is puzzling because the Torah itself has a few stories of angels. Perhaps they rejected only the more comprehensive schemes, current in the 1st century, of angels, archangels, demons, and archdemons. **23:11 *bear witness also in Rome*** See 25:10–12; 27–28. **23:12–31** On Jewish plots in *Acts*, see note to 9:22–24. The entire story of the plot, the intelligence from Paul's nephew, and the counterplan by the tribune adds a great deal of suspense to the narrative. Historians of this period were expected to include some measure of novel-like suspense. **23:16 *the son of Paul's sister*** This surprising reference (nothing else is said of Paul's sister or nephew elsewhere) assumes that Paul had relatives living in Jerusalem. This would fit the author's claim that Paul was educated in the city (22:3).

took him by the hand, drew him aside privately, and asked, "What is it that you have to report to me?" [20]He answered, "The Jews have agreed to ask you to bring Paul down to the council tomorrow, as though they were going to inquire more thoroughly into his case. [21]But do not be persuaded by them, for more than forty of their men are lying in ambush for him. They have bound themselves by an oath neither to eat nor drink until they kill him. They are ready now and are waiting for your consent." [22]So the tribune dismissed the young man, ordering him, "Tell no one that you have informed me of this."

Paul Sent to Felix the Governor

[23]Then he summoned two of the centurions and said, "Get ready to leave by nine o'clock tonight for Caesarea with two hundred soldiers, seventy horsemen, and two hundred spearmen. [24]Also provide mounts for Paul to ride, and take him safely to Felix the governor." [25]He wrote a letter to this effect:

[26]"Claudius Lysias to his Excellency the governor Felix, greetings. [27]This man was seized by the Jews and was about to be killed by them, but when I had learned that he was a Roman citizen, I came with the guard and rescued him. [28]Since I wanted to know the charge for which they accused him, I had him brought to their council. [29]I found that he was accused concerning questions of their law, but was charged with nothing deserving death or imprisonment. [30]When I was informed that there would be a plot against the man, I sent him to you at once, ordering his accusers also to state before you what they have against him.[p]"

[31]So the soldiers, according to their instructions, took Paul and brought him during the night to Antipatris. [32]The next day they let the horsemen go on with him, while they returned to the barracks. [33]When they came to Caesarea and delivered the letter to the governor, they presented Paul also before him. [34]On reading the letter, he asked what province he belonged to, and when he learned that he was from Cilicia, [35]he said, "I will give you a hearing when your accusers arrive." Then he ordered that he be kept under guard in Herod's headquarters.[q]

Paul before Felix at Caesarea

24 Five days later the high priest Ananias came down with some elders and an attorney, a certain Tertullus, and they reported their case against Paul to the governor. [2]When Paul[r] had been summoned, Tertullus began to accuse him, saying:

"Your Excellency,[s] because of you we have long enjoyed peace, and reforms have been made for this people because of your foresight. [3]We welcome this in every way and everywhere with utmost gratitude. [4]But, to detain you no further, I beg you to hear us briefly with your customary graciousness. [5]We have, in fact, found this man a pestilent fellow, an agitator among all the Jews throughout the world, and a ringleader of the sect of the Nazarenes.[t] [6]He even tried to

---

p Other ancient authorities add *Farewell*
q Gk *praetorium*
r Gk *he*
s Gk lacks *Your Excellency*
t Gk *Nazoreans*

23:24 Felix the governor Antonius or perhaps Claudius Felix. The exact dates of his tenure as procurator are uncertain, but 52–59/60 C.E. is widely accepted. He was a freedman (as his name, meaning "fortunate," also suggests) from the Emperor Claudius's household and had attained equestrian (lower-nobility) rank. Being made governor was an extraordinary honor for such a person. Under his tenure, political rebellion and banditry seem to have flourished in Judea. Josephus claims that he paid to have the high priest Jonathan murdered because of his constant criticisms (*Ant.* 20.162) and also that he violated Jewish laws by seducing another man's wife—Drusilla, daughter of King Agrippa—and then failed to be circumcised in order to marry her (*Ant.* 20.141–144). The aristocratic Roman historian Tacitus (*Histories* 5.9) complains that such a man was given a province.   **23:26 his Excellency** This common title for men of equestrian rank is the same as that used by the author for the patron Theophilus (*Luke* 1:3).   **23:27** Further humor: the tribune did *not* rescue Paul because he was a Roman citizen (21:31–36). The author portrays the tribune as misrepresenting himself, in a good light, to the governor. **23:29 nothing deserving death or imprisonment** See Pilate's words at Jesus' trial (*Luke* 23:1–25). The author stresses that Christianity, peculiar though it may seem, is not a threat to the Roman order.   **23:32 to Antipatris** Almost exactly halfway between Jerusalem and Caesarea, twenty-six miles (one day's journey on a march) from each. This was an extremely old site—more than three thousand years old in the 1st century—but it had been refounded by Herod the Great and renamed for his father, Antipater.   **23:35 Herod's headquarters** Herod's praetorium has not yet been discovered at Caesarea. **24:1 an attorney, a certain Tertullus** In Gk, this man with what might be considered a "fancy Latin name" is called a *rhētōr*, or orator. In the ancient world, this was not a compliment if it came from someone with a philosophical or historical bent, for rhetoric—by which one could make a case for anything one desired—was seen as the enemy of truth. This description of the man sets up the conditions for extreme sarcasm.   **24:2–4** This is biting humor. The orator, true to form, knows no limits to his obsequiousness. Everyone knows what a bad governor Felix is, but Tertullus has no qualms about praising him in the grandest of terms.   **24:5 the sect of the Nazarenes** Or better "the school of the Nazarenes." The author has this Jewish spokesman incidentally recognize the Christians as another school, alongside the Pharisees and Sadducees; see note to 15:5. **24:6** See 21:28.

profane the temple, and so we seized him.[u] [8]By examining him yourself you will be able to learn from him concerning everything of which we accuse him."

[9]The Jews also joined in the charge by asserting that all this was true.

Paul's Defense before Felix

[10]When the governor motioned to him to speak, Paul replied:

"I cheerfully make my defense, knowing that for many years you have been a judge over this nation. [11]As you can find out, it is not more than twelve days since I went up to worship in Jerusalem. [12]They did not find me disputing with anyone in the temple or stirring up a crowd either in the synagogues or throughout the city. [13]Neither can they prove to you the charge that they now bring against me. [14]But this I admit to you, that according to the Way, which they call a sect, I worship the God of our ancestors, believing everything laid down according to the law or written in the prophets. [15]I have a hope in God—a hope that they themselves also accept—that there will be a resurrection of both[v] the righteous and the unrighteous. [16]Therefore I do my best always to have a clear conscience toward God and all people. [17]Now after some years I came to bring alms to my nation and to offer sacrifices. [18]While I was doing this, they found me in the temple, completing the rite of purification, without any crowd or disturbance. [19]But there were some Jews from Asia—they ought to be here before you to make an accusation, if they have anything against me. [20]Or let these men here tell what crime they had found when I stood before the council, [21]unless it was this one sentence that I called out while standing before them, 'It is about the resurrection of the dead that I am on trial before you today.'"

[22]But Felix, who was rather well informed about the Way, adjourned the hearing with the comment, "When Lysias the tribune comes down, I will decide your case." [23]Then he ordered the centurion to keep him in custody, but to let him have some liberty and not to prevent any of his friends from taking care of his needs.

Paul Held in Custody

[24]Some days later when Felix came with his wife Drusilla, who was Jewish, he sent for Paul and heard him speak concerning faith in Christ Jesus. [25]And as he discussed justice, self-control, and the coming judgment, Felix became frightened and said, "Go away for the present; when I have an opportunity, I will send for you." [26]At the same time he hoped that money would be given him by Paul, and for that reason he used to send for him very often and converse with him.

[27]After two years had passed, Felix was succeeded by Porcius Festus; and since he wanted to grant the Jews a favor, Felix left Paul in prison.

Paul Appeals to the Emperor

25 Three days after Festus had arrived in the province, he went up from Caesarea to Jerusalem [2]where the chief priests and the leaders of the Jews gave him a report against Paul. They appealed to him [3]and requested, as a favor to them against Paul,[w] to have him transferred to Jerusalem. They were, in fact, planning an ambush to kill him along the way. [4]Festus replied that Paul was being kept at Caesarea, and that he himself intended to go there shortly. [5]"So," he said, "let those of you who have the authority come down with me, and if there is anything wrong about the man, let them accuse him."

[6]After he had stayed among them not more than eight or ten days, he went down to Caesarea; the next

---

u Other ancient authorities add *and we would have judged him according to our law.* [7]*But the chief captain Lysias came and with great violence took him out of our hands,* [8]*commanding his accusers to come before you.*

v Other ancient authorities read *of the dead, both of*

w Gk *him*

24:10 Paul's opening, although necessarily cordial, completely lacks any positive judgment about Felix's tenure; contrast Tertullus's. **24:14** *according to the Way, which they call a sect* For the author, Christian faith represents the only path, but he wants to portray the Jews as at least recognizing early Christians as a school within Judaism (see 24:5). The word translated "Way" could also be translated "Path" or "Road." **24:17** This is the only hint in *Acts* that Paul came to Jerusalem in order to bring an offering, although that offering largely preoccupies him in his letters (*1 Cor.* 16:2–4; *2 Cor.* 8–9; *Gal.* 2:10; *Rom.* 15:25–29). **24:21** Recalling 23:6. The author's Paul continues, disingenuously but humorously, to evade the charges by making the general question of resurrection the issue: he is on trial because he believes in a general resurrection and future judgment (24:15). **24:24–26** The humor continues as Felix, who was known for corruption and accepting bribes, meets briefly with Paul in the hope of receiving a bribe. Instead, while sitting with the wife whom he stole from another man, he hears a lecture about morality and future judgment. **24:27** Felix was succeeded by Porcius Festus, apparently in 59 or 60 C.E. He ruled only two years and died in office. Josephus portrays him as a relatively mild but unfortunately short-lived procurator (*Ant.* 20.188, 193–194, 197). **25:1–5** Once again the author sharply contrasts alleged Jewish malevolence with Roman justice; see note to 21:32. **25:6** *went down to Caesarea* See note to 12:19.

day he took his seat on the tribunal and ordered Paul to be brought. [7]When he arrived, the Jews who had gone down from Jerusalem surrounded him, bringing many serious charges against him, which they could not prove. [8]Paul said in his defense, "I have in no way committed an offense against the law of the Jews, or against the temple, or against the emperor." [9]But Festus, wishing to do the Jews a favor, asked Paul, "Do you wish to go up to Jerusalem and be tried there before me on these charges?" [10]Paul said, "I am appealing to the emperor's tribunal; this is where I should be tried. I have done no wrong to the Jews, as you very well know. [11]Now if I am in the wrong and have committed something for which I deserve to die, I am not trying to escape death; but if there is nothing to their charges against me, no one can turn me over to them. I appeal to the emperor." [12]Then Festus, after he had conferred with his council, replied, "You have appealed to the emperor; to the emperor you will go."

Festus Consults King Agrippa

[13]After several days had passed, King Agrippa and Bernice arrived at Caesarea to welcome Festus. [14]Since they were staying there several days, Festus laid Paul's case before the king, saying, "There is a man here who was left in prison by Felix. [15]When I was in Jerusalem, the chief priests and the elders of the Jews informed me about him and asked for a sentence against him. [16]I told them that it was not the custom of the Romans to hand over anyone before the accused had met the accusers face to face and had been given an opportunity to make a defense against the charge. [17]So when they met here, I lost no time, but on the next day took my seat on the tribunal and ordered the man to be brought. [18]When the accusers stood up, they did not charge him with any of the crimes[x] that I was expecting. [19]Instead they had cer-

tain points of disagreement with him about their own religion and about a certain Jesus, who had died, but whom Paul asserted to be alive. [20]Since I was at a loss how to investigate these questions, I asked whether he wished to go to Jerusalem and be tried there on these charges.[y] [21]But when Paul had appealed to be kept in custody for the decision of his Imperial Majesty, I ordered him to be held until I could send him to the emperor." [22]Agrippa said to Festus, "I would like to hear the man myself." "Tomorrow," he said, "you will hear him."

Paul Brought before Agrippa

[23]So on the next day Agrippa and Bernice came with great pomp, and they entered the audience hall with the military tribunes and the prominent men of the city. Then Festus gave the order and Paul was brought in. [24]And Festus said, "King Agrippa and all here present with us, you see this man about whom the whole Jewish community petitioned me, both in Jerusalem and here, shouting that he ought not to live any longer. [25]But I found that he had done nothing deserving death; and when he appealed to his Imperial Majesty, I decided to send him. [26]But I have nothing definite to write to our sovereign about him. Therefore I have brought him before all of you, and especially before you, King Agrippa, so that, after we have examined him, I may have something to write— [27]for it seems to me unreasonable to send a prisoner without indicating the charges against him."

Paul Defends Himself before Agrippa

26 Agrippa said to Paul, "You have permission to speak for yourself." Then Paul stretched out his hand and began to defend himself:

[2]"I consider myself fortunate that it is before you, King Agrippa, I am to make my defense today against all the accusations of the Jews, [3]because you are espe-

---

x Other ancient authorities read *with anything*

y Gk *on them*

---

seat on the tribunal This would be the same seat as that on which King Agrippa had accepted worship (12:21). See note to 18:12. **25:9–10** Festus changes his mind in order to win the favor of the local leaders (contrast 25:4–5). Paul exercises his citizen's right of appeal to the emperor (see note to 16:37–39) in order to avoid a trial in Jerusalem, which he suspects would turn out badly, and the reader knows that the Jews of the story would have killed Paul en route to Jerusalem (25:3). **25:13** *King Agrippa and Bernice* That is, Agrippa II, son of the Herod (Agrippa I), who died earlier in the story (12:1–23), and great-grandson of Herod the Great. Born in 27 C.E., he was too young to take over his father's kingdom when the latter died in 44 C.E. He was later made king, however, over some territories northeast of Judea. The date of his death is usually put at about 100 C.E., but it may have been as early as 93 C.E. Bernice was not his wife but his sister; she was also the sister of the Drusilla who married Felix. She was a widow. There were widespread rumors, however, that she and her brother had an incestuous relationship (Josephus, *Ant.* 20.145). That the author makes them a couple who stay together suggests either that he thought they were married or that he is deliberately setting the stage for further sarcasm—probably the latter, in view of his practice so far. **25:19** *about their own religion* See the response of Gallio in 18:14–15. **25:23** The author's emphasis on the pomp and circumstance with which Agrippa and his sister enter sets in sharp relief Paul's inner strength in addressing them. See the author's portraits of John the Baptist (*Luke* 7:24–35) and Jesus (23:3, 9). **25:25** *nothing deserving death* See note to 23:29. **26:3** Paul's remark about Agrippa's close familiarity with Jewish customs may be sarcastic, in view of the king's apparent relationship with his own sister (see note to 25:13).

cially familiar with all the customs and controversies of the Jews; therefore I beg of you to listen to me patiently. ⁴"All the Jews know my way of life from my youth, a life spent from the beginning among my own people and in Jerusalem. ⁵They have known for a long time, if they are willing to testify, that I have belonged to the strictest sect of our religion and lived as a Pharisee. ⁶And now I stand here on trial on account of my hope in the promise made by God to our ancestors, ⁷a promise that our twelve tribes hope to attain, as they earnestly worship day and night. It is for this hope, your Excellency,ᶻ that I am accused by Jews! ⁸Why is it thought incredible by any of you that God raises the dead?

⁹"Indeed, I myself was convinced that I ought to do many things against the name of Jesus of Nazareth.ᵃ ¹⁰And that is what I did in Jerusalem; with authority received from the chief priests, I not only locked up many of the saints in prison, but I also cast my vote against them when they were being condemned to death. ¹¹By punishing them often in all the synagogues I tried to force them to blaspheme; and since I was so furiously enraged at them, I pursued them even to foreign cities.

Paul Tells of His Conversion

¹²"With this in mind, I was traveling to Damascus with the authority and commission of the chief priests, ¹³when at midday along the road, your Excellency,ᶻ I saw a light from heaven, brighter than the sun, shining around me and my companions. ¹⁴When we had all fallen to the ground, I heard a voice saying to me in the Hebrewᵇ language, 'Saul, Saul, why are you persecuting me? It hurts you to kick against the goads.' ¹⁵I asked, 'Who are you, Lord?' The Lord answered, 'I am Jesus whom you are persecuting. ¹⁶But

get up and stand on your feet; for I have appeared to you for this purpose, to appoint you to serve and testify to the things in which you have seen meᶜ and to those in which I will appear to you. ¹⁷I will rescue you from your people and from the Gentiles—to whom I am sending you ¹⁸to open their eyes so that they may turn from darkness to light and from the power of Satan to God, so that they may receive forgiveness of sins and a place among those who are sanctified by faith in me.'

Paul Tells of His Preaching

¹⁹"After that, King Agrippa, I was not disobedient to the heavenly vision, ²⁰but declared first to those in Damascus, then in Jerusalem and throughout the countryside of Judea, and also to the Gentiles, that they should repent and turn to God and do deeds consistent with repentance. ²¹For this reason the Jews seized me in the temple and tried to kill me. ²²To this day I have had help from God, and so I stand here, testifying to both small and great, saying nothing but what the prophets and Moses said would take place: ²³that the Messiahᵈ must suffer, and that, by being the first to rise from the dead, he would proclaim light both to our people and to the Gentiles."

Paul Appeals to Agrippa to Believe

²⁴While he was making this defense, Festus exclaimed, "You are out of your mind, Paul! Too much learning is driving you insane!" ²⁵But Paul said, "I am not out of my mind, most excellent Festus, but I am speaking the sober truth. ²⁶Indeed the king knows about these things, and to him I speak freely; for I am certain that none of these things has escaped his notice, for this was not done in a corner. ²⁷King Agrippa, do you believe the prophets? I know that

---

ᶻ Gk *O king*
ᵃ Gk *the Nazorean*
ᵇ That is, *Aramaic*

ᶜ Other ancient authorities read *the things that you have seen*
ᵈ Or *the Christ*

26:4–23 Paul's speech before Agrippa resembles that given before the people of Jerusalem in 22:3–21. In both cases, Paul focuses on his former vigorous persecution of Christians and the inescapable divine revelation that he was compelled to obey. This is critical for the author: Christianity is not a new human concoction but a continuous development with the past, directed by God. Paul is the best possible witness to its truth because he had no motive to embrace it unless he was forced to do so by God. **26:4** See 22:3. **26:5** *I have belonged to the strictest sect of our religion and lived as a Pharisee* Interestingly, Josephus also says that the Pharisees were considered the strictest sect (or better "most precise school") among the Jews. See *J.W.* 2.162. **26:7** *your Excellency* See note to 23:26. **26:14** *It hurts you to kick against the goads* New information, showing again the author's freedom to change stories as he retells them. The image of kicking against goads had been made famous in Aeschylus, *Prometheus Bound* 324–326. **26:17** On Paul's call to the Gentiles, see note to 22:21. **26:18** *forgiveness of sins* See note to 2:38. **26:19** *I was not disobedient to the heavenly vision* That is, Paul could do nothing other than obey the divine revelation. See note to 26:4–23. **26:23** On the problem of the Messiah's suffering and resurrection, see note to 17:3. **26:25** *I am speaking the sober truth* This is the author's portrayal of the Christians throughout: truth is opposed by the massive forces of the establishment. **26:26** *I speak freely* Frank speaking in dangerous situations was considered the mark of the true philosopher. See note to 4:13.

you believe." [28]Agrippa said to Paul, "Are you so quickly persuading me to become a Christian?"[e] [29]Paul replied, "Whether quickly or not, I pray to God that not only you but also all who are listening to me today might become such as I am—except for these chains."

[30]Then the king got up, and with him the governor and Bernice and those who had been seated with them; [31]and as they were leaving, they said to one another, "This man is doing nothing to deserve death or imprisonment." [32]Agrippa said to Festus, "This man could have been set free if he had not appealed to the emperor."

Paul Sails for Rome

27When it was decided that we were to sail for Italy, they transferred Paul and some other prisoners to a centurion of the Augustan Cohort, named Julius. [2]Embarking on a ship of Adramyttium that was about to set sail to the ports along the coast

---

[e] Or *Quickly you will persuade me to play the Christian*

of Asia, we put to sea, accompanied by Aristarchus, a Macedonian from Thessalonica. [3]The next day we put in at Sidon; and Julius treated Paul kindly, and allowed him to go to his friends to be cared for. [4]Putting out to sea from there, we sailed under the lee of Cyprus, because the winds were against us. [5]After we had sailed across the sea that is off Cilicia and Pamphylia, we came to Myra in Lycia. [6]There the centurion found an Alexandrian ship bound for Italy and put us on board. [7]We sailed slowly for a number of days and arrived with difficulty off Cnidus, and as the wind was against us, we sailed under the lee of Crete off Salmone. [8]Sailing past it with difficulty, we came to a place called Fair Havens, near the city of Lasea.

[9]Since much time had been lost and sailing was now dangerous, because even the Fast had already gone by, Paul advised them, [10]saying, "Sirs, I can see that the voyage will be with danger and much heavy loss, not only of the cargo and the ship, but also of our lives." [11]But the centurion paid more attention to the pilot and to the owner of the ship than to what Paul said. [12]Since the harbor was not suitable for spending the winter, the majority was in favor of

---

26:28 Agrippa's words can be read as either a statement or a question and as either straightforward or sarcastic. **26:31** See note to 25:25; note to 23:29. **26:32** See 25:10–12. **27:1–28:14** This story of Paul's voyage to Rome is a sort of showpiece in *Acts*. Although much of the preceding narrative has involved travel around the eastern Mediterranean, nothing else compares to the concise detail of this story—detail concerning ship's parts and navigation as well as geography. Epic stories of adventure on ships, including obligatory shipwrecks and harrowing experiences on foreign islands, were a fundamental part of everyone's imaginative world because of the influence of Homer's *Odyssey* and Virgil's *Aeneid*. The author gives here a miniature *Odyssey* for Paul. Such stories were all the more compelling because every traveler knew the genuine risks of shipwreck (Josephus, *Life* 14–15). Each of the three vessels mentioned in this story was a cargo ship; passenger ships were unknown until the 19th century. They were driven by sail, which made travel extremely difficult. They did not have a complicated system of sails but one large rectangular sail made from flax, with at most a small triangular topsail and a rectangular foresail for added maneuverability. **27:1** *a centurion of the Augustan Cohort, named Julius* This was presumably an auxiliary, not legionary, cohort from Caesarea that had been honored with the title of the Emperor Augustus. Julius is a famous Roman name. He has the same kind of position as Cornelius (see note to 10:1), and he is another kindly Roman official in *Acts*. *a ship of Adramyttium* The ship was based in this coastal town near Assos and Troas in Mysia (see notes to 16:8; 20:13); the captain was going to sail home along the safe coastal route, stopping at ports along the way. **27:2** *Aristarchus* Introduced in 19:29, where he joins Paul's entourage in Ephesus. **27:3** *Sidon* See note to 11:19. **27:4** *under the lee of Cyprus* That is, on the side protected from the wind, which would be the north and east at this time of year. It was apparently late summer or early fall because 27:9 will claim that the Day of Atonement (usually in early October) has passed by that point. **27:5** They sailed along the south coast of Asia Minor. Myra was a good place to change ships because it was located near Patara (see 21:1), just before the ship would turn north, into the Aegean Sea, for Adramyttium (27:1). Although the town proper was inland about three miles, the name probably included its port of Andriace. **27:6** *an Alexandrian ship* This was a large ship because it carried (if the best manuscripts are right) more than 270 passengers (27:37). The cargo was evidently wheat (27:38). Ships carrying wheat on this route were common in the 1st century because Egypt was the principal supplier of grain to Rome. **27:7** Leaving Myra, they headed due west, the straightest route to Rome, and so passed Cnidus, a port town on the extreme western tip of a peninsula that projects from the mainland of Asia Minor. But unable to continue on this course because of headwinds, they turned south to find protection to the east and south of Crete. Salmone is on the eastern tip of Crete, a large island in the center of the eastern Mediterranean. **27:8** Neither place has been excavated or identified with absolute certainty, but most scholars accept that they were about five miles apart on the southern coast of Crete. **27:9** The ancient sailing season on the Mediterranean was normally from March to the beginning of November; the first and last six weeks of this period, however, were considered very dangerous. The danger was from both severe storms and increased cloud cover, which precluded navigation by sun and stars. Since *the Fast* probably refers to the Day of Atonement (Yom Kippur) in late September or early October—the only mandated fast in the Bible (*Lev.* 16:1–34)—sailing season was now effectively over. It seems that the centurion left Caesarea in ample time (presumably late summer) but the group was delayed. **27:12** *the harbor was not suitable for spending the winter* That is, Fair Havens, which seems to be vulnerable to winter winds from the north and northeast (see 27:14).

putting to sea from there, on the chance that somehow they could reach Phoenix, where they could spend the winter. It was a harbor of Crete, facing southwest and northwest.

The Storm at Sea

13When a moderate south wind began to blow, they thought they could achieve their purpose; so they weighed anchor and began to sail past Crete, close to the shore. 14But soon a violent wind, called the northeaster, rushed down from Crete.*f* 15Since the ship was caught and could not be turned head-on into the wind, we gave way to it and were driven. 16By running under the lee of a small island called Cauda*g* we were scarcely able to get the ship's boat under control. 17After hoisting it up they took measures*h* to undergird the ship; then, fearing that they would run on the Syrtis, they lowered the sea anchor and so were driven. 18We were being pounded by the storm so violently that on the next day they began to throw the cargo overboard, 19and on the third day with their own hands they threw the ship's tackle overboard. 20When neither sun nor stars appeared for many days, and no small tempest raged, all hope of our being saved was at last abandoned.

21Since they had been without food for a long time, Paul then stood up among them and said, "Men, you should have listened to me and not have set sail from Crete and thereby avoided this damage and loss. 22I urge you now to keep up your courage, for there will be no loss of life among you, but only of the ship. 23For last night there stood by me an angel of the God to whom I belong and whom I worship, 24and he said, 'Do not be afraid, Paul; you must stand before the emperor; and indeed, God has granted safety to all those who are sailing with you.' 25So keep up your courage, men, for I have faith in God that it will be exactly as I have been told. 26But we will have to run aground on some island."

27When the fourteenth night had come, as we were drifting across the sea of Adria, about midnight the sailors suspected that they were nearing land. 28So they took soundings and found twenty fathoms; a little farther on they took soundings again and found fifteen fathoms. 29Fearing that we might run on the rocks, they let down four anchors from the stern and prayed for day to come. 30But when the sailors tried to escape from the ship and had lowered the boat into the sea, on the pretext of putting out anchors from the bow, 31Paul said to the centurion and the soldiers, "Unless these men stay in the ship, you cannot be saved." 32Then the soldiers cut away the ropes of the boat and set it adrift.

33Just before daybreak, Paul urged all of them to take some food, saying, "Today is the fourteenth day that you have been in suspense and remaining without food, having eaten nothing. 34Therefore I urge you to take some food, for it will help you survive; for none of you will lose a hair from your heads." 35After he had said this, he took bread; and giving thanks to God in the presence of all, he broke it and began to eat. 36Then all of them were encouraged and took food for themselves. 37(We were in all two hundred seventy-six*i* persons in the ship.) 38After they had satisfied their hunger, they lightened the ship by throwing the wheat into the sea.

The Shipwreck

39In the morning they did not recognize the land, but they noticed a bay with a beach, on which they planned to run the ship ashore, if they could. 40So they cast off the anchors and left them in the sea. At the same time they loosened the ropes that tied the steering-oars; then hoisting the foresail to the wind, they made for the beach. 41But striking a reef,*j* they

---

f Gk *it*
g Other ancient authorities read *Clauda*
h Gk *helps*

i Other ancient authorities read *seventy-six*; others, *about seventy-six*
j Gk *place of two seas*

27:16 *a small island called Cauda* Located twenty-three miles south of Crete. Thus, the group was moving entirely off course. *the ship's boat* That is, the lifeboat, towed by ropes behind the ship. **27:17** *the Syrtis* Two dangerous, shallow gulfs off the coast of Libya (ancient Cyrenaica), which was still hundreds of miles away. *they lowered the sea anchor and so were driven* The crew dropped the anchor to act as a brake, to slow the ship down. But the Gk word rendered *anchor* here is vague ("object," "vessel," "instrument"), and it may refer to the lowering of some other items connected with the sails. **27:19** *ship's tackle* The Gk word is of the same root as the word translated "anchor" in 27:17, and is similarly vague. **27:20** *neither sun nor stars appeared* That is, because of cloud cover at that time of year; navigation was impossible. **27:21–26** Paul appears as the composed man in the face of chaos—not fearing death himself and able to encourage even these brave soldiers and sailors. **27:27** *the fourteenth night* Presumably since setting sail from Crete (27:21); see also 27:33. This means that it was now approaching November 1, when all ship travel should have ceased. **27:28** *Fathoms* A fathom is six feet. The Gk word means literally "stretched out [hands]." **27:29** *anchors* The proper word for "anchors" is used here, different from that used in 27:17. The anchors were intended as brakes. **27:30** This author is sensitive to the foibles and deceits of human nature; see 23:27. **27:34** *lose a hair from your heads* See Jesus' words in *Luke* 12:7; 21:8. **27:38** *throwing the wheat into the sea* See note to 27:6.

ran the ship aground; the bow stuck and remained immovable, but the stern was being broken up by the force of the waves. [42]The soldiers' plan was to kill the prisoners, so that none might swim away and escape; [43]but the centurion, wishing to save Paul, kept them from carrying out their plan. He ordered those who could swim to jump overboard first and make for the land, [44]and the rest to follow, some on planks and others on pieces of the ship. And so it was that all were brought safely to land.

Paul on the Island of Malta

28 After we had reached safety, we then learned that the island was called Malta. [2]The natives showed us unusual kindness. Since it had begun to rain and was cold, they kindled a fire and welcomed all of us around it. [3]Paul had gathered a bundle of brushwood and was putting it on the fire, when a viper, driven out by the heat, fastened itself on his hand. [4]When the natives saw the creature hanging from his hand, they said to one another, "This man must be a murderer; though he has escaped from the sea, justice has not allowed him to live." [5]He, however, shook off the creature into the fire and suffered no harm. [6]They were expecting him to swell up or drop dead, but after they had waited a long time and saw that nothing unusual had happened to him, they changed their minds and began to say that he was a god.

[7]Now in the neighborhood of that place were lands belonging to the leading man of the island, named Publius, who received us and entertained us hospitably for three days. [8]It so happened that the father of Publius lay sick in bed with fever and dysentery. Paul visited him and cured him by praying and putting his hands on him. [9]After this happened, the rest of the people on the island who had diseases also came and were cured. [10]They bestowed many honors on us, and when we were about to sail, they put on board all the provisions we needed.

Paul Arrives at Rome

[11]Three months later we set sail on a ship that had wintered at the island, an Alexandrian ship with the Twin Brothers as its figurehead. [12]We put in at Syracuse and stayed there for three days; [13]then we weighed anchor and came to Rhegium. After one day there a south wind sprang up, and on the second day we came to Puteoli. [14]There we found believers[k] and were invited to stay with them for seven days. And so we came to Rome. [15]The believers[k] from there, when they heard of us, came as far as the Forum of Appius and Three Taverns to meet us. On seeing them, Paul thanked God and took courage.

[16]When we came into Rome, Paul was allowed to live by himself, with the soldier who was guarding him.

Paul and Jewish Leaders in Rome

[17]Three days later he called together the local leaders of the Jews. When they had assembled, he said to them, "Brothers, though I had done nothing against

---

k Gk brothers

27:43 *the centurion, wishing to save Paul* See note to 27:1. **28:1** *Malta* A very small island province that had been inhabited for nearly four thousand years in Paul's day. Its defining period, apparently, was under the influence of Phoenicia and then Carthage; thus, it had a Semitic culture, and the Aramaic language evidently still flourished there (28:2). **28:2** *The natives showed us unusual kindness* The author uses the Gk word for "barbarians," which would normally mean only that they did not speak Greek (see previous note). But this translation is justified because the author presents this shipwreck as an adventure in an exotic place. One always feared that the natives of such a place might be cannibals or worse, such as the Cyclopes of Homer. In reality, the island had been civilized for a long time. **28:4** *justice has not allowed him to live* The construction here might well suggest that the goddess Justice (Dikē) is meant. **28:5–6** Paul thus fulfills Jesus' promise in *Luke* 10:19. A similar story is told of Rabbi Hanina ben Dosa; *y. Berakhot* 9a. Paul was also hailed as a god in 14:11. **28:7** *the leading man of the island, named Publius* This was a common Roman first name *(praenomen)*. Presumably, this man was the leading Roman official on the island; he would have been responsible for Roman soldiers and prisoners who came there. It appears from Maltese inscriptions that calling him the "leading man" accorded with local custom. **28:11** *Three months later we set sail* That is, to allow for the worst of the winter to pass. Even so, the group left at the earliest possible moment, apparently in February. See note to 27:9. *Alexandrian ship* See note to 27:6. *the Twin Brothers* These would be Castor and Pollux, often called the Dioscuri (lit. "sons of Zeus"). Although they were Greek gods (Castor and Polydeuces), they had played an important role in legendary early Roman history and so had a temple dedicated to them in the city; some remains still stand. After becoming identified with the constellation Gemini ("twins") they became the patron protectors of sailors. **28:12–14** *Syracuse ... Rhegium ... Puteoli* Three natural stops on the route north to Rome from Malta. Syracuse was the main city on the large island of Sicily, lying on its southeastern tip. Rhegium was on the Italian mainland, across the six- or seven-mile strait from Sicily. Puteoli was the major port in southern Italy, on its western coast. Grain from Alexandria was off-loaded either here or at Ostia, farther north. Here Paul and his group disembarked to travel to Rome by land. Puteoli had a significant Jewish community (Josephus, *J.W.* 2.104). **28:15** *the Forum of Appius and Three Taverns* Both towns were stops on the Appian Way leading to Rome, about forty-three miles and thirty-three miles, respectively, from the city. **28:17–31** In keeping with the major theme of the book, that Christians sought to remain connected with Judaism as long as possible, the apostle to the Gentiles makes a bold final effort to reach the Jews.

our people or the customs of our ancestors, yet I was arrested in Jerusalem and handed over to the Romans[l] [18]When they had examined me, the Romans wanted to release me, because there was no reason for the death penalty in my case. [19]But when the Jews objected, I was compelled to appeal to the emperor—even though I had no charge to bring against my nation. [20]For this reason therefore I have asked to see you and speak with you,[m] since it is for the sake of the hope of Israel that I am bound with this chain." [21]They replied, "We have received no letters from Judea about you, and none of the brothers coming here has reported or spoken anything evil about you. [22]But we would like to hear from you what you think, for with regard to this sect we know that everywhere it is spoken against."

Paul Preaches in Rome

[23]After they had set a day to meet with him, they came to him at his lodgings in great numbers. From morning until evening he explained the matter to them, testifying to the kingdom of God and trying to convince them about Jesus both from the law of Moses and from the prophets. [24]Some were con-

vinced by what he had said, while others refused to believe. [25]So they disagreed with each other; and as they were leaving, Paul made one further statement: "The Holy Spirit was right in saying to your ancestors through the prophet Isaiah,

[26] 'Go to this people and say,
    You will indeed listen, but never understand,
      and you will indeed look, but never perceive.
[27] For this people's heart has grown dull,
    and their ears are hard of hearing,
      and they have shut their eyes;
        so that they might not look with their
          eyes,
    and listen with their ears,
  and understand with their heart and turn—
    and I would heal them.'
[28]Let it be known to you then that this salvation of God has been sent to the Gentiles; they will listen."[n]

[30]He lived there two whole years at his own expense[o] and welcomed all who came to him, [31]proclaiming the kingdom of God and teaching about the Lord Jesus Christ with all boldness and without hindrance.

---

l Gk *they*
m Or *I have asked you to see me and speak with me*

n Other ancient authorities add verse 29, *And when he had said these words, the Jews departed, arguing vigorously among themselves.*
o Or *in his own hired dwelling*

28:23 *trying to convince them about Jesus both from the law of Moses and from the prophets* See Jesus' teaching about himself from Moses and the prophets in *Luke* 24:27. **28:24** Some Jews continued to convert, then, even though the author has generally taken to using "the Jews" of non-Christian Jews. See note to 9:22–24. **28:25–27** *Isa.* 6:8–10. *Acts* agrees exactly with the LXX, except that the Gk of *Acts* has *their* only in connection with the eyes (28:27), not with the ears, whereas the LXX is the reverse. Interestingly, *Matt.* 13:14–15 has the same version as *Acts*. This passage about Israel's stubbornness was a favorite among early Christians, and they may have known it mainly from a collection of such passages rather than from the biblical scrolls. **28:28** This brings to a finale the movement toward Gentiles anticipated in 13:46–47 and 18:6. The author has explained to Theophilus and others how the Christian movement gradually evolved from a group of Jesus' students, wholly within Judaism, to what it is at his time of writing: a largely non-Jewish group that lives separate from the Jewish community, is in conflict with it, and does not follow its laws or customs. **28:31 *with all boldness*** See note to 4:13.

The Secret Sayings of Jesus from Judas the Twin

GOSPEL OF THOMAS   Introduced by Stephen J. Patterson

T HE *GOSPEL OF THOMAS* is a collection of sayings attributed to Jesus. The single surviving copy of this text in its entirety was discovered in 1945 near the town of Nag Hammadi in Upper Egypt, part of a spectacular archaeological find known as the Nag Hammadi library. This copy of the *Gospel of Thomas* is written in Coptic, the language used by Christian missionaries to evangelize Egypt in the early Christian period. There are, however, fragments of *Thomas* in Greek, the language in which it was originally composed, that were also found in Egypt. Scholars knew of the existence of such a gospel for centuries, but until a farmer made his discovery in the sands of Egypt, this gospel was considered lost forever.

Setting

Though discovered in Egypt, the *Gospel of Thomas* is one of the earliest documents associated with the eastern Syrian branch of Christianity that grew up well to the north. The primary support for this setting is its opening line: "These are the secret sayings that the living Jesus spoke and Didymos Judas Thomas recorded." Didymos Judas Thomas was a popular legendary figure in Syria. In the third-century, Syrian *Acts of Thomas,* he is identified with the *Apostle* Thomas, who was also referred to as "the twin" (Gk *didymos;* see *John* 11:16; 14:5; 20:24–28; 21:2). This may account for the confusion between these two figures.

A number of texts from Syrian Christianity refer to Thomas, including *Thomas the Contender,* the Abgar legends, and the sermons of Ephraem, a famous leader of the Syrian church. But all these sources are probably much later than the *Gospel of Thomas.* This raises the question of whether the *Gospel of Thomas* was simply heir to the Syrian Thomas tradition, or in fact predates it, perhaps even bearing some of the responsibility for bringing this tradition to Syria in the first place. After all, as a collection of Jesus' sayings, much of the gospel's material would have originally come out of the early Jesus movement in Palestine. Furthermore, saying 12 departs from the dominant tradition of appealing to Thomas for authority and appeals instead to "James the just," that is, James the brother of Jesus, who was a leader in the early church in Jerusalem (*Gal.* 1:19). Thus, it may be that the *Gospel of Thomas* was originally assembled, not in Syria, but further west, among the Christian circles active in and around Jerusalem. Later it may have been transported to Syria, where it became the basis for the subsequent flowering of the Thomas tradition.

Overview

The *Gospel of Thomas* is unlike the early NT gospels in that it has no real narrative. It is simply a collection of sayings attributed to Jesus. It has no discernible structure. Rather, its sayings are presented *ad seriatim*, each introduced by the simple phrase "Jesus said." The only common structural device found in the *Gospel of Thomas* are catchwords. In this simple technique, a word near the end of a saying calls to mind the same word at the beginning of the next saying. Originally catchwords helped people memorize long lists. The catchwords in the *Gospel of Thomas* may have functioned in this way.

While there is no real structure to the *Gospel of Thomas*, occasionally one may detect small groups of sayings connected by form or theme. These smaller groupings may have their origin in earlier collections that have since been incorporated into the *Gospel* (see, for example, the beatitudes in 68–69 or the parables in 63–65). For the most part, however, *Thomas* may be read as a simple collection of sayings.

Purpose

Philosophical schools sometimes compiled the teachings of their founders. Such collections generally had a utilitarian aspect. They were used to instruct new students. More advanced students relied on them as a summary of the teacher's wisdom. Sometimes they were memorized, so that the philosopher might have a ready store of material to weave into extemporaneous public speeches.

They also served an important social function. They represented the gathered wisdom of the cultures of the ancient world. Jews, Greeks, Syrians, and Egyptians—all gathered the wise sayings of their sages as a cultural resource.

In the Jewish world of Christian origins, wisdom was the seat of an important theological tradition as well. More than just wise persons, sages were prophets of God's divine wisdom (Gk *sophia*). In early Judaism, *Sophia* was personified as a divine messenger, a companion and envoy of God. Wisdom's spokespersons delivered the word of God. Sometimes the words of *Sophia* were quite plain and proverbial (as in *Proverbs* 1–8). In other texts her words were mysterious and obtuse. They spoke of the secrets of the universe, of cosmic origins, of human depths, even the nature of God. When we look at the *Gospel of Thomas*, it is this sort of speculative wisdom that predominates. Its sayings are "secrets," whose interpretation holds the key to eternal life (saying 1). For this reason, the *Gospel of Thomas* was not conceived simply as a practical collection of wise sayings. Someone (or some group) felt it presented the divine words of "the living Jesus," secrets to be interpreted for the sake of their ultimate future.

Themes and Issues

Modern interpretation of the *Gospel of Thomas* is still in its infancy, but some initial observations may be ventured.

As a sayings collection, the *Gospel of Thomas* is an example of the genre *logoi sophon*, or "sayings of the wise." As such it automatically evokes a tradition current within the Jewish theological world of the first century: wisdom. It was in wisdom circles that collections such as *Proverbs, Ecclesiastes,* and the *Wisdom of Solomon* were produced. Like them, many of the *Gospel of Thomas*'s sayings speak of what is true about people, about life, and about the world. They consider what is worthwhile about the world, and what is wrong with it. They discuss human wisdom and human folly.

But wisdom, on the whole, tends to be rather conservative. It tends toward the conventional, the tried and true. By contrast, the *Gospel of Thomas* often voices an uncommon wisdom, a wisdom that is "not of this age" (*1 Cor.* 2:6). It enjoins the reader to renounce the world (*Gospel of Thomas* 110). Prudence is ridiculed in a parable (76). The savvy of the world are excluded from God's realm (64). Customary values, such as home and family (55, 99, 101), traditional piety (14), and respect for community leaders (3, 102), are sorely undermined. The wisdom one finds here is hardly conventional. In fact, if one is to view the *Gospel of Thomas*'s sagacity as wisdom at all, one must first cultivate a strictly countercultural way of thinking.

The theological underpinnings for the *Gospel of Thomas* also go beyond standard elements of wisdom theology. The truths the *Gospel* reveals about human nature extend beyond the ordinary observations that people tend to be selfish (41), vain (36), judgmental (26), foolish, and easily led astray (34). People are this way because they have forgotten who they are, where they have come from. In *Gos. Thom.* 28:1–4, Jesus speaks as one who has come from God to remind the "children of humanity" where they have come from and to where they will ultimately return:

> Jesus said, "I took my stand in the midst of the world, and in the flesh I appeared to them. I found them all drunk, and I did not find any of them thirsty. My soul ached for the children of humanity, because they are blind in their hearts and do not see, for they came into the world empty, and they also seek to depart from the world empty. But meanwhile they are drunk. When they shake off their wine, then they will repent."

The background for this way of thinking is found in gnosticism, a widespread religious movement of the same period as Christianity's rise. Gnosticism appears in myriad forms, including Greek and Egyptian, as well as Jewish and Christian. Gnosticism as a movement may have been diverse, but its theological orientation can be generally described as anti-cosmic. Gnostics believed that the world, the cosmos, is evil, a mistake in the divine order. Consequently, they did not hold themselves to be part of this world. Originally descending from God, they came into the world as the result of a tragic error, a fall, an entrapment. Over time, however, the world has worked its anesthetizing powers over them. They have forgotten their origins, their God, until such time as a savior, a revealer, comes to remind them once again of their heavenly home.

Not all of this, of course, may be found in the *Gospel of Thomas*. Neither are there any elaborate descriptions of the origins of the world, of humanity's fall, and of the journey back to the divine realm, all of which are typical of later Christian gnosticism. Still, the rudiments of this thinking recur throughout the book: the deprecation of the world and the flesh (56, 80); the tendency to remove oneself from the world (21:6); even perhaps a primitive catechism for the return home (49, 50). In the *Gospel of Thomas*, one sees an early Christian community taking its first steps in the direction of gnosticism, its countercultural wisdom modulating into the full-blown anti-cosmic gnostic orientation that would find its fullest expression among Christians only in the second century.

Religious practices accompanied the nascent Gnosticism of *Thomas*. As may be expected, distain for the world and the "flesh" probably gave rise to asceticism among *Thomas* Christians. Sayings such as 29 and 112 draw a sharp distinction between the body and the soul at the expense of the latter. *Gospel of Thomas* 27:1 is particularly evocative on that score: "If you do not fast from the world, you will not find the kingdom." At other points, however, the *Gospel of Thomas* seems to equivocate on traditional ascetic practices. Should one fast (104:1–3) or refrain from fasting (14:1)? Later, asceticism would emerge as a major feature of Christianity in Syria. Perhaps one sees in the *Gospel of Thomas* the very beginning of that tradition and the theological impulses with which it originated.

There may also be evidence in *Thomas* that those who used this gospel were given to mysticism and visionary experiences. These, too, belong to the general world of gnostic thinking, where the secrets of the universe are often revealed to the elect through visions. *Gospel of Thomas* 15 probably refers to the experience, common in Jewish mysticism, of ascending into heaven to behold God in a spectacular beatific vision: "Jesus said, 'When you see the one who was not born of woman, fall on your faces and worship. That one is your Father.'" Other sayings that may reflect such visionary experiences include *Gos. Thom.* 27:2; 83; 84; 59; and 37.

The *Gospel of Thomas* shares with gnosticism a basic concern for redeemable identity within a world that was widely perceived as brutal and mean. It presents us with a Jesus whose words call one out of the chaos into a quest to seek (2, 92, 94), and finally to discover, one's true identity as a child of God (3:4).

Date and Authorship

Like most early Christian writings, the *Gospel of Thomas* is pseudonymous, that is, it is attributed to a famous figure from Christian origins, but written anonymously. This was a common practice in the ancient world. To produce such a religious treatise in one's own name would have been considered a conceit. (See introduction to LETTERS ATTRIBUTED TO PAUL.)

It is not entirely clear to whom this gospel is attributed. As noted above, the opening lines credit the work to Didymos Judas Thomas. Initially this is how people would have referred to the book. The name appears elsewhere in this form only in the Syrian *Acts of Thomas* (ch. 1). "Judas Thomas" occurs in some Syrian manuscripts of *John* 14:22 and the *Book of Thomas the Contender*. Of the three, only Judas is a bona fide name; Didymos and Thomas (Hebrew *tô'ām*) are the Greek and Semitic words for "twin," respectively. Thus, the ascription may be to "Judas the twin."

There are many Judases in the early Christian tradition. Judas Iscariot betrayed Jesus. Another Judas is mentioned in *John* 14:22, "Judas, not the Iscariot." Curiously, in the later Syrian translation of *John*, this Judas is identified as Didymos Judas Thomas. This could be the same Judas the twin, but whose twin is he? There is yet another Judas in the gospels, namely Judas the brother of Jesus, mentioned in *Mark* 6:3 and *Matt.* 13:55. This series of connections has led Helmut Koester to suggest that the opening lines of this gospel may claim descent from none other than Judas, the twin brother of Jesus.

In Syrian tradition this connection would not have seemed at all far fetched. At some point in the history of the gospel, Didymos Judas Thomas was reduced simply to Thomas. A title, added later to the end of the book, reads "the gospel of Thomas," meaning the Apostle Thomas, who was thought by the early church to have evangelized eastern Syria and India. It is easy to see how this might have happened. Adding a title to the end of a book was customary in antiquity. Furthermore the Apostle Thomas is repeatedly referred to as "the twin" throughout the *Gospel of John* (11:16; 14:5; 20:24–28; 21:12). In Syria the names Judas Thomas and Thomas may have become confused over time, resulting in this conflation of the names. In a later Syrian text called the *Acts of Thomas*, Thomas is revealed as the twin brother of Jesus. Thus, the persons who used the *Gospel of Thomas* may well have considered it the gospel of Jesus' twin brother.

The date of the *Gospel of Thomas*'s composition is not known. As a sayings collection, it would have been much more malleable than other, narrative texts. Sayings may have been added or dropped from it throughout its long history. Some of its sayings come from Jesus himself. Others will have come from various persons and communities in the history of the early church. Exactly when someone first began to collect these diverse sayings cannot be determined with any certainty. Still, a few clues provide suggestions.

Gospel of Thomas 12 advises Jesus' followers to go to James the just after Jesus has departed from them. James the just was the brother of Jesus and a prominent leader in the Jerusalem church (*Gal.* 1:19). It may be that some early stage of this collection was associated with his authority. His martyrdom in 64 C.E. provides a time frame for such an early collection and an occasion for transferring authority to Didymos Judas Thomas (another brother of Jesus?). In any event, the collection probably grew over many years. When, exactly, it reached its present form, or whether the text we have now is unique, is not known. In fact, differences between the Coptic version and the extant Greek fragments suggest that there were indeed different versions of the *Gospel of Thomas* in circulation.

Relation to Other Early Christian Texts

One of the chief questions that have occupied *Gospel of Thomas* scholars over many decades is the question of its relationship to the canonical gospels, especially the Synoptics, with which it shares about half of its sayings. Early in the debate, many scholars argued or assumed that the author of *Thomas* must have taken these sayings from the Synoptic Gospels, editing them to suit his own theological agenda. Today, few scholars would defend this view. The Synoptics may be the source for a few of *Thomas*'s sayings, added to the collection relatively late after the Synoptic Gospels had gained ascendancy in Christian circles. But evidence for such borrowing is rare in *Thomas*. To the contrary, most of *Thomas*'s sayings appear to be earlier in form, or derived from forms earlier than their synoptic counterparts. Moreover, the dozens of sayings in *Thomas* that have no synoptic parallels show that *Thomas* derives from circles distinct from those that produced the Synoptics. For these and other reasons, most scholars today have come to view the *Gospel of Thomas* as basically autonomous, with its own distinctive sources and with its own distinctive flavor.

Value for the Study of Early Christianity

If this trend in scholarship turns out to stand the test of time, the significance of the *Gospel of Thomas* for the study of early Christianity may be considerable. On the one hand, the *Gospel of Thomas* would provide a textual window into a literary form that is quite different from what became canonical, but which nonetheless originated very early. This possibility lends support to Walter Bauer's hypothesis that the categories of "orthodoxy" and "heresy" cannot properly be applied to first century Christianity. Christian beginnings, rather, were marked by a diversity of theological interpretations of Jesus, a diversity that did not begin to settle out into "orthodox" and "heretical" views until later in the second century.

On the other hand, the possibility that the *Gospel of Thomas* represents a branch of the Jesus tradition that is essentially independent of the synoptic tradition has of late drawn the *Gospel of Thomas* into the historical Jesus discussion. The extensive overlap between the *Gospel of Thomas* and the Synoptics creates a pool of sayings and parables that are "multiply attested" in independent circles relatively early in the development of the Jesus tradition. Traditionally multiple attestation is a significant criterion in the attempt to identify authentic sayings of Jesus (see introduction to BIOGRAPHY, ANECDOTE, AND HISTORY). As a result, the *Gospel of Thomas* has become central to the latest phase of the quest for the historical Jesus. These are relatively high stakes. One is well advised to consider this when reading the sometimes highly polemical secondary literature that is gathering around this document.

For Further Reading

Bauer, Walter. *Orthodoxy and Heresy in Earliest Christianity*. Edited by Robert A. Kraft and Gerhard Krodel. Translated by the Philadelphia Seminary on Christian Origins. Philadelphia: Fortress, 1971.

Kloppenborg, John S., Marvin W. Meyer, Stephen J. Patterson, and Michael G. Steinhauser. *Q-Thomas Reader*. Sonoma: Polebridge, 1990.

Koester, Helmut. *Ancient Christian Gospels: Their History and Development*. Philadelphia: Trinity, 1990.

THE GOSPEL OF
THOMAS

Prologue

These are the secret sayings that the living Jesus spoke and Didymos Judas Thomas recorded.

1 And he said, "Whoever discovers the interpretation of these sayings will not taste death."

2 Jesus said, "Let them that seek not stop seeking until they find. ²When they find, they will be disturbed. ³When they are disturbed, they will marvel,*a* ⁴and will reign over all."*b*

3 Jesus said, "If your leaders say to you, 'Look, the kingdom is in the sky,' then the birds of the sky will precede you. ²If they say to you, 'It is in the sea,'*c* then the fish will precede you. ³Rather, the kingdom is inside you and it is outside you. ⁴When you know yourselves, then you will be known, and you will understand that you are children of the living Father. ⁵But if you do not know yourselves, then you live in poverty, and you are the poverty."

4 Jesus said, "The person old in days will not hesitate to ask a little child seven days old about the place of life, and that person will live. ²For many of the first will be last,*d* ³and will become a single one."

5 Jesus said, "Know what is in front of your face, and that which is hidden from you will be disclosed to you. ²For there is nothing hidden that will not be revealed."*e*

6 His disciples asked him and said to him, "Do you want us to fast? How should we pray? Should we give alms? What diet should we observe?" ²Jesus said, "Do not lie, ³and do not do what you hate, ⁴because

---

a Gk *they will rule*
b Gk *and when they rule*
c Gk *'It is under the earth,'*

d Gk adds *and the last first*
e Gk adds *and nothing buried that will not be raised*

TRANSLATION and NOTES by Stephen J. Patterson.

Prologue *living Jesus* This term occurs only here in *Thomas,* but is picked up in the title *living one* (37:3, 59, and 111:2). In later gnostic literature Jesus is often presented as returning after his death and resurrection to deliver fresh words to his followers. Some scholars think that the term *living Jesus* presupposes such a setting; however, *Thomas* never mentions the resurrection elsewhere. Therefore, Jesus may be presented here as the redeemer sent from God to bring lifesaving wisdom and knowledge to those who listen (1:1). The idea of the heaven-sent redeemer was widespread in ancient Near Eastern religions, but it does not necessarily include a resurrection concept. *Didymos Judas Thomas* See introduction to the *Gospel of Thomas.* **1** *not taste death* This concern for eternal life is pervasive in *Thomas* (see 18:3; 19:4; 85:2; 111:2). **2:1** See 92:1; 94; *Matt.* 7:8; *Luke* 11:10. **2:4** *reign* Since Jesus often spoke about the reign (or kingdom) of God, later Christians used this as a metaphor for achieving salvation. Very early in Christianity there was a disagreement over whether the reign of God was a future event or something accessible in the present. See, for example, *1 Cor.* 4:8, where Paul upbraids some at Corinth for thinking they already "reign" or "had become kings." Paul regarded this as something yet to come. *Thomas* presents the other view: the reign of God is already present (see esp. *Gospel of Thomas* 3). Later, the author of *2 Timothy* would take a position more akin to *Thomas* (*2 Tim.* 2:11–13). **3:1–3** *Mark* 13:21–23; *Matt.* 24:23–28; *Luke* 17:20–25; see 113:1–4. The idea of searching for insight in the farthest reaches of the cosmos derives from Jewish wisdom tradition (LXX *Job* 28:12–14, 20–22; *Bar.* 3:29–32, 35–37; LXX *Deut.* 30:11–14; and *Sir.* 1:1–3). Here it is probably intended as a mild parody of this tradition. **3:3** *Luke* 17:21. **4:1** *seven days old* See 22:1–3; 46:2. According to *Gen.* 17:12–13, Jewish males were to be circumcised on the 8th day. A child seven days old would be one who was not yet circumcised, and thus would have no standing in the community. **4:2** *Mark* 10:31; *Matt.* 19:30; 20:16; *Luke* 13:30. **4:3** See 22:5; 23:2; see also 16:4; 49:1; 75. *and will become a single one* Here this phrase designates a kind of soteriological status (see also 23:2). In 22:5, however, it is associated with androgyny. Some gnostic groups held that the origin of human sin was the creation of woman as distinct from man, a departure from the sexually nondifferentiated first human, Adam. Thus, the ultimate human destiny was to return to a primordial state of androgyny or divine perfection before the fall. **5:2** See 6:5–6; *Mark* 4:22; *Matt.* 10:26; *Luke* 8:17; 12:2. **6:1** *fasting* See 104:1–3; *Matt.* 6:16–18. *prayer* See *Matt.* 6:5–15; *Luke* 11:1–11. *giving alms* See *Matt.* 6:2–4. These formed the heart of ancient Jewish piety, along with dietary practice, and may be taken as summary questions about Jewish religious practice in general. The questions are not answered here. Rather, a warning against falsehood and hypocrisy is offered (6:2–3). In 14:1–3, all three are rejected. In 104:3, however, fasting and prayer are advocated. Clearly, the views of the *Thomas* community on these matters were in flux. **6:3** Christian and Jewish variations on the golden rule include *Luke* 6:31, *Matt.* 7:12, and *Tob.* 4:15. The latter reads, "And what you hate, do not do to anyone." *Thomas*'s saying, however, lacks the element of reciprocity and sounds more like a warning against hypocrisy.

all things are disclosed before heaven.*ƒ* ⁵For there is nothing hidden that will not be revealed, ⁶and there is nothing covered up that will remain undisclosed."

7 Jesus said, "Blessed is the lion that the human will eat, so that the lion becomes human. ²But foul is the human that the lion will eat; and the lion will become human."

8 And he said, "The human one is like a wise fisherman who cast his net into the sea and drew it up from the sea full of little fish. ²Among them the wise fisherman discovered a fine large fish. ³He threw all the little fish back into the sea, and easily chose the large fish. ⁴Whoever has ears to hear, let them hear."

9 Jesus said, "Look, the sower went out, took a handful (of seeds), and scattered them.*g* ²Some fell on the road, and the birds came and gathered them. ³Others fell on rock, and they did not take root in the soil and did not produce heads of grain. ⁴Others fell on thorns, and they choked the seeds and worms ate them. ⁵And others fell on good soil, and it produced a good crop: it yielded sixty per measure and one hundred twenty per measure."

10 Jesus said, "I have cast fire upon the world, and look, I'm guarding it until it blazes."

11 Jesus said, "This heaven will pass away, and the one above it will pass away. ²The dead are not alive, and the living will not die. ³During the days when you ate what is dead, you made it come alive. When you are in the light, what will you do? ⁴On the day when you were one, you became two. But when you become two, what will you do?"

12 The disciples said to Jesus, "We know that you are going to leave us. Who will be our leader?" ²Jesus said to them, "No matter where you are, you are to go to James the just, for whose sake heaven and earth came into being."

13 Jesus said to his disciples, "Compare me to something and tell me what I am like." ²Simon Peter said to him, "You are like a just angel." ³Matthew said to him, "You are like a wise philosopher." ⁴Thomas said to him, "Teacher, my mouth is utterly unable to say what you are like." ⁵Jesus said, "I am not your teacher. Because you have drunk, you have become intoxicated*h* from the bubbling spring that I

ƒ Gk *before truth*
g Coptic *took a handful and scattered*

h Or *"I am not your teacher, for you have drunk and have become intoxicated*

6:5–6 *Mark* 4:22; *Matt.* 10:26; *Luke* 8:17; 12:2; *Gos. Thom.* 5:2.   **7:1–2** See 11:3; *1 Pet.* 5:8–9. The meaning of this saying is obscure. In antiquity the lion often symbolized feelings of passion and pathos. To eat the lion may be to overcome such feelings. Likewise, to be consumed by the lion is to be overcome by them. 7:2 indicates that although the passions may temporarily dominate a person, ultimately he or she will overcome them.   **8:1–4** *wise fisherman* The fisherman is a commonly used metaphor in antiquity (Aesop, *Fables* 4; Philoxenus, *Homilies* 1.9). A similar parable is attributed to Jesus in *Matt.* 13:47–50. It is not certain whether this is ultimately the same parable and, if so, which version stands closer to the original. **8:1** *The human one* Lit. "The person" (Coptic *prōme*). The referent is unclear. There is a figure in some gnostic systems known as Anthropos, or Person, who is a primordial figure, the first person. Perhaps the *Thomas* text intends to render this title in Coptic.   **8:2** *a fine large fish* Thomas uses largeness to indicate desirability. In its version of the parable of the lost sheep, the sheep is "the largest" (107:2); in the parable of the leaven, "large loaves" are produced (96:2).   **8:4** See 21:10; 24:2; 63:4; 65:8; 96:3; *Mark* 4:9, 23; *Matt.* 11:15; 13:9, 43; *Luke* 8:8; 14:35; *Rev.* 2:7, 11, 17; 3:6, 13, 22; 13:9.   **9:1–5** *Mark* 4:2–9; *Matt.* 13:3–9; *Luke* 8:4–8. In antiquity, farmers sowed seed over a patch of ground, *then* worked it over with a simple implement. Initially, the sower might well toss seed onto paths, rocks, and thorns with the intention of working this poor soil into a respectable field.   **9:5** *sixty per measure and one hundred twenty per measure* Contemporary historians (Pliny, *Natural History* 18.21.95; Herodotus 1.193) report these yields as average.   **10** *fire* *Luke* 12:49. This image provokes and threatens. Fire was a constant menace in antiquity. Although apocalyptic visions often involve fiery conflagration, this need not be the sense here.   **11:1** See *Ps.* 102:25–27; *Isa.* 34:4; *Mark* 13:31; *Matt.* 5:18; 24:34–35; *Luke* 16:17; 21:33; *Gos. Thom.* 111:1–2; *2 Cor.* 12:2–4.   *This heaven . . . and the one above it* Ancient cosmology presupposed the existence of a number of heavenly spheres suspended above the earth's surface, enclosing it like thick layers of ethereal paint. Paul alludes to this in *2 Cor.* 12:2–4, where he refers to the Jewish mystical tradition of ascending through these heavenly realms, eventually to come into the presence of God. These multiple heavenly spheres were viewed as part of the created order. Hence, here their transitory nature is used to emphasize the transitory nature of the entire created order.   **11:2** See *Dialogue of the Savior* 56–57. **11:3** See note to 7:1–2.   **11:4** *when you were one, you became two* See note to 4:3.   **12:1** See *Mark* 9:33–34; *Matt.* 18:1; *Luke* 9:46; 22:24.   **12:2** *James the Just* The brother of Jesus (see *Mark* 6:3; *Matt.* 13:55; *Gal.* 1:19) was known as James "the just" in antiquity (Eusebius, *Eccl. Hist.* 2.23.4–7).   **13:1–8** Such scenes appear to demonstrate apostolic authority, passed along from an original disciple to those who would follow in his line. For example, in *Mark* Peter's authority is guaranteed by his confession at Caesarea Philippi (*Mark* 8:27–30; *Matt.* 16:13–20; *Luke* 9:18–22). Here the authority of Thomas, the gospel created as his legacy, and those who claimed to follow in his lineage is secured.   **13:5** See *Isa.* 43:19–21; *Ezek.* 47:1–12; *Joel* 3:18; *Zech.* 14:8; *Sir.* 15:3; *Gos. Thom.* 28:2; 108; *John* 4:13–15; 7:38.

have tended." 6And he took him, and withdrew, and spoke three sayings to him. 7When Thomas came back to his friends, they asked him, "What did Jesus say to you?" 8Thomas said to them, "If I tell you one of the sayings he spoke to me, you will pick up rocks and stone me, and fire will come from the rocks and devour you."

14 Jesus said to them, "If you fast, you will bring sin upon yourselves, 2and if you pray, you will be condemned, 3and if you give alms, you will harm your spirits. 4When you go into any region and walk about in the countryside, when people take you in, eat what they serve you and heal[i] the sick among them. 5For what goes into your mouth will not defile you; rather, it is what comes out of your mouth that will defile you."

15 Jesus said, "When you see one who was not born of woman, fall on your faces and worship. That one is your Father."

16 Jesus said, "Perhaps people think that I have come to cast peace upon the world. 2They do not know that I have come to cast conflicts upon the earth: fire, sword, war. 3For there will be five in a house: three will be three against two and two against three, father against son and son against father, 4and they will stand alone."

17 Jesus said, "I will give you what no eye has seen, what no ear has heard, what no hand has touched, what has not arisen in the human heart."

18 The disciples said to Jesus, "Tell us, how our end will come?" 2Jesus said, "Have you discovered the beginning, then, that you are looking for the end? You see, the end will be where the beginning is. 3Blessed is the one who stands at the beginning: that one will know the end and will not taste death."

19 Jesus said, "Blessed is the one who came into being before coming into being. 2If you become my disciples and pay attention to my sayings, these stones will serve you. 3For there are five trees in Paradise for you; they do not change, summer or winter, and their leaves do not fall. 4Whoever knows them will not taste death."

20 The disciples said to Jesus, "Tell us what the kingdom of heaven is like." 2He said to them, "It is like a mustard seed. 3It is the smallest of all seeds,[j] 4but when it falls on prepared soil, it produces a large plant and becomes a shelter for birds of the sky."

21 Mary said to Jesus, "What are your disciples like?" 2He said, "They are like little children[k] living in a field that is not theirs. 3When the owners

---

i Or *care for*

---

j Coptic verse 3 *smaller than all of the seeds*
k Possibly *servants*

14:1–3 fast . . . pray . . . give alms See note to 6:1. **14:1–4** See 104; *Mark* 6:7–13; *Matt.* 10:5–15; *Luke* 9:1–6; 10:1–12; *1 Cor.* 10:27. **14:4 countryside** The Gk word is ambiguous. When used in this way, it usually means places in the country as opposed to the city, but they could be either the rural areas in between small towns or the towns themselves. **14:5** *Mark* 7:14–23; *Matt.* 15:10–20. **15** See *John* 3:5–8; *Dialogue of the Savior* 59. **not born of woman** That is, not by natural childbirth. For some ancient religions, the passion associated with sexual intercourse was a sign of human fallenness. For example, in *John* becoming a child of God means not being born "of the will of the flesh or of the will of man, but of God" (1:12–13). Here the *one not born of woman* appears to be a divine figure, perhaps God or perhaps Jesus transformed into the likeness of God. The reference to *seeing* may indicate visionary experiences of mysticism. **16:1–4** *Matt.* 10:34–39; *Luke* 12:51–53. See 55, 101, 105; *Mark* 3:20–22; *Matt.* 12:46–50; *Luke* 8:19–21. **16:2 fire** See note to 10. **16:3** See *Mic.* 7:5–6. **16:4** See 4:3; 22:5; 23:2; 49:1; 75. **alone** The Coptic uses a Gk loan word here, *monachos*. In other texts this word may indicate a unique, solitary, or lonely person, an unmarried person, or later, as a technical term, a monk. Here discipleship probably entails the solitary life of the wandering ascetic. **17** *1 Cor.* 2:9. See *Matt.* 13:16–17; *Luke* 10:23–24; *Dialogue of the Savior* 57; *Isa.* 64:4. **18:2 the end will be where the beginning is** Basic to most forms of gnosticism was the notion that the world is evil, the result of the attempt by a rebellious angel (demiurge) to create something apart from God. The goal *(end)* of the gnostic's existence was to escape the created world and return to the state of perfection that existed in the *beginning*, before the creation of the world. **18:3** See 1; 19:4; 85:2; 111:2. **not taste death** *Thomas* is about the quest for immortality. This phrase appears several times in *Thomas*, reminding the reader of the focus of the text. **19:2** See *Matt.* 3:9; *Luke* 3:8; *Gos. Thom.* 77:3. **19:4** See 1; 18:3; 85:2; 111:2. **not taste death** See note to 18:3. **20:1–4** *Mark* 4:30–32; *Matt.* 13:31–32; *Luke* 13:18–19. **20:2 mustard** Mustard is a very prolific plant and so was considered unclean, a contaminant, and unfit for planting in any but the most controlled circumstances. A few seeds in tilled soil would quickly consume the entire field, crowding out any other, more desirable plant. On the other hand, it was renowned for its medicinal and other stimulative qualities. Inhaled, it was thought to clear the senses; ingested, it was thought to clear the bowels. It was also an antidote to snakebite and other poisonous substances. **20:4** LXX *Dan.* 4:20–21; LXX *Ezek.* 17:23 depict David's kingdom as great cedars of Lebanon. This parable alludes to and so parodies that kingdom.

of the field come, they will say, 'Give us back our field.' [4]They take off their clothes in front of them in order to give it back to them, and they return their field to them. [5]For this reason I say, if the owners of a house knows that a thief is coming, they will be on guard before the thief arrives, and will not let the thief break into their house, their domain, and steal their possessions. [6]As for you, then, be on guard against the world. [7]Prepare yourselves with great strength, so the robbers cannot find a way to get to you, for the trouble you expect will come. [8]Let there be among you a person who understands. [9]When the crop ripened, he came quickly carrying a sickle and harvested it. [10]Whoever has ears to hear, let them hear."

22 Jesus saw some babies nursing. [2]He said to his disciples, "These nursing babies are like those who enter the kingdom." [3]They said to him, "Then shall we enter the kingdom as babies?" [4]Jesus said to them, "When you make the two into one, and when you make[l] the inner like the outer and the outer like the inner, and the upper like the lower, [5]and when you make male and female into a single one, so that the male will not be male nor the female be female, [6]when you make eyes in place of an eye, a hand in place of a hand, a foot in place of a foot, an image in place of an image, [7]then you will enter the kingdom."[m]

23 Jesus said, "I shall choose you, one from a thousand and two from ten thousand, [2]and they will stand as a single one."

24 His disciples said, "Show us the place where you are, for we must seek it." [2]He said to them, "Whoever has ears to hear, let them hear. [3]There is light within a person of light, and it[n] shines on the whole world. If it does not shine, it is dark."

25 Jesus said, "Love your brother like your own soul,[o] [2]protect him like the pupil of your eye."

26 Jesus said, "You see the speck that is in your brother's eye, but you do not see the beam that is in your own eye. [2]When you take the beam out of your own eye, then you will see clearly to take the speck out of your brother's eye."

27[p] "If you do not fast from the world, you will not find the kingdom. [2]If you do not observe the sabbath as a sabbath, you will not see the Father."

28 Jesus said, "I took my stand in the midst of the world, and in flesh I appeared to them. [2]I found them all drunk, and I did not find any of them thirsty. [3]My soul ached for the children of humanity, because they are blind in their hearts and do not see, for they came into the world empty, and they also seek to depart from the world empty. [4]But meanwhile they are drunk. When they shake off their wine, then they will repent."

---

l Or *in order that you make*
m Coptic lacuna; *the kingdom* reconstructed from context

n Or *he*
o Or *life*
p Gk *Jesus said,*

21:4 See 37:2–3. *they take off their clothes* The phrase is obscure. Clues from later literature suggest several alternate interpretations: (a) Removal of one's clothing might indicate one's sexual indifference, sexual desire having been overcome through asceticism. (b) The phrase could refer to a baptismal ritual wherein the participants disrobe. Early Christian communicants were usually baptized in the nude. (c) It could refer symbolically to the platonic and later gnostic notion that upon death the soul sheds the body or "clothing" and proceeds upward to the heavenly realm from whence it has come (see 29; 87; 112). **21:5** *Matt.* 24:42–44; *Luke* 12:35–40. See 103; *1 Thess.* 5:1–2; *2 Pet.* 3:10. **21:9** *Mark* 4:29. See LXX *Joel* 3:13. **21:10** See note to 8:4. **22:1–3** See note to 4:1. **22:4–5** For the notion of primordial unity, see note to 4:3. **22:5** See note to 4:3. **22:6** See 50:1; 83:1–2. *image* The idea of replacing the various parts of the body until gradually one replaces the whole with a new *image* is rooted in platonic thought, which posits a heavenly, more perfect form corresponding to every earthly thing. The concept, like that expressed in 22:4–5, concerns replacing the inferior, earthly image with a more perfect heavenly image. It is possible that these ideas were enacted through asceticism. **23:1** See LXX *Deut.* 32:30; LXX *Eccl.* 7:28–29; *Matt.* 22:14; *John* 6:70; 13:18; 15:16, 19. **23:2** See note to 4:3. **24:1** See *John* 14:1–6; *Dialogue of the Savior* 77–78. **24:2** See note to 8:4. **24:3** *Matt.* 6:22–23; *Luke* 11:34–35. See *John* 8:12; 12:35–36; *2 Cor.* 4:6; *Matt.* 5:14–16; *Dialogue of the Savior* 8, 14. **25:1** *Lev.* 19:18; *Mark* 12:31; *Matt.* 22:39; 19:19; *Luke* 10:27. See *1 Sam.* 18:1; *Rom.* 13:8; *Jas.* 2:8. **25:2** See LXX *Ps.* 17:8; *Sir.* 17:22. **26:1–2** *Matt.* 7:3–5; *Luke* 6:41–42. **27:1** See 6:1; 14:1; 104; 110. *see the Father* The reference may indicate visionary experience or mysticism. **27:2** See LXX *Lev.* 23:32. *keep the sabbath a sabbath* The Coptic phrase is obscure. It probably means observing the Sabbath with integrity. Criticism of contemporary Sabbath observance is not unknown in the Jesus tradition (see *Mark* 2:27–28). **28:1–4** See *Prov.* 1:20–33; *Bar.* 3:37; *Luke* 21:34–36; *John* 1:14. Jesus speaks here as the heaven-sent redeemer. The language and imagery are typical of gnosticism, especially the metaphors of blindness and drunkenness. The redeemer seeks to open the eyes of the lost, to help them shake off their drowsiness, and ultimately to return to the heavenly home from which they have become estranged.

29 Jesus said, "If the flesh came into being because of spirit, that is a marvel, 2but if spirit came into being because of the body, that is a marvel of marvels. 3Yet I marvel at how this great wealth has come to dwell in this poverty."

30 Jesus said, "Where there are three deities, they are divine.q 2Where there are two orr one, I am with that one."s

31 Jesus said, "Prophets are not welcome in their own town; 2doctors do not heal those who know them."

32 Jesus said, "A city built upon a high hill and fortified cannot fall, nor can it be hidden."

33 Jesus said, "What you will hear in your ear,t into another ear proclaim from your rooftops. 2After all, no one lights a lamp and puts it under a basket, nor does one put it in a hidden place. 3Rather, one puts it on a lamp stand so that all who come and go will see its light."

34 Jesus said, "If a blind person leads a blind person, both of them will fall into a hole."

35 Jesus said, "One cannot enter a strong person's house and take it by force without tying his hands. 2Then one can loot his house."

36 Jesus said, "Do not fret, from morning to evening and from evening to morning, about what you are going to wear."u

37 His disciples said, "When will you appear to us, and when will we see you?" 2Jesus said, "When you strip without being ashamed, and you take your clothes and put them under your feet like little children and trample them, 3then you will see the son of the living one and you will not be afraid."

38 Jesus said, "Often you have desired to hear these sayings that I am speaking to you, and you have no one else from whom to hear them. 2There will be days when you will seek me and you will not find me."

39 Jesus said, "The Pharisees and the scribes have taken the keys of knowledge and have hidden them. 2They have not entered, nor have they allowed those who want to enterv to do so. 3As for you, be as wise as serpents and as innocent as doves."

40 Jesus said, "A grapevine has been planted apart from the Father. 2Since it is not strong, it will be pulled up by its root and will perish."

41 Jesus said, "Whoever has something in hand will be given more, 2and whoever has nothing will be deprived of even the little that they have."

42 Jesus said, "Be passersby."

43 His disciples said to him, "Who are you to say these things to us?" 2"You do not understandw who I am from what I say to you. 3Rather, you have become like the Jews, for they love the tree but hate its fruit, or they love the fruit but hate the tree."

---

q Gk God
r Gk where there is only
s Gk adds verses 3–4 "*Lift up the stone, and you will find me there. Split a piece of wood, and I am there.*"
t Gk *in one of your ears*
u Gk adds verses 2–4 *You are better than the lilies, which do not card nor spin. As for you, when you have no garment, what will you put on? Who might add to your stature? That very one will give you your garment.*"

v Gk *who are entering*
w Or "*Do you not understand*"

29:1–3 See 87; 112; *Gal.* 5:16–18; *Rom.* 8:3–11; *John* 3:6. **30:1–2** See *Matt.* 18:20. **30:2** See 77:2–3. **31:1–2** *Mark* 6:4–6; *Matt.* 13:57–58; *Luke* 4:23–24; *John* 4:44. **32** *Matt.* 5:14. See *Isa.* 2:2–3; *Mic.* 4:1–2. **33:1** *Matt.* 10:27; *Luke* 12:3. **into another ear** This difficult phrase may represent dittography—that is, a scribe's inadvertent duplication of words already transcribed. Otherwise, it may indicate the ear of another or perhaps one's own inner ear. **33:2–3** *Mark* 4:21; *Matt.* 5:15; *Luke* 8:16; 11:33. **34** *Matt.* 15:14; *Luke* 6:39. **35:1–2** *Mark* 3:27; *Matt.* 12:29; *Luke* 11:21–22. See *Gospel of Thomas* 98. **36** *Matt.* 6:25–33; *Luke* 12:22–31. **36:1–4** See *Dialogue of the Savior* 51–52; 84–85. **37:1 see you** The reference may indicate visionary experience or mysticism. **37:2** See 21:2–4; *Dialogue of the Savior* 84–85; *Gen.* 2:25 (LXX 3:1). **clothes . . . under your feet** On removing one's clothes see note to 21:4. **37:3 see the son** The reference may indicate visionary experience or mysticism. **38:1–2** See 59; *Matt.* 13:16–17; *Luke* 10:23–24; 17:22; *John* 8:21; 13:33. **38:2** *John* 7:33–36. **39:1–2** *Matt.* 23:13; *Luke* 11:52. See 102. **39:3** *Matt.* 10:16. **40:1–2** See *Matt.* 15:13; *John* 15:5–6. **41:1–2** *Mark* 4:24–25; *Matt.* 13:10–13; 25:29; *Luke* 8:18; 19:26. **42** See *Mark* 6:7–11; *Matt.* 10:5–15; *Luke* 9:1–5; 10:1–12. The saying may be taken literally, as a call to take up the itinerant life of the disciple. Some, however, have seen in it a call to pass through this world without becoming mired in it. **43:1–3** See *John* 14:8–11. **43:3** *Matt.* 7:17–18; *Luke* 6:43–44. See *Matt.* 12:33. The critical treatment of *the Jews* here is typical of early Christian writing, which reflects the point of view of a small, sectarian group securing its identity

44 Jesus said, "Whoever blasphemes against the Father will be forgiven, ²and whoever blasphemes against the Son will be forgiven, ³but whoever blasphemes against the Holy Spirit will not be forgiven, either on earth or in heaven."

45 Jesus said, "Grapes are not harvested from thorn trees, nor are figs gathered from thistles, for they yield no fruit. ²Good persons produce good from what they have stored up; ³bad persons produce evil from the wickedness they have stored up in their hearts, and say evil things. ⁴For from the overflow of the heart they produce evil."

46 Jesus said, "From Adam to John the Baptist, among those born of women, no one is so much greater than John the Baptist that their eyes should not be averted. ²But I have said that whoever among you becomes a child will recognize the kingdom and will become greater than John."

47 Jesus said, "A person cannot mount two horses or bend two bows. ²And slaves cannot serve two masters, otherwise they will honor the one and offend the other. ³Nobody drinks aged wine and immediately wants to drink young wine. ⁴Young wine is not poured into old wineskins, or they might break, and aged wine is not poured into a new wineskin, or it might spoil. ⁵An old patch is not sewn onto a new garment, since it would create a tear."

48 Jesus said, "If two make peace with each other in a single house, they will say to the mountain, 'Move from here!' and it will move."

49 Jesus said, "Blessed are those who are alone, the chosen, for you will find the Father's kingdom. ²For you have come from it, and you will return there again."

50 Jesus said, "If they say to you, 'Where have you come from?' say to them, 'We have come from the light, from the place where the light came into being by itself, established itself,ˣ and appeared in their image.' ²If they say to you, 'Is it you?' say, 'We are its children, and we are the chosen of the living Father.' ³If they ask you, 'What is the evidence of your Father in you?' say to them, 'It is motion and rest.'"

51 His disciples said to him, "When will the rest for the dead take place, and when will the new world come?" ²He said to them, "What you are looking forward to has come, but you do not know it."

52 His disciples said to him, "Twenty-four prophets have spoken in Israel, and they all spoke of you." ²He said to them, "You have disregarded the living one who is in your presence, and have spoken of the dead."

53 His disciples said to him, "Is circumcision useful or not?" ²He said to them, "If it were useful, their father would produce childrenʸ already circumcised from their mother. ³Rather, the true circumcision in spirit has become profitable in every respect."

---

x Coptic lacuna; *itself* reconstructed from context
y Coptic *them*

over against the majority culture. Since *Thomas* Christians themselves could well have been Jewish (see *Gospel of Thomas* 27), one should refrain from interpreting the saying in an anti-Semitic vein. **44:1–3** *Mark* 3:28–30; *Matt.* 12:31–32; *Luke* 12:10. **45:1–4** *Matt.* 7:15–20; 12:33–35; *Luke* 6:43–45. See *Jas.* 3:12. **46:1–2** *Matt.* 11:11; *Luke* 7:28. **46:1** *averted* Lit. "broken." The Coptic idiom is obscure. **46:2** See note to 4:1. **47:2** *Matt.* 6:24; *Luke* 16:13. **47:3–5** *Mark* 2:21–22; *Matt.* 9:16–17; *Luke* 5:36–39. **48a** See *Matt.* 18:19. **48b** *Gospel of Thomas* 106; *Mark* 11:22–23; *Matt.* 21:21; 17:20b; *Luke* 17:5–6; *1 Cor.* 13:2. **49:1–50:3** Gnosticism often speaks of human fallenness as a fall from heaven. The gnostic's goal is to return to heaven, a journey that may entail passage through gates and guardians on the way. *Gospel of Thomas* 50 provides a series of passwords to be used on the journey home. **49:1–2** See *Dialogue of the Savior* 1–2. *alone* See note to 16:4. **50:1** See *John* 1:4–5, 9; 3:19–21; 12:36. *We have come from the light* Ancient religions often employed dualistic schemes to express their understanding of the world as divided between good and evil. One finds this pair, for example, in *John*: "in him was life, and the life was the light of all people. The light shines in the darkness, and the darkness did not overcome it" (1:4–5). Here *light* stands for the place where *Thomas* readers began their cosmic journey. *image* See note to 22:6. **50:2** See 23. **50:3** See 2; 51:1; 60:6; 90; *Matt.* 11:28–29; *Dialogue of the Savior* 65–68; *Sir.* 51:26–27; 6:23–31. *motion and rest* The phrase is obscure. It has the ring of code language and thus may be intentionally opaque. *Motion* may refer to the movement of the *Thomas* Christian up through the heavenly spheres to the heavenly domain. Finding *rest* is tantamount to finding salvation in *Thomas* (P.Oxy. 654.9; *Gos. Thom.* 51:1; 60:6; 90). Its association with the quest for insight is reflective of its roots in the wisdom tradition (see esp. *Sir.* 51:26–27; 6:23–31). In *Thomas*, one achieves rest through insight in the present, not in a future existence (51:1). By contrast, later gnostic groups spoke of the hoped-for reunion of the gnostic soul with the God of heavenly remove as achieving "rest." In the NT "rest" is also associated with a future hope (e.g., *Rev.* 14:13). **51:1** *rest* See previous note. **51:2** See 3; 113; *Mark* 9:12–13; *Matt.* 17:11; *Luke* 17:20–21; *2 Tim.* 2:17–18. **52:1–2** See *John* 5:37–40; 8:52–53. **52:1** *twenty-four* Twenty-four is the number of books in the Hebrew scriptures (see *2 Esd.* 14:45). See also *Rev.* 4:4, where twenty-four elders appear. *of you* Lit. "in you." **53:1–3** See *Rom.* 2:25–29; *Phil.* 3:3; *1 Cor.* 7:17–19; *Gal.* 6:15; *Col.* 2:11–12.

54 Jesus said, "Blessed are the poor, for to you belongs the kingdom of heaven."

55 Jesus said, "Whoever does not hate father and mother cannot be my disciple, ²and whoever does not hate brothers and sisters, and carry the cross as I do, will not be worthy of me."

56 Jesus said, "Whoever has come to know the world has discovered a carcass, ²and whoever has discovered a carcass, of that person the world is not worthy."

57 Jesus said, "The Father's kingdom is like a person who had good*ᶻ* seed. ²His enemy came during the night and sowed weeds among the good seed. ³The person did not let the workers*ᵃ* pull up the weeds, but said to them, 'No, otherwise you might go to pull up the weeds and pull up the wheat along with them.' ⁴For on the day of the harvest, the weeds will be conspicuous, and will be pulled up and burned."

58 Jesus said, "Blessed is the person who has toiled*ᵇ* and has found life."

59 Jesus said, "Look to the living one as long as you live, otherwise you might die and then try to see the living one, and you will be unable to see."

60 He saw*ᶜ* a Samaritan carrying a lamb and going to Judea. ²He said to his disciples, "Why does that person carry around the lamb?"*ᵈ* ³They said to him, "So that he may kill it and eat it." ⁴He said to them, "He will not eat it while it is alive, but only after he has killed it and it has become a carcass." ⁵They said, "Otherwise he cannot do it." ⁶He said to

them, "So also with you, seek for yourselves a place for rest, or you might become a carcass and be eaten."

61 Jesus said, "Two will recline on a couch; one will die, one will live." ²Salome said, "Who are you, mister? You have climbed onto my couch and eaten from my table as if you are from someone." ³Jesus said to her, "I am the one who comes from what is whole.*ᵉ* I was granted from the things of my Father." ⁴"I am your disciple." ⁵"For this reason I say, if one is whole, one will be filled with light, but if one is divided, one will be filled with darkness."

62 Jesus said, "I disclose my mysteries to those who are worthy of my*ᶠ* mysteries. ²Do not let your left hand know what your right hand is doing."

63 Jesus said, "There was a rich person who had a great deal of money. ²He said, 'I shall invest my money so that I may sow, reap, plant, and fill my storehouses with produce, that I may lack nothing.' ³These were the things he was thinking in his heart, but that very night he died. ⁴Whoever has ears to hear, let them hear."

64 Jesus said, "A person was receiving guests. When he had prepared the dinner, he sent his slave to invite the guests. ²The slave went to the first and said to him, 'My master invites you.' ³He said, 'Some merchants owe me money; they are coming to me tonight. I have to go and give them instructions. Please excuse me from dinner.' ⁴The slave went to another and said to him, 'My master has invited you.' ⁵He said to the slave, 'I have bought a house, and I have been called away for a day. I shall have no

---

z Coptic lacuna; *good* reconstructed from context
a Coptic *them*
b Or *suffered*
c Or *They saw;* Coptic lacuna reconstructed from context
d Coptic *"That person is around the lamb."*

e Coptic reads *desolate*, probably in error
f Coptic lacuna; *who are worthy of my* reconstructed from context

---

54 *Matt.* 5:3; *Luke* 6:20b. See 63; 64; 81; 85; 110. **55:1–2** *Matt.* 10:37–38; *Luke* 14:26–27; *Gospel of Thomas* 101. See 16; 99; 105; *Mark* 3:20–22; *Matt.* 12:46–50; *Luke* 8:19–21; 12:52–53. **56:1–2** See 80, 111. This saying employs paradox. It may be advocating withdrawal from the world through ascetic practice. Verse 1 speaks of discovering the true nature of the world. Verse 2 speaks of discovering the true nature of the body, a discovery that will elevate one beyond the mundane world. **57:1–4** *Matt.* 13:24–30. See *Mark* 4:26–29. **57:3** See 58; *Matt.* 5:10–13; *Luke* 6:22–23; *Jas.* 1:12; *1 Pet.* 3:14; 4:13–14. **58** See *Wis.* 3:15; *Sir.* 51:26–27; *Matt.* 11:28–30. *life* See 1; 4; 111; *John* 8:51. **59** See 38:2; *Luke* 17:22; *John* 7:33–36; 8:21; 13:33. *see ... unable to see* The reference may indicate visionary experience or mysticism. *living one* Perhaps Jesus; see Prologue. **60:1–6** See 7; 11:3. **60:6** *rest* See note to 50:3. **61:1** *Matt.* 24:40–41; *Luke* 17:34–35. **61:2** *Salome* In the New Testament, Salome appears only in *Mark* (15:40; 16:1). Elsewhere in early Christian literature she surfaces in the *Protevangelium of James*, the *Secret Gospel of Mark*, the *Gospel of the Egyptians*, and in several gnostic works (*Pistis Sophia, First Apocalypse of James, Manichaean Psalm-Book*). *as if you are from someone* The meaning of the Coptic is unclear. It could mean "as if you are someone special" or perhaps "as if you are a stranger." **61:3** *Matt.* 11:27; *Luke* 10:22. See *John* 3:35; 6:37–39; 13:3–4. **61:5** See *Luke* 11:34–36; *John* 8:12. **62:1** See *Mark* 4:10–11; *Matt.* 13:10–11; *Luke* 8:9–10. **62:2** *Matt.* 6:3. **63:1–4** *Luke* 12:16–21. See *Sir.* 11:18–19. **63:4** See note to 8:4. **64:1–12** *Matt.* 22:1–10; *Luke* 14:16–24. See *Deut.* 20:5–7.

time.' 6The slave went to another and said to him, 'My master invites you.' 7He said to the slave, 'My friend is to be married, and I am to arrange the banquet. I shall not be able to come. Please excuse me from dinner.' 8The slave went to another and said to him, 'My master invites you.' 9He said to the slave, 'I have bought an estate, and I am going to collect the rent. I shall not be able to come. Please excuse me.' 10The slave returned and said to his master, 'Those whom you invited to dinner have asked to be excused.' 11The master said to his slave, 'Go out on the streets, and bring back whomever you find to have dinner.' 12"Buyers and merchants will not enter the places of my Father."

65 He said, "A person*g* owned a vineyard and rented it to some farmers, so that they might work it and he could collect its crop from them. 2He sent his slave so that the farmers would give him the vineyard's crop. 3They grabbed him, beat him, and almost killed him, and the slave returned and told his master. 4His master said, 'Perhaps he did not know them.' 5He sent another slave, and the farmers beat that one as well. 6Then the master sent his son and said, 'Perhaps they'll show my son some respect.' 7Because the farmers knew that he was the heir to the vineyard, they grabbed him and killed him. 8Whoever has ears to hear, let them hear."

66 Jesus said, "Show me the stone that the builders rejected: that is the keystone."

67 Jesus said, "Those who know all, but are lacking in themselves, are utterly lacking."

68 Jesus said, "Blessed are you when you are hated and persecuted; 2and no place will be found, wherever you have been persecuted."

69 Jesus said, "Blessed are those who have been persecuted in their hearts: they are the ones who have truly come to know the Father. 2Blessed are those who go hungry, so the stomach of the one in want may be filled."*h*

70 Jesus said, "If you bring forth what is within you, what you have will save you. 2If you do not have that within you, what you do not have within you will kill you."

71 Jesus said, "I will destroy this*i* house, and no one will be able to build it."

72 A person said*j* to him, "Tell my brothers to divide my father's possessions with me." 2He said to the person, "Mister, who made me a divider?" 3He turned to his disciples and said to them, "I am not a divider, am I?"

73 Jesus said, "The harvest is large but the workers are few, so beg the lord to dispatch workers to the harvest."

74 He said, "Lord, there are many around the drinking trough, but there is nothing in the well."*k*

75 Jesus said, "There are many standing at the door, but those who are alone will enter the bridal chamber."

---

g Coptic uncertain

h Or *for the stomach of the one who desires will be filled*
i Coptic lacuna; *this* reconstructed from context
j Coptic lacuna; *A person said* reconstructed from context
k Coptic uncertain

64:7 See *Deut.* 24:5. **64:12** See *Sir.* 26:29–27:2. **65:1–8** *Mark* 12:1–9; *Matt.* 21:33–41; *Luke* 20:9–16. **65:1 *A person*** A lacuna in the papyrus makes the Coptic here uncertain; it could read either "good" or "greedy" person. **65:4** Other scholars have suggested that the text be emended here to read "Perhaps they did not know him." **65:8** See note to 8:4. **66** *Ps.* 117:22; *Mark* 12:10–11; *Matt.* 21:42–43; *Luke* 20:17–18. See *Acts* 4:11–12; *1 Pet.* 2:4–8. **67** See *Mark* 8:36–37; *Matt.* 16:26; *Luke* 9:25. **68:1–2** *Matt.* 5:10, 11–12; *Luke* 6:22–23. See *Jas.* 1:12. **68:2 *no place*** This verse is obscure. *Place* may refer to the seat of knowledge in the heart of the gnostic. Thus, no such place is found where the *Thomas* Christians have been persecuted. Alternatively, the text could be corrupt, with a displaced negative, such that the original text would have read "a place will be found in which you will not be persecuted." **69:1** *Matt.* 5:10, 11–12; *Luke* 6:22–23. See *John* 4:23–24; 8:31–32; 14:6–7, 15–17; 17:17–19; 18:37–38; *Jas.* 1:12. ***in their hearts*** Probably referring to the inner struggle for insight (see *Gospel of Thomas* 2). **69:2** *Matt.* 5:6; *Luke* 6:21a. **71** *Mark* 14:58; 15:29; *Matt.* 26:61; 27:40; *John* 2:19. See *Mark* 13:2; *Acts* 6:14. ***house*** It is noteworthy that *Thomas* makes no direct reference to the temple. *House* could, however, here refer obliquely to the temple. It could also invite a number of other referents: the ruling Herodian house; a family household; or, metaphorically, the body as the house of the soul. ***build it*** Probably, *build it again.* **72:1–3** *Luke* 12:13–14. See 61:5. **73** *Matt.* 9:37–38; *Luke* 10:2. See 21:9; *John* 4:34–38. **74 *He*** This saying is not explicitly attributed to Jesus. It may form a dialogue together with 73 and/or 75. ***trough*** Some scholars think that the Coptic here has been misspelled and should read "well." **75 *alone*** See note to 16:4. ***bridal chamber*** See 104:3; *Dialogue of the Savior* 50. In antiquity it was customary for a marriage to be consummated soon after the wedding in a nuptial chamber. Some forms of gnostic Christianity included a cere-

76 Jesus said, "The kingdom of the Father is like a merchant who had a consignment of merchandise and then found a pearl. 2That merchant was prudent; he sold the merchandise and bought the single pearl for himself. 3So also with you, seek his treasure that is unfailing, that is enduring, where no moth comes to eat and no worm destroys."

77 Jesus said, "I am the light that is over all things. I am all: from me all came forth, and to me all attained. 2Split a piece of wood; I am there. 3Lift up the stone, and you will find me there."[l]

78 Jesus said, "Why have you come out to the countryside? To see a reed shaken by the wind? 2And to see a person dressed in soft clothes, like your[m] rulers and your powerful ones? 3They are dressed in soft clothes, and they cannot understand truth."

79 A woman in the crowd said to him, "Blessed are the womb that bore you and the breasts that fed you." 2He said to her,[n] "Blessed are those who have heard the word of the Father and have truly kept it. 3For there will be days when you will say, 'Blessed are the womb that has not conceived and the breasts that have not given milk.' "

80 Jesus said, "Whoever has come to know the world has discovered the body, 2and whoever has discovered the body, of that one the world is not worthy."

l Gk reads verse 3 before verse 2
m Coptic lacuna; *Like your* reconstructed from context
n Coptic lacuna; *to her* reconstructed from context

81 Jesus said, "Let one who has become wealthy reign, 2and let one who has power renounce it."[o]

82 Jesus said, "Whoever is near me is near the fire, 2and whoever is far from me is far from the kingdom."

83 Jesus said, "Images are visible to people, but the light within them is hidden in the image of the Father's light. 2He[p] will be disclosed, but his image is hidden by his light."

84 Jesus said, "When you see your likeness, you are happy. 2But when you see your images that came into being before you and that neither die nor become visible, how much you will have to bear!"

85 Jesus said, "Adam came from great power and great wealth, but he was not worthy of you. 2For had he been worthy, he would[q] not have tasted[r] death."

86 Jesus said, "Foxes have[s] their dens and birds have their nests, 2but human beings have no place to lay down and rest."

87 Jesus said, "How miserable is the body that depends on a body, 2and how miserable is the soul that depends on these two."

o Or *abdicate*
p Or *It*
q Coptic lacuna; *he would* reconstructed from context
r Coptic lacuna; *have tasted* reconstructed from context
s Coptic lacuna; *Foxes have* reconstructed from context

mony called the "bridal chamber." Both the content and the significance of the bridal chamber are obscure. It may have signified the union of the gnostic with his or her divine counterpart, or twin, who was said to reside in heaven awaiting his or her return. As such, the ceremony secured the fate of the gnostic after death. **76:1–2** *Matt.* 13:44–46. **76:3** *Matt.* 6:19–21; *Luke* 12:33–34. **77:1** See *Wis.* 7:24–30; *Rom.* 11:36; *1 Cor.* 8:6; *John* 8:12. **78:1–3** *Matt.* 11:7–9; *Luke* 7:24–26. **78:2** See *Rev.* 6:15; *Matt.* 20:25. **79:1–2** *Luke* 11: 27–28. See *John* 13:17. **79:3** *Luke* 23:28–29. **80:1–2** See note to 56. **81:1–2** *Gospel of Thomas* 110. See *Mark* 10:23; *Matt.* 19:23; *Luke* 18:24; *1 Cor.* 4:8. To reign or rule in *Thomas* can mean to attain the proper mind-set for salvation (2:4). One who is wealthy must learn to *reign.* The course to be followed is renunciation of *power.* The doublet of this saying in 110 is perhaps clearer. **82:1–2** See *Mark* 9:49; 12:34. The saying, known also from the early church leader Origen (*In Jerem., Hom.* XX, 3), among others, may be based loosely upon a proverb of Aesop (*Aesopica* 186): "Whoever is near to Zeus is near the thunderbolt." Likewise, here, the risks of discipleship are explored. **83:1–2** See 22:6; 83:1–2; 84:4; *2 Cor.* 4:4–6; *Gal.* 1:26–28. ***image*** See note to 22:6. For humans, the divine light is hidden. But with God, the platonic image is overwhelmed by the light. **84:1–2** See *Gen.* 1:26–28; *2 Cor.* 3:18; *1 Tim.* 6:14–16; *Gos. Thom.* 22:6; 83:1–2; 84:4. Here *image* is set in contrast to *likeness,* which seems to refer to the material nature or substance of a person. *Image* derives from the gnostic notion that each person has a heavenly twin, or image, that never perishes but awaits the moment of death, when the gnostic's soul is reunited with it. The saying speaks of the astonishment one experiences when one discovers this concealed world, perhaps through mysticism. **85:1–2** See *Gen.* 1:26–28; 3:17–19; *Rom.* 5:12–14; *1 Cor.* 15:21–22, 42–50. **85:2** ***not taste death*** See note to 18:3. **86:1–2** *Matt.* 8:20; *Luke* 9:58. ***human beings*** Lit. "son of man." Most scholars agree that this is not intended here as a title for Jesus. Occasionally, however, the phrase may be used self-referentially as a circumlocution for "I." **87:1–2** *Gospel of Thomas* 112. See 29; *Gal.* 5:16–18; *Rom.* 8:3–11; *John* 3:6. This saying comments on two levels of depravity, one in which the individual becomes mired in corporeal existence, and another in which even the soul fails to realize its freedom over against the body.

88 Jesus said, "The messengers and the prophets will come to you and give you what belongs to you. ²You, in turn, give them what you have, and say to yourselves, 'When will they come and take what belongs to them?'"

89 Jesus said, "Why do you wash the outside of the cup? ²Do you not understand that the one who made the inside is also the one who made the outside?"

90 Jesus said, "Come to me, for my yoke is easy and my lordship is gentle, ²and you will find rest for yourselves."

91 They said to him, "Tell us who you are so that we may believe in you." ²He said to them, "You examine the face of heaven and earth, but you have not come to know the one who is in your presence, and you do not know how to examine the present moment."

92 Jesus said, "Seek and you will find. ²In the past, however, I did not tell you the things about which you asked me then. Now I am willing to tell them, but you are not seeking them.

93 "Do not give what is holy to dogs, for they might throw them upon the manure pile. ²Do not throw pearls to swine, or they might bring it to naught."[t]

94 Jesus said,[u] "One who seeks will find, ²and for one who knocks[v] it will be opened."

95 Jesus said,[w] "If you have money, do not lend it at interest. ²Rather, give it to someone from whom you will not get it back."

96 Jesus said,[x] "The Father's kingdom is like a woman. ²She took a little yeast, hid[y] it in dough, and made it into large loaves of bread. ³Whoever has ears to hear, let them hear."

97 Jesus said, "The Father's[z] kingdom is like a woman who was carrying a jar[a] full of meal. ²While she was walking along a distant road,[b] the handle of the jar broke and the meal spilled behind her along[c] the road. ³She did not know it; she had not noticed a problem.[d] ⁴When she reached her house, she put the jar down and discovered that it was empty."

98 Jesus said, "The Father's kingdom is like a person who wanted to kill someone powerful. ²While still at home, he drew his sword and thrust it into the wall to find out whether his hand would go in. ³Then he killed the powerful one."

99 The disciples said to him, "Your brothers and your mother are standing outside." ²He said to them, "Those here who do the will of my Father are my brothers and my mother. ³They are the ones who will enter my Father's kingdom."

---

t Coptic ends *or they might*

u Coptic lacuna; *said* reconstructed from context
v Coptic lacuna; *one who knocks* reconstructed from context
w Coptic lacuna; *Jesus said* reconstructed from context
x Coptic lacuna; *said* reconstructed from context
y Coptic lacuna; *hid* reconstructed from context
z Coptic lacuna; *Father's* reconstructed from context
a Coptic lacuna; *jar* reconstructed from context
b Or *on the road, still far off*
c Coptic lacuna; *along* reconstructed from context
d Or *not understood how to toil*

88:1 messengers The Coptic here could also mean "angels" (heavenly messengers; see *Mark* 8:38). As in Gk, it may simply mean ordinary *messengers* (see *Luke* 9:51–52). Here it has been rendered in the latter sense because it is paired with *prophets*, a title assigned to people going from place to place in early Christianity (see *Did.* 11.3–6). **89:1–2** In *Matt.* 23:25–26 and *Luke* 11:39–41 the cup stands as a metaphor for Jesus' opponents, who give attention to outward appearances but allow inner corruption. **90:1–2** *Matt.* 11:28–30. See *Sir.* 51:26–27; 6:23–31. **90:2 rest** See note to 50:3. **91:2** *Matt.* 16:1–3; *Luke* 12:54–56. See *John* 6:30. **92:1** See 2:1; 94; *Matt.* 7:7–8; *Luke* 11:9–10; *Dialogue of the Savior* 10, 20. **92:2** See 38; *John* 16:4–5, 12–15, 22–28. **93:1–2** *Matt.* 7:6. See *Mark* 7:27–28; *Matt.* 15:26–27. **93:2 or they might** The text is damaged here. Among proposals for its restoration are "bring it [to naught]" and "grind it [to bits]." **94:1–2** See note to 90:2. **95:1–2** *Matt.* 5:42; *Luke* 6:30, 34–35. **96:1–2** *Matt.* 13:33; *Luke* 13:20–21. **96:2 yeast** In ancient literature, yeast can stand metaphorically for corruption and decay (see *Mark* 8:15; *1 Cor.* 5:6–8). As in *Gospel of Thomas* 20, the kingdom is likened to something unclean. **large** See note to 8:2. **96:3** See note to 8:4. **98:1–3** See 35; *Mark* 3:27; *Matt.* 12:29; 11:12–13; *Luke* 11:22; 16:16. While the use of violent imagery is not unknown in the Jesus tradition, the meaning of this parable is elusive. Perhaps "the underdog wins in the end" or "practice makes perfect." **98:2** The parable probably envisions a modest peasant home of mud brick, whose walls would serve well as a surface on which to practice one's thrust. **99:1–3** *Mark* 3:20–22; *Matt.* 12:46–50; *Luke* 8:19–21. See 16; 55; 101; 105; *Matt.* 10:36–38; *Luke* 14:26; 12:51–53.

100 They showed Jesus a gold coin and said to him, "The Roman emperor's people demand taxes from us." [2]He said to them, "Give the emperor what belongs to the emperor, [3]give God what belongs to God, [4]and give me what is mine.

101 "Whoever does not hate father[e] and mother as I do cannot be my disciple,[f] [2]and whoever does not[g] love father and[h] mother as I do cannot be my disciple.[i] [3]For my mother gave me falsehood,[j] but my true mother[k] gave me life."

102 Jesus said, "Woe to the Pharisees, for they are like a dog sleeping in a cattle trough, for it neither eats nor lets[l] the cattle eat."

103 Jesus said, "Blessed are those who know where the bandits are going to attack. They[m] may get going, bring together their resources,[n] and be prepared before the bandits arrive."

104 They said to Jesus, "Come, let us pray today, and let us fast." [2]Jesus said, "What sin have I committed, or how have I been undone? [3]Rather, when the groom leaves the bridal chamber, then let them fast and pray."

105 Jesus said, "Whoever knows the father and the mother will be called the child of a whore."

106 Jesus said, "When you make the two into one, you will become children of humanity, [2]and when you say, 'Mountain, move from here!' it will move."

107 Jesus said, "The kingdom is like a shepherd who had a hundred sheep. 2One of them, the largest, went astray. He left the ninety-nine and looked for the one until he found it. [3]After he had toiled, he said to the sheep, 'I love you more than the ninety-nine.' "

108 Jesus said, "Whoever drinks from my mouth will become like me; [2]I myself shall become that person, [3]and the hidden things will be revealed to them."

109 Jesus said, "The Father's kingdom is like a person who had a treasure hidden in his field but did not know it. [2]And when he[o] died he left it to his son. The son[p] did not know about it either.[q] He took over the field and sold it. [3]The buyer went plowing, discovered[r] the treasure, and began to lend money at interest to whomever he wished."

110 Jesus said, "Let one who has found the world, and has become wealthy, renounce the world."

e Coptic lacuna; *father* reconstructed from context
f Coptic lacuna; *disciple* reconstructed from context
g Coptic lacuna; *not* reconstructed from context
h Coptic lacuna; *father and* reconstructed from context
i Coptic lacuna; *disciple* reconstructed from context
j Coptic lacuna; *gave me falsehood* reconstructed from context
k Coptic lacuna; *mother* reconstructed from context
l Coptic lacuna; *Lets* reconstructed from context
m Coptic lacuna; *They* reconstructed from context
n Coptic uncertain

o Coptic lacuna; *when he* reconstructed from context
p Or *he left it. His son*
q Or *did not know.*
r Coptic lacuna; *discovered* reconstructed from context

100:1–4 *Mark* 12:13–17; *Matt.* 22:15–22; *Luke* 20:20–26. **101:1–3** *Matt.* 10:37–38; *Luke* 14:26–27; *Gospel of Thomas* 55. See 16; 99; 105; *Mark* 3:20–22; 10:28–30; *Matt.* 12:46–50; 19:27–29; *Luke* 8:19–21; 18:28–30; 12:52–53. **101:3** ***For my mother . . .*** The text is damaged here and cannot be restored with certainty. **102** See 39:1–2; *Matt.* 23:13; *Luke* 11:52. **103** See 21:5–7; *Matt.* 24:42–44; *Luke* 12:35–38; *1 Thess.* 5:1–2; *2 Pet.* 3:10; *Rev.* 3:3; 16:15. ***bring together their imperial rule*** The phrase is obscure. If an invasion is in view, the injunction may be for a ruler to muster his forces. **104:3** ***fast and pray*** See note to 6:1. ***bridal chamber*** See note to 75. **105** See 16; 55; 99; 105; *Mark* 3:20–22; *Matt.* 10:37–38; 12:46–50; *Luke* 8:19–21; 12:52–53; 14:26–27; *John* 8:39–42. ***child of a whore*** The origin of this phrase is obscure. Of possible relevance may be the charge, common in early Jewish-Christian debate, that Jesus was the illegitimate child of Mary and a Roman soldier. Or it may belong to a raft of sayings attributed to Jesus that seem to undercut family life. **106:1–2** *Gospel of Thomas* 48. See 22:4. **106:1** ***children of humanity*** Lit. "sons of men." The expression may read "sons of the Anthropos" or "sons of Adam." See note to 4:3. 106:2 See *Mark* 11:22–23; *Matt.* 17:19–20; 21:21; *Luke* 17:5–6; *1 Cor.* 13:2; *Gospel of Thomas* 42. **107:2** See note to 8:2. **107:3** ***toiled*** See note to 58. **108:1** See 13:5; *Sir.* 24:21; *John* 4:13–14; 7:37–39. Comparing revelation to water, from which the recipient drinks to his or her satisfaction, is common in wisdom and gnostic texts. The reference here to Jesus' mouth as the source of this satisfying drink is related to Jesus as one who speaks words of revelation. **108:3** See 5; 6:2–6; *Mark* 4:22; *Matt.* 10:26; *Luke* 8:17; 12:2. **109:1–3** *Matt.* 13:44. **109:1** ***hidden treasure*** Wisdom is sometimes likened to hidden treasure (see *Prov.* 2:1–5; *Sir.* 20:30–31). **110** See 27; 95. World renunciation is an important element in *Thomas.* See note to 81.

111 Jesus said, "The heavens and the earth will roll up in your presence, ²and whoever is living from the living one will not see death." ³Does not Jesus say, "Those who have found themselves, of them the world is not worthy"?

112 Jesus said, "Woe to the flesh that depends on the soul. ²Woe to the soul that depends on the flesh."

113 His disciples said to him, "When will the kingdom come?" ²"It will not come by watching for it. ³It will not be said,ˢ 'Look, here' or 'Look, there.' ⁴Rather, the Father's kingdom is spread out upon the earth, and people do not see it."

---

s Or *They will not say*

114 Simon Peter said to them, "Make Mary leave us, for females do not deserve life." ²Jesus said, "Look, I will guide her to make her male, so that she too may become a living spirit resembling you males. ³For every female who makes herself male will enter the kingdom of heaven."

111:1 *heavens* See note to 11:1. **111:2** See 1; 18:3; 19:4; 85:2; *Mark* 9:1; *Matt.* 16:28; *Luke* 9:27; *John* 8:51. **not see death** See note to 18:3. **111:3** See 56; 80. **112:1–2** *Gospel of Thomas* 87. See 29; *John* 3:6; *Gal.* 5:16–18; *Rom.* 8:3–11. The dualistic disconnection of body from soul is part of ancient asceticism. For the gnostic, the body is only an earthly prison from which the soul must escape if it is to reascend to the heavenly realm. Here the unfortunate fate of the flesh is ultimately to be destroyed. If it is not able to separate from the flesh the fate of the soul is lamentable. **113:1–4** See note to 3:1–3. **114:1** The Petrine tradition is notably unkind to women (*1 Pet.* 3:1–6). In the extracanonical tradition, Peter is portrayed as critical of Mary (e.g., in the *Gospel of Mary* 10:3–4 and the *Pistis Sophia* [146]). While some gnostic groups were egalitarian, many others were misogynist, identifying the origin of evil with the feminine. **114:2–3** See note to 4:3. Here the ideal is not to become androgynous but to "become male." In other texts (*Apocryphon of James* 41; 15–19; *Zostrianos* 131.2–10) the transition from female to male a metaphor for translation from earthly to heavenly existence, from mortality to immortality. There may also be a practical side to the saying. Women philosophers often disguised themselves as men as a way of participating in an intellectual and mendicant lifestyle that was largely the domain of men.

EARLY

CHRISTIAN

READER

WRITINGS ATTRIBUTED TO JOHN

THE JOHANNINE TRADITION

THE JOHANNINE CORPUS consists of a gospel and three brief letters, one of which is much more like a tract than a letter. Some scholars argue that the *Apocalypse* (commonly known as the *Revelation*) should be treated as part of the Johannine tradition too.[1] If these documents are really part of the same tradition, the Johannine material represents the widest spectrum of literary genre of any corpus in the New Testament (gospel, tract, letters, and apocalypse).

Although the collection is called "Johannine," only the *Apocalypse* bears the name "John" as author (stated three times within the opening few paragraphs: *Rev.* 1:1, 4, 9, and once in the closing: 22:8). The *Gospel* and the letters do not name their author, assuming, it seems, that the recipients know the source of the documents. By the latter part of the second century, all this material was linked to John the apostle, but a few ancient church voices rejected that attribution of authorship, and much of present scholarship has sided with these early critics.

The Intellectual Milieu

A century ago, Adolf von Harnack, a leading early church historian, stated: "The origin of the Johannine writings is, from the standpoint of a history of literature and dogma, the most marvelous enigma which the early history of Christianity presents."[2] That situation has not changed. Scholars still hotly debate the character and background of the Johannine tradition, as well as the relationship of the Johannine community to the other groups that comprised the early Christian church.

The Johannine literature is marked by its preference for special themes, which are often presented as contrasting pairs, such as "light" and "darkness," "truth" and "lies," and being of the "world" and not being of the "world." The primary word translated "light" occurs twenty-three times in the *Gospel of John* and six times in the

---

[1] We have placed the *Apocalypse* with the Johannine material in the *Reader*. Evidence for such grouping of this material can be found as early as the second century, though questions about Johannine authorship were raised early too. See the introduction to the *Apocalypse* for a detailed discussion of authorship.

[2] Adolf von Harnack, *History of Dogma*, 1.96.

letters, but only seven times in *Matthew* and *Luke* and only once in *Mark*. The primary cluster of cognates for "truth" occurs fifty-five times in the *Gospel* and twenty-eight times in the letters; this compares to six times in *Matthew* and *Mark* and eight times in *Luke*. Of the eleven occurrences of the word "liar" in our literature, seven are from the Johannine material. The word for "life" occurs thirty-six times in the *Gospel*, thirteen times in the letters, and seventeen times in the *Apocalypse;* this compares to seven occurrences in *Matthew,* four in *Mark,* and five in *Luke*. The word "world" (Gk *kosmos*) occurs seventy-eight times in the *Gospel* and twenty-four times in the letters, but only eight times in *Matthew* and three times in *Mark* and *Luke*.

Some scholars argue that Johannine thought was the peculiar expression of an isolated theological community; others contend that Johannine thought was the dominant theological perspective of Asia Minor, a leading center of the church during the second century. Both positions may be extreme. Most scholars prefer a middle position, recognizing the distinctiveness of the Johannine tradition but disallowing its isolation—in other words, positing some sort of productive tension between the Johannine group and other groups within the early church.

Also a matter of dispute is the pre-Christian religious milieu that provided the primary intellectual background of the Johannine tradition. Every possibility has been explored and proposed: Pauline, Qumran, Hermetic, Philonic, gnostic, Mandaean—running the gamut from conservative Judaism to radical Hellenism. One scholar of the Johannine material commented that "the novice is tempted to ask, with what intellectual milieu of the first century does the evangelist [John] *not* have some affinities?"[3]

It was once popular to think in terms of some kind of Hellenism[4] as the interpretive key for Johannine thought, thus largely removing John from roots in Judaism. That conclusion must be heavily qualified. On the one hand, it is now recognized that the Johannine perspective fits quite well within the range of religious options in first-century Judaism, even in *Palestinian* Judaism. That recognition has come about mainly as a result of our expanding knowledge of the range of options within first-century Judaism, especially illuminated by the discovery in the late 1940s of the Dead Sea Scrolls at Qumran.[5] On the other hand, we are now more aware that sharp lines cannot be drawn between Judaism and Hellenism or even between Palestinian Judaism and Diaspora Judaism. The Mediterranean world was Hellenistic in the first century, and Judaism, even in Palestine, was very much part of that world.

---

[3] Robert Kysar, *The Fourth Evangelist and His Gospel* (Minneapolis: Augsburg, 1975), 103.

[4] A good example of hellenized ideas is found in the work of the first-century Jewish philosopher, Philo of Alexandria. Many scholars have argued that the Johannine reference to the "logos" reflects a similar attempt to appropriate Greek (or Hellenistic) philosophy in the service of the Christian message.

[5] That does not mean that the Johannine tradition was influenced by the Qumran community, though some scholars have argued for that connection, especially on the basis of a shared dualism (e.g., light and darkness and good and evil). Rather, the Qumran literature helps to demonstrate that first-century Judaism was sufficiently diverse to have generated and accommodated a perspective such as that of the Johannine community.

Many scholars argue for the influence of gnostic thought on the Johannine tradition. This position owes much to the work of the noted twentieth-century New Testament theologian Rudolf Bultmann.[6] The dualistic language of the Johannine writings certainly has affinities with gnosticism, and some of the Johannine themes, such as knowledge, truth, the world, and being from above also reflect similarities with gnosticism.

The issue is complicated. For one thing, the shared language between gnosticism and the Johannine material is not so specifically gnostic as to demand gnostic influence, and the parallels are less striking when one examines the totality of the language of gnosticism. Another consideration is that the *Gospel of John,* which is the primary document of the Johannine tradition, may have gone through several stages of composition, and whatever the case for earlier forms, the final edition may be outside the orbit of the gnostic debate altogether, or as some have argued, antagonistic to gnosticism.

Later writings in the Johannine tradition, such as the letter called *1 John,* show that the community that preserved Johannine tradition became pointedly anti-docetic.[7] By extension, this would mark at least one branch of the Johannine community as antignostic, since docetism seems to have been largely an earlier form of the developed gnostic systems of the second century. That there may have been other branches of the Johannine community that developed in the direction of gnosticism is certainly possible, since the Johannine letters themselves reflect internal schism over a docetic understanding of Jesus. These schismatics—the "other side" in the Johannine letters—may well have had a life beyond that schism, even though we have no access to that community in the surviving literature of early Christianity.

Perhaps part of the ambiguity of the evidence for gnostic influence is that the original "edition" of the *Gospel of John* may have used language that could have been more easily appropriated by gnosticism than the language in the Synoptic Gospels. That could explain why the *Gospel of John* became a favorite of various gnostic circles in the second century. It could also explain why non-gnostic churches felt a vested interest in "rescuing" the Johannine gospel for their own use, which they do not seem to have been inclined to do for literature that was more distinctly gnostic.

The Johannine Genius

In the effort to identify the intellectual background of an author, scholars look for parallels of thought and language with other systems. This method can be illuminating, provided that we do not disallow all novelty, originality, and genius in the author we are trying to understand. The Johannine tradition, in particular, seems to reflect the impact of a theological genius who formulated a new under-

---

[6] Rudolf Bultmann, *The Gospel of John* (Philadelphia: Westminster, 1971). The German original was published in 1941.

[7] Docetism is discussed in the introduction to the letters of John.

standing of the Christian message. Although he may have borrowed widely for his theological images and idioms, the result should be recognized as distinctively his, and his originality should be given the same status as that of someone like Paul.

That some spark of genius lies behind the Johannine tradition is suggested both by the distinctiveness of the Johannine tradition and the possibility that a whole community or school was inspired by and took their identity from this perspective. We will see in the introduction to the *Gospel of John* just how distinctive the Johannine traditions about Jesus are when compared with the three Synoptic Gospels. Not only does the Johannine material offer different stories about Jesus; it offers a distinctive theological idiom as well. Whereas the Synoptic Gospels focused on the theme of the kingdom of God to describe God's resolution to the human dilemma, and Paul focused on the theme of salvation from sin or unrighteousness, John spoke of new life through belief in Jesus. Many of these images have become favorites of the Christian church.[8]

The Johannine community's choice of neither a Pauline nor a synoptic idiom is noteworthy, especially in light of the date of the fixing of the Johannine material in written form—widely placed in the last decade of the first century, when both the Pauline tradition and the synoptic tradition were already established. Why the Johannine circle chose a distinctive idiom when other idioms were available lies close to the heart of an understanding of the Johannine tradition.

The Break with the Synagogue

Many scholars who study the Johannine literature today are primarily interested in tracing the development of the community that produced or preserved these writings. One of the most convincing reconstructions locates the group's earliest history in the synagogue. It contends that, largely as a result of a forced break with the synagogue, the Johannine community became a self-conscious unit, producing its own literature.

In support of this view, scholars can point to numerous stories in the *Gospel* of Jewish hostility to the followers of Jesus,[9] and in particular to stories of expulsion from synagogues merely for believing in Jesus.[10] These stories, which on the surface recount a tension between Jesus and the Jews, really reflect the tension between the church and the synagogue at the time of the composition of the *Gospel of John*, ac-

---

[8] That is not to say that any author has a monopoly on particular language. The distinctive idiom of one author may be found somewhere within the works of another author. Nonetheless, authors do have favorite ways of speaking—cherished expressions that grasp the essence of the religious experience they wish to communicate and that mark the writing as theirs.

[9] Note the stories about Jesus' own conflicts with the Jews (*John* 6:41–59; 7:32–36; 8:21–59). In fact, most of the *Gospel of John* reflects some level of tension with the Jews, though it has been argued by some that the tension was not with Jews as a whole but more specifically with the Jewish leadership, or perhaps with Judeans (in contrast to Galileans, who were more receptive of Jesus' message).

[10] One can point specifically to stories such as the expulsion from the synagogue of a man healed by Jesus. The story takes up all of ch. 9. See too *John* 12:42 and 16:2.

cording to this view. Why else, these scholars argue, would the author be interested in dealing with this theme of tension between Christians and the synagogue? And why would his readers be interested in reading about it? The stories of tension with the Jews and of expulsion of followers of Jesus from the synagogue would seem to indicate that a formal break between the Johannine community and the synagogue had taken place—perhaps not long before the writing of the *Gospel* and while the wounds were still fresh. Some such reconstruction also helps to make sense of the more general anti-Jewish polemic in the *Fourth Gospel.*

Authorship

It is uncertain who wrote the Johannine material. On the one hand, many scholars are so skeptical about the association of John the disciple with the literature that came to bear his name that it has become common in scholarly circles to speak of the chief document of that tradition as the *Fourth Gospel,* rather than the *Gospel of John.* On the other hand, some scholars are prepared to consider the possibility that John the disciple was, if not the writer of the *Gospel,* at least the guarantor of the traditions behind the literature that has traditionally borne his name, and some argue this position with considerable vigor.

Early traditions place the apostle John in Ephesus toward the end of the first century.[11] It is disputed whether these traditions are reliable. Most scholars are prepared, however, to locate the main Johannine community in the area of Ephesus at the end of the first century, even though there is nothing within the Johannine gospel or letters that demand this.

A more detailed discussion of authorship follows in the introductions to the individual documents of the Johannine corpus.

For Further Reading

Ashton, John, ed. *The Interpretation of John.* Issues in Religion and Theology 9. Philadelphia: Fortress, 1986.

Brown, Raymond. *The Community of the Beloved Disciple.* Paramus, N.J.: Paulist, 1979.

Hengel, Martin. *The Johannine Question.* Translated by John Bowden. London: SCM/Philadelphia: Trinity Press, 1989).

---

[11] *The Acts of John* 19–55, 62–115 (mid-second century); Irenaeus, *Against Heresies* 3.1.1 (late-second century).

The Exposition of God by the Word Made Flesh

JOHN

John and the Synoptic Gospels: Common Traditions

Even a cursory reading of the gospels will uncover a number of differences between *John* and the Synoptic Gospels *(Mark, Matthew,* and *Luke)*. Scholars have generally focused on these differences. They are important and will be surveyed below. But such close analysis can sometimes cause us to overlook the striking similarities between the *Gospel of John* and the other gospels. In other words, were we to look at the entire range of world literature, the *Gospel of John* would most appropriately fit with the Synoptic Gospels.

Without dismissing any of the efforts to analyze the gospel records and to list the remarkable differences between *John* and the Synoptics, it is important first to get a sense of the remarkable similarities that exist.

Stories about Jesus could have been written in a number of ways. John and the synoptic writers choose what appears to be an unusual structure. First, their stories do not begin until Jesus is fully grown and about to embark on a career as a religious reformer of some sort. Thus much of Jesus' life, from childhood well into manhood, is passed over. Second, the latter half of *John* deals with the final few days of Jesus' life, with a detailed account of the trial and crucifixion. In some ways, the whole *Gospel* is little more than a story of Jesus' rejection and death. The striking feature is that the synoptic framework is not that different: the main story starts with the beginning of Jesus' career as a religious reformer and pays particular attention to the last week of his life.[1]

The recognition of such similarity of structure must be our starting point. Each author of the four canonical gospels builds the story of Jesus on that unusual structure, selecting and modifying, highlighting and qualifying various aspects of the tradition, with the result that each final product offers a distinctive understanding of Jesus. In the case of *John,* the author identifies the final cluster of events—the

---

[1] *Mark* generally is considered to be the oldest gospel. It begins with Jesus fully grown and about to begin his career; *Matthew* and *Luke* have stories of Jesus' birth (called "infancy narratives"), but these gospels then proceed immediately to the beginning of Jesus' career.

same events that are central to all the gospel writers—as *the hour.* Working with this term, he informs his readers of the progression toward that final scene (2:4; 7:30; 8:20), tipping them off about halfway through that what was anticipated has now arrived (12:23, 27; 13:1). With the announcement that "the hour has come," John begins his passion narrative.

John and the Synoptic Gospels: Distinctive Traditions

From the beginning, however, people have noticed that the *Gospel of John* differs starkly from the other three gospels. Its unique theological idiom as well as other features find no parallel in the synoptic tradition; introductions to the *Fourth Gospel* routinely list these differences. For convenience, these differences can be subdivided into geographical, chronological, literary, and theological details.

With regard to geography, the Synoptics report that Jesus worked exclusively in Galilee until his final Passover; the *Fourth Gospel,* however, portrays him as active in a much wider area, including Judea, Samaria, and Galilee.

With regard to chronology, four major differences are usually noted. (a) In the Synoptics, the career of Jesus begins after the arrest of John the Baptist (*Mark* 1:14), whereas in *John* it begins during the preaching activities of the Baptist, sometime prior to his arrest (3:24). (b) The length of Jesus' career covers about a one-year period, according to the synoptic reports, while according to *John* about three years seem to be required to take in all of the recorded events.[2] (c) The "cleansing" of the temple occurs in the final week of Jesus' career according to the Synoptics (*Mark* 11:15), but *John* places the event near the beginning (2:13). (d) The career of Jesus ends with a supper on Passover evening according to the synoptic traditions (*Mark* 14:1; 12–26), but *John* places that final meal before the Passover (13:1; 18:28), thus allowing the crucifixion of Jesus (who, according to John, is God's lamb) to occur at the precise time that lambs were being slaughtered for the Jewish Passover festival.

Various attempts have been made to explain these geographical and chronological differences. The importance of these differences will depend on the weight one places on such details in the gospel accounts. Form criticism, a methodology developed between the two world wars, tended to dismiss most geographical and chronological details as unrelated to the original stories, which had circulated orally as independent units, called pericopes. If the chronological and geographical details are rarely original to the stories, such details become merely the narrative glue by which the gospel authors joined their sources together, and disagreements at that level are expected.

The *Fourth Gospel* also differs from the Synoptics in literary style. *John*'s Jesus engages in lengthy discussions, employing allegories and images not used in the

---

[2] The length of the career of Jesus is determined by the number of Passover festivals mentioned in the gospels—useful information for the purpose since the Passover was an annual event. Only one Passover is mentioned in the Synoptics, and that occurred in the final week of Jesus' life. But in the *Fourth Gospel,* three Passovers are mentioned, and this requires about a three-year period.

other gospels. In contrast, the synoptic Jesus appears as a master of the "one-liner" and frequently makes his point with short parables, which *John*'s Jesus never uses.

John turns frequently to metaphor: living water, the true vine, the good shepherd, the bread of life, and the door are memorable images unique to the *Fourth Gospel*. Many of these images are introduced by the formula "I am," a charged phrase that does not appear in the Synoptics with this sense.

Even the selection of stories is different from that of the synoptic traditions. The miracle of water turned to wine (ch. 2), the discussion with Nicodemus (ch. 3), the Samaritan woman at the well (ch. 4), the man who carried his "bed" on the Sabbath (ch. 5), a healing of a blind man (ch. 6), the raising of Lazarus (ch. 11), the washing of the disciples' feet (ch. 13), and various post-resurrection stories (chs. 20 and 21) are all absent from the synoptic accounts.

But it is not a simple matter of the synoptic tradition's working with one set of stories and the Johannine tradition's working with another. In several stories, the common features are sufficiently striking to suggest that both *John* and the Synoptics reflect the same episode, however much the finer details of the stories might differ. The most obvious parallels are the accounts of the cleansing of the temple, the entry into Jerusalem, the feeding of the multitude, Jesus' walking on water, and various incidents in the passion narrative, along with numerous less specific parallels of language and event. So striking are some of the similarities that scholars have pondered the possibility of direct literary dependency of the Johannine author on the synoptic writings, or at least his access to the body of oral tradition from which the synoptic literature itself drew. This makes the development of the Johannine tradition and literature more complicated than perhaps would have been the case had the traditions been clearly and completely independent.

Finally, the *Fourth Gospel* differs from the Synoptics in terms of theology. The Jesus in *John* is a mirror image of the Jesus of the church's faith. All of the church's claims about Jesus are claims Jesus makes about himself: he is the Christ; he has come from the Father; eternal life comes through believing in and obeying him. The Synoptic Gospels, though just as certain as *John* is about the pivotal role of Jesus in God's program, portray Jesus as overshadowed by the message he announces—the good news of the coming of God's kingdom. In contrast, the kingdom of God is mentioned only twice in *John* (3:3, 5). On the other hand, the phrase "eternal life," a favorite in *John*, rarely occurs in the Synoptics.

Taken together, these differences are wide-ranging and striking. Much has been made of them by scholars who study the gospel traditions of the early church. But one must be careful not to dismiss the Johannine tradition simply because the synoptic tradition has the support of three gospels against one. For one thing, the Synoptic Gospels can hardly be viewed as three independent witnesses to a tradition— they are more closely related and mutually dependent than any other set of writings from the early church and represent basically one strand of early Christian tradition, although each of them interprets it distinctively. Further, the early church does not offer two traditions—a synoptic and a Johannine—from which a choice must be made. The early witness to Jesus was most diverse, which is clearly seen when we add the Pauline perspective to the equation—and various other tendencies that mark early Christian reflection about Jesus.

Setting

The setting of the *Gospel of John* is closely related to the process by which the *Gospel* reached its final form, for if the process was a long one, involving various "editions" before the final form was reached, we may need to speak not of one setting but several.

It seems necessary to admit at least one minor redaction, or editing, of *John*. Consider the last paragraph of chapter 20: "Now Jesus did many other signs in the presence of his disciples, which are not written in this book. But these are written so that you may come to believe that Jesus is the Messiah, the Son of God, and that through believing you may have life in his name." This reads like a formal closing of the story of Jesus, yet it is followed by an extended resurrection appearance account and a discussion of leadership in the church in chapter 21. The break at the end of chapter 20 makes chapter 21 look like an editorial comment attached to an earlier "version."

Since the final chapter seems to hint at the death of the disciple "whom Jesus loved" (21:20–23), many scholars contend that the final chapter reflects a new "edition" of *John,* made necessary by a crisis in the community that stemmed from the death of the disciple who was the guarantor of the traditions. Further, the death may have been unexpected—some even thinking that their leader would live until the return of Jesus at the end of the age (21:23).

Scholars find less common ground when they discuss the evidence for other levels of redactional (or editorial) activity. For example, *John* deals directly and frequently with the hostile relationship between Jesus and Jews who did not believe in him. Although most of the stories are set in the context of Jesus' own lifetime, many scholars believe that some of these stories of conflict with the Jews reflect more the strained and bitter relationship that the Johannine community itself had with the Jews. It has been suggested that an expulsion of Christians from synagogues shortly after the Jewish War (66–73 C.E.) may have given rise to the community's consciousness and self-understanding that we see reflected in *John*. Although the evidence of this expulsion is not without problems, it is considered an attractive hypothesis by many. Further, whether this tension was reflected in the original edition of *John* or is evidence of a later revision is not easily determined.

Some older theories saw the setting of the composition of the *Gospel of John* in terms of conflict with Docetism[3] or a dispute over authority in the community

---

[3] See the introduction to The Johannine Letters for a detailed discussion of Docetism.

(both of which are much clearer themes in the Johannine letters than in the *Gospel*, however); some have suggested the *Gospel* rose out of a mission to the Samaritans (chapter 4 deals largely with Samaritan expectations and the relation of Jesus to these). Other proposals, both ancient and recent, give the discussion a richness of speculation, though the consequence of this is that consensus is unlikely.

Themes and Issues

The *Gospel of John* portrays Jesus confronting his opponents in extended dialogues, which are marked by a number of recurring themes. In particular, various relationships are introduced and developed:[4] (a) between the Father (God) and the Son (Jesus); (b) between the Son and the world; (c) between the believer and the Father and his Son; and (d) between the believer and the world.

That between the Father and the Son is the most perfect relationship. The Son has come from Father and will return to the Father. He came to do the Father's will, and he does it. In fact, only *John* records the last words of the dying Jesus as "It is finished" (19:30)—most fitting "last words" for one whose purpose of coming into the world was to do his Father's will (4:34; 5:30; 6:38–39).

The Son's relationship with his Father contrasts sharply with the relationship that the Son has with the world (Gk *kosmos*). The world does not know the Son, even though the world is his world. Worse, the world hates the Son and will eventually kill him. This "world" is not clearly identified and probably is more effective as a polemical device precisely because it is not clearly identified. The readers sense the opposition; they experience the hostility. They do not need further definition of what that world is.

At times it seems that the Jews (or the leaders of the Jews, or perhaps the Judeans) are the opponents, but this, though true in part, is too narrow a definition of the opponents. The whole world is ignorant of the Father and is opposed to the Son. Yet the Father does not hate the world; in fact, in one of the best known passages in Christian literature, God is said to love the world (3:16). But that is not the final word; God will also judge the world if it rejects the Son.

A third relationship is that between the Father and those who are "not of the world"—that is, believers, or perhaps specifically, the Johannine Christians. These will not come under the Father's judgment of the world. In contrast to the world, these love the Son and abide in the Son, and so share in the Father's pleasure. Indeed, whatever they ask the Father in the Son's name, the Father will do.

Those who love the Son and are loved by the Son are hated by the world, for the world, in hating the Son, hates also those who belong to the Son. This is the fourth relationship of concern to the author.

---

[4] Other relationships can be identified. For example, Jesus speaks of the relationship between his opponents and the devil (8:39–47), but this, in some ways, is merely saying that the relationship between the Father and the world is a hostile one.

Connected to the theme of relationship are repeated statements about the place where Jesus is, or where he has been, or where he will be going. The secret shared by the author and the readers is that Jesus has come from the Father and will return to the Father. The world, not having understood that, fails to pursue a positive relationship with the Son. Such a relationship is necessary for establishing a positive relationship with the Father, which the world mistakenly thinks it already has.

Purpose

The author states his purpose near the end of the *Gospel:* "these things were written so that you might come to believe that Jesus is the Messiah" (20:31). That seems explicit enough. The document is a tool in the missionary thrust of the church, designed to lead its readers to conversion. But the matter is not so straightforward, for there is textual variation at this point: some manuscripts read *pisteusēte* (that you might come to believe); others read *pisteuēte* (that you might continue to believe)—a mere difference of the letter *s*. But the presence or absence of that *s* alters the meaning considerably, changing the purpose of the *Gospel* from a tool to produce converts to a guide for those already converted.

Whatever the author intended as his stated purpose, scholars generally see the document meeting at least two needs. One is to explain the tensions that the community has with Judaism; the second is to deal with the crisis that seems to have arisen from the unexpected death of the leader of the Johannine community and the guarantor of the traditions. Both matters are discussed in more detail elsewhere in this introduction.

Authorship

None of the four gospels names its author. Names are attached to *Matthew* and *Mark* by the earlier part of the second century, as is attested by the writings of Papias, the bishop of Hierapolis in Asia Minor. The first reference to John the disciple as the author of the *Fourth Gospel* is from the late second-century comment by Irenaeus, bishop of Lyons, in his work titled *Against Heresies* (3.1.2). Scholars have debated the historical worth of this attribution.

A possible clue about authorship is found in an unnamed character referred to as "the one whom Jesus loved" (13:23; 19:26; 20:2; 21:7; 20) or "the other disciple" (18:16; 20:2–4, 8).[5] This individual is popularly referred to as the "Beloved Disciple" in modern literature. This special unnamed disciple appears in various scenes of the passion narrative (the Last Supper, the crucifixion, the tomb, and in Galilee after the resurrection), and seems to have had a particularly close relationship to Jesus. At the end of *John*, Peter displays pointed concern about what the future holds for this disciple (21:20).

---

[5] Perhaps the comments at 11:3, 36 relate to this person too.

It is possible that the Beloved Disciple was the disciple John himself. In support of this is the surprising fact that, though John is mentioned prominently in the synoptic traditions and in other early Christian writings, he is never mentioned by name in the *Gospel of John*, though this mysterious anonymous disciple appears throughout the *Gospel*. Further, according to the *Gospel of John*, the first disciples to follow Jesus were Andrew and an associate, who is not named (a somewhat strange feature, since the author does not usually shy away from mentioning names). In the synoptic tradition, the brothers James and John are linked closely to the brothers Andrew and Peter (*Mark* 1:16–20; *Matt.* 4:18–22; *Luke* 5:1–11). Neither James nor John is named in the *Gospel of John*, and it is not until the final chapter, which is almost certainly an addition to the original *Gospel*, that mention is made of the "sons of Zebedee," the term by which James and John are sometimes identified in the Synoptic Gospels. Does this mean that this important pair were not known by the author of John, or, as some suggest, is the omission the key to the identity of the author?

The majority of scholars are sufficiently uncomfortable with the traditional attribution of the *Gospel* to John the disciple that they call this book simply the *Fourth Gospel*, indicating merely its canonical position in terms of the other gospels and demonstrating the general uncertainty about authorship. All that can be said with certainty is that there is more willingness today to think of the author as being Palestinian and Jewish than there was a few decades ago, when the author was viewed as the most thoroughly hellenized of the early Christian authors.

Although most have despaired in the quest to identify the author and the Beloved Disciple (assuming the two are identical—which is not the only conclusion possible from the evidence), some continue to propose new or to defend old hypotheses of authorship. Candidates can range from the traditional (John the disciple),[6] to the possible (John the Elder, known from Papias's comment, or Lazarus), to the unlikely (Nicodemus), and to the trendy (whatever that may happen to be).

Whoever the author was, the Johannine community believed that the traditions in the *Gospel* were guaranteed[7] by a highly respected member of their community, and they also believed that this person had roots in the apostolic community. Modern scholarship, in spite of its reservation about the traditional attribution of authorship to one of the leading disciples of Jesus, is generally willing to

---

[6]The Lazarus story is pivotal. Jewish leaders become concerned when people are attracted to Jesus because he raised Lazarus, so they plot to kill both Jesus and Lazarus (*John* 11:53; 12:9–10). This event divides the author's story into two main sections: before the *hour* has come, and the *hour*—which is how the author speaks of the death of Jesus, the crucial event in his story. Some see the comment that Jesus loved Lazarus (11:36) as a clue to the identity of the unnamed "Beloved Disciple" mentioned elsewhere in the story. Further, at the end of the *Gospel*, a crisis seems to have resulted from the death of the "Beloved Disciple," because a rumor had circulated that he would not die (21:20–23). Lazarus, having been resurrected from the dead, seems to some scholars to be the most likely subject of such a rumor.

[7] So the *Gospel* concludes (21:24): "This is the disciple who is bearing witness to these things, and who has written these things; and we know that his testimony is true."

admit that the author was a theological genius with a distinctive take on the beginnings of Christianity.

Date

We have already noted that the expulsion of Johannine Christians from the synagogue may have been the crucial event in shaping the self-understanding of the Johannine community. The composition of the *Gospel of John* probably would be some time after the Jewish War (66–73 C.E.), as the rabbis took steps to restructure Judaism against all competing interpretations. The most serious challenge may have come from Christianity. Some see confirmation for the expulsion of Christians from the synagogues in one of the "Eighteen Benedictions" of the Jewish liturgy. The intent of the Birkath ha-Minim, the "benediction" that condemns "heretics" in general, could have been designed to expose Christians and force them out of the synagogue. But this explanation is not without its problems, since both the date and the intention of this benediction can be otherwise argued. The specific situation prompting expulsion from the synagogue could have arisen from any number of crises other than the Jewish War.

The exalted status of Jesus in the *Gospel* could be evidence of its late date, but that argument, too, is weak, since the early church, even by the middle of the first century, worked with a range of views about Jesus and his relationship to God. Further, it must be recognized that "complex" or "developed" ideas are not necessarily the products of long periods of reflection and refinement; it is equally possible that such ideas emerged within a short period of time. The date for the *Gospel of John,* then, cannot be determined with the confidence that we enjoy with the letters of Paul, though a date in the final decade of the first century is accepted by most commentators and has no telling points against it.

Literary and Stylistic Devices

The style of the author is simple yet striking. The vocabulary is modest yet memorable. A strong thread of Semitic idiom and language comes through the writing, suggesting that the author was of Jewish background, and even convincing a few that the *Gospel* was originally composed in Aramaic, with the Greek text being a somewhat literal translation.

Whatever the conclusions reached regarding those issues, there is wide agreement that the author has literary skills and is adept at using irony, double meanings, and intentional ambiguities. For example, often what a character in the story has failed to understand is exactly what the believing reader already knows. The whole *Gospel* is something like a play in which the audience has a better grasp of what is going on than do the characters, who stumble along, making what the audience knows to be mistakes. Sometimes the characters of the story are informed of their mistakes; other times they are not. The Jews think that Jesus claimed that he could rebuild the temple in three days; the readers know that Jesus was speaking of his resurrection (2:19–21). Nicodemus thinks that Jesus spoke of a second physical birth; the readers know that Jesus was speaking of a spiritual birth (3:3–4). The Jews think that Jesus told his followers that they must eat his flesh and drink his blood; the readers know that Jesus was speaking of the Eucharist (6:52–53). The Jews think that Jesus is going to "close down shop" among the Jews and go to the Greeks; the readers know he is about to finish the work his Father gave him to do and return then to his Father (7:32–36).

Such ambiguities are commonly created by words with double meanings. For example, Jesus spoke of being born *anōthen,* a Greek word with a variety of meanings (3:3); in the passage, the meaning could be either "born again" or "born from above," which creates the ambiguity around which the scene advances. Another ambiguity is that Jesus spoke of being "lifted up," a term which was used in two radically different senses in Hellenistic Greek, "to be raised to high office" or "to be crucified." And around every corner, there is some touch of irony, some twist that makes the scene more comical or more sad than it seems on the surface, or that supplies a basis for the misunderstanding of the characters in the story, but not for the readers, who know the full story.

Relation to Other Early Christian Literature

In addition to the possible use of the synoptic material, various other sources have been proposed for the *Gospel of John,* but none has gained a wide reception, except for the "signs source" theory (also called *semeia* source, from the Greek word for sign).[8] The author's description of particular "wonder stories" or miracles as signs is intentional; he even numbers two of them (2:11; 4:54), and refers to numerous others. Further, he concludes his *Gospel* with a reference to them (20:30). But this interest in signs, in itself, need not suggest a previous collection of wonder stories from which the author drew; the collection could be part of the author's own contribution to the story he is telling. What has caused some scholars to propose a source from which the author drew these miracle stories is that the author seems at times to be offering a corrective to an undue emphasis on signs and miracles, qualifying them by associating them with the larger picture of rejection, suffering, and death. In other words, however much the author may refer to miracles and signs, they do not work! Jesus is still rejected; the Jews do not see more clearly.

John was not used nearly as widely by patristic writers as were the synoptic traditions; indeed, it seems to have had a far warmer reception among gnostic groups. It is customary to point out that the Valentinians, a gnostic group of the second century, used it widely and that the first commentary on *John* was by the gnostic Heracleon. But the issue is complicated. If the most natural home for the *Gospel of*

---

[8] The term appears frequently in *John* (sixteen times before ch. 13, and once after: 2:11, 18, 23; 3:2; 4:48, 54; 6:2, 14, 26, 30; 7:31; 9:16; 10:41; 11:47; 12:18; 12:37; 20:30). Some scholars have even argued that the present form of *John* is the result of bringing together a "signs" source and a "sayings" source.

John is within gnostic circles, then one must explain what it was about it that prompted the non-gnostic church to rescue this gospel from the gnostics for its own use. The non-gnostic church had the synoptic tradition; why salvage a variant gospel tradition that was at odds with the synoptic tradition and was identified with the opponent's camp? Generally, the church simply dismissed gnostic writings. Why did it not follow that policy here?

The main literary links of the *Gospel of John* are with the three letters commonly grouped under John's name (though his name does not appear in any of these letters). These letters demonstrate an early use of Johannine themes and language against gnostic ideas, whatever might be said of gnostic use of *John*. The long list of parallels between the Johannine gospel and the letters of John is considered in some detail in the notes to the letters, which follow this section.

Value for the Study of Early Christianity

The distinctive theology that characterizes the *Fourth Gospel* has led many to conclude that the Johannine perspective is the result of developed theological reflection. This judgment has often led to a dismissal of the historical worth of the traditions in this gospel. For example, given a choice between the Jesus who openly declares his divine status (as in the *Gospel of John*) and the Jesus who is reluctant to comment on his identity (as in the Synoptics), interpreters invariably take the latter to reflect the historical Jesus more faithfully.

They frequently have considered the synoptic tradition a reservoir of information about the historical Jesus, in contrast to the Johannine tradition, which has been viewed, at best, as a source of information about the "theological Christ," largely the creation of a community that had little interest in the historical Jesus. The Johannine gospel sometimes has been called the "Spiritual Gospel" (by friend and foe alike). Such a description of the *Fourth Gospel* is as old as Clement of Alexandria and Origen (second and third centuries). These early churchmen, of course, were not interested in the historical question in the way modern scholars are, and their description of *John* as a "spiritual" gospel had none of the derogatory tone that it does today.

The negative portrait of the historical worth of the Johannine tradition, a legacy of the early days of the rise of biblical criticism in the 1800s, still largely holds. Some, however, have asked whether some of the traditions behind *John* might not be more trustworthy than the synoptic counterparts. One reason for this reevaluation is that stories peculiar to *John*, such as the account of Jesus' baptizing alongside John the Baptist, are problematic from the perspective of the early church, and therefore are unlikely to have been created by the early church.[9] Although that kind

---

[9] The logic of this argument serves as a basis for one of the "criteria of authenticity" used by scholars to evaluate the historical worth of accounts about Jesus in the gospels. The criterion of discontinuity, which is appealed to in a story such as the one here, specifies that elements of a story that are

of logic alone cannot guarantee the historical worth of such stories, it does require more cautious reflection on the process and motivation that shaped specific stories, and it does caution against any general quick dismissal of the accounts in the *Fourth Gospel* for reconstructing the Jesus story. The question of the historical worth of at least some of the accounts in the *Gospel of John* is now more of an open matter than it has been since the rise of biblical criticism.

Questions about the nature and historical worth of the author's sources and the redactional levels reflected in the final form of the *Gospel* will occupy the attention of scholars for years to come.

For Further Reading

Brown, Raymond E. *The Gospel according to John.* 2 vols. Anchor Bible 29–29A. Garden City, N.Y.: Doubleday, 1966, 1970.

Dodd, C. H. *The Interpretation of the Fourth Gospel.* Cambridge: Cambridge University Press, 1953.

Kysar, Robert. "The Fourth Gospel: A Report on Recent Research." *Aufstieg und Niedergang der römischen Welt: Geschichte und Kultur Roms im Spiegel der neueren Forschung.* 25.3: 2391–480. Part 2, *Principat*, 25.3. Edited by H. Temporini and W. Haase. New York: W. de Gruyter, 1985. Pages 2391–2480.

Malina, Bruce J., and Richard L. Rohrbaugh. *Social-Science Commentary on the Gospel of John.* Minneapolis: Fortress, 1998.

Smith, D. Moody. *John among the Gospels: The Relationship in Twentieth-Century Research.* 2d ed. Columbia: University of South Carolina Press, 2001.

---

contrary to the practice of the community in which the story has been preserved are unlikely to have been the creation of that community. Had the community a prominent role in the shape of the story, one would have expected it to fit the community's purposes better. Thus, if the core of the story raises more questions for the community than it answers, scholars are prepared to be more open to the possibility that the story has authentic Jesus material. The *Gospel of John* has a few stories of this kind.

THE GOSPEL ACCORDING TO
JOHN

The Word Became Flesh

1 In the beginning was the Word, and the Word was with God, and the Word was God. [2]He was in the beginning with God. [3]All things came into being through him, and without him not one thing came into being. What has come into being [4]in him was life,[a] and the life was the light of all people. [5]The light shines in the darkness, and the darkness did not overcome it.

[6]There was a man sent from God, whose name was John. [7]He came as a witness to testify to the light, so that all might believe through him. [8]He himself was not the light, but he came to testify to the light. [9]The true light, which enlightens everyone, was coming into the world.[b]

[10]He was in the world, and the world came into being through him; yet the world did not know him. [11]He came to what was his own,[c] and his own people did not accept him. [12]But to all who received him, who believed in his name, he gave power to become children of God, [13]who were born, not of blood or of the will of the flesh or of the will of man, but of God.

[14]And the Word became flesh and lived among us, and we have seen his glory, the glory as of a father's only son,[d] full of grace and truth. [15](John testified to him and cried out, "This was he of whom I said, 'He who comes after me ranks ahead of me because he was before me.'") [16]From his fullness we have all received, grace upon grace. [17]The law indeed was given through Moses; grace and truth came through Jesus Christ. [18]No one has ever seen God. It is God the only Son,[e] who is close to the Father's heart,[f] who has made him known.

---

a Or [3]through him. And without him not one thing came into being that has come into being. [4]In him was life

b Or He was the true light that enlightens everyone coming into the world

c Or to his own home

d Or the Father's only Son

e Other ancient authorities read It is an only Son, God, or It is the only Son

f Gk bosom

1:1 *In the beginning* The author of *John* opens his gospel with the same words ("in the beginning") that open the Gk translation of the Hebrew Bible (Tanak) (*Gen.* 1:1). Both passages deal with creation. John says that all things came into being through the Word (1:3, 10), a point also made in the Tanak in another place (*Ps.* 33:6). Note that *Mark*, too, opens with the same word, "beginning." **Word** Gk *logos. Logos* had a wide range of meanings in Gk, and in some translations of the Bible, more than two dozen English words or phrases are used to translate its full range of meaning, with the choice determined by context. Greek philosophy of the period used the word to indicate the creative force of God or the wisdom of God, and the idea was borrowed by Jewish philosophers such as Philo, who may have influenced our author. **1:4** The variant translation listed in note *a* stems from a problem of punctuation, which ancient Gk did not usually indicate. Scholars can sometimes determine how early readers understood the punctuation by observing which section of the passage was quoted as a coherent unit in later Christian writings. *light* The theme of light and darkness, which also occurs in the first chapter of *Genesis,* is prominent in *John,* though only up to the Passion Narrative. It is also a feature of some writings found at Qumran. **1:5** The Gk word translated *overcome* could also be translated "understand" or "comprehend." **1:6** The reference is to John the Baptist, a preacher of some renown in Palestine at the time of Jesus. (The John connected to the Johannine literature is another John, a disciple of Jesus.) All four gospels mention John the Baptist, as does *Acts.* Josephus mentions John the Baptist briefly (*Ant.* 18.116). Scholars debate why John the Baptist is mentioned at all in the story of Jesus. Jesus must have been associated with the Baptist, and the church seems to have felt it necessary to explain this relationship. Many scholars think that John saw himself as the one who was to announce the arrival of God's kingdom and that Jesus was himself a disciple of John at the beginning. This would make the Christian movement a breakoff from the Baptist's movement rather than the culmination of it, as Christians claimed, and would force Christians to explain the early association of Jesus with John the Baptist. **1:9** The variant translation in note *b* results from an ambiguity in the Gk, where the verb *was coming* could have either *light* or *everyone* as its subject. Translators must choose. **1:12** *power* The Gk word has a wide range of meaning; two other possible readings are "right" and "authority." **1:14** *lived* The Gk word, rare in early Christian literature, literally means "tented." Here it may draw a parallel between Jesus' presence with his people and that of the tent (or tabernacle) that was God's dwelling place with Israel in its early period (*Exod.* 33:7–11). The image suggests a temporary stay. **1:17** The contrast between the law coming through Moses and grace and truth coming through Jesus sounds somewhat like the language of Paul in *Galatians* 3–4 and *Romans* 4–8. This contrast is featured very early in John's story. **1:18** *God the only Son* In most manuscripts, the reading is "the only begotten God" or "the only begotten Son." The phrase has become one of the more familiar in the Christian tradition, expressing Jesus' relationship to God, although only the Johannine tradition used it for Jesus (3:16; *1 John* 4:9). Other writers speak of the begotten Son, without the explicit modifier "only" (*Acts* 13:33; *Heb.* 1:5; 5:5).

The Testimony of John the Baptist

[19]This is the testimony given by John when the Jews sent priests and Levites from Jerusalem to ask him, "Who are you?" [20]He confessed and did not deny it, but confessed, "I am not the Messiah."[g] [21]And they asked him, "What then? Are you Elijah?" He said, "I am not." "Are you the prophet?" He answered, "No." [22]Then they said to him, "Who are you? Let us have an answer for those who sent us. What do you say about yourself?" [23]He said,

"I am the voice of one crying out in the wilderness,
'Make straight the way of the Lord,'"

as the prophet Isaiah said.

[24]Now they had been sent from the Pharisees. [25]They asked him, "Why then are you baptizing if you are neither the Messiah,[g] nor Elijah, nor the prophet?" [26]John answered them, "I baptize with water. Among you stands one whom you do not know, [27]the one who is coming after me; I am not worthy to untie the thong of his sandal." [28]This took place in Bethany across the Jordan where John was baptizing.

The Lamb of God

[29]The next day he saw Jesus coming toward him and declared, "Here is the Lamb of God who takes away the sin of the world! [30]This is he of whom I said, 'After me comes a man who ranks ahead of me because he was before me.' [31]I myself did not know him; but I came baptizing with water for this reason,

---

g Or *the Christ*

Father's heart The Gk reads "bosom," something like the use of the word in the English phrase "bosom buddies." It indicates the closest of associations. **1:19** *the Jews* John uses the phrase "the Jews" almost seventy times. This is a striking feature of *John,* for the Synoptics rarely use the term and, when they do, it is almost always in the phrase "King of the Jews" (four or five times for each of the Synoptic Gospels). *Mark* and *Matthew* have only one use of the word "Jews" by itself (*Mark* 7:3; *Matt.* 28:15), and *Luke* only two (7:3; 23:51). That *John* has so many and that most uses have a negative tone are important observations for understanding *John.* There is some debate whether *John's* references to Jews mean Jews as a people or something more limited, such as Judeans or Jewish leaders, to distinguish these persons from the Jews in Galilee who were perhaps more receptive to Jesus.   Only *John* says that the Baptist's comments about himself and his role are prompted by inquiries from the Jerusalem authorities. **Levites** The Levites were one of the twelve divisions, or "tribes," of Israel (*Deut.* 18:1–8) whose duty it was to serve in the temple, assisting the priests. This is *John's* only mention of Levites. **1:20** *Messiah* This English word is a transliteration of the Hebrew equivalent of *christos* ("Christ"), the Gk word used here. Both the Hebrew and the Gk mean "anointed." See note to 1:41. In *John,* the question of the messiahship of Jesus is raised early and answered explicitly. Every element in *John* 1 drives this point home (the Logos depiction; the various witnesses—John the Baptist, Andrew, Peter, Philip, and Nathanael). This is in contrast to the synoptic tradition, especially *Mark,* which handles the question of Jesus' messiahship less directly. **1:21** *Elijah* The return of Elijah was a popular expectation during this period, as can be seen in various documents of the intertestamental period (*1 Macc.* 4:46; 14:41; *4 Ezra* 2.18). The hope was based on the concluding comments of *Malachi* (4:5–6) and on the tradition that Elijah had not died but had been taken away in a heavenly chariot. All four gospels recognize the possible association of John to Elijah (*Matt.* 11:14; 17:13; *Luke* 1:17) although *Mark* is less explicit, simply describing the Baptist with the language used in the Jewish scriptures to describe Elijah (*Mark* 1:6; *2 Kgs.* 1:8).   *the prophet* A figure identified as "the prophet" was part of the messianic language of the 1st century. The Samaritans seemed to know of a coming prophet figure (4:19, 25), as did the Qumran community (1QS 9.11). The expectation was based on *Deut.* 18:15–18. Other 1st-century Christian authors worked with the idea (*Acts* 3:22), but the author of *John* seems to have had particular interest in the concept (1:25; 6:14; 7:40; 9:17), which may indicate that this was one of the disputes to which he or his community had to respond. **1:23** *make straight the way of the Lord* John uses the word for "road," as does the MT, but for the remainder of the quote, *John* follows the LXX. The synoptic tradition (*Mark* 1:3; *Matt.* 3:3) follows the LXX throughout, using "path" rather than "road" with the word "make straight." The synoptic tradition quotes more of the passage, including the part where a road is to be prepared. The quote, which is from *Isa.* 40:3, was applied by the Qumran community to itself—it was literally in the desert, preparing a way for the Lord. **1:27** The task of removing sandals and washing the guest's feet would have been done by a slave (13:12–16). *John, Mark,* and *Luke* all speak of the Baptist saying that he was unworthy to untie the sandals of Jesus (*Mark* 1:7; *Luke* 3:16), while *Matt.* 3:11 speaks of carrying the sandals. **1:28** *Bethany across the Jordan* There is variation in the manuscript tradition at this point. The differences seem to stem from an attempt to find a Bethany that was literally *across the Jordan* in relation to Jerusalem, the capital city. A better-known Bethany was two miles east of Jerusalem, on the road to Jericho, on the Jerusalem side of the Jordan, and thus not the Bethany across the Jordan. **1:29** The image of the Lamb of God (here and in 1:36) became common in Christian writing, but scholars are uncertain of the exact roots of this metaphor. It may draw on the descriptive language of *Isaiah* 53, a favorite passage for the early Christians, or on the image of the Passover lamb, or both. The problem is that offerings for sin normally required goats, bulls, or sheep—not lambs. **1:30** *This is he* In this gospel, the Baptist identifies Jesus as the Messiah early and unequivocally, in contrast to the synoptic tradition, which does not detail the Baptist's response to Jesus at the baptism, and the Q material (see APPENDIX E), which reports John's doubt from prison about Jesus' identity (*Matt.* 11:2–6; 7:18–23).

that he might be revealed to Israel." [32]And John testified, "I saw the Spirit descending from heaven like a dove, and it remained on him. [33]I myself did not know him, but the one who sent me to baptize with water said to me, 'He on whom you see the Spirit descend and remain is the one who baptizes with the Holy Spirit.' [34]And I myself have seen and have testified that this is the Son of God."[h]

The First Disciples of Jesus

[35]The next day John again was standing with two of his disciples, [36]and as he watched Jesus walk by, he exclaimed, "Look, here is the Lamb of God!" [37]The two disciples heard him say this, and they followed Jesus. [38]When Jesus turned and saw them following, he said to them, "What are you looking for?" They said to him, "Rabbi" (which translated means Teacher), "where are you staying?" [39]He said to them, "Come and see." They came and saw where he was staying, and they remained with him that day. It was about four o'clock in the afternoon. [40]One of the two who heard John speak and followed him was Andrew, Simon Peter's brother. [41]He first found his brother Simon and said to him, "We have found the Messiah" (which is translated Anointed[i]). [42]He brought Simon[j] to Jesus, who looked at him and said, "You are Simon son of John. You are to be called Cephas" (which is translated Peter[k]).

Jesus Calls Philip and Nathanael

[43]The next day Jesus decided to go to Galilee. He found Philip and said to him, "Follow me." [44]Now Philip was from Bethsaida, the city of Andrew and Peter. [45]Philip found Nathanael and said to him, "We have found him about whom Moses in the law and also the prophets wrote, Jesus son of Joseph from Nazareth." [46]Nathanael said to him, "Can anything good come out of Nazareth?" Philip said to him,

---

h Other ancient authorities read *is God's chosen one*

i Or *Christ*
j Gk *him*
k From the word for *rock* in Aramaic (*kepha*) and Greek (*petra*), respectively

---

1:32 A dove is mentioned in the synoptic tradition at the baptism of Jesus. But the Johannine account obscures the baptismal setting of the encounter between Jesus and John; indeed, *John* does not explicitly say that Jesus was baptized. The Johannine tradition differs too in omitting the report of a voice at the baptism and the story of the temptation of Jesus in the desert, which in the synoptic tradition follow Jesus' baptism. **1:34** The theme of testifying, or bearing witness, is prominent in all of the Johannine writings. **1:37** Only *John* claims that Jesus drew his 1st disciples from among the followers of John the Baptist. **1:38** *Rabbi* This is a common term in *John* (used nine times in a variety of contexts); use of the term in the Synoptics is less frequent and less varied. That the term is translated by the author provides a clue that the original readers did not know Aramaic. **1:39** *four o'clock in the afternoon* Lit. "tenth hour." The day was divided into twelve hours, beginning at roughly 6:00 A.M., thus making 4:00 P.M. the 10th hour. The night was divided into four watches, beginning about 6:00 P.M., but the lengths varied, depending on the time of year. **1:40** Only *John* reports that Peter (Simon) became a disciple because of his brother Andrew. *Mark* and *Matthew* have Jesus calling Peter and Andrew together (*Mark* 1:16; *Matt.* 4:18), and *Luke* omits any reference to Andrew in the call of Peter (*Luke* 5:1–11), mentioning Andrew only in the list of disciples (6:14), where *Mark* and Matthew also have mentioned Andrew. Andrew is slightly more visible in *John* (1:40, 44; 6:8; 12:22), and *Mark*'s 3d reference to Andrew (13:3) may be a hint of Andrew's importance. **1:41** In *John*, the first disciples attach themselves to Jesus with a full-blown confession of Jesus' messiahship. The synoptic account is briefer and lacks this confession (*Mark* 1:16–20; *Matt.* 4:18–22; *Luke* 5:10–11). *Messiah* Here the Gk transliterates the Hebrew word for "Messiah." The Gk *christos* is here translated *Anointed* (see note to 1:20). Only *John* uses the word "Messiah" (twice) in our literature (also in 4:25); all other writers use the translated word "Christ," which *John* uses nineteen times. Other strong marks of Semitic coloring in *John* led some scholars to suggest that it may have been originally written in Aramaic. In this short paragraph alone, three Semitic words ("Rabbi," "Messiah," and "Cephas") are translated for the Greek-speaking readership. **1:43** Both the synoptic and the Johannine traditions report an encounter between Jesus and John the Baptist in the area of the Jordan River, east of Jerusalem, at the beginning of Jesus' activity, and both traditions report that Jesus returned to Galilee after that. According to the synoptic tradition, John was imprisoned shortly after that meeting (*Mark* 1:14; *Matt.* 4:12), but in *John*, the Baptist is active much longer. The account in *Luke* is less definite (3:19–20). Philip is mentioned only once in each of the Synoptic Gospels, in the list of disciples (*Mark* 3:8; *Matt.* 10:3; *Luke* 3:1). He has a much more prominent role in *John* (1:43–48; 6:5–7; 12:21–22; 14:8–9). Andrew appears in all but the last incident (see 1:40). The disciple Thomas likewise receives a more extended treatment in *John* than he does in the Synoptics (see 11:16). **1:44** According to *Mark* 1:29, Peter and Andrew did not come from Bethsaida but from Capernaum, a town about three miles to the southwest. Bethsaida was the more significant center at the time. **1:45** Nathanael is mentioned only in *John*. Some scholars believe he is the Bartholomew of the synoptic tradition, because Philip is connected with Nathanael in *John* but with Bartholomew in the synoptic tradition. **1:46** Nazareth was nothing more than a small agricultural village, in contrast to Bethsaida, which recently had been built into a city under the tetrarch Philip (4 B.C.E.–34 C.E.).

"Come and see." 47When Jesus saw Nathanael coming toward him, he said of him, "Here is truly an Israelite in whom there is no deceit!" 48Nathanael asked him, "Where did you get to know me?" Jesus answered, "I saw you under the fig tree before Philip called you." 49Nathanael replied, "Rabbi, you are the Son of God! You are the King of Israel!" 50Jesus answered, "Do you believe because I told you that I saw you under the fig tree? You will see greater things than these." 51And he said to him, "Very truly, I tell you,*l* you will see heaven opened and the angels of God ascending and descending upon the Son of Man."

The Wedding at Cana

2 On the third day there was a wedding in Cana of Galilee, and the mother of Jesus was there. 2Jesus and his disciples had also been invited to the wedding. 3When the wine gave out, the mother of Jesus said to him, "They have no wine." 4And Jesus said to her, "Woman, what concern is that to you and to me? My hour has not yet come." 5His mother said to the servants, "Do whatever he tells you." 6Now standing there were six stone water jars for the Jewish rites of purification, each holding twenty or thirty gallons.

---

l Both instances of the Greek word for *you* in this verse are plural

7Jesus said to them, "Fill the jars with water." And they filled them up to the brim. 8He said to them, "Now draw some out, and take it to the chief steward." So they took it. 9When the steward tasted the water that had become wine, and did not know where it came from (though the servants who had drawn the water knew), the steward called the bridegroom 10and said to him, "Everyone serves the good wine first, and then the inferior wine after the guests have become drunk. But you have kept the good wine until now." 11Jesus did this, the first of his signs, in Cana of Galilee, and revealed his glory; and his disciples believed in him.

12After this he went down to Capernaum with his mother, his brothers, and his disciples; and they remained there a few days.

Jesus Cleanses the Temple

13The Passover of the Jews was near, and Jesus went up to Jerusalem. 14In the temple he found people selling cattle, sheep, and doves, and the money changers seated at their tables. 15Making a whip of cords, he drove all of them out of the temple, both the sheep and the cattle. He also poured out the coins of the money changers and overturned their tables. 16He told those who were selling the doves, "Take

1:51 This may be an allusion to the story of Jacob's ladder (*Gen.* 28:12). The title "Son of Man" may be an authentic label that Jesus applied to himself. It is striking that this phrase is frequently on the lips of Jesus in the gospels but is used only once in other NT documents (*Acts* 7:56). The phrase could carry at least two meanings: (a) the apocalyptic figure of *Dan.* 7:13–14 or (b) the more neutral use as merely a substitution for the personal pronoun "I." **2:1** John 1 reported three events occurring on three consecutive days (1:29, 35, 43). The third day mentioned here must have been intended to fit into this chronology. The town of Cana is mentioned only in *John.* There is uncertainty about its exact location, but it was no more than nine miles from Nazareth. The entire territory of Galilee is only about twenty-five miles square. Cana was the hometown of Nathanael (21:2), who appears only in *John* (see 1:45). Mary's role in *John* is limited to this episode of the marriage at Cana and the scene at the cross (19:25–27). In contrast to the Synoptic Gospels, Mary is never mentioned by name; since *John* tends to use personal names more often than the synoptic writers, it is worthy of note when he does not name a character. **2:4** *my hour has not yet come* The word "hour" (or "time") is *John*'s way of referring to the death of Jesus (7:30; 8:20; 12:23, 27; 13:1; 17:1). **2:6** Various Jewish groups emphasized washing as a means for gaining ritual purity. *John* displays some interest in such purifications (3:25). The author assumes that his audience needs some explanation of this Jewish practice. **2:8** The position of *chief steward* is otherwise unknown, but from the context it appears that the individual is the toastmaster or headwaiter. **2:11** This story, together with some of the other miracle stories in *John,* is not found in the synoptic tradition. Indeed, of the three dozen miracles mentioned in the gospels, *John* shares only two with the synoptic tradition (the walking on the water and the feeding of the five thousand). Unlike the Synoptic Gospels, *John* calls Jesus' miracles "signs" (see introduction to *John*). **2:13** This is the first mention of a Passover, an annual feast that occurred in March/April. References to Passover help us determine the number of years of Jesus' activities (see introduction to *John*). The Passover was one of three pilgrim festivals that pious Jewish males were expected to celebrate in Jerusalem. Jesus would have been part of a large crowd on the road going to the activities; some estimates suggest that as many as a hundred thousand people may have attended, and Josephus offers the improbable figure of three million. The synoptic tradition alludes to only one Passover, in the last week of Jesus' life; *John* mentions three (2:13; 6:4; 11:55). **2:14** The cleansing of the temple occurs in the final week of Jesus' life, according to the synoptic tradition, rather than at the beginning. Both traditions link it to the Passover (*Mark* 11:15; *Matt.* 21:12). Notice the differences in detail regarding what is being sold and what actions Jesus takes. **2:15** *money changers* Adult male Jews throughout the diaspora paid temple dues. These were collected annually for those unable to pay in person in the temple in Jerusalem. Dues had to be paid in the coinage of Tyre; thus, money changers played an important role in servicing pilgrims from the Diaspora, functioning somewhat like the currency exchange booths in modern-day international airports. **2:16** Jesus, by calling the temple his father's house, makes an exalted claim for himself. This kind of explicit and intimate association of Jesus with God is typical of the Johannine representation of Jesus.

these things out of here! Stop making my Father's house a marketplace!" [17]His disciples remembered that it was written, "Zeal for your house will consume me." [18]The Jews then said to him, "What sign can you show us for doing this?" [19]Jesus answered them, "Destroy this temple, and in three days I will raise it up." [20]The Jews then said, "This temple has been under construction for forty-six years, and will you raise it up in three days?" [21]But he was speaking of the temple of his body. [22]After he was raised from the dead, his disciples remembered that he had said this; and they believed the scripture and the word that Jesus had spoken.

[23]When he was in Jerusalem during the Passover festival, many believed in his name because they saw the signs that he was doing. [24]But Jesus on his part would not entrust himself to them, because he knew all people [25]and needed no one to testify about anyone; for he himself knew what was in everyone.

Nicodemus Visits Jesus

3 Now there was a Pharisee named Nicodemus, a leader of the Jews. [2]He came to Jesus[m] by night and said to him, "Rabbi, we know that you are a teacher who has come from God; for no one can do these signs that you do apart from the presence of God." [3]Jesus answered him, "Very truly, I tell you, no one can see the kingdom of God without being born from above."[n] [4]Nicodemus said to him, "How can anyone be born after having grown old? Can one enter a second time into the mother's womb and be born?" [5]Jesus answered, "Very truly, I tell you, no one can enter the kingdom of God without being born of water and Spirit. [6]What is born of the flesh is flesh, and what is born of the Spirit is spirit.[o] [7]Do not be astonished that I said to you, 'You[p] must be born from above.'[q] [8]The wind[o] blows where it chooses, and you hear the sound of it, but you do not know where it comes from or where it goes. So it is with everyone who is born of the Spirit." [9]Nicodemus said to him, "How can these things be?" [10]Jesus answered him, "Are you a teacher of Israel, and yet you do not understand these things?

[11]"Very truly, I tell you, we speak of what we know and testify to what we have seen; yet you[r] do not receive our testimony. [12]If I have told you about earthly things and you do not believe, how can you believe if I tell you about heavenly things? [13]No one has ascended into heaven except the one who descended from heaven, the Son of Man.[s] [14]And just as Moses lifted up the serpent in the wilderness, so must the Son of Man be lifted up, [15]that whoever believes in him may have eternal life.[t]

---

m Gk him

n Or *born anew*

o The same Greek word means both *wind* and *spirit*

p The Greek word for *you* here is plural

q Or *anew*

r The Greek word for *you* here and in verse 12 is plural

s Other ancient authorities add *who is in heaven*

t Some interpreters hold that the quotation concludes with verse 15

---

a marketplace *Zech.* 14:21. The synoptic tradition has a stronger rebuke, in which the temple is called a den of robbers (*Mark* 11:17; *Matt.* 21:13; *Luke* 19:46). **2:17** The quotation here is from *Ps.* 69:9. The MT and the LXX are almost identical here, except that the LXX uses a past tense. No reference is made to the Jewish scriptures at this point in the synoptic story. **2:19** This statement is missing from the synoptic account, but the synoptic tradition knows that Jesus was accused of having made such a charge (*Mark* 14:58; 15:29; *Matt.* 26:61; 27:40). **2:20** The rebuilding of the temple was begun in 20 B.C.E. by Herod the Great (thus the label, "Herod's temple"). The reference to forty-six years would date this incident to 26 C.E. Although the main sanctuary was completed within a few years, work continued on the larger complex until the 60s C.E., making the temple grounds a massive site by any Mediterranean standard. One of the causes for discontent and revolt in Palestine (66–73 C.E.) may have been the unemployment of thousands of workers after the completion of this temple. **3:1** Nicodemus is mentioned only in *John* (here and in 7:50; 19:39). The name is Gk and means "conqueror [or 'ruler'] of the people." This perhaps suggests that he was a member of the Jewish council, called the Sanhedrin, especially in light of other comments about Nicodemus in 7:45–52. Many Jewish names at the time, both in high Jewish circles and among Jesus' own Jewish disciples, were Greek. **3:3** *from above* Or "born anew." Either is a possible translation of the Gk *anōthen*. Nicodemus is caught by this ambiguity and asks how anyone could be born a second time. The ambiguity works only in Gk, and many scholars dismiss the historicity of this story on this basis, contending that a conversation between a Galilean preacher and a religious leader from Jerusalem would more likely have taken place in Aramaic. The inclusion of this story also suggests that the original readers of the gospel were Gk speaking and would have appreciated the wordplay. The same ambiguity is played out in 3:7. **3:10** *Are you a teacher of Israel?* Lit. "Are you the teacher of Israel?" **3:11** The use of the plural *we* rather than "I" may be intended to include the disciples or the church. **3:14** *Num.* 21:9. *John* uses the term "to lift up" with a double meaning: to indicate the death of Jesus by crucifixion, and to indicate the exaltation of Jesus through his dying. The Gk word can indicate the lifting up of someone physically or in terms of status (i.e., exalting), but only *John* makes use of the double meaning. See 8:28; 12:32–34; in the latter passage, the author explains the double meaning. See *Isa.* 52:13; *Acts* 5:30–31.

16"For God so loved the world that he gave his only Son, so that everyone who believes in him may not perish but may have eternal life.

17"Indeed, God did not send the Son into the world to condemn the world, but in order that the world might be saved through him. 18Those who believe in him are not condemned; but those who do not believe are condemned already, because they have not believed in the name of the only Son of God. 19And this is the judgment, that the light has come into the world, and people loved darkness rather than light because their deeds were evil. 20For all who do evil hate the light and do not come to the light, so that their deeds may not be exposed. 21But those who do what is true come to the light, so that it may be clearly seen that their deeds have been done in God."*u*

Jesus and John the Baptist

22After this Jesus and his disciples went into the Judean countryside, and he spent some time there with them and baptized. 23John also was baptizing at Aenon near Salim because water was abundant there; and people kept coming and were being baptized 24—John, of course, had not yet been thrown into prison.

25Now a discussion about purification arose between John's disciples and a Jew.*v* 26They came to John and said to him, "Rabbi, the one who was with you across the Jordan, to whom you testified, here he is baptizing, and all are going to him." 27John answered, "No one can receive anything except what has been given from heaven. 28You yourselves are my witnesses that I said, 'I am not the Messiah,*w* but I have been sent ahead of him.' 29He who has the bride is the bridegroom. The friend of the bridegroom, who stands and hears him, rejoices greatly at the bridegroom's voice. For this reason my joy has been fulfilled. 30He must increase, but I must decrease."*x*

The One Who Comes from Heaven

31The one who comes from above is above all; the one who is of the earth belongs to the earth and speaks about earthly things. The one who comes from heaven is above all. 32He testifies to what he has seen and heard, yet no one accepts his testimony. 33Whoever has accepted his testimony has certified*y* this, that God is true. 34He whom God has sent speaks the words of God, for he gives the Spirit without measure. 35The Father loves the Son and has placed all things in his hands. 36Whoever believes in the Son has eternal life; whoever disobeys the Son will not see life, but must endure God's wrath.

Jesus and the Woman of Samaria

4 Now when Jesus*z* learned that the Pharisees had heard, "Jesus is making and baptizing more disciples than John" 2—although it was not Jesus himself but his disciples who baptized— 3he left Judea and started back to Galilee. 4But he had to go through Samaria. 5So he came to a Samaritan city called Sychar, near the plot of ground that Jacob had given to his

---

u Some interpreters hold that the quotation concludes with verse 15
v Other ancient authorities read *the Jews*

w Or *the Christ*
x Some interpreters hold that the quotation continues through verse 36
y Gk *set a seal to*
z Other ancient authorities read *the Lord*

3:16 eternal life This is a striking Johannine idiom describing the mission of Jesus, shared with other literature in the Johannine corpus (*1 John* 4:9). The synoptic writers speak more often of Jesus' announcing the kingdom of God. **3:17 condemn** The Gk word means "to judge," but it can mean to judge negatively, as the translators render it here. In 3:19, the word rendered "judgment" could be translated "condemnation" as well. **3:22** Only *John* says that Jesus baptized, but the author later qualifies even this by saying that it was really the disciples of Jesus who baptized (4:1–2). Except for the final commission to the disciples of Jesus (*Mark* 16:16; *Matt.* 28:19), the Synoptics attribute water baptism only to John the Baptist. **3:23 Aenon near Salim** These locations have not been identified. Some scholars suggest that the names function symbolically—*Aenon* meaning "fountains" and *Salim* meaning "peace." **3:24** In the Synoptics, Jesus' ministry does not begin until John is imprisoned (*Mark* 1:14). **3:29** The image of Jesus as bridegroom is found also in the Synoptic Gospels but not on the lips of John the Baptist (*Mark* 2:19; *Matt.* 9:15; 25:1–10). **4:2** Some scholars think that this verse is not original but an early scribal addition. There is no manuscript support for this theory, however (see 3:22). **4:3–4** Note that in the synoptic tradition, Jesus' career is restricted to the area of Galilee until the last week of his life. The shortest route between Jerusalem and Galilee was through Samaria, and it was considerably shorter for those who lived in Nazareth. Another route, perhaps more commonly traveled by Jews, went east from Jerusalem to the Jordan River valley and turned north from there, thereby avoiding Samaria (see 4:9). The Samaritans, who had a form of worship based on the Pentateuch (the first five books of the Bible), had an old and serious conflict with Judean Jews (see 4:5–6). *Mark* has nothing to say about the Samaritans; *Matthew* offers nothing but a negative comment (10:5); *Luke* and *John* seem to recognize a greater role for this area in early Christian mission. **4:5–6** Sychar was a small town at the base of Mount Gerizim, about thirty miles north of Jerusalem and about halfway between Jerusalem and Nazareth. In earlier days it had been the site of the city of

son Joseph. 6Jacob's well was there, and Jesus, tired out by his journey, was sitting by the well. It was about noon.

7A Samaritan woman came to draw water, and Jesus said to her, "Give me a drink." 8(His disciples had gone to the city to buy food.) 9The Samaritan woman said to him, "How is it that you, a Jew, ask a drink of me, a woman of Samaria?" (Jews do not share things in common with Samaritans.)*a* 10Jesus answered her, "If you knew the gift of God, and who it is that is saying to you, 'Give me a drink,' you would have asked him, and he would have given you living water." 11The woman said to him, "Sir, you have no bucket, and the well is deep. Where do you get that living water? 12Are you greater than our ancestor Jacob, who gave us the well, and with his sons and his flocks drank from it?" 13Jesus said to her, "Everyone who drinks of this water will be thirsty again, 14but those who drink of the water that I will give them will never be thirsty. The water that I will give will become in them a spring of water gushing up to eternal life." 15The woman said to him, "Sir, give me this water, so that I may never be thirsty or have to keep coming here to draw water."

16Jesus said to her, "Go, call your husband, and come back." 17The woman answered him, "I have no husband." Jesus said to her, "You are right in saying, 'I have no husband'; 18for you have had five husbands, and the one you have now is not your husband. What you have said is true!" 19The woman said to him, "Sir, I see that you are a prophet. 20Our ancestors worshiped on this mountain, but you*b* say that the place where people must worship is in Jerusalem." 21Jesus said to her, "Woman, believe me, the hour is coming when you will worship the Father neither on this mountain nor in Jerusalem. 22You worship what you do not know; we worship what we know, for salvation is from the Jews. 23But the hour is coming, and is now here, when the true worshipers will worship the Father in spirit and truth, for the Father seeks such as these to worship him. 24God is spirit, and those who worship him must worship in spirit and truth." 25The woman said to him, "I know that Messiah is coming" (who is called Christ). "When he comes, he will proclaim all things to us." 26Jesus said to her, "I am he,*c* the one who is speaking to you."

27Just then his disciples came. They were astonished that he was speaking with a woman, but no one said, "What do you want?" or, "Why are you speaking with her?" 28Then the woman left her water jar and went back to the city. She said to the people, 29"Come and see a man who told me everything I have ever done! He cannot be the Messiah,*d* can he?" 30They left the city and were on their way to him.

31Meanwhile the disciples were urging him, "Rabbi, eat something." 32But he said to them, "I have food to eat that you do not know about." 33So the disciples said to one another, "Surely no one has brought him something to eat?" 34Jesus said to them, "My food is to do the will of him who sent me and to complete his work. 35Do you not say, 'Four months more, then comes the harvest'? But I tell you, look around you, and see how the fields are ripe for harvesting.

---

a Other ancient authorities lack this sentence
b The Greek word for *you* here and in verses 21 and 22 is plural

c Gk *I am*
d Or *the Christ*

Shechem (Gk *Sychem*). The Samaritans had built a temple on Mount Gerizim in the 4th century B.C.E. in opposition to the Jewish temple at Jerusalem. The conflict between the temple at Jerusalem and the alternative temple on Mount Gerizim was an old one. The Samaritans argued that Mount Gerizim, not one of the hills of Jerusalem, was the appointed site of the temple, and they could appeal to the Torah for support (*Deut.* 11:26–30; 27:1–13; *Josh.* 8:30–35). The Samaritan temple was destroyed by the Maccabean ruler John Hyrcanus in 128 B.C.E., but the location has remained sacred to the Samaritans even in the 21st century. Samaritans trace their biblical roots back to Jacob (*Gen.* 33:19; 48:22). The well itself is not mentioned in the Bible or elsewhere in early Christian literature. The traditional site is presently marked by a Greek Orthodox church. **4:6 noon** Lit. "the sixth hour." This would not have been the normal time for drawing water, since it was the hot part of the day. **4:9** The Samaritans were generally treated like Gentiles by Jews, even though they had roots in a culture and a religion shaped by the Torah. Little is mentioned about Samaria in early Christian literature, but the references are mainly positive (*Matt.* 10:5; *Luke* 9:52; 10:33; 17:16; *John* 4:9, 39, 40; 8:48; *Acts* 8:25). **4:19 prophet** Samaritans used only the first five books of the Bible, the Pentateuch. The Jewish images of a Messiah were informed mostly by the writings of the prophets. The Samaritans, lacking this influence, expected a prophet like Moses, on the basis of *Deut.* 18:15–18. This restorer was called *Taheb*, but little is known about this figure (see 1:21). **4:20** See 4:5–6. **4:26** This is the first of the so-called "I am" sayings (Gk *egō eimi*), a distinctive feature of *John*. The literal translation, "I am, who speak to you," sounds as strange in Gk as in English. Various parallels have been suggested for the "I am" sayings. They may serve to identify Jesus with the divine name—the name of the God of the Jews (see *Exod.* 3:14; *Isa.* 43:10–11). Other "I am" sayings occur in *John* at 4:26; 6:20, 35; 8:12, 28, 58; 10:11; 11:25; 13:19; 14:6; 15:1; 18:5–6. This gospel has Jesus claim explicitly and without reservation or caution that he is the Messiah. Note the more guarded admission in *Mark* 8:29–30, for example. **4:35** Sowing generally took place in November/December, just after the fields had been softened by the October rains (the "early rain"), and harvest was four or five months later, in April/May. It is difficult to use this comment to date the visit to Samaria, for *John*'s overall chronology seems to place the visit in the late spring or early summer, after the Passover (2:13; 4:45).

36The reaper is already receiving[e] wages and is gathering fruit for eternal life, so that sower and reaper may rejoice together. 37For here the saying holds true, 'One sows and another reaps.' 38I sent you to reap that for which you did not labor. Others have labored, and you have entered into their labor."

39Many Samaritans from that city believed in him because of the woman's testimony, "He told me everything I have ever done." 40So when the Samaritans came to him, they asked him to stay with them; and he stayed there two days. 41And many more believed because of his word. 42They said to the woman, "It is no longer because of what you said that we believe, for we have heard for ourselves, and we know that this is truly the Savior of the world."

Jesus Returns to Galilee

43When the two days were over, he went from that place to Galilee 44(for Jesus himself had testified that a prophet has no honor in the prophet's own country). 45When he came to Galilee, the Galileans welcomed him, since they had seen all that he had done in Jerusalem at the festival; for they too had gone to the festival.

Jesus Heals an Official's Son

46Then he came again to Cana in Galilee where he had changed the water into wine. Now there was a royal official whose son lay ill in Capernaum. 47When he heard that Jesus had come from Judea to Galilee,

he went and begged him to come down and heal his son, for he was at the point of death. 48Then Jesus said to him, "Unless you[f] see signs and wonders you will not believe." 49The official said to him, "Sir, come down before my little boy dies." 50Jesus said to him, "Go; your son will live." The man believed the word that Jesus spoke to him and started on his way. 51As he was going down, his slaves met him and told him that his child was alive. 52So he asked them the hour when he began to recover, and they said to him, "Yesterday at one in the afternoon the fever left him." 53The father realized that this was the hour when Jesus had said to him, "Your son will live." So he himself believed, along with his whole household. 54Now this was the second sign that Jesus did after coming from Judea to Galilee.

Jesus Heals on the Sabbath

5 After this there was a festival of the Jews, and Jesus went up to Jerusalem.

2Now in Jerusalem by the Sheep Gate there is a pool, called in Hebrew[g] Beth-zatha,[h] which has five porticoes. 3In these lay many invalids—blind, lame, and paralyzed.[i] 5One man was there who had been ill for thirty-eight years. 6When Jesus saw him lying there and knew that he had been there a long time, he said to him, "Do you want to be made well?" 7The sick man answered him, "Sir, I have no one to put me into the pool when the water is stirred up; and while I am making my way, someone else steps down ahead of me." 8Jesus said to him, "Stand up, take your mat

---

e Or 35 . . . the fields are already ripe for harvesting. 36The reaper is receiving

f Both instances of the Greek word for you in this verse are plural
g That is, Aramaic
h Other ancient authorities read Bethesda, others Bethsaida
i Other ancient authorities add, wholly or in part, waiting for the stirring of the water; 4for an angel of the Lord went down at certain seasons into the pool, and stirred up the water; whoever stepped in first after the stirring of the water was made well from whatever disease that person had.

4:44 John seems to imply that Jerusalem was the real home of Jesus. Jerusalem had just rejected Jesus (2:18–20, 23–25; 4:1–2), and Galilee was about to receive him (4:45). The synoptic tradition applies these words about a prophet's lack of status in his home country to Galilee (Mark 6:4; Matt. 13:57; Luke 4:24; see also Gospel of Thomas 31). **4:46** The royal official was probably an officer of Herod Antipas. Two Gk words are used for the official's child: one (huios) means "son"; the other (pais) has the wider meaning of "son" or "servant." The synoptic account does not use huios but words that could be translated as "servant" (pais, Matthew) or "slave" (doulos, Luke). John's account roughly parallels the healing of a centurion's servant in the Synoptics (Matt. 8:5–13; Luke 7:1–10). **4:54** second sign John describes many of the miracles of Jesus as "signs." The 1st sign was the turning of water in wine (2:11); although the miracle here is called the second sign, John assumes that Jesus has done many more signs (2:23; 3:2). Both the so-called 1st and 2d signs occur in Cana. **5:1** This is the 2d recorded journey to Jerusalem (2:13), but Jesus was in the area of Jerusalem at other times (1:43). The synoptic tradition restricts the activity of Jesus to Galilee until his final week. The occasion of the visit to Jerusalem mentioned here was a feast, probably a pilgrim feast. If it is a Passover, then John mentions four Passovers (see 2:14). Some scholars think John 5 is out of order, contending that if it were placed after John 6, the transitions between chapters would be neater. But there is no textual support for such a hypothesis (see 6:1). **5:2** Sheep Gate One variant reads "Sheep Pool." **Beth-zatha** There is considerable textual variation in the name. There is some archeological evidence that a double pool in the northeast corner of the city, just north of the temple, served as a healing center or health spa. **5:8** Compare Jesus' command with Mark 2:9–12; Matt. 9:1–8; Luke 5:17–26.

and walk." ⁹At once the man was made well, and he took up his mat and began to walk.

Now that day was a sabbath. ¹⁰So the Jews said to the man who had been cured, "It is the sabbath; it is not lawful for you to carry your mat." ¹¹But he answered them, "The man who made me well said to me, 'Take up your mat and walk.'" ¹²They asked him, "Who is the man who said to you, 'Take it up and walk'?" ¹³Now the man who had been healed did not know who it was, for Jesus had disappeared in*ʲ* the crowd that was there. ¹⁴Later Jesus found him in the temple and said to him, "See, you have been made well! Do not sin any more, so that nothing worse happens to you." ¹⁵The man went away and told the Jews that it was Jesus who had made him well. ¹⁶Therefore the Jews started persecuting Jesus, because he was doing such things on the sabbath. ¹⁷But Jesus answered them, "My Father is still working, and I also am working." ¹⁸For this reason the Jews were seeking all the more to kill him, because he was not only breaking the sabbath, but was also calling God his own Father, thereby making himself equal to God.

The Authority of the Son

¹⁹Jesus said to them, "Very truly, I tell you, the Son can do nothing on his own, but only what he sees the Father doing; for whatever the Father*ᵏ* does, the Son does likewise. ²⁰The Father loves the Son and shows him all that he himself is doing; and he will show him greater works than these, so that you will be astonished. ²¹Indeed, just as the Father raises the dead and gives them life, so also the Son gives life to whomever he wishes. ²²The Father judges no one but has given all judgment to the Son, ²³so that all may honor the Son just as they honor the Father. Anyone who does not honor the Son does not honor the Father who sent him. ²⁴Very truly, I tell you, anyone who hears my word and believes him who sent me has eternal life, and does not come under judgment, but has passed from death to life.

²⁵"Very truly, I tell you, the hour is coming, and is now here, when the dead will hear the voice of the Son of God, and those who hear will live. ²⁶For just as the Father has life in himself, so he has granted the Son also to have life in himself; ²⁷and he has given him authority to execute judgment, because he is the Son of Man. ²⁸Do not be astonished at this; for the hour is coming when all who are in their graves will hear his voice ²⁹and will come out—those who have done good, to the resurrection of life, and those who have done evil, to the resurrection of condemnation.

Witnesses to Jesus

³⁰"I can do nothing on my own. As I hear, I judge; and my judgment is just, because I seek to do not my own will but the will of him who sent me.

³¹"If I testify about myself, my testimony is not true. ³²There is another who testifies on my behalf, and I know that his testimony to me is true. ³³You sent messengers to John, and he testified to the truth. ³⁴Not that I accept such human testimony, but I say these things so that you may be saved. ³⁵He was a burning and shining lamp, and you were willing to rejoice for a while in his light. ³⁶But I have a testimony greater than John's. The works that the Father has given me to complete, the very works that I am doing, testify on my behalf that the Father has sent me. ³⁷And the Father who sent me has himself testified on my behalf. You have never heard his voice or seen his form, ³⁸and you do not have his word abiding in you, because you do not believe him whom he has sent.

³⁹"You search the scriptures because you think that in them you have eternal life; and it is they that testify on my behalf. ⁴⁰Yet you refuse to come to me to have life. ⁴¹I do not accept glory from human beings. ⁴²But I know that you do not have the love of God in*ˡ* you. ⁴³I have come in my Father's name, and you do not accept me; if another comes in his own name, you will accept him. ⁴⁴How can you believe when you accept glory from one another and do not seek the glory that comes from the one who alone is God? ⁴⁵Do not think that I will accuse you before the Father; your accuser is Moses, on whom you have set your hope. ⁴⁶If you believed Moses, you would believe me, for he wrote about me. ⁴⁷But if you do not

---

j Or *had left because of*
k Gk *that one*

l Or *among*

5:10 The Sabbath restrictions of the Jewish scriptures (*Exod.* 20:10; *Neh.* 13:19; *Jer.* 17:21) are expanded considerably in *m. Shab.* 7:2. **5:18 *equal to God*** This is one of a number of phrases or images that the author uses to claim exalted status for Jesus. Such statements have led scholars to speak of *John*'s Christology as "high," compared with the more muted language of the synoptic tradition. **5:3 *my testimony is not true*** But in 8:14 Jesus says that even if he testified on his own behalf, his testimony would be valid. **5:32 *I know*** Textual variants read "we know" and "you know." **5:34 *human testimony*** Lit. "testimony from a man" (perhaps pointedly indicating the witness of John the Baptist). **5:39 *You search*** The indicative and imperative forms for this verb in Gk are identical; it could thus be translated as a command: "Search." The approach here was typical of the early church's use of the Jewish scriptures, which were retained largely as a sourcebook of prophetic references about Jesus. See a similar treatment in 5:46, where Jesus states, "he wrote about me." **5:46** See 5:39.

believe what he wrote, how will you believe what I say?"

Feeding the Five Thousand

6 After this Jesus went to the other side of the Sea of Galilee, also called the Sea of Tiberias.[m] 2A large crowd kept following him, because they saw the signs that he was doing for the sick. 3Jesus went up the mountain and sat down there with his disciples. 4Now the Passover, the festival of the Jews, was near. 5When he looked up and saw a large crowd coming toward him, Jesus said to Philip, "Where are we to buy bread for these people to eat?" 6He said this to test him, for he himself knew what he was going to do. 7Philip answered him, "Six months' wages[n] would not buy enough bread for each of them to get a little." 8One of his disciples, Andrew, Simon Peter's brother, said to him, 9"There is a boy here who has five barley loaves and two fish. But what are they among so many people?" 10Jesus said, "Make the people sit down." Now there was a great deal of grass in the place; so they[o] sat down, about five thousand in all. 11Then Jesus took the loaves, and when he had given thanks, he distributed them to those who were seated; so also the fish, as much as they wanted. 12When they were satisfied, he told his disciples, "Gather up the fragments left over, so that nothing may be lost." 13So they gathered them up, and from the fragments of the five barley loaves, left by those who had eaten, they filled twelve baskets. 14When the people saw the sign that he had done, they began to say, "This is indeed the prophet who is to come into the world."

15When Jesus realized that they were about to come and take him by force to make him king, he withdrew again to the mountain by himself.

Jesus Walks on the Water

16When evening came, his disciples went down to the sea, 17got into a boat, and started across the sea to Capernaum. It was now dark, and Jesus had not yet come to them. 18The sea became rough because a strong wind was blowing. 19When they had rowed about three or four miles,[p] they saw Jesus walking on the sea and coming near the boat, and they were terrified. 20But he said to them, "It is I;[q] do not be afraid." 21Then they wanted to take him into the boat, and immediately the boat reached the land toward which they were going.

The Bread from Heaven

22The next day the crowd that had stayed on the other side of the sea saw that there had been only one boat there. They also saw that Jesus had not got into the boat with his disciples, but that his disciples had

---

m Gk of Galilee of Tiberias
n Gk Two hundred denarii; the denarius was the usual day's wage for a laborer
o Gk the men

p Gk about twenty-five or thirty stadia
q Gk I am

6:1 At the beginning of *John* 5, Jesus is said to have gone up to Jerusalem. There is no mention of a return to Galilee. To resolve this problem, some scholars have argued that *John* 6 originally belonged before *John* 5. A capital city was founded on the Sea of Chinnereth (or Galilee) by Herod Antipas around 20 C.E. and was named for the Roman emperor Tiberius. The Sea of Chinnereth sometimes was called the Sea of Tiberias because of this prominent city on its western shore. **6:4** This is the second mention of a Passover in *John*. See 2:13. **6:5** This is the first Johannine miracle found also in the synoptic accounts (*Mark* 6:32–44; *Matt.* 14:13–21; *Luke* 9:10–17). There are some differences. In the synoptic account, it seems that the crowd had spent the day with Jesus and it was becoming late; in *John*, as the crowd is coming, Jesus raises the question about food to test his disciples' faith. But there is agreement on a number of details: six months' wages (lit. "two hundred denarii"); five thousand people fed; five loaves and two fish; twelve baskets full of food left over. This is the second incident involving Philip (see 1:43). **6:8** *Andrew* See 1:40, 43. **6:9** The lad is not mentioned in the synoptic account. Only *John* mentions that these were *barley* loaves, a grain used for cattle feed and by the poor to make bread. **6:11** *given thanks* John uses the Gk word *eucharisteō*, which would immediately call to mind the Christian Eucharist for the original readers. The synoptic tradition uses the less evocative word *eulogeō*. *John* follows the story of the feeding of the multitude with an extended discussion of Jesus as the bread of life. The language is filled with eucharistic images, but the association with Jewish scripture is made not with the Passover, as might have been expected, but with the provision of bread in the wilderness. Further, *John* has no account of the institution of the Eucharist; the synoptic tradition does (see 6:35). **6:14** *prophet* See 1:21; 4:19. **6:17–18** Although roads circled the Sea of Galilee, it was considerably farther from the west side to the east by land than by boat. But since the lake was surrounded by mountains, bad storms and strong winds could arise quickly. **6:19** *Mark, Matthew*, and *John* record the story of Jesus' walking on the water, and all three place it immediately after the story of the feeding of the five thousand. Some scholars speculate that the two stories formed a unit in the oral tradition; others find evidence here for literary dependence between the Johannine and synoptic traditions. *John's* version is the least detailed. He does not include the stilling of the storm, simply saying that when Jesus entered the boat, immediately they reached the land to which they were going (6:21).

gone away alone. [23]Then some boats from Tiberias came near the place where they had eaten the bread after the Lord had given thanks.[r] [24]So when the crowd saw that neither Jesus nor his disciples were there, they themselves got into the boats and went to Capernaum looking for Jesus.

[25]When they found him on the other side of the sea, they said to him, "Rabbi, when did you come here?" [26]Jesus answered them, "Very truly, I tell you, you are looking for me, not because you saw signs, but because you ate your fill of the loaves. [27]Do not work for the food that perishes, but for the food that endures for eternal life, which the Son of Man will give you. For it is on him that God the Father has set his seal." [28]Then they said to him, "What must we do to perform the works of God?" [29]Jesus answered them, "This is the work of God, that you believe in him whom he has sent." [30]So they said to him, "What sign are you going to give us then, so that we may see it and believe you? What work are you performing? [31]Our ancestors ate the manna in the wilderness; as it is written, 'He gave them bread from heaven to eat.'" [32]Then Jesus said to them, "Very truly, I tell you, it was not Moses who gave you the bread from heaven, but it is my Father who gives you the true bread from heaven. [33]For the bread of God is that which[s] comes down from heaven and gives life to the world." [34]They said to him, "Sir, give us this bread always."

[35]Jesus said to them, "I am the bread of life. Whoever comes to me will never be hungry, and whoever believes in me will never be thirsty. [36]But I said to you that you have seen me and yet do not believe. [37]Everything that the Father gives me will come to me, and anyone who comes to me I will never drive

---

r Other ancient authorities lack *after the Lord had given thanks*
s Or *he who*

away; [38]for I have come down from heaven, not to do my own will, but the will of him who sent me. [39]And this is the will of him who sent me, that I should lose nothing of all that he has given me, but raise it up on the last day. [40]This is indeed the will of my Father, that all who see the Son and believe in him may have eternal life; and I will raise them up on the last day."

[41]Then the Jews began to complain about him because he said, "I am the bread that came down from heaven." [42]They were saying, "Is not this Jesus, the son of Joseph, whose father and mother we know? How can he now say, 'I have come down from heaven'?" [43]Jesus answered them, "Do not complain among yourselves. [44]No one can come to me unless drawn by the Father who sent me; and I will raise that person up on the last day. [45]It is written in the prophets, 'And they shall all be taught by God.' Everyone who has heard and learned from the Father comes to me. [46]Not that anyone has seen the Father except the one who is from God; he has seen the Father. [47]Very truly, I tell you, whoever believes has eternal life. [48]I am the bread of life. [49]Your ancestors ate the manna in the wilderness, and they died. [50]This is the bread that comes down from heaven, so that one may eat of it and not die. [51]I am the living bread that came down from heaven. Whoever eats of this bread will live forever; and the bread that I will give for the life of the world is my flesh."

[52]The Jews then disputed among themselves, saying, "How can this man give us his flesh to eat?" [53]So Jesus said to them, "Very truly, I tell you, unless you eat the flesh of the Son of Man and drink his blood, you have no life in you. [54]Those who eat my flesh and drink my blood have eternal life, and I will raise them up on the last day; [55]for my flesh is true food and my blood is true drink. [56]Those who eat my flesh and drink my blood abide in me, and I in them.

6:23 Some scholars think that this verse is a gloss, that is, a comment written by a copyist in the margin to explain the text, and that later it was accidentally incorporated into the text. The use of the singular *bread* (or "loaf") and the giving of thanks suggest the language of the Eucharist. **6:24** Capernaum was about ten miles north of Tiberias along the west coast of the Sea of Chinnereth. **6:31** *Ps.* 78:24 (LXX 77:24). The author follows the LXX in speaking of *bread;* the MT has "grain." See *Exod.* 16:15; *Num.* 11:8; *Neh.* 9:15. This becomes the opening for an extended discourse on the Eucharist. **6:32** This is characteristic of early Christian appropriation of the Jewish scriptures—applying an incident or comment from the Bible to the Christian community to emphasize its present fulfillment. Others in Judaism, particularly the authors of the Dead Sea Scrolls, treated the Jewish scriptures in the same way. **6:35–58** This entire passage has as its theme Jesus as the bread of life or the bread that came down from heaven. Although *John* does not describe the establishing of the sacrament of the Eucharist, his words here seem to point to the importance of the Eucharist for the Johannine community, for he speaks of Jesus' flesh as bread (6:52) and of eating flesh and drinking blood (6:53–58). **6:35** See note on 4:26. This is the first of a number of descriptions of Jesus introduced by the words "I am" (6:41, 48, 51; 10:7, 9, 11, 14; 14:6; 15:1, 5). The phrase "I am" occurs without qualification in 4:26; 6:20. **6:40** *the last day* That is, the day of the final judgment, when the righteous were to be resurrected, according to popular Jewish thinking of the time. **6:42** *Mark* does not mention Joseph; *Matthew* mentions him only in the nativity account; *Luke* mentions him in the nativity account and in one other passage (4:22), where, as in *John*, people ask whether Jesus is not Joseph's son. *John* repeats the question in one other passage (1:45), where there are, however, no negative overtones as there are here. This is another example of a touch of *John's* irony: the Jews say that Jesus cannot be from heaven because they know his father Joseph, but *John* and his readers know differently—Jesus is from heaven because God is his father. **6:45** *Isa.* 54:13; *Jer.* 31:34. **6:56** *abide* See 14:17.

57Just as the living Father sent me, and I live because of the Father, so whoever eats me will live because of me. 58This is the bread that came down from heaven, not like that which your ancestors ate, and they died. But the one who eats this bread will live forever." 59He said these things while he was teaching in the synagogue at Capernaum.

The Words of Eternal Life

60When many of his disciples heard it, they said, "This teaching is difficult; who can accept it?" 61But Jesus, being aware that his disciples were complaining about it, said to them, "Does this offend you? 62Then what if you were to see the Son of Man ascending to where he was before? 63It is the spirit that gives life; the flesh is useless. The words that I have spoken to you are spirit and life. 64But among you there are some who do not believe." For Jesus knew from the first who were the ones that did not believe, and who was the one that would betray him. 65And he said, "For this reason I have told you that no one can come to me unless it is granted by the Father."

66Because of this many of his disciples turned back and no longer went about with him. 67So Jesus asked the twelve, "Do you also wish to go away?" 68Simon Peter answered him, "Lord, to whom can we go? You have the words of eternal life. 69We have come to believe and know that you are the Holy One of God."t 70Jesus answered them, "Did I not choose you, the twelve? Yet one of you is a devil." 71He was speaking of Judas son of Simon Iscariot,u for he, though one of the twelve, was going to betray him.

The Unbelief of Jesus' Brothers

7After this Jesus went about in Galilee. He did not wishv to go about in Judea because the Jews were looking for an opportunity to kill him. 2Now the Jewish festival of Boothsw was near. 3So his brothers said to him, "Leave here and go to Judea so that your disciples also may see the works you are doing; 4for no one who wantsx to be widely known acts in secret. If you do these things, show yourself to the world." 5(For not even his brothers believed in him.) 6Jesus said to them, "My time has not yet come, but your time is always here. 7The world cannot hate you, but it hates me because I testify against it that its works are evil. 8Go to the festival yourselves. I am noty going to this festival, for my time has not yet fully come." 9After saying this, he remained in Galilee.

Jesus at the Festival of Booths

10But after his brothers had gone to the festival, then he also went, not publicly but as it werez in secret. 11The Jews were looking for him at the festival and saying, "Where is he?" 12And there was considerable complaining about him among the crowds. While some were saying, "He is a good man," others were saying, "No, he is deceiving the crowd." 13Yet no one would speak openly about him for fear of the Jews.

---

t Other ancient authorities read *the Christ, the Son of the living God*

u Other ancient authorities read *Judas Iscariot son of Simon;* others, *Judas son of Simon from Karyot* (Kerioth)

v Other ancient authorities read *was not at liberty*

w Or *Tabernacles*

x Other ancient authorities read *wants it*

y Other ancient authorities add *yet*

z Other ancient authorities lack *as it were*

6:62 Son of Man See 1:51. **6:69** The textual variant mentioned in note *t* stems partly from the slight difference in Gk between *Holy One* (*hagios*) and "Son" (*huios*). **6:71** All four gospels mention Judas as the betrayer of Jesus (*Mark* 3:19; 14:10; *Matt.* 10:4; 26:14; *Luke* 6:16; 22:3; *John* 6:71; 12:4; 13:2, 26–30; 14:22; 18:2–5). The name Iscariot probably indicates that Judas was from Kerioth, in southern Judea (making Judas possibly the only disciple from Judea). But a number of other theories have been proposed, a popular one being that the term links Judas to the Sicarii, a secretive group of dagger-wielding assassins active against Roman rule in Palestine; perhaps the name Iscariot was not used for Judas when he was a member of the band of disciples but was introduced later to mark him. *John* gives Judas a bit more attention than do the Synoptics. **7:2** The Festival of Booths was also called Tabernacles. This was the most popular and festive of the three major Jewish pilgrimage festivals, occurring in September or October, at the end of all the harvests, just before the beginning of the rains (see *Lev.* 23:33–43; *Deut.* 16:13–15). Jews would have filled the city of Jerusalem for this celebration. The festival lasted seven days, beginning on a Sabbath. By the 1st century, an eighth day, another Sabbath, appears to have been added. In *John,* Jesus seems to have traveled to Jerusalem frequently for the feasts. See APPENDIX C. **7:5** The brothers of Jesus are named in *Mark* 6:3. The most natural understanding of the word "brothers" is "children of the same parents," but the doctrine of the virginity of Mary led to other suggestions by the late 4th century: (a) these were cousins rather than brothers, and (b) these were older children of Joseph from a previous marriage. **7:8** The word "yet" in note *y* seems to be a scribal attempt to smooth out a problematic element in the story. Jesus did go to the feast (7:10); the plain statement that he was not going to the feast would be at odds with this. **7:13** The people in the festival crowd are afraid of *the Jews.* The sense must be the Jewish leaders, rather than Jews in general, since the pilgrims are themselves Jews (see 1:19). Or the writer slips by betraying his own non-Jewish perspective.

¹⁴About the middle of the festival Jesus went up into the temple and began to teach. ¹⁵The Jews were astonished at it, saying, "How does this man have such learning,ᵃ when he has never been taught?" ¹⁶Then Jesus answered them, "My teaching is not mine but his who sent me. ¹⁷Anyone who resolves to do the will of God will know whether the teaching is from God or whether I am speaking on my own. ¹⁸Those who speak on their own seek their own glory; but the one who seeks the glory of him who sent him is true, and there is nothing false in him.

¹⁹"Did not Moses give you the law? Yet none of you keeps the law. Why are you looking for an opportunity to kill me?" ²⁰The crowd answered, "You have a demon! Who is trying to kill you?" ²¹Jesus answered them, "I performed one work, and all of you are astonished. ²²Moses gave you circumcision (it is, of course, not from Moses, but from the patriarchs), and you circumcise a man on the sabbath. ²³If a man receives circumcision on the sabbath in order that the law of Moses may not be broken, are you angry with me because I healed a man's whole body on the sabbath? ²⁴Do not judge by appearances, but judge with right judgment."

Is This the Christ?

²⁵Now some of the people of Jerusalem were saying, "Is not this the man whom they are trying to kill? ²⁶And here he is, speaking openly, but they say nothing to him! Can it be that the authorities really know that this is the Messiah?ᵇ ²⁷Yet we know where this man is from; but when the Messiahᵇ comes, no one will know where he is from." ²⁸Then Jesus cried out as he was teaching in the temple, "You know me, and you know where I am from. I have not come on my own. But the one who sent me is true, and you do not know him. ²⁹I know him, because I am from him, and he sent me." ³⁰Then they tried to arrest him, but no one laid hands on him, because his hour had not yet come. ³¹Yet many in the crowd believed in him and were saying, "When the Messiahᵇ comes, will he do more signs than this man has done?"ᶜ

Officers Are Sent to Arrest Jesus

³²The Pharisees heard the crowd muttering such things about him, and the chief priests and Pharisees sent temple police to arrest him. ³³Jesus then said, "I will be with you a little while longer, and then I am going to him who sent me. ³⁴You will search for me, but you will not find me; and where I am, you cannot come." ³⁵The Jews said to one another, "Where does this man intend to go that we will not find him? Does he intend to go to the Dispersion among the Greeks and teach the Greeks? ³⁶What does he mean by saying, 'You will search for me and you will not find me' and 'Where I am, you cannot come'?"

Rivers of Living Water

³⁷On the last day of the festival, the great day, while Jesus was standing there, he cried out, "Let anyone who is thirsty come to me, ³⁸and let the one who believes in me drink. Asᵈ the scripture has said, 'Out of the believer's heartᵉ shall flow rivers of living water.'" ³⁹Now he said this about the Spirit, which believers in him were to receive; for as yet there was no Spirit,ᶠ because Jesus was not yet glorified.

---

a Or *this man know his letters*
b Or *the Christ*

c Other ancient authorities read *is doing*
d Or *come to me and drink.* ³⁸*The one who believes in me, as*
e Gk *out of his belly*
f Other ancient authorities read *for as yet the Spirit* (others, *Holy Spirit*) *had not been given*

7:15 The Synoptics report similar opinions about Jesus and his disciples being unlettered: *Mark* 1:22; 6:2; *Matt.* 7:28–29; 13:54; *Luke* 4:22, 32. The sense is often that Jesus' teaching has an authority more convincing than the scribes', or at least as convincing as theirs, although Jesus had not trained formally as a religious teacher. **7:20** Early Christian literature provides a number of accounts of demon possession. The term was used for various kinds of mental and other illness, from clear cases of insanity to conditions such as epilepsy. See the synoptic tradition, where similar charges are made (*Mark* 3:21–30; *Matt.* 9:34; 11:18; 12:24–28; *Luke* 7:33; 11:15–20; *John* 7:48–52; 10:20–21). **7:23** The issue is whether healing on the Sabbath is permitted. The logic of the Johannine argument is this: once it is established that some actions are allowed on the Sabbath (e.g., circumcision), and indeed even commanded by God to be done on the Sabbath, then it becomes possible that other actions are permitted. **7:32** *temple police* The Gk word is one of the words for "servant" (*hypēretēs*), which *John* uses consistently for the temple police (7:52; 18:3–19:6; see esp. 18:3). **7:35** *the Dispersion* Gk *diaspora*. The term refers either to *Jews* living outside Palestine or to the *land* beyond Palestine. The Gk word is used in two other places in our literature (*Jas.* 1:1; *1 Pet.* 1:1). The Johannine readers, if they are Jews, themselves fit the description of those who live in the dispersion among the Greeks, and this makes the comment more ironic—the opponents of Jesus are again mistaken. *John* frequently uses irony (e.g., 11:52; 12:20–26). *the Greeks* Used twice here by *John;* "Gentiles," a favorite word of the synoptic writers, is not used at all by *John.* **7:36** See *Gospel of Thomas* 38. **7:38** Although there seem to be partial parallels to this verse in *Isa.* 44:2–3; 58:11 and *Zechariah* 14, an exact source of the quotation as it now stands cannot be determined. The image of living water fits the scene of the festival, where each day water was carried from the Pool of Siloam to the temple. Similar imagery appears in 4:13–15. **7:39** *glorified* A term used to describe the vindication of Jesus in the resurrection event. The comment about the Spirit is puzzling but should be understood in light of 20:22.

Division among the People

[40]When they heard these words, some in the crowd said, "This is really the prophet." [41]Others said, "This is the Messiah."[g] But some asked, "Surely the Messiah[g] does not come from Galilee, does he? [42]Has not the scripture said that the Messiah[g] is descended from David and comes from Bethlehem, the village where David lived?" [43]So there was a division in the crowd because of him. [44]Some of them wanted to arrest him, but no one laid hands on him.

The Unbelief of Those in Authority

[45]Then the temple police went back to the chief priests and Pharisees, who asked them, "Why did you not arrest him?" [46]The police answered, "Never has anyone spoken like this!" [47]Then the Pharisees replied, "Surely you have not been deceived too, have you? [48]Has any one of the authorities or of the Pharisees believed in him? [49]But this crowd, which does not know the law—they are accursed." [50]Nicodemus, who had gone to Jesus[h] before, and who was one of them, asked, [51]"Our law does not judge people without first giving them a hearing to find out what they are doing, does it?" [52]They replied, "Surely you are not also from Galilee, are you? Search and you will see that no prophet is to arise from Galilee."

The Woman Caught in Adultery

[[[53]Then each of them went home,

8 [1]while Jesus went to the Mount of Olives. [2]Early in the morning he came again to the temple. All the people came to him and he sat down and began to teach them. [3]The scribes and the Pharisees brought a woman who had been caught in adultery; and making her stand before all of them, [4]they said to him, "Teacher, this woman was caught in the very act of committing adultery. [5]Now in the law Moses commanded us to stone such women. Now what do you say?" [6]They said this to test him, so that they might have some charge to bring against him. Jesus bent down and wrote with his finger on the ground. [7]When they kept on questioning him, he straightened up and said to them, "Let anyone among you who is without sin be the first to throw a stone at her." [8]And once again he bent down and wrote on the ground.[i] [9]When they heard it, they went away, one by one, beginning with the elders; and Jesus was left alone with the woman standing before him. [10]Jesus straightened up and said to her, "Woman, where are they? Has no one condemned you?" [11]She said, "No one, sir."[j] And Jesus said, "Neither do I condemn you. Go your way, and from now on do not sin again."]][k]

Jesus the Light of the World

[12]Again Jesus spoke to them, saying, "I am the light of the world. Whoever follows me will never

---

g Or *the Christ*
h Gk *him*

i Other ancient authorities add *the sins of each of them*
j Or *Lord*
k The most ancient authorities lack 7:53–8:11; other authorities add the passage here or after 7:36 or after 21:25 or after Luke 21:38, with variations of text; some mark the passage as doubtful.

7:40 *prophet* See 1:21. **7:41–42** This is another example of *John*'s use of irony. The readers know, at one level, of Jesus' disqualifying origins in Galilee, but they know, too, that Jesus, as God's Son, was from heaven. Jesus' opponents know only that Jesus is from Galilee and therefore fail to receive him (see 1:46). Whether the author knew about the stories of Jesus' birth in Bethlehem is uncertain; this would have been an ideal place to mention them if he did. Many scholars use this passage to show that the birth narratives in *Matthew* (2:1) and *Luke* (2:4) were late developments, taking shape after the Johannine tradition had been framed. The Bethlehem tradition is based on *Mic.* 5:2, a passage to which *Matthew* appeals in support of the Christian story (2:6). But no known Jewish literature of that time appeals to this passage as messianic. **7:49** The contrast is common in early Christian literature, where the law is seen in some way to work against the Christian movement. See 1:17. **7:50** *Nicodemus* See 3:1. **7:52** *arise from Galilee* The verb *arise* in the Gk is in the present tense, but the meaning can be future, as its sense is here. Some Hebrew prophets did indeed arise from Galilee. Jonah was from a town only three miles north of Nazareth (see also *Isa.* 9:1). **8:3** This is the only reference in *John* to scribes, experts in the law of Moses, in contrast to the frequent reference to them in the Synoptics. See 8:9. **8:5** *in the law* See *Lev.* 20:10; *Deut.* 22:22. Some commentators point out that the guilty man in the story was not brought before Jesus along with the woman as the law required. But *John* makes nothing of the absence of the guilty man. **8:7** A Jewish form of capital punishment was death by stoning (*Luke* 20:6; *John* 10:31; *Acts* 7:58; 14:5). In the case of such an execution, the witnesses were required to throw the first stone (*Deut.* 17:7). Such witnesses appear in the stoning of Stephen (*Acts* 7:58). **8:9** *elders* The Gk word, *presbyteros,* can be translated merely as "older man" or as the formal office of elder, as the NRSV translates it. This is its only occurrence in *John,* in contrast to the frequent mention (twenty-five times) of the formal group of elders in the Synoptics. The main opponents of Jesus in *John* are the chief priests and Pharisees or simply "the Jews," meaning, it seems, the Jewish leaders (see 1:19). The author of *John* may have in mind simply the older men at the scene, since he seems to have no conscious opposition to elders elsewhere in his gospel. **8:12** *light of the world* The phrase is used also in 9:5. *Matthew* too uses it, but of the followers of Jesus (5:14). Light is a favorite image in *John;* he mentions it nineteen times, several times referring to the light of the world (see 9:5; 11:9; 12:46).

walk in darkness but will have the light of life." [13]Then the Pharisees said to him, "You are testifying on your own behalf; your testimony is not valid." [14]Jesus answered, "Even if I testify on my own behalf, my testimony is valid because I know where I have come from and where I am going, but you do not know where I come from or where I am going. [15]You judge by human standards;[l] I judge no one. [16]Yet even if I do judge, my judgment is valid; for it is not I alone who judge, but I and the Father[m] who sent me. [17]In your law it is written that the testimony of two witnesses is valid. [18]I testify on my own behalf, and the Father who sent me testifies on my behalf." [19]Then they said to him, "Where is your Father?" Jesus answered, "You know neither me nor my Father. If you knew me, you would know my Father also." [20]He spoke these words while he was teaching in the treasury of the temple, but no one arrested him, because his hour had not yet come.

Jesus Foretells His Death

[21]Again he said to them, "I am going away, and you will search for me, but you will die in your sin. Where I am going, you cannot come." [22]Then the Jews said, "Is he going to kill himself? Is that what he means by saying, 'Where I am going, you cannot come'?" [23]He said to them, "You are from below, I am from above; you are of this world, I am not of this world. [24]I told you that you would die in your sins, for you will die in your sins unless you believe that I am he."[n] [25]They said to him, "Who are you?" Jesus said to them, "Why do I speak to you at all?[o] [26]I have much to say about you and much to condemn; but the one who sent me is true, and I declare to the world what I have heard from him." [27]They did not understand that he was speaking to them about the Father. [28]So Jesus said, "When you have lifted up the Son of Man, then you will realize that I am he,[n] and that I do nothing on my own, but I speak these things as the Father instructed me. [29]And the one who sent me is with me; he has not left me alone, for I always do what is pleasing to him." [30]As he was saying these things, many believed in him.

True Disciples

[31]Then Jesus said to the Jews who had believed in him, "If you continue in my word, you are truly my disciples; [32]and you will know the truth, and the truth will make you free." [33]They answered him, "We are descendants of Abraham and have never been slaves to anyone. What do you mean by saying, 'You will be made free'?"

[34]Jesus answered them, "Very truly, I tell you, everyone who commits sin is a slave to sin. [35]The slave does not have a permanent place in the household; the son has a place there forever. [36]So if the Son makes you free, you will be free indeed. [37]I know that you are descendants of Abraham; yet you look for an opportunity to kill me, because there is no place in you for my word. [38]I declare what I have seen in the Father's presence; as for you, you should do what you have heard from the Father."[p]

Jesus and Abraham

[39]They answered him, "Abraham is our father." Jesus said to them, "If you were Abraham's children, you would be doing[q] what Abraham did, [40]but now you are trying to kill me, a man who has told you the truth that I heard from God. This is not what Abraham did. [41]You are indeed doing what your father

---

l Gk *according to the flesh*
m Other ancient authorities read *he*
n Gk *I am*
o Or *What I have told you from the beginning*

p Other ancient authorities read *you do what you have heard from your father*
q Other ancient authorities read *If you are Abraham's children, then do*

8:14 *my testimony is valid* See 5:31.   **8:17** *two witnesses* Num. 35:30; *Deut.* 17:6; 19:15.   **8:20** The setting is probably near the chests in the Court of the Women used for collecting freewill offerings, not in the temple vaults or treasury itself. Secure vaults would have been present in many temples, since temples regularly served as banks and the priests of temples became guardians of deposits made there.   **8:24** *I am he* Lit. "I am." So also in 8:28. See 4:26.   **8:25** *Why* The Gk word for "why" can also be translated "what."   **8:28** *lifted up* That is, crucified. See 3:14   **8:33** This is a puzzling statement, since Jews had been frequently enslaved and in the 1st century lived under Roman rule, which in Palestine had become unbearable to many.   **8:34** *slave to sin* The Stoics used the same image of slavery. "Show me someone who is not a slave. One man is a slave to lust, another to greed" (Seneca, *Letters* 47).   **8:35** Both Jews and Gentiles would have been familiar with this principle. Indeed, the Jewish scriptures do not even bother to specify this as a law; it is simply taken for granted (see *Gen.* 21:10; *Prov.* 17:2). Adoption of a slave, however, was not unknown.   **8:39** *John* mentions Abraham only in this chapter. The argument is similar to Paul's treatment of Abraham's "true" children (*Rom.* 4:1, 11–19; *Gal.* 3:29; 4:28) and a comment in the Q material (*Matt.* 3:9; *Luke* 3:8).   The manuscripts vary in this verse; the differences stem from attempts to make the passage more grammatical.   **8:41** On the one hand, the comment about illegitimate children may be nothing more than a denial of the charge that Jesus leveled against the Jews—that Abraham was not their father. In response, they make an even greater claim: "God is our father." On the other hand, this comment is perhaps a slur on Jesus' own questionable birth. The

does." They said to him, "We are not illegitimate children; we have one father, God himself." [42]Jesus said to them, "If God were your Father, you would love me, for I came from God and now I am here. I did not come on my own, but he sent me. [43]Why do you not understand what I say? It is because you cannot accept my word. [44]You are from your father the devil, and you choose to do your father's desires. He was a murderer from the beginning and does not stand in the truth, because there is no truth in him. When he lies, he speaks according to his own nature, for he is a liar and the father of lies. [45]But because I tell the truth, you do not believe me. [46]Which of you convicts me of sin? If I tell the truth, why do you not believe me? [47]Whoever is from God hears the words of God. The reason you do not hear them is that you are not from God."

[48]The Jews answered him, "Are we not right in saying that you are a Samaritan and have a demon?" [49]Jesus answered, "I do not have a demon; but I honor my Father, and you dishonor me. [50]Yet I do not seek my own glory; there is one who seeks it and he is the judge. [51]Very truly, I tell you, whoever keeps my word will never see death." [52]The Jews said to him, "Now we know that you have a demon. Abraham died, and so did the prophets; yet you say, 'Whoever keeps my word will never taste death.' [53]Are you greater than our father Abraham, who died? The prophets also died. Who do you claim to be?" [54]Jesus answered, "If I glorify myself, my glory is nothing. It is my Father who glorifies me, he of whom you say, 'He is our God,' [55]though you do not know him. But I know him; if I would say that I do not know him, I would be a liar like you. But I do

know him and I keep his word. [56]Your ancestor Abraham rejoiced that he would see my day; he saw it and was glad." [57]Then the Jews said to him, "You are not yet fifty years old, and have you seen Abraham?"[r] [58]Jesus said to them, "Very truly, I tell you, before Abraham was, I am." [59]So they picked up stones to throw at him, but Jesus hid himself and went out of the temple.

A Man Born Blind Receives Sight

9 As he walked along, he saw a man blind from birth. [2]His disciples asked him, "Rabbi, who sinned, this man or his parents, that he was born blind?" [3]Jesus answered, "Neither this man nor his parents sinned; he was born blind so that God's works might be revealed in him. [4]We[s] must work the works of him who sent me[t] while it is day; night is coming when no one can work. [5]As long as I am in the world, I am the light of the world." [6]When he had said this, he spat on the ground and made mud with the saliva and spread the mud on the man's eyes, [7]saying to him, "Go, wash in the pool of Siloam" (which means Sent). Then he went and washed and came back able to see. [8]The neighbors and those who had seen him before as a beggar began to ask, "Is this not the man who used to sit and beg?" [9]Some were saying, "It is he." Others were saying, "No, but it is someone like him." He kept saying, "I am the man." [10]But they kept asking him, "Then how were your eyes opened?" [11]He answered, "The man called Jesus made mud, spread it

---

r Other ancient authorities read *has Abraham seen you?*
s Other ancient authorities read *I*
t Other ancient authorities read *us*

---

early church seems to have had to respond to charges that Jesus was illegitimate. Many scholars see the development of the doctrine of the virgin birth as a response to these charges. In the literature of this collection, reference to the virgin birth occurs only in the birth narratives of *Matthew* (1:23) and *Luke* (1:27, 34) and in Ign. *Eph.* 19.1; Ign. *Smyrn.* 1.12. **8:44** An allusion to the story of the murder of Abel by Cain (*Gen.* 4:1–14). **8:48** *Samaritan* A term of derision, especially in the context of a question of piety. See 4:9. **8:56** *would see my day* The statement puzzles the Jews. Whatever the author intended by this, it is clearly a grand claim regarding Jesus and a subordination of the Jewish patriarch Abraham to Jesus or his mission. **8:57** Levites retired from active service at age fifty. Perhaps the point of the comment on age here is that Jesus has not even reached retirement age. Such a statement could apply to persons of a wide age range and should not be used to determine the precise age of Jesus at the time. The only other comment about the age of Jesus is in *Luke* 3:23. Some copyists have tried to harmonize the two passages by changing *fifty* to "forty" here. **8:58** *I am* See 4:26; 8:24. **8:59** Parts of the temple were still under construction, and stones would have been readily available. **9:1** *blind* A common condition in the Middle East even today, and one of the common ailments in the healing stories of the gospels. Such people usually had no option but to beg (9:8). This is *John's* only account of such a healing, but the author makes much of it by referring back to it twice (10:21; 11:37). **9:2** The assumption was that illness is caused by sin. The question for the disciples was, "Whose sin?" The question makes sense in terms of some statements in the Jewish scripture (*Exod.* 20:5; 34:7; *Ps.* 109:13–15; *Isa.* 65:6–7), but note an alternative position in *Ezekiel* 18. **9:3** *he was born blind* These words are missing in the Gk but are borrowed by translators from the previous verse to make the passage clearer. **9:4** Most jobs had to be done during the day, and even theater events were held during the daytime. A few jobs, however, might be done at night, such as fishing (*Luke* 5:5; *John* 21:3). **9:5** *light of the world* See 8:12. **9:6** The use of saliva in cures was not unheard of in the ancient world. See *Mark* 7:33; 8:23. **9:7** Only *John* mentions the Pool of Siloam, located in the southeast corner of the city. The pool was connected to a spring by a 1750-foot tunnel built by King Hezekiah more than seven hundred years earlier (*1 Kgs.* 20:20; *2 Chr.* 32:30).

on my eyes, and said to me, 'Go to Siloam and wash.' Then I went and washed and received my sight." [12]They said to him, "Where is he?" He said, "I do not know."

The Pharisees Investigate the Healing

[13]They brought to the Pharisees the man who had formerly been blind. [14]Now it was a sabbath day when Jesus made the mud and opened his eyes. [15]Then the Pharisees also began to ask him how he had received his sight. He said to them, "He put mud on my eyes. Then I washed, and now I see." [16]Some of the Pharisees said, "This man is not from God, for he does not observe the sabbath." But others said, "How can a man who is a sinner perform such signs?" And they were divided. [17]So they said again to the blind man, "What do you say about him? It was your eyes he opened." He said, "He is a prophet."

[18]The Jews did not believe that he had been blind and had received his sight until they called the parents of the man who had received his sight [19]and asked them, "Is this your son, who you say was born blind? How then does he now see?" [20]His parents answered, "We know that this is our son, and that he was born blind; [21]but we do not know how it is that now he sees, nor do we know who opened his eyes. Ask him; he is of age. He will speak for himself." [22]His parents said this because they were afraid of the Jews; for the Jews had already agreed that anyone who confessed Jesus[u] to be the Messiah[v] would be put out of the synagogue. [23]Therefore his parents said, "He is of age; ask him."

[24]So for the second time they called the man who had been blind, and they said to him, "Give glory to God! We know that this man is a sinner." [25]He answered, "I do not know whether he is a sinner. One thing I do know, that though I was blind, now I see."

[26]They said to him, "What did he do to you? How did he open your eyes?" [27]He answered them, "I have told you already, and you would not listen. Why do you want to hear it again? Do you also want to become his disciples?" [28]Then they reviled him, saying, "You are his disciple, but we are disciples of Moses. [29]We know that God has spoken to Moses, but as for this man, we do not know where he comes from." [30]The man answered, "Here is an astonishing thing! You do not know where he comes from, and yet he opened my eyes. [31]We know that God does not listen to sinners, but he does listen to one who worships him and obeys his will. [32]Never since the world began has it been heard that anyone opened the eyes of a person born blind. [33]If this man were not from God, he could do nothing." [34]They answered him, "You were born entirely in sins, and are you trying to teach us?" And they drove him out.

Spiritual Blindness

[35]Jesus heard that they had driven him out, and when he found him, he said, "Do you believe in the Son of Man?"[w] [36]He answered, "And who is he, sir?[x] Tell me, so that I may believe in him." [37]Jesus said to him, "You have seen him, and the one speaking with you is he." [38]He said, "Lord,[x] I believe." And he worshiped him. [39]Jesus said, "I came into this world for judgment so that those who do not see may see, and those who do see may become blind." [40]Some of the Pharisees near him heard this and said to him, "Surely we are not blind, are we?" [41]Jesus said to them, "If you were blind, you would not have sin. But now that you say, 'We see,' your sin remains.

Jesus the Good Shepherd

10 "Very truly, I tell you, anyone who does not enter the sheepfold by the gate but climbs in by

---

u Gk *him*
v Or *the Christ*

w Other ancient authorities read *the Son of God*
x *Sir* and *Lord* translate the same Greek word

9:21 *he is of age* That is, he was at least thirteen, the age at which a male could legally give testimony, but he may have been considerably older. **9:22** All of *John* 9 is taken up with the healing of the blind man and the threat of expulsion from the synagogue by the synagogue leaders wherever they find expressions of faith in Jesus. The concern is repeated in 12:42 and 16:2. In all three passages, a new term is used—*aposynagōgos*, appearing nowhere else in early Christian texts. It is difficult not to conclude that the author comes back to this issue and includes this lengthy story because expulsion from the synagogue was one of the urgent issues faced by the author and his community. Most scholars argue that the cross-examination and responses in 9:24–34 seem to reflect the later struggle between Judaism and the Johannine community. **9:30** Here again is a bit of Johannine irony. The ones who are supposed to represent and know the ways of God do not recognize the messenger who comes from God. The original readers of *John* no doubt would have loved this caustic remark. **9:34** *born entirely in sins* Perhaps a reference to his being born blind (see 9:1). **9:35** *Son of Man* See 1:51. **9:38–41** More Johannine irony. The "seeing" Pharisees are blind to what the once blind man can now see—that Jesus is God's messenger. **10:1** *Very truly* Gk *Amēn, amēn.* *sheepfold* Sheep grazed during the day under the watchful eye of a shepherd and at night were kept in enclosures or courtyards, which were shared by a number of different flocks and guarded by a watchman. *bandit* (See also 10:8.) The Gk *lēstēs* probably implies more than "thief." It was a term sometimes used to describe those who rebelled against Roman rule. The convicts who were crucified with Jesus are called bandits (18:40), the same word used

another way is a thief and a bandit. ²The one who enters by the gate is the shepherd of the sheep. ³The gatekeeper opens the gate for him, and the sheep hear his voice. He calls his own sheep by name and leads them out. ⁴When he has brought out all his own, he goes ahead of them, and the sheep follow him because they know his voice. ⁵They will not follow a stranger, but they will run from him because they do not know the voice of strangers." ⁶Jesus used this figure of speech with them, but they did not understand what he was saying to them.

⁷So again Jesus said to them, "Very truly, I tell you, I am the gate for the sheep. ⁸All who came before me are thieves and bandits; but the sheep did not listen to them. ⁹I am the gate. Whoever enters by me will be saved, and will come in and go out and find pasture. ¹⁰The thief comes only to steal and kill and destroy. I came that they may have life, and have it abundantly.

¹¹"I am the good shepherd. The good shepherd lays down his life for the sheep. ¹²The hired hand, who is not the shepherd and does not own the sheep, sees the wolf coming and leaves the sheep and runs away—and the wolf snatches them and scatters them. ¹³The hired hand runs away because a hired hand does not care for the sheep. ¹⁴I am the good shepherd. I know my own and my own know me, ¹⁵just as the Father knows me and I know the Father. And I lay down my life for the sheep. ¹⁶I have other sheep that do not belong to this fold. I must bring them also, and they will listen to my voice. So there will be one flock, one shepherd. ¹⁷For this reason the Father loves me, because I lay down my life in order to take it up again. ¹⁸No one takes*y* it from me, but I lay it

down of my own accord. I have power to lay it down, and I have power to take it up again. I have received this command from my Father."

¹⁹Again the Jews were divided because of these words. ²⁰Many of them were saying, "He has a demon and is out of his mind. Why listen to him?" ²¹Others were saying, "These are not the words of one who has a demon. Can a demon open the eyes of the blind?"

Jesus Is Rejected by the Jews

²²At that time the festival of the Dedication took place in Jerusalem. It was winter, ²³and Jesus was walking in the temple, in the portico of Solomon. ²⁴So the Jews gathered around him and said to him, "How long will you keep us in suspense? If you are the Messiah,*z* tell us plainly." ²⁵Jesus answered, "I have told you, and you do not believe. The works that I do in my Father's name testify to me; ²⁶but you do not believe, because you do not belong to my sheep. ²⁷My sheep hear my voice. I know them, and they follow me. ²⁸I give them eternal life, and they will never perish. No one will snatch them out of my hand. ²⁹What my Father has given me is greater than all else, and no one can snatch it out of the Father's hand.*a* ³⁰The Father and I are one."

³¹The Jews took up stones again to stone him. ³²Jesus replied, "I have shown you many good works from the Father. For which of these are you going to stone me?" ³³The Jews answered, "It is not for a good work that we are going to stone you, but for blasphemy, because you, though only a human being, are

---

y Other ancient authorities read *has taken*

z Or *the Christ*
a Other ancient authorities read *My Father who has given them to me is greater than all, and no one can snatch them out of the Father's hand*

---

in the synoptic accounts (*Mark* 15:27; *Matt.* 27:38, 44). The author here may be intending to dismiss such messianic pretenders. Rebels are mentioned in *Acts* 5:36–37; fear of such persons is reflected in the arrest of Jesus (*Mark* 14:48; *Matt.* 26:55; *Luke* 22:52) and in the parable of the good Samaritan (*Luke* 10:30, 36). See 18:40. **10:6 figure of speech** The Gk *paroimia,* which occurs only four times in the early Christian texts (10:6; 16:25, 29; *2 Pet.* 2:22), is not the usual word for "parable" although it might be translated "proverb" or "parable." Unlike the Synoptics, in which parables are the characteristic form of Jesus' teaching, *John* rarely has Jesus teach in this way. This may be the only example. **10:10 have life** See 3:16. **10:11 I am** See 4:26. **lays down** Some manuscripts read "give" here and in 10:15. The meaning is the same. Only the Johannine literature uses the idiom "to lay down one's life" for death (10:15, 17–18; 13:37, 38, 15:13; *1 John* 3:16). **10:16** It is debated what *John* means by the phrase *other sheep;* possibly the Gentile mission is to be understood, or the Johannine community itself. See 7:35. **10:19 Jews were divided** The phrase is used in 7:43; 9:16. **10:20 He has a demon** See 7:20. **10:22** The Festival of the Dedication (also called the Feast of Lights, Hanukkah), celebrated in December, was the most recently established feast in the annual religious cycle of the Jews. It was instituted to commemorate the rededication of the temple after the victory of the Jewish leader Judas Maccabeus over the Seleucid (i.e., Syrian-Greek) King Antiochus IV Epiphanes in 164 B.C.E. (*1 Macc.* 4:36–59; *2 Macc.* 1–2; 10:1–8). **10:23 portico** Gk *stoa.* The temple was surrounded by covered columned areas, something like wide walkways. They were the setting for a variety of events, including religious instruction. According to *Acts,* early Christians met regularly in Solomon's portico (3:11; 5:12), on the east side of the temple. **10:25 The works that I do** See 10:37–39; 14:10. **10:31 to stone him** See 8:7. **10:33** The charge of blasphemy appears in several places in the accounts about Jesus: (a) here; (b) in the story of the healing of the paralyzed man (*Matt.* 9:3); and (c) in the trial narratives (*Mark* 14:64; *Matt.* 26:65). Scholars debate the grounds for the charge. See *Lev.* 24:16.

making yourself God." ³⁴Jesus answered, "Is it not written in your law,*ᵇ* 'I said, you are gods'? ³⁵If those to whom the word of God came were called 'gods'— and the scripture cannot be annulled— ³⁶can you say that the one whom the Father has sanctified and sent into the world is blaspheming because I said, 'I am God's Son'? ³⁷If I am not doing the works of my Father, then do not believe me. ³⁸But if I do them, even though you do not believe me, believe the works, so that you may know and understand*ᶜ* that the Father is in me and I am in the Father." ³⁹Then they tried to arrest him again, but he escaped from their hands.

⁴⁰He went away again across the Jordan to the place where John had been baptizing earlier, and he remained there. ⁴¹Many came to him, and they were saying, "John performed no sign, but everything that John said about this man was true." ⁴²And many believed in him there.

The Death of Lazarus

11 Now a certain man was ill, Lazarus of Bethany, the village of Mary and her sister Martha. ²Mary was the one who anointed the Lord with perfume and wiped his feet with her hair; her brother Lazarus was ill. ³So the sisters sent a message to Jesus,*ᵈ* "Lord, he whom you love is ill." ⁴But when Jesus heard it, he said, "This illness does not lead to death; rather it is for God's glory, so that the Son of God may be glorified through it." ⁵Accordingly, though Jesus loved Martha and her sister and Lazarus, ⁶after having heard that Lazarus*ᵉ* was ill, he stayed two days longer in the place where he was.

⁷Then after this he said to the disciples, "Let us go to Judea again." ⁸The disciples said to him, "Rabbi, the Jews were just now trying to stone you, and are you going there again?" ⁹Jesus answered, "Are there not twelve hours of daylight? Those who walk during the day do not stumble, because they see the light of this world. ¹⁰But those who walk at night stumble, because the light is not in them." ¹¹After saying this, he told them, "Our friend Lazarus has fallen asleep, but I am going there to awaken him." ¹²The disciples said to him, "Lord, if he has fallen asleep, he will be all right." ¹³Jesus, however, had been speaking about his death, but they thought that he was referring merely to sleep. ¹⁴Then Jesus told them plainly, "Lazarus is dead. ¹⁵For your sake I am glad I was not there, so that you may believe. But let us go to him." ¹⁶Thomas, who was called the Twin,*ᶠ* said to his fellow disciples, "Let us also go, that we may die with him."

Jesus the Resurrection and the Life

¹⁷When Jesus arrived, he found that Lazarus*ᵉ* had already been in the tomb four days. ¹⁸Now Bethany was near Jerusalem, some two miles*ᵍ* away, ¹⁹and

---

b Other ancient authorities read *in the law*
c Other ancient authorities lack *and understand*; others read *and believe*
d Gk *him*

e Gk *he*
f Gk *Didymus*
g Gk *fifteen stadia*

10:34 *in your law* That is, all of Jewish scripture, not just the Pentateuch, since the quotation is from the psalms, which was a part of the writings—a section of the Jewish scriptures that, according to some theories, was just establishing its place in the Jewish canon in the 1st century. The quotation is from LXX *Ps.* 82:6. **10:41** The reference is to John the Baptist and to his testimony as Christians understood it (1:19–34; 3:27–30). **11:1** *Lazarus* Lazarus is not mentioned in the synoptic accounts, but *Luke* may betray a knowledge of Jesus' friendship with Mary and Martha (10:38–42). Mary is a common name in our literature. If the synoptic and Johannine accounts refer to the same event, Mary, the sister of Martha and Lazarus, may be Mary Magdalene of the Synoptic Gospels (*Mark* 14:3; *Luke* 7:38). The required connection is that the woman of *Luke* 7:36–50 be the Mary mentioned immediately after this passage, in *Luke* 8:2; such a connection is not necessarily intended here. According to *Mark,* which agrees with *John,* the incident took place in Bethany (see *John* 12:2). **Bethany** This is *John*'s only mention of Bethany, a village just two miles outside Jerusalem (11:18), on the eastern side of the Mount of Olives. It appears that Jesus regularly stayed with friends there when he visited Jerusalem (*Mark* 11:11–12; 14:3; *Matt.* 21:17; 26:6). **11:3** *whom you love* (See too 11:36.) In the closing of *John,* the person who guarantees the Johannine traditions is identified simply by a phrase such as "the disciple whom Jesus loved" (19:26; 20:2; 21:7, 20). Linking this description to the description of Lazarus in the present story, some scholars have argued that Lazarus was the implied author of *John.* See notes on the "Beloved Disciple" in the section on authorship in the introduction to *John* (see 19:27). **11:7** This is another trip into Judea mentioned by *John* but not by the synoptic writers. **11:8** *the Jews* Perhaps "the Judeans." See 1:19. **11:9** *twelve hours of daylight* Daylight was divided into twelve equal units, called hours; the night into four watches. Some difference in the length of an hour or a watch occurred from winter to summer. **11:16** This is the first mention of Thomas in *John.* Thomas, whose name means "twin" in Aramaic, plays a prominent role in one of the final scenes of this gospel (20:24–28) and has a visible role in other scenes (14:5; 21:2). The Synoptic Gospels' only reference to Thomas is the mere inclusion of his name in their lists of disciples (*Mark* 3:18; *Matt.* 10:3; *Luke* 6:15). A later tradition *(Acts of Thomas)* portrays Thomas as the twin brother of Jesus, a development not suggested by the explanations of Thomas's name in *John* (20:24; 21:2) and in the *Gospel of Thomas* (prologue).

many of the Jews had come to Martha and Mary to console them about their brother. 20When Martha heard that Jesus was coming, she went and met him, while Mary stayed at home. 21Martha said to Jesus, "Lord, if you had been here, my brother would not have died. 22But even now I know that God will give you whatever you ask of him." 23Jesus said to her, "Your brother will rise again." 24Martha said to him, "I know that he will rise again in the resurrection on the last day." 25Jesus said to her, "I am the resurrection and the life.*h* Those who believe in me, even though they die, will live, 26and everyone who lives and believes in me will never die. Do you believe this?" 27She said to him, "Yes, Lord, I believe that you are the Messiah,*i* the Son of God, the one coming into the world."

Jesus Weeps

28When she had said this, she went back and called her sister Mary, and told her privately, "The Teacher is here and is calling for you." 29And when she heard it, she got up quickly and went to him. 30Now Jesus had not yet come to the village, but was still at the place where Martha had met him. 31The Jews who were with her in the house, consoling her, saw Mary get up quickly and go out. They followed her because they thought that she was going to the tomb to weep there. 32When Mary came where Jesus was and saw him, she knelt at his feet and said to him, "Lord, if you had been here, my brother would not have died." 33When Jesus saw her weeping, and the Jews who came with her also weeping, he was greatly disturbed in spirit and deeply moved. 34He said, "Where have you laid him?" They said to him, "Lord, come and see." 35Jesus began to weep. 36So the Jews said, "See how he loved him!" 37But some of them said, "Could not he who opened the eyes of the blind man have kept this man from dying?"

Jesus Raises Lazarus to Life

38Then Jesus, again greatly disturbed, came to the tomb. It was a cave, and a stone was lying against it. 39Jesus said, "Take away the stone." Martha, the sister of the dead man, said to him, "Lord, already there is a stench because he has been dead four days." 40Jesus said to her, "Did I not tell you that if you believed, you would see the glory of God?" 41So they took away the stone. And Jesus looked upward and said, "Father, I thank you for having heard me. 42I knew that you always hear me, but I have said this for the sake of the crowd standing here, so that they may believe that you sent me." 43When he had said this, he cried with a loud voice, "Lazarus, come out!" 44The dead man came out, his hands and feet bound with strips of cloth, and his face wrapped in a cloth. Jesus said to them, "Unbind him, and let him go."

The Plot to Kill Jesus

45Many of the Jews therefore, who had come with Mary and had seen what Jesus did, believed in him. 46But some of them went to the Pharisees and told them what he had done. 47So the chief priests and the Pharisees called a meeting of the council, and said, "What are we to do? This man is performing many signs. 48If we let him go on like this, everyone will believe in him, and the Romans will come and destroy both our holy place*j* and our nation." 49But one of them, Caiaphas, who was high priest that year, said to them, "You know nothing at all! 50You do not understand that it is better for you to have one man die for the people than to have the whole nation destroyed." 51He did not say this on his own, but being

---

h Other ancient authorities lack *and the life*
i Or *the Christ*

j Or *our temple*; Gk *our place*

11:31 *weep* Or "wail." A ritualized wailing was part of the mourning rites (*Mark* 5:38; *Matt.* 9:23; *Luke* 18:13; 23:48; *Sir.* 38:16–18). Similar mourning still occurs in some Middle Eastern societies. **11:38 *cave*** Burial usually was carried out on the day of death. Interment was in a trench grave or in a tomb. Caves often served as tombs, but the more wealthy could afford to have a sepulcher cut out of a rock face. Stone slabs would have been used to seal the opening. See the accounts of Jesus' burial (*Mark* 15:46; *John* 20:1). **11:44 *strips of cloth*** In the burial fashion of the day, the limbs would have been wrapped tightly to the body of the corpse (20:6–7). **11:47 *council*** Or "Sanhedrin," Gk *synedrion.* **11:48 *Romans will come*** Perhaps a touch of Johannine irony. At the probable time of *John*'s writing, Jerusalem and the temple had already been destroyed by the Roman armies. **11:49 *Caiaphas, who was high priest that year*** This need not suggest that the high priest served only a one-year term, although this practice could be found in some religions of the Mediterranean area, especially the imperial cult. The phrase may mean, as Origen suggested, "in that memorable year." Caiaphas was high priest from 18 to 36 C.E. He had an exceptionally long tenure during a period in which the holder of that office was secure only as long as he remained in favor with the governor. **11:51** A striking display of Johannine irony, which readers would have noticed immediately. The high priest who argues that Jesus should be killed to save the nation understands this in one way (i.e., his death would prevent the spread of revolutionary ideas that might provoke the Roman army); the Johannine community understood the death of Jesus as saving in a different way and no doubt read this passage with Jerusalem already ruined and the area occupied by the Roman army.

high priest that year he prophesied that Jesus was about to die for the nation, [52]and not for the nation only, but to gather into one the dispersed children of God. [53]So from that day on they planned to put him to death.

[54]Jesus therefore no longer walked about openly among the Jews, but went from there to a town called Ephraim in the region near the wilderness; and he remained there with the disciples.

[55]Now the Passover of the Jews was near, and many went up from the country to Jerusalem before the Passover to purify themselves. [56]They were looking for Jesus and were asking one another as they stood in the temple, "What do you think? Surely he will not come to the festival, will he?" [57]Now the chief priests and the Pharisees had given orders that anyone who knew where Jesus[k] was should let them know, so that they might arrest him.

Mary Anoints Jesus

12 Six days before the Passover Jesus came to Bethany, the home of Lazarus, whom he had raised from the dead. [2]There they gave a dinner for him. Martha served, and Lazarus was one of those at the table with him. [3]Mary took a pound of costly perfume made of pure nard, anointed Jesus' feet, and wiped them[l] with her hair. The house was filled with the fragrance of the perfume. [4]But Judas Iscariot, one of his disciples (the one who was about to betray him), said, [5]"Why was this perfume not sold for three hundred denarii[m] and the money given to the poor?"

[6](He said this not because he cared about the poor, but because he was a thief; he kept the common purse and used to steal what was put into it.) [7]Jesus said, "Leave her alone. She bought it[n] so that she might keep it for the day of my burial. [8]You always have the poor with you, but you do not always have me."

The Plot to Kill Lazarus

[9]When the great crowd of the Jews learned that he was there, they came not only because of Jesus but also to see Lazarus, whom he had raised from the dead. [10]So the chief priests planned to put Lazarus to death as well, [11]since it was on account of him that many of the Jews were deserting and were believing in Jesus.

Jesus' Triumphal Entry into Jerusalem

[12]The next day the great crowd that had come to the festival heard that Jesus was coming to Jerusalem. [13]So they took branches of palm trees and went out to meet him, shouting,

"Hosanna!
Blessed is the one who comes in
    the name of the Lord—
    the King of Israel!"

[14]Jesus found a young donkey and sat on it; as it is written:
[15] "Do not be afraid, daughter of Zion.
Look, your king is coming,
    sitting on a donkey's colt!"

---

k Gk *he*
l Gk *his feet*
m Three hundred denarii would be nearly a year's wages for a laborer

n Gk lacks *She bought it*

11:55 This is the third Passover mentioned in *John*. See 2:13.   **12:2–8** This is one of the few stories shared by *John* and the Synoptics, though with differences in detail (*Mark* 14:3–9; *Matt.* 26:6–13; *Luke* 7:36–50). Both *John* and the Synoptics place the incident in Bethany, but the synoptic tradition has it occur in Simon's house and *John* says it was in the home of Mary, Martha, and Lazarus. The woman is not named in the synoptic account, but the suggestion is that she was a prostitute; *John* calls her Mary and gives no hint of any impropriety in her conduct. Both accounts mention the expensive ointment, but the synoptic tradition reports that the woman poured it over the head of Jesus and *John* says it was over the feet (which agrees with *Luke*). Except for *Luke*, all agree that "the poor" were the reason that people objected to this "waste," and that it was a symbolic act pointing to the coming burial of Jesus (see 11:1). But the relationship of the various stories is complicated by the appearance of a similar story in *Luke* 7:36–50. There the anointing occurs in Galilee.   **12:3 *pound*** A Roman pound was roughly twelve ounces.   **12:4–6** See 6:71. Judas Iscariot comes off badly even in this account (12:4–6) before his act of betrayal. He is called a thief and is identified as the one who complains about the waste of the expensive ointment. In the synoptic tradition, others protest the waste.   **12:5 *three hundred denarii*** See APPENDIX A.   **12:6 *common purse*** (See 13:29.)   **12:13 *branches of palm tress*** *Mark* 11:8 and *Matt.* 21:8 mention branches, but each uses a different description: *Mark* says "leafy branches" and "cut in the fields"; *Matthew* says "branches from the trees." Palm branches were used at the Feast of Tabernacles; the feast here, however, is another feast, the Passover (*1 Macc.* 13:51). ***Hosanna!*** A Gk transliteration of an Aramaic expression meaning "Help, I pray" or "Save, I pray." The word comes from *Ps.* 118:32, a psalm sung during the Passover. The blessing is also found in the synoptic tradition, but *Luke* does not use the word "Hosanna." See *Mark* 11:9–10; *Matt.* 21:9; *Luke* 19:38. In Gentile churches, the expression came to be equivalent to the word "Praise."   ***King of Israel!*** *Ps.* 118:25–26.   **12:15 *donkey's colt*** Only *John* and *Matthew* connect the colt to a passage in the Bible (*Zech.* 9:9) although all four gospels mention the animal (*Mark* 11:1–7; *Matt.* 21:1–6; *Luke* 19:28–35).

[16]His disciples did not understand these things at first; but when Jesus was glorified, then they remembered that these things had been written of him and had been done to him. [17]So the crowd that had been with him when he called Lazarus out of the tomb and raised him from the dead continued to testify.[o] [18]It was also because they heard that he had performed this sign that the crowd went to meet him. [19]The Pharisees then said to one another, "You see, you can do nothing. Look, the world has gone after him!"

Some Greeks Wish to See Jesus

[20]Now among those who went up to worship at the festival were some Greeks. [21]They came to Philip, who was from Bethsaida in Galilee, and said to him, "Sir, we wish to see Jesus." [22]Philip went and told Andrew; then Andrew and Philip went and told Jesus. [23]Jesus answered them, "The hour has come for the Son of Man to be glorified. [24]Very truly, I tell you, unless a grain of wheat falls into the earth and dies, it remains just a single grain; but if it dies, it bears much fruit. [25]Those who love their life lose it, and those who hate their life in this world will keep it for eternal life. [26]Whoever serves me must follow me, and where I am, there will my servant be also. Whoever serves me, the Father will honor.

Jesus Speaks about His Death

[27]"Now my soul is troubled. And what should I say—'Father, save me from this hour'? No, it is for this reason that I have come to this hour. [28]Father, glorify your name." Then a voice came from heaven, "I have glorified it, and I will glorify it again." [29]The crowd standing there heard it and said that it was thunder. Others said, "An angel has spoken to him." [30]Jesus answered, "This voice has come for your sake, not for mine. [31]Now is the judgment of this world; now the ruler of this world will be driven out. [32]And I, when I am lifted up from the earth, will draw all people[p] to myself." [33]He said this to indicate the kind of death he was to die. [34]The crowd answered him, "We have heard from the law that the Messiah[q] remains forever. How can you say that the Son of Man must be lifted up? Who is this Son of Man?" [35]Jesus said to them, "The light is with you for a little longer. Walk while you have the light, so that the darkness may not overtake you. If you walk in the darkness, you do not know where you are going. [36]While you have the light, believe in the light, so that you may become children of light."

The Unbelief of the People

After Jesus had said this, he departed and hid from them. [37]Although he had performed so many signs in their presence, they did not believe in him. [38]This was to fulfill the word spoken by the prophet Isaiah:
    "Lord, who has believed our message,
        and to whom has the arm of the Lord been
            revealed?"
[39]And so they could not believe, because Isaiah also said,
[40]   "He has blinded their eyes
        and hardened their heart,
    so that they might not look with their eyes,
        and understand with their heart and turn—
            and I would heal them."
[41]Isaiah said this because[r] he saw his glory and spoke about him. [42]Nevertheless many, even of the authorities, believed in him. But because of the Pharisees they did not confess it, for fear that they would be put out of the synagogue; [43]for they loved human glory more than the glory that comes from God.

---

o Other ancient authorities read *with him began to testify that he had called . . . from the dead*

p Other ancient authorities read *all things*
q Or *the Christ*
r Other ancient witnesses read *when*

12:16 did not understand these things at first This comment shows that key elements of early Christian understanding developed after the death and, according to *John*, after the resurrection of Jesus. Much scholarship on the early church attempts to identify and separate the *historical* material in the gospels from the *theological* reflection of the church at the time the gospels were compiled about forty years after Jesus' life. **12:20 Greeks** See 7:35. **12:21–22 Philip** See 1:43. *Andrew.* See 1:40. **12:23 glorified** *John*'s word for the passion and vindication/resurrection of Jesus. **12:24** *1 Cor.* 15:36. **12:25** *Mark* 8:35; *Matt.* 10:39; *Luke* 17:33. **12:27** Although the context is different, the language is similar to Jesus' prayer in Gethsemane, recorded in *Mark* 14:32–36 and *Matt.* 26:36–39 (see *Luke* 22:41–42: the Mount of Olives) but unmentioned in *John* (18:1). **hour** See notes to 2:4; 13:1. **12:31** (See too 14:30; 16:11.) In the gospels, only *John* uses the expression *ruler of this world* for Satan. *John* often refers to the negative relationship between the world and God (see *Barn.* 4.13; Ign. *Trall.* 4.2; Ign. *Rom.* 7.1). **12:32 lifted up** See 3:14. **all people** Other ancient authorities read "all things." In Gk, the difference is slight: *all people* is *pantas;* "all things" is *panta.* **12:34 the law** See 10:34. **remains forever** *Ps.* 89:36; 110:4; *Isa.* 9:6–7; *Dan.* 7:14. **Son of Man** See 1:51. **12:35 light** See 1:4, 9; 12:46. **12:38** *Isa.* 53:1. The author probably is following the LXX here, which has the word "Lord," missing in the MT. *Rom.* 10:16. **12:40** LXX *Isa.* 6:9–10. See *Mark* 4:12; *Matt.* 13:15. **12:42** This is the 2d of three times when the author expresses a concern about being excommunicated from the synagogue. See 9:22.

Summary of Jesus' Teaching

44Then Jesus cried aloud: "Whoever believes in me believes not in me but in him who sent me. 45And whoever sees me sees him who sent me. 46I have come as light into the world, so that everyone who believes in me should not remain in the darkness. 47I do not judge anyone who hears my words and does not keep them, for I came not to judge the world, but to save the world. 48The one who rejects me and does not receive my word has a judge; on the last day the word that I have spoken will serve as judge, 49for I have not spoken on my own, but the Father who sent me has himself given me a commandment about what to say and what to speak. 50And I know that his commandment is eternal life. What I speak, therefore, I speak just as the Father has told me."

Jesus Washes the Disciples' Feet

13 Now before the festival of the Passover, Jesus knew that his hour had come to depart from this world and go to the Father. Having loved his own who were in the world, he loved them to the end. 2The devil had already put it into the heart of Judas son of Simon Iscariot to betray him. And during supper 3Jesus, knowing that the Father had given all things into his hands, and that he had come from God and was going to God, 4got up from the table,s took off his outer robe, and tied a towel around himself. 5Then he poured water into a basin and began to wash the disciples' feet and to wipe them with the towel that was tied around him. 6He came to Simon Peter, who said to him, "Lord, are you going to wash my feet?" 7Jesus answered, "You do not know now what I am doing, but later you will understand." 8Peter said to him, "You will never wash my feet." Jesus answered, "Unless I wash you, you have no share with me." 9Simon Peter said to him, "Lord, not my feet only but also my hands and my head!" 10Jesus said to him, "One who has bathed does not need to wash, except for the feet,t but is entirely clean. And youu are clean, though not all of you." 11For he knew who was to betray him; for this reason he said, "Not all of you are clean."

12After he had washed their feet, had put on his robe, and had returned to the table, he said to them, "Do you know what I have done to you? 13You call me Teacher and Lord—and you are right, for that is what I am. 14So if I, your Lord and Teacher, have washed your feet, you also ought to wash one another's feet. 15For I have set you an example, that you also should do as I have done to you. 16Very truly, I tell you, servantsv are not greater than their master, nor are messengers greater than the one who sent them. 17If you know these things, you are blessed if you do them. 18I am not speaking of all of you; I know whom I have chosen. But it is to fulfill the scripture, 'The one who ate my breadw has lifted his

---

s Gk *from supper*

---

t Other ancient authorities lack *except for the feet*
u The Greek word for *you* here is plural
v Gk *slaves*
w Other ancient authorities read *ate bread with me*

12:52 *dispersed children of God* See 7:35. **13:1** *John* differs from the synoptic tradition in placing the Last Supper on the evening before the Passover. Scholars have tried to reconcile the different dates, frequently appealing to the thesis that the authors were calculating dates on the basis of different calendars; this is not an impossible explanation, since different religious groups sometimes used different calendars (the evidence comes mainly from Qumran). The synoptic tradition views the Last Supper as a Passover meal; *John,* placing the Last Supper one day earlier, views the death of Jesus, which occurred the day after the Last Supper, as taking place at the time of the sacrifice of the Passover lambs, before the Passover meal. Thus, Jesus is implicitly presented as the true Passover lamb. This would recall the comment early in *John* attributed to John the Baptist, identifying Jesus as the Lamb of God (1:29), and the Eucharistic-like language of an earlier dispute in *John* (6:48–59). It is noteworthy, however, that, unlike the synoptic tradition, *John* gives no account of the institution of the Eucharist. See 18:28; 19:14. ***his hour had come*** Up to this point, Jesus has repeatedly said that his "hour" had not yet come (2:4; 7:30; 8:20). Now this changes. It has been argued that this declaration marks the significant division in *John.* The 1st half dealt with Jesus' ministry and public teaching; this 2d half deals largely with a one-day period: the night of the Last Supper, and the trial and execution that followed on the next day. It concludes with accounts of resurrection appearances. **13:2 *Judas*** See 6:71; 12:6. The account of Judas at the Last Supper is much more extensive in *John* than in the Synoptics (*Mark* 14:10–11; 18–21; *Matt.* 26:14–16, 21–25; *Luke* 22:3–6, 21–23). In *John,* Judas is mentioned by name or hinted at in 13:2, 11, 18, 21–31 in the Last Supper account and appears in other scenes noted above. The synoptic traditions indicate merely that the betrayer was at the table (*Luke* 22:21) or that he dipped at the same time as Jesus (*Mark* 14:20; *Matt.* 26:23). In *John,* Jesus specifically dips bread himself and hands it to Judas (13:26). **13:4–11** The story of Jesus' washing the disciples' feet is found only in *John,* and in considerable detail. Some trace of this story may be hinted at in *Luke* 22:27. It was customary to provide guests with the means to freshen up, and in a society where people walked on dusty roads in sandals, this meant providing water. But the host's slave, not the host, would have done the actual washing (*Luke* 7:44). **13:16 *messengers*** In the Gk, the singular form *apostolos* may be the better reading here. The word means simply "sent one." It is the only use of the word in *John.* The synoptic writers use the word "apostle" for the disciples; *John* does not. **13:18** *Ps.* 41:9.

heel against me.' [19]I tell you this now, before it occurs, so that when it does occur, you may believe that I am he.[x] [20]Very truly, I tell you, whoever receives one whom I send receives me; and whoever receives me receives him who sent me."

Jesus Foretells His Betrayal

[21]After saying this Jesus was troubled in spirit, and declared, "Very truly, I tell you, one of you will betray me." [22]The disciples looked at one another, uncertain of whom he was speaking. [23]One of his disciples—the one whom Jesus loved—was reclining next to him; [24]Simon Peter therefore motioned to him to ask Jesus of whom he was speaking. [25]So while reclining next to Jesus, he asked him, "Lord, who is it?" [26]Jesus answered, "It is the one to whom I give this piece of bread when I have dipped it in the dish."[y] So when he had dipped the piece of bread, he gave it to Judas son of Simon Iscariot.[z] [27]After he received the piece of bread,[a] Satan entered into him. Jesus said to him, "Do quickly what you are going to do." [28]Now no one at the table knew why he said this to him. [29]Some thought that, because Judas had the common purse, Jesus was telling him, "Buy what we need for the festival"; or, that he should give something to the poor. [30]So, after receiving the piece of bread, he immediately went out. And it was night.

The New Commandment

[31]When he had gone out, Jesus said, "Now the Son of Man has been glorified, and God has been glorified in him. [32]If God has been glorified in him,[b] God will also glorify him in himself and will glorify him at once. [33]Little children, I am with you only a little longer. You will look for me; and as I said to the Jews so now I say to you, 'Where I am going, you cannot come.' [34]I give you a new commandment, that you love one another. Just as I have loved you, you also should love one another. [35]By this everyone will know that you are my disciples, if you have love for one another."

Jesus Foretells Peter's Denial

[36]Simon Peter said to him, "Lord, where are you going?" Jesus answered, "Where I am going, you cannot follow me now; but you will follow afterward." [37]Peter said to him, "Lord, why can I not follow you now? I will lay down my life for you." [38]Jesus answered, "Will you lay down your life for me? Very truly, I tell you, before the cock crows, you will have denied me three times.

Jesus the Way to the Father

14 "Do not let your hearts be troubled. Believe[c] in God, believe also in me. [2]In my Father's house there are many dwelling places. If it were not so, would I have told you that I go to prepare a place for you?[d] [3]And if I go and prepare a place for you, I will come again and will take you to myself, so that where I am, there you may be also. [4]And you know the way to the place where I am going."[e] [5]Thomas said to him, "Lord, we do not know where you are going. How can we know the way?" [6]Jesus said to him, "I am the way, and the truth, and the life. No one comes to the Father except through me. [7]If you know me, you will know[f] my Father also. From now on you do know him and have seen him."

[8]Philip said to him, "Lord, show us the Father, and we will be satisfied." [9]Jesus said to him, "Have I been with you all this time, Philip, and you still do not know me? Whoever has seen me has seen the Father. How can you say, 'Show us the Father'? [10]Do you not believe that I am in the Father and the Father is in me? The words that I say to you I do not speak on my own; but the Father who dwells in me does his works. [11]Believe me that I am in the Father and the Father is in me; but if you do not, then believe me because of the works themselves. [12]Very truly, I tell you, the one who believes in me will also do the works that I do and, in fact, will do greater works than these, because I am going to the Father. [13]I will do whatever you ask in my name, so that the Father may be glorified in

---

x Gk I am
y Gk dipped it
z Other ancient authorities read Judas Iscariot son of Simon; others, Judas son of Simon from Karyot (Kerioth)
a Gk After the piece of bread
b Other ancient authorities lack If God has been glorified in him

c Or You believe
d Or If it were not so, I would have told you; for I go to prepare a place for you
e Other ancient authorities read Where I am going you know, and the way you know
f Other ancient authorities read If you had known me, you would have known

---

13:23 See 11:3. **13:26** See 13:2. **13:29** *common purse* See 12:6. **13:33** *Little children* This is a common phrase in *1 John* (2:1, 12, 28; 3:7, 18; 4:4; 5:21). **13:34** *love one another* This is a theme both in *John* and in the Johannine letters, suggesting perhaps a common tradition (*John* 15:12, 17; *1 John* 3:11, 14, 23). **13:38** *John* shares this prediction of denial with the synoptic writers (*Mark* 14:26–31; *Matt.* 26:30–35; *Luke* 22:31–34). The scene of the denial begins in 18:27. **14:1** *hearts be troubled* See 14:27. *Believe* Or "you believe." In Gk, the forms are identical. **14:5** *Thomas* See 11:16. **14:8** *Philip* See 1:43. **14:10** *Father is in me* See 10:30, 38; 14:11, 20; 17:11, 21–23. **14:13** *in my name* See 15:16; 16:23–26.

the Son. [14]If in my name you ask me[g] for anything, I will do it.

The Promise of the Holy Spirit

[15]"If you love me, you will keep[h] my commandments. [16]And I will ask the Father, and he will give you another Advocate,[i] to be with you forever. [17]This is the Spirit of truth, whom the world cannot receive, because it neither sees him nor knows him. You know him, because he abides with you, and he will be in[j] you.

[18]"I will not leave you orphaned; I am coming to you. [19]In a little while the world will no longer see me, but you will see me; because I live, you also will live. [20]On that day you will know that I am in my Father, and you in me, and I in you. [21]They who have my commandments and keep them are those who love me; and those who love me will be loved by my Father, and I will love them and reveal myself to them." [22]Judas (not Iscariot) said to him, "Lord, how is it that you will reveal yourself to us, and not to the world?" [23]Jesus answered him, "Those who love me will keep my word, and my Father will love them, and we will come to them and make our home with them. [24]Whoever does not love me does not keep my words; and the word that you hear is not mine, but is from the Father who sent me.

[25]"I have said these things to you while I am still with you. [26]But the Advocate,[i] the Holy Spirit, whom the Father will send in my name, will teach you everything, and remind you of all that I have said to you. [27]Peace I leave with you; my peace I give to you. I do not give to you as the world gives. Do not let your hearts be troubled, and do not let them be afraid. [28]You heard me say to you, 'I am going away, and I am coming to you.' If you loved me, you would rejoice that I am going to the Father, because the Father is greater than I. [29]And now I have told you this before it occurs, so that when it does occur, you may believe. [30]I will no longer talk much with you, for the ruler of this world is coming. He has no power over me; [31]but I do as the Father has commanded me, so that the world may know that I love the Father. Rise, let us be on our way.

Jesus the True Vine

15 "I am the true vine, and my Father is the vinegrower. [2]He removes every branch in me that bears no fruit. Every branch that bears fruit he prunes[k] to make it bear more fruit. [3]You have already been cleansed[k] by the word that I have spoken to you. [4]Abide in me as I abide in you. Just as the branch cannot bear fruit by itself unless it abides in the vine, neither can you unless you abide in me. [5]I am the

---

g Other ancient authorities lack *me*
h Other ancient authorities read *me, keep*
i Or *Helper*
j Or *among*

k The same Greek root refers to pruning and cleansing

14:15 *you will keep* Some Gk versions of the text have the imperative ("keep") in either the present or aorist form instead of the future tense, as it is translated here. In Gk, the difference is far less striking than in the English: the future is *tērēsete*, whereas the imperative is *tērēsēte* or *tērēsate*. Further, the pronounced forms (in contrast to the written forms) would have been almost indistinguishable, especially to a tired scribe copying a dictated text. This variant illustrates well some of the innocent differences found in the texts of early Christian literature, but even here one might wonder whether the change was more conscious, serving some theological agenda. ***keep my commandments*** 14:21–24; 15:10. This theme and various others in this passage are shared with *1 John*, perhaps suggesting a common tradition (*1 John* 2:3–4; 3:22, 24; 5:2–3; *2 John* 6). See the introduction to the Johannine letters. **14:16 *Advocate*** Gk *paraklētos*. The word is sometimes translated "Comforter" or "Helper." It is used for the Holy Spirit only in the Johannine literature (14:26; 15:26; 16:7; *1 John* 2:1). **14:17 *Spirit of Truth*** The phrase is found only in the Johannine literature in our collection (15:26; 16:13; *1 John* 4:6), but the Dead Sea Scrolls also use this term. ***abides with you*** The idea of abiding is the theme of an extended passage in the next chapter (15:4–10) and is mentioned in 6:56. The phrase occurs frequently in the Johannine letters (*1 John* 2:14, 24, 27; 3:9, 24; 4:15, 15; *2 John* 2, 9). **14:19 *no longer see me*** See 7:34, 36; 16:16–19. **14:22 *Judas*** See 6:71; 12:6; *Luke* 6:16; *Acts* 1:13. **14:27 *hearts be troubled*** The discourse ends much as it began (compare 14:1–3 with 14:27b–28a). **14:30 *ruler of this world*** See 12:31. **14:31 *be on our way*** The transition to the next passage is rough. Jesus seemingly has completed his message and is prepared to leave for the garden. But the next verse introduces more discourse, which is extensive. It is not until the beginning of *John* 18 that the scene moves to the garden. Note how much more fluid the transition is when one moves from the last verse of *John* 14 to the first verse of *John* 18: "'but I do as my Father has commanded me, so that the world may know that I love the Father. Rise, let us be on our way.' After Jesus had spoken these words, he went out with his disciples across the Kidron valley." Scholars sometimes attempt to restructure texts on the basis of such anomalies, which seem to give evidence of a seam or interpolation. Rarely is there manuscript evidence, however, for such breaks. Therefore, if there was an interpolation of material into an original document, the addition must have been inserted early. Just as likely an explanation for apparent interpolations is the roughness of an author's style or an author's limited organizational skills. **15:4 *abide*** See 14:17.

vine, you are the branches. Those who abide in me and I in them bear much fruit, because apart from me you can do nothing. 6Whoever does not abide in me is thrown away like a branch and withers; such branches are gathered, thrown into the fire, and burned. 7If you abide in me, and my words abide in you, ask for whatever you wish, and it will be done for you. 8My Father is glorified by this, that you bear much fruit and become*l* my disciples. 9As the Father has loved me, so I have loved you; abide in my love. 10If you keep my commandments, you will abide in my love, just as I have kept my Father's commandments and abide in his love. 11I have said these things to you so that my joy may be in you, and that your joy may be complete.

12"This is my commandment, that you love one another as I have loved you. 13No one has greater love than this, to lay down one's life for one's friends. 14You are my friends if you do what I command you. 15I do not call you servants*m* any longer, because the servant*n* does not know what the master is doing; but I have called you friends, because I have made known to you everything that I have heard from my Father. 16You did not choose me but I chose you. And I appointed you to go and bear fruit, fruit that will last, so that the Father will give you whatever you ask him in my name. 17I am giving you these commands so that you may love one another.

The World's Hatred

18"If the world hates you, be aware that it hated me before it hated you. 19If you belonged to the world,*o* the world would love you as its own. Because you do not belong to the world, but I have chosen you out of the world—therefore the world hates you. 20Remember the word that I said to you, 'Servants*p* are not greater than their master.' If they persecuted me, they will persecute you; if they kept my word, they will keep yours also. 21But they will do all these things to you on account of my name, because they do not know him who sent me. 22If I had not come and spoken to them, they would not have sin; but now they have no excuse for their sin. 23Whoever hates me hates my Father also. 24If I had not done

among them the works that no one else did, they would not have sin. But now they have seen and hated both me and my Father. 25It was to fulfill the word that is written in their law, 'They hated me without a cause.'

26"When the Advocate*q* comes, whom I will send to you from the Father, the Spirit of truth who comes from the Father, he will testify on my behalf. 27You also are to testify because you have been with me from the beginning.

16 "I have said these things to you to keep you from stumbling. 2They will put you out of the synagogues. Indeed, an hour is coming when those who kill you will think that by doing so they are offering worship to God. 3And they will do this because they have not known the Father or me. 4But I have said these things to you so that when their hour comes you may remember that I told you about them.

The Work of the Spirit

"I did not say these things to you from the beginning, because I was with you. 5But now I am going to him who sent me; yet none of you asks me, 'Where are you going?' 6But because I have said these things to you, sorrow has filled your hearts. 7Nevertheless I tell you the truth: it is to your advantage that I go away, for if I do not go away, the Advocate*q* will not come to you; but if I go, I will send him to you. 8And when he comes, he will prove the world wrong about*r* sin and righteousness and judgment: 9about sin, because they do not believe in me; 10about righteousness, because I am going to the Father and you will see me no longer; 11about judgment, because the ruler of this world has been condemned.

12"I still have many things to say to you, but you cannot bear them now. 13When the Spirit of truth comes, he will guide you into all the truth; for he will not speak on his own, but will speak whatever he hears, and he will declare to you the things that are to come. 14He will glorify me, because he will take what is mine and declare it to you. 15All that the Father has is mine. For this reason I said that he will take what is mine and declare it to you.

---

l Or *be*
m Gk *slaves*
n Gk *slave*
o Gk *were of the world*
p Gk *Slaves*

q Or *Helper*
r Or *convict the world of*

15:9 *Father has loved me* See 3:35; 5:20; 10:17. **15:11** *joy may be complete* This phrase is used in 16:24 and 17:13 and in two of the Johannine letters but not in the remainder of the literature in our collection (*1 John* 1:4; *2 John* 12). **15:12** *love one another* See 13:3. **15:13** *lay down one's life* That is, die. See 10:15. **15:18** *world hates you* See 7:7; 17:14; *1 John* 3:13. **15:19** *belong to the world* See 17:14–16. **15:25** *Ps.* 35:19; 69:4 **16:2** This is the third and final time that concern is expressed regarding expulsion from the synagogue. See 9:22.

Sorrow Will Turn into Joy

¹⁶"A little while, and you will no longer see me, and again a little while, and you will see me." ¹⁷Then some of his disciples said to one another, "What does he mean by saying to us, 'A little while, and you will no longer see me, and again a little while, and you will see me'; and 'Because I am going to the Father'?" ¹⁸They said, "What does he mean by this 'a little while'? We do not know what he is talking about." ¹⁹Jesus knew that they wanted to ask him, so he said to them, "Are you discussing among yourselves what I meant when I said, 'A little while, and you will no longer see me, and again a little while, and you will see me'? ²⁰Very truly, I tell you, you will weep and mourn, but the world will rejoice; you will have pain, but your pain will turn into joy. ²¹When a woman is in labor, she has pain, because her hour has come. But when her child is born, she no longer remembers the anguish because of the joy of having brought a human being into the world. ²²So you have pain now; but I will see you again, and your hearts will rejoice, and no one will take your joy from you. ²³On that day you will ask nothing of me.ˢ Very truly, I tell you, if you ask anything of the Father in my name, he will give it to you.ᵗ ²⁴Until now you have not asked for anything in my name. Ask and you will receive, so that your joy may be complete.

Peace for the Disciples

²⁵"I have said these things to you in figures of speech. The hour is coming when I will no longer speak to you in figures, but will tell you plainly of the Father. ²⁶On that day you will ask in my name. I do not say to you that I will ask the Father on your behalf; ²⁷for the Father himself loves you, because you have loved me and have believed that I came from God.ᵘ ²⁸I came from the Father and have come into the world; again, I am leaving the world and am going to the Father."

²⁹His disciples said, "Yes, now you are speaking plainly, not in any figure of speech! ³⁰Now we know that you know all things, and do not need to have anyone question you; by this we believe that you came from God." ³¹Jesus answered them, "Do you now believe? ³²The hour is coming, indeed it has come, when you will be scattered, each one to his home, and you will leave me alone. Yet I am not alone because the Father is with me. ³³I have said this to you, so that in me you may have peace. In the world you face persecution. But take courage; I have conquered the world!"

Jesus Prays for His Disciples

17 After Jesus had spoken these words, he looked up to heaven and said, "Father, the hour has come; glorify your Son so that the Son may glorify you, ²since you have given him authority over all people,ᵛ to give eternal life to all whom you have given him. ³And this is eternal life, that they may know you, the only true God, and Jesus Christ whom you have sent. ⁴I glorified you on earth by finishing the work that you gave me to do. ⁵So now, Father, glorify me in your own presence with the glory that I had in your presence before the world existed.

⁶"I have made your name known to those whom you gave me from the world. They were yours, and you gave them to me, and they have kept your word. ⁷Now they know that everything you have given me is from you; ⁸for the words that you gave to me I have given to them, and they have received them and know in truth that I came from you; and they have believed that you sent me. ⁹I am asking on their behalf; I am not asking on behalf of the world, but on behalf of those whom you gave me, because they are yours. ¹⁰All mine are yours, and yours are mine; and I have been glorified in them. ¹¹And now I am no longer in the world, but they are in the world, and I am coming to you. Holy Father, protect them in your name thatʷ you have given me, so that they may be one, as we are one. ¹²While I was with them, I protected them in your name thatʷ you have given me. I guarded them, and not one of them was lost except the one destined to be lost,ˣ so that the scripture

---

s Or *will ask me no question*

t Other ancient authorities read *Father, he will give it to you in my name*

u Other ancient authorities read *the Father*

---

v Gk *flesh*

w Other ancient authorities read *protected in your name those whom*

x Gk *except the son of destruction*

16:25 *figures of speech* See 10:6. **16:32** *will leave me alone* This seems to refer to the abandonment of Jesus at the time of his arrest, but only *Mark* 14:50 and *Matt.* 26:56 mention such a flight. **17:1–26** This prayer, for which there is no counterpart in the Synoptics, occurs before Jesus and his disciples go to a garden on the Mount of Olives (18:1). In *Mark* and *Matthew*, Jesus' prayer is in Gethsemane. But there may have been a break in the original text (see note to 14:31). *the hour has come* See 6:4; 12:27; 13:1. *glorify* The Gk word is sometimes used in *John* to indicate the death and resurrection of Jesus (12:16, 23; 21:19) **17:5** Here, as in the prologue (1:1), Christ is explicitly portrayed as having existed before the incarnation—that is, before the birth of Jesus. The theme occurs elsewhere in *John* (6:62; 8:58; 17:24). The synoptic tradition lacks these full-blown statements of Christ's divine origin. **17:6** *whom you gave me* See 6:39; 10:29; 17:7, 9, 11, 24; 18:9. **17:12** *destined to be lost* That is, Judas Iscariot. See 6:71.

might be fulfilled. [13]But now I am coming to you, and I speak these things in the world so that they may have my joy made complete in themselves.[y] [14]I have given them your word, and the world has hated them because they do not belong to the world, just as I do not belong to the world. [15]I am not asking you to take them out of the world, but I ask you to protect them from the evil one.[z] [16]They do not belong to the world, just as I do not belong to the world. [17]Sanctify them in the truth; your word is truth. [18]As you have sent me into the world, so I have sent them into the world. [19]And for their sakes I sanctify myself, so that they also may be sanctified in truth.

[20]"I ask not only on behalf of these, but also on behalf of those who will believe in me through their word, [21]that they may all be one. As you, Father, are in me and I am in you, may they also be in us,[a] so that the world may believe that you have sent me. [22]The glory that you have given me I have given them, so that they may be one, as we are one, [23]I in them and you in me, that they may become completely one, so that the world may know that you have sent me and have loved them even as you have loved me. [24]Father, I desire that those also, whom you have given me, may be with me where I am, to see my glory, which you have given me because you loved me before the foundation of the world.

[25]"Righteous Father, the world does not know you, but I know you; and these know that you have sent me. [26]I made your name known to them, and I will make it known, so that the love with which you have loved me may be in them, and I in them."

The Betrayal and Arrest of Jesus

18 After Jesus had spoken these words, he went out with his disciples across the Kidron valley to a place where there was a garden, which he and his disciples entered. [2]Now Judas, who betrayed him, also knew the place, because Jesus often met there with his disciples. [3]So Judas brought a detachment of soldiers together with police from the chief priests and the Pharisees, and they came there with lanterns and torches and weapons. [4]Then Jesus, knowing all that was to happen to him, came forward and asked them, "Whom are you looking for?" [5]They answered, "Jesus of Nazareth."[b] Jesus replied, "I am he."[c] Judas, who betrayed him, was standing with them. [6]When Jesus[d] said to them, "I am he,"[c] they stepped back and fell to the ground. [7]Again he asked them, "Whom are you looking for?" And they said, "Jesus of Nazareth."[b] [8]Jesus answered, "I told you that I am he.[c] So if you are looking for me, let these men go." [9]This was to fulfill the word that he had spoken, "I did not lose a single one of those whom you gave me." [10]Then

---

y Or *among themselves*
z Or *from evil*
a Other ancient authorities read *be one in us*

b Gk *the Nazorean*
c Gk *I am*
d Gk *he*

17:22 *we are one* See 10:30; 17:11.   **18:1** *Kidron valley* The area around Jerusalem is hilly; the main part of the city is on a hill just west of the Mount of Olives, separated from it by the steep Kidron valley.   *a garden* Only *John* mentions the garden; two synoptic writers name the place as Gethsemane (*Mark* 14:32; *Matt.* 26:36). *John* does not describe the agony of Jesus as the Synoptics do; the garden simply sets the scene for the arrest of Jesus. Contrast this to the synoptic Passion Narrative (*Mark* 14:32–42; *Matt.* 26:36–46; *Luke* 22:39–46), where the scene is the turning point of the story, with Jesus in agonizing prayer coming to the decision to die. See 17:1.   **18:3** *a detachment of soldiers* (See also 18:12.) Only *John* mentions the presence of this detachment in addition to the armed men under the temple authorities, reported also in the synoptic tradition. The Roman governor regularly stationed troops in Jerusalem for the Jewish festivals to be at the ready should anti-Roman agitators attempt to stir the swollen crowds of zealous pilgrims into revolt.   *police* Lit. "servants" or "assistants." There was no regular police force in the ancient world. Public order was kept by the magistrate and his assistants and, where necessary, by the army. The temple administration had various servants or assistants—not exactly what we think of as police, who are largely a creation of the 19th century.   *the Pharisees* (See also 7:32.) Only *John* includes the Pharisees in the Passion Narrative, and they are not mentioned again after this brief scene anywhere else during the trial and crucifixion. Although all the gospels charge that Pharisees were involved in loathsome opposition to Jesus, none makes them significant players in the trial itself.   *lanterns and torches* Not mentioned in the synoptic account. According to 18:18, it was cold. It was also the time of the full moon. The Passover occurred in the middle of the month of Nisan, and the Jewish calendar, being lunar, started the new month with the sighting of the new moon. This would have regularly placed the full moon in the middle of the month, at the very time of the Passover. The rainy season would have just been ending. For this time of year, in late March or early April, a cold, wild, and perhaps rainy night, with darkened sky and full moon obscured, would have been at least as likely as the serene scenes of the garden of Gethsemane featured in Christian art.   **18:4** This incident is not in the synoptic tradition. In the synoptic accounts, Jesus is identified by a kiss (a customary Middle Eastern greeting) from the betrayer, Judas. In *John,* Judas leads the group to Jesus but does not identify him. Rather, Jesus takes the initiative and asks, *"Whom are you looking for?"*   **18:5–6** *I am he* Lit. "I am." This is a charged expression in *John,* which helps explain the reaction of the soldiers and crowd. See 4:26.   **18:9** *whom you gave me* See 6:39; 10:28–30; 17:12.   **18:10** *Malchus* Only *John* mentions that Peter was the swordsman in this incident and that the victim's name was Malchus. Both *Luke* and *John* mention that it was the right ear of the servant (*Luke* 22:50).

Simon Peter, who had a sword, drew it, struck the high priest's slave, and cut off his right ear. The slave's name was Malchus. ¹¹Jesus said to Peter, "Put your sword back into its sheath. Am I not to drink the cup that the Father has given me?"

Jesus before the High Priest

¹²So the soldiers, their officer, and the Jewish police arrested Jesus and bound him. ¹³First they took him to Annas, who was the father-in-law of Caiaphas, the high priest that year. ¹⁴Caiaphas was the one who had advised the Jews that it was better to have one person die for the people.

Peter Denies Jesus

¹⁵Simon Peter and another disciple followed Jesus. Since that disciple was known to the high priest, he went with Jesus into the courtyard of the high priest, ¹⁶but Peter was standing outside at the gate. So the other disciple, who was known to the high priest, went out, spoke to the woman who guarded the gate, and brought Peter in. ¹⁷The woman said to Peter, "You are not also one of this man's disciples, are you?" He said, "I am not." ¹⁸Now the slaves and the police had made a charcoal fire because it was cold, and they were standing around it and warming themselves. Peter also was standing with them and warming himself.

The High Priest Questions Jesus

¹⁹Then the high priest questioned Jesus about his disciples and about his teaching. ²⁰Jesus answered, "I have spoken openly to the world; I have always taught in synagogues and in the temple, where all the Jews come together. I have said nothing in secret. ²¹Why do you ask me? Ask those who heard what I said to them; they know what I said." ²²When he had said this, one of the police standing nearby struck Jesus on the face, saying, "Is that how you answer the high priest?" ²³Jesus answered, "If I have spoken wrongly, testify to the wrong. But if I have spoken rightly, why do you strike me?" ²⁴Then Annas sent him bound to Caiaphas the high priest.

Peter Denies Jesus Again

²⁵Now Simon Peter was standing and warming himself. They asked him, "You are not also one of his disciples, are you?" He denied it and said, "I am not." ²⁶One of the slaves of the high priest, a relative of the man whose ear Peter had cut off, asked, "Did I not see you in the garden with him?" ²⁷Again Peter denied it, and at that moment the cock crowed.

18:11 drink the cup An idiom for doing a task (*Mark* 10:38; *Matt.* 20:22). **18:12 officer** Gk *chiliarchos*. This, the technical term for a tribune, literally means "a commander of a thousand men." **18:13–24** A hearing before Annas, the high priest's father-in-law, is not mentioned in the synoptic tradition, which instead has a trial before the Sanhedrin and the high priest. Annas had been high priest himself (6–15 C.E.) (*Luke* 3:2; *Acts* 4:6), and *John* calls him by this title in 18:19. The story of Peter's denial is located here in the Johannine account, but it is located in the hearing before the high priest and Sanhedrin in the synoptic accounts (*Mark* 14:53–65; *Matt.* 26:57–68; *Luke* 22:54–71). The accusation by the maid is shared, but other details differ. Although all accounts mention the crowing of the cock, *John* does not mention Peter's sorrowful reaction. **18:14** See 11:50. **18:15 another disciple** The second disciple is mentioned only by *John*. In many ancient manuscripts, the article is used, thus reading "the other disciple." This suggests that the readers were able to identify him by this description alone. Some scholars think that it refers to the "beloved disciple" (see introduction to *John*). The disciple has unusual access to the courtyard of the high priest because he is *known to the high priest,* a fact that the author mentions twice (18:15, 16), and that may indicate a connection to the Sanhedrin. Unfortunately, the author has provided enough information only to fuel speculation—not to resolve the identification. The Synoptic Gospels place only Peter at the scene and make no effort to explain how he might have had this kind of access. **18:16 the woman** Lit. "girl" or "young female slave." The same word is used in all four gospels. This person is mentioned in all the accounts, but some details differ, and *Mark* and *Matthew* mention a second accusation by a different maid (*Mark* 14:66–69; *Matt.* 26:69–72; *Luke* 22:56–57). **18:17** The accusation in the Johannine account is that Peter was one of Jesus' disciples (but note 18:26). In the synoptic account, the charge is that Peter had been with Jesus (*Mark* 14:67; *Matt.* 26:69; *Luke* 22:56) or was "one of them" (*Mark* 14:69; *Matt.* 26:73; *Luke* 22:58). The substance of the charge is the same. **18:18** Much of this sentence is repeated in 18:25 when the author returns to the scene involving Peter. The examination by the high priest separates the two scenes of denial. There is a bit of dramatic structuring of the narrative here. After Peter's first denial, the story shifts away from Peter to another scene, after which it shifts back; the setting is reestablished by repeating the final lines of the scene before the break. This is the second of three denials. **18:19 the high priest** The reference here is not to the official high priest, Caiaphas, but to the former high priest, Annas, who was still identified by the title (18:24; see 18:13). *John* mentions Caiaphas as high priest in 18:24. The sense here seems to be that the crowds of support that had been growing around Jesus were a matter of concern to the authorities, perhaps because of the potential for armed revolt (18:36). Jesus and his followers had to be sensitive to avoid this danger as much as possible, and in *John*'s portrayal of the trial of Jesus before Pilate, both Jesus and Pilate attempt to clarify the potentially explosive ideas of kingship (18:33–38). **18:27 the cock crowed** (See 13:38.) The synoptic tradition adds an account of Peter's sorrowful reaction (*Mark* 14:72; *Matt.* 26:75; *Luke* 22:61–62). *John* reports no reaction.

Jesus before Pilate

28Then they took Jesus from Caiaphas to Pilate's headquarters.*e* It was early in the morning. They themselves did not enter the headquarters,*e* so as to avoid ritual defilement and to be able to eat the Passover. 29So Pilate went out to them and said, "What accusation do you bring against this man?" 30They answered, "If this man were not a criminal, we would not have handed him over to you." 31Pilate said to them, "Take him yourselves and judge him according to your law." The Jews replied, "We are not permitted to put anyone to death." 32(This was to fulfill what Jesus had said when he indicated the kind of death he was to die.)

33Then Pilate entered the headquarters*e* again, summoned Jesus, and asked him, "Are you the King of the Jews?" 34Jesus answered, "Do you ask this on your own, or did others tell you about me?" 35Pilate replied, "I am not a Jew, am I? Your own nation and the chief priests have handed you over to me. What have you done?" 36Jesus answered, "My kingdom is not from this world. If my kingdom were from this world, my followers would be fighting to keep me

---
e Gk *the praetorium*

---

from being handed over to the Jews. But as it is, my kingdom is not from here." 37Pilate asked him, "So you are a king?" Jesus answered, "You say that I am a king. For this I was born, and for this I came into the world, to testify to the truth. Everyone who belongs to the truth listens to my voice." 38Pilate asked him, "What is truth?"

Jesus Sentenced to Death

After he had said this, he went out to the Jews again and told them, "I find no case against him. 39But you have a custom that I release someone for you at the Passover. Do you want me to release for you the King of the Jews?" 40They shouted in reply, "Not this man, but Barabbas!" Now Barabbas was a bandit.

19 Then Pilate took Jesus and had him flogged. 2And the soldiers wove a crown of thorns and put it on his head, and they dressed him in a purple robe. 3They kept coming up to him, saying, "Hail, King of the Jews!" and striking him on the face. 4Pilate went out again and said to them, "Look, I am bringing him out to you to let you know that I find no case against him." 5So Jesus came out, wearing the crown of thorns and the purple robe. Pilate said to them, "Here is the man!" 6When the chief priests and

---

18:28 headquarters Lit. "praetorium." This is the technical term for the procurator's official residence. It is unclear whether Pilate, the procurator (governor), would have stayed in Herod's palace or in the more central and secure Antonia fortress during the feast. **ritual defilement** Some Jews would have considered themselves made ritually impure by entering a Gentile house. **Passover** *John*'s chronology places the Passover the day after the Last Supper, contrary to the synoptic tradition, which makes the Last Supper a Passover meal (*Mark* 14:12; *Matt.* 26:17; *Luke* 22:7–8). In *John*'s chronology, the death of Jesus takes place at the time of the death of the Passover lambs, a significant theological point for *John*. See 13:1; 19:14. **18:29** Pilate was procurator 26–36 C.E. The trial before Pilate is central in all the Synoptics, as it is here (*Mark* 15:1–15; *Matt.* 27:1–2, 11–26; *Luke* 23:1–25). The initial dialogue between the Jewish leaders and Pilate (18:29–32) is not found in the synoptic accounts. **18:30 criminal** Lit. "doer of evil." There are several textual variants at this point. **18:31** Scholars disagree about the degree to which the Romans restricted the right of local authorities to impose capital punishment, but the evidence suggests that the Romans were extremely sensitive about this right, reserving it as one of their special prerogatives in client or conquered states. **18:32** See 12:32–33. **18:33 Are you the King of the Jews?** All four gospels record this as one of Pilate's primary questions to Jesus (*Mark* 15:2; *Matt.* 27:11; *Luke* 23:3). The conversation between Jesus and Pilate is more extended here than in the synoptic account, where Jesus is almost totally silent—to the amazement of the audience, given the seriousness of the charges against him (*Mark* 15:4–5; *Matt.* 27:12–14; *Luke* 23:9). **18:38** Both *Luke* (23:4, 13–16, 22) and *John* seem at pains to show that Pilate was unable to find a solid case against Jesus (*John* 19:4). According to these accounts, Pilate then tried to find a way to release Jesus; failing, he then gave in to the pressure of the Jews and sent Jesus to his death. Both *Mark* and *Matthew* present a similar portrait of Pilate but emphasize different details (*Mark* 15:10, 14; *Matt.* 27:18–19, 23). **18:39 you have a custom** Such a custom is mentioned also in the Synoptics (*Mark* 15:6; *Matt.* 27:15), but we have no evidence about this custom from other sources. **18:40 Barabbas** Mentioned in this role in all four gospels (*Mark* 15:6–14; *Matt.* 27:15–23; *Luke* 23:17–23) but otherwise unknown. The name Barabbas appears to be a Gk rendering of an Aramaic name—perhaps a nickname—"the son of Abba" or possibly "the son of the father." **bandit** Or "rebel" (*Mark* 15:7; *Luke* 19:23, 25). Rebels, or terrorist groups, even today often engage in robberies. In the years leading up to the Jewish revolt against Rome in 66 C.E., areas of Palestine became unsafe for foreigners and wealthy Jews. Many Jews with rural estates lived in towns or cities for protection. See 10:1. **19:1–3** This is a strange point in a trial to have a prisoner beaten. Under Roman law, a convicted prisoner, as punishment, might receive a "light" beating just before release. A person condemned to death might receive a beating as part of his more severe punishment. *John* has the beating take place before any conviction, unlike the synoptic tradition (*Mark* 15:15; *Matt.* 27:26). *Mark* and *Matthew* provide other details similar to those in *John*: the crown of thorns; the colored robe to indicate royalty; the mocking shout. The scene would have been a rowdy one, with the foreign soldiers making howling sport of their dazed prisoner. **19:4–15** This incident has no parallel in the synoptic tradition.

the police saw him, they shouted, "Crucify him! Crucify him!" Pilate said to them, "Take him yourselves and crucify him; I find no case against him." 7The Jews answered him, "We have a law, and according to that law he ought to die because he has claimed to be the Son of God."

8Now when Pilate heard this, he was more afraid than ever. 9He entered his headquarters*f* again and asked Jesus, "Where are you from?" But Jesus gave him no answer. 10Pilate therefore said to him, "Do you refuse to speak to me? Do you not know that I have power to release you, and power to crucify you?" 11Jesus answered him, "You would have no power over me unless it had been given you from above; therefore the one who handed me over to you is guilty of a greater sin." 12From then on Pilate tried to release him, but the Jews cried out, "If you release this man, you are no friend of the emperor. Everyone who claims to be a king sets himself against the emperor."

13When Pilate heard these words, he brought Jesus outside and sat*g* on the judge's bench at a place called The Stone Pavement, or in Hebrew*h* Gabbatha. 14Now it was the day of Preparation for the Passover; and it was about noon. He said to the Jews, "Here is your King!" 15They cried out, "Away with him! Away with him! Crucify him!" Pilate asked them, "Shall I crucify your King?" The chief priests answered, "We have no king but the emperor." 16Then he handed him over to them to be crucified.

The Crucifixion of Jesus

So they took Jesus; 17and carrying the cross by himself, he went out to what is called The Place of the Skull, which in Hebrew*h* is called Golgotha. 18There they crucified him, and with him two others, one on either side, with Jesus between them. 19Pilate also had an inscription written and put on the cross. It read, "Jesus of Nazareth,*i* the King of the Jews." 20Many of the Jews read this inscription, because the place where Jesus was crucified was near the city; and it was written in Hebrew,*h* in Latin, and in Greek. 21Then the chief priests of the Jews said to Pilate, "Do not write, 'The King of the Jews,' but, 'This man said, I am King of the Jews.'" 22Pilate answered, "What I have written I have written." 23When the soldiers had crucified Jesus, they took his clothes and divided them into four parts, one for each soldier. They also took his tunic; now the tunic was seamless, woven in one piece from the top. 24So they said to one another, "Let us not tear it, but cast lots for it to see who will get it." This was to fulfill what the scripture says,

"They divided my clothes among themselves,
    and for my clothing they cast lots."

25And that is what the soldiers did.

---

f Gk *the praetorium*
g Or *seated him*
h That is, *Aramaic*

i Gk *the Nazorean*

19:7 *the Son of God* See 10:33. **19:11** Unlike *John,* the synoptic tradition records no dialogue between Jesus and Pilate, other than Jesus' cryptic reply to Pilate's initial question (*Mark* 15:2–5; *Matt.* 27:11–14; *Luke* 23:3). Indeed, the accounts in *Mark* and *Matthew* state explicitly that Jesus did not further answer the charges. See note to *John* 18:33. *guilty* This is a difficult passage, but the author probably means the Jewish leaders rather than Judas here, since the author's purpose has been to put the blame for Jesus' death squarely on the shoulders of the leadership. **19:12** *friend of the emperor* This term was used officially to indicate a special recognized status. **19:14** *day of Preparation for the Passover John* places the crucifixion one day earlier than the synoptic writers; it seems designed to associate the killing of the Jewish Passover lambs with the death of Jesus. In the synoptic account, the Last Supper is the Passover meal, which requires a different chronology. See 13:1; 18:28. *noon* Lit. "the sixth hour." *Mark* says that Jesus was crucified at 9:00 A.M. and that darkness set in at noon (15:25, 33). **19:17–18** Condemned prisoners carried the cross-beam. This would be hoisted and nailed to the main stake. The main stake apparently was left in the ground permanently and could be reused. The Synoptic Gospels speak of a Simon of Cyrene, who was forced to carry Jesus' cross (*Mark* 15:21; *Matt.* 27:32; *Luke* 23:26). **19:17** *Golgotha* The Synoptics agree that the place of crucifixion was called Golgotha, or "the Skull," and that two others were crucified with Jesus. **19:19–22** *an inscription* Greek *titlos,* an official notice. The synoptic accounts simply mention the inscription's reading, "The King of the Jews." In *John,* the inscription includes the name of the convicted, *Jesus of Nazareth,* and the charge, which appears in three languages. Only *John* mentions a protest of the Jewish leaders to the inscription, but it lacks a scene in which the leaders and crowds taunt and mock Jesus as he dies. **19:23–24** Generally people wore two pieces of clothing: a long undershirt or tunic, for men knee or ankle length, and an outer wrap. It was the custom for the soldiers who carried out the execution to divide the personal effects of the victim among themselves. Only *John* mentions that the outer garment was divided (or cut into four pieces) while the soldiers gambled for the main tunic, which makes the scene reflect *Ps.* 22:18 (LXX 21:19), and only *John* connects this action to the fulfillment of scripture. The Synoptics simply indicate that the soldiers divided the clothes by casting lots (*Matt.* 27:35; *Luke* 23:34b); see also *Barn.* 6.24. The quote follows the LXX, which uses the past tense rather than the present. **19:25** *Mary Magdalene* All accounts except *Luke* mention the names of the women here; *Luke* names them later (24:10). All accounts agree that Mary Magdalene was present, along with at least one other Mary and other women, but it is difficult to work out

Meanwhile, standing near the cross of Jesus were his mother, and his mother's sister, Mary the wife of Clopas, and Mary Magdalene. [26]When Jesus saw his mother and the disciple whom he loved standing beside her, he said to his mother, "Woman, here is your son." [27]Then he said to the disciple, "Here is your mother." And from that hour the disciple took her into his own home.

[28]After this, when Jesus knew that all was now finished, he said (in order to fulfill the scripture), "I am thirsty." [29]A jar full of sour wine was standing there. So they put a sponge full of the wine on a branch of hyssop and held it to his mouth. [30]When Jesus had received the wine, he said, "It is finished." Then he bowed his head and gave up his spirit.

Jesus' Side Is Pierced

[31]Since it was the day of Preparation, the Jews did not want the bodies left on the cross during the sabbath, especially because that sabbath was a day of great solemnity. So they asked Pilate to have the legs of the crucified men broken and the bodies removed. [32]Then the soldiers came and broke the legs of the first and of the other who had been crucified with

him. [33]But when they came to Jesus and saw that he was already dead, they did not break his legs. [34]Instead, one of the soldiers pierced his side with a spear, and at once blood and water came out. [35](He who saw this has testified so that you also may believe. His testimony is true, and he knows[j] that he tells the truth.) [36]These things occurred so that the scripture might be fulfilled, "None of his bones shall be broken." [37]And again another passage of scripture says, "They will look on the one whom they have pierced."

The Burial of Jesus

[38]After these things, Joseph of Arimathea, who was a disciple of Jesus, though a secret one because of his fear of the Jews, asked Pilate to let him take away the body of Jesus. Pilate gave him permission; so he came and removed his body. [39]Nicodemus, who had at first come to Jesus by night, also came, bringing a mixture of myrrh and aloes, weighing about a hundred pounds. [40]They took the body of Jesus and wrapped it with the spices in linen cloths,

---

j Or *there is one who knows*

all the identities (*Mark* 40; *Matt.* 27:56). *John* never records the name of Jesus' mother, although she appears in two other places (2:1–5, 12; 6:42; see 20:1). **19:26–27** The scene in which the dying Jesus places his mother in the care of the beloved disciple does not appear in the synoptic tradition. A tradition developed that John the disciple became the guardian of Mary after Jesus' death. Further tradition places both John and Mary in Ephesus later in the century. A question arises about the apparent absence of Jesus' brothers at this time and their role as guardian of their mother. Jesus' brothers quickly assumed a leadership role in the Jerusalem church, but we can only speculate as to when they came to be involved in the Jesus movement. The gospels portray initial opposition to Jesus by his own family (7:5; *Mark* 3:21). **19:26 disciple whom he loved** This description has been used to identify John as the mysterious disciple who guarantees the tradition (19:35; see 11:3). See also the section on authorship in the introduction to John. **19:28** *Ps.* 69:21. The words *I am thirsty* do not occur in the synoptic account. **19:29 hyssop** Only *John* mentions the use of the hyssop here. The plant was used in the Passover ritual to sprinkle the door with blood from the sacrificial lamb (*Exod.* 12:22), and the author may be consciously connecting the Passover preparation and the crucifixion, both of which were occurring at the same time (see 13:1; 18:28; 19:14). The synoptic tradition oddly relates the drink to what they thought was a call for Elijah (*Mark* 15:36; *Matt.* 27:48–49). **19:30 It is finished** These words do not occur in the synoptic accounts. **19:31 day of Preparation** That is, the day before the Sabbath. This is not mentioned by the synoptic writers. All authors place the death of Jesus on the day before the Sabbath and the resurrection on Sunday. The synoptic authors make much of Jesus' resurrection "on the third day" or in "three days," and this tradition recurs in various early Christian writings (*Acts* 10:40; *1 Cor.* 15:4). Even *John* has one comment that suggests the author knows this tradition (2:19). See 19:14, where the phrase "day of Preparation" relates to the Passover. **19:33–37** Only *John* refers to the breaking of the other prisoners' legs and the thrusting of the spear into Jesus' side, although some early manuscripts of *Matthew* add this incident after 27:49. Both aspects are tied by *John* to the Jewish scriptures. For the breaking of the bones, *John* points to *Ps.* 34:20 but conforms it in some ways to the language of *Exod.* 12:46 or *Num.* 9:12. For the piercing of Jesus' side, the author has in mind *Zech.* 12:10. This image of Jesus later appears in *Rev.* 1:7. It is likely that the author consciously associated Jesus with the Passover lamb, whose bones could not be broken. Somewhat before *John* was written, Paul spoke of Jesus as the Passover lamb (*1 Cor.* 5:7). **19:38–39** Only Joseph of Arimathea is mentioned in the synoptic tradition; both he and Nicodemus are mentioned by *John*. *John* reports that Joseph was a secret disciple because of his "fear of the Jews," which is not hinted at in the Synoptics (*Mark* 15:43; *Matt.* 27:57–58; *Luke* 23:50–51). Fear of the Jews is a theme in *John,* perhaps reflecting the Johannine community's own experience (7:13; 9:22; 20:19). **19:39–40** The synoptic tradition does not mention at this point the spices used in the burial of Jesus; two of the synoptic writers later mention spices that the women bring after the Sabbath, not on the day of Preparation, to prepare the body (*Mark* 16:1; *Luke* 24:1). The quantity of spices mentioned by *John* is surprising (one Roman pound was about three-quarters of our pound). Regarding the material used to wrap the body, *John* seems to suggest the use of strips of cloth wrapped around the corpse and holding in the spices, as in the burial of Lazarus (11:44; 20:6–7). The synoptic writers suggest that a large linen sheet was used, similar to the shroud of Turin (*Mark* 15:46; *Matt.* 27:59; *Luke* 23:53).

according to the burial custom of the Jews. ⁴¹Now there was a garden in the place where he was crucified, and in the garden there was a new tomb in which no one had ever been laid. ⁴²And so, because it was the Jewish day of Preparation, and the tomb was nearby, they laid Jesus there.

The Resurrection of Jesus

20 Early on the first day of the week, while it was still dark, Mary Magdalene came to the tomb and saw that the stone had been removed from the tomb. ²So she ran and went to Simon Peter and the other disciple, the one whom Jesus loved, and said to them, "They have taken the Lord out of the tomb, and we do not know where they have laid him." ³Then Peter and the other disciple set out and went toward the tomb. ⁴The two were running together, but the other disciple outran Peter and reached the tomb first. ⁵He bent down to look in and saw the linen wrappings lying there, but he did not go in. ⁶Then Simon Peter came, following him, and went into the tomb. He saw the linen wrappings lying there, ⁷and the cloth that had been on Jesus' head, not lying with the linen wrappings but rolled up in a place by itself. ⁸Then the other disciple, who reached the tomb first, also went in, and he saw and believed; ⁹for as yet they did not understand the scripture, that he must rise from the dead. ¹⁰Then the disciples returned to their homes.

Jesus Appears to Mary Magdalene

¹¹But Mary stood weeping outside the tomb. As she wept, she bent over to look^k into the tomb; ¹²and she saw two angels in white, sitting where the body of Jesus had been lying, one at the head and the other at the feet. ¹³They said to her, "Woman, why are you weeping?" She said to them, "They have taken away my Lord, and I do not know where they have laid him." ¹⁴When she had said this, she turned around and saw Jesus standing there, but she did not know that it was Jesus. ¹⁵Jesus said to her, "Woman, why are you weeping? Whom are you looking for?" Supposing him to be the gardener, she said to him, "Sir, if you have carried him away, tell me where you have laid him, and I will take him away." ¹⁶Jesus said to her, "Mary!" She turned and said to him in Hebrew,^l "Rabbouni!" (which means Teacher). ¹⁷Jesus said to her, "Do not hold on to me, because I have not yet ascended to the Father. But go to my brothers and say to them, 'I am ascending to my Father and your Father, to my God and your God.'" ¹⁸Mary Magdalene went and announced to the disciples, "I have seen the Lord"; and she told them that he had said these things to her.

Jesus Appears to the Disciples

¹⁹When it was evening on that day, the first day of the week, and the doors of the house where the disciples had met were locked for fear of the Jews, Jesus came and stood among them and said, "Peace be with you." ²⁰After he said this, he showed them his hands and his side. Then the disciples rejoiced when they saw the Lord. ²¹Jesus said to them again, "Peace be with you. As the Father has sent me, so I send you." ²²When he had said this, he breathed on them and said to them, "Receive the Holy Spirit. ²³If you forgive the sins of any, they are forgiven them; if you retain the sins of any, they are retained."

---

k Gk lacks *to look*

l That is, *Aramaic*

19:41 Only *John* mentions that the tomb was near the place of crucifixion and that it was in a garden, but *Mark* and *Matthew* agree with *John* that the tomb was new—that is, previously unused (*Matt.* 27:60; *Luke* 23:53). The use of this tomb seems to have been made necessary by the approaching sundown and the beginning of the Sabbath (*John* 19:42). *John* makes nothing of the striking parallel in *Isa.* 53:9 although he, more than any other writer of the Passion Narratives, looks for parallels in the Jewish scriptures. **20:1** The synoptic tradition agrees with *John* regarding the presence of Mary Magdalene at the tomb. But the Synoptics mention the presence of other women: *Mark* 16:1 mentions Mary the mother of James, and Salome; *Matt.* 28:1 mentions only "the other Mary"; and *Luke* 23:55 mentions simply the women who had come with Jesus from Galilee. *Matthew*'s account has a different focus here, but the other three gospel writers agree that the resurrection occurred early on Sunday morning and that the stone had been removed (*Mark* 16:2–4; *Luke* 24:1; *John* 20:1). Mary Magdalene plays an important role in *John*: she is the 1st one at the tomb, carries the 1st word to the disciples about the empty tomb, and is the 1st to whom the resurrected Jesus appears (20:1–18). *Mark* 16:9 briefly states that the 1st appearance was to Mary, but this comment appears in a passage thought to have been later added to the text of *Mark*. See *John* 19:25. **20:2** *whom Jesus loved* Again a reference to the so-called beloved disciple (see 11:3). *Luke* 24:10–12 has a similar account of the race to the tomb, but only Peter is named specifically in that account. *John*'s account is much more detailed. **20:9** *John* does not specify the scripture that pointed to the resurrection, but both he and his readers would have been absolutely convinced that this act was the climax of all Jewish scripture. **20:11–18** This story is much more briefly told in the synoptic tradition (*Mark* 16:9–11; *Matt.* 28:9–10). *John* mentions two angels; the Synoptics speak of an angel or unusually attired men (*Mark* 16:5; *Matt.* 28:2–5; *Luke* 24:4). **20:19–29** *Luke* provides a similar account but lacks a role for Thomas (24:36–43), which *John* develops in some detail. **20:22** The theme of the Holy Spirit figures prominently in the Johannine literature; the *Gospel* presents this resurrection appearance as the occasion of the receiving of the Holy Spirit (7:39). In *Acts*, the Spirit comes on the day of Pentecost (*Acts* 2:4).

Jesus and Thomas

24But Thomas (who was called the Twin*m*), one of the twelve, was not with them when Jesus came. 25So the other disciples told him, "We have seen the Lord." But he said to them, "Unless I see the mark of the nails in his hands, and put my finger in the mark of the nails and my hand in his side, I will not believe."

26A week later his disciples were again in the house, and Thomas was with them. Although the doors were shut, Jesus came and stood among them and said, "Peace be with you." 27Then he said to Thomas, "Put your finger here and see my hands. Reach out your hand and put it in my side. Do not doubt but believe." 28Thomas answered him, "My Lord and my God!" 29Jesus said to him, "Have you believed because you have seen me? Blessed are those who have not seen and yet have come to believe."

The Purpose of This Book

30Now Jesus did many other signs in the presence of his disciples, which are not written in this book. 31But these are written so that you may come to believe*n* that Jesus is the Messiah,*o* the Son of God, and that through believing you may have life in his name.

Jesus Appears to Seven Disciples

21 After these things Jesus showed himself again to the disciples by the Sea of Tiberias; and he showed himself in this way. 2Gathered there together were Simon Peter, Thomas called the Twin,*m* Nathanael of Cana in Galilee, the sons of Zebedee, and two others of his disciples. 3Simon Peter said to them, "I am going fishing." They said to him, "We will go with you." They went out and got into the boat, but that night they caught nothing.

4Just after daybreak, Jesus stood on the beach; but the disciples did not know that it was Jesus. 5Jesus said to them, "Children, you have no fish, have you?" They answered him, "No." 6He said to them, "Cast the net to the right side of the boat, and you will find some." So they cast it, and now they were not able to haul it in because there were so many fish. 7That disciple whom Jesus loved said to Peter, "It is the Lord!" When Simon Peter heard that it was the Lord, he put on some clothes, for he was naked, and jumped into the sea. 8But the other disciples came in the boat, dragging the net full of fish, for they were not far from the land, only about a hundred yards*p* off.

9When they had gone ashore, they saw a charcoal fire there, with fish on it, and bread. 10Jesus said to them, "Bring some of the fish that you have just caught." 11So Simon Peter went aboard and hauled the net ashore, full of large fish, a hundred fifty-three of them; and though there were so many, the net was not torn. 12Jesus said to them, "Come and have breakfast." Now none of the disciples dared to ask him, "Who are you?" because they knew it was the Lord. 13Jesus came and took the bread and gave it to them, and did the same with the fish. 14This was now the third time that Jesus appeared to the disciples after he was raised from the dead.

Jesus and Peter

15When they had finished breakfast, Jesus said to Simon Peter, "Simon son of John, do you love me more than these?" He said to him, "Yes, Lord; you know that I love you." Jesus said to him, "Feed my lambs." 16A second time he said to him, "Simon son of John, do you love me?" He said to him, "Yes, Lord; you know that I love you." Jesus said to him, "Tend my sheep." 17He said to him the third time, "Simon son of John, do you love me?" Peter felt hurt because he said to him the third time, "Do you love me?" And

---

m Gk *Didymus*
n Other ancient authorities read *may continue to believe*

o Or *the Christ*

20:31 See note *n* above. In Gk, the difference in spelling between these two textual variants is slight: *may come to believe* is *pisteusēte;* "may continue to believe" is *pisteuēte.* See note on purpose in the introduction to *John.* Many scholars contend that this is the end of an earlier edition of this gospel, with *John* 21 added later, possibly after the death of the beloved disciple. Other scholars see this as merely another resurrection appearance story, having continuity with the rest of the document. **21:6** A similar story is related in *Luke* 5:4–7. **21:9** Fish and bread symbolized the Eucharist in early Christianity, and this may be what the author has in mind here. **21:15** Peter plays a prominent role in *John.* This is perhaps unexpected in a document in which the beloved disciple seems to be the authority behind the tradition. The importance of Peter is most sharply highlighted by the final chapter, in which Peter, not the beloved disciple, is the key player and the beloved disciple is little more than a passive player. This central role of Peter in *John* provides an intriguing puzzle, but we may not have adequate information to solve it. **21:15–17** There may be some play with the word *love* in this passage. In the Gk, two words are used *(phileō* and *agapaō).* Jesus uses *agapaō* the first two times he poses his question; the final time, he uses *phileō.* Peter uses only *phileō.* But we must be careful not to press the difference too much, for the words were widely interchangeable in Gk.

he said to him, "Lord, you know everything; you know that I love you." Jesus said to him, "Feed my sheep. [18]Very truly, I tell you, when you were younger, you used to fasten your own belt and to go wherever you wished. But when you grow old, you will stretch out your hands, and someone else will fasten a belt around you and take you where you do not wish to go." [19](He said this to indicate the kind of death by which he would glorify God.) After this he said to him, "Follow me."

Jesus and the Beloved Disciple

[20]Peter turned and saw the disciple whom Jesus loved following them; he was the one who had reclined next to Jesus at the supper and had said, "Lord, who is it that is going to betray you?" [21]When Peter saw him, he said to Jesus, "Lord, what about him?" [22]Jesus said to him, "If it is my will that he remain until I come, what is that to you? Follow me!" [23]So the rumor spread in the community[q] that this disciple would not die. Yet Jesus did not say to him that he would not die, but, "If it is my will that he remain until I come, what is that to you?"[r]

[24]This is the disciple who is testifying to these things and has written them, and we know that his testimony is true. [25]But there are also many other things that Jesus did; if every one of them were written down, I suppose that the world itself could not contain the books that would be written.

---

p Gk *two hundred cubits*
q Gk *among the brothers*

21:19 According to early tradition, Peter was fleeing Rome when, just a short distance south of the city walls, he was confronted by Jesus. Peter asked him where he was going (Latin: *Quo vadis,* "Where are you going?"); Jesus replied: "To Rome, to be crucified a second time." Convicted, Peter turned back to the city and was crucified upside down, so the story goes. An ancient church marks the supposed location of Peter's encounter with Jesus. **21:23** Many scholars think that this comment is intended to deal with the crisis in the Johannine community that resulted from the death of the beloved disciple.

The Johannine Letters

1 JOHN ✛ 2 JOHN ✛ 3 JOHN

The Johannine Corpus

The three Johannine letters will be considered together, since they have traditionally been treated as a unit and are generally so treated in modern scholarship as well. Specific questions will be addressed in shorter introductions to each letter.

The last two Johannine letters are comparatively short. The first, though longer, is more of an exhortation or sermon, and it lacks all the essential elements of a letter. Stylistically, the letters are too short for convincing linguistic analysis that might help to determine common authorship.

But the letters do share a number of elements that, when taken together, may serve as reasonable enough grounds for assuming common authorship. For example, the second letter has close parallels in the first. It could be described almost as an abstract of the first letter. The themes addressed in these two letters are not addressed elsewhere in quite the same way, suggesting at least that these two works came from the same author. The second letter is linked to the third letter by the description of the author as "the elder." All three share a number of phrases, and the pain of schism and exclusion has affected each. On the basis of such similarities, most attribute the three letters to the same author.

Setting

A schism lies at the heart of these letters. It is different from the schism reflected in the *Gospel of John,* which seems to have involved the expulsion of the Johannine community from the synagogue.[1] In the Johannine letters, the schism seems to involve one group of Johannine believers separating from the others. The schism and the letters stemming from it seem to date from after the rupture with the synagogue, though it is possible that the letters were earlier than the *Gospel.*

---

[1]See introduction to *John.*

Themes and Issues

The theological position confronted by the author of the Johannine letters is usually defined as *docetic*. That term comes from the Greek word meaning *to seem,* and it has become a popular label used to identify a proto-gnostic perspective, distinguishing it from the more developed and complex gnosticism of the second century.

Docetic belief, according to its opponents, questioned the physical reality of Jesus' life (birth, suffering, death, etc.). In other words, Jesus only *seemed* to be a real human, and the various human actions and experiences of Jesus was mere play-acting by a God in human disguise. This view may have derived from the philosophical principle that God, who is pure spirit, cannot truly suffer pain and death.

In *1 John,* the author labels as *antichrist* any view that denies that Jesus had *come in flesh.* These are strong words in a community whose primary claim is that Jesus was the *Christ*—an explicit theme also in the *Gospel of John.* To call the schismatic group *antichrist* is to dismiss them at the point of the fundamental confession they shared with the larger community prior to the schism.

We have little information about what happened to this group, though similar features seem to be characteristic of the theological position confronted by Ignatius in western Asia Minor a decade or so later.[2] The link would be particularly strong if the traditions that place the Johannine community in western Asia Minor are reliable.

A few decades after these letters were written, numerous gnostic systems dotted the Christian map, and there is enough similarity between docetism and gnosticism to link the two movements. Unfortunately, the precise nature of that link is unclear, as is almost everything else about the development of docetism and the origins of gnosticism. Irenaeus, a church leader who grew up in western Asia Minor in the middle of the second century, says that John the disciple, while in Ephesus, engaged in passionate opposition to a person by the name of Cerinthus (Eusebius, *Eccl. hist.* 3.28.6). From the little information we have about this Cerinthus, there do seem to be points of agreement between him and the schismatics of the Johannine letters, and both groups have points of agreement with the schismatics of the Ignatian letters. But it is unclear whether we should associate all three groups to a common schismatic movement.[3]

Authorship

The author calls himself simply "the elder" in the second and third letter, but in the first letter the author does not identify himself. Unfortunately, *elder* could refer to almost any leader of the early church, though we can assume the first readers were able to identify the author merely by that label. Papias, a Christian writer in the early second

---

[2]See the introduction to The Letters of Ignatius, and in particular, the letters to Tralles and Smyrna.

[3]In *3 John,* an otherwise unknown Diotrephes is accused by name; he had disregarded the author's authority and had refused to allow the author's associates access to his group. But the theological position of Diotrephes is not stated. It is only by linking all three letters to a common author and community that we have any grounds for thinking that Diotrephes was docetic.

century, knew of someone called John the elder. Some have identified that John with the author of these three letters (Eusebius, *Eccl. hist.* 3.39.5–6). Mainly, the lack of viable alternatives makes the John of Papias' comment an attractive possibility.

Thus the question of authorship is not one that is likely to be convincingly resolved. Even the three named in the third letter (Gaius, Diotrephes, and Demetrius) do not help; they are otherwise unknown in Christian tradition.

Date

Dating the Johannine letters has proved elusive, even with respect to their relationship to one another. Their thematic unity, however, suggests they were composed around the same time. One theory of dating stems from attempts to trace the development of a "Johannine community" and sees the writings as responses to two major splits in the community. The first split occurs when the community breaks from the synagogue (after 70 C.E.); this trauma is reflected in the *Gospel of John*. The second occurs later within the Johannine community and may have arisen as the community sought to restructure itself. A plausible time for this second schism, which concerned docetic interpretations of Jesus, would be in the late first or early second century.

A second theory of dating contends that the Johannine letters were responding to gnosticism, which had appropriated the *Gospel of John* for its own use. The letters, therefore, attempted to salvage the theology of the *Gospel* for a non-gnostic reading. According to this reconstruction, the letters would have been composed later in the second century.

These two theories as well as others remain speculative and should not unduly control the interpretation of the letters. Nonetheless, we can be fairly certain that a schism precipitated their writing and that they were likely composed after the *Gospel of John*.

Relation to Other Early Christian Writings

The Johannine letters share vocabulary and themes with the *Gospel of John* more than with any other document of early Christianity. The dualistic images of light and darkness, of love and hate, and of truth and lies figure prominently in both, as do the themes of eternal life, abiding, and the close relationship between the Father and the Son.

Further, the Johannine letters were possibly addressed to the same communities as the Ignatian letters. Certainly a similar problem was addressed: a docetic schism that threatened the stability of both communities. The evidence is particularly clear in the letters to Tralles and Smyrna.

Value for the Study of Early Christianity

The Johannine letters and the opposition revealed in these letters may provide a glimpse of two developments in the Johannine tradition: one, a docetic or proto-gnostic direction and, two, an anti-gnostic effort to rescue the *Gospel of John* from such gnostic use. Certainly these letters, particularly *1 John*, show a sharply anti-docetic perspective whose main theological images, nonetheless, are shared with the *Gospel of John*, a gospel that was to be a favorite in gnostic circles.

We must admit, however, that neither the path of development from docetism to mid-second-century gnosticism, nor the path from a distinct Johannine community to its incorporation into the larger church, is clear. Given the lack of relevant materials for the connecting period, scholars have generally been content to assume a link, though we have little idea what that association was.

1 John

The author wrote at a time when the community was still pained by a recent schism and still in danger of finding the other side attractive. The opposition has docetic markings, particularly in their denial of the physical dimension of Jesus' existence, or as the author put it, their denial that *Jesus is come in the flesh.* A similar theological disagreement may be reflected in *2 John,* where the author calls for caution regarding admission into the community.

Although he addresses specific matters, the author discusses almost every issue around the same set of themes. Thus the letter gives a sense of being a larger unit than it perhaps is. This impression is furthered by the author's willingness to introduce and then drop certain themes, only to pick them up again later to develop or repeat them. In doing so, the author makes some units less distinctive than they would have been had he addressed them fully in one place.

In some ways, *1 John* looks like the *written* message that the elder of *2 John* hoped to be able to deliver in person (*2 John* 12). At least, the elder's summary of his concerns in *2 John* (4–11) is as condensed an abstract of the themes of *1 John* as we are likely to find anywhere.

2 John

This shortest document in the Johannine corpus illustrates well the ancient letter form. Yet in some ways it is more a nonletter than a letter, for the author's purpose in writing was to tell the recipients that he would not be writing (v. 12) but would be visiting in person. Then he would tell them what would have otherwise been written.

The main purpose, then, of this our briefest letter is to inform the church of the author's approaching visit. The elder took the opportunity afforded by this note to summarize the important themes he was likely to expand in person and to warn the community to be on guard against docetic teachers (7–8).

Second John could be called the *Reader's Digest* version of *1 John.* All the major themes of the larger work are touched on in such a way that one can infer the substance of *1 John* by reading the much shorter *2 John.*

3 John

As with *2 John*, so with *3 John:* The main reason the elder wrote the letter was to announce that he was planning a visit to address matters in more detail (10, 13). But there was another reason. Gaius had rendered hospitality and financial support to some of the elder's people as they passed through. Such generosity on Gaius' part may have placed Gaius outside the goodwill of members of his own community; the elder wanted Gaius to know that he appreciated his generosity, however others may have reacted.

A number of things, though, are unclear about the situation. We do not know why the elder's people visited Gaius, nor why they were strangers to Gaius if both they and he were prominent players in churches under the influence of the elder. We do not know the purpose of their longer journey (v. 7), but it seems that they were not sent to Gaius's community to straighten out difficulties there; the visit with Gaius seems to have been only part of a more protracted journey, which would require financial support along the way. There is, as well, a puzzling comment that the elder's people would not accept support from nonbelievers—we have no idea what interest nonbelievers would have had in funding these people.

Further, the nature of the dispute between Diotrephes and the elder is a matter of debate. Some scholars see the situation as one in which the issue of the monarchical episcopate (bishop) had arisen. If this was the situation, it is unclear whether the elder or Diotrephes was the one who held this office. Certainly the elder believed that he had some right to speak in the church where Diotrephes had prevented representatives of the elder from being received. But the details are too unclear to establish the role of the players, though Diotrephes must have had considerable local support: he was able to prevent the circulation of the elder's writing addressed to the church (v. 9) and he had been able to cause others to refuse hospitality to the elder's people. Those who did, he was able to have removed from the church.

But *3 John* is only the middle of the story. The first part of the story was the elder's letter that was rejected.[4] The latter part of the story was the elder's announced visit, at which time he planned to confront Diotrephes. We do not know the outcome of that meeting, though it is clear that Diotrephes had the upper hand when *3 John* was written.

For Further Reading

Brown, Raymond. *The Epistles of John*. Anchor Bible 30. Garden City, N.Y.: Doubleday, 1982.

Bultmann, Rudolf. *The Johannine Epistles*. Hermeneia. Philadelphia: Fortress, 1973.

Marshall, I. Howard. *The Epistles of John*. New International Commentary on the New Testament. Grand Rapids: Eerdmans, 1978.

---

[4]The letter is mentioned in v. 9. It apparently did not survive—unless of course it is *1 John* itself.

THE FIRST LETTER OF JOHN

The Word of Life

1 We declare to you what was from the beginning, what we have heard, what we have seen with our eyes, what we have looked at and touched with our hands, concerning the word of life— 2this life was revealed, and we have seen it and testify to it, and declare to you the eternal life that was with the Father and was revealed to us— 3we declare to you what we have seen and heard so that you also may have fellowship with us; and truly our fellowship is with the Father and with his Son Jesus Christ. 4We are writing these things so that our*a* joy may be complete.

God Is Light

5This is the message we have heard from him and proclaim to you, that God is light and in him there is no darkness at all. 6If we say that we have fellowship with him while we are walking in darkness, we lie and do not do what is true; 7but if we walk in the light as he himself is in the light, we have fellowship with one another, and the blood of Jesus his Son cleanses us from all sin. 8If we say that we have no sin, we deceive ourselves, and the truth is not in us. 9If we confess our sins, he who is faithful and just will forgive us our sins and cleanse us from all unrighteousness. 10If we say that we have not sinned, we make him a liar, and his word is not in us.

Christ Our Advocate

2 My little children, I am writing these things to you so that you may not sin. But if anyone does sin, we have an advocate with the Father, Jesus Christ the righteous; 2and he is the atoning sacrifice for our sins, and not for ours only but also for the sins of the whole world.

3Now by this we may be sure that we know him, if we obey his commandments. 4Whoever says, "I have come to know him," but does not obey his commandments, is a liar, and in such a person the truth does not exist; 5but whoever obeys his word, truly in this person the love of God has reached

---

a Other ancient authorities read *your*

1:1 *from the beginning* See 2:13; 14; *John* 1:1. *touched with our hands* Only *Luke* (24:36–43) and *John* (20:24–29) have a post-resurrection scene in which the disciples are invited to touch Jesus. It is considerably more developed in *John*. *concerning the word* The concept of word (Gk *logos*) was introduced in the prologue of *John*. This, along with the phrase *from the beginning*, suggests that the author may be consciously recalling the beginning of the *Gospel*. The case becomes even stronger when the full list of striking parallels between *1 John* and the *Gospel* is examined. **1:2** *we have seen it* Three times in the opening three verses the author seems to speak of being an eyewitness to Jesus' ministry. There is a similar claim in *John* that the tradition was guaranteed by one who knew Jesus firsthand (21:20–24). *with the Father* Both the *Gospel* and this letter repeatedly emphasize the relationship between the Father and the Son; such reference is limited in the Synoptic Gospels to one or two passages. Even the extremely short *2 John* expresses this idea more than the Synoptic Gospels. **1:3** *fellowship* Gk *koinōnian*. The word is used four times in 1:3–7 but nowhere else in the Johannine material. The thought is similar to that expressed by the word "abiding," which is found much more frequently (see 2:5–6). **1:4** *our joy* Other ancient authorities read "your." In Gk the difference is slight: *our* is *hēmōn;* "your" is *hymōn*. *joy may be complete* The idea appears frequently in the Johannine writings (*John* 3:29; 15:11; 16:24; 17:13; *2 John* 12). **1:5** The theme of light and darkness occurs in the prologue of *John* (1:4–5, 9), in other key places in the *Gospel* (3:19–21; 8:12; 9:5; 12:35–36, 46), and in the 1st two chapters of *1 John*. **1:6–7** *walk in darkness . . . walk in light* (2:11; *John* 8:12; 11:10; 12:35). **1:6** *what is true* The themes of truth and lying occur frequently in the Johannine material. For example, the word "truth" occurs twenty-five times in the *Gospel* and twenty times in the letters; the Synoptic Gospels have only seven occurrences in total. Only Paul has such frequent use of the word. **1:8** There is some tension here between clear statements that believers sin (1:10; 2:1; 5:16) and that they should not (2:4; 3:3, 22, 24) or even do not (3:6–10; 5:18). **2:1** *I am writing* This phrase is formulaic here; it is used six times in the 1st half of this chapter (2:1, 7, 8, 12, 13 [twice]) but nowhere else in the Johannine literature. The perfect tense of the verb is also used frequently in a formulaic way (2:14 [three times], 26; 5:13; *3 John* 9). *advocate* Gk *paraklēton*. In our literature, this term is used only here and in *John* 14:16. **2:2** *atoning sacrifice* Gk *hilasmos*. The word is also used in 4:10 but nowhere else in our collection. It appears a few times in the LXX. *whole world* See *John* 1:29 **2:3** *know* This is another favorite word of the Johannine tradition. It occurs in *John* almost as often as it does in the three Synoptic Gospels combined (56 times compared with 60 times); it occurs in the Johannine letters 26 times. **2:5–6** The idea of being in Christ or in the Son is found in both *John* and the Johannine letters (see *John* 14:17). A favorite word to express this idea is "abide." It occurs forty times in the *Gospel* (but only 12 times in the Synoptics) and 27 times in the letters. Almost all of the uses of this word in the Johannine material are metaphorical, referring to abiding in Christ, whereas many of the uses in the Synoptic Gospels express merely the common idea of remaining in a particular physical location

perfection. By this we may be sure that we are in him: ⁶whoever says, "I abide in him," ought to walk just as he walked.

A New Commandment

⁷Beloved, I am writing you no new commandment, but an old commandment that you have had from the beginning; the old commandment is the word that you have heard. ⁸Yet I am writing you a new commandment that is true in him and in you, because[b] the darkness is passing away and the true light is already shining. ⁹Whoever says, "I am in the light," while hating a brother or sister,[c] is still in the darkness. ¹⁰Whoever loves a brother or sister[d] lives in the light, and in such a person[e] there is no cause for stumbling. ¹¹But whoever hates another believer[f] is in the darkness, walks in the darkness, and does not know the way to go, because the darkness has brought on blindness.

12   I am writing to you, little children,
      because your sins are forgiven on account of
        his name.
13   I am writing to you, fathers,
      because you know him who is from the
        beginning.
  I am writing to you, young people,
      because you have conquered the evil one.
14   I write to you, children,
      because you know the Father.
  I write to you, fathers,
      because you know him who is from the
        beginning.

I write to you, young people,
    because you are strong
  and the word of God abides in you,
    and you have overcome the evil one.
¹⁵Do not love the world or the things in the world. The love of the Father is not in those who love the world; ¹⁶for all that is in the world—the desire of the flesh, the desire of the eyes, the pride in riches—comes not from the Father but from the world. ¹⁷And the world and its desire[g] are passing away, but those who do the will of God live forever.

Warning against Antichrists

¹⁸Children, it is the last hour! As you have heard that antichrist is coming, so now many antichrists have come. From this we know that it is the last hour. ¹⁹They went out from us, but they did not belong to us; for if they had belonged to us, they would have remained with us. But by going out they made it plain that none of them belongs to us. ²⁰But you have been anointed by the Holy One, and all of you have knowledge.[h] ²¹I write to you, not because you do not know the truth, but because you know it, and you know that no lie comes from the truth. ²²Who is the liar but the one who denies that Jesus is the Christ?[i] This is the antichrist, the one who denies the Father and the Son. ²³No one who denies the Son has the Father; everyone who confesses the Son has the Father also. ²⁴Let what you heard from the beginning abide in you. If what you heard from the beginning abides in you, then you will abide in the Son and in the Father. ²⁵And this is what he has promised us,[j] eternal life.

---

b Or *that*
c Gk *hating a brother*
d Gk *loves a brother*
e Or *in it*
f Gk *hates a brother*

g Or *the desire for it*
h Other ancient authorities read *you know all things*
i Or *the Messiah*
j Other ancient authorities read *you*

2:7 new commandment (*John* 13:34; *2 John* 5). **2:8** *John* 1:9. **2:11** *John* 12:35. **2:12–14** There is considerable repetition in this brief passage, and some debate as to what the author intends by this repetition. The main difference is the change in the tense of the word "write" in otherwise nearly identical passages. Where the NRSV translators have rendered the passage *I am writing,* in Gk the tense is present; where the NRSV translators have rendered the passage *I write,* in Gk the tense is perfect (often translated "I have written" or "I wrote"). **2:14 word of God abides** *John* 5:38; 15:7. **2:15** The word "world" is another favorite in the Johannine material. It is used 78 times in *John* (but only 14 times in the Synoptics); it is used 24 times in the letters. The world is always set against God, and Christian association with the world is considered dangerous. **2:18 last hour** See *1 Pet.* 1:5. In our literature, the word "antichrist" is used only in the letters of John (*1 John* 2:18, 22; 4:3; *2 John* 1:7), but the idea of an evil opponent or usurper of Christ (either meaning is possible in the Gk) is widespread in apocalyptic literature. **2:19** This is the most explicit note about a schism within the community. We can assume that many of the issues raised in this letter relate directly to the issues of the schism, but we cannot confidently shape a full portrait of the schism from the issues of this letter. The author may be addressing other issues, too. **2:20 anointed by the Holy One** This anointing is probably a reference to the Holy Spirit. In the Gk a noun is used (*chrisma*), thus reading "you have an anointing." The noun is found also in 2:27 but nowhere else in our literature. **you have knowledge** Other ancient authorities read "you know all things." In Gk the difference in wording is slight; *oidate panta* requires the translation "you know all things," while *oidate pantes* requires *all of you have knowledge* (*John* 14:26). **2:25 has promised us** Other ancient authorities read "you." The difference in Gk is slight: *hēmin (us)* or *hymin* ("you").

[26]I write these things to you concerning those who would deceive you. [27]As for you, the anointing that you received from him abides in you, and so you do not need anyone to teach you. But as his anointing teaches you about all things, and is true and is not a lie, and just as it has taught you, abide in him.*k*

[28]And now, little children, abide in him, so that when he is revealed we may have confidence and not be put to shame before him at his coming.

Children of God

[29]If you know that he is righteous, you may be sure that everyone who does right has been born of him. **3** [1]See what love the Father has given us, that we should be called children of God; and that is what we are. The reason the world does not know us is that it did not know him. [2]Beloved, we are God's children now; what we will be has not yet been revealed. What we do know is this: when he*k* is revealed, we will be like him, for we will see him as he is. [3]And all who have this hope in him purify themselves, just as he is pure.

[4]Everyone who commits sin is guilty of lawlessness; sin is lawlessness. [5]You know that he was revealed to take away sins, and in him there is no sin. [6]No one who abides in him sins; no one who sins has either seen him or known him. [7]Little children, let no one deceive you. Everyone who does what is right is righteous, just as he is righteous. [8]Everyone who commits sin is a child of the devil; for the devil has been sinning from the beginning. The Son of God was revealed for this purpose, to destroy the works of the devil. [9]Those who have been born of God do not sin, because God's seed abides in them;*l* they cannot sin, because they have been born of God. [10]The children of God and the children of the devil are revealed in this way: all who do not do what is right are not from God, nor are those who do not love their brothers and sisters.*m*

Love One Another

[11]For this is the message you have heard from the beginning, that we should love one another. [12]We must not be like Cain who was from the evil one and murdered his brother. And why did he murder him? Because his own deeds were evil and his brother's righteous. [13]Do not be astonished, brothers and sisters,*n* that the world hates you. [14]We know that we have passed from death to life because we love one another. Whoever does not love abides in death. [15]All who hate a brother or sister*m* are murderers, and you know that murderers do not have eternal life abiding in them. [16]We know love by this, that he laid down his life for us—and we ought to lay down our lives for one another. [17]How does God's love abide in anyone who has the world's goods and sees a brother or sister*o* in need and yet refuses help?

[18]Little children, let us love, not in word or speech, but in truth and action. [19]And by this we will know that we are from the truth and will reassure our hearts before him [20]whenever our hearts condemn us; for God is greater than our hearts, and he knows everything. [21]Beloved, if our hearts do not condemn us, we have boldness before God; [22]and we receive from him whatever we ask, because we obey his commandments and do what pleases him.

[23]And this is his commandment, that we should believe in the name of his Son Jesus Christ and love one another, just as he has commanded us. [24]All who obey his commandments abide in him, and he abides in them. And by this we know that he abides in us, by the Spirit that he has given us.

Testing the Spirits

4 Beloved, do not believe every spirit, but test the spirits to see whether they are from God; for many false prophets have gone out into the world.

---

k Or *it*
l Or *because the children of God abide in him*
m Gk *his brother*

n Gk *brothers*
o Gk *brother*

---

eternal life See *John* 3:16; 17:3. Eternal life is a prominent theme in the Johannine literature and is uncharacteristic of the synoptic and the Pauline writings. The phrase is used 6 times in *1 John* and 17 times in *John* (compared with 8 occurrences in the Synoptics). **2:27 abide in him** Or "abide in it," referring to the anointing. The Gk forms are identical in this grammatical structure. The theme is also found in *John* (see *1 John* 2:5–6). **2:28 coming** Gk *parousia*. **3:1 children of God** *John* 1:12 **it did not know him** *John* 1:10; 16:3 **3:4–8** See 1:8. **3:8 sinning from the beginning** *John* 8:44. **3:10 children of the devil** *John* 8:44 **3:11** *John* 13:34–35. Love is another favorite theme of the Johannine literature. The verb and noun forms appear 43 times in *John* (compared with a total of 28 times in the Synoptics); the letters have 52 occurrences. It is also a favorite expression of Paul (108 times). From this point on in *1 John*, the theme of love dominates, but the discussion is not methodical. Frequently ideas are picked up, addressed briefly, and dropped, only to be picked up again. **3:12 Cain** Cain is mentioned elsewhere in our literature in *Jude* 11 and *1 Clement* 4. The story of Cain is in *Genesis* 4. **3:13 world hates you** *John* 15:18–19. **3:14 passed from death to life** *John* 5:24. **3:16** *John* 3:16. **3:17** Charity is a common theme in early Christian writings (see *Jas.* 1:10; 2:4). **3:23** *John* 13:34; 15:12, 17.

²By this you know the Spirit of God: every spirit that confesses that Jesus Christ has come in the flesh is from God, ³and every spirit that does not confess Jesus[p] is not from God. And this is the spirit of the antichrist, of which you have heard that it is coming; and now it is already in the world. ⁴Little children, you are from God, and have conquered them; for the one who is in you is greater than the one who is in the world. ⁵They are from the world; therefore what they say is from the world, and the world listens to them. ⁶We are from God. Whoever knows God listens to us, and whoever is not from God does not listen to us. From this we know the spirit of truth and the spirit of error.

God Is Love

⁷Beloved, let us love one another, because love is from God; everyone who loves is born of God and knows God. ⁸Whoever does not love does not know God, for God is love. ⁹God's love was revealed among us in this way: God sent his only Son into the world so that we might live through him. ¹⁰In this is love, not that we loved God but that he loved us and sent his Son to be the atoning sacrifice for our sins. ¹¹Beloved, since God loved us so much, we also ought to love one another. ¹²No one has ever seen God; if we love one another, God lives in us, and his love is perfected in us.

¹³By this we know that we abide in him and he in us, because he has given us of his Spirit. ¹⁴And we have seen and do testify that the Father has sent his Son as the Savior of the world. ¹⁵God abides in those who confess that Jesus is the Son of God, and they abide in God. ¹⁶So we have known and believe the love that God has for us.

God is love, and those who abide in love abide in God, and God abides in them. ¹⁷Love has been perfected among us in this: that we may have boldness on the day of judgment, because as he is, so are we in this world. ¹⁸There is no fear in love, but perfect love casts out fear; for fear has to do with punishment, and whoever fears has not reached perfection in love. ¹⁹We love[q] because he first loved us. ²⁰Those who say, "I love God," and hate their brothers or sisters,[r] are liars; for those who do not love a brother or sister[s] whom they have seen, cannot love God whom they have not seen. ²¹The commandment we have from him is this: those who love God must love their brothers and sisters[r] also.

Faith Conquers the World

5 Everyone who believes that Jesus is the Christ[t] has been born of God, and everyone who loves the parent loves the child. ²By this we know that we love the children of God, when we love God and obey his commandments. ³For the love of God is this, that we obey his commandments. And his commandments are not burdensome, ⁴for whatever is born of God conquers the world. And this is the victory that conquers the world, our faith. ⁵Who is it that conquers the world but the one who believes that Jesus is the Son of God?

Testimony concerning the Son of God

⁶This is the one who came by water and blood, Jesus Christ, not with the water only but with the water and the blood. And the Spirit is the one that testifies, for the Spirit is the truth. ⁷There are three that testify:[u] ⁸the Spirit and the water and the blood, and these three agree. ⁹If we receive human testimony, the testimony of God is greater; for this is the testimony of God that he has testified to his Son. ¹⁰Those who believe in the Son of God have the testimony in their hearts. Those who do not believe in God[v] have made him a liar by not believing in the testimony that God has given concerning his Son. ¹¹And this is the testimony: God gave us eternal life, and this life is in his Son. ¹²Whoever has the Son has life; whoever does not have the Son of God does not have life.

---

p Other ancient authorities read *does away with Jesus* (Gk *dissolves Jesus*)
q Other ancient authorities add *him*; others add *God*
r Gk *brothers*
s Gk *brother*
t Or *the Messiah*
u A few other authorities read (with variations) ⁷*There are three that testify in heaven, the Father, the Word, and the Holy Spirit, and these three are one.* ⁸*And there are three that testify on earth:*
v Other ancient authorities read *in the Son*

4:2 Jesus Christ has come in the flesh This is the most explicit statement identifying the opponents in this letter with the docetists. The opponents confronted by Ignatius are identified in similar language (see introduction to The Johannine Letters). **4:5** *John* 3:31. **4:8–11** Many of the themes here are brought together in *John* 3:16–21, which captures the heart of *1 John* as well as any six-verse passage in *1 John* itself. **4:12** *John* 1:18. **5:1 been born of God** *John* 1:12. **5:2–3 we obey his commandments** *John* 14:15–17. **5:4–5 conquers the world** *1 John* 2:13; 4:4; *John* 16:33. **5:6 water and blood** Although this may not be an intended allusion to the scene described in *John*'s passion narrative, it is noteworthy that only *John* (19:34) records the incident of the spear being thrust into the side of Jesus. **5:9** *John* 8:17–18. **5:10–12** *John* 3:18.

Epilogue

¹³I write these things to you who believe in the name of the Son of God, so that you may know that you have eternal life.

¹⁴And this is the boldness we have in him, that if we ask anything according to his will, he hears us. ¹⁵And if we know that he hears us in whatever we ask, we know that we have obtained the requests made of him. ¹⁶If you see your brother or sister^w committing what is not a mortal sin, you will ask, and God^x will give life to such a one—to those whose sin is not mortal. There is sin that is mortal; I do not say that you should pray about that. ¹⁷All wrongdoing is sin, but there is sin that is not mortal.

¹⁸We know that those who are born of God do not sin, but the one who was born of God protects them, and the evil one does not touch them. ¹⁹We know that we are God's children, and that the whole world lies under the power of the evil one. ²⁰And we know that the Son of God has come and has given us understanding so that we may know him who is true;^y and we are in him who is true, in his Son Jesus Christ. He is the true God and eternal life.

²¹Little children, keep yourselves from idols.^z

---

w Gk *your brother*
x Gk *he*

y Other ancient authorities read *know the true God*
z Other ancient authorities add *Amen*

5:13 *John* 20:31. Compare the conclusion of *John* with that of this letter. **5:14–15 ask** See 3:22; *John* 14:13–16; 15:7, 16; 16:23–26. **5:16–17 mortal sin** The exact meaning of the author is uncertain. **5:18** See 1:8. **5:20** *John* 17:3. **5:21** Although this verse may be connected to the previous sentence by the contrast between the "true God" and *idols,* it does not make this ending any less abrupt.

THE SECOND LETTER OF
JOHN

Salutation

[1]The elder to the elect lady and her children, whom I love in the truth, and not only I but also all who know the truth, [2]because of the truth that abides in us and will be with us forever:

[3]Grace, mercy, and peace will be with us from God the Father and from[a] Jesus Christ, the Father's Son, in truth and love.

Truth and Love

[4]I was overjoyed to find some of your children walking in the truth, just as we have been commanded by the Father. [5]But now, dear lady, I ask you, not as though I were writing you a new commandment, but one we have had from the beginning, let us love one another. [6]And this is love, that we walk according to his commandments; this is the commandment just as you have heard it from the beginning—you must walk in it.

[7]Many deceivers have gone out into the world, those who do not confess that Jesus Christ has come in the flesh; any such person is the deceiver and the antichrist! [8]Be on your guard, so that you do not lose what we[b] have worked for, but may receive a full reward. [9]Everyone who does not abide in the teaching of Christ, but goes beyond it, does not have God; whoever abides in the teaching has both the Father and the Son. [10]Do not receive into the house or welcome anyone who comes to you and does not bring this teaching; [11]for to welcome is to participate in the evil deeds of such a person.

Final Greetings

[12]Although I have much to write to you, I would rather not use paper and ink; instead I hope to come to you and talk with you face to face, so that our joy may be complete.

[13]The children of your elect sister send you their greetings.[c]

---

a Other ancient authorities add *the Lord*

b Other ancient authorities read *you*
c Other ancient authorities add *Amen*

1 *the elder* The same word is used to identify the author of *3 John* (v. 1). The author of *1 John,* though not identifying himself as "elder," writes as one in a position to instruct the whole church. *elect lady* Scholars differ on the meaning of this phrase, which identifies the recipient of this brief letter. Some say that it refers to a woman and some of her relatives, who have become Christians; others say that it is a reference to the local church, personified as a woman, in a similar way to that in which the church universal is called the "mother" church today. See also verses 5 and 13. The Gk words for "elect" and "church" are related. *know the truth* John 8:32. **2** *abides* See *1 John* 2:5–6. **3** *truth and love* These are the dominant themes of *1 John.* **4** *walking in the truth* 3 John 3, 4. **5** The commandment to love is discussed in *1 John* 2:7. **6** John 14:15–17, 23. *from the beginning* 1 John 2:7, 24; 3:11. **7** This charge has a docetic ring to it, but too little information is provided about the opponents to establish their identity with any certainty or even to vaguely outline their theological position (see *1 John* 4:2). *antichrist* See *1 John* 2:18, 22, 4:3. **8–11** The Johannine community has begun to draw lines to distinguish between acceptable and unacceptable belief. In an age when hospitality counted much, such exclusion of those who leaned toward a docetic position would have been an extreme measure. The language is harsh throughout, the tone uncompromising. In *3 John,* we may have a glimpse of the elder's opponents playing the same card, denying hospitality to the elder's own associates (*3 John* 10). See *3 John* 5. **12** The comment that the author has written only a short letter because he hoped to see his readers soon is somewhat formulaic, and the author repeats it almost word for word in *3 John* 13. *joy may be complete* See *1 John* 1:4. **13** *elect sister* See v. 1.

THE THIRD LETTER OF JOHN

Salutation

[1]The elder to the beloved Gaius, whom I love in truth.

Gaius Commended for His Hospitality

[2]Beloved, I pray that all may go well with you and that you may be in good health, just as it is well with your soul. [3]I was overjoyed when some of the friends[a] arrived and testified to your faithfulness to the truth, namely how you walk in the truth. [4]I have no greater joy than this, to hear that my children are walking in the truth.

[5]Beloved, you do faithfully whatever you do for the friends,[a] even though they are strangers to you; [6]they have testified to your love before the church. You will do well to send them on in a manner worthy of God; [7]for they began their journey for the sake of Christ,[b] accepting no support from non-believers.[c] [8]Therefore we ought to support such people, so that we may become co-workers with the truth.

Diotrephes and Demetrius

[9]I have written something to the church; but Diotrephes, who likes to put himself first, does not acknowledge our authority. [10]So if I come, I will call attention to what he is doing in spreading false charges against us. And not content with those charges, he refuses to welcome the friends,[a] and even prevents those who want to do so and expels them from the church.

[11]Beloved, do not imitate what is evil but imitate what is good. Whoever does good is from God; whoever does evil has not seen God. [12]Everyone has testified favorably about Demetrius, and so has the truth itself. We also testify for him,[d] and you know that our testimony is true.

Final Greetings

[13]I have much to write to you, but I would rather not write with pen and ink; [14]instead I hope to see you soon, and we will talk together face to face.

[15]Peace to you. The friends send you their greetings. Greet the friends there, each by name.

---

a Gk brothers
b Gk for the sake of the name
c Gk the Gentiles

d Gk lacks for him

---

1 *elder* See *2 John* 1. *love . . . truth* These are familiar themes from *1 John.* See *2 John* 3. *Gaius* This name was too common to allow an identification of this individual. A Gaius from Macedonia (*Acts* 19:29), a Gaius from Derbe (*Acts* 20:4), and a Gaius from Corinth (*1 Cor.* 1:14; *Rom.* 16:23) were associated with Paul. Another Gaius is mentioned by Ignatius (Ign. *Phld.* 11.1). **3–4** *walk in truth* 2 John 4. In *1 John* 1:6–7, the author speaks of walking in the light and walking in darkness. **4** *no greater joy* 1 John 1:4; 2 John 1:12. **5** The subject of the letter is hospitality. In the early days of the church, many local groups seem to have depended to some extent on the resources of traveling evangelists. Also, in any attempt to organize beyond the local level, representatives from a central church would find themselves in strange cities in need of accommodation, since inns were generally the places of last resort for the tired traveler. The Christian church encouraged hospitality. But the generosity could be abused, as comments in the *Didache* suggest (11.3–12.5), or could be extended to the wrong kind of people (*2 John* 10–11). **6** *send them on* Paul used this verb when he wrote to the church at Rome, requesting that it help fund his mission to Spain (*Rom.* 15:24). The use of the verb in *3 John* suggests that the visitors were en route to a destination beyond Gaius's hometown, even farther away from the elder's community. *in a manner worthy of God* This is a reference to financial support, but several items in this passage are unclear (see introduction to The Johannine Letters). **7** *accepting no support from unbelievers* It is not clear why nonbelievers would have supported the elder's people. Perhaps the comment is rhetorical, but such an explanation must be a last resort, since these letters do not show the author to be a master of such twists and wordplays. Could it be that some nonbelievers favored the elder's side and were willing to lend some support to his cause after the church, now under Diotrephes's control, shut the elder out? **9** *Diotrephes* This is the only mention of anyone by this name in our literature. Several things are known about him from the elder's brief letter (see introduction to The Johannine Letters). *does not acknowledge our authority* Lit. "does not welcome," as it is translated in verse 10. **10** There is no indication what these charges might have been and whether they were substantial or merely stock polemical charges. The matter, clearly serious, has deteriorated into vicious hostilities. **12** *Demetrius* Not the Demetrius of *Acts* 19:24, who resided in Ephesus and stirred up a riot against Paul. *testimony is true* John 21:24. **13** See *2 John* 12.

The Disclosure of Jesus Christ to John
REVELATION

The Apocalyptic Mindset

Compared to other material in the *Reader*, the *Apocalypse*[1] is filled with wild images, mysterious phenomena, codes, and numbers. A look at other apocalyptic literature from the period, however, shows that the language of the *Apocalypse* is not unusual at all.

Just as modern readers recognize from literary clues that they have stepped into the world of science fiction, murder mystery, trial transcript, or bedtime fairy tale, so it is with an apocalypse. There was a way of speaking, a specialized vocabulary, a particular stock of images; these told the first-century reader that the world of apocalyptic had been entered. And just as it is not possible to do justice to a murder mystery by reading it as a bedtime fairy tale, or to do justice to a cookbook by reading it as a work of science fiction, so apocalyptic works must be read with the appropriate glasses.

Christianity was born into a Jewish environment heavily influenced by apocalyptic thinking, where cosmic forces of destruction were seen tearing the fabric of the present age, bringing about the collapse of the human order. Even with this view of impending horrors, many Jews and Christians maintained an element of calm and confidence, resting in the certainty that God was in control, and that divine rule would prevail—God would defeat the forces of evil and bring in a golden age.

This ancient apocalyptic mindset has left its mark even on the modern world—with such images as the "thousand years of peace" (the millennium) or the more general ideas of a new or golden age, or an age of peace. The conviction that a new age was coming and that good would triumph, in spite of the present crisis, was to some extent built around the belief that God had disclosed (revealed) the details of the present distress well in advance of the situation. The explosion of the forces of evil in the end of the age was not, then, an element that God had failed to reckon with in his plans for the human race.

---

[1]The word "revelation" is a transliteration of the Latin *revelatio* (unveiling), a word with the same meaning as the Gk *apokalypsis*. When we transliterate the Gk, we get the word "apocalypse."

Apocalyptic thinking especially characterized those who suffered religious persecution. As their world collapsed under the wrath of their oppressors, they expected that God would rescue them and destroy their opponents. Evil and its allies, which seemed to triumph over the righteous, would suffer the greatest imaginable doom—eternal destruction. This would be the final victory in the war between good and evil.

These revelations or disclosures "in advance" were presented to the community in the form of written documents attributed to some ancient hero of the past.[2] Enoch, Shem, and Abraham—all heroes from the *Genesis* story—had apocalyptic works assigned to their hand, and one apocalypse was even attributed to Adam. In other cases, apocalyptic works were attributed to a figure from the heyday of prophecy (e.g., Elijah, Baruch, Ezekiel, Daniel). The learned scribe Ezra had special prominence as the "author" of apocalyptic works.

Some recent scholarship has distanced itself from the narrow eschatological ("end-time") definition of apocalyptic writings, attempting to link the genre to a broader "revelatory" literary tradition in the Greco-Roman world.

Purpose

Two matters affect our understanding of the purpose of the *Apocalypse*. First, since the work is of the apocalyptic genre, we assume that it shares to some extent a common purpose with the wider collection of apocalyptic writings from the period. This requires attention to the nature and purpose of apocalyptic literature. Second, we assume that some specific event or crisis prompted the author of *Revelation* to write his work. We must, therefore, investigate the particular setting of this work.

Setting and Date

The issue of persecution drives the *Apocalypse*. Its author, a leader of the churches of western Asia Minor, had already been exiled to a remote island for his Christian confession (1:9). This action was not an isolated intervention against a reckless preacher; it was, as he himself said, a danger he shared with those to whom he wrote (1:9). Further, he knew of at least one martyrdom (2:13), and perhaps of others (6:9–11; 20:4), and he expected the situation to grow worse—not better (2:10; 6:11). By the very act of writing the book, the author reveals the bleakness of the immediate situation.

Since we know both the issue (persecution of Christians) and the locale (the main centers in the Roman province of Asia, or present-day western Turkey), many scholars feel confident about the date of composition. When in western Asia Minor, they ask, did the church experience persecution? The most likely answer

---

[2]The second-century Christian apocalypses continue the older practice of attributing the work to one of the "ancients." The only real difference is that they now have their own distinctive heroes to choose from—Paul, Peter, James, and others from the age of the apostles.

appears to be some time in the reign of the Roman emperor Domitian (81–96 C.E.), and more probably in the latter years of his reign, when he became increasingly brutal. Ancient church traditions portray Domitian as a persecutor (Irenaeus, *Haer.* 5.30.3; Eusebius, *Eccl. hist.* 3.17), though we are not sure how reliable such traditions are. Evidence does point to the spread of the imperial cult in western Asia Minor around the time of Domitian, and this could have been the concrete cause that sparked the persecution experienced by John and his churches.[3]

But many doubt that Domitian singled out Christians for persecution. If they are right, and Christians fared no worse under Domitian than under most emperors, then the *Apocalypse* becomes more difficult to date, for nothing would link the writing to Domitian's or anyone else's reign.

Nonetheless, establishing the exact date is not necessary for understanding the soul of this document. Harassment of Christians by the authorities, which the document assumes, was common enough during the first three centuries, even though empirewide police actions did not occur before the mid-third century. Anyone could have brought forward a case against Christians; any magistrate could have yielded to local complaints. Such disciplinary actions (from the perspective of the authorities) were at least numerous enough to shape the early Christian self-consciousness with themes of martyrdom and persecution.[4] Such is clearly the context of the *Apocalypse.*

Overview

The *Apocalypse* has been carefully structured. The use of numbers and symbols, common in apocalyptic literature, help define the structure of *Revelation.* Other narrative writings and letters could not easily incorporate these.

---

[3]In the eastern provinces of the Roman Empire, a trend to deify the Roman emperors developed. Along with this, temples to Rome and to various Roman emperors were built. The literary and archaeological remains reflect the spread of the imperial cult in Asia Minor, and temples of the imperial cult figure prominently in the archaeological reconstructions of cities such as Ephesus, where temples of Domitian and Hadrian have been found, and in Pergamum, where the temple of Trajan dominates the scene. Sacrifices offered at such temples demonstrated one's loyalty to the Roman Empire, and Asia Minor seems to have been a center for this kind of devotion, which in many ways was primarily a display of civic loyalty. Christians, rooted in a monotheistic perspective, found it impossible to participate in any event that involved the worship of other divinities. But the refusal to sacrifice, even in some token way, could be taken as a sign of disloyalty to the empire. Rome was ever suspicious of revolt, and local administrations had every interest in ensuring that their city showed no hint of protest. Thus Christians stood out as a dangerous element in the society by their refusal to sacrifice, and though the motivations of the Christians were primarily religious, their actions often were misunderstood as political.

[4]We should not assume that every record of persecution of Christians has been preserved. There appears to have been a serious persecution around 111/112 C.E. in the area to the northeast of that addressed by the *Apocalypse.* We have record of this persecution only because Pliny, the Roman governor responsible for the action, wrote to the Emperor Trajan about the matter, and this correspondence was quite by chance preserved. There would have been a number of other such actions against Christians that were not recorded in any documents that have survived.

For the *Apocalypse,* the number seven is featured.[5] Some have identified four series of seven in the structure. In the first series, seven churches of Asia are addressed with individual letters (chs. 2–3). Then follow three series of seven, in which the seventh element of the series contains the next series of seven. Thus the seventh seal has within it the seven angels with seven trumpets (chs. 8–9), and the seventh angel with the seventh trumpet (ch. 11) has within it the seven golden bowls (chs. 15–16).

But other schemes have been suggested. One divides the revelation section between chapters 11 and 12, with the latter section being a recapitulation of the former. There does seem to be a case for various parallels and repetitions, but no consistently parallel structure is obvious. If the structure carries much of the meaning of the work, then we will find ourselves often puzzled or in disagreement.

Much energy has been expended over the years as various religious groups have attempted to find a key or code to the *Apocalypse* to unlock the "secrets" therein. Such quests have often been fueled by a sense that the end of the world was at hand. Contemporary events were believed to parallel scenes in the *Apocalypse* and various individuals were believed to correspond to the beast and false prophet found there. Such attempts to decode *Revelation* inevitably prove wrongheaded.

Authorship

The first Christian apocalypse differs from other apocalyptic writings of the time in that no attempt was made to attribute the work to a hero of the past. Perhaps the early Christian belief that prophecy was again "alive and well" allowed the community to grant considerable authority to the revelations of contemporary Christian prophets, rather than looking only to the prophets and heroes of the distant past. Whatever the case, no attempt was made in the *Apocalypse* to dignify the writing by disguising the identity of the real author.

The author presented himself simply as "John." That is stated explicitly three times in the first nine verses, and once toward the end of the book (22:8). Further, the author was still alive, and living in exile on an island not far from the churches to which his writing was addressed. These are hardly the impressive credentials that apocalyptic authors generally presented.

Although the author mentions himself by name, that information is not adequate for positively identifying the author. The name "John" was common, even within the Christian tradition, and there seem to have been at least two people by

---

[5]The following is a complete listing of the use of the number seven in the Apocalypse: seven churches of Asia (1:4); seven spirits (1:4); seven golden lampstands (1:12); seven stars (1:16); seven flaming torches (4:5); seven seals (5:1); seven horns (5:6); seven eyes (5:6); seven trumpets (8:2); seven thunders (10:3); seven heads (12:3); seven diadems (12:3); seven plagues (15:1); seven golden bowls (15:5); seven mountains (17:9); seven kings (17:9); and various groups of seven angels (1:20; 8:2; 15:1). There are less obvious uses of series of seven, and it is not clear whether the number seven was merely coincidental in such places: for example, seven *blessings* are prescribed: 1:3; 14:13; 16:15; 19:9; 20:6; 22:7, 14.

that name in leading positions in the church at Ephesus alone.[6] The general descriptions (servant and brother) do not point in any obvious way to John the disciple, which would have been the case had the word *apostle* been used. Therefore it is unlikely that a pseudonymous author is seeking to dignify his work with apostolic credentials. Of course, if John the apostle were the author, the unaffected terms *servant* and *brother* would be entirely fitting; some have argued for precisely that—John, one of the twelve disciples, as author. Traditions from the second century do link *Revelation* to John the disciple,[7] though that by no means went unchallenged even in the early period (Eusebius, *Eccl. hist.* 7.25.1–2).

In spite of our difficulty in identifying the particular John of this document, there is no reason to believe that the original recipients were confused about the identity of the author. The author wrote as though he knew his audience and they knew him. The only indication we have, however, that this author had status as a leader of the churches to whom he wrote is his very act of writing to them. One might be led to believe that the exile of the author resulted from civil action against the church, which probably would have been directly largely at the leadership. Little more than that can be said.

Another question of authorship which modern scholars address is whether the author of the *Apocalypse* could have written the *Gospel of John*. Although a few scholars do maintain common authorship for these documents, a number of features point to different authors. Indeed, even the ancients noted the striking difference in language and style and dismissed common authorship on this basis (Eusebius, *Eccl. hist.* 7.25.7–8).

Audience

After a short introduction in which the author identifies himself and encourages the recipients to read and obey the material in the book, the address of the work is given: "to the seven churches that are in Asia" (1:4). These are identified later as churches in prominent cities of the Roman province of Asia (1:11). Short messages to each follow in chapters 2 and 3, after which the author recounts the things "revealed" to him.

Of the seven cities named, five are mentioned for the first time in Christian literature. Of the other two, only Ephesus was prominent in the earlier literature, being the chief base for Paul's missionary work some forty years earlier. The other church of the *Apocalypse* mentioned in earlier literature is Laodicea. It is men-

---

[6]Papias, a bishop of Hierapolis in the early second century, mentioned two different Johns, though some scholars believed that he simply repeated himself in the list. Further, there were two graves of John in Ephesus, and Eusebius, the church historian, concluded that there must have been two Johns there. Having no sympathy for the perspective of the *Apocalypse*, Eusebius concluded that the second John, John the elder (rather than John the apostle), was its author (Eusebius, *Eccl. hist.* 3.39.4–7).

[7]Justin, *Dial.* 81.4; Melito of Sardis, cited in Eusebius, *Eccl. hist.* 4.26.2; Irenaeus, *Haer.* 4.20.11; Tertullian, *Marc.* 3.14.24; and it is listed under John the apostle's name in the Muratorian Canon, a canon list possibly from the late second century.

tioned only in *Col.* 4:16, from which we learn simply that a Pauline congregation existed there, and that Paul had sent a letter to them (*Col.* 4:16).[8] A few years after the *Apocalypse* was written, Ignatius wrote to several churches in the area: Smyrna, Philadelphia and Ephesus, as well as two other cities to the south not mentioned in the *Apocalypse*.

The seven cities named may be the main ones in the area, perhaps each serving as an administrative center for the surrounding area. Each city is close enough to other cities named so that almost every town in the more populated area of the province would have been no more than a day's journey from one of these centers. We cannot conclude from this list that there were no other cities or towns in the area with Christian churches, or that no other churches would have considered themselves included by such an address.

Relation to Other Early Christian Writings

The *Apocalypse* is the only Christian document of the first century that is a genuine literary apocalypse, though apocalyptic imagery does surface in a number of other early Christian works (*Mark* 13; *Matt.* 24; *Luke* 21). Also, apocalyptic material appears in Paul's writing[9] (especially his earlier writings); the air of apocalyptic permeates *2 Peter* and *Jude;* and hints of apocalyptic can be detected in the Johannine letters, in the last section of the *Didache,* and in the *Shepherd of Hermas.*

In the second century, a number of apocryphal apocalypses appeared, such as the *Apocalypse of Peter* and the *Apocalypse of Paul.* As well, Jewish apocalypses were sometimes revised by a Christian editor in order to appropriate them for the Christian cause. The *Sibylline Oracles* and *2 Enoch* are notable examples.

The quantity of parallels between the *Apocalypse* and other apocalypses of the time make it impossible to list anything more than a few to illustrate the general themes of apocalyptic thinking. The cross-references in the notes, then, should not be considered comprehensive.

Value for the Study of Early Christianity

The *Apocalypse,* however bizarre it might appear to modern readers, provides a glimpse of one important aspect of early Christian thought. And it is not some isolated and esoteric stream of the Christian movement that is represented in this literature, cut off and repudiated by the main Christian communities in Asia.

Although the apocalyptic perspective was not attractive to every Christian in the second and third centuries, believers in Asia Minor seem to have been

---

[8]We cannot be certain about the date of the founding of a church in Laodicea, because there is some question about the authenticity of *Colossians,* in which the first reference to a church in Laodicea is made (see note at *Col.* 4:16).

[9]Both *1 Thessalonians* and *2 Thessalonians* reflect apocalyptic thinking. *First Thessalonians* is usually attributed to Paul; the authorship of *2 Thessalonians* is debated.

enamored of this way of thinking, perhaps fostered by the *Apocalypse* itself. Papias, the early second-century bishop of Hierapolis, a city within view of Laodicea, is described in such terms by Eusebius (*Eccl. hist.* 3.39.11–13). Justin, who lived for some time in Ephesus in the first part of the second century, espoused aspects of an apocalyptic worldview (*Dial.* 80–81), as did Irenaeus, the bishop of Lyons, who grew up in Smyrna in the middle of the second century (*Haer.* 5.34–36). These were prominent men, and there is no reason to think that they were unrepresentative of popular Christian thinking in the Roman province of Asia in the second century. This may suggest just how influential John's *Apocalypse* became.

Apocalyptic ideas even gave rise to the Montanist movement, which, though ostracized by many in the mainstream, nonetheless attracted such leading minds as Tertullian of North Africa. Apocalyptic thought, then, was far more central in early Christian thinking than at any other point in the history of Christianity.

For Further Reading

Aune, David E. *Prophecy in Early Christianity and the Ancient Mediterranean World.* Grand Rapids: Eerdmans, 1983.

Caird, G. B. *The Revelation of St. John.* Black's New Testament Commentary. London: A & C Black, 1966. Repr., Peabody, Mass.: Hendrickson.

Charlesworth, James H., ed. *Old Testament Pseudepigrapha.* 2 vols. Garden City, N.Y.: Doubleday, 1985.

Hemer, Colin J. *The Letters to the Seven Churches of Asia in Their Local Setting.* Sheffield: JSOT Press, 1986.

THE REVELATION
TO JOHN

Introduction and Salutation

1 The revelation of Jesus Christ, which God gave him to show his servants[a] what must soon take place; he made[b] it known by sending his angel to his servant[c] John, 2who testified to the word of God and to the testimony of Jesus Christ, even to all that he saw.

3Blessed is the one who reads aloud the words of the prophecy, and blessed are those who hear and who keep what is written in it; for the time is near.

4John to the seven churches that are in Asia:

Grace to you and peace from him who is and who was and who is to come, and from the seven spirits who are before his throne, 5and from Jesus Christ, the faithful witness, the firstborn of the dead, and the ruler of the kings of the earth.

To him who loves us and freed[d] us from our sins by his blood, 6and made[b] us to be a kingdom, priests serving[e] his God and Father, to him be glory and dominion forever and ever. Amen.

7 Look! He is coming with the clouds;
    every eye will see him,
even those who pierced him;
    and on his account all the tribes of the earth
        will wail.
So it is to be. Amen.

8"I am the Alpha and the Omega," says the Lord God, who is and who was and who is to come, the Almighty.

A Vision of Christ

9I, John, your brother who share with you in Jesus the persecution and the kingdom and the patient endurance, was on the island called Patmos because of the word of God and the testimony of Jesus.[f]

---

a Gk *slaves*
b Gk *and he made*
c Gk *slave*
d Other ancient authorities read *washed*

e Gk *priests to*
f Or *testimony to Jesus*

1:1–3 These three verses serve almost as a cover page for the document. See note to 1:4. **1:1** *revelation* Gk *apocalypsis*. Transliterating rather than translating the Gk word created a new English word ("apocalypse"). "Revelation" and "apocalypse" mean the same thing, and either word can be used as the title of the present work. *what must soon take place* See 1:3. Apocalyptic literature was usually presented as something written in the distant past, which had been "sealed up" until the end of time, at which point its contents would be relevant and could be disclosed (*Dan.* 12:9, 13). This Christian apocalypse claims that the revelation itself comes at the end of time, and no sealing of the message is ordered (22:10, 12), except for a small part within the revelation (10:4). The link of apocalyptic literature to the final crisis is illustrated clearly in *4 Ezra* 4:26–52. Apocalyptic literature was presented as the revelation given to some ancient figure (Adam, Enoch, Moses, Ezra, etc.). This Christian apocalypse makes no such claim: a contemporary of the audience is the channel of the message. The framing of the revelation within a letter is also not conventional for apocalypses. **1:3** *prophecy* Some scholars believe that John functioned as an itinerant prophet such as those described in the *Didache* (11.3–12; 13.1–7). This might account for his familiarity with a number of churches within the province of Asia, but we cannot assume that only itinerant ministers would have been able to develop these kinds of contact. Indeed, the churches are grouped by a common name (the seven churches of Asia), and this may suggest that they themselves shared in a substantial formal relationship, apart from their connection to the author. **1:4** This verse is similar to the opening verses of many documents in our collection: the naming of the author and the recipients, and an extension of some blessing or good wishes. *the seven churches that are in Asia* It is unclear what is meant by this phrase (see introduction to *Revelation*). Asia was one of several Roman provinces established in Asia Minor (present-day Turkey). The province of Asia bordered the central part of the Aegean coast, whose booming ports and fertile valleys extending inland made it one of the wealthiest areas in the Roman Empire. *who is and who was* This reflects the rendering of *Exod.* 3:14 in the LXX, where the name for God (YHWH) is translated "He who is" instead of its more routine translation, "Lord" (Gk *Kyrios*). **1:5** *firstborn of the dead* Col. 1:18; 1 Cor. 15:20. *freed* Other ancient authorities read "washed." The difference in Gk is slight: *freed* is *lusanti*; "washed" is *lousanti*. The idea is found in *1 John* 1:7. **1:6** *a kingdom, priests . . .* See 5:10; 1 Pet. 2:9. **1:7** *with the clouds* Dan. 7:13. *who pierced him* Zech. 12:10. The portrayal of Jesus as having been pierced parallels the Johannine account of the crucifixion (*John* 19:37), a detail missing from the synoptic account. **1:8** *Alpha* is the first letter of the Gk alphabet; *omega* is the last. The phrase is also used in the conclusion of the *Apocalypse* (22:13), where the meaning is made clear, if indeed this was necessary: "I am the Alpha and Omega, the first and the last, the beginning and the end." The phrase "the first and the last" is found also in 1:17 and was used in Isa. 44:6; 48:12. **1:9** *Patmos* An island off the west coast of Turkey, in a group called the Sporades, southwest from Ephesus. Banishment, or exile, was one of the forms of Roman punishment, and islands in this group were used for this purpose. Such a serious sentence would have been pronounced by the provincial governor.

10I was in the spirit[g] on the Lord's day, and I heard behind me a loud voice like a trumpet 11saying, "Write in a book what you see and send it to the seven churches, to Ephesus, to Smyrna, to Pergamum, to Thyatira, to Sardis, to Philadelphia, and to Laodicea."

12Then I turned to see whose voice it was that spoke to me, and on turning I saw seven golden lampstands, 13and in the midst of the lampstands I saw one like the Son of Man, clothed with a long robe and with a golden sash across his chest. 14His head and his hair were white as white wool, white as snow; his eyes were like a flame of fire, 15his feet were like burnished bronze, refined as in a furnace, and his voice was like the sound of many waters. 16In his right hand he held seven stars, and from his mouth came a sharp, two-edged sword, and his face was like the sun shining with full force.

17When I saw him, I fell at his feet as though dead. But he placed his right hand on me, saying, "Do not be afraid; I am the first and the last, 18and the living one. I was dead, and see, I am alive forever and ever; and I have the keys of Death and of Hades. 19Now

write what you have seen, what is, and what is to take place after this. 20As for the mystery of the seven stars that you saw in my right hand, and the seven golden lampstands: the seven stars are the angels of the seven churches, and the seven lampstands are the seven churches.

The Message to Ephesus

2 "To the angel of the church in Ephesus write: These are the words of him who holds the seven stars in his right hand, who walks among the seven golden lampstands:

2"I know your works, your toil and your patient endurance. I know that you cannot tolerate evildoers; you have tested those who claim to be apostles but are not, and have found them to be false. 3I also know that you are enduring patiently and bearing up for the sake of my name, and that you have not grown weary. 4But I have this against you, that you have abandoned the love you had at first. 5Remember then from what you have fallen; repent, and do the works you did at first. If not, I will come to you and remove your lampstand from its place, unless you repent. 6Yet this is to your credit: you hate

g Or *in the Spirit*

1:10 *on the Lord's day* Christians came to call the 1st day of the week the Lord's day. The name "Sunday" reflects pagan use, for the day had been named in honor of the sun. A few scholars argue that the term *Lord's day* did not mean Sunday to the earliest Christians but rather Easter, the day of the resurrection. Which particular day does not seem crucial to the purpose or impact of the *Apocalypse*. **1:12** *golden lampstands* The image was central to the prophecy of *Zechariah* (ch. 4); other borrowing from *Zechariah* is found in 11:4, where the olive tree is mentioned. The seven-branched candlestick, known as the candelabra or menorah, was a symbol prominent in Judaism. When Domitian erected an arch in Rome to celebrate Titus's divinization after death, and depicted on it his brother's destruction of Jerusalem, the lampstand was a prominent feature of the frieze. It still is visible today, in rather good shape, just a minute's walk from the Coliseum in the center of Rome. **1:13** *Son of Man* Scholars are uncertain about the meaning of this term in the 1st century; the general opinion is that is was not a loaded or common messianic term until Christians developed it. The phrase itself comes from the book of *Daniel* (7:13), a mine of images for apocalyptic and messianic literature (*1 En.* 46–48; 62.5–9). The term *Son of Man* occurs regularly in the gospels (both synoptic and Johannine) but not in the letters. **1:13–16** The strange description of this apocalyptic figure is paralleled elsewhere (*Ezek.* 1:26–28; 43:2; *Dan.* 10:5–6). **1:14** *as white wool* A similar description of the "Ancient One" (Aramaic, "Ancient of Days") is found in *Dan.* 7:9. **1:20** *angels* Scholars disagree on the meaning of the word *angels* here. In Gk, the word means "messenger" (whether divine or human) and thus could refer to a local representative of the church (perhaps to a bishop) or to a divine messenger. In any case, the use of the word suggests that the local churches are comfortable thinking in terms of one representative for each local church, and this may indicate a tendency toward a monarchical (single-bishop) office. **2:1** *church in Ephesus* A church was founded in Ephesus by the early 50s C.E. Initially it seems to have been under Paul's influence, and according to *Acts* and Paul's own writings, Ephesus served as a base for his mission in Asia. In the later Pauline tradition, Ephesus still played a role; this is suggested by the connection of Paul's close associate Timothy to Ephesus in the Pastoral Letters. Some early evidence suggests that the area later came under John's influence, but it is impossible to determine how direct or how substantial this influence was. The city of Ephesus was ancient, founded by Greek colonists who had moved eastward, inhabiting the islands in the Aegean and the western part of what is modern Turkey a thousand years earlier. The city was one of the largest in the empire and one of the richest, being a port on a major east-west trading route. The great temple of Artemis (Diana), one of the seven wonders of the ancient world, was just northeast of Ephesus, on the road to Smyrna, and it became linked to the imperial cult in 29 B.C.E. The ancient ruins of the city are well preserved, and museums in Selçuk (near the old site), Vienna, and London display a wealth of artifacts from the city. The great temple itself is gone, with one lone pillar marking the place. **2:2** *claim to be apostles* John uses the term "apostle" in its technical sense (*Rev.* 21:14; probably 18:20). The term could also include a wider circle than the twelve apostles, as in Paul, for example (*1 Cor.* 15:7; *Gal.* 1:19; *Acts* 14:14). Some think that the word here means simply "messenger." The *Didache* presents a similar problem with use of the term "apostle" (*Did.* 11.3–6). **2:6** *Nicolaitans* See 2:15. Later tradition identified this group as the followers of Nicolas of Antioch (*Acts* 6:5; Eusebius, *Hist. eccl.* 3.29). We are unable to determine whether those who reported this connection had any evidence beyond what we ourselves have in the *Apocalypse,* whose information is inadequate for establishing such a connection.

the works of the Nicolaitans, which I also hate. [7]Let anyone who has an ear listen to what the Spirit is saying to the churches. To everyone who conquers, I will give permission to eat from the tree of life that is in the paradise of God.

The Message to Smyrna

[8]"And to the angel of the church in Smyrna write: These are the words of the first and the last, who was dead and came to life:

[9]"I know your affliction and your poverty, even though you are rich. I know the slander on the part of those who say that they are Jews and are not, but are a synagogue of Satan. [10]Do not fear what you are about to suffer. Beware, the devil is about to throw some of you into prison so that you may be tested, and for ten days you will have affliction. Be faithful until death, and I will give you the crown of life. [11]Let anyone who has an ear listen to what the Spirit is saying to the churches. Whoever conquers will not be harmed by the second death.

The Message to Pergamum

[12]"And to the angel of the church in Pergamum write: These are the words of him who has the sharp two-edged sword:

[13]"I know where you are living, where Satan's throne is. Yet you are holding fast to my name, and you did not deny your faith in me[h] even in the days of Antipas my witness, my faithful one, who was killed among you, where Satan lives. [14]But I have a few things against you: you have some there who hold to the teaching of Balaam, who taught Balak to put a stumbling block before the people of Israel, so that they would eat food sacrificed to idols and practice fornication. [15]So you also have some who hold to the teaching of the Nicolaitans. [16]Repent then. If not, I will come to you soon and make war against them with the sword of my mouth. [17]Let anyone who has an ear listen to what the Spirit is saying to the churches. To everyone who conquers I will give some of the hidden manna, and I will give a white stone, and on the white stone is written a new name that no one knows except the one who receives it.

The Message to Thyatira

[18]"And to the angel of the church in Thyatira write: These are the words of the Son of God, who

---

h Or *deny my faith*

2:8 *church in Smyrna* Smyrna (modern Izmir), a seaport north of Ephesus, was Ephesus's major competitor. This is the first mention in early Christian literature of a church there. A few years later, Ignatius wrote four of his letters from Smyrna, having stopped there for several days on his way to martyrdom in Rome. The church became famous under the leadership of Polycarp, himself a martyr about the middle of the 2d century. Little remains of the ancient city. **2:9** This indicates sharp tension with the local, influential Jewish population, which was well represented in all the large cities of Asia Minor. In the mid-2d century, Polycarp, the bishop of Smyrna, was executed in a plot that involved Jews, according to the Christian account (*Martyrdom of Polycarp* 12.2–3). John used similar language in his message to Philadelphia (see 3:9). **2:10** *for ten days* This may be recalling a period of testing specified in *Dan.* 1:12. *crown of life* The image is drawn from athletic competitions, which Christian writers often used to illustrate the ordeal of the martyr (see Ign. *Eph.* 3.1). **2:11** *second death* John uses the phrase also in *Rev.* 20:6, 14; 21:8. It means eternal death that is rendered as punishment in the final judgment. Other authors used a similar image (*Mark* 9:43–47; *Matt.* 10:28). **2:12** This is the 1st mention in early Christian literature of a church in Pergamum. Archaeological work has been under way at the ancient site for some years, and a museum in the city houses many of the finds. Pergamum was a serious competitor to Smyrna and Ephesus, but its status stemmed largely from its position as capital of an older kingdom bequeathed to Rome by its last king, Attalus III, in 133 B.C.E. The seaports of Smyrna and Ephesus had become the leading cities by the 1st century. **2:13** *where Satan's throne is* Perhaps a reference to the grand temple of Zeus, now reconstructed in the Pergamum Museum in Berlin. Parts of the base are visible in Pergamum still. *Antipas* He is called a faithful *witness*. The word "witness" in Gk is *martys*. As persistent Christian confession could lead to martyrdom, the word gradually came to mean "martyr," but most of the uses in our literature should be read simply as "witness." This passage, however, is a case where martyrdom seems to be implied. We cannot determine whether the death was the result of legal judgment or mob violence. Christians suffered both. **2:14** The story of Balaam, told in *Num.* 22–24, is used as a stock image of religious error (*1 Cor.* 9:25; *Jas.* 1:12). The teaching of Balaam is not described in detail. The charge that its adherents practiced fornication could be nothing more than polemical bad-mouthing. It is even possible that the reference to Balaam is merely a way to repudiate the Nicolaitans. The issue of eating meat sacrificed to idols is perhaps more concrete, for it was connected directly with the activities of local temples, whose sacrifices provided meat for the marketplace. The absence of Christians from these temples and from their economic net would have been noticed, as the evidence of Pliny, a Roman governor, confirms a few years later (Pliny the Younger, *Epistles* 10.96). Some have argued that the opponents in these letters were Christians who took a more accommodating stance to the state and the civic and religious expectations of society. **2:17** *manna Exod.* 16:4; *John* 6:31–34. *white stone* The meaning of this is disputed. Perhaps it was a protective amulet, popular in the ancient world, or a token for admission to an event. **2:18** The 1st mention of Thyatira (modern Akhisar) in early Christian literature is in the account of a woman of Thyatira who had a business in Philippi (*Acts* 16:14). It was mainly a commercial center.

has eyes like a flame of fire, and whose feet are like burnished bronze:

[19]"I know your works—your love, faith, service, and patient endurance. I know that your last works are greater than the first. [20]But I have this against you: you tolerate that woman Jezebel, who calls herself a prophet and is teaching and beguiling my servants[i] to practice fornication and to eat food sacrificed to idols. [21]I gave her time to repent, but she refuses to repent of her fornication. [22]Beware, I am throwing her on a bed, and those who commit adultery with her I am throwing into great distress, unless they repent of her doings; [23]and I will strike her children dead. And all the churches will know that I am the one who searches minds and hearts, and I will give to each of you as your works deserve. [24]But to the rest of you in Thyatira, who do not hold this teaching, who have not learned what some call 'the deep things of Satan,' to you I say, I do not lay on you any other burden; [25]only hold fast to what you have until I come. [26]To everyone who conquers and continues to do my works to the end,

I will give authority over the nations;
[27] to rule[j] them with an iron rod,
    as when clay pots are shattered—
[28]even as I also received authority from my Father. To the one who conquers I will also give the morning star. [29]Let anyone who has an ear listen to what the Spirit is saying to the churches.

---

i Gk *slaves*
j Or *to shepherd*

The Message to Sardis

3"And to the angel of the church in Sardis write: These are the words of him who has the seven spirits of God and the seven stars:

"I know your works; you have a name of being alive, but you are dead. [2]Wake up, and strengthen what remains and is on the point of death, for I have not found your works perfect in the sight of my God. [3]Remember then what you received and heard; obey it, and repent. If you do not wake up, I will come like a thief, and you will not know at what hour I will come to you. [4]Yet you have still a few persons in Sardis who have not soiled their clothes; they will walk with me, dressed in white, for they are worthy. [5]If you conquer, you will be clothed like them in white robes, and I will not blot your name out of the book of life; I will confess your name before my Father and before his angels. [6]Let anyone who has an ear listen to what the Spirit is saying to the churches.

The Message to Philadelphia

[7]"And to the angel of the church in Philadelphia write:

These are the words of the holy one, the true one,
    who has the key of David,
    who opens and no one will shut,
        who shuts and no one opens:
[8]"I know your works. Look, I have set before you an open door, which no one is able to shut. I know that you have but little power, and yet you have kept my word and have not denied my name. [9]I will make those of the synagogue of Satan who say that they are

---

burnished bronze The Gk word translated by this phrase is used only here in Greek literature. Some speculate that the word was used by the guild of local bronze smiths, thus reflecting the author's familiarity with the local situation. **2:20 *that woman Jezebel*** Jezebel was the wife of Ahab, a king in northern Israel. Hebrew prophets saw in her an opponent to the worship of Yahweh. Her name is probably used here in place of the name of the person intended. Again, as with the teaching of Balaam and the Nicolaitans, we know almost nothing of the beliefs or practices of these groups, but the charges of misconduct are the same as those leveled against the teaching of Balaam in Pergamum (2:15). Jezebel may be used here merely as a symbol of unspecified but grave religious failing (2:22–23). **2:24 *deep things of Satan*** Perhaps the group made such a claim. But there may be a touch of sarcasm here: the group may have claimed to know the deep things of God (a reasonable claim by a group of religious aspirants [*1 Cor.* 2:10; *1 En.* 52.1]); the author dismisses this claim by a caustic relabeling. **2:28 *morning star*** The planet Venus, which is visible in the morning sky after the stars are no longer visible (*Matt.* 2:2, 10). It became a title for Jesus (22:16). **3:1** This is the first mention in early Christian literature of a church in Sardis. Archaeological excavation has revealed a beautiful and massive synagogue in the center of Sardis, indicating a large and influential Jewish population in the 3d and 4th centuries. Many of the artifacts from Sardis are now housed in a museum in Manisa, Turkey. **3:3 *like a thief*** The theme of the need for watchfulness in the face of God's coming "like a thief in the night" is one that occurs frequently in the early Christian literature, and it is repeated in the *Apocalypse* itself (16:15; see *Matt.* 24:43; *Luke* 12:39; *2 Thess.* 2:5; *2 Pet.* 3:10). **3:5 *book of life*** The author frequently mentions this book, in which the names of the righteous are recorded (3:5; 13:8; 17:8; 20:12, 15; 21:27). It is also mentioned by Paul (*Phil.* 4:3), and a similar image is presented in *Testament of Abraham* 12. **3:7** *Isa.* 22:22. This is the first mention in early Christian literature of a church in Philadelphia. A short time after the writing of the *Apocalypse*, Ignatius passed through, leaving record of his visit there in a letter to the church. The city itself had been founded a little more than two hundred years earlier to promote Greek culture in the area. It, along with Sardis thirty miles to the west, had been devastated by an earthquake in 17 C.E. **3:9 *synagogue of Satan*** Not that there was a synagogue by that name—the author uses such language to dismiss his opponents. Scholars of the Johannine material generally recognize that the Christian community's identity was to some extent shaped by a broken relationship with the synagogue. See the description of Smyrna (2:9).

Jews and are not, but are lying—I will make them come and bow down before your feet, and they will learn that I have loved you. [10]Because you have kept my word of patient endurance, I will keep you from the hour of trial that is coming on the whole world to test the inhabitants of the earth. [11]I am coming soon; hold fast to what you have, so that no one may seize your crown. [12]If you conquer, I will make you a pillar in the temple of my God; you will never go out of it. I will write on you the name of my God, and the name of the city of my God, the new Jerusalem that comes down from my God out of heaven, and my own new name. [13]Let anyone who has an ear listen to what the Spirit is saying to the churches.

The Message to Laodicea

[14]"And to the angel of the church in Laodicea write: The words of the Amen, the faithful and true witness, the origin[k] of God's creation:

[15]"I know your works; you are neither cold nor hot. I wish that you were either cold or hot. [16]So, because you are lukewarm, and neither cold nor hot, I am about to spit you out of my mouth. [17]For you say, 'I am rich, I have prospered, and I need nothing.' You do not realize that you are wretched, pitiable, poor, blind, and naked. [18]Therefore I counsel you to buy from me gold refined by fire so that you may be rich; and white robes to clothe you and to keep the shame of your nakedness from being seen; and salve to anoint your eyes so that you may see. [19]I reprove and discipline those whom I love. Be earnest, therefore, and repent. [20]Listen! I am standing at the door, knocking; if you hear my voice and open the door, I will come in to you and eat with you, and you with me. [21]To the one who conquers I will give a place with me on my throne, just as I myself conquered and sat down with my Father on his throne. [22]Let anyone who has an ear listen to what the Spirit is saying to the churches."

The Heavenly Worship

4 After this I looked, and there in heaven a door stood open! And the first voice, which I had heard speaking to me like a trumpet, said, "Come up here, and I will show you what must take place after this." [2]At once I was in the spirit,[l] and there in heaven stood a throne, with one seated on the throne! [3]And the one seated there looks like jasper and carnelian, and around the throne is a rainbow that looks like an emerald. [4]Around the throne are twenty-four thrones, and seated on the thrones are twenty-four elders, dressed in white robes, with golden crowns on their heads. [5]Coming from the throne are flashes of lightning, and rumblings and peals of thunder, and in front of the throne burn seven flaming torches, which are the seven spirits of God; [6]and in front of the throne there is something like a sea of glass, like crystal.

Around the throne, and on each side of the throne, are four living creatures, full of eyes in front and behind: [7]the first living creature like a lion, the second living creature like an ox, the third living creature with a face like a human face, and the fourth living creature like a flying eagle. [8]And the four living creatures, each of them with six wings, are full of eyes all around and inside. Day and night without ceasing they sing,

"Holy, holy, holy,
the Lord God the Almighty,
who was and is and is to come."

[9]And whenever the living creatures give glory and honor and thanks to the one who is seated on the throne, who lives forever and ever, [10]the twenty-four elders fall before the one who is seated on the throne and worship the one who lives forever and ever; they cast their crowns before the throne, singing,

[11] "You are worthy, our Lord and God,
to receive glory and honor and power,
for you created all things,
and by your will they existed and were
created."

---

k Or *beginning*

l Or *in the Spirit*

3:14 **church in Laodicea** The church in Laodicea was mentioned in *Colossians* (4:15), which is attributed to Paul. Along with Colossae and Hierapolis, where tradition records that Philip the Evangelist and three of his daughters moved, the three cities formed a triangle in the wide Lycus valley. The ruins of Hierapolis are by far the most impressive, with little archaeological work done at Laodicea and the mound at Colossae still untouched. **Amen** This word is used nine times in the *Apocalypse*. It is a customary word in prayer, but here it seems to be used as a title. **3:15–16** The language perhaps recalls the poor quality of the water there, in contrast to the still impressive hot springs of Hierapolis and the clear water of Colossae. **3:17** Laodicea was a famous banking center and proudly refused routine imperial aid after the earthquake of 60 C.E. This would be similar, in the modern context, to refusing to be declared a disaster area. **3:18** *salve to anoint your eyes* Laodicea, which had a medical school, had become a center for pharmaceuticals and was particularly famous for eye salve. **4:1** Here begins the revelation proper. *first voice* See 1:10–11. **4:4** *twenty-four elders* It is unclear to what this refers; perhaps it indicates the twelve tribes of Israel and the twelve apostles. The author has used both groups separately elsewhere in his work. **4:6–8** *four living creatures* Isa. 6:2; Ezek. 1:5–14; 10:9–14. Strange creatures are stock images in apocalyptic works (*2 Enoch* 12). **4:8** Isa. 6:2–3.

The Scroll and the Lamb

5 Then I saw in the right hand of the one seated on the throne a scroll written on the inside and on the back, sealed[m] with seven seals; [2]and I saw a mighty angel proclaiming with a loud voice, "Who is worthy to open the scroll and break its seals?" [3]And no one in heaven or on earth or under the earth was able to open the scroll or to look into it. [4]And I began to weep bitterly because no one was found worthy to open the scroll or to look into it. [5]Then one of the elders said to me, "Do not weep. See, the Lion of the tribe of Judah, the Root of David, has conquered, so that he can open the scroll and its seven seals."

[6]Then I saw between the throne and the four living creatures and among the elders a Lamb standing as if it had been slaughtered, having seven horns and seven eyes, which are the seven spirits of God sent out into all the earth. [7]He went and took the scroll from the right hand of the one who was seated on the throne. [8]When he had taken the scroll, the four living creatures and the twenty-four elders fell before the Lamb, each holding a harp and golden bowls full of incense, which are the prayers of the saints. [9]They sing a new song:

"You are worthy to take the scroll
    and to open its seals,
for you were slaughtered and by your blood you
        ransomed for God
    saints from[n] every tribe and language and
        people and nation;
[10] you have made them to be a kingdom and
        priests serving[o] our God,
    and they will reign on earth."

[11]Then I looked, and I heard the voice of many angels surrounding the throne and the living creatures and the elders; they numbered myriads of myriads and thousands of thousands, [12]singing with full voice,

"Worthy is the Lamb that was slaughtered
to receive power and wealth and wisdom and
        might
and honor and glory and blessing!"

[13]Then I heard every creature in heaven and on earth and under the earth and in the sea, and all that is in them, singing,

"To the one seated on the throne and to the
        Lamb
be blessing and honor and glory and might
forever and ever!"

[14]And the four living creatures said, "Amen!" And the elders fell down and worshiped.

The Seven Seals

6 Then I saw the Lamb open one of the seven seals, and I heard one of the four living creatures call out, as with a voice of thunder, "Come!"[p] [2]I looked, and there was a white horse! Its rider had a bow; a crown was given to him, and he came out conquering and to conquer.

[3]When he opened the second seal, I heard the second living creature call out, "Come!"[p] [4]And out came[q] another horse, bright red; its rider was permitted to take peace from the earth, so that people would slaughter one another; and he was given a great sword.

[5]When he opened the third seal, I heard the third living creature call out, "Come!"[p] I looked, and there was a black horse! Its rider held a pair of scales in his hand, [6]and I heard what seemed to be a voice in the midst of the four living creatures saying, "A quart of wheat for a day's pay,[r] and three quarts of barley for a day's pay,[r] but do not damage the olive oil and the wine!"

[7]When he opened the fourth seal, I heard the voice of the fourth living creature call out, "Come!"[p] [8]I looked and there was a pale green horse! Its rider's name was Death, and Hades followed with him; they were given authority over a fourth of the earth, to kill with sword, famine, and pestilence, and by the wild animals of the earth.

[9]When he opened the fifth seal, I saw under the altar the souls of those who had been slaughtered for the word of God and for the testimony they had given; [10]they cried out with a loud voice, "Sovereign

---

m Or *written on the inside, and sealed on the back*
n Gk *ransomed for God from*
o Gk *priests to*

p Or *"Go!"*
q Or *went*
r Gk *a denarius*

5:1 A similar scroll, written on the front and back, is described in *Ezek.* 2:9–10. Since scrolls were designed to be written only on the inside, these scrolls are exceptional. **seven seals** An excessively sealed scroll. This was to protect the content from unauthorized, prying eyes and to attest its source. **5:5** 22:16. These links to David were used to point to the messianic qualifications of Jesus (*Gen.* 49:9; *Isa.* 11:1–10). King David was from the tribe of Judah, represented by a lion. **5:11** *Dan.* 7:10. **6:2–8** The image of the four horsemen of the Apocalypse is common in English literature. It is based on this passage, which itself is based on material in the Hebrew Bible (*Zech.* 1:7–11; 6:2–8). **6:6** *day's pay* Lit. "a denarius." This was a day's wage for a laborer. Various attempts were made in the empire to regulate prices and to prevent food riots. There had been a severe grain shortage perhaps just two or three years before John wrote (Suetonius, *Domitian* 7). **6:8** *Hades* Not hell but merely the abode of the dead (see 20:13). **6:10** This kind of question is raised often (*Isa.* 6:11; *Jer.* 47:6; *Zech.* 1:12).

Lord, holy and true, how long will it be before you judge and avenge our blood on the inhabitants of the earth?" [11]They were each given a white robe and told to rest a little longer, until the number would be complete both of their fellow servants[s] and of their brothers and sisters,[t] who were soon to be killed as they themselves had been killed.

[12]When he opened the sixth seal, I looked, and there came a great earthquake; the sun became black as sackcloth, the full moon became like blood, [13]and the stars of the sky fell to the earth as the fig tree drops its winter fruit when shaken by a gale. [14]The sky vanished like a scroll rolling itself up, and every mountain and island was removed from its place. [15]Then the kings of the earth and the magnates and the generals and the rich and the powerful, and everyone, slave and free, hid in the caves and among the rocks of the mountains, [16]calling to the mountains and rocks, "Fall on us and hide us from the face of the one seated on the throne and from the wrath of the Lamb; [17]for the great day of their wrath has come, and who is able to stand?"

The 144,000 of Israel Sealed

7After this I saw four angels standing at the four corners of the earth, holding back the four winds of the earth so that no wind could blow on earth or sea or against any tree. [2]I saw another angel ascending from the rising of the sun, having the seal of the living God, and he called with a loud voice to the four angels who had been given power to damage earth and sea, [3]saying, "Do not damage the earth or the sea or the trees, until we have marked the servants[s] of our God with a seal on their foreheads."

[4]And I heard the number of those who were sealed, one hundred forty-four thousand, sealed out of every tribe of the people of Israel:

[5] From the tribe of Judah twelve thousand sealed,
from the tribe of Reuben twelve thousand,
from the tribe of Gad twelve thousand,

[6] from the tribe of Asher twelve thousand,
from the tribe of Naphtali twelve thousand,
from the tribe of Manasseh twelve thousand,

[7] from the tribe of Simeon twelve thousand,
from the tribe of Levi twelve thousand,
from the tribe of Issachar twelve thousand,

[8] from the tribe of Zebulun twelve thousand,
from the tribe of Joseph twelve thousand,
from the tribe of Benjamin twelve thousand sealed.

The Multitude from Every Nation

[9]After this I looked, and there was a great multitude that no one could count, from every nation, from all tribes and peoples and languages, standing before the throne and before the Lamb, robed in white, with palm branches in their hands. [10]They cried out in a loud voice, saying,

"Salvation belongs to our God who is seated on
the throne, and to the Lamb!"

[11]And all the angels stood around the throne and around the elders and the four living creatures, and they fell on their faces before the throne and worshiped God, [12]singing,

"Amen! Blessing and glory and wisdom
and thanksgiving and honor
and power and might
be to our God forever and ever! Amen."

[13]Then one of the elders addressed me, saying, "Who are these, robed in white, and where have they come from?" [14]I said to him, "Sir, you are the one that knows." Then he said to me, "These are they who have come out of the great ordeal; they have washed their robes and made them white in the blood of the Lamb.

[15] For this reason they are before the throne of
God,
and worship him day and night within his
temple,
and the one who is seated on the throne will
shelter them.

[16] They will hunger no more, and thirst no more;
the sun will not strike them,
nor any scorching heat;

[17] for the Lamb at the center of the throne will be
their shepherd,
and he will guide them to springs of the
water of life,
and God will wipe away every tear from their
eyes."

The Seventh Seal and the Golden Censer

8When the Lamb opened the seventh seal, there was silence in heaven for about half an hour. [2]And I saw the seven angels who stand before God, and seven trumpets were given to them.

---

s Gk *slaves*
t Gk *brothers*

6:12–14 The images in these verses are standard apocalyptic language (see 8:12). **6:16** *Isa.* 2:10; 19; *Hos.* 10:8. **7:3** *Ezek.* 9:4. **7:4** The tribe of Dan is missing; Manasseh takes its place. The tribes may refer to the church, which often saw itself as the new Israel (*Rom.* 9:6–7; *Gal.* 4:26; 6:16). The omission of Dan may show that membership in Israel could be altered. **7:9 robed in white** *Zech.* 3:3–5; *1 En.* 62.16; *2 En.* 22.8 **7:16–17** *Isa.* 49:10; 25:8.

3Another angel with a golden censer came and stood at the altar; he was given a great quantity of incense to offer with the prayers of all the saints on the golden altar that is before the throne. 4And the smoke of the incense, with the prayers of the saints, rose before God from the hand of the angel. 5Then the angel took the censer and filled it with fire from the altar and threw it on the earth; and there were peals of thunder, rumblings, flashes of lightning, and an earthquake.

The Seven Trumpets

6Now the seven angels who had the seven trumpets made ready to blow them.

7The first angel blew his trumpet, and there came hail and fire, mixed with blood, and they were hurled to the earth; and a third of the earth was burned up, and a third of the trees were burned up, and all green grass was burned up.

8The second angel blew his trumpet, and something like a great mountain, burning with fire, was thrown into the sea. 9A third of the sea became blood, a third of the living creatures in the sea died, and a third of the ships were destroyed.

10The third angel blew his trumpet, and a great star fell from heaven, blazing like a torch, and it fell on a third of the rivers and on the springs of water. 11The name of the star is Wormwood. A third of the waters became wormwood, and many died from the water, because it was made bitter.

12The fourth angel blew his trumpet, and a third of the sun was struck, and a third of the moon, and a third of the stars, so that a third of their light was darkened; a third of the day was kept from shining, and likewise the night.

13Then I looked, and I heard an eagle crying with a loud voice as it flew in midheaven, "Woe, woe, woe to the inhabitants of the earth, at the blasts of the other trumpets that the three angels are about to blow!"

9And the fifth angel blew his trumpet, and I saw a star that had fallen from heaven to earth, and he was given the key to the shaft of the bottomless pit; 2he opened the shaft of the bottomless pit, and from the shaft rose smoke like the smoke of a great furnace, and the sun and the air were darkened with the smoke from the shaft. 3Then from the smoke came locusts on the earth, and they were given authority like the authority of scorpions of the earth. 4They were told not to damage the grass of the earth or any green growth or any tree, but only those people who do not have the seal of God on their foreheads. 5They were allowed to torture them for five months, but not to kill them, and their torture was like the torture of a scorpion when it stings someone. 6And in those days people will seek death but will not find it; they will long to die, but death will flee from them.

7In appearance the locusts were like horses equipped for battle. On their heads were what looked like crowns of gold; their faces were like human faces, 8their hair like women's hair, and their teeth like lions' teeth; 9they had scales like iron breastplates, and the noise of their wings was like the noise of many chariots with horses rushing into battle. 10They have tails like scorpions, with stingers, and in their tails is their power to harm people for five months. 11They have as king over them the angel of the bottomless pit; his name in Hebrew is Abaddon,u and in Greek he is called Apollyon.v

12The first woe has passed. There are still two woes to come.

13Then the sixth angel blew his trumpet, and I heard a voice from the fourw horns of the golden altar before God, 14saying to the sixth angel who had

---

u That is, *Destruction*
v That is, *Destroyer*
w Other ancient authorities lack *four*

8:7–12 The 1st four trumpets are set apart from the final three. The mention of plagues would immediately remind the readers of the classic plagues in Hebrew history—those that fell upon the Egyptians and resulted in the Hebrew escape from slavery (*Exod.* 7:14–11:1). The author has been influenced by the details of several of these plagues and by the images from *Joel*. **8:10** *Jer.* 51:25, 42; *1 En.* 18.13; *Sibylline Oracles* 5.158. **8:11** *Wormwood Jer.* 9:15; 23:15. It is possible that the image of a falling star recalls the myth of Helel (NRSV: "Day Star"), who tried to become king of heaven (*Isa.* 14:12–20). **8:12** The darkening of the sun and moon is a stock image of apocalyptic writing (*Joel* 2:10, 31; 3:15; *Isa.* 13:10; 34:4; *Sibylline Oracles* 8.203–204, 232–234) and also in early Christian apocalyptic (*Mark* 13:24; *Matt.* 24:29; *Acts* 2:20). **9:1** The star here must be Apollyon, the king over the bottomless pit (9:11). *bottomless pit* Gk *abyssos*. The abyss figured in many creation stories as the hostile element out of which creation came, and in the LXX *abyssos* translates the word usually rendered "the deep" (*Gen.* 1:2). The abyss was the home of the dead and of demons (*Ps.* 107:26; *1 En.* 18.9–12; 21.1–22.4). **9:3** *locusts* Not only the plague itself but numerous other details are taken from *Joel* 2:1–11. **9:11** *Abaddon* The name, meaning "destruction" in Hebrew, is used a few times in the Bible as a synonym for Sheol, the place of the dead. Apollyon means "destroyer" in Gk. Some believe that the author intended the reader to think of the god Apollo and the current emperor Domitian, who identified with this god. Greeks understood the name Apollo to relate to the word for "destruction" (Aeschylus, *Agamemnon* 1082; see *1 Cor.* 2:19). **9:13** *four horns of the golden altar* The altar used for sacrifice was square, each corner having a hornlike object that could be used to tie the sacrificial victim down. **9:14** *Euphrates* One of the two great rivers of Mesopotamia, it could easily call up memories of Babylon and exile for Jews. For the Romans, it could call to mind the troublesome Parthians on their eastern borders, the only serious threat to the Roman peace.

the trumpet, "Release the four angels who are bound at the great river Euphrates." 15So the four angels were released, who had been held ready for the hour, the day, the month, and the year, to kill a third of humankind. 16The number of the troops of cavalry was two hundred million; I heard their number. 17And this was how I saw the horses in my vision: the riders wore breastplates the color of fire and of sapphire*x* and of sulfur; the heads of the horses were like lions' heads, and fire and smoke and sulfur came out of their mouths. 18By these three plagues a third of humankind was killed, by the fire and smoke and sulfur coming out of their mouths. 19For the power of the horses is in their mouths and in their tails; their tails are like serpents, having heads; and with them they inflict harm.

20The rest of humankind, who were not killed by these plagues, did not repent of the works of their hands or give up worshiping demons and idols of gold and silver and bronze and stone and wood, which cannot see or hear or walk. 21And they did not repent of their murders or their sorceries or their fornication or their thefts.

The Angel with the Little Scroll

10And I saw another mighty angel coming down from heaven, wrapped in a cloud, with a rainbow over his head; his face was like the sun, and his legs like pillars of fire. 2He held a little scroll open in his hand. Setting his right foot on the sea and his left foot on the land, 3he gave a great shout, like a lion roaring. And when he shouted, the seven thunders sounded. 4And when the seven thunders had sounded, I was about to write, but I heard a voice from heaven saying, "Seal up what the seven thunders have said, and do not write it down." 5Then the angel whom I saw standing on the sea and the land

raised his right hand to heaven 6 and swore by him who lives forever and ever, who created heaven and what is in it, the earth and what is in it, and the sea and what is in it: "There will be no more delay, 7but in the days when the seventh angel is to blow his trumpet, the mystery of God will be fulfilled, as he announced to his servants*y* the prophets."

8Then the voice that I had heard from heaven spoke to me again, saying, "Go, take the scroll that is open in the hand of the angel who is standing on the sea and on the land." 9So I went to the angel and told him to give me the little scroll; and he said to me, "Take it, and eat; it will be bitter to your stomach, but sweet as honey in your mouth." 10So I took the little scroll from the hand of the angel and ate it; it was sweet as honey in my mouth, but when I had eaten it, my stomach was made bitter.

11Then they said to me, "You must prophesy again about many peoples and nations and languages and kings."

The Two Witnesses

11Then I was given a measuring rod like a staff, and I was told, "Come and measure the temple of God and the altar and those who worship there, 2but do not measure the court outside the temple; leave that out, for it is given over to the nations, and they will trample over the holy city for forty-two months. 3And I will grant my two witnesses authority to prophesy for one thousand two hundred sixty days, wearing sackcloth."

4These are the two olive trees and the two lampstands that stand before the Lord of the earth. 5And if anyone wants to harm them, fire pours from their mouth and consumes their foes; anyone who wants to harm them must be killed in this manner.

---

x Gk *hyacinth*

y Gk *slaves*

9:20 This is a standard Jewish and Christian critique of Greek religion (*Ps.* 115:4; 2:20; 20:19–20). **10:1–11** This seems to mark a digression, but it is unclear where it was intended to lead. The emphasis is on a remarkable angel and a little scroll; the scene is of description rather than action; and the result is hiding rather than disclosure. The passage does lead to a scene in which the author becomes the active participant; for the most part, he has been merely an observer. The angel is one of three angels identified as "mighty" (5:2; 18:21). **10:4** *seal up* See note to 1:3 above. **10:5–7** *Dan.* 12:6–7. **10:7** The 7th trumpet sounds in 11:15. *announced* Gk *euēngelisen,* from the same root from which the word for "gospel" comes. Ignatius included the prophets in a similar way (Ign. *Magn.* 2–9.2). **10:10** A similar scene is found in *Ezek.* 2:8–3:3. **11:1** *Ezekiel* 40 describes the measuring of the temple, as does *Zech.* 2:1–5. Whatever is measured seems to be assured protection. **11:2** *outer court* This was the part of the temple complex to which Gentiles were restricted. The angel announces that the Gentiles will indeed have this part, as Jesus himself warned (*Luke* 21:24). *forty-two months* Various ways are used to describe the same period of time: forty-two months; three and a half years; one thousand two hundred and sixty days; half a week (with each day signifying one year). The length of the time of distress is shaped by the phrase "time, two times, and half a time," taken from *Daniel* (7:25; 12:7, 14). The same measure of time is given in *Rev.* 12:6. For a slightly different measuring of time, see *2 Barn.* 26.1–28.2. There was no standard chronological scheme in apocalyptic literature. **11:4** *two olive trees* *Zech.* 4:3, 11, 14. See 1:12.

[6]They have authority to shut the sky, so that no rain may fall during the days of their prophesying, and they have authority over the waters to turn them into blood, and to strike the earth with every kind of plague, as often as they desire.

[7]When they have finished their testimony, the beast that comes up from the bottomless pit will make war on them and conquer them and kill them, [8]and their dead bodies will lie in the street of the great city that is prophetically[z] called Sodom and Egypt, where also their Lord was crucified. [9]For three and a half days members of the peoples and tribes and languages and nations will gaze at their dead bodies and refuse to let them be placed in a tomb; [10]and the inhabitants of the earth will gloat over them and celebrate and exchange presents, because these two prophets had been a torment to the inhabitants of the earth.

[11]But after the three and a half days, the breath[a] of life from God entered them, and they stood on their feet, and those who saw them were terrified. [12]Then they[b] heard a loud voice from heaven saying to them, "Come up here!" And they went up to heaven in a cloud while their enemies watched them. [13]At that moment there was a great earthquake, and a tenth of the city fell; seven thousand people were killed in the earthquake, and the rest were terrified and gave glory to the God of heaven.

[14]The second woe has passed. The third woe is coming very soon.

The Seventh Trumpet

[15]Then the seventh angel blew his trumpet, and there were loud voices in heaven, saying,

"The kingdom of the world has become the
   kingdom of our Lord
    and of his Messiah,[c]
and he will reign forever and ever."
[16]Then the twenty-four elders who sit on their thrones before God fell on their faces and worshiped God, [17]singing,

"We give you thanks, Lord God Almighty,
   who are and who were,
for you have taken your great power
   and begun to reign.
[18] The nations raged,
   but your wrath has come,
   and the time for judging the dead,
for rewarding your servants,[d] the prophets
   and saints and all who fear your name,
    both small and great,
and for destroying those who destroy the earth."

[19]Then God's temple in heaven was opened, and the ark of his covenant was seen within his temple; and there were flashes of lightning, rumblings, peals of thunder, an earthquake, and heavy hail.

The Woman and the Dragon

12 A great portent appeared in heaven: a woman clothed with the sun, with the moon under her feet, and on her head a crown of twelve stars. [2]She was pregnant and was crying out in birth pangs, in the agony of giving birth. [3]Then another portent appeared in heaven: a great red dragon, with seven heads and ten horns, and seven diadems on his heads. [4]His tail swept down a third of the stars of heaven and

---

z Or *allegorically;* Gk *spiritually*
a Or *the spirit*
b Other ancient authorities read *I*

---

c Gk *Christ*
d Gk *slaves*

11:6 The image of water turned to blood would call to mind traditions about Moses (*Exod.* 7:17). The image of the rain being held back would call to mind traditions about Elijah (*1 Kgs.* 17:1). Elijah's career was a well-known story in early Christian circles (*Luke* 4:25; *Jas.* 5:17). Here the length of the drought is altered slightly from a period of less than three years in the Bible to three and a half years. This fits John's scheme perfectly here. Some scholars think that such a change had already been made in Judaism itself. The return of Elijah at the end of the age was an aspect of apocalyptic speculation (*Mark* 9:11–13; *Matt.* 17:10–12; *Luke* 9:8; *John* 1:21, 25; *Sib. Or.* 2.186–189, where he is referred to merely as the Thesbite). Apparently, such speculation was based on a comment in *Mal.* 3:23. Moses and Elijah are linked in *Mark* 9:4; *Matt.* 17:3; *Luke* 9:30. **11:8** It is debated whether the author means Jerusalem or Rome. The statement that this was where the Lord was crucified might seem to point to Jerusalem, but the struggle for the author was with the Roman Empire, under whose authority Jesus had been killed and his followers were now being killed. In the seven other places where John speaks of "the great city," he means Rome, and it is possible that he means it here. (Paul speaks figuratively of Jerusalem in *Gal.* 4:25–26.) **11:12 they heard** Other ancient authorities read "I heard." The difference in Gk is slight: *they heard* is *ēkousan;* "I heard" is *ēkousa.* **11:15** The seventh trumpet does not announce doom but celebrates the heavenly victory that has come about, in part, because of the calamities of the previous trumpets. Similar language is found in *Dan.* 2:7; 7:14, 27 **11:16 twenty-four elders** See 4:4, 10; 5:8; 19:4. **12:1–6** The motif of the child prince destined for greatness but hunted by opponents is a popular theme in legend and mythology. **12:3 dragon** John uses the same Gk word nine times to describe Satan (see particularly 12:9). It is the same word the LXX uses for Leviathan, the mythic sea monster (*Job* 41:1 [LXX 40:25]; *Ps.* 74:14 [LXX 73:14]; *Isa.* 27:1). See *1 En.* 60.7–8; *2 Esd.* 6:49–52; *2 Bar.* 29:4 for stories of this creature. **ten horns** A ten-horned beast is mentioned in *Dan.* 7:7. The same beast is introduced in 17:3, where it clearly represents the Roman Empire. **12:4** *Dan.* 8:10 has a similar scene where the stars of the heavens are cast down.

threw them to the earth. Then the dragon stood before the woman who was about to bear a child, so that he might devour her child as soon as it was born. [5]And she gave birth to a son, a male child, who is to rule[e] all the nations with a rod of iron. But her child was snatched away and taken to God and to his throne; [6]and the woman fled into the wilderness, where she has a place prepared by God, so that there she can be nourished for one thousand two hundred sixty days.

Michael Defeats the Dragon

[7]And war broke out in heaven; Michael and his angels fought against the dragon. The dragon and his angels fought back, [8]but they were defeated, and there was no longer any place for them in heaven. [9]The great dragon was thrown down, that ancient serpent, who is called the Devil and Satan, the deceiver of the whole world—he was thrown down to the earth, and his angels were thrown down with him. [10]Then I heard a loud voice in heaven, proclaiming,

"Now have come the salvation and the power
 and the kingdom of our God
 and the authority of his Messiah,[f]
for the accuser of our comrades[g] has been
 thrown down,
 who accuses them day and night before our
 God.
[11] But they have conquered him by the blood of
 the Lamb
 and by the word of their testimony,
for they did not cling to life even in the face of
 death.
[12] Rejoice then, you heavens
 and those who dwell in them!

But woe to the earth and the sea,
 for the devil has come down to you
with great wrath,
 because he knows that his time is short!"

The Dragon Fights Again on Earth

[13]So when the dragon saw that he had been thrown down to the earth, he pursued[h] the woman who had given birth to the male child. [14]But the woman was given the two wings of the great eagle, so that she could fly from the serpent into the wilderness, to her place where she is nourished for a time, and times, and half a time. [15]Then from his mouth the serpent poured water like a river after the woman, to sweep her away with the flood. [16]But the earth came to the help of the woman; it opened its mouth and swallowed the river that the dragon had poured from his mouth. [17]Then the dragon was angry with the woman, and went off to make war on the rest of her children, those who keep the commandments of God and hold the testimony of Jesus.

The First Beast

[18]Then the dragon[i] took his stand on the sand of the seashore. **13** [1]And I saw a beast rising out of the sea, having ten horns and seven heads; and on its horns were ten diadems, and on its heads were blasphemous names. [2]And the beast that I saw was like a leopard, its feet were like a bear's, and its mouth was like a lion's mouth. And the dragon gave it his power and his throne and great authority. [3]One of its heads seemed to have received a death-blow, but its mortal wound[j] had been healed. In amazement the whole earth followed the beast. [4]They worshiped the

---

e Or to shepherd
f Gk Christ
g Gk brothers

h Or persecuted
i Gk Then he; other ancient authorities read Then I stood
j Gk the plague of its death

12:5 The description is based on *Ps.* 2:8–9, a passage applied to David's son, the Messiah. **12:6** *two hundred sixty days* See 11:2.; see also *Dan.* 7:25. **12:7** *Michael Dan.* 10:13. Michael was one of the chief angels, or archangels, and was a stock figure of apocalyptic literature (*Jude* 9; *1 En.* 9.1; *Sib. Or.* 2.215). **12:9** See 12:3. **12:10** This scene reflects the tradition of Satan's ejection from heaven (*Isa.* 14:12–15; *2 En.* 29.4–5), which Christians borrowed (*Luke* 10:18; *John* 12:31). **12:18** *the dragon* Lit. "he"; other ancient authorities read "I stood." The difference in Gk is slight: "he stood" is *estathē*; "I stood" is *estathēn.* **13:1** The beast rising out of the sea is similar to the beast introduced in 12:3, but it must be different, since the earlier beast is present in the scene as this second beast appears (12:18) and it later gives the second beast its authority (13:2). The beast arising out of the sea seems to be the same beast as arises out of the bottomless pit, or abyss (11:7) (on the meaning of "abyss," see note to 9:1.) *blasphemous names* The imperial cult used the titles "lord" and "savior," which Christians applied to Jesus. The use of the same terms may have sharpened the consciousness of Christians in areas where the imperial cult was popular—loyalty to one would be seen as stark disloyalty to the other. Also, coins bearing the imprint of the emperors had recently begun to carry the title *Divus,* declaring the divinity of living emperors. Domitian, the emperor at the time of the writing of the *Apocalypse,* may have pressed his claim even further, wanting to be called lord and god (Suetonius, *Domitian* 13), titles that, even when reserved for dead emperors, would have been offensive to Christians. **13:2** These beasts are somewhat similar to those in *Dan.* 7:3–7. **13:3** Most commentators believe that John is referring here to Nero, who committed suicide in 68 C.E., bringing to an end the Julio-Claudian dynasty. A belief circulated widely in the Roman world that the hated Nero was not really dead but would return (*Sibylline Oracles* 5.28–34, 93–110), and at least three impostors claimed to be Nero (Tacitus, *Histories* 1.2; 2.8; Suetonius, *Nero* 57).

dragon, for he had given his authority to the beast,
and they worshiped the beast, saying, "Who is like the
beast, and who can fight against it?"
5 The beast was given a mouth uttering haughty
and blasphemous words, and it was allowed to exercise authority for forty-two months. 6 It opened its
mouth to utter blasphemies against God, blaspheming his name and his dwelling, that is, those who dwell
in heaven. 7 Also it was allowed to make war on the
saints and to conquer them.[k] It was given authority
over every tribe and people and language and nation,
8 and all the inhabitants of the earth will worship it,
everyone whose name has not been written from the
foundation of the world in the book of life of the
Lamb that was slaughtered.[l]
9 Let anyone who has an ear listen:
10 If you are to be taken captive,
into captivity you go;
if you kill with the sword,
with the sword you must be killed.
Here is a call for the endurance and faith of the saints.

The Second Beast

11 Then I saw another beast that rose out of the
earth; it had two horns like a lamb and it spoke like
a dragon. 12 It exercises all the authority of the first
beast on its behalf, and it makes the earth and its
inhabitants worship the first beast, whose mortal
wound[m] had been healed. 13 It performs great signs,
even making fire come down from heaven to earth in
the sight of all; 14 and by the signs that it is allowed to
perform on behalf of the beast, it deceives the inhabitants of earth, telling them to make an image for the
beast that had been wounded by the sword[n] and yet
lived; 15 and it was allowed to give breath[o] to the
image of the beast so that the image of the beast
could even speak and cause those who would not
worship the image of the beast to be killed. 16 Also it
causes all, both small and great, both rich and poor,
both free and slave, to be marked on the right hand
or the forehead, 17 so that no one can buy or sell who
does not have the mark, that is, the name of the beast
or the number of its name. 18 This calls for wisdom:
let anyone with understanding calculate the number
of the beast, for it is the number of a person. Its number is six hundred sixty-six.[p]

The Lamb and the 144,000

14 Then I looked, and there was the Lamb, standing on Mount Zion! And with him were one
hundred forty-four thousand who had his name and
his Father's name written on their foreheads. 2 And I
heard a voice from heaven like the sound of many
waters and like the sound of loud thunder; the voice I
heard was like the sound of harpists playing on their
harps, 3 and they sing a new song before the throne and
before the four living creatures and before the elders.
No one could learn that song except the one hundred
forty-four thousand who have been redeemed from
the earth. 4 It is these who have not defiled themselves
with women, for they are virgins; these follow the Lamb
wherever he goes. They have been redeemed from
humankind as first fruits for God and the Lamb, 5 and
in their mouth no lie was found; they are blameless.

The Messages of the Three Angels

6 Then I saw another angel flying in midheaven,
with an eternal gospel to proclaim to those who live[q]

k Other ancient authorities lack this sentence
l Or *written in the book of life of the Lamb that was slaughtered from the foundation of the world*
m Gk *whose plague of its death*
n Or *that had received the plague of the sword*
o Or *spirit*
p Other ancient authorities read *six hundred sixteen*
q Gk *sit*

13:5–10 This may be the author's perception of the imperial cult: It fought against the saints, and it controlled all the world (see also 13:14–17). The threat of slavery or death hung over Christians caught by the authorities (13:10). The language provides a bleaker and more ironic twist to a passage in *Jer.* 15:2. **13:7** *Dan.* 7:21. **13:11–12** This new beast may represent the priesthood of the imperial cult, which was promoted in Asia Minor. This priesthood, to which wealthy citizens were elected for a period of one year, was more political than religious, almost a matter of civic duty and pride. Such priests were called Asiarchs. **13:14** ***image of the beast*** John probably has in mind the statues of the emperors used in the imperial cult. **13:15** In *Daniel,* those who did not worship the image of the king were killed (*Dan.* 3:5–6). **13:18** ***six hundred sixty-six*** See note *p* above. Both Jews and Greeks used letters of their alphabet to indicate numbers, not having a distinct numerical system; thus a name could have a number. This was calculated by taking the sum of all the letters of the word for which a numerical value was assigned, a process called gematria. Examples of the practice can be found in *Sib. Or.* 1.324–329; 5.12–42. Various attempts have been made, even from the early period, to discover the individual intended here by the number. Nero is a possibility. Some modern groups still attempt to identify an antichrist figure by this number. **14:1** ***Mount Zion*** That is, Jerusalem. ***one hundred and forty-four thousand*** The number is probably symbolic (7:1–8), as are most numbers in the *Apocalypse.* ***name . . . on their foreheads*** Those having the Lamb's and the Lamb's Father's name in their forehead stand in opposition to those who had received the mark of the beast in their forehead (13:16). **14:5** *Zeph.* 3:13.

on the earth—to every nation and tribe and language and people. ⁷He said in a loud voice, "Fear God and give him glory, for the hour of his judgment has come; and worship him who made heaven and earth, the sea and the springs of water."

⁸Then another angel, a second, followed, saying, "Fallen, fallen is Babylon the great! She has made all nations drink of the wine of the wrath of her fornication."

⁹Then another angel, a third, followed them, crying with a loud voice, "Those who worship the beast and its image, and receive a mark on their foreheads or on their hands, ¹⁰they will also drink the wine of God's wrath, poured unmixed into the cup of his anger, and they will be tormented with fire and sulfur in the presence of the holy angels and in the presence of the Lamb. ¹¹And the smoke of their torment goes up forever and ever. There is no rest day or night for those who worship the beast and its image and for anyone who receives the mark of its name."

¹²Here is a call for the endurance of the saints, those who keep the commandments of God and hold fast to the faith of* Jesus.

¹³And I heard a voice from heaven saying, "Write this: Blessed are the dead who from now on die in the Lord." "Yes," says the Spirit, "they will rest from their labors, for their deeds follow them."

Reaping the Earth's Harvest

¹⁴Then I looked, and there was a white cloud, and seated on the cloud was one like the Son of Man, with a golden crown on his head, and a sharp sickle in his hand! ¹⁵Another angel came out of the temple, calling with a loud voice to the one who sat on the cloud, "Use your sickle and reap, for the hour to reap has come, because the harvest of the earth is fully ripe." ¹⁶So the one who sat on the cloud swung his sickle over the earth, and the earth was reaped.

¹⁷Then another angel came out of the temple in heaven, and he too had a sharp sickle. ¹⁸Then another angel came out from the altar, the angel who has authority over fire, and he called with a loud voice to him who had the sharp sickle, "Use your sharp sickle and gather the clusters of the vine of the earth, for its grapes are ripe." ¹⁹So the angel swung his sickle over the earth and gathered the vintage of the earth, and he threw it into the great wine press of the wrath of God. ²⁰And the wine press was trodden outside the city, and blood flowed from the wine press, as high as a horse's bridle, for a distance of about two hundred miles.*

The Angels with the Seven Last Plagues

15 Then I saw another portent in heaven, great and amazing: seven angels with seven plagues, which are the last, for with them the wrath of God is ended.

²And I saw what appeared to be a sea of glass mixed with fire, and those who had conquered the beast and its image and the number of its name, standing beside the sea of glass with harps of God in their hands. ³And they sing the song of Moses, the servant* of God, and the song of the Lamb:

"Great and amazing are your deeds,
　Lord God the Almighty!
Just and true are your ways,
　King of the nations!*
⁴　Lord, who will not fear
　and glorify your name?
For you alone are holy.
　All nations will come
　and worship before you,
for your judgments have been revealed."

⁵After this I looked, and the temple of the tent* of witness in heaven was opened, ⁶and out of the temple came the seven angels with the seven plagues, robed in pure bright linen,* with golden sashes across

---

r Or *to their faith in*

s Gk *one thousand six hundred stadia*
t Gk *slave*
u Other ancient authorities read *the ages*
v Or *tabernacle*
w Other ancient authorities read *stone*

14:8 *Babylon the great* Isa. 21:9. **14:9–11** Here is a reversal of the story in 13:11–18. Those who had the mark of the beast escaped the beast's wrath, only to fall now under the wrath of God. **14:14** *a white cloud* Dan. 7:13. *Son of Man* See 1:13. **14:15** *fully ripe* Joel 3:13. Acts of harvesting were often employed as images of judgment and salvation (*Hos.* 6:11; *Jer.* 51:33; *Joel* 3:9–14; *Matt.* 13:30, 39; *Luke* 10:2; *John* 4:35–38). **14:19** Isa. 63:3. **14:20** *as high as a horse's bridle* 1 En. 100.3 talks of blood up to a horse's chest. *two hundred miles* Lit. *one thousand six hundred stadia.* The NRSV translators generally have converted ancient ways of measuring to modern ways. In the *Apocalypse,* however, the ancient units of measurement perhaps should be retained, since numbers were often part of the code of apocalyptic writing and can carry meaning (at least at times) as specific numbers. **15:1** Various plagues and disasters were recounted in *Revelation* 8–9. **15:3** *Song of Moses* Exod. 15:1–18; Deut. 32:1–47. The shared context is deliverance from severe oppression. **15:5** *tent of witness* The original Hebrew holy place for God, something like a portable temple (*Exod.* 25:9, 40; *Heb.* 8:2; 9:11). **15:6** *linen* Other ancient authorities read "stone." In Gk, the difference is slight: linen is *linon*; "stone" is *lithon*.

their chests. [7]Then one of the four living creatures gave the seven angels seven golden bowls full of the wrath of God, who lives forever and ever; [8]and the temple was filled with smoke from the glory of God and from his power, and no one could enter the temple until the seven plagues of the seven angels were ended.

The Bowls of God's Wrath

16 Then I heard a loud voice from the temple telling the seven angels, "Go and pour out on the earth the seven bowls of the wrath of God."

[2]So the first angel went and poured his bowl on the earth, and a foul and painful sore came on those who had the mark of the beast and who worshiped its image.

[3]The second angel poured his bowl into the sea, and it became like the blood of a corpse, and every living thing in the sea died.

[4]The third angel poured his bowl into the rivers and the springs of water, and they became blood. [5]And I heard the angel of the waters say,

"You are just, O Holy One, who are and were,
    for you have judged these things;
[6] because they shed the blood of saints and
        prophets,
    you have given them blood to drink.
It is what they deserve!"
[7]And I heard the altar respond,
"Yes, O Lord God, the Almighty,
    your judgments are true and just!"

[8]The fourth angel poured his bowl on the sun, and it was allowed to scorch them with fire; [9]they were scorched by the fierce heat, but they cursed the name of God, who had authority over these plagues, and they did not repent and give him glory.

[10]The fifth angel poured his bowl on the throne of the beast, and its kingdom was plunged into darkness; people gnawed their tongues in agony, [11]and cursed the God of heaven because of their pains and sores, and they did not repent of their deeds.

[12]The sixth angel poured his bowl on the great river Euphrates, and its water was dried up in order to prepare the way for the kings from the east. [13]And I saw three foul spirits like frogs coming from the mouth of the dragon, from the mouth of the beast, and from the mouth of the false prophet. [14]These are demonic spirits, performing signs, who go abroad to the kings of the whole world, to assemble them for battle on the great day of God the Almighty. [15]("See, I am coming like a thief! Blessed is the one who stays awake and is clothed,[x] not going about naked and exposed to shame.") [16]And they assembled them at the place that in Hebrew is called Harmagedon.

[17]The seventh angel poured his bowl into the air, and a loud voice came out of the temple, from the throne, saying, "It is done!" [18]And there came flashes of lightning, rumblings, peals of thunder, and a violent earthquake, such as had not occurred since people were upon the earth, so violent was that earthquake. [19]The great city was split into three parts, and the cities of the nations fell. God remembered great Babylon and gave her the wine-cup of the fury of his wrath. [20]And every island fled away, and no mountains were to be found; [21]and huge hailstones, each weighing about a hundred pounds,[y] dropped from heaven on people, until they cursed God for the plague of the hail, so fearful was that plague.

The Great Whore and the Beast

17 Then one of the seven angels who had the seven bowls came and said to me, "Come, I will show you the judgment of the great whore who is seated on many waters, [2]with whom the kings of the earth have committed fornication, and with the wine of whose fornication the inhabitants of the earth have become drunk." [3]So he carried me away in the spirit[z] into a wilderness, and I saw a woman sitting on a scarlet beast that was full of blasphemous names, and it had seven heads and ten horns. [4]The woman was clothed in purple and scarlet, and adorned with gold and jewels and pearls, holding in her hand a golden cup full of abominations and the impurities of her fornication; [5]and on her forehead was written a name, a mystery: "Babylon the great, mother of whores and of

---

x Gk *and keeps his robes*
y Gk *weighing about a talent*
z Or *in the Spirit*

15:8 *Isa.* 6:4 records a similar scene indicating the presence of God in his temple. The smoke could have come from burning incense, a regular feature of ancient religious ritual (*Rev.* 8:4). **16:2** Judgment had already been poured out on those with the mark of the beast (14:9–11). **16:3–4** A similar plague on the waters is recounted in 8:9. **16:10** A similar plague of darkness is recounted in 8:12. **16:12** The Euphrates River is mentioned in 9:14. **16:15** See 3:3. **16:16** *Harmagedon* The more commonly known form of this word is Armageddon, from earlier translations of the Bible. Armageddon has become the symbol of catastrophic war and destruction. The word is derived from Mount Megiddo, but the manuscripts offer a variety of spellings at this point and other meanings are possible. It is presented here as the site of the final cosmic battle between good and evil. Megiddo itself was a plain on the southern border of Galilee, set between hilly land and running in the direction of Mount Carmel. So situated, it became the site of many battles. **16:18** *Dan.* 12:1. **16:20** *Isa.* 40:4; *Ezek.* 38:20. **17:4** *abominations* The same word is used in an apocalyptic context in *Dan.* 9:27; 11:31; 12:11; *Mark* 13:14.

earth's abominations." [6]And I saw that the woman was drunk with the blood of the saints and the blood of the witnesses to Jesus.

When I saw her, I was greatly amazed. [7]But the angel said to me, "Why are you so amazed? I will tell you the mystery of the woman, and of the beast with seven heads and ten horns that carries her. [8]The beast that you saw was, and is not, and is about to ascend from the bottomless pit and go to destruction. And the inhabitants of the earth, whose names have not been written in the book of life from the foundation of the world, will be amazed when they see the beast, because it was and is not and is to come.

[9]"This calls for a mind that has wisdom: the seven heads are seven mountains on which the woman is seated; also, they are seven kings, [10]of whom five have fallen, one is living, and the other has not yet come; and when he comes, he must remain only a little while. [11]As for the beast that was and is not, it is an eighth but it belongs to the seven, and it goes to destruction. [12]And the ten horns that you saw are ten kings who have not yet received a kingdom, but they are to receive authority as kings for one hour, together with the beast. [13]These are united in yielding their power and authority to the beast; [14]they will make war on the Lamb, and the Lamb will conquer them, for he is Lord of lords and King of kings, and those with him are called and chosen and faithful."

[15]And he said to me, "The waters that you saw, where the whore is seated, are peoples and multitudes and nations and languages. [16]And the ten horns that you saw, they and the beast will hate the whore; they will make her desolate and naked; they will devour her flesh and burn her up with fire. [17]For God has put it into their hearts to carry out his purpose by agreeing to give their kingdom to the beast, until the words of God will be fulfilled. [18]The woman you saw is the great city that rules over the kings of the earth."

The Fall of Babylon

18 After this I saw another angel coming down from heaven, having great authority; and the earth was made bright with his splendor. [2]He called out with a mighty voice,

"Fallen, fallen is Babylon the great!
 It has become a dwelling place of demons,
a haunt of every foul spirit,
 a haunt of every foul bird,
 a haunt of every foul and hateful beast.[a]
[3] For all the nations have drunk[b]
 of the wine of the wrath of her fornication,
and the kings of the earth have committed
 fornication with her,
 and the merchants of the earth have grown
 rich from the power[c] of her luxury."

[4]Then I heard another voice from heaven saying,
"Come out of her, my people,
 so that you do not take part in her sins,
and so that you do not share
 in her plagues;
[5] for her sins are heaped high as heaven,
 and God has remembered her iniquities.
[6] Render to her as she herself has rendered,
 and repay her double for her deeds;
 mix a double draught for her in the cup she
 mixed.
[7] As she glorified herself and lived luxuriously,
 so give her a like measure of torment and
 grief.
Since in her heart she says,
 'I rule as a queen;
I am no widow,
 and I will never see grief,'

---

a Other ancient authorities lack the words *a haunt of every foul beast* and attach the words *and hateful* to the previous line so as to read *a haunt of every foul and hateful bird*
b Other ancient authorities read *she has made all nations drink*
c Or *resources*

17:8 See 1:4. **17:9–14** A slightly different and more explicit identification of the series of Roman emperors is provided in *Sib. Or.* 5.1–51. **17:9 seven mountains** This phrase would have pointed categorically to Rome, for by this time it had become a tag for Rome, just as "the windy city" is a tag for Chicago. Rome celebrated the enclosure of the seven hills within walls with an annual festival called the Septimontium (Suetonius, *Domitian* 4). John's use of the phrase is hardly coded language. It is so unambiguous that its veneer of coded speech is more an accommodation to the conventions of apocalyptic writing than an attempt to keep offensive or traitorous material concealed from the prying eyes of suspicious Roman investigators. **17:11** Various attempts have been made to identify the eighth king, who must be a Roman emperor (17:9). But there are difficulties in identifying the 8th. Counting from and including Julius Caesar, the 8th would be Domitian if the three failed emperors connected to the civil wars of 68–69 C.E. are not counted. The problem is that the author claims that the present time is in the reign of the 6th emperor. Some have claimed that only the deified emperors should be counted (Julius Caesar, Augustus, Claudius, Vespasian, Titus). The difficulty has not been resolved, and numerous hypotheses exist. **17:14** The combined titles used for Jesus here are found in reverse order in *1 Tim.* 6:15 and a few paragraphs later in the *Apocalypse* itself (19:16). The titles were usually applied to God. **17:18** An unmistakable reference to Rome. **18:1–24** Much of the language in this chapter comes from classic passages in the Hebrew Bible describing the destruction of Babylon six hundred years earlier. By linking Rome to Babylon, it was an easy step to borrow this description of catastrophic devastation for the church's own enemy, Rome. See *Isaiah* 21–23; *Ezekiel* 26–27; *Jeremiah* 50–51.

8   therefore her plagues will come in a single day—
      pestilence and mourning and famine—
  and she will be burned with fire;
      for mighty is the Lord God who judges her."

⁹And the kings of the earth, who committed fornication and lived in luxury with her, will weep and wail over her when they see the smoke of her burning; ¹⁰they will stand far off, in fear of her torment, and say,

  "Alas, alas, the great city,
    Babylon, the mighty city!
  For in one hour your judgment has come."

¹¹And the merchants of the earth weep and mourn for her, since no one buys their cargo anymore, ¹²cargo of gold, silver, jewels and pearls, fine linen, purple, silk and scarlet, all kinds of scented wood, all articles of ivory, all articles of costly wood, bronze, iron, and marble, ¹³cinnamon, spice, incense, myrrh, frankincense, wine, olive oil, choice flour and wheat, cattle and sheep, horses and chariots, slaves—and human lives.*d*

14   "The fruit for which your soul longed
      has gone from you,
  and all your dainties and your splendor
    are lost to you,
      never to be found again!"

¹⁵The merchants of these wares, who gained wealth from her, will stand far off, in fear of her torment, weeping and mourning aloud,

16   "Alas, alas, the great city,
    clothed in fine linen,
      in purple and scarlet,
    adorned with gold,
      with jewels, and with pearls!
17   For in one hour all this wealth has been laid
      waste!"

And all shipmasters and seafarers, sailors and all whose trade is on the sea, stood far off ¹⁸and cried out as they saw the smoke of her burning,

  "What city was like the great city?"

¹⁹And they threw dust on their heads, as they wept and mourned, crying out,

  "Alas, alas, the great city,

    where all who had ships at sea
      grew rich by her wealth!
  For in one hour she has been laid waste.
20 Rejoice over her, O heaven,
    you saints and apostles and prophets!
  For God has given judgment for you against
    her."

²¹Then a mighty angel took up a stone like a great millstone and threw it into the sea, saying,

  "With such violence Babylon the great city
    will be thrown down,
    and will be found no more;
22 and the sound of harpists and minstrels and of
      flutists and trumpeters
    will be heard in you no more;
  and an artisan of any trade
    will be found in you no more;
  and the sound of the millstone
    will be heard in you no more;
23 and the light of a lamp
    will shine in you no more;
  and the voice of bridegroom and bride
    will be heard in you no more;
  for your merchants were the magnates of the
    earth,
    and all nations were deceived by your
      sorcery.
24 And in you*e* was found the blood of prophets
    and of saints,
    and of all who have been slaughtered on
      earth."

The Rejoicing in Heaven

19 After this I heard what seemed to be the loud voice of a great multitude in heaven, saying, "Hallelujah!

  Salvation and glory and power to our God,
2   for his judgments are true and just;
  he has judged the great whore
    who corrupted the earth with her fornication,
  and he has avenged on her the blood of his
      servants."*f*

---

d Or *chariots, and human bodies and souls*

e Gk *her*
f Gk *slaves*

18:17–19 The reference to the shipping trade and to commerce comes naturally when the destruction of Rome is announced. Ships were generally the most convenient way to travel and the cheapest way to transport goods, particularly since Rome had cleared the Mediterranean of pirates as it expanded eastward in the 1st century B.C.E. With threatening pirates gone, trade and travel boomed. Only natural dangers made sea travel hazardous. The proclamation of the fall of Rome would fracture this security, hitting at the heart of commerce. **18:18** Rome had just been torched about thirty years earlier by Nero. It had been rebuilt with considerable splendor, but John is certain that the destroying fire that he foresaw will be permanent (18:21; 19:3). **18:20** The Gk is difficult here; one commentator suggests that the sense is, "God has imposed on her the sentence she passed against you." **18:21** *millstone* The image was used to describe the finality of the judgment against ancient Babylon (*Jer.* 51:60–63). **19:1** *Hallelujah* A word of praise to Yahweh, but the exact meaning is disputed. In our literature, it is used only in the *Apocalypse* (19:3, 4, 6).

³Once more they said,
"Hallelujah!
The smoke goes up from her forever and ever."
⁴And the twenty-four elders and the four living creatures fell down and worshiped God who is seated on the throne, saying,
"Amen. Hallelujah!"
⁵And from the throne came a voice saying,
"Praise our God,
all you his servants,ᵍ
and all who fear him,
small and great."
⁶Then I heard what seemed to be the voice of a great multitude, like the sound of many waters and like the sound of mighty thunderpeals, crying out,
"Hallelujah!
For the Lord our God
the Almighty reigns.
7 Let us rejoice and exult
and give him the glory,
for the marriage of the Lamb has come,
and his bride has made herself ready;
8 to her it has been granted to be clothed
with fine linen, bright and pure"—
for the fine linen is the righteous deeds of the saints.
⁹And the angel saidʰ to me, "Write this: Blessed are those who are invited to the marriage supper of the Lamb." And he said to me, "These are true words of God." ¹⁰Then I fell down at his feet to worship him, but he said to me, "You must not do that! I am a fellow servantⁱ with you and your comradesʲ who hold the testimony of Jesus.ᵏ Worship God! For the testimony of Jesusᵏ is the spirit of prophecy."

The Rider on the White Horse

¹¹Then I saw heaven opened, and there was a white horse! Its rider is called Faithful and True, and in righteousness he judges and makes war. ¹²His eyes are like a flame of fire, and on his head are many diadems; and he has a name inscribed that no one knows but himself. ¹³He is clothed in a robe dipped inˡ blood, and his name is called The Word of God. ¹⁴And the armies of heaven, wearing fine linen, white and pure, were following him on white horses. ¹⁵From his mouth comes a sharp sword with which to strike down the nations, and he will ruleᵐ them with a rod of iron; he will tread the wine press of the fury of the wrath of God the Almighty. ¹⁶On his robe and on his thigh he has a name inscribed, "King of kings and Lord of lords."

The Beast and Its Armies Defeated

¹⁷Then I saw an angel standing in the sun, and with a loud voice he called to all the birds that fly in midheaven, "Come, gather for the great supper of God, ¹⁸to eat the flesh of kings, the flesh of captains, the flesh of the mighty, the flesh of horses and their riders—flesh of all, both free and slave, both small and great." ¹⁹Then I saw the beast and the kings of the earth with their armies gathered to make war against the rider on the horse and against his army. ²⁰And the beast was captured, and with it the false prophet who had performed in its presence the signs by which he deceived those who had received the mark of the beast and those who worshiped its image. These two were thrown alive into the lake of fire that burns with sulfur. ²¹And the rest were killed by the sword of the rider on the horse, the sword that came from his mouth; and all the birds were gorged with their flesh.

The Thousand Years

20 Then I saw an angel coming down from heaven, holding in his hand the key to the bottomless pit and a great chain. ²He seized the dragon, that ancient serpent, who is the Devil and Satan, and bound him for a thousand years, ³and threw him into the pit, and locked and sealed it over him, so that he would deceive the nations no more, until the thousand years were ended. After that he must be let out for a little while.

---

g Gk *slaves*
h Gk *he said*
i Gk *slave*
j Gk *brothers*
k Or *to Jesus*

l Other ancient authorities read *sprinkled with*
m Or *will shepherd*

19:7 *marriage supper* Some early Christian writers spoke of the church as the bride of Christ (*2 Cor.* 11:2; *Eph.* 5:25–33). The image is borrowed from Judaism, where Israel's relationship with God is so described (*Isa.* 54:5). **19:9** The author employs two feast scenes here—that in which the righteous participate as guests of the lamb and that in which the wicked participate as the main course (19:17–18). See *Isa.* 25:6–8; *1 En.* 62.14. **19:11** Not the white horse of 6:2. **19:13** *Word of God* Both *John* and *1 John* open with this description of Jesus. **19:15** All the images used here have been used previously by *John* (1:16; 12:5; 14:19). **19:18** *Ezek.* 39:17–20. **19:20** *Dan.* 7:11. The place of eternal punishment, which sometimes is referred to as Gehenna. **20:3** In Gk, the word for thousand is *chilioi*. In Latin, it is *mille*. Both words have been transliterated into English, making two new words that relate to a golden age or a "thousand years of peace"—"chiliasm" and "millennium." After this golden age, according to the *Apocalypse,* there will be a brief death gasp of evil, after which the

4Then I saw thrones, and those seated on them were given authority to judge. I also saw the souls of those who had been beheaded for their testimony to Jesus[n] and for the word of God. They had not worshiped the beast or its image and had not received its mark on their foreheads or their hands. They came to life and reigned with Christ a thousand years. 5(The rest of the dead did not come to life until the thousand years were ended.) This is the first resurrection. 6Blessed and holy are those who share in the first resurrection. Over these the second death has no power, but they will be priests of God and of Christ, and they will reign with him a thousand years.

Satan's Doom

7When the thousand years are ended, Satan will be released from his prison 8and will come out to deceive the nations at the four corners of the earth, Gog and Magog, in order to gather them for battle; they are as numerous as the sands of the sea. 9They marched up over the breadth of the earth and surrounded the camp of the saints and the beloved city. And fire came down from heaven[o] and consumed them. 10And the devil who had deceived them was thrown into the lake of fire and sulfur, where the beast and the false prophet were, and they will be tormented day and night forever and ever.

The Dead Are Judged

11Then I saw a great white throne and the one who sat on it; the earth and the heaven fled from his presence, and no place was found for them. 12And I saw the dead, great and small, standing before the throne, and books were opened. Also another book was opened, the book of life. And the dead were judged according to their works, as recorded in the books. 13And the sea gave up the dead that were in it, Death and Hades gave up the dead that were in them, and all were judged according to what they had done. 14Then Death and Hades were thrown into the lake of fire. This is the second death, the lake of fire; 15and anyone whose name was not found written in the book of life was thrown into the lake of fire.

The New Heaven and the New Earth

21 Then I saw a new heaven and a new earth; for the first heaven and the first earth had passed away, and the sea was no more. 2And I saw the holy city, the new Jerusalem, coming down out of heaven from God, prepared as a bride adorned for her husband. 3And I heard a loud voice from the throne saying,

"See, the home[p] of God is among mortals.
He will dwell[p] with them as their God;[q]
they will be his peoples,[r]

---

n Or *for the testimony of Jesus*
o Other ancient authorities read *from God, out of heaven,* or *out of heaven from God*

p Gk *tabernacle*
q Other ancient authorities lack *as their God*
r Other ancient authorities read *people*

---

new and unending cosmos of peace will be established. In Judaism, there was a wide variety of schemes of cosmic chronology and speculation about the destruction of evil—themes at the heart of apocalyptic writing—but none reflects the scheme in the *Apocalypse*'s vision exactly (see *1 En.* 41.12–17; 43; *2 En.* 32.2–33.3). *Barnabas* 15 explains the scheme in part as a seven-thousand-year period, with each thousand years corresponding to one day of creation. The last one thousand years would reflect the Sabbath, a period of idealized peace and goodness. Many schemes, both Jewish and Christian, had no brief revival of evil after the new age had come; in the long discourse of *1 Enoch* 37–71, there is no millennium before the new age, nor is this idea reflected in Paul's writings (*1 Cor.* 15:24–28). The idea was popular throughout the 2d century, however, especially among the Christians of Asia Minor, the area addressed earlier by the *Apocalypse*. Eusebius had little appreciation for this perspective (*Hist. eccl.* 3.28). **20:4** *authority to judge Matt.* 19:28; *Luke* 22:29; *1 Cor.* 6:2. **beheaded** This swifter and less painful form of execution was reserved for people of status and wealth. John may have known of cases where Christians were so executed, or it may just be a way of speaking of execution generally, as some writers spoke of the sword, for example (*Rom.* 13:4; *Heb.* 11:34, 37; Ign. *Smyrn.* 4.2), including John himself (13:10). **its mark** See 13:6. **20:8** *Gog and Magog* Ezekiel 38 and 39 mentioned Gog of the land of Magog, but John saw two distinct nations here. They may have already been treated as separate in the Jewish tradition familiar to John. They are mentioned nowhere else in our literature, but they appear in some apocalyptic works (*Sib. Or.* 3.319) and became popular in rabbinic writings. **20:11–15** Scenes of a final judgment are regular features of apocalyptic literature (*1 Enoch* 100–102; *2 Enoch* 192–193; *Sibylline Oracles* 378–379). **20:13** Hades, or the underworld, was the shadowy abode of the dead. Death at sea was thought to prevent access to the underworld, leaving the wretched dead in an even less desirable abode. In Greek mythology, Zeus was the chief god who had overthrown the Titans. He shared his conquests with his brothers, assigning the underworld to Hades and the sea to Poseidon, and he became the god of the sky. The distinction made between the dead in Hades and the dead in the sea reflects this common division (see *2 Pet.* 2:4). **21:1** *new heaven and new earth Isa.* 65:17; *1 En.* 91.16. **21:2** *new Jerusalem* The new Jerusalem was mentioned in 3:12; now it is described in detail. In spite of their hostile relationship with the Jewish authorities in Jerusalem, Christians retained much of the theological structure of Judaism, even on the level of vocabulary, as we see in the positive use of the term "Jerusalem" both here and in other passages (*Gal.* 4:26; *Heb.* 12:22). **21:3** See note *p* above. The word "tabernacle" is used by the author of the *Gospel of John* to describe Jesus' incarnation (1:14).

and God himself will be with them;[s]

4 he will wipe every tear from their eyes.
  Death will be no more;
  mourning and crying and pain will be no more,
  for the first things have passed away."

[5]And the one who was seated on the throne said, "See, I am making all things new." Also he said, "Write this, for these words are trustworthy and true." [6]Then he said to me, "It is done! I am the Alpha and the Omega, the beginning and the end. To the thirsty I will give water as a gift from the spring of the water of life. [7]Those who conquer will inherit these things, and I will be their God and they will be my children. [8]But as for the cowardly, the faithless,[t] the polluted, the murderers, the fornicators, the sorcerers, the idolaters, and all liars, their place will be in the lake that burns with fire and sulfur, which is the second death."

Vision of the New Jerusalem

[9]Then one of the seven angels who had the seven bowls full of the seven last plagues came and said to me, "Come, I will show you the bride, the wife of the Lamb." [10]And in the spirit[u] he carried me away to a great, high mountain and showed me the holy city Jerusalem coming down out of heaven from God. [11]It has the glory of God and a radiance like a very rare jewel, like jasper, clear as crystal. [12]It has a great, high wall with twelve gates, and at the gates twelve angels, and on the gates are inscribed the names of the twelve tribes of the Israelites; [13]on the east three gates, on the north three gates, on the south three gates, and on the west three gates. [14]And the wall of the city has twelve foundations, and on them are the twelve names of the twelve apostles of the Lamb.

[15]The angel[v] who talked to me had a measuring rod of gold to measure the city and its gates and walls. [16]The city lies foursquare, its length the same as its width; and he measured the city with his rod, fifteen hundred miles;[w] its length and width and height are equal. [17]He also measured its wall, one hundred forty-four cubits[x] by human measurement, which the angel was using. [18]The wall is built of jas-

per, while the city is pure gold, clear as glass. [19]The foundations of the wall of the city are adorned with every jewel; the first was jasper, the second sapphire, the third agate, the fourth emerald, [20]the fifth onyx, the sixth carnelian, the seventh chrysolite, the eighth beryl, the ninth topaz, the tenth chrysoprase, the eleventh jacinth, the twelfth amethyst. [21]And the twelve gates are twelve pearls, each of the gates is a single pearl, and the street of the city is pure gold, transparent as glass.

[22]I saw no temple in the city, for its temple is the Lord God the Almighty and the Lamb. [23]And the city has no need of sun or moon to shine on it, for the glory of God is its light, and its lamp is the Lamb. [24]The nations will walk by its light, and the kings of the earth will bring their glory into it. [25]Its gates will never be shut by day—and there will be no night there. [26]People will bring into it the glory and the honor of the nations. [27]But nothing unclean will enter it, nor anyone who practices abomination or falsehood, but only those who are written in the Lamb's book of life.

The River of Life

22 Then the angel[y] showed me the river of the water of life, bright as crystal, flowing from the throne of God and of the Lamb [2]through the middle of the street of the city. On either side of the river is the tree of life[z] with its twelve kinds of fruit, producing its fruit each month; and the leaves of the tree are for the healing of the nations. [3]Nothing accursed will be found there any more. But the throne of God and of the Lamb will be in it, and his servants[a] will worship him; [4]they will see his face, and his name will be on their foreheads. [5]And there will be no more night; they need no light of lamp or sun, for the Lord God will be their light, and they will reign forever and ever.

[6]And he said to me, "These words are trustworthy and true, for the Lord, the God of the spirits of the prophets, has sent his angel to show his servants[a] what must soon take place."

[7]"See, I am coming soon! Blessed is the one who keeps the words of the prophecy of this book."

---

s Other ancient authorities add *and be their God*
t Or *the unbelieving*
u Or *in the Spirit*
v Gk *He*
w Gk *twelve thousand stadia*
x That is, almost seventy-five yards

y Gk *he*
z Or *the Lamb.* [2]*In the middle of the street of the city, and on either side of the river, is the tree of life*
a Gk *slaves*

21:6 *John* 4:10; 7:37–39. **21:10** *Ezek.* 40:2. **21:12** *tribes of the Israelites Ezek.* 48:31–34. See 7:4. **21:14** *twelve apostles* There were other views regarding the number of apostles. See 2:2. **21:15** The temple was measured in 11:1. **21:25** *Zech.* 14:7. **22:1–5** Many of the images of the new Jerusalem parallel the restoration mentioned in *Zech.* 14:6–8. See also *Ezek.* 47:1–12.

Epilogue and Benediction

[8]I, John, am the one who heard and saw these things. And when I heard and saw them, I fell down to worship at the feet of the angel who showed them to me; [9]but he said to me, "You must not do that! I am a fellow servant[b] with you and your comrades[c] the prophets, and with those who keep the words of this book. Worship God!"

[10]And he said to me, "Do not seal up the words of the prophecy of this book, for the time is near. [11]Let the evildoer still do evil, and the filthy still be filthy, and the righteous still do right, and the holy still be holy."

[12]"See, I am coming soon; my reward is with me, to repay according to everyone's work. [13]I am the Alpha and the Omega, the first and the last, the beginning and the end."

[14]Blessed are those who wash their robes,[d] so that they will have the right to the tree of life and may enter the city by the gates. [15]Outside are the dogs and sorcerers and fornicators and murderers and idolaters, and everyone who loves and practices falsehood.

[16]"It is I, Jesus, who sent my angel to you with this testimony for the churches. I am the root and the descendant of David, the bright morning star."
[17]   The Spirit and the bride say, "Come."
    And let everyone who hears say, "Come."
    And let everyone who is thirsty come.
    Let anyone who wishes take the water of life as a
        gift.

[18]I warn everyone who hears the words of the prophecy of this book: if anyone adds to them, God will add to that person the plagues described in this book; [19]if anyone takes away from the words of the book of this prophecy, God will take away that person's share in the tree of life and in the holy city, which are described in this book.

[20]The one who testifies to these things says, "Surely I am coming soon."
    Amen. Come, Lord Jesus!
[21]The grace of the Lord Jesus be with all the saints. Amen.[e]

---

b Gk *slave*
c Gk *brothers*
d Other ancient authorities read *do his commandments*

e Other ancient authorities lack *all;* others lack *the saints;* others lack *Amen*

22:10 See 1:3. **22:13** See 1:8. In the final few words, the author repeats the primary points stressed at the beginning. **22:16** *descendant of David* See note to 5:5. *morning star* See 2:28.

EARLY

CHRISTIAN

READER

OTHER EARLY WRITINGS

MOST OF THE DOCUMENTS from the first century of the Christian movement are "letters," in the broad sense of that term. Some were personal letters such as *Philemon*, *2 John*, and *3 John*. Most, however, were sermons or religious discourses in letter form, making them more widely useful than a typical letter. Such letters were preserved because of their sermonic and didactic character, and they circulated among a wide audience for the same reason.

Early Christian communities actively exchanged letters, and churches seem to have depended much on this kind of instruction, in addition to instruction provided by their permanent and itinerant leaders and teachers. Well over half of the pages of the *Reader* are "letters" of some sort. More than eighty percent of the individual documents of the *Reader* are letters. Indeed, most of the surviving documents from the first hundred years of the church's existence are in letter form. This leaves us with some clue as to the literary form of choice among the earliest Christians, for it is hardly likely that the predominance of the letter form is the result of chance preservation of an unrepresentative collection of early Christian writings. A letter is no more likely to survive than any other literary form—indeed, a letter might be less likely to survive than more official or "published" documents.

Although we have a considerable number of letters from early Christians, we know that far more simply did not survive. That does not mean that these letters were without merit; some letters may have been accidentally lost in the early days of the small, unorganized, and at times fractured communities. Some letters would have been too tied to peculiar local matters to be treasured beyond the addressed group. Other letters would have been neglected or destroyed by the forces of a developing "orthodoxy" in the church.

The Roman government itself may have played a role in the matter. In times of persecution, Christians were sometimes forced to hand over their sacred documents. This demand often became a crucial test of commitment to the Christian cause, and some died rather than hand over their scriptures. In such a situation, it became important to determine which documents deserved to be treated with that special kind of devotion and protection.

We do not know what a rich variety of literature may have been lost as a result of these factors, but we can glean some impression from the writings of Eusebius, especially from his *Ecclesiastical History,* written around the beginning of the fourth century. He said that large quantities of Christian materials were lost by his own day—he knew many only by title—and much of what he himself possessed has since been lost.

Even apart from hostile conditions threatening the survival of early Christian literature, we must consider the prohibitive costs involved in the production and preservation of documents. Each copy had to be handwritten (which is what the word "manuscript" literally means), an expensive process. Imagine what our books would cost today if the entire text had to be typed by hand for *each* copy produced—no printing presses, no photocopies, not even carbon paper! Only one copy of most documents and a few copies of the "best-sellers" would be made, and even fewer would be recopied as the originals wore out. Such was the situation in the past.

In spite of these obstacles, a large number of early Christian letters were preserved. Letters are found in most sections of the *Reader* and probably provide, better than any other literary form, a display of the full range of theological options in early Christian thought. The sections on the Pauline and Johannine traditions provide good examples of the letter form, as does the Ignatian material.

The Collection of Letters

Many letters purport to be from one of the first-century apostolic figures or one of their colleagues (Peter, Paul, John, James, Barnabas, or the obscure Jude), or from leaders of chief churches (Clement of Rome and Ignatius of Antioch). All these documents were cherished by the early Christians, but the letters attributed to Peter, Paul, James, John, and Jude are generally better known today because they came to be included in the Christian canon. This gave them a visibility that the others did not have.

In the New Testament arrangement, the letters collection was placed after the four gospels and *Acts,* with the Pauline letters first. Non-Pauline letters were called "general" or "catholic," indicating that they had been sent to Christian churches in general rather than to individual churches, as the letters of Paul had been. That distinction needs qualification, for at least one of Paul's letters, that to the Galatians, was written to *several* churches in the area of Galatia, while the second and third letters of John were addressed to a particular church or person and were less general than most of Paul's letters. The distinction and arrangement is even less useful when a wider range of early Christian correspondence is considered.

In this section, we have grouped several of these so-called general letters. They form a small part of the literature in the *Reader* but are important because they indicate the range of diversity and theological emphases that marked early Christian thinking. The letter of *James,* for example, may stand as a counterweight to some of

Paul's emphases; *Jude* and *2 Peter* have their own apocalyptic and ethical flavor, and *1 Peter,* once widely regarded as the work of a second-class Paulinist,[1] is now appreciated as a substantial contribution in its own right.

The Problem of the Letters

Two main questions about the letters attributed to apostles confront scholars: authorship and date. For the most part, these letters are not clearly tied to any historical incident that could help in determining the date—unlike the "undisputed" Pauline letters that are firmly tied to the 50s of the first century. Even the content and themes of these non-Pauline letters are so general that they are freed from the kinds of historical ties we find in other documents.

The second factor making the dating of these documents problematic is that their authorship is attributed to persons of the first-generation church, yet according to many scholars the content and perspective of these documents reflect a second-generation church. If these documents are from the late first century or later (as they would be if from a second-generation church), then apostolic authorship becomes difficult to maintain, since by that time the apostles likely would have already been dead.[2]

Paul's Importance to the Letter Form

It is possible that Paul's letters had gained sufficient importance that other Christian authors imitated their characteristic form (see *2 Thess.* 2:1–2). This relationship between Paul's letters and those by other authors deserves closer attention. It might provide one line of evidence that Paul's influence extended beyond his own communities. The letters associated with Peter follow the Pauline example most closely, whereas those connected with John follow it least. More detailed discussion of Paul's letter form is in the introduction to THE LETTERS OF PAUL.

The Recent Debate

Recently, scholars of early Christian literature have begun to reexamine the important role of the letter form in the Greco-Roman world. In previous studies of early Christian literary forms, some scholars had argued that a distinction should

---

[1] *First Peter* shows so many literary affinities with the letters of Paul that some scholars have argued that the author actually used Paul's letters in composing his own. But *1 Peter* has similar affinities with a wide range of early Christian literature, and may simply share a common world with other Christian writers.

[2] That is not to say that some of the disciples of Jesus could not have been living in the last decade or two of the first century. If some of the disciples joined Jesus when they were in their teens or early twenties, they would have been old by the latter part of the century (in their seventies and eighties), but not incapable of functioning as influential persons in the community. Early accounts speak of the martyrdom of various disciples, however, and provide evidence only of John surviving to the late first century—and one tradition recounts the early martyrdom of even John.

be made between the *letter* and the *epistle* (derived from the Gk word for "letter," *epistolē*), the former being more personal and private, the latter more formal and public. But it is now generally accepted that whatever differences might be detected between the "letter" and the "epistle," these are essentially varieties of the same form and share largely in style and even in purpose.

An examination of the letter form in early Christianity requires attention to the larger social and cultural world of the ancient Mediterranean. That world provided the church not only with converts but also with literary forms and conventions by which converts might be made and maintained. The letter form was particularly suited for the latter—the maintenance of converts—and was adopted quickly by early Christian leaders for that purpose.

For Further Reading

Aune, David E. *The New Testament in Its Literary Environment.* Library of Early Christianity. Philadelphia: Westminster, 1987.

Stowers, Stanley K. *Letter Writing in Greco-Roman Antiquity.* Library of Early Christianity. Philadelphia: Westminster, 1986.

White, John L. *Light from Ancient Letters.* Foundations and Facets Series. Philadelphia: Fortress, 1986.

To the Twelve Tribes of the Diaspora

JAMES

Authorship

The author identifies himself as James, a servant of God and of the Lord Jesus Christ, but this helps us little since James (Gk *Iakōbos* from its Hebrew form) was a common name and since "servant of God" is both too general and too widely used to pinpoint a particular individual.[1] The lack of anything more specific has suggested to most scholars that "James" was adequate identification of the author for readers. This indicates that not just any James, but a prominent James is implied. The scholarly consensus is that the name refers to the *preeminent* James of early church fame: James, the brother of Jesus, and leader of the Jerusalem church.[2] Ancient authorities who addressed the issue concluded this as well.

James is mentioned in a few key passages in early Christian literature. He holds a chief position in the Jerusalem church and in the pro-Torah party, according to Paul (*Gal.* 1:19; 2:9–12). Paul further recognizes the weight of James's authority when he argues for the resurrection of Jesus, counting James as a notable witness (*1 Cor.* 15:7). The author of *Acts,* too, presents James in a key role (12:17; 15:13; 21:18). Quite surprisingly, Josephus also comments on the death of James (c. 62 C.E.), the only Christian included in his review of the history of first-century Palestine (*Ant.* 20.200–202).

In spite of the broad agreement that the letter's introduction intends this prominent James, the brother of Jesus, we cannot simply assume this James was the

---

[1] Paul, on occasion, used the phrase "servant of God" in his salutation (*Rom.* 1:1; *Phil.* 1:1). The author of the letter to *Titus* used it, but that probably reflects dependence on Paul. The author of the letter of *Jude* used it (1:1), but that could be tied to the use of the phrase in the letter of *James,* since the author of *Jude* may have had that letter in mind when he composed his own letter (see the introduction to *Jude*).

[2] This James is sometimes called James "the Less" to distinguish him from James "the Greater," a brother of John the disciple, and a son of Zebedee, who was martyred under Herod Agrippa I in the early 40s (*Acts* 12:2). This James (the brother of Jesus) became the leader in the Jerusalem church and was not martyred until the 60s (Josephus, *J.W.* 20.200; Eusebius, *Eccl. hist.* 2.23.18). See *Mark* 3:31–35; 6:3; *Matt.* 13:55; *John* 7:3–10; *Acts* 1:14; *1 Cor.* 9:5; 15:7; *Gal.* 1:19. James "the Less" appears to have been a more significant figure in the early church than James "the Greater," who figured as a prominent disciple in the gospel accounts.

author. This problem faces scholars concerning much of ancient literature: Is the *named* author the *real* author, or is the name of the author a device of pseudonymous literature used to gain a hearing for the writing (see introduction to LETTERS ATTRIBUTED TO PAUL)? And if it is a literary device, how should it be viewed? Is it a relatively innocent and accepted practice, or is it a more negative, perhaps even intentionally misleading usage? Putting aside the latter question (which can be argued well from either side), we will consider only whether the attribution of authorship in this letter "of James" is accurate.

One of the first things that scholars look for in order to resolve questions of authorship and date is how the early church fathers (from the first half of the second century, or so) used a work. This is most clearly seen in direct quotes or unquestionable allusions to the writing. The second line of investigation is the status of a document in early canonical lists. On neither point does the letter of *James* have a solid case. It is little known, or at least little used, in the earliest period, and it was sometimes classed among the disputed works in early canonical lists. By the third century, however, Origen generally cites *James* as scripture,[3] and by the fourth century *James* was becoming widely accepted by eastern and western synods (church councils), but doubts about the authorship of *James* continued through the Middle Ages.

A number of other features offer possible clues to authorship and date of composition. The problem is that the evidence seems to point in conflicting directions. In defense of traditional views on authorship is the work's Palestinian flavor, the similarities to James's theology as it can be gleaned from other documents, and the primitive or early features.[4] Against traditional views on authorship is the polished quality of the Greek,[5] the marks of developed institutionalization,[6] and the lack of certain kinds of references to Jesus that might have been expected from a brother who came off rather badly in the gospel accounts, which portrayed James as unconvinced and critical of Jesus' sense of mission.[7] Such differing interpretations of the often ambiguous evidence makes a consensus on the question of authorship impossible.

---

[3] Origen, *Commentary on John* 8:24, gives the impression that the authorship of *James* is disputed.

[4] The reference to the early and the latter rains (5:7) reflects the Palestinian growing cycle, the sympathetic attitude to the Torah, characteristic of James in a wide variety of sources, the church structure (elders and teachers rather than bishops), the simple Christology, and the use of what appears to be a still flexible Jesus tradition are primitive characteristics (see comments in the notes at 1:1; 2:5, 8, 13; 3:6; 4:10; 5:3, 12).

[5] It is usually supposed that Jesus' family was not fluent in Greek, though that view has been challenged, partly on the strength of Paul's reference to the travels of Jesus' brothers, apparently in Greece (*1 Cor.* 9:3–7).

[6] The level of church structure depends on whether elders have exclusive claim on the charismatic gifts, for example, in healing (5:14). But compared to other documents that mention developed church structure more explicitly (especially promoting the office of bishop), the structure reflected in James does not seem developed, and could easily reflect a structure borrowed from the synagogue, which a Jewish form of Christianity might be expected to show.

[7] The word "Christ" or "Jesus" is used only once outside of the introduction (2:1). The significance of this is debated. Some scholars contend that the real James would have played up his connections to Jesus; others contend that a pseudonymous writer would have been the more likely to do that. On a re-

Date

The date depends somewhat on the decision about authorship. If James, the brother of Jesus, is the author, the letter must be dated before 62 C.E., the date of James's execution. But the work is not known by name until the 200s, and allusions to it before that are debatable. Therefore efforts to date the writing have often turned to the content.

Here again the matter is left unresolved. The content is mainly given to general exhortation, and that rarely helps in determining the date. Even the theme of faith and works that dominates sections of the document cannot tie it specifically to the first century, though many scholars argue from that theme that the letter is part of the debate between Paul and Jewish Christians. Certainly there are striking parallels in phrasing, as a comparison of *Jas.* 2:21–24 and *Rom.* 4:1–3 and 5:1 will show. Whether this information is helpful for dating the letter of *James* will depend on whether such a debate can be restricted to a particular period—specifically to the time of Paul's anti-Torah polemics—and whether Paul and *James* are talking about the same thing, which is denied by many who examine *James* closely.

Setting

Traditionally titled the *Letter of James,* this document uses the letter form only in the most peripheral way. The first two lines have characteristic features of a letter: Line one contains the salutation ("James, a servant of God and of the Lord Jesus Christ"). Line two contains the address ("to the twelve tribes scattered among the nations"). Nothing else is letterlike. The remainder consists of a series of brief and general exhortations. Not even a closing farewell is attached.

The address is too broad and the themes too general to help us specify a concrete historical setting for the writing. Parallels with the style of presentation and with specific illustrations can be found in the diatribe, a literary form, in the Greco-Roman world, and there are clear and numerous influences from Jewish proverbial and wisdom literature. Such parallels are too general for the modern investigator to determine a specific context for the document.

Overview

Any attempt to divide *James* into coherent sections tied together by intelligible transitions is probably doomed to fail. Themes are introduced, dropped, and picked up again, sometimes seeming to break up logical or thematic units.

---

lated issue, some scholars have suggested that the letter of James was a Jewish work, only slightly christianized. But the author uses the word "Lord" in an indisputably central way: as the coming one (5:7–8); the judge (5:9); the one in whose name the prophets spoke (5:10), and in whose name the sick are healed (5:14), which readers would identify with Jesus.

Probably the best way to get a sense of the letter is simply to note the range of topics, without attempting to place these into an overarching structure. In many ways, *James* seems to string together proverbs and wisdom sayings—sometimes with thematic connections and sometimes without. Indeed, we might say that the whole of *James* is *merely* the sum of its parts. There is no plot, no sustained argument, no ordered progression of ideas. Each part is on its own, something like the materials on a construction site, yet to be assembled into a building. That does not mean that the author has left his literary task undone; rather, that is an acceptable presentation for collections of proverbs and wise sayings.

Themes and Issues

This document is basically a sermon, and considerably less letterlike than the Pauline letters, for example. But we have yet to decide what kind of sermon it is. Martin Luther, the Protestant reformer, thought that *James* presented a misdirected message of works over faith—a counter-Pauline theology, so to speak. Given Luther's life-and-death struggle with sixteenth-century Catholicism, anything that seemed to lend support to a system of merit came in for caustic criticism. Thus the *Letter of James* gained a reputation in many Protestant circles as a "strawy" epistle—one of little value.

But the themes of *James* are not so focused. The considerable range of topics does not fit well under the general description of faith and works, though the topic of faith and works gets its share of attention (2:14–26). The letter is more aptly described as a collection of general wisdom statements on themes running the gamut from temptation, sin, riches, temper, pride, and partiality to charity, controlled speech, patience, mercy, and responsibility. Such a document is similar to *Proverbs* and *Ecclesiasticus*,[8] writings that early Christians would have known from the Septuagint.

Even the issue of faith and works must be set in the context of James's call for charity and the protection of the poor. This concern is largely a practical one, not a theological one as in Paul's writings. Thus we should read the comments of *James* on faith and works in light of the letter's own comments on wealth and responsibility rather than in comparison with Paul's discussion of faith and works. One of the guiding principles of critical interpretation is to make sense of specific statements within a document using the context of the document itself. Thus, if we can understand *James*'s statements about works and faith from the context of *James* itself, we should not appeal to other associations and documents for our primary sense of the author's concern.

---

[8]Not to be confused with *Ecclesiastes*. *Ecclesiasticus,* also known as the *Wisdom of Jesus ben Sirach,* or simply *Sirach,* is found in the collection called the Apocrypha, or the deutero-canonical writings. This collection was part of the Septuagint (often abbreviated LXX), the Gk translation of the Hebrew Bible that the early Christians used. It is found in modern Catholic and Orthodox Bibles, but generally excluded from Protestant versions.

Purpose

Since *James* lacks any overarching theme or encompassing structure, we must search for clues regarding the work's purpose in a consideration of smaller units. An initial place to look is in the introductory comments, which seem clear enough. Immediately after the greeting, the author writes: "My brothers and sisters, whenever you face trials of any kind, consider it nothing but joy, because you know that the testing of your faith produces endurance; and let endurance have its full effect, so that you may be mature and complete, lacking in nothing."

Such an emphasis on trials and testing might suggest a context of persecution, but there are problems with that conclusion. First, the author speaks of "trials of any kind," which, depending on what else he has to say, may indicate nothing beyond the everyday rigors of life. Second, though the author begins his letter with comments about trials and endurance, he drops the theme almost immediately and mentions it only briefly at the end of the letter. Further, it is often moral testing that is the concern—not testing by persecution. Finally, the author moves quickly from his initial theme to themes of wisdom, largely by word association (note the word "lack" in 1:4–5); then he moves from wisdom to the rich (1:10–11). Such ranging interests and logically unconnected themes help us little in finding an overall purpose to the documents, though the author had some purpose in mind.

Audience

Unlike Paul's letters, which were addressed to specific churches or individuals, this letter (if we can call it that) had a fairly general address—the twelve tribes of the Dispersion.[9] The term refers primarily to Jews living outside of Palestine— about eighty percent of the total Jewish population in the first century, according to some estimates. But the author of *James* had something more specific in mind. He either meant Jews who were Christians or Christians (including non-Jewish ones) who could understand their Christian identity within the terminology of Judaism. An audience of both Jews and Gentiles is probable, though not absolutely necessary.

According to some scholars, the address is later than the rest of the letter. If this is the case—and it is at best a hypothesis—then the document originally lacked any characteristic features of a letter, and the address of the letter offers no clue about the identity of the original audience. The document should probably be treated, then, simply as a tract.

---

[9]Besides *James,* a few others letters from early Christian writers were addressed to a wide audience, rather than to a particular city or person: *Jude, 1 Peter, 2 Peter.* Most letters, however, have more restricted audiences, though even these became widely known as they were shared with other churches.

As a tract, its themes are too general and wide-ranging to provide clues regarding the audience. It can even be argued that statements that might suggest something more specific, such as the polemic against the rich, reflect rhetorical convention rather than concrete engagement with specific incidents of abuse of the poor, though we must always be cautious lest we minimize the substance of charges, complaints, and concerns in a letter such as this by labeling them "rhetoric." We can safely say that the more general a letter is and the wider its audience, the less likely it is that concrete situations are being addressed, and thus less likely that we can reconstruct the setting or audience.

Relation to Other Early Christian Literature

It has been argued that this letter is the most Jewish and the least Christian of any writings from the early church. Some have even contended that James was originally a Jewish document, and that a few additions provide it with a Christian veneer. Jesus is mentioned at 1:1 and 2:1, and possibly in the reference to "the name of the Lord" in 5:14. But other uses of the word "Lord" could refer to God as easily as to Jesus. Indeed, very little material would need to be removed to make this into a wholly Jewish document of the wisdom literature type.[10]

That having been said, the document as we have it is nonetheless Christian. The author claims to be a slave of Jesus (1:1); he reflects a heavy influence from synopticlike Jesus material, particularly from the *Gospel of Matthew,* and he shares a number of striking similarities with *1 Peter,* a thoroughly Christian document.[11]

Value for the Study of Early Christianity

As the most thoroughly Jewish writing produced by the early church, the *Letter of James* reminds us of the deep ethical and theological roots that Christianity has in Judaism and the extent to which such thinking continued to shape Christianity even after its separation from its parent religion. Although *James* gives tantalizing hints about the social setting of this community, particularly with regard to tensions between the rich and the poor, but these clues are set in a context of rhetoric and common moralizing that makes the group being addressed difficult to reconstruct confidently.

For Further Reading

Dibelius, Martin. *James: A Commentary on the Epistle of James.* Translated by Michael A. Williams. Hermeneia. Philadelphia: Fortress, 1976.

---

[10]See E. M. Sidebottom, *James, Jude, 2 Peter* (NCBC; London: Nelson, 1967), 4–5.

[11]Sidebottom, *James, Jude, 2 Peter,* 6–11.

Laws, Sophie. *The Epistle of James.* Black's New Testament Commentary. London: A & C Black, 1980. Repr., Peabody, Mass.: Hendrickson, 1993.

Reicke, Bo. *The Epistles of James, Peter, and Jude.* Anchor Bible 37. Garden City, N.Y.: Doubleday, 1964.

Sidebottom, E. M. *James, Jude, 2 Peter.* New Century Bible Commentary. London: Nelson, 1967.

THE LETTER OF
JAMES

Salutation

1 James, a servant*a* of God and of the Lord Jesus Christ,

To the twelve tribes in the Dispersion:

Greetings.

Faith and Wisdom

²My brothers and sisters,*b* whenever you face trials of any kind, consider it nothing but joy, ³because you know that the testing of your faith produces endurance; ⁴and let endurance have its full effect, so that you may be mature and complete, lacking in nothing.

⁵If any of you is lacking in wisdom, ask God, who gives to all generously and ungrudgingly, and it will be given you. ⁶But ask in faith, never doubting, for the one who doubts is like a wave of the sea, driven and tossed by the wind; ⁷, ⁸for the doubter, being double-minded and unstable in every way, must not expect to receive anything from the Lord.

Poverty and Riches

⁹Let the believer*c* who is lowly boast in being raised up, ¹⁰and the rich in being brought low, because the rich will disappear like a flower in the field. ¹¹For the sun rises with its scorching heat and withers the field; its flower falls, and its beauty perishes. It is the same way with the rich; in the midst of a busy life, they will wither away.

Trial and Temptation

¹²Blessed is anyone who endures temptation. Such a one has stood the test and will receive the crown of life that the Lord*d* has promised to those who love him. ¹³No one, when tempted, should say, "I am being tempted by God"; for God cannot be tempted by evil and he himself tempts no one. ¹⁴But one is tempted by one's own desire, being lured and enticed by it; ¹⁵then, when that desire has conceived, it gives birth to sin, and that sin, when it is fully grown, gives birth to death. ¹⁶Do not be deceived, my beloved.*e*

¹⁷Every generous act of giving, with every perfect gift, is from above, coming down from the Father of

---

a Gk *slave*
b Gk *brothers*

c Gk *brother*
d Gk *he;* other ancient authorities read *God*
e Gk *my beloved brothers*

1:1 *servant* A number of early Christian writers introduced themselves by this term in their letters (*Rom.* 1:1; *Gal.* 1:10; *Phil.* 1:1; *Titus* 1:1; *2 Pet.* 1:1; *Jude* 1). **in the Dispersion** That is, the Diaspora. Jews were scattered throughout the Roman world, living as resident aliens. The image appears to have been one that Christians adopted for themselves (*1 Pet.* 1:1; 2:11; *1 Clem.* address; *Rom.* 9:6–7; 11:17–21; *Gal.* 6:16); thus, such a description is not helpful in determining whether the recipients were Jewish or Gentile. **Greetings** Gk *chairein.* This was a customary greeting in letters of the time (*Acts* 15:23; 23:26). Christian writers more often used *charis* ("grace"), perhaps under the influence of the Pauline letter form. See the introduction to The Letters of Ignatius. **1:2** *trials* A legal trial is probably not intended here although the idea of rejoicing in the face of persecution was widespread among early Christians (*Matt.* 5:10; *Luke* 6:22; Ign. *Trall.* 1.7; Ign. *Rom.* 5.5–7). The same word is translated "temptations" later (1:12). **1:3** *testing of your faith* *1 Pet.* 1:7. **1:5** *wisdom* A rich wisdom literature in Judaism informed aspects of early Christian thinking (e.g., *Proverbs, Sirach, Wisdom of Solomon*). *James* is indebted to this tradition (3:13–17), as are other early Christian writers (*Mark* 11:24; *Matt.* 7:7). **1:6** *never doubting* *Matt.* 21:21 *wave of the sea* *Jude* 13. **1:8** *double-minded* This appears to be the 1st use of the word in extant Gk literature (4:8). A number of other Christian writings composed about the same time also employ the term (*1 Clem.* 11.2; 23.2, 3; *Did.* 2.4; *Barn.* 19.5). **1:10** See 2:4. The author was concerned about the abuse of the poor by the rich and the apparent blindness of the poor to this abuse (2:2, 6, 15–16; 5:1, 3). The impermanence of wealth and the inequities between rich and poor were frequently addressed in early Christian literature (*Mark* 10:25; *1 Tim.* 6:9–10, 17; *1 Clem.* 13.2; 38.4). **1:10–11** Similar language is found in *Isa.* 40:6–9 (LXX 40:6–8), but the theme is different. The quotation is loose, but the LXX is more closely followed. The Hebrew reads "flowers of the field" and "flowers fade." **1:12** *endures temptation* The Gk root *(peir-)* has several meanings. In the Lord's Prayer, the root appears in the request not to be brought to the "time of *trial*" (*Matt.* 6:13; *Luke* 11:4). In *James,* the translators use the words "temptation" or "tempt." See 1:2–3; *Heb.* 12:7. *crown of life* In *Rev.* 2:10, it is Jesus who makes this promise. Some scholars have speculated that the promise, which is not preserved in the gospels, may be a lost saying of Jesus. **1:13** Satan, rather than God, is often described as the tempter. He tempted Jesus and now tempts believers (*Mark* 1:13; *Luke* 4:2; *1 Cor.* 7:5). **1:14** *desire* Gk *epithymia.* Desire was widely seen as leading to destruction, not only in Christian literature, but in Greek and Jewish as well. Greek mythology and legend provide the examples of Croesus and Midas. **1:15** *Rom.* 3:23. **1:17** *every perfect gift* Philo, *On the Confusion of Tongues* 36; Plato, *Republic* 3.379.

lights, with whom there is no variation or shadow due to change.*f* [18]In fulfillment of his own purpose he gave us birth by the word of truth, so that we would become a kind of first fruits of his creatures.

Hearing and Doing the Word

[19]You must understand this, my beloved:*g* let everyone be quick to listen, slow to speak, slow to anger; [20]for your anger does not produce God's righteousness. [21]Therefore rid yourselves of all sordidness and rank growth of wickedness, and welcome with meekness the implanted word that has the power to save your souls.

[22]But be doers of the word, and not merely hearers who deceive themselves. [23]For if any are hearers of the word and not doers, they are like those who look at themselves*h* in a mirror; [24]for they look at themselves and, on going away, immediately forget what they were like. [25]But those who look into the perfect law, the law of liberty, and persevere, being not hearers who forget but doers who act—they will be blessed in their doing.

[26]If any think they are religious, and do not bridle their tongues but deceive their hearts, their religion is worthless. [27]Religion that is pure and undefiled before God, the Father, is this: to care for orphans and widows in their distress, and to keep oneself unstained by the world.

Warning against Partiality

2 My brothers and sisters,*i* do you with your acts of favoritism really believe in our glorious Lord Jesus Christ?*j* [2]For if a person with gold rings and in fine clothes comes into your assembly, and if a poor person in dirty clothes also comes in, [3]and if you take notice of the one wearing the fine clothes and say, "Have a seat here, please," while to the one who is poor you say, "Stand there," or, "Sit at my feet,"*k* [4]have you not made distinctions among yourselves, and become judges with evil thoughts? [5]Listen, my beloved brothers and sisters.*l* Has not God chosen the poor in the world to be rich in faith and to be heirs of the kingdom that he has promised to those who love him? [6]But you have dishonored the poor. Is it not the rich who oppress you? Is it not they who

---

f Other ancient authorities read *variation due to a shadow of turning*

g Gk *my beloved brothers*

h Gk *at the face of his birth*

i Gk *My brothers*

j Or *hold the faith of our glorious Lord Jesus Christ without acts of favoritism*

k Gk *Sit under my footstool*

l Gk *brothers*

Father of lights Perhaps a reference to celestial bodies, such as planets and stars, since the three terms used immediately after this *(variation, shadow, change)* are all part of the language of ancient astronomy. **1:18 word of truth** *1 Pet.* 1:23. **first fruits** This term refers to the offering of the 1st part of the harvest and is used often by Paul (*Rom.* 8:23; *1 Cor.* 15:20; *2 Thess.* 2:13). It is also mentioned in *Rev.* 14:4, in *Didache* 13, and in *1 Clem.* 24.2; 29.6, where it is part of a quotation from the Bible. **1:19 slow to anger** *Eccl.* 7:9; *Sir.* 5:11; *Matt.* 5:22; *1 Clem.* 3.1; *Ign. Phld.* 8.2. Such restraint is idealized in most societies, and numerous passages from Greek and Latin writings could be cited. The control of emotions was a special concern of Stoics (Seneca, *An Essay about Anger*). **1:21 save your souls** Gk *psychē*. See 5:20. The word means "life" or "self." **1:22 doers of the word** A Hebraism for "those who obey the commandments." James uses the word "doers" three times in 1:22–25 and in 4:11. The word is used elsewhere in our literature only in *Rom.* 2:13. **1:24** Note *h* above. The meaning is disputed. **1:25 the law of liberty** See 2:8. The idea of the law as perfect can be found in *Ps.* 19:7. Positive statements can be found about the law in early Christian writings as well (*Rom.* 3:27; *John* 13:34; *1 Tim.* 1:7; *Barn.* 2.12). **doers who act** See 1:22. **1:26–27 religious** James uses a form of this word three times in 1:26–27. The word is used elsewhere only in *Acts* 26:5 and *Col.* 2:18 in our literature. A synonym is used on occasion elsewhere (*Acts* 17:22; 25:19; *1 Tim.* 3:16; 5:4; *1 Clem.* 62.1). **1:26 bridle their tongues** See 3:5. **1:27 orphans and widows** This is the only specific injunction in *James*'s summary statement and therefore should be an important element in any persuasive reconstruction of the audience, especially in light of his concern about differences between the rich and the poor (2:1–7; see 1:10). Such concern for orphans and widows was a mark of piety in Judaism and early Christianity (*1 Clem.* 8.4; *Ign. Smyrn.* 6.2; *Ign. Pol.* 4.1; *Barn.* 20.2). **2:1 acts of favoritism** Lit. "face-taking." See 2:9. A compound word meaning "partiality." The word (or a cognate) is also used in *Acts* 10:34; *Rom.* 2:11; *Eph.* 6:9; *Col.* 3:25; *Ign. Phld.* 6.1. **2:2 with gold rings** In Gk this is one word, perhaps coined by the author himself for effect. The phrase, "gold-ringed" man, may have produced an image similar to that produced by the phrase "silver-spooned" man in our society. Given what the author says about the rich in other places, it was hardly intended as a compliment (1:10). **assembly** Lit. "synagogue." This is a Gk word meaning a place of assembly. There is only one other place in our literature where this word is used for the Christian assembly (*Ign. Pol.* 4.2). Early Christian writings almost always use the Gk word *ekklēsia* for the church, and *James* also uses it in 5:14. **2:3 Stand . . . sit** In the Gk, emphasis is indicated here. We might translate it "*you* stand here . . . *you* sit there." **2:4 have you not made distinctions** Roman society was based on social distinctions, displayed most clearly in the network of patron-client relationships. It was not unusual for the host, or patron, to serve his clients food inferior to what he himself was eating at the next table. Such favoritism in regard to the rich is condemned in *Did.* 5.2 and *Barn.* 20.2. **2:5 chosen the poor** This is similar to one of the Jesus sayings in *Matt.* 5:3, 5 and *Luke* 6:20. **2:6 drag you into court** The specifics are unknown. It could be related to religious persecution, especially considering that the charge is followed by the accusation that the

drag you into court? [7]Is it not they who blaspheme the excellent name that was invoked over you?

[8]You do well if you really fulfill the royal law according to the scripture, "You shall love your neighbor as yourself." [9]But if you show partiality, you commit sin and are convicted by the law as transgressors. [10]For whoever keeps the whole law but fails in one point has become accountable for all of it. [11]For the one who said, "You shall not commit adultery," also said, "You shall not murder." Now if you do not commit adultery but if you murder, you have become a transgressor of the law. [12]So speak and so act as those who are to be judged by the law of liberty. [13]For judgment will be without mercy to anyone who has shown no mercy; mercy triumphs over judgment.

Faith without Works Is Dead

[14]What good is it, my brothers and sisters,[m] if you say you have faith but do not have works? Can faith save you? [15]If a brother or sister is naked and lacks daily food, [16]and one of you says to them, "Go in peace; keep warm and eat your fill," and yet you do not supply their bodily needs, what is the good of that? [17]So faith by itself, if it has no works, is dead.

[18]But someone will say, "You have faith and I have works." Show me your faith apart from your works, and I by my works will show you my faith. [19]You believe that God is one; you do well. Even the demons believe—and shudder. [20]Do you want to be shown, you senseless person, that faith apart from works is barren? [21]Was not our ancestor Abraham justified by works when he offered his son Isaac on the altar? [22]You see that faith was active along with his works, and faith was brought to completion by the works. [23]Thus the scripture was fulfilled that says, "Abraham believed God, and it was reckoned to him as righteousness," and he was called the friend of God. [24]You see that a person is justified by works and not by faith alone. [25]Likewise, was not Rahab the prostitute also justified by works when she welcomed the messengers and sent them out by another road? [26]For just as the body without the spirit is dead, so faith without works is also dead.

Taming the Tongue

3 Not many of you should become teachers, my brothers and sisters,[m] for you know that we who teach will be judged with greater strictness. [2]For all of us make many mistakes. Anyone who makes no mistakes in speaking is perfect, able to keep the whole body in check with a bridle. [3]If we put bits into the mouths of horses to make them obey us, we guide their whole bodies. [4]Or look at ships: though they are so large that it takes strong winds to drive them, yet they are guided by a very small rudder wherever the

---

m Gk *brothers*

rich blaspheme the name of Jesus (2:7). Note the particularly fierce condemnation of the rich in 5:1–6. (See also *1 Pet.* 3:15–17). **2:7** *name invoked over you* Probably a reference to Christian baptism. **2:8** *fulfill the royal law* There is no exact parallel for this phrase in Jewish literature. In the synoptic tradition, Jesus selected love for one's neighbor as the central commandment (*Mark* 12:31; *Did.* 1.3–4; *Barn.* 19.5), and that selection is paralleled in Jewish literature. *love your neighbor as yourself Lev.* 19:18. This is also the theme of one of the parables of Jesus, the parable of the good Samaritan (*Luke* 10:25–37). **2:10** *accountable for all of it Matt.* 5:19; *Gal.* 3:10; 5:3. **2:11** Both prohibitions are from the Ten Commandments (*Exod.* 20:13–14; *Deut.* 5:17–18). Much of the ethical system of Christianity was borrowed without revision from Judaism. See *Did.* 2.2. **2:13** The author is drawing on the parable of the unmerciful servant (*Matt.* 18:23–25; 5:7). **2:15** *naked and lacks daily food* This may not have exaggerated the plight of some members of this community. See 1:10; *Matt.* 25:36; *1 John* 3:17. **2:16** *Go in peace* A standard Jewish phrase meaning "good-bye." **2:17** See introduction to *James.* **2:19** *God is one* This is part of the principal Jewish confession, the Shema (see *Deut.* 6:4). *the demons believe Mark* 1:23–24; *Matt.* 8:29; *Luke* 4:34. **2:20** *senseless person* See 5:22; *1 Cor.* 15:36. This sounds more offensive to modern hearers than to the ancients, who would have been accustomed to this kind of language in the popular diatribe literary form used in philosophical teaching. *barren* Or "useless." Some manuscripts read "dead"; others read "empty." **2:21–23** *Heb.* 11:17–19; *1 Clem.* 12.1–8; 31.2. Paul does not mention this incident in his discussion of faith and the law, but he does appeal to Abraham as an example of faith (*Rom.* 4:3; *Gal.* 3:6). The original Abraham story takes up the middle part of the book of *Genesis.* **2:23** *friend of God 1 Clem.* 10.1; 17.3. The phrase is not found elsewhere in our literature. **2:24** *not by faith alone* Compare Paul's statements in *Rom.* 3:28 and *Gal.* 2:16, which seem to set forward the opposite proposition. It is difficult to determine whether one author was responding directly to the position of the other, although various attempts have been made to relate the two. See *1 Clem.* 32.4. **2:25** The story of Rahab is recorded in *Joshua* 2. Rahab is referred to in *Heb.* 11:13, and *1 Clem.* 12.1–8 repeats most of the details from the account in *Joshua.* Rahab is also mentioned in the genealogy of Jesus in *Matt.* 1:5. **3:1** *Rom.* 2:17–24; *Luke* 12:47–48; *John* 9:41. *brothers and sisters* The NRSV regularly translates the masculine nouns and pronouns as inclusive. Thus, for example, the Gk word *adelphoi* ("brothers") in this passage is rendered *brothers and sisters.* One cannot assume, however, that women held the position of teacher in *James*'s community. **3:2** *in check with a bridle* See 3:5. A standard metaphor of Hellenistic moral vocabulary. **3:4** Most ships used sails and depended upon the wind, making sea travel somewhat unpredictable and dangerous. Ships generally sailed near the coast rather than across open seas so that they could find a harbor when winds either failed or became too fierce. Since the sailing ship was a common mode of transportation, images of ships and shipwrecks

will of the pilot directs. 5So also the tongue is a small member, yet it boasts of great exploits.

How great a forest is set ablaze by a small fire! 6And the tongue is a fire. The tongue is placed among our members as a world of iniquity; it stains the whole body, sets on fire the cycle of nature,[n] and is itself set on fire by hell.[o] 7For every species of beast and bird, of reptile and sea creature, can be tamed and has been tamed by the human species, 8but no one can tame the tongue—a restless evil, full of deadly poison. 9With it we bless the Lord and Father, and with it we curse those who are made in the likeness of God. 10From the same mouth come blessing and cursing. My brothers and sisters,[p] this ought not to be so. 11Does a spring pour forth from the same opening both fresh and brackish water? 12Can a fig tree, my brothers and sisters,[q] yield olives, or a grapevine figs? No more can salt water yield fresh.

Two Kinds of Wisdom

13Who is wise and understanding among you? Show by your good life that your works are done with gentleness born of wisdom. 14But if you have bitter envy and selfish ambition in your hearts, do not be boastful and false to the truth. 15Such wisdom does not come down from above, but is earthly, unspiritual, devilish. 16For where there is envy and selfish ambition, there will also be disorder and wickedness of every kind. 17But the wisdom from above is first pure, then peaceable, gentle, willing to yield, full of mercy and good fruits, without a trace of partiality or hypocrisy. 18And a harvest of righteousness is sown in peace for[r] those who make peace.

Friendship with the World

4 Those conflicts and disputes among you, where do they come from? Do they not come from your cravings that are at war within you? 2You want something and do not have it; so you commit murder. And you covet[s] something and cannot obtain it; so you engage in disputes and conflicts. You do not have, because you do not ask. 3You ask and do not receive, because you ask wrongly, in order to spend what you get on your pleasures. 4Adulterers! Do you not know that friendship with the world is enmity with God? Therefore whoever wishes to be a friend of the world becomes an enemy of God. 5Or do you suppose that it is for nothing that the scripture says, "God[t] yearns jealously for the spirit that he has made to dwell in us"? 6But he gives all the more grace; therefore it says,

"God opposes the proud,
but gives grace to the humble."

7Submit yourselves therefore to God. Resist the devil, and he will flee from you. 8Draw near to God, and he

---

n Or *wheel of birth*
o Gk *Gehenna*
p Gk *My brothers*
q Gk *my brothers*
r Or *by*
s Or *you murder and you covet*
t Gk *He*

came to be used as illustrations of moral failure or inescapable fate, both among Christian (*1 Tim.* 1:19; *Barn.* 3.6) and Roman authors (Seneca, *Letters* 8.4; 85.33–34). ***pilot*** Lit. "the one who makes straight." **3:5** Uncontrolled speech was widely censured (1:26; *1 Pet.* 3:10; *Barn.* 19.8; *1 Clem.* 15.5; *Ps.* 12:3; *Prov.* 26:28; *Sir.* 14:1). The Gk employs alliteration here; it might be rendered into English as "the tongue is a *minor member* but boasts *major* things." **3:6** ***world of iniquity*** The Gk here for *world* is *kosmos,* which can sometimes be translated "ornament" or "adornment" (*1 Pet.* 3:3). The meaning is debated. ***stains*** See 1:27; *Mark* 7:20. ***the cycle of nature*** A concept popular in Hellenistic thinking, meaning here simply "life." ***hell*** Gk *Gehenna.* This is a Hebrew term transliterated into Greek. Outside this passage, it occurs only as a word of Jesus in our literature. **3:7** Such a four-part division was common in Hellenistic thinking (beast, bird, reptile, and sea creature). See *Gen.* 1:26 for a similar division. **3:9** ***made in the likeness of God*** *Gen.* 1:26–27. **3:11** ***fresh and brackish water*** Lit. "sweet and bitter." The author plays with these words in the verses immediately following: the word "fresh" is used in 3:12; the Gk word translated *brackish* here is translated "bitter"in 3:14. **3:15** In contrast to God's wisdom mentioned in 1:5–6 and 3:17. **3:17** *Wis.* 7:22. **3:18** ***those who make peace*** *Matt.* 5:9; *Col.* 1:20. **4:1** ***conflicts and disputes*** *1 Clem.* 46.1–5. The nature of the conflict is not clear. **4:2–4** *1 Pet.* 4:15. These concerns reflect elements in the Ten Commandments (*Exod.* 20:1–17). The charges are serious enough, but the historical situation cannot be determined. Such charges may be rhetorical devices, creating an atmosphere of seriousness. **4:2–3** ***ask*** See 1:5–8, where proper asking is discussed (*Matt.* 7:7–11). **4:4** ***friendship with the world*** James speaks of the "world" five times—twice in this verse and in 1:27; 2:5; 3:6. The word is used frequently in early Christian literature, almost always in a negative sense (*John* 12:25). **4:5** There is no quotation like this in Jewish scriptures although it seems to have been understood by the author as a scriptural citation. The author demonstrates a wide familiarity with the biblical materials, and his quotations and allusions are generally easily identifiable. Some scholars suggest that this passage may be a rough summary of various passages or of a general theme in Jewish scriptures. Others think the passage might refer to 4:6, with 4:5 as a parenthesis. **4:6–7** In both *Jas.* 4:6–7 and *1 Pet.* 5:5–9, the ideas of humility and resisting the devil are brought together. Perhaps this association comes naturally to mind when the word "resist" is used: God resists the proud; believers are to resist the devil. Or it may be evidence that one author is dependent on the other. **4:6** This quotation comes from the LXX (Prov. 3:34) and is cited in *1 Pet.* 5:5 and *1 Clem.* 30.2 as well. The Hebrew reads "At scoffers he scoffs, but to the lowly he shows grace." **4:8** *Zech.* 1:3; *Mal.* 3:7; *Ps.* 145:18.

will draw near to you. Cleanse your hands, you sinners, and purify your hearts, you double-minded. 9Lament and mourn and weep. Let your laughter be turned into mourning and your joy into dejection. 10Humble yourselves before the Lord, and he will exalt you.

Warning against Judging Another

11Do not speak evil against one another, brothers and sisters.*u* Whoever speaks evil against another or judges another, speaks evil against the law and judges the law; but if you judge the law, you are not a doer of the law but a judge. 12There is one lawgiver and judge who is able to save and to destroy. So who, then, are you to judge your neighbor?

Boasting about Tomorrow

13Come now, you who say, "Today or tomorrow we will go to such and such a town and spend a year there, doing business and making money." 14Yet you do not even know what tomorrow will bring. What is your life? For you are a mist that appears for a little while and then vanishes. 15Instead you ought to say, "If the Lord wishes, we will live and do this or that." 16As it is, you boast in your arrogance; all such boasting is evil. 17Anyone, then, who knows the right thing to do and fails to do it, commits sin.

Warning to Rich Oppressors

5 Come now, you rich people, weep and wail for the miseries that are coming to you. 2Your riches have rotted, and your clothes are moth-eaten. 3Your gold

and silver have rusted, and their rust will be evidence against you, and it will eat your flesh like fire. You have laid up treasure*v* for the last days. 4Listen! The wages of the laborers who mowed your fields, which you kept back by fraud, cry out, and the cries of the harvesters have reached the ears of the Lord of hosts. 5You have lived on the earth in luxury and in pleasure; you have fattened your hearts in a day of slaughter. 6You have condemned and murdered the righteous one, who does not resist you.

Patience in Suffering

7Be patient, therefore, beloved,*u* until the coming of the Lord. The farmer waits for the precious crop from the earth, being patient with it until it receives the early and the late rains. 8You also must be patient. Strengthen your hearts, for the coming of the Lord is near.*w* 9Beloved,*x* do not grumble against one another, so that you may not be judged. See, the Judge is standing at the doors! 10As an example of suffering and patience, beloved,*u* take the prophets who spoke in the name of the Lord. 11Indeed we call blessed those who showed endurance. You have heard of the endurance of Job, and you have seen the purpose of the Lord, how the Lord is compassionate and merciful.

12Above all, my beloved,*u* do not swear, either by heaven or by earth or by any other oath, but let your "Yes" be yes and your "No" be no, so that you may not fall under condemnation.

---

u Gk brothers

v Or will eat your flesh, since you have stored up fire
w Or is at hand
x Gk Brothers

---

double-minded See 1:8. **4:9** See 5:1; *Luke* 6:24; 16:15. **4:10** **he will exalt you** *Luke* 14:11. Or perhaps the author has in mind a comment in the story of Jesus' criticism of the Pharisees (*Matt.* 23:11). **4:11** **speaks evil** *1 Pet.* 2:1; *2 Cor.* 12:20; *Eph.* 4:11. **judges another** *Matt.* 7:1. **4:13–14** A similar illustration of the uncertainties of life for the rich is found in *Luke* 12:16–20. The uncertainties of the poor were too commonplace to need illustration or comment. **4:14** **mist...which vanishes** *1 Clem.* 17.6. *James* earlier used another illustration of the impermanence of life (1:9). **4:15** **If the Lord wishes** The idea of the need of divine favor for success was a feature of Hellenistic piety. **5:1** **you rich people** See 1:10; 2:4. **5:3** A similar combination of images (treasure, moth, and rust) appears in the Jesus tradition (*Matt.* 6:19–21). The gospels contend that the rich, by giving away wealth rather than storing it, will have treasure in the final accounting (*Mark* 10:21; *Matt.* 19:21; *Luke* 18:22). **5:4** **Listen!** The following list of charges has a prophetic ring (*Amos* 4:1; 5:11–12). **Lord of Hosts** Lit. "lord of *Sabaōth*." Several authors who quote this passage from LXX *Isa.* 5:9 do not translate the third word ("hosts") but merely transliterate it *(Sabaōth)*. Early Christian authors such as *James* and Paul (*Rom.* 9:29) follow the LXX. **5:7** **the late rains** *Joel* 2:23. Two heavy rains were needed in the normal cycle of planting and harvesting. One occurred at the beginning of the rainy season, softening the ground to make planting possible; the other at the end of the rainy season, bringing the crops to full head. **5:7–8** **coming of the Lord** The Gk word *parousia* is used often in our literature. In the gospels it is found only in Matthew's special material. The full phrase "coming of the Lord" is used elsewhere only in *1 Thess.* 3:13; 4:15; 5:23; *2 Thess.* 2:1 for the second coming of Christ. **5:11** The story of Job is detailed in a book by that name in the Bible. Otherwise Job is mentioned in the Bible only in *Ezek.* 14:14, 20 and, in our literature, here and in *1 Clem.* 17.3–4; 26.3. **5:12** **do not swear** The author clearly depends on the teaching of Jesus concerning swearing (*Matt.* 5:33–37). Judaism as a whole does not seem to have had such a blanket restriction on oaths.

The Prayer of Faith

[13]Are any among you suffering? They should pray. Are any cheerful? They should sing songs of praise. [14]Are any among you sick? They should call for the elders of the church and have them pray over them, anointing them with oil in the name of the Lord. [15]The prayer of faith will save the sick, and the Lord will raise them up; and anyone who has committed sins will be forgiven. [16]Therefore confess your sins to one another, and pray for one another, so that you may be healed. The prayer of the righteous is power-ful and effective. [17]Elijah was a human being like us, and he prayed fervently that it might not rain, and for three years and six months it did not rain on the earth. [18]Then he prayed again, and the heaven gave rain and the earth yielded its harvest.

[19]My brothers and sisters,[y] if anyone among you wanders from the truth and is brought back by another, [20]you should know that whoever brings back a sinner from wandering will save the sinner's[z] soul from death and will cover a multitude of sins.

---

y Gk *My brothers*
z Gk *his*

5:13 *songs of praise* Singing was an expected part of religious worship in both the Jewish and the Gentile worlds. **5:14** *anointing them with oil* This was a remedy used for some illnesses in the ancient world. Marcus Aurelius commented that because of his cold, he was going to pour oil on his head and go to sleep (Fronto, *Letters* 4.5). **5:15** *sins will be forgiven* See *John* 9:1–3 for a discussion of the connection between healing and the forgiveness of sins. **5:17** The incident is recorded at the beginning of the Elijah cycle of stories in *1 Kgs.* 17:1–22:53 and *2 Kgs.* 1:1–10:17. Elijah is otherwise mentioned in the Bible only at *2 Chr.* 21:12; *Ezek.* 10:21, 26; and *Mal.* 4:5. In early Christian literature, he is mentioned in the synoptic tradition and in *John* 1, *Rom.* 11:2, and *1 Clem.* 17.2. He was a popular character for much of the pseudepigraphical literature. **5:20** This is a strange, abrupt ending compared with most documents in our literature (but note the abrupt ending of *1 John*).

Paths to Follow and Paths to Avoid

DIDACHE

The Preservation of Early Christian Literature

Whereas most of the documents in this collection were preserved continuously from antiquity mainly because they gained for themselves a place in the New Testament canon, large quantities of early Christian literature went out of print, so to speak. A number of reasons might account for this. Papyrus and parchment writing materials were expensive. Then, someone had to be found to copy a book by hand. This required either substantial payment or voluntary effort. Some documents were simply judged not important enough to deserve such expenditure. These conditions would have applied in particular to the early church, a rapidly growing but not particularly wealthy movement, which, unlike most religious movement of the Mediterranean, made literature an important part of its framework.[1]

Perhaps partly in response to these conditions, churches began in the second century to identify the most important and authoritative texts. Although the mechanics are much disputed and the role of various individuals debated, the process undoubtedly involved decisions about which documents were to be favored, and which would receive less attention. Much of this process would have been based simply on the usefulness of particular documents to the communities which chose to preserve them.

In general, then, a document that did not survive was one that the early communities found they could live without.[2] Of course, some documents may have been destroyed by accident, though any literature having had wide impact and existing in many copies is not likely to have been lost for that reason. Some literature was suppressed in the political and other battles by which catholic, imperial "orthodoxy" took shape.

---

[1]Such interest in literature was more characteristic of philosophical movements of the day than of religious movements. Judaism and Christianity were exceptions.

[2]The matter changes after a document has begun to be treated as part of an authoritative canon. Some of the letters preserved in the NT must fit this category, their preservation being based more on past decision than on present usefulness. One need only compare the heavily theological letter of Paul to the *Romans* with this much shorter personal letter to *Philemon*.

With renewed interest in the world of antiquity, with a more methodical search for manuscripts, and with a good measure of luck, modern scholars have discovered some of the literature known only by name since the early period. One such document is the *Didache,* a text which was found little more than one hundred years ago.[3] The discovery of this long-lost text stirred the interest and imagination of the scholarly world of the late 1800s in a way similar to the discovery of the Dead Sea Scrolls and the Nag Hammadi library in the middle of the twentieth century.

Setting

The *Didache* seems to have presented itself initially as a corporate composition by the whole body of apostles, containing the teachings that Jesus had given to them. That is suggested by longer titles attached to this document, which read *The Teaching of the Twelve Apostles* and *The Lord's Teachings to the Gentiles through the Twelve Apostles.*

No one holds that this work came from the apostles' hands directly, though some would claim that it incorporates early Palestinian traditions of the church. Most scholars now see the document as a second-century composition from somewhere in Syria. It provides a summary of practical moral advice and proper conduct for the church.

Overview

The *Didache* falls clearly into two distinct parts. The first part is commonly called the Two Ways section (1–6). The document begins: "There are two ways, one of life and one of death, and there is a great difference between the two ways." Similar treatments of these contrasting ways can be found in other Jewish and Christian literature (including the *Letter of Barnabas*), where such sections are identified by the same terms.

The second section of the *Didache* offers guidelines for a wide range of Christian practices.

Themes and Issues

Issues involving Christian practice and church order make up the latter part of the document. Christians are to recite the Lord's Prayer three times a day (8.2); they are to fast on Wednesdays and Fridays (8.1); and they are to baptize according to a particular pattern, though some flexibility is allowed. These issues show some further influences from Judaism. Instructions for the Eucharist are included, and the role of bishops and deacons, who seem to be replacing apostles and prophets, is

---

[3]The eleventh-century manuscript (discovered in Constantinople in the late 1800s) contains two titles for this work: *The Teaching of the Twelve Apostles* and *The Lord's Teaching to the Gentiles by the Twelve Apostles.* We do not know how old these titles are, but we assume that this document is the same one referred to in the fourth century as *The Teaching of the Apostles.*

discussed at some length. A short apocalyptic exhortation concludes the work, further evidence of Jewish influence.

Purpose

The document functions as a church manual, but we cannot specify its purpose or use more clearly. Some have argued that the first part offers instructions that a recent convert might need, though what a recent convert might need to hear for the first time, an older convert might need to have refreshed. As the document stands, many Christian practices are detailed, and considerable attention is given to the nature of church leadership. This makes the document more than a manual for recent converts.

The *Didache* shares many of the key concerns found in Paul's writings and in the Synoptic Gospels. The primary difference, which might in part account for the creation of this document, is that the *Didache* seems to expand deliberately on important matters addressed more vaguely by other early literature. For example, the command made elsewhere to baptize simply specifies that it be done (*Matt.* 28:26). The *Didache* goes beyond that, specifying that the water, where possible, is to be running, cold, and in quantity;[4] but if necessary, hot water might be used, and water might simply be poured over the head three times (7.1–4).

Beyond this kind of expansion, there seems to be a specific concern about the leadership of the church. In particular, the resident bishops and deacons appear to have been neglected when itinerant "apostles" and "prophets" visited. The author is concerned that such wandering teachers could abuse their position of trust. He specifies how to distinguish between the authentic and inauthentic wandering prophets. The criteria are simple, concrete, and precise (11.8–12).

Audience

Although one of the titles by which the *Didache* is known suggests a Gentile audience, much of the work reflects a deep Jewish coloring. The Jewish coloring is seen in the Two Ways tradition that it has incorporated and in the many parallels with the *Gospel of Matthew,* perhaps the document most sensitive to Jewish concerns in our collection. Little else in the document demands a particular audience, and its contents are general enough to meet the needs of most any Christian community, which in part explains its popularity in the early church.

Authorship and Date

The term *didachē* is simply the Greek word for "teaching." The longer title of this work makes it clear what that teaching was—teaching from Jesus to the twelve apostles for Gentiles. If accepted as an accurate description of the content and ori-

---

[4]The requirements that the water be cold and running points to the use of streams or rivers.

gin of the work, this title would commend the *Didache* as an authoritative apostolic voice. But titles of documents are sometimes misleading, and the ascription of a document to some notable ancient figure or group in order to give it credibility is a well-attested literary practice in the Jewish, Christian, and Greco-Roman world. Church leaders were not unaware of this practice. Indeed, some also made use of it. (See introduction to LETTERS ATTRIBUTED TO PAUL.)

The modern scholar does not take ascriptions of authorship in ancient documents at face value. Sometimes, even the early church fathers expressed skepticism about the accuracy of an attribution of authorship. The apostolic authorship of the *Didache* was already rejected by the time we first find reference to the document in the fourth century.[5]

Although the "authenticity" of the *Didache* has no defenders, many recognize the presence of a substantial amount of very early material in it. They see the *Didache* largely as a composite of older sources. In particular, the instructions about the Eucharist and the description of church offices may be earlier than the second century. The Eucharist, for example, appears to be connected to a fellowship meal. There is evidence to suggest that this was the practice in at least some first-century Christian communities, but scholars think these two meals came to be separated early, with the Greek word *agapē* used to identify the fellowship meal.[6] Unfortunately, we know too little about the agape meal. All that we can say with certainty is that in the *Didache*, the Eucharist is part of a larger meal, and this strikes most investigators as an early tradition.

Primitive features are also found in the description of church offices. The *Didache* reflects some kind of struggle for prominence by bishops and deacons against apostles and prophets. The position of bishops and deacons in the *Didache* seems less secure than in the early second-century letters of Ignatius.[7] References to functioning apostles in the *Didache* seem out of place in the second century, from what we can glean in other writings of the period. Finally, the eschatological tone of the closing exhortation of the *Didache* recalls much of the literature of the first century. These observations have led many to conclude that the *Didache*, at least in places, reflects first-century Christian practice.

---

[5]The church historian Eusebius termed it the "so-called Teaching of the Apostles" (*Eccl. hist.* 3.25), and Athanasius, in the same century, listed it among the "disputed" books (*Festal Letter* 39).

[6]In Corinth, the Eucharist was celebrated as part of a larger meal. As a result of abuses (some people got drunk; in some cases the rich ate steak while the poor ate porridge, so to speak), Paul tried to regulate the practice by encouraging the celebration of the Eucharist in some other context than a fellowship meal (*1 Cor.* 11:20–34).

[7]Many scholars contend that the office of bishop, as distinct from the office of presbyter, was not fixed at the time of Ignatius (see the introduction to The Letters of Ignatius). The more important observation to make in regard to the *Didache* is that *both* offices (bishop and presbyter) are more securely established in the situation reflected in the Ignatian letters than in the *Didache*. There is not even a hint in the Ignatian letters that these offices were in some way clashing with the office of apostle or prophet. In fact, there is no evidence in Ignatius that apostles and prophets still existed. The *Didache* may thus reflect more primitive tradition at this point.

It is unwise, however, to date the *Didache* so early simply on the basis of apparently early features. For one thing, it is difficult to identify *early* features with any confidence, for not all areas of the Christian church would have developed at the same pace. The early church was in a process of development and change, and there is good reason to expect variety in many of the practices that later became more standardized and regulated.

Many scholars have even argued that the "primitive" aspects of the *Didache* are the work of a creative second-century writer who gives an apostolic flavor to his own production. This complicates the issue of date even further. As well, the final document appears to be a collection of disconnected materials, each reflecting a different date. For example, the instructions on baptism appear quite developed (ch. 7), as do the distinctions between Christians and Jews (ch. 8).

Though a convincing case probably cannot be made for a first-century date for the composition of the *Didache,* much of the material may reflect the primitive period. For that reason, we have included the *Didache* in our collection.

Value for the Study of Early Christianity

This early manual of church discipline is important evidence for the substantial appropriation of Judaism by those who shaped early Christianity. Even in his rejection of Jewish practice, the author of the *Didache* is influenced by Jewish piety and proposes alternatives that have a clearly Jewish stamp.[8] Further, the *Didache* may offer some glimpses into very primitive Christian practices.

Relation to Other Early Christian Documents

This document, though addressed to Gentiles according to its long title, reflects the heavy influence of Judaism at work in the shaping of the young Christian church. Scholars generally are convinced that the first third of the *Didache* (1.1–6.2) is based on a Jewish Two Ways tradition. The term Two Ways tradition refers to teaching that contrasts the way of life to the way of death, a theme that exists in other writings of the period.[9] This Jewish form of teaching, however, is clearly christianized in the *Didache* by a liberal sprinkling of synopticlike sayings of Jesus. In fact, much of the material throughout the *Didache* shows close parallels to material in the synoptic tradition, particularly to material in the *Gospel of Matthew.* This stands in stark contrast to a letter like *1 Clement,* which primarily depends on the Hebrew Bible for its images and instructions.

---

[8]We must be cautious about the kind of Jewish practices we associate with the first century. In most cases, the evidence we have comes from later centuries, primarily in writings of the rabbinic period. Many scholars now contend that so much development and standardization had occurred in these later texts that we can find little reliable witness to the practice of Jews in the first century in such documents.

[9]See *Barn.* 18.1–21.9. Also compare the parallels with the *Manual of Discipline* from Qumran.

For Further Reading

Kraft, Robert A. *Barnabas and the Didache.* Vol. 3 of *The Apostolic Fathers: A New Translation and Commentary.* New York: Nelson, 1965.

Draper, Jonathan A., ed. *The Didache in Modern Research.* Arbeiten zur Geschichte des Antiken Judentums und des Urchristentums 37. Leiden: Brill, 1996.

Niederwimmer, Kurt. *The Didache: A Commentary.* Hermeneia. Minneapolis, Minn.: Fortress, 1988.

van de Sandt, Hubb, and David Flusser. *The Didache: Its Jewish Sources and Its Place in Early Judaism and Christianity.* Compendia Rerum Iudaicarum ad Novum Testamentum 5. Minneapolis, Minn.: Fortress, 2002.

THE DIDACHE
or
THE TEACHING OF THE TWELVE APOSTLES

The teaching of the Lord to the Gentiles by the twelve apostles.

The Two Ways

1 There are two ways, one of life and one of death, and there is a great difference between these two ways.

The First Commandment of the Way of Life

2Now this is the way of life: first, "you shall love God, who made you"; second, "your neighbor as yourself"; and "whatever you do not wish to happen to you, do not do to another." 3The teaching of these words is this: "Bless those who curse you," and "pray for your enemies," and "fast for those who persecute you." "For what credit is it, if you love those who love you? Do not even the Gentiles do the same?" But "you must love those who hate you," and you will not have an enemy. 4Abstain from physical and bodily cravings. "If someone gives you a blow on your right cheek, turn to him the other as well," and you will be perfect. If someone "forces you to go one mile, go with him two miles"; "if someone takes your cloak, give him your tunic also"; "if someone takes from you what belongs to you, do not demand it back," for you cannot do so. 5Give to everyone who asks you, and do not demand it back," for the Father wants something from his own gifts to be given to everyone. Blessed is the one who gives according to the command, for such a person is innocent. Woe to the one who receives: if, on the one hand, someone who is in need receives, this person is innocent, but the one who does not have need will have to explain why and for what purpose he received, and upon being imprisoned will be interrogated about what he has done, and will not be released from there until he has repaid every last cent. 6But it has also been said concerning this: "Let your gift sweat in your hands until you know to whom to give it."

The Second Commandment of the Way of Life

2 The second commandment of the teaching is: 2"You shall not murder; you shall not commit

---

TRANSLATION by Michael W. Holmes after the earlier translation of J. B. Lightfoot and J. R. Harmer. TRANSLATION NOTES by Michael W. Holmes. Reprinted, with revisions, from *The Apostolic Fathers: Greek Texts and English Translations,* edited and revised by Michael W. Holmes (Grand Rapids: Baker Books, 1999). © 1992, 1999, 2003 by Michael W. Holmes. Used by permission of Baker Book House. All rights reserved. CONTENT NOTES are by the editors of this volume, with acknowledgment to Michael W. Holmes for his observations regarding a number of texts.

1.1 The Two Ways tradition recounted in 1.1–6.2 should be compared with that in *Barn.* 18.1–21.9. In several places, the parallels resemble the kind of relationship displayed by the Synoptic Gospels, with frequent word-for-word matches. **1.2** *your neighbour as yourself* The commands to love God and to love one's neighbor come from separate parts of the Bible (*Deut.* 6:5 and *Lev.* 19:18). The two are brought together in *Mark* 12:30–31, *Matt.* 22:37–39, and *Luke* 10:27, whose influence the *Didache* reflects here. *do not do to another* This is the negative form of the golden rule, found in its positive form in *Matt.* 7:12 and *Luke* 6:31. This idea is found in one form or another in Jewish (*Tob.* 4:15) and Hellenistic morality (Seneca, *Letters* 47.2–3). **1.3** *teaching* (Gk *didachē*). Here begins the 1st part of the teaching; the 2d part of the teaching runs from 2.1 to 4.14. Much of the material in the 1st part of the *Didache* comes from the Sermon on the Mount. The 3d paragraph of the *Didache* is roughly paralleled in *Matt.* 5:44–47 and *Luke* 6:27–36. But in this so-called Q material, the command is to pray, not fast, for one's persecutors, and nothing is mentioned there about having no enemies, although this may be implicit. **1.4** *physical and bodily cravings* 1 *Pet.* 2:11. *if someone gives you a blow* *Matt.* 5:39, 48. *if someone forces you* *Matt.* 5:41. *if someone takes your cloak* *Luke* 6:30. *you cannot do so* The text is puzzling here. Some scholars suggest that it may be a flippant scribal addition. **1.5** See 4.7–8 for the same theme. The 1st half of this paragraph recalls Q material, largely drawn from the parts of *Matthew* and *Luke* previously quoted. *every last cent* *Matt.* 5:26; *Luke* 12:59. Nothing is mentioned in the Q material about judgment on those who are the takers. The statement about paying the last cent is not there tied to giving and taking. It appears that some people have taken advantage of the generous hospitality of early Christian communities; this does not mean, however, that these communities are permitted to deny future hospitality (11.4–6, 9, 12.1–5). *cent* A *quadrans,* small coin of little worth. See APPENDIX A. **1.6** *let your gift sweat* Judaism and Christianity emphasize acts of charity, and this saying was probably one of many "wise words" about charity. For a similar theme, see *Sir.* 12:1–7; for similar language but a different theme, see *Matt.* 6:3. **2.1** *second commandment* See 1.3. The author does not mean the 2d of the Ten Commandments.

adultery"; you shall not corrupt boys; you shall not sexually promiscuous; "you shall not steal"; you shall not practice magic; you shall not engage in sorcery; you shall not abort a child or commit infanticide. "You shall not covet your neighbor's possessions; [3]you shall not commit perjury; you shall not give false testimony"; you shall not speak evil; you shall not hold a grudge. [4]You shall not be double-minded, or double-tongued, for the "double-tongue" is a deadly snare. [5]Your word must not be false or meaningless, but confirmed by action. [6]You shall not be greedy or avaricious, or a hypocrite or malicious or arrogant. You shall not hatch evil plots against your neighbor. [7]You shall not hate any one; instead you shall reprove some, and pray for some, and some you shall love more than your own life.

To Do and Not Do

3 My child, flee from evil of every kind and from everything resembling it. [2]Do not become angry, for anger leads to murder. Do not be jealous or quarrelsome or hot-tempered, for all these things breed murders. [3]My child, do not be lustful, for lust leads to fornication. Do not be foulmouthed or let your eyes roam, for all these things breed adultery. [4]My child, do not be an augur, since it leads to idolatry. Do not be an enchanter or an astrologer or a magician, or even desire to see[a] them, for all these things breed idolatry. [5]My child, do not be a liar, since lying leads to theft. Do not be avaricious or conceited, for all these things breed thefts. [6]My child, do not be a grumbler, since it leads to blasphemy. Do not be arrogant or evil-minded, for all these things breed blasphemies.

[7]Instead, be humble, for "the humble shall inherit the earth." [8]Be patient and merciful and innocent and quiet and good, and revere always the words which you have heard. [9]Do not exalt yourself or permit your soul to become arrogant. Your soul shall not associate with the lofty, but live with the righteous and the humble. [10]Accept as good the things that happen to you, knowing that nothing transpires apart from God.

4 My child, night and day remember the one who preaches God's word to you, and honor him as though he were the Lord. For wherever the Lord's nature is preached, there the Lord is. [2]Moreover, you shall seek out daily the presence of the saints, that you may find support in their words. [3]You shall not cause division, but shall make peace between those who quarrel. You shall judge righteously; you shall not show partiality when reproving transgressions. [4]You shall not waver with regard to your decisions.[b]

[5]Do not be one who stretches out his hands to receive but withdraws them when it comes to giving. [6]If you earn something by working with your hands, you shall give a ransom for your sins. [7]You shall not

---

a Some ancient authorities add *or hear*

b Gk *be of two minds whether it shall be or not*

2.2–7 Many of the things specifically forbidden in this paragraph come directly from Jewish sources such as the Ten Commandments (*Exod.* 20:1–17) and other codes. **2.2** In this sentence is a list of vices common in Greco-Roman society but forbidden by the author: homosexuality, magic, abortion, and infanticide. Magic was widely used and feared even by Jews and Christians. The Christian leadership fought against it (3.4). **engage in sorcery** The reference is to the use of magic potions or drugs of some sort. **infanticide** Unwanted babies (usually girls) were often simply exposed to the elements in the societies of the Mediterranean. Many were saved from death and raised as slaves or prostitutes. It was not only Jews and Christians who criticized the practice (see contemporary Musonius Rufus, *Whether One Should Rear All Children Born to Him*). On *homosexuality*, see note to *Rom.* 1:27. Many Greco-Roman moralists would have agreed in principle with the Christian attack. **2.3–7** Note the similar approach in *Matt.* 19:18–19, where the commandments are expanded to prohibit more familiar internal sins (e.g., hate as well as murder; the double tongue as well as the lying tongue). Given the heavy use of *Matthew*-like material in the *Didache*, *Matthew* may be the source of this comment. See 3.2–6 for a further example of the association of lesser evils with greater. **2.5** This sounds like the concern expressed in *Matt.* 5:33–37. **3.2–6** Here the injunctions are intensified to include the feelings that are the root of such actions. It is not just murder that is forbidden but anger and other emotions that might lead to murder, such as jealousy, quarreling, and a hot temper. Likewise, not only fornication is forbidden but also lust. This intensification of the commandments is part of the debate over the law. The strongest statements by Jesus in support of the law appear in *Matt.* 5:17–29. **3.3** In *Matt.* 5:27–29, adultery, lust, and the eye are mentioned together but in a slightly different way. **3.4** Obsession with omens and astrology marked the Mediterranean world of the 1st century. There is considerable evidence that some Jews were interested and even skilled in these arts. Some early Christians, too, found them attractive, and the Christians' interest in miracles led to charges that they practiced magic. Church leaders attempted to distinguish between magic and miracle, rejecting the former (5.1; *Barn.* 20; *Acts* 19:19). **augur** Lit. "watcher of birds." Observing the flight of wild birds or the feeding habits of tame birds was one way to predict the future. The term here may be intended to include all related activities designed to asertain the will of the gods, such as that of the *haruspices* (lit. "gut-gazers"), who examined the entrails of sacrifices, odd births, and other unusual phenomena by which the gods might communicate. **an enchanter** One who cast spells. **3.7 humble shall inherit the earth** *Matt.* 5:5. **3.10** This view was popularized by Stoic philosophers (Seneca, *Letters* 16.4–8). **4.1 remember . . . God's word** See *Heb.* 13:7. **4.3 partiality** *Deut.* 1:16; *Prov.* 31:9. The Stoics had a similar view (Seneca, *Letters* 47).

hesitate to give, nor shall you grumble when giving, for you shall yet come to know who is the good paymaster of the reward. [8]You shall not turn away from someone in need, but shall share everything with your brother, and not claim that anything is your own. For if you are sharers in what is imperishable, how much more so in perishable things!

[9]You shall not withhold your hand from[c] your son or your daughter, but from their youth you shall teach them the fear of God. [10]You shall not give orders to your slave or servant girl (who hope in the same God as you) when you are angry, lest they cease to fear the God who is over you both. For he comes to call not with regard to reputation but upon those whom the Spirit has prepared. [11]And you slaves shall be submissive to your masters in respect and fear, as to a symbol of God.

[12]You shall hate all hypocrisy and everything that is not pleasing to the Lord. [13]You must not forsake the Lord's commandments but must guard what you have received, neither adding nor subtracting anything. [14]In church you shall confess your transgressions, and you shall not approach your prayer with an evil conscience. This is the way of life.

The Way of Death

5 But the way of death is this: first of all, it is evil and completely cursed; murders, adulteries, lusts, fornications, thefts, idolatries, magic arts, sorceries, robberies, false testimonies, hypocrisy, duplicity, deceit, arrogance, malice, stubbornness, greed, foul speech, jealousy, audacity, pride, boastfulness. [2]It is the way of persecutors of good people, of those hating truth, loving a lie, not knowing the reward of righteousness, not adhering to what is good or to righteous judgment, being on the alert not for what is good but for what is evil, from whom gentleness and patience are

far away, loving worthless things, pursuing reward, having no mercy for the poor, not working on behalf of the oppressed, not knowing the one who made them, murderers of children, corrupters of God's creation, turning away from someone in need, oppressing the afflicted, advocates of the wealthy, lawless judges of the poor, utterly sinful. May you be delivered, children, from all these things!

The Right Choice

6 See that no one leads you astray from this way of the teaching, for such a person teaches you without regard for God. [2]For if you are able to bear the whole yoke of the Lord, you will be perfect. But if you are not able, then do what you can.

Concerning Food

[3]Now concerning food, bear what you are able, but in any case keep strictly away from meat sacrificed to idols, for it involves the worship of dead gods.

Concerning Baptism

7 Now concerning baptism, baptize as follows: after you have reviewed[d] all these things, baptize "in the name of the Father and of the Son and of the Holy Spirit" in running water. [2]But if you have no running water, then baptize in some other water; and if you are not able to baptize in cold water, then do so in warm. [3]But if you have neither, then pour water on the head three times "in the name of Father and Son and Holy Spirit." [4]And before the baptism, let the one baptizing and the one who is to be baptized fast, as well as any others who are able. Also, you must instruct the one who is to be baptized to fast for one or two days beforehand.

---

c I.e., *neglect your responsibility to*

d I.e., with those who are about to be baptized

4.8 *Acts* reports what might be called the Jerusalem experiment, in which the members of the young Christian community had all things in common (*Acts* 2:44–45; 4:32). This did not become the pattern of early Christian groups, but generosity was encouraged. **4.9** *not withhold your hand Barn.* 19.22; *Eph.* 6:4; *Heb.* 12:5–11; *1 Clem.* 56.23; a frequent theme in wisdom literature such as *Proverbs* and *Sirach.* **4.10–11** See *1 Pet.* 2:18. Seneca encourages masters to treat their slaves in such a way that the slaves will respect rather than fear them (*Letters* 47). **4.13** *Deut.* 4:2, 12:32 (LXX 13:1). **4.14** *This is the way of life* See 1.2. **5.1–2** This list is more detailed than, but not dissimilar to, the list in chs. 2–3. There the list was what a good person does not do; here it is what a bad person does. Paul provided a similar list in *Rom.* 1:29–30. **6.1** *leads you astray Matt.* 24:4. **6.3** *meat sacrificed to idols* Whether Christians should be permitted to eat meat offered as sacrifice in pagan temples was a question raised often among the early Christians. Eating such meat was generally forbidden, but there was some flexibility on the matter (*1 Cor.* 8:1–10; 10:19, 25; *Col.* 2:16; *1 Tim.* 4:3; *Heb.* 13:9; *Rev.* 2:14, 20). **7.1** *baptize in the name Matt.* 28:19. *in running water* Lit. "in living water"; also in 7.2. **7.3** *pour water on the head three times* This is the earliest reference to a mode of Christian baptism other than immersion, which the *Didache* also assumes to be the normal practice. **7.4** Baptism came to be carried out at Easter, and the prebaptismal fast gradually was extended into the period of abstinence now called Lent.

Concerning Fasts

8 But do not let your fasts coincide with those of the hypocrites. They fast on Monday and Thursday, so you must fast on Wednesday and Friday.

Concerning Prayer

2 Nor should you pray like the hypocrites. Instead, "pray like this," just as the Lord commanded in his gospel:
"Our Father in heaven,
hallowed be your name,
your kingdom come,
your will be done
    on earth as it is in heaven.
Give us today our daily bread,
and forgive us our debt,
    as we also forgive our debtors;
and do not lead us into temptation,
but deliver us from the evil one;*e*
for yours is the power and the glory forever."
3 Pray like this three times a day.

Concerning the Eucharist

9 Now concerning the Eucharist,*f* give thanks as follows. 2 First, concerning the cup:
We give you thanks, our Father,
for the holy vine of David your servant,
which you have made known to us
through Jesus, your servant;
to you be the glory forever.
3 And concerning the broken bread:
We give you thanks, our Father,
for the life and knowledge
which you have made known to us
through Jesus, your servant;
to you be the glory forever.

4   Just as this broken bread was scattered upon the
        mountains and then was gathered
        together and become one,
so may your church be gathered together from
        the ends of the earth into your kingdom;
for yours is the glory and the power
        through Jesus Christ forever.
5 But let no one eat or drink of your Eucharist except those who have been baptized into the name of the Lord, for the Lord has also spoken concerning this: "Do not give what is holy to dogs."

10 And after you have had enough, give thanks as follows:
2   We give you thanks, Holy Father,
    for your holy name which you
        have caused to dwell in our hearts,
    and for the knowledge and faith and immortality
        which you have made known to us
        through Jesus your servant;
    to you be the glory forever.
3   You, almighty Master, created all things for your
        name's sake,
    and gave food and drink to men to enjoy,
        that they might give you thanks;
    but to us you have graciously given
        spiritual food and drink,
    and eternal life through your servant.*g*
4   Above all we give thanks because you are
        mighty;
    to you be the glory forever.
5   Remember your church, Lord,
    to deliver it from all evil
    and to make it perfect in your love;
    and gather it, the one that has been sanctified,
    from the four winds into your kingdom,
    which you have prepared for it;
    for yours is the power and the glory forever.

---

e Or *from evil*
f Or *the thanksgiving*

g Some ancient authorities add *Jesus*

8.1 There is some ambiguity in the earliest Christian attitude to fasting (1.3; *Matt.* 6:16; 9:14; *Acts* 13:2; 14:23). The contrast here is with the Jews, who fasted on Mondays and Thursdays. Christians valued fasting, as Jews did. The change of fast days to Wednesdays and Fridays merely helped to provide a separate identity for a community that shared much with Judaism. **8.2–3** *Matt.* 6:9–13; *Luke* 11:1–4. The Jews had various fixed prayer forms in the 1st century. One, the *Tefillah,* was to be said three times a day, but we are not able to determine when this practice was instituted or became widespread. The custom of praying three times a day was itself an old tradition, but it is uncertain which prayer was used. Daniel is said to have prayed three times a day (*Dan.* 6:10); this story is usually dated to the 2d century B.C.E. *Acts* (1st century C.E.) reports a mid-afternoon prayer (3:1; 10:3, 30). It is likely that regular morning and evening prayers would have developed 1st, the midafternoon prayer bringing the count to three. **9.1–10.7** The instructions for the Eucharist presented here differ from the oldest extant form of the prayer (*1 Cor.* 11:23–26) and also from that in the synoptic tradition, which is close to the Pauline form (*Mark* 14:22–25; *Matt.* 26:26–29; *Luke* 22:19–24). The bread is usually first, then the cup, but *1 Cor.* 10:16 may suggest the reverse order. The prayers in the *Didache* seem to follow Jewish table prayers or graces more closely. **9.1** The Gk word for *Eucharist* simply means "thanksgiving." Christians made the word into a technical term quite early; see Ign. *Phld.* 4.1; Ign. *Smyrn.* 6.8–9; 8.5. **9.3** *give . . . thanks* The Gk for this expression, which occurs also in 10.1, 2, 3, is a verb form of the word "Eucharist." **9.5** *to the dogs Matt.* 7:6. **10.5** *you have prepared for it Matt.* 24:31.

6 May grace come, and may this world pass away. Hosanna to the God of David.
If anyone is holy, let him come; if anyone is not, let him repent.[h]
Maranatha! Amen.
[7]But permit the prophets to give thanks however they wish.[i]

Concerning Teachers

11 So, if anyone should come and teach you all these things that have just been mentioned above, welcome him. [2]But if the teacher himself goes astray and teaches a different teaching that undermines all this, do not listen to him. However, if his teaching contributes to righteousness and knowledge of the Lord, welcome him as you would the Lord.

Concerning Itinerant Apostles and Prophets

[3]Now concerning the apostles and prophets, deal with them as follows in accordance with the rule of the gospel. [4]Let every apostle who comes to you be welcomed as if he were the Lord. [5]But he is not to stay for more than one day, unless there is need, in which case he may stay another. But if he stays three days, he is a false prophet. [6]And when the apostle leaves, he is to take nothing except bread until he finds his next night's lodging. But if he asks for money, he is a false prophet.

[7]Also, do not test or evaluate any prophet who speaks in the Spirit, for every sin will be forgiven, but this sin will not be forgiven. [8]However, not everyone who speaks in the Spirit is a prophet, but only if he exhibits the Lord's ways. By his conduct, therefore, will the false prophet and the prophet be recognized. [9]Furthermore, any prophet who orders a meal in the Spirit shall not partake of it; if he does, he is a false prophet. [10]If any prophet teaches the truth, yet does not practice what he teaches, he is a false prophet. [11]But any prophet proven to be genuine who does something with a view to portraying in a worldly manner the symbolic meaning of the church[j] (provided that he does not teach you to do all that he himself does) is not to be judged by you, for his judgment is with God. Besides, the ancient prophets also acted in a similar manner. [12]But if anyone should say in the Spirit, "Give me money" or anything else, do not listen to him. But if he tells you to give on behalf of others who are in need, let no one judge him.

12 Everyone "who comes in the name of the Lord" is to be welcomed. But then examine him, and

---

h Or let him be converted
i Other ancient authorities add: And concerning the ointment, give thanks as follows: We give you thanks, Father, for the fragrant ointment which you have made known to us through Jesus your servant; to you be the glory forever. Amen.

j Or possibly who acts out in an earthly fashion the allegorical significance of the church; Gk who acts with a view to the earthly mystery of the church

---

10.6 Hosannah to the God of David See Matt. 21:9, 15 ("son of David"). **Maranatha** 1 Cor. 16:22. The word is a transliteration of the Aramaic words meaning "our Lord, come." It seems to have been a common saying in the early Christian communities and was taken over without translation even by Gk-speaking Christian groups. **10.7 prophets** From the detailed discussion that follows, it appears that prophets were an important part of the church leadership. They are to be distinguished from other leaders, such as bishops and deacons (15.1). The latter were local and permanent, but the prophets seem to have been largely itinerant, though the Didache offers evidence that some of the prophets chose to settle down in a local community (12.3–13.1). Further, these prophets are to be distinguished from the prophets of the Jewish scriptures, although early Christians may have thought that their prophets operated under the same inspiration. Generally in our literature, "prophets" refers to the Hebrew prophets. The Didache is the main exception, along with scattered passages in a few other writings (Acts 11:27; 13:1; 15:32; 21:10; 1 Cor. 12:28–29; 13:2; 14:29, 33, 37; Eph. 4:11; perhaps 2:20; 3:5; and some passages in Revelation, whose author considered his writing a prophecy [1:3]). **11.1** A reference to traveling prophets and teachers. In the early years, the local congregations did not have a full-time clergy. See the more detailed regulations that follow. **11.3 apostles and prophets** While the author introduces the case as involving apostles and prophets, he speaks only of prophets (11.3–13.7). Other Christian writers around this time routinely use "apostle" in a more restricted sense, to indicate the twelve disciples of Jesus, with this number frequently specified (Mark 3:14; Matt. 10:12; Luke 6:13; Acts 1:26; Rev. 21:14). The Pauline tradition has a slightly broader definition of "apostle" (1 Cor. 12:28–29; perhaps Eph. 4:11). It is possible that the author of the Didache used "apostle" in a nontechnical sense—meaning "messenger," rather than a formal office. **rule of the gospel** It is unclear what the author has in mind. **11.5–6** Abuses of hospitality must have been serious to prompt the author to restrict hospitality even to those called apostles. **11.7 speaks in the Spirit** See 1 Corinthians 14 for a fuller discussion of early Christian prophets. **this sin will not be forgiven** Matt. 12:31. **11.11 in a worldly manner the symbolic meaning** It is unclear what the author has in mind. **12.1–3** Matt. 21:9. The topic is still prophets (see 13.1). It is not clear, however, in what way these individuals differ from those mentioned in 10.4–6, although the permitted visit here was for three days rather than two. The difference may be related to the purpose of the visit. Here the individual is identified as a traveler who apparently has the full intention of stopping only briefly; thus, the abuses stemming from an extended stay would have been less of a concern. Nevertheless, precautions are to be taken should such a person decide to settle in the community (12.3–4). **12.1 true and false** Lit. "right and left understanding." This may reflect the influence of Jonah 4:11.

you will find out—for you will have insight—what is true and what is false. ²If the one who comes is merely passing through, assist him as much as you can. But he must not stay with you for more than two or, if necessary, three days. ³However, if he wishes to settle among you and is a craftsman, let him work for his living. ⁴But if he is not a craftsman, decide according to your own judgment how he shall live among you as a Christian, yet without being idle. ⁵But if he does not wish to cooperate in this way, then he is trading on Christ. Beware of such people.

13 But every genuine prophet who wishes to settle among you "is worthy of his food." ²Likewise, every genuine teacher is, like "the worker, worthy of his food." ³Take, therefore, all the firstfruits of the produce of the wine press and threshing floor, and of the cattle and sheep, and give these firstfruits to the prophets, for they are your high priests. ⁴But if you have no prophet, give them to the poor. ⁵If you make bread, take the firstfruit and give in accordance with the commandment. ⁶Similarly, when you open a jar of wine or oil, take the firstfruit and give it to the prophets. ⁷As for money and clothes and any other possessions, take the firstfruit that seems right to you and give in accordance with the commandment.

Concerning the Lord's Day

14 On the Lord's own day gather together and break bread and give thanks, having first confessed your sins so that your sacrifice may be pure.

²But let no one who has a quarrel with a companion join you until they have been reconciled, so that your sacrifice may not be defiled. ³For this is the sacrifice concerning which the Lord said, "In every place and time offer me a pure sacrifice, for I am a great king, says the Lord, and my name is marvelous among the nations."

Bishops and Deacons

15 Therefore appoint for yourselves bishops and deacons worthy of the Lord, men who are humble and not avaricious and true and approved, for they too carry out for you the ministry of the prophets and teachers. ²You must not, therefore, despise them, for they are your honored men, along with the prophets and teachers.

Call to Follow the Gospel

³Furthermore, correct one another not in anger but in peace, as you find in the gospel; and if anyone wrongs his neighbor, let no one speak to him, nor let him hear a word from you, until he repents. ⁴As for your prayers and acts of charity and all your actions, do them all just as you find it in the Gospel of our Lord.

16 "Watch" over your life: "do not let your lamps go out, and do not be unprepared, but be ready, for you do not know the hour when our Lord is coming." ²Gather together frequently, seeking the things that benefit your souls, for the all the time you have

---

12.5 trading on Christ The phrase is a compound word in Gk, *christemporos,* clearly meaning something negative here, such as "Christ-huckster." The author probably coined the word for the occasion. **13.1–2** The issue is salary for the clergy (*Matt.* 10:10; *Luke* 10:7; *1 Cor.* 9:13–14; *1 Tim.* 5:17–18). The church was expected to support its leaders. This indicates that the individuals discussed in 12.3–5 must have failed the test for being a prophet. Even so, they were to be accepted as members of the community, though not as part of the paid clergy. **13.3–7 firstfruits** Probably informed by the Jewish practice of giving the first part of the new crop to the priests in the temple, but readers could have been familiar with the practice in pagan religion as well. **13.3 high priests** The *Didache*'s use of the term "high priest" for Christian clergy is distinctive. Where the term is used elsewhere (mainly *Hebrews* and *1 Clement*), it is applied to Christ. See *1 Clem.* 36.1. **14.1 the Lord's own day** Probably Sunday, but there is considerable dispute. Scholars argue about whether the Christian use of Sunday came as a conscious break from the Jewish holy day (Saturday), called the Sabbath, or simply because it was the day of the resurrection of Jesus, according to early Christian tradition. Paul hints at a Sunday meeting (*1 Cor.* 16:2), and Justin, in the middle of the 2d century, refers to it explicitly (*1 Apology* 65–67), as does Ignatius at the beginning of the 2d century (Ign. *Magn.* 9.1); see also *Rev.* 1:10. Bishop Melito of Sardis wrote a tractate on the topic in the latter part of the 2d century (Eusebius, *Eccl. Hist.* 4.26). **14.2** *Matt.* 5:23–24. **14.3** *Mal.* 1:11, 14. **15.1** These requirements for bishops and deacons are less detailed than those specified in the Pastoral Letters (*1 Tim.* 3:2–13; *Titus* 1:7–9). In the *Didache,* bishops and deacons are viewed as substitutes for prophets and teachers. **bishops** Probably used in a descriptive sense, of a function, rather than as a formal office. This is the only mention of the term in the *Didache,* and it is in the plural; further, it nowhere mentions "presbyters." Here it might be better translated "overseers," indicating the group that in other literature is called the presbyters or elders. The Pastorals reflect a similar use of terms (see *1 Tim.* 3:1). **15.2** It seems that prophets had higher status than bishops. Some scholars have pointed to the *Didache* as evidence for tension between itinerant ministers (perhaps authenticated by dramatic displays of special powers or revelations) and an institutional ministry (perhaps elected to deal with the more practical or routine needs of the community). **15.4 find** Lit. "have." **Gospel of our Lord** It is not clear whether this comment refers to written gospels, oral traditions, or Jewish scriptures. The *Didache*'s familiarity with *Matthew*-like material makes it possible that an early written gospel is in view. **16.1–8** The language and theme of this final section recall *Matt.* 24:36–25:13, the apocalyptic discourse. The passage largely consists of catchwords and phrases from a variety of sources from Jewish scripture and early Christian writings, especially *Matthew.* **16.2** *Barn.* 4.9.

believed will be of no use to you if you are not found perfect in the last time.

Mini-Apocalypse

³For in the last days the false prophets and corrupters will abound, and the sheep will be turned into wolves, and love will be turned into hate. ⁴For as lawlessness increases, they will hate and persecute and betray one another. And then the deceiver of the world will appear as a son of God and "will perform signs and wonders," and the earth will be delivered into his hands, and he will commit abominations the likes of which have never happened before. ⁵Then all humankind will come to the fiery test, and "many will fall away" and perish; but "those who endure" in their faith "will be saved" by the accursed one himself. ⁶And "then there will appear the signs" of the truth: first the sign of an opening in heaven, then the sign of the sound of a trumpet, and third, the resurrection of the dead—⁷but not of all; rather, as it has been said, "The Lord will come, and all his saints with him." ⁸Then the world "will see the Lord coming upon the clouds of heaven."

16.3 Again the author parallels synoptic tradition, *Matt.* 24:11–12 in particular. The theme of coming *false prophets* occurs frequently in our literature (*Mark* 13:22; *Matt.* 24:11, 24; *1 John* 4:1; *Did.* 16.2; see *2 Tim.* 3:1; *1 Pet.* 1:5). **16.4** *as lawlessness increases* See *Matt.* 24:10–12. *the deceiver of the world* This is the image of an antichrist. An opponent of God is a theme in much of Christian apocalyptic literature, often having its roots in images from *Daniel* (*Dan.* 11:36–37; *2 Thess.* 2:3–4, 9; *Rev.* 13:2, 13). **16.5** *accursed one* The meaning is obscure. The reference could be to Christ, who became a curse, according to *Gal.* 3:13. **16.6** *trumpet* The sound of a trumpet is often associated with the final judgment (*1 Thess.* 4:16; *1 Cor.* 15:52). **16.7** *Zech.* 14:5. **16.8** *Matt.* 24:30, 26, 64. The text breaks off abruptly, and the manuscript tradition shows variation at this point. Final pages of a manuscript were most susceptible to damage or loss. See the apparently abrupt ending of *Mark* and the longer ending supplied by many manuscripts (*Mark* 16:8).

On the Interpretation of Scripture and the Two Ways

BARNABAS   Introduced by Jay C. Treat

T HE *LETTER OF BARNABAS* is an anonymous Greek treatise, one of the writings
now known as the Apostolic Fathers. The Apostolic Fathers are early Christian
writings that seventeenth-century scholarship treated as a group on the assumption that their authors were the successors of the apostles. Some of them have enjoyed canonical status in various times and places; for example, the *Letter of
Barnabas* is found in Codex Sinaiticus, an important fourth-century manuscript of
the Bible.

Author

Early church writers attributed this anonymous work to Barnabas, the companion of Paul. Most recent scholars disagree, partly because our author strongly
opposes a literal observance of circumcision, but the Barnabas of *Gal.* 2:13 acqui-
esced to it.

We can say little about the author. He is male and probably a Gentile (16.7). Despite his modest disclaimers, he is a teacher (1.8; 4.9; 9.9). He is part of a "school," a
living tradition of teachers who preserve traditional teaching materials, including
Jewish materials in Greek. He writes primarily as a transmitter of his tradition
("imparting to you a measure of what I have received," 1.5) rather than as a creative
authority such as Paul.

Setting and Date

The author's location is unknown. Recent suggestions include Egypt, Palestine,
Syria, and Asia Minor.

The occasion for writing is unknown. Although the author argues against Jewish or Christian rivals, his central intention is probably to pass on to his readers an
understanding of what God requires of them.

Since 16.3–5 presupposes that the temple is in ruins, *Barnabas* was most probably written sometime between Titus's destruction of the temple in 70 C.E. and
Hadrian's building of a Roman temple on the site in about 135 C.E. *Barnabas* 4.4–5

and 16.1–5 do not provide enough clues to narrow the time frame further. The letter uses traditions from several generations.

Literary Features

Most contemporary scholars agree that the *Letter of Barnabas* is not an actual letter written to real recipients, but rather a treatise in the form of a letter—much like *Hebrews*. Chapters 1, 17, and 21 form the letter's framework and are the author's own work. Two major sections of teaching are set in this framework.

The first major section (chs. 2–16) presents a "spiritual" interpretation of Jewish scripture. This section is meant to show that it is misguided to understand scripture as prescribing rituals like circumcision and fasting. Scripture points instead to Christ and his people and to ethical behavior. Like *Hebrews*, *Barnabas* interprets scripture in ways that show similarities to both allegorical and rabbinic methods.

The author forms this section by putting together blocks of traditional material (such as 2.4–3.6) with just enough cement to hold them together. These building blocks, which he takes from his school or tradition, typically contain a series of scriptural quotations combined with brief interpretations. The tradition has often reshaped quotations. Sometimes it quotes otherwise unknown writings as scriptural authorities.

The second major section of teaching (chs. 18–20) contains ethical instruction in a form known as the Two Ways. The author understands it to be an authoritative compilation of the Lord's requirements for ethical living (21.1).

Two Ways concepts in the Qumran *Community Rule* 3.13–4.26 show that a version of the tradition existed in a Semitic language form. In a Greek form, it evolved further in various settings. A version of the tradition similar to *Barnabas*'s appears in the *Didache*. Contemporary scholars tend to agree that the Two Ways sections in *Barnabas* and *Didache* derive from a common source. The version in *Barnabas* shows fewer specifically Christian developments than the version in *Didache* does.

Purposes, Themes, and Features

Barnabas is not systematic, but its primary purposes seem to be instruction and exhortation for practical Christian living. The author combines a concern for ethics with urgent eschatological expectation. The coming of the Lord in judgment is near (21.3). His people must make use of their time before the day of judgment to perform the will of God (4.9b; 19.10; 21.8), because they will be judged according to their conduct (4.12). They are not yet justified and should not live as if they were (4.10b; 15.7). They must pay attention to their conduct in these evil days, because Satan can use his power to drive them from the Lord's kingdom (2.1, 10b; 4.9–14). Those who persevere in obedience to God's righteous requirements will experience the end of evil and the renewal of all things (15.5–9).

Gnōsis, "special insight" or "knowledge," is a common term in *Barnabas. Barnabas*'s circle uses it in both an interpretive and an ethical sense. God grants interpretive gnosis to prophets (9.8b; 10.10a) and Christians (5.3; 13.7), so that they can interpret scripture and current events correctly. God also provides ethical gnosis so that they will know how to behave (5.4b; 18.1a; 19.1c; 21.5).[1] In the translation that follows, *gnōsis* is rendered "special knowledge."

Perhaps the most distinctive feature of *Barnabas* is its relation to Judaism. On the one hand, Jewish scripture plays a central authoritative role for the author's circle: They can derive everything they need from an allegorical interpretation of that scripture. On the other hand, they believe that Israel never actually received the covenant but was deceived by an evil angel (9.4) into interpreting God's requirements literally. Christians, the true heirs of the covenant, understand the scriptures in their intended sense. The author criticizes major aspects of Jewish ritual observance, but this critique probably derives from Jewish sources, themselves opposed to ritual.

Relation to Other Early Christian Texts

Barnabas 4.14 appears to quote *Matt.* 22:14. Otherwise, there is no clear evidence that the author knew any NT writings. Even in the case of *Barn.* 4.14, Helmut Koester has argued that the author may be quoting a saying of Jesus (or an unknown pre-Christian source), which he has mistakenly attributed to Jewish scripture.[2] Like other early church writings, *Barnabas* appears not to be dependent on written gospels but to stand near them in a living oral tradition.

Value for the Study of Early Judaism and Christianity

The *Letter of Barnabas* represents one of many early forms of Christianity. It preserves glimpses of a stage in Jewish tradition earlier than the Mishnah (see especially *Barnabas* 7–8) and glimpses of a stage in Christian tradition earlier than our written gospels (e.g., *Barn.* 7.3–5, 8).

For Further Reading

Jefford, Clayton N. "The Letter of Barnabas." Pages 11–31 in *Reading the Apostolic Fathers: An Introduction.* Peabody, Mass.: Hendrickson, 1996.

Kraft, Robert A. *Barnabas and the Didache.* Vol. 3 of *The Apostolic Fathers: A New Translation and Commentary.* New York: Nelson, 1965.

Treat, Jay. "Barnabas, Epistle of." Pages 611–14 in vol. 1 of *Anchor Bible Dictionary.* Edited by D. N. Freedman. 6 vols. New York: Doubleday, 1992.

---

[1] Although the author uses the term *gnōsis,* he is not a gnostic. He neither offers secrets for escaping the material world, nor sees the creator as an inferior divinity.

[2] *Synoptische Überlieferung bei den Apostolischen Vätern* (TU 65; Berlin: Akademie, 1957), 125–27, 157.

THE LETTER OF
BARNABAS

Salutation and Introduction

1 Greetings, sons and daughters, in the Name of the Lord who loved us, in peace.

[2]Seeing that God's righteous decrees[a] toward you are so extraordinary and abundant, my joy over your favored and illustrious spirits is unbounded. You have received such grace, such an implantation of the spiritual gift! [3]Wherefore I, who also hope to be saved, inwardly rejoice all the more because I can actually see that the spirit that is on you has been poured out in your midst from the abundance of the fountain of the Lord. My eagerly anticipated visit to you has so wonderfully exceeded all expectations concerning you!

[4]Therefore I am convinced of this—indeed, I am all the more conscious of it because I know that the one who spoke many things in your midst was my traveling companion in the way of righteousness, the Lord;[b] and for this reason I myself am constrained at all times to love you more than my own soul—for great faith and love dwell in you, with hope of obtaining the life he gives! [5]Therefore, since it has occurred to me that if I am diligent in imparting to you a measure of what I have received it will be to my credit for having ministered to such spirits, I have hastened to send you this brief communication so that along with your faith you may also have your special knowledge perfected.

[6]There are, then, three basic doctrines of the Lord of life: hope, the beginning and end of our faith; and righteousness, the beginning and end of judgment; [and] love, a witness of the joy and gladness of works done in righteousness.

[7]For the Master has made known to us through the prophets what already has come to pass and what is now occurring, and he has given us a foretaste of what is about to happen. Thus as we observe each of these things being worked out as he said, we ought all the more abundantly and enthusiastically to draw near in fear of him. [8]And now, not as a teacher but as one from your very midst, I will point out a few things that will enable you to rejoice in the present circumstances.

Correct Understanding of Scripture

2 Since, then, the present days are evil and the one who is now at work possesses the power, we ought to walk circumspectly and seek out the Lord's righteous requirements. [2]The auxiliaries of our faith, then, are fear and endurance, while patience and self-control also fight along at our side. [3]Thus while these allies remain in a pure state in relation to the Lord, there rejoice with them wisdom, understanding, knowledge, and gnosis.

What the Lord Requires

[4]For he made it clear to us through all the prophets that he needs neither sacrifices nor whole burnt offerings nor offerings in general—as he says in one place:

[5] "What good is the multitude of your sacrifices to
    me? says the Lord.
I am satiated with burnt offerings of rams and
    the fat of lambs,
    and I do not want the blood of bulls and
        goats—
not even if you come and appear before me!
    For who has required these things from your
        hands?
Do not continue to tread my [temple] court.
If you bring finely ground flour, it is vain;
    offering of incense is an abomination to me,
    I cannot bear your new moon festivals and
        sabbaths."

[6]Therefore he set these things aside, so that the new law of our Lord Jesus Christ, which is not tied to a

---

a Or *acts*; or *requirements*

b Another ancient authority reads *because I know that when I spoke many things in your midst, my traveling companion in the way of righteousness was the Lord.*

TRANSLATION by Robert A. Kraft, REVISED by Jay C. Treat and Robert A. Kraft. NOTES by Jay C. Treat.

1.1 sons and daughters Gk *huioi kai thygateres*, lit. *sons and daughters.* **1.2 righteous decrees** In the Gk, it is one word, *dikaiōmatōn*, a characteristic term in *Barnabas*. **spiritual** Gk *pneumatikēs*. This term means "characterized by the spirit [*pneuma*]" and often indicates the human faculty related to God and capable of receiving *gnōsis* (see introduction to *Barnabas*) or salvation. **1.4 faith . . . love . . . hope** See *1 Thess.* 1:3; 5:8; *1 Cor.* 13:13. **1.5 special knowledge** Gk *gnōsis*. This term, which has the sense of "special insight," is a basic concept in *Barnabas*. **1.8 not as a teacher** See 4.9. **2.1 the one who is now at work** That is, Satan. See 4.13; 18.2; *Eph.* 2:2. **2.5** *Isa.* 1:11–13. Polemic against rites and ritualism has a long history in Israelite and Jewish writings. **2.6 a yoke of necessity** See *Acts* 15:10; *Matt.* 11:29–30; *1 Clem.* 16.17; *Did.* 6.2.

yoke of necessity, might have as its offering one not humanly produced. 7And again he says to them: "Did I command your ancestors, when they were coming out of the land of Egypt, to offer burnt offerings and sacrifices to me? 8But, rather, this is what I commanded them —

'Let none of you hold a grudge in his heart
     against his neighbor,
     and love not a false oath.'"

9Therefore, since we are not without understanding, we ought to perceive the gracious intention of our Father. For he is speaking to us, desiring that we who are not misled as they were should seek how we might approach him with our offering. 10aTo us, then, he speaks thus:

"A sacrifice to God is a broken heart;
     An odor well-pleasing to the Lord is a heart
       that glorifies its creator."

10bTherefore, brothers and sisters,*c* we ought to pay strict attention to the matters that concern our salvation, lest the Wicked One cause error to slip in among us and hurl us away from our life!

3 Therefore he speaks to them again concerning these things:

"Why do you make a fast to me, says the Lord,
     so that today your voice is heard wailing?
This is not the sort of fast I have chosen, says the
     Lord,
     not humbling oneself.
2 Not even if you bend your neck in the shape of a
     circle,
     and deck yourselves out in sackcloth and
       ashes—
     you cannot even call such conduct an
       acceptable fast!"

3But to us he says:

"Behold, this is the fast that I have chosen, says
     the Lord:
Loose every bond of injustice,
     untie the knots of forcibly extracted
       agreements.
Release the downtrodden with forgiveness,
     and tear up every unjust contract.
Distribute your food to the hungry,

and if you see someone naked, clothe him.
Bring the homeless into your home,
     and if you see someone of lowly estate, do
       not despise him,
     nor [despise] anyone of your own household.
4 Then your light will break forth early,
     and your healing will arise quickly.
And your righteousness will go before you,
     and the glory of God will surround you.
5 Then you will cry out, and God will listen to
     you;
     While you are still speaking, he will say 'Here
       I am'—
     if you put away from you bonds and scornful
       gestures and words of complaint,
     and give your food to the hungry without
       hypocrisy,
     and have mercy on the person of lowly
       estate."

6So, for this reason, brothers and sisters, when he foresaw how the people whom he prepared in his Beloved One would believe in childlike innocence, the Patient One gave us a preview concerning everything, lest we be shattered to pieces as "proselytes" to their law.

Readiness in These Last Days

4 We must, then, carefully investigate the present situation and seek out the things that are able to save us.
1b Therefore let us completely flee from all the
     works of lawlessness,
     lest the works of lawlessness ensnare us;
And let us hate the error of the present age,
     so that we may be loved in the age to come.

2Let us give no leisure to our own soul so that it has opportunity to associate with the wicked and sinful—lest we become like them!

3aThe great final scandal is at hand, concerning which it has been written, as Enoch*d* says: 3b"For the Master cut short the times and the days for this reason, that his Beloved One might hasten and come into his inheritance." 4And the prophet speaks thus:

---

c Gk *brothers*

d One ancient authority reads *Daniel*

2.7–8 See *Jer.* 7:22–23. Not direct quotations of any known text, this and the next two citations probably come from a Jewish anthology of sources that dealt with true sacrifices. Many of the same texts are also used by other church writers. **2.8** *Let none of you . . . false oath* This is not a direct quotation of any known text. See *Zech.* 7:9–10; 8:16–17. **2.9** *Barnabas* characteristically contrasts Christians (*us*) with ritualistic Israelites (*them*). *They* have been misled. See 9.4. This contrast continues in the following verses. **2.10a** The 1st line is similar to *Ps.* 51:17. A marginal note in one ancient authority attributes the quotation to an *Apocalypse of Adam,* now lost (not that found at Nag Hammadi). **3.1–5** *Isa.* 58:4–10. The contrast between *us* and *them* continues. **4.3** *Enoch* See *Dan.* 8:13; 9:26–27; 11:31; 12:11. The reference to a *great final scandal* is not a direct quotation of any known Enoch text. See *1 En.* 89.61–64; 90.17–18; *2 En.* 34.1–3; *Jude* 14. **4.4–5a** Not direct quotations of any known text, these two citations probably come from contemporary developments of *Dan.* 7:7–8, 19–24. See *Revelation* 13; *4 Ezra* 11–12; Hippolytus, *Antichrist* 25; *Sib. Or.* 3.396–400.

"Ten kingdoms will reign on the earth.
And afterward there will arise a little king,
    who will humiliate three of the kingdoms
       simultaneously."

5aSimilarly, Daniel says concerning the same one:
"And I saw the fourth beast, wicked and
    powerful
    and more dangerous than all the beasts of the
       sea;
And how that ten horns sprouted from him,
    and from them budded a little offshoot of a
       horn;
And how that it humiliated three of the great
       horns simultaneously."

5bTherefore you ought to understand!

6Furthermore, I also urge you as one of your own, and especially as one who loves you all more than I love my own self, walk circumspectly and do not be like certain people, compounding your sins by claiming that our covenant is irrevocably ours.*e* 7aIt is ours. But they lost it completely in the following manner, after Moses already had received it. 7bFor the scripture says: "And Moses was on the mountain fasting for forty days and forty nights, and he received the covenant from the Lord, stone tablets inscribed by the finger of the Lord's hand."

7cBut when they turned to idols, they lost it. 8aFor the Lord speaks thus: "Moses, Moses, descend immediately, for your people whom you led out from the land of Egypt have sinned." 8bAnd Moses understood, and he hurled the two tablets from his hands. 8cAnd the covenant [of the tablets] was smashed to bits so that the covenant of Jesus, the Beloved One, might be sealed in our heart, in hope of his faith.

9aBut since I wish to write many things—not as a teacher would, but as is fitting for a friend to do—and to omit nothing of what we have received, I hurry along. I am your devoted slave. 9bWherefore let us walk circumspectly in these last days. For the entire period of our life and faith will be wasted unless now, in the lawless time and in the impending scandals, we resist as befits God's children.

10aTherefore, lest the darkling one make deceitful entrance, let us flee from all that is irrelevant, let us hate completely the works of the wicked way. 10bDo not live a separate existence by withdrawing to yourselves, as though you had already attained the righteous state, but assemble together to seek out what is to your mutual advantage. 11aFor the scripture says:
"Woe to those who are wise in their own eyes,
    and understanding in their own sight."

11bLet us be spiritual people; let us be a perfect temple to God. To the best of our ability let us meditate on the fear of God and strive to keep his commandments, so that we may rejoice in his ordinances. 12The Lord will judge the world impartially. Each person will receive payment in accord with his deeds: if he was good, his righteousness precedes him; if he was wicked, the reward of wickedness goes before him! 13Thus on no account should we slumber in our sins by relaxing as "those who have been called"—and the wicked ruler will take advantage of his power over us and push us away from the kingdom of the Lord. 14And finally, my brothers and sisters, understand this: when you notice what great signs and wonders were performed in Israel, and still they have been abandoned, let us take heed lest we be found to be, as it is written, "many called but few chosen."

Why the Lord Endured Suffering

5For it was for this reason that the Lord submitted to deliver his flesh to destruction, that by the forgiveness of sins we might be purified—that is, by the sprinkling [for purification] of his blood. 2For it is written concerning him—partly with reference to Israel and partly to us—and it says thus:
"He was wounded because of our lawless
       actions,
    and he was rendered helpless because of our
       sins;
    by his wounds we were healed.
As a sheep to the slaughter was he led,
    and as a lamb he was silent before his
       shearer."

---

e Another ancient authority reads *do not be like those who heap up your sins and say that their covenant is also ours.*

4.5b See *Mark* 13:14. The passage in 4.4–5 appears to identify a specific Roman emperor as the eleventh, *little*, king, but the imagery is so ambiguous that modern scholars have interpreted it to mean Vespasian, Domitian, Nerva, Hadrian, or even Nero reborn. Presumably, the interpretation was also unclear in late antiquity. **4.6–8** *Barn.* 14.1–4; both use the same traditional material. **4.7b** Not direct quotations of any known text, this and the next citation may come from a traditional Jewish paraphrase of the narratives in the Torah. See *Deut.* 9:9–16; *Exod.* 24:18; 31:18; 34:28. **4.7c** See *Exod.* 3:4; 32:7; *Deut.* 9:12. **4.9** *not as a teacher* See 1.8. **4.10** *the darkling one* The epithet may refer either to Satan's maliciousness or to the darkness in which he lurks. See 20.1. **4.10b** Compare *Heb.* 10:24–25. **4.11a** *Isa.* 5:21. **4.11b** *spiritual people* Gk *pneumatikoi*. See note on 1.2. **4.14** *many called but few chosen* See *Matt.* 22:14. This could be a quotation from the written gospel, from traditional gospel material mistakenly attributed to scripture, or from an older writing that did not survive. **5.2** *Isa.* 53:5, 7. *Prov.* 1:17 LXX. The Hebrew is problematic but probably means, "It is pointless to spread out nets for capturing birds."

³We ought, therefore, to give heartfelt thanks to the Lord because he has both given us special knowledge of the things which have come to pass and also given us wisdom in the present events; nor are we without understanding concerning what is about to happen. ⁴ᵃBut the scripture says, "It is not unjust to spread out nets for capturing birds." ⁴ᵇThis is what it is saying: it is just that a person should perish if, although he has special knowledge of the way of righteousness, he becomes ensnared in*ᶠ* the way of darkness.

⁵And furthermore, my brethren, consider this: if the Lord submitted to suffer for our souls—he who is Lord of the whole world, to whom God said at the foundation of the world, "Let us make humankind in accord with our image and likeness"—then how is it that he submitted to suffer at the hands of human beings? Learn! ⁶The prophets, after they had received special insight from him, prophesied concerning him. And he submitted so that he might break the power of death and demonstrate the resurrection from the dead. Thus it was necessary for him to be manifested in flesh. ⁷Also [he submitted] so that he might fulfill the promise to the ancestors and, while he was preparing the new people for himself and while he was still on earth, to prove that after he has brought about the resurrection he will judge.

⁸Furthermore, although he was teaching Israel and doing such great wonders and signs, the result was not that they loved him dearly for his preaching! ⁹But when he chose his own apostles, who were destined to preach his gospel—who were sinful beyond measure so that he might prove that he came not to call righteous but sinners—it was then that he revealed himself as God's Son. ¹⁰For if he had not come in flesh, how could human beings be saved by looking at him? They cannot even gaze directly into the rays of the sun, even though it is a work of his hands and is destined to cease existing!

¹¹Thus the Son of God came in flesh for this reason, that he might bring to summation the total of the sins of those who persecuted his prophets to death. ¹²ᵃSo also he submitted for this reason. ¹²ᵇFor God says that the afflicting of his flesh came from them:

"When they smite their own shepherd,

then the sheep of the flock will be lost."
¹³ᵃAnd he desired to suffer in such a manner, for it was necessary so that he might suffer on the wood. ¹³ᵇFor one who prophesies concerning him says:

"Spare my soul from the sword,
    and affix my flesh with nails,
for an assembly of evildoers has come upon me."
¹⁴And again he says:

"Behold, I have bared my back for stripes,
    and my cheeks for smiting,
but I have set my face as a solid rock."

6 When, therefore, he made the commandment, what does he say?

"Who disputes my judgment?
    Let him oppose me.
Or who vindicates himself in my presence?
    Let him draw near to the Lord's servant.
¹ᵇ Woe to you, for you all will grow old like a
    garment,
    and a moth will devour you!"

²ᵃAnd again, since he was established as a mighty stone that crushes, the prophet says of him: "Behold, I will insert into the foundations of Zion a stone that is precious, chosen, a cornerstone, prized." ²ᵇThen what does he say? "And whoever trusts in him will live forever." ³ᵃIs our hope, then, on a stone? Not in the least! But he speaks in such a way since the Lord has established his flesh in strength. ³ᵇFor he says, "And he established me as a solid rock." ⁴ᵃAnd again the prophet says, "The very stone that the builders rejected has become the cornerstone!" ⁴ᵇAnd again he says, "This is the great and awesome day that the Lord made."

⁵I write to you more clearly so that you may understand. I am a slave devoted to your love. ⁶ᵃWhat, then, does the prophet say again?

"An assembly of evildoers encompasses me,
    they surround me as bees around honey,
    and for my garments they cast lots."
⁶ᵇThus, since he was about to be manifested in flesh and to suffer, his passion was revealed beforehand. ⁷For the prophet says concerning Israel, "Woe to them, for they devised a wicked plot against themselves when they said, 'Let us bind the righteous one, for he is displeasing to us.'"

⁸What does the other prophet, Moses, say to them? "Behold, thus says the Lord God: Enter into the good land, which the Lord promised to Abraham and

---

ᶠ Or *keeps himself away for*

5.4b ***becomes ensnared in*** The Gk word for this phrase is found only here. **5.5** *Gen.* 1:26. **5.9** ***came not . . . sinners*** See *Mark* 2:17. **5.12b** See *Zech.* 13:7. **5.13b** ***Spare . . . sword*** *Ps.* 22:20. ***and affix . . . nails*** See *Ps.* 118:120 LXX: "Affix my flesh with nails from fear of You." MT 119:120: "My flesh creeps from fear of You." ***for an assembly . . . me*** or "for a synagogue" See *Ps.* 22:16. **5.14** *Isa.* 50:6, 7 **6.1–1b** *Isa.* 50:8–9. **6.2a** *Isa.* 28:16. **6.2b** The source is unknown. See 8.5b; 11.9–11. **6.3b** See *Isa.* 50:7. **6.4a** *Ps.* 118:22. **6.4b** *Ps.* 118:24. See *Ps.* 118:23. **6.6a** ***An assembly . . . encompasses me*** See note on 5.13b. ***they surround . . . honey*** *Ps.* 118:12. ***and for . . . lots*** *Ps.* 22:18. **6.7** *Isa.* 3:9–10 LXX. See *Wis.* 2:12. **6.8** See *Exod.* 33:1, 3; *Deut.* 6:18.

Isaac and Jacob, and make it your inheritance—a land flowing with milk and honey." 9aAnd what does special knowledge say? Learn! Hope, it says, on that Jesus who is about to appear to you in flesh. For a human being is land suffering, for Adam was formed from the face of the land. 9bWhat, then, does he say? "Into the good land—a land flowing milk and honey."

10aBlessed be our Lord, brothers and sisters, who has placed in us wisdom and understanding of his secrets. 10bFor the prophet says: "Who can understand a parable of the Lord, except one who is wise and understanding and who loves his Lord?"

11Since, then, he renovated us by the forgiveness [of sins], he made us to be another sort [of creation], as though we had a child's soul; he fashioned us again, as it were. 12aFor the scripture is speaking about us when he says to the Son: "Let us make humankind in accord with our image and likeness, and let them rule over the beasts of the earth and the birds of heaven and the fish of the sea." 12bAnd when he saw how well we were formed the Lord said: "Increase and multiply and fill the earth." These things [he said] to the Son.

13aAgain, I will show you how he says to us that he made a second fashioning in the last times. 13bAnd the Lord says, "Behold, I make the last things like the first." 13cIt is for this reason, therefore, that the prophet proclaimed: "Enter into the land flowing with milk and honey, and exercise lordship over it." 14aSee, then, we have been fashioned anew! 14bAs he says again in another prophet: "Behold, says the Lord, I will remove from them"—that is, from those on whom he foresaw the Lord's spiritᵍ—"their stony hearts, and I will insert fleshly hearts"—14cbecause he was about to be manifested in flesh and to dwell in us. 15For, my brethren, our heart being thus inhabited constitutes a holy temple to the Lord! 16aFor the Lord says again: "And in what manner shall I appear before the Lord my God and be glorified?" 16bHe says:

"I will confess you in the assembly of my
   brothers and sisters,

and I will praise you in the midst of the
   assembly of saints."

16cTherefore we are those whom he conducts into the good land!

17aWhat, then, is the "milk and honey"? The infant is initiated into life first by honey, then by milk. 17bThus also, in a similar way, when we have been initiated into life by faith in the promise and by the word, we will live exercising lordship over the land. 18aBut as it was already said above: "And let them increase, and multiply, and rule over the fish. . . ." 18bWho, then, is presently able to rule over beasts or fish or birds of heaven? For we ought to understand that "to rule" implies that one is in control, so that the one who gives the orders exercises dominion. 19If, then, this is not the present situation, he has told us when it will be—when we ourselves have been perfected as heirs of the Lord's covenant.

Lessons from the Atonement Ritual

7Understand, therefore, children of joy, that the good Lord revealed everything to us beforehand so that we might know whom we ought to praise continually with thanksgiving.

2If, then, the Son of God, who is Lord and is about to judge the living and dead, suffered so that his being afflicted might bring us life, let us believe that it was not possible for the Son of God to suffer except on our behalf.

3aBut he was also given vinegar and gall to drink when he was crucified. 3bHear how the priests of the temple made even this clear, when the commandment was written, "Whoever does not fast during the [atonement] fast must surely die." 3cThe Lord gave such a commandment since he was destined to offer the vessel of the spirit as a sacrifice for our sins, so that the type which is based on Isaac's having been offered up on the altar also might be fulfilled. 4What, then, does he say in the prophet? "And they shall eat from the goat which is offered up during the fast for all sins"—pay diligent attention—"and let all the priests alone eat the entrails unwashed, with vinegar." 5For what reason? "Since you [priests] are going to make me (who am destined to offer my flesh for the sins of my new people) drink gall mixed with

_____

ᵍ Or *from those whom the Lord's spirit foresaw*

6.9: a human being . . . of the land See *Gen.* 2:7, where the Hebrew *adam*, "human being," or "humankind," "Adam," sounds like *adamah*, "earth," or "ground." This play on words could have been available to a Gk-speaking community through an onomasticon, a list of etymological meanings of proper names. **6.10b** Source unknown. **6.12a** *Gen.* 1:26. **6.12b** *Gen.* 1:28. **6.13b** Source unknown. This is paralleled in *Didascalia* 26. See *Rev.* 21:5; Hippolytus, *Commentary on Daniel* 4.37. **6.14b their stony . . . fleshly hearts** See *Ezek.* 11:19; 36:26. **6.16a** See *Ps.* 42:2b. **6.16b** *Ps.* 22:22. **6.18a above** See 6.12. **7.3–11** This section probably uses a Jewish legal treatment, written in Gk, of the atonement fast, as transmitted in the *Barnabas* school. Mishnah, *Yoma* 4–8, contains some of the same nonbiblical details. **7.3** See *Ps.* 69:22. This gospel tradition is also preserved in *Gos. Pet.* 5.16. See *Matt.* 27:34, 48. **7.3b** See *Lev.* 23:29. **7.3c type** A model or pattern. **Isaac's . . . altar** *Gen.* 22:9. The offering of Isaac has been a significant theme in Judaism. See *Rom.* 8:32. **7.4 And they . . . sins** See *Lev.* 16:9, 27. **and let . . . vinegar** Source unknown.

vinegar, you alone will eat while the people fast and mourn in sackcloth and ashes." This is to demonstrate that he must suffer at their hands.

6aPay attention to what he commanded: "Take two goats that are handsome and alike, and present them; and let the priest take one for a burnt offering for sins." 6bBut what do they do with the other? "Accursed," he says, "is the other."

7Pay attention to how the type of Jesus is made clear! 8a"And you shall all spit on and prick [that goat], and encircle its head with scarlet wool, and thus let it be cast out into the desert." 8bAnd when this has been done, the one who bears the goat brings it into the desert and takes the wool and places it upon a bush which is called *rachē*, the buds of which we are accustomed to eat when we find them in the countryside. Thus of the *rachē* alone are the fruits sweet.

9aWhat, then, does it mean—pay attention!—that the one is placed on the altar and the other is accursed, and that the accursed one is crowned? 9bBecause they will see him then, on that day, wearing the scarlet robe around his flesh, and they will say, "Is not this he whom we once crucified, despising and piercing and spitting on him? Surely this was the one who then said he was God's Son!" 10aNow how is this like that situation? For this reason the goats were alike and handsome, equal, so that when they see it coming then, they will be amazed at the similarity of the goat. 10bTherefore notice here the type of Jesus, who was destined to suffer.

11aAnd what does it mean that they place the wool in the midst of the thorns? It is a type of Jesus placed in the church, so that whoever desires to snatch away the scarlet wool must suffer many things because the thornbush is treacherous, and he must obtain it through affliction. 11bIn such a way, he says, those who desire to see me and to take hold of my kingdom ought to take me through affliction and suffering.

Lessons from the Red Heifer Ritual

8 And what do you suppose is the type involved here, in that he commanded Israel that those men in whom sins are complete should offer a heifer; and when they had slaughtered it, burn it; and then the children should take the ashes and put them into containers; and the scarlet wool should be wrapped around a piece of wood—again, note the type of the cross, and the scarlet wool and the hyssop; and thus the children sprinkle the people individually in order to purify them from sins? 2Understand how it is told to you in such simplicity: the calf is Jesus; the sinful men who offer it are those who offered him to be slaughtered. Then men [appear] no longer, [it is] no longer [concerned with] the "glory" of sinners! 3aThe children who sprinkle are those who preach to us forgiveness of sins and purification of the heart, to whom he entrusted the authority to proclaim the gospel. 3bThere are twelve [of the latter], for a witness to the tribes, since there are twelve tribes of Israel. 4But why are there [only] three children who sprinkle? This is for a witness to Abraham, Isaac, and Jacob, because they are great before God.

5And the fact that the wool is on the wood signifies that the kingdom of Jesus is on the wood, and that those who hope on him will live forever. 6But why are the wool and the hyssop together? Because in his kingdom there shall be wicked and vile days, in which we shall be saved. For the one whose flesh is distressed is cured by means of the hyssop's vileness!

7Therefore the things that have come to pass are clear to us, but obscure to them, because they did not hearken to the Lord's voice.

Circumcised Understanding

9 For again, he speaks concerning the ears, how he circumcised the ears of[h] our heart. 1bThe Lord says in the prophet: "By listening with the ear, they hearkened to me." 1cAnd again he says:

"By hearing, those who are far off shall hearken;
the things I have done will become known."
And: "Circumcise, says the Lord, your hearts." 2And again he says: "Hear, Israel, for thus says the Lord your God: Who is he who desires to live forever? By hearing, let him hearken to the voice of my servant." 3aAnd again he says: "Hear, heaven, and give ear, earth; for the Lord has spoken"—these are mentioned as a witness. 3bAnd again he says, "Hear the Lord's word, rulers of this people." 3cAnd again he

---

h Latin; Gk omits

7.6a *Lev.* 16:7, 9.   **7.6b** See *Lev.* 16:8.   **7.8a** See *Lev.* 16:10. This tradition may appear in *Mark* 14:17–20; *Matt.* 27:28–31; *Gos. Pet.* 3.7–9.   **7.8b** *rachē* This untranslated word refers to a thorny bush, perhaps the caper bush or the blackberry. **7.9b** See *Mark* 15:39.   **7.11b** See *Acts* 14:22.   **8.1–7** See *Num.* 19:1–10; *Heb.* 9:13. *Barnabas* continues to use a Jewish legal source written in Gk. Surviving rabbinic writings contain almost no parallels to the traditions preserved here. **8.2** *Then men . . . sinners!* This sentence is obscure. The text may be corrupt.   **8.5** *the kingdom . . . wood* A variant, current in Christian circles, to *Ps.* 95:10 LXX reads "The Lord reigned from the tree [wood]." The MT (96:10) has: "The Lord reigns."   **9.1b** *Ps.* 18:44.   **9.1c** *The things . . . known* Isa. 33:13.   *And circumcise . . . hearts* See *Lev.* 26:41; *Deut.* 10:16; 30:6; *Jer.* 4:4; 9:26; *Ezek.* 44:7, 9; *Acts* 7:51.   **9.2** *Who is . . . forever?* See *Ps.* 34:12.   *hearken . . . servant* See *Isa.* 50:10. **9.3a** *Hear, . . . spoken* Isa. 1:2.   *these . . . witness* See *Deut.* 4:26.   **9.3b** *Isa.* 28:14; 1:10.   **9.3c** *Isa.* 40:3.

says, "Hear, children, a voice crying in the desert." [3d]Therefore he circumcised our ears, so that when we hear the word, we might believe.

[4a]But he also set aside the circumcision on which they relied. [4b]For he said that circumcision was not a matter of the flesh, but they became transgressors because a wicked angel "enlightened" them. [5a]And he says to them: "Thus says the Lord your God"—here I find a commandment—"Woe to those who sow among thorns; be circumcised to your Lord." [5b]And what is he saying? Circumcise the wickedness from your heart![i] [5c]And again he says:

"Behold, the Lord says, all the nations have uncircumcised foreskins,

but this people is uncircumcised in heart!"

[6]But you will say: And yet the people received circumcision as a special sign. But every Syrian and Arab, and all the priests of the idols also [are circumcised]. Are they also, then, from their covenant? But even the Egyptians are in circumcision!

[7]Learn, then, abundantly concerning everything, children of love; for when Abraham first gave circumcision, he circumcised while looking forward in the Spirit to Jesus, and he received the teachings of the three letters. [8a]For it says, "And Abraham circumcised the men of his household, eighteen and three hundred [in number]."

[8b]What, then, is the special knowledge that was given him? Learn! For the eighteen comes first, then after an interval it says three hundred. Now eighteen [is represented by two letters], J (ten) and E (eight)—thus you have "JEsus." And because the cross, represented by the letter T (three hundred), was destined to convey special significance, it also says three hundred. He makes clear, then, that "JEsus" is symbolized by the two letters, while in the one letter is symbolized the cross.

[9]The one who placed the implanted gift of his teaching[j] in us knows! No one has learned from me a more trustworthy lesson! But I know that you are worthy.

---

[i] Gk reads *Circumcise the hardness of your heart and do not stiffen your neck.*

[j] Other ancient authorities read *covenant*

10[1]Now in that Moses said, "Eat neither pig, nor eagle nor hawk nor crow, nor any fish that is without scales," he received in his understanding three doctrines. [2a]Further, he says to them in Deuteronomy: "And I will ordain as a covenant for this people my righteous ordinances." [2b]Therefore it is not God's commandment that they [literally] should not eat, but Moses spoke in the Spirit.

[3a]For this reason, then, he mentions the "pig": Do not associate, he is saying, with such people, who are like pigs. That is, they forget their Lord when they are well off, but when they are in need, they acknowledge the Lord; [3b]just as when the pig is feeding it ignores its keeper, but when it is hungry it makes a din, and after it partakes it is quiet again. [4a]"Neither eat the eagle nor the hawk nor the kite nor the crow." Do not, he is saying, associate with or be like such people. They do not know how to procure their own food by honest labor and sweat, but in their lawlessness they plunder the possessions of others, and they keep sharp watch as they walk around in apparent innocence, and spy out whom they might despoil by plundering; [4b]just as those birds are unique in not procuring their own food, but as they perch idly by, they seek how they might devour the flesh of others—pestilent creatures in their wickedness!

[5a]"And do not eat," he says, "sea eel nor octopus nor cuttlefish." Do not, he is saying, be like such people, who are completely impious and have already been condemned to death; [5b]just as those fish are uniquely cursed and loiter in the depths, not swimming about as do the rest but inhabiting the murky region beneath the deep water.

[6a]But neither shall you eat the hairy-footed animal. Why not? Neither be one who corrupts children, he is saying, nor be like such people; [6b]because the hare increases unduly its discharge each year, and thus has as many holes as it is years old.

[7a]But neither shall you eat the hyena. Be neither, he is saying, an adulterer nor a corrupter, nor be like such people. [7b]Why? Because this animal changes its nature each year, and at one time it is male while at another it is female.

[8a]But also he hated the weasel, fittingly. Do not, he is saying, be such a person. We hear of such

---

9.4b *enlightened* Or "deceived." **9.5a** *Jer.* 4:3–4. **9.5b** *Deut.* 10:16. **9.5c** See *Jer.* 9:26. **9.6** *sign* Gen. 17:11. *Egyptians . . . circumcision!* See *Jer.* 9:25–26. **9.8a** *And Abraham . . . household* Gen. 17:23. *eighteen and three hundred* Gen. 14:14. **9.8b** In Gk the letters are also used as numbers: *iota* = ten, *eta* = eight, *tau* = three hundred. The Gk letter *iota*, usually represented in English by the letter *i*, is often represented by *j* at the beginning of a name. The use of numerical values for interpretation is called gematria. **10.1–2** Similar ethical interpretations of food laws are found in Jewish sources written in Gk (*Letter of Aristeas* and Philo) and later became highly developed in Christian sources (esp. Clement of Alexandria). **10.1** See *Lev.* 11:7–15; *Deut.* 14:8–14. **10.2a** See *Deut.* 4:10, 13. **10.6–8** In this tradition, popular Hellenistic natural history has been adapted for ethical instruction. **10.6a** *hairy-footed animal* Lev. 11:5 LXX; *Deut.* 14:7 LXX. MT has "hare." The LXX uses "hairy-footed animal" as a circumlocution for "hare," possibly to avoid disrespect for the Ptolemies, whose ancestor's name (Lagus) sounded like the Gk word for "hare." **10.7a** *hyena* Mosaic law does not mention the hyena. See *Jer.* 12:9 LXX. **10.8a** *weasel* See *Lev.* 11:29.

men, who perform a lawless deed uncleanly with the mouth. Neither associate with those unclean women who perform the lawless deed with the mouth. 8bFor this animal conceives through its mouth.

9Concerning foods, then, when Moses received the three doctrines he spoke out thus, in the Spirit. But because of fleshly desires they accepted his words as though they concerned actual food.

10aAnd David also received special knowledge of the same three doctrines, and he says: 10b"Blessed is the one who has not walked according to the counsel of impious people," just as the fish which grope in darkness in the depths; 10c"nor stood in the way of sinners," just as those who appear to fear the Lord sin like the pig; 10d"nor sat in the seat of pests," just like the birds perched for plundering.

10eNow receive complete [understanding] concerning food. 11aMoses says again: "You may eat any split-hoofed and cud-chewing animal." 11bWhat is he saying [about the latter]? That [the animal] which receives fodder knows who feeds it, and while it relies on him, it seems content. He spoke fittingly in view of the commandment. 11cWhat, then is he saying? Associate with those who fear the Lord, with those who meditate in their heart on the subtleties of the matter, with those who proclaim the Lord's righteous ordinances and keep them, with those who realize that study is a joyful occupation, and who "ruminate" on the Lord's word. 11dAnd what does the "split-hoofed" mean? That the righteous person both walks in this world and anticipates the holy aeon.

11eSee how appropriately Moses legislated! 12aBut how could they perceive or understand these things? But since we rightly understand the commandments, we are speaking as the Lord desired. 12bThis is why he circumcised our ears and hearts, so that we might understand these things.

Baptism and the Cross Foreshadowed

11 But let us investigate whether the Lord was concerned to reveal beforehand concerning the water and concerning the cross.

2First, concerning the water, it is written with reference to Israel how they never will accept the baptism which conveys forgiveness of sins, but they will build [cisterns] for themselves. 3aFor the prophet says:
"Be astounded, heaven,
 and shudder greatly at this, earth,
For this people has committed two wicked acts:
They have forsaken me, the living fount of water,

and they have dug out for themselves a pit of
 death."
3b "Has my holy mount, Sinai, become an arid
 rock?
For you shall be as the fledglings of a bird,
 fluttering about when they are taken from the
 nest."
4And again the prophet says:
"I will go before you, and I will level mountains
 and shatter gates of brass and break iron bars,
And I will give you treasures—dark, hidden,
 unseen—
 that they may know that I am the Lord God."
5 "And you will dwell in an elevated cave made
 from solid rock,
 and its water supply is dependable.
You will see a king in his glory,
 and your soul will meditate on the fear of the
 Lord."
6aAnd again he says in another prophet:
"And the one who does these things will be like
 the tree
 planted by springs of waters,
which produces its fruit at the proper time,
 and has leaves that will not wither;
And everything he does will prosper.
6b The impious are not like this—not in the least.
 But rather, they are like the dust that the
  wind drives from the face of the earth.
For this reason, the impious will not appear for
 judgment,
 nor sinners in the council of the righteous.
For the Lord knows the way of the righteous,
 and the way of the impious will perish."
7Perceive how he specified the water and the cross together. 8aFor this is what he is saying: "Blessed" are those who, having placed their hope in the cross, descend into the water. For the reward, he says, comes "at the proper time"—then, he says, I will repay. 8bBut as for the present, what does he say? "The leaves will not wither." 8cHe is saying this, that every word that flows forth from you—through your mouth—in faith and love, will be a means of conversion and hope to many.

9And again, another prophet says, "And the Land of Jacob was praised more than any land." This says that he will glorify the vessel of his spirit. 10aThen what does he say?
"And there was a river flowing from the right
 side,
 and beautiful trees came up out of it;

---

lawless deed That is, oral sex. **10.10** *Ps.* 1:1. **10.11a** *Lev.* 11:3; *Deut.* 14:6. **10.11d** *the holy aeon* The age to come. **11.3a** *Jer.* 2:12–13. **11.3b** *Isa.* 16:1–2. **11.4** *Isa.* 45:2–3. **11.5** *Isa.* 33:16–18. **11.6** *Ps.* 1:3–6. **11.8** *Blessed Ps.* 1:1. **11.9–10** The text is quoted in two parts. The source is unknown, but the first part is also quoted in Clement, *Miscellanies* 3.12.86. It probably comes from an Ezekiel tradition. See *Ezek.* 20:6, 15; 47:1–12; *2 Bar.* 61.7.

and whoever eats of them will live forever."

10bHe is saying this: that we go down into the water full of sins and vileness, and we come up bearing fruit in our heart, having in the Spirit fear and hope in Jesus. 11a"And whoever eats from these will live forever." 11bHe is saying this: Whoever, he says, hears these things that are spoken and believes will live forever.

12 Similarly, he explains again concerning the cross in another prophet, who says:
"And when will these things come to pass,
    says the Lord?
When a tree falls down and rises up,
    and when blood drips from a tree."
1bAgain, you have [information] concerning the cross and the one who was destined to be crucified.

2aAnd again he says in the [book of] Moses, when Israel was under attack from foreigners—and so that he might remind those who were being attacked that they had been given over to death because of their sins—the Spirit says to Moses, in his heart, that he should make a type of the cross and of him who was destined to suffer. 2bIf they do not, he says, place their hope on him, they will be under attack forever. 2cThus Moses piled one shield upon another in the midst of the battle, and as he stood elevated above them all he stretched out his hands. And as long as he did so, Israel again prevailed; but whenever he let [his hands] drop, they were again being killed. 3Why? So that they might know that they could not be saved unless they hope on him.

4And again, in another prophet he says:
"The whole day I have stretched out my hands
    to a people who are disobedient
    and who oppose my righteous way."
5aAgain, Moses makes a type of Jesus—[signifying] that it was necessary for him to suffer and that he whom they supposed had perished would bestow life—in the standard [set up] when Israel was smitten [by a plague]. 5bFor the Lord made every serpent to bite them, and they were dying, so that he might demonstrate to them that it was because of their transgression—since transgression took root in Eve because of the serpent—that they would be given over to mortal affliction.

6aFurthermore, it is this same Moses, who commanded, "You shall have neither a cast-metal nor a carved image to your God"—he it is who makes [such an image] in order to provide a type of Jesus. 6bMoses, then, makes a bronze serpent and sets it up in a prominent place and calls the people together by means of a proclamation. 7aTherefore, when they came together they begged Moses to offer a prayer on their behalf, that they might be healed. 7bBut Moses said to them: "Whenever," he says, "anyone is bitten, let him come to the serpent that is erected on the wooden pole. And let him hope, believing that this dead object is able to bestow life, and he will be healed immediately." 7cAnd they did so. 7dAgain, you have also in these things the glory of Jesus, for all things take place in him and for his sake.

8aAgain, what does Moses say to Jesus son of Naue, when he had given this name to him who was a prophet so that all the people might hearken to him alone? 8bFor the Father is making all things clear concerning his Son Jesus. 9aThus Moses says to Jesus son of Naue, to whom he had given this name when he sent him to spy out the land: "Take a book in your hands and write what the Lord says, that Jesus the Son of God will cut off the entire house of Amalek by its roots at the end of days." 9bAgain, notice Jesus—not the son of a human being but the Son of God, and manifested in flesh by a type.

10Since, then, they were going to say that Messiah is David's Son, David himself—fearing and perceiving the error of the sinners—prophesies:
"The Lord said to my Lord,
    'Sit at my right hand
until I make your enemies a footstool for your
    feet.'"
11aAnd again, Isaiah says as follows:
"The Lord said to my Messiah, the Lord,
    whose right hand I held,
that nations would become obedient to him,
    and I will demolish the strength of kings."
11bNotice how David says he is "Lord," and does not say "Son."

The Covenant and Its Recipients

13 But let us see if this people is the heir or the former people, and if the covenant is for us or for them.

2Therefore, hear what the scripture says concerning "the people": "And Isaac was making entreaty for

11.11a From the unknown text of 11.9–10. **12.1** The source is unknown but is also quoted by Pseudo-Gregory, *Testimonies* 7. See *Job* 14:7–8; *Hab.* 2:11; *4 Ezra* 4.33; 5.5; *Ladder of Jacob* 7.5; *Sib. Or.* 3.683–684. **12.2** *Exod.* 17:8–15. **12.4** *Isa.* 65:2. See *Rom.* 10:21. **12.5a** *standard* See *Num.* 21:6–9. **12.5b** *transgression . . . serpent* Genesis 3. **12.6a** See *Lev.* 26:1; *Deut.* 27:15. **12.7b–7c** *Num.* 21:6–9. **12.7d** See *Rom.* 11:36. **12.8a** *given . . . him* Num. 13:16. The LXX translates "Joshua son of Nun" as "Jesus son of Naue." **12.9** See *Exod.* 17:14. **12.9b** *not the son of a human being* Or possibly "not the Son of Man." **12.10** *Ps.* 110:1. *Barnabas* argues against, not for, the position that Jesus is David's son. See *Mark* 12:35–37; *Luke* 20:41–44; *Acts* 2:34–35; *Heb.* 1:13; 10:13. **12.11** *Isa.* 45:1. The 2d *Lord* (Gk *kyrios*) is a corruption of "Cyrus" *(kyros)*. **13.2** *Gen.* 25:23.

Rebecca his wife, because she was barren. And she became pregnant. Then Rebecca also went to inquire of the Lord, and the Lord said to her:

'Two nations are in your womb,
     and two peoples in your belly.
And one of the people will dominate the other,
     and the greater will be subject to the lesser.'"

[3]You ought to perceive whom Isaac [represents] and whom Rebecca, and with reference to whom he had pointed out that "this people" is "greater" than "that."

[4]And in another prophecy Jacob says it even more clearly to his son Joseph, when he says: "Behold, the Lord has not [yet] deprived me of your presence. Bring your sons to me, so that I might bless them." [5a]And he brought Ephraim and Manasseh near, intending that Manasseh should receive the blessing, since he was older. Thus Joseph brought [the latter] to his father Jacob's right hand. [5b]But Jacob saw, in the Spirit, a type of "the people" which was to come afterward. [5c]And what does it say? "And Jacob crossed his hands and placed his right hand on the head of Ephraim, the second and younger [son], and blessed him. And Joseph said to Jacob: 'You should transpose your right hand to Manasseh's head, for he is my firstborn son.' And Jacob said to Joseph: 'I know, child, I know, but the greater will be subject to the lesser.'" And thus [Ephraim] received the blessing. [6]Note on which of them he placed [his right hand]—this "people" is to be first, and heir of the covenant!

[7a]Was, then, this situation also in view in the case of Abraham? We are receiving the perfection of our special knowledge! [7b]What, then, does he say to Abraham when for his belief alone he was established in righteousness? "Behold, I have established you, Abraham, as the father of nations which believe in God while uncircumcised."

14 Indeed, it was! [1b]But let us see if he has given the covenant that he promised the fathers he would give to "the people." [1c]He has given it, but they were not worthy to receive it because of their sins. [2]For the prophet says: "And Moses was fasting on Mount Sinai, when he was to receive the Lord's covenant with the people, for forty days and forty nights. And Moses received from the Lord the two tablets inscribed by the finger of the Lord's hand, in the Spirit. And when Moses received them, he brought them down to give to the

people. [3a]And the Lord said to Moses: 'Moses, Moses, descend immediately, because your people, whom you led out from the land of Egypt, have sinned.' [3b]And Moses understood, for they had again made molten images for themselves, and he hurled the tablets from [his] hands, and the tablets of the Lord's covenant were shattered." [3c]Moses, then, received it, but they did not prove worthy.

[4]And how did we receive it? Learn! Moses received it in the capacity of servant; but the Lord himself gave it to us, to a "people" of inheritance, by submitting for us. [5a]And he was made manifest so that they might fill up the measure of their sins, and we might receive it through Jesus, who inherits the Lord's covenant. [5b]He was prepared for this reason, that by appearing himself and liberating from darkness our hearts, which had already been paid over to death and given over to the lawlessness of error, he might establish a covenant in us by a word. [6]For it is written how the Father commanded him to prepare a holy people for himself when he had liberated us from the darkness. [7a]Therefore the prophet says:

"I, the Lord your God, have called you in
     righteousness,
     and I will grasp your hand and empower you;
And I have given you as a covenant to people, as
     a light for the nations,
     to open the eyes of the blind,
and to release from their bonds those who have
     been shackled,
     and to lead out from their prison house those
     sitting in darkness."

[7b]Know, then, whence we were liberated! [8]Again the prophet says:

"Behold, I have placed you as a light for the
     nations,
     that you might beam salvation to the end of
     the earth.
Thus says the Lord God who liberated you."

[9]Again the prophet says:

"The Lord's Spirit is on me,
     wherefore he anointed me to announce
     benefaction to the oppressed.
He sent me to heal those who are brokenhearted,
     to proclaim pardon to the captives and
     restoration of sight to the blind,
     to announce the acceptable year of the Lord,
     and the day of recompense,
     to comfort all those who are in mourning."

13.4 *Gen.* 48:9, 11. **13.5** *Gen.* 48:13–15, 18–20. **13.7b** See *Gen.* 15:6; 17:4–5. Agreement with *Rom.* 4:11 suggests that the interpretation is traditional. **14.2–3b** See 4.7–8. **14.4** *servant* See *Exod.* 14:31; *Heb.* 3:5. **14.7a** *Isa.* 42:6–7. **14.8** *Isa.* 49:6–7. **14.9** *Isa.* 61:1–2. See *Luke* 4:18–19.

The Sabbath

15 And furthermore, concerning the sabbath: It is written in the Ten Words by which [the Lord] spoke to Moses face to face on Mount Sinai: "And you shall keep the Lord's sabbath holy with clean hands and a clean heart." [2]And elsewhere he says, "If my sons guard the sabbath, then I will bestow my mercy on them." [3]He mentions "the sabbath" at the beginning of creation: "And God made the works of his hands in six days, and he finished on the seventh day. And he rested on it, and kept it holy."

[4a]Pay attention, children, to what he says: "He finished in six days." He is saying this, that in six thousand years the Lord will finish everything. For with him the "day" signifies a thousand years. [4b]And he bears me witness [on this point] saying: "Behold, a day of the Lord shall be as a thousand years." [4c]Therefore, children, "in six days"—in six thousand years—everything will be finished. [5]"And he rested on the seventh day." He is saying this: when his Son comes he will put an end to the time of the Lawless One, and judge the impious, and change the sun and moon and stars. Then he will truly rest "on the seventh day."

[6a]Furthermore he says: "Keep it holy with clean hands and a clean heart." [6b]If, then, anyone at present is able, by being clean in heart,[k] to keep holy the day that God hallowed, we have been deceived in everything! [7]But if he keeps it holy at that time by truly resting, when we ourselves are able [to do so] since we have been made righteous and have received the promise—when lawlessness is no more and all things have been made new by the Lord—at that time we will be able to keep it holy, when we ourselves first have been made holy.

[8a]Further, he says to them, "I cannot bear your new moon celebrations and sabbaths." [8b]See how he is saying that it is not your present sabbaths that are acceptable to me, but that [sabbath] which I have made, in which, when I have rested everything, I will make the beginning of an eighth day—that is, the beginning of another world. [9]Wherefore also we observe the eighth day as a time of rejoicing, for on it

---

Jesus both arose from the dead and, when he had appeared, ascended into the heavens.

The Temple

16 And finally, concerning the temple: I will show you how those wretches, when they went astray, placed their hope on the building and not on their God, who created them—as though God has a house! [2a]For, roughly speaking, they consecrated him by means of the temple, as the pagans do! [2b]But how does the Lord speak when he sets it aside? Learn!

"Who measured the heaven with a span,
    or the earth with a hand?
Was it not I, says the Lord?"
"The heaven is my throne,
    and the earth is the stool for my feet.
What sort of house will you erect for me,
    or what place for me to rest?"

[2c]You knew that their hope was vain! [3]Furthermore, he says again, "Behold, those who tore down this temple will themselves build it." [4]It is happening. For because of their fighting it was torn down by the enemies. And now the very servants of the enemies will themselves rebuild it.

[5a]Again, it was made clear that the city and the temple and the people of Israel were destined to be abandoned. [5b]For the scripture says, "And it shall be at the end of days that the Lord will abandon the sheep of the pasture, and the sheepfold, and their watchtower to destruction!" [5c]And it happened just as the Lord announced!

[6a]But let us inquire whether there is a temple of God? There is, where he himself says he makes and prepares it! [6b]For it is written: "And it shall come to pass when the week is finished, God's temple will be built gloriously in the Lord's name." [6c]Thus I find that there is a temple. [7]How, then, will it "be built in the Lord's name"? Learn! Before we believed in God, the dwelling place of our heart was corrupt and infirm—truly a temple built by human hands. For it was full of idolatry, and was a house of demons, through doing whatever things were contrary to God. [8a]But "it will be built in the Lord's name"—pay attention—so that the temple of the Lord may be "built gloriously." [8b]How? Learn! When we receive

---

k Other ancient authorities read *except him who is clean in heart*

15.1 Ten Words A standard Jewish name for the Ten Commandments. **face to face** See *Exod.* 33:11; *Deut.* 5:4; 34:10. **And you . . . holy** See *Exod.* 20:8; *Deut.* 5:12; *Jer.* 17:22. **with . . . heart** See *Ps.* 24:4; 51:10. **15.2 If my . . . sabbath** See *Exod.* 31:16. **then I . . . them** See *Isa.* 56:1–8. **15.3** See *Gen.* 2:2–3. **15.4b** See *Ps.* 90:4; *2 Pet.* 3:8; *Jub.* 4.30. **15.8a** *Isa.* 1:13. **15.9 eighth day** That is, Sunday, the day after the Sabbath. **16.2b Who measured . . . Lord?** *Isa.* 40:12. **The heaven is . . . rest?** *Isa.* 66:1. See *Acts* 7:49; *Sib. Or.* 4.8. **16.3** Source unknown. See 6.15–19; *Tob.* 14:5; *Isa.* 49:17. **16.4 was torn down . . . rebuild it** Romans destroyed the temple in 70 C.E. The writer of *Barnabas* expects their "servants" (Romans or Jews?) to rebuild a Jewish temple, but in about 135 C.E. the Roman emperor Hadrian erected a temple to Jupiter on the site. **16.5b** Source unknown. See 5.12b; *1 En.* 89.50–73; 90.28–29. **16.6b** Source unknown. See *1 En.* 91.13; *Tob.* 14:5; *Sib. Or.* 5.420–427; *Ezekiel* 40–48. **16.7 built by human hands** See 2.6; *Acts* 7:48.

the forgiveness of sins and place our hope on the name, we become new, created again from the beginning. Wherefore God truly dwells in our "dwelling place"—in us. 9In what way? The word of his faith, the invitation of his promise, the wisdom of his righteous ordinances, the commandments of his teaching; himself prophesying in us, himself dwelling in us—by opening for us the door of the temple, which is the mouth, and giving us repentance, he leads those who had been in bondage to death into the incorruptible temple. 10aFor the one who longs to be saved looks not to the [external] person, but to the one who dwells in him and speaks in him, and he is amazed at the fact that he never either had heard him speak such words from his mouth nor had himself ever desired to hear them! 10bThis is a spiritual temple built for the Lord!

Conclusion

17To the best of my ability, and in simplicity, [I have tried] to make [these things] clear to you. I hope that I have not neglected anything [vital]. 2aFor if I keep writing to you concerning things present or to come, you would never comprehend because they are contained in parables. 2bSo much for these matters.[l]

The Two Ways

18But let us move on to another special knowledge and teaching.
1b There are two ways of teaching and authority: that of light and that of darkness.
1c And there is a great difference between the two ways.
1d For over one are appointed light-bearing angels of God, but over the other, angels of Satan.
2 And the former is Lord from everlasting to everlasting, but the latter is ruler of the present time of lawlessness.

---

[l] One ancient authority ends the work here, substituting *Again you have [understanding] concerning the majesty of Christ, how all things take place in him and through him—to whom be honor, power, glory, now and forever.*

The Way of Light

19Therefore the way of light is this—1bif anyone who desires to traverse the way to the appointed place is diligent in his works. 1cTherefore, the special knowledge which is granted to us to walk in it is of this sort:
2a You shall love him who made you;
fear him who formed you;
glorify him who redeemed you from death.
2b Be upright in heart and rich in spirit.
2c Do not associate with those who are proceeding in the way of death.
2d Hate everything that is not pleasing to God.
2e Hate all hypocrisy.
2f Do not forsake the Lord's commandments.
3a Do not exalt yourself, but always be humble-minded.
3b Do not allow yourself to become arrogant.
3c Do not take glory on yourself.
3d Do not plot wickedly against your neighbor.
4a Do not be sexually promiscuous.
Do not commit adultery.
Do not be sexually perverted.
4b Let not the word of God depart from you with any sort of impurity.
4c Do not show partiality in reproving anyone for transgressions.
4d Be meek,
be quiet,
be one who fears the words which you have heard.
4e Do not take the Lord's name in vain.
4f Do not bear a grudge against your brother.
5a Do not be undecided as to whether or not a thing shall come to pass.
5b Love your neighbor more than yourself.
5c Do not murder a child by abortion,
nor, again, destroy that which is born.
5d Do not remove your control from your son or your daughter,
but from youth up, teach the fear of the Lord.
6a Be not desirous of the things of your neighbor.
6b Be not greedy, neither be yoked from your soul with the haughty;
but associate with the righteous and lowly.
6c Whatever befalls you, receive these experiences as good,
knowing that nothing happens without God.

16.10b *spiritual* See note to 1.2. **18.1–20.2** This section uses a large block of material called the Two Ways tradition. Another form of it appears in *Didache* 1–5. Two Ways concepts appear in a wide variety of Jewish and Christian writings. See especially 1QS 3.13–4.26. **18.1a** The first gnosis (*Barnabas* 2–16) uncovered the secrets of scripture. This 2d gnosis (*Barnabas* 18–20) reveals the behavior God requires. **19.2a** *You shall . . . made you* See *Deut.* 6:5; *Sir.* 7:29–30. **19.2b** *Be upright in heart* See *Ps.* 36:10. *rich in spirit* See "poor in spirit" in *Matt.* 5:3 and 1QM 14.7. **19.4e** See *Exod.* 20:7; *Deut.* 5:11; *Lev.* 19:12. **19.5b** *Lev.* 19:18.

7a Be not double-minded nor double-tongued
      for the double tongue is a snare of death.
7b Be subject to those over you as though to God,
      in reverence and fear.
7c Do not give an angry command to your slave or
      maid-servant, who trust in the same God,
      lest they fear not the God who is over you both;
Because he came not to call anyone according
      to status,
      but to call those in whom he prepared the
      spirit.
8a Share all things with your neighbor
      and do not claim that anything is exclusively
      yours;
For if you are sharers in what is imperishable,
      how much more so in what is perishable.
8b Be not overtalkative,
      for the mouth is death's snare
8c To the extent of your ability,
      be pure for your soul's sake.
9a Do not be one who stretches out his hands to
      receive
      but holds them back when it comes to giving.
9b Love as the apple of your eye
      all who proclaim the Lord's word to you.
10a Remember the day of judgment night and day,
10b   and pursue [the quest] each day
10c either by the word,
      by toiling and traveling in order to admonish
      and by taking pains to save a soul by the
      word,
10d or by your hands,
      by working to provide a ransom for your
      sins.
11a Do not hesitate to give nor grumble when you
      give,
      for you know who is the good paymaster of
      the reward.
11b Guard what you received,
      neither adding nor subtracting anything.
11c Hate evil completely.
11d Judge justly.
12a Do not cause divisions,
      but make peace with disputants by bringing
      them together.
12b Make confession for your sins.
12c Do not go to prayer with an evil conscience.
12d This is the Way of Light.

The Way of Darkness

20 But the way of the darkling one is crooked and
full of cursing.

1b For it is entirely a way of eternal death with
      punishment,
      in which lie the things which destroy the
      souls of those [on it]: 1c idolatry,
      arrogance, pride in power, hypocrisy,
      duplicity, adultery, murder, robbery,
      conceit, transgression, guile, malice,
      stubbornness, sorcery, magic, greed.
1d Without fear of God,
2a   persecutors of the good;
2b Hating truth,
      loving a lie;
2c Not knowing the reward of righteousness,
      not associating with what is good;
2d Not judging justly,
      not guarding the rights of the widow and
      orphan;
2e Being alert not with respect to the fear of God,
      but to that which is wicked;
      from whom courtesy and patience are far off
      and distant;
2f Loving what is worthless,
      pursuing reward;
2g Not showing mercy toward the poor,
      not laboring on behalf of the downtrodden;
2h Reckless with slanderous speech,
      not knowing him who made them;
2i Murderers of children,
      corrupters of God's creation;
2j Turning away from the needy,
      afflicting the oppressed;
2k Advocates of the rich,
      lawless judges of the poor—
2l   sinful through and through!

Conclusion

21 Therefore it is fitting that when one has learned
the ordinances of the Lord—as many as have
been written—one walks in them.
1b For the one who does these things will be
      glorified in God's kingdom;
      the one who chooses those will perish with
      his works.
1c For this reason there is resurrection,
      for this reason there is recompense.
2 I urge those who are in a high position—if you
accept any of my well-intentioned advice—to make
sure that there are among you those to whom you
may do that which is good. Do not fail in this.
3 The day is near in which all things will perish together with the wicked one. The Lord is near, and his
reward.

19.7b See *Col.* 3:22–24; *Eph.* 5:22; 6:5.   **20.1a** *the darkling one* This epithet suggests that the evil one is responsible for the darkness in which he lurks. See 4.10.

4Once more and again I urge you; be good lawgivers among yourselves, persevere as faithful advisers to each other, remove all hypocrisy from among you. 5And the God who has dominion over the whole universe will give you wisdom, insight, understanding, special knowledge of his ordinances, [and] endurance.

6Be taught by God, seeking out what the Lord seeks from you; and so act that you may find [what you seek] in the day of judgment. 7And if there is any remembrance of what is good, remember me as you meditate on these things, so that my earnest longing and my sleeplessness may lead to some good result.

8I urge you, begging your favor, while the "good vessel" is still with you do not fail in any respect, but continually seek out these things and fulfill every commandment, for they are worthy. 9Wherefore, I hastened all the more to write whatever I could. 9bMay you be saved, children of love and peace. 9cThe Lord of glory and of all grace be with your spirit.

On the Superiority of the Son of God

HEBREWS

Overview and Themes

The text traditionally known as the *Letter to the Hebrews* has no close parallel among the first-century Christian writings. Although preserved in ancient manuscripts (e.g., ℵ, A, C, B) along with Paul's letters, it does not claim to be written by Paul—indeed, it is anonymous—and it is more of an essay or sermon than a letter. It does not open with the customary greetings to identify sender and addressee, no health wish, and no thanksgiving. The only letterlike feature comes at the very end in a benediction and travel plans (13:20–25). But this looks more like a note appended to the essay, perhaps even a cover letter written by someone else, than an integral part of *Hebrews*. Unlike a letter, which discloses only one half of a conversation and requires that the other half be supplied by the reader, *Hebrews* fully elaborates a point and then proceeds to the next with plenty of logical connectives such as *since* and *therefore*. We find no obscure references to the author's opponents or events.

Because of its essay format, the main argument of *Hebrews* is quite easy to follow. The author wants to show that Christianity is superior to Judaism. At several points in the text he departs from this argument to insist that believers should persevere. A major problem for the modern reader is to determine precisely how these two points are related.

In good Hellenistic fashion, the author states his thesis in a preface (1:1–4): Jesus, as God's Son, supersedes all that went before him, and in particular the Jewish covenant. It is striking that, although his chosen topic is Jesus' relationship to Judaism, the author prefers to designate Jesus with the more Hellenistic term "Son of God," rather than the Jewish category "Messiah" (or Christ). This is one of many indications in the essay that the author comes from a Hellenistic-Jewish background.

The preface slides directly into the author's first argument for Jesus' supremacy, to the effect that Jesus is superior to the angels (1:4–2:18). This elaborately developed point is apt to seem irrelevant until one realizes its purpose, which is indicated in 2:2: The message declared by angels is therefore inferior to the message brought by the Son.

What was the "message declared by angels"? Although the Bible does not men-tion this event, some first-century Jews believed that the revelation of the Torah at Sinai was attended or even mediated by angels.[1] This scenario enhanced the gran-deur of the event, but these angelic mediators provided a ready target for some early Christian preachers, including Paul (*Gal.* 3:19–20) and the author of *Hebrews*. So the author contrasts Jesus with angels merely as a first step in his general argu-ment about the inferiority of the Jewish covenant to Christianity.

Oddly enough, the claim that Jesus surpasses the angels leads to the corollary that, if the Torah of the angels decreed punishments for disobedience, one should be even more wary of unfaithfulness to the new and better covenant (2:2–3). This practical application is puzzling. One can understand a preacher drawing briefly on some biblical example in order to teach a moral lesson, as Paul does (*1 Cor.* 10:1–13), but *Hebrews* devotes itself to a sustained critique of the Jewish covenant and then repeatedly uses that critique as a springboard for its admonitions to faith-fulness. What is the connection between argument and admonition?

The second step in the argument (3:1–4:13) compares Jesus and Moses. Al-though this section begins with a flat statement of Jesus' superiority, on the some-what strained analogy of a builder's superiority to his house (3:1–6), the author again moves quickly to his practical point. He recalls that the land of Canaan was offered to the Israelites when they left Egypt but that God prevented the first gener-ation from seeing the land because of their rebellion in the wilderness. Therefore, given Jesus' superiority to Moses, how much more should contemporary believers beware of "rebellion" if they wish to enter into God's "rest"? This *a fortiori* argu-ment is typical of the rabbis' interpretation of the Bible.

In the middle section of the essay (4:14–7:21) the author tries to show that Jesus is the ultimate high priest. In a noteworthy departure from Pauline imagery, he de-scribes Jesus' saving act, not as past resurrection or future return, but as a present activity in heaven, where Jesus has entered a heavenly sanctuary and pleads contin-ually on behalf of the faithful (7:25). Jesus' superiority to the Jewish priesthood is argued in several ways, but especially with the claim that he is the one referred to in *Ps.* 110:4, "You are a priest forever, after the order of Melchizedek." This connection enables the writer to say that Jesus' priesthood is eternal, unlike that of other priests, who must die, and that, since Abraham gave the priest-king Melchizedek a tenth of his war-spoils (*Gen.* 14:17–20), Melchizedek (and Jesus) must be greater than Abraham (and the Jewish covenant that he inaugurated).

Once again this seemingly abstruse argument is interrupted by a forthright practical injunction. Chapter 6 is an excursus on the necessity of perseverance with the Christian faith. It includes a dire warning to the effect that anyone who goes back on his or her confession crucifies the Son of God again and thereby loses all hope of salvation, even on a second repentance (6:4–8). The reader is encouraged

[1]*Gal.* 3:19; *Acts* 7:53; *Jub.* 1.29–2.1.

not to be "sluggish" but to go forward in the faith (6:12). Again, it seems odd that this injunction should be bounded on both sides by the Melchizedek argument.

The fourth section of the essay (8:1–10:39) both summarizes and broadens the general theme that Jesus has superseded Judaism. Now the author enlists some Greek philosophical categories in his aid, especially Plato's distinction between the true world of forms, on the one hand, and the transitory world of visible phenomena on the other. According to the argument, the earthly tabernacle (and subsequent temple in Jerusalem) was a mere "shadow" or pale "copy" of the true, heavenly sanctuary (8:2, 5; 9:1, 23–24), in which Jesus functions as high priest. The earthly sanctuary was fine for the past, but now that Jesus has offered his sacrifice and has begun his role as heavenly high priest, the earthly sanctuary is obsolete (9:11–14; 10:9–18). If the Jewish priesthood has been supplanted, then the entire covenant that it superintended—a shadow of the heavenly law (10:1)—has also passed away (see 7:12).

Yet again, however, all of this abstract argumentation is brought to a practical conclusion. *Hebrews* 10:26–31 repeats the dire warning of chapter 6 about those who abandon their Christian faith. The author then moves into an extended exhortation to persevere, which includes the famous catalogue of heroes of faith in chapter 11.[2] Chapter 12 is an urgent plea for faithfulness to the Christian proclamation. It appears that the first readers have encountered much hostility from outsiders (12:3, 7), though not to the point of death (12:4). The writer explains their suffering as God's fatherly discipline (12:7–11) and urges them to bear it with strength (12:12–17). After a final reminder of the superiority of Christianity to Judaism (12:18–24), he repeats his earlier warnings about forsaking the faith (12:25–29).

Chapter 13 offers the only typical features of a letter, for it comprises a list of miscellaneous ethical admonitions, not unlike Paul's, although the author also recalls his earlier themes (13:10–14).

Purpose

Any account of the purpose of *Hebrews* must explain its ongoing interplay between the theme of Christian superiority to Judaism and the admonition to persevere. This interplay is most easily explained if the writer believes that his readers, were they to defect from Christianity, would turn to Judaism. Thus the exhortation to Christian faithfulness and the critique of Judaism are two "prongs" of the same strategy. The author is saying both "Do stay here!" and "Do not go there!"

Notice that the readers' temptation to leave Christianity in favor of Judaism seems to be tied to the opposition that they face as Christians. They believe that this opposition will cease if they abandon Christianity for Judaism. How can this belief

---

[2]All the persons named are figures from the Bible, but it seems that the vaguer references at the end (11:36–38) are to characters from the apocrypha.

be explained? Judaism enjoyed a rather privileged position in the Roman empire. The great age of Judean culture and the early friendliness of Judea's rulers toward Rome had won for the Jews a certain recognition and a degree of legal protection. Christianity was not accorded this status and found itself increasingly vulnerable as it gradually distinguished itself from Judaism. It makes sense that Judaism would have appeared as an option to those who felt threatened as a result of their Christian identity. Although we are in no position to recover the readers' own view of their plight, the writer of *Hebrews* apparently believes that they will turn to Judaism if they leave the church on account of persecution.

Audience

This conclusion does not tell us, however, who the first readers of *Hebrews* were. It is conceivable that they were Gentile Christians who had been exposed to Judaism in various ways. For example, we know that in the first generation of the church many Christian preachers were still fully observant Jews who insisted on obedience to Torah (see *Gal.* 2:14). These preachers visited Paul's Gentile converts and tried to persuade them to become Jews.[3] We also know from various sources that non-Christian Judaism had a broad appeal in the Greco-Roman world; it may even have invited converts (e.g., Tacitus, *Hist.* 5.5). It is possible that the first readers of *Hebrews* were Gentile Christians who were introduced to Judaism in some way, like Paul's churches in Galatia and Corinth, and now found it an appealing alternative to their predicament of vulnerability to persecution. The other obvious possibility is that the first readers were Jews who had become Christians but then, after a time, came to wonder about their decision. In this case, the temptation to abandon Christianity for Judaism would have been simply a "return home."

The writer himself seems to have a Jewish background. He knows the details of the Torah and has some acquaintance with the Hebrew language (7:2). His allegorical style of biblical interpretation resembles that practiced by Philo of Alexandria, a first-century Jew. Other aspects of his arguments have parallels in rabbinic discussion. His use of Greek philosophical vocabulary has inclined most scholars to trace his roots to Alexandria, where members of the substantial Jewish community sought to understand and explain their faith in terms of Greek categories. If this proposal is correct, the author is a convert to Christianity from Alexandrian Judaism. At the time of writing, however, he may be in Rome (13:24).

Date

The date of *Hebrews* cannot be determined with precision. Although it often speaks as if the Jerusalem temple (destroyed in 70 C.E.) were still standing, we know from Josephus and rabbinic literature that people could still speak this way after the destruction. Nor should we assume that Jews who lived soon after 70 realized that

---

[3]See the introduction to *Galatians*.

their temple was permanently destroyed. This fact was probably not clear until well after the Bar Kochba revolt was quashed in 135 C.E., perhaps until after the fourth century. A writer at the end of the first century could, like Josephus, still speak of the temple service as a present reality.

Since *Hebrews* is referred to by Clement of Rome (c. 90 C.E.), it cannot have been written later than the 80s. On the other hand, its author seems broadly acquainted with strands of the Christian tradition. He evokes many Pauline themes[4] but also betrays a knowledge of the synoptic tradition[5] and perhaps of Luke's perspective.[6] The author's knowledge of these traditions (if not of the written gospels) seems to require that *Hebrews* be dated after about 70. This is confirmed by the author's notice that he learned about Jesus from "those who heard him" (2:3), which suggests that he is a generation or more removed from Jesus' lifetime. Most scholars would date the work to the 80s of the first century.

For Further Reading

Attridge, Harold W. *The Epistle to the Hebrews: A Commentary on the Epistle to the Hebrews*. Hermeneia. Philadelphia: Fortress, 1988.

———. "Hebrews, Epistle to the." Pages 97–105 in vol. 3 of *Anchor Bible Dictionary*. Edited by D. N. Freedman. 6 vols. New York: Doubleday, 1992.

Thompson, James W. *The Beginnings of Christian Philosophy: The Epistle to the Hebrews*. Catholic Biblical Quarterly Monograph Series 13. Washington, D.C.: Catholic Biblical Association, 1992.

---

[4]See 3:2–6 (*1 Cor.* 3:9–15); 3:7–4:13 (*1 Cor.* 10:1–13); 5:12–14 (*1 Cor.* 3:1–2); 8:6 (*2 Cor.* 3); 8:7 (*Gal.* 2:21; 3:21); 9:16–17 (*Gal.* 3:15–18).

[5]See 5:7 (*Mark* 14:35–36); 6:7–8 (*Mark* 4:13–20).

[6]As in *Luke-Acts,* Jesus often seems in *Hebrews* to have been "designated" or "appointed" Son of God as a consequence of his suffering (*Heb.* 1:2, 4; 5:5, 8–10; 7:28; 8:6; see *Acts* 2:36; 13:34). *Hebrews* also notes that Jesus "passed through the heavens" (4:14)—an apparent reference to the ascension, which only *Luke-Acts* describes. And finally, the author shares *Luke's* view that both Jesus and the early church were accredited by their miracles (*Heb.* 2:4; *Acts* 2:22, 43; 3:16; 4:9–10; 8:6).

THE LETTER TO THE
HEBREWS

God Has Spoken by His Son

1 Long ago God spoke to our ancestors in many and various ways by the prophets, ²but in these last days he has spoken to us by a Son,[a] whom he appointed heir of all things, through whom he also created the worlds. ³He is the reflection of God's glory and the exact imprint of God's very being, and he sustains[b] all things by his powerful word. When he had made purification for sins, he sat down at the right hand of the Majesty on high, ⁴having become as much superior to angels as the name he has inherited is more excellent than theirs.

The Son Is Superior to Angels

⁵For to which of the angels did God ever say,
"You are my Son;
    today I have begotten you"?
Or again,
"I will be his Father,
    and he will be my Son"?
⁶And again, when he brings the firstborn into the world, he says,
"Let all God's angels worship him."

⁷Of the angels he says,
"He makes his angels winds,
    and his servants flames of fire."
⁸But of the Son he says,
"Your throne, O God,[c] is forever and ever,
    and the righteous scepter is the scepter of
        your[d] kingdom.
⁹ You have loved righteousness and hated
        wickedness;
therefore God, your God, has anointed you
    with the oil of gladness beyond your
        companions."
¹⁰And,
"In the beginning, Lord, you founded the earth,
    and the heavens are the work of your hands;
¹¹ they will perish, but you remain;
    they will all wear out like clothing;
¹² like a cloak you will roll them up,
    and like clothing[e] they will be changed.
But you are the same,
    and your years will never end."
¹³But to which of the angels has he ever said,
"Sit at my right hand

---

a Or *the Son*
b Or *bears along*

c Or *God is your throne*
d Other ancient authorities read *his*
e Other ancient authorities lack *like clothing*

1:1 *our ancestors* This might seem to suggest that the author and readers were Jews, although (a) the Gk lacks *our* and (b) Paul writes to an apparently Gentile Christian audience of "our ancestors" (*1 Cor.* 10:1), meaning the biblical patriarchs. **1:2 *through whom he also created the worlds*** See *John* 1:2–3. The idea that creation was effected through Jesus seems to have resulted from Christian identification of him as the *logos*, or "reason," of the cosmos, as the wisdom of God, and thus as present at creation (*Proverbs* 8). See also the extended hymn to wisdom in *Wis.* 6–11, especially 7:22. **1:3 *sat down at the right hand of the Majesty on high*** An allusion to *Ps.* 110:1, the most quoted biblical passage in early Christian literature. Because it speaks of the Lord's instructing "my lord" to sit at his right hand, it became the basis for the Christian teaching that Jesus sits at the right hand of God. See *Luke* 20:42–43, 69; *Acts* 2:34–35. **1:4** This verse expresses the thesis: Jesus is vastly superior to the angels and to the covenant that they represent (Judaism). Thus, 1:1–4 serves as an effective prologue to the essay, in good Greek style. **1:5–14** One of the most extensive sets of proof texts in surviving Christian literature. All of these passages are adduced in support of Jesus' superiority to the angels. It is unclear whether the author has personally searched them out or whether he relies upon an anthology of proof texts. The Hebrew Bible did not speak much of angels, and many of these citations only make sense in the LXX. By the time of the Gk translation (LXX), angels had come to play a much larger role in popular Jewish thought. **1:5** Citing *Ps.* 2:7 and *2 Sam.* 7:14, both of which spoke originally of the king of Israel; many Christians interpreted them as speaking of Jesus. **1:6** *Ps.* 97:7 (LXX 96:7). The LXX has words cited by the author in Gk, but the *him* in question is simply God. The MT reads, "All divine beings bow down to Him" (*Ps.* 97:7). **1:7** *Ps.* 104:4. MT: "He makes the winds His messengers, / fiery flames His servants." The LXX (103:4) reads as *Hebrews*. **1:8–9** *Ps.* 45:6–7 (LXX 44:7–8). The psalmist addresses the king of Israel (45:2). The author views Jesus as someone who was rewarded by God and anointed *because of* his virtue; see *Acts* 2:36 and *Rom.* 1:4. Elsewhere the author describes Jesus as a preexistent being who took his place among humanity only for a specific purpose (1:2; 2:9, 17). **1:10–12** *Ps.* 102:26–28 (LXX 101:25–27). *Hebrews* follows the LXX almost exactly. The author begins to develop a major theme: the permanence of Christ over against the transience of Judaism. **1:13** Returning to *Ps.* 110:1 (LXX 109:1), which has already been alluded to (1:2). The scriptural argument comes full circle.

until I make your enemies a footstool for
your feet"?
[14]Are not all angels[f] spirits in the divine service, sent
to serve for the sake of those who are to inherit
salvation?

Warning to Pay Attention

2 Therefore we must pay greater attention to what
we have heard, so that we do not drift away from
it. [2]For if the message declared through angels was
valid, and every transgression or disobedience received a just penalty, [3]how can we escape if we neglect
so great a salvation? It was declared at first through
the Lord, and it was attested to us by those who heard
him, [4]while God added his testimony by signs and
wonders and various miracles, and by gifts of the
Holy Spirit, distributed according to his will.

Exaltation through Abasement

[5]Now God[g] did not subject the coming world,
about which we are speaking, to angels. [6]But someone has testified somewhere,
"What are human beings that you are mindful of
them,[h]
or mortals, that you care for them?[i]
[7] You have made them for a little while lower[j]
than the angels;
you have crowned them with glory and
honor,[k]
[8] subjecting all things under their feet."
Now in subjecting all things to them, God[g] left nothing outside their control. As it is, we do not yet see

everything in subjection to them, [9]but we do see
Jesus, who for a little while was made lower[l] than the
angels, now crowned with glory and honor because
of the suffering of death, so that by the grace of God[m]
he might taste death for everyone.
[10]It was fitting that God,[g] for whom and through
whom all things exist, in bringing many children to
glory, should make the pioneer of their salvation
perfect through sufferings. [11]For the one who sanctifies and those who are sanctified all have one Father.[n]
For this reason Jesus[g] is not ashamed to call them
brothers and sisters,[o] [12]saying,
"I will proclaim your name to my brothers and
sisters,[o]
in the midst of the congregation I will praise
you."
[13]And again,
"I will put my trust in him."
And again,
"Here am I and the children whom God has
given me."
[14]Since, therefore, the children share flesh and
blood, he himself likewise shared the same things, so
that through death he might destroy the one who has
the power of death, that is, the devil, [15]and free those
who all their lives were held in slavery by the fear of
death. [16]For it is clear that he did not come to help
angels, but the descendants of Abraham. [17]Therefore
he had to become like his brothers and sisters[o] in
every respect, so that he might be a merciful and
faithful high priest in the service of God, to make a
sacrifice of atonement for the sins of the people.

---

f Gk *all of them*
g Gk *he*
h Gk *What is man that you are mindful of him?*
i Gk *or the son of man that you care for him?* In the Hebrew of
Psalm 8:4–6 both *man* and *son of man* refer to all humankind
j Or *them only a little lower*
k Other ancient authorities add *and set them over the works of
your hands*

l Or *who was made a little lower*
m Other ancient authorities read *apart from God*
n Gk *are all of one*
o Gk *brothers*

2:1–4 The 1st of many movements from abstract argument to practical consequence *(therefore)*. Maintain Christian faith
because it is superior to Judaism. See introduction to *Hebrews*. **2:2 the message declared through angels** That is, the
"old" covenant from Sinai, upon which Judaism rests; see *Gal.* 3:19; *Acts* 7:53; *Jub.* 1.29–2.1. **2:3 attested to us by those
who heard him** See the similar language in *Luke* 1:1–2; both texts assume that a generation or more lies between Jesus' time
and their own. **2:4** The idea that God proved or testified to the truth of Christianity with *signs and wonders* from the Holy
Spirit is a prominent theme in *Luke-Acts*. See *Acts* 1:3 and note. **2:6–8** *Ps.* 8:4–6 (LXX 8:5–7) marvels at God's gifts to
humanity. **2:8–9** Although the author recognizes that this passage appears to be about human beings, he argues that it is not
yet fulfilled in general humanity but it suits Jesus, who first lived as a mortal and was then exalted. **2:10–13** Christians
share somewhat in the exalted status of Jesus, and they ought not to relinquish this for Judaism. **2:12** *Ps.* 22:22 (LXX 21:22).
The author agrees with the LXX except that he uses a different Gk verb for *proclaim*. *Congregation* is the Gk *ekklēsia*,
which is normally rendered "church" in translations of early Christian literature. **2:13** *Isa.* 8:17–18 (both quotations).
2:14–15 Christian freedom from enslavement to death is a prominent theme in Paul (*1 Cor.* 15:54–57; *Rom.* 8:31–39).
In popular philosophy, contempt for death was considered the greatest virtue. See Josephus, *Ag. Ap.* 2.232–235. **2:16 the
descendants of Abraham** Ordinarily, the Jews (see *Luke* 3:8), which might suggest that the author expects a Jewish audience.
But Paul could claim that Gentile Christians, too, were children of Abraham (see 3:29). **2:17 faithful high priest** The author introduces a major theme of the work: Jesus' role as eternal high priest in heaven (see introduction to *Hebrews*).

[18]Because he himself was tested by what he suffered, he is able to help those who are being tested.

Moses a Servant, Christ a Son

3 Therefore, brothers and sisters,[p] holy partners in a heavenly calling, consider that Jesus, the apostle and high priest of our confession, [2]was faithful to the one who appointed him, just as Moses also "was faithful in all[q] God's[r] house." [3]Yet Jesus[s] is worthy of more glory than Moses, just as the builder of a house has more honor than the house itself. [4](For every house is built by someone, but the builder of all things is God.) [5]Now Moses was faithful in all God's[r] house as a servant, to testify to the things that would be spoken later. [6]Christ, however, was faithful over God's[r] house as a son, and we are his house if we hold firm[t] the confidence and the pride that belong to hope.

Warning against Unbelief

[7]Therefore, as the Holy Spirit says,
"Today, if you hear his voice,
[8] do not harden your hearts as in the rebellion,
    as on the day of testing in the wilderness,
[9] where your ancestors put me to the test,
    though they had seen my works [10]for forty years.
Therefore I was angry with that generation,
and I said, 'They always go astray in their hearts,
    and they have not known my ways.'
[11] As in my anger I swore,
    'They will not enter my rest.'"
[12]Take care, brothers and sisters,[p] that none of you may have an evil, unbelieving heart that turns away from the living God. [13]But exhort one another every day, as long as it is called "today," so that none of you may be hardened by the deceitfulness of sin. [14]For we

have become partners of Christ, if only we hold our first confidence firm to the end. [15]As it is said,
"Today, if you hear his voice,
do not harden your hearts as in the rebellion."
[16]Now who were they who heard and yet were rebellious? Was it not all those who left Egypt under the leadership of Moses? [17]But with whom was he angry forty years? Was it not those who sinned, whose bodies fell in the wilderness? [18]And to whom did he swear that they would not enter his rest, if not to those who were disobedient? [19]So we see that they were unable to enter because of unbelief.

The Rest That God Promised

4 Therefore, while the promise of entering his rest is still open, let us take care that none of you should seem to have failed to reach it. [2]For indeed the good news came to us just as to them; but the message they heard did not benefit them, because they were not united by faith with those who listened.[u] [3]For we who have believed enter that rest, just as God[v] has said,
"As in my anger I swore,
'They shall not enter my rest,'"
though his works were finished at the foundation of the world. [4]For in one place it speaks about the seventh day as follows, "And God rested on the seventh day from all his works." [5]And again in this place it says, "They shall not enter my rest." [6]Since therefore it remains open for some to enter it, and those who formerly received the good news failed to enter because of disobedience, [7]again he sets a certain day— "today"—saying through David much later, in the words already quoted,
"Today, if you hear his voice,
do not harden your hearts."
[8]For if Joshua had given them rest, God[v] would not speak later about another day. [9]So then, a sabbath rest still remains for the people of God; [10]for those who

---

p Gk brothers
q Other ancient authorities lack all
r Gk his
s Gk this one
t Other ancient authorities add to the end

u Other ancient authorities read it did not meet with faith in those who listened
v Gk he

3:1–6 This author sees Jesus in part as a new Moses (see introduction to *Matthew*). Paul puts himself in this role, as bearer of a new covenant (*2 Cor.* 3:6–13). **3:2 was faithful in all God's house** An allusion to *Num.* 12:7. **3:7–11** *Ps.* 95:7–11 (LXX 94:8–11). MT has place names: "at Meribah" instead of "in the rebellion" and "Massah" instead of "testing." **3:12–15** The author continues to warn against desertion or falling away. **4:1–11** *rest* Distinguishing between the Sabbath rest enjoyed by God after creation and the rest promised to Israel, the author contends that there are different kinds of rests. Israel did not find rest, he claims, but it remains a possibility for believers. **4:3** The quotation refers back to 3:7–11. **4:4** *Gen.* 2:2. God has a rest, but the Israelites did not find it (4:5–6). The practice of comparing and contrasting two biblical verses with overlapping language, in order to draw out a new point not made in either one, was common among the rabbis (e.g., *t. Sanh.* 7.11). **4:7** See note to 3:7–11. **4:8–9** Joshua led Israel into the promised land after their exodus from Egypt. *Josh.* 21:44 claims that the people did find "rest on every side," but the author argues that since *Ps.* 95:7–11, holding out the promise of a future rest, was written long after Joshua's time, the psalm was not looking back to Joshua but to the future.

enter God's rest also cease from their labors as God did from his. [11]Let us therefore make every effort to enter that rest, so that no one may fall through such disobedience as theirs.

[12]Indeed, the word of God is living and active, sharper than any two-edged sword, piercing until it divides soul from spirit, joints from marrow; it is able to judge the thoughts and intentions of the heart. [13]And before him no creature is hidden, but all are naked and laid bare to the eyes of the one to whom we must render an account.

Jesus the Great High Priest

[14]Since, then, we have a great high priest who has passed through the heavens, Jesus, the Son of God, let us hold fast to our confession. [15]For we do not have a high priest who is unable to sympathize with our weaknesses, but we have one who in every respect has been tested[w] as we are, yet without sin. [16]Let us therefore approach the throne of grace with boldness, so that we may receive mercy and find grace to help in time of need.

5 Every high priest chosen from among mortals is put in charge of things pertaining to God on their behalf, to offer gifts and sacrifices for sins. [2]He is able to deal gently with the ignorant and wayward, since he himself is subject to weakness; [3]and because of this he must offer sacrifice for his own sins as well as for those of the people. [4]And one does not presume to take this honor, but takes it only when called by God, just as Aaron was.

[5]So also Christ did not glorify himself in becoming a high priest, but was appointed by the one who said to him,

"You are my Son,
today I have begotten you";
[6]as he says also in another place,
"You are a priest forever,
according to the order of Melchizedek."

[7]In the days of his flesh, Jesus[x] offered up prayers and supplications, with loud cries and tears, to the one who was able to save him from death, and he was heard because of his reverent submission. [8]Although he was a Son, he learned obedience through what he suffered; [9]and having been made perfect, he became the source of eternal salvation for all who obey him, [10]having been designated by God a high priest according to the order of Melchizedek.

Warning against Falling Away

[11]About this[y] we have much to say that is hard to explain, since you have become dull in understanding. [12]For though by this time you ought to be teachers, you need someone to teach you again the basic elements of the oracles of God. You need milk, not solid food; [13]for everyone who lives on milk, being still an infant, is unskilled in the word of righteousness. [14]But solid food is for the mature, for those whose faculties have been trained by practice to distinguish good from evil.

The Peril of Falling Away

6 Therefore let us go on toward perfection,[z] leaving behind the basic teaching about Christ, and not

---

w Or *tempted*

x Gk *he*
y Or *him*
z Or *toward maturity*

4:14 *a great high priest* Resuming the theme begun in 2:17. *who has passed through the heavens* This passage seems to refer to Jesus' ascension into heaven on clouds, which is described only in *Luke* 24:51 and *Acts* 1:9. **4:15** See 2:17–18. **5:3** On the Day of Atonement (Yom Kippur), the high priest offered sacrifice for himself and the nation; *Lev.* 16:1–34. **5:4** Aaron was the 1st high priest, according to biblical tradition; *Lev.* 8:1–9. **5:5** *Ps.* 2:7, already quoted (1:5). Jesus was appointed high priest only at a particular moment, at his resurrection and exaltation. See note to 1:8–9. **5:6** *Ps.* 110:4 (LXX 109:4). MT "a rightful king" or "king of righteousness." LXX "Melchizedek." The author assumes there was an *order* of Melchizedekian priests. In Hebrew, the name Melchizedek is composed of the words "king" and "right(ful)." Understood from the LXX as a reference to this particular king, *Psalm* 110 may well have been the source of his notions of Jesus as high priest and of Jesus' eternal service *(forever)* in this role. It also provides material for his argument about Jesus' superiority, since Abraham, the father of Judaism himself, paid tribute to Melchizedek. See *Heb.* 6:20–7:28. **5:7** See *Mark* 14:37; *Luke* 22:42–44. The author knows some version of the synoptic passion story. **5:11–6:3** This distinction between teaching for children and that for adults, as between milk and solid food, was a common image used by philosophers when speaking of the stages of education. See *1 Cor.* 3:1–2; Philo, *On the Preliminary Studies* 19; Epictetus, *Discourses* 3.24.53. **6:1–2** The author considers the rudiments of Christian faith to be repentance and faith in Christ, baptism, and future judgment. *laying on of hands* Either ordination (*Acts* 6:6; 13:3) or the imparting of the Holy Spirit, with consequent healing and wonder working (*Acts* 8:17–18; 9:12, 17; 19:6, 11; 28:8; see *Jas.* 5:14), more probably the latter. **6:1** *dead works and faith toward God* The faith-works contrast is reminiscent of *Gal.* 3:2–9, where Paul raises this issue in the context of a debate with Jewish Christians concerning "works" as obedience to Torah. It is likely that the audience here too was either Jewish or attracted to Judaism.

laying again the foundation: repentance from dead works and faith toward God, [2]instruction about baptisms, laying on of hands, resurrection of the dead, and eternal judgment. [3]And we will do[a] this, if God permits. [4]For it is impossible to restore again to repentance those who have once been enlightened, and have tasted the heavenly gift, and have shared in the Holy Spirit, [5]and have tasted the goodness of the word of God and the powers of the age to come, [6]and then have fallen away, since on their own they are crucifying again the Son of God and are holding him up to contempt. [7]Ground that drinks up the rain falling on it repeatedly, and that produces a crop useful to those for whom it is cultivated, receives a blessing from God. [8]But if it produces thorns and thistles, it is worthless and on the verge of being cursed; its end is to be burned over.

[9]Even though we speak in this way, beloved, we are confident of better things in your case, things that belong to salvation. [10]For God is not unjust; he will not overlook your work and the love that you showed for his sake[b] in serving the saints, as you still do. [11]And we want each one of you to show the same diligence so as to realize the full assurance of hope to the very end, [12]so that you may not become sluggish, but imitators of those who through faith and patience inherit the promises.

The Certainty of God's Promise

[13]When God made a promise to Abraham, because he had no one greater by whom to swear, he swore by himself, [14]saying, "I will surely bless you and multiply you." [15]And thus Abraham,[c] having patiently endured, obtained the promise. [16]Human beings, of course, swear by someone greater than themselves, and an oath given as confirmation puts an end to all dispute. [17]In the same way, when God desired to show even more clearly to the heirs of the promise the unchangeable character of his purpose, he guaranteed it by an oath, [18]so that through two unchangeable things, in which it is impossible that God would prove false, we who have taken refuge might be strongly encouraged to seize the hope set before us. [19]We have this hope, a sure and steadfast anchor of the soul, a hope that enters the inner shrine behind the curtain, [20]where Jesus, a forerunner on our behalf, has entered, having become a high priest forever according to the order of Melchizedek.

The Priestly Order of Melchizedek

7 This "King Melchizedek of Salem, priest of the Most High God, met Abraham as he was returning from defeating the kings and blessed him"; [2]and to him Abraham apportioned "one-tenth of

---

a Other ancient authorities read *let us do*
b Gk *for his name*

c Gk *he*

6:4–8 The 1st of three extremely dire warnings about falling away; see also 10:26–31; 12:14–29. Earlier warnings were not as vivid (2:1–4; 3:7–13). Apostasy was a serious problem for the young church in its second generation. Some would leave the Christian group and even renounce the faith when asked about it (see Pliny the Younger, *Letters* 10.96). The author of *Hebrews* holds that there is no 2d chance for such people.   **6:7–8** Jesus' teachings were used as sermon material in the young church and so were adapted to different situations even before they were written down in the gospels (see the introduction to BIOGRAPHY, ANECDOTE, AND HISTORY). This passage furnishes a good example of how Jesus' parable of the sower was used; see also *1 Clem.* 24.5, *Gospel of Thomas* 9, and the interpretation of the parable appended in *Mark* 4:13–20. See also Plutarch, *Education of Children, Mor.* 2.B–E for the philosophers' use of soil and seed imagery in education.   **6:11** *to the very end* That is, to the end of the age, when Jesus returns. The writer has a strong orientation toward the future, as did Paul (*1 Thess.* 1:9–10; 5:23).   **6:13–14** *Gen.* 22:15–17. Since he alludes to the biblical text without citing the relevant part ("By Myself I swear"), he must be assuming his audience's knowledge of the text.   **6:16–18** God's promise to Abraham and his oath in the *Gen.* 22:15–17 passage just cited provide a double guarantee. The promise was irrevocable, and it was fulfilled. This principle is then applied to the passage cited from *Ps.* 110:4 in 5:6 about the eternal priesthood of Melchizedek, which also begins with an oath from God (7:21). The eternal priesthood of Melchizedek is as sure a promise as the blessing of Abraham, on which the whole Jewish nation depends. This prepares for the author's further argument that Jesus fulfills this promise with his eternal priesthood (6:20–7:28).   **6:19** *sure and steadfast anchor of the soul* Ancient philosophy in general was looking for a secure basis for living, and philosophers used these same words. See *Luke* 1:4 and note to "truth" there. *the inner shrine behind the curtain* Presumably, the top surface ("mercy seat") on the box called the ark of the covenant, which was kept in the holy of holies, the inner chamber of the temple (*Exod.* 24:10–22; 26:34). Only the high priest could enter this chamber, and only once each year, on the Day of Atonement (Yom Kippur). See note to 5:3.   **6:20** *Jesus, a forerunner* This recalls Paul's description of the resurrected Jesus as the "first fruits" of resurrection; his followers will join him later (*1 Cor.* 15:21–23). The language contrasts with that of *Eph.* 2:6, where the believers have already been seated in heavenly places with Christ by sharing in his resurrection. *order of Melchizedek* Reverting to the theme introduced in 5:5–10. (See note to 6:16–18.)   **7:1–4** Melchizedek is the mysterious king of Salem and priest of "God Most High" (Hebrew *el elyon*) briefly mentioned in *Gen.* 14:18–20. He blesses Abraham, and then Abraham gives him one-tenth of "everything." His mention in LXX *Ps.* 109:4 shows that he had become a figure of speculation for later Jews. The author of *Genesis* and subsequent Jewish readers took "priest of *el elyon*" to indicate his remarkable status in relation to Israel's God, but the phrase may have

everything." His name, in the first place, means "king of righteousness"; next he is also king of Salem, that is, "king of peace." ³Without father, without mother, without genealogy, having neither beginning of days nor end of life, but resembling the Son of God, he remains a priest forever.

⁴See how great he is! Even*d* Abraham the patriarch gave him a tenth of the spoils. ⁵And those descendants of Levi who receive the priestly office have a commandment in the law to collect tithes*e* from the people, that is, from their kindred,*f* though these also are descended from Abraham. ⁶But this man, who does not belong to their ancestry, collected tithes*e* from Abraham and blessed him who had received the promises. ⁷It is beyond dispute that the inferior is blessed by the superior. ⁸In the one case, tithes are received by those who are mortal; in the other, by one of whom it is testified that he lives. ⁹One might even say that Levi himself, who receives tithes, paid tithes through Abraham, ¹⁰for he was still in the loins of his ancestor when Melchizedek met him.

Another Priest, Like Melchizedek

¹¹Now if perfection had been attainable through the levitical priesthood—for the people received the law under this priesthood—what further need would there have been to speak of another priest arising ac-

cording to the order of Melchizedek, rather than one according to the order of Aaron? ¹²For when there is a change in the priesthood, there is necessarily a change in the law as well. ¹³Now the one of whom these things are spoken belonged to another tribe, from which no one has ever served at the altar. ¹⁴For it is evident that our Lord was descended from Judah, and in connection with that tribe Moses said nothing about priests.

¹⁵It is even more obvious when another priest arises, resembling Melchizedek, ¹⁶one who has become a priest, not through a legal requirement concerning physical descent, but through the power of an indestructible life. ¹⁷For it is attested of him,

"You are a priest forever,
    according to the order of Melchizedek."

¹⁸There is, on the one hand, the abrogation of an earlier commandment because it was weak and ineffectual ¹⁹(for the law made nothing perfect); there is, on the other hand, the introduction of a better hope, through which we approach God.

²⁰This was confirmed with an oath; for others who became priests took their office without an oath, ²¹but this one became a priest with an oath, because of the one who said to him,

"The Lord has sworn
    and will not change his mind,
'You are a priest forever' "—

²²accordingly Jesus has also become the guarantee of a better covenant.

d Other ancient authorities lack *Even*
e Or *a tenth*
f Gk *brothers*

referred to a Canaanite god of that name. One of the Dead Sea Scrolls known as *Melchizedek* (11Q Melch) shows that some 1st-century Jews had come to view Melchizedek as a heavenly prince. **7:2 king of righteousness** The author seems to know some Hebrew; see note to 5:6. **king of peace** *Gen.* 14:18. *Salem* is the latter part of the name Jerusalem, and probably from an old name for the city before the Israelites arrived there under King David. See also *Ps.* 76:3. The author notes the clear parallel with the Hebrew word *shalom,* meaning "peace" (both words come from the root *sh-l-m*). He may also have in mind the hope in *Isa.* 9:5–6 for a descendant of David who will be the "prince of peace." **7:3** All of this is inferred from *Ps.* 110:4 and from the fact that the Bible says so little about Melchizedek. **7:4–28** The author continues the complex argument in three stages. Melchizedek's priesthood is superior to the Jewish Levitical and Aaronic priesthood. Jesus is identified as the new high priest of Melchizedek's order and supersedes the Jewish Levitical priesthood. Jesus' high priesthood is unique and eternal. **7:4–10** Melchizedek received tithes from Abraham (*Gen.* 14:19). Tithing was an ancient form of Israelite taxation, in which the people paid one 10th of their income to the central temple leadership, the Levites (*Num.* 18:23–32). In *Genesis,* which was written when Israel was well established in Jerusalem, this observation about Abraham's action when he was passing by the future site of Jerusalem may have been intended to foreshadow the payment of tithes to the Jerusalem priesthood. The author of *Hebrews* argues that since inferiors pay tribute to superiors (7:7), Abraham and the entire priestly complement that was *in his loins* (i.e., not yet born; 7:10) must have been inferior to Melchizedek. **7:6 this man, who does not belong to their ancestry** That is, Melchizedek was not part of the later high priesthood descended from Moses' brother Aaron. This observation prepares for the author's claim that Jesus, though not an Aaronic priest, represents the superior high priesthood of Melchizedek (7:14–15). **7:11–22** The argument runs thus: Scripture would not have commented about this other, eternal priesthood if the current priesthood had been adequate or permanent. Therefore it is not adequate or permanent. Jesus is a new high priest from Melchizedek's order because he comes from a non-Levitical tribe (Judah) and because his resurrection makes him alone suited to the qualification "eternal." Such a complete change in priesthood necessitates a complete change in the law administered by the priest(s). All of this has now happened, the author claims. **7:14 Lord was descended from Judah** Jesus was called Son of David by some Christians (see *Rom.* 1:3; *Matt.* 1:1), and David was from the tribe of Judah. This may be because he was considered the Messiah, not because he was in fact known to have been a descendant of David. Note the critique at *Mark* 12:35–37. **7:17** *Ps.* 110:4; see 5:6. **7:20–22** *Ps.* 110:4. See notes to 5:6; 6:16–18.

23Furthermore, the former priests were many in number, because they were prevented by death from continuing in office; 24but he holds his priesthood permanently, because he continues forever. 25Consequently he is able for all time to saveᵍ those who approach God through him, since he always lives to make intercession for them.

26For it was fitting that we should have such a high priest, holy, blameless, undefiled, separated from sinners, and exalted above the heavens. 27Unlike the otherʰ high priests, he has no need to offer sacrifices day after day, first for his own sins, and then for those of the people; this he did once for all when he offered himself. 28For the law appoints as high priests those who are subject to weakness, but the word of the oath, which came later than the law, appoints a Son who has been made perfect forever.

Mediator of a Better Covenant

8 Now the main point in what we are saying is this: we have such a high priest, one who is seated at the right hand of the throne of the Majesty in the heavens, 2a minister in the sanctuary and the true tentⁱ that the Lord, and not any mortal, has set up. 3For every high priest is appointed to offer gifts and sacrifices; hence it is necessary for this priest also to have something to offer. 4Now if he were on earth, he would not be a priest at all, since there are priests who offer gifts according to the law. 5They offer worship in a sanctuary that is a sketch and shadow of the heavenly one; for Moses, when he was about to erect the tent,ⁱ was warned, "See that you make everything according to the pattern that was shown you on the mountain." 6But Jesusʲ has now obtained a more ex-

cellent ministry, and to that degree he is the mediator of a better covenant, which has been enacted through better promises. 7For if that first covenant had been faultless, there would have been no need to look for a second one.

8Godᵏ finds fault with them when he says:
"The days are surely coming, says the Lord,
    when I will establish a new covenant with the house of Israel
    and with the house of Judah;
9   not like the covenant that I made with their ancestors,
    on the day when I took them by the hand to lead them out of the land of Egypt;
for they did not continue in my covenant,
    and so I had no concern for them, says the Lord.
10   This is the covenant that I will make with the house of Israel
    after those days, says the Lord:
I will put my laws in their minds,
    and write them on their hearts,
and I will be their God,
    and they shall be my people.
11   And they shall not teach one another
    or say to each other, 'Know the Lord,'
for they shall all know me,
    from the least of them to the greatest.
12   For I will be merciful toward their iniquities,
    and I will remember their sins no more."
13In speaking of "a new covenant," he has made the first one obsolete. And what is obsolete and growing old will soon disappear.

---

g Or *able to save completely*
h Gk lacks *other*
i Or *tabernacle*
j Gk *he*

k Gk *He*

7:23–28 Jesus is no longer susceptible to death, decay, and multiplicity. He is one and eternal. The author develops the distinction, made famous by Plato, between what is transient and material, on the one hand, and what is spiritual and eternal, on the other (*Resp.* 7.514–541). The temple of Judaism he places in the former category; Jesus' covenant in the latter. See *Phil.* 3:2–11, 17–21 and *Gal.* 3:1–4. **8:1–10:18** The author claims forthrightly that the imperfect, shadowy covenant of Judaism has been supplanted by a new, eternal, and perfect covenant. **8:1 *seated at the right hand*** *Ps.* 110:1. See 1:13. **8:2 *the true tent*** The temple in Jerusalem was preceded for hundreds of years by a moving sanctuary, a tent or tabernacle. God says that the instructions for building the tent come from a "pattern," or blueprint (*Exod.* 25:9, 40). Under the later influence of Plato's thinking, this pattern was considered a "form"—an eternally true idea not subject to imperfection or decay. This association, which had been made by other Jews of the period (*Wis.* 9:8), provides the basis for our author's contrast between an earthly and a heavenly sanctuary. **8:5** *Exod.* 25:40. **8:7** This verse (see also 7:11, 18–19) epitomizes Paul's critique of Torah observance. The critique reasons from the new to the old. Since Christ has come as Savior, the covenant of Torah must have been inadequate. If the biblical covenant was adequate, why did Christ need to come? See *Gal.* 2:21; 3:21. This author develops the point by showing that God himself promised a new covenant, finding fault with the old one (see next note). **8:8–12** *Jer.* 31:31–34; looked ahead to the days after the return from Babylonian captivity (6th century B.C.E.) as better times, when a *new covenant,* written on the heart, would be in place. *Hebrews* takes this to be a new *kind* of covenant, different from the Torah of Moses. This perspective recalls *2 Cor.* 3:1–18. **8:13** This is one of the strongest expressions in early Christian literature of the notion that Christianity has superseded Judaism. See also *Gal.* 3:19–29.

The Earthly and the Heavenly Sanctuaries

9 Now even the first covenant had regulations for worship and an earthly sanctuary. 2For a tent*l* was constructed, the first one, in which were the lampstand, the table, and the bread of the Presence;*m* this is called the Holy Place. 3Behind the second curtain was a tent*l* called the Holy of Holies. 4In it stood the golden altar of incense and the ark of the covenant overlaid on all sides with gold, in which there were a golden urn holding the manna, and Aaron's rod that budded, and the tablets of the covenant; 5above it were the cherubim of glory overshadowing the mercy seat.*n* Of these things we cannot speak now in detail.

6Such preparations having been made, the priests go continually into the first tent*l* to carry out their ritual duties; 7but only the high priest goes into the second, and he but once a year, and not without taking the blood that he offers for himself and for the sins committed unintentionally by the people. 8By this the Holy Spirit indicates that the way into the sanctuary has not yet been disclosed as long as the first tent*l* is still standing. 9This is a symbol*o* of the present time, during which gifts and sacrifices are offered that cannot perfect the conscience of the worshiper, 10but deal only with food and drink and various baptisms, regulations for the body imposed until the time comes to set things right.

11But when Christ came as a high priest of the good things that have come,*p* then through the greater and perfect*q* tent*l* (not made with hands, that is, not of this creation), 12he entered once for all into the Holy Place, not with the blood of goats and calves, but with his own blood, thus obtaining eternal redemption. 13For if the blood of goats and bulls, with the sprinkling of the ashes of a heifer, sanctifies those who have been defiled so that their flesh is purified, 14how much more will the blood of Christ, who through the eternal Spirit*r* offered himself without blemish to God, purify our*s* conscience from dead works to worship the living God!

15For this reason he is the mediator of a new covenant, so that those who are called may receive the promised eternal inheritance, because a death has occurred that redeems them from the transgressions under the first covenant.*t* 16Where a will*t* is involved, the death of the one who made it must be established. 17For a will*t* takes effect only at death, since it is not in force as long as the one who made it is alive. 18Hence not even the first covenant was inaugurated without blood. 19For when every commandment had been told to all the people by Moses in accordance with the law, he took the blood of calves and goats,*u* with water and scarlet wool and hyssop, and sprinkled both the scroll itself and all the people, 20saying, "This is the blood of the covenant that God has ordained for you." 21And in the same way he sprinkled with the blood both the tent*l* and all the vessels used in worship. 22Indeed, under the law almost everything is purified with blood, and without the shedding of blood there is no forgiveness of sins.

Christ's Sacrifice Takes Away Sin

23Thus it was necessary for the sketches of the heavenly things to be purified with these rites, but the heavenly things themselves need better sacrifices than these. 24For Christ did not enter a sanctuary made by human hands, a mere copy of the true one, but he entered into heaven itself, now to appear in the presence of God on our behalf. 25Nor was it to offer himself again and again, as the high priest enters the Holy Place year after year with blood that is not his own; 26for then he would have had to suffer again and again since the foundation of the world. But as it is, he has appeared once for all at the end of the age to remove sin by the sacrifice of himself. 27And just as it is appointed for mortals to die once, and after that the judgment, 28so Christ, having been offered once to bear the sins of many, will appear a second time, not to deal with sin, but to save those who are eagerly waiting for him.

---

l Or *tabernacle*
m Gk *the presentation of the loaves*
n Or *the place of atonement*
o Gk *parable*
p Other ancient authorities read *good things to come*
q Gk *more perfect*
r Other ancient authorities read *Holy Spirit*
s Other ancient authorities read *your*

t The Greek word used here means both *covenant* and *will*
u Other ancient authorities lack *and goats*

9:1–7 Summarizing the biblical regulations for the temple (tent) and its service; *Exod.* 25:9–30:38; *Lev.* 16:1–34. **9:8–10** The author argues that because the temple regimen needed constant repetition, it was imperfect. **9:11–15** See also *2 Cor.* 3:6. **9:16–28** The author first makes a play on the Gk word for "covenant" *(diathēkē)*, which can also mean "will" or "testament" (see also *Gal.* 3:15–18). Then, since a will requires death or *blood*, he moves by word association to discuss the supreme shedding of blood in Christ's death. **9:19–20** The author combines several different rituals: *Exod.* 24:8, from which the quoted words come; *Lev.* 14:4–7; 16:19; *Num.* 19:18, 20. **9:28** The author's orientation toward future salvation with Jesus' return from heaven recalls the early Paul (*1 Thess.* 1:9–10; 5:23).

Christ's Sacrifice Once for All

10 Since the law has only a shadow of the good things to come and not the true form of these realities, it[v] can never, by the same sacrifices that are continually offered year after year, make perfect those who approach. ²Otherwise, would they not have ceased being offered, since the worshipers, cleansed once for all, would no longer have any consciousness of sin? ³But in these sacrifices there is a reminder of sin year after year. ⁴For it is impossible for the blood of bulls and goats to take away sins. ⁵Consequently, when Christ[w] came into the world, he said,

"Sacrifices and offerings you have not desired,
 but a body you have prepared for me;
6   in burnt offerings and sin offerings
 you have taken no pleasure.
7   Then I said, 'See, God, I have come to do your
 will, O God'
 (in the scroll of the book[x] it is written of
 me)."

⁸When he said above, "You have neither desired nor taken pleasure in sacrifices and offerings and burnt offerings and sin offerings" (these are offered according to the law), ⁹then he added, "See, I have come to do your will." He abolishes the first in order to establish the second. ¹⁰And it is by God's will[y] that we have been sanctified through the offering of the body of Jesus Christ once for all.

¹¹And every priest stands day after day at his service, offering again and again the same sacrifices that can never take away sins. ¹²But when Christ[z] had offered for all time a single sacrifice for sins, "he sat down at the right hand of God," ¹³and since then has been waiting "until his enemies would be made a footstool for his feet." ¹⁴For by a single offering he has perfected for all time those who are sanctified. ¹⁵And the Holy Spirit also testifies to us, for after saying,

16   "This is the covenant that I will make with them

after those days, says the Lord:
 I will put my laws in their hearts,
 and I will write them on their minds,"
¹⁷he also adds,
 "I will remember[a] their sins and their lawless
 deeds no more."

¹⁸Where there is forgiveness of these, there is no longer any offering for sin.

A Call to Persevere

¹⁹Therefore, my friends,[b] since we have confidence to enter the sanctuary by the blood of Jesus, ²⁰by the new and living way that he opened for us through the curtain (that is, through his flesh), ²¹and since we have a great priest over the house of God, ²²let us approach with a true heart in full assurance of faith, with our hearts sprinkled clean from an evil conscience and our bodies washed with pure water. ²³Let us hold fast to the confession of our hope without wavering, for he who has promised is faithful. ²⁴And let us consider how to provoke one another to love and good deeds, ²⁵not neglecting to meet together, as is the habit of some, but encouraging one another, and all the more as you see the Day approaching.

²⁶For if we willfully persist in sin after having received the knowledge of the truth, there no longer remains a sacrifice for sins, ²⁷but a fearful prospect of judgment, and a fury of fire that will consume the adversaries. ²⁸Anyone who has violated the law of Moses dies without mercy "on the testimony of two or three witnesses." ²⁹How much worse punishment do you think will be deserved by those who have spurned the Son of God, profaned the blood of the covenant by which they were sanctified, and outraged the Spirit of grace? ³⁰For we know the one who said, "Vengeance is mine, I will repay." And again, "The Lord will judge his people." ³¹It is a fearful thing to fall into the hands of the living God.

---

v Other ancient authorities read *they*
w Gk *he*
x Meaning of Gk uncertain
y Gk *by that will*
z Gk *this one*

a Gk *on their minds and I will remember*
b Gk *Therefore, brothers*

10:1–4 Essentially repeating 9:23–28, on the unique perfection of Christ's sacrifice. **10:5–7** *not desired Ps.* 40:6–8 (LXX 39:7–8). LXX reads "not required" or "not sought." The passage itself says nothing about Christ's coming into the world; this is the author's application of it. **10:8–10** In rabbinic fashion, the author finds words in the scriptural passage to support his distinctions, here between God's will (the new covenant) and sacrifice of animals (the old covenant). **10:11–14** Repeating the claims of 9:15–28 but now with reference to *Ps.* 110:1 (1:2, 13; 8:1). The fact that Jesus is seated in heaven is meant to prove that he has given a single sacrifice for all time. **10:15–22** *Jer.* 31:31–34. See 8:8–12. Under the new (Christian) covenant, sins will be completely removed. **10:25** *not neglecting to meet together, as is the habit of some* This indifference on the part of some fits with the larger problem of falling away or apostasy, with which the entire document is concerned. *as you see the Day approaching* See note to 9:28 on the author's hope for Jesus' imminent return. **10:26–39** The second dire warning about leaving the Christian flock: there will be no further chance to avoid judgment. See note to 6:4–8. **10:28** *Deut.* 19:15. **10:30** *Deut.* 32:35–36.

[32]But recall those earlier days when, after you had been enlightened, you endured a hard struggle with sufferings, [33]sometimes being publicly exposed to abuse and persecution, and sometimes being partners with those so treated. [34]For you had compassion for those who were in prison, and you cheerfully accepted the plundering of your possessions, knowing that you yourselves possessed something better and more lasting. [35]Do not, therefore, abandon that confidence of yours; it brings a great reward. [36]For you need endurance, so that when you have done the will of God, you may receive what was promised.
[37] For yet "in a very little while,
> the one who is coming will come and will not delay;
[38] but my righteous one will live by faith.
> My soul takes no pleasure in anyone who shrinks back."
[39]But we are not among those who shrink back and so are lost, but among those who have faith and so are saved.

The Meaning of Faith

11 Now faith is the assurance of things hoped for, the conviction of things not seen. [2]Indeed, by faith[c] our ancestors received approval. [3]By faith we understand that the worlds were prepared by the word of God, so that what is seen was made from things that are not visible.[d]

The Examples of Abel, Enoch, and Noah

[4]By faith Abel offered to God a more acceptable[e] sacrifice than Cain's. Through this he received approval as righteous, God himself giving approval to his gifts; he died, but through his faith[f] he still speaks. [5]By faith Enoch was taken so that he did not experience death; and "he was not found, because God had taken him." For it was attested before he was taken away that "he had pleased God." [6]And without faith it is impossible to please God, for whoever would approach him must believe that he exists and that he rewards those who seek him. [7]By faith Noah, warned by God about events as yet unseen, respected the warning and built an ark to save his household; by this he condemned the world and became an heir to the righteousness that is in accordance with faith.

The Faith of Abraham

[8]By faith Abraham obeyed when he was called to set out for a place that he was to receive as an inheritance; and he set out, not knowing where he was going. [9]By faith he stayed for a time in the land he had been promised, as in a foreign land, living in tents, as did Isaac and Jacob, who were heirs with him of the same promise. [10]For he looked forward to the city that has foundations, whose architect and builder is God. [11]By faith he received power of procreation, even though he was too old—and Sarah herself was barren—because he considered him faithful who had promised.[g] [12]Therefore from one person, and this one as good as dead, descendants were born, "as many as the stars of heaven and as the innumerable grains of sand by the seashore."
[13]All of these died in faith without having received the promises, but from a distance they saw and greeted them. They confessed that they were strangers and foreigners on the earth, [14]for people who speak in this way make it clear that they are seeking a homeland. [15]If they had been thinking of the land that they had left behind, they would have had opportunity to return. [16]But as it is, they desire a better country, that is, a heavenly one. Therefore God is not

---

c Gk by this
d Or was not made out of visible things
e Gk greater
f Gk through it

g Other ancient authorities read By faith Sarah herself, though barren, received power to conceive, even when she was too old, because she considered him faithful who had promised.

10:32–39 This passage gives some insight into the community's history. In their early days, some time ago, they faced opposition and harassment with perseverance. Current persecution is linked in the author's mind to the desire of some to pull back from their Christian association. **10:37–38** Hab. 2:3–4. The 7th(?)-century prophet pleads with God to intervene, at a time when the wicked seem to prevail. God responds that he will come soon. Paul uses this passage to argue that one needs "faith [in Christ]," over against "works" (observance of Torah), to achieve life (Gal. 3:11; Rom. 1:17). The author of Hebrews, by contrast, maintains the original sense of faith as faithful perseverance, fidelity, and trust. In the following paragraphs he will develop this with a lengthy catalogue of mostly biblical figures who demonstrated such faithfulness (11:1–12:1). **11:1–12:1** The author's famous catalogue of faithful heroes is an integral part of his argument that his readers, too, must not abandon their Christian allegiance. See previous note. **11:3** See Gen. 1:1–5. **11:4** See Gen. 4:1–5. **11:5** See Gen. 5:18–24. The peculiar way in which Enoch's death is described ("he was no more, because God took him"; Gen. 5:24) gave rise to much speculation that he had gone to heaven without dying. Numerous books appeared under his name from the 3d century B.C.E. onward, now represented by 1, 2, and 3 Enoch. **11:7** See Genesis 6–9. **11:8–10** See Gen. 12:1–9. **11:11** See Gen. 18:9–15. **11:12** See Gen. 22:17. **11:13–16** In the Bible, these figures are presented as sojourners because their stories lead up to the eventual settlement of Israel in the promised land. The author reads this as waiting for a heavenly home.

ashamed to be called their God; indeed, he has prepared a city for them.

[17]By faith Abraham, when put to the test, offered up Isaac. He who had received the promises was ready to offer up his only son, [18]of whom he had been told, "It is through Isaac that descendants shall be named for you." [19]He considered the fact that God is able even to raise someone from the dead—and figuratively speaking, he did receive him back. [20]By faith Isaac invoked blessings for the future on Jacob and Esau. [21]By faith Jacob, when dying, blessed each of the sons of Joseph, "bowing in worship over the top of his staff." [22]By faith Joseph, at the end of his life, made mention of the exodus of the Israelites and gave instructions about his burial.[h]

The Faith of Moses

[23]By faith Moses was hidden by his parents for three months after his birth, because they saw that the child was beautiful; and they were not afraid of the king's edict.[i] [24]By faith Moses, when he was grown up, refused to be called a son of Pharaoh's daughter, [25]choosing rather to share ill-treatment with the people of God than to enjoy the fleeting pleasures of sin. [26]He considered abuse suffered for the Christ[j] to be greater wealth than the treasures of Egypt, for he was looking ahead to the reward. [27]By faith he left Egypt, unafraid of the king's anger; for he persevered as though[k] he saw him who is invisible. [28]By faith he kept the Passover and the sprinkling of blood, so that the destroyer of the firstborn would not touch the firstborn of Israel.[l]

The Faith of Other Israelite Heroes

[29]By faith the people passed through the Red Sea as if it were dry land, but when the Egyptians at-

tempted to do so they were drowned. [30]By faith the walls of Jericho fell after they had been encircled for seven days. [31]By faith Rahab the prostitute did not perish with those who were disobedient,[m] because she had received the spies in peace.

[32]And what more should I say? For time would fail me to tell of Gideon, Barak, Samson, Jephthah, of David and Samuel and the prophets— [33]who through faith conquered kingdoms, administered justice, obtained promises, shut the mouths of lions, [34]quenched raging fire, escaped the edge of the sword, won strength out of weakness, became mighty in war, put foreign armies to flight. [35]Women received their dead by resurrection. Others were tortured, refusing to accept release, in order to obtain a better resurrection. [36]Others suffered mocking and flogging, and even chains and imprisonment. [37]They were stoned to death, they were sawn in two,[n] they were killed by the sword; they went about in skins of sheep and goats, destitute, persecuted, tormented— [38]of whom the world was not worthy. They wandered in deserts and mountains, and in caves and holes in the ground.

[39]Yet all these, though they were commended for their faith, did not receive what was promised, [40]since God had provided something better so that they would not, apart from us, be made perfect.

The Example of Jesus

12 Therefore, since we are surrounded by so great a cloud of witnesses, let us also lay aside every weight and the sin that clings so closely,[o] and let us run with perseverance the race that is set before us, [2]looking to Jesus the pioneer and perfecter of our faith, who for the sake of[p] the joy that was set before

---

h Gk *his bones*

i Other ancient authorities add *By faith Moses, when he was grown up, killed the Egyptian, because he observed the humiliation of his people* (Gk *brothers*)

j Or *the Messiah*

k Or *because*

l Gk *would not touch them*

m Or *unbelieving*

n Other ancient authorities add *they were tempted*

o Other ancient authorities read *sin that easily distracts*

p Or *who instead of*

11:17 See *Gen.* 22:1–19. **11:18** *Gen.* 21:12. **11:20** See *Genesis* 27. **11:21** *Gen.* 49:1–28. The quotation is from LXX *Gen.* 47:31. The MT says simply that he "bowed at the head of the bed." **11:22** See *Gen.* 50:22–26. **11:23** See *Exod.* 1:15–2:2. **11:24–26** See *Exod.* 2:11–25. **11:27** See *Exod.* 2:11–25. This seems to refer to Moses' sojourn in Midian, rather than to the exodus, which follows later (11:29). **11:28** See *Exod.* 12:1–32. **11:29** See *Exod.* 14:1–31. **11:30** See *Josh.* 6:1–21. **11:31** See *Josh.* 6:22–27. **11:32** The stories of these leaders are told in *Judges* and *1–2 Samuel.* It is not clear what the author means by "prophets." See next note. **11:33** *shut the mouths of lions* See *Dan.* 6:6–28. At least in this context, this author considers *Daniel* among the prophets. Josephus agreed with this designation (*Ant.* 10.266). Later rabbinic Judaism, however, would consign this text to the writings *(ketuvim),* a final section of the Bible after the prophets *(nevi'im).* **11:35–38** The author appears to be referring to figures mentioned in the so-called apocryphal writings, especially *2 Maccabees* 7. **12:1–29** The 1st half deals with the problem of persecution, which seems to be a major motive in the wish to defect from the Christian fold. The 2d half is a stern warning not to trifle with God's grace. **12:1** Athletic imagery was extremely common in descriptions of the philosophical life. See Epictetus, *Discourses* 2.18.19–32. **12:2** *Jesus the pioneer and perfecter of our faith* Recalling 2:10. *his seat at the right hand* Ps. 110:1. See note to 1:3.

him endured the cross, disregarding its shame, and has taken his seat at the right hand of the throne of God.

3Consider him who endured such hostility against himself from sinners,[q] so that you may not grow weary or lose heart. 4In your struggle against sin you have not yet resisted to the point of shedding your blood. 5And you have forgotten the exhortation that addresses you as children—

"My child, do not regard lightly the discipline of
the Lord,
or lose heart when you are punished by him;
6 for the Lord disciplines those whom he loves,
and chastises every child whom he accepts."

7Endure trials for the sake of discipline. God is treating you as children; for what child is there whom a parent does not discipline? 8If you do not have that discipline in which all children share, then you are illegitimate and not his children. 9Moreover, we had human parents to discipline us, and we respected them. Should we not be even more willing to be subject to the Father of spirits and live? 10For they disciplined us for a short time as seemed best to them, but he disciplines us for our good, in order that we may share his holiness. 11Now, discipline always seems painful rather than pleasant at the time, but later it yields the peaceful fruit of righteousness to those who have been trained by it.

12Therefore lift your drooping hands and strengthen your weak knees, 13and make straight paths for your feet, so that what is lame may not be put out of joint, but rather be healed.

Warnings against Rejecting God's Grace

14Pursue peace with everyone, and the holiness without which no one will see the Lord. 15See to it that no one fails to obtain the grace of God; that no root of bitterness springs up and causes trouble, and through it many become defiled. 16See to it that no one becomes like Esau, an immoral and godless person, who sold his birthright for a single meal. 17You know that later, when he wanted to inherit the blessing, he was rejected, for he found no chance to repent,[r] even though he sought the blessing[s] with tears.

18You have not come to something[t] that can be touched, a blazing fire, and darkness, and gloom, and a tempest, 19and the sound of a trumpet, and a voice whose words made the hearers beg that not another word be spoken to them. 20(For they could not endure the order that was given, "If even an animal touches the mountain, it shall be stoned to death." 21Indeed, so terrifying was the sight that Moses said, "I tremble with fear.") 22But you have come to Mount Zion and to the city of the living God, the heavenly Jerusalem, and to innumerable angels in festal gathering, 23and to the assembly[u] of the firstborn who are enrolled in heaven, and to God the judge of all, and to the spirits of the righteous made perfect, 24and to Jesus, the mediator of a new covenant, and to the sprinkled blood that speaks a better word than the blood of Abel.

25See that you do not refuse the one who is speaking; for if they did not escape when they refused the one who warned them on earth, how much less will we escape if we reject the one who warns from heaven! 26At that time his voice shook the earth; but now he has promised, "Yet once more I will shake not only the earth but also the heaven." 27This phrase, "Yet once more," indicates the removal of what is shaken—that is, created things—so that what cannot be shaken may remain. 28Therefore, since we are receiving a kingdom that cannot be shaken, let us give thanks, by which we offer to God an acceptable worship with reverence and awe; 29for indeed our God is a consuming fire.

q Other ancient authorities read *such hostility from sinners against themselves*

r Or *no chance to change his father's mind*
s Gk *it*
t Other ancient authorities read *a mountain*
u Or *angels, and to the festal gathering* 23*and assembly*

12:4 ***not yet resisted to the point of shedding your blood*** An important observation about the severity of the perceived persecutions (see 10:32–34). **12:5–6** *Prov.* 3:11–12. ***My child*** LXX lacks My. The MT is similar, but its last line reads "as a father the son whom he favors." ***disciplines*** LXX reads "punishes." This may have sounded too harsh to the writer of *Hebrews.* **12:5–14** The persecution that some readers perceive (which may be the kind of police action described by Pliny, *Letters* 10.96) is one cause of their uncertainty about continuing a Christian allegiance. An inevitable question in such circumstances is, "Why does God allow this to happen to his chosen ones?" The author responds here that it can be a kind of discipline from God as parent. **12:9–20** *Exod.* 19:12–13. **12:15–29** The author's final warning about apostasy from Christian allegiance (see also 2:1–4; 3:7–4:13; 6:4–12; 10:19–39). **12:16–17** See *Gen.* 25:29–34; 27:30–40. **12:18–24** The author contrasts an allegedly material Judaism with a purely spiritual Christianity. The references are to well-known biblical events. The biblical prophets and many Jewish writers of the author's period, such as Philo of Alexandria, Josephus, and the authors of *Pseudo-Aristeas* and *Wisdom of Solomon* understood Judaism very much in spiritual terms. **12:21** *Deut.* 9:19. **12:22–24** The author brings together many themes from the preceding arguments. See 8:5–6; 9:13–15; 10:1–18. **12:25** ***the one who is speaking*** God. **12:26** *Hag.* 2:6 (LXX 2:7). **12:27–28** Judaism with its putatively material base will be (has been) shaken so that *what cannot be shaken* (a putatively spiritual and eternal Christianity) remains.

Service Well-Pleasing to God

13 Let mutual love continue. ²Do not neglect to show hospitality to strangers, for by doing that some have entertained angels without knowing it. ³Remember those who are in prison, as though you were in prison with them; those who are being tortured, as though you yourselves were being tortured.ᵛ ⁴Let marriage be held in honor by all, and let the marriage bed be kept undefiled; for God will judge fornicators and adulterers. ⁵Keep your lives free from the love of money, and be content with what you have; for he has said, "I will never leave you or forsake you." ⁶So we can say with confidence,

"The Lord is my helper;
  I will not be afraid.
What can anyone do to me?"

⁷Remember your leaders, those who spoke the word of God to you; consider the outcome of their way of life, and imitate their faith. ⁸Jesus Christ is the same yesterday and today and forever. ⁹Do not be carried away by all kinds of strange teachings; for it is well for the heart to be strengthened by grace, not by regulations about food,ʷ which have not benefited those who observe them. ¹⁰We have an altar from which those who officiate in the tentˣ have no right to eat. ¹¹For the bodies of those animals whose blood is brought into the sanctuary by the high priest as a sacrifice for sin are burned outside the camp. ¹²Therefore Jesus also suffered outside the city gate in order to sanctify the people by his own blood. ¹³Let us then go to him outside the camp and bear the abuse he endured. ¹⁴For here we have no lasting city, but we are looking for the city that is to come. ¹⁵Through him, then, let us continually offer a sacrifice of praise to God, that is, the fruit of lips that confess his name. ¹⁶Do not neglect to do good and to share what you have, for such sacrifices are pleasing to God.

¹⁷Obey your leaders and submit to them, for they are keeping watch over your souls and will give an account. Let them do this with joy and not with sighing—for that would be harmful to you.

¹⁸Pray for us; we are sure that we have a clear conscience, desiring to act honorably in all things. ¹⁹I urge you all the more to do this, so that I may be restored to you very soon.

Benediction

²⁰Now may the God of peace, who brought back from the dead our Lord Jesus, the great shepherd of the sheep, by the blood of the eternal covenant, ²¹make you complete in everything good so that you may do his will, working among usʸ that which is pleasing in his sight, through Jesus Christ, to whom be the glory forever and ever. Amen.

Final Exhortation and Greetings

²²I appeal to you, brothers and sisters,ᶻ bear with my word of exhortation, for I have written to you briefly. ²³I want you to know that our brother Timothy has been set free; and if he comes in time, he will be with me when I see you. ²⁴Greet all your leaders and all the saints. Those from Italy send you greetings. ²⁵Grace be with all of you.ᵃ

---

v Gk *were in the body*
w Gk *not by foods*
x Or *tabernacle*

y Other ancient authorities read *you*
z Gk *brothers*
a Other ancient authorities add *Amen*

13:1–19 The author concludes his argumentative "letter" with various exhortations. These seem random in places, but several pick up themes from the earlier discussion (esp. 13:9–15). **13:2** See, for example, *Gen.* 18:2–8. Hospitality to strangers was considered one of the most basic social obligations in ancient literature. **13:3** This suggests that imprisonment was becoming common for the author's circles; see also 10:32–34. **tortured** Physical beating was a common experience in ancient jails. **13:4** See also *1 Thess.* 4:3–8. **13:5–7** Freedom from the love of money was a common goal in ancient popular philosophy. See Lucian, *Nigrinus* 12–14, 20–21; *Matt.* 6:25–34. **13:5** *Deut.* 31:6, 8; *Josh.* 1:5. **13:6** *Ps.* 118:6 (LXX 117:6). **13:9–15** After several random ethical admonitions, the author returns to the main theme of his work: do not abandon the Christian faith on account of persecution, but persevere *because* it is far superior to Judaism. **13:9** *strange teachings* Inasmuch as they concern foods and sacrifices in the "tent," they all relate to Judaism. It may be that there is really only one teaching at issue. **13:18** These travel plans are the first clear indicator of the letter genre. The author seems to imply that he is being held on charges of activity that seems dishonorable to his prosecutors, although he considers it noble. Such a description would suit the most characteristic Christian behavior: meeting privately at night, men and women together, sharing the Eucharist (of body and blood), as well as holy kisses. **13:20–21** This benediction recalls those of Paul's letters (e.g., *1 Thess.* 3:11–13; *Rom.* 16:25–27), but the references to blood and the eternal covenant link this benediction with the foregoing text. **13:23–25** The final greetings are typical of a letter, and it is striking that the author mentions Paul's close associate Timothy (*1 Thess.* 1:1; 3:2, 6; *1 Cor.* 4:17). This reference is perhaps the primary reason why some Christians considered *Hebrews* Pauline. **13:24** *Those from Italy send you greetings* This could mean that the letter-essay was sent either to or from Rome. A connection with Rome is also suggested by the fact that *Hebrews* seems very familiar to the Roman author of *1 Clement* in the 90s C.E.

A Letter from the Romans to the Corinthians

1 CLEMENT

Setting

Forty to fifty years after its founding, the church at Corinth experienced a crisis of leadership (see introductions to *1* and *2 Corinthians*). The Roman church[1] wrote a long document to the Corinthian church, allying itself with the older leaders there who had lost, or were in danger of losing, their positions. The whole letter focuses on this revolt in Corinth, and even the extensive references to Bible stories are selected because of their relevance to the issue of submission to properly established leadership.

Although the revolt in Corinth is the ever-present concern of the document, almost nothing can be determined about the reason for the revolt, its extent, or its success. Nothing points to a theological issue as the root of the problem. The author's charges that the rebellious were "rash and self-willed" (1.1) or "worthless" (3.2) or proud and unruly (14.1) are standard features of polemical writing and tell us little about the concrete situation.

Perhaps the dispute arose merely because a younger group of gifted people felt excluded from positions of leadership, which were held by older men, whose appointments had been made by apostles or persons with apostolic association. These appointments apparently had been seen as lifetime positions (44.2), limiting the number of positions open to the second- and third-generation converts. But even on that point, we have ambiguous information.

Recent studies of *1 Clement* have applied sociological theory concerning the institutionalization of leadership in small groups. According to these studies, some of the major changes that took place in early Christianity resulted from tensions between charismatic or pneumatic (spiritually directed) ministry, and official, institutionalized office. This emergence of institutional leadership in the church is often labeled "early catholicism."

---

[1]Some manuscripts attribute the letter to Clement alone. *A Letter from the Romans to the Corinthians* is the title found at the conclusion of other manuscripts.

Others have argued that the tension was between gnostic and anti-gnostic tendencies that took root during Paul's lifetime in the earliest days of the Corinthian church. Still others suggest that Clement's comments are too rhetorical to provide any clue about the situation in Corinth, but that theory overlooks some rather specific comments (44.1; 47.6–7).

Overview

One might say that *1 Clement* is little more than an extended and diverse collection of illustrations concerning proper order interspersed with a call to emulate these fine examples. *First Clement* includes a broad range of illustrations from Jewish, Christian, and pagan sources, as well as illustrations from nature.

Purpose

The main purpose—indeed, we might say, the only purpose—of the letter was to counter the revolt in Corinth, in which some older leaders had been removed from office. The Roman church threw its support behind these deposed leaders, and the letter conveys that decision bluntly. Every point of the letter emphasizes that there is a proper order and sanctioned structure in all things, and violating this order affronts God. The church at Corinth was asked to recognize this order, restore the old leadership, and return to previously held views. The effort to reinstate the leaders is put forward in simple and uncompromising terms: The leaders had been properly appointed; there was no justification for their removal; they are to be restored.

There is a noticeable lack of defense for either the beliefs or the behaviors of the deposed leadership. Their behavior is blameless (45.3–7). Their belief is not an issue, for had theological or moral issues been the cause of removal, the letter should have addressed these in some way. There is not even a remote hint that this kind of support was needed.

Audience

The original audience was the Corinthian church in its most inclusive compass: the deposed leaders and the rebels, the clergy and the laity, the old and the young. The letter, like many in early Christian history, gained for itself an even wider circle of hearers. According to Bishop Dionysius of Corinth (ca. 170 C.E.), the letter continued to be read regularly in the Corinthian assembly itself some eighty years after it was written (Eusebius, *Eccl. hist.* 4.23.11). Other churches around the Mediterranean also found its message clear, constructive, and contemporary. According to Eusebius, the letter was still being read in some churches in the early 300s (*Eccl. hist.* 3.16). This popularity of *1 Clement* explains its place among the canonical documents in various canonical lists.

Themes and Issues

Clement summarizes the content of his letter in his closing comments. Although he lists a number of themes (62), his main concern is clear. He wants the church at Corinth to reinstate the old leadership and submit to them (63). Besides the necessary introduction and conclusion, which take up about fifteen percent of the work, the entire writing consists of calls to repentance and good order and illustrations of good order from a variety of sources, in particular from the Hebrew Bible.

For Clement, the old leadership in Corinth, being properly appointed, represented the proper structure. Since proper structure and order have been universally cherished by all who are pious, and God himself is the principal originator and sustainer of good order, the church at Corinth cannot hope to prosper by acting contrary to that well-established pattern. Their only recourse is to reinstate the old leadership and thereby to reestablish that order approved by God.

Style

It has been pointed out that *1 Clement* follows the pattern of a literary form popular in the Greco-Roman world called the *symboulē* or "counsel." Intended to discourage or encourage a particular course of action, such literature often reflects the same themes that dominate *1 Clement:* the cessation of faction and the restoration of concord.

Clement writes as an educated Greek. His style is clear and graceful. It leaves the translator with far fewer problems than the letters of Ignatius, for example, and many other early Christian documents.

Authorship

Officially, this letter was written by the church at Rome to the church at Corinth.[2] But the letter is commonly referred to as *1 Clement,* and there is little doubt that the principal author of this document was someone named Clement. More than two hundred years after the composition of this document, Eusebius simply called it *Clement's Letter to the Corinthians* (*Eccl. hist.* 4.22). Further, Eusebius preserved correspondence addressed to Rome from Dionysius, a bishop of Corinth in the latter half of the second century. Dionysius mentioned the frequent reading of this letter (by that time, an eighty-year-old letter) in the Corinthian assembly, and he referred to the document as the letter that Clement wrote on behalf of the Roman church (*Eccl. hist.* 4.23).

---

[2]Corinth lies as close to Rome as any city we know from early Christian literature. The church in Corinth is certainly the closest *large* church. Further, Corinth was founded as a Roman colony on the orders of the dying Julius Caesar (44 B.C.E.) and came to serve as a principal port for Roman trade. Such contacts may have made the churches of the two cities feel a special closeness.

But Clement was a common enough name. This makes identifying the author difficult, though as early as the second century, attempts have been made to identify the author with some other Clement mentioned in early Christian or secular records. One person of that name is mentioned in Paul's letter to the Philippians (4:3), but there is no way to establish a convincing connection between him and the author of *1 Clement*.

We are on more substantial footing with the Clement mentioned in the *Shepherd of Hermas* (a document written in Rome in the first half of the second century). The Clement mentioned there (Herm. *Vis.* 2.4) served in some capacity as the author of correspondence from the Roman church to foreign churches. Further, according to some early lists of bishops[3] (which may or may not be reliable), the third or fourth bishop of Rome was named Clement.[4] According to Eusebius (*Eccl. hist.* 3.15.34), Clement's episcopate lasted about ten years, from 92–101 C.E., but we have no way to determine the reliability of Eusebius's sources. A few scholars think that the Clement of the letter and the bishop list is the consul Titus Flavius Clemens, a member of the imperial family, who was executed in 95 or 96 C.E.,[5] but most hold this unlikely. Some argue that a freedman of Clemens's family, bearing the family name, may be our Clement. This person may have been a Jewish slave or a proselyte who became a Christian. This would explain Clement's rich reserve of biblical knowledge and his ability to write in Greek despite his Latin name.

Date

The letter addresses specific problems in the church at Corinth and mentions a few personal names.[6] But none of this helps in dating the document. The specific problem (a rebellion against the leadership) is otherwise unmentioned in any

---

[3]By the middle of the second century, some individuals were visiting churches to learn about the local history. One, Hegesippus, tried to establish lists of bishops from his day back to the apostles, based on the records and memory of the various churches. His five-volume work is now lost, but brief passages from it have been preserved in Eusebius's *Ecclesiastical History*. It is believed that the full works of Hegesippus had been preserved in some libraries until the sixteenth or seventeenth century. The discovery of his complete works would probably be more significant than the discovery of the Dead Sea Scrolls or the Nag Hammadi library for our understanding of early Christianity.

[4]Eusebius, *Eccl. hist.* 4.23.11, offers the following list of bishops: Peter, Linus, Anencletus, Clement. But it is anachronistic to list these men as bishops in Rome, since the episcopal office, with bishop separate from the presbytery, does not seem to have appeared in Rome until later. In fact, *1 Clement* itself does not distinguish between bishops and presbyters. Such a distinction is necessary, however, if one is to speak of a genuinely monarchical episcopate, where the primary office is filled by an individual rather than by a council.

[5]According to Dio Cassius, a Roman historian and politician in the early third century, Clemens was killed for atheism and following Jewish ways (*History of Rome* 67.14). Such charges could have applied either to followers of Judaism or Christianity. There is no way to determine which the author has in mind.

[6]No one from Corinth is named, but three people from Rome are mentioned in the closing: Claudius Ephebus, Valerius Bito, and Fortunatus.

independent record of the Corinthian church;[7] the persons named are otherwise unknown. This makes dating difficult, though the middle of the 90s is widely accepted, for the following reasons.

Some think that Clement refers to an official persecution of Christians when he speaks of "misfortunes and reverses" (ch. 1). Such a reference might help in determining the date, if we had other evidence of a persecution. Many contend that the last years of the reign of Emperor Domitian (d. 96) are in view here. Domitian was portrayed in other Christian literature as a persecutor of the church.[8] But there is some doubt that Domitian launched a deliberate persecution of Christians (see the introduction to *Revelation*). Some commentators doubt that the words cited here even refer to an official persecution. Thus the efforts to date the book by linking it to a persecution fall short.

Still, two other data in the document suggest a date in the 90s. First, the messengers sent from the Roman church to the Corinthian church (as carriers of the letter and as credible spokesmen for the Roman church's concerns) lived "from youth to old age" among the Christians at Rome. If Christianity came to Rome sometime in the 40s, young converts at that time would fit well the description "from youth to old age" by the end of Domitian's reign. Second, the writer notes that some of the recently deposed leadership had been appointed by the apostles themselves. The most likely apostles would have been Peter and Paul, who were martyred under Emperor Nero in the mid-60s.[9] Leaders appointed by them would have been reasonably old by the 90s. So the traditional date of this letter—in the last decade of the first century—seems plausible.

Relation to Other Early Christian Texts

The author assembles example after example of proper respect for leadership and authority. The main source of his examples is the Septuagint, from which he often quotes long passages. Although he is at home in the Septuagint, and quotes from it far more extensively than any other first-century Christian author, the author is heavily influenced by the new Christian writings of the first century as well.

---

[7]Factions were disrupting the church in Corinth when Paul wrote *1 Corinthians*. But they were formed in the earliest years—or months—of the church there, and they cannot be linked to the factions forty years later. First, Clement reminds the Corinthian church of their earlier problem (ch. 47), but he draws no connection between the earlier and the later. Second, Clement describes the rebellious party as "the young" (3.3). Whatever the rhetorical worth of that label, it is doubtful that it could have been totally inaccurate. Yet any faction with roots in the earliest period would be expected to have members from all age groups—from young to old—indistinguishable in age from other factions with similar roots in early disputes.

[8]Our primary evidence of a persecution under Domitian, specifically aimed at Christians, is the *Book of Revelation* (also called the *Apocalypse*). Domitian was noted for brutality in the latter years of his reign, having his cousin killed and his niece exiled. The charges against them were that they had "lapsed into Jewish customs" and "atheism." Both charges could have been leveled at Christians, but the evidence is too scanty to determine the degree and extent of the persecution of Christians.

[9]Clement is the first to mention the martyrdom of Peter and Paul.

He explicitly refers to Paul's *First Letter to the Corinthians,* and cites it often—an effective strategy when dealing with the very group who had received that letter from Paul some forty years earlier. He knows Paul's *Letter to the Romans* (as might be expected of someone writing from Rome). Somewhat more surprisingly, he knows *Ephesians*[10] and perhaps *1 Peter.* But *Hebrews* seems to have informed Clement's language the most.[11]

Further, Clement uses synopticlike material about Jesus. This raises questions about the spread and impact of the Synoptic Gospels themselves and the continuing influence of oral tradition on the early church. Oral tradition, rather than the written Synoptics, may be the source of most of Clement's Jesus material.

First Clement was known and used widely in the early church; in fact, it was a favorite. Polycarp was perhaps the first to quote from it. A Latin translation was made in the second century, and a body of Clementine pseudonymous literature arose after it, with various anonymous documents attributed to Clement *(2 Clement, Apostolic Constitutions and Canons,* and the *Martyrdom of Clement).* Some of the later literature became more popular than Clement's authentic first letter, which was not to regain some of its earlier popularity until the 1600s. In 1628, the patriarch of Constantinople gave Codex Alexandrinus to King Charles I of England. This fifth-century manuscript of the Bible contained the text of *1 Clement* and *2 Clement* and offered the only witness to the text of *1 Clement* until the nineteenth century.

Value for the Study of Early Christianity

First Clement was widely read in the early period, almost gaining for itself a place in the canon. Yet the modern age knew it only through one defective manuscript until 1873 when a complete eleventh-century manuscript was discovered.[12] For more than a century now, *1 Clement* has been an important source for the study of at least three critical issues regarding the early church: (a) the development of early church office and succession;[13] (b) the early role of the Roman church in the affairs of distant assemblies (an issue in the ultimate rise of the papacy); and (c) early liturgical developments. The document provides the earliest reference to Peter's residence in Rome (5.5) and to Paul's journey to Spain (5.7).

First Clement is also of use in tracing some Hellenistic influences on the early church. In particular, sections show influence from Stoic philosophy, though it

---

[10]Compare *Eph.* 4:4–6 and *1 Clem.* 46.6; *Eph.* 1:18 and *1 Clem.* 59.3.

[11]Eusebius recognized Clement's extensive use of *Hebrews* (from echoes to verbatim quotations), and on the basis of this use, argued that *Hebrews* must then have been early (*Eccl. hist.* 3.38). Major parallels between *1 Clement* and *Hebrews* will be listed in the notes following.

[12]This paucity of manuscripts for *1 Clement* and other early noncanonical Christian writings stands in sharp contrast to the rich manuscript tradition for those writings that were incorporated into the Christian canon.

[13]A passage in *1 Clement* is appealed to in support of the doctrine of "apostolic succession," in which the power of the apostles in transferred, generation by generation, to new leaders called bishops.

appears superficial. Such influence, significant as it was, shows just how much more massive was the influence of Jewish scriptures and early Christian writings, which color almost all of the text in a way that no other influence does. *First Clement* demonstrates the substantial debt of early Christianity to the Jewish Bible.

For Further Reading

The Apostolic Fathers. 2 vols. Translated by Kirsopp Lake. Cambridge, Mass.: Harvard University Press/London: Heinemann, 1976–1985.

Grant. R. M., and H. H. Graham. *First and Second Clement: A New Translation and Commentary*. Vol. 2 in *The Apostolic Fathers*. New York: Nelson, 1964–1968.

Jeffers, James S. *Conflict at Rome: Social Order and Hierarchy in Early Christianity*. Minneapolis: Fortress, 1991.

Lightfoot, J. B. S. *Clement of Rome*. 2 vols. Part I of *The Apostolic Fathers*. 2d ed. London: Macmillan, 1890. Repr., Grand Rapids: Baker, 1999.

Maier, Harry O. *The Social Setting of the Ministry as Reflected in the Writings of Hermas, Clement, and Ignatius*. Waterloo, Ont.: Wilfrid Laurier University Press, 1991.

THE LETTER OF THE ROMANS TO THE CORINTHIANS
commonly known as
FIRST CLEMENT

The Address

The church of God that sojourns in Rome to the church of God that sojourns[a] in Corinth, to those who are called and sanctified by the will of God through our Lord Jesus Christ. May grace and peace from almighty God through Jesus Christ be yours in abundance.

Corinth's History of Humility and Harmony

1 Because of the sudden and repeated misfortunes and reverses that have happened to us, brothers,[b] we acknowledge that we have been somewhat slow in giving attention to the matters in dispute among you, dear friends, especially the detestable and unholy schism, so alien and strange to those chosen by God, which a few reckless and arrogant persons have kindled to such a pitch of insanity that your good name, once so renowned and loved by all, has been greatly reviled. [2]For has anyone ever visited you who did not approve your most excellent and steadfast faith? Who did not admire your sober and magnanimous Christian piety? Who did not proclaim the magnificent character of your hospitality? Who did not congratulate you on your complete and sound knowledge? [3]For you did everything without partiality, and you lived in accordance with the laws of God, submitting yourselves to your leaders and giving to the older men among you the honor due them. You instructed the young to think temperate and proper thoughts; you charged the women to perform all their duties with a blameless, reverent,[c]

a Or *lives as an exile* or *lives as an alien*
b Or possibly *brothers and sisters,* as in the NRSV rendering

c Some ancient authorities omit *reverent*

TRANSLATION by Michael W. Holmes after the earlier translation of J. B. Lightfoot and J. R. Harmer. TRANSLATION NOTES by Michael W. Holmes. Reprinted, with revisions, from *The Apostolic Fathers: Greek Texts and English Translations,* edited and revised by Michael W. Holmes (Grand Rapids: Baker Books, 1999). © 1992, 1999, 2003 by Michael W. Holmes. Used by permission of Baker Book House. All rights reserved. CONTENT NOTES are by the editors, with acknowledgment to Michael W. Holmes for his observations regarding a number of texts.

Address sojourns "Lives as an alien." Various early Christian writers spoke of the alien and transient character of a Christian's life in the world (*Eph.* 2:19; *1 Pet.* 1:1; 17; 2:11). The word was often used in Greco-Roman society to indicate the status of resident aliens—in our terms, landed immigrants, or holders of green cards (*Luke* 24:18; *Acts* 7:6; 29; 13:17; *Heb.* 11:9). The same idea is expressed by another synonym at *1 Clem.* 1.2; *Heb.* 11:13; *1 Pet.* 1:1; 2:11. *called and sanctified* These are Pauline descriptions (*Rom.* 1:7; *1 Cor.* 1:2). *grace and peace* This is the most common greeting in the letters of our collection. Most of the Paulines, the two Petrine letters, and the *Revelation* use this form. **1.1** *misfortunes and reverses* This probably refers to persecution, but the specific persecution is a matter of dispute (see introduction to *1 Clement*). *brothers* Gk *adelphoi.* Unlike Paul, this writer may in fact be addressing the *brothers* rather than the community. **1.2** *piety* This positive description stands in sharp contrast to the image of Corinthian moral lapses reflected in Paul's correspondence and to the reputation Corinth had in the ancient world as a city without customary moral restraints. It is difficult to determine whether such praise for a church earlier castigated by Paul requires that *1 Clement* be written long after the church's early moral lapses. Regardless of how much its behavior may have improved, the circulation and popularity of Paul's letters helped tag the Corinthian church with a reputation for impiety. *knowledge* Gk *gnōsis.* Paul deals with knowledge in his correspondence with Corinth. It is not possible to determine whether Clement mentioned *knowledge* simply because he knew it to be a concern in the letters of Paul, whether the Corinthian church was, in fact, widely known for *perfect and secure knowledge,* or whether Clement was merely being polite. **1.3** *without partiality* In Paul's correspondence with the community, partisanship was perhaps the central problem of the young community (*1 Cor.* 1:10–13; 3:5–9). *lived in accordance with the laws of God* This would not have been a phrase that came readily to mind as the best description of the Corinthian church, from the portrait found in the Pauline letters. There Christian freedom without regard to any "law of God" characterized at least one prominent element in the church (*1 Cor.* 10). *the older men among you* Or "presbyters," a formal office in the church (47.8; 54.6; 57.1). See notes to *Titus* 2:2; *1 Tim.* 5:1. Often instructions to several groups are strung together, forming brief household codes (see note to *1 Tim.* 1:9). The instructions to women are the most detailed in this passage, and a similar emphasis is found in 21.6–7. But concern about the behavior of women is not particularly featured in the letter and probably does not enlighten us about the crisis in Corinth.

and pure conscience, cherishing their own husbands, as is right; and you taught them to abide by the rule of obedience, and to manage the affairs of their household with dignity and all discretion.

2Moreover, you were all humble and free from arrogance, submitting rather than demanding submission, "more glad to give than to receive," and content with the provisions that God[d] supplies. And giving heed to his words, you stored them up diligently in your hearts, and kept his sufferings before your eyes. 2Thus a profound and rich peace was given to all, together with an insatiable desire to do good, and an abundant outpouring of the Holy Spirit fell upon everyone as well. 3Being full of holy counsel, with excellent zeal and a devout confidence you stretched out your hands to almighty God, imploring him to be merciful if you had inadvertantly committed any sin. 4You struggled day and night on behalf of all the brotherhood, that through fear[e] and conscientiousness the number of his elect might be saved. 5You were sincere and innocent and free from malice one towards another. 6Every faction and every schism was abominable to you. You mourned for the transgressions of your neighbors: you considered their shortcomings to be your own. 7You never once regretted doing good, but were "ready for every good work." 8Being adorned with a virtuous and honorable manner of life, you performed all your duties in the fear of him. The commandments and the ordinances of the Lord were "written on the tablets of your hearts."

Corinth's Loss of Humility and Harmony

3All glory and growth were given to you, and then that which is written was fulfilled: "My beloved ate and drank and was enlarged and grew fat and kicked." 2From this came jealousy and envy, strife and sedition, persecution and anarchy, war and captivity. 3So people were stirred up: "those without honor against the honored," those of no repute against the

highly reputed, the foolish against the wise, "the young against the elders." 4For this reason "righteousness" and peace "stand at a distance," while each one has abandoned the fear of God and become nearly blind with respect to faith in him, neither walking according to the laws of his commandments nor living in accordance with his duty towards Christ. Instead, each follows the lusts of his evil heart, inasmuch as they have assumed that attitude of unrighteous and ungodly jealousy through which, in fact, "death entered into the world."

Ancient Examples of Jealousy

4For thus it is written: "And it came to pass after certain days that Cain offered from the fruits of the earth a sacrifice to God, and Abel also offered a sacrifice from the firstborn of the sheep and from their fat. 2And God looked with favor upon Abel and upon his gifts, but to Cain and his sacrifices he gave no heed. 3And Cain was greatly distressed and his face was downcast. 4And God said to Cain, 'Why are you so distressed and why is your face downcast? If you have offered correctly but not divided correctly, did you not sin? 5Be quiet; he shall turn to you, and you shall rule over him.' 6And Cain said to Abel his brother, 'Let us go out to the field.' And it came to pass, while they were in the field, that Cain rose up against Abel his brother and killed him." 7You see, brothers, jealousy and envy brought about a brother's murder. 8Because of jealousy our father Jacob ran away from the presence of Esau his brother. 9Jealousy caused Joseph to be persecuted nearly to death, and to be sold into slavery. 10Jealousy compelled Moses to flee from the presence of Pharaoh, king of Egypt, when he was asked by his own countryman, "Who made you a judge or a ruler over us? Do you want to kill me, just as you killed the Egyptian yesterday?" 11Because of jealousy Aaron and Miriam were excluded from the camp. 12Jealousy brought Dathan and Abiram down alive into Hades, because they revolted against Moses, the servant of God. 13Because of jealousy David not only was envied

d Most ancient authorities read Christ
e Some ancient authorities read compassion

2.1 more glad to give than to receive In Acts 20:35, this is quoted as a saying of Jesus, but we have no other text in which this statement is attributed to Jesus. **2.4 brotherhood** 1 Pet. 2:7; 5:9. **fear and conscientiousness** The text is corrupt at this point. Some manuscripts read "compassion" (eleous); one reads "fear" (deous). Some editors emend conscientiousness (syneidēseōs) to read "compassion" (synaistheseōs). **2.6** Possibly a reference to the problems reflected in 1 Corinthians 5. **2.7** Titus 3:1. **2.8** Prov. 7:3. **3.1** Deut. 32:15. **3.2–4** Stock polemical language. It tells us nothing about the opponents. **3.3 young against the elders** Isa. 3:5. The elders is translated from the Gk presbyteros, which could be translated "the old" or "presbyter." Rather than a mere description of age, a specific office is most likely intended here, since the removal of elders from office is the main focus of the letter. **3.4** Wis. 2:24; Isa. 59:14. **4.1–13** In this section the author offers seven biblical illustrations to support his arguments for proper order and his censure of schism. The story of Cain and Abel is from Gen. 4:3–8. **4.4** The meaning is a matter of debate among scholars. Even the Hebrew text, which is not closely followed here, is unintelligible. First Clement's use of Jewish scripture shows the influence of the LXX, the version that Gentiles and Gk-speaking Jews might be expected to use. **4.8** Gen. 27:41–28:6. **4.9** Gen. 37:2–28. **4.10** Exod. 2:14. **4.11** Numbers 12. **4.12** Numbers 16. **4.13** 1 Samuel 18.

by the Philistines but also was persecuted by Saul, king of Israel.*f*

Recent Examples of Jealousy

5 But to pass from the examples of ancient times, let us come to those champions who lived nearest to our time. Let us set before us the noble examples that belong to our own generation. ²Because of jealousy and envy the greatest and most righteous pillars were persecuted and fought to the death. ³Let us set before our eyes the good apostles. ⁴There was Peter, who, because of unrighteous jealousy, endured not one nor two but many trials, and thus having given his testimony went to his appointed place of glory. ⁵Because of jealousy and strife Paul by his example pointed out the way to the prize for patient endurance. ⁶After he had been seven times in chains, had been driven into exile, had been stoned, and had preached in the East and in the West, he won the genuine glory for his faith, ⁷having taught righteousness to the whole world and having reached the farthest limits of the West. Finally, when he had given his testimony before the rulers,

f One ancient authority omits *king of Israel*

he thus departed from the world and went to the holy place, having become an outstanding example of patient endurance.

6 To these men who lived holy lives there was joined a vast multitude of the elect who, having suffered many torments and tortures because of jealousy, set an illustrious example among us. ²Because of jealousy women were persecuted as Danaids and Dircae, suffering in this way terrible and unholy tortures, but they safely reached the goal in the race of faith and received a noble reward, their physical weakness notwithstanding. ³Jealousy has estranged wives from their husbands and annulled the saying of our father Adam, "This is now bone of my bones and flesh of my flesh." ⁴Jealousy and strife have overthrown great cities and uprooted great nations.

Call to Repent

7 We write these things, dear friends, not only to admonish you but also to remind ourselves. For we are in the same arena, and the same contest awaits us. ²Therefore let us abandon empty and futile thoughts, and let us conform to the glorious and holy rule of our tradition; ³indeed, let us note what is good and

5.1 those champions Gk *athlētas*. Early Christian writers frequently employed popular images of the athlete to describe their own struggles and victories (*2 Tim.* 2:5; Ign. *Pol.* 1.3; 2.3; 3.2; *4 Macc.* 6:10), and Philo describes the Essenes as athletes of virtue (*That Every Good Person Is Free*). Clement may have had in mind the actual persecution of Christians in the arena. In 7.1, he uses the words "arena" and "struggle" or "contest" together. The apostles (Peter and Paul are named) are offered as champions *of our own generation.* Clement could still speak in the 90s of Peter and Paul being of his own generation, given a context in which all other persons mentioned are from the ancient past. **5.2 pillars** The term is used by Paul for Peter and other church leaders (*Gal.* 2:9) although there is a negative overtone in his use. **5.4 Peter** Although many traditions about Peter developed in the 2d century, little information is found in the 1st-century literature. Nevertheless it shows an active and influential individual. (See introduction to LETTERS ASSOCIATED WITH PETER.) *First Clement* supplies no substantial information about Peter even though Clement wrote from Rome, where early tradition reports that Peter was martyred. **testimony** Gk *martyrēsas.* The usual meaning of this root is "testimony" or "witness," but early Christian writers shaped this word to specify those who gave the ultimate witness, with their life—what we call a martyr. In most cases in the early Christian literature, the sense of "martyr" is not intended (but see *Acts* 22:20; *1 Tim.* 6:13; *Rev.* 2:13). **5.5–7** From Paul's own accounts, we learn that he had been jailed often enough to raise the issue as a boast when confronted by those who wanted to discredit his efforts (*2 Cor.* 11:23). What is surprising about Paul's comment that he had "far more imprisonments" than his competitors is that the remark was made before any of the imprisonments that we know about from *Acts'* accounts of his ministry (except for a few hours' stay in a jail at Philippi). According to the accounts in *Acts,* Paul was jailed two other times: at Caesarea while awaiting trial, and then in Rome while awaiting his hearing before the emperor. Some scholars have argued for an Ephesian imprisonment also. In any case, *Clement's* reference to seven imprisonments *(in chains)* is mysterious. **5.6 exile** Paul regularly fled from cities in which he had preached; Damascus, Philippi, and Thessalonica are mentioned in his letters. Whether this is all that *Clement* meant is impossible to determine. We know of no formal exile. **stoned** Paul claims one stoning (*2 Cor.* 11:25). This is perhaps the one recounted by the author of *Acts* (14:19). **5.7 of the West** One tradition has Paul released from his first Roman imprisonment (recorded at the end of *Acts*), after which he traveled to Spain, the extreme western area of the empire. Such a tradition may be a legendary development from Paul's comment in *Rom.* 15:24 about his plans; there is no compelling evidence that he was able to carry out that intention. **testimony before the rulers** According to *Acts,* Paul appealed his case to Caesar (*Acts* 25:11; 28:19). **6.2 Danaids and Dircae** The persecution suffered by Christian women is communicated obliquely by reference to these women of Greek mythology. The Danaids were given as prizes to men who competed for them. Dirce was tied to the horns of a bull and so was killed. Lightfoot, who thinks that all the manuscripts are corrupt at this point, provides the reading "women, tender maidens, even slave girls, were persecuted." **physical weakness** 1 Pet. 3:7. **6.3** Gen. 2:23. **6.4** Stories of the fall of great cities and nations were the stuff of legend and reality in the ancient world—Troy, Carthage, and Jerusalem being but three examples. Nineveh is presented in the next section as an example of a city saved by repentance (7.7). **6.5** Wis. 12:10.

what is pleasing and what is acceptable in the sight of the one who made us. ⁴Let us fix our eyes on the blood of Christ and understand how precious it is to his Father, because, being poured out for our salvation, it won for the whole world the grace of repentance. ⁵Let us review all the generations in turn, and learn that from generation to generation the Master has given an opportunity for repentance to those who desire to turn to him. ⁶Noah preached repentance, and those who obeyed were saved. ⁷Jonah preached destruction to the people of Nineveh; but they, repenting of their sins, made atonement to God by their prayers and received salvation, even though they were alienated from God.

8 The ministers of the grace of God spoke about repentance through the Holy Spirit; ²indeed, the Master of the universe himself spoke about repentance with an oath: "For as I live, says the Lord, I do not desire the death of the sinner so much as his repentance." He also added this merciful declaration: ³"Repent, O house of Israel, of your iniquity; say to the sons of my people: Though your sins reach from the earth to heaven, and though they be redder than scarlet and blacker than sackcloth, yet if you turn to me with your whole heart and say 'Father,' I will listen to you as a holy people." ⁴And in another place he says this: "Wash and be clean; remove the wickedness from your souls out of my sight. Put an end to your wickedness; learn to do good; seek out justice; deliver the one who is wronged; give judgment on behalf of the orphan, and grant justice to the widow. And come, let us reason together, he says:*g* even though your sins be as crimson, I will make them white as snow; and though they be as scarlet, I will make them white as wool. And if you are willing and listen to me, you shall eat the good things of the earth; but if you are not willing and do not listen to me, a sword shall devour you, for the mouth of the Lord has spoken these things." ⁵Seeing, then, that he desires all his be-

loved to participate in repentance, he confirmed it by an act of his almighty will.

Ancient Examples of Proper Behavior

9 Therefore let us be obedient to his magnificent and glorious will, and presenting ourselves as suppliants of his mercy and goodness, let us fall down before him and return to his compassions, laying aside the fruitless toil and the strife and the jealousy that leads to death. ²Let us fix our eyes on those who perfectly served his magnificent glory. ³Let us take Enoch, for example, who was found righteous in obedience and so was taken up and did not experience death. ⁴Noah, being found faithful, proclaimed a second birth to the world by his ministry, and through him the Master saved the living creatures that entered into the ark in harmony.

10 Abraham, who was called "the friend," was found faithful in that he became obedient to the words of God. ²He obediently went forth from his country, from his people, and from his father's house, leaving a small country, a weak people, and an insignificant house in order that he might inherit the promises of God. ³For he says to him: "Go forth from your country and from your people and from your father's house to the land that I will show you, and I will make you into a great nation, and I will bless you and will make your name great, and you will be blessed. And I will bless those who bless you, and I will curse those who curse you, and in you all the tribes of the earth will be blessed." ⁴And again, when he separated from Lot, God said to him: "Lift up your eyes, and look from the place where you now are to the north and the south and the sunrise and the sea; for all the land that you see I will give to you and your seed forever. ⁵Furthermore, I will make your seed like the dust of the earth. If any one can count the dust of the earth, then your seed will be counted." ⁶And again he says: "God led Abraham forth and said to him, 'Look up to heaven and count the stars, if you are able to count them; so shall your seed be!' And Abraham

---

g Some ancient authorities read *the Lord says*

7.6 *Gen.* 6–9. **7.7–9.1** At this point, *Clement,* offering a word of hope to those who have rebelled, points to cases in which God forgave those who had been rebellious. **7.7** The short book of *Jonah* tells the story, which provided the most popular motifs in pre-Constantinian Christian art. **8.1** *ministers* Gk *leitourgoi.* Of the thirty-two occurrences of this term or a cognate in our literature, half are in *1 Clement,* and six others are in *Hebrews,* the document that *1 Clement* reflects most closely. **8.2–3** *Ezek.* 33:11. The source of the last phrase is not clear. It may be a loose paraphrase. **8.4** *Isa.* 1:16–20. **9.2** *Clement* now offers a long list of examples of obedience and faithfulness to be used against the schismatics in Corinth, who have not been obedient or faithful in the positions that God originally assigned to them. The author of *Hebrews,* with whom Clement has much in common, has a similar roll call of the faithful (*Heb.* 11:4–40), but for a different purpose. It is likely that Clement is dependent on *Hebrews* here. **9.3** *Gen.* 5:21–24; *Heb.* 11:5; *Barn.* 4.3. **9.4** *entered into the ark in harmony* There is no mention of harmony in the story of Noah, unless Clement has in mind that the animals entered the ark in pairs (*Gen.* 6:13–22). Clement makes the point here nonetheless; his whole purpose in writing this long letter is to restore concord under the properly appointed leaders. *Heb.* 11:7; *2 Pet.* 2:5. **10.1** *1 Clem.* 17.2; *2 Chr.* 20:7; *Isa.* 41:8; *Jas.* 2:23. **10.3** *Gen.* 12:1–3. **10.4** *sea* The Mediterranean Sea, forming the western boundary of Palestine. **10.4–5** *Gen.* 13:14–16. **10.6** *Gen.* 15:5–6; *Rom.* 4:3.

believed God, and it was reckoned to him as righteousness." 7Because of his faith and hospitality a son was given to him in his old age, and for the sake of obedience he offered him as a sacrifice to God on one of the mountains that he showed him.

11 Because of his hospitality and godliness Lot was saved from Sodom when the entire region was judged by fire and brimstone. In this way the Master clearly demonstrated that he does not forsake those who hope in him but destines to punishment and torment those who turn aside. 2Of this his wife was destined to be a sign, for after leaving with him she changed her mind and no longer agreed, and as a result she became a pillar of salt to this day, that it might be known to all that those who are double-minded and those who question the power of God fall under judgment and become a warning to all generations.

12 Because of her faith and hospitality Rahab the harlot was saved. 2For when the spies were sent to Jericho by Joshua the son of Nun, the king of the land realized that they had come to spy out his country, and so he sent out men to capture them, intending to put them to death as soon as they were caught. 3The hospitable Rahab, however, took them in and hid them in an upstairs room under some flax stalks. 4And when the king's men arrived and said, "The men spying on our land came to you; bring them out, for so the king commands," she answered, "Yes, the men whom you seek came to me, but they left immediately and are already on their way," and she pointed them in the opposite direction. 5Then she said to the men: "I am absolutely convinced that the Lord your God is handing this country over to you, for fear and terror of you have fallen upon all the inhabitants. Therefore, when you do take it, save me and my father's house." 6And they said to her: "It shall be exactly as you have said. Therefore, when you learn that we are coming, gather together all your family under your roof, and they will be saved. But anybody found outside the house will perish." 7And in addition they gave her a sign, that she should hang from her house something scarlet—making it clear that through the blood of the Lord redemption will come to all who believe and hope in God. 8You see, dear friends, not only faith but prophecy is found in this woman.

Call to Proper Behavior

13 Let us therefore be humble, brothers, laying aside all arrogance and conceit and foolishness and anger, and let us do what is written. For the Holy Spirit says: "Let not the wise man boast about his wisdom, nor the strong about his strength, nor the rich about his wealth; but let the one who boasts boast in the Lord, that he may seek him out, and do justice and righteousness." Most of all, let us remember the words of the Lord Jesus, which he spoke as he taught gentleness and patience. 2For he said this: "Show mercy, that you may receive mercy; forgive, that you may be forgiven. As you do, so shall it be done to you. As you give, so shall it be given to you. As you judge, so shall you be judged. As you show kindness, so shall kindness be shown to you. With the measure you use it will be measured to you." 3With this commandment and these precepts let us strengthen ourselves, that we may humbly walk in obedience to his holy words. For the holy word says, 4"Upon whom shall I look, except upon the one who is gentle and quiet and who trembles at my words?"

14 Therefore it is right and holy, brothers, that we should be obedient to God rather than follow those who in arrogance and unruliness have set themselves up as leaders in abominable jealousy. 2For we shall bring upon ourselves no ordinary harm, but rather great danger, if we recklessly surrender ourselves to the purposes of people who launch out into strife and dissension in order to alienate us from what is right. 3Let us be kind to them,*h* in accordance with the compassion and tenderness of the one who made us. 4For it is written: "The kind shall inhabit the land, and the innocent shall be left on it; but those who transgress shall be utterly destroyed from it." 5And again he says: "I saw the ungodly lifted up on high and exalted as the cedars of Lebanon. But I passed by, and behold, he was no more; I searched for his place, but I could not find it. Guard innocence and observe righteousness, for there is a remnant for the peaceful person."

---

h Some ancient authorities read *to one another*

10.7 *Gen.* 22:9–14; *Heb.* 11:7. The story of the sacrifice of Isaac was a popular one in early Christian art. Isaac was not actually sacrificed; a substitute was found. But this did not take away from the story as a compelling example of obedience. **11.1** Hospitality is a frequent theme in the literature of the early church. See *2 John, 3 John,* and the *Didache.* There are four references to hospitality in *1 Clement* 10–12 alone. Perhaps the schism involved some threat to hospitality. The story of Lot's hospitality is from *Genesis* 19; *2 Pet.* 2:6–7. **11.2 double-minded** *Jas.* 1:8; 4:8; *Did.* 4.4; *Barn.*19.5. Clement uses this word and a cognate at 23.2–3. **12.1–8** *Joshua* 2; *Heb.* 11:31; *Jas.* 2:25. **13.1** *1 Cor.* 1:31; *2 Cor.* 10:17; influenced by *Jer.* 9:23–24 and *1 Sam.* 2:10. **13.2** Citations by Clement are often very loose. Here it is difficult to determine whether Clement was quoting a written gospel (*Matt.* 5:7; 6:14; 7:1–2; *Luke* 6:31, 36–38) or oral tradition. **13.4** *Isa.* 66:2. **14.1** There is no clue in the letter itself showing how these *leaders* gained power, but the energy that Clement expended in addressing the issue shows that the rebels were to some extent successful. **14.4** *Prov.* 2:21–22; *Ps.* 37:9, 38 (LXX 36:9, 38). **14.5** *Ps.* 37:35–37 (LXX 36:35–37). **remnant** Posterity or descendents.

The Necessity of Sincere Humility

15 Therefore let us unite with those who devoutly practice peace, and not with those who hypocritically wish for peace. [2]For somewhere he says, "This people honors me with their lips, but their heart is far from me"; [3]and again, "They blessed with their mouth, but they cursed with their heart." [4]And again he says, "They loved him with their mouth, but with their tongue they lied to him; their heart was not right with him, nor were they faithful to his covenant." [5]Therefore, "let the deceitful lips that speak evil against the righteous be struck dumb." And again: "May the Lord utterly destroy all the deceitful lips, the boastful tongue, and those who say, 'Let us praise[i] our tongue; our lips are our own. Who is lord over us?' [6]Because of the misery of the needy and because of the groaning of the poor I will now arise, says the Lord. I will place him in safety; [7]I will deal boldly with him."

Christ As an Example of Humility

16 For Christ is with those who are humble, not with those who exalt themselves over his flock. [2]The majestic[j] scepter of God, our Lord Christ Jesus,[k] did not come with the pomp of arrogance or pride (though he could have done so), but in humility, just as the Holy Spirit spoke concerning him. [3]For he says: "Lord, who believed our report? And to whom was the arm of the Lord revealed? In his presence we announced that he was like a child, like a root in thirsty ground. He has no attractiveness or glory. We saw him, and he had no attractiveness or beauty; instead his 'attractiveness' was despised, inferior to that of humans. He was a man of stripes and of toil, knowing how to endure weakness, for his face is turned away; he was dishonored and not blessed. [4]This is the one who bears our sins and suffers pain for our sakes, and we regarded him as subject to toil and stripes and af-

fliction. [5]But he was wounded because of our sins and has been afflicted because of our transgressions. The chastisement that resulted in our peace fell upon him; by his wounds we were healed. [6]We all went astray like sheep, each one went astray in his own way; [7]and the Lord delivered him up for our sins. And he does not open his mouth, because he is afflicted; like a sheep he was led to slaughter, and as a lamb before his shearer is dumb, so he does not open his mouth. In his humiliation justice was denied him. [8]Who shall tell about his descendents? For his life was taken away from the earth. [9]For the transgressions of my people he came to his death. [10]But I will sacrifice the wicked for his burial, and the rich for his death; for he committed no sin, and no deceit was found in his mouth. And the Lord desires to cleanse him of his stripes. [11]If you make an offering for sin, your soul will see a long-lived posterity. [12]And the Lord desires to take away the torment of his soul, to show him light and to form him with understanding, to justify a Just One who is a good servant to many. And he will bear their sins. [13]Therefore he will inherit many, and will share the spoils of the strong, because his soul was delivered to death and he was reckoned as one of the transgressors; [14]and he bore the sins of many, and because of their sins he was delivered up." [15]And again he himself says: "But I am a worm and not a man, a reproach among men and an object of contempt to the people. [16]All those who saw me mocked me; 'they spoke with their lips'; they shook their heads, saying, 'He hoped in the Lord; let him deliver him, let him save him, because he takes pleasure in him.'" [17]You see, dear friends, the kind of pattern that has been given to us; for if the Lord so humbled himself, what should we do, who through him have come under the yoke of his grace?

Examples of Humility in the Hebrew Bible

17 Let us be imitators also of those who went about "in goatskins and sheepskins," preaching the coming of Christ. We mean Elijah and Elisha, and likewise Ezekiel, the prophets, and alongside them those men of renown as well. [2]Abraham was greatly

---

i Or *magnify*
j Some ancient authorities omit *majestic*
k Some ancient authorities read *the Lord Jesus Christ*

15.1 The issue is perhaps not clear-cut. Both parties wanted peace. Clement dismisses this concern on the part of his opponents by charging that they desire peace *hypocritically.* This may be little more than the language of polemics on Clement's part. **15.2** *Isa.* 29:13; *Mark* 7:6. **15.3** *Ps.* 62:4 (LXX 61:5). **15.4** *Ps.* 78:36–37 (LXX 77:36–37). **15.5** *Ps.* 31:18 (LXX 30:19); *Ps.* 12:4–6 (LXX 11:3–5). **16.1** *over his flock* 1 *Clem.* 44.5; 54.6; 57.3. The word "flock" is used by many early Christian writers for the church (*Luke* 12:32; *John* 10:16; *Acts* 20:28–29; *1 Pet.* 5:2–3; Ign. *Phld.* 2.3; Ign. *Rom.* 9.1). Israel is called God's flock and God is called Israel's shepherd (*Isa.* 40:11; 63:11; *Jer.* 13:17; 23:2–3; *Ezek.* 34:17, 22; *Mic.* 5:4; *Zech.* 9:16; 10:3; 11:4). **16.3–14** *Isa.* 53:1–12. This was a key passage in Jewish scripture to which Christians appealed. **16.15–16** *Ps.* 22:6–8 (LXX 21:7–9). **16.17** Many authors use the suffering and humility of Jesus as the primary example that Christians should emulate (*Rom.* 8:17; *1 Pet.* 2:21; see note to Ign. *Eph.* 1.1). **17.1** *Heb.* 11:37. Early Christians believed that the Hebrew prophets spoke about Christ, and they concentrated on Jewish scriptures where this kind of connection could be made. Apologists in the 2d century appealed to this material in their defense against Greek critics of Christianity. *Elijah and Elisha* 1 *Kings* 17–22; *2 Kings* 1–13. Little else is said of these men outside of that record except for a brief comment that Elijah would return

renowned and was called the friend of God; yet when he looked intently at the glory of God, he said humbly, "I am only dust and ashes." ³Moreover, concerning Job it is thus written: "And Job was righteous and blameless, one who was true and who honored God and avoided all evil." ⁴Yet he accuses himself, saying: "No one is clean from stain; no, not even if his life lasts but for a day." ⁵Moses was called "faithful in all his house," and through his ministry God judged Egypt with their plagues and the torments. But even he, though greatly glorified, did not boast but said, when an oracle was given to him at the bush, "Who am I, that you should send me? I have a feeble voice and a slow tongue." ⁶And again he says, "I am only steam from a pot."

18 And what shall we say about the illustrious David, to whom God said: "I have found a man after my own heart, David the son of Jesse; I have anointed him with eternal mercy." ²Yet he too says to God: "Have mercy upon me, O God, according to your great mercy; and according to the abundance of your compassion, blot out my iniquity. ³Wash me thoroughly from my transgression, and cleanse me from my sin. For I acknowledge my transgression, and my sin is always before me. ⁴Against you only have I sinned, and I have done evil in your sight, that you may be justified in your words, and may conquer when you contend. ⁵For in transgressions I was brought forth, and in sins my mother conceived me. ⁶For you have loved truth; the unseen and hidden things of your wisdom you have shown to me. ⁷You will sprinkle me with hyssop, and I will be cleansed; you will wash me, and I will become whiter than snow. ⁸You will make me hear joy and gladness; the bones that have been humbled will rejoice. ⁹Hide your face from my sins, and blot out all my transgressions. ¹⁰Create a clean heart within me, O God, and renew a right spirit within me. ¹¹Do not cast me away from your presence, and do not take your Holy Spirit from me. ¹²Restore to me the joy of your salvation, and strengthen me with a guiding spirit. ¹³I will teach sinners your ways, and the godless will turn

back to you. ¹⁴Deliver me from bloodguiltiness, O God, the God of my salvation. ¹⁵My tongue will rejoice in your righteousness. Lord, you will open my mouth, and my lips will proclaim your praise. ¹⁶For if you had desired sacrifice, I would have given it; but in whole burnt offerings you will take no pleasure. ¹⁷The sacrifice for God is a broken spirit; a broken and humbled heart God will not despise."

Learning from the Many Examples

19 Accordingly, the humility and subordination of so many people of such great renown have, through their obedience, improved not only us but also the generations before us, and likewise those who have received his oracles in fear and truth. ²Seeing, then, that we have a share in many great and glorious deeds, let us hasten on to the goal of peace, which has been handed down to us from the beginning; let us fix our eyes upon the Father and Maker of the whole world and hold fast to his magnificent and excellent gifts and benefits of peace. ³Let us see him in our mind, and let us look with the eyes of the soul on his patient will. Let us note how free from anger he is towards all his creation.

Harmony in Nature

20 The heavens move at his direction and obey him in peace. ²Day and night complete the course assigned by him, neither hindering the other. ³The sun and the moon and the choirs of stars circle in harmony within the courses assigned to them, according to his direction, without any deviation at all. ⁴The earth, bearing fruit in the proper seasons in fulfillment of his will, brings forth food in full abundance for both men and beasts and all living things that are upon it without dissention and without altering anything he has decreed. ⁵Moreover, the incomprehensible depths of the abysses and the indescribable judgments*ˡ* of the underworld are con-

---

l Or punishments.

---

before the final judgment (*Mal.* 4:5). From this one comment Elijah became an important figure in apocalyptic thought; one text of the Pseudepigrapha bears his name (*Apocalypse of Elijah*). Little is done with Elijah's apocalyptic role outside the gospels (*Mark* 9:4–13; *Matt.* 11:14; *Luke* 1:17; *John* 1:21, 25). See note to *Jas.* 5:17. **17.2** *Friend of God* 1 *Clem.* 10.1. ***dust and ashes*** *Gen.* 18:27. **17.3** *Job* 1:1. **17.4** *Job* 14:4–5. **17.5** *faithful in all his house* *Heb.* 3:2; *Num.* 12:7. *slow tongue* *Exod.* 3:11; 4:10. **17.6** The source of this quotation is unknown. **18.1** *Ps.* 89:20 (LXX 88:21); *1 Sam.* 13:14; *Acts* 13:22. **18.2–17** Most of *Psalm* 51 (LXX 50) is quoted here. **19.2** *Heb.* 12:1. **20.1** After providing examples of past heroes who lived in humility and obedience to God's will, Clement turns to the ordered elements of the natural world: seasons, boundaries of the ocean, etc. The fundamental ideas here have a Stoic flavor (Cicero, *On the Nature of the Gods* 2.47–57; 98–104). *First Clement* frequently uses the term "demiurge" or a cognate to describe God as creator (20.6, 10, 11; 26.1; 33.2; 35.3; 38.3; 59.2). It occurs elsewhere in our literature only in *Heb.* 11:10, but in Hellenistic thought it is a common description of the Creator. **20.5** *judgments* Lake's translation discards the Gk text at this point because he thinks it makes no sense. He emends the text to read "realms" (Gk *klimata*) rather than *judgments (krimata)*. Lightfoot suggests removing the word altogether. Some modern editors emend it to "things" or "regions."

strained by the same ordinances. ⁶The basin of the boundless sea, gathered together by his creative action "into its reservoirs," does not flow beyond the barriers surrounding it; instead it behaves just as he ordered it. ⁷For he said: "Thus far shall you come, and your waves shall break within you." ⁸The ocean—impassable by humans—and the worlds beyond it are directed by the same ordinances of the Master. ⁹The seasons, spring and summer and autumn and winter, give way in succession, one to the other, in peace. ¹⁰The winds from the different quarters fulfill their ministry in the proper season without disturbance; the everflowing springs, created for enjoyment and health, give without fail their life-sustaining breasts to mankind. Even the smallest living things come together in harmony and peace. ¹¹All these things the great Creator and Master of the universe ordered to exist in peace and harmony, thus doing good to all things, but especially abundantly to us who have taken refuge in his compassionate mercies through our Lord Jesus Christ, ¹²to whom be the glory and the majesty for ever and ever. Amen.

Call to Good Behavior

21 Take care, dear friends, lest his many benefits turn into a judgment upon all of us,[m] as will happen if we fail to live worthily of him and to do harmoniously those things that are good and well-pleasing in his sight. ²For he says somewhere, "The Spirit of the Lord is a lamp searching the depths of the heart." ³Let us realize how near he is, and that nothing escapes him, either of our thoughts or of the plans that we make. ⁴It is right, therefore, that we should not be deserters from his will. ⁵Let us offend foolish and senseless people, who exalt themselves and boast in the arrogance of their words, rather than God. ⁶Let us fear the Lord Jesus Christ,[n] whose blood was given for us. Let us respect our leaders; let us honor our elders;[o] let us instruct our young with instruction that leads to the fear of God. Let us guide our women toward that which is good: ⁷let them reveal a disposition to purity worthy of admiration; let them exhibit a sincere desire to be gentle; let them demonstrate by their silence the moderation of their tongue; let them show their love, without partiality and in holiness, equally towards all those who fear God. ⁸Let our chil-

dren receive the instruction that is in Christ: let them learn how strong humility is before God, what pure love is able to accomplish before God, how the fear of him is good and great and saves all those who live in it in holiness with a pure mind. ⁹For he is the searcher of thoughts and desires; his breath is in us, and when he so desires, he will take it away.

22 Now faith in Christ confirms all these things, for he himself through the Holy Spirit thus calls us: "Come, my children, listen to me; I will teach you the fear of the Lord. ²Who is the man who desires life, who loves to see good days? ³Keep your tongue from evil, and your lips from speaking deceit. ⁴Turn aside from evil and do good. ⁵Seek peace and pursue it. ⁶The eyes of the Lord are upon the righteous, and his ears are turned to their prayers. But the face of the Lord is against those who do evil, to destroy any remembrance of them from the earth. ⁷The righteous cried out, and the Lord heard him, and delivered him from all his troubles. Many are the troubles of the righteous, but the Lord shall deliver him from them all."[p] ⁸Furthermore,[q] "Many are the afflictions of the sinner, but mercy will surround those who set their hope on the Lord."

23 The Father, who is merciful in all things, and ready to do good, has compassion on those who fear him, and gently and lovingly bestows his favors on those who draw near to him with singleness of mind. ²Therefore, let us not be double-minded, nor let our soul indulge in false ideas about his excellent and glorious gifts. ³Let this scripture be far from us where he says, "Wretched are the double-minded, those who doubt in their soul and say, 'We heard these things even in the days of our fathers, and look, we have grown old, and none of these things have happened to us.' ⁴You fools, compare yourselves to a tree, or take a vine: first it sheds its leaves, then a shoot comes, then a leaf, then a flower, and after these a sour grape, and then a full ripe bunch." Notice that in a brief time the fruit of the tree reaches maturity. ⁵Truly his purpose will be accomplished quickly and suddenly, just as the scripture also testifies: "He will come quickly and not delay; and the Lord will come suddenly into his temple, even the Holy One whom you expect."

---

m Some ancient witnesses omit *all [of]*
n Some ancient witnesses omit *Christ*
o Or *the aged*

p Some ancient authorities omit *Many are . . . them all*
q Some ancient authorities omit *Furthermore;* others read *And again*

20.6 *Gen.* 1:9. **20.7** *Job* 38:11. **21.2** *Prov.* 20:27. **21.6** *honor our elders* Age rather than office seems to be intended, since the leaders have already been dealt with before this comment. **21.7** On the silence of women, see note to *1 Tim.* 2:11–12. **22.1–7** *Ps.* 34:11–17, 19 (LXX 33:12–18, 20). **22.7** *Ps.* 34:19 (LXX 33:20). **22.8** *Ps.* 32:10 (LXX 31:10). **23.3–4** The source of this quotation is unknown; it also appears in *2 Clem.* 11.2–3. **23.5** LXX *Isa.* 13:22; *Mal.* 3:1.

Proof of Resurrection

24 Let us consider, dear friends, how the Master continually points out to us the coming resurrection of which he made the Lord Jesus Christ the firstfruit when he raised him from the dead. ²Let us observe, dear friends, the resurrection that regularly occurs. ³Day and night show us the resurrection: the night falls asleep, and day arises; the day departs, and night returns. ⁴Let us take the crops: how and in what manner does the sowing take place? ⁵"The sower went forth" and cast into the earth each of the seeds. These seeds, falling to the earth dry and bare, decay; but then out of their decay the majesty of the Master's providence raises them up, and from the one seed many grow and bear fruit.

25 Let us observe the remarkable sign that is seen in the regions of the East, that is, in the vicinity of Arabia. ²There is a bird that is named the phoenix. This bird, the only one of its species, lives for five hundred years. When the time of its dissolution and death arrives, it makes for itself a coffin-like nest of frankincense and myrrh and the other spices, into which, its time being completed, it enters and dies. ³But as the flesh decays, a certain worm is born, which is nourished by the juices of the dead bird and eventually grows wings. Then, when it has grown strong, it takes up that coffin-like nest containing the bones of its parent, and carrying them away, it makes its way from the country of Arabia to Egypt, to the city called Heliopolis. ⁴There, in broad daylight in the sight of all, it flies to the altar of the sun and deposits them there, and then it sets out on its return. ⁵The priests then examine the public records of the dates, and they find that it has come at the end of the five hundredth year.

26 How, then, can we consider it to be some great and marvelous thing, if the Creator of the universe shall bring about the resurrection of those who have served him in holiness, in the assurance born of a good faith, when he shows us—by a bird, no less—the magnificence of his promise? ²For he says somewhere: "And you will raise me up, and I will praise you"; and, "I lay down and slept; I rose up, for you are with me." ³And again Job says: "And you will raise this flesh of mine, which has endured all these things."

Nothing Escapes God's Notice

27 With this hope, therefore, let our souls be bound to the one who is faithful in his promises and righteous in his judgments. ²The one who commanded us not to lie all the more will not lie himself, for nothing is impossible with God, except to lie. ³Therefore let our faith in him be rekindled within us, and let us understand that all things are near to him. ⁴By his majestic word he established the universe, and by a word he can destroy it. ⁵"Who will say to him, 'What have you done?' Or who will resist the might of his strength?" He will do all things when he wills and as he wills, and none of those things decreed by him will fail. ⁶All things are in his sight, and nothing escapes his will, ⁷seeing that "the heavens declare the glory of God, and the skies proclaim the work of his hands. Day pours forth speech to day, and night proclaims knowledge to night; and there are neither words nor speeches, whose voices are not heard."

28 Since, therefore, all things are seen and heard, let us fear him and abandon the abominable lusts that spawn evil works, in order that we may be shielded by his mercy from the coming judgments. ²For where can any of us escape from his mighty hand? And what world will receive any of those who desert him? For the scripture[r] says somewhere: ³"Where shall I go, and where shall I be hidden from your presence? If I ascend to heaven, you are there; if I depart to the ends of the earth, there is your right hand; if I make my bed in the depths, there is your Spirit." ⁴Where, then, can one go, or where can one flee from the one who embraces the universe?

Good Behavior, Faith, and God's Favor

29 Let us, therefore, approach him in holiness of soul, lifting up to him pure and undefiled hands, loving our gentle and compassionate Father who made us his chosen portion. ²For thus it is written: "When

---

r Or *writing*

24.1 Over the next three paragraphs, Clement offers various proofs for the resurrection. **firstfruit** *1 Cor.* 15:20. **24.5** *Mark* 4:3; *Matt.* 13:3; *Luke* 8:5; *1 Cor.* 15:36. **25.1–5** The story of the phoenix was well known in antiquity (Herodotus, *Histories* 2.73; Pliny the Elder, *Natural History* 10.2). However, in *Ps.* 92:12 (LXX 91:13), the Gk *phoinix* means "palm tree." Some early Christians thought that the psalm referred to the bird. Clement does not cite that verse here. **25.3** *Heliopolis* A compound word meaning "city of the sun." **26.2** *And you will raise Ps.* 28:7 (LXX 27:7). *I laid me down Ps.* 3:5 (LXX 3:6); see *Ps.* 23:4 (LXX 22:4). **26.3** *Job* 19:26. **27.2** *Heb.* 6:18. **27.5** *Wis.* 12:12. **27.7** *Ps.* 19:1–3 (LXX 18:2–4). **28.2** *the Scripture* Lit. "the writing." This could refer to the third division of Jewish scripture, or to scripture as a whole. **28.3** The quotation is from *Ps.* 139:7–10 (LXX 138:7–10), part of the 3d division of the Hebrew Bible. **29.2** Some scholars think that this comment showed that the other nations were under God's inferior ministers (i.e., *angels*), while Israel was directly under the care of God. Although this could be the general sense, Clement seems to refer to the passage only in order to add one more example of approved divine order. The quotation is from *Deut.* 32:8–9.

the Most High divided the nations, when he dispersed the sons of Adam, he fixed the boundaries of the nations according to the number of the angels of God. His people Jacob became the Lord's portion, and Israel his inherited allotment." [3]And in another place he says: "Behold, the Lord takes for himself a nation out of the midst of the nations, as a man takes the firstfruits of his threshing floor; and the Holy of Holies will come forth from that nation."

30 Seeing then that we are the portion of the Holy One,[s] let us do all the things that pertain to holiness, forsaking slander, disgusting and impure embraces, drunkenness and rioting and detestable lusts, abominable adultery, detestable pride. [2]"For God," he says, "resists the proud, but gives grace to the humble." [3]Let us therefore join with those to whom grace is given by God. Let us clothe ourselves in concord, being humble and self-controlled, keeping ourselves far from all backbiting and slander, being justified by works and not by words. [4]For he says: "He who speaks much shall hear much in reply. Or does the talkative person think that he is righteous? [5]Blessed is the one born of woman who has a short life. Do not be overly talkative." [6]Let our praise be with God, and not from ourselves, for God hates those who praise themselves. [7]Let the testimony to our good deeds be given by others, as it was given to our fathers who were righteous. [8]Boldness and arrogance and audacity are for those who are cursed by God; but graciousness and humility and gentleness are with those who are blessed by God.

31 Let us therefore cling to his blessing, and let us investigate what are the ways of blessing. Let us study the records of the things that have happened from the beginning. [2]Why was our father Abraham blessed? Was it not because he attained righteousness and truth through faith? [3]With confidence, Isaac, knowing the future, went willingly to be sacrificed. [4]With humility Jacob departed from his land because of his brother and went to Laban and served him, and the twelve tribes of Israel were given to him.

32 If anyone will consider them sincerely one by one, he will understand the magnificence of the gifts that are given by him. [2]For from Jacob[t] come all the priests and Levites who minister at the altar of God; from him comes the Lord Jesus according to the flesh; from him come the kings and rulers and governors in the line of Judah; and his other tribes are held in no small honor, seeing that God promised that "your seed shall be as the stars of heaven." [3]All, therefore, were glorified and magnified, not through themselves or their own works or the righteous actions that they did, but through his will. [4]And so we, having been called through his will in Christ Jesus, are not justified through ourselves or through our own wisdom or understanding or piety, or works that we have done in holiness of heart, but through faith, by which the Almighty God has justified all who have existed from the beginning; to whom be the glory for ever and ever. Amen.

The Value of Good Behavior and Harmony

33 What then shall we do, brothers? Shall we idly abstain from doing good, and forsake love? May the Master never allow this to happen, at least to us; but let us hasten with earnestness and zeal to accomplish every good work. [2]For the Creator and Master of the universe himself rejoices in his works.

---

[s] Some ancient authorities read *a holy portion* or *holy portions* or *a portion of holy ones*

[t] Gk *him*

29.3 Clement's precise source is difficult to determine although elements of the following passages are reflected here: *Deut.* 4:34; 14:2; *Num.* 18:27; *2 Chr.* 31:14; *Ezek.* 48:12. **30.1** It is difficult to determine whether the list of vices was merely drawn from a stock of polemical charges or is an accurate description of the behavior of the opposition in Corinth. Such abuses would seem strange after the high praise the church received in the introduction, unless such praise was merely a matter of epistolary politeness. **30.2** *Jas.* 4:6; *1 Pet.* 5:5; *Prov.* 3:34. **30.4–5** *Job* 11:2–3. **31.2–3** *Gen.* 15:5; 22:17; 26:4. Clement employed the example of Abraham at some length in 10.1–7 and 17.2. **31.3** Isaac is named only here, but his sacrifice is mentioned in 10.7. A more extensive treatment of Isaac appears in *Heb.* 11:9–20. See also *Jas.* 2:21; *Barn.* 7.3. **31.4** According to the biblical tradition, Jacob fled from his angered brother, Esau, after cheating Esau of his birthright. In exile with his uncle Laban, Jacob married Laban's two daughters and took two concubines. Their twelve sons figure in the biblical tradition as the founders of the twelve tribes of Israel (*Gen.* 28–32). **32.1–2** *him* Lake argues that the ch. division for 31 should run to 32.1, with ch. 32 beginning at 32.2. The last *him* of 32.1 would refer to God, who gave the gifts; the first *him* of 32.2 would refer to Jacob, as the present translation does. **32.2** *Levites* These were the temple assistants, from one of the twelve tribes, according to the Hebrew Bible. *according to the flesh Rom.* 9:3. *governors in the line of Judah* David, a member of the tribe of Judah, established a dynasty that was to become idealized after the collapse of the monarchy and the loss of independence. *as the stars of heaven Gen.* 15:5; 22:17; 26:4. **33.1** *Rom.* 6:1. In 32.4, Clement follows Paul's argument that the Christian is made righteous by faith rather than by piety or other accomplishments. Then he faces, as Paul did, the potential radical consequences—people ceased doing good works. The arguments are slightly different. Clement puts forward God's activity in creation as grounds for Christian piety (33.2–7). The details of such creative activity are from *Genesis* 1. *every good work Titus* 3:1.

³For by his infinitely great might he established the heavens, and in his incomprehensible wisdom he set them in order. Likewise he separated the earth from the water surrounding it, and set it firmly upon the sure foundation of his own will; and the living creatures that walk upon it he called into existence by his decree. Having already created the sea and the living creatures in it, he fixed its boundaries by his own power. ⁴Above all, as the most excellent and by far the greatest work of his intelligence,ᵘ with his holy and faultless hands he formed humankind as a representation of his own image. ⁵For thus spoke God: "Let us make humankind in our image and likeness. And God created humankind; male and female he created them." ⁶So, having finished all these things, he praised them and blessed them and said, "Increase and multiply." ⁷We have seenᵛ that all the righteous have been adorned with good works. Indeed, the Lord himself, having adorned himself with goodʷ works, rejoiced. ⁸So, since we have this pattern, let us unhesitatingly conform ourselves to his will; let us with all our strength do the work of righteousness.

34The good worker receives the bread of his labor confidently, but the lazy and careless dares not look his employer in the face. ²It is, therefore, necessary that we should be zealous to do good, for all things come from him. ³For he forewarns us: "Behold, the Lord comes, and his reward is with him, to pay each one according to his work." ⁴He exhorts us, therefore, who believe in him with our whole heart, not to be idle or careless about any good work. ⁵Let our boasting and our confidence be in him; let us submit ourselves to his will; let us consider the whole host of his angels, how they stand by and serve his will. ⁶For scripture says: "Ten thousand times ten thousand stood by him, and thousands of thousands served him, and they cried out, 'Holy, holy, holy is the Lord of Hosts; all creation is full of his glory.'" ⁷Let us also, then, being gathered together in harmony with intentness of heart, cry out to him earnestly, with one mouth, that we may come to share in his great and glorious promises. ⁸For he says: "Eye has not seen and ear has not heard, and it has not entered into the human heart, what great things he has prepared for those who patiently wait for him."

35How blessed and marvelous are the gifts of God, dear friends! ²Life in immortality, splendor in righteousness, truth with boldness, faith with confidence, self-control with holiness! And all these things fall within our comprehension. ³What, then, are the things being prepared for those who patiently wait for him? The Creator and Father of the ages, the all-holy one himself, knows their number and their beauty. ⁴Let us therefore make every effort to be found in the number of those who patiently wait for him, so that we may share in his promised gifts. ⁵But how shall this be, dear friends?—if our mind is fixed on God through faith;ˣ—if we seek out those things that are well-pleasing and acceptable to him;—if we accomplish those things that are in harmony with his faultless will, and follow the way of truth, casting off from ourselves all unrighteousness and lawlessness,ʸ covetousness, strife, malice and deceit, gossip and slander, hatred of God, pride and arrogance, vanity and inhospitality. ⁶For those who do these things are hateful to God; and not only those who do them, but also those who approve of them. ⁷For scripture says: "But to the sinner God said, 'Why do you recite my statutes, and take My covenant upon your lips? ⁸You hated instruction and threw away my words behind you. If you saw a thief, you joined with him, and with adulterers you threw in your lot. Your mouth produced wickedness abundantly, and your tongue wove deceit. You sat there and slandered your brother, and put a stumbling block in the way of your mother's son. ⁹These things you have done, and I kept silent. You thought, you unrighteous person, that I would be like you. ¹⁰I will convict you and set you face to face with yourself. ¹¹Now consider these things, you who forget God, lest he seize you like a lion, and there be no one to save you. ¹²The sacrifice of praise will glorify me, and that is the way by which I will show him the salvation of God.'"

Christ's Salvation

36This is the way, dear friends, in which we found our salvation, namely Jesus Christ, the high priest of our offerings, the guardian and

---

u Some ancient authorities omit *of his intelligence*
v Ancient authorities read *Let us observe*
w One ancient authority omits *good*

x One ancient authority reads *mind is fixed on God through faith;* another reads *mind of faith is fixed on God;* others read *mind is faithfully fixed on God*
y Some ancient authorities read *evil*

33.7 we have seen Gk *eidomen,* an editorial conjecture; the ancient manuscripts read "let us see" *(idōmen)*—only a slight difference in spelling. Modern editions emend to *we have seen.* **34.3** *Isa.* 40:10; 62:11; *Prov.* 24:12; *Rev.* 22:12. **34.4 any good work** *1 Clem.* 33.1. **34.6** *Dan.* 7:10; *Isa.* 6:3. **34.8** *1 Cor.* 2:9; *Isa.* 64:4. **35.5–6** *Rom.* 1:29–32. **35.7–12** *Ps.* 50:16–23 (LXX 49:16–23). **36.1 high priest** The description of Jesus as *high priest* (or simply "priest") runs throughout the book of *Hebrews.* Clement also uses the term often (36.1; 40.5; 41.2; 61.3; 64.3). Elsewhere in our literature, it is used only one other time for Jesus (Ign. *Phld.* 9.1), and in the only other occurrence of the term, it is applied to church leaders (*Did.* 13.3). This entire paragraph heavily reflects the language of *Hebrews.*

helper of our weakness. ²Through him let us look steadily[z] into the heights of heaven; through him we see as in a mirror his faultless and transcendent face; through him the eyes of our hearts have been opened; through him our foolish and darkened mind springs up into the[a] light; through him the Master has willed that we should taste immortal knowledge, for "he, being the radiance of his majesty, is as much superior to angels as the name he has inherited is more excellent." ³For so it is written: "He makes his angels winds and his ministers flames of fire." ⁴But of his Son the Master spoke thus: "You are my Son; today I have begotten you. Ask of me, and I will give you the Gentiles for your inheritance, and the ends of the earth for your possession." ⁵And again he says to him: "Sit at my right hand, until I make your enemies a footstool for your feet." ⁶Who, then, are these enemies? Those who are wicked and resist his will.

Christ's Soldiers and Their Service

37Let us, therefore, serve as soldiers, brothers, with all earnestness under his faultless orders. ²Let us consider the soldiers who serve under our commanders—how precisely, how readily, how obediently they execute orders. ³Not all are prefects or tribunes or centurions or captains of fifty and so forth, but each in his own rank executes the orders given by the emperor and the commanders. ⁴The great cannot exist without the small, nor the small without the great. There is a certain blending in everything, and therein lies the advantage. ⁵Let us take our body as an example. The head without the feet is nothing; likewise, the feet without the head are nothing. Even the smallest parts of our body are necessary and useful to the whole body, yet all the members work together and unite in mutual subjection, that the whole body may be saved.

38So in our case let the whole body be saved in Christ Jesus, and let each man be subject to his neighbor, to the degree determined by his spiritual gift. ²The strong must not neglect[b] the weak, and weak must respect the strong. Let the rich support the poor; and let the poor give thanks to God, because he has given him someone through whom his needs may be met. Let the wise display his wisdom not in words but in good works. The humble person should not testify to his own humility, but leave it to someone else to testify about him. Let the one who is physically pure remain so and[c] not boast, recognizing that it is someone else who grants this self-control. ³Let us acknowledge, brothers, from what matter we were made; who and what we were, when we came into the world; from what grave and what darkness he who made and created us brought us into his world, having prepared his benefits for us before we were born. ⁴Seeing, therefore, that we have all these things from him, we ought in every respect to give thanks to him, to whom be the glory for ever and ever. Amen.

No Boasting before God

39Senseless and stupid and foolish and ignorant people jeer and mock at us, wishing to exalt themselves in their own imaginations. ²For what can a mortal do? Or what strength does an earthborn creature have? ³For it is written: "There was no form before my eyes; I heard only a breath and a voice. ⁴What then? Shall a mortal be clean in the presence of the Lord? Or shall a man be blameless for his deeds, seeing that he does not trust his servants and has found some fault against his angels? ⁵Not even heaven is clean in his sight: away then, you who dwell in houses of clay, the very same clay of which we ourselves are made. He crushed them like a moth, and between morning and evening they cease to exist. Because they could not help themselves, they perished.

---

z Some ancient authorities read *we look steadily*
a One ancient authority adds *amazing*; another reads *his amazing* (see *1 Pet.* 2:9)

b Some ancient authorities read *must care for*
c Some ancient authorities omit *remain so and*

36.2 *into the light* See *1 Pet.* 2:9. **the name he has inherited** *Heb.* 1:3–4 **36.3** *Heb.* 1:7; *Ps.* 104:4. **36.4** *Heb.* 1:5; *Ps.* 2:7–8. **36.5** *Heb.* 1:13; *Ps.* 110:1. **37.1–3** Military images were used by many early Christian authors to describe aspects of Christian life (*1 Cor.* 15:23; *Eph.* 6:13–17; *1 Tim.* 1:18; Ign. *Pol.* 6.2). Clement argues here for a ranked order of leadership and relates one's responsibilities to the assigned duties of each rank. Armies work because there is rank and hierarchy, and each soldier, in doing his assigned duties, serves the emperor just as much as any other soldier, regardless of rank. **37.5** Clement moves to the image of a body, where each member has a valued and necessary function from which the whole body benefits. Clement's reuse of these Pauline images may have played on Paul's earlier critique of the Corinthians. From the image of the army and the body, Clement draws his conclusion (38.1); then he returns to other images of proper rank (40–41). **38.1** *spiritual gift* Gk *charisma*, a word used by Paul in *1 Cor.* 12–14. Of the twenty-one other occurrences of this term, two-thirds appear in Paul's letters to the churches at Rome and Corinth—the two churches linked by *1 Clement.* **38.2** Several themes of Paul's correspondence with the church at Corinth are mentioned here: weak and strong, rich and poor, the wise and the humble. *physically pure* This is a reference to celibacy, which was encouraged by a number of early Christian authors (*1 Cor.* 7:1, 6–9, 25–40; *Matt.* 19:11–12). It is the focus of the *Acts of Paul and Thecla,* a 2d-century apocryphal document. **39.3–9** *Job* 4:16–18; 15:15; 4:19–5:5.

6He breathed upon them and they died, because they had no wisdom. 7But call out, if some one should obey you, or if you should see one of the holy angels. For wrath kills the foolish person, and envy slays one who has gone astray. 8And I have seen fools putting down roots, but suddenly their house was consumed. 9May their sons be far from safety. May they be mocked at the doors of lesser men, and there will be none to deliver them. For the things prepared for them, the righteous shall eat; but they themselves will not be delivered from evil."

Following God's Proper Order

40 Since, therefore, these things are now clear to us and we have searched into the depths of the divine knowledge, we ought to do, in order, everything that the Master has commanded us to perform at the appointed times. 2Now he commanded the offerings and services to be performed diligently, and*d* not to be done carelessly or in disorder, but at designated times and seasons. 3Both where and by whom he wants them to be performed, he himself has determined by his supreme will, so that all things, being done devoutly according to his good pleasure, may be acceptable to his will. 4Those, therefore, who make their offerings at the appointed times are acceptable and blessed, for those who follow the instructions of the Master cannot go wrong. 5For to the high priest the proper services have been given, and to the priests the proper office has been assigned, and upon the Levites the proper ministries have been imposed. The layman is bound by the layman's rules.

41 Let each of you,*e* brothers, in his proper order give thanks to*f* God, maintaining a good conscience, not overstepping the designated rule of his ministry, but acting with reverence. 2Not just anywhere, brothers, are the continual daily sacrifices of-

fered, or the freewill offerings, or the offerings for sin and trespasses, but only in Jerusalem. And even there the offering is not made in every place, but in front of the sanctuary at the altar, the offering having been first inspected for blemishes by the high priest and the previously mentioned ministers. 3Those, therefore, who do any thing contrary to the duty imposed by his will receive death as the penalty. 4You see, brothers, as we have been considered worthy of greater knowledge, so much the more are we exposed to danger.

Proper Order: From Apostles to Bishops and Deacons

42 The apostles received the gospel for us from the Lord Jesus Christ; Jesus the Christ was sent forth from God. 2So then Christ is from God, and the apostles are from Christ. Both, therefore, came of the will of God in good order. 3Having therefore received their orders and being fully assured by the resurrection of our Lord Jesus Christ and full of faith in the word of God, they went forth with the firm assurance that the Holy Spirit gives,*g* preaching the good news that the kingdom of God was about to come. 4So, preaching both in the country and in the towns, they appointed their firstfruits, when they had tested them by the Spirit, to be bishops and deacons for the future believers. 5And this was no new thing they did, for indeed something had been written about bishops and deacons many years ago; for somewhere thus says the scripture: "I will appoint their bishops in righteousness and their deacons in faith."

43 And is it any wonder that those who in Christ were entrusted by God with such a work appointed the officials just mentioned? After all, the blessed Moses, "who was a faithful servant in all his house," recorded in the sacred books all the injunctions given to him, and the rest of the prophets

---

d Ancient authorities lack *diligently;* some also lack *to be performed . . . and*

e Some ancient authorities read *us*

f Some ancient authorities read *please*

---

g Or *with the fullness of the Holy Spirit*

40.1–5 The author is not arguing so much that the Christian ministry was like the Jewish priesthood but that the Christian ministry, like the Jewish priesthood, had a specific role to play in contrast to the role of the laity. The author is arguing for structure and order; he is not arguing for Jewish structure and order. So also in *1 Clement* 41. **40.2 diligently** Lightfoot's conjecture. **40.5 the Levites the proper ministries** The Gk word for *ministries (diakoniai)* is from the same root as that used for "deacons." This is the 1st Christian use of the term "layman." The contrast between the clergy and the laity in the context of Clement's argument against the schismatics may suggest that these new leaders had not previously held any office in the hierarchy. The same is suggested by Clement's general defense of elders. It is not one faction of elders against another faction of elders but the full body of elders against a new power structure. **41.1 give thanks** Gk *eucharisteō.* Perhaps meaning "join in the Eucharist." **41.2 Jerusalem** This need not mean that the temple in Jerusalem was still standing and being used for sacrifice. Jerusalem's role could still serve as an illustration after its fall to Roman armies in 70 C.E. **42.4** This is the most unequivocal statement in the early materials that bishops were appointed by the apostles. Clement mentions deacons, but not presbyters. This may reflect the influence of the scripture to which Clement appealed (42.5) rather than a reality of the hierarchical structure of the time, which we know revolved around presbyters from 47.6. It appears that in Clement's world, presbyters served as overseers—which is what the Gk word for "bishop" means. See especially 44.1–6. **42.5** See *Isa.* 60:17 LXX. **43.1** *Heb.* 3:5; *Num.* 12:7.

followed him, bearing witness with him to the laws that he enacted. ²For when jealousy arose concerning the priesthood, and the tribes were quarreling about which of them was to be decorated with the glorious title, he commanded the leaders of the twelve tribes to bring him rods inscribed with the name of each tribe. And taking them he tied and sealed them with the signet rings of the leaders of the tribes, and deposited them on the table of God in the tent of the testimony. ³Then, having shut the tent, he sealed the keys as well as the doors*h* ⁴and said to them, "Brothers, the tribe whose rod blossoms is the one God has chosen to be priests and to minister to him." ⁵Now when morning came, he called all Israel together, all six hundred thousand men, showed the seals to the leaders of the tribes, opened the tent of testimony, and brought out the rods. And the rod of Aaron was found not only to have blossomed, but also to be bearing fruit. ⁶What do you think, dear friends? Did not Moses know beforehand that this would happen? Of course he knew. But in order that disorder might not arise in Israel, he did it anyway, so that the name of the true and only God*i* might be glorified, to whom be the glory for ever and ever. Amen.

The Revolt against Order at Corinth

44 Our apostles likewise knew, through our Lord Jesus Christ, that there would be strife over the bishop's office. ²For this reason, therefore, having received complete foreknowledge, they appointed the officials mentioned earlier and afterwards they gave the offices a permanent character;*j* that is, if they should die, other approved men should succeed to their ministry.*k* ³These, therefore, who were appointed by them or, later on, by other reputable men with the consent of the whole church, and who have

ministered to the flock of Christ blamelessly, humbly, peaceably, and unselfishly, and for a long time have been well-spoken of by all—these we consider to be unjustly removed from their ministry. ⁴For it will be no small sin for us if we depose from the bishop's office those who have offered the gifts blamelessly and in holiness. ⁵Blessed are those presbyters who have gone on ahead, who took their departure at a mature and fruitful age, for they need no longer fear that someone may remove them from their established place. ⁶For we see that you have removed certain people, their good conduct notwithstanding, from the ministry that had been held in honor by them blamelessly.

Good and Bad Responses to God's Order

45 Be contentious*l* and zealous, brothers, but about the things that relate to salvation. ²You have searched the scriptures, which are true, which were given by the Holy Spirit; ³you know that nothing unrighteous or counterfeit is written in them. You will not find that righteous people have ever been thrust out by holy men. ⁴The righteous were persecuted, but it was by the lawless; they were imprisoned, but it was by the unholy. They were stoned by transgressors; they were slain by those who had conceived a detestable and unrighteous jealousy. ⁵Despite suffering these things, they endured nobly. ⁶For what shall we say, brothers? Was Daniel cast into the lions' den by those who feared God? ⁷Or were Ananias, Azarias, and Mishael shut up in the fiery furnace by those devoted to the magnificent and glorious worship of the Most High? Of course not! Who, then, were the people who did these things? Abominable people, full of all wickedness, who were stirred up to such a pitch of wrath that they tortured

---

h Some ancient authorities read *rods*
i Some ancient authorities read *Lord* or *One*
j Gk uncertain
k Translation attempts to preserve the ambiguity of the Gk.

l Or *You are contentious*

43.2 *Numbers* 17. **44.1** *bishop's office* Lit. "name of the bishop." See note to 42.4. **44.2** Several variants appear at this point in the manuscript tradition. In particular, there is debate about the meaning of the word *epinomēn,* translated here as *permanent character.* There is also debate about the group intended by the word *they (if they should die),* which, in Gk, is part of the verb. It may be interpreted at least three different ways. (a) *They* = the apostles: If the apostles themselves die, *other approved men* succeed to the apostolic office and the right to appoint local officials, and thus are the *other reputable men* of the following sentence. (b) *They* = those 1st appointed by the apostles. If these initial appointees should die, they are to be succeeded in office by others appointed by the apostles and, later on, by the *other reputable men* with apostolic status, such as Titus or Timothy. (c) *They* = the initial appointees, and *other reputable men* = the officials mentioned earlier. On this view, those appointed initially are responsible as a group for appointing their own successors; that is, upon the death of one of their number, the survivors appoint an "approved man" to fill the vacancy. It can be said with certainty, nonetheless, that some clear line of succession is envisioned, stemming from the apostles to the officials whom Clement supported. **44.6** *held in honor by them blamelessly* Lightfoot reads "which they preserved blamelessly"; this requires emending the text from *tetimēmenēs* to *tetērēmenēs.* Other editors emend it to read *"by them* that they had preserved *blamelessly."* **45.3–7** In another line of argument, Clement illustrates from scripture that the leaders who have been abused and removed are righteous and their persecutors are evil. Two specific examples are offered, both from the book of *Daniel* (chs. 6, 9).

cruelly those who served God with a holy and blameless resolve; they did not realize that the Most High is the champion and protector of those who with a pure conscience worship his excellent name. To him be the glory for ever and ever. Amen. 8But those who patiently endured with confidence inherited glory and honor; they were exalted and had their names recorded by God as their memorial[m] for ever and ever. Amen.

Senseless Schism in Corinth

46 Therefore we too, brothers, must follow examples such as these. 2For it is written: "Follow the saints, for those who follow them will be sanctified." 3And again it says in another place: "With the innocent man you will be innocent, and with the elect you will be elect, and with the perverse man you will deal perversely." 4Let us, therefore, join with the innocent and righteous, for these are the elect of God. 5Why is there strife and angry outbursts and dissension and schisms and conflict among you? 6Do we not have one God and one Christ and one Spirit of grace which was poured out upon us? And is there not one calling in Christ? 7Why do we tear and rip apart the members of Christ, and rebel against our own body, and reach such a level of insanity that we forget that we are members of one another? Remember the words of Jesus our Lord, 8for he said: "Woe to that person! It would have been good for him if he had not been born, than that he should cause one of my elect to sin. It would have been better for him to have been tied to a millstone and cast into the sea, than that he should pervert one of my elect." 9Your schism has perverted many; it has brought many to despair, plunged many into doubt, and caused all of us to sorrow. And yet your rebellion still continues!

47 Take up the epistle of the blessed Paul the apostle. 2What did he first write to you in the "beginning of the gospel"? 3Truly he wrote to you in the Spirit about himself and Cephas and Apollos, because even then you had split into factions. Yet that splitting into factions brought less sin upon you, for you were partisans of highly reputed apostles and of a man approved by them. 5In contrast now think about those who have perverted you and diminished the respect due your renowned love for the brotherhood. 6It is disgraceful, dear friends, yes, utterly disgraceful and unworthy of your conduct in Christ, that it should be reported that the well-established and ancient church of the Corinthians, because of one or two persons, is rebelling against its presbyters. 7And this report has reached not only us, but also those who differ from us, with the result that you heap blasphemies upon the name of the Lord because of your stupidity, and create danger for yourselves as well.

Schism Not the Christian Way

48 Let us therefore root this out quickly, and let us fall down before the Master and pray to him with tears, that he may be merciful and be reconciled to us, and restore us to the honorable and pure conduct that characterizes our love for the brotherhood. 2For this is an open gate of righteousness leading to life, as it is written: "Open to me the gates of righteousness, that I may enter through them and praise the Lord. 3This is the gate of the Lord; the righteous shall enter by it." 4Although many gates are opened, this righteous gate is the Christian gate; blessed are all those who have entered by it and direct their path in holiness and righteousness, doing everything without confusion. 5Let a person be faithful, let him be able to expound knowledge, let him be wise in the interpretation of discourses, let him be energetic in deeds, let him be pure;[n] 6for the greater he seems to be, the more he ought to be humble, and the more he ought to seek the common advantage of all, and not his own.

Love Unites, Not Divides

49 Let the one who has love in Christ fulfill the commandments of Christ. 2Who can describe the bond of God's love? 3Who is able to explain the majesty of its beauty? 4The height to which love leads

---

m Some ancient authorities read *and were inscribed by God in his memory*

n Some ancient authorities read *let him be pure in deeds*

46.2 The source of this quotation is unknown. **46.3** *Ps.* 18:25–26 (LXX 17:26–27). **46.5** *Eph.* 4:4–6. **46.8** *Woe unto that man Mark* 14:21; *Matt.* 26:24; *Luke* 22:22. *better for him Mark* 9:42; *Matt.* 18:6; *Luke* 17:2. **47.1–3** *1 Cor.* 1:10–17; 3:5–9. Clement seems to refer to the letter we know as *1 Corinthians* as the first correspondence of Paul to the church at Corinth. If this is the case, the lost letter to Corinth (written before *1 Corinthians*) was unknown to Clement at the end of the 1st century. See the introduction to *1 Corinthians*. **47:2** *beginning of the gospel Phil.* 4:15. **47.3–6** It is improbable that the factions in Clement's day were rooted in the factions of Paul's day. For one thing, Clement uses the factions in Paul's day as a contrast to the present factions. For another, Clement praised the Corinthian church for its earlier harmony (2.1, 6), which would hardly have been likely if the factions had continued from the days of Paul. **47.7** *those who differ from us* Not necessarily a reference to non-Christians; we know of various schisms within early Christian groups from the Pauline, Johannine, and Ignatian letters. **48.2–3** *Ps.* 118:19–20 (LXX 117:19–20).

is indescribable. [5]Love unites us with God; "love covers a multitude of sins"; love endures all things, is patient in all things. There is nothing coarse, nothing arrogant in love. Love knows nothing of schisms, love leads no rebellions, love does everything in harmony. In love all the elect of God were made perfect; without love nothing is pleasing to God. [6]In love the Master received us. Because of the love that he had for us, Jesus Christ our Lord, in accordance with God's will, gave his blood for us, and his flesh for our flesh, and his life for our lives.

50 You see, dear friends, how great and wonderful love is; its perfection is beyond description. [2]Who is worthy to be found in it, except those whom God considers worthy? Let us therefore ask and petition his mercy, that we may be found blameless in love, standing apart from the factiousness of men. [3]All the generations from Adam to this day have passed away, but those who by God's grace were perfected in love have a place among[o] the godly, who will be revealed when the kingdom of Christ[p] visits[q] us. [4]For it is written: "Enter into the innermost rooms for a very little while, until my anger and wrath shall pass away, and I will remember a good day and will raise you from your graves." [5]Blessed are we, dear friends, if we continue to keep God's commandments in the harmony of love, that our sins may be forgiven us through love. [6]For it is written: "Blessed are those whose iniquities are forgiven, and whose sins are covered. Blessed is the man to whom the Lord will reckon no sin, and in whose mouth there is no deceit." [7]This declaration of blessedness was pronounced upon those who have been chosen by God through Jesus Christ our Lord, to whom be the glory for ever and ever. Amen.

Call to Repentance and the End of Schism

51 So, then, for whatever sins we have committed and whatever we have done through any of the tricks of the adversary, let us ask that we may be forgiven. And those, too, who set themselves up as leaders of rebellion and dissension ought to look to the common ground of hope. [2]For those who walk in fear and love prefer that they themselves, rather than their neighbors, should fall into suffering, and they would rather bring condemnation upon themselves than upon the harmony that has been so nobly and righteously handed down to us. [3]For it is good for a person to confess his transgressions rather than to harden his heart, as the heart of those who rebelled against Moses the servant of God was hardened. Their condemnation was made very clear, [4]for they went down to Hades alive, and "Death will be their shepherd." [5]Pharaoh and his army and all the rulers of Egypt, "the chariots and their riders," were plunged into the Red Sea and perished, for no other reason than that their foolish hearts were hardened after the signs and the wonders had been accomplished in the land of Egypt[r] by Moses, the servant of God.

52 The Master, brothers, has no need of anything at all. He requires nothing of anyone except to make a confession to him. [2]For David, the chosen one, says: "I will confess to the Lord, and it will please him more than a young calf with horns and hoofs. Let the poor see this and rejoice." [3]And again he says: "Sacrifice to God a sacrifice of praise, and pay your vows to the Most High; call upon me in the day of your affliction, and I will deliver you, and you will glorify me. [4]For the sacrifice of God is a broken spirit."

53 For you know, and know well, the sacred scriptures, dear friends, and you have searched into the oracles of God. We write these things, therefore, merely as a reminder. [2]When Moses went up to the mountain and had spent forty days and forty nights in fasting and humiliation, God said to him: "Moses, Moses,[s] go down quickly from here, for your people, whom you led out of the land of Egypt, have broken the law. They have quickly turned away from the path which you established for them: they have cast for themselves some idols." [3]And the Lord said to him: "I have spoken to you time and again, saying, I have seen this people, and they are stiff-necked indeed! Let me destroy them completely, and I will wipe out their name from under heaven, and I will make you into a great and wonderful nation, far more numerous than this one." [4]And Moses said: "May it not be so, Lord. Forgive this people their sin, or else wipe me also out of the book of the living." [5]What mighty love! What unsurpassable perfection! The servant speaks boldly with his Master: he asks forgiveness for the multitude, or demands that he himself also be wiped out with them.

o Or *live in the abode of*
p Some ancient authorities read *God*
q Or *comes to*

r Some ancient authorities read *Egypt*
s Some ancient authorities omit *Moses, Moses*

49.5 *1 Pet.* 4:8. Much of this language about love is similar to that in the classic passage in *1 Corinthians* 13. **50.3** ***visits*** *1 Pet.* 2:12; *Luke* 19:44. **50.4** *Isa.* 26:20; *Ezek.* 37:12. **50.6** *Rom.* 4:7–9; *Ps.* 32:1–2 (LXX 31:1–2). **51.3–4** *Numbers* 16. See 4.12. **51.4** *Ps.* 49:14 (LXX 48:15). **51.5** *Exod.* 14:23. **52.2** ***young calf*** *Ps.* 69:30–32 (LXX 68:31–33). The reference is to animals used in sacrifice. **52.3** *Ps.* 50:14–15 (LXX 49:14–15); 51:17 (LXX 50:19). **53.2–5** *Exodus* 32.

Taking the Blame for the Common Good

54 Now, then, who among you is noble? Who is compassionate? Who is filled with love? [2]Let him say: "If it is my fault that there are rebellion and strife and schisms, I retire; I will go wherever you wish, and will do whatever is ordered by the people. Only let the flock of Christ be at peace with its duly appointed presbyters." [3]The one who does this will win for himself great fame in Christ, and every place will receive him, for "the earth is the Lord's, and all that is in it." [4]These are the things that those who live as citizens of the commonwealth of God—something not to be regretted—have done and will continue to do.

55 Let us, moreover, bring forward some examples of Gentiles as well: in times of pestilence, many kings and rulers, being prompted by some oracle, have given themselves over to death, that they might rescue their subjects through their own blood. Many have left their own cities, that there might be no more rebellions. [2]We know that many among us have had themselves imprisoned, that they might ransom others. Many have sold themselves into slavery, and with the price received for themselves have fed others. [3]Many women, being strengthened by the grace of God, have performed many manly deeds. [4]The blessed Judith, when the city was under siege, asked the elders to permit her to go to the enemy's camp. [5]So she exposed herself to peril and went out for love of her country and of her besieged people, and the Lord delivered Holophernes into the hand of a woman. [6]To no less danger did Esther, who was perfect in faith, expose herself, in order that she might deliver the twelve tribes of Israel when they were about to be destroyed. For through her fasting and her humiliation she entreated the all-seeing Master, the God[t] of the ages, and he, seeing the humility of her soul, rescued the people for whose sake she had faced the danger.

God's Discipline and God's Mercy

56 Therefore let us also intercede for those who are involved in some transgression, that forbearance and humility may be given them, so that they may submit, not to us but to the will of God. For in this way the merciful remembrance of them in the presence of God and the saints will be fruitful and perfect for them.[u] [2]Let us accept correction, which no one ought to resent, dear friends. The reproof that we give one to another is good and exceedingly useful, for it unites us with the will of God. [3]For thus says the holy word: "The Lord has indeed disciplined me but has not handed me over to death. [4]For whom the Lord loves he disciplines, and he punishes every son whom he accepts." [5]"For the righteous," it is said, "will discipline me in mercy and reprove me, but let not the oil[v] of sinners anoint my head." [6]And again it says: "Blessed is the person whom the Lord has reproved; do not reject the correction of the Almighty. For he causes pain, and he makes well again; [7]he has wounded, and his hands have healed. [8]Six times will he rescue you from distress, and in the seventh evil will not touch you. [9]In famine he will rescue you from death, and in war he will release you from the power of the sword. [10]From the scourge of the tongue he will hide you, and you will not be afraid when evils approach. [11]You will laugh at the unrighteous and wicked, [12]and of the wild beasts you will not be afraid, for wild beasts will be at peace with you. [13]Then you will know that your house will be at peace, and the tent in which you dwell will not fail. [14]And you will know that your seed will be many, and your children

---

t Some ancient authorities omit *the God*

u Or *in this way they will prove fruitful and perfect when God and the saints remember them with mercy*
v One ancient authority reads *mercy*

54.2 It may have been wishful thinking on Clement's part that the leaders of the revolt would step aside in order that the deposed presbyters might be reinstated. But the comments do suggest that Clement had no serious problem with the theological position of the new leaders. See similar comments in 57.1–2. **54.3** *Ps.* 24:1 (LXX 23:1). **54.4** *commonwealth of God* The word identifies citizens of a city. For other uses of the image of the church as a city, see *Gal.* 4:25–26; *Rev.* 21:9–27. **55.2** *ransom others* We do not know of specific instances in which this was done, but we know that churches sometimes used their funds to ransom people who might have fallen victim to pirates on the open seas, bandits on the roads, or slavery from war. A detailed story of such captivity is found in Achilles Tatius, *Leucippe and Cleitophon*. For reasons not specified, Ignatius warned Polycarp against the practice of ransoming slaves generally (Ign. *Pol.* 4.3). *slavery* One could become a slave because of debt, capture, kidnapping, conviction of certain crimes, or sale by one's own parents, often due to poverty. Here individuals sell themselves to gain the release of another. **55.3** It is not clear whether Clement has in mind particular women from his locale or generation. His two examples are from the Bible, but this need not mean that he could not produce contemporary examples of female valor. **55.4** The story of Judith is told in a book by that name in the LXX. This document, which is not found in Protestant Bibles, is part of the Apocrypha. **55.5** The story of Esther is told in a book by that name in the Bible. **56.3–4** *Heb.* 12:6; *Ps.* 118:18; *Prov.* 3:12. **56.5** *oil of sinners* There is a play on words. The mercy *(eleei)* of the righteous is contrasted with the oil *(elaion)* of sinners (*Ps.* 141:5; LXX 140:5). Lightfoot thinks a repetition of the word "mercy" may have been intended. **56.6–15** *Job* 5:17–26.

will be like the grass of the fields. 15And you will come to the grave like ripe wheat harvested at the proper time, or like a heap on the threshing floor gathered together at the right time." 16You see, dear friends, what great protection there is for those who are disciplined by the Master; because he is a kind Father, he disciplines us in order that we may obtain mercy through his holy discipline.

Pointed Warnings to the Leaders of the Revolt

57 You, therefore, who laid the foundation of the revolt, must submit to the presbyters and accept discipline leading to repentance, bending the knees of your heart. 2Learn how to subordinate yourselves, laying aside the arrogant and proud stubbornness of your tongue. For it is better for you to be found small but included in the flock of Christ than to have a preeminent reputation and yet be excluded from his hope. 3For thus says the all-virtuous Wisdom: "Listen! I will bring forth for you a saying of my spirit, and I will teach you my word. 4Because I called and you did not obey, and because I held out words and you paid no attention, but ignored my advice and disobeyed my correction, I therefore will laugh at your destruction and rejoice when ruin comes upon you, and when confusion suddenly overtakes you, and catastrophe arrives like a whirlwind, or when tribulation and distress come upon you. 5At that time, when you call upon me, I will not listen to you. Evil men will seek me but will not find me, for they hated wisdom and did not choose the fear of the Lord, nor did they desire to pay attention to my advice, but mocked my correction. 6Therefore they will eat the fruit of their own way and be filled with their own ungodliness. 7Because they wronged infants, they will be slain, and a searching inquiry will destroy the ungodly. But the one who hears me will dwell safely, trusting in hope, and will live quietly, free from fear of all evil."

58 Let us, therefore, obey his most holy and glorious name, thereby escaping the threats spoken by Wisdom long ago against those who disobey, that we may dwell safely, trusting in his most holy and majestic name. 2Accept our advice and you will have nothing to regret. For as God lives, and as the Lord Jesus Christ lives, and the Holy Spirit (who are the

faith and the hope of the elect), so surely will the one who with humility and constant gentleness has kept without regret the ordinances and commandments given by God be enrolled and included among the number of those who are saved through Jesus Christ, through whom is the glory to him for ever and ever. Amen.

Prayer for Peace and Forgiveness

59 But if certain people should disobey what has been said by him through us, let them understand that they will entangle themselves in no small sin and danger. 2We, however, will be innocent of this sin, and will ask, with earnest prayer and supplication, that the Creator of the universe may keep intact the specified number of his elect throughout the whole world, through his beloved servantʷ Jesus Christ, through whom he called us from darkness to light, from ignorance to the knowledge of the glory of his name. 3Grant us, Lord, to hope on your name,ˣ which is the primal source of all creation, and open the eyes of our hearts, that we may know you, who alone are "Highest among the high and remain Holy among the holy." You "humble the pride of the proud"; you "destroy the plans of nations"; you "exalt the humble" and "humble the exalted"; you "make rich and make poor"; you "kill and make alive." You alone are the Benefactor of spirits and the God of all flesh, who "looks into the depths," who scans the works of man; the Helper of those who are in peril, the "Savior of those in despair"; the Creator and Guardian of every spirit, who multiplies the nations upon the earth, and from among all of them have chosen those who love you through Jesus Christ, your beloved servant,ʷ through whom you instructed us, sanctified us, honored us. 4We ask you, Master, to be "our helper and protector." Save those among us who are in distress; have mercy on the humble;ʸ raise up the fallen; show yourself to those in need; heal the godless;ᶻ turn back those of your people who wander; feed the hungry; release our prisoners; raise up the

---

w Or *child*
x Gk lacks *Grant us, Lord*
y Some ancient authorities omit *have . . . humble*
z Some ancient authorities read *sick*

57.1–2 See note to 54:2. **57.1 bending the knees** In the ancient world, this was the position, not of prayer, but of submission and reverence. People usually prayed in the standing position, with arms outstretched and palms open to the heavens. **57.3 all-virtuous Wisdom** This was a title used of *Proverbs* or sometimes of the larger collection of which *Proverbs* was a part. **57.3–7** Prov. 1:23–33. **59.2 his beloved servant** So also in 59.3–4. See Acts 4:27. **59.3–61.3** Unlike other sections of Clement's writing, which appeal to well-known biblical stories or quote long passages of scripture, this prayer is largely made up of about fifty brief petitions from the whole range of Jewish scripture. **59.3 Grant us** The words do not appear in the Gk text but are supplied by translators to make sense of the passage. Lightfoot noticed that something must be missing because the text changes from the third person *(his name)* in 59.2 to the second person *(your name)* in 59.3 when referring to God—a switch from talk about God to prayer to God. **servant** See Acts 4:27.

weak; comfort the discouraged. "Let all the nations know that you are the only God," that Jesus Christ is your servant,[a] and that "we are your people and the sheep of your pasture."

60 For you through your works have revealed the everlasting structure of the world. You, Lord, created the earth. You are faithful throughout all generations, righteous in your judgments, marvelous in strength and majesty, wise in creating and prudent in establishing what exists, good in all that is observed, and faithful[b] to those who trust in you, merciful and compassionate: forgive us our sins and our injustices, our transgressions and our shortcomings. [2]Do not take into account every sin of your servants and slaves, but cleanse us with the cleansing of your truth, and "direct our steps to walk in holiness and righteousness and purity[c] of heart," and "to do what is good and pleasing in your sight" and in the sight of our rulers. [3]Yes, Lord, "let your face shine upon us" in peace "for our good," that we may be sheltered "by your mighty hand" and delivered from every sin "by your uplifted arm"; deliver us as well from those who hate us unjustly. [4]Give harmony and peace to us and to all who dwell on the earth, just as you did to our fathers when they reverently "called upon you in faith and truth," that we may be saved,[d] while we render obedience to your almighty and most excellent[e] name, and to our rulers and governors on earth.

61 You, Master, have given them the power of sovereignty through your majestic and inexpressable might, so that we, acknowledging the glory and honor that you have given them, may be subject to them, resisting your will in nothing. Grant to them, Lord, health, peace, harmony, and stability, that they may blamelessly administer the govenment that you have given them. [2]For you, heavenly Master, King of the ages, give to human beings glory and honor and authority over those upon the earth. Lord, direct their plans according to what is good and pleasing in your sight, so that by devoutly administering in peace and gentleness the authority that you have given them they may experience your mercy.

[3]You, who alone are able to do these and even greater good things for us, we praise through the high priest and guardian of our souls, Jesus Christ, through whom be the glory and the majesty to you both now and for all generations and for ever and ever. Amen.

Letter Summary; Repeated Requests

62 We have written enough to you, brothers, about the things which pertain to our religion and are particularly helpful for a virtuous life, at least for those who wish to guide their steps[f] in holiness and righteousness. [2]For we have touched upon every subject—faith, repentance, genuine love, self-control, sobriety, and patience—and have reminded you that you must reverently please Almighty God in righteousness and truth and steadfastness, living in harmony without bearing malice, in love and peace with constant gentleness, just as our fathers, of whom we spoke earlier, pleased him, by being humble towards the Father and God and Creator and towards all people. [3]And we have reminded you of these things all the more gladly, since we knew quite well that we were writing to men who are faithful and distinguished and have diligently studied the oracles of the teaching of God.

63 Therefore it is right for us, having studied so many and such great examples, to bow the neck and, adopting the attitude of obedience, to submit to those who are the leaders of our souls,[g] so that by ceasing from this futile dissension we may attain the goal that is truly set before us, free from all blame. [2]For you will give us great joy and gladness, if you obey what we have written through the Holy Spirit and root out the unlawful anger of your jealousy, in accordance with the appeal for peace and harmony that we have made in this letter. [3]We have also sent trustworthy and prudent men who from youth to old age have lived blameless lives among us, who will be witnesses between you and us. [4]This we have done in order that you may know that our only concern has been, and still is, that you should attain peace without delay.

---

a Or *child*
b Some ancient authorities read *kind*
c Some ancient authorities omit *and righteousness and purity*
d Gk lacks *that we may be saved*
e Some ancient authorities read *glorious*

f Or *helpful to those who wish to lead a virtuous life in holiness;* Gk lacks *their steps*
g Some ancient authorities read *and to adopt the attitude of obedience*, omitting *to submit . . . souls*

59.4 *servant* See *Acts* 4:27.   **60.2** See *1 Kgs.* 9:4; *Ps.* 40:2 (LXX 39:3).   **60.4–61.2** Clement reflects a positive attitude toward the state here, as do many other early Christian writers (see note to *1 Tim.* 2:2).   **61.3** *high priest* See note to 36.1. Here ends the prayer begun in 59.3.   **62.2–3** Clement summarizes the themes he has addressed: repentance, piety, and concord. These are supported here by numerous examples, largely from the Bible.   **63.1** *so many and such great examples* Clement explicitly states his purpose: He expects the hearers to respect these *examples*. He even clarifies what he means by respect: *bow the neck, and adopting the attitude of obedience, to submit*.   **63.3** See names in 65.1. The description of the agents of the Roman church may rule out an early date for the letter. See the discussion of the date in the introduction to *1 Clement*.

Final Prayer

64 Finally, may the all-seeing God and Master of spirits and Lord of all flesh, who chose the Lord Jesus Christ, and us through him to be his own special people, grant to every soul that has called upon his magnificent and holy name faith, fear, peace, patience, steadfastness, self-control, purity, and sobriety, that they may be pleasing to his name through our high priest and guardian, Jesus Christ, through whom be glory and majesty, might and honor to him, both now and for ever and ever. Amen.

Farewells and Parting Requests

65 Now send back to us without delay our messengers, Claudius Ephebus and Valerius Bito, together with Fortunatus, in peace and with joy, so that they may report as soon as possible the peace and concord that we have prayed for and desire, so that we too may all the more quickly rejoice over your good order. [2]The grace of our Lord Jesus Christ be with you and with all people everywhere who have been called by God through him, through whom be glory, honor, power, majesty, and eternal dominion to him, from everlasting to everlasting. Amen.

The letter of the Romans to the Corinthians.[h]

---

[h] So reads one ancient authority; the rest attribute it to Clement alone

---

64.1 *special people* Heb. 12:19; Num. 16:22; 27:16. **high priest** See note to 36.1. **65.1** These people are otherwise unknown. They were representatives of the Roman church who carried the letter from Rome to Corinth (63.3). **65.2** *of the Romans* See introduction to *1 Clement* for authorship.

The Letters of Ignatius

ROMANS ✣ EPHESIANS ✣ MAGNESIANS ✣ TRALLIANS
PHILADELPHIANS ✣ SMYRNAEANS ✣ POLYCARP

Setting and Audience

The seven letters of Ignatius were written within a few days of each other, and perhaps several were written on the same day. Thus the standard critical questions (date, occasion, setting, authorship, purpose, etc.) apply largely to the corpus as a whole, and will be discussed together in this general introduction. Each letter, however, has some unique features, which will be discussed in shorter introductions to follow.

Four of the letters were written from Smyrna and three from Troas a few days later. We have grouped them to reflect the locale of composition, since a change in circumstances between Smyrna and Troas has affected the tone of the letters. But whether written from Smyrna or from Troas, each of the six letters, addressed to churches in the Roman province of Asia,[1] is concerned with similar problems and governed by similar structures, matters that Ignatius addresses in detail. With each of these churches, Ignatius has had some kind of personal contact, either a face-to-face encounter (Philadelphia, Smyrna, and bishop Polycarp) or a visit from church representatives while he was delayed in Smyrna (Ephesus, Magnesia, and Tralles).

That he had face-to-face contact with some of the churches and not with others is explained by the route he took. Ephesus, Magnesia, and Tralles, the three Asian churches addressed from Smyrna, were situated to the south on one of two major valleys running from Laodicea to the Aegean coast. Ignatius wrote to thank these churches for their kindness, and the letters would have been carried back to the churches by their returning delegations. After leaving Smyrna, Ignatius seems to have been delayed again in Troas,[2] another port city, and from there he wrote to

---

[1]The churches of Roman Asia were about five hundred miles from Ignatius's home in Antioch. There is no evidence that he had visited any of these churches before this journey (though it is not impossible).

[2]This Troas, called Alexandria Troas, was about thirteen miles from the site of old Troy, which had itself continued to be inhabited until about 300 C.E. It lay 120 miles up the eastern Aegean coast from

Smyrna and Philadelphia, two churches he had already visited along the northern valley from Laodicea to the coast at Smyrna, and to Smyrna's bishop Polycarp.

The letter to the Romans, however, must be considered separately, since it is quite different in its content and concerns. Further, it was sent to a church which Ignatius had never visited, situated at the end of his journey (both in terms of his voyage and his life)—in the capital city of the empire, where he was to fight to the death with wild beasts for the entertainment of the crowds. Ignatius took the opportunity provided by the delay in Smyrna to write to the church at Rome, with which he apparently expected to have further contact once he reached Rome.

We are uncertain whether Ignatius's letters reflect the situation in Antioch, where he had been bishop and where his ideas and concerns would have been shaped, or the situation in Asia Minor, to which he addressed his letters and whose problems he made his own. In either case, common themes emerge: heresy and schism; persecution and martyrdom; church order and office. All these themes are interrelated in Ignatius's mind, though they have often become separate issues for modern scholars with their own agendas for the study of these letters.

Date

Although the letters themselves offer no clue about their date, and it is not possible to tie Ignatius to a specific persecution, most agree that they were written in the first or second decade of the second century. Eusebius places Ignatius's martyrdom at 107–108 C.E., in the tenth year of the reign of the emperor Trajan, and the legendary accounts of the martyrdom of Ignatius agree.[3]

In the letter to the Romans, Ignatius dated the letter: 24th of August. Of course, this does not tell us anything about the year, but it does place Ignatius's trip to Roman toward the end of the safe period for travel by ship.

Authorship

Little is known about Ignatius. The primary evidence for reconstructing the "historical" Ignatius comprises the seven letters that he wrote on his way to execution, but these contain little of biographical interest. Besides these seven letters, several others were attributed to Ignatius, but these are judged to be spurious (see discussion below). Moreover, the varying accounts of Ignatius's martyrdom are highly romanticized and fictional, without historical worth for information about Ignatius. Such accounts speak of Ignatius as a disciple of John the apostle, and a fellow-student with Polycarp. One account identifies Ignatius as the child Jesus took in his arms to bless (*Matt.* 18:2).

Smyrna. Ships normally traveled near the coast line, avoiding the more dangerous open seas as much as possible. Seneca spoke of the dangers of trying to save time by taking such shortcuts (*Letters* 53).

[3]Ignatius's arrest was tied to Emperor Trajan's visit to Antioch during an expedition against the Parthians. Such expeditions are dated to 107 and 116, with some dispute about further engagements.

Irenaeus (late second century), Origen (early third century), and Eusebius (early fourth century) all wrote about Ignatius and his letters, but their information seems to have come from the letters themselves.[4] Most modern investigators recognize that evidence for Ignatius is limited to his own correspondence, which reflects one brief moment in the life of the bishop.

Further, these letters were hastily written—all within a matter of a few days and under considerable pressure—to six unfamiliar congregations and one fellow bishop. We learn little more than that Ignatius was bishop in Antioch and that for some reason, which is not clear, he was sentenced to death by the authorities and was, at the time of his writing of the letters, on his way to public execution at the games in Rome.

The Situation in Antioch

Ignatius's plight has been the subject of considerable investigation. Many have argued that his arrest stemmed from an internal church conflict in Antioch, which rolled out into the streets, at which time the Roman authorities became involved for the public good. As a result of government intervention, Ignatius was forced to sacrifice himself to draw attention away from his church. Those who adopt this view argue that Ignatius's language reflects a more marked sense of unworthiness in the letters written from Smyrna than those from Troas, where he had learned that the church in Antioch was at peace.

Although that scenario is possible, it is not the only reasonable reconstruction. Early Christians frequently stood out as a puzzling, misunderstood, and offensive faction, and fell prey to various tensions within the society. We need not have corroborating evidence of an organized persecution of the church in Antioch at this time to conclude that Ignatius could have been a victim of non-Christian action rather than of interchurch politics that got out of hand.

The Integrity of the Seven-Letter Corpus

Scholars generally agree that only seven authentic letters from Ignatius have survived. Ignatius likely penned many others; at least, he turned readily to the letter form in the current situation. The real question is not whether Ignatius wrote more letters but whether he wrote additional letters during the difficult two-week period from which the seven surviving letters come. It is possible that the seven letters represent the full literary output of Ignatius during this brief period when he had the loan of Burrhus as secretary. Ignatius seemed to realize that his opportunity to write further letters would decrease when he left Troas, for he requested that Polycarp write in his stead to the churches before him (Ign. *Pol.* 8.1).

---

[4]Eusebius's account of Ignatius (*Eccl. hist.* 3.36) is taken entirely from Ignatius's own letters, and in one place when discussing Irenaeus's information about Ignatius, Eusebius says that Irenaeus drew the material "as usual" from Ignatius's letters (*Eccl. hist.* 5.8).

The question of the number of surviving authentic letters is complicated by the existence of various collections of Ignatian letters, some which contain several more,[5] or several fewer,[6] than the seven normally accepted. Confusing the matter further is the existence of shorter and longer recensions (editions) of the seven letters. After much debate, the matter has been settled in favor of the seven letters in their shorter versions. The case for this position was put forward as early as 1672 and convincingly defended by Bishop Lightfoot two hundred years later. These seven letters have been included in the *Reader*. A few scholars still dissent from this selection.

Literary Features

Ignatius uses many unusual words in his letters, perhaps coining many of the compounds himself. Further, he leaves a number of sentences incomplete. This may indicate time constraints or other restrictions, or it may reflect how letters were ordinarily written. The use of amanuenses (secretaries or scribes) could have meant that a letter was copied as dictated, thus reflecting the roughness of an unedited work; trained amanuenses may have been able to take a kind of "shorthand,"[7] and then compose a more polished letter later if time permitted.

Themes and Issues

Some disagreement about martyrdom (perhaps its value or its necessity) may lie close to the heart of what had divided the church in western Asia Minor. Otherwise it is puzzling why Ignatius repeatedly brought up his own martyrdom as relevant to the issue at hand. Further, he emphasized the reality of Jesus' death and the death of others.

There seem to be two sides to his appeal to the death of Jesus. Jesus truly died, Ignatius repeatedly states. That accounts for his own willingness to die. But, Ignatius asked, what of those who deny the reality of Jesus' death? With a number of different turns of phrase, Ignatius hammers home his conviction that it is on the issue of the reality of Jesus' humanity that his opponents were most grievously in error. It may even be that the opponents were presenting an argument for escape from martyrdom based on the claim that Jesus did not really die. We do know that some later gnostics were accused of running from martyrdom—indeed, even ideal-

---

[5]One was from Mary of Cassobelae with Ignatius's reply. One was to Hero, a deacon in Antioch. And one each was addressed to the churches at Tarsus, Antioch, and Philippi. Neither Eusebius (300s) nor Jerome (400s) mentions these eight in their discussion of Ignatius's letters.

[6]In 1845, William Cureton of the British Museum contended that only three letters were authentic—the ones to Polycarp, the Ephesians, and to Rome.

[7]About 150 years earlier, Cicero's secretary, Marcus Tullius Tiro, developed a shorthand system, and the method came to be spoken of as Tironian Notes, like a secretary today might speak of Gregg or Pitman. The art was lost during the medieval period, not to be developed again until the 1800s. Seneca speaks of this shorthand being able to keep up with the quickness of the tongue (*Letters* 90).

izing escape from martyrdom.[8] But that was a later accusation, not made specifically by Ignatius.

Scholars are far from agreement concerning the nature of the theological position that engaged and enraged Ignatius. Generally they find one of two heresies: one proto-gnostic or docetic (denying the humanity of Jesus), the other Jewish or judaizing. It is just as likely that the group being challenged by Ignatius reflected a mixture of both—a kind of Jewish gnosticism.

We do not know enough to answer convincingly basic questions about Ignatius and his letters. For example, How many distinct groups of opponents were addressed by Ignatius? What were the theological positions of the opponents? Why did martyrdom play a central role in Ignatius's attack on his opponents? Why is the authority of the bishops a recurring theme? Any satisfactory explanation of Ignatius's situation must do justice to all these issues.

Relation to Other Early Christian Literature

The *Reader* focuses largely on the Christian writings of the first century. Including the Ignatian letters and a few other documents takes us into the second century. We must remember that the early church (and the Roman world in general) did not have the same divisions of time that we are accustomed to, especially the divisions of centuries measured from the birth of Jesus. Such divisions are Christian creations of a later date.[9] For the earliest Christians, the difference between the letters of *Revelation* and the Ignatian letters, for example, would have been a difference of a few years, not a difference of "first-century letters" contrasted to "second-century letters."

Any line drawn between the first century and the second is largely theological in character and significance, not historical. That does not mean that such a line should not or cannot be drawn. The early church established a division like this when it spoke of an idealized age of the apostles. Nevertheless such a division was a construct built chiefly around a later conflict with "heretical" groups. "Orthodox" leaders contended for a pure apostolic age corrupted later by the heretics. This view was put forward, for the most part, after the fact. The idea of an apostolic age would have been a foreign concept to those who had participated in it.

---

[8]Gnosticism was not monolithic or unified. Some gnostics would have held different opinions. Marcionites, for example, did not flee martyrdom. In fact, the orthodox community was sometimes embarrassed by the willingness of the "heretics" who faced martyrdom, and in the case of the Montanists of Phrygia (in western Asia Minor) were clearly outdone by them in their zeal for martyrdom.

[9]The Christian calendar had its roots in the annual remembrance of saints on their days of martyrdom. The oldest extant calendar of this kind is from the fourth century after the conversion of Emperor Constantine to Christianity. It was not until the sixth century that Dionysius Exiguus (Denis, the Little, so named because of his humility or height) organized a calendar with the birth of Jesus in 1 C.E., with the new year starting on the date of the annunciation (that is, the conception).

Further, Christians living during this period had no fixed Christian canon—no New Testament. They cherished a variety of writings, from the Hebrew scriptures to documents written by Christian heroes of the more recent past and present. Without the fixed canon of later centuries, perhaps Christians would have read the letters of Ignatius with as much appreciation as they read *Revelation*. Men such as the Ignatius and Polycarp were revered, quite understandably, as members of the company of the apostles and early heroes. They were not seen as competitors or usurpers, nor were their writings dismissed as second-grade.

Only as the need grew to specify the boundary of canonical material (mainly in response to heretics, many of whom were producing their own writings) did the church attempt to isolate and elevate the apostolic documents to authoritative status.[10] Even then, the writings of the church fathers (church leaders after the apostles) were highly regarded and continued to be read and endorsed. The Ignatian letters, then, are a natural and necessary part of a collection of important early Christian writings and were treated so by early Christians. The first mention of the Ignatian letters is in a note from Polycarp to the church at Philippi, written perhaps before Ignatius had been martyred (Pol. *Phil.* 13.1–3).

We see in the Ignatian letters an increasing use of earlier Christian literature, a use reflected in *1 Clement* also. Clement's writing differs in that it appeals frequently to the Jewish scripture; such appeal is almost wholly lacking in the Ignatian letters, though there may be a number of stylistic influences from *4 Maccabees,* a book that had a similar interest in martyrdom.

Value for the Study of Early Christianity

The Ignatian letters are crucial for our reconstruction of the development of church office, in particular, the office of bishop. Monepiscopacy, in which a single bishop exercises primary authority, was ardently defended by Ignatius. But that office was not an end in itself. For Ignatius, this "episcopal" structure was the one effective tool by which apparently harmful theological tendencies might be checked, schismatic assemblies challenged, and apostolic truth preserved.

Independent or semi-independent groups that had distanced themselves from churches under the leadership of bishops figure prominently in Ignatius's concerns. Ignatius opposed such nonconformist groups, and directed his letters sharply against them. The bishops in the area were, as might be expected, allied with Ignatius, a bishop himself, and they found in this condemned man a fresh and weighty voice against the dissenters. This provides us with a picture of a developing church structure. Not only do bishops occupy the chief position of authority in the city churches, but these bishops are beginning to recognize the value of the support

---

[10]That is not to say that it was a late and arbitrary ecclesiastical action that gave documents authoritative status within the Christian communities. From the beginning, documents from respected leaders would have been treated with respect, and by the second century the issue of the authoritative status of documents was becoming prominent.

of their colleagues in other cities. This mutual support would grow considerably stronger in the next two centuries.

The Ignatian letters also give us a glimpse into the process by which at least one element in the church began to define itself and to exclude what it judged to be misrepresentations of the Christian message. This conflict used to be seen as a struggle between orthodoxy and heresy. Today, historians generally avoid such labels. The terms are theologically loaded, and their use may obscure the range of diversity that was tolerated in the early period.

Whatever label we use for Ignatius's opponents, these schismatics reflect thinking similar to, and perhaps the direct antecedent of, the gnostic systems of the second century, to which much recent scholarship on the early church has been directed. This makes the Ignatian material important, even if the sympathies of many modern scholars lie with the gnostics rather than with the bishop.

The Letters of Ignatius Written from Smyrna

Occasion

Earlier we learned that Ignatius had been visited in Smyrna by representatives of churches in the southern valley as he awaited passage to Rome. Delays were common enough, and Ignatius was traveling under guard (with ten soldiers, and perhaps other prisoners). It was August 24th when he wrote to the Romans (10.3),[11] and the dangerous winter sailing season was not far off.

Ignatius had traveled overland much of the way. At Laodicea,[12] the soldiers turned toward the Aegean Sea, traveling along the northern valley to Smyrna rather than along the southern valley to Ephesus. (The reason for this choice is not mentioned nor can it be ascertained.) The two valleys, running westward to the Aegean coast, were separated by the Messogis Mountains. A narrow valley joined the eastern end of the two routes at Laodicea.

Although we have no information about Ignatius's movements in Laodicea, we can infer certain details from what followed. The Ephesian, Trallian, and Magnesian churches at the Aegean end of the southern route sent representatives north to meet with Ignatius in Smyrna. It would seem, then, that after Ignatius left Laodicea for Smyrna, the church in Laodicea sent a messenger along the southern valley to inform the churches along the Meander River, perhaps ending in Tralles, of Ignatius's route. This messenger does not appear to have continued north to Smyrna with the other representatives, for Ignatius seems careful to list all who came to his aid in Smyrna, and no representative of Laodicea is mentioned.

---

[11]Perhaps the letter to the Romans was written first. It is different from all the other letters, and it conveys an urgent request from Ignatius to the Roman church that they not try to prevent his martyrdom. Since it is unlikely that this concern first came to mind in Smyrna, Ignatius may have taken his first opportunity (the pause in Smyrna) to send that message.

[12]Laodicea was one of three cities in the eastern end of the valleys. We know of early missionary success in all three cities—Laodicea, Hierapolis, and Colossae.

The bishop of the church at Tralles seems to have conveyed the news of Ignatius's journey to the churches at Magnesia and Ephesus as he passed through these cities on his way to meet Ignatius in Smyrna. Both of these churches hastily joined the church at Tralles in sending representatives to Smyrna. In all, ten people are named as members of this company—five from Ephesus (Ign. *Eph.* 2.1), four from Magnesia (Ign. *Magn.* 1.2), and one from Tralles (Ign. *Trall.* 1.1). This would have involved a considerable financial cost to the churches, for the members had to be away for several days.

Purpose

Ignatius took this opportunity to write to the churches that had sent representatives to visit and encourage him as he paused in Smyrna awaiting boat passage on his way to execution. He had at least three distinct reasons for writing. First, he wanted to express his gratitude for the effort and expense they had put themselves to in order to meet and encourage the convicted bishop face-to-face; he seems to have been genuinely touched by that display of friendship. Second, Ignatius had learned of "heresies" and "schisms": He wanted to warn the churches of these dangers, and to encourage them to seek the safety offered by their bishops. In doing this, he no doubt saw his letters as a tool by which to strengthen the authority of his fellow-bishops. Finally, he encouraged the churches to pray for the church at Antioch. Although it is a matter of considerable debate what the crisis in that church was, Ignatius's pressing concern was that it might have "peace."

Relationship to the Other Ignatian Letters

It has been argued that, though most of the themes are the same in all the letters to the churches in Asia, there is a marked change in one theme between the letters written from Smyrna and those written a few days later from Troas. In the letters written from Smyrna, Ignatius frequently mentions his "unworthiness," a concern that surfaces when he speaks of the church in Antioch over which he was bishop. It is contended that in the letters written from Troas, that sense of unworthiness is diminished, and the only change is that Ignatius has learned that the church at Antioch has gained its "peace." Thus the sense of unworthiness appears to be related to Ignatius's performance as bishop and the crisis that his church experienced under his leadership. But the matter is not that clear, as will be indicated in the notes.

To the Romans

The letter to the church at Rome is unlike any of those written to churches in Asia, though it was written at the same time. Several factors account for these differences.

Ignatius had not yet met the church in Rome, either in person or through visiting representatives. Further, it appears that the church in Rome was not troubled by the same issues that affected the churches of Asia. The intense concerns of the other letters—the dangers of heresy and the need of loyalty to the bishop and presbyters—do not surface, or they surface only in a superficial way that might be expected in any letter from a Christian leader to any church.

More important for understanding the unique concerns of Ignatius's letter to the Romans is the special position that the Roman church occupied. Ignatius believed that the Roman Christians might be able to prevent his martyrdom, which dismayed—rather than delighted—him. He wrote to prevent any such intervention.

Although we do not know what, if anything, the Roman church could have done to gain Ignatius's release, it is clear that Ignatius feared that they had some means at their disposal. His unwillingness to take advantage of whatever rescue might be secured seems puzzling and unreasonable to the modern reader, and it could not have been much different for the letter's first readers. Some sense can be made of this somewhat surprising reaction to the possibility of release if we understand that Ignatius had already embraced martyrdom as the mark of a true disciple. It was in terms of true discipleship that he most vividly described his condemnation and coming execution in Rome when he wrote to the Asian churches. Now to have martyrdom denied him seemed to steal the opportunity to become in action what he had been in word—a true disciple.

To prevent interference by the concerned Roman church, Ignatius delivers his rhetorical best immediately after the customary greetings and praise—epistolary politeness at least, though perhaps an expression of genuine fondness and respect. Ignatius tells them, "I am afraid of your love" (1.2). He implores them to "Let me be eaten by the beasts" (4.1). Twisting everyone's concern around, he adds, "Hinder me not from living; do not wish me to die" (6.2). Finally, near the closing he writes, "If I suffer, it was your favor. If I be rejected [that is, be delivered from martyrdom], it was your hatred" (8.3).

Ignatius's letter to the Romans seems not to have been a part of the letter collection that someone in Smyrna initially made for the benefit of area churches. Once that letter had been written and sent, it was gone from Asia. The other Ignatian letters remained, cherished by churches with an established network of communication and support among themselves. Early on they may have shared and copied the letters. However, Ignatius's letter to the Romans became the most quoted of his letters. This could be due in part to its content and in part to the ease of copying and distributing one letter versus a six-letter corpus.

To the Ephesians

This is the longest of Ignatius's letters, written to the church due south of Smyrna. This church had sent five representatives to visit Ignatius, and two of these, Burrhus and Croccus, were singled out for special mention because of their service to Ignatius (2.1). Ignatius wanted the services of the deacon Burrhus for a while longer, and his letter to the Ephesians was, at least in part, a request for that. The decision to grant the request must have been made by the Ephesian bishop and the delegates with him, for the larger church learned of the request only after the fact, upon the return of their representatives from Smyrna with the letter and without Burrhus. Burrhus seems to have returned when Ignatius sailed from Troas, for Ignatius then requested that Polycarp take over the task of letter writing—a strange request if Burrhus had been continuing with him to Rome (Ign. *Pol.* 8.1).

Perhaps this is the first letter Ignatius wrote in Smyrna. It is longer than the other letters. Further, at the end of the letter, Ignatius mentioned the possibility of writing a second letter (20.1), suggesting that he did not feel particularly pressed for time. The other letters are shorter, however, and none mentions the possibly of a second letter. Further, from a comment made to Polycarp, it seems that Ignatius had intended to write to various other churches, but was prevented from doing that by the sailing schedule (Ign. *Pol.* 8.1).

It is probably not accidental that the letter to the Ephesians appears at the beginning of the collection of the Ignatian letters. Ephesus has the same pride of place in the seven letters to the churches in *Revelation* (1:11; 2:1), and some scholars have argued that Paul's *Letter to the Ephesians* actually stood at the beginning of the original collection of Paul's letters. The city was important as the center from which Paul's mission to the province of Asia emanated, and the various comments of Ignatius in his letter to Ephesus reflect the continuing prominence of the church there.

To the Magnesians

Magnesia, on the Maeander, was about fifteen miles southeast of Ephesus, the first city on the route from Ephesus to Laodicea. Distance and traveling time in the ancient world corresponded less closely than in the modern world. When travel is by foot or animal, the terrain is more important than the actual distance. While most of the roads of Roman Asia, which were traveled by Ignatius or his visitors, were level and straight, the short section of the road from Magnesia to Ephesus involved a steep climb, which even today can bring a bus to a crawl. It would have been a strenuous full-day trip in either direction between these two cities over this mountain ridge.

We cannot determine when a church was first established in Magnesia. Being close to Ephesus, one might expect an early mission there. Certainly there would have been close contact between Magnesia and Ephesus; the southern gate of Ephesus is called the Magnesian Gate. Further, from several comments made by Ignatius in his letter, there seems to be a Jewish presence of some kind in Magnesia, perhaps suggesting further possible contacts for the early Christian mission. Finally, given Paul's three-year residence in Ephesus (*Acts* 19:8–10), and the success of his mission during that time throughout the province of Asia, it seems unlikely that the church in Magnesia was much younger than the mother-church of the region at Ephesus.

Written some forty years after Paul's stay in Ephesus and about ten or fifteen years before Ignatius's letters, the *Revelation* to "the seven churches of Asia" does not list Magnesia. This omission cannot be taken as evidence that no church existed in Magnesia at this time. The "seven churches of Asia" seem to be representative churches, with Magnesia included in the address to Ephesus, just as churches at Hierapolis and Colossae were probably included in the address to Laodicea.

Four representatives of the Magnesian church journeyed to meet Ignatius: their young bishop Damas, along with the presbyters Bassus and Apollonius, and the deacon Zotion. Nothing else is known about these people, though the youth of Damas is noted, which for the modern scholar poses a problem. The young bishop apparently did not rise to the bishop's office through the ranks of the presbytery (a body of elders). All we can say is that a possible parallel to that situation may be reflected in the *Pastoral Letters* regarding Timothy's youth (*1 Tim.* 4:10). There are hints that some people may have resisted the young bishop's leadership (3.1–4.1; 6.1–7.1)

Some form of Judaism seems to be at the heart of what Ignatius dismisses as a deviant form of Christianity, which someone had tried to propagate in Magnesia—unsuccessfully, according to Ignatius (11.1), but still a matter of some concern to him. The exact nature of this Judaism is unclear; there may have been features of docetic belief mixed with the Jewish elements, though it is the Jewish features that seem to concern Ignatius most. A similar concern is reflected in Ignatius's discussion of the opponents in Philadelphia (Ignatius, *Philadelphians* 5–9). Some have argued that Ignatius dealt with two groups of opponents: Jewish ones in Magnesia and Philadelphia, and docetic ones elsewhere, particularly in Tralles and Smyrna.

To the Trallians

Tralles was about seventeen or eighteen miles from Magnesia, on the road from Ephesus to Laodicea. The road runs north of the Meander River along the fertile plain and south of the Messogis mountain range. Lightfoot notes Cicero's comment about a trip he had made along the same road about the same time of year as Ignatius's visitors—the hottest time of the year (July/August). Cicero described it as a "boiling and dusty journey" (*ad Att.* 5.14).

Tralles, chosen for its defensive position, was set on a plateau some distance from the river. The modern city of Aydin lies on the plain at the southern base of this plateau, a heartland of bountiful orchards, as it was in ancient times. The city may have been particularly wealthy, for a number of its citizens were Asiarchs, the highest title given in Asia, from whom the priest of the imperial cult was chosen. At one time the city had also competed for the right to build a temple to the emperor. Becoming Asiarch and building a temple were expensive undertakings.

Ignatius praises the church, but there is a hint that at least some members had not acted properly toward their bishop, Polybius (3.1; 12.3). Ignatius is concerned here, as in other letters, that separate assemblies not be held (7.2). It is unclear whether the situation in Tralles had reached that point or whether Ignatius merely anticipated it, which is what he seems to say (8.1)

Docetism also seems to be a problem, and Ignatius addresses it directly in a number of places. Judaism, which he mentions several times in his letter to the Magnesians, is not alluded to at all in this letter. However, one might question the likelihood of Tralles, with its docetic problem, and nearby Magnesia, with its Judaism problem, *not* tainting one another with these problems. It seems at least as likely that the opposition is the same, with a mixture of Jewish and docetic elements, different sides of which are mentioned in each letter.

The Letters of Ignatius Written from Troas

Purpose

After leaving the port of Smyrna in late August, the boat carrying Ignatius was delayed long enough in Troas for him to write to his hosts in Smyrna (the church and the bishop) to thank them for their hospitality. He writes a third letter to Philadelphia, after learning more news about the situation there from recent visitors.

These letters share less than the three letters written from Smyrna, and are treated separately below. Unlike the letters to the churches of Ephesus, Magnesia and Tralles, of which Ignatius had no firsthand knowledge, these letters address specific needs that Ignatius observed while visiting Philadelphia and Smyrna.

To the Philadelphians

Ignatius had passed through the city of Philadelphia on his way from Laodicea to Smyrna, probably spending no more than a night there. In spite of being under armed guard and escorted in chains, Ignatius was able to meet with a number of the Christians there and apparently waded into a conflict involving some kind of schism.

The nature of the schism is difficult to describe, because it appears that members of the schismatic faction were present in the bishop's company when the assembly met with Ignatius. Further, the schism could not have been obvious to a visitor, because Ignatius claimed that he learned of the schism from the Holy Spirit, which would have been a hollow claim had the schism been obvious to any observer. Finally, Ignatius charged that the schismatics had tried to deceive him, and though we are not able to determine *how* they accomplished this, the fact that they *could* adds to the puzzle (7.1–2).

As usual, Ignatius took the bishop's side. That does not necessarily mean that Ignatius blindly supported the episcopal structure, regardless of the situation. Ignatius supported certain theological perspectives, and he must have found substantial theological allies in these bishops.

How Ignatius could assume that the bishops would sympathize with his theological perspective continues to divide scholars. It opens issues concerning the nature of earliest Christianity and the diversity versus unity in which the early church developed.

His call for submission to the bishop and his censure of schism is more sustained here than in any of his other letters. The schism involved elements of Judaism—again more intensely engaged here than in any of the other letters. Similar concerns were expressed in the *Letter to the Magnesians.*

To the Smyrnaeans

Ignatius's difficult trip to his death in Rome was met with some special kindness in Smyrna as his guards arranged passage. The church there and its bishop Polycarp made his stay as comfortable as possible, providing him with secretarial help and probably hosting him and his ill-mannered guards. One senses Ignatius's deep gratitude for this time in the touching closing remarks in the letters to the church and to Polycarp.

The standard range of themes in Ignatius's other letters is found here, but he attacks the docetic position more vigorously here than elsewhere though the theme does receive special attention in the *Letter to the Trallians* (9.1–10.1). In this letter to the Smyrnaeans he is at his rhetorical best, turning the opponents' position against themselves. While not always offering the most tightly logical argument, Ignatius had some cutting one-liners that must have had an appreciative audience among his many supporters. The problem of the opponents is so pressing that, after a brief greeting (a matter of epistolary politeness), he immediately engages the opponents, and he sustains the attack through most of the first half.

Ignatius closes his letter with a request that the church in Smyrna participate in a congratulatory visit to the church in Antioch, sharing in the celebration of the peace that church attained. The request is even more detailed in the letter to Polycarp, in which he delegates Polycarp to promote similar visits to Antioch by other churches.

It remains a matter of considerable debate what the crisis in Antioch was, how it was resolved, and why such a massive and expensive response to its resolution seemed to Ignatius a reasonable and necessary request.

To Polycarp

Whereas the other letters are addressed to churches, this one is addressed to Polycarp, the bishop, and it bears the most personal touch. Although most of the instruction is specifically intended for Polycarp, it appears that Ignatius expected the letter to be read to the church also. He directs at least one comment to the church rather than to the bishop (6), and in others places he instructs Polycarp regarding the duties of slaves (4), wives (5.1), husbands (5.1), and celibates (5.2). The letter closes with a number of personal greetings, three by name (8.2). Indeed, the latter half of the letter jumps back and forth from second person singular to second person plural. Nevertheless, Polycarp is foremost in Ignatius's mind, and issues addressed primarily to the church are placed in the more formal letter. This is Polycarp's letter and should be read as such.

Ignatius brings a number of matters to Polycarp's attention—much of it advice that an older bishop might pass on to a younger: to act meekly (2.1); to care for widows (4.1); to know the members of the church by name (4.2); to treat slaves with respect (4.3); to be the advisor in sexual matters, from marriage to periods of celibacy that a married couple might choose (5.2).

Ignatius also has more specific and immediate requests, which probably necessitate this additional letter. For one thing, he has received word that the church in Antioch has gained its "peace," and he wishes Polycarp to arrange a "courier" to travel from Smyrna to Antioch (8.1), a point which he discusses more fully in his letter to the church at Smyrna (Ign. *Smyrn.* 11.1–3). Further, Ignatius intended to write to various churches "on the road in front" of him (Ign. *Pol.* 8.1), but was unable to do so because of his sudden sailing from Troas—at which point Burrhus, his borrowed scribe, returned to Ephesus. Ignatius now places the task of writing to these churches in Polycarp's hands.

Other than what we learn about Polycarp from Ignatius's letters (basically that he was bishop of Smyrna), we know little about him until his old age, though a number of authors report stories concerning him, and the young Irenaeus was his pupil. Polycarp was martyred in 155 C.E. (there is some dispute about the date) at the age of eighty-six. If Ignatius passed through Smyrna around 110, Polycarp would have been around forty years old. Some traditions claim that Polycarp was himself a disciple of John the apostle, which is chronologically not impossible if John lived into the last decade of the first century.

For Further Reading

The Apostolic Fathers. 2 vols. Translated by Kirsopp Lake. Cambridge, Mass.: Harvard University Press/London: Heinemann, 1976–1985.

Brown, Charles Thomas. *The Gospel and Ignatius of Antioch.* New York: Lang, 2000.

Grant, Robert M. *Ignatius of Antioch.* Vol. 4 of *The Apostolic Fathers: A New Translation and Commentary.* New York: Nelson, 1966.

Lightfoot, J. B. *S. Ignatius, S. Polycarp.* 3 vols. Part II of *The Apostolic Fathers.* 2d ed. London: Macmillan, 1890. Repr., Grand Rapids: Baker, 1999.

Schoedel, William R. *Ignatius of Antioch: A Commentary on the Letters of Ignatius of Antioch.* Hermeneia. Philadelphia: Fortress, 1985.

Trevett, Christine. *A Study of Ignatius of Antioch in Syria and Asia.* Lewiston, N.Y.: Mellen, 1992.

THE LETTER OF IGNATIUS
TO THE ROMANS

Salutation

Ignatius, who is also called Theophorus, to the church that has found mercy in the majesty of the Father Most High and Jesus Christ his only son, beloved and enlightened through the will of the one who willed all things that exist, in accordance with faith in and love for Jesus[a] Christ our God, which also presides in the place of the district of the Romans, worthy of God, worthy of honor, worthy of blessing, worthy of praise, worthy of success, worthy of sanctification, and presiding over[b] love, observing the law of Christ,[c] bearing the name of the Father, which I also greet in the name of Jesus Christ, son of the Father; to those who are united in flesh and spirit to every commandment of his, who have been filled with the grace of God without wavering and filtered clear of every alien color: heartiest greetings blamelessly in Jesus Christ our God.

Request Not to Prevent His Martyrdom

1 Since by praying to God I have succeeded in seeing your godly faces, so that I have received more than I asked[d]—for I hope to greet you in chains for Jesus Christ, if it is his will for me to be reckoned worthy to reach the goal. [2]For the beginning is auspicious, provided that I attain the grace[e] to receive my fate without interference. For I am afraid of your love, in that it may do me wrong; for it is easy for you to do what you want, but it is difficult for me to reach God, unless you spare me.

2 For I do not want you to please people, but to please God, as you in fact are doing. For I will never again have an opportunity such as this to reach

---

a Or *faith and love of Jesus;* other ancient authorities omit *faith* [*in*] *and*

b Or *preeminent in*

c Other ancient authorities read *bearing the name of Christ*

d Most ancient authorities read *faces, even as I have been asking to receive yet more*

e Other ancient authorities read *goal*

TRANSLATION by Michael W. Holmes after the earlier translation of J. B. Lightfoot and J. R. Harmer. TRANSLATION NOTES by Michael W. Holmes. Reprinted, with revisions, from *The Apostolic Fathers: Greek Texts and English Translations*, edited and revised by Michael W. Holmes (Grand Rapids: Baker Books, 1999). © 1992, 1999, 2003 by Michael W. Holmes. Used by permission of Baker Book House. All rights reserved. CONTENT NOTES are by the editors of this volume, with acknowledgment to Michael W. Holmes for his observations regarding a number of texts.

Salutation *Jesus Christ our God* Ignatius makes stark claims that Jesus is God. He even speaks of the blood of God (Ign. *Eph.* 1.1) and the suffering of God (Ign. *Rom.* 6.3) and uses the phrase "Jesus Christ our God" twice in this introductory paragraph. See Ign. *Eph.* salutation. *presides in the place of the district of the Romans* This is both a recognition of the importance of the church at Rome and a polite epistolary introduction. Nothing leads us to conclude that a church in the capital, founded about seventy years earlier, would not have promoted missionary endeavors beyond its own city. Some earlier Protestant scholars attempted to qualify the meaning of the word "presides," which they thought gave special status to the church at Rome. *worthy* In the Gk, six compound words in this sentence begin with the prefix *axi-*, meaning "worthy." Two of these words may have been coined by Ignatius; they occur nowhere else in Gk literature. *observing the law of Christ* In Gk this is one word *(christonomos)*; the variant "bearing the name of Christ" differs only slightly *(christōnymos). filtered* Filtering was a common method for removing impurities from a variety of substances (Ign. *Phld.* 3.1; *Isa.* 25:6; *Matt.* 23:24). **1.1** *more than I asked* A bit of irony. Ignatius says that he has prayed to visit the Roman church; now his prayer has been answered—in fact, answered more than he asked—for he is coming as a chained and condemned convict to be martyred in their presence. *I hope to greet you* Ignatius thinks that he will be able to meet with the church at Rome as he did with the Christians from several churches along the way—Smyrna and perhaps Philadelphia, Troas, and Philippi. **1.2** *do me wrong* This is Ignatius's first request to the Romans, telling them not interfere in his approaching martyrdom, and he makes this the primary theme of his letter. We do not know how the Roman church might have been able to secure Ignatius's release from the death sentence. We are certain that Ignatius wanted to die, and he considered his death in the arena as the final mark of true discipleship (see notes to Ign. *Eph.* 1.1; Ign. *Trall.* 4.2; 5.2). He does not want to be denied this final test. *unless you spare me* Again a touch of irony. If the Roman church acted to spare Ignatius from execution, it would have prevented him from being a true disciple. As he says in the previous sentence, *For I am afraid of your love, in that it may do wrong.* **2.1** *please people* Gk compound word, *anthrōpareskēsai*, which occurs also in *Col.* 3:22 and *Eph.* 6:6. It is clearly negative, and the translation "men-pleasers" or "people-pleasers" probably catches the sense better (see *Gal.* 1:10 and *1 Thess.* 2:4, where the two words are used separately in the phrase *anthrōpois areskō*).

God, nor can you, if you remain silent, be credited with a greater accomplishment. For if you remain silent and leave me alone, I will be a word of God, but if you love my flesh, then I will again be a mere voice. ²Grant me nothing more than to be poured out as an offering to God while there is still an altar ready, so that in love you may form a chorus and sing to the Father in Jesus Christ, because God has judged the bishop from Syria worthy to be found in the West, having summoned him from the East.ᶠ It is good to be setting from the world to God in order that I may rise to him.

Martyrdom: The True Test of a Christian

3 You have never envied anyone; you taught others. And my wish is that those instructions that you issue when teaching disciples will remain in force. ²Just pray that I will have strength both outwardly and inwardly so that I may not just talk about it but want to do it, that I may not merely be called a Christian but actually prove to be one. For if I prove to be one, I can also be called one, and then I will be faithful when I am no longer visible to the world. ³Nothing that is visible is good. For our God Jesus Christ is more visible now that he is in the Father. The work is not a matter of persuasive rhetoric; rather, Christianity is greatest when it is hated by the world.

Sacrifice As True Discipleship

4 I am writing to all the churches and am insisting to everyone that I die for God of my own free will—unless you hinder me. I implore you: do not be "unseasonably kind" to me. Let me be foodᵍ for the wild beasts, through whom I can reach God. I am God's wheat, and I am being ground by the teeth of the wild beasts, that I may prove to be pure bread.ʰ ²Better yet, coax the wild beasts, that they may become my tomb and leave nothing of my body behind, lest I become a burden to anyone once I have fallen asleep. Then I will truly be a disciple of Jesus Christ, when the world will no longer see my body. Pray to the Lordⁱ on my behalf, that through these instruments I may prove to be a sacrifice to God. ³I do not give you orders like Peter and Paul: they were apostles, I am a convict; they were free, but I am even now still a slave. But if I suffer, I will be a freedman of Jesus Christ and will rise up free in him. In the meantime, as a prisoner I am learning to desire nothing.

Desire to Face, Not Flee, Martyrdom

5 From Syria all the way to Rome I am fighting with wild beasts, on land and sea, by night and day, chained amidst ten leopards (that is, a company of soldiers) who only get worse when they are well

---

ᶠ Gk *in the setting* [of the sun] . . . *from the rising* [of the sun]

ᵍ Other ancient authorities omit *food*
ʰ Other ancient authorities read *bread of God;* others read *bread of Christ*
ⁱ Other ancient authorities read *Pray to Christ*

---

if you remain silent Again Ignatius appeals to the Roman church not to interfere. Perhaps they could have offered in his defense information that might have prevented his martyrdom. Ignatius plays with two words: *word (logos)* and *voice (phōnē),* which can be translated "sound." If Ignatius is permitted to die, he will be a *word of God.* If he is rescued, he will be merely a "sound" of some kind. Ignatius clearly intends the latter to be negative. **2.2 chorus** As one might find at pagan sacrifices and ceremonies (Ign. *Eph.* 19.2). **bishop from Syria** Ignatius describes himself here as the bishop from Syria and in another place as a member of the church there (Ign. *Magn.* 14.1). Regarding his church, he has two ways of describing it: the church in Syria (Ign. *Eph.* 21.2; Ign. *Magn.* 14.1; Ign. *Trall.* 13.1; *Ign. Rom.* 9.1) and the church in Antioch of Syria (Ign. *Phld.* 10.1; Ign. *Smyrn.* 11.1; Ign. *Pol.* 7.1), but never Antioch alone. **the West** Rome. The rising of the sun in the next clause refers to Antioch. He plays with this image—setting to the world and rising to God, a reference to the resurrection. **3.2–3 Christian . . . Christianity** See Ign. *Eph.* 11.2. **3.2 when I am no longer visible to the world** Ignatius speaks here of his death. It is only after he has proven his faith by enduring martyrdom that he will truly deserve the name *Christian* (see Ign. *Eph.* 1.1; Ign. *Magn.* 4.2). **3.3 our God Jesus Christ** See the note to the salutation, where Ignatius twice speaks of Jesus as God. **The work** See Ign. *Eph.* 14.2. **4.1–3** This is perhaps the most vivid description of the link between discipleship and martyrdom in Ignatius's writings. See notes to Ign. *Eph.* 1.1; Ign. *Trall.* 4.2; 5.2. Other vivid language occurs in Ign. *Rom.* 5.2–3. **4.1** Ignatius says that he is writing to all the churches. At this time he has written only to three others that we know of (Ephesus, Magnesia, and Tralles). There is some indication that he intended to write to many more churches but was prevented because of his unexpected departure from Troas. He then assigned the responsibility to complete this task to Polycarp (Ign. *Pol.* 8.2). **unseasonably kind** The phrase is thought to be part of a proverb recorded by Zenobius (*Paroem.* 1.50). **bread** This term could recall the Eucharist, for Ignatius does see his death as a sacrifice (4.2) See Ign. *Eph.* 5.2. **4.3** This is one of only two passages in our literature where Peter and Paul are mentioned together. The earliest evidence seems to indicate a degree of tension, if not competition, between the two. Compare this passage and *1 Clem.* 5.4–5 with comments made by Paul himself in *Gal.* 2:11–14 and *1 Cor.* 1:12. As for Ignatius's comment about Peter, it is not clear in what way Peter "gave orders to" the church at Rome; Paul, at least, had written a letter to the Romans. For Ignatius's reference to his convict status, see Ign. *Eph.* 1.2. **freedman of Jesus Christ** *1 Cor.* 7:22. **5.1 on land and sea** This suggests that the first leg of Ignatius's trip was by ship from Antioch, landing perhaps at Attalia on the southern coast of Turkey, then by an overland route north through the area of Colossae, then on through Philadelphia to Smyrna. **leopards** Ignatius gives us some

treated. Yet because of their mistreatment I am becoming more of a disciple; nevertheless "I am not thereby justified." [2]May I have the pleasure of the wild beasts that have been prepared for me; and I pray that they prove to be prompt with me. I will even coax them to devour me promptly, not as they have done with some, whom they were too timid to touch. And if when I am willing and ready they are not, I will force them. [3]Bear with me—I know what is best for me. Now at last I am beginning to be a disciple. May nothing visible or invisible envy me, so that I may reach Jesus Christ. Fire and cross and battles with wild beasts, mutilation, mangling,[j] wrenching of bones, the hacking of limbs, the crushing of my whole body, cruel tortures of the devil—let these come upon me, only let me reach Jesus Christ!

6 Neither the ends of the earth nor the kingdoms of this age are of any use to me. It is better for me to die for Jesus Christ than to rule over the ends of the earth. Him I seek, who died on our behalf; him I long for, who rose again for our sake. The pains of birth are upon me.

Longing for Life through Death

[2]Bear with me, brothers and sisters: do not keep me from living; do not desire my death. Do not give to the world one who wants to belong to God, nor tempt[k] him with material things. Let me receive the pure light, for when I arrive there I will be a man.

[3]Allow me to be an imitator of the suffering of my God. If anyone has him within himself, let him understand what I long for and sympathize with me, knowing what constrains me.

7 The ruler of this age wants to take me captive and corrupt my godly intentions. Therefore none of you who are present must help him. Instead take my side, that is, God's. Do not talk about Jesus Christ while you desire the world. [2]Do not let envy dwell among you. And if upon my arrival I myself should appeal to you, do not be persuaded by me; believe instead[l] these things that I am writing to you. For though I am still alive, I am passionately in love with death as I write to you. My passionate love has been crucified and there is no fire of material longing within me, but only water living and speaking[m] in me, saying within me, "Come to the Father." [3]I take no pleasure in corruptible food or the pleasures of this life. I want the bread of God, which is the flesh of Christ who is of the seed of David; and for drink I want his blood, which is incorruptible love.

8 I no longer want to live according to human standards. And such will be the case, if you so desire. Do so desire, that you also may be desired! [2]With these brief lines I am making my request of you. Do believe me! And Jesus Christ, the unerring mouth by whom the Father has spoken truly, will make it clear to you that I am speaking truly. [3]Pray for me, that I may reach the goal.[n] I write to you not according to

---

j Other ancient authorities read *wild beasts, mutilation, and wrenching;* others read *wild beasts, wrenching*

k Gk is corrupt; one ancient authority reads *deceive*

l Other ancient authorities read *be persuaded instead by*

m Another ancient authority reads *living;* other ancient authorities vary widely

n Other ancient authorities add *through the Holy Spirit*

---

sense of the ill treatment he has received from his armed escort. He calls them *wild beasts* and *leopards;* the latter term appears here for the first time in Gk or Latin literature. **I am not thereby justified** 1 Cor. 4:4. **5.2** Ignatius seems to have been aware of incidents where the wild beasts did not attack the condemned prisoners. It is unclear whether these victims were Christians or others. **5.3** The list of possible tortures, including the cross, was designed for all condemned alike, whether Christian or non-Christian. **6.1** *the pains of birth are upon me* A touch of irony here. Ignatius is on his way to martyrdom in Rome; the church he is addressing knows his approaching fate, and he has pleaded with them not to rescue him from this horror. Clearly, he is to die. But this he considers a *birth.* Later, Christians began to count the day of a person's martyrdom as the day of the person's birth—birth into God's presence—and they celebrated this date of martyrdom annually. Out of such celebrations came the Christian calendar we know today, marked by saints' days. **6.2** *do not keep me from living* The irony continues. Ignatius fears that the church in Rome will prevent his martyrdom, but he twists this concern to say that they would be hindering him *from living* were they to save him from death. He continues with the same logic and striking irony through the next two sections (7–8). **6.3** *suffering of my God* See Ign. *Eph.* salutation. **7.1** See 6.2. If Ignatius is rescued the beasts of the arena, he will have been torn to pieces by the *ruler of this age.* And if this rescue is made possible by the intervention of the Roman Christians, they will have helped the devil. These outrageous statements must have surprised his Roman readers. *ruler of this age* Meaning the devil. See Ign. *Eph.* 17.1. **7.2** Ignatius fears that when he arrives in Rome and faces the grim reality of his fate, he might change his mind and request that the Roman Christians intervene. To prevent this, he asks them to follow his instructions in this letter, regardless of what he might say after he arrives in Rome. *My passionate love has been crucified* His love for "the world" has died with Christ. See *Gal.* 6:14. **7.2–3** *water living . . . bread of God . . . drink . . . his blood* The images here parallel those in *John* 6–7, and they have their primary force in the environment of the Eucharist. **7.3** *seed of David* See notes to Ign. *Eph.* 20.2; Ign. *Trall.* 9.1. *love* Gk *agapē.* Some scholars think that Ignatius has the Eucharist or the agape feast in mind. See Ign. *Smyrn.* 8.2 regarding the agape feast. **8.3** See notes to 6.2 and 7.1. The wording of the sentence is puzzling, but the sense is clear enough: "If you love me, let me die; if you hate me, let me live."

human perspective but in accordance with the mind of God. If I suffer, you will have wanted it; if I am rejected, you will have hated me.

Personal Greetings and Parting Requests

9 Remember in your prayers the church in Syria, which has God for its shepherd in my place. Jesus Christ alone will be its bishop—as will your love. [2]But I myself am ashamed to be counted among them, for I am not worthy, since I am the very last of them and an untimely birth. But I have been granted the mercy to be someone, if I reach God. [3]My spirit greets you, as does the love of the churches that welcomed me in the name of Jesus Christ, rather than as a mere transient. For even churches that did not lie on my way (that is, my physical route) went before me from city to city.

10 I write these things to you from Smyrna through the Ephesians, who are most worthy of blessing. With me, along with many others, is Crocus, a name very dear to me. [2]Regarding those who preceded me from Syria to Rome to the glory of God, I believe that you have information. Let them know that I am near, for they are all worthy of God and of you, and it is quite proper for you to refresh them in every respect. [3]I am writing these things to you on the ninth day before the calends of September. Farewell to the end, in the patient endurance of Jesus Christ.

9.1 *shepherd . . . bishop* The two terms are also linked in *Acts* 20:28 and *1 Pet.* 2:25. **9.2** *I am not worthy* See notes to Ign. *Eph.* 1.2; Ign. *Magn.* 1.2. **untimely birth** *1 Cor.* 15:8–9. It is uncertain what Ignatius means. **9.3** The reference must be at least to the churches of Ephesus, Magnesia, and Tralles, but visitors from churches situated nearer the northern route that Ignatius traveled cannot be ruled out. **10.1** Crocus served as the scribe, or amanuensis, of this letter. Ign. *Eph.* 2.1. **10.2** Individuals from Syria—probably from Ignatius's own church in Antioch—are already in Rome. The phrase *to the glory of God* may suggest that they, too, were sent for execution, but Ignatius seems to think that they are not yet dead. Perhaps when the church at Antioch learned that Ignatius was being sent to Rome, it sent people on ahead, thus bringing news of Ignatius's plight to churches on the way and informing the Roman church. Certainly Ignatius seems to assume that the Roman church knows the details of his fate. **10.3** *ninth day before the calends of September* August 24. The safest period for shipping and sea travel was coming to an end.

THE LETTER OF IGNATIUS
TO THE EPHESIANS

Salutation

Ignatius, who is also called Theophorus, to the church at Ephesus in Asia, blessed with greatness through the fullness of God the Father, predestined before the ages for lasting and unchangeable glory forever, united and elect through genuine suffering by the will of the Father and of Jesus Christ our God, a church most worthy of blessing: heartiest greetings in Jesus Christ and in blameless joy.

1 I welcomed in God your well-beloved name, which you possess by reason of your righteous na-ture,[a] characterized by faith in and love of Christ Jesus our Savior. Being imitators of God, once you took on new life through the blood of God you completed perfectly the task so natural to you. ²For when you heard that I was on my way from Syria in chains for the sake of our common name and hope, and was hoping through your prayers to succeed in fighting with wild beasts in Rome—in order that by so succeeding I might be able to be a disciple—you hurried to visit me. ³Since, therefore, I have received

---

a Other ancient authorities read *possess by natural right in an upright and righteous mind*

TRANSLATION by Michael W. Holmes after the earlier translation of J. B. Lightfoot and J. R. Harmer. TRANSLATION NOTES by Michael W. Holmes. Reprinted, with revisions, from *The Apostolic Fathers: Greek Texts and English Translations,* edited and revised by Michael W. Holmes (Grand Rapids: Baker Books, 1999). © 1992, 1999, 2003 by Michael W. Holmes. Used by permission of Baker Book House. All rights reserved. CONTENT NOTES are by the editors of this volume, with acknowledgment to Michael W. Holmes for his observations regarding a number of texts.

Salutation The numerous parallels between this and the introduction to the *Letter to the Ephesians* attributed to Paul may point to Ignatius's familiarity with that letter and his imitation of it. **Theophorus** Lit. "God-bearer," apparently a nickname for Ignatius. Ignatius uses the word as an adjective in 9.2. **Asia** The Roman province of Asia (modern western Turkey), not to be confused with Asia Minor, which included several Roman provinces. **fullness of God** Gk *plērōma*, a term found in other early Christian literature (*John* 1:16; *Rom.* 15:29; *Eph.* 1:23). This term becomes significant in gnostic thought in the 2d century. **genuine suffering** This idea is repeated and developed throughout the Ignatian letters. The suffering of Jesus was real, as was Ignatius's own suffering and approaching martyrdom, and it was by such suffering that true discipleship was determined. This position has an antidocetic ring (see introduction to The Letters of Ignatius). **greetings** Ignatius uses the common Gk word for letter greetings, *chairein* (*Acts* 15:23; *Jas.* 1:1). Many Christian writers, however, used the word *charis* ("grace"), perhaps under the influence of Paul's letters. **Christ our God** Ignatius repeatedly called Jesus God, using such language as "the blood of God" (1.1) and "the suffering of my God" (Ign. *Rom.* 6.3). This kind of language was judged unacceptable in the trinitarian and christological controversies of later centuries. **1.1 well-beloved name** Ephesus was the chief city of Paul's mission, and the church there held a leading position until Constantine shifted the center of the empire to Constantinople. Although the importance of Ephesus then began to decline, one of the important early councils was held there in 431 C.E. **imitators** Paul spoke much of imitation (*1 Cor.* 4:16; 11:1; *Eph.* 5:1; *1 Thess.* 1:6; 2:14). For Ignatius, the term served to express true discipleship, even to the point of imitating the death of Jesus by actual martyrdom (10.3; Ign. *Trall.* 1.2; Ign. *Rom.* 4.1–3; 6.3; Ign. *Phld.* 7.2). The idea occurs in other Christian literature too (*Heb.* 6:12; *1 Clem.* 17.1). **1.2 in chains** A number of the leaders of the early Christian movement experienced prosecution and imprisonment and, in extreme cases, received the death sentence for their Christian activity. They frequently spoke of their chains, much as we might speak of handcuffs. Ignatius was well aware of his status as a prisoner (see 21.2) and the shame that would normally accompany this (11.2; Ign. *Magn.* 1.2; Ign. *Trall.* 1.1; Ign. *Rom.* 1.1; Ign. *Phld.* 5.1; Ign. *Smyrn.* 4.2; Ign. *Pol.* 2.3). Paul, or those writing in Paul's name, likewise spoke of imprisonments (*Rom.* 16:1; *Eph.* 3:1; *Col.* 4:3, 10, 18; *2 Tim.* 1:8, 16; *Phlm.* 9, 23). The author of *Acts* used forms of the Gk words for "prison" and "chains" more than thirty times in his account of the early church. **common name** See note at 11.2. "The Name" came to be a label used by Christians to identify themselves. See 3.1; 7.1; Ign. *Phld.* 10.1; *Acts* 5:41; *1 Pet.* 4:14–16; *3 John* 7. Christians were persecuted as an undesirable group in the Roman Empire in the 2d and 3d centuries. A common complaint of Christian writers was that Christians were condemned in the Roman courts simply because they called themselves Christian, whereas normally people were not condemned unless they had committed a specific crime. See *1 Pet.* 4:14–16. **fighting with wild beasts** Ignatius appears to have been condemned to death in the arena, part of the regular entertainment of urban residents, at which criminals and other condemned persons were pitted against a variety of wild animals or against professional gladiators. Death was certain (Ign. *Trall.* 10.1; Ign. *Rom.* 4.1–2; Ign. *Smyrn.* 4.2). **in Rome** The colosseum, built by the Flavian emperors, mainly Trajan, was completed shortly before Ignatius's death. **disciple** For Ignatius, any claim to be a true disciple seemed an arrogant and dangerous boast until it was put to the ultimate test—martyrdom. He was cautious not to claim such status too early (3.1; Ign. *Pol.* 2.1; Ign. *Magn.* 9.2; see Ign. *Magn.* 1.2). **you hurried to visit me** The decision of the churches at Tralles, Magnesia, and Ephesus to send a delegation to meet Ignatius in Smyrna must have been made in haste. One of these

in God's name your whole congregation in the person of Onesimus, a man of inexpressible love who is also your earthly[b] bishop, I pray that you will love him in accordance with the standard set by Jesus Christ and that all of you will be like him. For blessed is the one who has graciously allowed you, worthy as‘ you are, to have such a bishop.

Thanks for Visit and Assistance

2 Now concerning my fellow servant Burrhus, who is by God's will your deacon, blessed in every respect, I pray[c] that he may remain with me both for your honor and the bishop's. And Crocus also, who is worthy of God and of you, whom I received as a living example of your love, has refreshed me in every way; may the Father of Jesus Christ likewise refresh him, together with Onesimus, Burrhus, Euplus, and Fronto, in whom I saw all of you with respect to love. 2May I always have joy in you—if, that is, I am worthy. It is proper, therefore, in every way to glorify Jesus Christ, who has glorified you, so that

---

b Other ancient authorities omit *earthly*
c Or *beg* or *wish*

---

you, joined together in a united obedience and subject to the bishop and the presbytery, may be sanctified in every respect.

3 I am not commanding you, as though I were someone important. For even though I am in chains for the sake of the name, I have not yet been perfected in Jesus Christ. For now I am only beginning to be a disciple, and I speak to you as my fellow students. For I need to be trained by you in faith, instruction, endurance, and patience. 2But since love does not allow me to be silent concerning you, I have therefore taken the initiative to encourage you, so that you may run together in harmony with the mind of God. For Jesus Christ, our inseparable life, is the mind of the Father, just as the bishops appointed throughout the world are in the mind of Christ.

Obedience to the Bishop

4 Thus it is proper for you to act together in harmony with the mind of the bishop, as you are in fact doing. For your presbytery, which is worthy of its name and worthy of God, is attuned to the bishop as strings to a lyre. Therefore in your unanimity and harmonious love Jesus Christ is sung. 2You must join

---

churches was able to dispatch five men to spend several days away from their work, and this may tell us something about the financial health of these communities. The church at Magnesia sent four men for an even longer trip (Ign. *Magnesians* 2), and the church at Tralles sent its bishop (Ign. *Trall.* 1.1). **1.3 *Onesimus*** The name is too common to warrant concluding, as some have done, that this Onesimus was the slave from the city of Colossae mentioned by Paul fifty years earlier (*Phlm.* 10; *Col.* 4:9). ***I pray that you will love him*** The call to submit to or to follow the bishop is at the heart of Ignatius's correspondence to the churches in Asia; the theme does not appear in the letter to the church in Rome, where the more pressing issue of his approaching martyrdom overshadows everything else. **2.1 *fellow servant*** Ign. *Magn.* 2.1; Ign. *Phld.* 4.1; Ign. *Smyrn.* 12.2; *Col.* 1:7; 4:7; *Rev.* 6:11. ***remain with me*** We do not know how long Burrhus stayed with Ignatius. Ignatius seems to be aware that Burrhus's service would involve some cost to the Ephesians, and he praises them for their support when he writes to the church at Philadelphia (Ign. *Phld.* 11.2). The church at Smyrna has helped the church at Ephesus with the expense (Ign. *Smyrn.* 12.1). Burrhus, valued by Ignatius because of his service as a scribe, probably had a good education that had provided him with other administrative skills, which may have propelled him into the position of deacon in the Ephesian church. Such a person was unlikely to be a day laborer, and his absence for a few weeks from the workforce would surely have been missed. ***refreshed*** 2 *Tim.* 1:16. The five people mentioned here are from Ephesus. We know nothing more about them, except that Burrhus continued on with Ignatius (Ign. *Phld.* 11.2; Ign. *Smyrn.* 12.1), perhaps mainly to assist him in his correspondence (Ign. *Smyrn.* 12.1), and that Crocus, too, was singled out for special mention (Ign. *Rom.* 10.1). **2.2 *if ... I am worthy*** Ignatius frequently raises the issue of his own worthiness. Many scholars believe that he was so self-deprecating because he blamed himself for the difficulties that the church at Antioch had experienced when he had been bishop there. It is just as possible that his sense of unworthiness was connected to his understanding of true discipleship, which he felt was not assured until his actual martyrdom (3.1). See introduction to The Letters of Ignatius. **3.1 *fellow students*** A compound Gk word found only in Ignatius. Ignatius was fond of rare compound terms and may have coined many himself. ***I need to be trained*** Lit. "anointed." Oil was used to prepare athletes for their contests. Christians often used the language of brutal gladiatorial sport to describe their spiritual preparation, which, ironically, often resulted in their deaths in Roman sports arenas (*1 Clem.* 5.1; Ign. *Pol.* 1.3). With some repulsion, Seneca describes such entertainment (*Letters* 7.2–5). **3.2 *throughout the world*** We have no evidence outside Antioch and western Asia Minor that bishops, as officials distinct from presbyters and having authority over presbyters, were prominent fixtures of church organization in the early 2d century. **4.1–2** For other uses of musical imagery in Ignatius, see 5.1; Ign. *Rom.* 2.2; Ign. *Phld.* 1.2. Greek authors frequently used musical images to describe harmony and unity (Seneca, *Letters* 88.9). **4.1 *presbytery*** Ignatius uses this word thirteen times; it is used in only one other place in our literature for a body of Christian elders (*1 Tim.* 4:14) and twice for the Jewish council (*Luke* 22:66; *Acts* 22:5). Most references are to "presbyters" rather than to "a presbytery," although an identifiable body is often assumed. This may show the development of technical vocabulary, reflecting a shift from a group of older men (presbyters) to a more formal body (presbytery). ***Jesus Christ is sung*** This may refer to a practice in Christian worship of singing hymns to Christ (*Eph.* 5:9). Pliny, a Roman governor who investigated the Christian movement, spoke of this practice among Christians in Roman Bithynia and Pontus around this time (*Letters* 10.96.7).

this chorus, every one of you, so that by being harmonious in unanimity and taking your pitch from God you may sing in unison with one voice through Jesus Christ to the Father, in order that he may both hear you and, on the basis of what you do well, acknowledge that you are members of his Son. It is, therefore, advantageous for you to be in perfect unity, in order that you may always have a share in God.

5 For if I in a short time experienced such fellowship with your bishop, which was not merely human but spiritual, how much more do I congratulate you who are united with him, as the church is with Jesus Christ and as Jesus Christ is with the Father, that all things may be harmonious in unity. ²Let no one be misled: if anyone is not within the sanctuary, he lacks the bread of God. For if the prayer of one or two has such power, how much more that of the bishop together with the whole church! ³Therefore whoever does not meet with the congregation thereby demonstrates his arrogance and has separated*d* himself, for it is written: "God opposes the arrogant." Let us, therefore, be careful not to oppose the bishop, in order that we may be obedient to God.*e*

6 Furthermore, the more anyone observes that the bishop is silent, the more one should fear him. For

everyone whom the Master of the house sends to manage his own house we must welcome as we would the one who sent him. It is obvious, therefore, that we must regard the bishop as the Lord himself. ²Now Onesimus himself highly praises your orderly conduct in God, reporting that you all live in accordance with the truth and that no heresy*f* has found a home among you. Indeed, you do not so much as listen to anyone unless he speaks truthfully about Jesus Christ.*g*

Warnings about Teachers of Error

7 For there are some who are accustomed to carrying about the name maliciously and deceitfully while doing other things unworthy of God. You must avoid them as wild beasts. For they are mad dogs that bite by stealth; you must be on your guard against them, for their bite is hard to heal. ²There is only one physician, who is both flesh and spirit, born and unborn, God in man,*h* true life in death, both from Mary and from God, first subject to suffering and then beyond it, Jesus Christ our Lord.

8 Therefore let no one deceive you, just as you are not now deceived, seeing that you belong entirely

---

d Or *judged*
e One ancient authority reads *belong to God by our subjugation*

f Or *faction*
g One ancient authority reads *except Jesus Christ speaking in truth;* another has a grammatically impossible reading
h Other ancient authorities read *God come in flesh*

5.2 sanctuary Gk *thysiastērion*. This common term was used mainly to identify the Jewish temple or altar or to speak of the altar in an abstract way, as a place for sacrifice. Ignatius uses the word as a synonym for "church" (Ign. *Magn.* 7.2; Ign. *Trall.* 7.2; Ign. *Phld.* 4.1), though he uses *ekklēsia* much more frequently. **lacks the bread of God** See John 6:33. There had been schisms in western Asia Minor. Ign. *Phld.* 4.1; 7.2; Ign. *Smyrn.* 7.1; 8.1. Ignatius mentions that separate Eucharists were conducted. The reference in this passage may be to such Eucharists. According to Ignatius, one gains the benefits of Christ through membership in the bishop's church, a point he also made in 4.2 above. **prayer of one or two** Matt. 18:18–20. **5.3 congregation** Ignatius judges all activity conducted outside the bishop's authority to be invalid (20.2; Ign. *Magn.* 7.1, 3; Ign. *Trall.* 2.2; Ign. *Phld.* 7.2; Ign. *Smyrn.* 9.1). **opposes the arrogant** Jas. 4:6; 1 Pet. 5:5. **6.1 bishop is silent** It is not clear what Ignatius means by this comment. For whatever reason, it is an important issue to him (15.1–2; 19.1; Ign. *Phld.* 1.1). Some scholars believe that it indicates a lack of charismatic qualities (e.g., prophecy) in the bishop. For Ignatius the criticism is groundless, since God himself works in silence (Ign. *Eph.* 15.1–2; Ign. *Magn.* 8.2). For a different criticism of the bishop, see Ign. *Magn.* 3.1. **6.2 heresy** Or "faction." Gk *hairesis*. In later Christian writings, the word comes to mean a dangerous and devilish system of thinking that stands in fundamental opposition to God and truth—more than a mere faction. Ignatius's use of the word may have been partly responsible for this change (4.1; Ign. *Magn.* 8.1; Ign. *Trall.* 6.1). **7.1 doing other things unworthy of God** This language may be a stock polemical charge, indicating nothing specific or tainting generally whatever the opponents are doing. In the 1st half of the 2d century, Christians were slandered for the most repulsive kinds of activities—baby eating and incest. Although these charges probably arose from misunderstandings of the language of the Eucharist and of the *agapē*, or love feast, some Christian groups may have been involved in abhorrent behavior. **dogs that bite by stealth** Other Christian writers used the word "dog" for their opponents (*Phil.* 3:2; *Rev.* 22:15). This was a popular usage in the Mediterranean world (Josephus, *J.W.* 6.196; *Odes of Solomon* 28.13; Zenobius, *Cent* 4.90; *Paroem. Gr.* 1.109). **7.2** This passage has a creedal or hymnlike quality. **God in man** See John 1:14. **both flesh and spirit** This summarizes many of Ignatius's concerns—in particular, the suffering and the reality of Jesus' humanity (see introduction to The Letters of Ignatius). **Mary** See 18.2; 19.1; Ign. *Trall.* 9.1. Outside the gospels and Acts 1:14, these are the only passages where Mary, the mother of Jesus, is mentioned by name in our literature. **subject to suffering** Lit. "passible." The word indicates a capacity to suffer or experience human emotions. Greek philosophy argued that God was impassible—not subject to suffering and, in particular, not subject to death. Christians, who spoke of Jesus as God and for whom the suffering and death of Jesus were fundamental events, had to defend this paradoxical position often. **8.1 deceive you** Eph. 5:6; 2 Thess. 2:3.

to God. For when no dissension[i] capable of tormenting you is established among you, then you indeed live God's way. I am a humble sacrifice for you and I dedicate myself to you Ephesians, a church that is famous forever. [2]Those who are carnal cannot do spiritual things, nor can those who are spiritual do carnal things, just as faith cannot do the things of unfaithfulness, nor unfaithfulness the things of faith. Moreover, even those things that you do carnally are in fact spiritual, for you do everything in Jesus Christ.

9But I have learned that certain people from elsewhere have passed your way[j] with evil doctrine, but you did not allow them to sow it among you. You covered up your ears in order to avoid receiving the things being sown by them, because you are stones of a temple, prepared beforehand[k] for the building of God the Father, hoisted up to the heights by the crane of Jesus Christ, which is the cross, using as a rope the Holy Spirit; your faith is what lifts you up, and love is the way that leads up to God.

[2]So you are all fellow pilgrims, carrying your God and your shrine, your Christ and your holy things, adorned in every respect with the commandments of Jesus Christ. I too celebrate with you, since I have been judged worthy to speak with you through this letter, and to rejoice with you because you love nothing in human life, only God.[l]

---

i Other ancient authorities read *lust*
j Or *certain people from there have passed by*
k Some ancient authorities read *temple of the Father, prepared*
l Ancient authorities may be translated *you love nothing in your new way of life except God*

Response to Maltreatment

10Pray continually for the rest of humankind as well, that they may find God, for there is in them hope for repentance. Therefore allow them to be instructed by you, at least by your deeds. [2]In response to their anger, be gentle; in response to their boasts, be humble; in response to their slander, offer prayers; in response to their errors, be "steadfast in the faith"; in response to their cruelty, be gentle; do not be eager to retaliate against them. [3]Let us show ourselves their brothers by our forbearance, and let us be eager to be imitators of the Lord, to see who can be the more wronged, who the more cheated, who the more rejected, in order that no weed of the devil may be found among you, but that with complete purity and self-control you may abide in Christ Jesus physically and spiritually.

The Last Times: Both Cosmic and Personal

11These are the last times. Therefore let us be reverent, let us fear the patience of God, lest it become a judgment against us. For let us either fear the wrath to come or love the grace that is present, one of the two; only let us be found in Christ Jesus, which leads to true life. [2]Let nothing appeal to you apart from him, in whom I carry around these chains (my spiritual pearls!), by which I hope, through your prayers, to rise again. May I always share in them, in order that I may be found in the company of the Christians of Ephesus, who have always been in agreement with the apostles, by the power of Jesus Christ.

12I know who I am and to whom I am writing. I am a convict; you have received mercy. I am in

---

humble sacrifice See 18.1. This term literally means something much more negative—"scum," "dirt," "rubbish"—but it came to express epistolary politeness (*Barn.* 4.9; 6.5). A more negative use is found in *1 Cor.* 4:13 ("dregs"). **8.2** *Rom.* 8:5, 8. **9.1 certain people from elsewhere** A possible translation is "some from where you are," which would mean that opponents had come from Ephesus to Smyrna, where Ignatius then was. Lightfoot suggested that they were from Philadelphia. **crane** Gk *mēchanē.* Having mentioned the church as building stones (see *1 Pet.* 2:5), Ignatius introduces various parallels with the devices used in ancient construction. **9.2 fellow pilgrims** A compound word, *synodoi,* from *syn* ("with") and *hodos.* Gk writers tend to use such repetition of cognate forms more often than English writers. Having mentioned love as the road (or "way," Gk *hodos*) to God in 9.1, Ignatius makes a rough transition from construction to travel. **carrying your God . . . and holy things** Each idea is represented by a compound word in the Gk, literally meaning "God-carrying," "temple-carrying," "Christ-carrying," and "holiness-carrying," respectively. Theophoros ("God-carrying") is Ignatius's own nickname (see the salutation). Ignatius coins compound words frequently to suit his purposes. **carrying . . . your shrine** Ignatius may have been thinking of the religious processions in the ancient world, in which holy objects and images were carried from the temple along a parade route and then back to the temple. For Ephesus, small shrines of Diana's temple would have been among the sacred objects carried in the procession (*Acts* 19:24). **10.1 pray continually** *1 Thess.* 5:17. **10.2 anger** *Matt.* 5:43–44. **10.3** *1 Cor.* 6:7. **11.1 last times** The themes of the end of the world and the coming kingdom of God marked much of early Christian preaching (see *1 Pet.* 1:5). **patience of God** *1 Pet.* 3:20; *2 Pet.* 3:9. **11.2** Ignatius's zeal for martyrdom must be seen in the context of two factors: his desire to be a true disciple by following the example of Jesus, the supreme martyr, and his certainty of the resurrection of the righteous dead. Here he speaks of his chains becoming pearls in the resurrection (19.3; 20.2). Seneca (*Letters* 77) reflects at length on reasoned suicide, which is probably as close to Christian martyrdom as we are likely to find among philosophers. See also Seneca, *Letters* 26. **Christians** Ign. *Magn.* 4.1; Ign. *Trall.* 6.1; Ign. *Rom.* 3.2; Ign. *Phld.* 6.1; Ign. *Pol.* 7.3. Often Ignatius spoke simply of "the name," by which he meant "Christian" or "Christ" (see Ign. *Eph.* 1.2).

danger; you are secure. ²You are the highway of those who are being killed for God's sake; you are fellow initiates of Paul, who was sanctified, who was approved, who is deservedly blessed—may I be found in his footsteps when I reach God!—who in every letter remembers you in Christ Jesus.

Frequent and Harmonious Meetings

13 Therefore make every effort to come together more frequently to give thanks and glory to God.*ᵐ* For when you meet together frequently, the powers of Satan are overthrown and his destructiveness is nullified by the unanimity of your faith. ²There is nothing better than peace, by which all warfare among those in heaven and those on earth is abolished.

Words and Actions

14 None of these things escapes your notice, if you have perfect faith and love toward Jesus Christ. For these are the beginning and the end of life: faith is the beginning, and love is the end, and the two, when they exist in unity, are God. Everything else that contributes to excellence follows from them. ²No one professing faith sins, nor does anyone possessing love hate. "The tree is known by its fruit"; thus those who profess to be Christ's will be recognized by their actions. For the work is a matter not of what one promises now, but of persevering to the end in the power of faith.

15 It is better to be silent and be real than to talk and not be real. It is good to teach, if one does what one says. Now there is one teacher, who "spoke and it happened"; indeed, even the things that he has done in silence are worthy of the Father. ²The one who truly possesses the word of Jesus is also able to hear his silence, that he may be perfect, that he may act through what he says and be known through his silence. ³Nothing is hidden from the Lord; even our secrets are close to him. Therefore let us do everything with the knowledge that he dwells in us, in order that we may be his temples, and he may be in us as our*ⁿ* God—as, in fact, he really is, as will be made clear in our sight by the love that we justly have for him.

The Stench of Evil Teaching

16 Do not be misled, my brothers and sisters: those who adulterously corrupt households "will not inherit the kingdom of God." ²Now if those who do such things physically are put to death, how much more if by evil teaching someone corrupts faith in God, for which Jesus Christ was crucified! Such a person, having polluted himself, will go to the unquenchable fire, as will also the one who listens to him.

17 The Lord accepted the ointment upon his head for this reason: that he might breathe incorruptibility upon the church. Do not be anointed with the stench of the teaching of the ruler of this age, lest he take you captive and rob you of the life set before you. ²Why do we not all become wise by receiving

---

m Or *frequently for the Eucharist and glory of God*   *n* Other ancient authorities omit *our*

12.2 you are the highway A number of martyrs may have passed through Ephesus on their way to martyrdom in Rome. Both Ephesus and Smyrna were primary seaports for the road running from from the East to Rome. There is no other mention in our literature of such martyrs. **footsteps** This is perhaps an allusion to the tradition about the death of Paul in Rome, where Ignatius was to find himself within a matter of weeks. Paul, too, reached Rome as a prisoner. For Ignatius, his "reaching God" depended on his faithfulness to the death. **every letter** A puzzling statement in that Paul mentions the Ephesians or Ephesus only in *1 Corinthians* (15:32; 16:8, 19; *1 Tim.* 1:3; *2 Tim.* 4:12). For the most part, all these passages merely indicate location, with no comment on the church itself. **13.1 give thanks** This may be a reference to the Eucharist. In Gk, the word for Eucharist meant "thanksgiving"; through Christian use, it became a technical term for one of the primary sacraments. Ignatius was distressed when separate Eucharists were held (see 5.2). **13.2 peace** Many scholars believe that Ignatius intends internal harmony when he expresses his concern that the church in Antioch gain peace. But others see "peace" in Antioch as meaning the end of civil persecution (see introduction to The Letters of Ignatius). **14.2 by its fruit** Matt. 12:33. **the work** Meaning Christianity. See Ign. *Rom.* 3.3. **to the end** Mark 13:13; *Matt.* 10:22; 24:13. **15.1** Here silence seems to be contrasted with teaching. Silence is better although teaching is good. This may show some tension between the bishop and more eloquent teachers (see 6.1). **spoke and it happened** Ps. 33:9 (LXX 32:9); 148:5. **15.3 secrets** Rom. 2:16; *1 Cor.* 4:5; 14:25; *2 Cor.* 4:2. **his temples** See 9.1 **our God** The image of God being in God's temple fits the common expectation of the Mediterranean world. Ephesian readers would have thought of their famous temple with the image of Artemis. Because Christians did not have a physical temple, they were frequently labeled "atheists" and derided. But early Christian writers saw themselves as God's temple (*1 Cor.* 3:16–17; *2 Cor.* 6:16; *Eph.* 2:21; Ign. *Phld.* 7.2; *Barn.* 4.11). Seneca, the Stoic, also expressed the idea that God dwells within (*Letters* 41). **16.1** *1 Cor.* 6:9–10; *Gal.* 5:21; *Eph.* 5:5. **unquenchable** Gk asbeston. Mark 9:43; *Matt.* 3:12; *Luke* 3:17. **17.1 ointment upon His head** Matt. 26:7; *John* 12:3. **ruler of this age** Meaning the devil. The plural form of this expression occurs in *1 Cor.* 2:6, 8. See 19.1; Ign. *Magn.* 1.2; Ign. *Trall.* 4.2; Ign. *Rom.* 7.1; Ign. *Phld.* 6.2; *John* 12:31; *Eph.* 2:2.

God's knowledge, which is Jesus Christ? Why do we foolishly perish, ignoring the gracious gift that the Lord has truly sent?

The Mystery of Jesus' Death

18 My spirit is a humble sacrifice for the cross, which is a stumbling block to unbelievers but salvation and eternal life to us. "Where is the wise? Where is the debater?" Where is the boasting of those who are thought to be intelligent? ²For our God, Jesus the Christ, was conceived by Mary according to God's*ᵒ* plan, both from the seed of David and of the Holy Spirit. He was born and was baptized in order that by his suffering he might cleanse the water.

19 Now the virginity of Mary and her giving birth were hidden from the ruler of this age, as was also the death of the Lord—three mysteries to be loudly proclaimed, yet which were accomplished in the silence of God. ²How, then, were they revealed to the ages? A star shone forth in heaven brighter than all the stars; its light was indescribable and its strangeness caused amazement. All the rest of the constellations, together with the sun and moon, formed a chorus around the star, yet the star itself far outshone them all, and there was perplexity about the origin of this strange phenomenon, which was so unlike the others. ³Consequently all magic and every kind of spell were dissolved, the ignorance so characteristic of wickedness vanished, and the ancient kingdom was abolished,*ᵖ* when God appeared in human form to bring the newness of eternal life; and what had been prepared by God began to take effect. As a re-

sult, all things were thrown into ferment, because the abolition of death was being carried out.

Promise of a Second Letter

20 If Jesus Christ, in response to your prayer, should reckon me worthy, and if it is his will, in a second letter that I intend to write to you I will further explain to you the subject about which I have begun to speak, namely, the divine plan with respect to the new man Jesus Christ, involving faith in him and love for him,*q* his suffering and resurrection, ²especially if the Lord reveals anything to me. All of you, individually and collectively, gather*r* together in grace, by name, in one faith and one*s* Jesus Christ, who physically was a descendent of David, who is Son of Man and Son of God, in order that you may obey the bishop and the presbytery with an undisturbed mind, breaking one bread, which is the medicine of immortality, the antidote we take in order not to die but to live forever in Jesus Christ.

Personal Greetings and Parting Requests

21 I am devoted to you and to those whom for the honor of God you sent to Smyrna, from where I am writing to you, with thanksgiving to the Lord and love for Polycarp as well as for you. Remember me, as Jesus Christ does you. ²Pray for the church in Syria, from where I am being led to Rome in chains, as I—the very least of the faithful there—have been judged worthy of serving the glory of God. Farewell in God the Father and in Jesus Christ, our common hope.

---

o One ancient authority omits *God's*
p Other ancient authorities read *magic was dissolved and every wicked spell vanished; ignorance was abolished and the ancient kingdom was destroyed*

q Or *involving his faith and his love*
r Ancient authorities read *especially if the Lord reveals to me that all of you, individually and collectively, continue to gather*
s Other ancient authorities read *in*

18.1 *humble sacrifice* See note at 8.1. *stumbling block* Gk *skandalon* (*Gal.* 5:11; *1 Cor.* 1:23). **18.2** *our God, Jesus the Christ* Ignatius calls Jesus God without reservation. In Ign. *Rom.* 6.3 he speaks of the "suffering of my God" and in Ign. *Eph.* 1.1 of the "blood of God." Ignatius contributed some of the most elevated language for describing Jesus. *by his suffering* Lake thinks that the entire reference is to baptism, not to the death of Jesus. *the water* Meaning the water of baptism. **19.1** *the virginity of Mary* *Matt.* 1:23 and *Luke* 1:27 independently mention the virginity of Mary. Their birth narratives are otherwise quite different. *ruler of this age* See 17.1. **19.2** *a star shone* The star of Bethlehem, a detail from *Matthew's* Christmas story (*Matt.* 2:1–12). Clearly, Ignatius has expanded the description. **19.3** *all magic and every kind of spell* Ephesus was a center of the magical arts (*Acts* 19:19), and magical texts were referred to as "Ephesian letters." *newness Rom.* 6:4. **20.1** *a second letter* Lit. "little book" or "scroll." Ignatius means simply "another letter." There is a letter called the *Second Epistle to the Ephesians,* but scholars judge it, together with a number of other letters attributed to Ignatius, to be the work of an anonymous author who took the opportunity to supply the intended letter to which this passage refers. **20.2** *reveals anything to me* Editors emend the Gk to read *hoti* ("that") rather than *ti* ("anything"). The *ho* sound is represented by a small mark over the initial vowel in a word. *one Jesus Christ* Some authorities read "in" rather than "one." The difference in Gk between the words "one" (*heni*) and "in" (*en*) is minor, given that there is no letter *h* in Gk. *descendant of David* Gk *sperma* ("seed") is used rather than *genos* ("family") as in 18.2. The meaning is the same. *breaking one bread* The reference is to the Eucharist (see 5.2). **21.1** *I am devoted to you* Possibly the sense is of a life given as a ransom. See Ign. *Smyrn.* 10.2; Ign. *Pol.* 2.3; 6.1. **21.2** *least of the faithful* Ignatius sometimes mentions his unworthiness when he speaks of the church at Antioch (Ign. *Magn.* 14.1; Ign. *Trall.* 13.1; Ign. *Smyrn.* 11.1), but it is difficult to determine the exact link between the two concerns (see introduction to The Letters of Ignatius). This kind of self-deprecating comment is similar to statements made by Paul himself or by others regarding Paul (*1 Cor.* 15:9; *Eph.* 3:8).

THE LETTER OF IGNATIUS
TO THE MAGNESIANS

Salutation

Ignatius, who is also called Theophorus, to the church at Magnesia on the Maeander, which has been blessed through the grace of God the Father in Christ Jesus our Savior, in whom I greet her and wish her heartiest greetings in God the Father and in Jesus Christ.

Chains and Worthiness

1 When I learned how well ordered your love toward God is, I rejoiced and resolved to address you in the faith of Jesus Christ. ²For inasmuch as I have been judged worthy to bear a most godly name, in these chains that I bear I sing the praises of the churches, and I pray that in them there may be a union of flesh and spirit that comes from Jesus Christ, our never-failing*a* life, and of faith and love, to which nothing is preferable, and—what is more important—of Jesus and the Father. In him we will, if we patiently endure all the abuse of the ruler of this age and escape, reach God.

Obedience to the Bishop

2 So, then, I was permitted to see you in the persons of Damas, your godly bishop, and your worthy presbyters Bassus and Apollonius, and my fellow servant, the deacon Zotion; may I enjoy his company, because he is subject to the bishop as to the grace of God, and to the presbytery as to the law of Jesus Christ.

3 Indeed, it is right for you also not to take advantage of the youthfulness of your bishop but to give him all the respect due him in accordance with the power of God the Father, just as I know that the holy presbyters likewise have not taken advantage of his youthful appearance but yield to him as one who is wise*b* in God; yet not really to him, but to the Father of Jesus Christ, the bishop of all. ²For the honor, therefore, of the one who loved you*c* it is right to be obedient without any hypocrisy, for it is not so much a matter of deceiving this bishop who is seen but of cheating the one who is unseen. In such a case he must reckon not with the flesh but with God, who knows our secrets.

4 It is right, therefore, that we not just be called Christians, but that we actually be Christians, unlike some who call a man bishop but do everything without regard for him. Such people do not appear to me to act in good conscience, inasmuch as they

---

a Or *everlasting* or *continual*

b Other ancient authorities read *ones who are wise*
c Other ancient authorities read *us*

TRANSLATION by Michael W. Holmes after the earlier translation of J. B. Lightfoot and J. R. Harmer. TRANSLATION NOTES by Michael W. Holmes. Reprinted, with revisions, from *The Apostolic Fathers: Greek Texts and English Translations,* edited and revised by Michael W. Holmes (Grand Rapids: Baker Books, 1999). © 1992, 1999, 2003 by Michael W. Holmes. Used by permission of Baker Book House. All rights reserved. CONTENT NOTES are by the editors of this volume, with acknowledgment to Michael W. Holmes for his observations regarding a number of texts.

1.2 *judged worthy* Ignatius associated his status as a condemned prisoner—in particular, the martyrdom he would endure in Rome—with worthiness and true discipleship (see Ign. *Eph.* 1.2; 3.1; Ign. *Magn.* 9.1; Ign. *Trall.* 4.2; 5.2; Ign. *Rom.* 1.1; Ign. *Pol.* 7.1). *bear a most godly name* See notes to Ign. *Eph.* salutation; 9.2. *in these chains* See Ign. *Eph.* salutation. *I pray that in them* Refers to *the churches* (rather than to *the chains*); the Gk makes this clear by the use of the feminine form of the pronoun. *ruler of this age* Meaning the devil. See Ign. *Eph.* 17.1. **2.1** In the Gk, this is not a complete sentence. Schoedel suggests that it is picked up again at 6.1. **3.1** *youthfulness of your bishop* Young Damas seems not to have been selected from the body of elders (presbyters). A similar situation may be reflected in *1 Tim.* 4:11. The presence of such a young bishop indicates that bishops were not appointed exclusively from among the presbyters. Perhaps a younger assistant of a bishop sometimes succeeded to the bishop's office. *the bishop of all* In Ignatius's letters, bishops are usually compared to God. In this passage, God is called a *bishop*. Although the word could mean simply "overseer," Ignatius seems to be using it in a fairly technical sense. See Ign. *Trall.* 2.2. **3.2** *obedient without any hypocrisy . . . deceiving this bishop* This may suggest that opposition to the bishop was somewhat hidden. At least, there does not appear to have been open rebellion; there was still token respect, if not more. A situation of open rebellion would not make good sense of the language Ignatius uses here (4.1). *unseen* To speak of God as invisible is more characteristic of Gk philosophical thought than of the Jewish scriptures or much of the early Christian literature (Ign. *Pol.* 3.2; *Rom.* 1:20; *Col.* 1:15–16; *1 Tim.* 1:17; *Heb.* 11:27). **4.1** *Christians* See 10.1; Ign. *Eph.* 4.1. *do everything without regard for him* Lit. "do everything without him." See 7.1; Ign. *Trall.* 2.2; Ign. *Phld.* 7.2; Ign. *Smyrn.* 8.2; Ign. *Pol.* 4.1.

do not validly meet together in accordance with the commandment.

Two Ways

5 Seeing then that all things have an end, two things together lie before us, death and life, and everyone will go to his own place. [2]For just as there are two coinages, the one of God and the other of the world, and each of them has its own stamp impressed upon it, so the unbelievers bear the stamp of this world, but the faithful in love bear the stamp of God the Father through Jesus Christ, whose life is not in us unless we voluntarily choose to die into his suffering.

Further Comments about Obedience to the Bishop

6 Since, therefore, in the persons mentioned above I have by faith seen and loved the whole congregation, I have this advice: Be eager to do everything in godly harmony, the bishop presiding in the place of God and the presbyters in the place of the council[d] of the apostles and the deacons, who are most dear to me, since they have been entrusted with the service of Jesus Christ, who before the ages was with the Father and appeared at the end of time. [2]Let all, therefore,

---

d Other ancient authorities read *the bishop presiding after the model of God and the presbyters after the model of the council*

accept the same attitude as God and respect one another, and let no one regard his neighbor in merely human terms, but in Jesus Christ love one another always. Let there be nothing among you that is capable of dividing you, but be united with the bishop and with those who lead, as an example and a lesson of incorruptibility.

7 Therefore as the Lord did nothing without the Father, either by himself or through the apostles (for he was united with him), so you must not do anything without the bishop and the presbyters. Do not attempt to convince yourselves that anything done apart from the others is right, but, gathering together, let there be one prayer, one petition, one mind, one hope, with love and blameless joy, which is Jesus Christ, than whom nothing is better. [2]Let all of you run together as to one temple of God, as to one altar, to one Jesus Christ, who came forth from one Father and remained with the One and returned to the One.

Judaism and Christianity

8 Do not be deceived by strange doctrines or antiquated myths, since they are worthless. For if we continue to live in accordance with Judaism, we admit that we have not received grace. [2]For the most godly prophets lived in accordance with Christ Jesus. This is why they were persecuted, being inspired as

---

do not validly meet together This refers to separate assemblies, yet there appears to still be a level of recognition for the local bishop by such schismatics. The puzzle is why the group would go on recognizing the bishop in some way while having almost no association with him. See 3.2. **accordance with the commandment** Apparently not a specific commandment but a principle of good order. **5.1 death and life** Compare *Didache* 1–6 and *Barnabas* 18–20, where the Two Ways tradition is more explicit. **to his own place** *Acts* 1:25; *1 Clem.* 5.7. **5.2 coinages** *Matt.* 22:19. **unless we vountarily choose to die into his suffering** Perhaps a reference to the Pauline theme of dying with Christ in baptism (*Rom.* 6:4–5; *Gal.* 2:20; 3:27), but it could also be a reference to martyrdom. Martyrdom is perhaps the central theme in Ignatius's letters. Ignatius tests faithfulness in terms of willingness to submit to martyrdom. **6.1 in the place** Gk *topon*. Variant *(typon)* translated "type" or "model." The word *typos* appears also in 6.2, where it is translated "example." **council of the apostles** All three uses of *synedrion* (council) to describe a Christian body are in Ignatius (Ign. *Trall.* 3.1; Ign. *Phld.* 8.1). Otherwise the word is used for the chief Jewish council, the Sanhedrin. A more common word for "council"—*symboulion*—is used in Ign. *Pol.* 7.2. **deacons ... entrusted with the service** The wordplay concerns the Gk *diakonoi* (deacons) and *diakonia* (service). The counterpart provided here for bishops and elders is not provided for deacons (bishops = God; presbyters = council of the apostles). See Ign. *Trall.* 2.2. **before the ages was with the Father** The language emphasizes the divine status of Jesus. Here we have a clear statement of preexistence (*John* 1:1; *Phil.* 2:5–7). **at the end of time** Many early Christian writings reflect the view that the end of the age (sometimes "last days") had come (see *1 Pet.* 1:5). **7.1–2** This section begins and ends with statements about Jesus' unity with the Father. Some form of the Gk word for "one" occurs twelve times in this paragraph. This heavy use emphasizes that there are no other options—all activity must be conducted under the one bishop. *John* 5:19, 30; 8:28; 10:30. **7.2 came forth from one Father** Some argue that the language of "coming from the Father" and "going to the Father" here and in *John* reflects gnostic influence. More likely this is a shared vocabulary that has been shaped in profoundly different ways. **8.1 strange doctrines** Gk *heterodoxiai*. Lit. "different doctrines" although it was hardly a neutral word. Ignatius clearly intends to dismiss this teaching and uses unequivocal language elsewhere for the position of the opponents (10.1–3). The term is roughly the equivalent to "heresy" elsewhere in Ignatius (see Ign. *Eph.* 6.2; *1 Tim.* 1:3). **antiquated myths** This charge is made elsewhere in *1 Tim.* 1:4; 4:7; *Titus* 1:14. The link of these myths to Judaism is unclear. Ignatius charges that they belong to what he calls *Judaism*. At the time, philosophers either rejected the Gk myths outright or subjected them to more sober interpretation. **in accordance with Judaism** Christians competed against, and were threatened by, the Jewish world at every step in their mission in the Roman Empire, particularly in the area of Asia Minor. Ephesus, a short distance from Magnesia, was a major Jewish center during this time. The letters of *Revelation* 2–3, addressed to the seven churches of Asia, reflect tensions with Jews, and the Pastoral Letters (roughly from the same time

they were by his grace in order that those who are disobedient might be fully convinced that there is one
God who revealed himself through Jesus Christ his
Son, who is his Word that came forth from^e silence,
who in every respect pleased him who sent him.

9 If, then, those who had lived in antiquated practices came to newness of hope, no longer keeping
the sabbath but living in accordance with the Lord's
day, on which our life also arose through him and his
death (which some deny), the mystery through which
we came to believe, and because of which we patiently
endure, in order that we may be found to be disciples
of Jesus Christ, our only teacher, ²how can we possibly live without him, whom even the prophets, who
were his disciples in the Spirit, were expecting as their
teacher? Because of this, he for whom they rightly
waited raised them from the dead when he came.

10 Therefore let us not be unaware of his goodness. For if he were to imitate the way we act, we
are lost. Therefore, having become his disciples, let us
learn to live in accordance with Christianity. For
whoever is called by any other name than this one
does not belong to God. ²Throw out, therefore, the
bad leaven, which has become stale and sour, and
reach for the new leaven, which is Jesus Christ. Be
salted with him, so that none of you become rotten,
for by your odor you will be convicted. ³It is utterly
absurd to profess Jesus Christ and to practice Judaism. For Christianity did not believe in Judaism, but
Judaism in Christianity, in which "every tongue" believed and "was brought together" to God.

The Reality of Jesus' Human Experiences

11 Now I write these things, my dear friends, not
because I have learned that any of you are actually like that, but, as one who is less than you, I want
to forewarn you not to get snagged on the hooks of
worthless opinions but instead to be fully convinced
about the birth and the suffering and the resurrection
that took place during the time of the governorship of
Pontius Pilate. These things were truly and most as-
suredly done by Jesus Christ, our hope, from which
may none of you ever be turned aside.

Obedience to the Bishop

12 May I have joy in you in every respect—if,
that is, I am worthy. For even though I am in
chains, I cannot be compared to one of you who are
at liberty. I know that you are not conceited, for you
have Jesus Christ within you. Moreover, I know that
when I praise you, you feel ashamed, as it is written:
"the righteous is his own accuser."

13 Be eager, therefore, to be firmly grounded in
the precepts of the Lord and the apostles, in
order that "in whatever you do, you may prosper,"
physically and spiritually, in faith and love, in the Son
and the Father and in the Spirit, in the beginning and
at the end, together with your most distinguished
bishop and that beautifully woven spiritual crown
which is your presbytery and the godly deacons. ²Be
subject to the bishop and to one another, as Jesus
Christ in the flesh^f was to the Father, and as the

---

e Other ancient authorities read *not from*

f Some ancient authorities omit *in the flesh*

---

and place) confront similar issues. Ignatius shows little sensitivity or hesitation in his rejection of Judaism (10.3; Ign. *Phld.*
6.1). **8.2** Early Christians identified with the Hebrew prophets. They, too, were persecuted, criticized the ritual aspects of
temple and cult, and shared in some way the revelation about the Christ (9.1–2; Ign. *Phld.* 5.2; *Matt.* 5:12; *Luke* 11:47–51; *Acts*
7:51–52). *from silence* Some scholars argue that Ignatius here reflects gnostic thought, in which silence occupies an important place. But this is not a key concept for Ignatius, and his antidocetic stance mutes the significance of any shared terminology with gnostic thought. **9.1** *Lord's day* Christians came to set aside the first day of the week as their special day,
replacing the Jewish Sabbath (*1 Cor.* 16:2; *Acts* 20:7; *Rev.* 1:10; *Did.* 14.1; *Barn.* 15.9). Sunday became important because it
was considered to be the day of Jesus' resurrection. Ignatius seems to be arguing that the prophets kept Sunday rather than
Saturday as their holy day (*Isa.* 1:13). Other Christian authors made similar claims. Possibly, though, Ignatius is referring to
the first disciples. Modern scholars disagree over a number of issues related to this development. Some contend that *Lord's
day* indicates Easter, not Sunday. *found to be disciples* Ignatius frequently connects discipleship to suffering (10.1; see
Ign. *Eph.* 1.1). **9.2** *raised them from the dead* *1 Pet.* 3:19–20. There was a tradition that Jesus descended into Hades and
freed the dead. This may stem from a report that some dead people were raised at the time of Jesus' death (*Matt.* 27:52–53).
The belief is especially developed in the *Gospel of Nicodemus* and the *Acts of Pilate.* Ignatius seems to have something like this
in mind, but it is not possible to determine his source. **10.2** *bad leaven* *1 Cor.* 5:7; *Heb.* 8:13. *practice Judaism* See 8.1.
10.3 *every tongue* *Phil.* 2:11; *Isa.* 45:23; 66:18. **11.1** *Pontius Pilate* The Roman governor of Judea, who sentenced Jesus
to death. In our literature, outside the gospels and *Acts,* Pilate is mentioned only by Ignatius (Ign. *Magn.* 11.1; Ign. *Trall.* 9.1;
Ign. *Smyrn.* 1.2) although he becomes a figure of interest in the 2d-century apocryphal writings. *truly and most assur-
edly* The emphasis on the reality of these experiences is an antidocetic attack. **12.1** *worthy* Ignatius prides himself on his
chains (see notes to 1.2 and Ign. *Eph.* 2.2). *the righteous . . . accuser* LXX *Prov.* 18:17. **13.1** *3 John* 2; *Ps.* 1:3. **13.2** *in the
flesh* This phrase may have been added by a scribe who did not wish Ignatius to seem to be subordinating the Son to the
Father. *and to the Father* The addition of "and to the Spirit" in some manuscripts may have been meant to support trinitarian doctrine.

apostles were to Christ and to the Father,[g] that there may be unity, both physical and spiritual.

Personal Greetings and Parting Requests

14Knowing as I do that you are full of God, I have only briefly exhorted you. Remember me in your prayers, in order that I may reach God; remember also the church in Syria, of which I am not worthy to be called a member.[h] For I need your united prayer and love in God, that the church in Syria may be judged worthy of being refreshed by the dew of your fervent prayers.[i]

15The Ephesians greet you from Smyrna, from where I am writing you. They, like you, are here for the glory of God, and have refreshed me in every respect, together with Polycarp, bishop of the Smyrnaeans. All the other churches also greet you in honor of Jesus Christ. Farewell in godly harmony to you who possess an undivided spirit, which is Jesus Christ.

---

[g] Gk is corrupt; some ancient authorities add *and to the Spirit*
[h] Gk lacks *member*

[i] Some ancient authorities read *with dew by means of your church*

14.1 *not worthy* See Ign. *Eph.* 2.2. **15.1** *refreshed me in every respect* Perhaps a reference to financial support. **undivided spirit** The meaning is not clear.

THE LETTER OF IGNATIUS
TO THE TRALLIANS

Salutation

Ignatius, who is also called Theophorus, to the holy church at Tralles in Asia, dearly loved by God the Father of Jesus Christ, elect and worthy of God, at peace in flesh and spirit*a* through the suffering of Jesus Christ, who is our hope when we rise to be with him, which I greet in the fullness of God in the apostolic manner and offer heartiest greetings.

Praise for the Trallians

1 I know that you have a disposition that is blameless and unwavering in patient endurance, not from habit but by nature, inasmuch as Polybius your bishop informed me when, by the will of God and Jesus Christ, he visited me in Smyrna; so heartily did he rejoice with me, a prisoner in Christ Jesus, that in him I saw your entire congregation. ²Having received, therefore, your godly good will through him, I praised God when I found out that you were, as I had learned, imitators of God.

Obedience to the Bishop

2 For when you are subject to the bishop as to Jesus Christ, it is evident to me that you are living not in accordance with human standards but in accordance with Jesus Christ, who died for us in order that by believing in his death you might escape death. ²It is essential, therefore, that you continue your current practice and do nothing without the bishop, but be subject also to the presbytery as to the apostles of Jesus Christ, our hope, in whom we shall be found, if we so live.*b* ³Furthermore, it is necessary that those who are deacons of the mysteries of Jesus Christ please everyone in every respect. For they are not merely deacons*c* of food and drink but ministers of God's church. Therefore they must avoid criticism as though it were fire.

3 Similarly, let everyone respect the deacons as Jesus Christ, just as they should respect the bishop, who is a model of the Father, and the presbyters as God's council and as the band of the apostles. Without these no group can be called a church. ²I am sure that you agree with me regarding these matters, for I received a living example of your love and still have it with me in the person of your bishop, whose very demeanor is a great lesson and whose gentleness is his power; I think that even the godless respect him. ³Because I love you I am sparing you, though I could write more sharply on his behalf. But I did not think myself

---

a Other ancient authorities read *blood*

b Other ancient authorities add *in him*
c Or *servers*

TRANSLATION by Michael W. Holmes after the earlier translation of J. B. Lightfoot and J. R. Harmer. TRANSLATION NOTES by Michael W. Holmes. Reprinted, with revisions, from *The Apostolic Fathers: Greek Texts and English Translations*, edited and revised by Michael W. Holmes (Grand Rapids: Baker Books, 1999). © 1992, 1999, 2003 by Michael W. Holmes. Used by permission of Baker Book House. All rights reserved. CONTENT NOTES are by the editors of this volume, with acknowledgment to Michael W. Holmes for his observations regarding a number of texts.

Salutation *apostolic manner* This could mean "in a letter, as the apostles did" or "according to apostolic teaching." **1.1** *prisoner* See Ign. *Eph.* 1.2. **1.2** *godly good will* Perhaps financial support. *imitators of God* 1 *Cor.* 4:16; 11:1; *Eph.* 5:1. Ignatius frequently speaks of discipleship as imitation of Christ, particularly regarding suffering (see Ign. *Eph.* 1.1). **2.2** *nothing without the bishop* This is a stock phrase in Ignatius (7.2; Ign. *Magn.* 7.2; Ign. *Phld.* 7.2; Ign. *Smyrn.* 9.1). *subject also to the presbytery* Ignatius called for submission to the presbytery (13.2) as well as to the bishop. This seems to indicate that the presbytery was generally supportive of the bishop. Some modern discussions have suggested that the presbytery was fractured, allowing for the rise of a bishop to chief power. There may be a hint of such conflict in 12.2–12.3. Still, Ignatius is extremely generous in his comments about the presbytery and the support it should receive. *as to the apostles* The link between presbyters and apostles is standard in Ignatius's writings (3.1; Ign. *Magn.* 6.1; 7.1; Ign. *Phld.* 5.1; Ign. *Smyrn.* 8.1). He usually connects bishops with God. Only toward the end of the 2d century was the bishop more closely identified with the apostles as the doctrine of apostolic succession developed. *Christ, our hope* 1 *Tim.* 1:1. **2.3** *deacons* A technical term for the office. Its nontechnical meaning is "one who serves," including such humble tasks as waiting on tables. Ignatius tells deacons that they are "servers" not merely of food but of the mysteries of the faith. **3.1** Deacons are here associated with Christ. Ignatius seems to speak of the deacons with a special fondness (Ign. *Magn.* 2.1; 6.1; Ign. *Phld.* 4.1; Ign. *Smyrn.* 12.2). **3.3** The text is corrupt at various points. It is unclear what information Ignatius has that prompts him to make such a statement. The meekness of Bishop Polybius is singled out; some may have taken advantage of this meekness and challenged his authority (12.3).

qualified[d] for this, that I, a convict, should give you orders as though I were an apostle.

Suffering and True Discipleship

4 I have many deep thoughts in union with God, but I take my own measure, lest I perish by boasting. For now I must be more careful and not pay attention to those who flatter me, for those who speak to me in this manner torture me. [2]For while I strongly desire to suffer, I do not know whether I am worthy, for the envy, though not apparent to many, wages war against me all the more. Therefore I need gentleness, by which the ruler of this age is destroyed.

5 Am I not able to write to you about heavenly things? But I am afraid to, lest I should cause harm to you, who are mere babes. So bear with me, lest you be choked by what you are unable to swallow. [2]For I myself, though I am in chains and can comprehend heavenly things, the ranks of the angels and the hierarchy of principalities, things visible and invisible, for all this I am not yet a disciple. For we still lack many things, that we may not lack God.

The Danger of False Teaching

6 I urge you, therefore—yet not I, but the love of Jesus Christ—partake only of Christian food, and keep away from every strange plant, which is heresy. [2]These people, while pretending to be trustworthy, mix Jesus Christ with themselves[e]—like those who administer a deadly drug with honeyed wine, which

the unsuspecting victim accepts without fear,[f] and so with fatal pleasure drinks down death.

Safety under the Bishop

7 Therefore be on your guard against such people. And you will be, provided that you are not puffed up with pride and that you cling inseparably to Jesus Christ[g] and to the bishop and to the commandments of the apostles. [2]The one who is within the sanctuary is clean, but the one who is outside the sanctuary is not clean. That is, whoever does anything without bishop and presbytery and deacons does not have a clean conscience.

Advanced Warning against Error

8 Not that I know of any such thing among you; rather, I am guarding you in advance because you are very dear to me and I foresee the snares of the devil. You, therefore, must arm yourselves with gentleness and regain your strength[h] in faith (which is the flesh of the Lord) and in love (which is the blood of Jesus Christ). [2]Let none of you hold a grudge against his neighbor. Do not give any opportunity to the pagans, lest the godly majority be blasphemed on account of a few foolish people. For "woe to the one through whose folly my name is blasphemed among any."

The Reality of Jesus' Human Experiences

9 Be deaf, therefore, whenever anyone speaks to you apart from Jesus Christ, who was of the family of

---

d Gk is corrupt; or *But I was not empowered*
e Gk is corrupt

f Some ancient authorities read *accepts gladly*
g Other ancient authorities read *God, Jesus Christ*
h Some ancient authorities read *and renew yourselves*

4.2 desire to suffer Lit. "love to suffer." Some modern scholars find this to be evidence of mental instability in Ignatius, but perhaps it is the mental state of martyrs in general that confounds the modern reader. For Ignatius, Christ's own death and the death of others who followed Christ had become templates for Christian discipleship (see Ign. *Eph.* 1.1). **whether I am worthy** Ignatius is cautious about receiving prior to his martyrdom any special treatment or praise reserved for martyrs, for he realizes that he has yet to endure that final trial (5.2; Ign. *Rom.* 4.1–3; Ign. *Phld.* 5.1). The Christians he meets on the way seem to have praised him as a martyr already. **ruler of this age** Meaning the devil. See Ign. *Eph.* 17.1. **5.1–2** Ignatius appears to be appealing to charismatic gifts or special visions he has had, as he does also in Ign. *Phld.* 7.1. The nature or content of these special revelations is not known. **5.1 mere babes** 1 *Cor.* 3:1–2. **5.2** Being a chained convict for his Christian profession is a positive image for Ignatius, but he is cautious not to count this as the highest accomplishment. He will be truly a disciple when he has not only faced death but endured it (see 4.2). **things visible and invisible** Col. 1:16. **6.1 heresy** See 8.1; Ign. *Eph.* 6.2. **6.2 deadly drug** Ignatius sometimes labels the beliefs of his opponents poison or dismisses their ideas by some other negative image, such as "wicked offshoots" or "deadly fruit" (11.1). **7.2 within the sanctuary** See Ign. *Eph.* 5.2. **8.1** Ignatius claims that his warning about heresy and dangerous teachers is not prompted by knowledge that the church at Tralles already has been infected by heresy. If these teachers were already in the church, such a comment would have defeated his purposes by exonerating the very people he had hoped to censure. **flesh . . . blood** This reference recalls the elements of the Eucharist. **8.2 opportunity to the pagans** Ignatius is aware that strife (e.g., a grudge against one's neighbor) could discredit the Christian movement. Many Christian authors from this period repeat the theme. **godly majority** Lit. "the many in God." Ignatius sets up a contrast between the *few foolish people* and the *godly majority*. **Woe to him** Isa. 52:5. **9.1 family of David** Ign. *Eph.* 20.2. The genealogies of Jesus in *Matt.* 1:1–17 and *Luke* 3:23–38, though different, both trace the line back through David. This ancestry is cited in the Christian argument for the messiahship of Jesus (*Acts* 13:34–36; 15:16; *Rom.* 1:3; *2 Tim.* 2:8; *Rev.* 3:7; 5:5; 22:16; *Did.* 9.1; *Barn.* 12.10).

David, who was the son of Mary; who really was born, who both ate and drank; who really was persecuted under Pontius Pilate, who really was crucified and died while those in heaven and on earth and under the earth looked on; ²who, moreover, really was raised from the dead when his Father raised him up, who—his Father, that is—in the same way will likewise also raise us up in Christ Jesus who believe in him, apart from whom we have no true life.

10 But if, as some atheists (that is, unbelievers) say, he suffered in appearance only (while they exist in appearance only!), why am I in chains? And why do I want to fight with wild beasts? If that is the case, I die for no reason; what is more, I am telling lies about the Lord.

11 Flee, therefore, from these wicked offshoots that bear deadly fruit; if anyone even tastes it, he dies on the spot. These people are not the Father's planting. ²For if they were, they would appear as branches of the cross, and their fruit would be imperishable—the same cross by which he, through his suffering, calls you who are his members. The head, therefore, cannot be born without members, since God promises unity, which he himself is.

Personal Greetings and Parting Requests

12 I greet you from Smyrna together with the churches of God that are present with me, people who have refreshed me in every respect, phys-ically as well as spiritually. ²My chains, which I carry around for the sake of Jesus Christ while praying that I may reach God, exhort you: persevere in your unanimity and in prayer with one another. For it is right for each one of you, and especially the presbyters, to encourage the bishop, to the honor of the Father and to the honor of Jesus Christ[i] and of the apostles. ³I pray that you will listen to me in love, so that I may not by virtue of having written to you become a witness against you. But also pray for me, for I need your love in the mercy of God so that I may be reckoned worthy of the fate that I am eager[j] to obtain, lest I be found disqualified.

13 The love of the Smyrnaeans and of the Ephesians greets you. Remember in your prayers the church in Syria, of which I am not worthy to be considered a member, being as I am the very least of them. ²Farewell in Jesus Christ. Be subject to the bishop as to the commandment, and likewise to the presbytery. And love one another, each one of you, with an undivided heart. ³My spirit is dedicated to you, not only now but also when I reach God. For I am still in danger, but the Father is faithful: he will fulfill my prayer and yours in Jesus Christ. May we[k] be found blameless in him.

---

i Other ancient authorities read *of the Father and of Jesus Christ*; others read *of the Father of Jesus Christ*
j Text and meaning are uncertain
k Other ancient authorities read *you*

Mary See Ign. *Eph.* 7.2. **really** Or *truly*. Ignatius repeats the word to emphasize the reality of Jesus' human life and death (see Ign. *Smyrn.* 1.2). In this paragraph, this word or a cognate occurs five times. **Pontius Pilate** See Ign. *Magn.* 11.1. **9.2 moreover** Or "in the same manner." Paul used the same expression when he compared the resurrection of believers with the resurrection of Jesus (*1 Cor.* 15:12; 32). **true life** By using cognates of *true*, Ignatius links *true life* with the statements that Jesus *truly* or *really* lived, died, and was raised from the dead. In the next paragraph Ignatius works with a similar association. **10.1 atheists** Gk *atheoi*. Some translations read "godless." **suffered in appearance only** Lit. "he seemed to suffer." That is, he did not really suffer. The Gk word for "seem" here is *dokeō*, from which comes the technical term for this position, "Docetism." **fight with wild beasts** Ignatius points to the reality of his own situation—a prisoner on his way to martyrdom—as an argument against docetic belief that claimed Jesus' sufferings were not real. Everyone knew that the beasts facing Ignatius would be real, as would be his death. **11.1 not the Father's planting** See Matt. 15:13; *Gospel of Thomas* 40. **11.2 branches of the cross** A few early Christian writers attempted to expand some aspect of the cross symbol (Ign. *Eph.* 9.1; Ign. *Smyrn.* 1.2; 2.4; *Barn.* 9.8; 11.1–12.6). **12.2 especially the presbyters** Some have argued that this comment hints at opposition to the bishop within the presbytery (see 2.2). **12.3 a witness against you** Ignatius seems to be aware of some tension in Tralles (see 3.3). **am eager to obtain** An emendation renders this passage "I eagerly press on." In Gk, this would require the text to read *houper enkeimai* rather than *perikeimai*, perhaps not an impossible mistake for a tired scribe to make, particularly given that Gk used only a small mark for the letter *h* and had no space between words. **lest I be found disqualified** Ignatius is careful not to boast in his status as "near martyr." Only when he finally has given his life up in the arena will he truly be worthy (see notes at Ign. *Eph.* 1.2; Ign. *Magn.* 1.2; 4.2). See *1 Cor.* 9:27. **13.1 not worthy** See Ign. *Eph.* 2.2. **13.3 spirit is dedicated** See Ign. *Eph.* 8.1. **I am still in danger** Not that he might be killed but that he might not be. To be released from martyrdom—for whatever reason—would have been a defeat, for then Ignatius could not have achieved full discipleship (see 12.3). Ignatius often plays with this kind of irony, especially in *To the Romans.*

THE LETTER OF IGNATIUS
TO THE PHILADELPHIANS

Salutation

Ignatius, who is also called Theophorus, to the church of God the Father and of Jesus[a] Christ at Philadelphia in Asia, one that has found mercy and is firmly established in godly harmony and unwaveringly rejoices in the suffering of our Lord, fully convinced of his resurrection in all mercy, which I greet in the blood of Jesus Christ, which is eternal and lasting joy, especially if they are at one with the bishop and the presbyters and deacons who are with him, who have been appointed by the mind of Jesus Christ, whom he, in accordance with his own will, securely established by his Holy Spirit.

Praise for the Bishop

1 I know that the bishop obtained a ministry (which is for the whole community) not by his own efforts nor through people nor out of vanity, but in the love of God the Father and the Lord Jesus Christ. I am impressed by his forbearance; he accomplishes more through silence than others do by talking.[b] 2For he is attuned to the commandments as a harp to its strings. Therefore my soul blesses his godly mind (well aware that it is virtuous and perfect), his steadfast character, and his lack of anger, as one living with all godly gentleness.[c]

Warnings about Divisions

2 Therefore as children of the light of truth flee from division and false teaching. Where the shepherd is, there follow like sheep. 2For many seemingly trustworthy wolves attempt, by means of wicked pleasure, to take captive the runners in God's race; but in your unity they will find no opportunity.

3 Stay away from the evil plants, which are not cultivated by Jesus Christ, because they are not the Father's planting. Not that I found any division among you: instead, I found that there had been a purification. 2For all those who belong to God and Jesus Christ are with the bishop, and all those who repent and enter into the unity of the church will belong to God, that they may be living in accordance with Jesus Christ. 3Do not be misled, my brothers and sisters: if

---

a Other ancient authorities read *Lord Jesus*
b Other ancient authorities add *purposelessly*

c Or *anger, in all gentleness of the living God*

TRANSLATION by Michael W. Holmes after the earlier translation of J. B. Lightfoot and J. R. Harmer. TRANSLATION NOTES by Michael W. Holmes. Reprinted, with revisions, from *The Apostolic Fathers: Greek Texts and English Translations,* edited and revised by Michael W. Holmes (Grand Rapids: Baker Books, 1999). © 1992, 1999, 2003 by Michael W. Holmes. Used by permission of Baker Book House. All rights reserved. CONTENT NOTES are by the editors of this volume, with acknowledgment to Michael W. Holmes for his observations regarding a number of texts.

Salutation The theme of unity with the bishop (and with the presbytery and deacons) is found in all six letters written to the churches of western Asia Minor. The seventh letter of Ignatius, written to the church at Rome, does not address this topic. **1.1 ministry** Gk *diakonia.* Although this word, with its cognates, came to be used as a technical term for the office of deacon, it was also used in a nontechnical sense, as in this case, describing the function of the office of bishop. **silence** On the silence of bishops, see Ign. *Eph.* 6.1. Ignatius seems to have valued gentleness in bishops (1.2; Ign. *Trall.* 3.1; Ign. *Pol.* 2.1). **1.2 harp** Ign. *Eph.* 4.1–2. **2.1 false teaching** A compound word in the Gk. In Ign. *Eph.* 16.2, the words occur in the uncompounded form. **where the shepherd is** A clear reference to the bishop and the church under his supervision. There was a schism in the church (see 3.1), and Ignatius draws attention to it throughout his short letter. **2.1–2 shepherd... sheep** Only here does Ignatius use the image of sheep, and in only one other place the image of a shepherd (Ign. *Rom.* 9.1); this passage contains the only mention of wolves in his writings. The false teacher as a wolf is also found in *Matt.* 7:15; *Acts* 20:29. **2.2 runners in God's race** A compound word in the Gk—another word coined by Ignatius, a frequent feature of his writings. **3.1–3** Some modern scholars have accused Ignatius of being responsible for drawing sharp lines between orthodoxy and heresy, thus fracturing the church and tainting it with intolerance. Ignatius certainly gave no quarter to docetic views. How tolerant he was to diversity on other matters is impossible to determine from his writings. **3.1 Father's planting** *Matt.* 15:13. **purification** Although Ignatius says here that he has not found division in the church at Philadelphia, everything else in the letter indicates that there was division (3.1; 4.1; 7.1–8.1). Obviously, he is playing with words. Rather than calling the schism a *division,* he caustically calls it a *purification* (lit. "filtering"). Both terms imply a separation, which everyone knew had taken place. Ignatius says that the church is purer without the schismatics; he almost washes his hands of them (but see 3.2). **3.3 Do not be misled** 1 *Cor.* 6:9–10.

anyone follows a schismatic, he will not inherit the kingdom of God. If anyone holds to alien views, he disassociates himself from the passion.

4 Take care, therefore, to participate in one Eucharist (for there is one flesh of our Lord Jesus Christ, and one cup that leads to unity through his blood; there is one altar, just as there is one bishop, together with the presbytery and the deacons, my fellow servants), in order that whatever you do, you do in accordance with God.

Safety in the Gospel and in the Church

5 My brothers and sisters, I am overflowing with love for you, and greatly rejoice as I watch out for your safety—yet not I, but Jesus Christ. Though I am in chains for his sake, I am all the more afraid, because I am still imperfect. But your prayer to God[d] will make me perfect, that I may attain the fate by which I have received mercy, since I have taken refuge in the gospel as the flesh of Jesus and in the apostles as the presbytery of the church. [2]And we also love the prophets, because they anticipated the gospel in their preaching and set their hope on him and waited for him; because they also believed in him, they were saved, since they belong to the unity centered in Jesus Christ, saints worthy of love and admiration, approved by Jesus Christ and included in the gospel of our common hope.

Warnings about Judaism

6 But if anyone expounds Judaism to you, do not listen to him. For it is better to hear about Christianity from a man who is circumcised than Judaism from one who is not. But if either of them fails to speak about Jesus Christ, I look on them as tombstones and graves of the dead, upon which only the names of people are inscribed. [2]Flee, therefore, the evil tricks and traps of the ruler of this age, lest you be

---

[d] Other ancient authorities omit *to God*

worn out by his schemes and grow weak in love. Instead gather together, all of you, with an undivided heart.

Dealings with the Church at Philadelphia

[3]Now I give thanks to my God that I have clear conscience in my dealings with you, and that no one can boast, either privately or publicly, that I was a burden to anyone in any respect, small or great. Moreover, I pray that all those to whom I spoke will not cause what I said to become a witness against them.

7 For even though certain people wanted to deceive me, humanly speaking, nevertheless the Spirit is not deceived, because it is from God; for it knows from where it comes and where it is going, and exposes the hidden things. I called out when I was with you; I was speaking with a loud voice, God's voice: "Pay attention to the bishop and to the presbytery and deacons." [2]To be sure, there were those who suspected that I said these things because I knew in advance about the division caused by certain people. But the one for whose sake I am in chains is my witness that I did not learn this from any human being. No, the Spirit itself was preaching, saying these words: "Do nothing without the bishop. Guard your bodies as the temple of God. Love unity. Flee from divisions. Become imitators of Jesus Christ, just as he is of his Father."

8 I was doing my part, therefore, as a man set on unity. But God does not dwell where there is division and anger. The Lord, however, forgives all who repent, if in repenting they return to the unity of God and the council of the bishop. I believe in the grace of Jesus Christ, who will free you from every bond.

The Gospel versus Judaism

[2]Moreover, I urge you to do nothing in a spirit of contentiousness, but in accordance with the teaching of Christ. For I heard some people say, "If I do not find it in the archives, I do not believe it in the

---

disassociates himself from the passion Usually the debate about the passion is engaged with docetists, but in this letter the Jewish character of the opponents seems to be highlighted. **4.1 one Eucharist** This is another indication of schism. Elsewhere Ignatius speaks of a dispute regarding the Eucharist, which seemed for Ignatius to be the concrete expression of unity with the bishop. See notes to Ign. *Eph.* 5.2; Ign. *Smyrn.* 7.1; see also *1 Cor.* 10:17, where Paul uses the phrase "one bread" to describe the Eucharist. **5.1** Ignatius links his imprisonment and approaching martyrdom with true discipleship (see Ign. *Eph.* 1.2). **5.2 prophets** Some scholars think this refers to Christian prophets (such as those encountered in the *Didache*). But this letter focuses on the witness of Judaism to the gospel, a theme that Ignatius picks up immediately after speaking of prophets. It would be strange for Ignatius to raise the issue of Christian prophets, for his concern with Christian leaders had always been focused on bishops, presbyters, and deacons. **6.3** Perhaps this passage means that he did not receive financial support from them. **7.1–2** Ignatius apparently made a plea for unity under the bishop while he was in Philadelphia. The schismatics were offended because they thought he had allowed himself to be used as a tool of the local supporters of the bishop. Ignatius denies this and claims the Spirit, not the bishop's supporters, made him aware of the schism. **7.1 knows from where it comes** John 3:8. **8.2 archives** Most scholars believe these are the Jewish scriptures (Josephus, *Ag. Ap.* 1.29). Ignatius subordinates the Jewish scriptures to the Christian message; his explicit preference is the gospel (9.2).

gospel." And when I said to them, "It is written," they answered me, "That is precisely the question." But for me, the "archives" are Jesus Christ, the inviolable archives are his cross and death and his resurrection and the faith that comes through him; by these things I want, through your prayers, to be justified.

9 The priests, too, were good, but the High Priest, entrusted with the Holy of Holies, is better; he alone has been entrusted with the hidden things of God, for he himself is the door of the Father, through which Abraham and Isaac and Jacob and the prophets and the apostles and the church enter in. All these come together in the unity of God. ²But the gospel possesses something distinctive, namely the coming of the Savior, our Lord Jesus Christ, his suffering, and the resurrection. For the beloved prophets preached in anticipation of him, but the gospel is the imperishable finished work. All these things together are good, if you believe with love.

Personal Greetings and Parting Requests

10 Since it has been reported to me that in answer to your prayer and the compassion that you have in Christ Jesus the church at Antioch in Syria is at peace, it is appropriate for you, as a church of God, to appoint a deacon to go there on a mission as God's ambassador, to congratulate them when they have assembled together and to glorify the name. ²Blessed in Christ Jesus^e is the one who will be judged worthy of such ministry, and you yourselves will be glorified. It is certainly not impossible for you to do this for the name of God, if you are willing; indeed, the neighboring churches have sent bishops, and others presbyters and deacons.

11 Now concerning Philo, the deacon from Cilicia, a man with a good reputation, who even now assists me in the word of God, along with Rhaius^f Agathopus, a chosen man who followed me from Syria, having renounced this life: they speak well of you, and I give thanks to God on your behalf, because you received them as the Lord received you. But may those who dishonored them be redeemed by the grace of Jesus Christ.

²The love of the brothers in Troas greets you. I am writing you from there through Burrhus, who was sent with me by the Ephesians and Smyrnaeans as a mark of honor. The Lord Jesus Christ will honor them, on whom they set their hope in body, soul, and spirit with faith, love, and harmony. Farewell in Christ Jesus, our common hope.

---

e Other ancient authorities read *Jesus Christ*
f Some ancient authorities read *Rheus,* others *Gaius*

The lack of punctuation in the Gk has made this passage ambiguous: Is Ignatius identifying the *charters* as the gospel, or is he distinguishing the two? **9.1–2** Ignatius claims the Hebrew forefathers and the Hebrew prophets for the Christian cause. They are joined in unity with the Christian apostles. Yet Ignatius uses the Bible less often than any of the writers in our collection (8.2). **the gospel possesses something distinctive** Ignatius means the death and resurrection of Jesus, not the written gospels. **9.1 High Priest** Jesus. See *Heb.* 4:14–5:10. The Jewish priestly office had little influence on the Christian structures of authority (see *1 Clem.* 36.1). **the door** See *John* 10:7, 9, where "gate" translates the same Gk word. **10.1** Ignatius received word in Troas that the problem in his church at Antioch had been resolved. In the letters written from Troas (of which *To the Philadelphians* is one), he speaks of the "peace" of the church at Antioch. The problem in Antioch may have concerned an internal church schism or an external persecution. Perhaps both (see introduction to The Letters of Ignatius). **appoint a deacon to go** The request is for the churches of Asia to send representatives to *congratulate* the church at Antioch. Sending messengers would have been expensive, and Ignatius's request may show how serious the problem had been. See previous note. **10.2 neighboring churches** Ignatius probably means churches in the neighborhood of Antioch, not of Philadelphia. This information must have come from Philo or Rhaius (11.1), and it appears that many churches were involved. **11.1 Rhaius** See the note at Ign. *Smyrn.* 10.1. These men would have carried news of the improved situation in Antioch. Whether they were also on their way to martyrdom is not clear, but the comment that Rhaius had *renounced this life* seems to suggest this. Philo is mentioned in Ign. *Smyrn.* 13.1. Perhaps the same people who confronted Ignatius in Philadelphia challenged Philo and Rhaius as they passed through (7.2). **11.2 Troas** The church at Troas appears to have hosted Ignatius in the same way as the church at Smyrna when he was there a few days earlier. **Burrhus** See Ign. *Eph.* 2.1.

THE LETTER OF IGNATIUS
TO THE SMYRNAEANS

Salutation

Ignatius, who is also called Theophorus, to the church of God the Father and of the beloved Jesus Christ at Smyrna in Asia, mercifully endowed with every spiritual gift, filled with faith and love, not lacking in any spiritual gift, most worthy of God, bearing holy things: heartiest greetings in a blameless spirit and the word of God.

The Reality of Jesus' Human Experiences

1 I glorify Jesus Christ, the God who made you so wise, for I observed that you are established in an unshakable faith, having been nailed, as it were, to the cross of the Lord Jesus Christ in both body and spirit, and firmly established in love by the blood of Christ, totally convinced with regard to our Lord that he is truly of the family of David with respect to human descent, Son of God with respect to the divine will and power,[a] truly born of a virgin, baptized by John in order that all righteousness might be fulfilled by him, ²truly nailed in the flesh for us under Pontius Pilate and Herod the tetarch (from its fruit we derive our existence, that is, from his divinely blessed suffering), in order that he might raise a banner for the ages through his resurrection for his saints and faithful people, whether among Jews or among Gentiles, in the one body of his church.

2 For he suffered all these things for our sakes, in order that we might be saved;[b] and he truly suffered just as he truly raised himself—not, as certain unbelievers say, that he suffered in appearance only (it is they who exist in appearance only!). Indeed, their fate will be determined by what they think: they will become disembodied and demonic.

3 For I know and believe that he was in the flesh even after the resurrection; ²and when he came to Peter and those with him, he said to them: "Take hold of me; handle me and see that I am not a disembodied demon." And immediately they touched him and believed, being closely united with his flesh and blood.[c] For this reason they too despised death; indeed, they proved to be greater than death. ³And after his resurrection he ate and drank with them like one who is composed of flesh, although spiritually he was united with the Father.

---

a Gk *to the will and power;* some ancient authorities read *to God's will and power*

b Other ancient authorities omit *in order . . . saved*

c Other ancient authorities read *flesh and spirit*

TRANSLATION by Michael W. Holmes after the earlier translation of J. B. Lightfoot and J. R. Harmer. TRANSLATION NOTES by Michael W. Holmes. Reprinted, with revisions, from *The Apostolic Fathers: Greek Texts and English Translations,* edited and revised by Michael W. Holmes (Grand Rapids: Baker Books, 1999). © 1992, 1999, 2003 by Michael W. Holmes. Used by permission of Baker Book House. All rights reserved. CONTENT NOTES are by the editors of this volume, with acknowledgment to Michael W. Holmes for his observations regarding a number of texts.

Salutation *Smyrna* Ignatius has stayed at Smyrna for some days, enjoying the hospitality of certain people in the church, while waiting for a ship to Rome or for favorable winds. Ships tended to sail along the coasts rather than taking the more direct, dangerous route across open seas (Seneca, *Letters* 53.1–4). Ignatius's next stop after Smyrna was Troas, another port along this coastal route, from where he wrote this letter. *most worthy of God, bearing holy things* Gk two compound words. Ignatius is particularly fond of such constructions. **1.1** *family of David* See notes to Ign. *Eph.* 20.2; Ign. *Trall.* 9.1. *born of a virgin* See Ign. *Eph.* 19.1. *might be fulfilled by him* The baptism of Jesus is explained with the same terms in *Matt.* 3:15. **1.2** *truly nailed in the flesh* This is part of the strong antidocetic theme in much of Ignatius's thought. Ignatius prefixes the word "truly" to a number of elements in the life of Jesus that he feels compelled to emphasize against his opponents. *its fruit* The cross's fruit. *Pilate and Herod* See Ign. *Magn.* 11.1. This is the only mention of Herod in our literature outside the gospels and *Acts. raise a banner Isa.* 5:26. *one body of his church Eph.* 2:16. **2.1** With polemical skill Ignatius turns his opponents' denial of the physical dimension of Jesus' existence into a denial of their own physical existence. Having denied the real resurrection of Jesus, they will not themselves experience the real resurrection; they will be mere phantoms. Ignatius's opponents may have developed a scheme in which physical resurrection was not important, and Ignatius's comment therefore may have meant little to them. Note a similar twist in 5.2. **3.1** *Luke* 24:39. **3.2** Ignatius links the real death of Jesus to a number of other real deaths, which no one, not even Ignatius's opponents, could credibly deny. By this time stories about Peter and other disciples' martyrdoms were circulating. Ignatius calls attention to his own approaching martyrdom in the following paragraph.

Warnings about Teachers of Error

4 Now I am advising you of these things, dear friends, knowing that you are of the same mind. But I am guarding you in advance against wild beasts in human form—people whom you must not only not welcome but, if possible, not even meet. Nevertheless, do pray for them, if somehow they might repent, difficult though it may be. But Jesus Christ, our true life, has power over this.

Martyrdom Motivated by Jesus' Real Passion

²For if these things were done by our Lord in appearance only, then I am in chains in appearance only. Why, moreover, have I surrendered myself to death, to fire, to sword, to beasts? But in any case, "near the sword" means "near to God"; "with the beasts" means "with God." Only let it be in the name of Jesus Christ, that I may suffer together with him! I endure everything because he himself, who is*d* the perfect human being, empowers me.

5 Certain people ignorantly deny him, or rather have been denied by him, for they are advocates of death rather than of the truth. Neither the prophecies nor the law of Moses have persuaded them, nor, thus far, the gospel nor our own individual suffering; ²for they think the same thing about us. For what good does it do me if someone praises me but blasphemes my Lord by not confessing that he was clothed in flesh? Anyone who does not acknowledge this thereby denies him completely and is clothed in a corpse. ³Given that they are unbelievers, it did not seem worthwhile to me to record their names. Indeed, far be it from me even to remember them, until such time as they change their mind in regard to the passion, which is our resurrection.

Bad Teachers and Bad Beliefs

6 Let no one be misled. Even the heavenly beings and the glory of angels and the rulers, both visible and invisible, are also subject to judgment if they do not believe in the blood of Christ.*e* "The one who accepts this, let him accept it." Do not let a high position make anyone proud, for faith and love are everything; nothing is preferable to them.

²Now note well those who hold heretical opinions about the grace of Jesus Christ that came to us; note how contrary they are to the mind of God. They have no concern for love, none for the widow, none for the orphan, none for the oppressed, none for the prisoner or the one released,*f* none for the hungry or thirsty.*g* They abstain from Eucharist and prayer because they refuse to acknowledge that the Eucharist is the flesh of our savior Jesus Christ, which suffered for our sins and which the Father by his goodness raised up.

7 Therefore those who deny the good gift of God perish in their contentiousness. It would be more to their advantage to love, in order that they might also rise up. ²It is proper, therefore, to avoid such people and not speak about them either privately or publicly. Do pay attention, however, to the prophets and especially to the gospel, in which the passion has been made clear to us and the resurrection has been accomplished.

---

d Other ancient authorities read *became*

e One ancient authority adds *who is God*
f Other ancient authorities omit *or the one released*
g Some editions begin chapter 7 here

4.2 Ignatius uses his own approaching martyrdom as an argument against his opponents' position. Real suffering is a mark of discipleship (see Ign. *Eph.* 1.2; Ign. *Magn.* 9.1; Ign. *Trall.* 4.2; Ign. *Rom.* 1.1; Ign. *Pol.* 7.1).   **5.2** *praises me but blasphemes my Lord* It appears that some of the people against whom Ignatius wrote were willing to welcome him. Some scholars accuse Ignatius of drawing harsher lines of exclusion than the churches of Asia had.   *clothed in a corpse* This is the point against which Ignatius argues repeatedly. By denying that Jesus was clothed in flesh, his opponents themselves become clothed in a corpse. Far better to be clothed in living flesh than in dead flesh!   **5.3** Ignatius nowhere names any of the opponents. We do not know why he omitted such names nor how helpful they would be had he supplied them.   **6.1** *let him accept it* The words are from *Matt.* 19:12, but the context is different.   *a high position* Lit. "a place." Some translators have rendered it "rank" or "office." See Ign. *Magn.* 6.1. This statement does not provide clear evidence of error or revolt in the ranks of the presbytery; elsewhere Ignatius has high praise for the clergy (8.1).   **6.2** Ignatius condemns his opponents for their general lack of charity. It is not clear whether he knew a specific dereliction in this area or whether he assumed it from their separation from the common assembly of the bishop, who had the responsibility along with the deacons to distribute charity for his church. The list supplied here may shed some light on the kinds of charity cases for which the church considered itself responsible.   *abstain from Eucharist* Ignatius explains why the schismatics are unable to participate in the Eucharist. In other places, however, Ignatius seems to assume that schismatic groups have continued the Eucharist (8.1; Ign. *Eph.* 5.2; Ign. *Phld.* 4.1).   **7.2** *the prophets* Ignatius probably used this word for the whole of Jewish scriptures rather than a specific section of the Bible.   *especially to the gospel* The reference is not to written gospels but to the story of Jesus that formed the center of early Christian preaching. This is not to say that local congregations did not have a manuscript of one or more of the written gospels. See Ign. *Phld.* 8.2.

Obedience to the Bishop

8 Flee from divisions, as the beginning of evils.[h] You must all follow the bishop, as Jesus Christ followed the Father, and follow the presbytery as you would the apostles; respect the deacons as the commandment of God. Let no one do anything that has to do with the church without the bishop. Only that Eucharist which is under the authority of the bishop (or whomever he himself designates) is to be considered valid. [2]Wherever the bishop appears, there let the congregation be; just as wherever Jesus Christ is, there is the catholic church. It is not permissible either to baptize or to hold a love feast without the bishop. But whatever he approves is also pleasing to God, in order that everything you do may be trustworthy and valid.

9 Finally, it is reasonable for us to come to our senses while we still have time to repent and turn to God. It is good to acknowledge God and the bishop. The one who honors the bishop has been honored by God; the one who does anything without the bishop's knowledge serves the devil.

Thanks for Services Rendered

[2]May all things, therefore, be yours in abundance in grace, for you are worthy. You refreshed me in every respect, and Jesus Christ will refresh you. In my absence and in my presence you loved me. God is

your reward;[i] if you endure everything for his sake, you will reach him.

10 You did well to welcome Philo and Rhaius[j] Agathopus, who followed me for God's sake, as deacons[k] of God.[l] They too give thanks to the Lord on your behalf because you refreshed them in every way. You will certainly not lose any of this! [2]May my spirit be a ransom on your behalf, and my bonds as well, which you did not despise, nor were you ashamed of them. Nor will the perfect hope,[m] Jesus Christ, be ashamed of you.

Detailed News about Antioch

11 Your prayer reached the church at Antioch in Syria; having come from there bound in the most God-pleasing chains I greet everyone, even though I am not worthy to be from there, for I am the very least of them. Nevertheless in accordance with the divine will I was judged worthy, not because of the witness of my own conscience, but by the grace of God, which I pray may be given to me in perfection, that by your prayer I may reach God. [2]Therefore, in order that your work may become perfect both on earth and in heaven, it is appropriate that your church appoint, for the honor of God, a godly ambassador to go to Syria to congratulate them, because they are at peace and have regained their proper stature and their corporate life has been restored to its proper state. [3]It seemed to me, therefore, to be a deed

---

h Some editions end chapter 7 here

i Other ancient authorities read *God will reward you*
j Some ancient authorities read *Rheus,* others *Gaius*
k Or *ministers* or *servants*
l Other ancient authorities read *Christ God*
m Other ancient authorities read *faith*

8.1 *Flee from divisions* The high praise for all elements of the clergy here suggests that they were not involved in the factions Ignatius attacks. *Eucharist . . . considered valid* See 7.1. **8.2** *catholic church* This is the first occurrence of the term "catholic" in Christian literature. The Gk term is a compound word, lit. "according to the whole," usually translated "universal," without any of the religious weight that it has come to possess. Soon after this early period, and perhaps stemming from Ignatius's use, the idea developed that the authentic church throughout the world possessed a common faith and practice. Ignatius uses the term here as a contrast to the separate assemblies operating beyond the bishop's authority. *love feast* Gk *agapē*. One of several Gk terms for "love," this word is often translated "love feast" in Christian texts because in some places it plainly refers to a communal meal. Some translators prefer to keep the Gk work as a technical term. Originally, the *agapē* seems to have been closely linked with the Eucharist (*1 Cor.* 11:17–34), but by the mid-2d century the two meals were separate events. It is uncertain whether this passage refers to the Eucharist or to a separate meal. **9.1** *The one who honors . . . devil* The Gk of the 1st part is clear, with the wordplay: the one who "honors" has been "honored." The 2d part contains a play of sounds obscured in the English translation: *lathra* (without one's knowledge) . . . *latreuei* (serves). **10.1** *Philo and Rhaius Agathopus* The name of the 2d person is confused in the manuscript tradition. Some translators read "Rheus," and others "Gaius." In Gk, the capital letters *R* and *G* are similar. A tired scribe or a worn manuscript could account for inaccurate copying. Most words can be judged to be correct or incorrect by the context, but there is nothing in the context to recommend Rhaius over Rheus or Gaius (Ign. *Phld.* 11.1). These men have caught up to Ignatius in Troas, following along the same route through Philadelphia and Smyrna. It is not clear whether they are on their way to martyrdom also; the phrases *followed me for God's sake* and *renounced this life* (Ign. *Phld.* 11.1) may suggest this. *deacons* Gk *diakonos*. It may mean merely "servant," rather than a formal office. **10.2** *bonds.* See Ign. *Eph.* 1.2. **11.1** *not worthy* See Ign. *Eph.* 2.2. **11.2** This request, made to a number of churches, would have involved considerable expense and a trip requiring several weeks. It is debated why Ignatius made such a request when finally the church at Antioch was at peace. See Ign. *Pol.* 7.2.

worthy of God[n] for you to send one of your own people with a letter, that he might join in glorifying the tranquility which by God's will has come to them, and because they have now reached, thanks to your prayers, a safe harbor. Inasmuch as you are perfect, let your intentions also be[o] perfect, for if you want to do well, God is ready to help you.

Personal Greetings and Parting Requests

12 The love of the brothers in Troas greets you. I am writing you from there through Burrhus, whom you, together with your Ephesian brothers, sent with me. He has refreshed me in every respect. Would that all were imitators of him, for he is a model of service to God. Grace will reward him in every respect. [2]I greet the bishop, so worthy of God, and the godly presbytery, and my fellow servants, the deacons, and all of you, individually and collectively, in the name of Jesus Christ and in his flesh and blood, his suffering and resurrection (which was both physical and spiritual), in unity with God and with you. Grace, mercy, peace, patience to you always.

13 I greet the households of my brothers with their wives and children, and the virgins who are called widows. I bid you farewell in the power of the Father.[p] Philo, who is with me, greets you. [2]I greet the household of Gavia,[q] and pray that she may be firmly grounded in faith and love both physically and spiritually. I greet Alce, a name very dear to me, and the incomparable Daphnus, and Eutecnus and everyone else individually. Farewell in the grace of God.

---

n Other ancient authorities read *to be a worthy deed*
o Or *are perfect, aim at what is*

p Other ancient authorities read *Spirit*
q Other ancient authorities read *Tavia*

12.1 *Burrhus* See Ign. *Eph.* 2.1. *service* Gk *diakonia.* **13.2** *Gavia* Another variant reads "Tavia," a change of only the initial letter in Gk (*T* rather than *G*), almost identical in Gk uppercase letters. *Eutecnus* Some scholars have suggested that this is not a personal name but a word meaning "with good children."

THE LETTER OF IGNATIUS
TO POLYCARP

Salutation

Ignatius, who is also called Theophorus, to Polycarp, bishop of the church of the Smyrnaeans, or rather who has God the Father and the Lord[a] Jesus Christ as his bishop, heartiest greetings.

1 So approving am I of your godly mind, which is grounded, as it were, upon an unmovable rock, that my praise exceeds all bounds, inasmuch as I was judged worthy of seeing your blameless face. May it bring me joy in God.

General Instructions for a Bishop

[2]I urge you, by the grace with which you are clothed, to press on in your race and to exhort all people, that they may be saved. Do justice to your office with constant care for both physical and spiritual concerns. Focus on unity, for there is nothing better. Bear with all people, even as the Lord bears with you; endure all in love, just as you now do. [3]Devote yourself to unceasing prayers; ask for greater understanding than you have. Keep on the alert with an unresting spirit. Speak to the people individually, in accordance with God's example.[b] Bear the diseases of all, as a perfect athlete. Where there is more work, there is much gain.

---

a One ancient authority omits *the Lord*
b Or *in a godly agreement of convictions*

2 If you love good disciples, it is no credit to you; rather with gentleness bring the more troublesome ones into submission. "Not every wound is healed by the same treatment"; "relieve inflammations with cold compresses." [2]"Be as shrewd as a snake" in all circumstances, yet always "innocent as a dove." You are both physical and spiritual in nature for this reason, that you may treat gently whatever appears before you; but ask, in order that the unseen things may be revealed to you, that you may be lacking in nothing and abound in every spiritual gift. [3]The time needs you (as pilots need winds and as a storm-tossed sailor needs a harbor) in order to reach God. Be sober, as God's athlete; the prize is incorruptibility and eternal life, about which you are already convinced. May I be a ransom on your behalf in every respect, and my bonds as well, which you loved.

Dealing with Teachers of Error

3 Do not let those who appear to be trustworthy yet who teach strange doctrines baffle you. Stand firm, like an anvil being struck with a hammer. It is the mark of a great athlete to be bruised, yet still conquer. But especially we must, for God's sake, patiently put up with all things, that he may also put up with us. [2]Be more diligent than you are. Understand the times. Wait expectantly for the one who is above time: the Eternal, the Invisible, who for our sake

TRANSLATION by Michael W. Holmes after the earlier translation of J. B. Lightfoot and J. R. Harmer. TRANSLATION NOTES by Michael W. Holmes. Reprinted, with revisions, from *The Apostolic Fathers: Greek Texts and English Translations,* edited and revised by Michael W. Holmes (Grand Rapids: Baker Books, 1999). © 1992, 1999, 2003 by Michael W. Holmes. Used by permission of Baker Book House. All rights reserved. CONTENT NOTES are by the editors of this volume, with acknowledgment to Michael W. Holmes for his observations regarding a number of texts.

Salutation *Polycarp* Ign. *Eph.* 21.1; Ign. *Magn.* 15.3. **as his bishop** Lit. "is being bishoped by" or "is being overseen by." Ignatius refers to God (Ign. *Magn.* 3.1) and Jesus (Ign. *Rom.* 9.1) as bishop. **1.2 office** Lit. "place" or "position." Ignatius has used this common word for physical location to describe a position in the church, that is, an office (Ign. *Magn.* 6.1; Ign. *Smyrn.* 6.1). **Focus on unity** Unity under the authority of the bishop. Ignatius uses Gk *henōsis* ("unity") eight times; it does not appear elsewhere in our literature (5.2; Ign. *Magn.* 1.2; 13.2; Ign. *Trall.* 11.2; Ign. *Phld.* 4.1; 7.2; 8.1). **endure all in love** *Eph.* 4:2. **1.3 Bear the diseases** *Isa.* 53:4; *Matt.* 8:17. **athlete** Ignatius uses the term in 2.3 and 3.1 but not in his other letters. The image is used in *2 Tim.* 2:5; *Heb.* 10:32; *1 Clem.* 5.1–2. See Ign. *Eph.* 3.1. **Where there is more work there is much gain** This aphorism may have been coined by Ignatius. Gk *hopou pleiōn kopos, poly kerdos.* "Where greatest pain, much gain." **2.1 If you love good disciples** *Luke* 6:32; *1 Pet.* 2:18–19; *Did.* 1.3. Ignatius may have learned about troublesome persons from Polycarp himself, or he may simply be giving general advice on the basis of his own experience as a bishop. **cold compresses** Some mixture used to soothe (see Seneca, *Letters* 53.5). **innocent as a dove** *Matt.* 10:16. **2.3 pilots need winds** See Ign. *Smyrn.* salutation. **athlete** See 1.3. **bonds . . . which you loved** Or "which you kissed," though that meaning of the verb *agapaō* is disputed. Early Christians had a practice of kissing the chains of the condemned as they made their way to martyrdom. **3.2 above time: the Eternal, . . . the Unsuffering** This description of God fits well the Hellenistic philosophical view of God, which Ignatius accepted. Ignatius has one qualification: His God has indeed suffered. This is a main point of contention between Ignatius and his docetic opponents.

became visible; the Intangible, the Unsuffering, who for our sake suffered, who for our sake endured in every way.

Protecting the Weak

4 Do not let the widows be neglected. After the Lord, you be their guardian. Let nothing be done without your consent, nor do anything yourself without God's consent,[c] as indeed you do not. Stand firm. [2]Let meetings be held more frequently; seek out everyone by name. [3]Do not treat slaves, whether male or female, contemptuously, but neither let them become conceited; instead, let them serve all the more faithfully to the glory of God, that they may obtain from God a better freedom. They should not have a strong desire to be set free at the church's expense, lest they be found to be slaves of lust.

Duties of the Married

5 Flee from wicked practices; better yet, preach sermons about them. Tell my sisters to love the Lord and to be content with their husbands physically and spiritually. In the same way command my brothers in the name of Jesus Christ to love their wives, as the Lord loves the church. [2]If anyone is able to remain

chaste to the honor of the flesh of the Lord, let him so remain without boasting. If he boasts, he is lost; and if it is made known to anyone other than the bishop, he is ruined. And it is proper for men and women who marry to be united with the consent of the bishop, that the marriage may be in accordance with the Lord and not due to lustful passions. Let all things be done for the honor of God.

Obedience to the Bishop; Harmonious Work

6 Pay attention to the bishop, in order that God may pay attention to you. I am a ransom on behalf of those who are obedient to the bishop, presbyters, and deacons; may it be granted to me to have a place among them in the presence of God![d] Train together with one another: struggle together, run together, suffer together, rest together, get up together, as God's managers, assistants, and servants. [2]Please him whom you serve as soldiers, from whom you receive[e] your wages. Let none of you be found a deserter. Let your baptism serve as a shield, faith as a helmet, love as a spear, endurance as armor. Let your deeds be your deposits, in order that you may eventually receive the savings that are due you. Be, therefore, patient and gentle with one another, as God is with you. May I always have joy in you.

---

c Other ancient authorities read *without God*

d Other ancient authorities read *among them in God*
e One ancient authority reads *will receive*

4.1 widows Ign. *Smyrn.* 13.1; *Acts* 6:1; 9:39–41; *1 Cor.* 7:8; *1 Tim.* 5:3–15; *Jas.* 1:27; Pol. *Phil.* 4.3; 6.1; *Barn.* 20.2; *1 Clem.* 8.4. Perhaps this mention of widows, which seems to begin a new thought, should be linked with the command to Polycarp not to let anything be done without his approval. Bishops were the chief financial officers of the church, a major responsibility of which involved the support of widows. It also involved buying the freedom of slaves, which Ignatius addresses in 4.3. **guardian** This is the only use of the Gk term in our literature. According to Lightfoot, it was a semiofficial term. **4.2 meetings** Lit. "synagogues." See notes to Ign. *Eph.* 5.2; *Jas.* 2:2. We do not know how often Christians met regularly. **seek out everyone by name** It is uncertain whether this statement suggests a small Christian group, in which such intimacy would have been possible, or a large group, in which the bishop was removed from close contact with many in the church and needed to be encouraged to make himself more accessible. **4.3** *1 Tim.* 6:2. See notes to *Titus* 2:9; *1 Pet.* 2:18. **church's expense** Lit. "from the common [*or* public] treasury." See *Apostolic Constitutions and Canons* 4.9 for the practice of ransoming slaves. **5.1 wicked practices** Ign. *Phld.* 6.2. Perhaps a reference to witchcraft (*Acts* 19:19), although more specific terms were available to identify such activities. It could refer to an entire range of activities judged to be evil. **content with their husbands** *1 Cor.* 7; *Eph.* 5:22–24; *Col.* 3:18; *Titus* 2:4–5; *1 Pet.* 3:1–5; *1 Clem.* 1.3; Pol. *Phil.* 4.2. **loves the church** *Eph.* 5:25, 29. **5.2** Ignatius does not praise celibacy as an ideal, and he rejects it if it becomes a matter for boasting. Ignatius refers to celibacy (perpetual or for a specific period) practiced by a married couple; the unmarried would have been expected to be celibate. The practice of celibate marriage, known from 2d- and 3d-century writings, was probably influenced by *1 Cor.* 7:1, 8, 25. **be united with the consent of the bishop** The 1st reference in our literature to the involvement of church officials in Christian marriages. Roman marriages generally had a ceremony in which the god Hymen was featured. One wedding song repeats the refrain "Without your blessing, Hymen . . . without your rites." It is uncertain whether the Christian blessing is meant as a substitute for pagan practices. **6.1** Here Ignatius begins to direct his instructions to the church rather than specifically to the bishop. **Train together** Ignatius uses a series of six compound words beginning with a prefix from the preposition *syn* ("with"), to express the unity of action undertaken together. **6.2** Ignatius uses military terms to illustrate unity of purpose, with each person serving in their appropriate rank. Those who fail are guilty of deserting, a serious charge. **shield . . . helmet . . . spear . . . armor** The equipment of a foot soldier. See *Eph.* 6:13–17 for a similar use of military vocabulary. **savings** Lake translates this as "back pay." Soldiers were paid half their wage during service, the other half upon retirement, allowing for some comforts during the periods of both service and retirement. Ignatius uses three Latin technical terms in this passage, all of which have come into English in some way (*desertor, deposita,* and *accepta*). Deserters would have lost their back pay. Such words, as well as the comparisons of Christian qualities to armor, may have

Request for Delegate to Antioch

7 Since (as I have been informed) the church at Antioch in Syria is at peace through your prayer, I too have become more encouraged in a God-given freedom from anxiety—provided, of course, that through suffering I reach God, that I may prove to be a disciple by means of your prayer.*f* 2It is certainly appropriate, Polycarp (how blessed by God you are!), to convene a council that will be most pleasing to God and to appoint someone whom you*g* consider to be especially dear and resolute, who is qualified to be called God's courier; commission him to go to Syria, that he may glorify your resolute love, to the glory of God. 3A Christian has no authority over himself; rather he devotes his time to God. This is God's work, and will be yours, when you complete it. For by grace I trust that you are ready for a good work in the service of God. Knowing the intensity of your sincerity, I have exhorted you only briefly.

Personal Greetings and Parting Requests

8 Since*h* I have not been able to write to all the churches because I am sailing at once from Troas to Neapolis, as the divine will commands, you*i* must write, as one possessing the mind of God, to the churches on this side, so that they too may do likewise—those who can should send messengers, the rest letters through the people being sent by you,*i* that you*j* may be glorified by an eternal deed—for you*i* are worthy of such a thing.

2I greet everyone by name, including the widow of Epitropus with her whole household and those of the children. I greet Attalus, my dear friend. I greet the one who is about to be commissioned to go to Syria. Grace will be with him always, and with Polycarp, who sends him. 3I bid you*j* farewell always in our God Jesus Christ; may you remain in him, in the unity and care of God. I greet Alce, a name very dear to me. Farewell in the Lord.

---

f Other ancient authorities read *be your disciple in the resurrection*
g Gk *you* and *your* are plural throughout chapter 7

---

h Other ancient authorities read *Therefore since*
i Gk singular *you*
j Gk plural *you*

---

been impressed upon Ignatius from conversations he overheard from his armed escort, with whom he had been chained for several weeks. **7.1 *at Antioch*** Lit. "in Antioch of Syria." See Ign. *Rom.* 2.2. ***I have been informed*** Some scholars contend that, as a result of the information that Ignatius received, there was a substantial change of tone between the letters written from Smyrna and those written from Troas (see introduction to the Letters of Ignatius). ***through suffering I reach God*** See notes to Ign. *Rom.* 4.1–3; 5.2–3; Ign. *Eph.* salutation; Ign. *Trall.* 4.2; 5.2. ***by means of your prayer*** There is a textual variant here, reading "resurrection" in place of "intercession." **7.2** Ignatius is sensitive to the cost to the churches when their clergy are away from their day-to-day duties in order to visit him (see Ign. *Eph.* 2.1). Yet he asks that the church in Smyrna, which has just shared in funding Burrhus to assist Ignatius as far as Troas (or possibly farther), now fund a far more expensive mission to carry congratulations to the church in Antioch in person. He further requests that churches on the road before him be encouraged by Polycarp to send messengers if they can; otherwise they are to send letters. ***council*** Gk *symboulion*. See Ign. *Magn.* 6.1. ***God's courier*** Lit. "God-runner." Another compound word, possibly coined by Ignatius. **7.3 *Christian*** See Ign. *Eph.* 11.2. **8.1** Ignatius planned to write to more churches, but a sudden sailing prevented him. Burrhus may have returned to Smyrna and Ephesus, leaving Ignatius without scribal assistance. ***Neapolis*** Modern Kavalla, a port on the road between Rome and the East. The Roman colony of Philippi was a few miles to the north. ***churches on this side*** The churches intended by this phrase are not clear. The expression could indicate churches in front of Ignatius (those in Macedonia and Achaia—modern Greece), for we know of churches there that Paul and his associates had established (Philippi, Thessalonica, Beroea, and Corinth). We also know of a letter written by the church at Philippi, which expressed an interest in Ignatius's situation. That letter is lost, but Polycarp's reply is preserved. The expression could also indicate churches Ignatius had passed through *earlier* (those between Antioch and Smyrna). ***you are worthy*** In 8.1, the 1st, 2d, and 4th instances of *you* are singular, apparently referring to Polycarp the bishop, whereas the 3d instance is plural, apparently referring to the congregation. This shift from singular to plural and then back is both odd and awkward. One early translation (the Latin) relieved the awkwardness by making all four instances singular, while another (the Armenian) rendered all four as plurals. **8.2 *Epitropus*** The Gk could be translated as a personal name, "Epitropus," or literally as "governor."

EARLY

CHRISTIAN

READER

Coins and Money

APPENDIX A

	JEWISH	GREEK	ROMAN
copper coins			
the very last penny (*Luke* 12:59)		**lepton** = 1/2 perutah	
the last penny (*Matt.* 5:26) a widow's mite (*Mark* 12:42)	**perutah** = 1 quadrans		**quadrans** = 1/64 denarius
two sparrows sold for a penny (*Matt.* 10:29)			**assarion** = 1/16 denarius
silver coins*			
the usual daily wage (*Matt.* 20:9) the tax to Caesar (*Matt.* 22:19)			**denarius** = 1 drachma
the widow's lost coin (*Luke* 15:9)		**drachma** = 1 denarius	
temple tax (*Matt.* 17:24)		**didrachmon** = 2 drachmai	
a coin in the mouth of the fish (*Matt.* 17:27)	**shekel** = 1 stater	**stater** (tetradrachmon) = 4 drachmai	
thirty pieces of silver (*Matt.* 26:15) books worth fifty thousand silver coins (*Acts* 19:19)		**argirion** = 32 drachmai = 8 statera	
gold coin			
the man with one pound (*Luke* 19:20)		**mina** = 100 denarii	
measure of money			
the man with one talent (*Matt.* 25:15)		**talent** = 6,000 denarii	

*Sometimes writers do not specify among the silver coins. Often the most valuable silver piece is intended when the exact coin is not indicated.

Major Figures in the Herodian Family

APPENDIX B

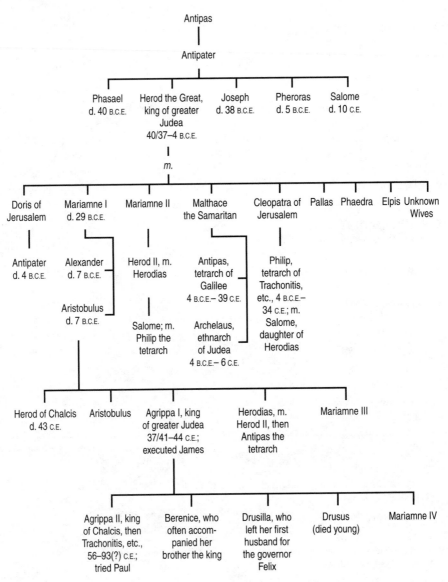

Antipas
|
Antipater
|

Phasael	Herod the Great,	Joseph	Pheroras	Salome
d. 40 B.C.E.	king of greater Judea 40/37–4 B.C.E.	d. 38 B.C.E.	d. 5 B.C.E.	d. 10 C.E.

m.

Doris of Jerusalem	Mariamne I d. 29 B.C.E.	Mariamne II	Malthace the Samaritan	Cleopatra of Jerusalem	Pallas	Phaedra	Elpis	Unknown Wives

Antipater d. 4 B.C.E.	Alexander d. 7 B.C.E.	Herod II, m. Herodias	Antipas, tetrarch of Galilee 4 B.C.E.– 39 C.E.	Philip, tetrarch of Trachonitis, etc., 4 B.C.E.– 34 C.E.; m. Salome, daughter of Herodias
	Aristobulus d. 7 B.C.E.	Salome; m. Philip the tetrarch	Archelaus, ethnarch of Judea 4 B.C.E.– 6 C.E.	

Herod of Chalcis d. 43 C.E.	Aristobulus	Agrippa I, king of greater Judea 37/41–44 C.E.; executed James	Herodias, m. Herod II, then Antipas the tetrarch	Mariamne III

Agrippa II, king of Chalcis, then Trachonitis, etc., 56–93(?) C.E.; tried Paul	Berenice, who often accompanied her brother the king	Drusilla, who left her first husband for the governor Felix	Drusus (died young)	Mariamne IV

The Jewish Civil Year
APPENDIX C

GREGORIAN CALENDAR	EVENT	JEWISH CALENDAR
	TRUMPETS (Rosh Hashanah)	Tishri 1, 2
	DAY OF ATONEMENT (Yom Kippur)	10
October	**TABERNACLES (Booths/Ingathering)**	15–22
	beginning of planting season	
November		Marchesvan
	DEDICATION (Lights/Hanukkah)	Chislev 25
December		
		Tebeth
January		
		Shebat
February		
	PURIM (Lots)	Adar 14, 15
March	beginning of the harvest	
	PASSOVER (Unleavened Bread)	Nisan 14–21
April	barley	
		Iyyar
May	wheat	
	PENTECOST (Firstfruits/Weeks)	Sivan 6
June		
	grapes	Tammuz
July		
	figs and dates	Ab
August		
	olives	Elul
September	end of the harvest	
	TRUMPETS (Rosh Hashanah)	Tishri 1, 2
	DAY OF ATONEMENT (Yom Kippur)	10
	TABERNACLES (Booths/Ingathering)	15–22

Early Christian Use of the Jewish Bible

APPENDIX D

The only Bible known to Jesus, Paul, and their contemporaries was the Jewish Bible, which later Christians would call the "Old Testament." In the first century, of course, there was nothing old about this Bible, even if Christians insisted that it be read through the lens of Jesus' resurrection and with the guidance of the Spirit (*2 Cor.* 3:14), and if for some of them it was a book of mysterious codes that pertained to the world's final generation (*1 Cor.* 9:10; 10:6). Still, for all of them it was an important text.

Any assertion that Christians used the Jewish Bible must be tempered, however, by our uncertainty about the exact scope and precise wording of the Bible they used. One reason for this uncertainty is that we no longer possess the original biblical texts that were available in the first century. All we have are copies from later periods or other locales. Because all ancient writing materials, like modern ones, were bound to decay over time, significant documents had to be preserved by copying. But copying by hand, in different places and from different master texts, inevitably produced slightly different readings. It is the job of "textual criticism" to reconstruct as well as possible the original text that produced our many copies.

The Jewish scriptures used by the Christians were originally composed in Hebrew, with a few brief passages in the related language, Aramaic. Before 1947, our earliest manuscripts of these ancient books were from the ninth century C.E., the so-called Masoretic text (MT). The discovery of the Dead Sea Scrolls (DSS) at Qumran, from 1947 onward, has produced both complete texts and fragments of most Jewish scriptures. These manuscripts are about a thousand years older than the MT. Some of the Qumran versions agree quite closely with the MT, but most differ significantly in some passages. These differences illustrate that even when texts are copied with great care, both accidental error and deliberate change ("correction") are bound to occur. Some scholars despair of ever finding the original Hebrew text, if there was a single original. In a predominantly oral culture, such as that of the first century and before, it is hard to think of a single written prototype.

The problem of identifying the exact wording of the Jewish scriptures is complicated further by the fact that Christians generally preferred Greek translations of the Bible, not the Hebrew originals. One of the first Greek translations had been made by Jews living Alexandria in the third and second centuries B.C.E. This version came to be called the "Septuagint" (LXX) because of the tradition that it was translated with divine aid by seventy (or seventy-two in some stories) Jewish elders. Once again, we do not possess original manuscripts of the Greek Jewish scriptures. In this case we must rely on fourth-century manuscripts, which are sure to differ from the originals in some respects. Different Greek versions likely circulated during the first century. Still, we often find sufficient similarity between an early Christian's reference to the scripture and the verse in the LXX, but not in the MT, to conclude that Christians preferred the LXX. This was natural since they were writing in Greek.

Anyone who knows more than one language understands that translation always involves interpretation. There is no single way of rendering one language into another. Words in one culture overlap in meaning with words from another, but there are always slight differences. Translators must choose between a range of alternatives for vocabulary, sentence structure, and rhetorical emphasis. (Compare the New International Version, New Revised Standard Version, and New American Standard Bible translations of the New Testament.) The LXX was not immune from such human constraints, and its translators apparently intended more than wooden translation. Much of the LXX differs substantially from the Hebrew tradition represented by either the DSS or the MT.

Differences between the Hebrew and Greek textual traditions became a source of controversy between Jews and early Christians, who competed for rights to the Jewish scriptures. When Christians cited passages in Greek and claimed that these supported their interpretation (i.e., their view of Jesus), Jews could respond that such readings were not possible in the original Hebrew and so could not have been divinely intended. Some favorite Christian texts that depend on the Greek, but lack any basis in the Hebrew text, are: (a) the gospels' citation of *Isa.* 40:3 to certify John the Baptist as the "voice crying in the wilderness"; (b) Paul's interpretation of *Deut.* 27:26 to mean that anyone who fails to fulfill "all" the things written in the law is under a curse (*Gal.* 3:10); and (c) *Matthew's* use of *Isa.* 7:14 to show that the prophet foretold a "virgin" birth (*Matt.* 1:23). Compare the senses of the original Hebrew in the passages cited below. In some cases, we know that the Hebrew/Greek disagreement existed already in the earliest manuscripts because the verses had become points of dispute by the second century.

A final cause of our uncertainty about what constituted "Jewish scripture" in the first century is the possibility that the scope of the Bible was not entirely settled. To be sure, many sources describe the scripture as consisting of (a) "Torah" or "Moses" or "law," (b) "prophets," and (c) in some cases, a third category of "psalms" or other writings. Virtually all Jewish writers are committed to the observance of God's teaching (Torah) as revealed through Moses, and many evoke the themes of the prophets. Nevertheless, it seems that many Jewish groups were quite impressed by books that did not ultimately find a home in the Jewish canon—books such as *1 Enoch, Jubilees,* and *Tobit.* The discovery of these and many other nonbiblical texts at Qumran has reminded scholars how wide the range of authoritative reading was for some Jews. Early Christian writers, too, regarded many of these books with reverence. Maccabean literature as well as the falsely attributed *Wisdom of Solomon* and *1 Enoch* were especially popular—the first two finding a place in the Bible that the Catholic Church still uses. Ancient writings were in scroll form usually with each text occupying its own roll. That system may have made it less obvious where the dividing line was, though it is worth noting that Josephus, a contemporary of the gospel writers, who also dealt with scrolls, nonetheless insists that a fixed Jewish Bible had been around for a long time (*Ag. Ap.* 1.37–43).

In sum, early Christian authors relied heavily on the Jewish scriptures to interpret Jesus' meaning for the world. We have a fairly good idea of the mainstream texts read by Jews everywhere, of the broad shape of the Jewish canon, and of the passages favored by Christians. Yet we do not know the exact perimeter or wording (in many places) of either the Hebrew or Greek Jewish Bible as it circulated in the first century. And we are sure that some passages had different senses in the two textual traditions.

However broad the scope of the Jewish canon, it was not all of equal interest to the young church. Those Christians whose basic belief was that the crucified man Jesus had been raised from the dead and supremely honored by God scanned the biblical texts looking for passages that would help to elucidate the meaning of this event. Favored verses spoke of God's vindication of a sufferer, for these could be seen as anticipating the greatest such reversal: Jesus' resurrection. Thus *Isaiah 53* and several of the psalms became the stuff of this kind of Christian preaching. Christians also used these passages in their efforts to persuade Jews of Jesus' messianic status. When that effort largely failed, they could draw on still other biblical texts (e.g., *Isa.* 6:9–10) that chastised Israel for its stubbornness and blindness.

It is most unlikely that Christian authors examined the text of the Bible each and every time they quoted from it. Rather, as several scholars have proposed, early Christians must have had their own collections of preferred proof-texts from which they could draw at will. Evidence for this conclusion is as follows.

First, the physical form of the biblical texts made them rather difficult of access. Each book of the Bible had its own papyrus or parchment scroll(s), and these scrolls, without chapter, verse, or even word divisions, must have been rather difficult to consult quickly. Indeed, it is possible that Christians developed the *codex* ("book") form in the second century partly to facilitate access to the scriptures, which had not been widely used earlier. Since the early Christians were not equally interested in all of the scriptural narrative, one would expect them to make their own compilations of the passages that interested them.

Second, the reader of early Christian writings quickly discovers that the same, relatively few, scriptural passages—like *Isa.* 6:9–10; *Pss.* 2:7; 8:4–6; 110:1; 118:22—

turn up in different texts by different authors. Since Paul's letters, the gospels, *Acts*, and *Hebrews*, for example, all quote or allude to the same texts, it seems that the authors did not coincidentally draw out the same passages from the mass of biblical material but rather drew on some common lists that circulated in the church.

Perhaps the strongest evidence for lists of proof-texts in early Christianity is the evident confusion with which the writers sometimes quote passages, indicating that they are unaware of the original contexts. For example, authors sometimes combine two different passages and attribute them to the same author, as when *Mark* conflates *Mal.* 3:1 with *Isa.* 40:3 and presents the result as if it were a single passage from *Isaiah* (*Mark* 1:2). *Matthew*, similarly, joins a line from *Isaiah* with one form *Zechariah* to produce a single prophecy (*Matt.* 21:5). In *Matt.* 27:9–10, the same author generates an entirely new "prophecy," which he attributes to *Jeremiah*, by combining elements from *Zechariah* 11 (predominantly) with words from *Jeremiah* 18 and 32. This apparent confusion about the original biblical text, which might also account for the author's belief that the "prophets" had foretold Jesus' upbringing in Nazareth (*Matt.* 2:23),[1] seems best explained on the supposition that the first Christian authors often used an intermediate source—an anthology of proof-texts—rather than the Bible itself.

However the early Christians gained access to the Bible, there can be little doubt that it shaped their belief about Jesus to a large degree. The author of *Matthew*, for example, was willing to change the story of Jesus' life, as he found it in his sources, better to accord with prophecy. Thus he has Jesus riding into Jerusalem on two animals—a donkey *and* a colt—in supposed fulfillment of *Zech.* 9:9 (*Matt.* 21:1–11). Since *Mark* (11:1–10) and *Luke* (19:28–40) use only one animal in their stories, and since only *Matthew* explicitly cites the passage from *Zechariah*, it seems that the author has shaped his account to fit the prophecy.

It is worth asking whether the biblical proof-texts also set the framework for larger stretches of narrative in the gospels. The question arises particularly with the stories of Jesus' trial and crucifixion. *John* is the only text that cites *Psalm* 22 in this connection (*John* 19:24), but all of the trial narratives in the gospels are replete with the language of that psalm. They refer to the "wagging of heads" of the passers-by (*Ps.* 22:7), the taunt about God's failure to deliver Jesus (22:8), the piercing of Jesus' hands and feet (22:16), the dividing of his garments by lot (22:18), and Jesus' plea, "My God, my God, why hast thou forsaken me?" (22:1). The close parallels between the trial narratives and *Psalm* 22 raise the historical question: Is it more likely that the events really happened this way, and that the Christian writers simply noticed

---

[1] Although ingenious explanations of this absent prophecy have been proposed, usually offering alternative explanations of the underlying Hebrew word for "Nazarene," the fact remains that *Matthew* wanted readers to believe that Jesus' settling in Galilee fulfilled prophecy, even though no such prophecy exists. There is no evidence that he expected his readers to understand some Hebrew play on words. On the contrary, in view of his rather inept handling of *Zechariah* 9:9 (see *Matt.* 21:5), it is most unlikely that he was himself sensitive to such nuances.

the extensive parallels with *Psalm* 22 after recording the events independently, or is it more likely that the story of Jesus' trial was shaped from the beginning by this psalm of distress? If the latter scenario seems probable, then the biblical prophecies have influenced early Christian thinking to an extraordinary degree.

Some would argue that such influence extends to early Christian theology. An example is the belief that Jesus, once he had been exalted to heaven, would remain there until "all things" were subject to him (see *1 Cor.* 15:24–28; *Heb.* 2:5–9). It seems likely that Christians took over this view from *Pss.* 8:4–6 and 110:1 (cited below), which spoke originally of God's exaltation of humanity (*Psalm* 8) and of the Israelite king (*Psalm* 110). Once these passages had been applied to Jesus, because of their theme of exaltation, their further remarks about the subjection of all things were also naturally applied to him.

The vast number of passages from the Bible that were pressed into service by the early Christians, in either direct quotation or allusion, prevents us from offering an exhaustive collection here. But it is possible to give the reader some idea of the decisive passages—those few that entered the Christian tradition early and exercised a formative influence. A first-generation Gentile Christian, though not necessarily knowing the Bible firsthand, might well have heard the following excerpts in the church's preaching. Note the emphasis on the prophets and some psalms, in contrast to the predominant interest of contemporary Jewish writers in the Torah.

THE JEWISH BIBLE IN EARLY CHRISTIAN WRITINGS

from the Law (Torah)

Genesis 15:6	*Gal.* 3:6; *Rom.* 4:9 • *Jas.* 2:23; *1 Clem.* 10.6
Leviticus 19:18	*Gal.* 5:14; *Rom.* 12:9 • *Mark* 12:31, 33; *Matt.* 5:43; 19:19; 22:39; *Luke* 10:27 • *Jas.* 2:8; *Did.* 1.2
Deuteronomy 18:15, 19	*Mark* 9:4, 7; *Matt.* 17:5; *Luke* 7:39; 9:35; 24:25; *Acts* 3:22–23 • *John* 1:21; 5:46

from the Prophets (Nevi'im)

2 Samuel 7:14	*2 Cor.* 6:18 • *Acts* 21:7 • *John* 1:49 • *Heb.* 1:5
Isaiah 6:9–10	*Rom.* 11:8 • *Mark* 4:12; *Matt.* 13:14–15; *Luke* 8:10; *Acts* 28:26–27
Isaiah 8:14	*Rom.* 9:32–33 • *1 Pet.* 2:8 • *Matt.* 16:23; 21:42; *Luke* 2:34
Isaiah 28:16	*Rom.* 9:33; 10:11 • *Eph.* 2:20; *2 Tim.* 2:19 • *1 Pet.* 2:4, 6 • *Matt.* 21:42; *Luke* 20:17
Isaiah 40:3, LXX	*Mark* 1:3; *Matt.* 3:3; *Luke* 1:76; 3:4–6 • *John* 1:23
Isaiah 42:1–4	*Matt.* 3:17; 12:18–21; *Luke* 3:22; 9:35; 23:35

from the Prophets (Nevi'im)

Isaiah 52:7	*Rom.* 10:15 • *Eph.* 2:17; 6:15 • *Acts* 10:36
Isaiah 53:1–12	*1 Cor.* 15:3; *Phil.* 2:7; *Rom.* 4:24–25; 5:1, 15, 19; 10:16 • *1 Pet.* 2:24–25 • *Mark* 9:12; 10:45; 14:24, 49, 61; 15:27; *Matt.* 8:17; 12:29; 20:28; 26:28; 27:12, 38; *Luke* 11:22; 22:37; 23:34; 24:25; *Acts* 5:6, 9; 8:32–33 • *Heb.* 9:28; *1 Clem.* 16.3–14 • *John* 1:29; 12:38; *1 John* 3:5; *Rev.* 14:5
Isaiah 61:1–3	*Matt.* 5:3; 11:5; *Luke* 6:20; 7:22; *Acts* 4:27; 10:38 • *Rev.* 5:10
Jeremiah 31:31–34	*1 Cor.* 11:25; *2 Cor.* 3:3, 6; *Rom.* 2:15; 11:27 • *Mark* 14:24; *Matt.* 23:8; 26:28; *Luke* 22:20 • *John* 6:45 • *Heb.* 8:8–12; 9:15; 10:16–17
Joel 2:28–32 (MT 3:1–5)	*1 Cor.* 1:2; *Rom.* 10:13 • *Titus* 3:6 • *Mark* 13:24; *Luke* 21:25; *Acts* 2:17–21; 6:12, 17 • *Rev.* 8:7; 14:1
Habakkuk 2:4b	*Gal.* 3:11; *Rom.* 1:17 • *Heb.* 10:38
Malachi 3:1	*Mark* 1:2; *Matt.* 11:3, 10; *Luke* 1:17; 7:27 • *Rev.* 22:16 • *1 Clem.* 23.5
Malachi 4:5–6 (MT 3:23–24)	*Mark* 9:11–12; *Matt.* 11:14; 17:10–11; *Luke* 1:17; 9:8; *Acts* 1:6

from the Writings (Ketuvim)

Psalm 2:7	*Matt.* 3:17; 4:3; *Luke* 3:22; *Acts* 13:33 • *John* 1:49 • *Heb.* 1:5; 5:5; *1 Clem.* 36.4
Psalm 8:4–6	*1 Cor.* 15:27 • *Eph.* 1:22 • *Heb.* 2:6–7
Psalm 16:10–11	*Acts* 2:25–28, 31; 13:35
Psalm 22:1 (MT 22:2)	*Mark* 15:34; *Matt.* 27:46
Psalm 22:7–8 (MT 22:8–9)	*Mark* 15:29; *Matt.* 27:29, 39, 43; *Luke* 23:35 • *1 Clem.* 16.16
Psalm 22:16–18 (MT 22:17–19)	*Mark* 15:24; *Matt.* 27:35; *Luke* 23:34 • *John* 19:24
Psalm 110:1	*1 Cor.* 15:25; *Rom.* 8:34 • *Col.* 3:1; *Eph.* 1:20 • *Mark* 12:36; 14:62; 16:19; *Matt.* 22:44; 26:64; *Luke* 20:42–43; 22:69; *Acts* 2:34–35 • *Heb.* 1:3, 13; 8:1; 10:12
Psalm 110:4	*Rom.* 11:29 • *Heb.* 5:6, 10; 6:20; 7:3–21
Psalm 118:22–23	*1 Pet.* 2:4, 7 • *Mark* 8:31; 12:10–11; *Matt.* 21:42; *Luke* 20:17; *Acts* 4:11
Psalm 118:25–26	*Mark* 11:9; *Matt.* 11:3; 21:9; 23:39; *Luke* 7:19; 13:35; 19:38 • *John* 12:13

The Lost Sayings Source: "Q"

APPENDIX E

In the introduction to BIOGRAPHY, ANECDOTE, AND HISTORY we discussed the reasons for the common scholarly view that an early gospel constructed mainly of Jesus' sayings was soon lost to Western history. In a nutshell: Although it appears that *Matthew* and *Luke* used *Mark* as a source, those two gospels share much material that is not in *Mark*. Since it also appears that neither gospel took this mostly-sayings material from the other, one must posit a shared source text or texts. Not everyone who knows the evidence well accepts this "Q" hypothesis as the best solution to the problem; some consider it more likely that either *Matthew* or *Luke* was the source for the other. Nevertheless, the Two-Document Hypothesis is the dominant theory of synoptic relationships.

To reconstruct the hypothetical Q is, however, no trivial task. Aside from the major questions, whether it is one text or many (or oral traditions and texts combined), whether all of it is represented in *Matthew* and *Luke,* and whether it is sometimes reflected in material that only *Matthew* or *Luke* happens to preserve, one must speculate on the degree to which *Mark*/Q overlaps explain the many agreements between *Matthew* and *Luke* against *Mark* in material that they are supposed to have taken from *Mark* (see the introduction to BIOGRAPHY, ANECDOTE, AND HISTORY). A maximalist solution to this problem would make Q much more than a "sayings source." And then, once one has resolved these fundamental issues, there remains the task of trying to distill the original Q from *Matthew*'s and *Luke*'s (often rather different) appropriations of it. For every single word, one must ask whether one of these texts preserves the original or whether Q had something different from both. If the latter, how can one know what it was?

In view of these obstacles, there seemed little point in our attempting to provide the student with yet another guess about the precise contents and shape of Q. One can find such an attempt in Part II of Burton Mack, *The Lost Gospel Q: The Book of Christian Origins* (San Francisco: Harper Collins, 1993). The full parallels, with discussion, may be found in John S. Kloppenborg, *Q Parallels: Synopsis, Critical Notes and Concordance* (Sonoma: Polebridge, 1988), and a complete student's edition now exists in James M. Robinson, Paul Hoffmann, and John S. Kloppenborg, eds., *The Sayings Gospel Q in Greek and English* (Minneapolis: Fortress, 2002). Still, because it is helpful to have some notion of what Q might have looked like, if it existed, we include here a list of the parallel passages in *Matthew* and *Luke* that gave rise to the Q hypothesis. It is customary to follow *Luke*'s order for this material. It will be an illuminating exercise for the student to look up these passages in a synopsis.

PARALLEL PASSAGES IN MATTHEW AND LUKE

Matthew	Luke	Matthew	Luke
3:7–10	3:7–14	23:1–39	11:37–54
3:11–12	3:15–17	10:26–33; 12:32	12:2–10
3:13–17	3:21–22	10:19–20	12:11–12
4:1–11	4:1–13	6:25–33	12:22–32
5:3–12	6:20–23	6:19–21	12:-33–34
5:38–48; 7:12	6:27–36	24:43–51	12:39–46
15:14; 10:24–25	6:39–40	10:34–36	12:49–53
7:1–5	6:37–42	16:2–3	12:54–56
7:15–20; 12:33–35	6:43–45	5:25–26	12:57–59
7:21–27	6:46–49	13:31–33	13:18–21
8:5–13	7:1–10	7:13–14, 22–23	13:22–27
11:2–6	7:18–23	8:11–12	13:28–30
11:7–11	7:24–28	23:37–39	13:34–35
21:32	7:29–30	12:11–12	14:5
11:16–19	7:31–35	22:2–10	14:16–23
8:18–22	9:57–62	10:37–39	14:26–27; 17:33
9:36–38; 10:7–16	10:1–12	5:13	14:34–35
11:21–23, 40	10:13–16	18:12–14	15:1–7
11:25–27	10:21–22	6:24	16:13
13:16–17	10:23–24	11:12; 5:18, 32	16:16–18
6:9–13	11:2–4	18:21–22	17:4
7:7–11	11:9–13	17:20	17:6
12:22–30; 9:32–34	11:14–23	24:26–28, 37–41	17:22–37
12:43–45	11:24–26	25:14–30	19:12–27
12:38–42	11:16, 29–32	19:28	22:28–30
5:15; 6:22–23	11:33–36		

Dating the Early Christian Texts

APPENDIX F

The following table will indicate something of the range of scholarly opinion concerning the dates of the early Christian texts. This is not an exhaustive summary, but the six works chosen represent some of the main constituencies, perspectives, and assumptions. Please note that each author includes fuller discussion of possibilities and alternative dates, which cannot be shown in this tabular form. We have chosen only the date range most favored by the author. We recommend that readers consult the original books for the context of each proposal.

Because the dating of some texts depends upon judgments concerning their authenticity, we have included the codes "i" and "a," for "inauthentic" and "authentic" respectively, for those texts that claim a certain authorship but whose authenticity is in dispute. A slash mark indicates "or"—where an author does not obviously favor one alternative.

Students will find detailed discussion of the chronology of Paul's career (including the dates of his letters) in Robert Jewett, *A Chronology of Paul's Life* (Philadelphia: Fortress, 1979) and Gerd Lüdemann, *Paul: Apostle to the Gentiles, Studies in Chronology*, translated by F. Stanley Jones (Philadelphia: Fortress, 1984).

For Further Reading

Brown, Raymond E. *An Introduction to the New Testament.* New York: Doubleday, 1997.

Guthrie, Donald. *New Testament Introduction.* Downers Grove, Ill.: InterVarsity, 1970.

Koester, Helmut. *Introduction to the New Testament.* 2 vols. Berlin: de Gruyter, 1982.

Kümmel, Werner Georg. *Introduction to the New Testament.* Nashville: Abingdon, 1979.

Robinson, John A. T. *Redating the New Testament.* London: SCM, 1976.

Tyson, Joseph B. *The New Testament and Early Christianity.* New York: Macmillan, 1984.

	KÜMMEL	KOESTER	ROBINSON	TYSON	GUTHRIE	BROWN
1 Thessalonians	50	50	50 early	40–51	50–51	50–51/41–43
1 Corinthians	54–55	52–55	55 spring	40–51	57	56–57/54–55
Philippians	53–55 / 56–58	54–55	58 spring	51–54	±60	54–56
Philemon	56–60	54–55	58 summer	51–54	–60	±55
2 Corinthians	55–56	54–55	56 early	51–54	57	late 57/55–56
Galatians	54–55	52–55	56 late	51–54	49	54–55
Romans	55–56	55/56	57 early	51–54	57–59	57–58/55–56
Colossians	56–60(a)	60–70+(i)	58 summer(a)	51–54(a)	±60(a)	80s(i)/61–63(a)
Ephesians	80–100	±100(i)	58 summer(a)	90(i)	±60(a)	90s(i)/60s(a)
2 Thessalonians	50–51(a)	–90(i)	50/51(a)	40–51(a)	51(a)	51–52(a)/–100(i)
1 Peter	90–95	±112(i)	65 spring(a)	98–117(i)	62–64(a)	70–90(i)
Hebrews	80–90	–100	±67	90–95	–64	80s
James	–100	70+(i)	47–48(a)	II C.E.(i)	50(a)	80–100(i)
Mark	±70	70+	45–60	±70	40–50+	68–73
Q	–50–70 or	mid-I C.E.	—	mid-I C.E.	50	60s
Matthew	80–100	80–100	40–60+	±80	50+	±80–90
1 Clement	90s	96–97	70 early	95	—	96–120
John	90–100	–100	40–65+	90–100	–70	80–110
1 John	90–110	±100	60–65	±100	–100	±100
2 John	90–110	±100	60–65	±100	–100	±100
3 John	90–110	±100	60–65	±100	–100	100–110
Thomas	—	mid-I C.E.	—	II C.E.	—	II C.E.
Revelation	90–95	90–96	68 late (–70)	95–96	90–96	92–96
Ignatius	early II C.E.	±110	—	115	—	–110
1 Timothy	100+(i)	120–60(i)	55 fall(a)	90–185(i)	61–64(a)	80–100(i)
2 Timothy	100+(i)	120–60(i)	58 fall(a)	90–185(i)	61–64(a)	late 60s(i)
Titus	100+(i)	120–60(i)	57 spring(a)	90–185(i)	61–64(a)	80–100(i)
Luke	70–90	II C.E.	57–60+	80–85	60–63	±85
Acts	80–90 /100	II C.E.	57–62+	80–85	60–63	±85
Jude	±100(i)	–100(i)	61–62(a)	±140(i)	65–80(a)	90–100(i/a)
2 Peter	125–50(i)	–150(i)	61–62(a)	±150(i)	–68(a)	±130(i)
Didache	–150	–100	40–60	mid-II C.E.	—	early II C.E.
Barnabas	—	±100 C.E.	±75	132+(?)	—	–135

The Literary Context of the Early Christians

APPENDIX G

	HEBREW	GREEK	ROMAN (LATIN)	CHRISTIAN
	Earliest Bible (J and E?) Sources of Samuel/Kings?			
900				
800				
700	Isaiah	Homer, *Iliad, Odyssey* Hesiod		
600				
500	Jeremiah, Ezekiel 2 Isaiah	Heraclitus Aeschylus, Aristophanes		
	Genesis-Joshua(?)	Herodotus, Euripides, Sophocles		
	Ezra-Nehemiah	Thucydides, Socrates		
400		Plato Aristotle, Diogenes, Isocrates Alexander the Great		
300		Euhemerus Septuagint		
	Ecclesiastes/Qohelet			
200			Plautus Terence	
	Daniel Dead Sea Scrolls (DSS)	Polybius		
100				
		Dionysius of Halicarnassus	Cicero, Varro, Catullus, Sallust, Lucretius Livy, Ovid, Virgil	
0	DSS continue		Horace, Elder Seneca	Jesus
		Philo of Alexandria		Paul, Q
			Petronius	Gospels & Acts, Hebrews, Revelation, 1 Clement,
		Flavius Josephus, Epictetus	Seneca, Lucan, Elder Pliny Martial	Thomas(?)
		Plutarch, Dio of Prusa	Pliny the Younger, Tacitus, Suetonius	Ignatius, Polycarp
100				
		Lucian	Juvenal	Marcion, Justin Martyr Irenaeus, Clement of
		Pausanius, Celsus	Apuleius, Marcus Aurelius	Alexandria
200	Mishnah	Cassius Dio	Paulus	Tertullian
	Tosefta	Diogenes Laertius(?)		Origen
	Midrash Halakhah	Plotinus		
300		Porphyry		Arius, Eusebius, Athanasius
				Gregory Nazianzus
400				
	Jerusalem Talmud(?) Midrash Rabbah			Augustine
500				
	Babylonian Talmud(?)		Justinian, Digest	

EARLY

CHRISTIAN

READER

Judea in Context
(first century C.E.)
25-mile (40-km) square grid

- Sidon
- Damascus

SYRIA

▲ Mt. Hermon
- Tyre
- Caesarea Philippi

- Gischala
Lake Semechonitis

GALILEE
- Ptolemais Chorazin
  Capernaum
- Bethsaida Gamala

▲Mt. Carmel
- Magdala
Sea of Galilee
- Sepphoris
- Tiberias
- Hippos

Mediterranean Sea
- Nazareth
- Gadara

- Dora

- Caesarea
Scythopolis
DECAPOLIS
- Pella

SAMARIA
- Sebaste
- Gerasa

- Apollonia
▲ Mt. Gerizim

- Antipatris
PEREA
- Joppa

- Lydda
- Philadelphia

JUDEA
Jericho
- Emmaus

- Jamnia
Jerusalem - Bethany
- Azotus
Qumran
- Bethlehem
- Herodium

- Ascalon
- Marisa
- Machaerus

- Gaza **IDUMEA** - Hebron
- Adora En-Gedi Dead Sea

Masada ▲

- Beersheba
NABATEA **NABATEA**

© 2013 Tom Robinson

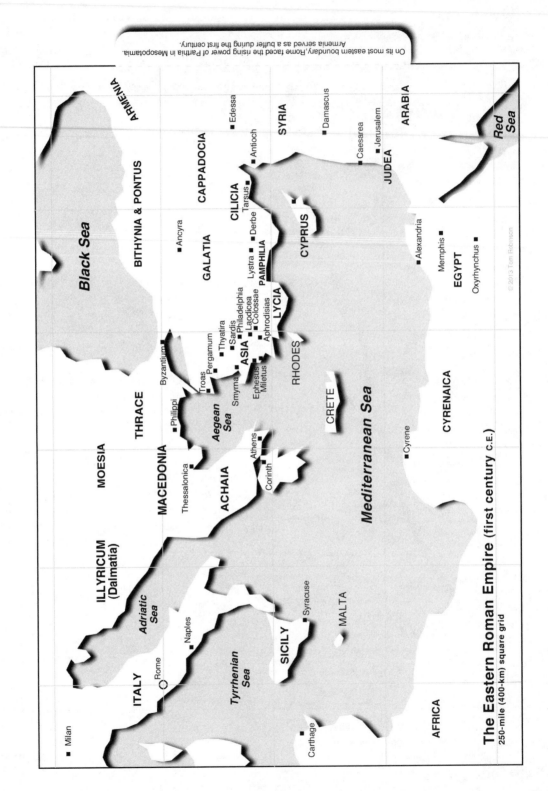

On its most eastern boundary, Rome faced the rising power of Parthia in Mesopotamia. Armenia served as a buffer during the first century.

ARMENIA

Edessa

SYRIA

Damascus

ARABIA

Red Sea

CAPPADOCIA

BITHYNIA & PONTUS

Antioch

Caesarea

JUDEA

Jerusalem

Black Sea

Tarsus

CILICIA

Ancyra

GALATIA

Derbe

CYPRUS

Lystra

PAMPHILIA

Alexandria

Memphis

Philadelphia

LYCIA

EGYPT

Thyatira

Sardis

Laodicea

Oxyrhynchus

Pergamum

ASIA

Colossae

Aphrodisias

Byzantium

Troas

Ephesus

RHODES

Smyrna

Miletus

THRACE

Aegean Sea

CRETE

Mediterranean Sea

Philippi

MOESIA

MACEDONIA

Athens

Thessalonica

ACHAIA

Corinth

CYRENAICA

ILLYRICUM
(Dalmatia)

Cyrene

Adriatic Sea

Syracuse

Naples

MALTA

Tyrrhenian Sea

SICILY

ITALY

Rome

AFRICA

Milan

Carthage

The Eastern Roman Empire (first century C.E.)
250-mile (400-km) square grid

©2013 Tom Robinson

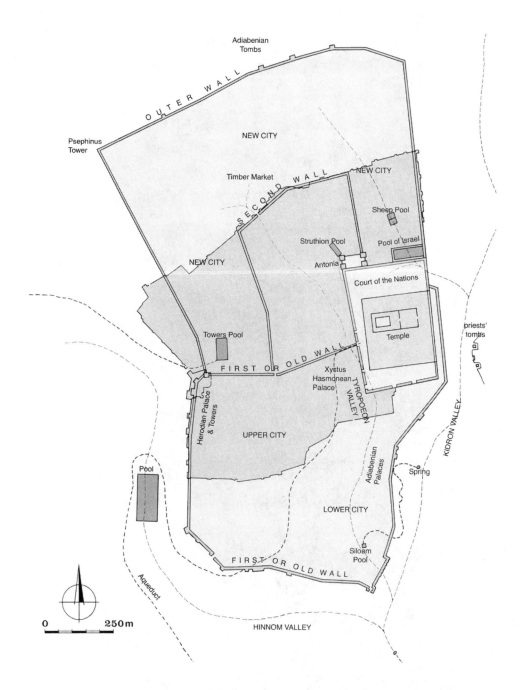

Jerusalem in the First Century C.E.

Figures on pages 779 and 780 © Leen Ritmeyer,
all rights reserved; used with permission

JERUSALEM
Herod's Temple Mount
A reconstruction based on
archaeological and historical evidence

L. RITMEYER

Mount of Olives

Mount Scopus

Court of the Nations

Upper City

Antonia